Genealogy of the Child,

Childs and Childe families,

of the past and present in the United States

and the Canadas, from 1630 to 1881

Elias Child

Alpha Editions

This edition published in 2020

ISBN : 9789354023262

Design and Setting By
Alpha Editions
email - alphaedis@gmail.com

DEDICATION.

TO THE DESCENDANTS NOW ON THE STAGE, AND THOSE COMING AFTER,
OF A WORTHY ANCESTRY TRACED IN THE SEVERAL LINES
BEARING THE NAME OF CHILD, CHILDS AND CHILDE,
THIS WORK IS RESPECTFULLY DEDICATED;
WITH THE EARNEST WISH AND CONFIDENT HOPE THAT THE RESULTS
OF A PATIENT AND PERPLEXING SERVICE OF MORE THAN THREE
YEARS, MAY MEET THE CORDIAL APPROVAL OF THOSE
FOR WHOSE PLEASURE AND BENEFIT THE WORK
HAS BEEN UNDERTAKEN.

———

Honour thy father and thy mother, that thy days may be long upon the land which the Lord
thy God giveth thee."—Exodus xx. 13

THE CHILD COAT OF ARMS

PREFACE.

We would earnestly request all to read the Introduction (so termed) to this work, as opening the plan pursued in its arrangement. Selecting the Emigrant, the date of whose arrival in America is most definitely ascertained, as the pioneer in our Genealogy, we have traced his descendants as far as attainable to the present time. The next line is kindred to that first given, the emigration, also, supposed to be about the same time; and thus with each line the same order is observed in reference to arrangement. These differing lines are followed by some incomplete families now in the United States who have not as yet been able to find the clues to their early ancestry in America; and two ancestors and their descendants who have come to this country within the present century; the whole supplemented by some names not linked to any line, and some statistics pertaining to lines previously recorded, which came to hand too late to be placed in their due position. Such matter is so marked as to be easily placed where it belongs. There is another point we wish may early attract attention, namely, the articles on the "Origin and Etymology of the surname Child," and "Sketches and Incidents of English Families." That we may escape the charge of any purpose to force the use of a form in the name, which some discard, we wish it to be distinctly understood that our aim has been to write the name in all cases as desired by its bearer. Any failure has been unintentional. It has been exceedingly difficult to discriminate, when in the same family a part write the name with, and a part without the "s". Further on we think it is clearly shown that the name was originally written without the "s." We are aware that some feel indifferent, and others regret

the use of the " s " as a terminal in their own case, and have requested that it be left off in the printing of their record. Others
still are quite tenacious to have the " s ",attached. We cannot
but express the belief that when the article on the origin of the
name, furnished by one who has devoted much time in its preparation, is carefully read, there will be a common feeling of
regret that the " s " should ever have been added. Its use or
omission will not vitally affect the identity of any one in this
work. No very serious embarrassment will arise in tracing the
lines. Our method of recording the different branches by generations in due chronological order, will generally render it easy
for one to trace his or her line of ascent. In this place it is
pertinent to emphasize the advantages of a well prepared Genealogy—one of which is that it preserves the identity of families
and individuals, even with such changes in the spelling of the
name, in any manner to please the fancy. The importance
of preserving this identity is apparent in questions of legal titles
to an estate, a point perhaps to which many have not given
serious thought. A no less important consideration is that
Genealogical records show how far we are indebted to our ancestors for our physical, mental and moral proclivities—an inheritance we cannot escape if we would. It is folly therefore to attempt to ignore our ancestry, as we are held by a law
higher than ourselves. It is the dictate of wisdom to recognize
the existence of relations which affect our destinies, and cherish
what are beneficent, while we guard against those that are baneful in their tendencies. Much of the moral evil and physical
suffering of this life might be avoided or remedied by giving
heed to the laws of transmission. The medical man in the
treatment of physical diseases has gained a point often when
he has learned the antecedents of his patient. This law applies
to mental and moral tendencies with equal force. Instead of
alliances and associations fruitful of baneful results, more
healthful ones could be inaugurated, bearing sweeter fruits,
were not fundamental laws set aside.

TABLE OF CONTENTS.

CONTENTS. XI.

xii. CONTENTS.

ILLUSTRATIONS.

EXPLANATIONS.

To the name of each individual is attached a number   This number will indicate that individual wherever found, proving an additional means of identification; necessary where names are so often repeated.

The following abreviations have been used b. for born; m. for married; d. for died; yg. for young; da. or dau. for daughter.

ERRATA.

Page 147. No. 28.—Read Ruth Curtis, not Ruth *Ammidown*, as found twice on this page; again No. 641.

Page 417. No. 641.—Read Dudley, not *Daniel* Chase. This marriage linked the family with the U. S. Senator Dudley Chase, Bishop Philander Chase, both brothers of Mercy Chase, who married Stephen Child No. 641, and a later generation, the late Chief Justice Salmon Chase who was a nephew of Mercy Chase Child. Ruth Child, No. 646, not *Harris* left one son Samuel M. Chase.

Page 148.—Read Abner Palmer, not *Abraham Chas. Palmer.*

"   151.—Read in line 17, Meteorology, not *Metallurgie.*

"   126. xxx.—Read Alfred DeForest Childs, not *Arthur C.*

"   238. No. 1449.—Read Ida, not *Ada*

"   226.—Foot note, read Mrs. Sylvina Thorp Child's family.

"   182. No. 938—Read Louisa, not *Loisa.*

"   285. No. 1851 —Read Hannah B. Holmes.

"   485. No. 4449 —Read Mary Blanchard Malcom.

"   723. 7078.—Read Samuel Capen, not *Chapin Child.*

"   418. No. 3566.—Read Mildred Lee, not *Milinda.* She was the daughter of the distinguished General Henry Lee, of revolutionary fame of Virginia, and sister of Robert E. Lee, the late Confederate general; the same change from Milinda to Mildred should be observed when repeated.

Page 404. No. 3427.—Read Fitz Henry Morse, not *Fitzhugh.* Same change should be observed where Fitzhugh is repeated, page 405, Nos. 3435, 3436, 3437.

Page 210. No. 1234.—Should read Hale, not *Hall.*

"   233. No. 1403.—Read Angeline Coats, not *Augusta.*

"   285. No. 1850.—Read Hannah Holmes, not *Howes,* and again 1851, where William Childs is taken over read Hannah Holmes.

"   485. No. 4449.—Read Mary Blanchard Malcom.

"   508. Read No. 4747.—Josiah Child.

"   510. No. 4762.—Read Mehitable Flagg, not *Taft.*

"   578. No. 5491.—Read Freeman Childs, not *Truman.*

"   496. No. 4549.—Read Sarah Platt, not Sarah *Norcross.*

"   723. No. 7078.—Read Capen, not *Chapin.* Same page read Mary Burditt, not *Burdell.*

"   634. No. 6240.—Read Mrs. Hitchcock, not *Alvord.*

"   473. Nos 4291, 4292.—Read Brigham, not *Bingham.*

"   396. No. 3331.—Read William Bennett, not *Burnett.*

"   332. No. 2454 —Date of birth of Ellen Louisa Child read 1845.

INTRODUCTION.

Not infrequently concurrent influences draw one into a line of activities unsought and unlooked for. By such a method I have been led to undertake the work of preparing a Genealogy of the Child, Childe or Childs family, and alliances by marriage, in the United States and the Canadas.

The name has been variously spelled in this country for years, taking on sometimes the terminal "e," but more often the terminal "s." For the first two generations in this country the name was written *Child*. Occasionally at an early period the terminal "e" was used. But later the "s" has been more frequently employed. Upon whatever principle the change may be explained, it seems unfortunate for the preservation of the integrity of the family, as the effect is sometimes to lead members of the same branch to lose sight of their kindred. We have aimed scrupulously to write the name in this volume as written by those who have furnished their record; deeming it our duty however, to be governed by the public records where the fathers of the lines have observed the English method of spelling the name. Not a few using the terminal "s" have expressed to me regret that it had been added to their name. In this connection it occurs to us to suggest a return to the original mode of spelling the name with the terminal "e" as written upon its translation in Great Britain from its Norman Frank form, might now be accomplished, as the different branches are awakened to an interest in their family history. This would meet the objection felt by some as to the brevity of the name, and its easy confusion with the common noun. This proposed change has been spoken of to some of the leading ones of different branches who are quite ready to fall in with it.

It is approaching three years since I was first made acquainted with the fact that Mr. Isaac Child of Boston, Mass., a descendant in direct line like myself from Benjamin Child, the emigrant, had for many years been gathering the statistics of the early

B

families of the New England emigrants of our name and their descendants. This information was given me by Hon. William Graves Child, M. D., of Bath, Grafton county, N. H., whose special interest in behalf of a Genealogy of the *family* name was awakened by the connection of his immediate branch with the Dwight *family*, and whose family record is extensively recorded in Dr. Dwight's Genealogy: an early ancestor of Dr. Child having married a daughter of Rev. Josiah Dwight, who was ordained and settled as the first Congregational minister of Woodstock, Ct., in 1690. It was upon the suggestion of Dr. Child that I was led to entertain the purpose of attempting a Genealogy on the *basis* of Mr. Isaac Child's material. After much deliberate reflection, I decided to undertake the task of reviving the memories of those who had passed away, and placing their names with those now upon the stage, in a form of permanent record. In the incipient stages of the work, a slumbering affection for the memory of those whom in childhood I had been taught to revere was quickened, and incidents of early and later life, almost forgotten, or thought of occasionally as of no great significance, began to be recalled. I could see in them a *moral*, conveying thoughts noble, inspiring, and instructive. To bring these memories into a form, and weave these incidents into a web of sufficient interest to attract intelligent members of the great fraternity, seemed indeed a work of much labor and not a little delicacy, yet not without some compensating pleasure. The circle of family friends of near kinship, with whom I found myself allied at the commencement, has been enlarging, till almost thousands are now numbered in a quasi kinship, with many of whom, by a daily handshaking through epistolary correspondence, I seem to be brought into bonds of warmest friendship. There is much of common interest, so much of sentiment and sympathy in common, our experiences are found to run naturally in a common channel.

Correspondence was opened with Mr. Child of Boston, who had hitherto been unknown to me, which led to an arrangement with him for placing in my hands the material which he had, to be incorporated in the proposed Genealogy. His matter forms the *nucleus* of this work; not that it constitutes the larger amount, nor that it was arranged, as incorporated in this work. The filling up of many branches, partially traced by Mr. Isaac

Child, and the discovery of many new lines, will swell the volume to threefold or more beyond his material. Yet had it not been for his industry and perseverance, it is probable the present work would not have been undertaken.

The scope of my plan takes a wider range than that embraced in his manuscript. His record has not gone outside of the New England emigrants and their descendants; nor does it extend, with but few exceptions, to the female members of the family and their descendants. The present plan embraces all of the name, whether traceable to New England emigrants, or to ancestors known to have come to our shores at other points, and at later periods. I trace also the descendants of the female members, as well as the males to the latest dates.

It was not possible to foresee the amount of labor and expenditure of money which would be required, nor the numberless occasions of delay, before the work could be completed. Much is due to the earnest desires expressed by many prominent in the branches they represent, that the work should go on to completion, that it has not been abandoned long ago as a hopeless task. For it was early discovered that a superficial production would not only prove unsatisfactory, but be held, as one member expressed it, "with intolerable loathing." There is no lack of intelligence in this widespread family. It would be worse than folly in an enterprise of this kind to ignore this intelligence; and it is with not a little pride and self-gratulation that I record the fact that words of cheer have reached me from outside the family name,—from those who view such works as a benefaction to the race: among these is one of New York's most enlightened and patriotic statesmen—Hon. Horatio Seymour, Ex-Governor of this State. In a letter dated Utica, July 10, 1879, he writes:

DEAR SIR: I am glad that you mean to get up a record of your family. I have known some of its branches, and held them in high regard. Genealogies do not merely gratify curiosity. They tend to elevate, because they keep in men's minds the character of the best of their race; and these become standards of morals and positions, which men aim to equal. The commandment that we should honor our fathers has purposes more wide and far reaching than is usually supposed. I hope you will go on with your work. I am truly yours, &c.,

Elias Child, Esq., Utica. HORATIO SEYMOUR.

In the earlier stages of the work I received, unsolicited, the following generous note from Rev. Theophilus Packard, who was for fifty years a citizen of Shelburne, Mass., and twenty-five years of that time pastor of the Congregational Church in that town:

DEAR SIR:—I have had sufficient experience in such work (Genealogies) to sympathise with you in the difficulties and delays which must have tried your patience. Yours is a worthy undertaking; and will, if completed, be more highly appreciated by future generations than by those now living. I shall be glad to assist in your work. I have many valuable statistics as to the tribes of Childses, and will gladly and *gratuitously* furnish them to you if you deem them suited to your profound work.

Wishing you success in your enterprise, I am, respectfully, yours, &c.,

THEOPHILUS PACKARD.

Additional encouragement is derived from a monthly *Journal* published in New York city by the "American College of Heraldry and Genealogical Registry," brief extracts from which I quote:

There is an importance attached to carefully written accounts of the origin and dispersion of the individuals of a family, becoming more essential as population increases in this vast country, the asylum of all nationalities.

Often the rights of heritage, through a neglect of records systematically kept in the family, or public documents properly guarded and certified to by qualified officials, are imperiled or utterly lost. Great estates in Europe are lost entirely to heirs who might have had wealth and position had their parents been careful to bring with them when emigrating to the United States, documentary evidence of their lineage in their fatherland.

A few have been fortunate in securing a rich competency to which they had never supposed themselves entitled on account of the many heirs between themselves and an estate; but who in the revolutions of society have suddenly and unexpectedly emerged from poverty to wealth, on the strength of the testimony of a record in a long forgotten book, hardly known to exist, in which was chronicled their descent from a remote ancestry; only known to them through the declarations of a court of chancery.

The indifference of some, and the positive aversion of others, to Genealogies, may break the force of such testimony as these extracts afford, yet they are the views of men of experience and sound judgment. The wisdom of the cautionary language here employed to guard against indifference and neglect on this point, finds confirmation in actual cases of estates waiting for claimants of our own family name. There are credits in the

Bank of England, in stocks and money, against the following names:

ELIZABETH CHILD,
JANE CHILD,
HENRY CHILDS,   All dating back to 1513-1818.
RICHARD CHILD,
MARTHA CHILD,

Also in the Bank of England, there have long been credits waiting for claimants in the heirs of Ann Child, John Child, Sarah Child, Anthony Child, Thomas Child, William Child, Mary Child. These properties have been several times advertised, as attested by J. P. Jayne, Commissioner.

We are seldom indifferent to the opinions of our friends, and when they coincide with ours, or may be somewhat in advance, they lend encouragement and force to our schemes; and it is a pleasure to place them on record, when in form to be preserved. From one of the many communications from the pen of Judge William Child of Fairlee, Vt., the following extract warmly endorses our enterprise:

I would say there is a pleasure in erecting monuments of marble or granite or other material to the memory of our relatives. Why may not our pleasure or gratification be greatly increased by the possession of a volume containing a brief mention of all the families of our name, whether near or remote, to which we can at any time refer, and ponder upon their good qualities of head and heart therein recorded, and try to emulate or excel in all the virtues that pertain to any individual or family of our name. Sums great and small are continually being expended in erecting memorials to our departed relatives; the smallest of such sums would probably purchase many volumes of the work upon which you are engaged, and which would be as valuable as inscriptions on monumental marble.

Professor Francis Joseph Child, LL. D., of Harvard University, who does not claim to have made the Genealogy of his family a special study, says:

I do not see how a human being should not be glad to know what was his kith and kin, when some one is able to tell him. For one, I thank you and Mr. Isaac Child for the interesting information I have derived, and expect to derive, from the volume preparing.

The almost universal approval of the object set forth in the circulars and letters sent out, renders it difficult to draw a line that may not seem to undervalue the kindly offices of many in helping in our common enterprise. Yet we fail not to appreciate the smallest service, while we specially note the more marked efforts of a goodly number of the friends:

Daniel B. Childs, Esq. of New York city, was among the earliest who prepared a lengthy and lucid record of the prolific branch to which he belongs. Mrs. Alice Walker Child of East Woodstock, Ct., whose fourscore years are a storehouse of useful memories, is entitled to special recognition for her voluntary and effective services in gathering material for this book. George Walker, Esq. of Northford, Ct., who has the blood of two most worthy families in his veins, has poured out the riches of a mind well stored with historical facts and chronological statistics to enrich the volume. Mrs. E. M. Childs Haskins of Brattleboro, Vt., has been indefatigable in collecting records and tracing different lines in the branches of her own and other families. Mrs. William G. Child of North Woodstock, Ct., has been an earnest and untiring worker in this enterprise. Mrs. Cynthia Child May of North Woodstock, Ct., has manifested a laudable interest and rendered valuable service in hunting up records and supplying interesting incidents. Mr. Elias Child of East Woodstock, Ct., who has passed away since this work commenced, greatly facilitated our labor by putting into our hands a transcript of the Woodstock records, as far as relating to the Child family. Wm. H. Childs, Esq. of Niagara Falls, N. Y., was an early and zealous advocate and helper, whose earnestness gave much impulse to the work. Miss Alma Childs, daughter of Hon. Aaron Childs of Ypsilanti, Mich., has wrought cheerfully and effectively in the work. Mrs. E. A. B. Child Rice of Lyons, N. Y., an octogenarian, has devoted much time with good results. Franklin S. Childs, Esq. of Grinnell, Iowa, has been a faithful gleaner of essential material. Roswell Child, Esq. of Moretown, Vt., has done much. Alexander B. Child, Esq. of Granville, Vt., has done good service. Hon. A. L. Childs of Waterloo, N. Y., editor of the *Seneca News*, has rendered kindly aid through the channels of his popular weekly. Albert Baxter, Esq., editor of *Grand Rapids Eagle*, Michigan, has rendered aid through his columns and otherwise. Jonathan Child, Esq. of Rochester, Lewis J. Child, Esq. of Philadelphia, Jeff. Co., N. Y., Nathaniel Childs of Washington, D. C., Warren Gould Child, Esq., Ogden City, Moses R. Chamberlain, Esq., Bradford, Vt., Miss Jennie Child of Bath, N. H., and many others whose friendly offices might be named, we sincerely thank.

To Mr. Addison Child of Boston, is due an especial and hearty tribute. His scholarly researches in the United States and Great Britain have furnished us the fascinating and instructive article upon the "Origin of the Name" and very largely the resumé of the "English Families."

I should fail in my duty did I neglect to recognize before the public the efficient aid rendered by my wife, Mrs. S. P. Cleaveland Child, whose autograph has so often appeared in the copious correspondence demanded in the preparation of this volume, and who has been a judicious counsellor and essential helper in its compilation. I have no censures for any who confess they feel no interest in a family Genealogy. Our tastes and judgments are formed from different surroundings, and must necessarily differ somewhat in their character. What to one is a pleasure, to another may be an object of aversion or indifference. So if any have neglected to reply to our courteous requests for family record, or sent a curt response, we accept their estimate.

To meet a feeling that may have obtained to some extent that this enterprise is purely a business affair, entered upon from mercenary motives: and that honorable business rules have been ignored, I desire here more fully to explain my position.

The work was commenced under the impression that six months, or at most one year only, would be required to complete it. It was supposed that the material was already collected; that it only needed proper arrangement, historically and chronologically, to be ready for the press. But it was early apparent that much remained to be done by way of collecting material, if anything like a satisfactory Genealogy was to be prepared. Having advanced to a point where the field could be more fully surveyed, it was seen that a work had been entered upon whose end lay far in the distant future. To abandon the work would disappoint many whose efforts had placed in our hands much valuable material, and, whose enthusiasm had inspired in us sanguine hopes of ultimate success, though the road should prove long in reaching the end. There seemed to be no alternative but to continue the work, relying upon the magnanimity of a *family* with whom it is our pride to be connected, and whose interest for our success had been so often and distinctly announced, to shield us from essential loss.

Under the impression, presumably, that the sale of the book would reimburse outlays and compensate fairly for time spent, the pecuniary responsibility has been left to myself. I have assumed it not from my abundant wealth, but from a confidence that the many embraced in the *family* who would want a book would make the burden light.

The estimated cost of the book at $5.00 per copy was made upon the basis of an issue of five hundred copies and of more than one hundred pages less than the present volume contains. And although only about two hundred copies have been ordered, I have decided to publish, trusting there will be, after its issue, the full compliment of five hundred copies called for.

While my pecuniary circumstances would not justify indifference to the results of my labors and expenditures, I have never allowed myself to ignore legitimate business principles. The doctrine of a *quid pro quo* I fully recognize. But I have been shut up to the necessity of the utmost economy, (not understanding in the beginning what the burdens were to be,) in order to make the enterprise pay the necessary outlay. I have asked no service, however, of such as were not known or supposed to be interested equally with myself in preserving the records of the family name and alliances by marriage, for which I have not paid or offered a full compensation. Those of the family name and those allied by marriage, I have treated in my correspondence more as *allies* embarked with me in a common cause: such I have found, with few exceptions, ready coadjutors. In two or three instances I have accidentally come upon those that are allied who were preparing some history of the special branch with which they were connected, but with all due defference have refrained from unfriendly interference with their rights. I say this much because I have been misapprehended, and consequently unjustly censured.

Our friends may look for greater perfection in the compilation of this work than it is possible for ordinary intelligence to produce. Errors in dates and names and possibly in incidents will occur, while special care has been taken on our part to secure the greatest exactitude. These errors may arise in some instances from oversight on our part, or they may occur from illegible chirography, or from differences in the reports of different members of a family widely separated and unable to compare notes previous to sending their records; reliance on memory and erroneous tradition may bring out a false record. In view of the manifold difficulties it would be a marvel if no errors were discovered.

Failures to find a *complete* record will appear in almost any branch. This should not be chargeable to us. We have written and waited long for returns, which either do not come or if sent in part it is with the announcement that the records have been lost or have never been kept; and memory and tradition can supply but imperfectly. Such incidents show the value of a family Genealogy deposited where casualties could not destroy the entire record; scattered among a numerous family and placed, as copies usually are, in public libraries.

Our efforts to bring out a Genealogy that should meet the reasonable expectations of those who are interested have not been limited to letter correspondence; this has been extensive and ought to have accomplished a great deal more. We have visited in person, or by paid agents, state and city libraries, county and town records, in several different states, and spent many days in searching records to discover missing links in branches of families whose records have been given to us incomplete, or to establish some important historical point.

Our sincere thanks are due and heartily tendered to the librarians of the following public libraries: New York State Library, at Albany, N. Y.; Astor and Mercantile Libraries, New York City; State Library, at Hartford, Conn.; Springfield and Worcester, Mass., public libraries; Historical Library, of Worcester, Mass. We also recognize the gentlemanly attentions of county and town clerks, who have rendered us ready facilities for examining such records as could afford us aid in our work.

All sources of information known to hold out promise of success we have explored and exhausted to make the work complete. Any failure to secure the most satisfactory results cannot be more a matter of regret with others than with ourselves. Future research may reveal the link connecting the American emigrants with the English ancestor. The friends can not fail to appreciate the difficulties lying in the way of securing a complete record.

CHARACTERISTICS.

A brief resumé of some of the prominent characteristics of the family may afford pleasant reflections to the reader. If we have not failed to form just opinions from the examinations of early public records, and the historical sketches sent us by descendants of ancestors, and of cotemporaries, there is not a little to admire and imitate.

A spirit of enterprise is a feature of the family which will not escape the notice of the reader. A desire to improve their condition draws them on in new enterprises and efforts to make the most of life. They possess enough of the impulsive element to defy dangers and to grapple with difficulties to obtain a manly independence. As pioneers, no class of men can show a better record. There has been a constant migration of successive generations till, from the Atlantic shores, they have spread over the continent. Sober, industrious, frugal, and with a good degree of intelligence, they have known how to use the appliances of life wisely and effectively to construct comfortable homes and rear intelligent and virtuous families.

One may well be amazed at the incidents in the histories of not a few recorded in this volume. The determination and perseverance with which many have met and overcome difficulties, and the boldness and daring in adventure displayed in others, will thrill the reader and awaken his admiration, if he has a spark of enthusiasm in his composition.

In pursuits, the family is largely agricultural : yet it has its representatives in the various industries of the country. In every generation there are found shrewd and prosperous tradesmen. Men of inventive genius in the mechanic arts, successful manufacturers, and men of thrift in the lesser trades. While few can boast of large fortunes, as measured by present standards, the conditions of medium wealth are usually attained.

For general intelligence and virtue it has a fair record. Education and high culture have been regarded as essential in every generation. The number who have enjoyed the opportunity of a liberal education will favorably compare with most other American families. The proportion who have been employed as public teachers is strikingly large.

Among the educated class there have been those who have risen to prominence in all the learned professions. The legal, the medical and the clerical representatives of the family, in many cases, have attained to no mean eminence. Literary ability and acquirements are by no means lacking. We often find the love of knowledge drawing them away from the bustle and ambitions of life into the quiet seclusions of the study, where they find their sweetest companionship with some history, romance, or philosophical treatise.

Another prominent feature of this family is its patriotism. None have been more ready to expose themselves to the hardships of the camp and the dangers of the battle field than the emigrants and their descendants. They have often risked and sacrificed their all to save their country. Military fame has followed not a few from the battle field, while many from the rank and file have borne for life the scars of many a hard-fought battle. Many of the early emigrants were in the Indian and French wars; their descendants were in the revolutionary struggles; then again in the war of 1812; later in the Mexican war, and finally in the civil war, from 1861 to 1865, which closed a bloody era in the nation's history. In the revolutionary period twenty-two (22) of the family name were of the first company of volunteers and minute men, on the outbreak of hostilities, when Lexington, Mass., was attacked by the British, April 19, 1775. In the following list, which embraces the above twenty-two Massachusetts patriots, many of the descendants will recognize their ancestral head:

AARON CHILD.	JONATHAN CHILD.
ABEL CHILD.	JOSHUA CHILD.
ABIJAH CHILD.	JOSIAH CHILD.
ABRAHAM CHILD.	LEMUEL CHILD,
DANIEL CHILD.	MOSES CHILD.
DAVID CHILD,	PHINEAS CHILD.
ELIJAH CHILD.	REUBEN CHILD.
ELISHA CHILD.	SILAS CHILD.
ISAAC CHILD.	SAMUEL CHILD.
JOHN CHILD.	SOLOMON CHILD,
JONAH CHILD.	TIMOTHY CHILD.

A manly independence has ever been more to the race than fame or wealth or position, while none of these would be despised or rejected if they were the legitimate rewards of industry and virtue.

As benefactors of their race they are usually sympathetic and active; they abhor oppression; they are earnest advocates of equal rights. No wrong stirs their blood so certainly as that which is inflicted by the exercise of irresponsible and arbitrary power. Their philanthropy is not limited to that form of oppression which draws its life from organized agencies. It reaches to its subtler forms as found in individual character and in social life. It is not less their mission as benefactors to employ such appliances as Providence has placed in their hands to rescue their fellow men from ignorance, degradation and crime. Their benefactions are distributed upon the broadest principles of Christianity.

It is a family of decided religious tendencies. The early emigrants came to this western world with essentially just religious ideas; with longings for freedom of conscience denied them in the fatherland. Their deep religious convictions are evinced in the conscientious observance of the institutions of our Christian religion. A spirit of toleration has marked its religious history. Independent thought has had full scope; and different religious creeds and philosophical theories have come to exist, yet the mass have built their religious opinions upon the Bible, substantially as interpreted by the Reformers of the 16th and 17th centuries. They have a profound reverence for the Bible. While some of the opinions of the early ancestors are received in a modified form at the present period, the essential truth, as taught in the Divine Book, is warmly cherished and insisted on as constituting the only true basis of sound morality, and a rational theory of accountability to the Divine Lawgiver.

In politics they have distinct and differing opinions, which are maintained with characteristic earnestness and persistency.

It may be of interest to know the impression of a thoughtful and observing member belonging to one of the largest and most intelligent branches as to some of the characteristics of the family. I take pleasure, therefore, in giving an extract from a recent letter from Rev. Increase Child of Frewsburgh, Chautauqua county, N. Y.:

I should like to give you some of my impressions in regard to the Child family. I hope, too, you will somewhere in your work endeavor to give some of the more prominent characteristics of our family. I would say that during my early life I was told over and over again that I was not a Child, but a Deake, my *mother's* boy. So that I used to think of the Child family as almost another family. For that reason I have thought that I could think and speak of them somewhat impartially and independently; and I have often taken a foolish pride in trying to do so. As I have grown older, friends have often said to me, "You are getting to be more of a Child than you used to be;" and it seems so to me also. However this may be, I feel a great aversion to being made conspicuous. Sometimes I suffer very much from this feeling. I like to see and hear all that is going on, but give me a quiet seat in the corner. I think this is characteristic of our family. Perhaps our natural love of ease is at the bottom of it. I have heard my father say many times that the Child family were *lazy*. I do not admit *that*, as we commonly use language, but perhaps there is some ground for it, especially if it be true, as old Dr. Wayland used to say, that mankind are as lazy as they *can* be. Of the family, my impressions are derived, first, from my grandfather, Judge Salmon Child and his brothers; and second, from my own observation. My impression is that they are a benevolent, virtuous and intelligent people; not particularly ambitious, loving ease and quiet, but possessed of a considerable degree of latent power, which has never been developed as it should have been. They are a people who love to read and speculate; love their friends, love to have friends and serve them, and are not particularly adapted to the accumulation of property. My impression is that they love order and a good style of things, and are sufficiently conservative to keep them from an extreme radicalism or fanaticism. At the same time they wish to know the reason of things too well to follow a blind orthodoxy; in other words, there is a certain tendency to rationalism. Hence, instead of the old New England orthodoxy, you find Baptists, Methodists and Universalists, even, among them. So far as I know the Child family, they love liberty and have a deep-seated hatred of oppression of every form; a people of quick sympathies and impulsive nature, capable of enjoying much and suffering much. A people who have accomplished much, but who ought to have accomplished much more. Their love of ease and of the pleasures of knowledge and refinement, as well as love of home has often prevented them from achieving what they were capable of.

This estimate accords with my own convictions, derived from my correspondence and personal knowledge of many members of the family.

In a brief recapitulation of some of the characteristics of this family, viz., its robust character, mentally and physically, its general intelligence, its enterprise, its independence in thought and action, its sobriety and industry, its patriotism and philanthropy, and its reverence for divine authority—it will be found that it is a fair inference that these elements aptly constitute the family a valuable factor in rearing the structures of prosperous communities, for which they challenge the respect and confidence of their fellow citizens.

Carlyle says, "the writers of newspapers, pamphlets, books, poems—these are the real working, effective church of a modern country." The compilers of this book feeling the desirability that all persons should be made acquainted with the characters, noble deeds and experiences of their ancestry, and recognizing the fact that such knowledge is not born with a person, but must come by cultivation on these topics, have sought so to embody the results of their explorations and collations, as to make the work as truly instructive and elevating as it can be entertaining, or suitable for mere matter of reference.

The tradition handed down in many branches as we have found, that from three emigrant brothers have sprung all of the name, must be overturned by the record as we find it. A like tradition has been widespread in other families, with no better foundation.

Our pleasant labor is ended; its results you have. That our success will be variously estimated is a matter of course. We deprecate no fair criticism, but crave your acceptance of our honest effort to give a true report of our honest, honorable family (whose nobility is that of the higher nature), in plain ungarnished Anglo-Saxon phrase.

ELIAS CHILD.

Origin and Etymology of the Surname Child.

The name Child. in common with many other modern names. is derived from Hildr of the Norse mythology. The name of this deity can in turn be traced to the rudimental and interchangeable *al. el, il, ol,* the feracious root of many terms and words expressive of holiness, power, and supernatural attributes in all the languages and religions derived from the Aryans. This would include the *Solar* and He*llenic* myths from which the Norse came, and the Jewish Hagiology. *Hild* became synonymous with *Bel* with the Scandinavians, and hence a popular protonym with their be*lligerent* descendants in the early warlike centuries. It also became a V*al*kyrian term for maiden. and a fertile root in the nomenclature of the Norse sagas.

Its dual significance and its descent from mythic to historical times can be traced in that beautiful epic. the Nebelungen Lied. the *Il*iad of the north.

After the "Love breathing Kreim*hild.*" has supplanted the "Flower maiden Bryn*hild*" and immolated her entire family, she is herself taken off by *Hild*ebrand (war sword). [The *etymon* has been *italicized* throughout and quotations made from the saga, to show its constant use.]

> "The King sat at the festive board beside the Queen Bryn*hild*"
> "Who never felt injured pang as when she saw Kreim*hild.*"
>   *   *   *   *   *   *   *   *
> "It happened in those quiet times when good Queen He*lcha* died,
> That Etz*el* ru*l*er of the Huns desiring other bride.
> Was by his friends and courtiers, told of Burgund's widow famed
> For lofty mind and perfect form, Kreim*hild* was she named."

Etz*el* is supposed to have been At*al*a the "Scourge of God." He afterwards, according to Goldsmith, married I*l*dica (beautiful maid). and died on their nuptial night. *Childe* is first used as a title for King in this saga,

> "Doth*il*der the youthful Margravine, now gave her lily hand
> To Gish*el*der, the youngest King of famous Burgund land."

or. as rendered in a more graceful version,

> "This done, with gentle gesture the damsel meek and mild
> By the hand yet trembling. took Gish*el*der the *Childe.*"

C

A son. of Brynhilde. the "Flower maiden." assumed the Burgundian throne in A. D. 466. under the title of Childperic (Battle Empire). His ponderous sword (almost as large as the wonderful Gram or Bahmang of his ancestor. forged by Voland. the Norse Vulcan) was taken from his tomb in the last century. and is now preserved in the Louvre. A brother of Merovens had previously. in A. D. 451. aided by Atila. made himself King of the Ripuarian Franks and taken the title of Childeric (Battle Splendor). He was converted from heathenism by his wife Clothilde. baptized Clochilde. whereupon the Pope bestowed upon him the title of "first Christian King." and "eldest son of the church." which the legitimate kings of France proudly retained. He was succeeded by Childeric. the father of Childebert (Bright Warrior). who became King of the Parigii. Amalric. King of the Visigoths. married Childebert's sister. and was by him assassinated for his cruelty to her.

Gaidoz. in his "French Folk Lore." published in 1878. says that this sister was the heroine of the "Chanson de Clothilde." from which Perrault founded his story of La Barbe Bleue.

Many of the kings of France prefixed Childe to their cognomens, from the fifth to the tenth centuries. after which the title descended to the eldest son. A large number of the kings. queens, and allodial rulers of Europe during this time. derived their appellation from this root. The Goths carried it to Spain. The great Visigothic King Pelayo. named his son Hildefans (Eager in war). but southern tongues refused to pronounce the harsh aspirate. and softened it into Alfonso, a title borne by some scores of kings since. The belligerent monk Hildebrand (war sword) carried his warlike name and sword (literally) to Italy. in the eleventh century. and by the help of the imperial Mathilde, seated himself on the Papal throne. The Tuscans euphonized his Gallic name into Aldovrandino. since borne by the Counts D'Este. While the Goths and Vandals were blending their Norse terms with the Latin and Romance idioms of the south. hordes of Scandinavian and Teutonic adventurers were carrying their sharp swords and aspirated words to the shores of Great Britain. There is no pantographical history of Britain from the egress of the Romans to the ingress of the Teutons, or to the advent of the Norman French. The blurred record of the race-struggles. and the persistence of the fittest. is written in the idiomatic names of their battlefields, bretwalds, and abiding places. The Norse war term *Hild* from the bellicose spirit of the times, became a popular patronym. Doomesday Book[1] (A. D. 1083) registers over three hundred towns, and wapentakes (hundreds) bearing this synonym, with suffices indicating their environments and the tribe that adopted it, as *Childe*wolde, *Child*ness, *Child*thorpe, cote, ton, *Child*han, by, bre, dale, ford, &c., besides many Latin terminations. *Ciltecomb*, now *Childcomb*, near Winchester, had nine churches at the time of the Domesday survey. But like the protographs of the palimsests, these allodial records have been so rewritten, overwritten, overgrown and buried by newer accretions, that most of them are now veiled to all except to the skilled eye of the archæologist. Although four out of the five British authors who wrote before the Conquest, *Gildas*, *Aldhelm*, *Hilda* of Lindisfarne, and *Alcuin*, wore Thor's mark in their names, they were soldiers of the cross only, and wrote but little secular history. Some legends that floated down the stream of time were gathered by the early English writers. ROBERT of Gloucester preserved the legend of "Chylde Waween, King Lothe's son." Lotus was a British king converted to Christianity about A. D. 650. MORGAN, in his *England under the Normans*, p. 135, says that "there are several persons in Domesday book, bearing the surname or title of *Child*, and among them the Kentish *Alnod*, and Godewin, Abbot of Westminster," and that the "great Thanes of Kent, *Child Alnod* and his peers, guarded the king (Eduuard)[2] when he rode into Canterbury." He also says that, "Edmard Child of Domesday Book, had a third part of the Archbishop of York's Church at Wyne in Lancashire;" and SPORLEY says, that "Edunius, called Goduinus Childe, suc-

<hr/>

[1] Domesday or Doomesday Book, a very ancient record, made in the time of William the Conqueror, which is now in the exchequer, in two volumes. The larger contains a survey of all the lands in most of the counties in England, and the less, some counties not at first surveyed. The Book of Domesday was begun by five justices, assigned for that purpose in each county, in the year 1081, and finished in 1086. It was of such authority that the Conqueror himself submitted, in some cases wherein he was concerned, to be governed by it. Camden calls this book the *Tax Book of King William*: and it was further called *Magna Rolla*. There is a third volume, made by order of the same king; and a fourth—an abridgement of the other books."

[2] The dual letter, double u, is used throughout Doomesday Book.

ceeded his cousin Uualnoth as Abbott of Westminster, in 1049," and that "in his time the church of Westminster was pulled down and rebuilt in more splendid style by Eduuard the Confessor," that he was of English descent and called *Alguui* in one of the conqueror's charters and PALGRAVE, that "Uualnothe Childe of Sussex, sometimes called Thane of Sussex, was father of Godunin who went with Canute to Denmark, afterwards the powerful Earl Godwin of Wessex." He married Gytha, *Alf* Jarl's sister, and their daughter Edgytha married Eduuard, who gained the sobriquet of Saint, or Confessor, by abjuring his marital right too continently." HASTED, in his History of Kent, says that *Alnod Cyld* was a younger brother of King Harold, who from the royalty of his kindred, had the addition of *Cild*," and that "one of his manors was given by William the Conqueror to Battle Abbey." KILHAM and others assert that Leuuric Child of Doomesday Book, was Earl Leofric of Mercia and Coventry, the husband of Lady Godiva, whose irresistible charms proved so fatal to poor *Peeping Tom.* Her personal merits are commemorated in song, stone, and statute, and revived yearly by a civic procession in which her *naiveté* is personated *modo et formo.* The term Childe is generally used as a title in Doomesday Book : indeed surnames were almost unknown to Anglo-Saxon England, and were introduced by the Norman French during the last Saxon and first Norman reigns. The French prefix *sur* is a contraction from the Latin *super*, over, and the surname, as it indicates, was not at first written on the line with, but over the Christian name, between the lines, in smaller letters. It is so written over these names in

Cild   Cild   Cild   Cild

Doomesday Book; Eduuinus, Brixi, Leuuinus, Ulft. Ulft held wapentakes in Lincolns'cire, Snottings'cire (Nottingham), and Derbys'cire. This would indicate that in these cases it was used as a *sur,* or over-name. It was used as the equivalent of prince and knight by the earliest writers. NARES says, prince, LOWER, knight, and both that it was a title held by the eldest son of a king or earl, "until he inherited the title of his ancestors or gained new honors by his prowess."

> " And yonder lives the Childe of Elle,
> A young and comely Knight."

Percy's Reliques, 1–109.

"Chylde Rowland to the dark tower came."
Lear iii. 4.
"Chylde Tristam prayed that he might go," &c.
Fairie Queen, vi. 34.

A manuscript by Chaucer, now in the British Museum, quaintly commemorates the legend of "Childe Bristow," who gained his title not by noble descent or prowess in arms, but by devoting his patrimony in restitution of that wrongfully gotten, and in prayers for the redemption of his father's soul from purgatory, after which new riches flowed in upon him: he "First was rich and Sithen bare, and Sithen richer than ever he were."

Byron's fictitious application of the historic *Childe Harold* to his hero, in fact to himself, is a euphemism:

"Childe Harold was he hight; but whence his name
And lineage long, it suits me not to say;
Suffice it that perchance they were of fame,
And had been glorious in another day."

The title, profession, calling, location, or some characteristic of the individual was generally adopted as the surname. As the title Childe became gradually obsolete it was generally adopted as a surname by descendants or dependants. Etymology indicates and former usage requires that the name should be written Childe. If the original or correct spelling is ever generally restored, it will distinguish the name from the noun. The percentage of families of the name, retaining the original final "e," is larger in England than America, while those adding a final "s" is much less. None of the legitimate or higher families in England use the "s." About one in four of the name, graduates of Oxford University since 1856, have used "e" final, while none have added the "s." Of sixty-four of the names in the London Commercial Directory and twenty-six in the Court Directory for 1878, fourteen and seven, respectively, add the final "s." The latter spelling is a solecism, and Childs is a misnomer of modern growth and uncertain origin. Probably it arose from a negligent retention of the apostrophic "s" after the elision of the object and mark of the genitive case, as Childs for Child's (House), Childs broder for Child's brother, and Child's cote (side) appear as names in Doomesday Book

Eadulf Evilchild was made Thane of Northumbria by Edgar, in 971. We gather from the *Camden Publications*, that Walter

Childe was living near Hereford in 1294, and was granted an annuity for life by Bishop Swinefield; that Thomas Childe was tenant of the Priory of St. Mary's, Worcester, in 1304; that Johani Childe lived near Finchdale, Durham, in 1362; and that Lawrence Child was Bishop of St. Asaph's in 1382; "That Thomas Childe presented the judges of Wigorn (Worcester) assizes with a lambe and vi. artichokes valued at 12 pence, in 1601;" that Robert Chylde received a legacy from Sir Robert Cook, Vicar of Hawley, near Bury, Suffolk, in 1587. There are several instances in the early history of England where the name took the French form, L'Enfant. Indeed, although the term undoubtedly came to the Anglo-Saxon through the Frankish form of the Scandinavian, there are indications that it was also brought to Anglo-Norman England in the Latinized French names of the conqueror's followers. In 1350, Roger Baldwin, a descendant of the Bawdwins of the Roll of Battle Abbey married Jane, daughter of Wm. de Wigley by Alice LeChilde, great granddaughter of John L'Enfant, who married Emblema, daughter of Richard Acheley, descendant of William Achilles, named in the Festa de Nevelle of Henry Third's time.

Having traced this Teutonic term from its apotheosis in the Norse mythology through a gradual avatar to a common surname in England and America, we will now trace its further descent and differentiation from a name to a noun, the correlative to parent, and follow it through some of its inflections. There has always been a tendency to appropriate and assimilate titles and words of dignity from the specific to the generic. Such may have been the process whereby Child came to be a generic term for the young of the human species of either sex, and a declinable word. From an Ethnic term for Deity, it became that of supernatural attributes, and descended by divine right to kings: by primogeniture to their eldest sons, by etiquette to other sons, by usage to all sons, and by convenience to all human progeny, regardless of sex. The fact that this term was primarily restricted to males in England, would strengthen this view, if its equivalents in other dialects did not sometimes limit it to females. Some authorities, not very reliable, have asserted that it was so used in Warwickshire. The fact that Shakespeare, in the "Winter's Tale," makes the old shepherd exclaim on finding Perdita, "What have we here?

Mercy on's, a barne, a very pretty barne: a boy or a child,
I wonder?" has not much weight when it is remembered
that the scene of that drama was laid in a foreign country, of
Slavonic origin, filiated with the Teutonic.   If Prof. Caro is
correct in his exhaustive commentary on that drama, recently
published (1878), Shakespeare founded it upon an old Lithu-
rian ballad, brought to England in the fourteenth century.   In
this case he may have followed the original text.   It is more
than probable that the use of the word child, for progeny, came
from an earlier and similar differentiation in the Keltic and
Gothic tongues.   There was an unipersonal blending of the
generative principle inherent in all cosmologies, and especially
those of the sun or nature myths.   The scheme and nomenclature of the northern mythologies was derived from Aryan
roots.

Terms denoting both muliebrity and virility have been derived from those androgynous roots, and applied arbitrarily
and interchangeably by different nations.   The Teutons called
the sun female and the moon male.   _Hild_ was a Norse term
for both hero and maiden : from the latter came Kulla, meaning a maid and a brood, in Danish, and Hilda and Hulda, almost
generic terms for maiden, in English. Cen, cyn, kyn, in cymric
are allied words of kindred meaning.   Some etymologists have
derived child (offspring) from Anglo-Saxon cenned or Danish
kulla, the past participle of kennen, and kullden, to bring forth,
while others trace it to the Gothic kilthei (womb) and Latin
cyma, from the Greek, a sprout or embryo.   However derived,
early English writers use the word freely, and with some inflections rarely used now. WYCLIF uses the phrase "Eve chylded,"
&c., in his translation of the Bible, 1380. CHAUCER uses chylded
and kinded for begotten—"chosen of Joseph whom he took
to wive, unknowing him childed by miracle." DRAYTON
writes,

"Who having in her youth her childing felt the woe,
 Her lord's embraces she never more would know."

ADDISON CHILD.

It may interest some to know that in the various works of Heraldry, in which we have made diligent and exhaustive search for the establishment of the line, the arms, and the name, of which the more prominent are Clark, DeBret, Lodge, and numerous editions of Burke, we have never found the name written with the terminal "*s*." For the curiously inclined we append this list of names in the differing spelling, as culled from these works :

L'Enfant,	Chylde.
Infans,	Chyld,
Le Chylde,	Child,
Le Child,	Child—Villiers.

Hooke—Child,
Child—Pemberton.

Sketches and Incidents of English Families.

Sir John Child of Surat. E. I.; Sir Josiah Child and Sir Francis Child of London. Eng.

These three men were, perhaps, the most noteworthy and distinguished individuals of any bearing the name of Child. They all raised themselves to eminence, occupied prominent positions, both in public and private life, and became the founders of opulent families in the last half of the seventeenth century. The first as a civic and military ruler, the second as a merchant, political economist and philanthropist, and the latter as a banker, goldsmith and sociologist.

They were descendants of a family whose chief was among the first to adopt a surname, and probably assumed his Saxon title (Childe) as such, towards the end of the Saxon domination in England. Following the usage of the higher classes, after the Norman-French conquest, members of the family took the Latinized French form of the name (L'Enfant) for some generations.[1] Several individuals of the name were concerned in Henry Second's conquest of Ireland and its subsequent government in the twelfth century;[2] and others seated themselves at Shrewsbury, Salop county, and Pool-Court, Pennock and Northwick, in the county of Worcester.[3] Baldwin Childe and Robert L'Enfant are mentioned in the Cartulary of St. Nicholas, Essex, and the latter was Provost of Shrewsbury in Henry Third's time, and signed Robert L'Enfant as a witness, and Le Childe to other documents.[4] Richard Le Child was lord of the manor of Northwick in 1320, and was succeeded by his two sons—William Le Childe in 1350, and Thomas Le Childe in 1353, and by his grandson, Thomas Le Childe, who was escheater for the county in 1428. The latter was the progenitor of William

---

[1] Bourne's London Merchants.
[2] Lodge's Peerage of Ireland.
[3] Fuller.
[4] Collectanea Genealogica.

Childe of Northwick, Edmund Childe of the same, and Wm. Child high sheriff of Worcestershire, in 1586, and William Child of Pensax, high sheriff in 1599, and William, lord of the manor of Northwick, in 1634. The sons of the latter, Thomas of Northwick, William and John Child, one' or more of whom, probably the two younger, migrated to the neighborhood of London previous to Charles First's time.[5] They intermarried with the Wheeler family, originally of Wiltshire, but goldsmiths of "The Marygold," Temple Bar, Fleet street, London, in James First's time. A son, Richard Childe, the father of Sir John and Sir Josiah Child of this article, became a merchant of London, trading with the West Indies and the American colonies, and high sheriff of Bedfordshire at the commencement of the long Parliament in 1640.[6] He was the great grandson of the second high sheriff of Queen Bess' time.

There is some diversity in statements regarding the parentage of Sir John Child. Both Collins[7] and Betham[8] state that he was a son of John of London, gentleman, by Frances, daughter of Francis Goodyear of Hereford. Macaulay,[9] Bourne, and later writers say he was a brother of Sir Josiah, whose father was Richard, and as they quote from his contemporaries, White, Carey, Pierce, Butler, Hamilton, Papillion, and the records of the House of Commons, they are most likely to be right. Palfrey[10] speaks of "that astute London merchant, Sir Josiah Child," as the brother of the "factious Dr. Child, whose experience in Massachusetts was not likely to have made his brother friendly to that colony." If they bore this relationship, the subject of this article must have been the Maj. John Child who defended his brother (the Doctor) so ably in the "Jonah cast up in London," 1647, and who subsequently sought a more independent field of action in the infant English colony of the east. Dr. Robert Child was a distinguished graduate of Bennet's College, of the University of Cambridge, and of the most renowned medical school of the world, that of Padua. Italy, from which he received his medical diploma.[11] He came to Boston by the advice of such men as Emanuel Downing, John Winthrop, Jr. and Hugh Peters, with other capitalists, to assist

[5] Bourne's Celebrated London Merchants.   [6] Ibid.
[7] Wotten's Ed. British Baronetage, London, 1741   [8] English Families.
[9] History of England.   [10] His. New Eng.   [11] Winthrop's His. New Eng

in developing the mineral wealth of the new country. He investigated, at that early day, the deposit of black lead in Worcester county, Mass., and of iron at Braintree and Saugus, Mass., and was one of the original proprietors of the iron works at the latter places, the first established in America.

He purchased of Sir Richard Vines, in 1645, the site of Biddeford, Me., and was invested with the Patent, "livery and seisin" of the same, which William Phillips of Boston subsequently acquired.[12] That same year the notable Rev. Hugh Peters wrote Gov. John Winthrop: "Dr. Child is come: that honest man, who will be of exceeding great use, if the country know how to improve him: indeed he is very, very useful. I pray let us not play tricks with such men by our jealousyes."[13] How necessary, but disregarded, this admonition was, subsequent events proved. Having enlarged views, he held that the Charter guaranteed political and religious liberties, that were arbitrarily abridged by the Puritan rulers. His claiming the right of petition, and resorting to it for redress, so roused the ire, hatred and fear of the colonial magistrates, that they not only traduced, amerced, imprisoned and expelled him from the country, but invoked the vengeance of God upon his head, and did not hesitate to ascribe the accidental stumble and injury of a messenger carrying his petition, the burning of a house, and the natural phenomenon of a storm at sea, to his special intervention.[14] John Cotton, in his sermon, compared his petition to a Jonah, and precatorily exhorted passengers by sea, in case they perceived God's special anger rising, to search for the hidden petition, appease Him and exorcise their ship by giving it to the clamorous waves."[15] This they afterwards alleged they piously affected, and "God stilled the troubled waters." They and the All-Seeing were imposed upon, however, by a counterfeit. The *bona fide* Jonah (petition) arrived with them safely in London. These incidents suggested the title to Major John Child's disquisition, "New England's Jonah cast up at London."

Gov. Winthrop says Dr. Child's "hopes and endeavors had been blasted by the special providence of the Lord."[16] He remained in England, but retained the friendship and became

[12] Mass. His. Collections.   [13] *Ibid.*   [14] Strong.
[15] Mass. His. Collections.   [16] His. New Eng.

a valued correspondent of John Winthrop, Jr., imparting to him the developments made in the world of science, to which he henceforth devoted himself.[17]   The names of these two individuals seldom appear in the annals of New England after this, but that of their younger brother, Josiah, is often referred to. Little else is known of Maj. John Child, except that he had command of a regiment in Kent,[18] until he went to India, in 1653, and was subsequently made Governor of Bombay and Calcutta, and commander of all the land and naval forces of England in the East.   The title of "His Excellency" was conferred upon him by Parliament, in 1682,[19] and King James II. made him a baronet as "Sir John Child of Surat," in 1684. He was a powerful coadjutor of his brother, Sir Josiah, executing his imperious instructions with a swift, sure hand.   His enemies asserted that he was grasping and violent, ruling arbitrarily, and that he assumed sovereign powers, declaring war and governing by martial law upon his own responsibility.[20] This his friends justified upon the ground that it required twelve months to transmit instruction from the home government, and while surrounded by powerful and warlike enemies, there were times when there was not a government armed vessel within ten thousand miles.[21]   He was much blamed as all English Colonial Governors have ever been since, under similar circumstances, for becoming at war with the Great Mogul, King Aurengzebe, but history has shown that it was made necessary by the machinations of his political enemies.   All recriminations were ended by his death, in 1691, just after he had signed a protocol of peace.[22]   Later writers say "he had the reputation of being a person of sobriety, wisdom, truth, and courage, esteemed and beloved by all the people of all the nations of the East."[23]   He had two sisters married to members of the East Indian Company at Bombay.[24]   He married Mary, daughter of John Shackston, deputy governor, and had issue—John who died in 1718, and Sir Cæsar, who married Hester, daughter of John Vance of London, goldsmith, by whom he had Sir Cæsar, the father of Sir Cæsar, with whom the baronetcy became extinct, in 1753.[25]

[17] Winthrop's Letters.   [18] Winthrop.   [19] Macaulay.   [20] Pierce Butler.   [21] Macaulay.   [22] Ibid,   [23] Bourne's Great London Merchants.   [24] Burke's Irish Peers.   [25] Ibid.

Sir Josiah Child, born in 1630, younger brother of Governor John Child, and son of the London merchant, Richard Child, succeeded to his father's business. He became the first royal contractor for supplying the naval docks at Portsmouth, England, with ship timber from the coasts of North America. British archives show that government furnished his ships with convoys through the pirate-infested English Channel, and that they awarded him, in 1665, £25 and £33 each for masts, twenty and twenty-five inches in diameter.[26] He also engaged in brewing, and at the death of Timothy Alsop, he succeeded him as brewer to the King. In 1666 Charles II. recommended him to the "Honorable Company of London Brewers," as "having done faithful service in supplying the royal household and navy with beer."[27] But his greatest achievement was in the East. The wealth and importance of the Indies were concressive and concurrent with his own. Thornbury styles him the "eminent political economist, president and formulator of the first East India Company."[28] The two cities which he practically founded, Calcutta and Bombay, aggregate more inhabitants to-day than the prefounded cities of New York and Boston. "Sir George Gough attributes his wealth and elevation to having had while young the advice of the great Sir Josiah Child."[29] But his sound judgment, liberal views, commercial enterprise and personal patronage were not unrecognized in the Western Hemisphere. William Vaughn, a wealthy merchant of Portsmouth, N. H., when unjustly imprisoned by Governor Cranfield, in writing his friend, William Weare, who had escaped to London says: "I send you a letter to my master, Sir Josiah Child; wait on him while he reads it, and attend to his directions, if God moves his heart to do aught for us."[30]

Palfrey says: "Sir Josiah was not an acknowledged nonconformist, but had always upheld religious liberty, and was a judicious counselor for the colonies;" that "he was one of that class of active and important traders whose stubborn character and whose heavy purse had for fifty years prolonged the doubtful conflict,"[31] meaning that waged between the colony

[26]Green's Callender State Papers.   [27]Bourne.
[28]Old London and New.   [29]Wotten's English Baronets.
[30]Bouton's Provincial Papers of N. H. [31]History New England.

and the home government.   He questioned the expediency of enacting the Navigation Act, which required all British colonies to confine their commerce to the ships and ports of the mother country, and which proved so obnoxious to the colonies;[32] and doubted whether the inconvenience it brought with it be not greater than the convenience;[33] but he upheld its principles, and urged that a "country was better off without, than with, a colony competing with home interests."[34]   In his "New Descource on Trade" he compared the colonies of the Round Heads in New England with those of the Cavaliers in Virginia and Antigua, and showed the superiority of the first, and warned his countrymen "that New England was the most prejudicial plantation to the kingdom, for the reason of its competition in articles produced in England, its capacity for building ships and raising seamen, and consequent growing naval strength, and because of its comparative freedom from negro slavery."[35]

Sir Josiah was the first to perceive and warn his government of the correlation between the stubborn bigotry, self-will and obstinacy of the Puritan character and the event that climaxed at Bunker Hill a century afterwards, in religious, commercial and political independence.   Sir Josiah's national sympathies were always with the New England colonies and unaffected by the narrow bigotry and petty tyrannies of their rulers; but his large grasp of commercial polity made him cosmopolitan, and when the colonies differentiated their interests from those of the mother country his patriotism led him to uphold the latter. Thornbury[36] states that Sir Josiah was once a partner—and others, that he was a brother—of Sir Francis Child, founder of the banking firm of Child & Co., but T. G. H. Price,[37] a present member of that firm, who has access to their early books, says that both these statements are incorrect, but that he was closely related to him through his father, and also through the Wheelers.   He was born May 7, 1630,[38] and must, with all his other enterprises, have become interested in oriental trade early in life.   Tyndal says that "He applied himself chiefly to the East India trade, which, by his management, was

[32] Palfrey's Hist. New England.   [35] New Discourse on Trade.
[34] Ibid.   [35] Ibid.   [36] Old London and New.
[37] London and Middlesex Archæ. Soc. 1875.
[38] Morant's Hist. and Antiquity of Essex.

raised so high that it drew much envy and jealousy upon himself and the company." The shares in the East India Company advanced during his presidency from £70 in 1664, to £370 in 1691. Macaulay[39] says: "There was one great man pointed out on the Royal Exchange, as having by judicious or lucky purchases of stock, created in no long time, an estate of twenty thousand a year. This commercial grandee, who in wealth and in the influence that attend wealth, vied with the greatest nobles of his time, was Sir Josiah Child." He was by far the richest member of the East India Company, with one-third of its stock on his own hands and that of his dependents." Bourne[41] says: "From the time of Charles Second's accession Sir Josiah became a favorite at Court, doing his share of money lending to the spendthrift king, and gaining esteem by the honest deporment, which even the most dishonest well knew how to appreciate." Macaulay devotes many pages to him in his History of England, Vol. IV., pp. 108 to 119, describing his immense wealth, superior talent, great force of character and potency in controlling not only his associates, but "opposing majorities in Parliament, kings, queens, and the powers of the East." Sir Josiah had always been a whig, and won the special hatred of the Duke of York by his tolerant spirit and bold defence of schismatics : but on the dissolution of the Oxford Parliament he separated from his old friends and formed a close alliance with the tories. "When the Court was all powerful in the state, he became all powerful at the Court."

He distributed his wealth with a judicious prodigality. Charles II. accepted a present of 10,000 guineas and his brother, the Duke of York, a like sum of 10,000 guineas, and readily became a stockholder in his company. "All who could help or hurt at Court, ministers, mistresses, priests, were kept in good humor by presents of shawls and silks, bird's nests and attar of roses, purses of diamonds and bags of guineas."[42] Very soon, however, all was changed, the revolution of '88 brought in a whig government : the connections that had been his boasts were now its weakness. The king was in exile, the judge who had decreed his doings legitimate was a prisoner, the great whig merchants whom he had expelled from the direction

[39] History of England.
[41] Celebrated London Merchants.
[4] Peirce Butler's Tale, 1680
[42] Macaulay's Hist. of Eng.

of the company demanded justice and vengeance."[13] But his indomitable courage and persistent will quailed not, and prevailed. He began with William and Mary, and his enemies reported that he gave the leaders in Parliment 100,000 pounds sterling to stave off the repeal of the charter of his company. These political opponents accused both himself and his brother, Sir John, Governor of the East Indies, of the most frightful atrocities, usurpations and ponderous briberies in the administrations of the company's affairs. Scores of volumes of speeches, letters and essays upon the exciting subject were printed and read. During all this the most exalted families in the realm were seeking alliance with his, and William III. conferred a baronetcy on his son Josiah."[14] His powerful enemies went so far as to demand his dismissal forever from the direction of the company, and reported that the Great Mogul had made a like degradation of his brother, Sir John, a condition of peace. But before any action was taken death relieved the latter, leaving Sir Josiah to climb successfully the excelsior heights of his ambition alone.

He seems to have been the best hated man of his day. But after the political animosities of the day had been assuaged by time, and all jealousy and envy put to rest by his death, most authorities agree in characterizing him as a man of great probity and enlightened views. Macaulay[15] says that his success in accumulating great wealth and in forwarding the interests of the company of which he was the head, made him somewhat haughty and imperious, and gave color to some of the envious charges brought against him by his enemies: but that all conceded "that with all his love of money making his main object was to establish the sovereignty of England in the East: and to him, more than any other man is this due."[16] Even at that early day he was assiduous in urging the Japanese ambassadors, then in London, to open the trade of their country to England. Tyndal says that "he had a compass of knowledge and apprehension unusual to men of his profession." His "Observations Concerning Trade and Interest on Money," written at his country seat, Wanstead, during a leisure forced upon him by the prevalence of the great plague of 1665, contain ideas far in advance of his day and generation. At that

[13] Butler's Tale.   [14] Burke.   [15] History of England.   [16] Ibid

time the commerce of England was in the hands of the opulent
Netherlanders. He gave fifteen reasons why his countrymen
should imitate their policy, the soundness of which the course
of trade since has proven.   Only the most advanced commercial nations have yet arrived at the truth of the ideas he evolved
on the use and interest of money.   He wrote an Essay on the
best practical methods of elevating the lower classes of London,
and did much personally to ameliorate their condition.   He
was a patron and large benefactor of Christ Hospital.   The advanced thoughts which he put forth were combatted by the
conservatives of the day, especially those on the science of
money, in a paper war that continued long after his death.

Evelyn's[47] assertion "that there were those who remembered
him as a merchant's apprentice, sweeping out one of the count-
ing-houses of the city," was probably true, but that implied no
menial service, for in those days every young aspirant for commercial eminence, had to begin at the bottom round and mount
the ladder through a regular apprenticeship, however well born.
While looking after his royal contracts for shiptimber at Portsmouth, England, in early life, he met with and married Anne
Boul[48] of that city, by whom he had two sons who died young,
and one daughter who "nobly wedded."   He married second
Mary Atwood of Hackney, by whom he had a son, baroneted
as Sir Josiah Child by William III., 1692, who died without
issue, in 1704, and two daughters, who also "nobly wedded."
He took for his third wife Emma, daughter of Sir Henry Bernard, and had by her Bernard Child, who died in 1698, and
Sir Richard Child, made Baron of Newton and Viscount Cas-
tlemaine in 1718, and Earl Tylney in 1732.   Sir Richard mar-
ried Dorothy, daughter of John Glynne, and granddaughter of
Francis Tylney of Rotherwick, and added Tylney to his name.
He had Richard, first Earl Tylney, and John, second Earl Tyl-
ney, both of whom died childless, and a daughter Emma, who
married Sir Robert Long of Dracott, and had Sir James Tylney
Long, who died without issue, and Catherine, who married
"William the Worthless," Viscount Wellesley, fifth Earl of
Mornington, who assumed the name Tylney Long.   His son,
William Richard Arthur Pole Tylney Long Wellesley, sixth

47 Evelyn's Diary.   48 Macaulay's Hist. and Antiq. of Essex.

Earl of Wellsley, "ended the richest merchant family of the seventeenth century."

The first Sir Josiah's third wife. Emma, survived her husband twenty-six years. dying in 1725. "at which time she was so nearly allied to so many of the prime nobility, that eleven dukes and duchesses used to ask her blessing, and above fifty great families went into mourning for her." [50]

Soon after his first marriage Sir Josiah purchased Wanstead House, where eighty years before the Earl of Leicester entertained most devotedly his royal mistress, Queen Elizabeth. [51] Here the great merchant "expended immense sums in excavating fish ponds and in planting whole square miles of barren land with walnut trees." [52]   He was made a baronet by Charles II. in 1678, and died at Wanstead, in 1699.

While Sir Josiah was acquiring distinction in unfolding the maxims and laying the foundations of modern commerce, successfully contending with and controlling whig cabals and tory cabinets, amassing wealth, with his hand on the rudder of his fortune ten thousand miles away, his cousin. Sir Francis Child, was gaining a like distinction by initiating, and opulency by practicing, the system of modern banking.

Descending from the same ancient stock. his immediate progenitors seated themselves at Heddington. Wiltshire, from whence Francis migrated to London, in Charles First's reign. [53] He was apprenticed to a goldsmith's firm whose business had been conducted by his relatives, the Wheelers, at the sign of " Yᵉ Marrigold, Temple Bar, No. 1 Fleet street," from time immemorial.   Francis [54] says "the books of Child & Co. go back to 1620, and refer to previous documents."   He married his cousin Elizabeth, only daughter and heiress of his uncle, the second William Wheeler, [55] of the firm of which he and his descendants subsequently became the head.

Previous to the introduction and manufacture of fictile wares in Europe, in the eighteenth century, the lower classes used wooden, the middle pewter, and the higher classes and nobility used services of gold and silver: articles of the latter for the

[49] Bourne's Celebrated London Merchants.   [50] *Ibid.*
[51] Morant's Hist. and Antiq. of Essex.   [52] Macaulay.
[53] Price's London and Middlesex Archæological Society, 187.
[54] History of Bank of England.   [55] Evelyn's Diary.

toilet and table, costing pounds where the same in porcelain cost shillings now. This made the goldsmith's craft an important and lucrative one. Formerly the nobility and wealthy classes kept their money and valuables in "cash boxes," in their castles and domiciles, but as their wealth increased and their armed retainers decreased, this became unsafe. They then used the mint in the Tower of London as a safe deposit. But Charles I. perfidiously seized and confiscated all those deposits. They then made the rich goldsmiths their custodians. This led the latter to keeping "running cashes" and to making interest bearing loans to tradespeople, and others, on pawns or pledges, thus adding incipient banking to their craft. Child & Co. are inserted in the little London Directory for 1677, as "goldsmiths keeping running cashes." They were the first to separate the two callings. Francis[56] states "that the celebrity of the first banking-house belongs by common consent to Mr. Francis Child." There is an account on their ledgers opened in 1669, before they divorced the two vocations, under the head of "Pawns," changed a few years later to "P," which has been brought forward from ledger to ledger under this title as their collateral loan account, for two hundred and ten years.

The record of this family of bankers is so interwoven, warp and woof, with that of Temple Bar, the Marygold and their environs, that any narrative of either, without frequent reference to the others would be perfunctory indeed. Many of their customers addressed their cheques to "Mr. Alderman Child and partner, at ye Marygold, next door to Temple Bar;" sometimes "next door to the Devil Taverne." When the heads of the firm were lord mayors of London, the Earl of Oxford addressed his cheques "To the Worshipful the Lord Mayor & Co., at Temple Bar."[57] Like most of the distinctive appellations of the goldsmiths of London, the sign of the Marygold originated in that of a tavern. It was the usage for succeeding occupants to retain the sign, without reference to the vocation. "Messrs. Child's banking house was in King James First's reign, a public ordinary, the sign being the Marygold."[58] When it came into the occupation of the goldsmiths is not definitely known, but probably about 1620, as the last mention of it as a public house was on St. Thomas' day, December 21, 1619,

[56] History Bank of England.   [57] Price.   [58] Beaufoy's Tokens.

D

when it was presented to the ward-mote "for disturbing its next neighbors late in the nights, from time to time, by ill disorders."[59] The goldsmiths held it on a ground rent. Sir Francis Child put the present front to the Marygold in 1666, the year of the great fire of London, although the conflagration did not reach it. An old document, still extant, shows that Sir Francis *renewed* his lease of the Marygold from the "Feast of St. Michael the archangel, 1707, and the Sugar Loaf and Green Lettuce, 1714, at a yearly rental of £60 for sixty-one years." The Sugar Loaf was an old London tavern, directly in the rear of the Marygold. Sir Francis repaired it in 1707 and added it to his banking premises. He subsequently purchased for £2,800 the famous tavern popularly called the "Old Devil" from its sign. "St. Dunstan pulling the Devil's nose," which adjoined, and erected a block of houses now known as "Child's Place."[60] The "Old Devil" was the favorite resort of Ben Jonson, where he lorded it over his confrères that were "sealed of the tribe of Ben." Here he sometimes met Shakespeare. He wrote "Drink to me with thine eyes," &c., at this famous resort. Child & Co. have with characteristic conservativeness preserved many very interesting relics of these three historical houses. They have the original sign of the Marygold and Sun, made of oak, stained green, with gilt border, with the motto "*Ainsi mon ame*," now put up over the door between the front and back office, and retain it on the water-mark of their cheques, &c.

The old passageways of the Sugar Loaf, with their wooden hat pegs, the old dining rooms, kitchens and larders, with their wooden meat hooks, are preserved as they were two and three centuries ago. In one of the rooms over the old kitchen may be seen the bust of Apollo, and the tablet on which the lines of welcome to the Apollo Room, by Ben Jonson, are engraved in gold letters.[61] Those were on the chimney piece of the great room. When Sir Christopher Wren rebuilt Temple Bar, in 1666, Child & Co. rented the chambers over the arcade adjoining their premises, of the city of London, at a yearly rental of £20, which they used as a sort of muniment room for the safe keeping of their old papers and books of accounts, until the excavations for the foundations of the new Inner Courts of Law, in 1875, caused Temple Bar to settle so much that, in

[59] Beaufoy.   [60] Price.   [61] See Tatler, No. 79.

1877, the city gave them notice to vacate on "next midsummer's day;"[62] what a notice to give and receive: a notice to quit forever premises filled with the familiar associations and the daily records of one's ancestors for centuries! The widening of Fleet street demanded for public convenience the demolition of the time-honored banking house, and the erection of another, one door east, covering the site of Child's place, anciently that of the "Old Devil," to which the firm moved on next bank holiday, April 15, 1879.[63] They are still on ancestral ground. Among the many interesting pre-Elizabethan relics found in excavating the foundations of Sugar Loaf and the Old Devil taverns, in 1878, the most curious is an ancient flagon, filled with a ruby wine, intact, the glass of which has been oxidized into iridescent colors by contact with the earth for centuries.

During a larger part of their tenancy the heads or quarters of those who suffered for political offences were exposed upon Temple Bar, directly opposite the windows of the bank. It sometimes happened that the bankers were obliged to look daily upon the ghastly features of a former friend and client for long years after the procurator of the crown had covered in to the public treasury the forfeited balances of their accounts. Dickens[64] characteristically described Child & Co. under the pseudonym of Tellson & Co., as they were in the days of the French revolution. Up to that time crimes against property, theft, forgery, false coining, the unauthorized opening of a letter, were punished by death. He says "that their bank had taken so many lives in its day, that if the heads laid low by it had been ranged on Temple Bar, they would probably have excluded what little light the ground floor had in a rather significant manner." He hardly exaggerates when he says: "The house was founded a hundred and fifty years previously," or caricatures in saying, "their bank by Temple Bar was an old-fashioned place, even in the year one thousand seven hundred and eighty. It was very small, very dark, very ugly, very incommodious. It was an old-fashioned place, moreover in the moral attribute that the partners in the house were proud of smallness, proud of its darkness, proud of its ugliness, proud of its incommodiousness. They were even boastful of its emi-

[62] *London Times*, February 22, 1877.
[63] *London Telegraph*, January 28, 1879.   [64] *Tales of Two Cities*.

nence in those particulars, and were fired by an express conviction that if it were less objectionable, it would be less respectable. This was no passive belief, but an active weapon
which they flashed at more convenient places of business.
Tellson's (they said) wanted no elbow-room, Tellson's wanted
no light, Tellson's wanted no embellishment. Noakes and Co.'s
might, or Snooks Bros. might; but Tellson's, thank Heaven!—

" Any one of these partners would have disinherited his son
on the question of rebuilding Tellson's. In this respect the
house was much on a par with the Country; which did very
often disinherit its sons for suggesting improvements in laws
and customs that had long been highly objectionable, but were
only the more respectable.

" Thus it had come to pass, that Tellson's was the triumphant
perfection of inconvenience. After bursting open a door of
idiotic obstinacy with a weak rattle in its throat, you fell into
Tellson's down two steps, and came to your senses in a miserable little shop, with two little counters, where the oldest of
men made your check shake as if the wind rustled it, while
they examined the signature by the dingiest of windows, which
were always under a shower-bath of mud from Fleet street,
and which were made the dingier by their own iron bars proper,
and the heavy shadow of Temple Bar. If your business necessitated your seeing 'the House,' you were put into a species
of Condemned Hold at the back, where you meditated on a
misspent life, until the House came with its hands in its pockets, and you could hardly blink at it in the dismal twilight.
Your money came out of, or went into, wormy old wooden
drawers, particles of which flew up your nose and down your
throat when they were opened and shut. Your bank notes
had a musty odor, as if they were fast decomposing into rags
again. Your plate was stowed away among the neighboring
cesspools, and evil communications corrupted its good polish
in a day or two. Your deeds got into extemporized strong
rooms made of kitchens and sculleries, and fretted all the fat
out of their parchments into the banking house air. Your
lighter boxes of family papers went up stairs into a Barmecide
room, that always had a great dining table in it and never had
a dinner, and where, even in the year one thousand seven hundred and eighty, the first letters written to you by your old

love, or by your little children, were but newly released from
the horror of being ogled through the windows, by the heads
exposed on Temple Bar with an insensate brutality and ferocity
worthy of Abyssinia or Ashantee.

"Cramped in all kinds of dim cupboards and hatches at
Tellson's, the oldest of men carried on the business gravely.
When they took a young man into Tellson's London House
they hid him somewhere till he was old. They kept him in a
dark place, like a cheese, until he had the full Tellson flavor
and blue-mould upon him. Then only was he permitted to
be seen, spectacularly poring over large books, and casting his
breeches and gaiters into the general weight of the establishment."

Child & Co. had a branch house in Paris, with the accounts
of the noblesse which were transferred to London during the
revolution, together with their valuables, to be used to eke out
a miserable existence, or to to be settled *sans compté rendu par
Les États exécutifs*, the guillotine.

The Marygold became the headquarters of the *Émigrés* during
the reign of terror, and its secret couriers were constantly passing between the two cities. So great was the crowd anxious to
get the latest news from Paris, that bulletins were posted in its
windows giving the names of the daily victims of the guillotine.

The banking firm retain many old time usages, probably inherited from their ancestors, the goldsmiths. They call their
front office "the shop," and that in the rear, where the ledgers
are kept, "the counting house," where they "cast up the shop"
once a year. Use cheques written (never printed) on paper bearing their trade-mark, the Marygold, in its water mark. They
adhere to the good old fashioned rule now too little practiced,
of advancing their clerks by seniority and merit, and eventu-
ally admitting them as partners.

The firm has usually consisted of a head and five or six active partners, restricted, as a rule, to one of a family at a time,
but open to hereditary succession, other things being equal. A
member of the Child family has always succeeded to the first
position, and the gaps made by time among other partners have
been filled from the well seasoned stock of head clerks, selected
in the sapling and carefully bred in the soil favorable to the

best growth.   This selection and survival of the fittest, together
with inherited conservativeness, seems to have been favorable
to longevity.   Eight head partners of four generations, presided
from 1663 to 1867.   The last was of the fourth from the first
Sir Francis Child, while he was of the sixth generation from
his contemporary, Vere Fane, third Earl of Westmoreland, who
opened an account with their bank in 1678.   During these two
centuries there were about fifty active partners, with an average
tenure of about thirty years, and nearly as many more as clerks.
There were three John Wormalds, father, son and grandson,
partners in the firm collectively eighty-nine years, and clerks
ninety-four years.   The last died in 1874, having been taken
ill on the sixtieth anniversary of the day he began his apprenticeship.   Ralph and George Addison averaged about the same
time as partners, and Robert Dent was a partner forty-three
years.

The exceptional prosperity and continuity of this banking
firm is largely due to the wisdom and forethought with which
the first Sir Francis Child laid its broad foundations.   The con-
sensus that he evolved and the remarkable clauses that he inserted in his will, together with their innate conservativeness,
have enabled his descendants to conduct a large and increasing
business successfully through the perturbations of two centuries
and more.   This is probably an unique instance of a vocation
having descended from one generation to the next, without a
consanguinal break, in the same building, for more than two
hundred years !

> " Within that time how many an empire hoar
> And young republic flushed with wealth and war
> Alike hath changed the ermine for the shroud."

The first Sir Francis Child was a careful, shrewd man of
affairs, conservative in many things, but the originator of many
of the maxims and forms of modern banking.   That he was a
man of little political or religious bias, is shown by his popularity with men differing widely on these subjects.   His old
ledgers show that he had the accounts of Oliver Cromwell,
Charles II., his queen, his mother, his ministers, his mistresses,
his natural sons, the Dukes of Richmond and Monmouth, his
brother, James II., William and Mary, and the leading men of
their several reigns.   The Middlesex and London Archæologi-

cal Society published a list, in 1875, of some scores of noblemen and leading men who opened accounts with his bank previous to 1700, whose descendants are still keeping their bank accounts there. Among the many valuable autographs and relics preserved in the bank is a cheque drawn by the Duke of Bolton to the order of, and endorsed by the notorious Titus Oats; one signed "Ellen $\overset{\text{her}}{\times}$ Gwin," a bond signed by four dukes and earls agreeing to pay her indebtedness $\overset{\text{mark}}{}$ to the firm, by overdrawing her account £6,000, after deducting her plate, 14,400 ounces turned in; Dr. Hurrell's receipt "in full for all remedies and medicines delivered to Miss Ellen Gwin, deceased," dated 1699, twelve years after her exit; a cheque for £200, payable "upon producing and delivering to them, the King's pardon to James Hooper for high treason;" an autograph note of the Duke of Leeds, dated 1694, praying "his very good friend, Sir Francis Child, goldsmith, neare Temple Bar," "to subscribe foure thousand pounds for mee to the stock of the Bank of England," then forming; a school receipt dated 1685, for £2.18.5 tuition for his sons Robert and John at a private school, which small sum includes their books, "a Cato and Corderius, a Horace, a Livy, a Cornelius Nepos, and a French master;" another for £2.5.10 for John, including the above and "dinners for ten weeks less five holidays."   His son James' bill for 1702, including "books, light, fire, coach hire, pocket money, gloves, mending clothes, cutting hair, tuition, pole money, and full board for six months" was £12.2.6; another, including all the above and "the board and expenses of a private tutor, writing, French and dancing masters, powder, oyl and church dues," £23.16.8.

There is a spirited caricature by Hogarth, extant, of the Duchess of Marlboro' as she appeared at the bank, Temple Bar, followed by porters carrying the most remarkable articles of silver and gold plate which she had hastily collected, on hearing of a threatened run on Child's bank, to tide them over.   During a panic in 1663, Pepys[a] says: "I cannot have my two hundred pieces of gold again for silver, all being bought up last night that were to be had, and sold for twenty-four and twenty-five shillings, so I must keep my silver by me."   Forgetting that similar acts had brought the "grey crowned head" of his father

[a] Pepys' Diary.

to the block, Charles II. treacherously closed the exchequer in 1672, entailing ruin, bankruptcy and want upon all classes, especially the goldsmiths, who had large amounts deposited there, and among them Alderman Backwell, of "the Grasshopper," Lombard street, to whom the Crown owed £296,000. After great distress, the King issued six per cent. annuity bonds to Backwell and others, but repudiated them before any interest was paid, and Backwell died in prison. After many years, William III. reinstated those debts which Charles' prodigality had caused, and this was the beginning of the present public debt of England. A late number of the *British Review* naively remarks, that "Barbara Villiers was the foundation of this public debt."

After Alderman Backwell's failure, his son married a daughter of Sir Francis Child, and became a partner in that bank, taking his books and valuable accounts with him, many of which are still on their books. "Sir Francis acted as messenger and banker of the lottery of Prince Rupert's jewels, valued at £20,000, at which the King himself took part, counting out the tickets among the lords and ladies." [66] There was much jealousy and rivalry between Child & Co. and the Bank of England. Previous to the establishment of the latter, the former had found it popular and lucrative to issue notes of circulation, which privilege the bank's charter took from them, within sixty-five miles of London. They then put their certificates of deposit into circulation, which soon commanded a premium, while the notes of the bank were at a discount. Stung by this, and to retaliate, the bank secretly bought up a large amount of their certificates, hoping to break Child & Co. by presenting them all at once. Hearing of this, the latter applied to their sure friend, the Duchess of Marlboro', who loaned them £700,000 in a single cheque on the Bank of England. Holding this until the certificates were presented, a preconcerted signal caused a clerk to draw the bills for it, and return with them long before the cool headed banker had summed up the total of the certificates, when he paid them off with the bills. He was able to buy them the next day (to pay the Duchess back), at a large discount. [67] Some time after this, Sir Francis attempted to break the bank, by refusing publicly to receive its notes: not succeed-

[66] *London Gazette*, Dec. 3, 1683.   [67] Francis' Hist. Bank of England.

ing in this, he essayed to effect it by their own device, quietly collecting £100,000 of their bills and demanding their redemption; they tided over this by paying out only sixpences, miscounting, and keeping their counters thronged by their own servants, who returned the silver privately to the bank after drawing it.

Sir Francis was arraigned in parliament, of which he was then a member, for injuring the government and helping its enemies, by trying to break the Bank of England.[68]   He carried it off with a high hand, saying every "tub must stand on its own bottom," or fall.   This rivalry and warfare was kept up for half a century, and long after the first and second Sir Francis were dead.   In the year (1745) that the Stewarts made their last, most brilliant, and almost successful attempt to recover the crown of their ancestor, under the guidance of the youthful and comely Charles Edward, the notes of the Bank of England were at a fearful discount.   "The directors, alarmed at the great depreciation of their paper, and attributing it to the high estimation in which the house of Child & Co. still remained, attempted, by very unfair artifices, to ruin their reputation.[69]   But like that of the Pretender, the assault ended in strengthening the assailed.   Smiles[70] says that when the Duke of Bridgewater became embarrassed in the construction of his great canal, in 1760, "taking the road to the city on horseback, attended only by his groom, to try what could be done with his London bankers, Child & Co., Temple Bar, then the principal banking house in the metropolis, as it is the oldest, and where most of the aristocratic families kept their accounts."   He effected a loan on hypothecating the revenues of the canal, that enabled him to complete it.

The first Sir Francis Child was a man of great executive ability, public spirit, and benevolence.   Besides conducting his business through four rather panicy reigns, with much sagacity and success, discounting revolutions, holding the "sinews" and patronage of whig or tory alike, he held respectively the offices of alderman, high sheriff, colonel of the honorable artillery company,[71] and lord mayor of London.[72]   He represented the city in Queen Anne's first parliament,[73] and was president and

[68] Francis' Hist. of Bank of England.   [69] Ibid.
[70] Lives of the Engineers.   [71] Highmore.   [72] I. B. Firth.
[73] Falkner's Hist. Falkner, &c.

a large benefactor of Christ's Hospital, rebuilding the ward over the east cloisters," which bears a marble tablet inscribed "Anno. 1705. This ward was rebuilt at the sole charge of Sir Francis Child. Knt., some time lord mayor, and now president of this house." [75] Full length portraits of Sir Francis, and his son Sir Francis, who was also president of the institution and lord mayor of London, adorn the centre of the great hall, opposite to the fine portrait of its founder, Edward VI. [76]

Sir Francis purchased the magnificent estate, Osterly House, in 1711, but died, two years later, without occupying it, in a mansion which he built, called East End House. The "Beauties of England and Wales" has a fine view of Osterly House. Sir Francis had three brothers: Daniel, who lived with him, at Parson's Green: Edward, who lived at Burghley, and John, at Devizes, and twelve sons and three daughters. Sir Robert, Sir Francis and Sir Samuel succeeded their father *puri-passu* as heads of the banking house. Stephen Child founded a separate banking house previous to 1713, under the name of Stephen Child & Co., which has been doing business ever since at the "Crown," near Pope's Head Alley, under varying titles, but as Willis, Percival & Co. for several generations, and has had dealings and an open account with Child & Co. for one hundred and sixty-six years, as shown by their books." [77] John was a clerk in his father's bank, where the following undertaker's bill is still preserved: "For the burial of John Child of the Marygold, Esq., in the vault of the Temple Church, February, 1702," total, £6.10.00 of which the principal items are "for candles for the church, £0.2.6;" "for the six bearers in gowns, £2.0.0." George was in holy orders; Thomas a merchant; James and William died early, and were buried in Falham churchyard, with their father and sister Martha, who married A. Collins; Jane died young, and Elizabeth married Tyrringham Backwell, who became a partner in Child's bank, as did his two sons, Barnaby and William; what became of Leonard and the other two sons, is not known.

The eldest son, Robert, as has been said, succeeded his father as head of the firm: he was also alderman, and colonel of the honorable artillery company, and was one of the four citizens knighted by George I. on his accession, in 1714, in compliment

74 Trollop's Hist. Christ's Hospital.   75 *Ibid.*
76 Allen's Hist. of London.   77 Price.

to the city of London," yet he paid, according to his cash book
of 25th September, " £86.11.6 for the honor of knighthood."
He was the first of the family who resided at Osterly, where he
died without issue, in 1721, and where his portrait, by Michael
Dahl, can be seen. His next brother, Francis, alderman 1721,
high sheriff 1722, lord mayor and baronet 1732, president
Christ Hospital, or "blue coat school" 1727–1740; member of
parliament for the city, and director in the East India Company,
lived at Osterly, to which he added Northall, in 1726, at a cost
of £19,501, and died there, in 1740. Full length portraits of
himself and his father, both in the robes of lord mayor, may be
seen there."

He was succeeded as head of the bank and at Osterley by
his younger brother, Sir Samuel Child, baronet and member
of parliament. He lived in Lincoln's Inn Field, and married
Miss Agatha Edgar, by whom he had two sons, Francis and
Robert, and a daughter. There is a beautiful group of these
three children at Osterley, by Dandridge, and also of Sir Samuel and Lady Child, by I. Vanderbank. Sir Samuel was succeeded as head of the firm at his death, in 1752, by his widow,
Mrs. Agatha Child, until her decease in 1763, when her eldest
son, Francis, took her place. He, however, died the same year,
leaving two of his partners, Devon and Lovelace, £20,000 each,
and £20 each to their seven clerks for mourning. It is remarkable that, under the good old rule of the house, all these seven
clerks became partners in the firm within the next twenty-seven
years, the youngest reaching that goal in 1790. Francis Child
was a man of cultivated taste and refined discrimination. He
expended large sums in rebuilding Osterley House in 1760,[50]
preserving the ancient ground plan generally, but covering the
square court in front by a spacious portico, and changing Osterley chapel, where the beautiful Anne Waller was married to
Sir Philip Harcourt, in 1661, into the present servants' hall."
He purchased a fine painting, by Rubens, in Holland; which
ornaments the grand staircase; subject, "The Apotheosis of
William I., Prince of Orange."

Osterley Manor, according to Lyson, was a fine old place in
Edward First's reign, in the thirteenth century. Having be-

---

[38] Allen's Hist. of London.
[50] Lyson's Environs of London.
[54] Lyson.
[51] Lyson.

longed to the convents of Sheen and of Sion, it reverted to the
Crown on the suppression of the monasteries, and was granted
successively to the Marquis of Exeter and the Duke of Somerset, and was forfeited by both on their attainders.[2] Coming into
the possession of Sir Thomas Gresham, the founder of the Royal
Exchange, he enclosed the park, rebuilt the Manor House, and
entertained Queen Elizabeth there in 1578 most sumptuously.
The Queen having remarked that the great court "would look
handsomer if divided by a wall in the centre," Sir Thomas, when
the Queen retired for the night, procured workmen from London and had the wall built before she rose in the morning."[3]
Result, a pun, that it was "no wonder that a man who could
build a 'Change could change a building." [4] Like unto "rain
water sherry," one wonders how such a weak pun could have
been preserved so long.

Osterley House stands in the centre of a fine park of three
hundred and fifty acres. It is 140 by 117 feet.   "The interior,
which is fitted up with great taste and magnificence, was finished by Robert Child, who succeeded to his brother Francis'
estates in 1763." [5]   The most remarkable of the rooms are a
noble gallery, 130 feet in height, (sic) containing a good collection of pictures by the old masters, and some valuable portraits,
"The state bedroom, very magnificently furnished, and a dining room hung with beautiful tapestry, procured at a great expense from the Gobelins manufactory in 1775." [6]   "The library
contains a large and most valuable collection of books, of which
there is a printed catalogue, drawn up by Dr. Morell, in 1771."

Robert Child succeeded his brother as head of the firm, and
amassed the largest private fortune of the eighteenth century.
He sold his house in Lincoln's Inn Field, and purchased that
of the Duke of Manchester, in Berkley square, in 1767, for
£10,500. This is still the town residence of the family. With
all his magnificent expenditures, he was a close, penurious man.
He once asked Sheridan, who lived neighbor at Osterley, to
write him a sermon. He took for his text, "A Rich Man,"
and described his neighbor's (the banker's) characteristic foibles
so accurately, that it was patent to every one whom the subject
of the discourse was intended for. He married Sarah, daughter

[2] Lyson.   [3] Wolton's English Baronets.   [4] *Ibid.*
                [5] Lyson.   [6] *Ibid.*

of Gilbert and Mary (Craddock) Jodrell, of Ankerwicke Priory.[57] (This Priory, on the banks of the Thames, was the refuge of King John the night before he was compelled to sign Magna-Charta of Runnymede.) Their only child, Sarah Anne, eloped from her father's house in Berkley square on the night of the 17th January, 1782, with John Fane, tenth Earl of Westmoreland, causing a great sensation at the time. Her father took post-chaise and pressed the lovers so closely in Northamptonshire, " that the Earl was obliged to stand up in his carriage and shoot the leading horse of the pursuers, capsizing the vehicle, thereby causing a delay that enabled the lovers to reach Gretna Green and be married by the blacksmith before the father arrived."[58] The incensed father never forgave his daughter, but disinherited her and debarred her right of succession to the firm, bequeathing that valuable right and his immense estates to her eldest daughter. He died within the year, when his widow, Mrs. Sarah Child, succeeded him as head of the firm. She subsequently married Lord Ducie, who signed the balance sheet with her on the " casting up of the shop," in 1791, and receipted for her at her death, in 1793, from which time to the majority of her granddaughter, Lady Sophia Child Fane, in 1806, the headship of the firm was held in abeyance for the first time.

Lady Ducie was an accomplished artist, and many of her paintings are to be found at Osterley, where she continued to live. There are to be seen there several paintings of her, and a joint one of her as Lady Ducie and her daughter, the Countess of Westmoreland; and also several of Robert Child; one by Romney, which is considered his best work. He is commemorated by a fine monument of white marble in the south chancel of Heston Church, near Osterley, designed by Adams, architect.

The Earl of Westmoreland was of the fifth generation from Vere Fane 3d Earl, who opened an account with his contemporary, the first Sir Francis, in 1678, which account he still kept open. He was dining with Robert Child at the bank, Temple Bar, a few days before the elopement, when he asked the banker confidentially what he would do " if he was in love with a girl,

[57] Lyson's Beauties of Buckinghamshire.
[58] *London Gazette*, July, 1782.

whose parents, he had good reason for believing, would not consent to the marriage," and was answered, "run away with her, of course," the banker little thinking that "the girl" was his own daughter. She had one son, John, the eleventh Earl, who married Priscilla Ann Wellesley, neice of the great Duke of Wellington, and sister of the fifth Earl of Mornington, who married Catherine, daughter of Sir James Tylney Long, and great granddaughter of Sir Josiah Child," and three daughters, the second of whom married Earl Morey, and for her second husband Sir Arthur Paget; and the third married the Earl of Bessborough. The eldest daughter, Lady Sophia Child Fane, became the head of the firm of Child & Co. at her majority, March, 4, 1806. When they "cast up the shop," as they still term it, the head of the firm visits their counting house, examines and signs the "balance sheet," concurrently with all the partners, and afterwards dines with them in the old Sugar Loaf dining room, up one flight of stairs, at the Marygold.

On the occasion of Lady Sophia's assuming her hereditary position at the head of the table and firm, a full-length portrait of her, by Sir Thomas Laurence, was placed over the Elizabethan chimney piece of the old dining room, where it has since remained, and the old-time day of reckoning changed from October 3d to March 4th, in honor of her birthday. This slip of Gretna Green proved of thoroughbred tissue. She presided longest of any of her blood—sixty-one years. She became a reigning beauty of the Court of George IV., "succeeded by bequest to the immense fortune of her grandfather, Robert Child, and married George Villiers, fifth Earl of Jersey, who was twice lord chamberlain of George IV., and twice master of horse to Victoria." He was enabled, by act of parliament, to assume the additional arms and surname of Child, in 1812. He died in 1859." Issue: George Augustus Frederick Child-Villiers, sixth Earl of Jersey; Augustus John, who married a daughter of Viscount Keith; F. W. Child-Villiers, who married a sister of the Earl of Athlone; Francis and three daughters, one of whom married Prince Esterhazy. George, sixth Earl, married a daughter of the late Sir Robert Peel, and predeceased his mother, who was succeeded as head of the firm, at her death in 1867, by his eldest son, Victor Albert George Villiers-Child,

⁸⁹ Burke's Peerage.   ⁹⁰ Burke's Peerage.

seventh Earl of Jersey, who married a daughter of Lord Leigh, of Stone Leigh, and has a son, Henry George Child-Villiers, born 1873, who is heir apparent to his father's position as head of the family and Child & Co.'s bank. The present Earl was born in 1845, educated at Eton and Oxford; is Baron Hoo and Viscount Grandison, Magistrate for Oxen, Lord of Middleton Park, Bicester, and Osterley Park, Hounslow, where he has country seats, and resides in Berkley square, city. He is a direct descendant of several noble families, who opened accounts with his great ancestor, Sir Francis Child, previous to 1700, and of Edward Villiers, Governor of Ireland, father of the beautiful Barbara Villiers, mistress of Charles II., Duchess of Cleveland, Countess of Castlemaine, who kept an account with Child & Co., and whose autograph cheque that firm still hold, beginning, " Pray paye Fifty Ginneys to berer," dated 1689, and of the lineage of the Earls of Bridgewater, Derby, Cumberland, descendants of the Duke of Suffold, who married Mary, sister of Henry VIII., through whom he has the right to quarter the royal arms.

If any apology is due for the prominence given to the commercial relations of the family herein imperfectly sketched, it may be found in the fact that it was eminently a commercial family : that its members were potent factors in the establishment of an important commercial colony, now grown to be a great political empire, with hundreds of millions of subjects, and the founders and are the managers of the first and now the oldest bank among English-speaking people: that these relations have been the prime source of wealth and eminence, and are so interwoven with its history that if less accentuated this article would have been more imperfect.

NOTE.—The writer of the above sketch is indebted for many of the incidents of the family and bank to an article thereon written by a present member of the firm of Child & Co., F. Hilton Price, and published in the proceedings of the London and Middlesex Archaeological Society, for 1875.

ADDISON CHILD.

Some fragmentary items of various persons of the name are herewith given. One is a metrical account of an *affaire de cœur*, published some years ago in England, which I found in the ".Book of Days." In the same book was found the item in regard to Lady Child. These are of an amusing character.

In 1750, Charles Baldwin married a daughter of Sir William Lacon Childe, and assumed the name and arms of Childe. Their present representative is William Lacon Childe, of Shropshire. SYMONDS' DIARY says that, "Charles I. encamped at Childley, an ancient house near Oxford ; also at Childton. near Hungerford, in 1644, and in 1645 at Child's, Wickham, Glos'-tershire.

John Child was in the secret service of Charles II. and James II., and was sent by the latter to St. Christopher's as chaplain, in 1685. He may have been the son of Sir Francis Child of London, who died in 1703.

ROWLAND DAVIS speaks of William of Orange lodging at Child's house at Cullen, near Tipperary, Ireland, in 1690.

From the BOOK OF DAYS we quote : "Dr. Plott in his Natural History of Shropshire, 1686, gives many instances of centenarians of his time." After citing some of these, he says : "This is much the same that Zuingerus reports of a noble matron of the family of Dolburger. the archbishop of Mentz, who could thus speak to her daughter :

> "(1) *Mater ait* (2) *natar*, *Die* (3) *natar*, *Filia*, (4) *natam*
> *Ut moveat*, (5) *natar flangere* (6) *filiolam!*"

That is, the "Mother said to her daughter, daughter, bid thy daughter tell her daughter that her daughter's daughter cries!" He adduces as proof how far this case is from being difficult of belief, that a Lady Child of Shropshire, being married at *twelve*, her first child was born before she was complete *thirteen :* this being repeated in the second generation, Lady Child found herself a grandmother at *twenty-seven*. At the same rate she might have been a *beldam*[22] at *sixty six*, and had she reached one hundred and twenty, as has been done by others, it was possible that *nine* generations might have existed together." It will be found that Lady Child of Shropshire, is not the only matron in the Child family at the age of

---

[22] One who sees the sixth generation.

twelve, as Benjamin Child, son of the emigrant of that name, married Grace Morris when she was only twelve.[1]

In this same BOOK OF DAYS we find an extract from "The Berkshire Lady's Garland:" "March 29th, 1679, is the date of a baronetcy conferred on a Berkshire gentleman, William Kenrick of Whitley, which, however, expired with the second generation, about the close of the century. The *second* baronet left his property to an only daughter, who is understood to have soon after disposed of herself in marriage, in a very extraordinary manner. Tradition and a contemporary broadside ballad concur in representing this young gentlewoman as paid court to by many, but refusing all, and keeping herself disengaged, until attending a wedding at Reading, she met a young and handsome, but poor, attorney, named Benjamin Child, with whom she fell violently in love on the spot. For some days she reasoned with herself on the subject, trying to shake herself free of this sudden passion, but all in vain. Then feeling that something must be done, but unable, from confusion of mind, to devise a proper course, she took the extraordinary course of sending the young man a letter, demanding satisfaction for injuries she alleged he had inflicted on her, and appointing time and place for a hostile meeting. Mr. Child was much surprised, and quite at a loss to conceive who the challenger could be. By the advice of a friend, however, he resolved to attend. The meeting may be described in the words of the ballad:

> " Early on a summer's morning,
> When bright Phoebus was adorning
> Every bower with his beams,
> The fair lady came, it seems.
>
> At the bottom of a mountain,
> Near a pleasant crystal fountain,
> There she left her gilded coach,
> While the grove she did approach.
>
> Covered with her mask and walking,
> There she met her lover, talking—
> With a friend that he had brought
> So she asked him whom he sought."
>
> " I am challenged by a gallant
> Who resolves to try my talent,
> Who he is I cannot say,
> But I hope to show him play."
>
> " It is I that did invite you:
> You shall wed me, or I'll fight you

[1] An error, as later record proves.

E

Underneath these spreading trees;
Wherefore choose from which you please.

You shall find I do not vapour;
I have sought my trusty rapier;
Therefore take your choice," said she:
"Either fight, or marry me!"

Said he, "Madam, pray what mean you?
In my life I've never seen you;
Pray unmask, your visage shew
Then I'll tell you aye or no."

"I will not my face uncover
Till the marriage ties are over;
Therefore choose you which you will,
Wed me, sir, or try your skill.

Step within that pleasant bower
With your friend one single hour;
Strive your thoughts to reconcile,
And I'll wander here the while."

While the beauteous lady waited,
The young bachelor debated
What was best for to be done,
Quoth his friend, "The hazard run.

If my judgment can be trusted,
Wed her first, you can't be worsted;
If she's rich, you'll rise to fame,
If she's poor, why you're the same."

He consented to be married;
All three in a coach were carried
To a church without delay,
Where he weds the lady gay.

Though sweet pretty cupids hovered
Round her eyes, her face was covered
With a mask,—he took her thus,
Just "for better or for worse."

.   .   .   .

Now he clothed in rich attire,
Not inferior to a Squire;
Beauty, honor, riches' store,
What can man desire more?

The ballad goes on to state that the pair went in her coach to
the lady's elegant mansion, where leaving him in a parlor, she
retired to dress herself in her finest attire, and by-and-by broke
upon his vision, as a young and handsome woman, and his devoted wife.

It appears that Mr. Child took a position in society suitable
to the fortune thus conferred upon him, and was high sheriff of
the county, in 1714.[92]

[92] Entire ballad, with notes, in "Ancient Ballads and Songs of the Peas-
antry," edited by Robert Bell, 1857.

Of the Coat of Arms.

That a Coat of Arms should be represented in the Genealogy of a family long residing in a republic, may to some seem
incongruous: indeed we have in our intercourse with this wide-
spread household, found those who have expressed more than
indifference to this matter. Those who think highly of such
memorials, will not need the following resumé of the original
use of such heraldic devices, but we believe we can make it
apparent that if we are truly entitled to cherish these favors
long ago conferred upon some unknown ancestor, we shall find
all, eager for their preservation. I shall therefore make extracts
from Burke, and DeBrete, (indisputable and well known authorities on such matters,) and from a very admirable little
compilation, by Hugh Clarke, entitled "Introduction to Heraldry:"

"Heraldic devices, truly so called, make their first appearance in Europe in the middle of the twelfth century, and about
one hundred years later we find Heraldry a science in high repute, without being able to trace its intermediate progress, or
discover the names of those who first laid down its laws, or
subsequently promulgated them. The earliest Heraldic document of which even a copy has come down to us is a Roll of
Arms, that is, a catalogue of armorial bearings of the Kings of
England, and the principal barons, knights, &c., in the reign of
Henry Third, and from internal evidence, supposed to have
been compiled between the years 1240 and 1245." In the
reign of Henry Third armorial ensigns became hereditary,
marks of cadency distinguishing various members of a family.

The use of *arms* at that period was to distinguish persons and
property, and record descent and alliance, and no modern invention has been found to supersede it. Only the members of
a particular family can lawfully bear certain armorial ensigns,
and the various branches of that family have their separate
differences to distinguish one from the other.

The shield, or escutcheon, (from the Latin word *scutum*, a hide, of which shields are supposed to have been originally made,) represents the defensive implement of that name used in war, and on which armorial ensigns were originally borne. The ground, or surface, is called a *field*, and here are depicted the figures which make up the coat of arms. The *position* of these different figures mark the distinct and different arms.

Crests were anciently marks of great honor, because they were worn only by heroes of great valor and high rank, that they might be the better distinguished in an engagement; and thereby rally their men if dispersed. Crests appear on the helmets of knights as early as the thirteenth century; and after the institution of the Order of the Garter, and in imitation of Edward III., who was the first King of England that bore a crest on his helmet, all knights companions of the Order began to wear crests. This practice soon became more general, until at length they were assumed at discretion, by all who considered themselves entitled to bear arms. They are at present considered mere ornaments. The crest is the highest part of the ornaments of a coat of arms, and is placed upon a wreath, unless it is issuant from a coronet, or standing on a chapeau. In the middle ages, no man who was under the degree of knight had his crest on a wreath, which is composed of two rolls of silk twisted together, and of the color or metal of the arms.

Mottoes are not always hereditary, and have been changed, varied, and relinquished at the pleasure of the bearer. As many now in use have been originally war cries, and most are presumably associated with some deed of prowess or noble aspiration, it would seem desirable to retain those handed down.

Arms are divided into eleven classes: 1st. Arms of Dominion, such as kings and emperors bear constantly on coins, standards, seals, etc. 2d. Arms of Pretension, as the quartering of the arms of France with those of England, until 1801. 3d. Arms of Community, as those of bishoprics, cities, universities, etc. 4th. Arms of Assumption, formerly allowed when one captured a prisoner of higher rank than himself, he took his arms. 5th. Arms of Patronage, such as governors of provinces, patrons of benefices, add to their family arms. 6th. Arms of Succession, taken by those who inherit lands, manors, &c., by will, entail, and donation, and which they add to their own.

7th. Arms of Alliance, as when heiresses marry into families, are taken by their issue, to show their descent, paternal and maternal. 8th. Arms of Adoption, like arms of succession, called "of adoption" because the last of a family may, by will, adopt a stranger to possess his name, estate, and arms. 9th. Arms Paternal and Hereditary, such as are transmitted from the first possessor to his son, grandson, and succeeding generations. 10th. Arms of Concession, are augmentations granted by the sovereign, of part of his ensigns, or regalia, to such persons as he pleaseth to honor therewith. 11th. Canting or Allusive Arms, are coats of arms whose figures allude to the names, professions, &c., of the bearer, as three *herrings* for Herring, a *camel* for Camel, three covered *cups* for Butler, a *pine tree* for Pine, etc. Such arms have been mistakenly supposed by some to be of an inferior order, whereas there can scarcely be greater proof of their antiquity, and highly honorable character."

There are other distinctive marks attached to arms to mark the different sons of a house, and descent therefrom: the duplication or combination of these distinguishing figures carries on the ratio and line of descent. There are nine of these defining figures: that of the eldest son is of this form and is termed a label: the second is a crescent: the third is called a mullet: the fourth a martlett (or small martin). We give the marks of distinction so far, for a reason apparent farther on. We think what we have quoted from these authorities will be a sufficient explanation of the desire, if we may lawfully do so, to hold as a memento of past worth, a coat of arms.

We have found in the American families, what may be called three coats of arms, or more strictly, two. One bears upon its field three doves, the motto being " *Imitari Quam Invidere.*"[20] The other has three eagles, in the same positions, with the same crest, and motto; the third is a variation of the second, in having in its centre a small shield with a martlett, indicating the bearer to be the fourth son of the first house. Had the researches prosecuted years since through Mr. Horatio G. Somerby, and later by some members of the family,

[20] Imitate rather than envy.

succeeded in establishing the line from which the American families are descended, we could doubtless know with measurable certainty to which we were entitled. Failing this, we give the grounds upon which we base our decision, and preface, with the fact that about the time of the Revolution, and later, a John Cole and his son made it their business to furnish families who desired them, coats of arms: these were not wholly plagiarisms, as they generally, if not always, gave those which were borne by some family of the same name in Great Britain. Later research has shown many of these works to be spurious.

The great grandfather of the compiler of this book, Mr. Henry Child of Woodstock, Ct., built in the years 1761–2 a large and commodious house for his family, and as it stood upon a principal thoroughfare, and removed from the town, he opened therein an Inn, and hung out for his Inn-sign a transcript of a coat of arms; this sign, now in preservation (though it ceased to swing out its welcome to the wayfarer many years ago), bears unmistakably the doves, and an octogenarian relative tells us, that "it was always called the family coat of arms, and the figures were meant for doves." Rev. Dr Willard Child (my uncle) found some years since, in the old homestead, a torn copy of a coat of arms, upon which the figures are evidently doves. These escape the condemnation of Cole's manufactures, as they antedate his operations. We shall farther on give the coat of arms of an English family, resident in that county of England in which the New England emigrants have been thought to have originated, bearing doves, upon its field.

Indeed we have found copies of a coat of arms in several families and lines. Among the descendants of Edward and Margaret Weld Child are found two copies alike in main points, but with some slight variations. In the Watertown branch, in the family of Ephraim Child, Jr., of Rutland, and West Boylston, Mass. In the Barnstable branch in the family of Dr. Timothy Childs; and in a family of one of the southern branches.

Mr. Addison Child, who has aided us much in furnishing the scholarly articles over his signature, has given much thought to this matter, and we have, upon consultation with him, accepted his view, which we thus sum up.

The percentage of families bearing the arms with the eagles upon the field is so very much the larger, that any other form is but an occasional exception, therefore, presumably the coat of arms of the family would bear the eagles. 2d. Each advance we have made in establishing a link between the American and English families has pointed more and more strongly towards a family bearing the eagles upon their arms, circumstantially indicating a kinship with Richard Child, father of Sir John and Sir Josiah Child, whose notable careers are so graphically outlined for us. Sir Josiah Child had *Arms* "*Gules, a chevron engrailed ermine, between three eagles close argent. Crest, an eagle wings expanded argent enveloped with a snake proper.*" *Motto* " Imitari Quam Invidere."

Sir John Child had *Arms*, "*Vert two bars engrailed, between three leopard's faces or. Crest a leopard's face or, between two laurel branches proper.*" *Motto*, "Spes Alit." We do not know when he took these Arms, but his baronetcy was conferred upon him in 1684, while he was resident in the East Indies. He might then have adopted the leopard's faces, as the leopard was a frequent enemy, and some deed of prowess may easily have led to this assumption, always such arms are regarded as most honorable. His title became extinct in 1753, and his Arms are not at present borne by any of the name, or others quartering the Child arms with their own.

As some persons have a deep interest in armorial bearings, we give a condensed and abbreviated summary of facts on this point, gathered in our exhaustive search in the best collections of Heraldic lore available in America. In Burke's "General Armory of England, Scotland, Ireland and Wales," we found eighteen families of the name, with their arms, &c.; with eight the motto was given, and five had, " *Imitari Quam Invideri.*"

In Berry's " Encyclopedia Heraldic and Dictionary of Heraldry," of eleven families Child, we find but one marked difference in the arms: " *Ermine on a chief indented gules, three escallops or.*" Of the larger number the *Arms* are "*Gules, a chevron engrailed ermine, between three eagles close argent. Crest, an eagle, wings expanded or elevated argent enveloped with a snake proper.*" *Motto* "Imitari Quam Invideri." This is the coat of arms we present as that which we may accept with large confidence.

In the account by Burke of the family of the present Sir Smith Child, who was made baronet in 1868, we find his grandfather to have been "Admiral of the Blue," and that "he entered the navy in 1747, under Earl Gower's auspices, and eminently distinguished himself in the service. He commanded the 'Europe' in the two actions off the Chesapeake; subsequently, in 1795, he took command of the 'Commerce de Marseilles,' one hundred and twenty (120)guns, and attained his flag in 1799." He may have been accompanied by his son, Smith Child, whom we find to have married Miss Elizabeth Parsons, daughter of Timothy Parsons, Esq., of Massachusetts, U. S. He died early, leaving one son, the present baronet.

The family of Child, Northwick, Worcestershire, (as found in the 38th edition of Burke's "Baronetage and Peerage of Great Britain,") have *Arms, "Gules a fesse ermine, between three doves argent. Crest a dove, wings expanded argent, with a snake twining about her neck and body or."*

Should any desire to have a copy of these arms blazoned to hang in their homes, we append herewith the proper tinctures or colors for the Child arms, in such terms as will be readily apprehended :

Shield *gules* (or red) in the groundwork, chevron white, engrailed black, ermine black, outlines of the shield gilt, eagles *argent* (or silver), the coils of the wreath alternate red and gilt, eagle silver, snake black. We give also a brief glossary of the heraldic terms used :

TINCTURES.

Or—Gold, or yellow.
Argent—Silver, or white.
Gules—Red.
Azure—Blue.
Sable—Black.
Vert—Green.

The *Chevron* is formed of two lines placed in the form of a pyramid, and descending in form of a pair of compasses to the extremities of the shield.

The *Fesse* is formed by two horizontal lines across the shield comprising the centre third part of the escutcheon, emblematic of the military girdle worn over the armor. The *Bar*, a diminutive of fesse.

Engrailed. , *ermine*, sable spots on a white field, the tail terminating in three hairs; *erminois*, black spots on gold field. *Nebulée*, *Indented* *Cross croslet*, is a cross crossed again at the extremities, at a small distance from each of the ends; cross croslet fitchée, so termed when the under limb of the cross ends in a sharp point.

AMERICAN FAMILIES.

CHAPTER I.

1. EPHRAIM CHILD.

Could we give the parentage of this first emigrant, Ephraim Child, it would be exceedingly gratifying. Since prosecuting this work, we have learned that the same uncertainty as to the paternity of the emigrants, has perplexed the chronicler of other families, arising as we have said elsewhere from the necessity for a quiet embarkation. The difficulty of restoring these lost links may be more easily understood, when it is remembered that many of the early emigrants were led to come from the motherland for greater freedom in their religious faith, and often sailed from some minor port, and no list of passengers was made or desired. That this was true of our emigrating ancestry, we do not know, it may have been, as but few of the name are found on any preserved list. A Michael Child and Thomas Child sailed from London to Virginia, and in connection with their names it is stated that they took the oath of allegiance to the established church.

Ephraim Child, born in England in 1593, came to America in 1630, accompanied as seems probable by his nephew, Benjamin Child.

The marriage of Ephraim Child to a widow, the Mrs. Elizabeth Palmer, is recorded at Nayland, Suffolk county, England, on the 8th of February, 1625. Mrs. Palmer is presumed to be the daughter of Jonas Bond of Bury St. Edmunds, of the same county. Ephraim Child was admitted freeman May 18th, 1631, applied therefor the year previous.

By virtue of his seniority and prominence in colonial affairs, Ephraim Childs takes precedence in the Genealogy, though not generally believed to .ave left descendants to bear his name or

retain his honors. He is known as the personal friend of
Governor John Winthrop of Massachusetts, and from this
circumstance may have arisen the impression that, like Gov.
Winthrop, Mr. Child was a native of Suffolk county, England.

Mr. Ephraim Child occupied a leading position in Watertown, Massachusetts; a man of property, and piety, he was
often chosen to places of trust and responsibility in town and
county affairs; and held office in the church as one of the first
deacons. For twelve years he is found a representative at the
General Court, a post, then, bestowed only upon those of known
integrity, mental power, and financial ability.

His judgment is also attested in his appointment by the
County Court one of the Commissioners to "end small causes;"
and from the esteem of his fellow-citizens he was elected one of
the selectmen of the town for fifteen years.

His death occurred on the thirteenth of February 1663, when
seventy years of age. His will dated, the tenth of November,
1662, is given as of interest, and from the fact that we gather
therefrom certain clues to further record. Bond, one of our
authorities, says, "the appraisal of his homestall and the amount
of his inventory (£770 15) show that he was one of the most
affluent of the settlers, and the distribution of his widow's
wardrobe and furniture by her will, show that she had some of
the elegancies as well as the comforts of life."

Will of Ephraim Child.

November 20th   I give unto William Bond, father, forty acres of my Lands
1662.   on the hither Plain, and I give unto Richard Child and John
                Child all the rest of that Land with all other lands abroad,
namely, my remote meadow, my Farm any upon the further plain, with the
land called Township-land, to the end that before my estate be broken, care
and endeavour be used, either by improving or by sale, my Debts may be secured and all have their own, and withal my will is that there be twenty
cord of Wood cut out every year if it be there for the use of my wife, so long
as she lives. I give unto my dear and loving wife my dwelling house and
Lott with all that appertains thereunto, also my Divident, Dorchester Field,
and my meadow upon the other side of the river, with all my Goods and
Chattels for her maintenance as long as she lives, and allow her Te—[oblit-
erated] pounds of that Estate then in being to dispose of as she pleases pr
de—[obliterated] being dead. My will is that Ephraim Child the son of
Benjamin Child should inhabit my dwelling-house and Lott; with one half
my Divident and Dorchester field, my coz. William Bond, the Father the
other half of my Divident and the meadow upon the other side of the river,
and the remainder of the Estate which then shall be, be equally divided,

both Goods within (as nothing be defaced, but all that is nailed fast remain to the house) and all the Chattels abroad unto Richard Child, John Child, Ephraim Child, and William Bond above named. And to that end I do appoint my dear wife and my loving Coz. William Bond to be my executors.

I give unto my dearly beloved Pastour ten pounds, to Mary Rowles wife to John Parker a Cow with Clf. I give forty shillings a year forever to be paid out of my lands towards the maintenance of a Schoolmaster in Watertown. I give my servant David one Cow, *bullocks* and unto Samuel Burk two Ewes.

This is the will of me,

EPHRAIM CHILD.

BENJAMIN CHILD.

[First Generation.]

2. BENJAMIN CHILD. who emigrated from Great Britain to America, and became the head of the larger number of the families of the name on this side of the Atlantic, from strong presumptive evidence was the nephew of Ephraim Child of Watertown, with whom we commence this Genealogy. Patriarchal in the best sense, we find Mr. Child to have been earnest in character, and in the promotion of that puritan stamp of piety for which the Massachusetts settlers were especially distinguished. Mr. Benjamin Child was of that order of nobility bearing the stamp affixed at the departure from Eden. Methodical and exact in habit Mr. Child is known to have been: and legal manuscripts carefully preserved at the present time by some of his descendants, attest his familiarity with affairs, and fine standing in the community.

In the records of Roxbury, Mr. Benjamin Child is stated to have been of the thirty who contributed the joint sum of £104. 6s. for the erection of the First Church of Roxbury: one of the customs peculiar to the period connected with the building of this "meeting-house," was a "raising," the bill of expenses and provisions amounting to £20 15s. 10d. and £9 5s. "to the hands for et ceteras."

Bearing the name of the youngest son of the Head of the Israelites, Mr. Benjamin Child, like that patriarch, "in the land wherein he was a stranger," became the father of twelve children, an example his descendants have satisfactorily emulated. We are very glad also to say in this connection, that the probity, sterling integrity, and devout conscientiousness of their progenitor, are found to have been transmitted, in complete verification of the strong assurances of the Decalogue.

Of the time or place of Mr. Benjamin Child's marriage, we are ignorant, and only know that his wife bore the sweet name, Mary, was like her scriptural predecessors a follower of the Master: "was admitted to the Church of Roxbury in 1658;" she survived her husband, though we know not for what length of time. Mr. Benjamin Child died the fourteenth day of October, 1678, residing at that time in Roxbury, near Jamaica Pond (or the Great Pond), as it was then called; and his estate there has been the homestead of his direct descendants until a few years since.

The accompanying inventory of his estate and effects, the original of which, complete and clear, is held in choice keeping in the family, is appended, that his posterity, scattered through nearly every State in the Union, may be informed of the exact fortune left by their greatest grandfather in America:

1679.

BENJAMIN CHILD, HIS INVENTORY.

[Copy.]

An Inventory of the Estate of Benjamin Child, late of Roxbury, who dyed 14th October, in the year of our Lord 1678.

	£	s.	d.
A House and Barne	80	00	00
80 acres of Land conveniently adjoining to y³ 3d housing	320	00	00
12 acres in the thousand acres	3	00	00
2 cows at 50s. per cow, and more at 40s.: 2 yearling heifers at 40s.	9	00	00
One horse and a mare at 40s. y² each and one sow at 16s.	4	16	00
Money in the House and in good hands	13	00	00
In the parlor: 3 silver spoons and one wine cup	1	14	00
One standing w⁰ʰ curtains, valines, old rug, 2 blankets, bolster and pillow	5	00	00
One trundle bedstead w⁰ʰ a feather bed, bolster, blankets and covering	2	00	00
One old court cupboard, 10s.: 3 chests, 20s.	1	10	00
8 pair of sheets at 8s.	3	04	00
3 fine Table cloths, being worne, 10s.: 11 napkins, 7s.: 3 pair pillow bears, 10s.	1	07	00
All his wearing clothes, woolen & linen, shoes, stockings, and hats	7	00	00
One carbine 12s., one fowling piece 18s., one Rapier 5s.	1	15	00
Parlor chamber: one feather bed and a flock bed under it, w⁰ʰ bolsters to them and pillows to the feather bed: 2 old blankets and an old Rug	3	00	00

10lb of Flax.. . ...   10 00

In the Kitchin: Brass 4/. 10s, Pewtar 35s, spoons & timers ware 3s,   6 08 00
    fire pan-tongs, 1 old spit, 2 pair tramels, an old frying   15 00
    pan, an old Iron pot and two pair of poot hookes........ \

A kneading trough 2s., and old table 2s., 2 chaires and a woolen   08 00
    wheel 4s.. \

A powdering tubb, butter churn, old pailes, wooden bottle,   12 00
    trenchers and other Lumber....................... \

Bridle and saddle 7s.; an axe and a bill 3s................ ....   10 00

A cart with shod wheeles (3 yeares old), tackling for horses   4 00 00
    draught and a piece of an old timber chain .... \

An acre and halfe of salt marsh............................   10 00 00

5½ acres of Land at the pond plains........ ....   25 00 00

One Horse more......................................   2 10 00

                                             £506 19 00

Inventoryed and apprized this 24 day of October, in the yeare of our Lord one thousand six hundred seventy and eight, by John Weld Sen, John Gore, John Weld and Mary Childe, admitt Adm made Oath in Court pr. May 1679, to the truth of the above Inventory, and that when more appeares they will adde it. Attests, Is Addington, Cler.

Vera Copia of its Original on ye file of Inventorys Ann 1679.

                         Atteste: Is Addington, Cler.

[Second Generation.] Children:

3. i. EPHRAIM CHILD, b. in Roxbury, Mass. 1654, killed in battle.

4. ii. BENJAMIN CHILD, b. in Roxbury, Mass. 1656, m. Mar. 7, 1683, Grace Morris.

5. iii. JOSHUA CHILD, b. in Roxbury, Mass. 1658, m. May, 9, 1685, Elizabeth Morris.

6. iv. MARY CHILD, b. in Roxbury, Mass. Aug. 8, 1660, m. Jan. 24, 1683, Jacob Chamberlain.

7. v. An infant, no name, b. 1662.

8. vi. ELIZABETH CHILD, b. in Roxbury, Mass. Dec. 2, 1663, num.

9. vii. MARGARET CHILD, b. in Roxbury, Mass. Dec. 21, 1665, unmarried. d. July 15, 1712.

10. viii. JOHN CHILD, b. in Roxbury, Mass. Jan. 8, 1667, d. yg.

11. ix. MEHITABLE CHILD, b. in Roxbury, Mass. June 29, 1669, m. Samuel Perrin.

12. x. JOHN CHILD 2D, b. in Roxbury, Mass. Aug. 1, 1671, m.

13. xi. JOSEPH CHILD, b. in Roxbury, Mass. June 1, 1678, d. yg.

14. xii. JOSEPH CHILD 2D, b. in Roxbury, Mass. Dec. 10, 1674.

[Second Generation.]

3. i. EPHRAIM CHILD, second of the name in America, and eldest son of Benjamin Child of Roxbury, was born in Roxbury in 1654. He was baptized a few years later with two younger brothers, by the Rev. John Elliot, pastor of the Church in Roxbury, of which his parents were members. He was made, by his great uncle, Mr. Ephraim Child of Watertown,

heir to a large portion of his estate: he had not long entered upon these possessions when the Massachusetts colony was distracted and devastated by the relentless slaughter of many of its inhabitants, in combats known as "Phillip's War." Ephraim Child, with other valiant young men under command of Capt. Beers, was slain by the Indians at Northfield, Massachusetts, on the 23d of September, 1675.

Thus was Mr. Benjamin Child called to seal his faith in the consecration of his eldest born upon the altar of patriotism; and the young man, though leaving no wife or child to mourn his early death, has yet bequeathed to those of his race an heritage of honorable self-sacrifice, for native land and for the right. His property was shared by his brothers and sisters.

[Second Generation.]

4.   ii. BENJAMIN, second son and child of Benjamin and Mary Child of Roxbury, was born in Roxbury, in 1656. The death of his elder brother, Ephraim Child, gave him the seniority in his father's family, and the British laws of primogeniture being then in force in the colonies, he was thereby the inheritor of the larger share of his father's property, or the Benjamic "double portion"

He remained at the homestead, and we believe felt constrained to follow in all good ways the example of his parents. Moved by the charms of a fair young maiden, he asked her hand in marriage, and on the 7th of March, 1683, he was united in holy wedlock to Grace Morris, who was born Feb. 17, 1661, a daughter of Deacon Edward and Grace Bett Morris. "Dea. Morris was one of the projectors and early settlers of the town of Woodstock, Ct. From 1677 to 1684, he was one of the selectmen of Roxbury, and during the same period was also a deputy from that town to the General Court of Massachusetts, and during part of the time Colonial Auditor. Grace Morris was admitted to the church June 21, 1681." The goodly number of twelve sons and daughters again made cheery the Puritan's demure household. Deed of sale of the property of his brother Ephraim, is on record in the name of Benjamin Child, who acted for the heirs. We give the quaint document accompanying—wherein he settles with brothers and sisters in the partition of the paternal heritage, as many will be interested to look in this way into the past.[1] This union, so complete, was broken by death, but for an exceedingly brief period. Mrs. Grace Morris Child died on the 10th of December, 1723, and her husband joined her on the 24th of January, 1724.

[Third Generation.] Children:

15. i. EPHRAIM CHILD, b. in Roxbury, Mass. Dec. 18, 1683, m. 1710, Priscilla Harris.

16. ii. BENJAMIN CHILD, Jun., b. in Roxbury, Mass., July 19, 1685, m. 1712, Patience Thayer.

17. iii. EDWARD CHILD, b. in Roxbury, Mass., Nov. 1, 1687, m. 1712, Margaret Weld.

18. iv. GRACE CHILD, b. in Roxbury, Mass. Oct. 27, 1689, m. Timothy Walker.

19. v. MARY CHILD, b. in Roxbury, Mass. Oct. 25, 1691, m. June 9, 1715, Peter Walker.

20. vi. EBENEZER CHILD, b. in Roxbury, Mass. Sept. 7, 1692, m. 1720, Elizabeth Bacon.

21. vii. MEHITABLE CHILD, b. in Roxbury, Mass. Jan. 5, 1695.

22. viii. WILLIAM CHILD, b. in Roxbury, Mass. Oct. 14, 1697, m. 1723, Deborah Goddard.

23. ix. PENUEL CHILD, b. in Roxbury, Mass. Sept. 3, 1699, m. March 7, 1724, Dorothy Dwight.

24. x. RICHARD CHILD, b. in Roxbury, Mass. Oct. 22, 1701, d. May 18, 1759.

25. xi. THOMAS CHILD, b. in Roxbury, Mass. Nov. 10, 1703, m. Sep. 27, 1729, Anna Morris, dau. of Ebenezer Morris, and gr. dau. of Dea. Edward Morris.

26. xii. MARGARET CHILD, b. in Roxbury, Mass. May 26, 1706.

---

[1] This account is given by a descendant of Dea. Edward Morris.

[2] Given on two following pages.

JACOB CHAM-
BERLAIN and others
release to BENJA-
MIN CHILD.

Articles of Agreement and Settlement. Indented, made, & fully concluded and agreed upon, this Fif . teenth — Day of May, Anno Dm. One thousand Six hundred Ninety and Nine, Amongᵭ R:R•, Gulielmᵉ Z. une Anglæ — Cᵃ Undecimo. Between Jacob Chamberlain and Mary his wife, Elizabeth Child, Spinster, Margaret Child, Spinster, Samuel Perrin and Mehetabel his wife, and John Child of the one part, And Benjamin Child on the other part, all Children and heirs of Benjamin Child, sometime of Roxbury, within the County of Suffolk and Province of the Massachusetts Bay in New-England, yeoman, decᵈ Intestate.

Whereas the said Benjamin Child, the Father, dyed seized containing by Estimation about Forty Six — acres, Township of Roxbury, and partly within the Township of Boston, Partition, and to be divided to and among all his Children. It is mutually consented, concluded and agreed upon, by and Son of the said deceased, shall have and enjoy to him, his heires Tenement, and all the lands thereto adjoining and belonging, paying thereout unto his Brother and Sister above named, and value aforesaid, of the said Farme lands. That is to to each of them within the space of Six months next Benjamin Child, the Father, or at any time within or before interim, after the rate of five pounds ⅌ Centum ⅌ therefore these presents, That the said Jacob Chamberlain, and Mary Mehetabel his said wife, and John Child, and each and given, granted, assigned, released and forever quitclaimed, every of them respectively, give, grant, assigne, release, Brother, his heires and assignes forevever (in his actual share, Interest. Title, claim and Demand tfices, Buildings, rights, members, hereditaments, appertaining, and Estate wherever not already actuall Seized To. have and to

[Obliterated.]

riv   n   ment,   mentioned
least.   Let,   denial,   interruption,   claim.
them, their any or either of their heires.   And the said bind and oblige himselfe, his heires, Execrs and Admrs for and and truly to pay, or cause to be paid unto the said Jacob, Child, Samuel Perrin and Mehetabel his said wife, and heires, or assignes, in manner and time as above expressed, in currant money of New-England (amounting in the whole Together with Interest or allowance for the same, after the

of a certain Messuage, or Tenemeot Farme and Land thereto belonging, be the same more or less, situate, lying and being partly within the said in the County aforesaid; which is . not capable to admit of without great prejudice to and spoyling of the whole: And whereas between the parties to these presents, that the sᵈ Benjamin Child, eldest and assignes for ever, the said whole Farme messuage, or at the rate or value of Two hundred seventy Five pounds. He their respective single portions, ratable parts and shares of the price say, the sum of thirty-nine pounds, five shillings and eight pence after the decease of their mother, Mary Child, Relict widow of the said am. until the said payments respectively be made. Witnesseth, his said wife, Elizabeth Child, Margaret Child, Samuel Perrin and every of them, respectively, do for themselves and their heires, and each and and by these puts Do for themselves and their heires, and each and confirme, and — forever quitclaime unto the said Benjamin Child, their possession now being), all and singular their several and respective of, in, to, and out of the af   meot Farme
                                                                 ces

hold all and singular   nd appurᵗˢ thereto belonging,
rights, members, profits, priv   o his and their onely proper
Benjamin Child, his heires and ass   and quietly to use, occupy, possess and enjoy the same, without any the eviction, challenge or demand of them, the said Granter, any or either of Benjamin Child, party to these presents, doth hereby covenant, promise in consideration of the said granted and released premises, well Chamberlain and Mary his said wife, Elizabeth Child. Margaret John Child, and to each of them respectively, their several respective each the sum of Thirty Nine pounds, five shillings & eight pence unto. one hundred ninety six pounds, Eight Shillings and eight pence rate of Five pounds ⅌ Centum ⅌ annum from the day of the date hereof

[Obliterated.]   [Obliterated.]

ed and released premises with the
crᵃms of the same unto the said
loofe forever.   Freely,   peaceably
molestation,   claim,

until the said principal sum be paid, the Interest to proportionably from time to time, as any part of the principal shall be paid. In Witness whereof, the said partys to these present Articles have interchangably Set their hands & seals the day and year first above written. Signed, Sealed and Deliv'd

in presence of us,
(by Jacob Chamberlain, Eliz: Child, Samuel Perrin, Mehetable Perrin and John Child, & also the memorand'm by Joshua Child).

SAM: SEWALL.
EDW'd SURREBY.

JACOB CHAMBERLAIN.
Signed.
MARY CHAMBERLAIN.
Signed.
ELIZABETH . . CHILD.
Signed.
MARGARET CHILD.
SAMUEL PERRIN.
Signed.
MEHETABEL . . . PERRIN.
JOHN CHILD.

Memorand'm }

That I, Joshua Child, one of the Children & heirs of Benjamin Child, above named, late of Roxbury, deced, having formerly had & received my full part, share and portion of the Estate left by my s'd Father, In consideration thereof, Do for me & my heirs, remise, release, & forever quitclaim unto my Brother, Benjamin Child, his heirs and assignes for ever, all right, Interest, claim & demand whatsoever, of me or my heirs, of, in & unto the Messuage or Tenement Farme & Lands with y'e members, & and appurtenances thereof above mentioned, to be granted to my s'd Brother, Benjamin Child, To have & to hold to him, his heirs & assignes forever. Witness my hand & seal hereunto set the 15th day of May, Anno Domini 1699—

JOSHUA CHILD { Seal. }

[On the back.]

BOSTON, May 15th 1699.

The within named Jacob Chamberlain, Elizabeth Child, Samuel Perrin, Mehetable Perrin, and John Child personally appearing before me, the Subscriber, one of the Council and Justice of the Peace within his Maj's Province of the Massachusetts Bay in New-England, acknowledged the within Instrument to be their act and Deed, and also Joshua Child, appearing at the same time, acknowledged the Memorandum thereunder written, to be his act and Deed.

ISA: ADDINGTON.

[On the back.]

May 15th 1699.

We underwritten do hereby acknowledge to have received of our Brother, Benjamin Child, the sum of Twenty shillings in money, each, towards payment of the sum of Thirty nine pounds, five shillings & eight pence, payable to each of us as within mentioned—

JACOB CHAMBERLAIN,
Signed.
ELIZABETH . . CHILD.
Signed.
MARG: CHILD,
SAMUEL PERRIN,
Signed.
MEHETABEL . . . PERRIN.
JOHN CHILD.

CHAPTER II.

WOODSTOCK FAMILIES.

It will be found by a close observation of the records, that a restless spirit has moved upon the family at intervals, resulting in an emigration of numbers. The first movement of this kind in America was made from Roxbury, Mass. to the new settlement of New Roxbury, made as it was supposed. within the bounds of the Massachusetts colony. "Need for more extended pasturage," awakened the residents of Roxbury to action, and resulted in accordance with the custom of the period, in referring the matter to the minister, the Rev. John Elliot, first pastor of the Roxbury church: a man whose labors on behalf of the Indians has consecrated his name forever. In the various journeyings Mr. Elliot had made in this missionary work, he had noted very correctly the soil and climate of the Massachusetts and Connecticut colonies, and upon his commendation the selectmen of Roxbury petitioned the General Court of the Massachusetts colony for a grant of land, then supposed to be within the boundaries of that colony, which was awarded them, and some thirteen of their number were appointed "to spy out and take possession." The section within which selection was made at that period was known as the "Nipmuck, or Nipmung country;" but few Indians remained in the immediate vicinity, the larger number had been slain in "King Phillip's War." The Indian name for the location was "Wabquassit, or Wappaquassit." Here the "Apostle Elliot" had preached to the Indians on the 16th of September, 1674, and the colonists felt a blessing must attend a place thus consecrated.

Reluctant to unlink them from the homesteads, the new settlement was for a period called New Roxbury, but from this it would seem some conflicting claims arose, and petition was had to the General Court for a change of name, granted to them on the eighteenth of March, 1690. The private diary of Judge

Samuel Sewall of Boston, says, "I gave New Roxbury the name of Woodstock, because of its nearness to Oxford, for the sake of Queen Elizabeth, and the notable meetings that have been held at that place bearing the name in England." Woodstock, Connecticut, lying eight miles apart from Oxford, Massachusetts, as do the old towns of the names in Great Britain. A brief enumeration of some of the historical associations clustering in and about the old town of Woodstock in the motherland, may not be amiss for the instruction of the younger members of this clan, resident in Connecticut, or claiming descent therefrom. The Saxon and Norman kings made this place a royal residence: here King Alfred, whose religious and literary culture was so superior for the time, pursued his studies; here Princess Elizabeth was retired to escape the intriguing machinations of Queen Mary's suspicious advisers. Sir Walter Scott founds one of his Waverley novels upon a legend of the town.

An amusingly brief and explicit classification of the people of Roxbury is made in the records of transfer to the new settlement: those emigrating were termed "Goers," those remaining "Stayers." The division of the land was made by lot, at a meeting held for the purpose, the minister opening with prayer. After appropriating a certain number of acres for a site for the "meeting house" and the "burial ground," with a reserved quarry for "hearth and building stone," a portion of twenty acres for each householder was made, the exact location of this homestead being attained by the lot. We find the minister drew the third lot. The local name given to this village location was "Plain Hill," now known as the "South Parish Hill of Woodstock." The erection of a pastor's house was decided upon at a town meeting on the 27th of October, 1690, with the details of size, "four stacks of chimneys and gables," the building to be sufficiently completed for use within two years. As a defence from the ravages of fire, each inhabitant was ordered to provide a ladder and buckets for his house before a stated day, and "Jonathan Peak was to see that this was done." This ordinance for ladders and buckets we find to have been made six years before the establishment of the first fire insurance company in England. Mr. John Chandler, Jr., by an act at a regular town meeting, "was requested and procured to teach the children to read, write and cipher." [1]   The colony thus sent out into the wilderness was never forgotten by those remaining in Roxbury, but was "the constant subject of prayer by the Roxbury church, the Rev. Mr. Elliot being wont on every Sabbath in his public prayers in the church uniformly to pray for the 'colony in New Roxbury.'"   But on one occasion, when the congregation had assembled on the Sabbath for worship, the pious Elliot neglected to mention in his prayers the "colony of New Roxbury," closed and took his seat.   This neglect of the minister was noticed by the goodly fathers and mothers of the church with great pain, and they began to fear the children at New Roxbury would be devoured by the wild beasts or destroyed by the Indians, and the iniquity of the fathers visit their children, because they had been omitted by the godly Elliot.   While the good mothers were thus sitting depressed in spirit at so great a neglect, it occurred to the minister that he had not made mention of the New Roxbury colony in his prayer, and he immediately arose in his pulpit and exclaimed: "Alas! alas! I forgot to pray for our sons and daughters at New Roxbury, and therefore let us again pray!" He made a most fervent prayer, especially for the colony, much to the comfort and relief of the congregation.

We do not find any of the Child name on the list of the first "goers," but a few years later the name occurs frequently upon the town records, as actors in the differing posts of honor and toil, in affairs of the town, and in the defence of colony and country from internal and external foes.   At this early period, we find seven brothers of the Child name settled in the north part of the town.   The scarcity of "neat cattle" in the new world limited the supply so that many who would wish to do so were unable to own any.   One cow was owned by these seven brothers, Child, and they took turns in the use of her, one week at a time, except immediately before the Thanksgiving Day, when the elder brother was allowed to keep the cow long enough to accumulate a supply of milk which should suffice to enable the gathered households to enjoy a "Thanksgiving Supper of hasty pudding and milk."   On one occasion of the annual gathering of the seven households, beneath the elder brother's roof

---

[1] The major portion of these facts were culled from a work by Holmes Ammidown, Esq., entitled "Historical Collections."

the supper was duly prepared, and set forth upon a large "fall-leaf-table," each family provided with their wooden bowls and wooden spoons. According to their custom, all were standing around the frugal supper, while the elder brother, as patriarch, asked the Divine blessing; while thus solemnly engaged, the large watch dog, in passing under the table, moved the leg upholding the leaf, and down went table, milk and pudding. The younger brother saw the table falling, and cried out, "Stop, brother! Stop! stop! The pudding is gone, and the milk is gone, and of what use is the blessing now; *but kill the dog!*" The Puritan training, though thoroughly observed and reverenced, could not wholly subdue the natural temper, or exclude all humor from the occasional gatherings of young or old.

In 1690, a Congregational Church and Society was organized, and religious services maintained for several years without a settled minister, when the Rev. Josiah Dwight was installed as pastor, which relation he held for thirty-seven years with mutual satisfaction of pastor and people, when an unfortunate difference with regard to church discipline and some other matters sprung up which led to the termination of the pastorate. Mr. Dwight was esteemed as a man of decided talents, and religiously devoted to the interests of his charge during his long pastorate. The revolution in this church led to the organization of the church and society in "Muddi Brook," now East Woodstock, in the year 1759, by the majority who claimed to be the first church of Woodstock. A new house of worship was erected in this parish; the church records were retained by this majority, and a pastor, Rev. William Graves, was installed, while the minority remained undisturbed in their original place of worship, and in possession of the Society's property.

[Third Generation.]

15. i. EPHRAIM CHILD, first child of Benjamin and Grace Morris Child, b. in Roxbury, Mass., Dec. 18, 1683, m. 1710, Priscilla Harris, dau. of Dan'l Harris of Brookline, Mass. He d. Nov. 22, 1759. She was b. June 4, 1684. She d. June 26, 1780, æt. 96.

Ephraim Child was the eldest of the seven brothers who migrated from Roxbury, Mass., to "New Roxbury," Ct. (afterwards called Woodstock). He removed shortly before or immediately after his marriage, in 1710, and settled in that part of the town now called East Woodstock (anciently known as Muddi Brook), erecting for himself a house, which, with some additions, has been retained in the line of his male descendants till the present time, covering a period of quite 170 years. Its enlargement, at a somewhat early period, made it as it now stands, a commodious and attractive home. Its site is in a beautiful vale, about half a mile east of East Woodstock village. It was probably at this house where occurred the amusing incident on a Thanksgiving occasion, which is found recorded in the early part of this chapter. Many pleasant memories cluster around this ancient home. It has been the birthplace of sons and daughters, whose history, with that of a long line of descendants, it is pleasant to trace. In this house hospitalities for many generations have been liberally dispensed to kindred and aliens, particularly on the Sabbath, when, in the interval between the morning and afternoon religious service, numbers of worshippers living remote from the place of worship, accepted as an accorded right, a hearty meal of boiled meats and vegetables, or a soporific lunch of hasty pudding and milk : this latter being the favorite repast, particularly of *one*, who could not resist the luxury of a quiet nap under the afternoon sermon.

These were the good old times which the elder men of the present age like to recall, and which link them to the memory of uncles, aunts, grandfathers and grandmothers.

Before this ancient dwelling stands a magnificent elm, whose trunk and outspreading branches are emblematical of a noble ancestor and his sturdy descendants. In 1876 this stately elm was christened the "Centennial Tree." More than one hundred years had passed since man and beast had rested beneath its grateful shade.

Mr. Ephraim Child was a prominent man of his day. He was intelligent, patriotic, enterprising, generous and self-sacrificing. His patriotism was kindled by the stirring incidents of the times, and he was among the first of the early defenders of colonial interests. In 1753 he held a commission as Lieutenant in Company 17, in 11th Regiment of Infantry, in Connecticut, and was active in the revolutionary struggles for independence. He was a man of broad views, of a warm and sympathetic nature, living for others quite as much as for himself. Earnest

ERECTED BY EPHRAIM CHILD. 1735.

in efforts for the public good, he drew around him men less brave, who shared in his sympathies and profited by his counsels. In church affairs he was conscientious, steadfast and reliable, a leader whose integrity and wisdom secured the confidence of his Christian brethren, and rendered him a fit man to transmit to posterity, attractive and valuable characteristics.

[Fourth Generation.] Children:

27. i. EPHRAIM CHILD, Jr., b. in Woodstock, Jan. 15, 1711, m. Jan. 20, 1734, Mary Lyon.

28. ii. DANIEL CHILD, b. in Woodstock, Ct., Jan. 1, 1713, m. first Jan. 1, 1747, to Ruth Ammidown Curtis, second m. to Abigail Bridges.

29. iii. PRISCILLA CHILD, b. in Woodstock, Ct., Mar. 7, 1715, d. Sep. 6, 1736.

30. iv. HENRY CHILD, b. in Woodstock, Ct., May 28, 1717, m. twice, first 1742 Rebecca Bacon. She d. Nov. 2, 1772. His second m. was July 6, 1757, to Dorothy Child.

31. v. MEHITABLE CHILD, b. in Woodstock, Ct., June 8, 1718, m. July 3, 1741, Nehemiah Lyon.

32. vi. MARY CHILD, b. in Woodstock, Ct., April 12, 1721, m. first March 20, 1746, Job Revere, m. second June 11, 1747, Stephen May.

33. vii. ESTHER CHILD, b. in Woodstock, Ct., Sept. 6, 1722. Not known. whether she married. Died April 9, 1789.

34. viii. ELISHA CHILD, b. in Woodstock, Ct, Feb. 11, 1725, m. Jan. 20, 1750, Alice Manning.

35. ix. PETER CHILD, b. in Woodstock, Ct., July 6, 1727, m. Dec. 10, 1756, Susanna Child.

36. x. JOHANNA CHILD, twin sister of Peter, b. July 6, 1727, d. Mar. 21, 1756.

[Fourth Generation.]

27. i. EPHRAIM CHILD, first child of Ephraim and Priscilla Harris Child, b. in Woodstock Ct., Jan. 15, 1711, m. June 20, 1734, Mary Lyon. He d. Sept. 12, 1775. She d. April 21, 1790. They had four children. Residence in Woodstock, Ct.

[Fifth Generation.] Children:

37. i. PRISCILLA CHILD, b. 1737, m. Jonathan Bacon.

38. ii. INCREASE CHILD, b. Dec. 13, 1740, m. Nov. 3, 1762, Olive Pease.

39. iii. ASA CHILD, b. April 6, 1743, m. Nov. 16, 1793, Elizabeth Murray.

40. iv. THEODA CHILD, bapt. April 7, 1745, d. Dec. 12, 1748.

[Fifth Generation.]

38. ii. INCREASE CHILD, second child of Ephraim and Mary Lyon Child, b. in Woodstock, Ct., Dec. 13, 1740, m. Olive Pease of Somers, Ct. Nov. 3, 1762. She was b. March 10, 1738, d. July 5, 1822, in Greenfield, Saratoga Co., N. Y. He d. June 10, 1810, in the same town. They had nine children.

From papers furnished by one of the descendants of Increase
Child, we obtain items of his history which reveal a somewhat
eventful life, showing manliness, patriotism, and personal virtues. Captain Increase, as he comes to our notice, is a lusty,
burly youth, of a mercurial temperament, of an adventurous
disposition, not content with the monotony of a home devoid of
excitements, bent upon knowing and seeing what was going on
in the world. At scarcely sixteen years of age, when Israel
Putnam was commissioned by the Connecticut colony as captain, in 1755, in the French war, young Increase, in response
to the call for volunteers, was among the first to be enrolled,
and served through the seven years' campaign of this war. He
fought in the battles at Crown Point and Ticondaroga. At the
time of Putnam's capture, in 1756, young Child was marching
near him. The Indians seized Putnam and bound him to a
tree, where he was exposed to the fire of both friends and foes.
How Putnam was extricated from his position, our informant
does not tell. But he lived, as we know, to fight the battles
of the Revolution. Returning to the old homestead at the close
of this war, he tarried but a short time, when he left and went
to Dutchess county, N. Y., and engaged in school teaching in a
place called "Oblong," deriving its name probably from its
peculiar shape, as a point of land adjacent to the Hudson river.
After spending a few years in teaching, he returned to Woodstock, Ct., and married Miss Pease of Somers He made Woodstock, Ct., his home for a number of years, rearing some of his
children, if not all, in this town, when the attractions of the then
west brought him back to the borders of the Hudson river.
Taking his eldest son (Salmon Child), then a lad, on horseback
behind him, he went to Dutchess county, N. Y., provided a
home, and brought over his family, and settled there.

When the Revolutionary war broke out, he enlisted under
General Schuyler, as captain. Under Generals Schuyler and
Gates he served through the war and obtained an honorable
discharge. In this campaign his son (Salmon) acted at first as
a waiter for his father, being too young at the commencement
of the war to be taken as a soldier, but before its close his
name was enrolled on the list of volunteers. The excitements
and hardships of war during an eight years' service were not
sufficient to break the force of will and purpose in Captain In-

crease Child. The northern section of the State of New York, through which the army of Schuyler and Gates had been led, presented such attractions to Captain Child that he resolved to make it his future home. His settlement was in Milton, Saratoga county, N. Y., where he became a permanent and useful citizen. The early opportunities of Captain Increase Child for a substantial education, that should qualify him for practical life, had been well improved. He was an excellent penman, and a competent surveyor and conveyancer, and a man of excellent general business capacity. The inherent force of character evinced by Increase Child in budding youth did not expend itself in riper years; nor did it expire at his death and leave no traces in the long line of descendants of this remarkable man. As we trace the history of this branch of the family name, there lies along the entire line, at not very wide intervals, the most robust and sturdy qualities of mental and physical manliness and moral worth. The children of Captain Increase Child were among the best and most enlightened citizens of their day. Nor have succeeding generations exhibited less noble, manly, patriotic and intelligent characteristics.

[Sixth Generation.] Children:

41. i. HAVILAN CHILD, b. in Woodstock, Ct., Aug. 13, 1763, d. Aug. 19, 1766.

42. ii. SALMON CHILD, b. in Woodstock, Ct., Sep. 19, 1765, m. Jan. 7, 1787, Olive Rose.

43. iii. ROXALANA CHILD, b in Woodstock, Ct., June 17, 1767, d. young.

44. iv. ROXALANA CHILD, 2d, b. in Woodstock, Ct., May 3, 1769, m. Robert Ackerman, d. at Pillar Point, N. Y.

45. v. MARK ANTHONY CHILD, b. in Woodstock, Ct., May 10, 1771, m. Dec. 8, 1793, Hannah Benedict, m. 2d 1819, Submit Peacock.

46 vi. EPHRAIM CHILD, b. May 10, 1773, m. Jan. 1, 1796, Mary Woodworth.

47. vii. OLIVE CHILD, b. Mar. 11, 1775, m. 1798, Alfred Bosworth.

48. viii WILLIAM CHILD, b Jan. 4, 1777, m. Feb. 5, 1820, Polly Weed.

49. ix. ASA CHILD, b. May 21, 1780, m. 1806, Lois Foote.

[Sixth Generation.]

42. ii. Judge SALMON CHILD, second child of Captain Increase and Olive Pease Child, b. in Woodstock, Ct., Sept. 19, 1765, m. Jan. 7, 1787, Olive Rose. She was b. Oct. 23, 1763, and died May 2, 1825. He died at East Troy, Walworth Co., Wisconsin, Jan. 28, 1856. They had five children.

Judge Salmon Child in his boyhood received his education amid the stirring scenes of the Colonial Revolution. His surroundings in his youth were of a character to foster manly sentiments and noble aspirations. His contact with men of large ideas and elevated purposes helped to develop him into the man he was in after life. When his father, Captain Increase Child, returned from the French War, with experiences full of stirring incident, the son could but catch the spirit and imbibe the sentiments of the father. Thus was laid the foundation of a noble character in the great and good man he came to be in after life. As already related in his father's history, he entered the Revolutionary army at an early age, serving as his father's waiter, being too young for regular service. When arrived at the proper age, he put on the trappings of the soldier, and fought the battles of freedom by the side of his patriot sire. At the close of the war he went with his father to Saratoga county, N. Y., and effected an independent settlement in the town of Greenfield in that county. In 1787 he married Olive Rose, and entered upon a new career of life. His experiences in the army, conjoined with inherent qualities of sound sense and uncommon sagacity, fitted him for the duties of civil life. His influence as a leading citizen in town and county was early acknowledged, and the confidence reposed in him by his fellow citizens is clearly indicated by the official positions to which he was elected by their suffrages. But it was not in a civil capacity alone that Judge Child contributed a healthful influence to the conditions of society. Few men could be found at that period more truly conscientious, and who comprehended more clearly the importance of educational and religious institutions in establishing a prosperous community. The estimate in which Judge Child was held in the town and county where he spent a long life will be seen in an obituary notice, taken from a Saratoga, N. Y., weekly paper, which we give in this connection:

DIED.—January 28, 1856, in Walworth county, Wisconsin, Hon. SALMON CHILD.

Judge Salmon Child was for a long time a resident of Saratoga county, N. Y. He was one of the first settlers in West Greenfield, more than seventy years ago, and resided there until a few years since, when he and his family removed West. He was a pensioner, having when quite young gone out with his father, who was a captain in the Revolutionary war. He was a prominent member of the Baptist Church, and had much to do in its formation and maintenance where he resided. He was one of the six or eight men in Greenfield who formed one of the first temperance societies in this county, in 1809. He was a plain farmer, a plain common-sense man, and ever sustained an irreproachable, moral and religious character; the great weight of which brought him into public life. He was twice elected as Member of Assembly from this county, and was appointed and served for a number of years as first judge of the county. He was elected in 1821 a member of the convention to amend the Constitution of the State of New York. Perhaps no non-professional man ever received a greater share of public offices in the county. He has served out a long life (91 yrs.) of usefulness. He died calmly and in peace, and has entered upon the rest prepared for the people of God.

We append the following quotations from the writings of Judge Salmon Child, as illustrating his times and himself. In part, they are from a long letter addressed to his granddaughter and her husband, when the Judge was eighty-five years of age, and from an article prepared for a newspaper publication called the *Repository*. The letter begins with a clear statement of his religious faith, especially his strong belief in the Trinity, quoting from the Old and New Testaments, passages elucidating and verifying his deductions, bringing out with unmistakable emphasis the doctrines of free will and moral responsibility, closing this portion of the letter with these words:

The history both of the Old Testament and the New, and of the Church of Christ down to the present day, teaches us that settling down on a form of Godliness, without the spirit or power thereof, God abhors. And it is the stronghold, the foundation of anti-Christ's kingdom. As long as a Christian or a Christian church live in the faith, in the love, spirit and obedience of the Gospel of Christ, they will grow in grace and in knowledge daily, and become the "salt of the earth," the light of the world, a "city set on a hill that cannot be hid."

He then gives some account of his early life:

My parents and grandparents lived in Woodstock, Connecticut. My grandfather belonged to what was then called the "Standing Order," since, "Congregationalists." They were very strict in keeping the Sabbath and all the forms of religion, as they understood them. They kept Saturday night. All kind of labor, in doors and out, was laid aside as soon as the sun set, and if it was necessary they should boil victuals for the Sabbath, every thing was prepared and put into the pot before the sun set. They took the whole family to meeting, and after returning, and supper was over, the children were taught the Westminster catechism, or other religious exercises, until the sun set, which was watched very closely by us children, and not forgotten by the elders. The moment it was said, "It is sundown," the men were out preparing for the week's work, the women making all things ready for the wash-tub, and the children all hilarity. When I was about six years old my father moved into Dutchess county, New York, about one mile from the west line of Connecticut. The Stamp Act had been passed and repealed before this time, but a number of other oppressive laws had been passed. There was at that time very little paper made in America, and no contract, even to a note of hand, could be collected, or was lawful, unless written on stamped paper, sent from England. Boston was the center-place of opposition to these oppressions, and regular troops were sent there to enforce these laws. Under these circumstances, the patriotic neighborhood where my father resided, formed into a minute company, to be ready at all times, when called for in defence of their country.

Soon after the battle of Bunker Hill my father was called to the City of New York, received a captain's commission to enlist a company for one year, from the following first of April. He did so, and rendezvoused with his company on Constitution Island, opposite West Point, for the purpose of fortifying that place, so as to stop navigation on the Hudson, of British shipping going up to the head of navigation, which would leave but 50 or 60 miles of land for an army to cross to the head of Lake Champlain. It was so important to fortify West Point and the Highlands, that a number of the officers took their sons (under 14 years) for waiters, that all the able-bodied men might serve. My father took me only in my eleventh year, I served only ten months. On the 1st of April, 1777, all my father's resources were spent, and he involved in debt. In 1777, the British sent an army from New York up the Hudson and another from Montreal to meet at Albany. The one from the south took Fort Montgomery. Had the British succeeded in their plans of cutting off the New England States from the Southern, the declaration of '76 would have continued to be treated with contempt. Soon after, my father became captain of a company of volunteers, raised to stop the progress of Burgoyne. The company joined Gates' army at Stillwater, Saratoga county, where they stayed until the surrender of the British army. My father was so well suited with the land in Stillwater, he bargained for a farm, about three miles from where the battles were fought, and he and myself went there in March, prepared for and put in some grain, and a garden, and he returned for the family.

It being a wooded country, and but little of the farm cleared, in the spring a number of the bodies of men were found. They had been buried in so shallow a grave, the covering so light, the wolves had dug them up and partially devoured them. Some parts of the battles had been fought in the woods. I think it was the next winter a negro, sent to the woods with his axe to chop trees, not returning, he was searched for, and it was found he had fought a large number of wolves, killed two with his axe, but they were too numerous and had killed and partly eaten him. Wolves were so plenty sheep could be kept only by shutting them in a close pen at night.

My father was a well-read man and had as good an education as any at that period, who had not enjoyed collegiate advantages. Was with General Putnam (then Major) in two campaigns of the French war, and was within a few feet of him when the Indians captured him. My father was a whig, and lived in a neighborhood of whigs. I, of course, heard much said about the whig and tory parties in the British parliament, and although a boy, I turned to an old English dictionary to find the meaning of those words so closely connected with the serious and fearful anxieties that appeared on the countenances of the more aged. The original meaning of whig I found to be whey, buttermilk, or small beer, and was first applied to those in Scotland who held their meetings in the fields, their food being buttermilk; afterwards a nickname given those who opposed the court and high church party in the times of King Charles and James II. The word tory was used in Ireland to signify robbers, murderers, who stood outlawed for their crimes; subsequently a name given the opulent, overbearing, ecclesiastical and political aristocracy of the British Government. I, of course, venerated the whig party, and abhorred the other. There was another source from which I learned much. At that time there was published a small weekly newspaper, under the heading *Common Sense*, several articles appeared, giving a very clear and discriminating view of the principles of the British Government and contrasting them with a republican. From these sources, I formed the opinions which have been my polar star through my three score years and ten. Great honors have been bestowed on the patriot soldiers of the Revolution; but the mothers, wives and daughters of those noble men bore their full share of the sufferings of those times, and are equally with them entitled to the gratitude of the present and future generations.

[Seventh Generation.] Children:

50. i. INCREASE W. CHILD, b. in Greenfield, Saratoga Co., N. Y., Oct. 9, 1787, m. Jan 12, 1810, Desire Frink.

51. ii. ESTHER CHILD, b. in Greenfield, N. Y. Dec. 27, 1790, d. July 24 1796.

52. iii. OLIVE CHILD, b. in Greenfield, N. Y., Jan. 21, 1795, d. young.

53. iv. WILLIAM CHILD, b. in Greenfield, N. Y., Jan. 4, 1798, m. Feb. 5, 1820, Susan Deake.

54. v. PRISCILLA CHILD, b. in Greenfield, N. Y. Sep. 3, 1800, m. Mr. Petit, d. April 1, 1877.

[Seventh Generation.]

50. i. Dr. INCREASE W. CHILD, eldest child and son of Judge Salmon and Olive Rose Child, b. in Greenfield, N. Y., Oct. 9, 1787, m. Jan. 12, 1810, Desire Frink, dau. of Colonel Henry Frink of Milton, Saratoga Co., N. Y. She was b. Feb. 10, 1791, d. Sep. 23, 1824. He d. in Fayette, Seneca Co., N. Y., Feb. 1, 1846.

As a physician and surgeon, Dr. Child was eminent not only in Saratoga county, for many years his field of practice, but attained a high standing in the state. His medical associates held him in great esteem for his personal qualities as well as superior skill in his profession. His services as a lecturer in his profession were often sought and obtained by the medical colleges in the country, and his opinions in critical cases were deferred to by the medical fraternity. His private virtues secured for him the confidence of all classes, and gave him commanding influence. His patrons were not altogether among the rich and influential; the humble dwellings of the poor and lowly were never shunned by Dr. Child. Endowed by nature with noble and generous feelings, expanded and deepened by the force of a Christian faith, he was drawn to the needy, on whom he freely expended his counsels and aid without fee or reward. As a public benefactor, he early espoused the temperance reform, and from his personal popularity, reclaimed some from habits of intemperance, and saved many by his persuasions and his methods for prescribing for his patients from falling into these habits. Seldom, if ever, did he prescribe alcoholic liquors as a tonic.

Mrs. Child was scarcely less popular among her extensive acquaintances and her husband's patients. By nature and culture, she was a lady of great personal attractions. Her qualities of heart were among her greatest charms. She seems to have been the counterpart of her noble husband. One of her daughters says of her, "by her ladylike qualities and kindness of heart she gained many friends. Many a time have I seen her fill a basket with delicacies, provisions and clothing for poor families, the patients of my father, to be conveyed by him in his round of visits to their humble abodes." In speaking of her mother, in the portrayal of her excellencies, another daughter says, "I cannot say enough in her praise." And at her burial, her clergyman speaks of her as embodying all that is lovely and attractive.

[Eighth Generation.]   Children:

55. i. HENRY FRINK CHILD, b. in Milton, Saratoga Co., N. Y., Oct. 25, 1811.

56. ii SALMON CHILD, b. in Milton, N. Y., Oct. 25, 1812, m. Catharine Lewis.

57. iii MARION CHILD, b. in Milton, N. Y., March 2, 1814, m. Adam Wynkoop.

58. iv. CAROLINE CHILD, b. in Milton, N. Y., Sep. 7, 1815, m. Dan'l Barrett.

59. v. HANNAH FRINK CHILD, b. in Milton, N. Y., Dec. 17, 1816, m. Israel Howe.

60. vi. OLIVE CHILD, b in Milton, N. Y., June 1, 1818, d. Aug. 1854, unm.

61. vii. BENJAMIN R. CHILD, b. in Milton, N. Y., Oct. 2, 1819, m. Catharine Cole.

62. viii. MARY CHILD, b. in Milton, N. Y., Aug. 8, 1821, lives with Mrs. Barret at Fairfax, C. H., Va. unmarried.

63. ix. SARAH CHILD, b. in Milton, N. Y., Jan. 27, 1823, m. Nov. 2, 1850, Paris Pettit

64. x. MARTHA CHILD, b. in Milton, N. Y., June, 20, 1825, m. Nov. 25, 1848, Andrew Van Gieson

65. xi. MELINDA CHILD, b. in Milton, N. Y., May 7, 1827, m. Nov. 2, 1851, Bernard M Madden

66. xii. FRANCES FRINK CHILD, b. in Milton, N. Y., Jan. 18, 1829, m. Nov. 17, 1847, William Gates.

67. xiii. DESIRE FRINK CHILD, b. in Milton, N. Y., Dec. 5, 1830, m. Dan'l Barrett, her brother-in-law, at Falls Church, Fairfax Co., Va.

68. xiv. ISAAC FRINK CHILD, b. in Milton, N. Y., June 21, 1832, m. Oct. 11, 1862, Jennie E. Kellogg.

69. xv. INCREASE W. CHILD, Jr., b. in Milton, N. Y., Nov. 12, 1835, d. 1872. Was a merchant in New York city, unmarried.

[Eighth Generation.]

55. i. HENRY FRINK CHILD, eldest child of Dr. Increase W. and Olive Rose Child, b. in Milton, N. Y., Oct. 25, 1811, was a physician, and established himself in Poughkeepsie, N. Y., where he had an extensive practice: was popular as a man, and acquired a high reputation in his profession. He died Sept. 1871, much lamented by his friends and acquaintances. He never married.

[Eighth Generation.]

56. ii. SALMON CHILD, second child and son of Dr. Increase W. and Olive Rose Child, b. in Milton, N. Y., Oct. 25, 1812, m. Catharine Lewis of Ontario Co., N. Y., moved to Virginia, purchased a large tract of land six miles from Georgetown, and became a successful planter. He died Dec. 29, 1860, leaving a wife, but no children.

[Eighth Generation.]

57. iii. MARION CHILD, eldest dau. and third child of Dr. Increase W. and Desire Frink Child, b. in Milton, N. Y., March 2, 1814, m. Adam Wynkoop, a wealthy farmer of Hopewell, Ontario Co., N. Y.

[Ninth Generation.] Children:

70. i. CARA C. WYNKOOP.
71. ii. DESIRE F. WYNKOOP.
72. iii. JOHN WYNKOOP.

[Eighth Generation.]

58. iv. CAROLINE CHILD, second dau. and fourth child of Dr. Increase W. and Desire Frink Child, b. Sep. 7, 1815. She had a thorough education. Started a young ladies' seminary in Dutchess Co., N. Y., of which she was for some years principal.

She married Daniel Barrett in that county, and they removed
to Fairfax Co., Va. Mr. Barrett became an extensive planter.
Mrs. Barrett died in 1862. Mr. Barrett married, second, Desire
Frink Child, sister of his first wife. There were no children
by this marriage. He died in 1874. Mr. Barrett's house was
often the headquarters of Gen. McClellan and staff. Mrs. Barrett resides at Fairfax, C. H., Va.

[Ninth Generation.] Children of Caroline Child and Daniel Barrett:
    73. i. HENRY BARRETT,
    74. ii. SAMUEL BARRETT.
    75. iii. CAROLINE BARRETT.
    76. iv. KATHARINE BARRETT.

[Eighth Generation.]

    59. v. HANNAH FRINK CHILD, third dau. and fifth child of
Dr. Increase W. and Desire Frink Child, b. in Milton, N. Y.,
Dec. 17, 1816, m. Israel Howe of Gorham, Ontario Co., N. Y.;
removed to Sanford, Broome Co., N. Y.

[Ninth Generation.] Children:
    77. i. PHILO HOWE, b. in Gorham, Ontario Co., N. Y., Feb. 13, 1843, m.
Dec. 25, 1872, Della Baker.
    78. ii. EMMA P. HOWE, b. in Gorham, Ontario Co., N. Y., Oct. 21, 1844,
m. Aug. 1862, Jno. E. Freleigh, reside in Floyd Co., Iowa.
    79. iii. ALVIN RUSH HOWE, b. in Gorham, Ontario Co., N. Y., April 30,
1847, m. May 11, 1870, Patience A. Seward.
    80. iv. ANNE D. HOWE, b. in Gorham, Ontario Co., N. Y., Aug. 7, 1851;
is a teacher in a ladies' school at Dobb's Ferry, on the Hudson river.

[Eighth Generation.]

    61. vii. BENJAMIN R. CHILD, seventh child of Dr. Increase
W. and Desire Frink Child, b. in Milton, N. Y., Oct. 2, 1819,
m. Catharine Cole, dau. of Judge Cole, of New York City.

[Ninth Generation.] Children:
    81. i. HENRY CHILD.
    82. ii. HENRIETTA CHILD.

[Eighth Generation.]

    63. ix. SARAH H. CHILD, sixth dau. and ninth child of Dr.
Increase W. and Desire Frink Child, b. in Milton, N. Y., Jan.
27, 1823, m. Nov. 2, 1850, Paris Pettit, son of William Riley
and Priscilla Child Pettit, (the mother of Paris P. was dau.
of Judge Salmon Child,) by Rev. John J. Stearns, in Gorham, Ontario Co., N. Y. They reside at Fort Atkinson, Jefferson county, Wis. Mrs. Pettit is by profession a teacher.

[Ninth Generation.] Children:

83. i. AGNES CHILD PETTIT, b. in Troy, Wis., Aug. 19, 1852, d. April 22, 1853.

84. ii. MARION CORNELIA PETTIT, b. in Troy, Wis., April 15, 1854.

85. iii. FANNIE FRINK PETTIT, b. in Troy, Wis., March 9, 1856.

86. iv. ALICE SMITH PETTIT, b. in Troy, Wis., June 3, 1858, d. Nov. 5, 1863.

87. v. HENRY PARIS PETTIT, b. in Troy, Wis., July 25, 1862.

[Eighth Generation.]

64. x. MARTHA CHILD, seventh dau. and tenth child of Dr. Increase W. and Desire Frink Child. b. in Milton, N. Y., June 2, 1825, m. Nov. 2, 1848, Andrew Van Gieson, son of John and Cynthia Bush Van Gieson of Lodi, Washtenaw Co., Michigan, by Rev. Mr. Tozer, in Fayette N. Y.   Mr. Van G. is a farmer, Mrs. Van G. is a teacher.   They Reside in Beloit, Rock Co., Wis.

[Ninth Generation.] Children:

88. i. FRED L. VAN GIESON, b. Feb. 6, 1854, in Broome Co., N. Y.

89. ii. CHARLES BUSH VAN GIESON, b. March 25, 1860, in Rock Co., Wis.

90. iii. CLARA BELL VAN GIESON, b. Nov. 7, 1866, in Rock Co., Wis.

[Eighth Generation.]

65. xi. MELINDA FRINK CHILD, eighth dau. and eleventh child of Dr. Increase W. and Desire Frink Child, b. in Milton, N. Y., May 7, 1827, m. Nov. 2, 1851, Bernard M. Madden of Seneca Co., N. Y., now residents in Elkhorn, Walworth Co., Wis.

[Ninth Generation.] Children:

91. i. FRANCES LILLIAN C. MADDEN, b. in Elkhorn, Wis., Jan. 15, 1854.   She is principal of the high school in Elkhorn.

92. ii. MARY CHILD MADDEN, b. in Elkhorn, Wis., July 10, 1856.

93. iii. ISAAC CHILD MADDEN, b. in Elkhorn, Wis., Oct. 13, 1860.   Is a law student.

94. iv. MELINDA CHILD MADDEN, b. in Elkhorn, Wis., May 22, 1863.

[Eighth Generation.]

66. xii. FRANCES FRINK CHILD, ninth dau. and twelfth child of Dr. Increase W. and Desire Frink Child, b. in Milton, N. Y., Jan. 18, 1829, m. Nov. 17, 1847, William Gates, son of Cyrus and Jane Wycoff Gates of La Crosse, Wis., by Rev. John G. Stearns.   Reside in Beloit. Wis.

[Ninth Generation.] Children:

95. i. ADELBERT GATES, b. in Tuttle, Rock Co., Wis., June 27, 1849, d. by railroad accident Aug. 27, 1877.

96. ii. JENNIE GATES, b. in Tuttle, Rock Co., Wis., July 3, 1851.

97. iii. HARRY ELWOOD GATES, b. in Tuttle, Rock Co., Wis., Apr. 18, 1857,

G

98. iv. Oscar Elmore Gates, b in Tuttle, Rock Co., Wis., Dec. 29, 1859, d. Oct. 31, 1860.

99. v. Edna S. Gates, b in Tuttle, Rock Co., Wis., Jan. 14, 1869.

100. vi. Lois C. Gates, b. in Tuttle, Rock Co., Wis., Sep. 14, 1870.

[Eighth Generation.]

68. xiv. Isaac Frink Child, fourth son and fourteenth child of Dr. Increase W. and Desire Frink Child, b. in Milton, N. Y., Jan. 21, 1832, m. Oct. 10, 1862, by Jack Lynes, Esq., Jennie E. Kellogg, dau. of Helmont and Electa Washburn Kellogg of New Bloomfield, Callaway Co., Mo.

Mr. Child was a dry goods merchant at Dryersburg, Tennessee. His death has occurred but recently, (March 9, 1879,) and was very sudden. Mrs. Child writes us that "He died of a congestive chill fever. A few days previous to his death, while in health, he received your letter asking for his family record, when he expressed himself greatly pleased at the prospect of a genealogy of the Child family, and had set apart the very day of his death for preparing his family record," the melancholy duty falling upon his wife, which she has faithfully performed. Mr. Child was popular as a citizen in Dryersburg, once Mayor of the city, and esteemed for his probity, magnanimity and generosity. He removed to Tennessee in 1859, and through the sectional strife adhered to the old flag of the Union, affording ample proof that the blood of his Puritan ancestry was running in his veins not less warmly than in the veins of the fathers in the days of the Revolution.

[Ninth Generation.]   Children:

101. i. Madge Child, b. Oct. 3, 1864.

102. ii. Gerold Child, b. Aug. 18, 1865.

103. iii. Gretchen Child, b. March 15, 1868.

104. iv. Stamford Child, b. Oct. 5, 1870.

105. v. Guy Child, b. June 6, 1873.

106. vi. May Tenth Child, b. May 10, 1875.

107. vii. Mac Child, b. April 25, 1878.

[Seventh Generation.]

53. iv. William Child, second son and fourth child of Judge Salmon and Olive Rose Child, was b. in Greenfield, Saratoga Co., N. Y., Jan. 4, 1798, m. Feb. 5, 1820, to Susan Deake. She was b. Dec. 25, 1798. On the 14th of May, 1861, Mr. Child writes to his cousin Olive, dau. of Dr. Increase W. Child, sending to her a copy of the family record from the old

family Bible,—"Wm. Child, b. Jan. 4, 1798, m. to Susan Deake Feb. 5, 1820, and are this day living joyfully together, through the mercy of God, May 14, 1861."

Mr. William Child was the youngest son, and the home son, until the spring of 1836, when he moved to Gorham, Ontario county, where he resided some eleven years. In 1847, he again moved with his family to Walworth county, Wis., and here remained until his death. His children were born in Greenfield, Saratoga county, N. Y. In stature five feet ten inches, like his mother's family (the Rose) he was spare, but with the Child complexion and eyes. Fragile in health in early years, he used to say of himself that, "he grew up a puny, petted and spoiled child," owing some unusual indulgence to the frequent absence from home upon public affairs of his father, Judge Child. He was kind and tender in heart, impulsive, and sometimes irritable in temper, but never retaining ill-will. Of hunting and fishing, he was passionately fond, and always loved his dog and gun. An admirer of Burns and Shakespeare, whom he read effectively, and thus instructed and entertained his children in the long winter evenings; with his family, he shared all his pursuits and pleasures in a marked degree. Indeed, he attributed his conversion to the lovely christian life and daily prayers of his wife, though he had an inheritance of godliness. After his removal to the west, he became an earnest Christian worker. Linked with the Baptist denomination, he served almost gratuitously the "Wisconsin Baptist State Missionary Convention," for some time in a quiet and effective manner, collecting and dispensing funds and awakening a strong sympathy between the different Baptist churches in the State. With equal enthusiasm he regarded the causes of education and politics. The last outside activities of this fond husband and wife, were ministrations in the household of a poor German family, who were all sick. Mrs. Child caught the fever, and her death from it occurred on the 17th of April, 1865; two days previous President Lincoln had been assassinated. Mr. Child was an ardent admirer of President Lincoln, and the shock of these two deaths was too severe. With no organic disease, he succumbed on the 24th of the same month. Walking from the fire to his bed, he lay down, waved his hand to his son James standing near, and smiling said, "Good-bye." These incidents are related by his son, Rev. Increase Child.

[Eighth Generation.]   Children:

108 i. JAMES CHILD, b. Aug. 23, 1823, m. Sep. 15, 1847, Esther Dinsmore.
109. ii. OLIVE CHILD, b. May 6, 1825, m. Feb. 14, 1850, Alfred Payne.
110, iii. INCREASE CHILD, b. Dec. 10, 1827, m June 5, 1850, Artimesia Lincoln, m. 2d Sept. 2. 1875. Adaline Flagg.
111. iv. DEXTER CHILD, b. Nov. 7, 1829, d. May 3, 1852, beloved by all who knew him.
112 v. ABBEY CHILD, b. May 4, 1836, m. Nov. 12, 1856, to Cyrus S. Phillips.

[Eighth Generation]

108. i. JAMES CHILD, first child of William and Susan Deake Child, b. Aug. 23, 1823, m. Sep. 15, 1847, Esther Dinsmore. She was b. March 4, 1827. They reside in East Troy, Walworth Co., Wis.

[Ninth Generation]   Children:

113. i. MELZAR CHILD, b. Aug. 26, 1848, d, Sep. 29, 1849.
114. ii. HULDAH CHILD, b April 6, 1850, m. T. H. Conklin. She d. Nov. 29, 1872.
115. iii. SUSAN CHILD, b. March 7, 1852, d. April 22, 1869.
116. iv. WILLIAM CHILD, b. Feb. 14, 1854, d. Oct. 3, 1855.
117. v. WILLIAM CHILD, 2d, b. June 27, 1856.
118. vi. HENRY DEXTER CHILD, b. Oct. 25, 1858, d. Sep. 1, 1866.
119. vii. EMMA CHILD, b. March 17, 1861.
120. viii. CHAUNCEY CHILD, b. May 6, 1863, d. Sep. 5, 1864.
121. ix. ABBEY L. CHILD, b. Sep. 9. 1864.
122. x. ESTHER M. CHILD, b. Feb. 13, 1869, d. Sep. 21, 1869.

[Eighth Generation.]

109. ii. OLIVE CHILD, eldest dau. and second child of William and Susan Deake Child, b. in Milton N. Y., May 6, 1825, m. Feb. 14, 1850, at Spring Prairie, Wis., Alfred Payne of Piqua, O., a portrait and landscape painter. They reside in Hinsdale, Ill.

[Ninth Generation.]   Children:

123. i. SUSAN PAYNE, b. in Hinsdale, Ill., Feb. 23, 1851, is a teacher of English Literature in the Latin High School, Chicago, Ill.
124. ii. EMMA PAYNE, b. in Hinsdale, Ill., May 10, 1853, m. April 9, 1874, Charles E. Erskine, of the firm of Chase & Co., manf. of threshing machines and portable furnaces.
125. iii. HENRY PAYNE, b. in Hinsdale, Ill., Oct. 23, 1855, is a teacher in Hinsdale, Ill.
126. iv. WILLIAM CHILD PAYNE, b. in Hinsdale, Ill., July 28, 1861.
127. v. ELSIE PAYNE, b. in Hinsdale, Ill., April 27, 1864.
128. vi. BERTHA PAYNE, b. in Hinsdale, Ill., January 20, 1867.

[Ninth Generation.]

124. ii. EMMA PAYNE, second dau. and second child of Olive Child and Alfred Payne, b. in Hinsdale, Ill., May 10, 1853, m. April 9, 1874, Charles E. Erskine.

[Tenth Generation.] Child:

129. i. ALFRED M. ERSKINE, b. June 12, 1875.

[Eighth Generation.]

110. iii. Rev. INCREASE CHILD, second son and third child of William and Susan Deake Child, b. Dec. 10, 1827, m. 1st Artimesia Lincoln, June 5, 1850. She was b. Dec. 31, 1829, d. June 21, 1875; m. 2nd Sept. 2, 1875, Adaline Flagg. She was b. Nov. 6, 1838.

Rev. Mr. Child is an inheritor from his paternal and maternal ancestry, of that "mercy unto thousands of them that love Me and keep my Commandments," and lives to perpetuate the promise to future generations. The wonderful transmission of characteristics peculiar to different families, has found in him a dual manifestation. In early life he seemed to partake entirely of the mental features of his mother's family; with advancing years these were largely overgrown by the Child qualities. In the work of the ministry, Mr. Child has found his sphere, and by it has been compelled to conquer that *vis inertia* which is thought to be a Child characteristic, often hindering them from being and doing all they might. Chastened by afflictions, he is the true consoler of the sorrowing; craving knowledge, he is fitted to instruct and elevate others; loving his Master, he labors untiringly to win his flock into the fold of the good Shepherd. Quick in his sympathies, he has been earnest in his efforts to aid in this memorial work of a noble ancestry.

[Ninth Generation.] Children:

130. i. HENRY LINCOLN CHILD, b. Aug. 10, 1851, d. Feb. 11, 1852.

131. ii. MARY LINCOLN CHILD, b. March 18, 1854, d. July 8, 1854.

132. iii. ELLEN LOVISA CHILD, b. June 20, 1855, m. Feb. 6, 1875, d. Clinton Ransom.

133. iv. JULIA L. CHILD, b. February 1, 1858, d. June 11, 1861.

134. v. CHARLES M. CHILD, b. April 11, 1866, d. April 13, 1866.

135. vi. CLEMENT DEXTER CHILD, b. May 15, 1868.

[Eighth Generation.]

112. v. ABBEY CHILD, second dau. and fifth child of William and Susan Deake Child, b. May 4, 1836, m. Nov. 12, 1856, Cyrus

S. Phillips. He was b. April 18, 1828. Resides in Tecumseh, Johnson Co., Nebraska.

[Ninth Generation.]   Child:

    136. i. LOTTIE PHILLIPS, b. Dec. 15, 1868.

[Sixth Generation.]

    45. v. MARK ANTHONY CHILD, third son and fifth child of Increase and Olive Pease Child, b. in Stillwater, Saratoga Co., N. Y,, May 10, 1771, d. in St. Lawrence Co., N. Y., Feb. 1843, m. Hannah Benedict, Dec. 8, 1793. She was b. Jan. 1, 1774, d. 1818; m. 2nd about 1819, Submit Peacock. Had eleven children by the first wife, and five by the second.

[Seventh Generation.]   Children:

    137. i. MARY CHILD, b. February 5, 1795, d. same day.

    138. ii. ALFRED BOSWORTH CHILD, b. in Greenfield, N. Y., Nov. 19, 1796, m. March 19, 1817, Polly Barber.

    139. iii. EPHRAIM CHILD, b. in Milton, N. Y., May 15, 1798, m. about 1819, Margaret Van Tassel.

    140. iv. JOHN CHILD, b. in Milton, N. Y., Jan. 18, 1800, m. Jan. 18, 1824, Betsey Harris.

    141. v. BETSEY CHILD, b. Sept. 5, 1802. m. Wm. Harris, 1823.

    142. vi. PAULINA CHILD, b. Nov. 8, 1803. m. Walter Hewitt.

    143. vii. PAMELIA CHILD, b. Aug. 28, 1804, m. Lyman Wooster, March 9, 1850.

    144. viii. RENSSELAER CHILD, b. Oct. 17, 1809, m. Charlotte Burnham, Sept. 1, 1831.

    145. ix. HANNAH CHILD, b. Oct. 16, 1810, m. Amos H. Burnham, 1834.

    146. x. EMELINE CHILD, b. Jan. 19, 1815, m. Jan. 27, 1835, Alanson Barber, m. 2nd, March 11, 1862, Amos Burnham.

    147. xi. MARK ANTHONY CHILD, JR., b. Jan. 13, 1817, m. 1837, Lydia Robinson.

[By second Marriage]:

    148. xii. POLLY B. CHILD, b. in Milton, N. Y., Nov. 9, 1820, m. May 10, 1838, Charles Porter Bennett.

    149. xiii. HARRIET CHILD, b. 1823, m. James Purdy who lives in Ionia, Mich, she d. 1871.

    150. xiv. WALTER CHILD, d. at 17 years.

    151. xv. HENRIETTA CHILD, m. Edmund Robinson.

    152. xvi. CHARLOTTE CHILD, b. Nov. 18, 1833, m. Nov. 17,1864, Mr. Riddle.

[Seventh Generation.]

    138. ii. ALFRED BOSWORTH CHILD, second child and first son of Mark Anthony and Hannah Benedict Child, b. in the town of Greenfield, Saratoga Co., N. Y., Nov. 19, 1796, m. March 19, 1817, Polly Barber who was b. March 30, 1799. She was the daughter of Ichabod and Anne Deake Barber. He died Dec. 22, 1852. They had twelve children.

The somewhat eventful history of Mr. Alfred Bosworth
Child, which we here annex, is furnished by one of his sons,
Warren Gould Child, who passed through many of the experiences of the father, and has much of his zeal for the Mormon
faith:

Alfred Bosworth Child, my father, was married to Polly, daughter of
Ichabod and Anne Deake Barber. He soon after his marriage moved to
the town of Morristown, St. Lawrence county, New York, where he purchased a small farm, of which he cleared and cultivated some thirty acres,
and through economy and industry acquired a limited amount of property.
It was here, in the year 1837, that the principles of Mormonism were sounded
in his ears, and after a careful investigation of the same he embraced Mormonism, sold his farm and moved West to Kirtland, Ohio. Staying there
but a few months, he then left with his family for Caldwell county, Missouri,
where he arrived in the fall of the same year having made the entire journey
with only one team consisting of two horses.

The family had been settled upon a farm purchased by them, when the
persecutions commenced upon the Mormons. We were compelled to leave
in the following spring. The farm and one horse were taken and confiscated by the mob.

He next settled in Lee county, Iowa, in the year 1840, taking up and improving a farm on what was known as the half breed track, remaining there
about seven years. In 1841, he accepted the position of postmaster at what
is known as Spring Prairie post office, which position he held as long as he
remained in the county, which he left through the persecutions of the Mormon people, in 1847. He then started further West, travelling through that
portion of the state which at that time was inhabited by the Pottowattamie
Indians. He settled again at or near where Council Bluffs City, Iowa, now
stands, taking up and improving another farm on which he lived about
five years.

Salt Lake Valley having been selected as a last resort for the more peaceful settlement of the Mormon people, he again, now the fourth time, left
all he had. On the 8th day of July, 1852, he started for Salt Lake Valley,
where he arrived on the first day of the following October, having travelled
in wagons drawn by oxen and cows over one thousand miles across uninhab-
ited desert and mountainous country. On the 22nd day of the next December he died of disease of the lungs, brought on through exposure and the
hardships of his journeyings. His age was 56 years, 1 mo. and 7 days. He
left a wife with four sons and three daughters.

[Eighth Generation.] Children:

    153. i. ICHABOD CHILD, b. April 20, 1818, d. young.
    154. ii. MARY CHILD, b. March 15, 1819, d. young.
    155. iii. JOSEPH CHILD, b. January 19, 1820, d. young.
    156. iv. POLLY ANN CHILD, b. July 20, 1822, m. R. E. Richardson.
    157. v. MARK ALFRED CHILD, b. October 19, 1823, d. unmarried.

Mark Alfred Child enlisted in the U. S. Army at Fort Leavenworth, Mo., in 1844. He marched overland to Mexico as one of

Gen. Kearney's staff, which position he held during the war with Mexico, where he received a lance wound in the neck, and a ball wound in the instep, which disabled him from active service. At the close of the war he was discharged with a pension. After recovering from his wounds he went to Upper California: was there in the great gold excitement, where he engaged in the ranching business, was very successful for a time, when the Indians made a raid on his stock driving it off. He with a posse went in pursuit, in which they were ambushed in a cañon and their entire party killed.

158. vi. MYRON BARBER CHILD, b. Nov. 25, 1825, m. Feb. 14, 1846, Emeline Elmer

159. vii. HANNAH POLINA CHILD, b. Jan. 24, 1828, m. March 26, 1846, William Elmer.

160. viii. JOHN LONSON CHILD, b. Oct. 26, 1830, m. Jan. 24, 1850, Eliza Curtiss.

161. ix. PHEBE WOOSTER CHILD, b. Jan. 17, 1833, m. May 14, 1848, C. Richardson.

162. x. WARREN GOULD CHILD, b. Feb. 21, 1835, m. Jan. 6, 1853, Hannah A. Wilder.

163. xi. ORVILLE RENSSELAER CHILD, b. Oct. 11, 1838, m. Feb. 13, 1859, Urinda Rawson.

164. xii. ASA THOMAS CHILD, b. July 28, 1841, d. May 3, 1848. Lived and died in Lee county, Iowa.

[Eighth Generation.]

156. iv. POLLY ANN CHILD, second dau., and fourth child of Alfred Bosworth and Polly Barber Child, b. July 20, 1822, m. R. E. Richardson about 1847.

[Ninth Generation.]   Children:

165. i. ALFRED BOSWORTH RICHARDSON, b. in Pottawottamie Co., Iowa, Feb. 18, 1848, d. May 16, 1848.

166. ii. WARREN CHILD BOSWORTH RICHARDSON, b. May 4, 1850, m. about 1871, Olive E. Singleton.

167. iii. EBENEZER RICHARDSON, b. Oct. 11, 1852, m. about 1877, Miss Singleton.

168. iv. ANGELINE RICHARDSON, b. Aug. 21, 1857, in Ogden City, U. Ter., m. S. Draney.

169. v. LEVI RICHARDSON, b. Oct. 16, 1860, in Ogden City, U. Ter.

170. vi. ORVILLE RICHARDSON, b. July 11, 1862, in Ogden City, U. Ter., d. January 8, 1865.

[Ninth Generation.]

166. ii. WARREN CHILD BOSWORTH RICHARDSON, second child of Polly Ann Child and R. E. Richardson, b. May 4, 1850, m. Olive E. Singleton, about 1871.

[Tenth Generation.] Children:
171. i. OLIVE RICHARDSON, b. July 17, 1872.
172. ii. HARRIET W. RICHARDSON, b. November 7, 1874.
173. iii. THOMAS E RICHARDSON, b. August 25, 1876.
174. iv. ANNIE RICHARDSON, b. April 29, 1878.

[Ninth Generation.]

167. iii. EBENEZER RICHARDSON, third child of Polly Ann Child and R. E. Richardson, b. Oct. 11, 1852, m. about 1877, Miss Singleton. Lives in Eldorado Co., Cal.
[Tenth Generation.] Child:
175. i. EMMA ERINDA RICHARDSON, b. October 25, 1878.

[Ninth Generation.]

168. iv. ANGELINE RICHARDSON, fourth child of Polly Ann Child and R. E. Richardson, b. Aug. 21, 1857, m. S. Draney. Residence, Ogden City, Utah.
[Tenth Generation.] Children:
176. i. SAMUEL E. DRANEY, b. August 9, 1874.
177. ii. JOHN H. DRANEY, b. August 5, 1876.
178. iii. JOSEPH O. DRANEY, b. August 6, 1878.

[Eighth Generation.]

158. vi. MYRON BARBER CHILD, sixth child of Alfred Bosworth and Polly Barber Child, b. Nov. 25, 1825, m. Feb. 14. 1846, Emeline Elmer, who was b. July 27, 1828, in Chittenden county, Vt.

Warren G. Child writes of M. B. Child:

M. B. Child, now in his 54th year, crossed the plains to Utah in 1850, and settled in or near Ogden. Is a farmer and a prominent citizen; has held various offices of profit and trust, and, like all bearing the name of Child, with whom we have formed any acquaintance, stands high and unblemished in society. Is in stature of medium height, active and jovial, and rather inclined to be corpulent.

[Ninth Generation.] Children:
179. i. WILLIAM WARREN CHILD, b. in Lee county, Iowa, Feb. 26, 1848, m 1868, Jennette Fife.
180. ii. ASA LONSON CHILD, b in Lee county, Iowa, Dec. 29, 1849, unm.
181 iii. ALFRED BOSWORTH CHILD, b. in Pottawattamie county, Iowa, July 8, 1852, m. S. J. Stonebraker.
182. iv. MYRON BARBER CHILD, b. in Pottawattamie county, Iowa, July 3, 1854 d. Nov. 4, 1854.
183. v. MARK ANTHONY CHILD, b. in Weber county, Utah Ter., Dec. 22, 1855.
184. vi. EMELINE LUCINA CHILD, b. in Weber county, Utah Ter., Nov. 21, 1858, m. Alexander Patterson.

185. vii. CYNTHIA LOUISA CHILD, b. in Weber county, Utah Ter., Dec. 14 1861.

186. viii. JOHN SQUIER CHILD, b. in Weber county, Utah Ter., July 4, 1863.

187. ix. CHAUNCEY CHILD, b. in Weber county, Utah Ter., Aug. 13, 1865, d. Aug. 6, 1878.

188. x. POLLY CHILD, b. in Weber county, Utah Ter., Nov. 13, 1868.

189. xi. HENRY INCREASE CHILD, b. in Weber county, Utah Ter., Sept. 2, 1870.

[By second wife, Serepta Cole]:

190. xii. NATHAN CHILD, b. Oct. 24, 1865, in Ogden City, Utah Ter.

191. xiii. HANNAH S. CHILD, b. July 12, 1868, in Ogden City, Utah Ter.

192. xiv. MYRON BARBER CHILD, b. March 7, 1872, in Ogden City, Utah T.

193. xv. GEORGE C. CHILD, b. July 22, 1877, in Ogden City, Utah Ter.

[Ninth Generation,]

179. i. WILLIAM WARREN CHILD, eldest child of Myron Barber and Emeline Elmer Child, b. in Lee county, Iowa, Feb. 26, 1848, m. 1868, Jennette Fife of Ogden City, Utah Ter.

[Tenth Generation.] Children:

194. i. WILLIAM WARREN CHILD, JR., b. Aug. 31, 1869, d. 1878.

195. ii. MYRON BARBER CHILD, b. Sept. 1, 1869, at Riverdale, Utah.

196. iii. NETTIE ELLEN CHILD, b. April 4, 1873, at Hooper City, Utah.

197. iv. JOHN ABRAM CHILD, b. Nov. 21, 1875, d. Oct. 6, 1876, at Hooper City, Utah.

198. v. MARY A. CHILD, b. 1877.

****, vi. LOUISA EMELINE CHILD, b. June, 1879.

[Ninth Generation.]

181. iii. ALFRED BOSWORTH CHILD, third child of Myron Barber and Emeline Elmer Child, b. July 8, 1852, m. Oct. 8, 1872, S. J. Stonebraker.

[Tenth Generation.] Children:

199. i. ALFRED CHILD, b. Sept. 13, 1874.

200. ii. NETTIE PEARL CHILD, b. Oct. 11, 1876.

201. iii. ADELE CHILD, b. Nov. 22, 1878.

[Ninth Generation.]

184. vi. EMELINE L. CHILD, sixth child of Myron Barber and Emeline Elmer Child, b. Nov. 21, 1858, m. Alexander Patterson, about 1875.

[Tenth Generation.] Children:

202. i. ALEXANDER PATTERSON, JR., b. Dec. 28, 1876, in Utah Ter.

203. ii. LUCY E. PATTERSON, b. May 26, 1878, in Utah Ter.

[Eighth Generation.]

159. vii. HANNAH POLINA CHILD, seventh child of Alfred
Bosworth and Polly Barber Child, b. Jan. 24, 1828, m. March
26, 1846, William Elmer, son of John and Sallie Reque Elmer.
He was b. Sept. 16, 1820, in Norwich, Vt.

[Ninth Generation.] Children:

204. i. JOHN SAMUEL ELMER, b. Oct. 13, 1847, d. 1858, in Utah Ter.

205. ii. MARK ALFRED ELMER, b. in Pottawatamie Co. Iowa, Dec. 10, 1848,
m. Minnie Jost.

206. iii. WILLIAM W. ELMER, b. in Pottawatamie Co. Iowa, Jan. 10, 1850,
m. A. Hall.

207. iv. CYNTHIA TRIPHENIA ELMER, b. in Ogden, U. Ter. Dec. 16, 1852,
m. John Leavitt.

208. v. HANNAH PAULINA ELMER, b. in Ogden, U. Ter. Feb. 13, 1853, d.
Dec. 1856.

209. vi. POLLY ANN ELMER, b. in Ogden, U. Ter. Dec. 6, 1856, m. 1876,
J. M. Taylor.

210. vii. PHEBE WOOSTER ELMER, b. in Payson, U. Ter. Sept. 19, 1858,
m M. Hall, Jun.

211. viii. ROSABELL ELMER, b. in Ogden, U. Ter. Nov. 1, 1861.

212. ix. SARAH J. ELMER, b. in Ogden, U. Ter. April 15, 1863.

213. x. DELECTA ANN ELMER, b. in Ogden, U. Ter. Jan. 20, 1866, d. in
Ogden.

214. xi. CHARLES A. ELMER, b. in Ogden, U. Ter. Aug. 1867, d. July 3,
1870.

215. xii. HIRAM B. ELMER, b in Ogden, U. Ter. 1871, d. 1872.

[Ninth Generation.]

205. ii. MARK ALFRED ELMER, second child of Hannah Polina Child and William Elmer, b. Dec. 10, 1848, m. Minnie
Jost, about 1872.

[Tenth Generation.] Children:

216. i. MINNIE M. ELMER, b. Nov. 1873.

217. ii. ELLA M. ELMER, b. July 18, 1875.

218 iii. JOHN A. ELMER, b. 1877.

219. iv. IDA A. ELMER, b. 1878.

[Ninth Generation.]

206. iii. William W. Elmer, third child of Hannah Polina
Child and William Elmer, b. in Pottawatamie Co. Iowa, Jan.
10, 1850, m. A. Hall, about 1873.

[Tenth Generation.] Children:

220. i. MARTHA A. ELMER, b. 1874.

221, ii. WILLIAM W. ELMER, Jun. b. 1877.

[Ninth Generation.]

207. iv. CYNTHIA TRIPHENIA ELMER, fourth child of Hannah Polina Child and William Elmer, b. Dec. 16, 1852, m. 1872, John Leavitt.

[Tenth Generation.] Children.
 222. i. JOHN LEAVITT, Jr, b. Dec. 4, 1873.
 223. ii. ADELE LEAVITT, b. Aug. 22, 1875.
 224. iii. MINNIE LEAVITT, b. June 27, 1878.

[Ninth Generation.]

209. vi. POLLY ANN ELMER, sixth child of Hannah Polina Child and Wm. Elmer, b. Dec. 6, 1856, m. J. M. Taylor, 1876.

[Tenth Generation.] Children:
 225. i. ELIZABETH TAYLOR, b. 1876.
 226. ii. JOHN TAYLOR, b. July 1, 1879.

[Ninth Generation.]

210. vii. PHEBE W. ELMER, seventh child of Hannah Polina Child and Wm. Elmer, b. Sept. 19, 1858, m. 1874, M. Hall, Jr.

[Tenth Generation.] Children:
 227. i. MARK HALL, b. Sept. 1875, d. July 25, 1878.
 228. ii. CHARLES HALL, b. March 12, 1877, d. March 29, 1877.
 229. iii. JOHN HALL, b. Feb. 12, 1878, d. at birth.

[Eighth Generation.]

160. viii. JOHN LONSON CHILD, eighth child of Alfred Bosworth and Polly Barber Child, b. probably in Greenfield, N. Y. Oct. 26, 1830, m. Jan. 24, 1850, Eliza J. Curtiss, dau. of Uriah and Phebe Martin Curtiss of Pottawattamie Co. Iowa. She was b. April 30, 1830, in Fountain county, Ind. Second m. to Mary M. Curtiss.

[Ninth Generation.] Children:
 230. i. SARAH ANN CHILD, b. in Pottawattamie Co. Iowa, Nov. 8, 1850, d. in Ogden City, U. Ter. Jan. 3, 1854.
 231. ii. JOHN COLUMBUS CHILD, b. in Pottawattamie Co. Iowa, March 3, 1852, m. Miss Patterson.
 232. iii. MARY ROSALIE CHILD, b. in Weber Co. U. Ter. Jan. 2, 1854, m. July 28, 1869, C. T. Richardson.
 233. iv. CHARLES URIAH CHILD, b. in Weber Co. U. Ter, Nov. 2, 1855, m. Sept. 10, 1877, Atelia Thompson.
 234. v. LESTER AARON CHILD, b. in Weber Co, U. Ter., Feb. 8, 1862.
    [By second marriage—Mary M. Curtiss.]
 235. vi. EMMA C. CHILD, b. Nov. 2, 1861, m. 1879, A. Bybee.
 236. vii. PHEBE PAULINA CHILD, b. April, 1863.

[Ninth Generation.]

231. ii. JOHN COLUMBUS CHILD, second child and eldest son of John Lonson and Eliza J. Curtiss Child, b. in Pottawattamie Co. Iowa, March 3, 1852, m. Mary Patterson, Oct. 1875, Riverdale, Utah.

[Tenth Generation.] Children:
237. i. LETTIE CHILD, b. Aug. 28, 1876.
238. ii. MARY ELIZA CHILD, b. May 12, 1878.

[Ninth Generation.]

232. iii. MARY ROSALIE CHILD, third child of John Lonson and Eliza J. Curtiss Child, b. in Weber Co. Utah Ter., Jan. 2, 1854, m. July 28, 1869, to C. T. Richardson.

[Tenth Generation.] Children:
239. i. CARRIE RICHARDSON, b. July 22, 1874.
240. ii. MARTHA RICHARDSON, b. Nov. 26, 1875.
241 iii. JOHN RICHARDSON, b. April 17, 1877.
242 iv. DEAN RICHMOND RICHARDSON, b. Dec. 11, 1878.

[Ninth Generation.]

233. iv. CHARLES URIAH CHILD, fourth child of John Lonson and Eliza J. Curtiss Child, b. Nov. 2, 1855, in Weber Co. Utah Ter. m. Atelia Thompson, Sept. 10, 1877.

[Tenth Generation.] Child:
243. i. CLARENCE CHILD, b. June 5, 1878, Riverdale, Utah.

[Eighth Generation.]

161. ix. PHEBE WOOSTER CHILD, ninth child and fourth daughter of Alfred Bosworth and Polly Barber Child, b. in Greenfield, N. Y., Jan. 17, 1833, m. May 14, 1848, C. Richardson of Pottawattamie county, Iowa.

[Ninth Generation.] Children:
244. i. AMANDA MALVINA RICHARDSON, b. Aug. 24, 1849, in Pottawattamie county, Iowa, m. Dudley Chase, August 15, 1868.
245. ii. CHARLES CHILD RICHARDSON, b. in Ogden City, Utah Ter., May 23, 1851, m. Oct. 27, 1873, A. Allred.
246. iii. FRANKLIN RICHARDSON, b. in Ogden City, Utah Ter., May 9, 1853, m. Oct. 25, 1875, Louisa L. Shurtleff.
247. iv. CORNELIUS RICHARDSON, b. in Ogden City, Utah Ter., Mar. 20, 1855.
248. v. CHAUNCEY RICHARDSON, b. in Ogden City, Utah Ter., Apr. 5, 1858.
249. vi. ALFRED RICHARDSON, b. in Ogden City, Utah Ter., Apr. 12, 1861.
250. vii. JOHN LYMAN RICHARDSON, b. in Ogden City, Utah Ter., March 8, 1863, d. 1866.
251. viii. MYRON RICHARDSON, b. in Ogden City, Utah Ter., Feb. 21, 1865.

252. ix. WILLIAM RICHARDSON, b. in Ogden City, Utah Ter., April 1, 1867.
253. x. EZRA CHASE RICHARDSON, b. in Ogden City, Utah Ter., May 26, 1869.
254. xi. JOSEPH RICHARDSON, b. in Ogden City, Utah Ter., July 1, 1871.

[Ninth Generation.]

244. i. AMANDA MALVINA RICHARDSON, eldest child of Phebe Wooster Child and C. Richardson, b. Aug. 24, 1849, m. Aug. 15, 1868, Dudley Chase. Reside in Ogden City, Utah.
[Tenth Generation.]   Children:
   255 i. TERZA CHASE, b. Jan. 3, 1870.
   256. ii. EZRA CHASE, b. March 10, 1871.
   257. iii. DUDLEY CHASE, b. Dec. 27, 1872.
   258. iv. LOLY ANN CHASE, b. July 8, 1874.
   259. v. ELSIE CHASE, b. Dec. 2, 1875.
   260. vi. NANCY A. CHASE, b. May 22, 1878.

[Ninth Generation.]

245. ii. CHARLES CHILD RICHARDSON, second child of Phebe Wooster Child and C. Richardson, b. in Ogden City, Utah, May 23, 1851, m. Oct. 27, 1873, A. Allred.
[Tenth Generation.]   Children:
   261. i. CHARLES D. RICHARDSON, b. Aug. 20, 1874.
   262. ii. JOSEPH F. RICHARDSON, b. May 29, 1876.
   263. iii. LOLY ANN RICHARDSON, b. June 19, 1878.

[Ninth Generation.]

246. iii. FRANKLIN RICHARDSON, third child of Phebe Wooster Child and C. Richardson, b. in Ogden City, Utah Ter. May 9, 1853, m. Oct. 25, 1875, Louise L. Shurtliff.
[Tenth Generation.]   Children:
   264. i. PHEBE L. RICHARDSON, b. Oct. 15, 1876.
   265. ii. LAURA A. RICHARDSON, b. Oct. 16, 1878.

[Eighth Generation.]

162. x. WARREN GOULD CHILD, tenth child and sixth son of Alfred Bosworth and Polly Barber Child, b. in Greenfield, Saratoga county, N. Y., Feb. 21, 1835. His first marriage was on Jan. 6, 1853, to Hannah A. Wilder, daughter of Austin and Sally M. B. Wilder of Elba, Genesee county, N. Y. His second marriage was to Martha Jane Elmer, daughter of David and Wealthy Elmer, who was b. March 2, 1838, in the state of Indiana. His third marriage was to Jane Bybee, daughter of Lee and Nancy Bybee. She d. Jan. 19, 1878.

W. G. Child.

We have already intimated that Mr. Warren Gould Child is a mormon. While having no sympathy whatever with those addicted to such false views of social life and progress, as we deem them, it is yet quite in accordance with our plan of doing justice to all so far as it is possible, to let each one make his own presentation of himself and his family from his own standpoint of thought and feeling. It is easy to see from his history in Utah, that he is a man of robust constitution, of great physical endurance, bold, fearless and of untiring energy; shrewd, sagacious, far seeing in business, and persistent and determined in his undertakings. The following incidents are from his own pen:

Warren G. Child, now engaged in the mercantile business at Ogden, besides the various travels with his father's family, has crossed the plains to and from Utah, nine different times, five times with ox, cow and horse power. Was one of the early settlers of Utah, settling in Ogden City in 1852; married Miss Hannah A. Wilder of Elba, N. Y., in the winter of 1853. In the spring of '54, accompanied by his wife, he crossed the plains and visited their friends in the State of New York. While on the desert our small party was attacked by Indians, who, except for the interposition of a friendly Indian actuated by a higher power, would doubtless have massacred the whole of our party. Our losses were provisions and other valuables. Having lost our provisions, death by starvation strongly presented itself to our view, for we were several hundred miles from any settlement. But again, like the children of Israel who, through the providence of God, were provided for, we too, were met by a party of emigrants of whom we procured sufficient food to last us to the nearest settlement.

We remained with our friends in the East nearly two years and again returned to Utah, crossing the plains with five wagons drawn by ox and cow power. During this tedious journey of three months duration and about midway, near the foot of the Black Hills, our second son was given us, five hundred miles from the nearest settlement. This almost proved too much for my wife and child, being exposed to the broiling sun by day and the cold mountain breezes by night, with only canvas covers to shelter them, but they both survived. We arrived at and settled in Ogden, and engaged in farming under many disadvantages, having our crops (raised only by artificial irrigation) for several years in succession destroyed by locusts and crickets, and for a time famine was at our doors. Flour could only be had at the price of twenty to thirty dollars per sack of one hundred pounds, and but little at these figures; many were compelled to live on roots, herbs, etc. The winter following being of such a severe character, and so much snow having fallen, we could obtain no food for our stock (which had been by this time reduced to mere skeletons) except that browsed from felled trees, and famine throughout our land, with even more serious results seemed imminent.

The locusts and pests that did not deposit themselves in the Great Salt Lake, left our pastures for others more green, and we were enabled to raise bountiful crops which commanded good prices, this being a recruiting point for the Overland California and Oregon Emigration. Rich mines of gold, silver and lead were discovered in all parts of our territory, demanding more easy transit to and through our country. Soon the great Continental and other railroads were built, making Ogden the centre of four different railroads and the junction of the U. P. & S. P. Railroads.

But a few years ago our country a desert, and pronounced unproductive, is now dotted for three hundred miles south and one hundred and fifty miles north, with towns and villages and rich fields of grain, making a pleasant and healthful resort for eastern tourists and invalids. The population of Utah now numbers some 160,000, three-fourths of which number are that peculiar people called Mormons, with whom the writer of this is numbered. He is 44 years old at this writing, 1879, is the father of twenty-five children, twenty of whom are now living, four of them are married, he has nine grandchildren. His mother, now living, has had near two hundred grand and great grandchildren, all of whom are located in Utah Territory.

Since my arrival in Utah, my travels have been various. In the spring of '58, I was called with a number of others to go north to Salmon River, Idaho, where a settlement had been formed by people of our faith, which had been beseiged by Indians, who had killed some three or four of their number. Upon our arrival we were placed on the defensive, but before any further troubles arose we effected a settlement with the " Reds," recovering from them part of our lost property. Our party then started for their homes in the south, and on our way we were attacked by Indians, who killed and scalped one of our number. Other and like scenes I have gone through, but my scalp has been and is to-day my own property.

Not wishing to occupy too much space, I do not wish to say more only by way of advice, and encouragement to those of our family following after. I would have them first learn the characters of their forefathers, and then strive with all their powers to keep up the reputation which has been so dearly bought and maintained up to the present.

[Ninth Generation.]   Children:

266. i. AUSTIN WILDER CHILD, b. in Ogden City, Utah. Ter., Feb. 11, 1854., m. Nov. 1, 1872, Mrs. Mary Thompson, of Riverdale, Utah Ter.

267. ii. WARREN GOULD CHILD, Jr. b. in Nebraska, Aug. 15, 1856, m. Dec. 27, 1877, Luella Chase.

268. iii. HANNAH MARIA CHILD, b. in Payson, Utah. Ter., Aug. 20, 1858, m. Adam Russell of Scotland, 1874.

269. iv. RACHEL TERESA CHILD, b. in Ogden City, Utah Ter., Sept. 14, 1860, m. J. M. Browning.

270. v. HENRY HARRISON CHILD, b. in Ogden City, Jan. 22, 1863.

271. vi. HEBER THOMAS CHILD, b. in Ogden City, May 29, 1865.

272. vii. JULIA ADELAIDE CHILD, b. in Ogden City, May 2, 1868.

273. viii. NELLA DORA CHILD, b in Ogden City, Oct. 11, 1870.

274. ix. JESSE CHILD, b in Ogden City, July 22, 1872.

275. x. ZILPHA A. CHILD, b. in Ogden City, April 12, 1875. d. young.

[By second marriage—Martha Jane Elmer.]

276. xi. ROSETTA JANE CHILD, b. in Ogden City, March 26, 1859, m. Ambrose Shaw.

277. xii. SUSAN W. CHILD, b. in Ogden City, Sept. 28, 1860.

278. xiii. CHARLES A. CHILD, b. in Ogden City, July 28, 1863.

279. xiv. ELIZA L. CHILD, b. in Ogden City, Aug. 31, 1864, d. Feb. 1865.

280. xv. WILLIAM W. CHILD, b. in Ogden City, Oct 14 1865.

281. xvi. DAVID J. CHILD, b. in Ogden City, Aug. 31, 1857, d. March 3, 1868.

282. xvii. SYLVIA A. CHILD, b. in Ogden City, April 11, 1869.

283. xviii. THEODORE F. CHILD, b. in Ogden City, April 24, 1871.

284. xix. SIMON CHILD, b. in Ogden City, July 24, 1873, ⎰ Twins,
285. xx. ELLIOTT CHILD, " " " ⎱ d. Jan. 1874.

286. xxi. LILLY EDITH CHILD, b. in Ogden City, April 30, 1876, d. July, 1878.

287. xxii. Infant, not named, b. in Ogden City, July 11, 1879.

[By third marriage—Jane Bybee.]

288. xxiii. EFFA BELL CHILD, b. in Ogden City, Jan 6, 1874.

289. xxiv. WARREN LEE CHILD, b. in Ogden City, Oct. 4, 1875.

290. xxv. JOHN A. CHILD, b. in Ogden City, July 5, 1877.

[Ninth Generation.]

266. i. AUSTIN WILDER CHILD, first child of Warren Gould and Hannah Wilder Child, b. in Ogden City, Utah Ter., Feb. 11, 1854, m. Mary Thompson.

[Tenth Generation.] Children:

291. i. ANN G. CHILD, b. Feb. 18, 1876.

292. ii. HANNAH E. CHILD, b. Nov. 22, 1878.

293. iii. AUSTIN CHILD, b. Sept. 8, 1877, d. young.

294. iv. JOHN FRANCIS CHILD, b. Feb. 8, 1879.

[Ninth Generation.]

267. ii. WARREN G. CHILD, Jr., second child of Warren Gould and Hannah A. Wilder Child, b. Aug. 15, 1856, m. Dec. 27, 1877, Luelle Chase.

[Tenth Generation.] Child:

295. i. LUELLE C. CHILD, b. 1878.

[Ninth Generation.]

268. iii. HANNAH MARIA CHILD, third child of Warren Gould and Hannah Wilder Child, b. Aug. 20, 1858, m. Oct. 13, 1874, Adam Russell.

[Tenth Generation.] Children:

296. i. HANNAH E. RUSSELL, b. July 23, 1875, d. Nov. 27, 1876, in Riverdale.

297. ii. WARREN A. RUSSELL, b. May 31, 1877, in Riverdale.

298. iii. WILLIAM FRANCIS RUSSELL, b. April 26, 1879.

H

[Ninth Generation.]

269. iv. RACHEL CHILD, fourth child of Warren Gould and Hannah A. Wilder Child, b. Sept. 1860, m. J. M. Browning.
[Tenth Generation.] One child (not named), b. 1879.

[Eighth Generation.]

163. xi. ORVILLE RENSSELAER CHILD, eleventh child of Alfred Bosworth and Polly Barber Child, b. Oct. 11, 1838, m. in Hancock Co., Ill., Feb. 13, 1859, Urinda Rawson, dau. of Cyrus S. and Eliza Coffin Rawson. She was b. in New York, Feb. 8, 1844.
[Ninth Generation.] Children:
299. i. ORVILLE RENSSELAER CHILD, Jr., b. Jan. 8, 1860, in Ogden City, Utah Ter.
300. ii. SARAH ANN CHILD, b. Nov. 14, 1861, in Ogden City.
301. iii. WILLIAM ALFRED CHILD, b. April 3, 1864, in Ogden City.
302. iv. POLLY Y. CHILD, b. May 5, 1866, in Ogden City.
303. v. ELIZABETH CHILD, b. Aug. 11, 1868, in Ogden City.
304. vi. MARY ELIZA CHILD, b. April 11, 1872, in Ogden City.
305. vii. HANNAH L. CHILD, b. March 30, 1874, in Ogden City.

[Ninth Generation.]

300. ii. SARAH ANN CHILD, second child of Orville Rensselaer and Urinda Rawson Child, b. Nov. 14, 1861, m. John Dewey.
[Tenth Generation.] Child:
306. i. Name not given.

[Seventh Generation.]

139. iii. EPHRAIM CHILD, third child and second son of Mark Anthony and Hannah Benedict Child, b. in Milton, Saratoga Co., N. Y., May 15, 1798, m. about 1819, Margaret Van Tassel, who was b. Feb. 26, 1799.

Mr. Child was a man of large stature and great strength. It is said he could raise a thirty-two gallon cask of cider from the ground, with ease, and drink from the bung. He was a mason by trade, and resided at Saratoga Springs, N. Y. He died in Saratoga Springs, N. Y., Feb. 8, 1880, æt. 82 yrs. 8 mos.
[Eighth Generation.] Children:
307. i. HANNAH LAVINA CHILD, b. in Greenfield, Saratoga Co., N. Y., March 30, 1820, m. Feb. 3, 1848, Isaac Dunwick.
308. ii. ALMON CHILD, b. in Greenfield, Saratoga Co., N. Y., March 25, 1822, d. date not given.
309. iii. EMILY CHILD, b. in Greenfield, Saratoga Co., N. Y., July 12, 1825
310. iv. MARIETTA CHILD, b. in Greenfield, N. Y., Oct. 12, 1829, m. Eli Burgess, Jan. 28, 1852.

311. v. VESTA ANN CHILD, b. in Greenfield, N. Y., March 4, 1836, m. Nov. 30, 1858, William S. Balch.

312. vi. DELIA ADELAIDE CHILD, b. in Greenfield, N. Y., Oct. 21, 1838, d. June 13, 1859.

[Eighth Generation.]

307. i. HANNAH LAVINA CHILD, eldest child of Ephraim and Margaret Van Tassel Child, b. in Greenfield, N. Y., March 30, 1820, m. Feb. 3, 1848, Isaac Dunwick.

[Ninth Generation.] Children:

313. i. WILLIAM DUNWICK, b. July 18, 1849.

314. ii. MARY LOUISA DUNWICK, b. Aug. 29, 1851.

315. iii. FREDERICK JOHNSON DUNWICK, b. Jan. 31, 1853.

[Eighth Generation.]

310. iv. MARIETTA CHILD, fourth child of Ephraim and Margaret Van Tassel Child, b. Oct. 12, 1829, m. Jan. 28, 1852, Eli Burgess.

Ninth Generation.] Children:

316. i. EDWARD A. BURGESS, b. Dec. 5, 1852.

317. ii. AUSTIN C. BURGESS, b. Jan 19, 1856.

318. iii WILLIAM E. BURGESS, b. June 6, 1859.

319. iv. ELWOOD W. BURGESS, b. Nov. 3, 1865.

[Eighth Generation.]

311. v. VESTA ANN CHILD, fifth child of Ephraim and Margaret Van Tassel Child, b. in Greenfield, N. Y., March 4, 1836, m. Nov. 30, 1858, Wm. S. Balch, RR. conductor. Resides at Saratoga, N. Y.

[Ninth Generation.] Children:

320. i. CARRIE VESTA BALCH, b. in Saratoga, N. Y., June 24, 1860.

321. ii. NELLIE W. BALCH, b. in Saratoga, N. Y., Feb. 21, 1865.

322. iii. LILLIE EMILY BALCH, b in Saratoga, N. Y., Mar. 24, 1868, d Feb. 8, 1869.

[Seventh Generation.]

140. iv. JOHN CHILD, fourth child of Mark Anthony and Hannah Benedict Child, b. in Milton, Saratoga Co., N. Y. Jan. 18, 1800, m. Jan. 18, 1821, Betsey Harris; m. 2nd, Sarah Kelsey.

He was a hotel keeper, industrious, and a prominent man in Milton, N. Y., and in Rock Co., Ill., to which place he removed from Milton. He was large of stature,—about six feet high,—of great physical strength, weighing about two hundred pounds.

[Eighth Generation.]   Children:

323. i BARNEY CHILD, b. in Saratoga Co., Aug. 4, 1821, d. in Rock Co., Wis. 1855.

324. ii. LEWIS CHILD, b. Sept. 23, 1824, in Milton, Saratoga Co. N. Y.; m. first, Rhoda Fraser; second m. Sophronia Conrad.

325. iii HANNAH H. CHILD, b. Jan. 5, 1828, d. July, 1832.

326. iv. EMELINE B. CHILD, b. Mar. 21, 1831, unm , resides with her mother.

327. v. ALFRED CHILD, b. April, 1833, in Saratoga Co , N. Y., d. 1849, in Wisconsin.

328. vi. BETSEY CHILD, b. Sept. 17, 1835, d. early.

329. vii. BETSEY AMELIA CHILD, (by second marriage, no date of birth given,) m. a Mr. Maxon of Lima Centre, Wis.

[Eighth Generation.]

324. ii. LEWIS CHILD, second child and second son of John Child and Betsey Harris, b. Sept. 23, 1824, in Saratoga Co., N.Y. m. 1st about 1857, Rhoda Frazer; m. 2d, Sophronia Conrad. Resided in Morristown, St. Lawrence Co., N. Y. Commenced life as a merchant.

[Ninth Generation.]   Children:

330. i. HENRY JOHN CHILD, b in Rock Co., Wis., 1858.

331. ii. ALLEN CHILD, b. in Rock Co., Wis., 1860.

332. iii. ADAM CHILD, b. in Rock Co., Wis., 1867. d. young.

[Seventh Generation.]

141. v. BETSEY CHILD, fifth child and second dau. of Mark Anthony and Hannah Benedict Child, b. in Milton, N. Y., Sept. 15, 1802, m. 1823, Wm. Harris of Saratoga Co., N. Y.

[Eighth Generation.]   Children:

333. i. BENJAMIN FRANKLIN HARRIS, b. April 6, 1824, m. Polly Jewett.

334. ii. HANNAH POLINA HARRIS, b. July 9, 1827, m. Jonathan Mills.

335. iii. JOHN RENSSELAER HARRIS, b. Dec. 18, 1834.

336. iv. PAMELIA HARRIS, b. April 19, 1836.

337. v. MARK HARRIS, b. Oct. 16, 1842.

[Eighth Generation.]

333. i. BENJAMIN FRANKLIN HARRIS, eldest child of Betsey Child and William Harris, b. April 6, 1824, m. Polly Jewett about 1848. She was b. Dec. 9, 1828.

[Ninth Generation.]   Children:

338. i. LYMAN WOOSTER HARRIS, b. Nov. 3, 1849, d. Dec. 31, 1863.

339. ii. WM. HENRY HARRIS, b. Oct. 19, 1851, d. Dec. 26, 1852.

340. iii. ALICE HARRIS, b. Nov. 15, 1853.

341. iv. FREDERICK HARRIS, b. Oct. 19, 1854.

342. v. ALFRED HARRIS, b July 4, 1855.

[Eighth Generation.]

334. ii. HANNAH POLINA HARRIS, eldest daughter and second child of Betsey Child and Wm. Harris, b. July 9, 1827, m. about 1854, Jonathan Mills, who was b. 1846, in Saratoga Co., N. Y., now of Austin, Moore Co., Wis.

[Ninth Generation.] Children:

343. i. ALBERT MILLS, b. 1855.
344. ii EMMA MILLS, b. June 25, 1857, d. young.
345. iii. BYRON BARNARD MILLS, b. Nov. 18, 1859.

[Seventh Generation.]

142. vi. PAULINA CHILD, sixth child of Mark Anthony and Hannah Benedict Child, b. Nov. 8, 1803, m. Walter Hewitt, of Stillwater, Saratoga Co., N. Y.

Mr. H. went early to Detroit, Mich., with his family, and finally to Ypsilanti, where he has resided for many years. He has been engaged in mercantile business, prosperous and successful. His children were born in Detroit.

[Eighth Generation.] Children:

346. i. EDMUND HEWITT, b. in Detroit, Mich., Nov. 14, 1829, m. Lucy Post.
347. ii. MARY HEWITT, b. in Detroit, Mich., 1831, m. Wm. Cheever.
348. iii. LOUIS HEWITT, b. in Detroit, Mich., July 23, 1834.
349. iv. CHARLES HEWITT, b. in Detroit, Mich., Oct. 3, 1836.
350. v. WALTER HEWITT, b. in Detroit, Mich., Sept. 28, 1839, m. Carrie Cook.

[Eighth Generation.]

346. i. EDMUND HEWITT, eldest son of Paulina Child and Walter Hewitt, b. Nov. 14, 1829, m. Lucy Post of Ypsilanti, Mich.

[Ninth Generation.] Children:

351. i. LUCY HEWITT, d. at birth.
352. ii. ARTHUR CHILD HEWITT, d. young.
353. iii. MARY HEWITT.
354. iv. HELEN HEWITT.

[Eighth Generation.]

347. ii. MARY HEWITT, dau. and second child of Paulina Child and Walter Hewitt, b. 1831, m. Wm. E. Cheever, son of Rev. Mr. Cheever. He was b. 1835. Mr. Cheever resides in Ypsilanti, does business in Detroit.

[Ninth Generation.] Children:

355. i. WALTER HEWITT CHEEVER, b. Feb. 27, 1859.
356. ii. FANNY CHEEVER, b. July 9, 1862.

[Eighth Generation.]

350. v. WALTER HEWITT, son of Paulina Child and Walter
Hewitt, b. Sept. 28, 1839, m. Carrie Cook.
[Ninth Generation.] Children:
  357. i. WALTER HEWITT, b. May 18, 1868.
  358. ii. FLORENCE PAULINA HEWITT, b. 1870.

[Seventh Generation.]

143. vii. PAMELIA CHILD, seventh child of Mark Anthony
and Hannah Benedict Child, b. Aug. 28, 1804, m. March 9,
1830, Lyman Wooster of Morristown, St. Lawrence Co., N. Y.
Removed to North Hammond, N. Y.

Mr. Wooster d. Feb. 22, 1849. His sons continued in North
Hammond, St. Lawrence Co., N. Y., managing the estate till
1855, when most of the family removed to Rock county, Wisconsin. Now reside at Fort Atkinson, Jefferson county, Wis.

Mr. Wooster is a descendant of an honorable family of early
emigrants from Worcestershire, England, who settled in Worcester, Mass. The name was originally Worcester. Gradually, from an easier pronunciation, it was shortened to Wooster.
It was a family some branches of which flourished in the Revolution. An early member was a General in the army, and fell
in battle, in honor of whom government has appropriated
$25,000 for a monument. On the mother's side the family
alliance is with the Barber family of Rhode Island, and of
French descent. This alliance connects with the Gould family,
from which has descended the great railway king, Jay Gould.
Among the descendants of these early English emigrants, we
find many active and enterprising citizens of the present as
well as past generations.

Charles Abram Wooster of Hammond, St. Lawrence county,
N. Y., is a worthy scion of this stock. His father, Abram
Wooster, was a native of Oneida county, N. Y., born in 1800.
While yet a boy, he went from his father's home to North
Hammond, N. Y., then a wilderness, and commenced business
for himself. His outfit consisted of a rifle (of which he was
very proud as "a dead shot"), an axe, an extra shirt, and five
or six dollars of money. He engaged in the business of lum-
bering, taking his lumber and timber in rafts to Quebec, Canada. From this business and successful farming operations he
has become quite wealthy, and is enjoying a happy old age

(now 80), hale and hearty, in the town of Hammond. His rifle is still his pet, and his boast is that he can yet bring down a deer at forty rods. He had a brother, David Wooster, who was popularly known for thirty years as a hotel keeper in Oneida county, N. Y.

Charles Abram Wooster, from whom we obtain this account of the Wooster family, is a son of Abram and Phebe Wooster, a prominent citizen of Hammond, a man of much general intelligence, of large enterprise, connected with railways, banking, &c., in St. Lawrence county. He married Ellen A. Savage of Hammond, and has the following children :

   1. CHARLES CHANDLER WOOSTER, b. Sept. 17, 1867, d. 1874.
   2. LENA LAOLA WOOSTER, b. May 6, 1873.
   3 EVA LOELLA WOOSTER, b. May 7, 1876.

[Eighth Generation.] Children:
   359. i. LYDIA ELIZABETH WOOSTER, b. Jan. 27, 1831, d. Aug. 21, 1848.
   360. ii. LYMAN AUGUSTUS WOOSTER, b. Feb. 10, 1833, m. Henrietta Foltz.
   361. iii. WM. HARRIS WOOSTER, b. Jan. 22, 1835. Mr. Wooster enlisted in the Union Army on the breaking out of the late rebellion, where by exposure he was prostrated and sent home, and died on the 3rd of March, 1862, at Quindaro, Kansas. Was a farmer.
   362. iv. GEORGE WASHINGTON WOOSTER, b. April 10, 1837, m. Annie M. Cornell.
   363. v. HANNAH MARIA WOOSTER, b. Sept. 3, 1839, m. Chas. Edward Green.
   364. vi. SARAH AMELIA WOOSTER, b. Dec. 14, 1843, m. James M. Coakley, M.D.
   365. vii. JOHN CHILD WOOSTER, b. Feb. 3, 1846, d. May 2, 1847, in Hammond, N. Y.
   366. viii. LYMAN CHILD WOOSTER, b. Aug. 1, 1849. Resides with his mother at Whitewater, Wis.

[Eighth Generation.]

   360. ii. LYMAN AUGUSTUS WOOSTER, eldest son and second child of Pamelia Child and Lyman Wooster, b. Feb. 10, 1833, m. Henrietta Foltz, d. Dec. 27, 1878, at Fort Atkinson, Wis. Carpenter.

[Ninth Generation.] Child:
   367. i. MARY WOOSTER, b. March 7, 1868, in Lima, Rock county, Wis.

[Eighth Generation.]

   362. iv. GEORGE WASHINGTON WOOSTER, son of Pamelia Child, and Lyman Wooster, m. Annie M. Cromwell, Nov. 1860

[Ninth Generation.] Children:
   368. i. MYRTIE WOOSTER, b. Nov. 5, 1862.
   369. ii. GEORGE HENRY WOOSTER, b. Dec. 18, 1864.

[Eighth Generation.]

363. v. HANNAH MARIA WOOSTER, fifth child, and second
dau. of Pamelia Child, and Lyman Wooster, b. Sept. 3, 1839, m.
Sept. 25, 1858, Charles E. Green.   Reside in Whitewater, Wis.
[Ninth Generation.] Child:
    370. i. NELLIE AMELIA GREEN, b. Dec. 18, 1869.

[Eighth Generation.]

366. viii. LYMAN CHILD WOOSTER, eighth child of Pamelia
Child and Lyman Wooster, b. Aug. 1, 1849, m. Aug. 6, 1877,
Ellen Ada Basset, of Whitewater, Wis.   Is a teacher in the State
Normal School, in Whitewater, Wis.
[Ninth Generation.] Child:
    371. i. CHARLES BASSETT WOOSTER, b. in Whitewater, June 26, 1878.

[Seventh Generation.]

144. viii. RENSSELAER CHILD, eighth child of Mark Anthony
and Hannah Benedict Child, b. Oct. 16, 1809, m. Sept. 1, 1831,
Charlotte Burnham, of Morristown, St. Lawrence county, N. Y.
She was b. in the Province of Upper Canada, April 14, 1812, d.
Feb. 11, 1875. Mr. C. d. in Whitewater, Wis., April 1, 1874.
[Eighth Generation.] Children:
    372. i. OLIVE BURNHAM CHILD, b. in Morristown, St. Lawrence county,
N. Y., June 2, 1832, m. Oct. 28, 1854, Joseph Green.
    373. ii. NANCY CHILD, b. in Morristown, N. Y., June 9, 1835, d. Nov. 8,
1843.
    374. iii. ELIJAH CHILD, b. in Morristown, N. Y., Nov. 13, 1838, d. April
11, 1842.
    375. iv. JAMES CHILD, b. in Morristown, N. Y., Dec. 25, 1841, d. Oct. 1,
1848.
    376. v. MARY FERN CHILD, b. in Hebron, Wis., Dec. 10, 1845, d. April
15, 1860.
    377. vi. JOHN J. CHILD, b. in Lima, Wis., Dec. 3, 1847, d. April 15, 1863.

[Eighth Generation.]

372. i. OLIVE BURNHAM CHILD, eldest child of Rensselaer
and Charlotte Burnham Child, b. Jan. 2, 1832, m. Oct. 28, 1854,
Joseph Green, of Lima, Wis.   Mr. Green is a dentist.
[Ninth Generation.] Children:
    378. i. ELLA GREEN, b in Palmyra, Wis., Dec. 12, 1856, d. in Lakeland,
Minn, June 20, 1858.
    379. ii. OSCAR GREEN, b. in Hudson, St. Croix county, Wis., June 3, 1859.
Is a member of the U. S. Military Academy at West Point.
    380. iii. MARY C. GREEN, b. in Whitewater, Walworth county, Wis, July
2, 1867.

[Seventh Generation.]

145. ix. HANNAH CHILD, ninth child and fifth dau. of Mark Anthony and Hannah Benedict Child, b. in Milton, Saratoga county, N. Y., Oct. 16, 1816, m. 1834, Amos H. Burnham, who was b. Jan. 22, 1811. Soon after marriage they removed from Saratoga county, N. Y., to Hebron, Jefferson county, Wis. Mrs. Burnham died Feb. 25, 1861, leaving six children.

[Eighth Generation.] Children:

381. i. JAMES M. BURNHAM, b. in Hebron, Wis., June 9, 1836, m. Aug. 13, 1865, Eveline Abbey.

382. ii. GEORGE C. BURNHAM, b. in Hebron, Wis., June 10, 1839, m. April 17, 1867, Charlotte Stagg.

383. iii. CHARLES BURNHAM, b. in Hebron, Wis., March 26, 1841, m Jan. 1, 1868, Almira Torrey.

384. iv. CHARLOTTE I. BURNHAM, b. in Hebron, Wis., May 9, 1843.

385. v. RENSSELAER BURNHAM, b. in Hebron, Wis., May 12, 1845, m. May 22, 1870, Mary Garlock. Was in the Union Army for the suppression of the Rebellion, in the 33d Vol. Infantry of Wisconsin. Was in many battles and skirmishes—at Holly Springs, Vicksburg, Red River, Nashville and Mobile, besides many smaller engagements. In all these battles, he never received a wound. He served under Gen'ls Grant, A. J. Smith and Thomas. No children given of this marriage.

386. vi. OLIVE T. BURNHAM, b. in Hebron, Wis., Aug. 8, 1851.

[Eighth Generation.]

381. i. JAMES N. BURNHAM, eldest son of Hannah Child and Amos H. Burnham, b. June, 1836, in Hebron, Wis., m. Aug. 13, 1865, Eveline Abbey.

Mr. Burnham served in the Union Army through the entire war of the Rebellion. He was captured by the rebel forces and imprisoned for nine months in a prison, where the suffering and barbarity were almost equal to those endured by our men in Andersonville prison. Mr. Burnham was in the 13th Wis. Vol. Infantry. He served under Gen'ls Grant, Rosecrans and Sherman, and was in the battle at Athens, Ala., and in the fight at Donaldsonville, and Lookout Mountain.

[Ninth Generation.] Children:

387. i. HANNAH D. BURNHAM, b. Aug. 2, 1867.

388. ii. FRANK D. BURNHAM, b. Nov., 1869.

389. iii. MAUD M. BURNHAM, b. Sept. 14, 1871.

390. iv. ANNIE E. BURNHAN, b. Aug. 15, 1875.

[Eighth Generation.]

382. ii. GEORGE BURNHAM, second child of Hannah Child and Amos H. Burnham, b. June 10, 1839, m. April 17, 1867, Charlotte Stagg.

[Ninth Generation.] Children:

391. i. FLORA M. BURNHAM, b. Aug. 27, 1868.
392. ii. OLIVE E. BURNHAM, b. Dec. 12, 1869.
393. iii FRED B. BURNHAM, b. April 18, 1872.
394. iv. CHARLIE J. BURNHAM, b. April 27, 1874.

[Eighth Generation.]

383. iii. CHARLES BURNHAM, third child of Hannah Child
and Amos H. Burnham. b. in Hebron, Wis., March 26, 1841,
m. Jan. 1, 1868. Almira Torrey.

[Ninth Generation.] Children:

395. i. ALBERT E. BURNHAM, b. Oct. 15, 1868.
396. ii. AMOS H BURNHAN, b. July 14, 1870.
397. iii. EMMA E BURNHAM, b. Sept. 10, 1872.
398. iv. ALICE M. BURNHAM, b. May 1, 1875.

[Eighth Generation.]

386. vi. OLIVE T. BURNHAM, sixth child of Hannah Child
and Amos H. Burnham. b. Aug. 8, 1851, m. Nov. 13, 1872.
Will. Marshall.

[Ninth Generation] Children:

399. i. WILL OTIS MARSHALL, b. Sept. 3, 1775.
400 ii. CURTIS W. MARSHALL, b. May 27, 1879.

[Seventh Generation]

146. x. EMELINE CHILD, tenth child of Mark Anthony and
Hannah Benedict Child, b. Jan. 19, 1815, m. 1st. Alanson Barber,
m. 2nd. Amos H. Burnham, the former husband of her sister
Hannah. All her children were by her first marriage. Mr.
Burnham died May 10, 1878, leaving his family in good circum-
stances.

[Eighth Generation] Children of Mrs. Emeline Barber, now Mrs. Burnham.

401. i. POLLY BARBER, b. March 4, 1835, d. Sept. 4, 1835.

402. ii. BENJAMIN FRANKLIN BARBER, b. July 31, 1837. Was in the
Union Army for suppressing the Rebellion, in 1861, died early in the war

403. iii. MARIAN E. BARBER, b. Jan. 12, 1839, m. Nov. 15, 1857, John
Hillsmade.

404. iv. MYRON CHILD BARBER, b. Nov. 9, 1840.

405. v. WARREN GOULD BARBER, b. Dec. 12, 1842   He enlisted in the
Union Army at the commencement of the Rebellion, but through exposure
and sickness lost his sight, and returned home and died in 1863.

406. vi. JOHN CHILD BARBER, b. Dec. 12, 1844, m. May 4, 1868, Mary
Frances Craig   He is by occupation a master car builder, now of Missouri,
Kansas and Texas Railway.

407. vii LYMAN WOOSTER BARBER, b. April 7, 1845.

408. viii. JOSEPH LAWRENCE BARBER, b. Jan. 2, 1847.

409. ix. ANN ELIZABETH BARBER, b. Jan. 12, 1852.

[Eighth Generation.]

403. iii. MARIAN E. BARBER, third child of Emeline Child and Alanson Barber, b. Jan. 12, 1849, in North Hammond, N. Y., m. Nov. 15, 1857, John Hillsmade, of Sedalia, Mo.

[Ninth Generation] Children:

410. i. NELLIE EMELINE HILLSMADE, b. Nov. 4, 1858.
411. ii. MYRON WARREN HILLSMADE, b. Dec. 17, 1860.
412. iii. JOHN SALLS HILLSMADE, b. Jan. 22, 1862.

[Seventh Generation.]

147. xi. MARK ANTHONY CHILD, Jr., eleventh child of Mark Anthony and Hannah Benedict Child, b. in Milton, Saratoga Co., N. Y., Jan. 13, 1817, m. in 1837 Lydia Robinson, of Vermont, who was b. April 27, 1818 ; they reside at Lima Centre, Rock Co., Wis.

Mr. Child is of full stature, of about 190 lbs. weight: has been deputy postmaster in Lima Centre for six or seven years past.

[Eighth Generation.] Children:

413. i. ADALINE DEMARIUS CHILD, b. in Morristown, St. Lawrence Co., N. Y., Nov. 17, 1840, m. Orson Freeman.
414. ii. CLINTON DEMARIUS CHILD, b. in Morristown, N. Y., Dec. 29, 1842, m. July 1, 1863, Sarah King.
415. iii. MARTHA JANE CHILD, b. in Morristown, N. Y., Aug. 28, 1844, m. Dec. 21, 1865, William Freeman.
416. iv. JOHN RENSSELAER CHILD, b. in Morristown, N. Y., Jan. 14, 1848, d. Aug. 19, 1852.
417. v. MARK ALONZO CHILD, b. Oct. 5, 1849, m. Dec. 22, 1877, Mary Mc-Coneghy.
418. vi. GEORGE WASHINGTON CHILD, b. Sep. 28, 1852, in Lima Centre, Wis.
419. vii. LOUISA AMELIA CHILD, b. Sep. 29, 1854, in Lima Centre.
420. viii. VESTA A. CHILD, b. Aug. 11, 1856, in Lima Centre.
421. ix. CHARLES HERBERT CHILD, b. Dec. 12, 1858, in Lima Centre.
422. x. FREDDIE BOARDMAN CHILD, b. April 13, 1864, in Lima Centre.

[Eighth Generation.]

414. ii. CLINTON DEMARIUS CHILD, second child of Mark Anthony, Jr., and Lydia Robinson Child, b. in Morristown, N. Y., Dec. 29, 1842, m. July 18, 1864, Sarah King, who was b. in Plymouth, Vt., Jan. 5, 1845.

Mr. Child served two years in the Union Army in the war of the Rebellion. He is in the mercantile business, and is postmaster at Lima Centre, Wis.

[Ninth Generation.] Child:

423. i. ALABEL CHILD, b. in Plymouth, Vt., April 17, 1865.

[Eighth Generation.]

415. iii. MARTHA JANE CHILD, third child of Mark Anthony, Jr., and Lydia Robinson Child, b. in Morristown, N. Y., Aug. 28, 1844, m. Dec. 21, 1865, William Freeman.

Mr. Freeman served in the Union Army in the war of the Rebellion. He is a blacksmith.

[Ninth Generation] Children:

423½ i. ORION EUGENE FREEMAN, b. May 10, 1867.

424. ii. MEDORA ETTA FREEMAN, b. May 9, 1871

[Seventh Generation.]

148. xii. POLLY B. CHILD, twelfth child (and first by Submit Peacock) of Mark Anthony and Submit Peacock Child, b. in Greenfield, Saratoga Co., N. Y., Nov, 9, 1820, m May 10, 1838, Charles Porter Bennett, who was born in the village of Mickleton, Gloucestershire, England, July 8, 1812. Reside in Ypsilanti, Mich.

[Eighth Generation.] Children:

425. i. MARK BENNETT, b. in Ypsilanti, Washtenaw Co., Mich., May 19, 1841, d. Aug. 12, 1841.

426. ii. CHARLES BENNETT, b in Ypsilanti, Mich., April 10, 1843, d. Oct. 3, 1845.

427. iii. HANNAH FRANCES BENNETT, b. in Ypsilanti, Mich., April 26, 1846, m. March 11, 1867, John Atkin, Jr.

428. iv. MARY PORTER BENNETT, b. in Ypsilanti, Mich, Aug. 5, 1848, m. Charles M. Phillips.

429. v. WALTER BENNETT, b. in Ypsilanti, Mich., May 29, 1852, d. March 16, 1855.

430. vi. CHARLES WALTER BENNETT, b. in Ypsilanti, Mich., Feb. 16, 1858.

[Eighth Generation]

427, iii. HANNAH FRANCES BENNETT, dau. of Polly B. Child and Charles Porter Bennett, b. in Ypsilanti, Mich , April 26, 1846, m. March 11, 1867, John Atkins, Jr., in the town of Milford, Oakland Co., Mich.

[Ninth Generation.] Children:

431. i. MARY BENNETT ATKINS, b. in Milford, Oakland Co., Mich., Sept. 5, 1868.

432. ii. CHARLES BENNETT ATKINS, b. in Milford, Mich., May 22, 1871.

433. iii. ALICE POLLY ATKINS, b. in Milford, Mich., April 6, 1874.

[Eighth Generation.]

428. iv. MARY P. BENNETT, dau. of Polly B. Child and Charles Porter Bennett, b. in Ypsilanti, Mich , Aug. 5, 1848,

m. June 6, 1876, Charles M. Phillips, of Milford, Oakland Co., Mich.

[Ninth Generation.] Child:

434. i FANNY ELIZA PHILLIPS, b. in Mason, Ingham Co., Mich., Oct. 21, 1877.

[Seventh Generation.]

151. XV. HENRIETTA CHILD, dau. of Mark Anthony and Submit Peacock Child, m. Edmund Robinson. Mrs. Robinson d. in Milton, Rock Co., Wis., 1865, where Mr. R. lived in 1873.

[Eighth Generation.] Children:

435. i. SYLVESTER ROBINSON.
436. ii. DEXTER ROBINSON.
437. iii EDMUND ROBINSON, b. July 27, 1849.
438. iv. WALTER HEWIT ROBINSON, b. 1853.
439. v. AUGUSTA ROBINSON, b. 1856.
440. vi. WILLIE ROBINSON, b. 1861.
441. vii. HERBERT ROBINSON, b. 1863.

[Seventh Generation.]

152. xvi. CHARLOTTE CHILD, sixteenth child of Mark Anthony and fifth by Submit Peacock, b. Nov. 18, 1833, m. Nov. 17, 1864, Mr. Riddle.

[Eighth Generation] Child:

442. i. (Name not given.)

[Sixth Generation.]

46. vi. DR. EPHRAIM CHILD, sixth child of Capt. Increase and Olive Pease Child, b. in Woodstock, Ct., May 10, 1773, m. Mary Woodworth, youngest child of Ephraim and Anna More Woodworth of Stillwater, Saratoga Co., N. Y., Jan. 1, 1796. She was b. Feb. 2, 1781, and d. July 18, 1843, at Syracuse, N.Y. He was a physician, and practiced his profession in Stillwater, N. Y., where he d. June 10, 1830. They had ten children.

Dr. Ephraim Child was a cousin of the celebrated lawyer, Ambrose C. Spencer. The mothers of Mr. Spencer and Mrs. Child were sisters. Ambrose C. Spencer's first two wives were sisters of Governor DeWitt Clinton: his third wife was a Norton. He survived them all.

[Seventh Generation.] Children:

443. i. ELIZA ANN BLEEKER CHILD, b. in Stillwater, N. Y., May 18, 1799, m. Sept. 20, 1841, Zalmon Rice, who d. July 6, 1844. No children.

444. ii. EPHRAIM CHILD, b. in Stillwater, April 10, 1801, m. 1st, Jan. 25, 1825, Elizabeth Curd Redford; m. 2nd, Betsey Jewell; m. 3rd, Ann Eliza Olmstead.

445. iii. ORVILLE WHITMORE CHILD, b. in Stillwater, Dec. 29, 1803, m. about 1828, Mary G. Eno.

446. iv. THERESA PEASE CHILD, b. in Stillwater, Jan. 25, 1805, m. about 1828, Col. John Fitzgerald, deceased.

447. v. NOADIAH MOODY CHILD, b. in Stillwater, Dec. 20, 1806, m. 1st October, 1839, Martha Brewer; m. 2nd, Jan. 26, 1865, Sarah Elizabeth Dawes.

448. vi. HENRY DAVIS CHILD, b. in Stillwater, Dec., 1808, m. Julia Ann Perkins.

449. vii. HENRIETTA SCHUYLER CHILD, b. in Stillwater, Dec. 22, 1810, m. Nov. 12, 1834, Luke Alvord.

450. viii MARY ANN HOLLAND CHILD, b. in Stillwater, Oct. 18, 1813, m. 1844, Jacob A. Staats of Louisville, Ky., d. July 4, 1850.

451. ix. RENETTA WILLARD CHILD, b. in Stillwater, Jan. 19, 1817, m. John H. Pope. Lived at the cor. State and Magazine sts., 6th District, New Orleans.

452. x. CAROLINE CANFIELD CHILD, b. in Stillwater, Aug. 13, 1821, m. Capt. Charles Barger, July 6, 1848. He d. March 4, 1856. She m. 2nd, G. W. Gerrish, now of San Francisco, Cal.

[Seventh Generation.]

443. i. Miss ELIZA A. B. CHILD was early betrothed to Mr. Cyrenius W. Canfield of Rochester, New York. The acquaintance was made when Miss Child was a pupil of the Academy, and Mr. Canfield a student of Union College, Schenectady, N. Y. The engagement was a long one, for both were young, and Mr. Canfield had his collegiate course to finish, and his professional one to pursue, and then to enter upon its duties and emoluments before they could expect their union. But each was true, and the golden hopes of success illumined the years of waiting.

Earnest study and courageous toil were opening the doors to an honorable and gifted manhood,—fond parents rejoicing in fulfilled expectations,—friends prophesying high attainments and a prominent career,—a bright and loving maiden putting on the festive robes; suddenly the end came; a few days illness, and the life of earth was left for the life of eternity. Parents' hopes crushed, friends' bright anticipations overthrown, sable garments exchanged for bridal sheen, the marriage week became that of entombment. Comforted by the ready and full recognition of her lover's talents and acquirements, made by his friends and legal associates, Miss Child in time could smile again. In September, 1841, she became the wife of Mr. Zalmon Rice a merchant of Lyons, Wayne Co.,

New York, whom she has survived many years. But the glowing tints of her morning have not wholly faded from the evening of her life, and to meet the chosen one of early days, is one of the joys of anticipation crowning the future existence.

[Seventh Generation.]

444. ii. EPHRAIM CHILD, second child of Dr. Ephraim and Mary Woodworth Child, b. April 10, 1801, m. first, Jan. 25, 1825, Elizabeth Curd Redford; m. second to Betsey Jewell; m. third to Ann Eliza Olmstead. Resides in Weedsport, N. Y.

[Eighth Generation.] Children:

453. i. ORVILLE CHILD, b. in Troy, N. Y., Feb. 9, 1827. Resides in Syracuse

454. ii. WALLACE CHILD, b. Feb. 22, 1831, d. June 9, 1831.

455. iii. MARTHA RENETTA CHILD, b. June, 1822, m. Floyd Johnson.

456. iv. DeWITT CLINTON CHILD, b. June, 1834, d. Oct. 21, 1844

457. v. ELIZA ANN CHILD, b. April 23, 1836, m. Dec. 27, 1853, Samuel Everhart.

458. vi GEORGE W. CHILD, b. Dec. 1, 1839, in Lysander, Oswego Co., N. Y., m. April 23, 1865, Mary Cordelia La Fever.

[Eighth Generation.]

457. v. ELIZA ANN CHILD, fifth child of Ephraim and Elizabeth Curd Redford Child, b. April 23, 1836, m. Dec. 27, 1853, Samuel Everhart of Lyons, N. Y.; he was b. Nov. 10, 1829, in Newfield, Tompkins Co., N. Y.; removed to Berlin, Mich.

[Ninth Generation.] Children:

459. i. FLOYD JOHNSON EVERHART,) Twins. (b. at Nayland, Allegan-
460. ii. EPHRAIM EVERHART,) (Co., Mich., Apr. 11, 1855.
461. iii. CARRIE ESTELLA EVERHART, b. at Berlin, Mich., Nov. 24, 1857.
462. iv. GEO. WRIGHT EVERHART, b. at Berlin, Mich., Oct. 29, 1863.

[Eighth Generation.]

458. vi. GEORGE W. CHILD, sixth child of Ephraim and Elizabeth Curd Redford Child, b. Dec. 1, 1839, m. April 23, 1865, Mary Cordelia La Fever. She was b. August, 1848, at Hector, N. Y. Reside at Grand Rapids, Mich.

[Ninth Generation.] Children:

463. i. CHARLES SANFORD CHILD, b. at Muskegon, Mich., Feb. 17, 1867.
464. ii. WM. ORVILLE CHILD, b. Jan. 5, 1869, in Muskegon, Mich.

[Seventh Generation]

445. iii. ORVILLE WHITMORE CHILDS, third child and second son of Dr. Ephraim and Mary Woodworth Child, b. in Stillwater, N. Y., Dec. 29, 1803, m. Mary G. Eno. (The date of

the marriage or birth of children we have been unable to ascertain.)

Orville W. Childs was one of the foremost and ablest practical civil engineers in this country. He was early in the employ of the State of New York, and our magnificent public works attest his genius and his skill. His labors and accomplishments were not confined to this State alone, but were extended to and embraced other gigantic enterprises and works of national interest and renown.

He had charge of a large amount of work, and was engaged in the survey and construction of the Champlain canal improvement, in 1824–5, and the building of the Oswego canal in 1826–8. He made the survey and plans for the improvement and navigation of the Oneida river in 1829–30, which were adopted, and the work was completed in 1850. He was next engaged with John B. Jervis in constructing the Chenango canal, in 1833–6, and in the latter year commenced his labors on the Erie canal enlargement, which was divided into three divisions, he being the chief engineer of the middle division of that work, which extended from Syracuse to Rochester. He was occupied upon this enlargement during most of the many years it took to complete that great work; but not as a division engineer only, for in 1840 he was appointed chief engineer of the New York State works entire, which position he held and filled with signal ability and honor for a period of seven years.

In 1848 he was the Democratic candidate for the office of state engineer, then created, but was defeated with the rest of the ticket. He was the companion, adviser and trusted friend of Governor William C. Bouck, Azariah C. Flagg, Henry Seymour, Jonas Earll, Jr., Michael Hoffman, Stephen Van Rensselaer and their contemporaries, and shared with John B. Jervis and William J. McAlpine the celebrity and honors arising from the plans upon which the enlarged Erie canal were based. Of those eminent engineers who grew up with him or under him and reached prominence in their profession are Van R. Richmond and Sylvanus H. Sweet, each having filled the office of state engineer several different times, and John D. Fay, the eminent canal commissioner.

In 1848-9 he was chief engineer in the survey and construction of the N. Y. Central RR. from Syracuse to Rochester (direct road). He left this to accept a like position at the instance of the American Atlantic and Pacific Ship Canal Co., of which Cornelius Vanderbilt and others were at the head, and who had a grant from the government of Nicaraugua, Central America, to build an inter-oceanic ship canal across that country, and in this gigantic enterprise he was occupied in 1850-52. His reports, maps, surveys and estimates of this work attracted universal attention throughout this country and Europe, and are regarded as models of thorough, exact and reliable scientific and practical skill. It was and is still held to be the most feasible and perfect survey of that route, which extended from the harbor of Greytown on the Atlantic, to that of Brito on the Pacific. The difficulties which were overcome, both of an engineering and physical character, to accomplish this work, together with the prominence of the enterprise and the ability with which it was conducted, established and confirmed his high rank in his profession. He also surveyed the route across the country from Lake Nicaraugua to the Pacific, of the Accessory Transit Co.'s passenger route, and afterwards visited Europe with Commodore Vanderbilt and others in relation to raising the necessary capital for constructing this ship canal, and was received there with marked attentions and honor. The above reports made by him have now become scarce, out of print, and are highly valued.

Subsequently he became chief engineer, and surveyed and constructed the Terre Haute and Alton RR. in 1855-8; was one of a commission of three to report on the practicability of putting a tunnel under the Hudson river at Albany, and made a survey and important investigation in behalf of the State of New York, for the purpose of designating and fixing the limits and boundaries of the City and County of New York, and to determine the extent of the encroachments thereon, and afterwards was engaged in the matter of the harbor defences about that city.

He removed from Syracuse, N. Y., where he had resided for the greater part of his life, to Philadelphia, Pa., about 1860, where he was engaged as one of the patentees and proprietors of the sleeping cars, then newly invented, and in other railroad interests. Was president of the Central Transportation Co.,

I

and the Philadelphia Car Works, and died in that city Sept. 6, 1870.

His name was synonymous with integrity, unflagging industry and high moral and intellectual worth. He was a close, hard student, persevering, and of high and exalted ideas as to his profession, in which he took great pride, and sought by every means in his power to elevate its standard to the highest pitch. He had profound contempt for all who were idle, shiftless, dishonest or unambitious. He was indefatigable in accomplishing whatever he undertook, and was upright, honest and incorruptible, without the shadow of a blemish in his whole professional career. The labors of his pen will be found scattered through the public documents and statute books of this State during a period of forty years prior to his death, and he contributed much to professional literature. He prepared the majority of the canal reports to the Legislature during his time. Always careful, considerate and exact to the minutest point, these habits of thought and action made him a safe counsellor and guide, and his opinion and advice was much sought after. In all these qualities he left a noble example in his profession as well as out of it. He was of dignified, impressive bearing, and unusually fine looking, of full habit and excellent features, and left a handsome fortune. His conversation was deeply interesting, his manner forcible and sincere, and his utterances always carried weight. Vigorous, inflexible in his convictions and accustomed to push all his undertakings to a successful issue, he justly earned the appellation, "an extraordinary man."

[Eighth Generation.]   Children:

****   i. CAROLINE MARY CHILDS, b. 1833, m. 1st, William T. Shear, 2d, John H. Nye, 3d, M. B. Weaver. Mrs. Weaver resides at Waverly, N. Y.

****   ii. JOHN HINMAN CHILDS, b. 1839, m. Oct. 7, 1863, Frances Amelia Burton, dau. of Burr and Laura M. Burton, at Syracuse, N. Y. She was b. at Syracuse, Feb. 8, 1844.

[Ninth Generation.]   Children of John Hinman and Frances Burton Childs:

****   i. ORVILLE BURTON CHILDS, b. June 3, 1864, d. July 26, 1865.

****   ii. FANNIE CHILDS, b. Aug. 19, 1865.

****   iii. MARY G. CHILDS, b. Dec. 13, 1866.

****   iv. JOHN CHILDS, b. June 19, 1868.

****   v. CARRIE CHILDS, b. Aug. 26, 1874.

****   vi. FLORENCE CHILDS, b. Sept. 6, 1877.

[Seventh Generation.]

446. iv. THERESA PEASE CHILD, fourth child and second dau of Dr. Ephraim and Mary Woodworth Child, b. in Stillwater, Saratoga county, N. Y., Jan. 25, 1805, m. about 1828, Col. John Fitzgerald. Col. Fitzgerald died at Phœnix, N. Y., where Mrs. F. still resides.

[Eighth Generation.] Children:

465. i. EPHRAIM FITZGERALD, b. in Stillwater, N. Y., Oct. 28, 1830, m. Ella Alvord.

466. ii. CYRENIUS CANFIELD FITZGERALD, b. in Clifton, Saratoga county, N. Y., March 19, 1832: m. 1st, Maria Gonez, m. 2nd, Mary Porter: m. 3rd, Willie M. Graves.

467. iii. FRANKLIN ALVORD FITZGERALD, b. May 28, 1834, m. 1854, Ada H. Leland.

468. iv. GEORGE FITZGERALD, b. 1843, d. at 8 months.

[Eighth Generation.]

465. i. EPHRAIM FITZGERALD, eldest child of Theresa Pease Child and Col. John Fitzgerald, b. in Stillwater, N. Y., Oct. 28 1830, m. Jan. 20, 1854, Ella Alvord, dau. of Thomas Alvord, Esq., of Homer, N. Y., at one time Lieut. Gov. of New York, Mr. Fitzgerald was a hardware merchant in Phœnix, N. Y.

[Ninth Generation.] Child:

469. i. ELIZABETH FITZGERALD, b. Sept. 28, 1860.

[Eighth Generation.]

466. ii. CYRENIUS CANFIELD FITZGERALD, second child of Theresa Pease Child and Col. John Fitzgerald, b. in Clifton, N. Y., March 19, 1832, m. Dec. 1858, Maria Gonez, of Leon, Nicaragua, Central America. She died in Chenondaga, Central America, Nov. 30, 1867. He m. second, Mary Porter, dau. of John K. Porter, of Albany, N. Y. She lived but three months after marriage. He married third, in 1870, Willie M. Graves of New Haven, Ct. They reside at Venezuela, South America. Mr. Fitzgerald is a mining engineer, on a salary of twenty thousand dollars a year.

[Ninth Generation.] Children:

470. i. RINALDO FITZGERALD, b. in Chenandoga, Cent. America, Sept. 14, 1860.

471. ii. GEO. EDWIN FITZGERALD, b. in Chenandoga, Cent. America, Aug. 14, 1862.

472. iii. THERESA FITZGERALD, b. in Chenandoga, Cent. America, Aug. 17, 1864.

473. iv. DONNIE FELIPE FITZGERALD, b. in Chenandoga, Cent. America, Nov. 29, 1867.

Three of these children are now in Claverick College, N. Y., and one in school at New Orleans, La.

[Eighth Generation.]

467. iii. FRANKLIN ALVORD FITZGERALD, third child of Theresa Pease Child and Col. John Fitzgerald, b. in Salina, Onondaga county, N. Y., May 28, 1834, m. 1854, Ada H. Le. land, dau. of Judge Leland of Steuben county, N. Y.

[Ninth Generation.] Children:

474. i. L. AMELIA THERESA FITZGERALD, b. Sept. 28, 1855, in Oswego county, N. Y.

475. ii. JOHN L. FITZGERALD, b. Sept. 28, 1859, member of Union College, and will graduate 1880.

476. iii. NELLIE FITZGERALD, b. in Half Moon, N. Y., Sept. 28, 1861.

477. iv. LOUISA STILLMAN FITZGERALD, b. in Brunswick, Ga., July 15, 1875.

[Seventh Generation.]

447. v. NOADIAH MOODY CHILDS, fifth child and third son of Dr. Ephraim and Mary Woodworth Child, b. in Stillwater, Sar. atoga county, N. Y., Dec. 6, 1806, m. first Oct. 1839, Martha Brewer, dau. of Simeon and Eunice Brewer of Providence, R. I. She was b. Aug. 23, 1821, and d. at Syracuse, N. Y., Aug. 31, 1863. His second m. was in Jan. 26, 1865, to Sarah Elizabeth Dawes, dau. of Ebenezer Dawes, Esq.

During the first half of his life, Mr. N. M. Childs was a civil engineer like his brother Orville W., and with him assisted in the running and construction of the Oswego canal, in 1828-9, the Oneida river improvement in 1829-30, and the Chenango canal in 1835. He was then appointed superintendent of the Oswego canal, which office he filled until 1839, and had charge of the extraordinary repairs and improvements made in this canal during that time. He was engaged as an engineer on the Erie canal enlargement from Syracuse to Lyons in 1839-40. In 1841, he entered into mercantile business, and the manufacture of salt at Syracuse, (then Salina) taking up his residence there, and has ever since been so engaged to quite a large extent. He was one of the commissioners of public schools of Syracuse, and was president of the board of education in 1855. He was one of the trustees of the Syracuse Salt Company, and was president of that company in 1872, and a prominent citizen of Syracuse, where he still resides.

Martha Brewer, the first wife of Noadiah M. Childs, (born 1821, died 1863) was a woman of remarkable sweetness of character, deep piety, and good deeds. She practiced a liberal charity, was quiet, unobtrusive, and took a prominent part in church matters. She was one of those who first organized Plymouth Church at Syracuse, and died in the midst of her useful life, deeply bereaved by all who knew her.

[Eighth Generation.]   Children:

478. i. ELIZABETH BELL CHILDS, b. in Syracuse, N. Y., Oct. 29, 1840, m. Feb. 9, 1869, Theodore L. Scott.

479. ii. DANIEL BREWER CHILDS, b. in Syracuse, May 5, 1843, m. Dec. 24, 1867, Mary F. Powers Vanderworker, of Waterford, N. Y.

480. iii. WILLIAM AUGUSTUS CHILDS, b. in Syracuse, March 9, 1846.

481. iv. FRANKLIN EARL CHILDS, b. in Syracuse, Oct. 16, 1848.

482. v. ANNA LOUISA CHILD, b. in Syracuse, Sept. 3, 1855, m. June, 1877, Henry D. Dillaye, Esq., attorney at law, of the firm of Vann, McClennan & Dillaye; reside in Syracuse, N. Y.

[Eighth Generation.]

478. i. ELIZABETH BELL CHILDS, eldest child of Noadiah and Martha Brewer Childs, b. in Syracuse, N.Y., Oct. 29, 1840, m. Feb. 9, 1869, Theodore L. Scott, Esq., cashier of the National Albany Exchange Bank, at Albany, N. Y.

[Ninth Generation.]   Child:

483. i. MARTHA BELL SCOTT, b. in Syracuse, N. Y., Nov. 29, 1876.

[Eighth Generation.]

479. ii. DANIEL BREWER CHILDS, second child and eldest son of Noadiah Moody and Martha Brewer Childs, b. in Syracuse, N. Y., May 5, 1843, m. Dec. 24, 1867, Mary F. Powers Vanderwerker, dau. of Robert and Margaret Vanderwerker of Waterford, N. Y.

Mr. Childs* graduated at Yale College, in 1863, and at the Albany Law School, in 1864. He entered the law office of Sedgwick, Andrews & Kennedy, at Syracuse, N. Y., and removed to the City of New York, January 1st, 1866, where he entered into partnership with the Hon. Amos G. Hull, and practiced law under the name of Hull & Childs for four years. His health becoming impaired, he suspended practice for a year, when he resumed under his own name, in 1871. In 1874 he formed a partnership with Hon. Herbert G. Hull, subse-

---

* We are indebted to the kindness of Daniel B. Child, Esq., of New York City (195 Broadway), for brief notices of some of the members of his branch of the family. In connection therewith, he remarks: "I will add that my uncle, Orville W., and my father were the first to add the final "s" to our name, in our line, a thing I regret."

quently Assistant U. S. District Attorney, under the name of
Childs & Hull, which firm still continues, having its office in
the Western Union Building, 195 Broadway, N. Y., he residing at Englewood, New Jersey. The firm has been engaged
in many important and prominent suits in that city, and does
a large civil business.

He was a director in the Manhattan Quotation Telegraph
Co., in 1874 and 1875, and was one of the original projectors
of the Law Telegraph Co., in 1874, by which lawyers and their
clients, and merchants generally, were put into telegraphic communication with each other, the courts and public buildings in
New York and Brooklyn, and in which telephones are now used,
and he has been from its organization a director, and the vice
president of that company.

[Eighth Generation.]

480. iii. WILLIAM AUGUSTUS CHILDS, third child and sec-
ond son of Noadiah Moody and Martha Brewer Childs, b. at
Syracuse, N. Y., March 9, 1846, m. Dec. 5, 1878, Julia Maria
Selleck, dau. of James W. and Elizabeth Selleck of Englewood,
N. Y. She was b. at Brooklyn, N. Y., Jan. 25, 1850.

Mr. Childs studied at the University of Michigan, at Ann
Arbor, and removed from Syracuse to the City of New York,
early in 1866. He entered the wholesale woolen house of Hull,
Holmes & Ingersoll, in Walker street, and after remaining there
a few years, he went into the employ of the Standard Life Insurance Co., of which he was made assistant secretary. In
1871 he received the appointment of superintendent of agencies of the Manhattan Life Insurance Co., and in 1874, became
interested with his brother Daniel, in projecting the Law Telegraph Co., heretofore described, and devoted his entire time and
energies to building it up to its present successful condition.
From its organization he has been a director, its treasurer and
manager.

The office of the Company is at 140 Fulton street, N. Y.,
and he resides at Englewood, N. J.

[Ninth Generation.]   Child:

**** i. ARTHUR CHILDS, b. at Englewood, N. Y., Sept. 15, 1879.

[Eighth Generation.]

481. iv. FRANKLIN EARL CHILDS, fourth child and third son
of Noadiah Moody and Martha Brewer Childs, b. in Syracuse,

N. Y., Oct. 16, 1848, m. Nov. 20, 1878, Mary Irene Sabin, dau. of John and Cora Irene Scranton Sabin, b. Jan. 8, 1853. She is the granddaughter of Edwin Scranton, Esq., who was editor of the first newspaper published in Rochester, N. Y. Mr. Childs graduated at Hamilton College, Clinton, N. Y., class of '59. Residence Bay City, Mich.

[Ninth Generation.] Child:

**** i. EMALITA PHILLIPS CHILDS, b. in Bay City, Mich., Oct. 21, 1879.

[Seventh Generation.]

448. vi. HENRY DAVIS CHILD, sixth child of Dr. Ephraim and Mary Woodworth Child, b. Nov. 16, 1808, in Stillwater, N. Y., m. Aug. 1832, Julia Ann Perkins. She d. in Wilmington. Will Co., Ill. July 17, 1878. He was a farmer, and died in W.

[Eighth Generation.] Children:

484. i CELIA ANN CHILD, b. Nov. 24, 1834, m. 1st, Z. F. Hanford, m. 2nd, A. Wilkins.

485. ii. HELEN CHILD, b. May 20, 1841, m. R. D. Loudon, farmer.

486. iii. FRANK CHILD, (adopted.)

[Eighth Generation.]

484. i. CELIA ANN CHILD, first child of Henry Davis and Julia Ann Perkins Child, b. Nov. 24, 1834, m. first, Nov. 24, 1852, Zalmon F. Hanford, at Wilmington, Ill. m. second April 11, 1872, Abraham Wilkins, of Wilmington, Ill.

[Ninth Generation.] Children:

487. i. HARRIET HANFORD, b. at Rockville, Kankee Co., Ill , Oct. 21, 1853,

488. ii. ABBIE J. HANFORD, b. at Manteno, Kankee Co., Oct. 7, 1863.

[Ninth Generation]

487. i. HARRIET HANFORD, first child of Celia Ann Child and Zalmon F. Hanford, m. Sep. 3, 1872, at Chicago, Ill., Eugene Sue Kimball.

[Tenth Generation.] Children:

489. i. MARK REESE KIMBALL, b. at Chicago, Ill., July 15, 1873.

490. ii. HARRIET SUE KIMBALL, b. at Chicago, Ill., Dec. 7, 1874.

491 iii. HELEN ELIZABETH KIMBALL, b. at Chicago, Ill., Sep. 19, 1876.

492. iv. EUGENE SUE KIMBALL, b at Chicago, Ill., March 19, 1879.

[Eighth Generation.]

485. ii. HELEN CHILD, second child of Henry Davis and Julia Ann Perkins Child, b. May 20, 1841, m. at Wilmington, Ill., March 13, 1862, Rodney D. Loudon.

[Ninth Generation.]　Children:

493. i. MARY LOUDON, b. at Wilmington, Ill., April 13, 1863, d May 9, 1864.

494. ii. FRED LOUDON, b. at Wilmington, Ill., Jan. 27, 1866.

[Seventh Generation.]

449. vii. HENRIETTA SCHUYLER CHILD, seventh child of Dr. Ephraim and Mary Woodworth Child, b. at Stillwater, Saratoga Co., N. Y., Oct. 22, 1810. m. at Syracuse, N. Y., Nov. 12, 1834, Luke Alvord, eldest son of Dioclesian Alvord. He is an architect, and resides at Vallejo, Cal.

[Eighth Generation.]　Children:

495. i. CASS L. ALVORD, b. at Syracuse, N. Y., Sep. 13, 1836, m. Martha Taylor.

496. ii. HELEN BURNETT ALVORD, b. at Syracuse, N. Y., Aug. 30, 1845. m. at Vallejo, Cal., July 9, 1867, William H. Tripp.

[Eighth Generation.]

495. i. CASS L. ALVORD, son of Henrietta S. Child and Luke Alvord, b. Sept. 13, 1836, m. Martha Taylor, neice of Gen. Zachary Taylor. Mr. Alvord is a civil engineer, and resides at Springfield, Ill. (1879.)

[Ninth Generation.]　Children:

497. i. LUKE EDWARD ALVORD, b March 22, 1867, at Springfield, Ill.

498. ii. HORACE ALVORD, b. April 3, 1869, at Springfield, Ill.

499. iii. MARY ALVORD, b. May 4, 1873. at Springfield, Ill.

[Eighth Generation.]

496. ii. HELEN BURNETT ALVORD, dau. of Henrietta S. Child and Luke Alvord, b. at Syracuse, N. Y., Aug. 20, 1845, m. Wm. H. Tripp of Vallejo, Cal., July 9, 1867. Mr. Tripp is professor of Penmanship, and resides with his family at Vallejo, Cal.

[Ninth Generation.]　Children:

500. i. SPENCER L. TRIPP, b. at Vallejo, California. July 25, 1870.

501. ii. DON EVERETT TRIPP, b. at Vallejo, California, June 2, 1877.

[Seventh Generation.]

450. viii. MARY ANN HOLLAND CHILD, dau. of Dr. Ephraim and Mary Woodworth Child, b. Oct. 16, 1818, at Stillwater, N. Y., m. Feb., 1831, Samuel McCleary, superintendent of public works. Mr. McCleary was b. May 13, 1809, at Watervliet, Albany county, N. Y. They had one child who died in infancy. Mrs. McCleary m. 1844, Jacob Staats. She was a successful teacher of French, possessed excellent musical ability,

and was the organist of the church. Religious in sentiment, she cordially gave her aid as an instructor in the Sabbath school. She was a member of an order termed the "Federal Arch." Her death was sudden, from an attack of the cholera, and occurred upon a steamer on which she had taken passage at Cincinnati, Ohio, for Galena, Ill. All care and attention were rendered by the captain of the steamer, in her illness, and death; he caused her to be honorably buried with the service of the Episcopal church at Leavenworth, Ind.

[Seventh Generation.]

452. x. CAROLINE CANFIELD CHILD, dau. of Dr. Ephraim and Mary Woodworth Child, b. Aug. 13, 1821, m. July 6, 1848, Capt. Charles Barger, at Galena, Ill. Capt. Barger died at New Orleans, at the residence of his cousin, Dr. Jones, Feb. 22, 1857. A Galena paper gives the following: "Capt. Chas. Barger has been for many years past, extensively known as one of the best and most accomplished steamboat captains on the Mississippi river, both on the upper and lower trade, and by his gentlemanly deportment, by his decision of character, by his upright and honorable action and bearing on all occasions, he won universal confidence and esteem. His sickness was long and painful, terminating in consumption. He died in the full assurance of Christian faith, leaving a devoted wife and friends everywhere to mourn his loss. The funeral of Capt. Barger was attended by many of our citizens at the Episcopal church. He was buried with the honors of Odd Fellowship." Mrs. Caroline C. Barger was again married some years afterwards, May 16, 1868, at the residence of her sister, Mrs. John H. Pope, in New Orleans, to G. M. Gerrish, Professor of Metallurgy, of San Francisco, Cal. His native place is Portland, Maine.

[Sixth Generation.]

47. vii. OLIVE CHILD, seventh child of Capt. Increase and Olive Pease Child, b. in "Oblong," town of Armenia, Dutchess Co., N. Y., March 11, 1775, m. 1798, Alfred Bosworth, of English ancestory, his earliest ancestor in this country came sometime after the year 1630, and settled in or near Bristol, R. I. Alfred Bosworth was b. in Bristol, R. I., Feb. 26, 1773, and removed to Saratoga Co., N. Y., about 1797. He died July 11, 1861, at Dundee, Ill. They had six children. She died Aug. 20, 1847.

[Seventh Generation.] Children:

502. i. MARY CHURCH BOSWORTH, b. in Milton, Saratoga Co., N. Y.,
Oct. 17, 1799, m. Sep. 13, 1818, Harry Weed.

503. ii. BENJAMIN F. BOSWORTH, b. in Greenfield, N. Y., Oct. 7, 1801,
m. 1st, Almira Smith, m. 2nd, Elizabeth Nixon.

504. iii. OLIVER C. BOSWORTH, b. in Greenfield, Saratoga Co., N. Y.,
Dec. 30, 1803.

505. iv. LUCINDA S. BOSWORTH, b. in Greenfield, N. Y., March 29, 1806,
m. Alfred Edwards.

506. v. ABIGAIL M. BOSWORTH, m. Benjamin Simonds; have no children.

507. vi. INCREASE BOSWORTH, b. in Greenfield, Saratoga Co., N. Y.,
April 2, 1812.

[Seventh Generation.]

502. i. MARY CHURCH BOSWORTH, eldest child of Olive
Child and Alfred Bosworth, b. in Milton, Saratoga Co., N. Y.,
Oct 13, 1799, m. Sep. 13, 1818, Harry Weed. She d. Sep. 19.
1846.

[Eighth Generation.] Children:

508. i. ALFRED BOSWORTH WEED, b. Dec. 9, 1820, m. May 2, 1841, Betsey
Rice.

509. ii. MARY ANN WEED, b. Nov. 6, 1822, m. Samuel J. Smith, Oct. 17,
1843.

510. iii. OSCAR FITZALLAN WEED, b. Nov. 26, 1824. m. Jan. 16, 1845,
Laura Conger.

[Eighth Generation.]

508. i. ALFRED BOSWORTH WEED, eldest child of Mary
Church Bosworth and Harry Weed, b. Dec. 9, 1820, m. May
2, 1841, Betsey Rice. He d. Feb. 25, 1850.

[Ninth Generation.] Children:

511. i. GEORGE CROMWELL WEED, b. Feb. 5, 1842, m. Jan. 7, 1866, Ellen
White.

512. ii. HELEN M. WEED, b. June 25, 1844, m. Feb. 22, 1860, Francis
Rafferty.

513. iii. CHARLES S. WEED, b. Nov. 5, 1846. m. Dec. 23, 1875, Ada Rossman.

[Ninth Generation.]

511. i. GEORGE CROMWELL WEED, eldest child of Alfred
Bosworth and Betsey Rice Weed, b. Feb. 5, 1842, m. Jan. 7,
1866, Ellen White.

[Tenth Generation.] Children:

514. i. MINNIE H. WEED, b. Oct 9, 1869.

515. ii. ETTA M. WEED, b. May 1, 1871.

516. iii. NORA WEED, b. April 30, 1874.

517. iv. EDITH WEED, b. Oct. 28, 1776.

[Ninth Generation.]

512. ii. HELEN M. WEED, second child of Alfred Bosworth and Betsey Rice Weed, b. June 25, 1844. m. Feb. 22. 1860, Francis Rafferty.

[Tenth Generation.]   Children:

518. i. ALBOURNE ELEANOR RAFFERTY, b. July 23, 1861.
519. ii. ESTELLA RAFFERTY, b. April 22, 1863.
520. iii. FRANK RAFFERTY, b. Oct. 23, 1866.
521. iv. CORA RAFFERTY, b. June 7, 1870.
522. v. THOMAS RAFFERTY, b. July 8, 1872.
523. vi. NELLIE RAFFERTY, b. April 3, 1876.
524. vii. MARIETTA RAFFERTY, b. Aug. 13, 1878.

[Ninth Generation.]

513. iii. CHARLES S. WEED, third son of Alfred B. Weed and Betsey Rice Weed, b. Nov. 5, 1846, m. Dec. 23, 1875, Ada Rossman.

[Tenth Generation.]   Child:

525. i. DELLA LEONA WEED, b. Jan. 13, 1877.

[Eighth Generation.]

509. ii. MARY ANN WEED, second child of Mary Church Bosworth and Harry Weed, b. Nov. 1, 1822, m. Oct. 17, 1843, Samuel Smith   Mr. Smith died in 1849.   She m. 2nd, Nov. 6, 1858, Henry B. Reeves.

[Ninth Generation.]   Children:

526. i. FRANKLIN B. SMITH, b. Feb. 7, 1846, d. June 6, 1847.
527. ii. GEORGE M. SMITH, b Nov. 29, 1847, d. Nov. 14, 1848

[Eighth Generation.]

510. iii. OSCAR F. WEED, third child of Mary Church Bosworth and Harry Weed, b. Nov. 26, 1824. m. Jan. 16, 1845, Laura Conger.

[Ninth Generation.]   Children:

528. i. ALFRED BOSWORTH WEED, b. Aug. 5, 1850.
529. ii. FREDERICK C. WEED, b. April 1, 1854, m. Belle Stowe, 1874.
530. iii. DELLA M. WEED, b. April 16, 1856, m. Oct. 16, 1873, Edson E. Gordon.

[Tenth Generation.]   Children of Della M. Weed and Edson Gordon:

531. i. LAURA L. GORDON, b. May 9, 1875.
532. ii. ALFRED WEED GORDON, b. Feb. 27, 1878.

[Seventh Generation.]

503. ii. BENJAMIN F. BOSWORTH, second child of Olive Child and Alfred Bosworth, b. in Greenfield, N.Y., Oct. 7, 1801, m. first to Almira Smith; m. second, Elizabeth Nixon.   He died Sept. 8, 1843, in McHenry Co., Ill.

[Eighth Generation.]   Child, by Almira Smith:

533. i. FRANKLIN S. BOSWORTH, b. Dec. 17, 1832, m. Sarah E. Hunt.

[Eighth Generation.]

533. i. FRANKLIN S. BOSWORTH. eldest and probably only child of Benjamin F. Bosworth and Almira Smith, b. Dec. 17, 1832, m. 1858, Sarah E. Hunt.

[Ninth Generation.] Children:

534. i. EDWARD INCREASE BOSWORTH, b. Jan. 10, 1861.
535. ii. MARY A. BOSWORTH, b. Sept. 22, 1867.
536. iii. FRANK H. BOSWORTH, b. Sept. 3, 1870.

[Seventh Generation.]

504. iii. OLIVER C. BOSWORTH, third child of Olive Child and Alfred Bosworth, b. in Greenfield, N. Y., Dec. 30, 1803, m. —; d. in Nashville, Chautauqua Co., N. Y., July 15, 1835.

[Eighth Generation.] Children:

537. i. FRANKLIN H. BOSWORTH, b. —; m. Feb. 23, 1851, Mary Waxham.
538. ii. WILLIAM A. BOSWORTH.
539. iii. JULIA BOSWORTH, b. Dec. 3, 1834; m. Sept. 23, 1857, A. L. Bishop.

[Eighth Generation.]

537. i. FRANKLIN H. BOSWORTH, eldest child of Oliver C. Bosworth, b. —; m. Feb. 23, 1851, Mary Waxham.

[Ninth Generation.] Children:

540. i. FREDERICK A. BOSWORTH, b. May 15, 1857.
541. ii. ALFRED B. BOSWORTH, b. June 17, 1859.
542. iii. OLIVE C. BOSWORTH, b. Mar. 23, 1868.

[Eighth Generation.]

539. iii. JULIA BOSWORTH, third child of Oliver C. Bosworth and ——, b. Dec. 3, 1834, m. Sept. 23, 1857, A. L. Bishop.

[Ninth Generation.] Child:

543. i. MARY BISHOP, b. July 16, 1868.

[Seventh Generation.]

505. iv. LUCINDA BOSWORTH, fourth child of Olive Child and Alfred Bosworth, b. in Greenfield, Saratoga Co., N. Y., Mar. 29, 1806, m. July 8, 1829, Alfred Edwards of Greenfield, N. Y. Mrs. Edwards d. July 12, 1849.

[Eighth Generation.] Children:

544. i. ESTHER LUCINDA EDWARDS, b. Jan. 17, 1831.
545. ii. MARY EDWARDS, b. Aug. 19, 1832. m. April 26, 1852, J. A. Carpenter.
546. iii. GEORGE EDWARDS, b. Mar. 20, 1834.
547. iv. HENRY EDWARDS, b. July 14, 1835, m. April 17, 1866, Adelaide Dunton.
548. v. ELIZABETH B. EDWARDS, b. March 2, 1838 m. Feb. 23, 1860, J. C. Wilder.

549. vi. OLIVIA ADELAIDE EDWARDS, b. March 2, 1840.
550. vii. ABBEY ANNETTE EDWARDS, b. May 22, 1845.
551. viii. LOUISA STILLMAN EDWARDS, b. Aug. 27, 1846.
552. ix. ELLA LUCINDA EDWARDS, b. June 27, 1849, m. Sept. 20, 1870, E. F. Cleveland, M. D.

[Eighth Generation.]

545. ii. MARY EDWARDS, second child of Lucinda Bosworth and Alfred Edwards, b. Aug. 19, 1832, m. April 26, 1852 Julius Angelo Carpenter of Dundee, Ill.

[Ninth Generation.] Children:
553. i. ELLA CARPENTER, b. Dec. 27, 1854.
554. ii. ALICE MAY CARPENTER, b. May 17, 1860.
555. iii Infant son, b. Dec. 27, 1872.

[Eighth Generation.]

547. iv. HENRY EDWARDS, fourth child of Lucinda Bosworth and Alfred Edwards, b. July 14, 1835, m. April 17, 1866, Adelaide Dunton of Dundee, Ill.

[Ninth Generation.] Children:
556. i. ALFRED DUNTON EDWARDS, b. Feb. 18, 1867.
557. ii. FLORENCE EDWARDS, b. June 2, 1869.
558. iii. MAY EDWARDS, b. May 26, 1872.
559. iv. LUCINDA EDWARDS, b. Feb., 1868.

[Eighth Generation.]

548. v. ELIZABETH B. EDWARDS, fifth child of Lucinda and Alfred Edwards, b. March 2, 1838, m. Feb. 23, 1860, Jedediah Charles Wilder.

[Ninth Generation.] Children:
560. i. CHARLES E. WILDER, b. Jan. 11, 1861.
561. ii. ELLA MAY WILDER, b. March 21, 1867.

[Eighth Generation.]

552. ix. ELLA LUCINDA EDWARDS, ninth child of Lucinda and Alfred Edwards, b. June 27, 1849, m. Sept. 20, 1870, Edmund Francis Cleveland, M. D., of Dundee, Ill.

[Ninth Generation.] Children:
562. i. ANNABEL CLEVELAND, b. Oct. 6, 1871.
563. ii. MAY ELIZABETH CLEVELAND, b. Dec. 10, 1875.

[Seventh Generation.]

507. vi. INCREASE C. BOSWORTH, sixth child of Olive Child and Alfred Bosworth, b. April, 1812, in Greenfield, N. Y., m. about 1844.

[Eighth Generation.] Children:
564. i. ALFRED BOSWORTH, b. April 1, 1846, m. Sept. 10, 1872, Eleanor Wheeler.

565. ii. WILLIAM EUGENE BOSWORTH, b. Oct. 8, 1848, m. May 12, 1874, Ida Woodruff.

566. iii. ABBEY L. BOSWORTH, b. June 1, 1851.

567. iv. HENRY I. BOSWORTH, b. Sept. 20, 1854.

[Eighth Generation.]

564. i. ALFRED BOSWORTH, eldest child of Increase C. Bosworth, b. April 1, 1846, m. Sept. 10, 1872, Eleanor Wheeler.
[Ninth Generation.]　Children:

568. i. ELEANOR BOSWORTH, b. Sept. 2, 1873.

569. ii. NEIL BOSWORTH, b. May 25, 1878.

[Eighth Generation.]

565. ii. WILLIAM EUGENE BOSWORTH, second child of Increase C. Bosworth, m. May 12, 1874, Ida Woodruff.
[Ninth Generation.]　Children:

570. i. CYRUS INCREASE BOSWORTH, b. March 29, 1875.

571. ii. CHARLES E. BOSWORTH, b. Jan. 29, 1878.

[Sixth Generation.]

48. viii. WILLIAM CHILD, eighth child of Increase and Olive Pease Child, b. in Woodstock, Ct., June 25, 1777, m. Polly Weed, "a pretty orphan girl." He d. 1840, in Jefferson, Hillsdale Co., Mich.

The following obituary notice of Mr. William Child is furnished by Mrs. Dr. Jones of Chicago, Ill., his niece, taken from a Michigan paper:

The death of William Child, Esq., at Jefferson, Hillsdale county, Mich., occurred on the 31st of March, 1840, in the sixty-third year of his age. More than merely "he is dead" is due to the memory of Mr. Child. He was connected with the newspaper press of New York State many years. He served his apprenticeship with Solomon Southwick, then Southwick & Barber, printers, in Albany. He first conducted a paper in Saratoga Co., in Jefferson's exciting times, and warmly espoused his cause. He afterwards removed to Johnstown and conducted the Montgomery *Republican*, with his brother Asa, after which he published the Ballston Spa *Gazette*. In 1810 he removed to Seneca Co., N. Y., and for several years directed his attention to agricultural pursuits. But his pen was not idle: he contributed freely to the columns of one or more papers—*Plow Boy* among the rest, on agricultural and other subjects. He was one of the earlier advocates of temperance, in print, having in 1818 or 1819 prepared a pamphlet called "A Blow at the Bottle," setting forth the alarming effects of the all-prevailing vice, which he printed and gratuitously and liberally circulated. In 1823 he purchased one of the newspaper establishments in Genesee Co., N. Y., which he conducted with great ability till 1837. He also edited an anti-masonic paper, which was the cause of great commotion, and made him many enemies among the masons. It is no more than justice to say that few papers in Western New York were edited with more ability than the *Genesee Farmer*, by William Child. In the fall of 1838, Mr. Child came to Penn Yan, and for some months conducted the *Democratic Whig*; but finding himself too far advanced in years to endure the fatigues and perplexities attending the publication of a political paper, he determined to retire from the bustle of a printing office and seek in Michigan a quiet retreat for his old age. Soon after his arrival in that state he was appointed one of the judges of Ingham Co. He was elected judge with a large majority. His friends called upon him in the evening to congratulate him, and staid till a late hour. Shortly after retiring he spoke to his wife and said, "I am dying." Before a physician could arrive he was speechless, and lived but a short time. To say that William Child was an *honest man* in the full import of the words is an all-sufficient epitaph, and those who knew him will readily bear testimony to its truth. His principles were not purchasable. His patriotism had *no price*. What was right in his view must be done, even at a sacrifice. As a husband, parent and friend, he was kind and affectionate and warm hearted. So he lived and so he died, suddenly, in a moment, as it were, one of the noblest works of his Creator. But when the summons came he was ready, long having cherished and professed a well-grounded hope of a glorious resurrection and acceptance in and through the merits of his Saviour Jesus Christ.

[Seventh Generation.] Children:

572. i. JENNETTE CHILD, m. Rev. Mr. Lewis, a Baptist clergyman, in Seneca Co., N. Y.

573. ii. WILLIAM CHILD; he was a printer and editor; first lived in Lyons, Wayne Co., N. Y.; m.; left Seneca Co; it is not known to what place he went.

574. iii. MARY ANN CHILD, m. a Mr. Sylvester, a druggist who lived, in 1833, in Waterloo, N. Y.

575. iv. GEORGE CHILD.

576. v. JOHN CHILD.

577. vi. FABER CHILD.

[Sixth Generation.]

49. ix. ASA CHILD, sixth son and ninth child of Increase and Olive Pease Child, b. in Woodstock, Ct., May 21, 1780, m. in 1806, Lois Foote of Kingsborough, Fulton Co., N. Y. He d. in 1828, in the City of New York. Mrs. C. was b. in 1783, and d. in Chicago in 1875, in the home of her daughter, Mrs. Dr. Jones, æt. ninety-two years.

Mr. Child was the youngest of the nine children of Captain Increase and Olive Pease Child. His life was spent as a journalist. He was a genuine man, of solid physical proportions, and of marked intellectual force. The manliness of Mr. Child was conspicuous in his varied relations in life. Just in his feelings, conscientious, transparent, his bearing was dignified and winning. While serving the public at the head of a weekly

journal, he was actuated by the most honorable motives, and
gave currency to what he deemed the soundest principles of
good government. No flattery or denunciation could alter in
him an honest conviction. By nature unobtrusive and retiring, he studiously avoided collision with those differing from
him on questions of public concern. But he was not pusillan-
imous or craven. Occasions sometimes brought out the grit
and force of character which lay hidden ordinarily beneath an
unruffled surface. It is related of him that on one occasion in
a time of high political excitement, a man who felt himself
aggrieved at a published article in Mr. Child's paper, went to
the office, and in bitter, offensive language denounced Mr.
Child, whose quiet, unruffled temper so increased the anger of
his assailant as to provoke an assault. A violent blow across
his shoulders from the cane of the angered man brought Mr.
Child to his feet, when he seized his assailant and pitched him
headlong into the street. He could teach his enemies to fear
his strength and respect his opinions. But he by no means
lacked magnanimity. He was warm hearted, socially attractive, sympathetic and benevolent, drawing to his side men of
like instincts, whom he entertained by his wit and humor.
But with all his natural excellences, his aims in life were
prompted by higher impulses than mere natural instincts. The
power of a Christian faith transformed the inner and controlled
the outer life. His death in the meridian of life was a public
loss, and sincerely mourned by his friends and those who knew
his worth. An obituary notice at the time of his death, written by Rev. Dr. Samuel Hanson Cox, of whose church Mr.
Child was a member, published in the *New York Statesman*, is
a just tribute to his memory, and is worthy of preservation in
this record:

DIED.—In New York City, on the 19th of March, 1827, after a distress-
ing sickness of six months, Asa Child, printer, and formerly editor of the
Montgomery Republican of Johnstown, N. Y. Mr. Child was in his forty-
seventh year, and has left a widow and four children to mourn the loss of an
affectionate husband and tender father. For fourteen years he had been
a professor of the religion of Jesus Christ, in whom a deep sense of his own
sinfulness and wants had brought him to trust as his Saviour and his righteousness. Mr. Child always evinced a low and abasing conception of himself. Self-distrust was a trait in his Christian character which resulted
from an enlightened conviction of the perfidy of the human heart and of
the real grandeur and excellency of a true disciple. In the first stage of his

illness this diffidence seemed oppressive and painful, owing much perhaps to the nature of his disease and the medicines administered; but in its concluding scenes the prospects brightened for immortality. His mind rose by faith above the ruins it was soon to leave; it acquired calmness, confidence and hope in Jesus Christ our Lord. His bodily strength gradually wasted away, while his soul serenely waited for the signal of its release. He gently sunk into the embraces of death, without a struggle or a groan, in the spirit of submission and the consolation of hope; leaving to a large circle of relatives and friends a legacy, of all the most desirable and precious, the legacy of a Christian hope, a happy death-bed and a good name. "Henceforth there is laid up for me a crown of righteousness, which the Lord the righteous judge shall give me at that day, and not to me only, but unto all them also that love his appearing."

Mrs. Dr. Jones, a daughter of Mr. Child, says:

He (Dr. Cox) not knowing the history of my father, did not give particulars of his life. I think my father with his brother William were in Solomon Southwick's office in Albany, N. Y. I well remember the time when politics were running so high in Governor Clinton's day. The Democrats had no press in Johnstown at that time, and were obliged to get their printing done at my father's office. And one night they went in and demolished the form that was ready for the press in the morning, and scattered the type in every direction. The excitement was so great, we trembled for my father's life. Judge Cady of Johnstown was one of the leading spirits of the Whig party, and was constantly upholding and defending the rights of the party to which he belonged; and I believe he was one of Governor Clinton's personal friends, as he was of my father.

[Seventh Generation.] Children:

578. i. OLIVE PEASE CHILD, b. in Waterloo, Seneca Co., N. Y., in 1808, m. in 1843 to Dr. Elijah Jones of Bristol, Mich., moved to Galena, Ill., in 1844, thence to Chicago, 1872, where they now reside; no children.

579. ii. CAROLINE CHILD, b. in Johnstown, N. Y., Jan. 18, 1810, d. Oct. 4, 1812.

580. iii. CHAUNCEY CHILD, b. in Johnstown, N. Y., May 17, 1812, d. 1813.

581. iv. CAROLINE CHILD, 2d, b. in Johnstown, N. Y., Nov. 7, 1815, m. Julius Peck. Reside in Zumbrota, Min.

582. v. WILLIAM CHAUNCEY CHILD, b. in Johnstown, Montgomery Co., N. Y., Aug. 16, 1817, m. Dec. 1846, Phebe W. Sanford.

583. vi. LOUISA CHILD, b. in Johnstown, N. Y., Nov. 5, 1819, m. in New York City to Nelson Stillman.

584. vii. ASA BARNES CHILD, b. in Johnstown, N. Y., March. 1824, d. in New York City, Feb. 25, 1826.

[Seventh Generation.]

582. v. Rev. WILLIAM CHAUNCEY CHILD, D. D., second son and fifth child of Asa and Lois Foote Child, b. in Johnstown, N. Y., Aug. 16, 1817, m. Dec., 1846, Phebe W. Sanford, dau. of Giles Sanford of Albany, N. Y. Dr. Child died Jan. 14, 1876.

K

The youth of Dr. Child gave promise of a future which was fully realized in the development of some of the most attractive and useful characteristics. Nature in the bestowment of her gifts upon him was not parsimonious. Inheriting the best qualities of intelligent and Christian parents, he commenced life under most favorable circumstances, which happily shaped his course in maturer years. Gifted with more than ordinary intellect, endowed with a disposition of peculiar sweetness, he readily secured warm and lasting friendships. His public life leaves record of his wisdom and Christian activities. A thorough education fitted him for positions in the higher spheres of life. At twenty-four years of age he was honorably graduated from Union College, Schenectady, N. Y. He at once entered upon his professional studies at the Baptist Theological Seminary, in Newton, Mass. The honorary degree of Doctor of Divinity was conferred upon him by his Alma Mater.

His public service was commenced by his settlement as pastor of the First Baptist Church in Charlestown, Mass. Later he was installed over the Baptist Church of Framingham, Mass. Some years after, he became connected with the American Tract Society, as one of its officers. He was also connected with a widely circulated Baptist weekly journal, bearing the title of *Watchman and Reflector*, published in Boston, Mass. The varied experiences of Dr. Child gave to him that completeness of character which lacked nothing of attractiveness, and increased greatly his efficiency in his public career. His estimable wife, whose companionship contributed much to his domestic happiness, as well as his ministerial usefulness, says in a note to us, as indicative of the secret of his success in life: "My esteemed husband was characterized by an unusually genial temperament. He was gentle, affectionate and courteous. The Rev. Dr. Kirk of Boston, once spoke of him at a public meeting of the Tract Society, as being 'a sweet Child among us.' The expression was so appropriate it made me remember it. He encouraged the unfortunate, strengthened the weak, and caused many to admire the source from whence he drew his spiritual comfort."

[Eighth Generation.] Children:

585. i. ANNA GERTRUDE CHILD, b. March 21, 1851, in Boston, Mass., m. April 26, 1871, Samson D. Whittemore.

586. ii. WILLIS SANFORD CHILD, b. Aug. 2, 1857, m. June 8, 1879, Nettie Griffin of Newbury, Kansas. Mr. Child is engaged in stock raising in Kansas: resides at Newbury.

[Eighth Generation]

585. i. ANNA GERTRUDE CHILD, eldest child of Rev. Dr. Chauncey and Phebe W. Sanford Child, b. in Boston, Mass., March 21, 1851, m. April 26, 1871, Samson D. Whittemore of Boston, Mass., son of Alvin and Sophia Whittemore of Paris, Me. He was b. Dec. 18, 1842, in Paris Hill, Me.

[Ninth Generation] Children:
**** i. GRACE WHITTEMORE, b. Sep. 13, 1873.
**·* ii. WILLIAM CHILD WHITTEMORE, b. Sep. 6, 1874.

[Seventh Generation.]

583. vi. LOUISA CHILD, dau. of Asa and Lois Foote Child, b. in Johnstown, N. Y., Nov. 5, 1819, m. Feb. 25, 1839, in New York City, Nelson Stillman of Colebrook, Ct. Mr. Stillman was a merchant. He died Aug. 31, 1871. Mrs. Stillman lives in Zumbrota, Minn.

[Eighth Generation.] Children:
587. i. MARY L. STILLMAN, b. in Galena Ill., Dec. 6, 1845.
588. ii. CHARLES PHELPS STILLMAN, b. in Galena, Ill., June 25, 1852.
589. iii. ISABELLE STILLMAN, b. in Galena, Ill., July 17, 1857.

[Fifth Generation.]

39. iii. ASA CHILD, second son and third child of Ephraim and Mary Lyon Child, b. in Woodstock, Ct., April 6, 1742, m. Nov. 26, 1762, Elizabeth Murray. He d. Oct. 20, 1826, of old age: his wife was b. Sept. 15, 1741, d. April 28, 1790.

[Sixth Generation.] Children:
590. i. THEDE CHILD, b. in Woodstock, Ct., Aug. 24, 1763, d. unm., Jan 25, 1833.
591. ii. DEXTER CHILD, b. in Woodstock, Ct., Jan. 19, 1766, d. unm., April 19, 1833.
592. iii. RENSSELAER CHILD, b. in Woodstock, Ct., Sept. 15, 1769, m. Nov. 28, 1797, Priscilla Corbin.

[Sixth Generation.]

592. iii. RENSSELAER CHILD, b. in Woodstock, Sept. 15, 1769, m. Nov. 28, 1797, Priscilla Corbin of Thompson, Conn.

Mr. Child bore the sobriquet of "Master Rans" for his prominence as a teacher at one time, he was a man of much native talent, and well educated for the times. He was influential, and esteemed for his personal worth, and justly intrusted with public offices.   The following extract is from "H. Ammidown's Historical Collections:"

Rensselaer Child was largely engaged as surveyor and conveyancer over a circuit of country of considerable extent in that vicinity; and as the records will show, this class of business, for a number of years among the farming community, was monopolized by him: he was a man of large stature, and possessed more than the ordinary powers of intellect.

[Seventh Generation.]   Children:

593. i. ASA CHILD, b. in Woodstock, Ct., Dec. 2, 1798, m. Feb. 13, 1826, Alice H. Goddard.

594. ii. PELEG CORBIN CHILD, b. in Woodstock, Ct., July 11, 1800, m. Sept. 16, 1829, Abigail Bullock.

595. iii. LINUS CHILD, b. in Woodstock, Ct., Feb. 27, 1803, m. Oct. 27, 1827, Berenthia Mason.

596. iv. MYRA CHILD, b. in Woodstock, Ct., Feb. 18, 1804, d. unm. Dec. 15, 1825.

597. v. LEVINIA CHILD, b. in Woodstock, Ct., Nov. 4, 1806, m. May 3, 1832, Henry Ingalls.

598. vi. CLARISSA CHILD, b. in Woodstock, Ct., Sept. 26, 1810, m. July 18, 1841, Charles Chandler.

599. vii. PRISCILLA CHILD, b. in Woodstock, Ct., Oct. 2, 1812, m. April 27, 1840, Rensselaer Woodruff. She d. Oct. 10, 1841, she left no children.

600. viii. EPHRAIM CHILD, b. in Woodstock, Ct., May 31, 1818, d. Dec. 30, 1827.

601. ix. RENSSELAER CHILD, JR., b. in Ct., Woodstock, March 6, 1820, m. Aug., 1842, Maria Marcy.

[Seventh Generation.]

593. i. HON. ASA CHILD, eldest child of Rensselaer and Priscilla Corbin Child, b. in Woodstock, Ct., Dec. 2, 1798, m. Feb. 13, 1826, Alice Hart Goddard, dau. of the Hon. Calvin Goddard of Norwich, Ct. Judge Goddard was an eminent lawyer in Connecticut. He was twice elected to Congress when the Federal party was in power,—was for many years Mayor of the City of Norwich, Ct.,—Speaker of the House of Representatives in the Connecticut Legislature,—Judge of the Superior Court and of the Supreme Court of Errors in Connecticut,—his wife was the daughter of the Rev. Levi Hart, D.D., of Preston, Ct., and granddaughter of the Rev. Joseph Bellamy, D.D., of Bethlehem, Ct., who d. May 12, 1832.

Hon. Asa Child was in stature six feet, of full habit and fine personal appearance. Descended from a stock talented and influential, his early life commenced with very favorable surroundings. Possessed of more than ordinary intellectual abilities, with a thorough education, he became prominent in public life.

He was graduated at Yale College, New Haven, Ct., in 1821, pursued his preparatory studies for the law in the office of Hon. Calvin Goddard of Norwich, Ct. He was prominent as a lawyer in Connecticut, afterwards in Baltimore, Maryland, and later in New York City. He held at one time the office of United States District Attorney for Connecticut, under the administration of President Jackson. He died at Norwich, Ct., May 11, 1858.

[Eighth Generation.] Children:

602. i. JULIA GODDARD CHILD, b. at Norwich, Ct., April 20, 1828, m. May 12, 1852, Levi W. Allen.

603. ii. EDWARD CHILD, b. in Hartford, Ct., Oct. 11, 1829, d. Aug. 23, 1830.

604. iii. ALICE HART CHILD, b. in Norwich, Ct., Aug. 23, 1832, d. at Stamford, Ct., April 27, 1873.

605. iv. CALVIN GODDARD CHILD, b. in Norwich, Ct., April 6, 1834, m. Sept. 16, 1858, Kate Godfrey.

[Eighth Generation.]

602. i. JULIA GODDARD CHILD, eldest child of Hon. Asa and Alice Hart Goddard Child, b. in Norwich, Ct., April 20, 1825, m. May 12, 1852, Levi W. Allen of South Hadley, Mass. He was b. Oct. 12, 1817, and d. May 22, 1872. His parents were Peter and Abby Wright Goodrich Allen of Weathersfield, Ct. His mother was granddaughter of Oliver Wolcott, Governor of Connecticut, and one of the signers of the "Declaration of Independence."

[Ninth Generation.] Children:

606. i. CHARLES GODDARD ALLEN, b. in South Hadley, Mass., July 22, 1853, d. Feb. 13, 1858.

607. ii. ABBY WRIGHT ALLEN, b. at South Hadley, Jan. 24, 1856.

[Eighth Generation.]

605. iv. HON. CALVIN GODDARD CHILD, second son and fourth child of Hon. Asa and Alice Hart Goddard Child, b. in Norwich, Ct., April 6, 1834, m. Sept. 16, 1858, Kate Godfrey, dau. of Jonathan and Elizabeth Hubbell Godfrey. Mrs. K. G. Child was born Dec. 12th, 1837. Residence Stamford, Ct.

The prominent positions occupied by Hon. Calvin Goddard Child, furnish ample proof of the confidence reposed in him as a public servant. His early surroundings were favorable to the development of the proper elements of character for success and usefulness in life. Graduated with honors at Yale College, New Haven, Ct., in 1855, he chose for his profession the law.

for which his taste and talents eminently fitted him. Since 1870 he has held the office of United States District Attorney for the State of Connecticut; receiving his first appointment from President Grant, and his present appointment from President Hayes.

As a citizen, Mr. Child has the respect and esteem of the community where his influence contributes largely to promote the moral and material interests of his adopted home.

[Ninth Generation.] Children:

608. i. KATE GODFREY CHILD, b. in Norwich, Ct., Aug. 21, 1859.
609. ii. CALVIN GODDARD CHILD, JR., b. in Norwich, Ct., Aug. 27, 1862.
610. iii. WILLIAM BUCKINGHAM CHILD, b. in Stamford, Ct., Nov., 1865.
611. iv. ELIZABETH CHILD, b. in Stamford, Ct., Aug. 20, 1868.

[Seventh Generation.]

594. ii. PELEG CHILD, second child and second son of Rensselaer and Priscilla Corbin Child, b. in Woodstock, Ct., July 11, 1800, m. Sept. 16, 1829, Abigail Bullock. He died Oct. 20, 1861, on the old homestead of his father. Mrs. Child did not long survive him. They had only one child—an adopted daughter—who was an amiable and intelligent girl, and the light of their dwelling for many years, when the frosts of death cut down the flower in its full bloom, and filled their cheerful home with sadness.

Mr. Peleg Child was of a stalwart frame, whose avoirdupois would overleap two hundred pounds. In intellect he was much above mediocrity; was fond of reading, and well posted in matters of Church and State. He was specially interested in the politics of the country—a pronounced Democrat. Kinship was no barrier to his onslaught upon his opponents. He was remorselessly severe and unrelenting in his attacks upon men and measures opposed to his views. His neighbors were often entertained and amused when listening to the earnest debates on political questions between him and his brother, the Hon. Linus Child, who had as little sympathy with the Democratic party as Peleg had for the Old Whig, and later Republican. Both equally tenacious of their opinions, waxed warm as the discussion progressed, till both were ready to adopt the language of Macbeth,

"Lay on, McDuff,
And damn'd be him who first cries, Hold! enough!"

The storm of words having expended itself, calm was soon restored in each breast, and fraternal relations remained undisturbed.   Mr. Child was a valuable member of society, identified with all its interests.   He resided on his father's homestead, north of Village Corners, in the town of Woodstock, and was a thrifty farmer.

[Seventh Generation.]

595. iii. Hon. LINUS CHILD, third child and third son of Rensselaer and Priscilla Corbin Child, b. in Woodstock, Ct., Feb. 27, 1803, m. Oct. 27, 1827, Berenthia Mason.

"Hon. Mr. Child passed his early years on his father's farm, with the usual attendance upon the public school.   He began his preparation for College under the tuition of Rev. Samuel Backus of East Woodstock, and completed his preparatory studies at Bacon Academy, in Colchester, Connecticut, in the autumn of 1820.   The following winter he entered Yale College, New Haven, whence he graduated in 1824.   Mr. Child did not reach the highest rank in college as a scholar; but for honest, actual mastery of the prescribed course, few were before him.   After he graduated, he became a member of the Law School in New Haven, and studied in the office of S. P. Staples. He was also under Judge Daggett's instruction.   Six months later he became a student in the office of Hon. Ebenezer Stoddard, in the west parish of his native town, and after eighteen months' study there, was admitted to the bar in Connecticut. He spent a year in the office of Hon. George A. Tufts of Dudley, Mass., when he was admitted to practice in the courts of Worcester county, upon this he established himself in Southbridge, Worc. Co., Mass.   He resided in Southbridge some eighteen years, during this period he was six times elected Senator from Worcester county to the State Legislature.   In 1845 he removed to Lowell, and held the agency of one or two of the large manufacturing corporations of that city." [1]   He possessed the unusual stature and frame of his father and grandfather, was cordial and genial in look and manner.   Earnest in the promotion of all efforts for the public weal, and prominent in church and missionary interests, a member of the American Board of Foreign Missions.   In 1862, Mr. Child removed

[1] H. Ammidown's Historical Collection.

to Boston, and resumed his professional duties, associating with him his son, Linus M. Child. Hon. Mr. Child died in Hingham, Mass., after a short illness, on the 26th August, 1870.

[Eighth Generation.]   Children:

    612. i. MYRA BERENTHIA CHILD, b. in Southbridge, Mass., Nov. 26, 1830.

    613. ii. LINUS MASON CHILD, b. in Southbridge, Mass., March 13, 1835, m. Oct., 1862, Helen A. Barnes.

    614. iii. ABBIE BULLOCK CHILD, b. in Southbridge, Mass., April 3, 1840.

[Eighth Generation.]

    613. ii. LINUS MASON CHILD, Esq., second child and only son of Hon. Linus and Berenthea Mason Child, b. March 13, 1835, m. Oct., 1862, Helen A. Barnes. Mr. Child graduated at Yale College, New Haven, Ct., in 1855, and is a lawyer in Boston, Mass.

We will preface a brief sketch of Mr. Child, having had no personal acquaintance with him, by saying, we have aimed in the compilation of this work, on the one hand, to avoid the charge of flattery, and on the other, to escape the suspicion of detraction. To place on record in a pleasing light every member in every branch, truthfully, is our pleasant office. From what one says and does, history is made, this is the basis of what we say of Mr. Child. From a late "*Boston Herald*," which has just fallen into our hands, (March 26, 1880) containing an argument by Linus M. Child, Esq., of Boston, before a Massachusetts Legislative Committee, in support of a petition for a charter from the legislature for an elevated railway in Boston, may be gathered some elements of his character, which entitle him to be placed in our record in a pleasant light. From a cursory perusal of his argument, we are impressed with the fact that Mr. Child must have attained to a very commendable rank in his profession, to have been entrusted with matters of so much magnitude. His argument evinces a knowledge of facts which none but a close observer would have treasured up. His deductions are logical and forcible, while sound judgment, legal acumen, and broad financial views, are so clearly evinced as to entitle him to the confidence reposed in him by his clients. Descended from a stock possessing sturdy physical and mental qualities, and having enjoyed the best opportunities for mental culture, and with more than ordinary natural abilities, a failure to reach an enviable eminence, could hardly be looked for.

[Ninth Generation.]　Children:
615. i. HELEN LOUISA CHILD, b. in Boston, Mass., Oct. 9, 1863.
616. ii. LINUS MASON CHILD, JR., b. in Boston, Dec. 21, 1865.
617. iii. MYRA LIND CHILD, b. in Boston, March, 17, 1870.

[Seventh Generation.]

597. v. LAVINIA LYON CHILD, fifth child and second dau. of Rensselaer and Priscilla Corbin Child, b. in Woodstock, Ct., Nov. 1, 1808, m. May 3, 1832, Henry Ingalls, who was born in Abington, Ct. They moved immediately after their marriage to Illinois, and reside now in North Branch Station, Chisago county, Minnesota. Their children were born in Illinois.

From a letter to me since my work of preparation commenced, from Mrs. Lavinia Child Ingalls, we give the following extract, which will interest many:

"My great grandfather, Ephraim Child, was one of seven brothers who emigrated from Roxbury, Mass., to Woodstock, Windham county, Ct. I think they laid out the town and located themselves in different parts of the same." [From other data we think the town had been surveyed and bounded. —Ed.] "I have no dates that I can rely upon with regard to this early history. I will give to you from memory, what I have heard my father and my grandfather say. The town of Woodstock, where these stalwart men (we infer from other record, they were of large stature) and women, commenced their new homes, was seven miles long and five miles wide. It was no prairie country, the tall trees had to be leveled. These noble men and women were inured day by day to privations and hardships, and their children were trained to endurance, like the ancient Spartans. Notwithstanding their laborious duties, they did not neglect the education of their children. As soon as they got their own cabins tenantable, they built a cabin schoolhouse as near central as they could, and started a school for the winter months. The children who could make their way through the deep snows, boarded at home. Those who could not, boarded at the nearest uncle's. My grandfather used to tell me many reminiscences of those early days. My grandfather (Asa) and his brother Increase Child, were among those that boarded out (Ephraim Child, who married Mary Lyon, was their father.) The average number of boarders was from twelve to fifteen, and on stormy nights, the number increased to twenty or twenty-five. The "brindle" cow had not come in yet, and bean porridge and the brown loaf, were the supper and the breakfast, and potatoes roasted in the ashes for the dinner. A great round bowl that some of the most ingenious ones had dug out of a big log, that would hold a plump pailfull, was the common dish. As many boys and girls as could, gathered around this festive board, each with his wooden spoon, and when sufficed would give place to others. Thus were laid the foundations of a prosperous society."

[Eighth Generation.]　Children:
618. i. LINUS CHILD INGALLS, b. Aug. 16, 1833, d. Nov., 1833.
619. ii. EPHRAIM CHILD INGALLS, b. Oct, 25, 1835, m. Cordelia ———.

620. iii. HENRY FRANCIS INGALLS, b. Aug. 28, 1837, d. in Chisago, March 15, 1863, and is buried at the family home in Minnesota.

621. iv. RENSSELAER C. INGALLS, b. January 15, 1839.

622. v. EDMUND INGALLS, b. June 4, 1841. m. Sept. 29, 1872, Ruth A. Pennock.

[Eighth Generation.]

619. ii. EPHRAIM CHILD INGALLS, second son of Lavinia Lyon Child and Henry Ingalls, b. Oct. 25, 1835, m. Cordelia ———.

[Ninth Generation.] Child:

623. i. ANNA CHILD INGALLS, b. 1860.

[Eighth Generation.]

622. v. EDMUND INGALLS, fifth son of Lavinia Lyon Child and Henry Ingalls, b. June 4, 1841, m. Sept. 29, 1872, Ruth A. Pennock, who was b. Aug. 9, 1847. Mr. Ingalls is a prominent business man, residing in Duluth, St. Louis county, Minnesota,—a citizen highly esteemed for his activity and integrity.

[Ninth Generation.] Children:

624. i. RUTH LAVINIA INGALLS, b. Oct. 5, 1873.

625. ii. LILLIE ALMIRA INGALLS, b. July 2, 1875.

626. iii. FLORENCE ELIZABETH INGALLS, b. April 13, 1877.

627. iv. EDMUND INGALLS, JR., b. Aug. 5, 1878.

[Seventh Generation.]

598. vi. CLARISSA CHILD, sixth child and third dau. of Rensselaer and Priscilla Corbin Child, b. in Woodstock, Ct., Sept. 26, 1810, m. in 1842, Dr. Charles Chandler. She died March 13, 1874.   Dr. Chandler is a prominent man and physician in Chandlerville, Cass county, Illnois.

[Eighth Generation.] Children:

628. i. ALICE CHILD CHANDLER, b. in Chandlerville, Ill., Sept., 1842. d. May 1, 1852.

629. ii. JOHN THOMAS CHANDLER, b. in Chandlerville, April 26, 1845.

630. iii. LINUS CHILD CHANDLER, b. in Chandlerville, Aug. 9, 1846. m. Sarah L. Beane, Sept. 5, 1873.

[Eighth Generation.]

629. ii. JOHN THOMAS CHANDLER, second child and eldest son of Clarissa Child and Dr. Charles Chandler, b. in Chandlerville, Ill., April 26, 1845. m. 1st, Mary C. Ricard, Oct. 12, 1852, m. 2d, Emma Morse, July 1st, 1849, dau. of Almira and John H. Morse, and granddaughter of Elias Child, of West Woodstock, Connecticut.

[Ninth Generation.]   Children:
    631. i. CHARLES CHANDLER, b. June 27, 1870.
    632. ii. MYRTIS CHILD CHANDLER, b. May 27, 1873.

[Eighth Generation.]

    630. iii. LINUS CHILD CHANDLER, third and youngest child of Clarissa Child and Dr. Charles Chandler, b. Aug. 9, 1846, m. Sept. 5, 1873, Sarah L. Beane of Lisbon, N. H. He graduated at Harvard University Law School, Cambridge Mass., June 1871, is a lawyer in Chandlerville, Ill., has been District Attorney for Cass County, Ill., for four years.

[Ninth Generation.]   Children:
    633. i. CARL BEANE CHANDLER, b. Feb. 16, 1876.
    634. ii. WILLIAM CHARLES CHANDLER, b. Feb. 21, 1879.

[Seventh Generation.]

    601. ix. RENSSELAER CHILD, JR., youngest child, and fifth son of Rensselaer and Priscilla Corbin Child, b. in Woodstock, Ct., March 6, 1820, m. 1841, Maria Marcy of Southbridge, Mass. She was b. July 2, 1824. He died 1864, in the Union Army.

[Eighth Generation.]   Children:
    635. i. PELEG CHILD, b. in Chandlerville, Ill., July 10, 1842.
    636. ii. DWIGHT STACY CHILD, b. in Chandlerville, Ill. Jan. 2, 1845.
    637. iii. MARY LOIS CHILD, b. in Chandlerville, Ill., Aug. 29, 1847.
    638. iv. JOHNSON CORBIN CHILD, b. in Chandlerville, Ill., Dec. 1, 1849.

[Fourth Generation.]

    28. ii. DANIEL CHILD, second child and second son of Ephraim and Priscilla Harris Child, b. in Woodstock, Ct., Jan. 1, 1713, m. 1st, Ruth Ammidown, Jan. 1, 1747, m. 2d, Abigail Bridges. He died 1776.

[Fifth Generation.]   Children:
    639. i. DANIEL CHILD, JR., b. in Woodstock, Ct., Oct. 8, 1747, d. young.
    640. ii. ZEREIAH CHILD, bapt. in Woodstock, Ct., Dec. 12, 1748.
    641. iii. STEPHEN CHILD, b. in Woodstock, Ct., Nov. 27, 1749, m. Sept. 7, 1778, Mercy Chase.
    642. iv. ABEL CHILD, b. in Woodstock, Ct., Oct. 15, 1752, m. March 11, 1779, Rebecca Allard.
    643. v. ABIGAIL CHILD, b. in Woodstock. Ct.
    644. vi. DANIEL CHILD, 2d, b. in Woodstock. Ct.

[Fifth Generation.]

    641. iii. STEPHEN CHILD, third child and third son of Daniel and Ruth Ammidown Child, b. in Woodstock, Ct., Nov. 27, 1749, m. Sept. 7, 1778, Mercy Chase of Sutton, Mass., dau. of Daniel and Alice Corbit Chase. She d. Dec. 27, 1835, æt. 80 yrs. He d. May 24, 1831, æt. 82 yrs, in Cornish, N. H., to which

town he early emigrated from Woodstock, Ct. Mr. Child was one of the early proprietors of Bethel, Vt., but never became a resident of the town.

[Sixth Generation.]   Children:

645. i. DANIEL CHILD, b. in Cornish, N. H., Aug. 6, 1779, m. Nov. 11, 1804, Appama Lyman.

646. ii. RUTH HARRIS CHILD, b. in Cornish, N. H., Dec. 25, 1780, m. 1804, Samuel March Chase, who was b. Nov. 13, 1772, at Walpole, N. H., and d. March 11, 1866, at Jubilee, Colorado.

647. iii. ENOS CHILD, b. in Cornish, N. H., Jan. 10, 1783, m. Aug. 23, 1806, Sarah Bemis.

648. iv. URSULA CHILD, b. in Cornish, N. H., June 2, 1785, m. Nov. 2, 1806, Ebenezer Cummings.

649. v. ALICE CHILD, b. April 2, 1787, in Cornish, N. H., m. Dec. 24, 1812, Bela Chase.

650. vi. EUDOCIA CHILD, b. in Cornish, N. H., Jan. 27, 1789, m. June 8, 1806, Benjamin Freeman.

651. vii. ARAMINTA CHILD, b. in Cornish, N. H., Sept. 3, 1791, d. Oct. 6 1791.

652. viii. STEPHEN CHILD, b. in Cornish, N. H., Aug. 30, 1792, m. March 20, 1822, Eliza Atwood.

653. ix. MERCY CHILD, b. in Cornish, N. H., May 10, 1794, m. March 18, 1819, Abraham Chase Palmer, at Langdon, Vt.

654. x. JANE CHILD, b. in Cornish, N. H., Nov. 4, 1797, m. March 12, 1820, Jacob Johnson Safford.

655. xi. PRUDENTIA CHILD, b. in Cornish, N. H., March 7, 1800, d. Aug. 25, 1802.

[Sixth Generation.]

645. i. DANIEL CHILD, eldest child of Stephen and Mercy Chase Child, b. in Cornish, N. H., Aug. 6, 1779, m. Appama Lyman, Nov. 11, 1804. She was the dau. of Josiah and Eunice Tiffany Lyman, and niece of Rev. Elijah Lyman, a well known clergyman of the Congregational church of that period. She was b. Sept. 15, 1783, at Lebanon, N. H., d. in Bethel, Vt., Sept. 21, 1854. He d. Jan. 7, 1853. They had nine children.

Daniel, with his brother Enos, early settled in the town of Bethel, Vt. When a young man he went to Brookfield, Vt., and started a mercantile business. After marrying, he settled in Rochester Hollow, Vt., as a farmer. Here he made a beginning in the wilderness. In the autumn of 1818 he moved to Bethel, Vt., where he lived until his death, in 1853. His place was the home of the Child family during his life. Mr. Child died very suddenly, dropping dead upon the street in Bethel village. He built the house on the home farm in 1827. Illustrative of the times, the contract for building the house was let to two parties for a specified sum, including what *rum* they could drink! Two of the boys were deputed to bring the rum from the village, which they did in an old-fashioned gallon measure, carried on a stick between them, making a trip almost daily! During his life in Bethel, Mr. Child was a man of some prominence in local public affairs. He was the clerk of the district in which he lived; clerk of the Episcopal church of which he was a member, and was very careful and methodical in making and preserving all the records with which he had anything to do. His care in these respects is specially noticeable, and it is owing to it that the town and church are now in possession of some valuable records of an early date. He was town clerk for some years. He was well known as a surveyor of lands in all these parts, and he knew better than any one else all the old land marks, in fact, his word came to be authority in all such matters; and the records of surveys, "notes" and "field books" which he left are even now appealed to, to settle the location of disputed corners and lines. He was careful to preserve all his papers, and when he died, left a large quantity which he had accumulated. The *Woodstock* (Vt.) *Mercury*, used to be the local paper. Mr. Child was accustomed to visit the post office on each Friday, take the papers belonging to the subscribers in the north part of the town, carry them up to the church on Sunday morning, and before service scatter them through the pews for their respective owners. And so constant and regular was he in the performance of this duty, that it came to be associated in the mind of the postmaster as an inseparable part of Friday, and in the minds of the subscribers who received their papers in this way, an inseparable part of Sunday. It nearly answered the purpose of a calendar. [1]

[Seventh Generation.] Children:

656. i. EMILY MARY FRANCES CHILD, b. at Rochester, Vt. Aug. 23, 1806, m. March 1, 1829, Richard W. Roche.

657. ii. LAURA CHILD, b. in Rochester, Vt., Nov. 11, 1808, m. Dec. 28, 1826, Jay Wilson.

658. iii. DOCT. ABEL LYMAN CHILD, b. in Rochester, Vt., Aug. 9, 1810, m. 1st, Oct. 3, 1833, Margaret Tozier: m. 2d, Dec. 25, 1847, Rebecca Coates: m. 3d, April 25, 1849, Eliza Hampton: m. 4th, Aug. 16, 1856, Cora Woodward.

[1] The above is from a printed record furnished by Dr. Abel L. Child, a son.

659. iv. Philander C. Child, b. in Rochester, Vt., July 13, 1812, d. March 12, 1816.

660. v. Eliza A. Child, b. in Rochester, Vt., July 16, 1814, m. Seth Sterling.

661. vi. Elijah Lyman Child, b. in Rochester, Vt., July 31, 1816, m. June 26, 1838, Eliza B. Blanchard.

662. vii. Lucy C. Child, b. in Rochester, Vt., June 23, 1818, m. Jan. 23, 1841, Levi Devoll, at Albany, N. Y. He was accidentally shot. They left no children.

663. viii. Rev. Stephen R. Child, b. in Bethel, Vt., Dec. 31, 1819, m. Nov. 23, 1849, Mary S. Belcher, at Brimfield, Ill. He was an Episcopal clergyman. He d. at Decatur, Ill., 1854. They had three children, names are not given.

664. ix. Unity R. Child, b. at Bethel, Vt., March 1, 1822, m. Oct. 30, 1844, Charles W. Lillie.

[Seventh Generation.]

656. i. Emily Mary Frances Child, eldest child of Daniel and Appama Lyman Child, b. in Rochester, Vt., Aug. 23, 1806, m. March 1, 1829, Richard W. Roche of Boston, Mass. He d. at Chicopee, Mass., Oct. 16, 1839. She d. of a disease supposed to be yellow fever, communicated from bales of cotton when opened in the mills in that place. Mr. and Mrs. Roche were Romanists in their religious belief.

[Eighth Generation.]   Children:

665. i. Joanna Roche, b. in Charlestown, Mass., 1830, now Lady Abbess in a convent in Montreal, Canada.

666. ii. Constantine Roche, b. at Cabotsville, Mass., now in California.

667. iii. Franklin Roche, b. at Cabotsville, Mass., now in Missouri.

[Seventh Generation.]

657. ii. Laura Child, second child and second dau. of Daniel and Appama Lyman Child, b. in Rochester, Vt., Nov. 11, 1808, m. Dec. 28, 1826, Jay Wilson. Reside in Bethel, Vt.

[Eighth Generation.]   Children:

668. i. James J. Wilson, b. 1831, m. Jane Flynn of Bethel, Vt., has seven children, but no names given. Mrs. Jane Flynn Wilson died, and Mr. Wilson married Mary L. McCoy of Louisiana. Mr. Wilson is an attorney by profession, conversant with the affairs of state, was elected from Windsor Co., Vt., to the state senate. He resides in Bethel, Vt.

669. ii. March Chase Wilson, b. May 4, 1834, d. in 1852.

670. iii. Oliver S. Wilson, b. Sept. 13, 1838.

671. iv. Laura C. Wilson, b. Oct. 30, 1840, d. June 16, 1862.

672. v. Dudley F. Wilson, b. March 25, 1844, d. Feb. 3, 1854.

673. vi. Harriet E. Wilson, b. Aug. 13, 1849.

658. iii. Dr. ABEL L. CHILD, third child and eldest son of Daniel and Appama Lyman Child, b. in Rochester, Vt., Aug. 9, 1810, m. 1st, Oct. 3, 1833, Margaret Tosier, at Manchester, Ind., m. 2d, Dec. 25, 1847, Rebecca Coates, at Cincinnati, O., m. 3d, April 25, 1849, Eliza Hampton, at Munroe, O., m. 4th, Aug. 16, 1856, Cora Woodward, at Walnut Hills, O.

Dr. Child left Vermont in the summer of 1833, and commenced the study of medicine at Manchester, Ind.; thence he went to Cincinnati and attended lectures in the old Ohio Medical College, and afterwards practiced for several years in Indiana. In 1839 he left his profession and took charge of the Portsmouth, O., public schools, as superintendent. In 1848, he removed to Cincinnati and took charge of the Cincinnati High School (colored). In 1850 he became principal of the Walnut Hills High School. In the spring of 1857 he removed to Nebraska, bought land, and became a farmer, at the same time commenced metallurgic observations and reporting to the Smithsonian Institute. These observations are still continued, and reports made to the U. S. Signal Office. In 1867 he was elected a member of a constitutional convention of the state, and in 1869, elected probate judge of Cass county, which office he still holds (1880).

The experiences of Dr. Child have been in many respects most remarkable. His life has been one of great activity. Following the bent of an inquisitive mind, he has seen and known much of men and things. The natural force of character and versatility of talent which have marked his career have been important elements in reaching results. As a pioneer, future generations will read his history with interest and profit. His reminiscences of the town of Plattsmouth and county of Cass, in Nebraska, contained in a little pamphlet entitled "Centennial History of Plattsmouth City," &c., are instructive and amusing, exhibiting much of wit and humor in the author; and as a book of reference, will always be valuable. His indomitable courage and power of endurance are striking features in his history, and such as are always prime elements in pioneer life. Of boldness and daring in adventure, we have a thrilling illustration in a narrative from his pen, which we here insert:

A REMINISCENCE OF NIAGARA FALLS, OR, THE OLD INDIAN LADDER.

During a residence of several months at Niagara Falls, in the summer of 1832, much of my time was spent in wandering about, above, below and under the Falls, searching out the various grand views, recesses and curiosities of the vicinity. One morning in June I had descended the old spiral stairway to the foot of the American Fall, and after a time spent among the rocks and spray, was about to return, when a legend occurred to me of an old Indian ladder, said by some to exist, or to have existed in former times, by which ascent had been made from the river to the top of the cliffs above (some 200 feet), and to be located from one-half mile to one mile below the Falls. The existence of such a ladder had been disputed in my hearing several times by the oldest residents, and often sought for from the cliffs above by others as well as by myself, but nothing had been discovered indicating its existence.

The search from below on the river bank had not been attempted, as it was held to be impossible for a human being to pass down the river between the cliffs and water, as in places the rocks projected to the very margin of the rapid tumultuous torrent, and the portions where the solid walls receded were filled either with broken, jagged rocks or densely matted with thorny bushes and brush, living and dead, forming a barrier hardly penetrable to any animal larger than a squirrel or rabbit.

With but very little thought or consideration, I resolved at once to attempt the impassable (?) and search from below. I soon learned from sore experience that the difficulties of the path had not been magnified. It was indeed a fearfully hard road to travel. But I persevered till the *certainty* of the fearful track to be retraced, in case of retreat, overshadowed the possibilities of the advance. I therefore continued to press forward. At length, after, to me, a very long half mile's travel, I was rewarded with a sight of something like a ladder. It looked ancient and much decayed, many of the rounds broken out and gone. It was some 25 feet long, and stood with its top resting against a shelf or table projected from the face of the perpendicular wall, extending some fifty or sixty feet above it.

The ladder seemed weak and dangerous, and the rough and ragged rocks about its foot argued no pleasant bed in case of even a slight fall. But it was the *ladder* or *retreat;* and, with some hesitation, I took to the ladder. With bated breath—touching each round *so carefully*—changing from one side to the other, as the one seemed more decayed, or cracked under my weight, I slowly worked my way up. It was with extreme difficulty that I passed over the missing rounds, and off from two which broke under my feet without shocks and jars which might send the ladder and myself in a crash to the rocks below. But over all I reached the top and could then see that the shelf against which the ladder rested was from twelve to fifteen inches in width. To the right it decreased in width till, at some twenty feet distance, it disappeared. On the left it ran with unequal widths from ten to twelve inches, about the same distance, and was then lost behind a sharp angle of the rock. Escape to the right there was none; to the left— could I possibly succeed in reaching the angle? was there a path beyond? If not, why was this ladder ever placed here? The presumption was in favor of a passage, and I would try it. But to leave the ladder for an upright position on the shelf, as also to traverse this narrow ledge, with the perpendicular rock above crowding you off, when once on it, was a work of peril. A slight touch of the rock above might upset my balance, when nothing could save me from the ragged rocks twenty-five feet below. That every movement was calculated, timed and measured previous to actual motion, I need not say.

At length my feet rested on the shelf. And, then, as I gradually raised myself, a part of the shelf under my foot crumbled and fell. I also fell, with my face to the shelf. But in my struggle to save myself I pressed my foot so hard against the ladder that it was displaced, and with a terrific crash it lay in fragments on the rocks below, leaving me with all *retreat utterly cut off*. Completely exhausted and unnerved, I lay like one dead for several minutes, when the question of a passage around the angle of the rock occurred to my mind, and instantly rebraced every nerve and muscle. Cautiously I raised myself on to my hands and knees and crept along a few feet, till the shelf became so narrow that there was not room for both knees. Slowly and carefully I rose to my feet, grasping with thumb and finger ends upon the small projections, crevices, &c., of the rocks above me, and advancing one foot a few inches and then bringing the other up behind, as there was no room to pass one by the other.

Thus at last I reached the dreaded angle. But there, the light blazed out upon me. Around the angle, and a couple of steps, and I was lying at rest on a beautiful but slightly inclined greensward. Luxurious as my couch was, it was not devoid of thorns, as I could not forget that I had yet some one hundred and seventy-five feet more to climb, and some barrier must be interposed, somewhere, else this place would have been discovered from above. I noticed while lying here, for the first time, that my finger ends were badly cut, by the intensity of my grip on the rocks over my narrow path.

My anxiety increasing as to what I had still to encounter above, I arose and commenced my upward way. Evidently I was on a large slide of former days, arrested in its movement. On a very crooked track I found no difficulty in ascending to about twenty feet from the top of the cliffs, but here I met the apprehended barrier, in a solid perpendicular wall of about twenty feet. I followed this wall to the right till the slide joined it in a sheer descent of one hundred feet. No escape there. Then to the left with a like result, only fifty feet worse. The Old Bastile of France was not a safer prison. The remains of another old ladder, utterly decayed, showed how formerly travelers had ascended. But hold, a ray of light produces a throb of hope. In the angle produced by the wall and slide on the left, grows a small white birch tree, with the roots inserted partly in the crevices of the wall, and partly in the earth of the slide. It rose some thirty feet, leaning from both the wall and the slide at an angle of some ten degrees, and over the fearful abyss below of one hundred and fifty feet. Its diameter at the foot was some four or five inches. Again, an old log of about one foot in diameter (but how long I could not see), projected from the slightly sloping bank above, the lower end nearly reaching the white birch tree, some eighteen feet from the root. Here was a bridge that a squirrel might pass over in safety, but *could I?*

My weight upon the tree must bear it down, and away from the end of the log, and probably out of reach of it, and suspend me over the terrible

L

abyss below. No, no! I could never travel over *that road*. But, what then? What other resource? There was really no other way of escape from my prison, and to remain there, was only a long lingering death from starvation. I well knew that the road from the Falls, down the river to the whirlpool, passed a full half mile distant. It was a lonely, out of the way place, and hardly a chance of a human being coming within reach of the sound of my voice at any time.

A full examination of all my resources, showed clearly that the only choice there was in the matter, was death by starvation, long and cruel, or a sudden, yet fearful one, on the rocks below. If I chose the latter, there was a barely *possible* chance of escape. The love of life was then strong with me, and the almost infinitely small chance for it, sent me to the foot of the tree. The small limbs were frequent, and up I climbed. My anticipations were realized. By the time I was up twelve feet on the tree, it had bent over so as to be entirely out of reach of the log above, and one glance into the fearful depths below induced such giddiness, sickness, and intense fear, that it was with the utmost difficulty that I held to the tree, as I hastened to the ground. I dropped to the earth in a dull, stupified despair. All hope was dead.   .   .   .   .   .   .

I have no recollection of any process of thought or reason. I knew nothing—but a sensation of *utter hopelessness*. How long I lay in this state, I know not, time was forgotten. But at length I found myself upon my feet, and making for the tree again; why, or for what, I knew not. Simply as a machine I went to the tree, and recommenced its ascent. Devoid of all fear or nervousness, I reached the height of the log on the bank, now some three feet from my extended hand and arm. Next I found myself swaying the tree back and forth, to bring it within reach of the log—over and over, down and *down* I went toward that awful abyss, again and again before the reaction brought me within reach of the log. As I reached it, I threw my arm over it, and thus for an instant I hung. The recoil of the tree, assisted by my weight, was pulling upon my arm with a force it could not endure. At that instant a full consciousness of my position and its fearful peril broke upon me, and as full a sense that *then* and *there* was no time or place for thought or consideration. I let the tree loose, and with a desperate effort, threw my other arm over the log, and then, after two fruitless efforts, locked my feet around the log above my hands.

And then I felt that the *log was slowly sliding down over the bank*. Yes —it was surely going—I could feel it and see it move—it was all but over— that would be—annihilation—. All fear, fatigue, and nervous weakness left me, I was at perfect ease. Time again utterly failed me. How long I was thus suspended I have no knowledge. But at last, I became conscious that the log had stopped. I could see where it had rubbed and ground along on the edge of the rock about a foot, and then caught on a knot. Then I tried to move myself up toward the bank, but found, suspended as I was, and with the inclination of the log (some ten degrees), I could not. I *must* get on top of the log—and I did so—but *how* I have no recollection. From thence I reached the bank and fell upon the grass. There memory ceased, and all was blank.   .   .   .   .   As consciousness slowly returned, I began to realize that if I had a body, it was utterly dead. I was surrounded by the blackest of darkness, and could neither move or stir any member of my body, if I had one. By degrees I recalled the perilous scenes through which I had passed, and a somewhat indefinite conclusion followed that by some means I had fallen from the cliff, and that the body was dead.

But the old habit of controlling the body through the mind was still strong, and in my continued efforts in that direction, one of my hands fell from my body to the ground, producing a cold and wet sensation. This produced a shock and upset my conclusion as to my death, and I worked away more vigorously to get control over the body. In a few minutes, I so far succeeded as to find myself lying on the wet grass. With still further effort I found a log near by, lying much as I recollected the one did on which I reached the bank, and knowing that the higher end lay *from* the precipice, and in the direction of the road, I followed it on my hands and knees to the end, and then succeeded in getting on to my feet and started in the direction of the road.

After several mishaps, from contact with brush, stumps, trees, &c., and several falls, with the returning circulation, my sight also began to return. I began to see stars, but of course no sun. The day had passed and it was some time in the night. At last I found the road, and reached my boarding house at the Falls, at 2 o'clock A. M.

[Eighth Generation.]　Children.

[By Margaret Tozier.]

674. i. LUCY MARION CHILD, b. at Manchester, Indiana, Aug. 12, 1834, m. July 4, 1853, Washington Walts.

675. ii. ROLLIN ALMANZOR CHILD, b. at Manchester, Ind., Aug. 6, 1836, d. same day.

676. iii. PHILANDER RONALD CHILD, b. at Campbell, Ind., Nov. 10, 1837, m. Jan., 1860, Lizzie Zeodorski.

677. iv. LAURA ALMIRA CHILD, b. at Portsmouth, O., July 11, 1840, m. Mar. 14, 1856, William Simmons.

678. v. EVERARD SEYMOUR CHILD, b. at Portsmouth, O., Jan. 7, 1842, m. Aug. 6, 1865, Hannah E. Thorndike.

679. vi. ELLA OLIVIA CHILD, b. at Portsmouth, O., Dec. 14, 1843, d. June 19, 1845.

[By Rebecca Coates Child.]

680. vii. HARRY PRESTON CHILD, b. at Clermont Phalanx, O., Oct. 2, 1848; for some ten years past yard master of Kansas City, Mo., stock yards.

[By Eliza Hampton Child.]

681. viii. JULIA E. CHILD, b. Nov. 10, 1850, at Walnut Hills, O., m. June 29, 1879, James W. Thomas, at Plattsmouth, Neb.

[Eighth Generation.]

674. i. LUCY MARION CHILD, eldest child of Dr. Abel Lyman and Margaret Tozier Child, b. in Manchester, Ind., Aug. 12, 1834, m. at Harmonia, Ind., July 4, 1853, Washington Walts. She d. in Oregon, Feb. 12, 1855. Mr. Walts resides in Oregon with his two sons.

[Ninth Generation.]   Children:
   682. i. ALONZO L. WALTS, b. at New Albany, Ind., 1854, d. 1857.
   683. ii. HENRY WALTS, b. at Sugar Grove, Ind., Aug. 10, 1856.
   684. iii. MARCUS WALTS, b. at Glendale, Neb., Jan. 1860.

[Eighth Generation.]

   676. iii. PHILANDER RONALD CHILD, third child and second son of Dr. Abel L. and Margaret Tozier Child, b. at Campbell, Ind., Nov. 10, 1837, m. Jan., 1860, at St. Louis, Mo., Lizzie Zeodorski. He was engaged in a railroad tunnel in California, in April, 1875, since which time he has not been heard from; it is presumed he is dead. He served in the late civil war in the Union army.
[Ninth Generation.]   Children:
   685. i. MICHAEL CHILD, b. at St Louis, Mo., 1861.
   686. ii. BENON CHILD, b. at St. Louis, Mo., 1863.
   687. iii. WILLIE CHILD, b. at Glendale, Neb., 1866.

   These three children are living in Saunders Co., Nebraska.

[Eighth Generation.]

   677. iv. LAURA ALMIRA CHILD, fourth child and second dau. of Dr. Abel L. and Margaret Tozier Child, b. in Portsmouth, O., July 11, 1840, m. March 14, 1856, William Simmons, at Lafayette, Ind. They reside at Lafayette, Ind.
[Ninth Generation.]   Children:
   688. i. GEORGE SIMMONS, b. at Lafayette, Ind., April 22, 1858, d. same day.
   689. ii. HENRY L. SIMMONS, b. at Lafayette, Ind, Feb. 1, 1860, d. Aug. 10, 1864, at St. Louis, Mo.
   690 iii. LUCY E SIMMONS, b. at Lafayette, Ind., May 13, 1863, d. Feb. 13, 1865.
   691. iv. WILLIAM E. SIMMONS, b. at Lafayette, Ind, March 24, 1865.
   692. v. MINNIE ISABEL SIMMONS, b. at Lafayette, Ind., Jan. 24 1869.
   693. vi. MARGARET JANETTE SIMMONS, b. in Glendale, Neb., July 20, 1872
   694. vii. CHARLES LESTER SIMMONS, b. in Glendale, Jan. 22, 1875.
   695. viii. EARL CHASE SIMMONS, b. at Lafayette, Ind., Sept. 18, 1877.

[Eighth Generation.]

   678. v. EVERARD SEYMOUR CHILD, fifth child and third son of Dr. Abel L. and Margaret Tozier Child, b. in Portsmouth, O., Jan. 7, 1842, m. Aug. 6, 1865, Hannah E. Thorndike. Reside at Afton, Neb. Mr. Child served through the civil war: is postmaster and county surveyor.
[Ninth Generation.]   Children:
   696 i. LORENA P. CHILD, b. June 2, 1866, at Glendale, Neb.
   697. ii. EARL L. CHILD, b. Feb. 15, 1869, at Glendale, Neb.

[Seventh Generation.]

660. v. ELIZA AUGUSTIN CHILD, fifth child and third dau. of Daniel and Appama Lyman Child, b. in Rochester, Vt., July 6, 1814, m. about 1843, Seth Sterling.

[Eighth Generation.] Children:

698. i. MAURICE STERLING, b. in Warren, Vt., 1844, m. Elmina Freeman of Warren.

699. ii EMILY STERLING, b. in Warren, Vt, 1847, m. Godfrey Sumner of Braintree, Vt. Lives in Warren.

700. iii. GEORGE STERLING, b in Warren, Vt., 1849, m. Mary Bucklin. Lives in Warren, Vt.

701 iv. LAURA STERLING, b. in Warren, Vt, 1854, m. Wm. Prosser of Hancock, Vt.

702. v. IDA STERLING, b. 1859.

[Seventh Generation.]

661. vi. ELIJAH LYMAN CHILD, sixth child and third son of Daniel and Appama Lyman Child, b. in Rochester, Vt., July 31, 1816, m. June 20, 1838, Elizabeth Blanchard, at Woodstock, Vt. He lives in Bethel, Vt., a merchant there for thirty years.

[Eighth Generation.] Children:

703. i. ELIZABETH JANETTE CHILD, b. July 1, 1840, lives in Bethel, Vt.

704. ii. DANIEL LYMAN CHILD, b. June 25, 1852, lives in Bethel, Vt.

[Seventh Generation.]

664. ix. UNITY R. CHILD, ninth child and fifth daughter of Daniel and Appama Lyman Child, b. in Bethel, Vt., March 1, 1822, m. Oct. 30, 1844, Charles W. Lillie, at Bethel, Vt.

[Eighth Generation.] Children:

705. i JULIETTE A. LILLIE, b. in Bethel, Vt, Dec. 3, 1845, m. Sept. 17, 1863, E. C. Belt. Reside at Corning, Iowa.

706. ii. CHARLES W. LILLIE, JR., b. in Bethel, Vt., April 7, 1849, d. May 5 1863.

707. iii. ELBERT RAY LILLIE, b. in Bethel, Vt., April 11, 1851, d. in California, Aug. 18, 1875.

708. iv. SAMUEL LILLIE, b. in Bethel, Vt., Dec. 3, 1853, d. same day.

709. v. DANIEL LILLIE, b. in Sugar Grove, Ills., Nov. 17, 1854, d. Oct. 6, 1860.

710. vi. LIZZIE A. LILLIE, b. in Hazleton, Iowa, Dec., 1857.

711. vii EDWIN LILLIE, b. in Hazleton, Iowa, Mar. 1, 1862

712. viii. FRANCIS G. LILLIE, b. in Independence, Iowa, Feb. 14, 1865.

[Sixth Generation.]

647. iii. ENOS CHILD, third child and second son of Stephen and Mercy Chase Child, b. in Cornish, N. H., Jan. 10, 1783, m. Aug. 23, 1806, Sarah Bemis, who was b. in Spencer, Mass., Sept. 3, 1783. He removed from Cornish to Bethel, Vt., 1812 or 1813, where he d. Jan. 30, 1839.

[Seventh Generation] Children:

713. i. ABIGAIL MARY CHILD, b. in Bethel, Vt., May, 24, 1807, m. Jan. 18, 1829, Benjamin Rice of Royalton, Vt. They lived in Royalton. He d. May 12, 1867: she d. April 25, 1868.

714. ii. W. CHASE CHILD, b. in Bethel, Vt., June 24, 1808, d. March 13, 1813.

715. iii. ALICE CORBIT CHILD. b. in Bethel, Vt., Feb. 26, 1810, m. 1839, Hiram Twichell.

716. iv. MERCY CHILD, b. in Bethel, Vt., Oct. 12, 1811, m. May 4, 1833, Justin Lilly.

717. v. ASAPH BEMIS CHILD, b. in Bethel, Vt., Aug. 22, 1813, m. Jan. 7, 1840, Eusebia Sabine.

718. vi. SARAH CHILD b. in Bethel, Vt., Aug. 17, 1815, m. Sept. 14, 1854. John Nasely, in Randolph, Vt. She d. Sept. 18, 1856.

719. vii RUTH CHILD, b. in Bethel, Vt., Nov. 22, 1817, m. Sept. 12, 1837, Wm. Bass.

720. viii. RACHEL DAWSON CHILD, b. in Bethel, Vt., Nov. 4, 1819, d. 1822.

721. ix ENOS DENNISON CHILD, b. in Bethel, Vt., May 7, 1822, m. June 7, 1846, Ellen Williams, b. April 14, 1829. Settled in Ironton, O., in 1844, and died there. No children.

722. x RACHEL CHILD, 2D, b. in Bethel, Vt., June 25, 1824, m. May 7, 1844, Dr. David G. Williams.

[Seventh Generation.]

715. iii. ALICE CORBIT CHILD, third child and second dau. of Enos and Sarah Bemis Child, b. in Bethel, Vt., Feb. 26, 1810, m. 1839, Hiram Twichell of Bethel, b. March 3, 1813. Four children.

[Eighth Generation.] Children:

723. i. ALICE CHILD TWICHELL, b. in Bethel, Vt., March 27, 1840.
724. ii. MARY JANETTE TWICHELL, b. in Bethel, Vt., July 18, 1842.
725. iii. SARAH TWICHELL, b. in Bethel, Vt., Oct. 23, 1843.
726. iv. FRANK TWICHELL, b. in Bethel, Vt., Sept. 7, 1848.

[Seventh Generation.]

716. iv. MERCY CHILD, fourth child and third dau. of Enos and Sarah Bemis Child, b. Oct. 12, 1811, in Bethel, Vt., m. May 4, 1833, Justin Lilly, b. Oct. 5, 1807. She d. Feb. 27, 1838. Lived in Barnard, Vt.

[Eighth Generation.] Children:

727. i. DUDLEY CHILD LILLY, b. Oct. 19, 1834.
728. ii. ALICE CHILD LILLY, b. June 7, 1836.
729. iii. DANIEL LILLY, b. Jan. 31, 1838.

[Seventh Generation.]

717. v. ASAPH BEMIS CHILD, fifth child and second son of Enos and Sarah Bemis Child, b. in Bethel, Vt., Aug. 22, 1813, m. Jan. 7, 1840, Eusebia Sabine, who was born Feb. 20, 1813,

d. Sept 15, 1873. Mr. Child d. March, 1879, in the 66th year of his age.

Soon after the birth of Asaph Bemis Child, his parents moved into Bethel, Vt., then comparatively new and wild, where he led a truly pioneer life. Asaph Bemis grew to be a stalwart boy by the exercise of his muscular powers in helping to bring into culture the new home. He came to be a power, ere he had reached the age of twenty-one, in clearing the farm and sustaining the household. At an early day the elements of a strong mind, and a robust constitution, began to be developed. While his hands were industriously and efficiently employed in the field, his leisure hours were spent in reading and study, till his knowledge of the primary branches of education was sufficient to qualify him to teach a common school. For several winters, while in his minority, he taught school, and returned to work on his father's farm in the summer. After reaching his majority, he spent two winters at the Academy in Randolph, Vt., boarding with his uncle, Judge Chase, Chief Justice of the State of Vermont; working for his board. So faithful and efficient was he, that his uncle declared he accomplished more than any other laborer on the farm, and that he was so studious he kept his standing in his class. Such was the force of character, and the unflagging mental application exhibited at this period, foreshadowing what the future would be in attainments and efficiency.

Having passed his twenty-second year, and acquired such knowledge as his limited means would allow, he commenced the study of medicine, and attended a course of medical lectures at Dartmouth College, N. H. Afterwards he attended a medical course in Boston, Mass., when he returned to Bethel, Vt., and read and practiced with Dr. Alfred Page of that town, and gained much favor among the people for skill and urbanity. To complete his medical studies he went to Burlington, Vt., and graduated, receiving his medical diploma from that institution. His thoroughness as a student cannot be questioned. But he was not satisfied with the medical practice. He went to Boston and connected himself with the office of Messrs. Ellis & Dana, leading dentists in that city. For two years he industriously applied himself, and became a skillful dentist. He then opened an office of his own, and proved himself to be one of the most popular dentists of the city. Naturally of a speculative turn of mind, he began at this period to write and publish articles on questions of public interest. His first dissertation was a treatise on the "Care and Preservation of the Teeth." These literary efforts led to the publication of a monthly magazine called *The Athenæum*. He was much interested in the subject of education, and for some time was an active member of the Public School committee of Boston. He finally became much interested in the new philosophies and spiritualistic manifestations, so called. In support of these he was very earnest, and is thought to have made many converts.

The development of his philosophies is before the public, and the fruits will be judged of variously, as the opinions of men approximate to or diverge from his own.

[Eighth Generation.] Children:

730. i. JOHN THEODORE CHILD, b. June 13, 1841, m. June 4, 1863, Sarah Gerry.

731. ii. HENRY CHILD, b. Jan. 16, 1847, in Boston, Mass.

732. iii. CHARLES EDWARD CHILD, b. July 31, 1853, in Boston, Mass.

[Eighth Generation.]

730. i. JOHN THEODORE CHILD, eldest child of Asaph Bemis and Eusebia Sabine Child, b. June 13, 1841, m. June 4, 1863, Sarah Gerry.

[Ninth Generation.] Children:

733. i. SARAH GERTRUDE CHILD, b. 1864.

734. ii. MADALINE ELIZABETH CHILD, b. 1867.

735. iii. RUTH LAVINIA CHILD, b. Dec. 7, 1868.

736. iv. BERNICE THEODORE CHILD, b. Feb. 1, 1872.

[Seventh Generation.]

719. vii. RUTH CHILD, seventh child and fifth dau. of Enos and Sarah Bemis Child, b. in Bethel, Vt., Nov. 22, 1817, m. Sept. 12, 1837, Wm. Bass of Braintree, Vt., b. March 14, 1810. She died at Jefferson City, Mo., 1861.

[Eighth Generation.] Children:

737. i. WM. EDWARD BASS, b. Aug. 16, 1838, in Braintree, Vt.

738. ii. ENOS CHILD BASS, b. in Braintree, Vt., July 26, 1840.

739. iii. DUDLEY CHASE BASS, b. in Braintree, Vt., Aug. 10, 1842.

740. iv. SARAH AGNES BASS, b. in Braintree, Vt., Dec. 2, 1844.

741. v. CHARLES HENRY BASS, b. in Braintree, Vt., July 23, 1848.

[Seventh Generation.]

722. x. RACHEL CHILD, 2D, tenth child and seventh dau. of Enos and Sarah Bemis Child, b. in Bethel, Vt., June 25, 1824,

m. May 7, 1844. Dr. Gardner Williams. She d. May 17, 1868, in Boston, Mass.

[Eighth Generation.] Children:

742. i. EUSEBIA SABINE WILLIAMS, b. March 3, 1845.

743. ii. GRACE WILLIAMS, b. Feb. 6, 1849.

744. iii. CLARIE WILLIAMS, b. Sept. 26, 1851.

745. iv. ULEYETTE WILLIAMS, b. Jan. 27, 1855.

746. v. ALICE CHILD WILLIAMS, b. May 24, 1858.

[Sixth Generation]

648. iv. URSULA CHILD, fourth child and second dau. of Stephen and Mercy Chase, b. in Cornish, N. H., June 2, 1785. m. Nov. 2, 1806, Ebenezer Cummings, at Cornish, N. H. He was b. June 24, 1779. She d. Jan. 29, 1834, in Cornish.

[Seventh Generation.] Child:

747. i. DUDLEY CUMMINGS, resides at Palmyra, Mo.

Sixth Generation.]

650. vi. EUDOCIA CHILD, sixth child and fourth dau. of Stephen and Mercy Chase Child, b. in Cornish, N. H., Jan. 27, 1789. m. June 8, 1806, Benjamin Freeman, who was born Aug. 6, 1781, at Plainfield, N. H.

[Seventh Generation.] Children:

748. i. PHILANDER CHASE FREEMAN, b. in Plainfield, N. H., Aug., 1807, m. May, 1838, Sarah Norton.

749. ii. JAMES FREEMAN, b. in Plainfield, N. H., Aug., 1812, d. May, 1877.

750. iii. MERCY FREEMAN, b. in Plainfield, N. H., Oct., 1814, m. 1837, March Chase.

751. iv. LUCIA FREEMAN, b. in Plainfield, N. H., Nov., 1817, m. 1843, Benj. C. Daniels.

752. v. CLARA FREEMAN, b. in Plainfield, N. H., Dec., 1820. Lives in Plainfield, N. H.

753. vi. JOHN FREEMAN, b. in Plainfield, N. H., April, 1825.

[Seventh Generation.]

748. i. PHILANDER CHASE FREEMAN, eldest child of Eudocia Child and Benjamin Freeman, b. in Plainfield, N. H., Aug., 1807, m. May, 1838, Sarah Norton of Plainfield, N. H.

[Eighth Generation.] Children:

754. i. FREDERICK FREEMAN, b. in Claremont, N. H., March, 1839, d. in Newburgh, N. Y., 1867.

755. ii. FRANK GRANNIS FREEMAN, b. in Claremont, N. H., April, 1844, d. Nov. 1844.

[Seventh Generation.]

750. iii. MERCY FREEMAN, third child and eldest dau. of Eudocia Child and Benjamin Freeman, b. in Plainfield, N. H., Oct., 1814, m. Jan., 1837, March Chase of Langdon, N. H.

[Eighth Generation.]   Child:

756. i. JOHN CHASE, b. in Langdon, N. H., Oct., 1840, m. April, 1864, Eleanor G. Spaulding in Lebanon, N. H.   They had one child.

[Ninth Generation.]   Child:

757. i. LUCY CHASE, b. in Langdon, N. H., March, 1867.

[Seventh Generation.]

751. iv. LUCIA FREEMAN, fourth child and second dau. of Eudocia Child and Benjamin Freeman, b. Nov., 1817, m. June, 1843, Benjamin C. Daniels.   She died June, 1847.

[Eighth Generation]   Children:

758. i. NELLIS K. DANIELS, b. March, 1844, m. Oct., 1874, Emma J. Hall.

759. ii. JAMES MORRIS DANIELS, b. Aug., 1846, d. Jan., 1862.

[Eighth Generation.]

758. i. NELLIS K. DANIELS, eldest child of Lucia Freeman and Benjamin C. Daniels, and grandson of Eudocia Child Freeman, b. March, 1844, m. Oct., 1874, Emma J. Hall in Lebanon, N. H.

[Ninth Generation.]   Child:

760. i. BLANCHE L. DANIELS, b. Aug, 1879.

[Sixth Generation.]

652. viii. STEPHEN CHILD, JR., eighth child and third son of Stephen and Mercy Chase Child, b. in Cornish, N. H., Aug., 20, 1792, m. March 20, 1822, Eliza Atwood, at Cornish Flats, N. H.   She was born April 21, 1801, at Pelham, N. H.   Mr. Child lived and died in Cornish.

[Seventh Generation.]   Children:

761. i. ELIZA JANE CHILD, b. in Cornish, N. H., June 23, 1823, m. May 4, 1868, Freeman Woodward of Greenfield, Mass.

762. ii. PHILANDER CHASE CHILD, b. in Cornish, N. H., Sept. 30, 1824, m. Sept. 20, 1846, Sarah Hodge of Cornish.

763. iii. GEORGE FRANKLIN CHILD, b. in Cornish, N. H , July 18, 1827, d. Aug. 22, 1834.

764. iv. WILLIAM HENRY CHILD, b. in Cornish, N. H., Dec. 22, 1832, m. Jan. 1, 1857, Ellen Frances Leighton.

765. v. MARION ELLA CHILD, b. in Cornish, N. H., Oct. 6, 1834, m. July 10, 1867, Gen. Joseph Hartlinger of Hungary, Europe, now of Dover, N. H.

[Seventh Generation.]

764. iv. WILLIAM HENRY CHILD, fourth child and third son of Stephen and Eliza Atwood Child, b. in Cornish, N. H., Dec.

22, 1832, m. Jan. 1, 1837, Ellen Frances Leighton of Hartford, Vt. A farmer, lives at Cornish Flat, N. H.

[Eighth Generation.] Children:

766. i. WILLIAM PALMER CHILD, b. Nov. 15, 1857, in Cornish, N. H.

767. ii. FRANK EUGENE CHILD, b. April 19, 1859, in Cornish, N. H., d. 1860.

768. iii. HATTIE LILLIAN CHILD, b. Dec. 28, 1863, in Cornish, N. H.

769. iv. EDWIN LEIGHTON CHILD, b. May 28, 1867, in Cornish, N. H.

770. v. EVA CHILD.

[Sixth Generation.]

654. x. JANE CHILD, tenth child and seventh dau. of Stephen and Mercy Chase Child, b. in Cornish, N. H., m. Jacob J. Safford. They lived at Royalton, Vermont, a few years and then moved to Coldwater, Mich., and resided there till the time of their death. Their children were all born in Royalton, Vt.

[Seventh Generation.] Children:

771. i. HENRY SAFFORD, was a clergyman of the Episcopal church; has been settled in Vermont, Michigan and Indiana.

772. ii. HEBER CHASE SAFFORD.

773. iii. PHILANDER SAFFORD.

774. iv. PRUDENTIA SAFFORD.

[Fifth Generation.]

642. iv. ABEL CHILD, fourth child and fourth son of Daniel and Ruth Ammidown Child, b. in Woodstock, Ct., Oct. 18, 1752, m. March 11, 1779, Rebecca Allard. She was b. 1760, d. 1820, in Woodstock. He d. Nov. 12, 1807, in Woodstock, Ct., where he had always lived. They had eight children.

[Sixth Generation.] Children:

775. i. URIAH CHILD, b. in Woodstock, Ct., Dec. 5, 1779, m. April 2, 1807, Polly Carpenter.

776. ii. SALOME CHILD, b. July 8, 1781, m. Sept. 3, 1803, Abiel Chamberlain.

777. iii. STEPHEN CHILD, b. in Woodstock, Ct., April 21, 1783, m. Abigail Carter.

778. iv. NABBY BRIDGES CHILD, b. in Woodstock, Ct., March 28, 1785, unmarried.

779. v. REBECCA CHILD, b. in Woodstock, Ct., May 6, 1790, m. Jan. 28, 1822, Nathan Morse.

780. vi. ABEL CHILD, JR, b. in Woodstock, Ct., May 6, 1792, m. 1st, March 16, 1826, Dorothea Child, m. 2d, Feb. 16, 1831, Sophia Child.

781. vii. ALVIN CHILD, b. in Woodstock Ct., April 23, 1795, m. May 3, 1824, Mary May.

782. viii. DANIEL CHILD, b. in Woodstock, Ct., Dec. 2, 1797, m. April 9, 1827, Lucy Carpenter.

[Sixth Generation.]

775. i. URIAH CHILD, first child of Abel and Rebecca Allard Child, b. in Woodstock, Ct., Dec. 5, 1779, m. April 2, 1807, Polly Carpenter. Soon after his marriage he removed to Norwich, Chenango county, N. Y., and settled on a farm a few miles from the village of Norwich. He died July 4, 1812, leaving a wife and three young children. For several years, previous to his marriage, he was a school teacher; with some military aspirations, he held a captain's commission in a company of Infantry, which he supported with credit to his skill as an officer. At his death, Mrs. Child was left to cultivate the farm and care for the children. Being a woman of great energy, and possessing a vigorous constitution, under many discouragements, succeeded, in managing successfully the farm till her sons grew to manhood, and relieved her of much of her burdens. She died in Norwich, 1834.

[Seventh Generation.]   Children:

783 i. ABEL CHILD, b. in Norwich, Chen. county, N. Y., Dec. 20, 1807. He never married. He held the office of captain in a company of Infantry. He died Sept. 24, 1864.

784. ii. ANN CELIA CHILD, b. in Norwich, N. Y., Dec. 12, 1809. m. March 10, 1846, Samuel Aldrich. He died Jan. 25, 1873, leaving no children. Mrs. Aldrich lives in the village of Norwich, N. Y.

785. iii. JOSEPH URIAH CHILD, b in Norwich, N. Y., Feb. 12, 1812, m. 1st, Dec 5, 1850, Luanna Page. She died Jan. 30, 1858, and he m. 2d, Olive Eccleston, whose maiden name was Benedict. He died May 6, 1879. Mr. Child was a farmer, and resided in Preston, N. Y.

[Eighth Generation.]   Children of Joseph Uriah Child, by his first wife:

786. i. CELIA L. CHILD, b. April 15, 1855.

787. ii. JOHN P. CHILD, b. Jan. 25, 1858.

[Sixth Generation.

776. ii. SALOME CHILD, second child of Abel and Rebecca Allard Child, b. in Woodstock, July 8, 1781, m. Sept. 3, 1803, Abiel Chamberlain.

[Seventh Generation.]   Child:

788. i. JOHN NEWTON CHAMBERLAIN, b May 26, 1812, m. 1838, Persis Plympton. Had seven children.

[Eighth Generation.]   Children:

789. i. REBECCA PLYMPTON CHAMBERLAIN, b. Nov. 12, 1839, m 1859, T. H. Baker. Had five children.

790. ii. JOHN NEWTON CHAMBERLAIN, b. Feb. 20, 1841, m. Abbie Buck.

791. iii. ALVIN BOND CHAMBERLAIN, b. Dec. 16, 1842, m. Oct. 10, 1867, Mary L. Frink.

792. iv. ELLEN S. CHAMBERLAIN, b. Jan. 13, 1846, m. Nov. 30, 1867, Emery Andrews. Have two children.

793. v. EMILY L. CHAMBERLAIN, b. May 3, 1847, m. 1868, Warren Howard. Have one child.

794. vi. MARY D. CHAMBERLAIN, b. April 24, 1849.

795. vii. EDWIN H. CHAMBERLAIN, b. Feb. 2, 1852, m. 1876, Clara C. Wallace. Have one child.

[Sixth Generation.]

777. iii. STEPHEN CHILD, second son, and third child of Abel and Rebecca Allard Child, b. in Woodstock, Ct., April 21, 1783, m. Abgail Carter, of Dudley, Mass., who was b. March 22, 1783. She lives in Woodstock, Ct., in the home to which she was taken at her marriage, which must have been in 1811, or 1812, her age being 96 years.

[Seventh Generation.] Children:

796. i. ELIZABETH M. CHILD, b. in Woodstock, Ct., in 1813, m. April 4, 1848, Rev. L. Burleigh.

797. ii. CAROLINE CHILD, b. in Woodstock, Ct., in 1816, m. William Chandler.

798. iii. ABBEY CHILD, b. in Woodstock, Ct., 1818, m. Ashley Mills.

799. iv. ABEL CHILD, b. in Woodstock, Ct., 1821, m. Ellen Bugbee.

800. v. HARRIET F. CHILD, b. in Woodstock, Ct., 1827, m. Harris May.

[Seventh Generation]

796. i. ELIZABETH MORSE CHILD, eldest child of Stephen and Abigail Carter Child, b. in Woodstock, Ct., 1813, m. by Rev. Thomas Boutwell, April 4, 1848, to Rev Lucien Burleigh.

This Burleigh family, into which Elizabeth Morse Child married, is one of such prominence, from their unusual ability and devotion to the great reforms of the day, we are glad their alliance to the Child name permits us to sketch them, briefly though it must be. Their lives are of such as we gladly offer the youth of our kindred for ensamples. Rev. Lucien Burleigh is the son of Rinaldo and Lydia Bradford Burleigh. Mrs. Lydia B. Burleigh was a direct descendant of Governor Bradford, who came to the new world with the first band of emigrants in 1620, on board the May-flower. Of the family of nine children given Mr. and Mrs. Rinaldo Burleigh, two died in infancy, the other seven attained mature years, six sons and one daughter. The physical development of these sons was so remarkable, they were sometimes termed "The thirty-six feet of Burleigh boys." The eldest son, John Oscar Burleigh, was born in Plainfield, Ct., where his father, who was a graduate of

Yale College, was residing, being the principal of the Plainfield Academy. Mr. John O. Burleigh was educated at the Plainfield Academy, and at the Connecticut Literary Institute at Suffield. He became a teacher in the public schools of Killingly, Ct., Oxford and Brookline, Mass. While principal of the high school at Oxford Plains, he married Miss Evaline Moore, of that place. He had four children. The second child of Rinaldo and L. B. Burleigh, was a daughter. Frances Mary Bradford Burleigh, who married Jesse Arms, and resided in Vineland, New Jersey. The third child was Charles Calister Burleigh. "He was a bright scholar at an early age; was fitted for college before he was twelve; commenced teaching when he was fourteen. He was admitted to the bar as a lawyer, in Windham county, Ct." At this time he gave promise of great brilliancy and distinction in this profession. For two years before his admission to the bar, in the years 1833 and '34, he edited the first anti-slavery paper in Connecticut. From a deep sense of duty, he gave up his legal aspirations, and devoted himself to the cause of the slave, which he plead with unequaled logic, and great eloquence, until the hour of emancipation. He then became a preacher and ministered to an "Independent Congregational Society" in Florence, Mass., a position he held for most of the remaining years of his life. He was injured by a passing train when at a railway station, resulting in his death ten days later. The highest testimony to his intellectual and moral worth, was rendered by his friends, Samuel May, William Lloyd Garrison, and other able men at the time of his decease. The fourth child in the family, was William Henry Burleigh; as a boy, possessed of a sunny, mirthful temper, which dubbed him the "rogue" in boyhood, and cheered and sweetened his manhood. With less academical training than his brothers, he made for himself, nevertheless, a place in the ranks of reformers. He became a printer and editor, and bravely and effectively labored in the temperance and anti-slavery causes. In 1837, he removed to Pittsburgh, Pa., and published there the *Christian Witness*, and later the *Temperance Banner*. The years of his residence in Pennsylvania, were busy, useful, honorable and honored. In 1843, he returned to Connecticut, and in Hartford edited the *Christian Freeman*, soon changed to *Charter Oak*. One who knew

him well, and was capable of judging wisely, says of him: "He
had few equals, and no superiors, as a writer, speaker, editor,
poet, reformer, friend, associate; it was the universal testimony
of those knowing him best, and esteeming him most truly, that
he stood in the forefront of his generation."[1]

In 1849, Mr. W. H. Burleigh went to Syracuse, N. Y., in
the employ of the New York State Temperance Society, as
lecturer, secretary, and editor of their paper, which position
he held five years. In 1855, he received the unsolicited appointment of harbor master from Gov. Myron H. Clark. In
1863, heavy afflictions came upon him, and the loss of father,
wife, daughter and grandson in rapid succession, so told upon
his health, he was speedily compelled to seek restoration in
change of scene. Somewhat more than a year after, he was
invited to attend a silver wedding in Syracuse; unable to be
present, he sent the accompanying little poem of regrets:

"On this auspicious day, could all my wishes
　　That peace be yours, and happiness, and health,—
Assume the varied form of silver dishes,
　　How would your tables glitter with their wealth.

But since no sprite can work this transformation,
　　I send my simple blessing in this rhyme:
With hearty love, and honest admiration
　　That still grows stronger with the passing time.

May the good angels evermore attend you
　　And make your days all beautiful and fair,
And since no other silver can I send you,
　　I send a lock of my own silver hair."

He passed away on the 18th March, 1871: John Chadwick
said of him, at his funeral, "He loved everything, from rocks,
woods, and waters, up to truth and God."

The fifth child of Rinaldo and Lydia B. Burleigh was Lucian, who married Elizabeth (or "Betsey") Morse Child; he
was born in Plainfield, Ct., on the 3d February, 1817, and is
yet living in the house where he was born. He studied for the
ministry, and became a Baptist clergyman; he was, however,
early inspired with the reformatory bias of his family. At sixteen years of age made his maiden speech, upon temperance,
and years of his life have found him devoting time and talent

---

[1] Hon. Francis Gillette, M. C.

to the promotion of this reform.   In 1850, he became secretary
of the "Society for the Suppression of Gambling."   In 1854,
he was again in his native place, engaged in teaching, much of
the time, in the Plainfield Academy, of which institution he
has published an extended history.   For a number of years he
has resided upon the ancestral farm, cultivating the soil, and
acting as agent for the Conn. Temperance Union, also preaching when called upon.[1]

The fifth son of this line was Cyrus Moses Burleigh, born in
Plainfield, Ct., 8th Feb., 1820, dying at Sunnyside, Pa., 7th
March, 1855.   "Though ending life in the richness and
strength of his mental manhood, the years he had lived were
full of earnest, hearty toil for the amelioration of the colored
race, for the release of the intemperate from the thraldom of
vice, and for the advance of all efforts to uplift his fellow-beings."   The last years of his life were spent in the State of
Pennsylvania, editing the *Pennsylvania Freeman.*

The youngest of these sons was George Shepard Burleigh,
who was born in Plainfield, in 1822: he is now in the full maturity of a noble physical and mental manhood, and is widely
known as a poet of much strength and beauty of thought.
Several years since he published in Philadelphia, Pa., a volume
of poems, entitled, "The Maniac, and other Poems."   At the
time of the Fremont campaign he published a volume of poems, on incidents in the life of J. C. Fremont, called, "Signal
Fires on the Trail of the Path-Finder."   He has written many
articles for periodicals, which would fill several volumes if collected.   He married Miss Ruth Burgess of Little Compton,
R. I., where he now resides.

Of the succeeding generation we say but a few words.   There
seems a remarkable development of artistic taste and talent, from
which we may hope such good work, in the promotion of
æsthetic culture, as the parents have wrought in reform.

[Eighth Generation]   Children:

801. i. GERTRUDE ELIZABETH BURLEIGH, b. in Woodstock, Ct., March
10, 1844.

802. ii. HARRIET FRANCES BURLEIGH, b. in Plainfield, Ct., July 10, 1846.

803. iii. CAROLINE ELLA BURLEIGH, b. in Plainfield, Ct., July 28, 1848,
m. Frank Tyler.   She resides in Danielsonville, Ct.

[1] To him we are indebted for the main facts given of this band of brothers.

804. iv. LUCIEN RINALDO BURLEIGH, b. in Plainfield, Ct., Feb. 6, 1853.
805. v. WM. BRADFORD BURLEIGH, b. in Plainfield, Ct., July 18, 1855.
806. vi. JOHN CARTER BURLEIGH, b. in Plainfield, Ct., May 18, 1857.

[Seventh Generation.]

797. ii. CAROLINE CHILD, second dau. and child of Stephen and Abigail Carter Child, b. in Woodstock, Ct., 1816, m. Jan. 1, 1844, William Chandler, son of Capt. John and Deborah Eddy Chandler of Dudley, Mass. Mr. and Mrs. William Chandler were married by Rev. Thomas Boutwell.

William Chandler is one of a family of ten children—nine sons and one daughter. His eldest brother, John Chandler, went as a missionary to India, in Oct., 1846, and has continued there till the present time. He has had nine children, two of whom have died; the others have received an education in this country; three married and returned to India—two as missionaries. Joseph Chandler, another brother of William, is a clergyman settled in Minnesota, and has had six children, three of whom are living. Augustus Chandler, the youngest brother of William, is a clergyman, preaching in Brattleboro, Vt., till compelled by failing health to relinquish his charge, and is now editor of a paper in Vermont.[1] Of the two remaining brothers of William Chandler now living, one, Daman, is a farmer in Woodstock, Ct.; the other, Amasa, is the proprietor of a hotel on Woodstock Hill, Ct. He has four children: the two eldest are graduates from Yale College, New Haven, Ct. The sister of Mr. William Chandler married Royal Hatch of Strafford, Vermont, and has had nine children. The farm owned at the present time by Mr. William Chandler, has for several generations past been in the Child name. Mrs. Stephen Child came to this place on her marriage, and is still living, at the age of ninety-six. At the annual gathering at this ancient home on Thanksgiving days, four generations have been represented for several years past.

[Eighth Generation.] Children:
807. i. J. F. CHANDLER, b. in Woodstock, Ct., June 27, 1845.
808. ii. HATTIE E. CHANDLER, b. in Woodstock, Ct., April 22, 1849, m. Sept. 14, 1870, Chauncey Morse.
809. iii. ABBIE C. CHANDLER, b. in Woodstock, Vt., Feb. 14, 1852, m. May 15, 1873, Monroe Ide.

[1] Rev. Mr. A. Chandler has deceased since the writing of the above.
M

810. iv. ALICE C. CHANDLER, b. in Woodstock, Ct., July 31, 1855.
811. v. WM. H. CHANDLER, b. in Woodstock, Ct., Aug. 18, 1857.
812. vi. AGNES E. CHANDLER, b. in Woodstock, Ct., May 6, 1859.

[Eighth Generation.]

808. ii. HATTIE E. CHANDLER, dau. of Caroline Child and William Chandler, b. April 22, 1849, m. Sept. 14, 1870, Chauncey Morse. Reside in Millbury, Mass.

[Ninth Generation.] Children:
813. i. CLARA ESTELLA MORSE, b Dec. 21, 1871.
814. ii. ERNEST CHANDLER MORSE, b. Aug. 16, 1875.
815. iii. ALICE MORSE, b. Sept. 23, 1877.

[Eighth Generation.]

809. iii. ABBIE C. CHANDLER, dau. of Caroline Child and Wm. Chandler, b. Feb. 14, 1852, m. May 15, 1873, Monroe Ide. She died April 26, 1877. Resided in Woodstock, Ct.

[Ninth Generation] Child:
816. i. HERBERT CHAUNCY IDE, b. Oct. 21, 1874.

[Seventh Generation.]

798. iii. ABBEY CHILD (Abigail Eleanor), dau. of Stephen and Abigail Carter Child, b. in Woodstock, Ct., Aug. 11, 1818, m. April 6, 1842, Ashley Mills, son of Nathaniel and Polly Tourtelotte Mills of Thompson, Ct. Married by Rev. Thomas Boutwell.

[Eighth Generation.] Children:
817. i. ABIGAIL ELEANOR MILLS, b. in Thompson, Ct., Feb. 15, 1843, d. Aug. 22, 1848.
818. ii. NATHANIEL CHILD MILLS, b. in Thompson, Ct., April 21, 1845, d. in Boston, Oct. 13, 1872.
819. iii. ASHLEY P. MILLS, b. in Thompson, Ct., Sept. 25, 1847.
820. iv. STEPHEN CHILD MILLS, b. in Thompson, Ct., Aug. 29, 1850, d. Sept. 29, 1850.
821. v. CHARLES EUGENE MILLS, b. in Thompson, Ct., Jan. 12, 1852.
822. vi. WM. CARTER MILLS, b. in Thompson, Ct., Nov., 1854.

[Seventh Generation.]

799. iv. DEA. ABEL CHILD, son of Stephen and Abigail Carter Child, b. in Woodstock, Ct., July 27, 1821, m. April 2, 1851, Ellen Matilda Bugbee, dau. of Hezekiah and Jemima Harding Bugbee. She was b. Nov. 27, 1831. Reside in So. Woodstock, Ct.

[Eighth Generation.] Children:
  823. i. CLARENCE HARDING CHILD, b. in Woodstock, Ct., May 14, 1855.
  824. ii. CHARLES CARTER CHILD, b. in Woodstock, Ct., Sept. 30, 1861, d. Sept. 12, 1866.
  825. iii ELLEN MARIA CHILD, b. in Woodstock, Ct., May 16, 1866.
  826. iv. HERBERT CHAUNCY CHILD, b. in Woodstock, Ct., Dec. 18, 1868, d. March 12, 1872.

[Seventh Generation.]

800. v. HARRIET F. CHILD, fourth dau. and fifth child of Stephen and Abigail Carter Child, b. in Woodstock, Ct., Jan. 7, 1826, m. March 13, 1856, Charles Harris May, son of Asa and Sally May; he was b. Sept. 2, 1823.

[Eighth Generation.] Children:
  827. i. JULIA A. MAY, b. in Woodstock, Ct., March 25, 1857.
  828. ii. CHARLES H. MAY, b. in Woodstock, Ct., July 1, 1858.
  829. iii. HERBERT MAY, b. in Woodstock, Ct., Dec. 27, 1860.
  830. iv. ASA L. MAY, b. in Woodstock, Ct., Jan. 6, 1864.
  831. v. MARION F. MAY, b. in Woodstock, Ct., Feb. 18, 1866.
  832. vi. JOHN S. MAY, b. in Woodstock, Ct., Feb. 25, 1868.
  833. vii. EVERETT MAY, b. in Woodstock, Ct., April 22, 1870.

[Sixth Generation.]

779. v. REBECCA CHILD, fifth child of Abel and Rebecca Allard Child, b. in Woodstock, Ct., 1790, m. Jan. 28, 1822, Nathan Morse of Woodstock, Ct: he was b. 1785, d. 1853.

[Seventh Generation.] Child:
  834. i. GEORGE MORSE, b. in Wookstock, Ct, March 29, 1825, m. April 5, 1852, Sylvia Child May, dau. of Trenck and Cynthia Child May of North Woodstock, Ct. They have no children.

[Sixth Generation.]

780. vi. ABEL CHILD, JR., third son and sixth child of Abel and Rebecca Allard Child, b. in Woodstock, Ct., July 1, 1792, m. 1st, March 16, 1826, Dorothea Child, dau. of Capt. Elias and Sophia Morse Child. She d. July 4, 1829. He m. 2d, Feb. 16, 1831, Sophia Child, sister of his first wife. He d. in Woodstock, Ct., May 4, 1878, æt. 86. His widow resides in Boston, with one of her sons.

[Seventh Generation,] Children:
(By his first wife, Dorothea,)
  835 i. EDWARD CHILD, b. Dec. 17, 1826, in Woodstock, Ct., m. April 6, 1851, Maria Child.
  836. ii. FREDERICK NEWMAN CHILD, b. March 19, 1829, in Woodstock, Ct. Was killed in battle at Spottsylvania, Va., in the War of the Rebellion, May 10, 1864.

(By his second wife, Sophia, he had:)

837. iii. SPENCER CHILD, b. in Woodstock, Ct, May 19, 1832, m. April, 1861, Eliza Goodrich.

838. iv. ELLEN DOROTHEA CHILD, b. in Woodstock, Ct., Dec. 5, 1833, m. April 29, 1858, Henry May.

839. v. ANDREW JACKSON CHILD, b. in Woodstock, Ct, Jan. 19, 1838, m. April 21, Anne E. Brown.

[Seventh Generation.]

835. i. EDWARD CHILD, son of Abel and Dorothea Child, b. Dec. 17, 1826, m. April 16, 1851, Maria Child, dau. of Lemuel Child, who was the son of Moses Child. He d. April 10, 1862. Mrs. Child resides in North Woodstock, Ct.

[Eighth Generation.]   Children:

840. i. EUGENE CHILD, b. May 18, 1853.

841. ii. EDWARD CHILD, b. Jan. 28, 1862, d. April 10, 1862.

[Seventh Generation.]

837. iii. SPENCER CHILD, son of Abel and Sophia Child, b. May 19, 1832, m. April 3, 1861, Eliza Goodrich, dau. of Sam'l A. and Elizabeth Wheeler Goodrich. She was b. July 2, 1838. Reside at 226 Broadway, Cambridgeport, Mass. Business 172 State street, Boston.

[Eighth Generation.]   Children:

842. i. LOUISE E. CHILD, b. March 14, 1862.

843. ii. ERNEST G. CHILD, b. July 6, 1868.

844. iii. HOWARD CHILD, b. Nov. 4, 1871, d. Jan. 3, 1872.

845. iv. WALLACE SPENCER CHILD, b. 1872, d. Dec. 13, 1874.

846. v. ALICE MAY CHILD, b. 1874, d. Nov. 10, 1875.

[Seventh Generation.]

838. iv. ELLEN DOROTHEA CHILD, only dau. of Abel and Sophia Child, b. in Woodstock, Ct., Dec. 5, 1833, m. April 29, 1858, Henry May, son of Trenck and Cynthia Child May of North Woodstock. Mr. May was appointed, under President Lincoln's administration, as commercial agent at Gaboon, Africa.

[Eighth Generation.]   Children:

847. i. FLORENCE E. MAY, b. June 14, 1861.

848. ii. GEORGE H. MAY, b. April 3, 1867.

[Sixth Generation.]

781. vii. ALVIN CHILD, fourth son and seventh child of Abel and Rebecca Allard Child, b. in Woodstock, Ct., April 23, 1795, m. May 3, 1824, Mary May, dau. of Ephraim May. Met his death by accidental burning.

[Seventh Generation.]   Child:

849. i. ALVIN CHILD, b. 1825.

ERECTED BY HENRY CHILD, 1760.

[Sixth Generation.]

782. viii. DANIEL CHILD, son, eighth child of Abel and Rebecca Allard Child, b. in Woodstock, Ct., Dec. 3, 1797, m. April 9, 1827, Lucy Carpenter, dau. of Cyril Carpenter. She was b. May 12, 1802, d. July, 1863.

[Seventh Generation.] Children:

850. i. CYRIL CARPENTER CHILD, b. in Woodstock, Ct., Feb. 20, 1828, lives in Boston.

851. ii. OSCAR HERBERT CHILD, b. in Woodstock, Ct., March 8, 1831, m. Dec. 25, 1857, Mary L. Appleton.

852. iii. FOSTER DANIEL CHILD, b. in Woodstock, Ct., Aug. 13, 1834, m. Eliza A. Ormsby.

853. iv. SUSAN RICHMOND CHILD, b. in Woodstock, Ct., March 11, 1836. Has spent many years in teaching. In the winter of 1869-70, she taught in Savannah, Ga. Also, in Wilmington, N. C. After teaching two seasons in the South, she taught one year in Illinois; thence returned to her home in W., and m. May 30, 1877, Joseph W. Cliff of Marshfield, Mass.

854. v. FREEMAN W. CHILD, b. in Woodstock, Ct, Dec. 15, 1839, d. at Ottawa, Ills., 1867. } Twins.

855. vi. AMASA C. CHILD, b. in Woodstock, Ct., Dec. 15, 1839, m. Jan. 13, 1869, Anna L. Emery, d. May 9, 1874, in San Francisco, Cal.

856. vii. HENRY S. CHILD, b in Woodstock, Ct., Jan. 19, 1844, lives in North Woodstock, with his brother, Foster Child.

[Seventh Generation.]

851. ii. OSCAR HERBERT CHILD, second son of Daniel and Lucy Carpenter Child, b. in Woodstock, Ct., March 8, 1831, m. Dec. 25, 1857, Mary L. Appleton.

[Eighth Generation.] Children:

857. i. ARTHUR APPLETON CHILD, b. in Woodstock, Ct., Dec. 18, 1859.

858. ii. MARY E. CHILD, b. in Woodstock, Ct., Jan. 13, 1865.

859. iii. JOHN APPLETON CHILD, b. in Woodstock, Ct, June 28, 1866.

[Fourth Generation.]

30. iv. HENRY CHILD, fourth child of Ephraim and Priscilla Harris Child, b. in Woodstock, Ct., May 28, 1717, m. twice: 1st, in 1742, to Rebecca Bacon, who was b. Oct. 9, 1722, and d. Nov. 17, 1753, æt. 31; 2nd, July 6, 1757, to Dorothy Child, dau. of Nathaniel Child, of Thompson, Ct.; she was b. Sept. 18, 1730, and d. April 17, 1794. He d. Jan. 17, 1795, æt. 78 yrs.

Henry Child was one of the ten of the name of Child, who took the Freeman's Oath on the transfer of the town of Woodstock, from the colony of Massachusetts to the colony of Connecticut. Very little written record has been left of his life. From tradition, he was esteemed as a man of much character and influence in Woodstock. The character of his descendants, of whom more is known, will certainly justify the opinion, that physically and intellectually, he ranked among the best class of citizens of that town. Immediately on his marriage, he went with his brother, Peter, from Muddy Brook, now East Woodstock, to the Northwest part of the town, known afterwards as the "English neighbourhood." This part of the town was then mostly forest, and had been the hunting ground of the Indians, and the habitation of bears and other wild beasts; and still continued to be frequented by the Indians. This gave rise to many fears of the mother of these youthful pioneers, lest they should be eaten by bears or murdered by Indians. Henry and Peter located lots adjoining. Henry, after spending some years in a small cabin, erected in the year 1760, a commodious house which still stands in good condition upon the original site, owned and occupied by one of his descendants. This house Mr. Child kept many years as an Inn. Around this early home cluster interesting memories. It stood on the great thoroughfare from the Western settlements of the colony to the seaboard, and afforded shelter and rest to many a weary traveller. Often it became the resting place of the patriot soldier in his marches to and from the battlefield during the Revolutionary struggle, when the hospitalities of the patriotic landlord were unstintedly dealt out. Often the floors of the parlor, kitchen and barroom were covered for the night with sturdy soldiers. Sometimes it was used as a hall of justice. On one occasion an exciting trial of one Bugbee, who had headed a town riot, took place there. He resisted the legal authorities in collecting the town taxes. The trial ended in his conviction and punishment.

Of late years the quiet hospitalities of successive heads of families of the *line* have been cheerfully dispensed, and the frequent gatherings of descendants, to the fifth generation from the patriarch Henry, have kept alive the memories of the past. One, as memorable among them, was the gathering in honor of Capt. Willard Child, a son of Henry and successor to the homestead, which occurred in 1842, when the venerable father, then in his eighty third year, sat as priest amidst children, grandchildren and great grandchildren to the number of 130, pronouncing the coveted benediction upon the waiting and happy throng. The closing scene was one of song and thanksgiving: recognizing the beneficent Providence which had ever vouchsafed His guardianship to this numerous household.

[Fifth Generation.] Children:

860. i. Infant, not named, b. 1742, d. young.

861. ii. AMASA CHILD, b. in Woodstock, Ct., June 13, 1745, m. Feb. 1, 1770, Joanna Carpenter.

862. iii. LEVI CHILD, b. in Woodstock, Ct., Jan. 10, 1747. Was a soldier in the Revolutionary war, and died in the army at New Castle, N. Y., Nov. 15, 1776.

863. iv. CYNTHIA CHILD, b. in Woodstock, Ct., Jan. 19, 1749, m. Jan. 11, 1770, Amasa Carpenter.

864. v. DINAH CHILD, b. in Woodstock, Ct., Oct. 21, 1751, d. unmarried.

865. vi. WILLARD CHILD, b. in Woodstock, Ct., May 7, 1758, m. 1st, Jan. 10, 1781, Lydia Morse, m. 2nd, May 7, 1795, Sylvia Child.

866. vii. EPHRAIM CHILD, b. in Woodstock, Ct., June 7, 1760, m. June 12, 1792, Betsey Bacon, died without issue. His widow married Minerva Cushman, of Exeter, Otsego county, N.Y.

867. viii. JOANNA Child, b. in Woodstock, Ct., Aug. 26, 1762, died Nov. 27, 1762.

868. ix. REBECCA CHILD, b. in Woodstock, Ct., Aug. 26, 1762, m. Nov. 27, 1794, Luther Baldwin.

} Twins.

[Fifth Generation.]

861. ii. AMASA CHILD, eldest son and second child of Henry and Rebecca Bacon Child, b. in Woodstock, Ct., Jan. 13, 1745, m. Feb. 1, 1770, Joanna Carpenter. He d. Sept. 8, 1820.

[Sixth Generation.] Children:

869. i. ROYAL CHILD, b. in Woodstock, Ct., 1770, bap. Oct. 17, 1772, d. 1775.

870. ii. DOROTHY CHILD, b. in Woodstock, Ct., Oct. 4, 1772, bapt. May 26, 1776, d. unmarried.

871. iii. AARON CHILD, b. in Woodstock, Ct., June 19, 1794, m. 1st, Lucy Burnham; m. 2nd, Mary Spring.

872. iv. SALLY CHILD, b. in Woodstock, Ct., June 9, 1796, m. William Duncan, and resided in New York City.

873. v. LEVI CHILD, b. in Woodstock, Ct., March 8, 1778, d. young.

874. vi. LEVI CHILD, 2D, b. in Woodstock, Ct., June 13, 1779.

875. vii. POLLY CHILD, b. in Woodstock Ct., Aug. 19, 1781, d. unm.

876. viii. BETTY CHILD, b. in Woodstock, Ct., Sept. 4, 1783, d. Feb. 1795.

877. ix. IRENE CHILD, b. in Woodstock, Ct., Sept. 4, 1785.

878. x. PERSIS CHILD, b. in Woodstock, Ct., March 25, 1787.

[Sixth Generation.]

871. iii. Capt. AARON CHILD, third child and eldest son of Amasa and Joanna Carpenter Child, b. in Woodstock, Ct., June 19, 1794, m. 1st, about 1804, to Lucy Burnham, dau. of Capt. Jotham Burnham, of Ashford, Ct. By her he had one child. Mrs. Child died soon after the birth of this child. He

m. 2nd, about 1814, Mary Spring of Petersham, Mass.   She d.
in Woodstock, June 1, 1857.   He d. in Woodstock, Ct. April
18, 1851.   He held a captain's commission in a company of Infantry for many years.   Like many others who are not born
with a silver spoon in their mouth, he struggled hard through life
to obtain it, without success.   He possessed a kindly nature,
full of good humor, and given to hospitality ; so that his social
life brought and conferred compensating pleasures.   As a neighbor, none were more ready to confer friendly offices, and even to
make sacrifices for the benefit of others.   As an instance of
pleasant humor, on one occasion his neighbor employed him to
do a piece of work.   When the job was finished, he received as
compensation only the employers' thanks.   Taking it all in
good part, he spoke of it humorously, and frequently to his
neighbors as a generous compensation, and as the first instance
of prompt pay for his services since he had resided in the town.
He was a whig in politics, patriotic in his feelings and a warm
advocate for the emancipation of the enslaved colored race.

[Seventh Generation.]   Children :

879. i. HIRAM BURNHAM CHILD, b. in Woodstock, Ct., Dec. 5, 1805, m.
Oct. 8, 1828, Fannie Nye.

[By his second marriage :]

880. ii. LUCY BURNHAM CHILD, b. in Woodstock, Ct., Oct. 21, 1815, m.
1st, 1834, Ralph Russell ; m. 2nd, 1844, Charles T. Wortley.

881. iii. GEORGE WASHINGTON CHILD, b. in Woodstock, Ct., April 19,
1818, d. Feb. 9, 1843.

882. iv. LEVI LINCOLN CHILD, b. in Woodstock, Ct., Sept. 16, 1820, m.
Charlotte Sheldon, of Somers, Ct.   They reside in New London, Ct.

883. v. CAROLINE AMANDA CHILD, b. March 31, 1823, m. George Baylies,
of Southbridge, Mass.

884. vi. AMASA CHILD, b. in Woodstock, Ct., Dec. 16, 1825, m. Feb. 28,
1851, Sarah L. Child.

885. vii. AARON CHILD, JR., b. in Woodstock, Ct., Oct. 30, 1827, m. Nov.
14, 1876, Mary Carpenter.

[Seventh Generation.]

879. i. HIRAM BURNHAM CHILD, eldest child of Capt. Aaron
and Lucy Burnham Child, b. in Woodstock, Ct., Dec. 5, 1805,
m. Oct. 8, 1828, Fanny Nye, of Keene, N. H.

[Eighth Generation.]   Children.

886. i. CHARLES CHILD, b. in Woodstock, Ct., Aug. 8, 1829, resides in
Atco, Camden county, N. J.

887. ii. LURA IRENE CHILD, b. in Woodstock, Ct., April 1, 1831, m. Dec.
1, 1852, James Alton, of Atco, Camden county, N. J.

888. iii. LYDIA BENSON CHILD, b. in Woodstock, Ct., June 3, 1833, d. in Dudley, Mass., June 27, 1855.

889. iv. LUCY BURNHAM CHILD, b. in Woodstock, Aug. 12, 1837, unm. Resides in Danbury, Ct.

890. v. LOUISA MARIA CHILD, b. in Woodstock, Ct., Sept. 6, 1843, m. July, 1863, Walter W. Kimball. Resides in New York City.

891. vi. SARAH ELIZABETH CHILD, b. in Webster, Mass., June 18, 1846, m. Oct. 2, 1874, Geo. S. Purdy. Resides in Danbury, Ct.

[Seventh Generation.]

880. ii. LUCY BURNHAM CHILD, second child of Capt. Aaron Child, by his second wife, Mary Spring, b. in Woodstock, Ct., Oct. 21, 1815, m. 1st, 1834, Ralph Russell; m. 2nd, 1844, Charles T. Wortley.

[Eighth Generation.] Children. By Ralph Russell:

892. i. MARY RUSSELL, m. 1859, Ephraim Snyder.

893. ii. JANE RUSSELL.

[By Mr. Wortley:]

894. iii. HERBERT C. WORTLEY, b. Aug. 13, 1846.

895. iv. LIZZIE C. WORTLEY, b. Oct. 3, 1852.

896. v. WILLIE J. WORTLEY, b. April 18, 1856.

[Eighth Generation.]

887. i. MARY RUSSELL, eldest child of Lucy Burnham Child and Ralph Russell, m. Ephraim Snyder about 1859.

[Ninth Generation.] Children:

897. i. ALANTHIA SNYDER, b. 1860.

898. ii. HARRIS SNYDER, b. 1863.

899. iii. FREDERICK SNYDER, b. 1867.

900. iv. RALPH SNYDER, b. 1869.

[Seventh Generation.]

884. iv. AMASA CHILD, sixth child and fourth son of Capt. Aaron Child, b. in Woodstock, Ct., Dec. 16, 1825, m. Feb. 28, 1851, Sarah L. Child, dau. of Charles and Almira Holmes Child. Mr. Child is a farmer. He removed from Woodstock, Ct., in 1839, to Adams county, Iowa, thence to the town of Jefferson, Green county, Iowa, where he now resides.

[Eighth Generation.] Children:

901. i. MARY ELLA CHILD, b. in East Woodstock, Ct., June 14, 1852.

902. ii. EMMA ALMIRA CHILD, b. in East Woodstock, Ct., Dec. 9, 1857.

903. iii. EVA FLORETTA CHILD, b. in East Woodstock, Ct., Feb. 15, 1857.

904. iv. CHARLES FREEMAN CHILD, b. in East Woodstock, Ct., Feb. 9, 1863.

905. v. LEONARD HOLMES CHILD, b. in East Woodstock, Ct., Oct. 9, 1865.

865. vi. Capt. WILLARD CHILD, sixth child and third son of Henry and Dorothy (Child) Child—she was the daughter of Nathaniel and Dorothy Johnson Child—b. in Woodstock, Ct., in the northwestern part of the town, known as the "English neighbourhood," May 7, 1758, m. 1st, Jan. 10, 1781, Lydia Morse, dau. of Deacon Jedediah and Sarah Child Morse, and the sister of Rev. Dr. Jedediah Morse of Charlestown, Mass. The account of the Morse family as allied to the Child family, is fully treated in another place. Mrs. Willard Child was b. in Woodstock, Ct., June 22, 1759; she d. Dec. 9, 1792. He m. 2d, 1795, Sylvia Child, dau. of Capt. Elisha and Alice Manning Child of East Woodstock, Ct.; she was b. Oct. 28, 1762, d. 1824. Capt. Willard d. Nov. 1, 1844.

Capt. Willard Child was descended from a stock both intelligent and enterprising. He was also allied by marriage with intelligence and moral worth; consequently his surroundings were of a healthful and elevating tone. He belonged to a class of thoughtful and substantial men who gave character and dignity to the age in which they lived. Measured by the standard of intelligence, morality and practical Christianity of that age, which was by no means of an indifferent character, few men stood on a higher plane. He was prominent and influential in private and public affairs. His opinions were sought in determining difficult matters in church and state. His wisdom, probity and sagacity gave him deserved prominence among his fellow townsmen.

He lived in warlike times. At an early age his surroundings were such as to awaken patriotic feelings. The spirit of independence in governmental affairs in the colonies then prevalent was aroused in his own breast, and in the ardor of robust youth he enlisted in the service of his country, and served through the Revolutionary War.

Army life has its amusing incidents, as well as its more serious and trying experiences. The following anecdote was many years ago related to me by one of my grandfather's comrades: The hour of supper in the camp was approaching. The time had come for filling their pitchers with milk for the evening repast, from the cows in a field adjoining the camp. The owner of the herd kept a close lookout for the army boys. Aware of this fact, a roguish comrade fell behind his companions on the way, and paused while they filled their pitchers. As they were leaving the field, he stealthily approached within gunshot, and with an old root, resembling in the twilight a musket, took steady aim at young Child, and with the click of his tongue he aroused his attention—who seeing, as he supposed, the old farmer with his gun sighting for a deadly shot, started on the double quick for the camp. In great fright he reached his tent with an empty pitcher. Discovering that he had been made the victim of a joke, and taking it all in good part, he returned and obtained the needed supply of milk, and enjoyed a good supper as well as a good joke!

[Sixth Generation.] Children:

905. i. NANCY CHILD, b. in Woodstock, Ct., Dec. 3, 1782, m. 1st, 1802, Elisha Child, m. 2d, Sept. 29, 1831, Dea. Dudley Child.

(*For record of children, see Elisha Child, No. 1340.*)

906. ii. HANNAH CHILD, b. in Woodstock, Ct., April 2, 1785, m. Jan. 24, 1804, David Morse, Jr.

907. iii. CLARISSA CHILD, b. in Woodstock, Ct., March 5, 1787, m. Jan. 21, 1808, Charles Thompson Child.

(*For record of children, see Charles Thompson Child, No. 1342.*)

908. iv. HENRY CHILD, b. in Woodstock, Ct., Jan. 3, 1789, m. 1st, 1813, Lucretia Child; 2d, April 3, 1818, Henrietta May; 3d, Nov. 10, 1823, Lucy May; 4th, Betsey Buel.

909. v. LUTHER CHILD, b. in Woodstock, Ct., Mar. 19, 1791, m. 1st, Jan. 25, 1815, Pamelia Child, 2d, Miss Susan Walker.

[By Sylvia Child.]

910. vi. WILLARD CHILD, b. in Woodstock, Ct., Nov. 14, 1796, m. Sept. 13, 1827, Katharine Griswold Kent.

911. vii. LYDIA CHILD, b. in Woodstock, Ct., July 29, 1798, m. Nov. 11, 1821, Erastus May.

912. viii. SYLVIA CHILD, b. in Woodstock, Ct., Jan. 28, 1800, m Elisha Walker.

913. ix. CYNTHIA CHILD, b. in Woodstock, Ct., April 2, 1804, m. Dec. 16, 1828, Trenck May

[Sixth Generation]

906. ii. HANNAH CHILD, second child of Capt. Willard and Lydia Morse Child, b. in Woodstock, Ct., April 2, 1785, m. Jan. 24, 1804, David Morse, son of Dr. David and Anna Newman Morse of Woodstock, Ct. He was b. in Woodstock, Ct., Jan. 29, 1777. His father was the son of Dr. Parker Morse, A. M., and Hannah Hughes. The father of Dr. Parker Morse was Capt Abel Morse, of the fourth generation of the Morses; he was a member of the Colonial Legislature one or more terms;

was b. Oct. 5, 1792, m. 1st, Grace Parker, 1714, 2d, Mary Kimball, 1757. His father, Benjamin Morse, of the third generation, b. 1668, m. Susanna, dau. of Abel Merrill, and granddaughter of Aquilla Chase of Cornwall, Eng. His father was Deacon Benjamin Morse of the second generation, b. March 4, 1640, and married Ruth Sawyer. Benjamin Morse's father was Anthony Morse, of the first generation in America, and emigrated to America in 1635, and settled in Newbury, Mass.

Immediately on their marriage, Mr. and Mrs. David Morse removed from Woodstock to Exeter, Otsego Co., N. Y., and settled on a farm in the southeast part of the town, where they lived till 1822, when they removed to Barrington, Yates Co., N. Y., where they both died—Mr. Morse Sept. 27, 1828, and Mrs. Morse in 1842. Mr. Morse was a man of unusual energy of character, sound judgment and executive ability, of sterling integrity and of decided Christian principles. He was a wise and affectionate father, and a kind husband. He was an earnest and consistent member of the Congregational church, and when his work was finished, died in the Christian faith, in the full belief of a glorious resurrection.

[Seventh Generation.]   Children:

914. i. LYDIA MORSE, b. in Exeter, N. Y., Jan. 21, 1805, m. March 1, 1831, Cameron Goff.

915. ii. Infant, unchristened, b. in Exeter, N. Y., Jan. 21, 1805, d. yg.

916. iii. EARL MORSE, b. in Exeter, Otsego Co., N. Y., Sept. 27, 1806, d. Nov. 1, 1833.

917. iv. ROSCIUS MORSE, b. in Exeter, Otsego Co., N. Y., April 29, 1808, m. in 1837, Mary Ann Hill.

918. v. LINUS MORSE, b. in Exeter, Otsego Co., N. Y., April 20, 1810, m. July 18, 1839, Jane McCain.

919. vi. HENRY CHILD MORSE, b in Exeter, N. Y., May 22, 1811, m. 1st, 1843, Sarah May Child, 2d, 1858, Caroline Lincoln (Hammond).

920. vii. HANNAH MORSE, b. in Exeter, N. Y, Oct. 23, 1813, m. Nov. 7, 1839, William Egbert Crane.

921. viii. NANCY MORSE, b. in Exeter, N. Y., Dec. 8, 1815, d. unm., Feb. 7, 1845.

922. ix. MARY MORSE, b. in Exeter, N. Y., July 12, 1817, lives at Ridgefield, Ills.

923. x. EMILY MORSE, b. in Exeter, N. Y., Aug. 13, 1818, d. Oct. 11, 1851.

924. xi. CELINA MORSE, b. in Exeter, N. Y., Mar. 16, 1820, lives at Ridgefield, Ills.

925. xii. SHERMAN MORSE, b. in Exeter, N. Y., Mar. 12, 1821, m. Nov. 29, 1872, Sarah O. Halcom.

926. xiii. ALBERT MORSE, b. in Exeter, N. Y., April 19, 1822, farmer in Ridgefield, Ills.

927. xiv. Infant, unchristened, d. young.

928. xv. FLOYD MORSE, b. in Barrington, Yates Co., N. Y., Oct. 20, 1825, m. Mary Amanda Pierce.

929. xvi. WILLARD CHILD MORSE, b. in Barrington, Yates Co., N Y., Oct. 20, 1826, m. April 6, 1853, Mary Erwin Cooper.

[Seventh Generation.]

914. i. LYDIA MORSE, eldest child of Hannah Child and David Morse, b. in Exeter, Otsego Co., N. Y., Jan. 2, 1805, m. March 1, 1831, Cameron W. Goff of Howard, Steuben Co., N. Y.; removed to Nunda, Ill., where she died Feb., 1878.

They had five children ; two only lived.

[Eighth Generation.] Children:

930. i. HENRIETTA GOFF, b. 1832, m. Columbus Howe.

931. ii. WILLIAM WATSON GOFF, b. in 1837, m. Laura Paine of Nunda, Ills. Have four children, names not given.

[Eighth Generation]

930. i. HENRIETTA GOFF, eldest child of Lydia Morse and Cameron Goff, and grand dau. of Hannah Child Morse, b. 1832, m. Columbus Howe, and live in Osage, Iowa.

[Ninth Generation.] Children:

932. i. BARNETT HOWE.

933. ii. EGBERT HOWE.

934. iii. WILLARD HOWE.

935. iv. LIZZIE HOWE.

[Seventh Generation.]

917. iv. DR. ROSCIUS MORSE, fourth child and second son of Hannah Child and David Morse, b. in Exeter, N. Y., April 29, 1808, m. April, 1837, Mary Ann Hill. She d. Dec. 30, 1870. He d. March 26, 1877, in Elmira, N. Y.

In his boyhood Dr. Morse enjoyed the advantages of a common school education, by which he was fitted for teaching in early youth : an occupation which he followed for several seasons, when he commenced the study of medicine with Dr. Carr of Canandaigua, N. Y. Completing his medical studies, he entered upon the practice in Barrington, Yates Co., N. Y.; thence he went to Penn Yan, in the same county, where he gained more than a local reputation in his profession. After a number of years of successful practice in Penn Yan, he removen to Elmira, Chemung Co., N. Y. His success as a physician having preceded him, he readily secured an extensive and lucrative practice, extending over some fifteen years, at the close of which he died a happy death, much lamented by his family and a numerous circle of friends. A touching incident which occurred in his last hours is worthy of record. The Doctor had become much attached to a horse, which had for many years been his faithful servant, carrying him safely over rough paths and dangerous places, amid tempests of rain and driving snow-storms. That he might take a farewell look, and bid a final adieu to this noble animal, the Doctor directed him to be brought from his stall, after he had been neatly groomed, and to be led by the window of the room where he was lying. As the animal passed by and returned, the Doctor waived his white handkerchief and said, "good-bye, old friend." Dr. Morse was a thorough business man, as well as a successful practitioner, a conscientious Christian, an esteemed and useful citizen, a true and sincere friend.

[Eighth Generation.] Children:
936. i. BARNET W. MORSE, m. Henrietta Scott.
937. ii. ROSCIUS MORSE, died early.
938. iii ROSCIUS C. MORSE, m. Louisa Westlake.
939. iv. MARY MORSE, m. Junius R. Clark.
940. v. HENRY CHILD MORSE.
941. vi. LUCIA BENTON MORSE.
942. vii. JENNIE MORSE.
*** viii. An infant unbaptized.

[Eighth Generation.]
936. i. Dr. BARNET W. MORSE, eldest child of Dr. Roscius and Mary Hill Morse, m. Henrietta Scott of Southport, Chemung Co., N. Y. He was educated a physician, and is practicing in Elmira, N. Y. He was a surgeon in the Union army in the late civil war.

[Ninth Generation] Children:
943. i. LUCIA BENTON MORSE.
944. ii. FANNIE MORSE.
945. iii. JESSIE MORSE, d. yg.

[Eighth Generation]
938. iii. ROSCIUS C. MORSE, third child and third son of Dr. Roscius and Mary Hill Morse, m. Loisa Westlake of Cleveland. O. Mr. Morse is a merchant in Elmira, N. Y. They have three children : names not given.

[Eighth Generation.]
939. iv. MARY HASTINGS MORSE, fourth child and eldest dau. of Dr. Roscius and Mary Hill Morse, m. Sept. 25. 1875. Junius R. Clark, Esq., a lawyer of Warren, Pa.

[Ninth Generation.] Child:
949. i. Son, b. March 19, 1877.

[Seventh Generation.]

918. v. LINUS MORSE, fifth child and third son of Hannah Child and David Morse, b. in Exeter, Otsego Co., N. Y., April 20, 1810, m. July 18, 1839, Jane McCain, dau. of Joseph McCain of Barrington, Yates Co., N. Y. Mr. Morse moved from Barrington to Nunda, Ill., thence to Nebraska. He served in the Union army in the war of the Rebellion.

[Eighth Generation.] Children:

950. i. ELIZABETH MORSE, m. Martin Kellogg of Ridgefield, Ill. Have four children.

951. ii. ALFRED MORSE, served in the army of the Union in the late war of the Rebellion. At the close of the war he settled in Nebraska, on a soldier's claim; is a conductor on a western railroad.

952. iii. WEBSTER MORSE, m. a Miss Stickney of Nunda, Ill. They reside in Nunda. He is a mail agent from Chicago, Ill., to St. Paul, Minn.

953. iv. FRANCES MORSE, m. Mr. Friend; have several children, names and dates of birth not given.

954. v. MARY MORSE, m. Mr. Jenkins, and settled in Nebraska.

955. vi. HELEN MORSE, unmarried.

[Seventh Generation.]

919. vi. Rev. HENRY CHILD MORSE, six child and fourth son of Hannah Child and David Morse, b. in Exeter, Otsego Co., N. Y., March 22, 1811.

Mr. Morse was graduated at Yale College, New Haven, Ct., in 1839. During the three following years he was principal of Nichols Academy, Dudley, Mass. He studied theology in Andover, Mass., and in Auburn, N. Y.; was licensed to preach by Windham County Association, Ct.; soon after settled over a church in Lima, Ind. Afterwards removed to Tyrone, Steuben Co., N. Y.; thence to Union City, Mich., where he held the pastorate of the Congregational Church for five years, when he was called to take charge, as principal, of La Grange Institute, Ind. During his connection with the Institute, he supplied destitute churches in the vicinity of La Grange as opportunity offered. A year and a half later he returned to Union City, and settled on a farm, where he has since resided, beloved by a large circle of friends. His Christian activities have not been relaxed. The Sabbath schools in Union City and feeble churches in the vicinity, have largely profited by his labors. The personal qualities of Mr. Morse have won for him many friends. Open-hearted, frank, and benevolent, he readily finds his way to the hearts of the people and commands their confidence and respect.

Mr. Morse has been twice married : first in May, 1843, to Sarah May Child. dau. of Deacon Luther and Pamelia Child of Woodstock, Ct. She died in Union City, Mich., 1848, leaving no children. His second marriage was in 1858, to Caroline Lincoln (Hammond), widow of Samuel J. Mills Hammond, Esq., attorney at law, and son of Judge Chester Hammond, an early settler, an influential and much esteemed citizen of Union City.

[Eighth Generation.] Child:

956. i. HENRY MILLS MORSE, b. in Union City, Mich., Dec., 1855.

[Seventh Generation.]

920. vii. HANNAH MORSE, seventh child and second dau. of Hannah Child and David Morse, b. in Exeter, Otsego Co., N. Y., Oct. 23, 1813, m. Nov. 7, 1839, William Egbert Crane, son of Ira Crane of Barrington, Yates Co., N. Y. Soon after their marriage they moved to Bradford, Steuben Co., N. Y., where they still reside. Mr. Crane has been an extensive and successful farmer, and accumulated a handsome property, upon which he has retired to spend his declining years in independence and ease. They have but one child.

[Eighth Generation.] Child:

957. i. GEORGIANA CRANE, b. in Bradford, N. Y., June 30, 1846, m. May 22, 1867, Cyrus M. Merriman.

[Eighth Generation.]

957. i. GEORGIANA CRANE, only child of Hannah Morse and William Egbert Crane, b. in Bradford, N. Y., June 30, 1846, m. May 22, 1867, Cyrus M. Merriman, son of Hiram Merriman, a lumber merchant in Williamsport, Pa. Mr. Cyrus M. Merriman possesses fine business talents, and holds the office of justice of the peace in Bradford, N. Y.

[Ninth Generation.] Children:

958. i. EGBERT CRANE MERRIMAN, b. in Bradford, N. Y., May 18, 1868.
959. ii. AUGUSTA CURTISS MERRIMAN, b. in Bradford, N. Y., June 15, 1870.

[Seventh Generation.]

925. xii. Dr. SHERMAN MORSE, twelfth child and fifth son of Hannah Child and David Morse, b. in Exeter, N. Y., March 12, 1821, m. Nov. 9, 1872, Sarah Orthonett Halcom of Langdon, N. H. He was in the Union army in the late civil war,

as physician and surgeon; afterwards settled in Ridgefield, Ill.,
where he now resides, following his profession, and farming.
[Eighth Generation.] Children:
 960. i. ANNIE H. MORSE.
 961. ii. FLOYD S. MORSE.

[Seventh Generation.]

 928. xv. Dr. FLOYD MORSE, fifteenth child and seventh son
of Hannah Child and David Morse, b. in Barrington, Yates
Co., N. Y., April 11, 1825, m. Mary Amanda Pierce, dau. of
Dea. Allanson and Sylvia Pierce of Cooper's Plains, Chemung
Co., N. Y. Dr. Morse entered upon his practice in Tuscarora,
Livingston Co., N. Y., afterwards removed to Painted Post,
Steuben Co., N. Y., where he died, Sept. 20, 1858.
[Eighth Generation.] Children,
 962. i. EMMA PIERCE MORSE, b. Oct. 31, 1850, m. Sept. 1, 1875, Rev.
Giles H. Hubbard, a Baptist Clergyman.
 963. ii. BENJAMIN RUSH MORSE, b. Oct. 21, 1852.
 964. iii. FLOYD HERBERT MORSE, b. Aug. 31, 1854.
 965. iv. ANNIE L. MORSE, b. May 23, 1856.

[Seventh Generation.]

 929. xvi. WILLARD CHILD MORSE, youngest child and
eighth son of Hannah Child and David Morse, b. in Barrington, Yates Co., N. Y., Oct. 20, 1826, m. April 6, 1853, Mary
Erwin Cooper, dau. of Dr. John Cooper of Cooper's Plains,
Steuben Co., N. Y. Mr. Morse is a well-to-do farmer and an
esteemed citizen of Painted Post, Steuben Co., N. Y.
[Eighth Generation.] Children:
 966. i. JOHN COOPER MORSE, b. in Painted Post, Sept. 22, 1854.
 967. ii. LIZZIE EVANS MORSE, b. in Painted Post, Feb. 19, 1857, d. Oct.
21, 1864, at Cooper's Plains.

[Sixth Generation.]

 908. iv. HENRY CHILD, fourth child and eldest son of Capt.
Willard and Lydia Morse Child, b. in Woodstock, Ct., Jan. 3,
1789, m. Oct. 1, 1813, Lucretia Child, dau. of Nehemiah and
Eliza Shipman Child. She d. April 3, 1816: he m. 2d, April
3, 1818, Henrietta May, dau. of Ephraim and Abigail Chan-
dler May. She d. Jan. 28, 1822; he m. 3d, Nov. 10, 1823,
Lucy May, dau. of Asa and Anna Fillebrowne May. She d.
March 20, 1843; he m. 4th, April 28, 1845, Betsey Buel. She
d. June 18, 1877. Mr. Child was a farmer in West Fairlee,
Orange Co., Vt., where he died April 8, 1861.

 N

Mr. Child was a man of fine constitution, of ruddy complexion, in stature nearly or quite six feet, broad shouldered, deep chested, weighing nearly 200 pounds. He first settled in Woodstock, Ct., afterwards removed to West Fairlee, Vt., where he spent the balance of his days. He was a citizen of much public spirit, of earnest purposes, sound in judgment, which gave efficiency to a life of usefulness and gained the esteem of his fellow townsmen. He was an intelligent man, well informed on the topics of the times, a true patriot and philanthropist, and a sincere Christian. He died in the seventy-second year of his age.

[Seventh Generation.]   Children:

[By first marriage.]

968. i. ELEANOR LUCRETIA CHILD, b. in Woodstock, Ct., April 1, 1816, m. Ralph Perry.

[By second marriage.]

969. ii. ABBIE CHANDLER CHILD, b. in Woodstock, Ct., April 22, 1819, m. Calvin M Holbrook.

970. iii. EPHRAIM CHILD, b. in West Fairlee, Vt., Aug. 1, 1821, d. Sept. 24, 1823.

[By third marriage.]

971. iv. ASA MAY CHILD, b. in West Fairlee, Vt., Nov. 8. 1824, m. Oct. 22, 1857, Mary E. Wadleigh.

972. v. HENRY CHILD, Jr., b. in West Fairlee, Vt, March 31, 1826, d. March 24, 1875. No children.

973. vi. GEORGE MAY CHILD, b. in West Fairlee, Vt., April 24, 1831, m. Rosina Falls.

[Seventh Generation.]

968. i. ELEANOR LUCRETIA CHILD, eldest child of Henry and Lucretia (Child) Child, b. in Woodstock, Ct., April 1, 1816, m. Dec. 26, 1838, Ralph Perry, a farmer of Chester, Vt.

[Eighth Generation.]   Children:

974. i. MARY LUCRETIA PERRY, b Sept 2, 1839, m. Sept. 7, 1872, Eugene Fred Bigelow.

975. ii. NEWSOME PERRY, b. April 14, 1841, d. Aug. 3, 1848.

976. iii. GEORGE WILSON PERRY, b Aug. 4, 1842.

977. iv. ANNA PERRY, b. Sept. 13, 1844, d. Dec. 10, 1845.

978. v. ELIZABETH PERRY, b. July 24, 1846, d. Nov 30, 1850.

979 vi. HENRY CHILD PERRY, b Jan. 25, 1848, m. Jan 30, 1873, Rosa Duklee.   She d. Jan. 26, 1875.

980. vii. LUCY MAY PERRY, b. Aug. 30, 1850.

981. viii. ELMIRA ROSETTA PERRY, b. Feb. 15, 1852, m. Nov. 9, 1878, Wallace Miles Knowlton.

982. ix. JOHN PERRY, b. May 5, 1853, d. July, 1854.

983. x. ALICE SOPHIA PERRY, b May 29, 1855, d. Nov. 16, 1863.

984. xi. JAMES MADISON PERRY, b. June 17, 1857, m. June 28, 1879, Lura Annette Perry.

985. xii. EDGAR EVERETT PERRY b. Aug. 21, 1859, d. Nov. 6, 1863.

[Seventh Generation.

969. ii. ABBIE CHANDLER CHILD, second child and second dau. of Henry Child, by Henrietta May, b in Woodstock, Ct., April 22, 1819, m. Sept. 22, 1848, Calvin M. Holbrook, of West Fairlee, Vt. She d. Feb. 11, 1852. He died Dec. 29, 1870.

[Eighth Generation.] Children:

986. i. ABBIE CHILD HOLBROOK, b. in West Fairlee, Vt., July 14, 1849.

987. ii HENRIETTA MAY HOLBROOK, b. in West Fairlee, Vt., Oct. 5, 1851.

[Seventh Generation.]

971. iv. ASA MAY CHILD, fourth child and second son of Henry Child, by Lucy May, b. in West Fairlee, Vt., Nov. 8, 1824, m. Oct. 20, 1857, Mary E. Wadleigh, of Lyme, N. H. Mr. Child is a farmer in West Fairlee, Vt.

[Eighth Generation.] Children:

988. i. ALICE MAY CHILD, b. it West Fairlee, Vt., Aug. 1, 1863.

989. ii. NELLIE MAY CHILD, b. in West Fairlee, Vt., April 17, 1866

990. iii. ASA IRVING CHILD, b. in West Fairlee, Vt., Jan. 11, 1868, d. April 13, 1879.

991 iv. LUCY MAY CHILD, b. in West Fairlee, Vt., Oct 4, 1872.

[Seventh Generation.]

973. vi. GEORGE MAY CHILD, sixth child and third son of Henry Child, by Lucy May, b. in West Fairlee, Vt., April 24, 1831, m. Rosina Falls, of Westford, Mass. They reside at Ayer, Middlesex county, Mass.

[Eighth Generation.] Child:

992. i. GEORGE HENRY CHILD, b. in Ayer, Mass., Sept. 26, 1863.

[Sixth Generation.]

969. v. DEA. LUTHER CHILD, fifth child and second son of Capt. Willard and Lydia Morse Child, b. in Woodstock, Ct., March 19, 1791, m. twice: 1st, Jan. 25, 1815, to Pamelia Child, dau. of Col. Chester and Sarah May Child, of Woodstock, Ct.: she was b. 1790, d. April 15, 1851: 2nd, to Susan Walker, dau. of Leonard and Chloe Child Walker, of Stafford, Vt. She was b. May 22, 1792. She still lives at 88 years of age. He died Jan. 30, 1860, on the old homestead, when the ownership went into the hands of one of his children. Deacon Child was a man of much intelligence, and active in the affairs of life. His can-

der, amiable disposition and clear judgment, rendered him a safe and reliable counsellor. In 1824, he was elected Deacon in the Congregational church, which he held till his death. His cheerful hospitality rendered his home a place of pleasant resort for kindred and friends, while the stranger was treated with consideration and kindness. His memory is warmly cherished by a large circle of acquaintances.

[Seventh Generation.] Children:

993. i. CLINTON CHILD, b. in Woodstock, Ct., May. 3, 1817, lives unm. in the old homestead.

984. ii. SARAH MAY CHILD, b. in Woodstock, Ct., Oct. 18, 1818, m Rev. Henry Morse, d. in Union City, Mich , without children.

995. iii. ASA THURSTON CHILD, b. in Woodstock, Ct., June 7, 1820, m. March 11, 1845, Roxana Lyon.

996. iv. EDWARD MORSE CHILD, b. in Woodstock, Ct , April 15, 1822, d. young.

997. v LUTHER S. CHILD, b. in Woodstock, Ct . May 12, 1824, d young.

998. vi. MARY ANN CHILD, b. in Woodstock, Ct., May 16, 1826, m. Mar. 12, 1852, J . W. Leavitt.

990. vii. PAMELIA HARRIS CHILD, b, in Woodstock, Ct., July 12, 1829.

1000 viii. EZRA CHILD, b. in Woodstock, Ct., April 6, 1830, d. young.

1001. ix. SUSAN A. CHILD, b. in Woodstock, Ct., Oct. 3, 1831, unm., resides in Woodstock.

1002. x. LYDIA MORSE CHILD, b. in Woodstock, Ct , April 4, 1834, d yg.

[Seventh Generation.]

995. iii. DEA. ASA THURSTON CHILD, third child and second son of Dea. Luther and Pamelia Child, b. in Woodstock, Ct., June 7, 1820, m. by Rev. Mr. Marsh, March 11, 1845, to Roxana Lyon, dau. of Dea. Moses and Tryphena Lyon, of Woodstock, Ct. He died Feb. 10, 1859. Mrs. Child resides in South Woodstock, Ct. The substantial characteristics of an honored father seem to have been the inheritance of a worthy son. Intelligent and earnest purposes, gave impulse to his activities. After his marriage he settled as a farmer in South Woodstock, Ct., and identified himself in the moral and material interests of the parish. The wisdom of his counsels was manifest by the esteem and confidence in which he was held by his fellow citizens. He was specially valued as a pillar in the church of which he was an esteemed officer, having been early chosen as one of its deacons.

[Eighth Generation.] Children:

1003. i. HENRY THURSTON CHILD, b. in South Woodstock, Ct., June 26, 1846, m. May 5, 1875, Ella E. Fitts.

1004. ii. MARY ELIZABETH CHILD, b. in South Woodstock, Ct., March 26, 1849, m. Nov. 29, 1875, John Newton Green.

1005. iii. EDWARD MOSES CHILD, b. in South Woodstock, Ct., Aug. 24, 1851. A physician in Meriden, Ct.

1006. iv. FLORENCE AUGUSTA CHILD, b. in South Woodstock, Ct., Oct. 31, 1858.

[Eighth Generation.]

1003. i. HENRY THURSTON CHILD, eldest child of Dea. Asa Thurston and Roxana Lyon Child, b. in South Woodstock, Ct., June 26, 1846, m. by Rev. H. Hyde, in Pomfret, Ct., May 5, 1875, to Ella E. Fitts, dau. of Lyman and Harriet Fitts, of Pomfret, Ct. Mr. Child resides in South Woodstock, Ct., on his father's homestead. A man held in high esteem by his fellow townsmen, as honorable and upright, intelligent, enterprising and successful in business. A warm supporter of educational and religious institutions; and like his father and grandfather, a worthy office bearer in the Congregational church.

[Ninth Generation.] Children:

1007. i. ALFRED THURSTON CHILD, b. in South Woodstock, Ct., March 10, 1876.

1008. ii. EDWARD LYMAN CHILD, b. in South Woodstock, Ct., Oct. 6, 1877.

1009. iii. RICHARD LYON CHILD, b. in South Woodstock, Ct., March 3, 1879.

[Eighth Generation.)

1004. ii. MARY ELIZABETH CHILD, second child, eldest dau. of Dea. Asa Thurston and Roxana Lyon Child, b. in South Woodstock, Ct., March 26, 1849, m. by Rev. N. Beach, Nov. 29, 1875, to John Newton Green, son of John J. and Hannah Green, of Putnam, Ct. They reside in Greenboro, North Carolina.

[Ninth Generation.] Child:

1010. i. HENRY JEWETT GREEN, b. 1878.

[Seventh Generation.]

998. vi. MARY ANN CHILD, sixth child and second dau. of Dea. Luther and Pamelia Child, b. in Woodstock, Ct., May 16, 1826, m. March 10, 1852, J. W. Leavitt. He d. Dec. 4, 1864. Mrs. Leavitt resides on the old homestead, built by Henry Child, her great-grandfather, the ownership having been retained by his direct descendants to the present date.

[Eighth Generation.]   Children:
    1011. i. HERBERT LEAVITT. b. Woodstock, Ct., May 26. 1853, m. Aug.
19. 1874. Evelyn L. Hebbard.
    1012. ii. LUTHER LEAVITT. b. in Woodstock, Ct., Feb. 26. 1855.
    1013. iii. SUSAN A. LEAVITT, b. in Woodstock. Ct., May 21. 1858.

[Eighth Generation.]

    1011. i. HERBERT LEAVITT, eldest child of Mary Ann Child
and J. W. Leavitt, b. may 26, 1851, m. Aug. 19, 1874, Evelyn
L. Hebbard.
[Ninth Generation.]   Child:
    1014. i. WALLACE HERBERT LEAVITT. b. May 28. 1878.

[Sixth Generation.]

    910. vi. Rev. WILLARD CHILD, D.D., sixth child of Capt.
Willard Child, by Sylvia Child, (2nd m.) third son, b. in Woodstock, Ct., Nov. 14, 1796, m. Sept. 13, 1827, Katherine Griswold Kent, dau. of Rev. Dan and Betsey Griswold Kent, of
Benson, Vt. She was b. in Benson, Feb. 7, 1805, and d. Feb.
26, 1851. He d. Nov. 13, 1877, 81 years of age. He graduated at Yale College, New Haven. Ct, the year we are not able to
state.

    Dr. Child was a man of quiet and easy dignity ; justly admir-
ed for his attractive personel. In stature he was nearly six feet,
possessing a fine physical development. His muscular power
in early youth was unusual. In his school-boy days, he was
the pride of his associates : he stood at their head as an athletic,
and usually won the victory in warmly contested games. In
riper manhood, his strength was vigorously tested in resisting
an attack by an insane man of great muscular power, which occurred on his father's farm on the occasion of one of his visits to
the ancestral home, being suddenly attacked while in the field
near his father's laborers, by the man alluded to. The men
were astonished at the ease with which the Dr. held his assailant,
till he was bound with cords and rendered harmless. There
was a charm of great fascination about Dr. Child. His large
blue eye, beaming with the light of intelligence : his benignant
countenance, and his deep and mellow voice, invested him with
a power to win those who came within the reach of his magnetic
presence. The simplicity of his manners. his graceful and
easy bearing, his sympathetic nature, his abounding good will,
were elements of his power over men. Buoyant, hopeful. rich in

anecdote, he was always a welcome guest among friends and acquaintances. By his personal attractions, he drew to his side such as valued the instructions of a wise and intelligent teacher. His intellectual grasp was of high order. His native powers, which were of no ordinary cast, received a culture which gave him rank among scholars and statesmen.

As a public man, he was admired, honored and trusted: he was without ostentation and undue ambition. To his social nature all ambitious longings were subordinated. Life was much more to him in the quiet circle of appreciative friends, than in the glare of public fame. To serve the Master in humble private homes, in ministration to the sick and bereaved, was far more congenial to his feelings than to receive the adulations of an admiring, popular assembly; and his power to hold the attention of an audience was scarcely excelled. In pulpit oratory, in which he was by no means deficient, there was nothing of the florid and gushing method. Language, simple and direct, conveyed his thoughts to the conscience and the understanding of his audience with great effect. But the social element in Dr. Child was the secret of his success. His free and kindly manner with all classes gave him influence over men, and won to his confidence a large element in the community. Entering, as he readily did, into the sympathies of men in their varied pursuits and experiences, he easily touched the springs of their nature and drew them into sympathy with sentiments of high morality and christian obligation. Among the marked characteristics of Dr. Child, was his love of nature.

But the great work of his profession was paramount. His ministry was a prolonged one, covering a period of more than half a century. The obituary, written by one unknown to us, taken from the *Congregationalist*, briefly sums up the fields of his labors, and pays a just and beautiful tribute to his memory:

Willard Child, D. D., born at Woodstock, Ct., Nov. 14, 1796; graduated at Yale College and Andover Seminary; settled as pastor successively in Pittsford, Vt., Norwich, Ct., Lowel, Mass., and Castleton, Vt; performing subsequently several years' ministerial labor in North Brookfield, Mass., Crown Point and Mooers, N. Y., and dying at the last named place Nov. 13, 1877 (lacking thus but one day of eighty-one years)—such are the chief outward facts of the history of a man affectionately remembered by all to whom he ever ministered in the gospel, or who came within the sphere of his personal acquaintance.

These mere facts give evidence of a long life and a varied and protracted ministry. He graduated from college and seminary at a younger age than is common, and he was able to fulfill some ministerial labor to within comparatively few months of his death. His, therefore, has been a service in our churches which, on the ground of its continuity and extent alone, is worthy of public notice.

But Dr. Child's ministerial service is not to be estimated by its duration only. Its quality was more marked than its continuance. Few, if any, men have brought into our Congregational service a richer nature than his. Whether looked at on its intellectual or emotional side; whether considered in respect to the extent and quality of its cultivation, or its various power to influence and touch other men, his was a spirit of unusual opulence of endowment.

And this large, rich nature was well habited in a singularly pleasing and commanding bodily presence. Indeed, when the present writer looks back twenty-five years, and calls up to his mind the *tout ensemble* of Dr. Child's presence, manner, voice, and substantial utterance, as he then remembers him in the pulpit, he is free to say that the whole was as near perfection as he has ever known.

His felicity of expression, his aptness of quotation, his delicacy of allusion, betrayed a familiarity, quite unusual in even our most cultivated clergy, with the whole range of general literature, and especially its poetic department. He was in truth a poet, without the habit of verse. Yet his preaching wanted nothing of the vigor and manliness more common to natures less refined.

With such qualifications, it is not surprising that Dr. Child should have been a widely admired preacher. Yet unquestionably a wider and more enduring repute would have belonged to him had he been a more ambitious man, and not as easily contented with the satisfactions of friendship and of books as he was. He lacked something of that strenuousness which was necessary to bring out the best possibilities of his reputation.

But to himself, and to his immediate acquaintance, any such loss may well have been made good by the enjoyment given and received in that social intercourse, which was at once a pleasure and a power. Through this channel went out from him not a little portion of his best efficiency in helping others. And by it hundreds who have known him will remember him affectionately and long, as one of the most attractive and inspiring men and ministers they have ever met.

His remains were brought from Mooers to Pittsford, the scene of his earliest ministry, and buried beside those of his earliest friends:

> " Among familiar names to rest,
> And in the places of his youth."

G. L. W.

[Seventh Generation.]   Children:

1015. i. WILLARD A. CHILD, b. in Pittsford, Vt., Sept. 16, 1828, m. March 26, 1863, Emma Knapp.

1016. ii. CEPHUS H. CHILD, b. in Pittsford, Vt., Jan. 17, 1830, d. Aug. 31, 1831.

1017. iii. KATHARINE KENT CHILD, b. in Pittsford, Vt., Feb. 8, 1833, m. Rev. Edward Ashley Walker, March 25, 1863.

1018. iv. FANNIE F. G. CHILD, b. in Pittsford, Vt., Oct. 1, 1838, d. Nov. 23, 1843.

1019. v. CHARLES H. CHILD, b. in Pittsford, Vt., Dec. 20, 1840, d. Nov. 14, 1843.

1020. vi. EMMA JULIETTE CHILD, b. in Pittsford Vt., Jan. 25, 1846, d. Aug. 14, 1847.

[Seventh Generation.]

1015. i. WILLARD A. CHILD. M. D., eldest child of Rev. Dr. Willard and Katharine Kent Child, b. in Pittsford, Vt., Sept. 16, 1828, m. March 26, 1863, Emma Knapp, dau. of Abel Knapp, Esq., of Mooers, Clinton Co., N. Y. Esq. Knapp went to Mooers at an early day and established himself in the mercantile and lumber trade, which he still successfully pursues.

Dr. Willard A. Child was graduated at the Medical College at Castleton, Vt., in 1857, and commenced his practice in the town of Mooers, N. Y., afterwards removed to Pittsford, Vt., his native town. Previous to his medical course he made several sea voyages, one of which was around the world. At the breaking out of the civil war, Dr. W. A. Child was the first in the town of Pittsford, Vt., to enroll for volunteer service in the Union Army. He was immediately appointed assistant surgeon in the 4th Volunteer Regiment of Infantry of Vermont. At the expiration of the three months' service he returned to his home, but soon after went back to the army, and was again appointed assistant surgeon of the 4th Regiment. Shortly after he was promoted to surgeon in the 10th Vol. Reg't, Vt., then to brigadier surgeon, and finally to the post of division surgeon, and served through the entire war. He performed the first surgical operation on the field, which took place at Big Bethel. His army record is a highly honorable one. He was in twenty-eight or twenty-nine battles. After his marriage in 1863, his wife was with him during the greater part of the remaining campaign, rendering sympathy and aid to wounded and dying soldiers. At the close of the war, Dr. W. A. Child resumed his practice in the town of Mooers, N. Y., where he spent the balance of his life. His health was impaired by exposure in the camp, and his days were much shortened in consequence. His professional life was a busy one, and one which secured him flattering regard among his patrons. Dr. W. A. Child was talented and well educated. His opportunities for general knowledge were unusually favorable and well appropriated. He formed intelligent opinions from observation and reading, which made him at home among literary as well as business men. While he possessed the characteristics and qualifications that fitted him for manly duties in his profession and as a citizen, the finer feelings, developed only in the sanctuary of the domestic circle, were not lacking. His love for his revered and aged father prompted the tender ministries which filial affection only can supply. The last years of his father were spent in his family, where he enjoyed the attentions and loving sympathies of a dutiful son, and not less self-sacrificing and cheerful ministrations of a much loved daughter-in-law, whose devotion could not have been more earnest and loving in an own child. It was in his last sickness only that Dr. W. A. Child learned of our enterprise of publishing a Genealogy of the Child Family. In a communication from his surviving companion, which was received soon after his decease, she informed me that her husband expressed much interest in the success of the work, and that it had been his purpose to contribute some incidents and experiences in his own history,--a failure which we sincerely regret.

[Eighth Generation.] Child:

1021. i. EDWARD WILLARD LEVI CHILD, b. in Mooers, Clinton Co., N. Y., Dec. 29, 1863.

[Seventh Generation.]

1017. iii. KATHARINE KENT CHILD, third child and eldest dau. of Rev. Dr. Willard and Katharine Griswold Kent Child, b. in Pittsford, Vt., Feb. 8, 1833, m. March 25, 1863. Rev. Edward Ashley Walker, son of Alfred and Eunice Minor Walker of New Haven, Ct.

Mr. Walker was a clergyman of the Congregational church ; settled in Worcester, Mass., and died of consumption a few years after his settlement. Mrs. Katharine Child Walker is a lady of much talent, of some literary taste and ability, and has written several juvenile books for Sabbath schools, and contributed occasionally articles for the monthlies. She resides in New Haven, Ct.

[Eighth Generation.] Child:

1022. i. ETHEL C. WALKER, b. Feb. 25, 1864.

[Sixth Generation.]

911. vii. LYDIA CHILD, seventh child and fourth dau. of Capt. Willard (by Sylvia) Child, b. in Woodstock, Ct., July 29, 1798, m. Nov. 11, 1821, Erastus May of Woodstock. He was b. Nov. 2, 1796, d. May 3, 1873. She d. Jan. 14, 1871.

[Seventh Generation.] Children:

1023. i. GEORGE M. MAY, b. in Woodstock, Ct., June 14, 1823, d. Jan. 11, 1825.

1024. ii. BETSEY MAY, b. in Woodstock, Ct., Nov. 14, 1825.

1025. iii. EDWARD MAY, b. in Woodstock, Ct., May 23, 1828.

1026. iv. IRVING MAY, b. in Woodstock, Ct., March 27, 1830.

[Sixth Generation.]

912. viii. SYLVIA CHILD, eighth child and fifth dau. of Capt. Willard (by Sylvia) Child, b. in Woodstock, Ct., June 28, 1800, m. Sept. 30, 1824, Elisha C. Walker, son of Capt. Alfred and Betsey Child Walker. He was b. Sept., 1797, d. March 28, 1871. Mrs. Walker died—date not given.

Mr. Walker was a man of earnest and honest purposes, and devoted to every public enterprise looking to the benefit of society; a man of decided temperance principles, and a warm advocate for the abolition of slavery; a man whose aims in life were broad and benevolent—living for others quite as much as for himself.

[Seventh Generation.] Children:

1027. i. HENRY KIRK WALKER, b. Aug. 7, 1827, m. June, 1854, Mary Northrop.

1028. ii. MARY ANN WALKER, b. Aug. 5, 1829, unm., resides with her brother in New Haven, Ct.

1029. iii. ALFRED ASHLEY WALKER, b. Sept. 5, 1831, shot through the chest in the late civil war, at Vicksburg, Miss., May 22, 1863.

1030. iv. JAMES WALKER, b. March 18, 1834, m. Aug. 30, 1864, Martha Johnson.

1031. v. SYLVIA ELIZABETH WALKER, b. May 18, 1837, teacher in Chicago, Ill.

1032. vi. FRANCIS ELISHA WALKER, b. Jan. 22, 1840, m. 1867, Lucy R. Pitney.

[Seventh Generation.]

1027. i. HENRY KIRK WALKER, eldest child of Sylvia Child and Elisha Walker, b. Aug. 27, 1827, m. June, 1854, Mary Northrop. Mr. Walker is a cabinet ware dealer in New Haven, Ct.

[Eighth Generation.]   Children:
   1033. i. ALFRED ELISHA WALKER, b. Aug. 27, 1855.
   1034. ii. MARY NORTHROP WALKER, b. Aug. 31, 1857.
   1035. iii. LIZZIE MAUDE WALKER, b. July 15, 1859.
   1036. iv. HENRY KIRKE WALKER, JR., b. Jan. 16, 1864.
   1037. v. VIOLETTE WALKER, b. Oct. 18, 1871.
   1038. vi. EMILY SMITH WALKER, b. Sept. 28, 1872.

[Seventh Generation.]

   1030. iv. JAMES WALKER, fourth child and third son of Sylvia Child and Elisha Walker. b. March 18, 1834. m. Aug. 30, 1864, Martha Johnson. Mr. Walker is a partner with his brother, Henry Kirk Walker, in the cabinet business. Resides in New Haven, Ct.

[Eighth Generation.]   Children:
   1039. i. EDITH CHILD WALKER. b. July 6, 1865.
   1040. ii. CORNELIA HOWE WALKER, b. June, 1868.
   1041. iii. MARGARET ASHLEY WALKER, b. Sept. 1, 1869.
   1042. iv. ALICE JOHNSON WALKER, b Aug. 13, 1871
   1043. v JAMES WALKER, JR., b. Jan. 25, 1874.
   1044. vi. CURTIS HOWE WALKER, b. 1877.

[Seventh Generation.]

   1032. vi. FRANCIS ELISHA WALKER, sixth child and fourth son of Sylvia Child and Elisha Walker, b. Jan. 22, 1840, m. 1867, Lucy R. Pitney. Mr. Walker is a very energetic and reliable citizen, in Chicago, Ill.: a bridge and car builder.

[Eighth Generation.]   Children:
   1045. i. FRANK ASHLEY WALKER, b. April 8, 1869.
   1046. ii. ERNST LEIGHTON WALKER, b. June 31, 1871.
   1047. iii. AMY WALKER, b. June 1, 1873.

[Sixth Generation.]

   913. ix. CYNTHIA CHILD, ninth child and sixth dau. of Capt. Willard and Sylvia Child, b. in Woodstock. Ct., April 12, 1804, m. Dec. 16, 1828. Trenck May, son of Nehemiah and Nancy Morse May: he was b. in Woodstock, Ct., Oct. 19, 1800, and d. April 27, 1876. As his father before him, Mr. May was an extensive cattle dealer, as well as successful farmer. Boston. Albany and New York were his principal markets. Mrs. Cynthia Child May is the youngest child of Capt. Willard and Sylvia Child, and the last representative in her generation of her father's family. As a mother and friend, she is loved for her affectionate disposition and her gentleness of manners: personally attractive, her charms are crowned with sincere and consistent piety.

[Seventh Generation.] Children:

1048. i. HENRY MAY, b. in Woodstock, Ct., Oct. 13, 1829, m. Ellen D. Child. [Children given in connection with the mother, No. 838.]

1049. ii. SYLVIA CHILD MAY, b. in Woodstock, Ct., Nov. 25, 1831, m. George Morse. They have no children.

1050. iii. WILLARD CHILD MAY, b. in Woodstock, Ct., May 1, 1834, d. July 2, 1840.

1051. iv. ELLEN MAY, b. in Woodstock, Ct., Oct. 4, 1836, m. Rev. Henry Francis Hyde.

1052. v. WILLARD MAY, b. in Woodstock, Ct., Sept. 23, 1840; lives, unm., on the homestead.

1053. vi. MATILDA JANE MAY, b. in Woodstock, Ct., June 21, 1843.

1054. vii. ANNA CYNTHIA MAY, b. in Woodstock, April 15, 1847, m. June 21, 1877, Darius Mathewson Adams, a farmer of Pomfret, Ct.

[Seventh Generation.]

1051. iv. ELLEN MAY, second dau. and fourth child of Cynthia Child and Trenck May, b. in Woodstock, Ct., Oct. 4, 1836, m. about 1862, Rev. Henry Francis Hyde, son of Wm. Henry and Harriet Young Hyde of Brookline, Ct. He graduated from Amherst College, Mass, in 1859, studied Theology in Union Theological Seminary, New York City, and at East Windsor, Ct.; now settled over the Congregational church in Rockville, Tolland county, Conn.

[Eighth Generation.] Children:

1055. i. ARTHUR MAY HYDE, b. Sept. 14, 1864.

1056. ii. ERNEST ALFRED HYDE, b. March 27, 1867, d. Dec., 1867.

1057. iii. CLARA ANNA HYDE, b. Dec. 11, 1868.

1058. iv. MARGARET ELLEN HYDE, b. Dec. 14, 1870.

1059. v. BERTHA CHILD HYDE, b. June 17, 1874.

1060. vi. MABEL HARRIET HYDE, b. Dec. 7, 1877.

[Fifth Generation.]

868. ix. REBECCA CHILD, ninth child and fifth dau. of Henry and Dorothy Child (Dorothy a dau. of Nathaniel Child), b. in Woodstock, Ct., Aug. 26, 1762, m. Nov. 27, 1794, Luther Baldwin.

[Sixth Generation.] Children:

1061. i. DOLLY CHILD BALDWIN, b. Sept. 13, 1795, lives, unm., in North Woodstock, Ct.

1062. ii. HENRY BALDWIN, b. in Woodstock, Ct., Sept. 12, 1797, d. Aug. 15, 1863.

1063. iii. LEVI BALDWIN, b. Jan. 8, 1798, d. Aug. 11, 1870.

1064. iv. SALLY BALDWIN, b. Nov. 26, 1800, unm., resides in North Woodstock, Ct.

1065. v. LUTHER BALDWIN, JR., b. July 14, 1803, d. Oct., 1876.

1066. vi. THOMAS BALDWIN, b. Feb. 25, 1805, d. Aug., 1866.

[Fourth Generation.]

31. v. MEHITABLE CHILD, fifth child and second dau. of
Ephraim and Priscilla Harris Child, b. in Woodstock, Ct., June
8, 1718, m. July 3, 1741, Nehemiah Lyon, b. 1719, in Woodstock, Ct.

[Fifth Generation.]   Children:

1067. i. MARTHA LYON, b. in Woodstock, Ct., 1742, m. Eliakim May.

1068. ii. ELISHA LYON, b. in Woodstock, Ct., 1744, d. 1767, by the accidental discharge of a gun at a military training.

1069. iii. AMASA LYON, b. in Woodstock, Ct., 1745, m. Martha Dana.

1070. iv. AARON LYON, b. in Woodstock, Ct., 1748, m. Elizabeth May;
no children.

1071. v. LEVINA LYON, b in Woodstock, Ct., 1750, m. Peleg Corbin; d.
1788.

1072. vi LYMAN LYON, b in Woodstock, Ct., 1853, m. Hannah Corbin,
1777.

1073. vii. MEHITABLE LYON, b. in Woodstock, Ct., 1758, m. Samuel
Corbin.

[Fifth Generation.]

1067. i. MARTHA LYON, eldest child of Mehitable Child and
Nehemiah Lyon, b. in Woodstock, Ct., 1742, m. Eliakim May,
March, 1770, d. 1815.

[Sixth Generation.]   Children:

1074. i. MARY MAY, b. in Woodstock, Ct., 1772, m. Jerry Sheppard

1075. ii. NEHEMIAH MAY, b. in Woodstock, Ct., 1773, m. Nancy Morse,
dau. of Dr. David Morse of Woodstock, Ct., who removed with his son, David Morse, Jr., to Exeter, Otsego county, N. Y.

1076. iii. MEHITABLE MAY, b in Woodstock, Ct., 1774, m. John Phillips.

1077. iv. ELIAKIM MAY, b. in Woodstock, Ct., 1776, m. Hannah Bradford.

1078. v. EZRA MAY, b. in Woodstock, Ct., 1780, m Chloe Plumb.

1079. vi. AMASA MAY, b. in Woodstock, Ct., 1782, m. Betsey Clark.

[Sixth Generation.]

1074. i. MARY MAY, eldest child of Martha Lyon and Eliakim May, and grandchild of Mehitable Child and Nehemiah
Lyon, b. in Woodstock, Ct., 1772, m. Jerry Sheppard, who settled in Exeter, Otsego county, N. Y.

[Seventh Generation.]   Children:

1080. i. ELISHA SHEPPARD, m. Jerusha Angell of Exeter, N. Y.

1081. ii. MARTHA LYON SHEPPARD, m. Copeland, both dead.

1082. iii. OLIVE SHEPPARD, d. unm.

1083. iv. ELIAKIM SHEPPARD, m. Miss Coates.

1084. v. JERRY SHEPPARD, JR., m. Laura Curtiss, dau. of Agur Curtiss.

1085. vi. DAVID SHEPPARD, m. a Miss Bailey.

1086. vii. MARY SHEPPARD, m. Jos. Robinson.

1087. viii. CAROLINE SHEPPARD, d. unm.

1088. ix. ASA SHEPPARD, m.

1089. x. PARSENIA SHEPPARD, m. a Mr. Richards.

[Sixth Generation.]

1075. ii. NEHEMIAH MAY, eldest son and second child of Martha Lyon and Eliakim May, and grandchild of Mehitable Child Lyon, b. in Woodstock, Ct., 1773, m. Nancy Morse, dau. of Dr. David Morse of Woodstock, Ct.

[Seventh Generation.] Children:

1090. i. DON MAY, b. in Woodstock, Ct., 1799.

1091. ii. TRENCK MAY, b. in Woodstock, Ct., 1800, m, Cynthia Child.

[See general No. 1048.]

1092. iii. PITT MAY, b. in Woodstock, Ct.

1093. iv. MALONA MAY, b. in Woodstock, Ct.

1094. v. MARTHA MAY, b. in Woodstock, Ct.

1095. vi. MATILDA MAY, b. in Woodstock, Ct.

[Sixth Generation.]

1076. iii. MEHITABLE MAY, third child of Martha Lyon and Eliakim May, granddau. of Mehitable Child and Nehemiah Lyon, b. in Woodstock, Ct., 1774, m. 1794, John Phillips, who settled in Exeter, Otsego Co., N. Y., soon after his marriage. He had ten children, two eldest born in Woodstock, Ct., the others were born in Exeter, N. Y. He died in 1843.

[Seventh Generation.] Children:

1096. i. POLLY PHILLIPS, b. in Woodstock, Ct., Aug., 1795, m. 1818, Nathan Tucker.

1097. ii. TEMPA PHILLIPS, b. in Woodstock, Ct., July, 1796, d. unm., in Exeter, 1823.

1098. iii. JOHN PHILLIPS, JR., b. in Exeter, Otsego Co., N. Y., Oct., 1798, m. 1832, Olive Babcock.

1099. iv. EZRA PHILLIPS, b. in Exeter, Otsego Co., N. Y., 1800, d. 1804.

1100. v. CHRISTIANA PHILLIPS, b. in Exeter, Otsego Co., N. Y., 1802, lives in Binghamton, unm.

1101. vi. MANDANA PHILLIPS, b. in Exeter, Otsego Co., N. Y., Dec., 1804, d. July, 1863, unm.

1102. vii. MARIETTA PHILLIPS, b. in Exeter, Otsego Co., N. Y., July, 1807, m. Dr. John C. Gorton.

1103. viii. SETH PHILLIPS, b. in Exeter, Otsego Co., N. Y., 1809, m. 1st, 1834, Mary Carver, 2d, ——.

1104. ix. MARCIA MARIA PHILLIPS, b. in Exeter, Otsego Co., N. Y., March, 1811, m. April, 1832, Edward McKinney.

1105. x. LEVANTIA PHILLIPS, b. in Exeter, N. Y., Nov. 15, 1815, m. Aug., 1849, James Dobbin. He d. ——. She resides in Providence, R. I., with an only child, a son.

[Seventh Generation.]

1096. i. POLLY PHILLIPS, eldest child of Mehitable May and
John Phillips, and great-grandchild of Mehitable Child Lyon,
b. in Woodstock, Ct., Aug., 1795, m. 1818, Nathan Tucker,
who was born in Woodstock, Ct., 1790. Mrs. Tucker died in
Binghamton, N. Y., 1875.

[Eighth Generation.]   Children:

1106. i. CARLOSS TUCKER, b. in Exeter, N. Y., in 1822, is married, (name
not given,) has children: is a practicing physician in New York.

1107. ii. PITT L. TUCKER, b. in Exeter, N. Y., 1836, m. 1860, Cornelia
Stagg of Stratford, Ct.   He is editor of the *Binghamton Daily Republican*.

[Seventh Generation.]

1098. iii. JOHN PHILLIPS, third child and eldest son of Mehitable May and John Phillips, and great grandchild of Mehitable Child Lyon, b. in Exeter, N. Y., Oct., 1798, m. May 22,
1832, Olive Babcock, dau. of Dea. Jonas Babcock of Westford,
N. Y.   She was born May 5, 1805, in Westford, N. Y.   Mr.
Phillips d. in Exeter, Dec. 9, 1861.

Mr. Phillips spent his days in Exeter, living on the old homestead: was an influential and valuable citizen in the town and
county.   He was specially efficient in promoting the interests
of the Presbyterian church, in which he was a respected elder
and deacon for nearly thirty years.   Mrs. Phillips was not less
esteemed for estimable qualities as a mother and neighbor, as
well as for her Christian consistency and fidelity.   Mrs. Phillips
resides in Oneonta, N. Y.

[Eighth Generation.]   Children:

1108. i. WARD IRVING PHILLIPS, b. in Exeter, Otsego Co., N. Y., Sept.
11, 1833.

1109. ii. OWEN PHILLIPS, b in Exeter, Otsego Co., N. Y., April 27, 1837.

1110. iii. JUDITH CAMPBELL PHILLIPS, b. in Exeter, Otsego Co., N Y.,
May 22, 1839, m. April,1872, David Thompson, and resides at Mt. Pleasant,
Iowa.

1111. iv. JULIA ELLEN PHILLIPS, b. in Exeter, N. Y., Nov. 8, 1842.

1112. v AMELIA PHILLIPS, b. in Exeter, N Y., Feb. 6, 1845.

1113. vi. EDWARD PHILLIPS, b. in Exeter, N. Y., July 14, 1847, is a civil
engineer.

1114. vii. ELIZABETH CHESTER PHILLIPS, b. in Exeter, N. Y., Nov. 14,
1849, d. Jan. 29, 1857.

1115. viii. MARY ELLEN PHILLIPS, b. in Exeter, N. Y., Dec. 24, 1851.

[Seventh Generation.]

1102. vii. MARIETTA PHILLIPS, seventh child of Mehitable
May and John Phillips, and great-grandchild of Mehitable Child

Lyon, b. in Exeter, Otsego Co., N. Y., July, 1807, m. Dr. John
C. Gorton, Nov., 1828. She d. Dec., 1842. Dr. Gorton was
for many years a practicing physician in Gilbertsville, Otsego
county, N. Y., and Norwich, Chenango county, N. Y., but subsequently removed to Detroit, Mich.

[Eighth Generation.] Child:

1116. i. HELEN M. GORTON, b. ——, m. Israel Holmes, a lawyer, now in
Chicago, Ill.

[Seventh Generation.]

1103. viii. SETH PHILLIPS, eighth child and third son of
Mehitable May and John Phillips, and great grandchild of Mehitable Child Lyon, b. in Exeter, Otsego Co., N. Y., in 1809, m.
1st, 1834, Mary Carver, 2d, Mrs. Amelia (Bradley) Beebe.

After his first marriage, Mr. Phillips settled at Chenango
Forks, N. Y. Some years afterwards he removed to Exeter,
Otsego Co., N. Y., his native place, and was for many years an
influential citizen in the town, as well as in the county, holding
the office of justice of the peace many years. Since his second
marriage, his home has been in Mt. Upton, Chenango Co., N.Y.

[Eighth Generation.] Children:

1117. i. JOHN PHILLIPS, b. June 5, 1839, m. Feb. 20, 1862, Mary S. Scribner.

1118. ii. HANNAH REBECCA PHILLIPS, b. Jan., 1841, m. Sept., 1868, Andrew P Merchant.

1119. iii. MANDANA AMELIA PHILLIPS, b. Sept., 1843, m. 1861, Alonzo
H. Sumner.

1120. iv. MARIETTA PHILLIPS, b. 1845, m. 1862, Judah Colt.

1121. v. SARAH E. PHILLIPS, b. 1847, m. Dec., 1868, Geo. W. Robinson.

1122. vi. SCEVA PHILLIPS, b. 1849, unm.

1123. vii. WILLIAM HENRY PHILLIPS, b. 1851, unm.

1124. viii. HARRIET ANN PHILLIPS, b. 1853, m. 1878, Franklin Noyes.

[Eighth Generation.]

1117. i. JOHN PHILLIPS, eldest child of Seth and Mary Carver Phillips, b. June 5, 1839, m. Feb. 20, 1862, Mary S. Scribner, dau. of John and Kate Scribner, b. in 1841. Mr. Phillips
resides in Utica, N. Y.: is a carpenter and joiner by trade.

[Ninth Generation.] Children:

1125. i. KATE MARY PHILLIPS, b. July 15, 1866.

1126. ii. JOHN TEFT PHILLIPS, b. May 5, 1879.

[Eighth Generation.]

1118. ii. HANNAH REBECCA PHILLIPS, second child of Seth
Phillips and Mary Carver, b. Jan., 1841, m. Sept., 1868, Andrew P. Merchant.

O

[Ninth Generation.] Child:
    1127. i. PELEG ANDREW MERCHANT, b. Sept., 1870.

[Eighth Generation.]
    1119. iii. MANDANA AMELIA PHILLIPS, third child of Seth and Mary Carver Phillips, b. Sept., 1843, m. 1861, Alonzo H. Sumner, son of Charles Sumner and Martha Lyon Sumner. He resides in Ilion, N. Y.

[Ninth Generation.] Child:
    1128. i. ALBERT E. SUMNER, b. Sept., 1867.

[Eighth Generation.]
    1120. iv. MARIETTA PHILLIPS, fourth child of Seth and Mary Carver Phillips, b. in 1845, m. in 1862, Judah Colt of Exeter, Otsego Co., N. Y.

[Ninth Generation.] Children:
    1129. i. LILLIAN COLT, b. July, 1864.
    1130. ii. NELLIE COLT, b. 1868.
    1131. iii. MARY ANN COLT, b. 1871.

[Seventh Generation.]
    1104. ix. MARCIA MARIA PHILLIPS, ninth child and sixth dau. of Mehitable May and John Phillips, and great grandchild of Mehitable Child Lyon, b. March, 1811, m. April, 1832, Edward McKinney, a merchant. Mr. McKinney died many years since. Mrs. McKinney resides in Binghamton.

[Eighth Generation.] Children:
    1132. i. EDWARD McKINNEY, Jr., a graduate of Yale College, is engaged in mercantile business in Binghamton, N. Y.; is married and has three children; names not given.
    1133. ii. WM. A. McKINNEY, a graduate of Yale College, is a practicing attorney in Binghamton, N. Y.

[Sixth Generation.]
    1078. v. EZRA MAY, fifth child of Martha Lyon and Eliakim May, and grandchild of Mehitable Child and Nehemiah Lyon, b. in Woodstock, Ct., May 8, 1780, m. about 1804 to Chloe Plumb, dau. of Joseph Plumb of New Haven, Ct. They settled in the town of Otsego, Otsego Co., N. Y., at the foot of Schuyler's Lake. This part of the town was afterwards attached to Exeter in Otsego Co., N. Y. Mrs. May died Nov. 24, 1816. Mr. May died Nov. 22, 1826.

[Seventh Generation.] Children:
    1134. i. MARTHA LYON MAY, b. in Otsego, N. Y., May 29, 1806, m. May 25, 1828, Charles Sumner.
    1135. ii. EZRA MAY, Jr., b. in Otsego, N. Y., May 20, 1808, m. Juliette Terry.

1136. iii. CHLOE ANN MAY, b. June 8, 1810, d. 1868, unm.

1137. iv. JENNETTE MAY, b. Oct. 3, 1812, m. Alfred Furman.

1138. v. EARL MAY, b. in Otsego, N. Y., June 6, 1816, d. Oct. 25, 1816.

[Seventh Generation.]

1134. i. MARTHA LYON MAY, eldest child of Ezra and Chloe Plumb May, b. in Otsego, N. Y., May 29, 1806, m. May 25, 1828, Charles Sumner, son of Dea. Moses Sumner of Burlington, Otsego Co., N. Y. Mr. Charles Sumner was b. in 1795, d. March 12, 1872. Mrs. Sumner resides in the village of Mohawk, Herkimer Co., N. Y.

[Eighth Generation.] Children:

1139. i. AMBROSE D. SUMNER, b. in Otsego, N. Y., Sept. 29, 1829, m. Gertrude Van Volkenburg.

1140. ii. ALONZO H. SUMNER, b. Nov 12, 1831, m. 1861, Mandana Phillips.

1141. iii. JULIETTE SUMNER, b. in Otsego, N. Y., March 3, 1834, resides in Mohawk, unm.

1142. iv. GEORGE B. SUMNER, b. in Otsego, N. Y., Sept. 6, 1836, m. Alzin Angell.

1143. v. ERASMUS E. SUMNER, b. in Otsego, N. Y., Aug. 20, 1840, d. Oct. 3, 1868.

[Eighth Generation.]

1139. i. AMBROSE D. SUMNER, eldest child of Martha Lyon May and Charles Sumner, b. in Otsego, N. Y., Sept. 24, 1829, m. 1857, Gertrude Van Volkenburg, dau. of Rev. Daniel Van Volkenburg of Exeter, Otsego Co., N. Y. Mr. Van Volkenburg was for many years the much esteemed pastor of the Presbyterian Church in Exeter, N. Y.

[Ninth Generation.] Children:

1144. i. HELEN NORTON SUMNER, b. Sept., 1858.

1145. ii. WILLIAM SUMNER, b. April, 1860, d. early.

1146. iii. SARA SUMNER, b. April, 1862, d. early.

1147. iv. CHARLES SUMNER, b. April, 1864.

1148. v. JULIA TRACY SUMNER, b. Dec., 1868.

1149. vi. MARY GERTRUDE SUMNER, b. July 8, 1874.

[Eighth Generation.]

1142. iv. GEORGE B. SUMNER, fourth child of Martha Lyon May and Charles Sumner, b. in Otsego, N. Y., 6, 1836, m. March 19, 1866, Alzina Angell, dau. ngell of Exeter, N. Y.

Mr. Angell was a son of one of the   rs of the town of Exeter, N. Y., and like his fathe   ngell, was greatly esteemed as one of the leading citi   t town. The name suggests a curious incident which occurred many years since, in the locality where many of the name resided. It was a marriage between two of the name of remote kinship, and recorded in the *Cooperstown Journal* as follows: " MARRIED—On — inst., on Angell Hill, by Hon. William Angell, Mr. Ira Angell to Miss Lucy Angell, in the presence of seventy Angells."

[Ninth Generation.]   Children:

1150. i. AGNES E. SUMNER, b. Dec. 30, 1862.

1151. ii. ARTHUR M. SUMNER,) twins, { b. April 27, 1870
1152. iii. ANNIE M. SUMNER,   )   ..   "

[Sixth Generation.]

1079. vi. AMASA MAY, sixth child of Martha Lyon and Eliakim May, b. in Woodstock, Ct., 1783, m. about 1810, Betsey Clark of Schuyler's Lake, Otsego Co., N. Y.

[Seventh Generation.]   Children:

1153. i. ELIZA JANE MAY, b. in Otsego, N. Y., May, 1812, m. 1818, Richard Tunniclif of Schuyler's Lake.

1154. ii. ABELARD MAY, b. in Otsego, N. Y., May 6, 1813, m.

[Seventh Generation.]

1154. ii. ABELARD MAY, second child of Amasa May and Martha Lyon, b. May 6, 1813, m.

[Eighth Generation.]   Child:

1155. i. GEORGE A. MAY, keeps a hotel in Boonville, N. Y.

[Fifth Generation.]

1069. iii. AMASA LYON, third child of Mehitable Child and Nehemiah Lyon, b. in Woodstock, Ct., 1745, m. Martha Dana. He died in the Revolutionary War.

[Sixth Generation.]   Children:

1156. i. SALLY LYON, b. in Woodstock, Ct.

1157. ii. JUDAH LYON, b. in Woodstock, Ct., m. Feb. 18, 1802, Mehitable Child, dau. of Dea. Charles Child of East Woodstock.   (For children see No. 1235.)

1158. iii. AMASA LYON, Jr., b. in Woodstock, Ct., 1777, m. a Penniman.

[Sixth Generation.]

1156. i. SALLY LYON, first child of Amasa Lyon and Martha Dana, granddaughter of Mehitable Child (general No. 31), b. in Woodstock, Ct., m. Ebenezer Bishop. She d. 1832.

[Seventh Generation.]   Children:

1158½. i. AMASA BISHOP.

1159. ii. ELISHA BISHOP.

1160. iii. ADALINE BISHOP.

1161. iv. HEZEKIAH BISHOP.

1162. v. TABITHA BISHOP.

1163. vi. EBENEZER BISHOP, Jr.

[Sixth Generation.]

1158. iii. AMASA LYON, Jr., third child of Amasa and Martha Dana Lyon. and grandson of Mehitable Child Lyon, b. 1777. m. 1802, —— Penniman of Woodstock, Ct. He d. 1840.
[Seventh Generation.] Children:
 1164 i. SARAH WINCHESTER LYON, b. in Woodstock, Ct., in 1803.
 1165. ii. AARON M. LYON.
 1166. iii. JESSE P. LYON.
 1167. iv. AMASA P. LYON.

[Fifth Generation.]

1071. v. LEVINA LYON, fifth child of Mehitable Child and Nehemiah Lyon, b. in Woodstock, Ct., 1750. m. 1773, Peleg Corbin. She d. 1778.
[Sixth Generation.] Children:
 1168. i. PATTY CORBIN, b. in Woodstock, Ct., 1774, d. 1844. unm.
 1169. ii. PRISCILLA CORBIN, b. in Woodstock, Ct., 1776, m. Rensselaer Child. (See No. 592.)
 1170. iii. ELIAKIM CORBIN, b. in Woodstock, Ct., 1777, m.
 1171. iv. ICHABOD CORBIN, b in Woodstock, Ct., 1780: had no children.
 1172. v. AARON CORBIN, b. in Woodstock, Ct., 1781, m. Betsey Johnson.
 1173. vi LEVINA CORBIN, b. in Woodstock, Ct , 1786, m. —— Perrin.

[Sixth Generation]

1170. iii. ELIAKIM CORBIN, third child of Levina Lyon and Peleg Corbin, b. in Woodstock, Ct., 1777, m.
[Seventh Generation] Children:
 1174. i. ARIAN CORBIN, m Rev. Amos Hollister.
 1175. ii. ABEL CORBIN.
 1176. iii HORACE CORBIN.
 1177. iv. LEVINA CORBIN.
 1178. v. ELI CORBIN.
 1179. vi. AMANDA CORBIN.

[Sixth Generation.]

1172. v. AARON CORBIN. b. in Woodstock, Ct., 1781, m. Betsey Johnson. Aaron was the fifth child of Levina Lyon and Peleg Corbin, and grandchild of Mehitable Child and Nehemiah Lyon.
[Seventh Generation.] Child:
 1180. i. JOHNSON CORBIN.

[Sixth Generation.]

1173. vi. LEVINA CORBIN, sixth child of Levina Lyon and Peleg Corbin, and grandchild of Mehitable Child and Nehemiah Lyon, b. 1786, m. —— Perrin.
[Seventh Generation.] Child:
 1181. i. POLLY PERRIN.

[Fifth Generation.]

1072. vi. Lyman Lyon, sixth child of Mehitable Child and Nehemiah Lyon, b. in Wooodstock, Ct., 1753, m. 1777, Hannah Corbin; m. 2nd, Nov.. 1801, Philina ——

[Sixth Generation.] Children:

1182. i. Eliakim Lyon, b. in Woodstock. Ct., Nov. 3, 1779, d. June 20, 1856.

1183. ii. Samuel Lyon. b. in Woodstock, Ct., Sept. 17, 1784, d. April 16, 1848.

1184. iii. Nehemiah Lyon, Jr., b. in Woodstock. Ct., Oct. 15, 1786, d. April 4, 1840.

1185. iv. Lyman Lyon, b. in Woodstock. Ct., Aug., 1794, d. April 18, 1860.

1186. v. Mehitable Lyon, b. in Woodstock, Ct., Dec. 25, 1779.

1187. vi. Patty Lyon. b. in Woodstock, Ct., Sept. 17, 1781, d. Sept. 26, 1807.

1188. vii. Hannah Lyon, b. in Woodstock, Ct., Sept. 6, 1789. d. July 3, 1850.

1189. viii. Nancy Lyon. b. in Woodstock. Ct., June 23. 1792.

[By his second wife:]

1190. iv. Willard Lyon, b. in Woodstock. Ct., Aug. 9, 1802. Mrs. Lyon, d. 1805.

[Fourth Generation.]

32. vi. Mary Child, sixth child of Ephraim and Priscilla Harris Child, b. in Woodstock, Ct., April 12, 1711, m. June 16, 1747, Stephen May, of Woodstock. Ct. He was b. Nov. 10, 1721.

[Fifth Generation.] Children:

1191. i. Elizabeth May, b. in Woodstock, Ct., Nov. 10, 1748, m. 1770, Deac. Aaron Lyon, son of Nehemiah Lyon and Mehitable Child.

1192. ii. Lucy May, b. in Woodstock, Ct., 1750, d. unmarried.

1193. iii. Molly (Mary) May, b. in Woodstock, Ct., Aug. 25, 1752, m. Alpha Child, son of Nathaniel Child. (Alpha was the father of Darius Griffin and Spencer Child. (See 1193 repeated.)

1194. iv. Stephen May, Jr., b. May 23, 1755, in Woodstock. Ct., m. —— Lived in Fairlee, Vt.; left a family.

1195. v. Joanna May, b. Feb. 8, 1757, d. unmarried.

1196. vi. Ephraim May, b. Nov. 22, 1759, m. Abigail Chandler.

1197. vii. Sarah May, b. Nov. 30, 1761, m. Col. Chester Child, of North Woodstock, Ct.

1198. viii. Asa May, b. in Woodstock. Ct., Sept. 4, 1764. Lived in Fairlee, Vt.

[Fifth Generation.]

1196. vi. Ephraim May, sixth child of Mary Child and Stephen May, b. in Woodstock, Ct., Nov. 22, 1759, m. Abigail Chandler, about 1790.

[Sixth Generation.] Children:

1199. i. HENRIETTA MAY, b. in Woodstock. Ct., Nov. 18, 1791. m. Henry Child. (See his general No., 908.)

1200. ii. ASA MAY. b. in Woodstock, Ct., Aug. 24, 1793. m. Sally May, dau. of John May.

1201 iii. STEPHEN MAY, b. in Woodstock, Ct., 1796, d. 1800.

1202. iv. SETH MAY, b. in Woodstock, Ct., 1798, d. 1801.

1203. v. ELIZABETH MAY, b. in Woodstock, Ct., 1800, m. Elias Mason.

1204. vi. MARY MAY. b. in Woodstock, Ct., 1803.

1205. vii. JULIA ANNA MAY, b. in Woodstock, Ct., 1809. d. 1832. umm.

[Sixth Generation.]

1200. ii. ASA MAY, second child of Ephraim and Abigail Chandler May, and grandson of Mary Child and Stephen May, b. in Woodstock. Ct., Aug. 24, 1793, m. about 1820, Sally May, dau. of John and Sally May.

[Seventh Generation.] Children:

1206. i. ELIZABETH MAY, b. in Woodstock, Ct., July 10, 1821. m. Erasmus Rawson: had no children.

1207. ii CHARLES HARRIS MAY, b. in Woodstock, Ct., Sept. 2, 1823. m. Harriet F. Child. (For children of Harris May, see No. 827.)

1208. iii. EZRA C. MAY, b. in Woodstock, Ct., Oct. 13, 1825, m. Abbey E. Chandler. She died leaving no children.

1209. iv. CARLO MAY, b. in Woodstock, Ct., Sept. 3, 1839, m. March 23, 1853, Sarah M. Child, dau. of Dea. Wm. Child, of East Woodstock, Ct. (For children, see under Dea. William Child.)

[Sixth Generation.]

1203. v. ELIZABETH MAY, fifth child of Ephraim and Abigail Chandler May, b. in 1800, in Woodstock, Ct., m. 1824, Elias Mason.

[Seventh Generation.] Children:

1210. i. LUCY MASON, b. in Woodstock, Ct., in 1825, m. Augustus Mason, d. 1848.

1211. ii. ABBEY C. MASON, b. in Woodstock, Ct., 1829.

[Fourth Generation.]

34. viii. Capt. ELISHA CHILD, eighth child and fourth son of Ephraim and Priscilla Harris Child, b. in Woodstock, Ct., Feb. 11. 1725, m. Jan. 6, 1750, Alice Manning, who was born 1728, d. 1798. He d. Nov. 22. 1796.

Captain Elisha Child was a man of strong character and much intelligence, and was everywhere prominent in affairs of town, state and church. A man of quick perceptions, cool and accurate judgment. withal of that kindly spirit which wins and retains firm friendship. His abilities found ready recognition, and he held various offices of responsibility and honor most creditable to himself and fellow citizens. Capt. Child represented the town of Woodstock in the General Court of the Colony of Connecticut for several terms. The patriotic enthusiasm of the people of this town, kindled with the first watch-fires of the revolution.

"At a very full meeting of the inhabitants of the town of Woodstock, legally warned and held at said Woodstock, on the 21st day of June, A. D. 1774, Nathaniel Child, Esq., was chosen Moderator. The resolves of the House of Representatives were presented by a committee of this corporated body, for their consenting to and voting the above resolves, in conjunction with the other representatives of this Colony, in General Court assembled. As said resolves do honor to the worthy representatives of a free, loyal and virtuous people, are very expressive of the sentiments of the inhabitants of this town, and by them judged necessary in such a day as this, when we have the most convincing proofs of a fixed and determined plan of the British administration, to overthrow the liberties of America and subject these colonies to a bondage that our father's did not, would not,—and fled into the wilderness that they might not—and God grant that we, their posterity, never may—bear.

2ndly. Being animated from the consideration of the absolute importance of adopting every rational and probable means in our power for the political salvation of our country, we engage to contribute our utmost exertions in defence of our American liberties and privileges, and stand ready to join our brethren in this and the other American colonies in every possible measure that may influence Great Britian to withdraw her oppressive hand; at the same time we apprehend that a General Congress consisting of delegates from each colony on the Continent is necessary, speedily to be formed that the sentiments of the whole may be known and such an unity in measures be established as may constitute a strength invincible by tyranny, and break out in one general burst against the attempts that are made and making to destroy the Constitution of these Governments.

3rdly. And inasmuch as the promotion of industry, frugality, economy, arts and manufactures among ourselves is of great importance to the good of a community, we determine from this very day to live as much within ourselves, and purchase as few British goods, wares, and merchandises as possible, and give all due encouragement to every useful art among us.

4thly. It having been judged needful at this alarming crisis, and generally come into, that committees of correspondence be appointed, etc., etc, voted that Capt. Elisha Child, Charles C. Chandler, Jedediah Morse, Esq., Capt. Samuel McLellan, and Nathaniel Child, Esq., be a committee for maintaining a correspondence with the towns of this and the neighboring colonies.

5thly. Voted, that a copy of these votes be printed in the *New London Gazette*, to manifest the deep sense we have of the parliamentary invasion of the constitutional rights of British America.

(A true copy,)

Attest. ELISHA CHILD, *Town Clerk.*

On the requisition of the Contenental Congress, troops were raised in all the colonies. Connecticut was prompt to furnish her quota. Capt. Elisha Child was placed in command of one of the first companies organized. On the news reaching Connecticut of the rencontre at Lexington, Mass., Woodstock sent several companies, one under Capt. Child, also one under Capt. Benjamin Lyon, one under Capt. E. Manning, one under Capt. Daniel Lyon, and a troop of horse under command of Capt. Samuel McLellan.

We first find Capt. Elisha Child recorded as a member of the General Court in the Session of 1775, when Jonathan Trumbull was Governor, and Mathew Griswold Lient. Governor. During this Session. "Capt. Elisha Child, Col. Samuel Chapman, Capt. Henry Allyn, Joseph Hopkins, and Mr. Isaac Doolittle were appointed a committee severally or in conjunction, to search after lead mines in the colony, and directed to inform the Governor if any were discovered, that the Governor might inform the Continental Congress in the summer session of 1776."

At the same meeting of the General Court, we find Capt. Child and others were added to a committee previously appointed "to procure fire-arms, and gun locks to supply the State Militia in the war."

[Fifth Generation.] Children:

1212. i. CHARLES CHILD, b. in Woodstock, Ct., then Muddy Brook Parish, now East Woodstock, Sept. 15, 1750, d. young.

1213. ii. CHARLES CHILD, 2d, b. in East Woodstock,Ct., Nov. 22, 1751, m. April 13, 1777, Eliza May.

1214. iii. ALICE CHILD, b. in Woodstock, Ct., Nov. 11, 1753, d. Oct. 25, 1756.

1215. iv. CAPT. ELIAS CHILD, b. in Woodstock, Ct., Dec. 28, 1755, m 1st, March 18, 1779, Dorothea Morse, dau. of Dr. Parker Morse; m. 2nd, Mar. 18, 1790, Sophia Morse, dau. of Dr. David Morse.

1216. v. THOMPSON CHILD, b. in Woodstock, Ct., Feb. 12, 1758, d. May 12, 1760.

1217. vi. ALICE CHILD, 2nd, b. in Woodstock, Ct., June 15, 1760, d. Nov. 1, 1781.

1218. vii. SYLVIA CHILD, b. in Woodstock, Ct., Oct. 31, 1762, m. May 7, 1795, Capt. Willard Child. For her children, see Capt. Willard, No. 865.

1219. viii. BETSEY CHILD, b. in Woodstock, Ct., Dec. 23, 1764, d. early.

1220. ix. CHLOE CHILD, b. in Woodstock, Ct., March 28, 1767, m. March 3, 1790, Leonard Walker.

1221. x. PRISCILLA CHILD, b. in Woodstock, Ct., Nov. 19, 1769, d. Oct. 3, 1775.

1222. xi. BETSEY CHILD, 2nd, b. in Woodstock, Ct., 1773, m. Feb. 21, 1797, Alfred Walker.

1223. xii. A daughter: name not given.

[Fifth Generation.]

1213. ii. Dea. CHARLES CHILD, son of Capt. Elisha and Alice Manning Child, b. in Woodstock, Ct., Nov. 22, 1751, m. April 13, 1777, Eliza May. She was b. 1756, d. 1838, in Woodstock, Ct. She was the daughter of Caleb May, of Woodstock.

Dea. Charles Child marks an era in family descent as the inheritor of the homestead of two preceding generations. He was a man of fine appearance in his prime, and in old age the stamp of youth had not altogether disappeared. He was a staid and substantial citizen : a worthy deacon in the Congregational church. Social, hospitable and benevolent. His descendants are numerous, and occupying honorable positions in various callings in life.

[Sixth Generation.]   Children:

1224. i. MEHITABLE CHILD, b. in Woodstock, Ct., Aug. 22, 1779, m. Feb. 18, 1802, Capt. Judah Lyon, of Woodstock, Ct.

1225. ii. CALEB CHILD, b. in Woodstock, Ct., Sept 30, 1781, d. June 11, 1853, unmarried.

1226. iii. ALICE CHILD, b. in Woodstock, Ct., Oct. 21, 1783, m. Oct. 16, 1806, George Potter, of Woodstock.

1227. iv. HANNAH MAY CHILD, b. in Woodstock, Ct., April 29, 1786, d. in 1817, unmarried.

1229. v. SALLY SUMNER CHILD, b. in Woodstock, Ct., March 9, 1787, d. Jan. 11, 1792.

1229½ vi. JOHN CHILD, b. in Woodstock, Ct., 1789, m. Sept 11, 1831, Alice Manning Walker.

1230. vii. CHARLES CHILD, JR., b. in Woodstock, Ct., 1791, m. March 20, 1817, Almira Holmes.

1231. viii. ELIZA CHILD, b. in Woodstock, Ct., May 24, 1793, m. April 23, 1863, Rensselaer Coombs.

1232. ix. SALLY SUMNER CHILD, 2nd, b. in Woodstock, Ct., Aug. 19, 1795, d. July 20, 1859, unmarried.

1233. x. ELIAS CHILD, b. in Woodstock, Ct., Oct. 30, 1797, m. April 19, 1827, Sophronia Meacham.

1234. xi. ABIEL CHILD, b. in Woodstock, Ct., Nov. 6, 1799, m. Feb. 18, 1831, Henrietta Hall.

[Sixth Generation.]

1224. i. MEHITABLE CHILD, eldest child of Dea. Charles and Eliza May Child, b. Aug. 22, 1779, in East Woodstock, Ct., m. Feb. 18, 1802, Judah Lyon, son of Amasa and Martha Dana

Lyon of Woodstock, Ct., and grandson of Mehitable Child, who
m. Nehemiah Lyon.

[Seventh Generation.] Children:

1235. i. ELISHA LYON, b. in Woodstock, Ct., 1803, m. Lucy May, 1832.

1236. ii. ELIZA LYON, b. in Woodstock, Ct., 1804, m. Dr. Witter.

1237. iii. MARTHA D. LYON, b. in Woodstock, Ct., 1806, m. —— Bishop.

1238. iv. MEHITABLE LYON, b. in Woodstock, Ct., 1810, m. Anson Fowler.
She died early, and left no children.

[Seventh Generation.]

1235. i. ELISHA LYON, eldest child of Mehitable Child and
Judah Lyon, m. 1st, Lucy May, 1832. She d. soon after the
birth of her only child, and Mr. Lyon m. 2d, Rebecca Rice.

[Eighth Generation.] Children:

(By first marriage.)

1239. i. ELISHA MAY LYON, b. May 11, 1839, m. Oct. 3, 1872, Charlotte
W. Day; had no children.

(By second marriage.)

1240. ii. LUCY MAY LYON, b. in Woodstock, Ct., May 5, 1842, m. Dec. 7,
1865, Geo. P. Whitney.

1241. iii. ABBIE LYON, b. in Woodstock, Ct., Jan. 5, 1844, d. young.

1242. iv. CHARLES E. LYON, b. in Woodstock, Ct., Feb. 28, 1845, m. Mar.
9, 1868, Mary M. Spaulding.

1243. v. OLIVER P. LYON, b. in Woodstock, Ct., March 3, 1847, m. Dec. 2,
1874, Ellen M. Spaulding.

1244. vi. WILLIAM P. LYON, b. in Woodstock, Ct., Oct. 19, 1852, unm.

1245. vii. SARAH E. LYON, b. in Woodstock, Ct., April 25, 1854, m. Nov.
18, 1874, John B. Morse.

1246. viii. HATTIE E. LYON, b. in Woodstock, Ct., Sept. 14, 1855, unm.

[Eighth Generation.]

1240. ii. LUCY MAY LYON, second child of Elisha Lyon
and Rebecca Rice, b. in Woodstock, Ct., June 5, 1842, m. Dec.
7, 1865, Geo. P. Whitney.

[Ninth Generation.] Child:

1247. i. ERNEST W. WHITNEY, b. Aug. 11, 1877.

[Eighth Generation.]

1242. iv. CHARLES E. LYON, fourth child and second son of
Elisha and Rebecca Rice Lyon, b. Feb. 28, 1845, m. March 9,
1868, Mary M. Spaulding.

[Ninth Generation.] Child:

1248. i. EDWARD SUMNER LYON, b. Feb. 21, 1874.

[Eighth Generation.]

1243. v. OLIVER P. LYON, fifth child and third son of Elisha
and Rebecca Spaulding Lyon, b. March 3, 1847, m. Ellen W.
Spaulding, Dec., 1874.

[Ninth Generation.] Child:
    1249. i. Mabel R. Lyon, b. March 26, 1877.

[Eighth Generation.]

    1245. vii. Sarah E. Lyon, sixth child of Elisha and Rebecca Rice Lyon, b. April 25, 1854, m. Nov. 18, 1874, John B. Morse.
[Ninth Generation.] Child:
    1250. i. Josie E. Morse, b. March 19, 1876.

[Seventh Generation.]

    1236. ii. Eliza Lyon, second child of Mehitable Child and Judah Lyon, and granddaughter of Dea. Charles Child, b. in Woodstock, Ct., 1814, m. 1827, Dr. Asa Witter of Woodstock, Ct., who settled in East Woodstock, Ct., as physician and surgeon, and gained much reputation for his skill as a practitioner. He was highly esteemed and greatly beloved by citizens of Woodstock and vicinity. Mrs Alice W. Child of East Woodstock, Ct., says in one of her many helpful letters to us, "Doctor Asa Witter was our physician here in East Woodstock for a good many years, very much beloved. Three of his sons are physicians and men of character, viz., John, Ebenezer, and Wilber Fisk Witter, men of ability in their profession, and highly esteemed as citizens in their respective communities."
[Eighth Generation.] Children:
    1251. i. John Witter, b. in Woodstock, Ct., Dec. 31, 1831, m. Mary E. Paine.
    1252. ii. Judah L. Witter, b. in Woodstock, Ct., 1833, m. Ruth Richardson.
    1253. iii. Martha Jane Witter, b. in Woodstock, Ct., 1837, unm.
    1254. iv. Ebenezer Witter, b. in Woodstock, Ct , 1839, m. Ellen S. Wright.
    1255. v. Asa Witter, Jr., b. in Woodstock, Ct., 1846.
    1256. vi. Wilber Fisk Witter, b. in Woodstock, Ct., 1849.

[Eighth Generation.]

    1251. i. John Witter, M. D., eldest child of Dr. Asa Witter and Eliza Lyon, b. 1831, m. April 13, 1856, Mary E. Paine ; she was b. 1835. He is a physician, settled in Putnam, Ct.
[Ninth Generation.] Children:
    1257. i. Wm. Paine Witter, b. July 23, 1858.
    1258 ii. Frank E. Witter, b. May 21, 1861.
    1259. iii. Mary Agnes Witter, b. Feb. 26, 1863.
    1260. iv. Eliza Lyon Witter, b. March 9, 1865.   } Twins.
    1261. v. Abbie Ricard Witter, b. Mar. 9, 1865, d. Sept. 17. 1867. }
    1262. vi. Henry Paine Witter, b. Aug. 29, 1869.

[Eighth Generation.]

1252. ii. JUDAH L. WITTER, second child of Dr. Asa Witter and Eliza Lyon, b. in Woodstock, 1833, m. Ruth Richardson, 1864.

[Ninth Generation.] Children:
1263. i. WENDELL WITTER, b. 1867.
1264. ii. FRANK WITTER, b. 1869.
1265. iii. GRACIE WITTER, b. 1874.

[Eighth Generation.]

1254. iv. EBENEZER WITTER, M. D., fourth child and third son of Dr. Asa Witter and Eliza Lyon, b. 1839, m. 1867, Ellen S. Wright. Is a physician, and settled in Sturbridge, Mass.

[Ninth Generation.] Child:
1266. i. NELLIE WITTER, b. 1868.

[Eighth Generation.]

1256. vi. WILBER FISK WITTER, M. D., sixth child and fourth son of Dr. Asa Witter and Eliza Lyon, b. in Woodstock, Ct., 1849, m. 1874, Sally Hooker. They have two children— no names given. Dr. Wilber F. Witter resides in Brookfield, Mass.

[Seventh Generation.]

1237. iii. MARTHA D. LYON, dau. and third child of Mehitable Child and Judah Lyon, b. in Woodstock, Ct., 1806, m. Hezekiah Bishop, son of Dr. Ebenezer Bishop and Sarah Lyon. Dr. Bishop settled in East Woodstock in 1800, or before, and was practicing when Dr. Witter entered upon the profession in the same parish, in 1825 or 6. Mrs. Bishop d. Dec. 23, 1877.

[Eighth Generation.] Children:
1267. i. SARAH BISHOP, b. in Woodstock, Ct., 1839.
1268. ii. EBENEZER BISHOP, b. in Woodstock, Ct., 1841.
1269. iii. ANNA BISHOP, b. in Woodstock, Ct., 1844.
1270. iv. ESTHER BISHOP, b. in Woodstock, Ct., 1845.
1271. v. MARTHA H. BISHOP, b. in Woodstock, Ct., 1850.

[Sixth Generation.]

1226. iii. ALICE CHILD, third child and second dau. of Dea. Charles and Eliza May Child, b. in Woodstock, Ct., Oct. 21, 1783, m. Oct. 6, 1806, Geo. Potter of Woodstock. She d. 1878, in her 95th year. He d. 1816.

[Seventh Generation.] Children:
1272. i. STEPHEN L. POTTER, b. in Woodstock, Ct., 1808, m. Sarah C. Morse.
1273. ii. BENJAMIN POTTER, b. in Woodstock, Ct., 1810, m. Mary Chamberlain.

1274. iii. CHARLES C. POTTER, b. in Woodstock, Ct., 1812.
1275. iv. GEORGE POTTER, b. in Woodstock, Ct., 1814, d. 1836.
1276. v. RHODES W. POTTER, b. in Woodstock, Ct., 1816, d. 1836.

[Seventh Generation.]

1272. i. STEPHEN L. POTTER, eldest child of Alice Child and Geo. Potter, b. in Woodstock, Ct., 1808, m. Sarah C. Morse.
[Eighth Generation.] Children:
1277. 1. GEORGE M. POTTER, b. 1836, m.   Lives in Minnesota.
1278. ii. WM. RHODES POTTER, b. 1837, d. in the U. S. service, 1863, in the War of the Rebellion.
1279. iii. MARY E. POTTER, b. in 1838.
1280. iv. ALBERT E. POTTER, b. 1839, m. Mary E. Sumner, 1869.
1281. v. CHARLES H. POTTER, b. 1842, m.; no children; served in U. S. army in late rebellion; lives in Nebraska.
1282. vi. S. DWIGHT POTTER, b. 1844, d. 1874.
1283. vii. CALEB C. POTTER, b. 1846, m. Isadore Brown; no children; lives in Fall River, Mass.
1284. viii. SARAH ALICE POTTER, b. 1848, d. 1867.
1285. ix. HENRY J. POTTER, b. 1850.
1286. x. NEWTON R. POTTER, b. 1853.

[Seventh Generation.]

1273. ii. BENJAMIN POTTER, second child and second son of Alice Child and George Potter, b. in Woodstock, Ct., 1810, m. Mary Chamberlain.
[Eighth Generation.] Children:
1287. i. MARY E. POTTER.
1288. ii. ELISHA POTTER, m. lives in N. Y. City.
1289. iii. CYRUS D. POTTER, m. Emma Dean.
1290. iv. FRANK POTTER, is a clergyman.
1291. v. HARRIS POTTER.
1292. vi. MILTON POTTER, lives in Chicago.
1293. vii. CHARLES H. POTTER.

[Seventh Generation.]

1274. iii. CHARLES C. POTTER, son of Alice Child and Geo. Potter, b. in Woodstock, Ct., 1812, m. 1838, Maria Walker. She d. 1843.
[Eighth Generation.] Child:
1294. i. MARIA ELIZABETH POTTER, b. 1842.

[Eighth Generation.]

1280. iv. ALBERT E. POTTER, son of Stephen L. and Sarah C. Morse, b. 1839, m. Mary Elizabeth Sumner, 1869.
[Ninth Generation.] Children:
1295. i. GEO. SUMNER POTTER, b. 1870.
1296. ii. SARAH ALICE POTTER, b. 1874.

[Sixth Generation.]

1229. vi. JOHN CHILD, sixth child and second son of Dea. Charles and Eliza May Child, b. in East Woodstock, Ct., 1789, m. Sept. 11, 1831, Alice Manning Walker, dau. of Leonard and Chloe Child Walker of Stafford, Vt. Mrs. C. was b. in Stafford, Vt., Nov. 23, 1791.

Mr. Child has been a successful farmer in this parish for many years—a citizen esteemed for his probity of character—of clear and discriminating judgment in all practical matters, whose influence has always been found on the side of right ; an early and persistent supporter of the temperance reform. His patriotism placed him in the foremost ranks of his country's helpers when threatened with domestic invasion : and without a murmur he surrendered to the uncertainties and dangers of warfare, the son on whom he was relying for support in his waning years. Ninety years of life have been given him, not in vain.

Mrs. Child, inheriting the characteristics of parents remarkable for intellectual strength and physical vigor, to which are added excellent qualities of heart not less inherited, of pleasing and commanding personal appearance, lives in the midst of a large domestic circle, a central figure, surrounded by children and grandchildren, ministering in kind and motherly offices to all around her. Our recognition of her as a cheerful and efficient helper in our work, is noticed elsewhere. They reside in East Woodstock, Ct.—Mr. Child in his 91st year, and Mrs. Child in her 89th year.

[Seventh Generation.] Children :

1297. i. JOHN SPENCER CHILD, b. in Woodstock, Ct., Sept. 30, 1833, m. 1859, Lydia Lyon.

1298. ii. GEO. WALKER CHILD, b. in Woodstock, Ct., Dec. 1836, m. Dec. 18, 1861, Martha Agnes Child, dau. of Erastus and Rhoda Ricard Child of Woodstock, Ct.

[Seventh Generation.]

1297. i. JOHN SPENCER CHILD, eldest child of John and Alice Manning Walker Child, b. in Woodstock, Ct., Sept. 30, 1833, m. 1858, Lydia Lyon. Mr. Child resides in Rockford, Iowa.

[Eighth Generation.] Children :

1299. i. HARRIS MANNING CHILD, b. in Woodstock, Ct., June 24, 1859.

1300. ii. ALICE SABRA CHILD, b. in Woodstock, Ct., June 15, 1861.

1301. iii. MARY LYON CHILD, b. in Woodstock, Ct., Jan. 19, 1864.

1302. iv. ANNA GERTRUDE CHILD, b. in Woodstock, Ct., Aug. 22, 1867.

1303. v. LEONARD WALKER CHILD, b. in Woodstock, Ct., Sept. 29, 1874.

[Seventh Generation.]

1298. ii. GEORGE WALKER CHILD, second child of John and Alice Manning Walker Child, b. in Woodstock, Ct., Dec. 18, 1836, m. Dec. 18, 1861, Martha Agnes Child, dau. of Erastus and Rhoda Ricard Child of Woodstock, Ct.

Capt. George W. Child had the honor of serving his country in the Union army in the late war of the rebellion. He raised a company of infantry in his native place, over which he was appointed captain. He was in several engagements and showed himself worthy of his honors. He came out unharmed and returned at the close of the war to his home and his farm, which he found quite as congenial as the strife of battles.

[Eighth Generation.] Children:

1304. i. JOHN ERASTUS CHILD, b. in Woodstock. Ct., July 5, 1868.

1305. ii. ALICE RHODA CHILD, b. in Woodstock, Ct., Aug. 7, 1870.

1306. iii. AGNES CHILD, b. in Woodstock, Ct., April 11, 1874.

[Sixth Generation.]

1230. vii. CHARLES CHILD, third son and seventh child of Dea. Charles and Elizabeth May Child of Woodstock, Ct., b. in Woodstock, Ct., 1791, m. March 20, 1817, Almira Holmes, cousin of Oliver Wendell Holmes, the poet physician of Cambridge, Mass.

Mr. Child was a thrifty and skillful farmer in East Woodstock, Ct. In stature he was six feet, and of stalwart frame, with somewhat florid complexion; a man of correct and sober habits. Like many of his kinsmen bearing the Child name, he was tenacious of his own opinions, acting from his own convictions rather than upon the opinions of others, a trait of character to be commended when based upon enlightened views; never yielding a point to please one differing from him in opinions. Such an one must necessarily make his way through the world by warm encounters with opponents, but with the approval of friends.

[Seventh Generation.] Children:

1307. i. LEONARD HOLMES CHILD. b. in Woodstock, Ct., April 24, 1818, d. May 1, 1819.

1308. ii. ABIEL CHILD, b. in Woodstock, Ct., May 28, 1820, d. young.

1309. iii. SARAH TEMPERANCE CHILD, b. in Woodstock, Ct., Dec. 8, 1822, d. young.

1310. iv. MARY ELIZABETH CHILD, b. in Woodstock, Ct., July 25, 1826, m. Feb. 25, 1851, John Bacon Healy, son of Jedediah and Abigail Bacon Healy of Brimfield, Mass. Mr. Healy is a farmer. They have no children.

1311. v. SARAH LUCINDA CHILD, b. in Woodstock, Ct., May 14, 1829, m. Feb. 28, 1851, Amasa Child, son of Capt. Aaron Child of Woodstock, Ct. For children see No. 901.

1312. vi. HANNAH ALMIRA CHILD, b. in Woodstock, Ct., Feb 28, 1831, m. April 15, 1851, Edward Killam.

1313. vii. EMMA MARIAH CHILD, b. in Woodstock, Ct., June 23, 1833, m. Dec. 18, 1867, Geo. Child Phillips.

1314. viii. SUSAN ELLEN CHILD, b. in Woodstock, Ct., April 4, 1836, unm.

1315. ix. ANNETTE MATILDA CHILD, b. in Woodstock, Ct., Nov. 8, 1838, m. May 10, 1865, Samuel Gildersleeve, of New York City.

[Seventh Generation.]

1312. vi. HANNAH ALMIRA CHILD, sixth child and fourth dau. of Charles and Almira Holmes Child. b. in Woodstock, Ct., Feb. 28, 1831, m. April 15, 1851, Edward Killam. Mrs. Killam died Dec. 10, 1872.

[Eighth Generation.] Children:
1316. i. CHARLES HENRY KILLAM, b. March 19, 1852, m. March 19, 1878.
1317. ii. JULIA ELIZABETH KILLAM, b. Dec. 26, 1854, unm.

[Seventh Generation.]

1313. vii. EMMA MARIAH CHILD, seventh child and fifth dau. of Charles and Almira Holmes Child, b. in Woodstock, Ct., June 23, 1833, m. Dec. 18, 1867, by Rev. D. G. Ashley, George Child Phillips, son of Jeremiah and Zuriah Phillips, he was b. 4th April, 1836. Removed to West Woodstock, Jan., 1873.

[Eighth Generation.] Children:
1318. i. GEORGE CHILD PHILLIPS, Jr., b. March 15, 1873.
1319. ii. ANNETTE ZURIAH PHILLIPS, b. Feb. 15, 1875.

[Seventh Generation.]

1315. ix. ANNETTE MATILDA CHILD, seventh dau. and youngest child of Charles and Almira Holmes Child, b. in Woodstock, Ct., Nov. 8, 1838, m. May 10, 1865, by Rev. S. Bourne, Samuel Gildersleeve of New York City. Mr. and Mrs. Gildersleeve are connected with the House of Refuge in New York City.

[Eighth Generation.] Children:
1320. i. CHARLES CHILD GILDERSLEEVE, b. in Northport, Long Island, N. Y., April 28, 1866.
1321. ii. SUSIE ALMIRA GILDERSLEEVE, b. in Northport, Long Island, N. Y., March 26, 1869.

P

[Sixth Generation.]

1233. x. ELIAS CHILD, tenth child and fourth son of Dea. Charles and Eliza May Child, b. in Woodstock, Ct., Oct. 30, 1797, m. April 19, 1827, Sophronia Meacham. She d. Jan. 31, 1875. Mr. Child d. Oct. 20, 1879.

Mr. Child was the successor of his father, Dea. Charles Child, to the ownership of the old homestead, the fourth generation from the original owner, Ephraim Child, who came from Roxbury, Mass., to Woodstock about 1710. Mr. Elias Child belonged to the old school class of men, who feel that the former days are better than the present, and he was not easily drawn into any reforms or changes of the present day. He was a laborious and thrifty farmer when in his prime, and left a handsome property to his only child, John H. Child, who succeeds to the ownership of the old homestead, now in possession of the fifth generation from Ephraim Child, the first occupant.

[Seventh Generation.] Child:

1322. i. JOHN HOLBROOK CHILD, b. in East Woodstock, Ct., April 3, 1830, m. 1st, April 30, 1851, Julia Sanger. She d. Aug. 1879. He m. 2d, March 29, 1880, Ruth Witter.

[Eighth Generation.] Children:

1323. i. JENNIE E. CHILD, b. in East Woodstock, Ct., 1860, m. Aug. 20, 1879, Henry Pratt.

1324. ii. JOHN FRANK CHILD, b. in East Woodstock. Ct., 1863.

[Sixth Generation.]

1234. xi. ABIEL CHILD, eleventh child and fifth son of Dea. Charles and Eliza May Child, b. in Woodstock. Ct., Nov. 6, 1799, m. Feb. 18, 1826 or 1827, Henrietta Hale. He d. July 4, 1859.

[Seventh Generation.] Children:

1325. i. HANNAH ELIZABETH CHILD, b. April 1, 1828, m. Jerome Pomeroy.

1326. ii CHARLES DICKERMAN CHILD, b. June 29, 1830, m. 1st Cornelia Munson, 2d, Emily Jones.

1327. iii. CALEB HARRIS CHILD, b. May 25, 1834, m. May 22, 1861, Emily M. Robbins.

1328. iv. DELLA H. CHILD, b. in Suffield, Ct., Oct. 26, 1848, m. Oct. 19, 1869, Samuel T. Buel.

[Seventh Generation.]

1325. i. HANNAH ELIZABETH CHILD, eldest child of Abiel and Henrietta Hale Child, b. April 1, 1828, m. June 2, 1852, Jerome Pomeroy. Residence, Brooklyn, N. Y.

[Eighth Generation.] Children:

    1329. i. HENRIETTA CHILD POMEROY, b. April 8, 1855.
    1330. ii. HENRY CHILD POMEROY, b. Nov. 8, 1859.
    1331. iii. JOHN MINER POMEROY, b. May 31, 1864.

[Seventh Generation.]

    1326. ii. CHARLES DICKERMAN CHILD, second child and eldest son of Abiel and Henrietta Hale Child, b. June 29, 1830, m. 1st, abt. 1854, Cornelia Munson, m. 2d, Jan. 1, 1868, Emily Jones of Wallingford, Vt.

[Eighth Generation.] Children:

    1329½. i. MARY CORNELIA CHILD, b. in Wallingford, Vt., May 17, 1855.
    1330½. ii. CHARLES MUNSON CHILD, b. in Wallingford, Vt., Nov. 17, 1856, d. 1857.
    1331½. iii. EMELINE MUNSON CHILD, b. in Wallingford, Vt., Sept. 13, 1859.
    1332. iv. WILLIAM DAY CHILD, b. in Wallingford, Vt., April 13, 1864.

[Seventh Generation.]

    1327. iii. CALEB HARRIS CHILD, third child and second son of Abiel and Henrietta Hale Child, b. May 25, 1834, m. May 22, 1861, Emily M. Robbins of Hartford, Ct. Mr. Child is descended from a vigorous and robust stock physically and mentally, is well developed, standing six feet, of good proportions, of florid complexion of regular and comely features, wears a countenance full of vitality, and vigor marks his movements. He is a prosperous jobber in dry goods at No. 87 Worth St., New York City.

The genealogy of Mrs. Child was written by her little daughter of twelve years, at my request, whose sweet little note it is our pleasure here to insert:

NEW YORK CITY, Nov. 8, 1879.

DEAR MR. CHILD:—I received your letter, and I am very sorry I have not answered it before. My great-grandmother's maiden name was Emily Hollister. She first married my great-grandfather, Mr. Strickland, and on his death, Mr. Savage. My grandmother's maiden name was Emily Malvina Strickland; she married my grandfather, Philemon F. Robbins, who is still living. My mother's maiden name was Emily Malvina Robbins; she married my father, Harris Child, and my name is Emily Robbins Child. The last time we sat down at the same table together was at a Thanksgiving dinner at Hartford, Ct., at my grandmother's, in 1873. My great-grandmother was hale and hearty as ever. She died in 1874, and my grandmother in 1877. From your little friend,

EMILY R. CHILD,

No. 50 East 68th St.

[Eighth Generation.]   Children:

    1333. i. Infant, unchristened.

    1334. ii. EMILY ROBBINS CHILD, b. in Hartford, Ct., July 15, 1867.

    1335. iii. CAROLINE ADELAIDE CHILD, b in New York City, June, 21, 1870

    1336. iv. HARRIS ROBBINS CHILD, b. in New York City, March 28, 1872.

    1337. v. MARY HALL CHILD, b. in New York City, Feb. 18, 1874.

    1338 vi. LOUISA ROBBINS CHILD, b. in New York City, Jan. 21, 1876.

[Seventh Generation.]

    1328. iv. DELLA H. CHILD, fourth child and second dau. of Abiel and Henrietta Hale Child, b. in Suffield, Ct., Oct. 26, 1848, m. Oct. 19, 1869, Samuel T. Buel.   Reside in Mechanicsville, Cedar Co., Iowa.

[Eighth Generation.]   Children:

    1339. i. SAMUEL KENNETH BUEL, b. in Mechanicsville, Iowa, Nov. 16, 1872.

    1340 ii. Son, unchristened b. July 10, 1879.

[Fifth Generation.]

    1215. iv. Capt. ELIAS CHILD, the fourth child of Capt. Elisha and Alice Manning Child, b. Dec. 28, 1755, m. 1st, March 18, 1779, Dorothea Morse, b. July 24, 1760, dau. of Doct. Parker and Hannah Huse Morse.   She d. 1786.   He m. 2d, March 18, 1790, Sophia Morse, dau. of Doct. David and Anna Newman Morse, a niece of his first wife.   She d. Feb. 28, 1826   Those interested in the genealogy of the wives of Capt. Elias Child, will find it more fully treated in connection with David Morse, who married Hannah Child, (No. 906) dau. of Capt. Willard Child, on page 179, and in connection with No. 1480, where the marriage of Sarah Child to Jedediah Morse, Esq., first allies the two families afterwards so repeatedly linked.

    It may be noticed that military titles are often affixed to the names of men who lived in colonial times.   The title meant something in that period—for those who bore it were in actual service, or in training as minute men, liable to be called to the field at any moment.   They were patriotic men, ready to peril life and property in defence of American liberty.   We are, therefore, particular to give the title as handed down to us in the record.   Capt. Elias Child was the son of a man in whom the Colonial Government reposed confidence for his abilities and his devotion to the American cause.   This son partook largely of his father's spirit and his ideas, and bore some of his father's honors.   Less in public life than his father, because the fruits of the Revolution were being quietly enjoyed he was content with less military honor, and more absorbed with civil pursuits. Capt. Elias Child ranked among the best of citizens, and was recognized by his neighbors as a man of sound and discriminating judgment, and upright in all his business transactions. He was known in his time as a prosperous and wealthy farmer, a warm supporter of moral and religious institutions, and was a consistent member of the Congregational Church. He died April 3, 1834.

[Sixth Generation.] Children. By first wife—four children:

1340½. i. ELISHA CHILD, b. in Woodstock, Ct., Feb. 11, 1780, m. 1802, Nancy Child.

1341. ii. PARKER MORSE CHILD, b. March 13, 1782, d. Aug. 6, 1795.

1342. iii. CHARLES THOMPSON CHILD, b. in North Woodstock, Ct., Feb. 15, 1784, m. Jan. 21, 1808, Clarrissa Child.

1343. iv. ELIAS SEWALL CHILD, b. in North Woodstock, Ct., Mar. 2, 1786, d. Mar. 18, 1786.

[By second marriage—four children.]

1344. v. ELIAS CHILD, b. in Woodstock, Ct., Sept. 19, 1791, d. Feb. 15, 1793

1345. vi. ERASTUS CHILD, b. in Woodstock, Ct., Sept. 3, 1793, m. Feb. 24, 1824, Rhoda Ricard.

1346. vii. DOROTHEA MORSE CHILD, b. in Woodstock, Ct., Aug. 2, 1797, m March 16, 1826, Abel Child.

1347. viii. SOPHIA CHILD, b. in Woodstock, Ct., May 2, 1800, m. Feb. 16, 1831, Abel Child. (See *Abel Child's record*—780.)

[Sixth Generation.]

1340½. i. ELISHA CHILD, eldest child of Capt. Elias and Dorothea Morse Child, b. Feb. 11, 1780, m. 1802, Nancy Child, eldest dau. and child of Capt. Willard and Lydia Morse Child, of North Woodstock. He d. Oct. 13, 1822. She d. March 25, 1853, the widow of a second husband.

As the accredited compiler of this genealogy it will not be deemed an offence against good taste, if in this connection I adopt the use of the first person while chronicling my father and family. In opening correspondence for this genealogy my name to many was unfamiliar; by others, while familiar, it was not readily traced to its legitimate branch. It will possibly gratify an innocent curiosity if I introduce the reader to my immediate ancestor.

My father Elisha Child, son of Capt. Elias Child, of North Woodstock, Ct., was among the early settlers (about 1805) in

the town of Exeter, Otsego County, N. Y. My earliest recollections place me in a sparsely settled neighborhood composed
mostly of New England people. The pioneers of the town
were the Tunniclifs and the Herkimers; soon after the Cush-
mans, Williamses, Brookses, Curtisses and the Sumners; then
the Childes and the Morses. My father and my uncle, Charles
Thompson Child, and David Morse, their brother-in-law, came
very nearly together. These later pioneers were from Connecticut. To them the school house and the house of worship
were of the first importance. Thus early were laid the foundations of a moral and Christian community. These fathers
and their children constituted a substantial society, observant
of religious institutions, and zealous promoters of all enterprises
that promised permanency and prosperity. My father was
reared a farmer and continued to cultivate the soil during his
life. In stature he was six feet high and well proportioned, of
fine personal appearance and bearing, of sanguine temperament, of a well balanced mind, of sound judgment, of good
executive ability, of strict integrity, and a sincere Christian.
He was a man of average intelligence for the times and was
held in much esteem by his neighbors and acquaintances for
his manly bearing and stability of character; and was often the
arbitrator in church and secular differences. His excellent
musical abilities rendered his position in church affairs one of
much importance. As my father passed away before I was of
sufficient age to fully appreciate his characteristics, I write the
account as given by those who were cotemporary with him,
and some of whom were intimately associated with him in the
affairs of life. It will not be out of place to mention a pleasing incident which occurred some few years since. On the occasion, I was brought into company with an intelligent and
leading citizen of one of the towns adjoining my native town,
(myself a stranger to him) who was an intimate associate of my
father. Incidentally our family name was mentioned, but in
no way to indicate that I bore the name. The gentleman remarked that in earlier life (he was now quite aged) he had
"had a very pleasant acquaintance with Elisha Child, of
Exeter; he was a superior man and one who was highly
esteemed as a citizen." As the compliment was paid to the
memory of my father, in ignorance of my relationship, I have
ever cherished it with peculiar satisfaction.

My mother, Nancy Child, was the eldest child of Capt. Willard and Lydia Morse Child. Her mother was the sister of Rev. Dr. Jedediah Morse, the great American Geographer, who was the father of Samuel F. B. Morse, LL. D., the inventor of the "Morse Telegraph." She was in stature somewhat above the average of her sex, of fair complexion and comely features. Her younger brother, the late Rev. Dr. Willard Child, once said to me, "your mother when a young lady was in my youthful eye the perfection of a beautiful girl." Her characteristics were such as might be looked for in a descendant of a good family of Puritan stock. She was marked with much strength of intellect : her intelligent ideas upon matters of church and public interest are found in her diary, which for many years she was accustomed to keep. The religious element was prominent in her character. The education of her family in high, moral principles, with a view to meet the practical duties of life, was to her a matter of first importance. Her children cherish her memory with warm affection, veneration and gratitude, for her tender and faithful devotion to their happiness and usefulness in life. Some years after my father's death she married Dea. Dudley Child, of Bath, N. H.

[Seventh Generation.] Children:

1348. i. PARKER MORSE CHILD, b. in North Woodstock, Ct., March 27, 1803, m. March 27, 1824, Sabrina Robinson.

1349. ii. HARRIET CHILD, b. in North Woodstock, Ct., Nov. 18, 1804, m. March 28, 1827, Lemuel Southard.

1350. iii. ELIAS CHILD, b. in Exeter, Otsego Co., N. Y., Sept. 3, 1806, m. 1st, Aug. 29, 1831, Melissa Hollister; m. 2d, May 14, 1833, Sylvina Thorp; m. 3d, Oct. 16, 1867, Susan P. Cleaveland.

1351. iv. WILLARD CHILD, b. in Exeter, N. Y., April 17, 1808, m. Dec. 31, 1833, Dorothea Child.

1352. v. CHARLES CHILD, b. in Exeter, N. Y., April 27, 1810, m. 1st, Oct. 7, 1846, Diantha Cushman; m. 2d, July 3, 1866, M. Augusta Thorp.

1353. vi. ELISHA CHILD, b. in Exeter, N. Y., June 14, 1812, m. Lucia Whitney.

1354. vii. NANCY MAY CHILD, b. in Exeter, N. Y., April 8, 1814, m. May 16, 1833, Dwight P. Child. (For children, see record Dwight P. Child, of Bath, N. H.)

1355. viii. HANNAH CHILD, b in Exeter, N. Y., May 21, 1816, m. Nov. 17, 1837, Bradley Child. (For children, see record Bradley Child, of Bath, N. H.

1356. ix. WILLIAM GRAVES CHILD, b. in Exeter, N. Y., June 23, 1818, m. Dec. 6, 1840, Jane Simpson.

1357. x. HORATIO HENRY CHILD, b. in Exeter, N. Y., July 16, 1820, m. 1849, Betsey Brand.

1358. xi. HENRIETTA AMELIA CHILD, b. in Exeter, N. Y., May 28, 1823, youngest and posthumous: m. Geo. Minot, of Bath, N. H. They removed to Coventry, Vermont, where Mr. Minot died some years before his wife She died Nov. 20, 1856. They had no children.

[Seventh Generation.]

1348. i. PARKER MORSE CHILD, eldest child of Elisha and Nancy (Child) Child, b. in Woodstock, Ct., March 27, 1803, m. March 27, 1824, Sabrina Robinson, of Exeter, N. Y., dau. of Lemuel Robinson, Sr., late of Barre, Mass. She was b. in Barre, Mass., July 15, 1805, d. Jan. 1, 1880, in Utica, N. Y., at the house of her son, Lucius C. Childs. Mr. P. M. Child d. Sept. 10, 1837, in Exeter, N. Y.

[Eighth Generation.] Children:

1359. i. MARY ANN CHILD, b. in Exeter, N. Y., Feb. 4, 1825, m. Nov. 13, 1844, Henry Hatch Curtiss.

1360. ii. LUCIUS CURTISS CHILD, b. in Exeter, N. Y., Nov. 24, 1831, m. Jan 13, 1853, Anna Jane Tapping.

[Eighth Generation.]

1359. i. MARY ANN CHILD, eldest child of Parker Morse and Sabrina Robinson Child, b. in Exeter, Otsego Co., N. Y., Feb. 4, 1825, m. Nov. 13, 1844, Henry Hatch Curtiss, son of Abel Curtiss, an early settler in Otsego County, N. Y. Mr. Curtiss came to Utica nearly forty years ago, and established himself in the printing business, which he has successfully conducted till the present time, now the head of the firm of Curtiss & Childs. He is among the most respected citizens of the city, and has long been an esteemed and efficient elder in the Westminster Presbyterian church of Utica. He has been twice married. His first wife dying Aug. 6, 1849 : he m. 2d, Oct. 16, 1850, Mary Burt Cooley, dau. of John and Sabra Cooley, of Longmeadow, Mass. She was b. Oct. 10, 1814, and d. March 12, 1879.

[Eighth Generation.] Children:

1361. i. MARY STORRS CURTISS, b. in Utica, N. Y., March 1, 1845. Immediately upon her graduation from the High School of her native city, Miss Mary S. Curtiss began to teach in one of the public schools, and has made herself a most successful and esteemed instructor, bringing to her work a conscientious fidelity and thoroughness, carried often beyond her physical strength in her toils, by a sincere enthusiasm.

1362. ii. HARRIET AMANDA CURTISS, b. in Utica, N. Y., Oct. 26, 1848.

[By Mr. Curtiss' second marriage.]

1363. iii. CLARA EVERTS CURTISS, b. in Utica, N. Y., Jan. 9, 1853.

Elias Child

[Eighth Generation.]

1360. ii. LUCIUS CURTISS CHILDS,[1] second child of Parker Morse and Sabrina Robinson Child, b. in Exeter, Otsego Co., N. Y., Nov. 24, 1831, m. Jan. 13, 1853, Anna Jane Tapping, dau. of Isaac and Jane Tapping, of Utica, N. Y. Having acquired his trade, Mr. Childs first established himself in business in Boonville, N. Y., becoming the editor and publisher of the Boonville *Herald*, a local paper in the interest of the old Whig party. After several years continuance in this connection he disposed of his interests in Boonville, and established a business in Utica. Four years later he formed a partnership with his brother-in-law, Henry H. Curtiss, where they have built up and still conduct a prosperous business. Commencing with but little capital, except a thorough knowledge of his trade, Mr. Childs has risen to the status of a successful and popular business man; having the public confidence for his thoroughness and unswerving integrity.

[Ninth Generation.] Children:

1364. i. CHARLES PARKER CHILDS, b. in Utica, N. Y., Oct. 10, 1854, d. July 30, 1862. This child was much endeared to his parents by his precociousness and future promise, had he lived to mature manhood. At the tender age of eight years he gave pleasing proof of his ripeness for a higher and happier state of existence.

1365. ii. ALICE JANE CHILDS, b. in Boonville, Oneida Co., N. Y., Aug. 20, 1857.

1366. iii. WILLIAM TAPPING CHILDS, b. in Utica, N. Y., July 1, 1862.

1367 iv. CARRIE LOUISA CHILDS, b. in Utica, N Y., Dec. 17, 1867.

[Seventh Generation.]

1349. ii. HARRIET CHILD, second child of Elisha and Nancy (Child) Child, b. in North Woodstock, Ct., Nov. 18, 1804, m. March 28, 1827, Lemuel Southard, of West Fairlee, Vt. He d. 1876 or 1877. She d. March 29, 1833. They had two children.

[Eighth Generation.] Children:

1368. i. ELIAS CHILD SOUTHARD, b. in West Fairlee, Vt., Aug. 10, 1828, d. Jan 31, 1850.

1369. ii. LINUS SOUTHARD, b. in West Fairlee, Vt., Jan. 24 1832, d. ——

[Seventh Generation.]

1350. iii. ELIAS CHILD, third child and second son of Elisha and Nancy (Child) Child, was born in Exeter, Otsego Co.,

[1] Mr. L. C. Childs adopted the terminal (s.)

New York, on the 3d September, 1806. Has been three times married, first marriage on the 29th August, 1831, by Rev. Dr. M. L. Perrine, Prof. of Auburn Seminary, to Melissa Hollister. Second marriage on the 11th of May, 1833, by the Rev. Chauncey Goodrich, to Sylvina Thorp. Third marriage by Rev. J. P. Cleaveland D. D., on the 16th October, 1867, to Susan P. Cleaveland.

Mr. Child's first wife, Miss Hollister, was the daughter of Roswell and Esther Guernsey Hollister, of South Ballston, Saratoga Co., N. Y. Possessed of an unusually attractive face, her large, soft, dark eye, and broad brow, betokened the sweetness of disposition, and strength of intellect, which especially characterized her. Even at the time of her marriage, her health was impaired by pulmonary difficulty, and her wedded life was very brief, after the birth of an infant, who did not survive her. Mrs. M. H. Child died in Tompkins, Delaware Co., N. Y., on the 18th of July, 1832.[1] Miss Thorp, the second wife, was the daughter of Edward and Sylvina Tremaine Thorp, of Butternuts, Otsego Co,. N. Y. Inheriting from her father a strong love for reading, and fine intellectual abilities, Miss Thorp had a highly cultivated mind, and entered upon the life of a clergyman's wife, with unusual qualifications to fill the position. Notwithstanding many cares and occupations, Mrs S. T. Child found always time for reading, indeed, she ever preferred a book or her pen to society, though possessed of rare conversational powers. Mrs. Child left in manuscript some fine products of her ready pen. Her death occurred in New York City, on the 5th of October, 1865.[2]

The third wife is the daughter of Rev. Dr. J. P. and S. H. D. Cleaveland. Dr. Cleaveland was a clergyman of the Presbyterian church ; settled first in Salem, Essex Co., Mass., and from thence removed to Detroit, Michigan. While in Michigan he was connected as President with Marshall College, afterwards, we believe, merged with the University at Ann Arbor Later Dr. Cleaveland was settled in Cincinnati, Ohio, and Providence, R. I. At the time of the late war, Dr. C. became chaplain of a regiment of the Gulf Squadron. Dr. Cleaveland

[1] Further record of the Hollister family in the Appendix.
[2] Further notice of Mrs. Thorp Child's family is found in the appendix.

died at his home in Newburyport, Mass., on the 7th of March, 1873.

Mrs. S. P. Cleaveland Child was educated under the careful supervision of her father, and at the Ingham University at Le Roy, Genesee Co., N. Y., and at Andover, Mass., in the Abbott Female Seminary. Her signature has become familiar to many of the name, as the amenuensis of her husband in the preparation of this genealogy.[1]

"Mr. Elias Child was early consecrated by his parents in baptism, and as was so often the custom of New England families, dedicated to the ministry should his spirit thus incline him with increasing years. With this in view, he was sent to fit for college at an academy in Stockbridge, Mass. Here he was encompassed with the best possible influences for mental and moral growth. Boarding in the family of the parents of Prof. Hopkins, his room-mate was the "Bob" Hopkins of boyhood, who became in after years the honored Prof. Hopkins of Williams College. The society of this town was composed and controlled by the New England aristocracy of cultured refinement: the influence of which was felt by young Child, and never forgotten. During this period of preparatory study, Mr. Child's father died, and henceforth he knew little of home. He entered Union College, Schenectady, in 1824, graduating in 1828, under the presidency of Eliphalet Nott, D. D., and went soon to the Theological Seminary at Auburn, N.Y., where he studied with the Rev. Drs. Richards, Mills and Perrine, men eminent in their denomination. Mr. Child was settled in two parishes of his native state, from whence he removed to Michigan, being called to Albion, Calhoun Co. A very earnest and studious man, he devoted himself to his profession, and was considered a chaste and able sermonizer. Enthusiastic by nature, he became early in life the zealous friend of the slave, at a period when such friendship was not popular. A bronchial difficulty resulted in a withdrawal from the active service of the ministry. Business life has been intermitted by the superintendency of two charitable educational institutions, the only links to the early professional life, which his reverence for the office would permit. Excellent natural abilities are shrouded by an extremely modest estimate of himself, arising in part from a proud

[1] In the appendix will also be found further notice of the Cleaveland family.

sensitiveness of spirit, and the sketch so brief here given of
him, would never have appeared in this genealogy of his com-
piling, had not a friend who knew him well, offered to prepare
a notice, due to him and his descendants."   *   *   *

[Eighth Generation.]   Children.   By first marriage:

1370. i. Infant, unchristened, b. July 18, 1832, d. same day.

[By second marriage:]

1371. ii. CHARLES HENRY CHILD, b. in Unadilla, Otsego Co., N. Y., Aug.
9, 1835, d. in Albion, Mich., March 16, 1841.

1372. iii. CAROLINE CLEAVELAND CHILD, b. in Albion, Calhoun Co., Mich.,
Jan. 30, 1842, d. in Batavia, N. Y., July 4, 1848.   A sweet and lovely child
of great promise.

1373. iv. CHARLES HENRY CHILD, 2D, b. in Clinton, Mich., March 21,
1843, d. March 22, 1843.

1374. v. CHARLES HENRY CHILD, 3D, b. in Oaksville, Otsego Co., N. Y.,
Aug. 24, 1844, m. July 28, 1876, Charlotte C. Leland.

[Eighth Generation.]

1374. v. CHARLES HENRY CHILDS,[1] son of Elias and Sylvina
Thorp Child, b. in Oaksville, Otsego Co., N.Y., Aug. 24, 1844,
m. July 28, 1876, Charlotte, dau. of Henry and Elizabeth M.
Conkling Calhoun,[2] of New York City.   Mr. Childs is agency
clerk in the publishing house of Ivison, Blakeman, Taylor & Co.,
New York City, where he has been the last fifteen years.

[Ninth Generation.]   Children:

1375. i. CLEAVELAND CHILDS, b. at Fort Lee, N. J., Sept. 17, 1877.

1376. ii. ETHEL THORPE CHILDS, b. in New York City, Jan. 5, 1879.

[Seventh Generation.]

1351. iv. WILLARD CHILD, fourth child and third son of
Elisha and Nancy (Child) Child, b. in Exeter, Otsego Co., N.Y.,
April 17, 1808, m. Dec. 31, 1833, Dorothea Morse Child, dau.
of Charles Thompson and Clarissa (Child) Child, of Exeter,
N. Y.   He was a farmer in the town of Bradford, Steuben Co.,
N.Y.; and d. March, 1842.   His widow m. Dea. Cyril Sumner,
of East Pharsalia, N. Y., and both still survive.

[Eighth Generation.]   Children:

1377. i. EDWARD CHILD, b. in Bradford, N. Y., Aug. 3, 1836, d. Sept. 12,
1850, in Woodstock, Ct.

1378. ii CLARISSA ELIZABETH CHILD, b. in Bradford, N. Y., Nov. 15, 1839.

1379. iii. LORETTA FIDELIA CHILD, b. in Bradford, N. Y., Feb. 24, 1842,

[1] C. H. C. adds the terminal " s " to his name.

[2] See appendix for further account of the Calhoun family.

m. Sept. 26, 1860, Samuel Reed, of Osco, Henry Co., Ill. They had one child which died young.

[Seventh Generation.]

1352. v. CHARLES CHILD,[1] fifth child and fourth son of Elisha and Nancy (Child) Child, b. in Exeter, N. Y., April 27, 1810, m. 1st, Oct. 7, 1846, Diantha Cushman, eldest child of David and Hetty Curtiss Cushman, of Exeter, N. Y. She was b. Nov. 16, 1819, d. Aug. 18, 1861. He m. 2d, July 5, 1866, Mary Augusta Thorp, dau. of Hon. Henry and Mary Buckley Thorp, of Butternuts, N. Y.

Passing the period of childhood and early youth with the ordinary educational advantages obtained in common schools of that period, Mr. Child commenced business as a clerk in a country store. After a term of service in this capacity, he purchased a part interest in a line of stages, with U. S. mail contract. Later he became connected with a cotton manufacturing business in Oaksville, Otsego Co., N. Y. After several years in this connection, he disposed of his interest and turned his attention to farming, connecting it with the produce commission business. He has for thirty years been a resident of Oaksville, Otsego Co., N. Y. Possessing good business talents, he has shared the public confidence in the several official positions, entrusted to him in town and county. He held for many successive years the office of post-master; for six years he was R. R. commissioner for the town of Otsego, N. Y.; for several years one of the Directors of the Cooperstown and Susquehanna R. R.,—and for many years he has been an officer of the Otsego County Agricultural Society. In all public interests relating to district, town and county affairs, he has always been a cheerful and liberal supporter.

[Eighth Generation.] Children by 1st marriage:

1379½. Infant son, unchristened.

By second marriage:

1380. i. HELEN AUGUSTA CHILD, b. in Oaksville, Otsego Co., N. Y., Feb. 14, 1868.

[Seventh Generation.]

1353. vi. Dea. ELISHA CHILD, sixth child, add fourth son of Elisha and Nancy (Child) Child, b. in Exeter, Otsego Co., N.Y., June 14, 1812, m. March 4, 1839, Lucia D. Whitney, dau. of Dea. Job and Nabby R. Whitney, of Woodstock, Ct.

[1] Mr. Charles Child adds the (s.)

Mr. Child early made his home at North Woodstock, and in mature manhood settled on the farm where he now resides. A staid and thoughtful man, his position has been an honorable and useful one in town and church affairs. The office of deacon in the Congregational church in North Woodstock, he has for many years faithfully and acceptably maintained. His chosen life-long companion is among the best loved of her sex, for her many amiable and excellent personal qualities. Her musical endowments have enlarged the circle of her friends and made her for years an essential element in the choir of the Congregational church. The rare christian grace of loving devotion and self-sacrifice to aged parents and kinsfolk, illumined their later days and secured the gracious promise of the fifth Commandment.

[Eighth Generation.] Children:

1381. i. NANCY CHILD, b. in Woodstock, Ct., April 26, 1841, m. 1864, Daniel James Whitney.

1382. ii. ABBEY E. CHILD, b. in Woodstock, Ct., April 17, 1843, m. Jan. 1868, Ezra C. Child. (*For children see No.* 1471.)

1383. iii. RUTH KNAPP CHILD, b. in Woodstock, Ct. March 1, 1849.

1384. iv. Son—unchristened, b. in Woodstock, Ct., 1851.

1385. v. HENRIETTA AMELIA CHILD, b. in Woodstock, Ct., Dec. 26, 1856.

[Eighth Generation]

1381. i. NANCY CHILD, eldest child of Deac. Elisha and Lucia D. Whitney Child, b. April 26, 1841, m. 1864, Daniel James Whitney. She d. Dec. 25, 1868.

[Ninth Generation.] Child:

1386. i. NANCY WHITNEY, b. in 1865.

[Seventh Generation.]

1356. ix. WILLIAM GRAVES CHILD, ninth child and sixth son of Elisha and Nancy (Child) Child, b. in Exeter, Otsego Co., N. Y., Jan. 23, 1818, m. Dec. 16, 1840, Jane M. Simpson, dau. of Robert and Esther Simpson, of Belfast, Ireland. She was b. Aug. 18, 1818.

Mr. Child went to Woodstock in his early boyhood, where he has since resided. On reaching manhood, he established himself in business as a wheel-wright, but later as a farmer, an occupation better suited to his taste and genius. Interested and active in the material interests of parish and town, his influence is salutary and efficient. Mrs. Child was a successful teacher before her marriage: her untiring energy of character and earnest resolution to educate her children, has enabled her to triumph over delicate health and accomplish marvels. She justly draws from us our warmest esteem and gratitude for her cheerful and indefatigable efforts to advance our work. Intelligent, thoughtful and energetic, she has been quick to comprehend and supply needed information.

[Eighth Generation.] Children:

1387. i. ESTHER SIMPSON CHILD, b. in Woodstock, Ct, Jan. 25, 1842. With great energy and success has devoted herself to teaching.

1388. ii. MARY JANE CHILD, b. Jan. 30, 1844, d. young.

1389. iii. CASSIUS M. CHILD, b. in Woodstock, Ct., Sept. 13, 1845, m. Sept. 14, 1873. Rachel P. Swisher.

1390. iv. SARAH PAMELIA CHILD, b. in Woodstock, Ct., July 4, 1851, m. May 30, 1879, Thomas Meek, cashier for Collins Axe Company, of East Douglass, Mass.

[Eighth Generation.]

1389. iii. CASSIUS M. CHILD, third child and eldest son of Wm. Graves and Jane M. Simpson Child, b. in Woodstock, Ct., Sept. 13, 1845, m. Sept. 14, 1873. Rachel P. Swisher, of Rowlandsville, Md. Mr. Child is a traveling agent for a mercantile house of Baltimore, Maryland, resides in Rowlandsville, Md.

[Ninth Generation] Children:

1391. i. PHILLIPS JEREMIAH CHILD, b. in Rowlandsville, Md., Sept. 11, 1874.

1392. ii. MAUD MARYLAND CHILD, b. in Rowlandsville, Md., Aug. 30, 1877.

1393. iii. FREDERICK WILLIAM CHILD, b. in Rowlandsville, Md., Sept. 27, 1879.

[Seventh Generation.]

1357. x. HORATIO HENRY CHILD, seventh son and tenth child of Elisha and Nancy (Child) Child, was b. in Exeter, Otsego Co., N. Y., 16th of July, 1820, m. 7th of August, 1849, Betsey Brand, dau. of Samuel and Sally Brand, of Leonardsville, Madison Co., N. Y. She was born May 15th, 1822, in Leonardsville.

Mr. Child had naturally a mechanical genius, and was engaged in the manufacture of agricultural implements. After several years of earnest application in this calling, failure of health necessitated a change; when with characteristic enthusiasm, he established himself in the insurance business, in which he is now employed, in connection with a commission agency in produce. He is of sanguine temperament, of earnest purposes, fond of reading, interested in the passing events of the day, holds posi-

tive and distinct opinions upon political and religious matters.
He is esteemed as an honorable and worthy citizen of Leonardsville, N. Y., his present residence.

[Eighth Generation.]   Children:

1394. i. ARTHUR CHILD, b. in Leonardsville, N. Y., May 14, 1850, d. Aug.
2, 1870. He was an amiable, bright and intelligent youth; in a course of
education for the legal profession, when he was attacked with malignant
fever, which in a few days terminated his life.

1395. ii. FRANK SAMUEL CHILD, b. in Leonardsville, N. Y., May 20, 1854.
Rev. F. S. Child inherited a somewhat fragile constitution, with the general mental characteristics and tastes of his mother. Fond of his book from
early childhood, the quietude resulting from not vigorous health, was happily spent in reading. Every available book was devoured, and fortunately
the love for a desirable class of literature was formed, leading to the decided
penchant for belles-lettres which appeared in his student life. Mr. Child fitted for college at the Whitestown Seminary in Oneida Co., N. Y., where he
graduated in 1871. He entered Hamilton College, Clinton, N. Y., graduating in the class of '75, with a most honorable standing. He graduated from
Union Theological Seminary in 1878. In January, 1879, Mr. Child was
installed pastor of the Congregational church in Greenwich, Ct., his present
charge.

[Sixth Generation.]

1342. iii. CHARLES THOMPSON CHILD, third child and third
son of Capt. Elias Child, b. in North Woodstock, Ct., Feb. 15,
1784, m. Jan. 21, 1808, Clarissa Child, second dau. of Capt.
Willard Child, of North Woodstock, Ct. She d. in Exeter,
N. Y., March 14, 1847, æ 60 years. He d. in Exeter, N. Y.,
April 19, 1854, æ 74.

Soon after their marriage they removed from Woodstock to
Exeter, Otsego Co., N. Y., and settled on a farm, where they
spent the balance of their days, and where their children were
born and reared to manhood and womanhood. Mr. Child was
a man of a most kindly nature, of genial temperament, fond
of his friends, of untiring industry, noted for his probity and
conscientiousness in all his business transactions; a supporter of
all useful reforms, and a devout christian. With a life-long
companion in full sympathy with him in domestic, social and
religious life, the mother of thirteen children, twelve of whom
grew up to manhood and womanhood under her sweet maternal
influence, and settled in life.

[Seventh Generation.]   Children:

1399. i. EPHRAIM CHILD, b. in Exeter, N. Y., Nov. 1, 1808, m. Nov. 25,
1830, Armenia Higgins.

1400. ii. ELIZABETH CHILD, b. in Exeter, N. Y., April 11, 1810, m. 1834, Harmon Edmunds.

1401. iii. MARCUS CHILD, b. in Exeter, N. Y., Dec. 16, 1811, m. 1st May, 25, 1836, Elmira Eaton; m. 2d, Cynthia Sillick.

1402. iv. DOROTHEA MORSE CHILD, b. in Exeter, Otsego Co., N. Y., m. 1st, Dec. 31, 1833, Williard Child; m. 2d, Cyril Sumner. (*For children, see Williard*—1351.)

1403 v. LUTHER CHILD, b. in Exeter, N. Y., July 19, 1815, m. Jan. 10, 1841, Augusta Coates.

1404. vi. ERASTUS CHILD, b. in Exeter, N. Y., Oct. 4, 1817, m. April 29, 1846, Rachel Foster.

1405. vii. CLARISSA PAMELIA CHILD, b. in Exeter, N. Y., Dec. 30, 1818, m. Oct. 3, 1847, Chas. Hill, d. June, 29 1853. No children.

1406. viii. FINLEY BREESE CHILD, b in Exeter, N. Y., Jan. 22, 1821, m. 1st, Feb. 15, 1848, Emeline Adkins; m. 2d, March 6, 1851, Libbie Denton; m. 3d, June 18, 1876, Nancy M. Dixon.

1407 ix. CHARLES MASON CHILD, b. in Exeter, N. Y., Nov. 1, 1822, m. March 6, 1851, Seba Ann Carr.

1408. x. HETTY CURTIS CHILD, b. in Exeter, N. Y., Dec. 5, 1824, d. Feb. 2, 1826

1409. xi. AARON PUTNAM CHILD, b. in Exeter, N. Y., Jan. 25, 1827, m. Sept. 2, 1855, Emily L. Babcock.

1410. xii. FIDELIA TODD CHILD, b. in Exeter, N. Y., Nov. 11, 1828, m. Dec. 7, 1865, Lyman B. Ferris.

1411. xiii. FLOYD CUSHMAN CHILD, b. in Exeter, N. Y., Nov. 19, 1831, m. Feb. 24, 1869, Sarah Felton.

[Seventh Generation.]

1399. i. EPHRAIM CHILD, first child of Charles Thompson and Clarissa (Child) Child, b. in Exeter, N. Y., Nov. 1, 1808, m. Nov. 25, 1830, Armenia Higgins, dau. of Darius Higgins, of Exeter, Otsego Co., N. Y. He d. Feb. 6, 1833, leaving two children.

[Eighth Generation.] Children:

1412. i. CELESTIA ESMINA CHILD, b. —— 20, 1831, m. Aug. 17, 1849, Benjamin Child, of Lenox, N. Y., They had three children. (*See Benjamin Child, of Lenox, N. Y.*)

1413. ii. LUCY MELISSA CHILD, b. July 26, 1833, m. John Cancross; resides in Iowa.

[Seventh Generation.]

1400. ii. ELIZABETH CHILD, eldest daughter and second child of Charles Thompson and Clarissa (Child) Child, b. in Exeter, Otsego Co., N. Y., April 11, 1810, m. 1834, Harmon Edmunds, of Exeter, N. Y. Mr. Edmunds is a hotel keeper, now in Sangerfield, N. Y. Has been sheriff of Otsego Co., N. Y., one term, and quite popular as a politician.

R

[Eighth Generation.] Children.

1414. i. LEVERET EDMUNDS, b. in Exeter, N. Y., July 4, 1836, m. Nov. 11, 1856, Julia Hatch.
1415. ii. PITT EDMUNDS, b. Dec. 21, 1841, d. early.

[Eighth Generation.]

1414. i. LEVERET EDMUNDS, son of Elizabeth Child and Harmon Edmunds. of Exeter, N. Y., b. July 4, 1836, m. Nov. 11, 1856, Julia Hatch, dau. of widow Elizabeth Hatch, of Cooperstown, N. Y. Residence, Sangerfield, N. Y.

[Ninth Generation.] Children:

1416. i. FLORA E. EDMUNDS, b. in Cooperstown, Otsego Co., N. Y., Aug. 15, 1858, m. June 14, 1876, Frederick Terry.
1417. ii. EDDIE EDMUNDS, b. in Cooperstown. Otsego Co., N. Y., Dec. 23, 1863.
1418. iii. LULU MAUD EDMUNDS. } Twins, b. Nov. 22, 1867, d. Oct 2, 1868.
1419. iv. LELA MAY EDMUNDS. } Twins, b. Nov. 22, 1867, d. Aug. 3, 1868.
1420. v. LILLIAN MAY EDMUNDS. b. in Cooperstown. Otsego Co., N. Y., Dec. 31, 1870.
1421. vi. HANNAH EDMUNDS. b. in Cooperstown. Otsego Co., N. Y., July 11, 1873.

[Ninth Generation]

1416. i. FLORA E. EDMUNDS. eldest child of Leveret and Julia Hatch Edmunds, grand-daughter of Elizabeth Child Edmunds. b. in Cooperstown. N. Y., Aug. 15, 1858, m. June 14, 1876, Frederick Terry, son of Delos Terry, a wealthy farmer in the town of Sangerfield, Oneida Co., N. Y.

[Tenth Generation.] Child:

1422. i. HARRIET TERRY. b. in Sangerfield. N. Y., June 20, 1877.

[Seventh Generation.]

1401. iii. MARCUS CHILD, third child, second son of Charles Thompson Child and Clarissa, his wife, b. in Exeter, N. Y., Dec. 16, 1811, m. 1st, Elmira Eaton, May 25, 1836 ; m. 2d, Cynthia Sillick, of Schenectady, N. Y. Settled in Saratoga, N. Y., where he died in 1866. Mr. and Mrs. Marcus Child have one adopted daughter, Anna Child.

[Eighth Generation.] Children. By first wife:

1423. i. EATON CHILD, b. Aug. 3, 1837, d. Feb. 16, 1857.
1424. ii. LAWRENCE ALLEN CHILD, b. Feb. 3, 1848, d. Oct., 1848.

[Seventh Generation.]

1403. v. LUTHER CHILD, third son, and fifth child of Charles Thompson and Clarissa (Child) Child, b. in Exeter, N. Y., July 19, 1815, m. by Rev. Mr. Wall, Jan. 10, 1841, Angeline Coates dau. of Ransome and Patience Coates, of Bradford, Steuben Co., N. Y. She was b. May 11. 1816, d. April 10, 1863.

Mr. Child removed from Steuben Co., N.Y., in the year 1855, to the State of Michigan, and finally settled in Fowlersville, Livingston Co., Mich., where he now resides, a thrifty farmer.

[Eighth Generation.] Children:

1425. i. AMANDA JANE CHILD, b. in Bradford, Steuben Co., N. Y., Dec. 6, 1841, d June 25, 1869, unmarried.

1426. ii. FIDELIA CHILD, b. in Woodhull, Steuben Co., N. Y., April 27, 1843, d. April 6, 1849.

1427. iii. ELLEN CHILD, b. in Bradford, N. Y., July 25, 1844, d. June 6, 1849.

1428. iv. MARY CHILD, b. in Bradford, N. Y., Nov. 28, 1845, m. Feb. 10, 1863, Nathaniel Brayton.

1429. v. MARCUS CHILD, b. in Bradford, N. Y., March 24, 1847, m. Nov. 23, 1867, Adella Tanner.

1430. vi. PATIENCE CHILD, b. in Bradford, N. Y., Feb. 26, 1849, m. Jan. 24, 1872, Myron Green.

1431. vii. LORETTA CHILD, b. in Bradford, N. Y., Feb. 14, 1852.

1432. viii. MATILDA CHILD, b. in Bradford, N. Y., Nov. 14, 1854.

1433. ix. FRANK CHILD, b. in Plymouth, Wayne Co., Mich., March 16, 1858.

[Eighth Generation.]

1428, iv. MARY CHILD, fourth dau. and child of Luther and Angeline Coates Child, b. in Bradford, N. Y., Nov. 28, 1845, m. Feb. 10 1863, in Howell, Livingston Co., Mich. Nathaniel Brayton, a miller by trade.

[Ninth Generation.] Children:

1434. i. FRANK BRAYTON, b. in Howell, Mich., July 2, 1868.

1435 ii. LEON BRAYTON, b. in Howell, Mich., March 1, 1871, d. young.

1436. iii. BERTIE BRAYTON, b. in Howell, Mich., July 8, 1873.

[Eighth Generation.]

1429. v. MARCUS CHILD, eldest son and fifth child of Luther and Angeline Coates Child, b. March 24, 1847, m. Nov. 21, 1867, Adella Tanner, of Conway, Livingston Co., Mich. She d. Feb. 21, 1874. Mr. C. is a miller, a man of enterprise, and with his brother-in-law, Nathaniel Brayton is a mill builder in Kent Co., Mich.

[Ninth Generation.] Child:

1437. i. LENA CHILD, b. in Conway, Livingston. Co., Mich., Dec. 14, 1870.

[Eighth Generation.]

1430. vi. PATIENCE CHILD, fifth dau. and sixth child of Luther and Angeline Coates Child, b. Feb. 26, 1849, m. Jan. 24, 1872, Myron Green, of Handy, Livingston Co., Mich.

[Ninth Generation.]　Child:

1438. i. ANGIE GREEN, b. in Handy, Mich., Aug. 21, 1873.

[Seventh Generation.]

1414. vi. ERASTUS CHILD, fourth son and sixth child of
Charles Thompson and Clarissa (Child) Child, b. in Exeter,
Otsego Co., N. Y., Oct. 4, 1817, m. by Rev. Beriah Green,
April 29, 1846, Rachel Foster, of Whitesboro, Oneida Co., N. Y.

Mr. Child evinced a love of books, and very early resolved
on obtaining an education that should fit him for professional
life. His mature youth was devoted to school teaching. Later,
he entered Oneida Institute at Whitesboro, N. Y., where
he continued for some years, acquiring a fair education, and
graduated in 1841. He then pursued a course of theological
studies under the late Rev. Beriah Green. He became thoroughly
imbued with the views of his teacher on questions of slavery,
then agitating the country, and identified himself with the party
that held no church fellowship with slaveholders or their sympathizers. With characteristic earnestness and sincerity, he sought
to bring public sentiment to his views. The success of the
party was not great. Though licensed as a clergyman, his public services in his profession were brief. Failure of health made
it necessary for him to seek other employment, and after a brief
residence in Whitesboro, N. Y., in secular pursuits, he removed
to Oneida, Knox County, Ill., where he now resides, acting as
reporter for a weekly paper in Galesburg, Ill., and cultivating
and adorning his beautiful home. His life has been marked
with usefulness in the community where he resides; and his
upright and conscientious course has won the confidence and
esteem of all who knew him. A christian mother's training in
his childhood has largely shaped his moral feelings, and given
him the deepest abhorance of immoralities of every kind. Not
long since he wrote me that a profane word had never escaped
his lips, that the remembrance of *one rough* word, not profane,
to an elder sister, when a small boy, always gives him pain.

[Eighth Generation.]　Children:

1439. i. SARAH ELIZABETH CHILD, b. in Whitesboro, N. Y., May 14, 1849,
m. Nov. 28, 1877, by Rev. A. W. Chamberlain, Fielding Bradford Webb, of
Bedford, Taylor Co., Iowa. Mr. Webb was b. in Maquoin, Ill., April 30,
1851; he is a miller, resides in Bedford, Taylor Co., Iowa.

1440 ii. CHARLES T. CHILD, b. in Whitesboro, N Y., April 4, 1852, d. July
1, 1854, by scalding.

1441. iii JULIA IRENA CHILD, b. in Oneida, Knox Co., Ill., May 30, 1869.

[Seventh Generation.]

1406. viii. FINLEY BREESE CHILD, eighth child and fifth son of Charles Thompson and Clarissa (Child) Child, b. in Exeter, Otsego Co., N. Y., Jan. 22, 1821, m. 1st, Feb. 16, 1848, Emeline Adkins of Burlington, Otsego Co., N. Y. She d. April 7, 1868; m. 2d, Libbie Denton. She d. Feb. 16, 1874; m. 3d, June 18, 1876, Nancy Dixon, who was b. March 7, 1846, in Bloomington, Grant Co., Ill.

Passing his boyhood, without special incident, except such as sometimes crops out in boys in whom is pent up an exuberant store of fun, in advancing years he showed courage and independence in grappling with the realities of life, and was not easily daunted by failures in his plans. He commenced life as a farmer in Steuben County, N. Y. From thence he removed to Springville, Erie Co., N. Y., thence to Oneida, Knox Co., Ill. Twelve years later, he removed to the town of Oak, Nuckolls Co., Nebraska, where, with grown up sons, he established his home for the balance of life. He possessed the essential elements of a pioneer. He was energetic, persevering, self sacrificing, hopeful. He was a man of sterling integrity, and a useful man in society, often caring more for others than himself. His death occurred at his sister's, Mrs. Ferris, in Oneida, Knox Co., Ill., on the 2nd of July, 1880, of a pulmonary difficulty, which had long been undermining his once vigorous constitution. A portion of the last years of his life was spent as a colportuer and Sabbath school agent.

[Eighth Generation.] Children. By first marriage:

1442. i. ADELBERT CHILD, b. July 11, 1850.

1443. ii. HERBERT CHILD, b. Sept. 19, 1853.

[By third marriage:]

1444. iii. CHARLES TRACY CHILD, b. May 30, 1877.

1445. iv. THERON FLOYD CHILD, b. Sept. 17, 1878.

[Seventh Generation.]

1407. ix. CHARLES MASON CHILD, ninth child and sixth son of Charles Thompson and Clarissa (Child) Child, b. in Exeter, Otsego Co., N. Y., Nov. 1, 1822, m. March 6, 1851, Seba Ann Carr.

On attaining his majority, the California gold fever carried him across the plains and mountains to the gold mines, where a few years of hard toil secured for him moderate gains, when he returned, married and commenced life as a miller in the village of Millville, Mass., his present residence. Industrious, conscientious and upright, he is esteemed as a worthy and useful citizen.

[Eighth Generation.] Children:

1446. i. CLARENCE MERRIMAN CHILD, b. Feb. 18, 1852, d. Sept. 6, 1868, by accidental drowning in the mill pond.

1447. ii Horace Edward Child, b. Dec. 11, 1857, m. 1878, Harriet E· White.

1448. iii. Geo. Mason Child, (adopted) b. Nov. 24, 1866.

[Eighth Generation.]

1447. ii. HORACE EDWARD CHILD, second child of Charles Mason and Seba Ann Carr Child, b. Dec. 11, 1857, m. 1878, Harriet E. White.

[Ninth Generation.] Child:

1449. i. ADA BARTLET CHILD, b. April 18, 1879.

[Seventh Generation.]

1409. xi. AARON PUTNAM CHILD, eleventh child and seventh son of Charles Thompson and Clarissa (Child) Child, b. in Exeter, N. Y., Jan. 25, 1827. m. Sept. 2, 1855, Emily L. Babcock. dau. of Lester and Amelia Manning Babcock, of Westford, Otsego Co., N. Y. She was b. May 16, 1831.

Mr. Child was reared a farmer; commenced active life as a teacher, in which capacity he was popular and successful. Soon after marrying he removed to the town of Oneida, Knox Co., Ill., and commenced farming. After a few years of success and accumulation, he removed to Creston, Iowa, where he now resides. Here his occupation is farming in connection with the harness making business. He is energetic and sagacious and usually compasses his plans and is known as a successful business man. Inheriting the best instincts of a worthy ancestry, his aims are elevated and his practical bearing is beneficent and christian.

[Eighth Generation.] Children:

1450. i. CHARLES LESTER CHILD, b. in Oneida, Ill., Oct. 22, 1856, d. Sept. 12, 1875.

1451. ii. FLORA ELMIRA CHILD, b. in Oneida, Ill., March 6, 1860.

1452. iii. KATE KENT CHILD, b. in Oneida, Ill., June 6, 1868.

[Seventh Generation.]

1410. xii. FIDELIA TODD CHILD, twelfth child and fifth dau. of Charles Thompson and Clarissa (Child) Child, b. in Exeter, N. Y., Nov. 11, 1828, m. Dec. 7, 1865, Dea. Lyman B. Ferris, a well-to-do farmer in Walnut Grove, Oneida, Ill. He was b. in Huntington, O., Feb. 16, 1820.

[Eighth Generation.] Child:

1453. i. MARY FERRIS, b. in Oneida, Ill., Feb. 17, 1868.

[Seventh Generation.]

1411. xiii. FLOYD CUSHMAN CHILD, thirteenth child and eighth son of Charles Thompson and Clarissa (Child) Child, b. in Exeter, Otsego Co., N. Y., Nov. 19, 1831, m. Feb. 24, 1869, Sarah Felton, of Marlboro, Mass. She was b. Sept. 3, 1842.

Mr. Child was the Benjamin of the family. For several years he staid on the homestead, caring for aged parents and a widowed sister with two young daughters. When the rebellion broke out he was drafted into the U. S. service. The alternative was before him, to obey the summons in person or procure a substitute. His duties under the paternal roof seemed imperative: hence he procured a substitute. His parents passing away, and his sister remarrying, he removed to Iowa and settled in Creston, his present home.

[Eighth Generation.] Child:

1454. i. ETTA CHILD, b. May 22, 1870.

[Sixth Generation.]

1345. vi. ERASTUS CHILD, sixth child of Capt. Elias and Sophia Morse Child. b. in Woodstock, Ct., Sept. 3, 1793, m. Feb. 24, 1824, Rhoda M. Rickard. She was b. in Dudley, Mass., Feb. 1, 1801. He d. Aug. 13, 1853. Mrs. Child lives in North Woodstock, Ct.

Mr. Child was a farmer and the possessor of the old homestead of his father; and ranked among the intelligent and worthy citizens of the town: a man of sound and discriminating judgment, a nice sense of right and of strict probity. As a neighbor, he was kind and obliging, genial and happy in his domestic relations; his home was ever open for cheerful hospitality. An under current of humor was a characteristic which frequently cropped out, as well in his family as among his neighbors. Mrs. Child did not always escape his facetious bantering. Her good humour, however, was equal to her husband's, and her wit was always at her command, when needed to parry a joke. A standing panacea was "Erastus, the only evidence of superior judgment in the Child family I ever saw, was that exhibited in the choice of their wives." But the milk of human kindness flowed perpetually through their kindly natures, and domestic happiness was uninterrupted through a long life. Mrs. Child was of French descent. Her ancestors may have been of those Huguenot Refugees who found an asylum from persecution in the New World. She possesses that sparkling, piquant vivacity characteristic of that nation; thoroughly lovable and domestic in her character, genial, affable and courteous, she is a universal favorite in the neighborhood and circle of her acquaintance, and withal a sincere christian woman.

[Seventh Generation.]   Children:

1455. i. NEWMAN GERRISH CHILD, b. in Woodstock, Ct., Sept. 10, 1825, d. Sept. 1, 1826.

1456. ii. PETER HAMILTON CHILD, b. in Woodstock, Ct., Jan. 6, 1827, m. Jan 5. 1865, Mary Ann Stetson.

1457. iii. MARTHA AGNES CHILD, b. Oct. 19, 1840, m. Dec. 1861. Geo. Walker Child. (*For children, see page* 216, *No.* 1298.)

[Seventh Generation.]

1456. ii. PETER HAMILTON CHILD, second son and second child of Erastus and Rhoda Rickard Child, b. January 6, 1827, m. Jan. 5, 1865, Mary Ann Stetson, of Woodstock, Ct. Mr. Child succeeded to the homestead of his father, where he died, July 11, 1872.

[Eighth Generation.]   Children:

1458. i. MARY AGNES CHILD, b. in Woodstock, Ct., April 1, 1866.

1459. ii. ABBIE RICKARD CHILD, b. in Woodstock, Ct., Jan. 21, 1868, d. Oct. 22, 1879.

1460. iii. HENRY HAMILTON CHILD, b. in Woodstock, Ct., Nov. 21, 1872.

[*For Nos.* ix. *and* xi. *Children of Capt. Elisha Child, see the Walker branch at the end of chapter III.*]

[Fourth Generation.]

35. ix. PETER CHILD, ninth child and fifth son of Ephraim and Priscilla Harris Child, b. in Woodstock, Ct. July 6, 1727, m. Dec. 30, 1756, Susanna Child, dau. of Nathaniel Child, who was probably one of the eldest sons of John and Elizabeth Child. Peter Child d. in 1810, æ. 83. She died Aug. 12, 1806.

[Fifth Generation.]   Children:

1461. i. CHESTER CHILD, b. in Woodstock, Ct., Oct. 7, 1757, m. Feb. 11, 1790, Sarah May.

1462. ii. EZRA CHILD, b in Woodstock, Ct., June 1, 1759, m. March 20, 1783, Hannah Child, b. July 14, 1762, dau. of Richard Child, and sister of Capt. John and Dea. Dudley Child, of Bath, N. H. Mr. Child was one of the pioneer settlers of the town of Bath. A man of good intellectual abilities and generally well informed: was a man of a good deal of prominence, and a useful member of society; date of his death or wife's death not ascertained. They died childless.

1463. iii WINSLOW CHILD, b. in Woodstock, Oct. 7, 1763, d. Dec. 30, 1765.

1464. iv. JOANNA CHILD, b. in Woodstock, June 16, 1765.

[Fifth Generation.]

1461. i. Col. CHESTER CHILD, eldest child of Peter and Susanna (Child) Child, b. in Woodstock, Ct., Oct. 7, 1757, m. Feb. 11, 1790, Sarah May, dau. of Sarah Child and Stephen May. He d. April, 12, 1823.

[Sixth Generation.] Children:

1465. i. PAMELIA CHILD, b. in Woodstock, Ct., Dec. 9, 1790, m. July 25 1816, Dea. Luther Child, son of Capt. Willard Child. She d. April 15, 1851 (*For children, see page* 188, *No.* 993.)

1466. ii. EZRA CHILD, b. in Woodstock, Ct., Sept. 6, 1792, m. March 25, 1820, Betsey May, dau. of Caleb May. He d. Nov. 17, 1860, æ. 68. They had no children.

Mr. Child was one of the prominent business men of the town; of much energy of character, self-reliant, and of positive opinions; was usually successful in carrying out his purposes. A worthy citizen, and for many years a justice of the peace. He enjoyed the esteem of his fellow townsmen.

1467. iii. SUSAN CHILD, b. June 7, 1796, m. May 20, 1828, Spencer Child, son of Alpha and Mary May Child. He d. in Woodstock, July 25, 1832. She d. 1870, in Woodstock. No children.

1468. iv. MARY ANN CHILD, b. Aug. 27, 1798, d. July 15, 1823.

1469. v. CHESTER CHILD, JR., b. June 24, 1802, m. Feb. 24, 1831, Prudence Carpenter.

[Sixth Generation.]

1469. v. Dea. CHESTER CHILD, second son and youngest child of Col. Chester Child, m. Feb. 24, 1831, Prudence Carpenter, dau. of Cyril Carpenter, of Woodstock, Ct. He was a man much esteemed in the community for his excellent qualities. Twenty-one years he held the office of Deacon, in the Congregational church; and was prominent in town affairs. He lived on the homestead of his father and grandfather in that part of the town of Woodstock, known as the English neighborhood.

[Seventh Generation.] Children:

1470. i. CHESTER EDWARD CHILD, b. Oct. 13, 1836. He served in the Union Army in the war of the Rebellion of 1861-65, in the 26th Connecticut Regt. of Infantry, under Capt. Geo. Walker Child. He d. Aug. 10, 1863, of disease contracted in the army.

1471. ii. EZRA CARPENTER CHILD, b. April 15, 1841, m. Jan. 1, 1868, Abbie E. Child.

1472. iii. ABBIE PRUDENCE CHILD, b. April 21, 1843, m. Feb. 6, 1873, Merrick Paine.

1473. iv. BRAINARD WINSLOW CHILD, b. in Woodstock, Ct., Aug. 29 1846. He served in the Union Army in the war of the Rebellion. Resides in the West.

[Seventh Generation.]

1471. ii. EZRA CARPENTER CHILD, second child and second son of Dea. Chester and Prudence Carpenter Child, b. in Woodstock, Ct., April 15, 1841, m. Jan. 1, 1868, Abbie E. Child, dau. of Dea. Elisha and Lucia Whitney Child. He d. May 13, 1876.

Mr. Child was justly held in high esteem by his fellow townsmen. At his death he had served three years on the board of the selectmen of the town of Woodstock. For a number of years he was the efficient superintendent of the Sabbath school in the congregation of which he was an active member, and but a short time before his death he was elected deacon of the church. The elements of an influential man were largely developed. His companion, not less esteemed, was in full sympathy with her husband in all that pertained to home and society.

[Eighth Generation.] Children.
  1474. i. LIZZIE CARPENTER CHILD, b. in Woodstock, Ct., April 23, 1870.
  1475. ii. CHESTER ELISHA CHILD, b. in Woodstock, Ct., Aug. 1, 1872.
  1476. iii. GRACE ANNIE CHILD, b. in Woodstock, Ct., June 6, 1875.

[Seventh Generation.]

1472. iii. ABBIE PRUDENCE CHILD, third child and only dau. of Dea. Chester and Prudence Carpenter Child, b. in Woodstock, Ct., April 21, 1843, m. Feb. 6, 1873, Merrick Paine, son of John Paine, of East Woodstock, Ct.

[Eighth Generation.] Children:
  1477. i. ROBERT PAINE, b. Dec. 13, 1874.
  1478. ii. JOHN BRAINARD PAINE, b. Feb. 6, 1877, d. Oct. 8, 1877.

CHAPTER III.

[Third Generation.]

16. ii. Capt. BENJAMIN CHILD, second child and second son of Benjamin and Grace Morris Child, b. in Roxbury, Mass., July 19, 1685, m. Sept. 1712, Patience Thayer, of Mendon, Mass. They removed soon after to Woodstock, Ct., then called "New Roxbury." "They joined the church in Woodstock in 1740; Patience joined by letter." She d. March 15, 1764.

[Fourth Generation.] Children:

1479. i. BENJAMIN CHILD, b. in Roxbury, Mass., Aug. 28, 1713, m. Patience ———, 1740.

1480. ii. GRACE CHILD, b. in Woodstock, Ct., July 22, 1716, m. 1737, Moses Lyon.

1481. iii. NATHANIEL CHILD, b. in Woodstock, Ct., April 13, 1717, m. 1st, April 3, 1747, Jemima Bugbee: m. 2d, Sept. 19, 1776, Mrs. Eleanor Fox.

1482. iv. ELIJAH CHILD, b. in Woodstock, Ct., Aug. 5, 1719, d. Sept. 5, 1736.

1483. v. PATIENCE CHILD, b. in Woodstock, Ct, June 22, 1721, pub. Oct. 18, 1746, with Joseph Wild, of Boston, Mass.

1484. vi. SARAH CHILD, b. in Woodstock, Ct., Nov. 19, 1722, m. Feb. 19, 1746, Dea. Jedediah Morse.

1485. vii. MOSES CHILD, b. in Woodstock, Ct., Oct. 27, 1725, m. June 24, 1752, Mary Payson.

[Fourth Generation.]

1479. i. BENJAMIN CHILD, JR., eldest child of Capt. Benjamin and Patience Thayer Child, b. in Roxbury, Mass., Aug. 28, 1713, m. about 1740, Patience ———.

[Fifth Generation.] Children:

1486. i. CHLOE CHILD, b. in Woodstock, Ct., March 9, 1741, m. Oct. 3, 1764, Luther Cady.

1487. ii. SARAH CHILD, b. in Woodstock, Ct., Dec. 20, 1742, d. early.

1488. iii. ELIJAH CHILD, b. in Woodstock, Ct., Dec. 3, 1744, m. Hannah Harris.

1489. iv. PHINEAS CHILD, bapt. Sept. 21, 1746, m. ———.

1490. v. MARY CHILD, bapt. Jan. 22, 1748, m. April 9, 1767, Parker Bacon.

1491. vi. LEVINA CHILD, b. Jan. 24, 1851, m. March 10, 1774, Eleazer Jackson.

1492. vii. SARAH CHILD, 2D, b. Jan. 16, 1753.

1493. viii. CEPHAS CHILD, b. Sept. 7, 1755, m. Feb. 18, 1782, Martha Child.

1494. ix. ZILLAH CHILD, b. Aug. 27, 1757.

1495. x. LYMAN CHILD, b. Oct. 29, 1759, m. ———.

1496. xi. FREEMAN CHILD, b. Nov. 16, 1762. All the children of Benjamin and Patience were born in Woodstock, Ct.

[Fifth Generation.]

1488. iii. ELIJAH CHILD, third child and eldest son of Benjamin, Jr.. and Patience —— Child. bapt. in Woodstock, Ct., Dec. 3, 1744. m. Hannah Harris, dau. of Timothy and Elizabeth Stevens Harris, of Brookline, Ct. She was b. Aug. 14, 1754, d. June 5, 1808. He d. July 14, 1825.

[Sixth Generation.] Child:

1497. i. TIMOTHY HARRIS CHILD, b. Feb. 14, 1784, d. July 19, 1856, unm.

[Fifth Generation.]

1493. viii. CEPHAS CHILD, third son and eighth child of Benjamin, Jr., and Patience Child, was b. Sept. 7, 1756, in Connecticut. He with a brother, Lyman Child, removed to Vermont at an early period of their lives. Mr. Lyman Child settling in Hartford, Vt., while Mr. Cephas Child made his home in West Fairlee. Orange Co., Vt., where he married on the 18th of February, 1782, Martha Child. Mrs. Martha Child died in West Fairlee, Vt., on the 6th of February, 1795. After her decease, Mr. Child resided in the family of his daughter, Mrs. Moses Chamberlain, in Bradford, Vt., until his own death, which occurred the 30th of April, 1836. Mr. Child was a Revolutionary soldier, and in his later years drew a pension for his services.

[Sixth Generation.] Children:

1498. i. NANCY CHILD, b. June 15, 1784, in West Fairlee, Vt., m. Thule Williard, of Hartland, Vt. She died there June 26, 1838. Left no children.

1499. ii. MARTHA CHILD, b. in West Fairlee. Vt., 1786. m. Jan. 1806, Capt. Moses Chamberlain.

1500. iii. SALLY CHILD, b. Sept. 7, 1788. m. Andrew Luce.[1]

1501. iv. MARY CHILD, b Nov. 20, 1793, m. Feb. 20, 1814, Col. Moody Chamberlain.

1502. v. BENJAMIN CHILD, b. March 30, 1794, d. May 30, 1813, in the army.

[Sixth Generation.]

1499. ii. MARTHA CHILD, second dau. and third child of Cephas and Martha (Child) Child, was b. in West Fairlee, Vt., in 1786. m. Capt. Moses Chamberlain, January, 1806. Resided in Bradford. Vt. Capt. Moses Chamberlain and his brother, Col. Moody Chamberlain, who married Mary Child, the fourth daughter of Cephas Child, were sons of Col. Remembrance Chamberlain, an early emigrant from Connecticut to Vermont: himself the son of Dea. Moses and Jemima Wright Chamberlain, of Connecticut. "There's many a true word

[1] Record of this family will be found in the appendix if obtained.

spoken in jest," is a proverb finding such fulfillment in the life of Col. Remembrance Chamberlain, we believe others beside the family will be interested in its relation. Coming to Newbury, Vt., in 1770, he settled in the southern part of that town, and boarded with a Mr. Johnson, who used to ask him, in a joking way, why he did not marry. In like spirit, he would reply, "I am waiting for your widow." 1775, Mr. Johnson died. Threatened by an invasion of Tories and Indians from Canada, Mrs. Johnson took her three sons, the youngest an infant of months, upon a horse with her, and rode to Chester, New Hampshire, to the home of her parents. The next year she returned to Newbury, and became the wife of Col. Remembrance Chamberlain, and the mother of eight Chamberlain children. That blessings should attend this line, we can but believe, so thoroughly have they obeyed the command to "Honor father and mother." We find Col. R. Chamberlain brought to Vermont his parents and in his large household, they held honored and honorable positions, until called to their heavenly home. The same chivalric courtesies were extended to Mr. Cephas Child by his son-in-law, Capt. Moses Chamberlain. Capt. Chamberlain died in Bradford, Vt., in November, 1854, aged 77 years. Mrs. Martha Child Chamberlain, his wife, having died some fifteen years before, on the 25th of November, 1839.

[Seventh Generation.] Children:

1503. i. JOHN E. CHAMBERLAIN, b. Nov. 4. 1806, m. March, 1831, Laura Willard.

1504. ii. CEPHAS CHILD CHAMBERLAIN, b. Jan. 28, 1809, m. Alice Mallen.

1505. iii. MARTHA C. CHAMBERLAIN, b. April 10, 1811, m. Oct. 1839, John G. Cross. Mrs Cross died on January 30, 1843.

1506. iv. MARY C. CHAMBERLAIN, b. Aug. 9, 1813, m. March 9, 1837, Benjamin Chamberlain.

1507. v. MOSES R. CHAMBERLAIN, b. April 28, 1816, m. Sept. 25, 1849, Ruby S. Johnson.

1508. vi. ELIZABETH A. CHAMBERLAIN, b. Aug. 1, 1818, d. March. 20, 1821.

1509. vii. BENJAMIN F. CHAMBERLAIN, b. Dec. 21, 1821, d. April 2, 1845.

1510. viii. ELIZABETH E. CHAMBERLAIN, b. Aug. 16, 1823, m. March 26, 1855, Jared M. Hazeltine.

1511. ix. AMANDA N. CHAMBERLAIN, b. May 22, 1826, m. May 23, 1849, Henry E. Sawyer.

1512. x. AZUBA A. W. CHAMBERLAIN, b. Sept. 2, 1831, m. Oct. 20, 1853, Luther S. Grover.

[Seventh Generation.]

1503, i. JOHN E. CHAMBERLAIN, eldest son and child of Martha Child and Capt. Moses Chamberlain, b. in Bradford, Vt., 4th November, 1806, m. March, 1831, Laura Willard. Residence, Newbury. Vt.

[Eighth Generation.] Children:

1513. i. GEORGE W. CHAMBERLAIN, b. March 9, 1832, m. Mrs. Eliza Harrison.

1514. ii. HORACE E. CHAMBERLAIN, b. Nov. 30, 1834.

1515. iii REMEMBRANCE W. CHAMBERLAIN, b. March 31, 1837, m. Helen Corliss. Two children.

1516. iv. LAURA EVALYN CHAMBERLAIN. b. April 9, 1842, m. John W. Currier, of West Troy, Vt.

1517. v. ELLEN A. CHAMBERLAIN, b. Aug. 1, 1845, m. George B. Harriman, of Bradford, Vt.

1518. vi. CHARLES W. CHAMBERLAIN, b. Nov. 4, 1849.

[Seventh Generation.]

1504. ii. CEPHAS CHILD CHAMBERLAIN, second son and child of Martha Child and Capt. Moses Chamberlain, b. in Bradford, Vt., 28th January, 1809, m. abt. 1835, Alice Mallen, of Boston, Mass., where they resided until Mr. Chamberlain's death, in that city, on the 1st of February, 1876.

[Eighth Generation.] Children:

1519. i. ALFRED W. CHAMBERLAIN, b.——————— in Boston, Mass.

1520 ii SUSAN E CHAMBERLAIN, b. Sept. 23, 1840, in Boston, Mass,, m. a Mr. Bartlett, of same city.

[Seventh Generation.]

1506. iv. MARY CHILD CHAMBERLAIN, second dau. and fourth child of Martha Child and Capt. Moses Chamberlain, b. in Bradford, Vt., 9th August, 1813, m. 9th March, 1837, Benjamin Chamberlain. Residence, Bradford, Vt.

[Eighth Generation.] Children:

1521. i. ELLEN A. CHAMBERLAIN, b. Sept. 8, 1838, m. Sept. 26, 1860, Nelson R. Doe.

1522. ii. MARTHA A. CHAMBERLAIN, b. Dec. 29. 1840, m. Nov. 21, 1866, Benjamin F. Pillsbury.

1523 iii. GEORGE Z. CHAMBERLAIN. b. Feb. 28, 1843. d. April 1, 1844.

1524. iv. BENJAMIN F. CHAMBERLAIN, b. July 30, 1845.

[Eighth Generation]

1521. i. ELLEN A. CHAMBERLAIN, eldest dau. and child of Mary Child Chamberlain and Benjamin F. Chamberlain, b. 8th of September, 1838, m. 26th September, 1860, Nelson R. Doe.

[Ninth Generation.] Children:

1525. i. FRED E. DOE, b. Sept. 29, 1863.

1526. ii. LONISON WESLEY DOE, b. July 10, 1865.

[Eighth Generation.]

1522. ii. MARTHA A. CHAMBERLAIN, second dau. and child of Mary Child Chamberlain and Benjamin F. Chamberlain. b. Dec. 29th, 1840. m. 21st November, 1866, Benjamin T. Pillsbury.

[Ninth Generation.] Children:

1527. i. ALICE Z. PILLSBURY, b. Jan. 12, 1868.

1528. ii. MARY CHILD PILLSBURY, b. Aug. 12, 1871.

[Seventh Generation.]

1507. v. MOSES R. CHAMBERLAIN, third son and fifth child of Martha Child and Capt. Moses Chamberlain, b. in Bradford, Orange Co., Vt., 28th April, 1816. m. 25th September, 1841, Ruby S. Johnson. Mr. Chamberlain is a farmer, of the energetic, progressive order. seeking to improve and elevate this most noble calling. Is an extensive dealer in fine stock: in swine, sheep and cattle. He resides upon the homestead of his grandfather, Col. Remembrance Chamberlain.

[Eighth Generation.] Children:

1529. i. MARTHA E. CHAMBERLAIN, b. Oct. 7, 1842. d. May 13, 1845.

1530. ii. FRANK R. CHAMBERLAIN, b. May 15, 1844. m. Feb. 9, 1868, Abbie F. Manser.

1531. iii. MARTHA E. CHAMBERLAIN, 2D. b. July 26, 1847, unm.

1532. iv. JOHN W. CHAMBERLAIN, b. Dec. 5, 1848. d. May 25, 1864.

1533. v. RUBY J. CHAMBERLAIN, b. Nov. 16, 1856, unm.

[Eighth Generation.]

1530. ii. FRANK R. CHAMBERLAIN, eldest son and second child of Moses R. and Ruby S. Johnson Chamberlain, and grandson of Martha Child Chamberlain, was born on the ancestral farm Bradford, Vt., 15th May, 1844, married 9th February, 1868, Abbie F. Manser. Mr. Chamberlain is associated with his father in the culture of the old home estate, and in the rearing of blooded stock, at Bradford. Vt.

Ninth Generation.] Children:

1534. i. JOHN W. CHAMBERLAIN, b. Sept. 18, 1870.

1535. ii GERTIE M. CHAMBERLAIN, b. March 21, 1876.

1536. iii. SARAH S. CHAMBERLAIN, b. Aug. 29, 1878.

[Seventh Generation.]

1510. viii. ELIZABETH E. CHAMBERLAIN, fourth dau. and eighth child of Martha Child and Capt. Moses Chamberlain, b. in Bradford, Vt., 16th August, 1823, m. 26th March, 1855, Jared M. Hazeltine. Reside in Janesville, Wis.

[Eighth Generation.]   Children:

  1537. i. CHARLES H. HAZELTINE, b. Jan. 1856, in Janesville. Wis.
  1538. ii. HYATT SMITH HAZELTINE, b. Jan. 1857, in Janesville. Wis.
  1539. iii. FRANKLIN C. HAZELTINE, b. March 17. 1864, in Janesville. Wis.

[Seventh Generation.]

  1511. ix. AMANDA N. CHAMBERLAIN, fifth dau. and ninth
child of Martha Child and Capt. Moses Chamberlain, b. in Bradford, Vt.. 22d May, 1826, m. May 23d, 1849, Henry E. Sawyer.
Residence, Chicago. Ill.

[Eighth Generation.]   Child:

  1540. i. HARRY C. SAWYER, b. Nov. 21. 1854, in Janesville. Wis.

[Seventh Generation.]

  1512. x. AZUBA A. W. CHAMBERLAIN, eighth dau. and
tenth child of Martha Child and Capt. Moses Chamberlain, b.
in Bradford, Vt., September 2d, 1831, m. Oct. 20th, 1853,
Luther S. Grover.   Residence, White River Junction. Vt.

[Eighth Generation.]   Children:

  1541. i EDWARD MAITLAND GROVER, b. Aug. 26, 1854, in Burlington.
Vt., m, Miss Clark. Resides in Boston, Mass.; one child.
  1542. ii. CHARLES F. GROVER, b. Dec. 13, 1858, in Lebanon, N. H., unm
  1543. iii. MARY E. GROVER, b. June 2, 1863.
  1544 iv. GEORGE B. GROVER, b. July 9, 1869.

[Sixth Generation.]

  1501. iv. MARY CHILD, fourth child and dau. of Cephas and
Martha Child, b. in West Fairlee, Vt.. 20th November, 1793, m.
20th February, 1814, Col. Moody Chamberlain, of Newbury,
Vt. Mrs. Mary Child Chamberlain died 8th August, 1838.
Col. Chamberlain died at Newbury, Vt., July 24, 1863.

[Seventh Generation.]   Children:

  1545. i. JOHNSON CHAMBERLAIN, b. Nov. 16, 1814. m. Oct. 12, 1838, Olive
Ann Hazeltine.
  1546. ii. HARRIET CHAMBERLAIN, b. July 19, 1816, m. May 18, 1836,
James M. Chadwick.
  1547. iii. MOODY CHAMBERLAIN, JR., b. Nov. 28, 1818.
  1548. iv. EZRA B. CHAMBERLAIN, b. May 9, 1821, d. young.
  1549. v. ELIZABETH E. CHAMBERLAIN, b. March 9, 1823, m. July 11, 1850,
William B. Hibbard.
  1550. vi. EZRA B CHAMBERLAIN, 2D, b. June 14, 1825, m. Nov. 25, 1852,
Elizabeth H. Bayley.
  1551. vii. EMELINE B. CHAMBERLAIN, b. Feb. 4, 1828, m. Nov. 25, 1852,
Harry Fox.
  1552. viii. MARY CHILD CHAMBERLAIN, b. Sept. 21, 1830.

[Seventh Generation.]

  1545. i. JOHNSON CHAMBERLAIN, eldest son and child of
Mary Child and Col. Moody Chamberlain, b. in Newbury, Vt.,

16th November, 1814. m. 12th October. 1838, Olive Ann
Hazeltine.

[Eighth Generation.] Children:

1553. i. CHARLES CHAMBERLAIN, b. July 14, 1840, d. young.

1554. ii. WRIGHT CHAMBERLAIN, b. Aug. 27, 1843, m. Nov. 25, 1868, Abbie
F. Smith.

1555. iii. FRANCIS CHAMBERLAIN, b. Feb. 4, 1845.

1556. iv. CHARLES CHAMBERLAIN, 2d, b. Jan. 13, 1849.

[Eighth Generation.]

1554. ii. WRIGHT CHAMBERLAIN, second son and child of
Johnson and Olive A. Hazeltine Chamberlain, and grandson of
Mary Child Chamberlain, b. 27th August, 1843, m. 25th November, 1868, Abbie F. Smith, dau. of Charles E. and Susan
Smith, of Corinth, Vt. Resides in Lancaster, Coos Co., New
Hampshire.

[Eighth Generation] Children:

1557. i. AMELIA K. CHAMBERLAIN, } Twins, { b. Aug. 27, 1869, Amelia d.
1558. ii. ALICE S. CHAMBERLAIN, } { Mar. 10, 1878.

1559. iii. SUSIE O. CHAMBERLAIN, b. Jan. 28, 1871, d. Feb. 18, 1878.

[Seventh Generation.]

1546. ii. HARRIET CHAMBERLAIN, eldest dau. and second
child of Mary Child and Col. Moody Chamberlain b. in Newbury, Vt., 19th, July, 1816, m. 18th May 1836, James M. Chadwick.

[Eighth Generation.] Child:

1560. i. ELLEN F. CHADWICK, b. June 11, 1839.

[Seventh Generation.]

1549. v. ELIZABETH E. CHAMBERLAIN, second dau. and
fifth child of Mary Child and Col. Moody Chamberlain, b. in
Newbury, Vt., 9th March, 1823, m. July 11th, 1850, William
B. Hibbard.

[Eighth Generation.] Children:

1561. i. ELIZABETH CHAMBERLAIN HIBBARD, b. April 30, 1851, m. Feb. 24,
1874, J. W. Baxter.

1562. ii. MARY EMELINE HIBBARD, b. April 15, 1856, in Elkhart, Ind., m.
April 15, 1879, Franklin W. Hall.

1563. iii. CARRIE FRANCES HIBBARD, b. Jan. 10, 1863, in Chicago.

[Eighth Generation.]

1561. i. ELIZABETH CHAMBERLAIN HIBBARD, eldest child
of Elizabeth E. Chamberlain and William B. Hibbard, and
granddaughter of Mary Child Chamberlain, b. 30th April, 1851,
m. 24th February, 1874, J. Walter Baxter, son of John and
Rosa Ann Baxter. Reside in Clinton, Iowa.

S

[Ninth Generation.] Children:

    1564. i. ROSE MAY BAXTER, b. Nov. 30, 1874, d. March 4, 1877.
    1565. ii. WILLIAM WALTER BAXTER, b. Feb. 20, 1875.
    1566. iii. MAUD IRENE BAXTER, b. May 10, 1878

[Seventh Generation.]

    1550. vi. EZRA B. CHAMBERLAIN, fourth son and eighth child of Mary Child and Col. Moody Chamberlain, b. in Newbury, Vt., 4th June, 1825, m. 25th November, 1852, Elizabeth H. Bayley. Reside in Newbury, Vt.

[Eighth Generation.] Children:

    1567. i. SARAH B. CHAMBERLAIN, b. Jan. 16, 1858.
    1568. ii. HARRY B. CHAMBERLAIN, b. Nov. 1, 1862.
    1569. iii. MARTHA P. CHAMBERLAIN, b. Nov. 24, 1866

[Seventh Generation.]

    1551. vii. EMELINE BUXTON CHAMBERLAIN, third dau. and seventh child of Mary Child and Col. Moody Chamberlain, b. in Newbury, Vt., February 4th, 1828, m. 25th November, 1852, Harry Fox, who was born Sept. 29th, 1826. Residence Chicago, Ill.

[Eighth Generation.] Children:

    1570. i. HARRY CHAMBERLAIN FOX, b. April 30, 1856, d. July 29, 1856.
    1571. ii. HARRIOT AMORET FOX, b. Feb. 10, 1858.
    1572. iii. ALICE ELIZABETH FOX, b. Dec. 13, 1860, d. May 30, 1861.
    1573. iv. FREDERICK HURLBURT FOX, b. March 24, 1862.
    1574. v. Infant son, unchristened, b. March 20, 1864, d. June 29, 1864.
    1575. vi. Baby HARRY FOX b. Nov. 6, 1866, d. Feb. 28, 1867.

[Fifth Generation.]

    1495. x. LYMAN CHILD, fourth son and tenth child of Benjamin, Jr., and Patience Child, b. in Woodstock, Ct., 29th Oct. 1759. Removed to the State of Vermont when quite young, with his brother, Cephas Child. Like his brother, he served in the army of the Revolution, and drew a pension in his latter days. Mr. Lyman Child married and resided in Hartford and Hartland, finally settled in Sharon, Windsor Co., Vt., but we have been unable to ascertain to whom he was married. He had several daughters and one son. One daughter married a Dimmick, and removed to the State of New York. Another married James Elliott, of Newbury, Vt., they removed to Canada; are said to have had several children. The son is said to have died in Sharon, Vt., but we are not able to trace the line further.

[Fourth Generation.]

1481. iii. NATHANEL CHILD, third child and second son of Capt. Benjamin and Patience Thayer, b. in Woodstock, Ct., April 13, 1717, m. 1st, May 28, 1747, Jemima Bugbee, b. 1726, d. Oct. 29, 1769; m. 2d. Sept. 19, 1776, Mrs. Eleanor Fox. He d. June 19, 1791, æ. 74. Mrs. Eleanor F. Childs d. Nov. 1822, æ. 94.

[Fifth Generation.] Children:

1576. i. DARIUS CHILD, b in Woodstock, Ct., April 25, 1748, d. May 29, 1759.

1577. ii. NEHEMIAH CHILD, b. in Woodstock, Ct., Feb. 3, 1751, m. 1st, May 24, 1774, Elizabeth Shipman; m. 2d. 1785, Mary McClellan.

1578. iii. ALPHA CHILD, b. in Woodstock, Ct., Aug. 19, 1753, m. March 21, 1777, Mary May.

1579. iv. SPENCER CHILD, b in Woodstock, Ct., April 11, 1756. A soldier in the Revolution, and d. 1784.

1580. v. JEMIMA CHILD, b. in Woodstock, Ct., May 28, 1760, m. 1st, Dec 19, 1782, Samuel Jones; m. 2d, a Mr. Bacon. She d. April 18, 1788.

1581. vi. CHARITY CHILD, b. in Woodstock, Ct., Oct. 31, 1762, d. Nov. 18, 1764.

1582. vii. CYRIL CHILD, b. in Woodstock, Ct., Sept, 23, 1771.

[Fifth Generation.]

1577. ii. NEHEMIAH CHILD, second son and second child of Nathaniel and Jemima Bugbee Child, b. in Woodstock, Ct., Feb. 3, 1751, m. 1st, May 24, 1774, Elizabeth Shipman; m. 2d, 1785, Mary McClellan. He d. Jan. 2, 1838.

[Sixth Generation.] Children. By first marriage:

1583. i. CHARITY CHILD, b. 1775, m. Eleazer Clark, of Belchertown, Mass.

[By second marriage:]

1584. ii. WILLIAM CHILD, b. in Woodstock Sept. 24, 1786, m. 1st, Jan. 23, 1812, Sally Lyon; m. 2d, Oct. 21, 1818, Sally Moore; m. 3d, June 28, 1829, Sophia Selby.

1585. iii. FAITH CHILD, b. in Woodstock, Ct., March 10, 1790, d. Aug. 12, 1824, unmarried.

1586. iv. LUCRETIA CHILD, b. in Woodstock, Ct., April 2, 1791, m. Oct. 1813, Henry Child. [See page 185, No. 908, for Children.]

1587. v. MARY CHILD, b. in Woodstock, Ct., Aug. 8, 1793, d. March 5, 1859, unmarried.

1588. vi. NATHANIEL CHILD, b. in Woodstock, Ct., Feb. 15, 1796, d. 1824. unmarried.

1589. vii. BETSEY CHILD, b. in Woodstock, Ct., 1800, d. 1848, unm

[Sixth Generation]

1584. ii. Dea. WILLIAM CHILD, second child and eldest son of Nehemiah and Mary McClellan Child, b. in Woodstock, Ct., Sep. 24, 1786, married three times—1st, Jan. 23, 1812, Sally

Lyon. She d. April 4, 1816; m. 2d, Oct. 2, 1818, Sally Moore. She d. June 2, 1821: m. 3d, June 28, 1829, Sophia Selby. She d. May 10, 1874. Date of his death not ascertained.

[Seventh Generation.] Children. By first marriage:

1590. i. SAMUEL CHILD, b. in Woodstock, Ct , Aug. 1815.

[By third marriage.]

1591. ii. SARAH M. CHILD, b. June 5, 1830, m. March 23, 1853, Carlo May.

1592. iii. NATHANIEL CHILD, b. in Woodstock, Ct , March 5, 1833, m. 1st, Georgiana Sholes, m. 2d, October 27, 1858, Nancy May.

1593. iv. WM. L. CHILD. b. in Woodstock, Ct., Aug. 15, 1835.

[Seventh Generation.]

1591. ii. SARAH M. CHILD, second child, and only dau. of Dea. William and Sophia Selby Child, b. June 18, 1830, m. March 23, 1853, Carlo May, son of Maj. Asa May, of Woodstock, Ct.

[Eighth Generation.] Children:

1594 i. LILLIAN MAY, b. Aug. 18, 1855, in Woodstock, Ct., d. March 27, 1868.

1595. ii. EZRA MAY, b. Sept. 9, 1857, in Woodstock, Ct.

1596. iii. MARY L. MAY, b. April 9, 1860, in Woodstock, Ct.

1597. iv. FRANK N. MAY, b. July 20. 1868, in Woodstock, Ct.

[Seventh Generation.]

1592. iii. NATHANIEL CHILD, third child, second son of Dea. William and Sophia Selby Child, b. March 5, 1833, married twice—1st, March 20, 1856, Georgiana Sholes, of Brookline, Ct. She was b. June 13, 1837, d. March, 1857; m. 2d, Oct. 27, 1858, Nancy May, dau. of Chester May, b. March 18, 1833.

[Eighth Generation.] Child:

1598. i. WILHEMINA CHILD, b. Oct. 5, 1857, m. Sept. 1, 1874, Geo. A. Paine, son of John Paine, d. Aug. 4, 1875.

[Fifth Generation.]

1578. iii. ALPHA CHILD, third child and third son of Nathaniel and Jemima Bugbee Child, b. in Woodstock, Ct., Aug. 19, 1753, m. March 21, 1777, Mary May, dau. of Stephen and Mary Child May, of Woodstock, Ct. He d. Jan. 20, 1809.

[Sixth Generation.] Children:

1599. i. DARIUS CHILD, b. in Woodstock, Ct., Dec. 26, 1777, m. Feb. 2, 1802, Letitia Morris.

1600. ii. PAMELIA CHILD, b. in Woodstock, Ct., April 15, 1780, d. July 27, 1782.

1601. iii. SPENCER CHILD, b. in Woodstock, Ct., May 15, 1782, m. March 20, 1828, Susan Child, dau. of Col. Chester Child, of Woodstock. He d. July 21, 1832. She d. 1870. No children.

1602. iv. GRIFFIN CHILD, b. in Woodstock, Ct., Jan. 25, 1784, m. twice, 1st, Aug. 15, 1811, Nancy Peck; 2d, Sarah Field.

[Sixth Generation.]

1599. i. DARIUS CHILD, eldest child of Alpha and Mary May Child, b. in Woodstock, Ct., Dec. 26, 1779, m. Feb. 2, 1802, Letitia Morris. Mr. Child was a large, portly man, of 200 lbs. weight, and of fine personal appearance. The record of Mr. Child and descendants brings out some points of interest worthy of note. Soon after marrying he removed from Woodstock, Ct., to Fairlee, Orange County, Vt., where he spent his long and active life. The country was mostly covered with forests, and required many a sturdy blow to bring the soil into a productive state. There was no lack of muscle or energy in Mr. Child to reach results that should afford adequate support for a growing family. He possessed a vigorous mind and powerful physical constitution. His enterprise, industry and probity secured him prominence among his fellow townsmen, by whom he was often promoted to official stations in the town and the commonwealth. He attained to easy pecuniary circumstances, and closed his days peacefully in his cherished home, Dec. 10, 1862, at the advanced age of 85 years.

[Seventh Generation.] Children:

1603. i. ALPHA CHILD, b. in Fairlee, Vt., Nov. 15, 1802. He was a promising youth, but died in early manhood, Aug. 21, 1824.

1604. ii. ALMIRA CHILD, b. in Fairlee, Vt., May 28, 1805, d. July 13, 1805.

1605 iii. WILLIAM CHILD, b. in Fairlee, Vt., June 14, 1806, m. June 1, 1831, Lucretia Fulton.

1606 iv. MARY MAY CHILD, b. in Fairlee, Vt., May 3, 1808, m. Hon. Alexander Gilmore.

1607. v. PAMELIA CHILD, b. in Fairlee, Vt., Nov. 21, 1811, m. Rev. Daniel Blodgett. Of him, his brother-in-law, Judge Child, says: "He prepared for college at the academy in his native town. Entered Dartmouth college from which he graduated in 1818. Was soon licensed to preach as a Congregational minister. Was ordained by the Royalton Association of Ministers in 1825. Settled as pastor in three or four different parishes; died in Randolph, Vt., 1855. One incident in college life is perhaps worthy of mention. At the time of the battle at Plattsburg, (1814) Mr. Blodgett, with four other members of his class, in obedience to his country's call, enlisted in the U. S. service for the common defence. Went to the scene of action and remained until honorably discharged, and returned to his Alma Mater." No issue from this marriage.

1608. vi. EDWIN SPENCER CHILD, b. Oct. 20, 1814, m. Aug. 1843, Juliette Richmonds. He d. July 5, 1844, leaving no children. Says Judge Child, "His widow is a lady of fine qualities, respectably connected, a genial, social companion with all her associates."

1609 vii. EPHRAIM MAY CHILD, b. in Fairlee, Vt., Nov. 8, 1874, d. April 17, 1830.

[Seventh Generation.]

1605. iii. Judge WILLIAM CHILD, third child, and second son of Darius and Letitia Morris Child, b. in Fairlee, Vt., June 15, 1806, m. Jan. 1, 1831, Lucretia Fulton, dau. of Alexander and Sarah Blair Fulton, of Deering, N. H. She was b. in 1808. They had six children.

In stature, Judge Child is six feet, of spare proportions, bearing more the type of his mother's family than the father's, with strong marked features indicating strength and decision of character. He has been an influential citizen in town, county and state from early manhood. A man esteemed for his qualities of heart and mind ; justly entrusted with official responsibilities, he has rendered much public service. Three years he represented his town in the State Legislature. Two years he held the Governor's commission, as Associate Judge of the County Court of Orange; he has held a commission as Justice of the Peace for thirty-five or forty years.

While the Judge claims to be a plain farmer, it has neither dwarfed his intellect nor blunted his sensibilities, his liberal and enlightened opinions bear the stamp of wisdom and justice. In our frequent correspondence with him in the progress of this work, we have been impressed with a manliness and dignity of bearing which are the result of cultivation of heart and intellect. The following extract from one of his letters to us, reveals among other things, the effect of his early training under a pious grandmother. He remarks :

"You allude to my residence in Muddy Brook parish in Woodstock, Ct. Many recollections of my short stay in that strictly Puritan locality frequently return to my mind. It was there I was first inducted (under a good grandmother's instructions) into the mysteries of the Westminster catechism, although in my then unripe years I understood no more about " the chief end of man " than I did about the statutes of Patagonia; but it served as an exercise to my mind, and left an impression of scripture truths that will never be effaced while reason lasts."

[Eighth Generation.] Children :

1610. i. ALPHA CHILD, b. in Fairlee, Vt., in 1831. Died of a fever at Northfield, Vt., Jan. 26, 1853, æ. 22.

1611. ii. LUCY JANE CHILD, b. Nov. 1833, m. Charles Hartshorn.

1612. iii. Lieut. DARIUS GRIFFIN CHILD, b. in Fairlee, Vt., in 1836, d. July 20, 1862, at New Orleans. in U. S. army. in war of Rebellion, æ 26.

1613. iv. Lieut. LEWIS CHILD, b. in Fairlee, Vt., in 1838, m. Dec . 1865, Sarah F. Mathewson.

1614. v. WILLARD H. CHILD, b. in Fairlee, Vt., in 1840, m. Dec. 25, 1866, Julia A. Mann. Was in the Union army.

1615. vi. ELLA S. CHILD, b. in Fairlee, Vt., in 1848, d. ——.

[Eighth Generation.]

1611. ii. LUCY JANE CHILD, second child and eldest dau. of Judge William and Lucretia Fulton Child, b. in Fairlee, Vt., Nov. 1833, m. Charles Hartshorn, of Littletown N. H.

[Ninth Generation.] Children:

1616. i. CHARLES C. HARTSHORN, b. (date not ascertained.) Killed while coasting on an icy hill.

1617. ii. WILLIAM C. HARTSHORN, b. (date not ascertained.) Is fitting (1879) for college under Rev. Wm. Spencer Child, Newport, R. I.

1618. iii. HARRY HARTSHORN. Said to be a bright, active boy of much promise and of fine talents.

[Eighth Generation.

1613. iv. LIEUT. LEWIS CHILD, fourth child and third son of Judge William and Lucretia Fulton Child, b. in Fairlee, Vt., in 1838, m. Dec. 6, 1865, Sarah F. Mathewson, grand-daughter of Griffin Child, of Providence, R. I.

[Ninth Generation.] Children

1619. i. LEWIS F. CHILD, b. in Fairlee, Vt., 1867, d. 1868.

1620. ii. ANNA M. CHILD, b. in Fairlee, Vt., 1869.

[Eighth Generation]

1614. v. WILLARD H. CHILD, fifth child and fourth son of Hon. Wm. and Lucretia Fulton Child, b. in Fairlee, Vt., 1840, m. Dec. 25, 1866, Julia A. Mann.

[Ninth Generation.] Children:

1621. i HOWARD F. CHILD, b. in Bradford, Vt., May, 1868, d. Sept. 1868.

1622. ii. ROBERT A. CHILD, b. in Bradford, Vt., May, 1871.

1623. iii. CHARLES H. CHILD, b. in Bradford, Vt., Feb. 1874, d. July, 1875, at Newport, Vt.

1624. iv. LEWIS A. CHILD, b. at Newport, Vt., Feb. 1876, d. at Fairlee, Sept. 1876.

[Seventh Generation.]

1606. iv. MARY MAY CHILD, fourth child and second dau. of Darius and Letitia Morris Child, b. in Fairlee, Vt., May 3, 1808, m. Hon. Alexander H. Gilmore, who was born at Acworth, N. H., 1804, d. at Fairlee, 1873. Mr. Gilmore was a farmer by occupation, and in that calling accumulated a handsome estate. Being a man of more than ordinary ability and intelligence he arose to prominent positions in public affairs. He served five terms as a member of the Vermont State Legislature; held the office of Judge of Probate for eight years in succession; was one year County Judge.

[Eighth Generation.] Children:

1625. i. LETICIA JANE GILMORE, b. Sept. 1831, d. 1847.

1626. ii. SPENCER C. GILMORE, b. 1833, d. 1855.

1627. iii. EDWIN A. GILMORE, b. 1835, m. Mary B. Russell, of Oxford, N. H. Went to Delhi, Iowa, and soon after died of consumption, in 1859.

1628. iv. JAMES H. GILMORE, b. 1837, m. 1869. Maria Aldrich: have three children, names not ascertained. Residence, Topeka, Kansas.

1629. v. WM. H. GILMORE, b. in 1839, m. Mary T. Haseltine, of Oxford, N. H. They live on the old homestead in Fairlee, Vt., with the mother of Mr. Gilmore. They have a son and daughter, names not ascertained.

1630. vi. MARY A. GILMORE, b. 1841, d. 1852.

1631. vii. PAMELIA C. GILMORE, b. 1844, d. 1851

1632 viii. JANE CATHIE GILMORE, b. 1849, d. 1865. All the deaths in in this family are from consumption.

[Sixth Generation.]

1602. iv. GRIFFIN CHILD, fourth child and third son of Alpha and Mary May Child, b. in Woodstock, Ct., Jan. 25, 1784, married twice—1st, Aug. 15, 1811, Nancy Peck, b. 1775, d. April 15, 1816; m. 2d, Jan. 22, 1818, Sarah Field, b. June 23, 1796, d. 1855. He d. Feb. 12, 1862, æ. 78.

Mr. Child was a man of imposing appearance, being six feet in height and of solid proportions, his weight, when in health, being 200 lbs. or over; of a florid complexion, with dignified bearing, he looked the man of mark he was, having the unmistakable signs of intellectual strength and decision of character. He possessed a clear and logical mind, and was usually successful in maintaining his positions. He was a man of much culture and for a number of years, in early manhood, a successful educator, popular and influential among the intelligent and cultured classes, and held in high esteem by all his acquaintances. On relinquishing his profession as a teacher, he established himself in the mercantile business in Providence, R. I., where he spent the balance of his life, becoming quite opulent.

[Seventh Generation.]   Children:

1633. i. LEWIS PECK CHILD, b. in Providence, R. I., Nov. 28, 1812, unm.

1634. ii. JAMES GRIFFIN CHILD, b. in Providence, R. I., Aug. 15, 1815, d. Aug. 15, 1821.

1635. iii. WM. SPENCER CHILD, b. in Providence, R. I., Nov. 14, 1818, m. July 27, 1841, Georgiana Clough Jones, m. 2d, Jessie Isabella Davis.

1636. iv. ANNA MARIA CHILD, b. in Newport, R. I., Oct. 17, 1820, m. Jan. 13, 1841, Geo. Mathewson.

1637. v. JAMES GRIFFIN CHILD, 2D, b. in Providence, R. I., Jan. 24, 1825.

1638. vi Infant, unchristened, b. Aug. 3, 1827, d. Aug. 10, 1827.

1639. vii. SARAH FIELD WASHINGTON CHILD, b. in Providence, R. I., Feb. 22, 1835, d. Dec. 19, 1836.

[Seventh Generation.]

1635. iii. Rev. WILLIAM SPENCER CHILD, D. D., third child and third son of Griffin and Sarah Field, b. Nov. 14, 1818, m.

Georgiana Clough Jones, by whom he had six children. She died and he married second, Jessie Isabella Davis, and by her he had three children.

Mr. Child is a prominent clergyman of the Episcopal church, and resides in Newport, R. I. He is a graduate of Brown University, and has received the honorary degree S. T. D.

Rev. Dr. William Spencer Child has established in Newport, Rhode Island, a school for young men, called the "St. John's School," the standard of whose scholarship is so high that none can graduate therefrom without honorable and thorough attainments. In the report of the school year, ending 14th of July, 1880, we find the committee on compositions, stated in their written report, that they "commend with especial emphasis three features in the essays, namely, their marked originality; their extraordinary accuracy of spelling; and their ease and clearness of style, rising in some instances to genuine elegance." Elsewhere we read: "None receive a first testimonial unless the average of his scholarship for the year is 95 per cent. or upwards; or a second testimonial unless 90 per cent. or upwards." Several prizes were competed for, some offered by the Rector, Dr. Child, others by friends of the institution, Dr. Batterson, of Philadelphia, and Dr. Malcolm. We are pleased also, to record the promise for the future of the Child name, that a Miss Edith Child, and a son, Clarence G. Child, of the Rector, were awarded prizes for declamation and Latin. The school is finely located on the Point, near the bay in this most healthful, attractive watering place.

[Eighth Generation.] Children:

1640. i. WM. POPE CHILD, b. in Newport, R. I. Dec. 10, 1843, d. Jan. 29, 1845.

1641. ii. LEWIS PECK CHILD, b. in Newport, R. I., June 14, 1847. Business 26 Exchange Place, New York City.

1642. iii. SPENCER CHILD, b. in Newport, R. I., Nov. 22, 1849, d. Nov. 12, 1852.

1643. iv. SAMUEL PENNY CHILD, b. in Newport, R. I., Dec. 3, 1854.

1644. v. ANNIE MARIA CHILD, b. in Newport, R. I., Nov. 21, 1855.

1645. vi. WM. SPENCER CHILD, JR., b. in Newport, R. I., Dec. 23, 1856.

1646. vii. HERBERT DOANE CHILD, b. in Newport, R. I., May 26, 1862.

1647. viii. CLARENCE GRIFFIN CHILD, b. in Newport, R. I., March 22, 1864.

1648. ix. JOHN CHILD, b. in Newport, R. I., Dec. 14, 1865.

[Seventh Generation.]

1636. iv. ANNA MARIA CHILD, fourth child and eldest dau. of Griffin and Sarah Field Child, b. in Newport, R. I., Oct. 17, 1820, m. Jan. 13, 1841, Geo. Mathewson.

[Eighth Generation.]   Children:

1649. i. SARAH FIELD MATHEWSON, b. in Newport, R. I., Nov. 5, 1841, m. Dec. 6, 1865, Lieut. Lewis Child.

1650. ii. AMY MATHEWSON, b. in Newport, R. I., May 11, 1843.

1651. iii BROCKHOLST MATHEWSON, b. in Newport, R. I., Oct. 17, 1844.

1652. iv. MARY WAITE MATHEWSON, b. in Newport, R. I., May 23, 1846.

1653. v. ANN MARIA MATHEWSON, b. in Newport, R. I., Nov. 20, 1847, d. Aug. 27, 1848.

1654. vi. GEORGE MATHEWSON, b. in Newport, R. I., Sept. 19, 1849, d. May 2, 1850.

1655. vii. WM. SPENCER MATHEWSON, b. in Newport, R. I., Feb. 20, 1851, d. Jan. 1, 1853.

1656. viii. LEWIS CHILD MATHEWSON, b. in Newport, R. I., June 28, 1854.

[Fourth Generation.]

1484 viii. SARAH CHILD, sixth child and third dau. of Capt. Benjamin and Patience Thayer Child, b. in Woodstock, Ct., Nov. 19, 1722, m. Feb. 19, 1746, Jedediah Morse, of Woodstock. This family became distinguished, and frequently allied to the Child family in subsequent years.

Deacon Jedediah Morse was a man of very strong individuality of character, he was born in Woodstock, Ct., in 1726. In 1763, we find he was chosen a deacon of the church, at or near the same time, another deacon was chosen, they had been married at very nearly the same date, and together they served the church for over fifty years; the wives of each deceased about the same time, after being married nearly sixty years—and the closely united friends after surviving their wives some fourteen years, were scarce separated in death. Dea. Jedediah Morse was chosen selectman in 1763, and in 1764, representative to the General Court of Connecticut, a position he held for thirty one years. In 1764, he was chosen town clerk, and held this office twenty-seven years. He was made Justice of the Peace in 1774, and continued in this office until 1801. He was a man very methodical in all his modes of thought and act, and a quaint resumé of his life, recapitulating his numerous official acts in the differing offices held by him, with sundry comments thereon, in the same measured, singular phraseology, is yet in the custody of a descendant. Mrs. Sarah Child Morse died on the 5th of April, 1805, aged 83, having been married fifty-eight years. Dea. Morse died in 1819, aged 93.

[Fifth Generation.] Children:

1657. i. DOROTHY MORSE, b. Dec. 20, 1747, d. April, 1755.

1658. ii. JONATHAN MORSE, b. April 30, 1850, m. Azubah Lyon.

1659. iii. CALVIN MORSE, b. June 30, 1852, m. Sophia Mason.

1660. iv. AMOS MORSE, b. 1755–6, d. young.

1661. v. DOROTHEA MORSE, b. April 29, 1757, married twice—1st, Silas May; 2d, a Mr. Bliss.

1662. vi. LYDIA MORSE, b. June 22, 1759, m. Jan. 10, 1781, Capt. Willard Child. [*See page 179 for children.*]

1663. vii. JEDEDIAH MORSE, b. Aug. 23, 1761, m. March 14, 1789, Elizabeth Ann Breese.

1664. viii. LEONARD MORSE, b. Nov. 11, 1763, d. Dec. 16, 1763.

1665. ix. SARAH MORSE, b. Jan. 2. 1765, d. Feb. 5, 1765.

[Fifth Generation.]

1663. vii. Rev. JEDEDIAH MORSE, D.D., fourth son and seventh child of Sarah Child and Dea. Jedediah Morse, b. in Woodstock. Ct., Aug. 23, 1761, m. March 14, 1789, to Miss Elizabeth Ann Breese, of Shrewsbury, N. J. He was a graduate of Yale College, New Haven, Ct., in 1783.

Dr. Morse was a prominent clergyman of the Congregational denomination during a long settlement at Charlestown, Mass. He was, however, better and more widely known as the "Father of American Geography." His first work on this subject, and the first of the kind published in America, he prepared and printed while yet a tutor in Yale College, in 1784. This was succeeded by larger works on Geography, also several gazetteers. But not alone was Dr. Morse absorbed in these geographical and historical studies; he was also a noted polemic—in opposing the Unitarian belief. He was sole editor of the *Panoplist*, a magazine published in Massachusetts for several years. Dr. Morse's life was one of unusual activity for a clergyman of that period; we find he was at one time under appointment of the United States Government, sent to the Northwest to examine into the condition of the Indians, as a result of this tour he published a volume entitled "Indian Report." He also published a "History of New England." The University of Edinburgh, Scotland, in recognition of his scholarly attainments conferred upon him his Doctorate. At the age of sixty-five Dr. Morse closed his full and respected life in New Haven, Ct., June 9, 1826, leaving a family honorably sustaining the father's repute; two of his sons possessed marked literary and scientific ability, with unusual inventive genius.

[Sixth Generation.] Children:

1666. i. Samuel Finley Breese Morse, b. April 27, 1791, m. twice—1st, Oct. 6, 1818, Lucretia Walker; m. 2d, Aug. 10, 1848, Sarah Griswold.

1667. ii. Edwards Morse, b. Oct. 4, 1792, d. 1793.

1668. iii. Edwards Sidney Morse, b. Feb. 7, 1794, m. April 1, 1841, Catherine Livingston.

1669. iv. Richard Cary Morse, b. May 6, 1797, m. twice—1st, 1828, Louisa Davis; m. 2d, Aug. 1856, Harriet Messenger.

1670. v. Elizabeth A. Morse, b July 12, 1798, d. 1804.

1671. vi. James R. Morse, b. June 20, 1801, d. young.

1672. vii. Elizabeth Morse, b. Jan. 27, 1803, d. in infancy.

[Sixth Generation.]

1666. i. Prof. Samuel Finley Breese Morse, LL. D., eldest son and child of Rev. Dr. Jedediah and Elizabeth A. Breese Morse, and grandson of Sarah Child and Dea. Jedediah Morse, was born in Charlestown, Mass., on the 27th April, 1791, was twice married, his first marriage to Miss Lucretia Walker, daughter of Mr. Charles Walker, of Concord, N. H., on the 6th October, 1818. Mrs. L. W. Morse died on the 7th February, 1827. Prof. Morse was married on the 10th August, 1828, to Miss Sarah Griswold.

Dr. Morse's name is so prominently linked with the application of magnetism to telegraphy, as almost to obscure the other talents of this distinguished man. He was a graduate of Yale College, New Haven, Ct., in 1810. The year following he went to England, in the company of Washington Allston, the artist; and while there became the pupil of the celebrated Benjamin West, in painting, to which pursuit he devoted many years; was so successful while yet in Great Britain as to enter one of his pictures, "The Dying Hercules," at an exhibition of the Royal Academy. In 1813 he received the gold medal of the Adelphi Society of Arts, at the hands of the Duke of Norfolk. Prof. Morse returned to America in 1815 and spent most of his time for the succeeding ten or twelve years in portrait painting. In 1829 Prof. Morse again crossed the Atlantic, remaining abroad some years; upon his return voyage, in 1832, the "idea of a permanent recording telegraph was suggested to him by a fellow voyager, Dr. Jackson." From this time Prof. Morse was absorbed by this project until, in 1844, his

Sam F. B. Morse

labors were crowned with success by the establishment of the first electric telegraph in the United States. The history of his toils and disappointments cannot be written, but the final triumph compensated. Dr. Morse's invention was accepted in Germany, and ready recognition, with due honors, were bestowed upon him by the sovereigns and literary and scientific associations of Europe. From his Alma Mater, Prof. Morse received the Doctorate of Laws in 1846. Dr. Morse lived to see the world almost girdled with the magic wires of telegraphy. He died in New York City on the 2d April, 1872. National honors in memoriam were accorded him in the Hall of Representatives, at the Capitol in Washington, D. C., on the night of Tuesday, the 16th April, 1872, on which occasion we received as relatives the following invitation:

The National Telegraph Memorial Association
Requests the honor of your presence at the
Memorial Services in honor of the late Sam'l F. B. Morse,
to be held in the Hall of Representatives,
Tuesday evening, April 16th, 1872, at 7½ o'clock.

Committee of Arrangements.

On the part of the Congress of the United States.

E. H. ROBERTS, N. Y.   F. W. PALMER, Iowa.   F. E. SHOBER, N. C.

C. F. STANSBURY,	H. D. COOKE,	M. G. EMERY,
C. C. COX,	J. E. KERR,	D. W. BLISS,
L. A. GOBRIGHT,	A. J. MYER,	O. E. BABCOCK,
HORATIO KING,	S. A. DUNCAN,	B. S. HEDRICK,
RICH'D WALLACH,	R. M. CORWINE,	
H. AMIDON, Sec'y.		A. S. SOLOMONS, Chairman.

Seats will be provided for the invited guests of the Association and the ladies accompanying them.

The services were of unusual interest, nothing commonplace or trite was uttered, the accompanying programme of services but epitomises, we can do no more. The marvellous invention was its own testimony on the occasion from in front the speaker's desk, the ticking so slight as not to interrupt the speeches, tolled off its weird, sibyllistic characters, flashing words of greeting to all the principal cities of the Union, and, most strange of all, was the sending to His Honor, the Mayor of London, and the immediate response, dated London, Wednesday morning, one o'clock the 17th April, received in the Hall on *Tuesday evening,* the 16th, before eleven P. M.

Order of Memorial Services

IN HONOR OF THE LATE

SAMUEL F. B. MORSE,

IN THE

Hall of the House of Representatives, Tuesday Ev'g, April 16, 1872.

Chairman, MR. SPEAKER BLAINE,

ASSISTED BY THE VICE PRESIDENT OF THE UNITED STATES.

Prayer by the REV. DR. W. ADAMS, D. D., of New York.

MR. SPEAKER BLAINE will announce the Order of Proceedings.

Music by the Marine Band.

Presentation of Resolutions by HON. C. C. COX, M. D., of Washington, D. C.

Address by HON. J. W. PATTERSON, of New Hampshire.

Address by HON. FERNANDO WOOD, of New York.

Vocal Music by the Choral Society of Washington.

Address by HON. J. A. GARFIELD, of Ohio.

Address by HON. S. S. COX, of New York.

Music by the Marine Band.

Address by HON. D. W. VOORHEES, of Indiana.

Address by HON. N. P. BANKS, of Massachusetts.

Vocal Music by the Choral Society of Washington.

Benediction by the REV. DR. WHEELER, of Poughkeepsie, New York.

Committee of Arrangements.

ON THE PART OF THE CONGRESS OF THE UNITED STATES

E. H. ROBERTS, New York.   F. W. PALMER, Iowa.   F. E. SHOBER, North Carolina.

C. F. STANSBURY,	H. D. COOKE,	M. G. EMERY,	C. C. COX,	J. B. KERR,
D. W. BLISS.	L. A. GOBRIGHT.	O. E. BABCOCK,	A. J. MYER,	HORATIO KING,
RICH'D WALLACH,	S. A. DUNCAN,	R. M. CORWINE,	B. S. HEDRICK.	

H. AMIDON, *Secretary.*   A. S. SOLOMONS, *Chairman.*

[Seventh Generation.]   Children.

1673. i. SUSAN WALKER MORSE. b. Sept. 2, 1819, m. about 1839 Edward Lind.

1674. ii. CHARLES WALKER MORSE. b. March 17, 1823, m. June 15; 1849, Mannette Lansing.

1675. iii. JAMES FINLEY MORSE. b. Jan. 20. 1825.

1676. iv. SAMUEL ARTHUR BREESE MORSE, b. July 24, 1849, d. July 17, 1876, in New Orleans, La.

1677. v. CORNELIA LIVINGSTON MORSE. b. April 8, 1851.

1678. vi. WILLIAM GOODRICH MORSE, b. Jan. 31, 1853, m. Oct. 2, 1873, Katherine Crabbe.

1679. vii. EDWARD LIND MORSE, b. March 29, 1857.

[Seventh Generation.]

1673. i. SUSAN WALKER MORSE, eldest daughter and child of Prof. S. F. B. Morse, LL. D., was born on the 2d September 1819, about 1839 was married to Mr. Edward Lind, a merchant and planter in Arroyo, Porto Rico, West Indies.

[Eighth Generation.] Child.

1680. i. CHARLES WALKER LIND, b. about 1840. Business agent of sugar estates in Arroyo, Porto Rico, W. I.

[Seventh Generation.]

1674. ii. CHARLES WALKER MORSE, eldest son and second child of Prof. S. F. B. Morse, LL. D., was born March 17, 1823, and 15th June, 1849, married Miss Mannette Lansing, who was born 3d April, 1830, a daughter of Bleecker B. Lansing.

[Eighth Generation.] Children :

1681. i. BLEECKER LANSING MORSE, b. Sept. 29, 1850, m. Sept. 29, 1879, in Texas.

1682. ii. SAMUEL FINLEY B. MORSE, b. Nov. 24, 1854.

1683. iii HENRY LIND MORSE, b. Jan. 4, 1860, d. April 4, 1863.

1684. iv. SUSAN LIND MORSE, b. Jan 26, 1863.

[Seventh Generation.]

1678. vi. WILLIAM G. MORSE, fourth son and sixth child of Prof. S. F. B. Morse, LL. D., b. January 31, 1853, m. October 2, 1873, Katherine Crabbe, of Havana, Cuba.

[Eighth Generation.] Child:

1684½. i. LEILA LIVINGSTON MORSE, b. June 25, 1878.

[Sixth Generation]

1668. iii. SIDNEY EDWARDS MORSE, third son and child of Dr. Jedediah and Elizabeth A. Breese Morse, and grandson of Sarah Child and Dea. Jedediah Morse, was born in Charlestown, Mass., on the 7th February, 1794, married on the 1st April, 1841, Catherine Livingston, dau. of Rev. Dr. Gilbert R. Livingston, of Philadelphia, Pa. She was born on the 24th September, 1813. Mr Morse graduated at Yale College, New Haven, Ct., in 1811 ; was associated with his brother, Prof. S. F. B. Morse, in the development of several of his mechanical inventions. He was, however, known widely as a journalist, first in 1815 establishing a weekly religious paper in Boston, Mass., called the Boston *Recorder*; with this paper his connection was brief, and in 1823, he united with his younger brother, Rev. Richard Morse, in establishing the New York *Observer*, the earliest religious paper in the State. He inherited the literary tastes of his father, and was himself the compiler of works upon physical and political geography. "In June, 1839, he in connection with Henry A. Munson, produced by a new art termed, Cerography, map

prints superior to those hitherto known." His death occurred
in the City of New York, on the 23d December, 1871.

[Seventh Generation.]   Children:

1685. i. GILBERT LIVINGSTON MORSE, b. Feb. 8, 1842, m. Feb. 8, 1871,
Mary Coles.

1686. ii. LUCRETIA MORSE, b. Dec. 28, 1843, m. Oct. 2, 1862, Charles K.
Herrick.

[Seventh Generation.]

1685. i. GILBERT LIVINGSTON MORSE, eldest child of Sidney
E. and Catherine Livingston Morse, b. in New York City, on
the 8th February, 1842, married on the 8th February, 1871,
Mary Coles, dau. of John Coles, of Worthing, England. She
was b. May 18th, 1850. Mr. Morse's business, rentier, on Nassau
street, New York City. Residence in Yonkers, Westchester,
Co., N. Y.

[Eighth Generation.]   Children:

1687. i. MAUD LIVINGSTON MORSE, b. Dec. 17, 1871.
1688. ii. SIDNEY E. MORSE, b. Jan. 29, 1874.
1689. iii. MAY MORSE, b. May 3, 1876.
1690. iv. ELSIE MORSE, b. Oct. 8, 1878.

[Seventh Generation.]

1686. ii. LUCRETIA MORSE, only dau. of Sidney Edwards
and Catherine Livingston Morse, was born in the City of New
York, on the 28th December, 1843, married on the 2d October,
1862, to Charles K. Herrick: separated, she resumes her paternal
name, as do her children.

[Eighth Generation.]   Children:

1691. i. LIVINGSTON B. MORSE, b. Aug. 29, 1863.
1692. ii. LUCRETIA MORSE, d. in infancy.
1693. iii. KATE MORSE, d. in infancy.
1694. iv. EDNA MORSE, b. Aug. 23, 1869.

[Sixth Generation.]

1669. iv. RICHARD CARY MORSE, fourth son and child of
Rev. Dr. Jedediah and Catherine Breese Morse, and grandson
of Sarah Child and Dea. Jedediah Morse, was born in Charlestown, Mass., on the 6th May, 1797, married twice—1st, in 1828,
to Louise Davis: married 2d, in August 1856, Harriet Mess-
inger.

Rev. Mr. Morse graduated from Yale College, New Haven,
Ct., in 1812. Studied for the ministry and received his licensure,
but was not long occupied with the duties of that profession.
In 1823, he became the partner of his brother, Sidney E. Morse,

in publishing the widely circulated journal, the New York *Observer*, a pioneer enterprise in this State, now a fixed fact. The possession by this family of such distinctive and unusual talents, verify the theories of transmission.

[Seventh Generation.] Children:

1695. i. ELIZABETH MORSE, b. Aug. 5, 1829, m. 1853, Samuel Colgate.
1696. ii. CHARLOTTE MORSE, b. 1831, m. Aspinwall Hodge.
1697. iii. SIDNEY E. MORSE, b. Nov. 25, 1835, m. Nov. 1, 1859, Annie Church.

[Seventh Generation.]

1695. i. ELIZABETH MORSE, eldest dau. and child of Rev. Richard Cary and Louisa Davis Morse, b. 5th Aug. 1829, m. in 1853, Samuel Colgate.

[Eighth Generation.] Children:

1697½. i. RICHARD MORSE COLGATE.
1698. ii. GILBERT COLGATE.
1699. iii. SIDNEY COLGATE.
1700. iv. AUSTEN COLGATE.
1701. v. SAMUEL COLGATE, JR.
1802. vi. RUSSEL COLGATE.

[Seventh Generation.

1696. ii. CHARLOTTE MORSE, second dau. and child of Rev. Richard Cary and Louisa Davis Morse, b. in 1831, m. Aspinwall Hodge.

[Eighth Generation.] Children:

1703. i. BAYARD HODGE, d. in infancy.
1704. ii. ASPINWALL HODGE, JR.
1705. iii. RICHARD HODGE.
1706. iv. HUGH HODGE.
1707. v. SAMUEL C. HODGE.

[Seventh Generation.

1697. iii. SIDNEY E. MORSE, eldest son and third child of Rev. Richard Cary and Louisa Davis Morse, b. 26th November, 1835, m. 1st November, 1859, by Stephen H. Tyng, D D., Miss Anna Matilda Church, dau. of John Bartsee and Maria Trumbull Silliman Church, and grand-daughter of Prof. Silliman, of Yale College, New Haven, Ct. She was b. August 8th, 1839. Mr. Morse's business, rentier 140 Nassau St., New York City.

[Eighth Generation.] Children:

1708. i. MARY TRUMBULL MORSE, b. Dec. 7, 1862.
1709. ii. ELIZABETH BREESE MORSE, b. June 16, 1864.

T

[Fourth Generation.]

1485. vii. MOSES CHILD, seventh child and fourth son of Capt. Benjamin and Patience Thayer Child, b. in Woodstock, Ct., Oct. 27, 1725, m. June 24, 1752, Mary Payson.

[Fifth Generation.] Children.

    1710. i. LUCRETIA CHILD b. in Woodstock, Ct., Aug. 17, 1756, d. young.
    1711. ii RUFUS CHILD, b. in Woodstock, Ct., Aug 30, 1762, m. twice—
1st, Miss Marcy, she died Feb. 2, 1789, m. 2d, Jan. 18, 1795, Anna Barnum.
    1712. iii. JOHN PAYSON CHILD, b. in Woodstock, Ct., 1763.
    1713. iv. OLIVER CHILD, b in Woodstock, Ct., July 12, 1764.

[Fifth Generation.]

1711. ii. RUFUS CHILD, eldest child of Moses and Mary Payson Child, b. Aug. 30, 1762, m. 1st, Miss Marcy, she d. Feb. 2, 1789; he m. 2d, Anna Barnum.

[Sixth Generation.] Child.

    1714. i. LUCRETIA ANN CHILD, b. in Woodstock, Ct., Aug 6, 1796,

[Fifth Generation.]

1220. ix. CHLOE CHILD, fifth daughter and ninth child of Capt. Elisha and Alice Manning Child of Woodstock, Conn., b. in Woodstock, March 28th, 1767, m. March 31st, 1790, Leonard Walker, eldest son of Phineas and Susanna Hyde Walker, of Woodstock.

Mr. Leonard Walker was a mechanic and his ingenuity was remarkably versatile. His father being a blacksmith, he could not well avoid that trade. He learned also the art of card making, which was then after a most primitive fashion: each tooth of the card being made singly, and by hand, and the holes in the leather for the insertion of the teeth were made in the same slow and laborious manner. After the leather and teeth were prepared, they were sent to all the families in the region who would receive them, that the women and children might push the teeth into their place in the leather. Mr. Leonard Walker was a pioneer in devising a method to accomplish this work by machinery. Mr. and Mrs. Walker, with their family, at that time consisting of four children, in the year 1797 removed from Woodstock, Conn., to Strafford, Vt. In this new settlement, where mechanics were few, his ingenuity had ample range, for not only everything that could by any possibility come under the name of blacksmithing was done by him, but clocks, fowling-pieces, spinning-wheels, pocket-knives, brass-kettles, trunk-locks, jews-harps, tin horns and teapots, when out of order, were brought to him; and he felt as much at home in soldering a gold finger-ring, or ear-ring, as he did in splicing a crow-bar. As a citizen he was active in every enterprise that was a benefit to a new country, took a deep interest in having the best schools; was foremost in the erection of the meeting-house, whose beautiful situation on the knoll at the north end of the green is unsurpassed. He made the vane for the steeple in that "universal manufactory," and his son Charles, (afterward the Rev. Charles Walker, D. D.,) then eight years old, sawed the laths for the plastering. His whole influence was in favor of law and order; he early embraced the cause of temperance, and gave up his much loved pipe. In all these good ways and works Mrs. Walker was a thorough help-meet. Guiding her children and her whole household in paths of pleasantness and peace, a true "Mother in Israel." For about twenty years Mrs Walker read Scott's Family Bible through each year, with all the notes and observations. Never had a numerous family a more excellent mother. Mr. George Walker, the eighth child of Mr. and Mrs. Leonard Walker, remained at home until he was of age, and does not remember ever hearing an angry word pass his mother's lips. Mrs. Walker died on September 1st, 1843, her husband survived her seven years, passed from earth on the 9th September, 1851. [This sketch of Mr. and Mrs. L. Walker is furnished us by Mr. Geo. Walker, of Northford, Ct.]

[Sixth Generation.] Children:

1715. i Charles Walker, b. Feb. 1, 1791, m. Sept. 22. 1823, Lucretia Ambrose.

1716. ii. Susan Walker, b. May 22, 1792, m. Dea. Luther Child.

1717. iii. Benjamin Walker, b. Oct. 11, 1793, d. young.

1718. iv. Leonard Walker, b. Oct. 1, 1794, m. Sept. 11, 1822, Hannah Child. (See descendants of Capt. John Child, of Bath, N. H., for children.)

1719. v. Alice Walker, b. March 23. 1796, m. Sept. 3, 1831, John Child. (See page 215, No 1229, for children.)

1720. vi Sylvia Walker, b. March 13, 1798, d. April 28, 1874.

1721. vii. Chloe Walker, b. Nov. 30, 1799, "a sweet singer," d. Sept. 30, 1832.

1722. viii. George Walker, b. March 8, 1802, m. Jan. 2, 1832, Minerva Hoadley.

1723. ix. Freeman Walker, b. Feb. 4, 1804, d. Sept. 21, 1827.

1724. x. Eliza Walker, b. June 5, 1805, m. March 29, 1825, Andrew Chandler, d. Dec. 9, 1827, one child.

1725. xi. PHINEAS WALKER, b. Jan. 13, 1807. m. Aug. 19, 1839, Mahala Walker.

1726. xii. LUCIUS WALKER, b. Feb. 1. 1809. m. Jan. 1, 1837, Henrietta Davenport, d. June 30, 1878.

1727. xiii. ALDACE WALKER, b. July 20, 1812. m. April 30, 1841, Mary A. Baker, d. July 24, 1878.

[Sixth Generation.]

1715. i. Rev. CHARLES WALKER, D. D., eldest son of Chloe Child and Leonard Walker, b. in Woodstock, Conn., 1st February, 1791, was a vigorous, active and wide awake youth, fond of sports and athletic games, but loving books better; often he would leave his playmates to sit happily beside his mother, reading such old standard works as Doddridge, Milton, Young and Baxter. But he had little leisure for play or reading, for the exigencies of a new settlement left small space for pastime. The saw-mill, shop and farm kept him (and his younger brothers) busy, and his labors were performed with a willing mind and deft hand. When he was of age he went to Woodstock, Conn., among the friends of his parents, and his own infant days; through the influence of these relatives he obtained a position in a woolen mill, and such was his dexterity, inherited from his father, with the training of the "universal manufactory" of the home in Vermont, that he was soon at the head of the establishment, where he continued a few years, giving entire satisfaction to his employers. Under the preaching of the Rev. Samuel Backus, he was led to embrace the truth in Jesus the Christ, and, like Paul, the first question was "Lord, what wilt Thou have me to do?" He decided to devote himself to saving others, and he never lost sight of that aim, keeping to it most singly through a long and very useful life.

Mr. Walker devoted himself to study for the ministry of the Congregationalist order. His first settlement was at Rutland, Vermont, and hither he brought his bride. Miss Lucretia Ambrose, of Concord. New Hampshire, to whom he was married on the twenty-second of September, 1823. Mr. Walker remained with the church in Rutland for ten years. After a period of unusual labor, his voice failed utterly and he was compelled to resign his parish. Mr. Walker took charge of the high school in Castleton, Vermont, and in about two years recovered his voice and was settled over a Congregational church in Brattleboro, Vermont, in January, 1835,

where for eleven years he was a beloved and successful pastor.
A very decided stand taken on the temperance question gave
offence to some of the parish, and lest injury should befall the
church Mr. Walker withdrew, preferring the good of others to
his own ease—though firm in his views of the right in his
position. In August, 1846. Dr. Walker was installed as pastor
of a church in Pittsford, Vermont, where he continued till, from
advanced age, he felt impelled to resign—a ministry of more
than eighteen years had greatly endeared him to this people.
In the words of one who knew him well, "Dr. Walker was
endowed by nature with a mind of vigorous and substantial
power. He was clear, consecutive and strong. Few men saw
better than he did the main points on which the truth of an
argument depended. Few men could put those points into
statements more simple, logical and convincing. His intellect
was healthful. There was nothing morbid, still less senti-
mental, in his constitution. The robustness of his physical
health, as well as the practical character of his early training
contributed, doubtless, to this sound quality of his mental
action. This characteristic gave his judgment great weight.
He was a man strong for counsel. In the decision of vexed
questions of controversy, in ecclesiastical or social matters, his
verdict was pretty certain to be right. Hence few men were
oftener called into requisition when difficulties arose in
churches. His service upon councils was no small or unim-
portant part of his work. Without being a strenuous or intense thinker, his mind was active and retained its alertness to
the last. He lived in his age. He looked with always interested eye upon the progress of affairs in state and society. He
read history for its lessons of practical and present instruction.
He had definite opinions in politics. He applied the principles
of the gospel to public affairs. Hence his occasional dis-
courses, drawn out by events in the social and political world,
were always instructive and interesting. As a sermonizer he
was marked by some signal merits. His style of composition
was singularly clear and chaste. He wrote good English. No
one ever mistook his meaning. This directness and effective-
ness of address was aided by a pulpit manner in a high degree impressive. Dr. Walker was a large, dignified and handsome man, a man whose presence commanded respect and

attention. His voice was penetrating and powerful. It was also expressive of tender and strong emotions, so that in his more earnest passages he held his hearers in an intense and solemn grasp. In his social character Dr. Walker was genial and affectionate. Not a great talker, he was fond of good conversation. He was loved by all the children. The success of others pleased him. He did not think that wisdom was dead, or the world growing worse all the time. But perhaps the most characteristic trait of Dr. Walker was his simplicity. He was a man utterly incapable of finesse or duplicity. Few men ever carried such demonstration of sincerity in all they did. Of exceedingly few could it be said with equal truth, he was a 'man in whom there was no guile.'" Dr. and Mrs. Walker had six children. His death occurred on the 28th of November, 1870, at Pittsford, Vermont.

[Seventh Generation.]   Children:
     1728. i. CHARLES A. WALKER, b. Sept. 10, 1824, d. Aug. 12, 1838.
     1729. ii. ANNE A. WALKER, b. Aug. 26, 1826, m. Aug. 15, 1866, to George N. Boardman, Prof. in the Theo. Sem. in Chicago.
     1730. iii. GEORGE LEON WALKER, b. April 10, 1830, m. Sept. 16, 1858, Maria Williston.
     1731. iv. LUCRETIA A. WALKER, b. May 4, 1832, d. July 18, 1833.
     1732. v. STEPHEN A. WALKER, b. Nov. 2, 1835, unm. Lawyer in New York.
     1733. vi. HENRY F. WALKER, b. July 3, 1838. Physician; unm.

[Seventh Generation.]

     1730. iii. Rev. GEORGE LEON WALKER, D. D., son of Rev. Dr. Charles and Lucretia Ambrose Walker, born in Rutland, Vermont, married Sept. 16, 1858, Miss Maria Williston. Dr. Walker is a clergyman of the Congregationalist order. Settled in Hartford, Ct. He has never known vigorous health, yet has been able to sustain himself well as a sermonizer ; is an interesting, not to say fascinating preacher. The lawyer and the child being equally attracted. Dr. Walker's health has been so frail as to compel the resignation of several settlements, but as strength permits, he still labors for the Master. Dr. and Mrs. Walker have had two children.

[Eighth Generation.]   Children:
     1734. i. WILLISTON WALKER, b. July 1, 1860.
     1735. ii. CHARLES A. WALKER, b. Sept. 27, 1861, d. July 22, 1869.

     1722. viii. GEORGE WALKER, eighth child of Chloe Child and Leonard Walker, b. in Strafford, Vt., 8th March, 1802,

m. Miss Minerva Hoadley, daughter of Jairus Hoadley, Esq., of Northford, Ct., 2d January, 1832.

Mr. Walker was a mechanic and manufacturer. He spent his youth upon the home farm, in the saw-mill, and more pleasurably in the "universal manufactory" of his father, and inherited largely the peculiar gifts of his father of brain and hand. Upon attaining his majority he left home, and was fully and successfully employed for some eight years in various machine shops. Upon his marriage he settled in New Haven, Conn., where he established a lucrative business in stoves, etc. Mr. George Walker was the first to introduce patent warm air furnaces into churches and dwellings in that city. After residing in New Haven about fourteen years, Mr. Walker in the year 1844, removed with his family to the City of New York, and for fifteen years his was the leading house in the city for warming dwellings and public buildings. He sold out and occupied the next ten years in many kindly acts of service for others, making this his business as it was truly his pleasure; this included the investigation of the mining and metal resources of the country, involving three journeys to the Rocky Mountains of Colorado, made by mule teams. Not being a writer, Mr. Walker has never published an account of these trips,—though the home-fireside and social board are often enlivened by reminiscences of the varied and amusing experiences of those long journeys. Not unremunerative were they either to Mr. Walker or his associates. The evening of life is spent by Mr. and Mrs. Walker in the home of Mrs. Walker's infancy, where, as in all the years of their united life, happiness gilds their unselfish lives, and competence gives ease.

[Sixth Generation.]

1724. x. ELIZA WALKER, fifth daughter and ninth child of Chloe and Leonard Walker, b. in Strafford, Vermont, June 5, 1805, m. 29th March, 1825, Andrew Chandler. Mr. and Mrs. Chandler had one child, a daughter, who married and has several children. Mr. Chandler died 19th Dec., 1827.

[Seventh Generation.] Child:

1736. i. ELMINA CHANDLER, married to Mr. Richard Lakeman, of Boston.

[Seventh Generation.]

1736. i. ELMINA CHANDLER, only child of Andrew and Eliza Walker Chandler, and granddaughter of Chloe Child Walker, married about 1853, Richard Lakeman.

[Eighth Generation.] Children:
   1737. i. FRANK LAKEMAN, b. July 14, 1854.
   1738. ii. EMMA J. LAKEMAN, b. Nov. 24, 1857.
   1739. iii. RICHARD J. LAKEMAN, b. Jan. 17, 1861.
[Sixth Generation.]

   1725. xi. PHINEAS WALKER, sixth son and eleventh child
of Chloe Child and Leonard Walker, b. in Strafford, Vermont,
13th January, 1807, m. 19th August, 1839, Miss Mahala
Walker, daughter of Freeman Walker, of Connecticut.

   Mr. Phineas Walker was the home-son, and was such a son
to his parents in their years of infirmity through age, as we are
warranted to expect a son to be, whose training is that of scriptural command. It is only a truthful, though high praise to
say of him. "He is a good specimen of honest New England
character: is a deacon in the church, and a substantial supporter of those things that are of good report." Mr. Walker
combines the farm pursuits with mechanical as did his father.
This fertility of brain power seems a frequent possession of
the genuine New Englander. Three children were given them
of whom only one remains.
[Seventh Generation.] Children:
   1740. i. LEONARD WALKER, b. May 1. 1836, d. July 1, 1841.
   1741. ii HARRIET WALKER, b. Jan. 2, 1838, d. Dec. 15, 1858.
   1742. iii. SUSAN WALKER, b. July 7, 1842, m. Perley Chandler.
[Seventh Generation.]

   1742. iii. SUSAN WALKER, third child of Phineas and Mahala
(Walker) Walker, b. 7th July, 1842, m. Perley Chandler, a
jeweler of Barre, Vermont, November 11, 1867. Has two
children.
[Eighth Generation.] Children:
   1743. i. HATTIE CHANDLER, b. May 9, 1869.
   1744. ii. MINERVA CHANDLER, b. May 24, 1875, d. Sept. 5. 1875.

[Sixth Generation.]
   1726. xii. LUCIUS WALKER, seventh son and twelfth child
of Chloe Child and Leonard Walker, b. in Strafford, Vermont,
Feb. 1, 1809, m. Miss Henrietta Davenport, Jan. 1st, 1837. Of
four children granted to them, only one is now living. Two
noble sons of rare intellectual powers in early manhood rested
from their labors, and went home almost on the threshold of
their young manhood. Mr. L. Walker d. June 30, 1878.
[Seventh Generation.] Children:
   1745. i. ALDACE ATWOOD WALKER, b. Jan. 30, 1839, d. Oct. 23, 1861.
   1746. ii. ALICE H. WALKER, b. Feb. 10, 1841, d. April 12, 1845.

1747. ii. EDNA MINERVA WALKER, b. Oct. 23, 1843, m. Fitzhugh M. Dibble
1748. iv. LUCIUS PIERPONT WALKER, b. March 29, 1845, d. July 13, 1872.

[Seventh Generation.]

1745. i. ALDACE ATWOOD WALKER, eldest son of Lucius and Henrietta Davenport Walker, b. January 30, 1839. Was a genuine scholar, educated at the Free academy in New York City. He was a young man of great promise, and though so young when called home, had already become a successful teacher. He died of consumption, on the 23d of Oct. 1861.

[Seventh Generation.]

1748. iv. LUCIUS PIERPONT WALKER, fourth child and second son of Lucius and Henrietta Davenport Walker, b. March 29, 1845.

Lucius was in some respects a remarkable child. When only four years old he would repeat on his sister's melodeon any tune she would play : simple airs of course, as she was young ; at first not keeping time, but would touch every note, and soon would get the time. At eight years of age he did not incline to music at all, but was wholly absorbed in his studies. He would give the diameter of each planet, with its distance from the sun, the length of its day and year, with the relative size of each, and number of their moons, as fast as he could speak. And on the blackboard he would make a diagram of the whole, and in doing it he would make the chalk fly rapidly. At fifteen years of age he was a sly rogue, manifested in sundry ways beside running away and enlisting in the 2d Connecticut Heavy Artillery, under the assumed name of Charley Morris, so that his parents could not find him. But when once with the army, he wrote to his parents, and ever after was as regular in his correspondence with the home friends as the exigencies of war would permit. He was, what he looked, a mere boy, but he carried his musket, haversack and other accoutrements like a veteran, and never flinched, though marching twenty-four and even thirty-six hours consecutively. He was with Gen. Sheridan in all the battles of the Shenandoah Valley. In his own words we give an incident of his Shenandoah experience :

"At that time I was stationed at Corps Headquarters in the capacity of 'Provost Guard,' and in company with others of the guard used frequently to go into the country on foraging expeditions. On such occasions we generally went ten or twelve miles from the camp, and were of course liable to the attacks of guerrillas with whom the country swarmed. At this time we started with the teams about daylight, and after travelling about four hours, halted at a barn, which stood near the road; the main part of our squad (about twenty in all) commenced loading the wagons with hay, sending out six of us 'sheep-hunting,' which always formed an important part of our expeditions; having the reputation of a good shot, I was chosen one of the six. We did not find any until we had gone fully half a mile from the wagons, when we saw a large flock in an inclosed lot. When sufficiently near, we opened fire.' The echoing reports of our pieces had scarcely died away when we suddenly saw three puffs of white smoke arise from a belt of wood directly before us, about two hundred yards distant, and three bullets with their peculiar zip, zip, zip, flew past our heads. As our muskets were discharged we could not return the fire, but started for the wagons at full speed, followed by a scattering volley of musketry from at least twenty mounted guerrillas, whom we could now see emerging from the wood on the gallop toward us. As we were on foot we knew it would be useless to try to outrun them, and consequently determined to fight it out. For this purpose we selected an old building composed of huge pine logs, which Providentially stood near. On arriving here we loaded our pieces, and as the guerrillas came within fifty yards we fired into the m, which knocked one man over and brought the rest to a halt. For a few moments all was quiet. Then one of them approached waving a handkerchief and calling on us to surrender if we did not want our d—d throats cut; we told him we could not see the point, when he departed cursing like a pirate, in which he was assisted by his comrades, who all tried to see who could vituperate the —— Yankees the worst, treating us with an occasional bullet, but not dari g to advance. We kept up a random fight for a short time, but fearing our ammunition would become exhausted, resolved to cease firing until they made some new hostile demonstration. In a few moments we saw they were trying to flank us, about half of them going on our right, and the rest on our left. Presently we saw they were preparing for a charge; accordingly, three of us took one side and three the other, fixed our bayonets and resolved to sell our lives dearly. Soon they advanced, receiving our fire which killed two of them when within twenty yards we rose and prepared to give them cold steel, when suddenly an overwhelming volley was poured into them by a party of our cavalry, which were out on a scout. At this new turn of affairs the surviving ruffians instantly made tracks, but were pursued and taken prisoners before they could reach their horses. Among the nine prisoners was the notorious Dick Saunders. Thirteen other guerrillas lay on the ground killed and wounded. After this we left for our wagons, not however forgetting our sheep."

In his sketch of his army life, he thus describes the battle of Cedar Creek :

"Just before morning we heard several volleys of musketry, but at first paid little attention to it, as we thought it picket-firing. We were soon informed of our mistake for orders came to pack up and fall in. We formed in line and marched toward the firing, halting in the road just in front of a ravine. The morning was foggy, and we could not see far, but presently discovered two lines of battle in front of us, which we took to be our own men. But on receiving a volley from them learned our mistake. We replied to their fire for about fifteen minutes, and then being ordered to fall back, a panic seemed to seize everybody, and for about two miles we made quick time, until we were stopped by a line of our cavalry, when we (the 6th corps) halted and soon after gave the Rebels two tremendous volleys which had the effect of making them stop quite suddenly. We then were put on the skirmish line for about three hours, when the arrival of Sheridan fixed things up by forming for a charge which was soon done, and in all my army life, I never saw a more desperate charge. The Johnnies stood as long as they could and then left, and when night came we found ourselves in our old camp, and thus ended the battle of Cedar Creek."

After Lee's surrender he had an honorable discharge. He had not grown much in his three years' service, and his musket shoulder was drawn down so much we feared it might prove a permanent deformity. But he soon began to grow, his shoulder obtained its right position, and he became a good-sized, well formed man. The family moving from New Haven, Conn., to Louisville, Kentucky, and his four year old passion for music reviving, he was soon at the head of the musical profession in Louisville; and was by a unanimous vote elected leader of the Organist Club. He composed several airs. He never used tobacco, never took intoxicating drinks, though both were so common in the army. He became a communicant of the church, and was in every respect an exemplary young man. His death was sudden and unaccountable. He was bathing with others in the Ohio river, sank and did not rise. His death was upon the 14th July, 1872, when in his twenty-fifth year.[1]

[Sixth Generation.]

1727. xiii. Rev. ALDACE WALKER, D. D., thirteenth child and eighth son of Chloe Child and Leonard Walker, was born in Strafford, Vermont, 10th July, 1812. He was an exceedingly pleasant boy and a studious youth. At the age of eighteen he was converted, and immediately commenced preparation for the ministry. He graduated from Dartmouth College, Hanover, New Hampshire, in 1837; and from the Theological Seminary in Andover, Mass., in 1840. In the same year he was called to settle over the Congregational church in West Rutland, Vermont, where he remained until 1862, when failing health compelled him to give up the pastorate, to the lasting regret of his people. After two years his health was so far restored as to permit him to accept a call to Wallingford, Vermont, where he remained until his death.

[1] We are indebted to his Uncle Mr George Walker for this sketch.

Early in his ministry he was elected a member of the corporation of Middlebury College, to whose interests he was ever after devoted. He was for many years a corporate member of the "American Board of Foreign Missions." In the language of one who knew him well, "The character of Dr. Aldace Walker was a harmonious one, centered upon an abiding purpose, and distinguished by sound judgment, such as usually comes from absence of selfishness, and devotion to a great cause. Such a character drew to itself duties as well as dignities. In the general convention and in the councils of the church, as well as in the affairs of his own parish, his wise advice was sought and followed. He was a leader by the divine right of superior wisdom, tact and fidelity. It was impossible to come within the reach of his character without being impressed with its sincerity; its entire freedom from disturbing ambition, and the depressing influence of a conflict between the outward surroundings of life and its inward purpose. In his ministry of twenty-one years in West Rutland, he became identified with his parish in an unwonted degree. His words were received with respect by his people who always trusted him. Revivals marked his ministry, which had no drawback to its success. It stands a monument of his life. He was happy in his work, which never fretted him. He had a faculty of saying and doing things easily. His power was in the pulpit, where he showed his capacity to lead men. He never misled his hearers or left them in doubt, that it was best for them to accept the truth. As trustee of Middlebury College he was always self-possessed, and never doubted that a way would open out of all difficulties. No one had a calmer head, or firmer decision." Dr. Aldace Walker was married to Miss Mary A. Baker, April 30th, 1841, in the same year of his graduation from the Theological Seminary and settlement at West Rutland, Vermont. Dr. Walker's death occurred at Wallingford, Vermont, the place of his last parochial charge, 24th July, 1878.

[Seventh Generation.] Children:

1749. i. ALDACE F. WALKER, b. May 11, 1842, m. April 6, 1868, Katie M. Shaw.

1750. ii. LEONARD BAKER WALKER, b. Oct. 5, 1845, d. Aug. 6, 1846.

1751. iii. MARY MALVINA WALKER, b. Nov. 18, 1851, is a teacher in Brattleborough, Vermont.

[Seventh Generation]

1749. i. ALDACE F. WALKER, eldest child of Rev. Dr. Aldace and Mary A. Baker Walker, b. in West Rutland, Vermont, m. Miss Katie M. Shaw, April 6, 1868. Mr. Walker is a lawyer and resides in Rutland, Vt.

[Eighth Generation.] Children:

1752. i. RICHARD WALKER, b. Oct. 25, 1872, d. Jan. 19, 1876.

1753. ii. ROBERT WALKER, b. Aug. 24, 1874.

1754 iii. HAROLD WALKER, b. June 5, 1876.

[Fifth Generation.]

1222. xi. BETSEY CHILD, seventh dau. and eleventh child of Capt. Elisha and Alice Manning Child, b. in Woodstock, Ct., 1773, m. Feb. 21, 1797, Alfred Walker, son of Phineas and Susannah Hyde Walker. An excellent mechanic doing business in East Woodstock, Ct., the place of his birth. A man of genial disposition, affable, hospitable, of strict integrity, and a most excellent citizen. A worthy father of seven children, who have not failed to honor their parentage. Mr. Walker was born March 29, 1774, d. ——

[Sixth Generation.] Children:

1755. i. EMILY WALKER, b. in Woodstock, Ct., Feb. 3, 1797, m. 1833, Isaac E. Smith.

1756. ii. ELISHA CHILD WALKER, b. Sept. 1799, m. Sept. 30, 1824, Sylvia Child. (For children see No. 912, p. 195.)

1757. iii. ADALINE WALKER, b. in Woodstock, Ct., 1801, m. August 14, 1821, John Hibbard.

1758. iv. ELVIRA WALKER, b. in Woodstock, Ct., Aug. 5, 1803, d. 1830, unmarried. Much admired for personal beauty, loveliness of character and accomplishments as a singer.

1759. v. ALFRED WALKER, b. in Woodstock, Ct., July 29, 1805, m. Eunice Minor. Mr. W. is a real estate and loan broker in New Haven, Ct. Had several children.

1760. vi. JAMES WALKER, b. in Woodstock, Ct., March 12, 1808, m. Isabel Hibbard. Farmer and mechanic, resides in Woodstock, Ct. Had two daughters, not living.

1761. vii. WILLIAM WALKER, b. in Woodstock, Ct., May 15, 1810, m. Marie Dunham in 1836, d. March 27, 1870.

[Sixth Generation.]

1755. i. EMILY WALKER, eldest dau. and child of Betsey Child and Alfred Walker, b. in Woodstock, Ct., Feb. 3, 1797, m. 1833, Isaac E. Smith, a lumber merchant of New York City. She d. October 29, 1870.

[Seventh Generation.] Children:

1762. i. EDWARD A. SMITH, b. in New York, July 25, 1835, m. March 3, 1868, Mrs. Melissa Heath.

1763. ii. ERNEST L. SMITH, b. in New York, Nov. 29, 1837, m. April 18, 1866. Caroline W. Marther; have no children. Mr. Smith is in the lumber business with his father in New York City.

[Seventh Generation.]

1762. i. Rev. EDWARD A. SMITH, eldest son of Emily Walker and Isaac E. Smith, and grandson of Betsey Child Walker, b. July 25, 1835, m. March 3, 1868, Mrs. Melissa Heath (neé Knox), dau. of Charles W. Knox of Chester, Mass. Rev. Mr. Smith is pastor of the Congregational church in Farmington, Ct.; have two children.

[Eighth Generation.] Children:
    1764. i. HERBERT KNOX SMITH, b. in Chester, Mass., Nov. 7, 1869.
    1765. ii. EARNEST WALKER SMITH, b in Farmington, Ct., June 5, 1878.

[Sixth Generation.]

1757. iii. ADALINE WALKER, third child of Betsey Child and Capt. Alfred Walker of East Woodstock, Ct., b. 1801, m. Aug. 14, 1821, John Hibbard, moved to Dundee, Ill., d. July 24, 1857.

[Seventh Generation.] Children:
    1766. i. JOHN HIBBARD, b. Dec. 24, 1826, m. Nov. 18, 1851, Catharine Thompson.
    1767. ii. ADELINE HIBBARD, b. about 1828, m. Nov. 8, 1865, L. D. Kendall.
    1768. iii. ELVIRA HIBBARD, b. Dec. 25, 1831, m. Jan. 15, 1852, Geo. E. Slade.
    1769. iv. EMILY HIBBARD, b. Dec. 25, 1831, d. May 7, 1857.
    1770. v. MINERVA HIBBARD, b. Jan. 23, 1836, m. Sept. 20, 1859, Frank Slade.

[Seventh Generation.]

1766. i. JOHN HIBBARD, first child of Adaline Walker and John Hibbard, and grandson of Betsey Child Walker, b. Dec. 24, 1826, m. Nov. 18, 1851, Catharine Thompson, she d. July 6, 1857; m. 2d, Elizabeth Goodwin, she d. 1869; m. 3d, Levantia Richards.

[Eighth Generation.] Children:
By first marriage.
    1771. i. JOHN LAWRENCE HIBBARD, b. July 2, 1857.
By second marriage.
    1772. ii FRANK G. HIBBARD, b. May 15, 1867.
By third marriage.
    1773. iii. LOUIS R. HIBBARD, b July 8, 1874.
    1774. iv. KATE E. HIBBARD, b. Sept. 12, 1877.

[Seventh Generation.]

1767. ii. ADELINE HIBBARD, second child of Adaline Walker and John Hibbard, and granddaughter of Betsey Child Walker, b. about 1828, m. L. D. Kendall, Nov. 8, 1850.

[Eighth Generation.] Child:

1775. i. ARTHUR D. KENDALL, b. July 3, 1852.

[Seventh Generation.]

1768. iii. ELVIRA HIBBARD, third child of Adaline Walker and John Hibbard, and granddaughter of Betsey Child Walker, m. Jan. 15, 1852, Geo. E. Slade.

[Eighth Generation.] Children:

1776. i. EMILY SLADE, b. Nov. 8, 1852, m. Dec. 25, 1872, Emmet O'Connell.

1777. ii. CHARLES W. SLADE, b. March 18, 1857.

1778. iii. ADDIE W. SLADE, b. May 1, 1861.

[Seventh Generation.]

1770. v. MINERVA HIBBARD, fifth child of Adaline Walker and John Hibbard, and granddaughter of Betsey Child Walker, b. Jan. 23, 1836, m. Sept. 20, 1859, Frank Slade.

[Eighth Generation.] Children:

1779. i. HARRY G. SLADE, b. March 22, 1861.

1780. ii. SUSIE SLADE, b. April 17, 1867.

CHAPTER II.

Edward Child, the third child of Capt. Benjamin and Grace Morris Child, was not of the families that went to Woodstock, Ct. He remained on the old homestead and raised a family in Roxbury, Mass. We note this fact, as we give the other sons as emigrating to Woodstock, under head of WOODSTOCK FAMILIES.

[Third Generation.]

17. iii. EDWARD CHILD, third child and son of Benjamin and Grace Morris Child, and grandson of the Emigrant Benjamin Child, b. in Roxbury, Mass., Nov. 1, 1687, m. 1712 Margaret Weld. He was the possessor of the old homestead, the successor of his father Benjamin Child, Jr. He was well known as a glazier and as a farmer, and noted as a large landholder, holding grants in numerous deeds, copies of which and a number of originals are in the possession of David Weld Child, of Boston, and later of Auburndale, Mass., of the seventh generation.

[Fourth Generation.] Children.

1781. i. HANNAH CHILD, b. in Roxbury, Mass., Dec. 7, 1712, m. April 18, 1734, Thomas Baker, Jr.

1782. ii. JOHN CHILD, b. in Roxbury, Mass., Jan. 26, 1714, m. Jan. 26, 1742, Esther Child.

1783. iii. ELEAZER CHILD, b. in Roxbury, Mass., March 11, 1717, d. yg.

1784. iv. STEPHEN CHILD, b. in Roxbury, Mass., Aug. 19, 1719, m.———

1785. v. EDWARD CHILD, JR., b. in Roxbury, Mass., Sept. 13, 1721, m Miss Perrin.

[Fourth Generation.]

1782. ii. JOHN CHILD, second child and eldest son of Edward and Margaret Weld Child, b. in Roxbury, Mass., Jan. 26, 1714, m. Jan. 26, 1742, Esther Child.

[Fifth Generation] Children.

1786. i. HANNAH CHILD, b. in Roxbury, Mass., April 20, 1743, d. young.

1787. ii. MARGARET CHILD, b. in Roxbury, Mass., April 8, 1745, d. April 26, 1775.

1788. iii. PRISCILLA CHILD, b. in Roxbury, Mass., Dec. 20, 1748, d. April 14, 1750.

1789. iv. HANNAH CHILD, 2D, b. in Roxbury, Mass., Jan. 30, 1750, m. March 17, 1774, Abner Craft.

1790. v. ESTHER CHILD, b. in Roxbury, Mass., March 2, 1753, d. young.

1791. vi. JOHN CHILD, JR., b. in Roxbury, Mass., June 16, 1756. He was successor to Edward Child, his grandfather, to the old homestead of Benjamin Child. He also was well known as a glazier, as well as a large possessor of landed estates, there being twenty or more original deeds and copies of which he was the grantee. He died unmarried at Wrentham, Sept. 2, 1825.

1792. vii. STEPHEN CHILD, b. in Roxbury, Mass., Aug. 10, 1758, m. May 25, 1786, Sarah Weld.

1793. viii. JOHANNA CHILD, b. in Roxbury, Mass., Oct. 10, 1760.

1794. ix. ANN CHILD, b. in Roxbury, Mass., Jan. 22, 1762 unmarried.

1795. x. CATHARINE CHILD, b. in Roxbury, Mass., Sept. 3, 1764, m. John Dale.

[Fifth Generation.]

1792. vii. STEPHEN CHILD, seventh child and second son of John and Esther Child, b. in Roxbury, Mass., Aug. 10, 1758, m. May 25, 1786, Sarah Weld.

[Sixth Generation.] Children.

1796. i. STEPHEN CHILD, JR., b. in Roxbury, Mass., March 16, 1787, m. Dec. 2, 1813, Hepzebah Coburn Richards.

1797. ii. JOHN WELD CHILD, b. in Roxbury, Mass., Feb. 8, 1789, m. April 24, 1817, Sarah Richards.

1798. iii. MARGARET CHILD, b. in Roxbury, Mass., March 11, 1791, m. Feb. 9, 1814, Benjamin Williams.

1799. iv. HARRIET CHILD, b. April 11, 1793, m. Augustus Perrin.

1800. v. SARAH WELD CHILD, b. in Roxbury, Mass., June 9, 1795, d. 1811.

1801. vi. DAVID WELD CHILD, b. in Roxbury, Mass., June 27, 1798, d. Sept. 20, 1798.

1802. vii. DAVID WELD CHILD, 2D, b. in Roxbury, Mass., Aug. 2, 1799, d. 1816, by a fall which fractured the spine.

1803. viii. EDWARD AUGUSTINE CHILD,) b. Aug. 3, 1804, m. Sarah Wales.
〉 Twins.
1804. ix. ESTHER CHILD, ） b. Aug. 3, 1804, d. 1805.

1805. x. ELIZABETH CHILD, b. in Roxbury, Mass., July 23, 1805, d. Aug. 7, 1805.

1806. xi. BENJAMIN FRANKLIN CHILD, b. in Roxbury, Mass., Oct. 12, 1806, m. Aug. 17, 1836, Helen Brown.

[Sixth Generation.]

1796. i. STEPHEN CHILD, JR., eldest child of Stephen and Sarah Weld Child, b. in Roxbury, Mass., March 16, 1787, m. Dec. 2, 1813, Hepzebah Coburn Richards. Mr. Child was a coal and lumber dealer in Boston.

[Seventh Generation.] Children.

1807. i. SARAH CHILD, b. in Boston, Mass., Jan. 6, 1815, m. Dec., 1840, Elbridge Gerry Dudley, by Rev. John Pierrepont.

1808. ii. WILLIAM HENRY CHILD, b. in Boston, Mass., Oct. 8, 1816, d. Nov. 28, 1816.

U

1809. iii. MARGARET CHILD, b. in Boston, Mass., Jan. 4, 1818, m. June 14, 1854, John Albree.

1810. iv. MARTHA ANN CHILD, b. in Boston, Mass., Oct. 10, 1820, m. Nov. 19, 1857. E. G. Dudley.

1811. v. DAVID WELD CHILD, b. in Boston, Mass., Aug. 7, 1822, m. Jan. 13, 1848, Olive Turner Thayer

1812. vi. STEPHEN FRANKLIN CHILD, b. in Boston, Mass., Dec. 8, 1824, m. March 27, 1851, Mary E. Follett.

1813. vii. DANIEL WELD CHILD, b. in Boston, Mass. Jan. 25, 1828, m. May 5, 1859, Ellen B. Cunningham.

1814. viii. MARY RICHARDS CHILD, b. in Boston, Mass. Nov. 7, 1831.

1815. ix. ELIZABETH RICHARDS CHILD, b. in Boston, Mass. March 4, 1835, d. Nov. 27, 1835.

[Seventh Generation.]

1811. v. DAVID WELD CHILD, fifth child and second son of Stephen, Jr., and Hepzebah Coburn Child, b. in Boston, Mass., Aug. 7, 1822, m. by Rev. Dr. N. Adams, Jan. 13, 1848, Olive Turner Thayer, dau. of Geo. W. Thayer, a merchant of Boston. Mrs. C. was b. May 7, 1823. Mr. Child was formerly a grain dealer; later a real estate broker in Boston. Resides in West Newton, Mass.

[Eighth Generation.] Children:

1816. i. LUCY CHILD.   ) b. in Boston, Dec. 28, 1848, d. soon.
                          } Twins.
1817. ii. WALTER CHILD,   ) b. in Boston, Dec. 28, 1848, d Nov. 5, 1862.

1818. iii. CAROLINE CHILD, b June 23, 1852, in Boston, Mass.

1819. iv. HARRIET CHILD, b. in Boston, July 25, 1854

1820. v. GEO. STEPHEN CHILD,) b. in Boston, Ap. 17, '58, d. Ap. 21, '58.
                             } Twins.
1821. vi. GRACE MORRIS CHILD.) b. in Boston, Ap. 17, '58, d. Ap. 18, '58.

1822. vii. FRANCES CHILD, b. in Boston, Aug. 21, 1859.

1823. viii. STEPHEN CHILD, b. in Boston, Aug. 14, 1866.

[Seventh Generation.]

1813. vii. DANIEL WELD CHILD, seventh child and fourth son of Stephen, Jr., and Hepzebah Coburn Richards Child, b. in Boston, Jan. 25, 1828, m. 1859, Ellen B. Cunningham.

[Eighth Generation.] Children:

1824. i. EDITH CHILD, b. in Boston, Mass, Oct. 31, 1859.

1825. ii. MARGARET CHILD, b. in Boston, Mass., Oct. 21, 1862.

[Sixth Generation.]

1797. ii. JOHN WELD CHILD, second child and second son of Stephen Child, Jr., and Sarah Weld Child, b. in Roxbury, Mass., Feb. 8, 1789, m. April 24, 1817, Sarah Richards. She was born Aug. 9, 1794, d. 1832; he d. March 21, 1864.

[Seventh Generation.] Children:

1826. i. MARY CAROLINE CHILD, b. in Roxbury, Mass., Jan. 15, 1818, m. May 2, 1840, Stephen Jenks.

1827. ii. ESTHER MARIA CHILD, b. in Roxbury, Mass., May 12, 1819, m. Feb. 10, 1842, J. Metcalf.

1828 iii. JOHN AVERY RICHARDS CHILD, b. in Roxbury, Mass., Aug. 29, 1821, lives in Dorchester, Mass.

1829. iv. JOHN WELD CHILD, JR., b. in Roxbury, Mass., June 6, 1823, d. 1840.

1830. v. EDWARD AUGUSTUS CHILD, b. in Roxbury, Mass., Feb. 28, 1825, m. 1854, Amanda Peet.

1831. vi. SARAH RICHARDSON CHILD, b. in Roxbury, Mass., Oct. 24, 1827. She was a popular teacher in the public schools of Dorchester, to which she was for many years attached. Her death was much lamented.

1832. vii. STEPHEN CHILD, b. Oct. 5, 1831, d. young.

[Sixth Generation.]

1806. xi. BENJAMIN FRANKLIN CHILD, ninth child and sixth son of Stephen and Sarah Weld Child, b. in Roxbury, Mass., Oct. 12, 1806, m. Aug. 17, 1836, Helen Brown. He resided at Hardin, Calhoun county, Ill., where he died (date of death not ascertained).

[Seventh Generation.] Children:

1833. i. MARGARET CHILD, b. in Hardin, Calhoun Co., Ill., June 3, 1838, d. Aug. 17, 1839.

1834. ii. STEPHEN CHILD, b. in Hardin, Calhoun Co., Ill., June 20, 1840.

1835. iii. BENJAMIN FRANKLIN CHILD, JR., b. in Hardin, Calhoun Co., Ill., July 11, 1842, d. Jan. 22, 1848.

1836. iv. THOMAS BROWN CHILD, b. in Hardin, Calhoun Co., Ill., June 25, 1844, d. Sept. 3, 1845.

1837. v. JOSEPH PERRIN CHILD, b. in Hardin, Calhoun Co., Ill., Oct. 9, 1845, d. Sept. 28, 1846.

1838. vi. EDWARD CHILD, b. in Hardin, Calhoun Co., Ill., May 2, 1849, d. of cholera, Aug. 8, 1851.

1839. vii. HARRIET HELEN CHILD, b. in Hardin, Calhoun Co., Ill., June 14, 1849, d. Aug. 22, 1851.

1840. viii. GEORGE BROWN CHILD, b. in Hardin, Calhoun Co., Ill., June 12, 1851.

1841. ix. SARAH CHILD, b. in Hardin, Calhoun Co., Ill., Oct. 30, 1853.

1842. x. FRANK CHILD, b. in Hardin, Calhoun Co., Ill., Aug. 27, 1855.

The unusual mortality in this family is remarkable, the cause or causes of which in most instances are not reported.

[Fourth Generation.]

1784. iv. STEPHEN CHILD, fourth child and third son of Edward and Margaret Weld Child, b. in Roxbury, Mass., Aug. 17, 1719. Was a soldier in the successful expedition under General Pepperell, (afterwards Sir William Pepperell, made Baronet for his prowess, the first of the American Colonists to receive a title ;) mostly from Boston and vicinity—to Port Royal, in 1745, at a period when England was disputing claims with the French. Port Royal then in possession of the French, was captured and became a British Province, under the name of Nova Scotia. When Louisburg, which had been called the Gibraltar of America, was taken, and the army had entered the city, the soldiers were filled with amazement at the ease with which they had possessed it. The fortifications had cost five millions of dollars, and had been regarded as impregnable. Yet an undisciplined army of four thousand farmers and fishermen had gained an easy possession. They seemed inspired with the words of Whitefield, then in Boston, to the little army as it was about to set sail: "Nothing is to be despaired of when Christ is the leader."

Having no date by which to determine with certainty the fact and time of Stephens Child's marriage, our knowledge of his descendants is inferential rather than positive. But there is strong circumstantial evidence that Aaron Child, born in Roxbury, Mass., in 1741, was the son of this Stephen Child, of the Port Royal expedition. We think that perfect assurance may sometime be obtained.[*]   Lemuel Child who kept the famous Peacock tavern in Roxbury, Mass., is known to have been a brother to this Aaron Child.

An amusing incident is related as occurring at this popular place of resort. "When the British officers were in Boston, Mass., they frequently made up skating parties for suppers, and after exercising at the pond, would ride over and partake of the good cheer of the *Peacock*. Upon one of these occasions, so says tradition, the "pretty maid" of the *inn*, afterwards Mrs. Williams, a niece of the inn-keeper, was followed by one of the gay young bloods into the cellar, whither she had gone for supplies for the table. Being familiar with the premises, she blew out the lighted candle she held in her hand and made her escape, not forgetting to fasten the cellar door behind her. After thumping his head against the rafters in the vain effort to follow her, her persecutor was finally obliged to alarm the house before

* If any of Lemuel Child's descendants should see this volume and have in their possession any data relative to the ancestry of Aaron Child, born 1741, they will confer a favor by communicating with Stephen Child of New Hartford, Oneida county, New York.

he could be released from his awkward position." Washington and other distinguished officers were frequent visitors here during the siege. Lemuel Child led the minute men of the third parish in the Lexington battle.—(*Roxbury paper.*)

[Fifth Generation.]

1843. AARON CHILD, son of Stephen Child of Roxbury, Mass., b. in Roxbury. Mass., in 1741. m. Nov. 9, 1869, Susannah Gridley, who was b. in Roxbury, in 1746, died Jan. 10, 1835. Mr. Aaron Child died Aug. 6, 1795.

[Sixth Generation.] Children:

1844. i. AARON CHILD, JR., b. Jan. 1, 1770, m. Mary Hall.

1845 ii. STEPHEN CHILD, b. July 17, 1771, m. Dec. 22, 1803, Rebecca Williams.

1846. iii. SUSANNAH CHILD, b. Aug. 22, 1776, m. 1804, William Blake.

1847 iv. ANNA CHILD, b. Sept. 3, 1779, in Brookline, Mass., d. Oct. 14, 1866.

1848. v. MARY CHILD, b. Feb. 4, 1788, m. about 1808, Rufus Babcock. Four other children were born to this couple, two named Lemuel, one Samuel, and one William, but they died in infancy, and neither the dates of their births or deaths are known.

[Sixth Generation.]

1844. i. AARON CHILD, JR., eldest son and child of Aaron and Susannah Gridley Child, b. in Brookline, Mass., Jan. 1, 1770, m. about 1794, Miss Mary Hall, who was b. Oct. 21, 1772, in Newton, Mass., and died July 26, 1847. Mr. Child died May 11, 1847.

[Seventh Generation.] Children:

1849. i. AARON CHILD, JR., b. Dec. 21, 1795, d. Aug. 3, 1839, æ. 44.

1850. ii. MARY MILLER CHILD, b. Oct. 16, 1799, m. David Hall.

1851. iii. WILLIAM CHILD, b. Aug. 21, 1802, m. abt. 1826, Hannah Howes.

1852. iv. CATHERINE ELIZA CHILD, b. Feb. 2, 1805, d. June 11, 1859, æ. 54.

1853. v. EDWARD HALL CHILD, b. April 11, 1808, m. Miss Haskell, d. in Boston, Sept. 16, 1826.

1854. vi. EMILY CHILD, b. March 15, 1811, m. 1st, George Hodges; m. 2d, Mr. Ripley.

1855. vii. REBECCA B. CHILD, b. Aug. 8, 1815, m. abt. 1842, Hiram Hall.

[Seventh Generation.]

1851. iii. WILLIAM CHILDS, third child and second son of Aaron and Mary Hall Child, b. in Roxbury, Mass., Aug. 21, 1802, m. about 1826, Hannah Bradford Holmes, who was b. Aug. 16, 1804. Mrs. H. B. H. Child d. Dec. 7, 1875. Mr. Wm. Child was a real estate broker in Boston. Residence, Dorchester, Mass., where he died April 22, 1878, æ. 76.

[Eighth Generation.] Children:
    1856. i. WILLIAM CHILDS, JR., b. 1827, unm. Resides in California.
    1857. ii. MARY ANN CHILDS, b. March 11, 1831, m. 1853, Isaac W. Pierce.
    1858. iii. CURTIS CHILDS, b. March 4, 1835, m. 1860, Louisa Eveleth.
    1859. iv. AARON CHILDS, d. at 17 years of age.
    1860. v. GEORGE CHILDS, d. at 10 years of age.
    1861. vi. ABNER CURTIS CHILDS, d. one year old.

[Eighth Generation.]

    1857. ii. MARY ANN CHILDS, eldest dau. and second child of William and Hannah B. Holmes Childs, b. March 11, 1831, m. 1852, Isaac W. Pierce, who was born July 24, 1827, and died April 20, 1876.

[Ninth Generation.] Children:
    1862. i. JAMES PIERCE, b. Feb. 6, 1853.
    1863. ii. LIZZIE PIERCE, b. June 19, 1862.

[Eighth Generation.]

    1858. iii. CURTIS CHILDS, second son and third child of William and Hannah B. Holmes Childs, b. May 4, 1835, m. 1860, Louisa Eveleth, who was born June, 1837.

[Ninth Generation.] Children:
    1864. i. JENNIE CHILDS, b. March 22, 1862.
    1865. ii. LUCY CHILDS, b. Dec. 17, 1864.
    1866. iii. HANNAH CHILDS, b. May 16, 1867.

[Seventh Generation.]

    1855. vii. REBECCA B. CHILDS, fourth dau. and seventh child of Aaron and Mary Hall Child, b. Aug. 8, 1815, m. Hiram Hall, abt. 1842. Mrs. R. B. Child Hall died in Jamaica Plains, on the 19th January, 1873.

[Eighth Generation.] Children.
    1867. i. EDWARD C. HALL, b. April 3, 1843.
    1868. ii. HIRAM HALL, JR., b. Dec. 17, 1844.
    1869. iii. HENRY G. HALL, b. Jan. 23, 1849.
    1870. iv. EMMA R. HALL, b. Aug. 23, 1853.
    1871. v. WALTER D. HALL, b. Dec. 13, 1855.
    1872. vi. ALBERT B. HALL, b. April 13, 1858.

[Sixth Generation.]

    1845. ii. STEPHEN CHILDS, second son and child of Aaron and Susannah Gridley Child. b. in Brookline, Mass., July 17, 1771, m. Dec. 22, 1803, Rebecca Williams, of Dorchester. She was b. at Roxbury, Mass., March 29, 1781, and d. Jan. 3, 1865. Mrs. Rebecca W. Childs was a descendant of Gov. Winslow, of Massachusetts, her mother's maiden name being Rebecca Winslow. He d. Jan. 16, 1863, aged 91.

[Seventh Generation.] Children:

1873. i. REBECCA WINSLOW CHILDS, b. 1804, m. June 12, 1832, Reuben M. Stackpole.

1874. ii. SUSANNAH CHILDS, b. March 2, 1806, m. Feb. 10, 1836, Galen V. Bowditch.

1875 iii. STEPHEN CHILDS, JR., b. Jan. 25, 1808, m. Oct. 1, 1845, Harriet Richardson.

1876. iv. HENRY CHILDS, b. Dec. 31, 1809, m. May 10, 1853, Ellen J. Neal.

1877. v. MARTHA WILLIAMS CHILDS, b. Feb. 7, 1812, m. June 12, 1833, Galen V. Bowditch.

1878. vi. NATHANIEL RUGGLES CHILDS, b. July 15, 1814, m. 1st, April 30, 1846, Eliza Etta Stone; m. 2d, Nov. 9, 1859, Caroline D. Hayden.

1879. vii. SAMUEL GRIDLEY CHILDS, b. May 20, 1817, d. Jan. 19, 1818.

1880. viii. SARAH WINSLOW CHILDS, b. Dec. 5, 1818, m. June 1, 1848, Wm. J. Hyde.

1881. ix. ALBERT CHILDS, b. May 3, 1821, m. Dec. 3, 1856, Anna M. Dudley.

1882. x. GEORGE CHILDS, b. Dec. 27, 1823, d. Feb. 15, 1869, unm.

[Seventh Generation.]

1873. i. REBECCA WINSLOW CHILDS, eldest child of Stephen and Rebecca Williams Childs, b. in Roxbury, Mass., in 1804, m. June 12, 1832, Reuben Markham Stackpole, who was b. April 8, 1792. Reside at Boston Highlands.

[Eighth Generation.] Children:

1883. i. CHARLES MARKHAM STACKPOLE, b. Sept. 23, 1833, d. Aug. 24, 1834.

1884. ii. HORACE MARKHAM STACKPOLE, b. March 16, 1835, d. Sept. 7, 1837.

1885. iii. ANNA WINSLOW STACKPOLE, b. Jan. 2, 1838, m. July 28, 1864 Edward Moulton Lancaster.

1886. iv. GEORGE REUBEN STACKPOLE, b. Sept. 23, 1839, d. Sept. 15, 1853.

1887. v. FREDERICK WILLIAM STACKPOLE, b. Aug. 20, 1841.

1888. vi. STEPHEN HENRY STACKPOLE, b. July 24, 1843, m. Oct. 18, 1871, Julia Langley Faunce.

[Eighth Generation.]

1885. iii. ANNA WINSLOW STACKPOLE, eldest dau. and third child of Rebecca W. Childs and Reuben M. Stackpole, b. in Roxbury, Mass., Jan. 2, 1838, m. July 28, 1864, Prof. Edward Moulton Lancaster, who was b. March 29, 1832. Prof. Lancaster is the Principal of the High School, at Hyde Park, Mass., he has recently edited a "History of England" for schools.

[Ninth Generation.] Children:

1889. i. EDWARD WINSLOW LANCASTER, b. March 2, 1866.

1890. ii. ALICE REBECCA LANCASTER, b. Oct. 15, 1869.

1891. iii. HELEN ABBIE LANCASTER, b. July 29, 1879.

[Eighth Generation.]

1888. vi. Rev. STEPHEN HENRY STACKPOLE, youngest son and child of Rebecca Winslow Childs and Reuben M. Stackpole, b. in Roxbury, Mass., July 24, 1843, m. Oct. 18, 1871, Julia Langley Faunce, who was b. Feb. 1843. Rev. Mr. S. H. Stackpole is a clergyman of the Baptist church, and now resident at Saxtons River, Windham Co., Vt.

[Ninth Generation.] Children:

1892. i. MARKHAM WINSLOW STACKPOLE, b. June 5, 1873.

1893. ii. PIERPONT LANGLEY STACKPOLE, b. Feb. 16, 1875.

[Seventh Generation.]

1874. ii. SUSANNAH CHILDS, second dau. and child of Stephen and Rebecca Williams Childs, b. in Roxbury, Mass., Mch. 2, 1806, m. Feb. 10, 1836, Galen V. Bowditch. Mrs. Susannah C. Bowditch was the second wife of Mr. G. V. Bowditch, his first wife was her younger sister, Martha Williams Childs, to whom Mr. Bowditch was m. June 12, 1833. She d. Feb. 22, 1834. Mrs. Susannah C. Bowditch d. Oct. 17, 1869.

[Eighth Generation.] Children.:

1894. i. SUSAN BOWDITCH, d. in infancy

1895. ii GALEN BOWDITCH, b. Nov. 23. 1837, in Roxbury, Mass

1896. iii. MARTHA CHILDS BOWDITCH, b. Jan. 5, 1840, in Roxbury, Mass.

1897. iv. JOSEPH ESTY BOWDITCH, b. Mch, 1843, d. Jan. 5, 1871.

[Seventh Generation.]

1875. iii. STEPHEN CHILDS, JR., eldest son and third child of Stephen and Rebecca Williams Childs, b. in Roxbury, Mass., Jan. 25, 1808, m. Oct. 1st, 1845, Harriet Richardson, dau. of Jonathan and Lois Parker Richardson. She was b. Sept. 25, 1820. Mr. Stephen Childs, Jr., removed to New Hartford, Oneida Co., New York, in 1830, and carried on the tanning and currying business for many years with much success. Mr. Childs is a man of pleasing presence, and much esteemed. Mrs. Childs belongs to a family of high respectability, and is a lady of most noble qualities. Residence New Hartford, Oneida Co., N. Y.

[Eighth Generation.] Children:

1898. i. STEPHEN HENRY CHILDS, b. Sept. 7, 1846, m. 1876, Mary Elizabeth Jenkins.

1899 ii. ALBERT NATHANIEL CHILDS, b. Feb. 20, 1850, d. April 9, 1850.

1900. iii. EMILY LOIS CHILDS, b. July 9, 1852.

1901. iv. SARAH ELIZABETH CHILDS, b. Feb. 5, 1854, d. June 16, 1856.

1902. v. WILLIAM RICHARDSON CHILDS, b. Dec. 18, 1856, d. June 25, 1873.

1903. vi. EDWARD WINSLOW CHILDS, b. May 30, 1859.

[Eighth Generation.]

1898. i. STEPHEN HENRY CHILDS, eldest son and child of Stephen and Harriet Richardson Childs, b. in New Hartford, New

York, Sept. 7, 1846, m. in 1876, Mary Elizabeth Jenkins, dau. of William and Delia Hall Jenkins. She was b. in New York City, Sept. 13, 1854.

[Ninth Generation.] Children:

1904. i. WILLIE RICHARDSON CHILDS, b. April 30, 1877.

1905. ii. EDITH MAY CHILDS, b. Feb. 21, 1880, in New Hartford, Oneida Co., N. Y.

[Seventh Generation.]

1876. iv. HENRY CHILDS, second son and fourth child of Stephen and Rebecca Williams Childs, b. in Roxbury, Mass., Dec. 31, 1809, m. May 10, 1853, Ellen Jane Neal. Mr. Henry Childs d. Jan. 25, 1876. Resided in Boston, and Cambridge-port. He was a printer.

[Eighth Generation.] Child:

1906. i. HARRY NEAL CHILD, b. Nov. 8, 1854.

[Seventh Generation.]

1878. vi. NATHANIEL RUGGLES CHILDS, third son and sixth child of Stephen and Rebecca Williams Childs, b. in Roxbury, Mass., July 15, 1814, m. April 30, 1846, Eliza Etta Stone, who d. June 12, 1857. Mr. Childs m. 2d, Nov. 9, 1859, Caroline D. Hayden. Resided in Dorchester, New Bedford and Rox-bury, Mass.; engaged largely in the shoe and leather business.

[Eighth Generation.] Children:

1907. i. MARTHA WINSLOW CHILDS, b. Jan. 25, 1847, m. Dec. 27, 1870, Edward W. Nash.

1908 ... NATHANIEL RUGGLES CHILDS, JR., b. Jan. 1849, resides in Elgin, Ill.

1909. iii. MARY STONE CHILDS, b Aug. 18, 1850, d. Feb. 20, 1854.

1910. iv. ELIZA ETTA CHILDS, b. May 16, 1852.

1911. v. FRANCES STONE CHILDS, b. Nov. 6, 1853, d. March 25, 1854.

[Seventh Generation.]

1880. viii. SARAH WINSLOW CHILDS, fourth daughter and eighth child of Stephen and Rebecca Williams Childs, b. in Roxbury, Mass., Dec. 5, 1818, m. June 1, 1848, William J. Hyde. Reside in Brookline, Mass.; bricklayer by occupation.

[Eighth Generation] Children:

1912. i. MARY ELIZABETH HYDE, b. May 11, 1849.

1913. ii. REBECCA WILLIAMS HYDE, b. March 19, 1851.

1914. iii. HARRIET CHILDS HYDE, b. March 19, 1854, m. June 15, 1876, Robert Watson Standart.

1915. iv. ALBERT CHILDS HYDE, b. Oct. 18, 1858, d. May 9, 1864.

1916. v. GEORGE WILLIAM HYDE, b. June 4, 1861.

[Eighth Generation.]

1914. iii. HARRIET CHILDS HYDE, third dau. and child of
Sarah Winslow Childs and William J. Hyde, b. March 19,
1854, m. June 15, 1876, Robert Watson Standart of Detroit,
Mich. Hardware merchant, of the firm of "Standart Brothers," in Detroit.

[Ninth Generation.] Children:

1917. i. SARAH WINSLOW STANDART, b. Sept. 23, 1877. d. July 5, 1878, in
Detroit, Mich.

1918. ii. WILLIAM ESTY STANDART, b. Oct. 25, 1879, in Detroit, Mich.

[Seventh Generation.]

1881. ix. ALBERT CHILDS, fifth son and ninth child of
Stephen and Rebecca Williams Childs, b. in Roxbury, Mass.,
May 3, 1821, m. Dec. 3, 1856, Anna M. Dudley. Reside in
Roxbury, Mass.; leather merchant, Boston.

[Eighth Generation.] Children:

1919. i. ALBERT WALTER CHILDS, b. April 11, 1861, in Roxbury, Mass.

1920. ii. FREDERICK TRACY CHILDS, b. April 16, 1866, in Roxbury, Mass.

[Sixth Generation.]

1846. iii. SUSANNAH CHILD, eldest dau. and third child of
Aaron and Susannah Gridley Child, b. in Brookline, Mass.,
Aug. 22, 1776, m. 1804, William Blake. She d. in Boston,
Mass., Aug. 31, 1866, æ. 90 years.

[Seventh Generation.] Children:

1921. i. WILLIAM BLAKE, JR., [date of birth not given] d. 1839.

1922. ii. JAMES BLAKE, [date of birth not given] went to Indiana.

1923. iii. JOHN BLAKE,   "   "   "   m. abt. 1833 Lucretia —

[Seventh Generation.]

1923. iii. JOHN BLAKE, third son and child of Susannah
Child and William Blake, m. about 1833 Lucretia ———

[Eighth Generation.] Children:

1924. i. ANNA M. BLAKE, b. Nov. 2, 1834, m. Sept. 6, 1854, Francis H.
Holton.

1925. ii. WALTER F. BLAKE, b June 13, 1836.

1926. iii. EDWIN H. BLAKE, b. Nov. 2, 1838, m. June 1, 1862, Mary E.
Parkhurst.

1927. iv. CLARA M. BLAKE, b. Aug. 31, 1841, m. June 23, 1874, Dr. Byron
R. Harmon.

1928. v. THEODORE E. BLAKE, b. Dec. 30, 1843.

1929. vi. EVELYN AMELIA BLAKE, b. Jan. 13, 1845, m. Nov. 2, 1866, Eben.
Pratt.

1930. vii. FREDERICK WILLIAM BLAKE, b. May 1, 1848.

1931. viii. ARTHUR WELLESLEY BLAKE, b. Oct. 14, 1851.

1932. ix. IRENE ADELIA BLAKE, b. April 13, 1854, d. July 30, 1876.

1933. x. JOSIAH QUINCY BLAKE, b. March 30, 1856, d. Sept. 9, 1858.

1934. xi. GEORGE WASHINGTON BLAKE, b. Feb. 4, 1861.

[Eighth Generation.]

1924. i. ANNA M. BLAKE, eldest child of John and Lucretia Blake, and granddaughter of Susannah Child Blake, b. Nov. 2, 1834, m. Sept. 6, 1854, Francis H. Holton.

[Ninth Generation.] Children:

1935. i. FRANCIS H. HOLTON, JR., b. Feb. 27, 1856.
1936. ii. FREDERICK BLAKE HOLTON, b. Dec. 23, 1858, d. April 1, 1864.
1937. iii. ANNA M. HOLTON, b. Nov. 30, 1864, d. Feb. 18, 1866.
1938. iv. EDWARD L. HOLTON, b. May 4, 1867, d. Aug. 1, 1868.

[Eighth Generation.]

1926. iii. EDWIN H. BLAKE, third child and second son of John and Lucretia Blake, and grandson of Susannah Child Blake, b. Nov. 2, 1838, m. June 1, 1862, Mary E. Parkhurst.

[Ninth Generation.] Children:

1939. i. CHARLEY EARNEST BLAKE, b. June 4, 1863, d. Oct. 26, 1863.
1940. ii. EDDIELENA MARION BLAKE, b. Aug. 7, 1864, d. Aug. 27, 1864.
1941. iii. ALFRED ELMA BLAKE, b. May 27, 1866.
1942. iv. CLARENCE WILLFRED BLAKE, b. July 27, 1869.
1943. v. JOHN QUINCY BLAKE, b. Oct. 14, 1874.
1944. vi. EDWINA MAY BLAKE, b. Dec. 11, 1875.

[Eighth Generation.]

1927. iv. CLARA M. BLAKE, second dau. and fourth child of John and Lucretia Blake, and granddaughter of Susannah Child Blake, b. Aug. 31, 1841, m. June 23, 1874, Dr. Byron R. Harmon.

[Ninth Generation.] Child:

1945. i. BERTIE CLAYTON HARMON, b. Aug. 15, 1876, d. April 10, 1878.

[Eighth Generation.]

1929. vi. EVELYN AMELIA BLAKE, third dau. and sixth child of John and Lucretia Blake, and granddaughter of Susannah Child Blake, b. Jan. 29, 1845, m. Nov. 2, 1866, Eben. Pratt.

[Ninth Generation.] Children:

1946. i. FREDERIC LINCOLN PRATT, b. Jan. 9, 1867.
1947. ii. ALICE EVELYN PRATT, b. Feb. 16, 1873.
1948. iii. SUSAN WHEATON PRATT, b. Feb. 16, 1875.
1949. iv. WILLIAM EARNEST PRATT, b. Nov. 21, 1878.

[Sixth Generation.]

1848. v. MARY CHILDS, third dau. and fifth child of Aaron and Susannah Gridley Childs, b. in Brookline, Mass., Feb. 4, 1788, m. abt. 1808, Rufus Babcock, of Boston. She d. in Melrose, Mass., Sept. 2, 1864.

[Seventh Generation.] Child:
1950. i. CAROLINE A BABCOCK, b. Sept. 6, 1809, m April 20, 1834, Joseph H. Greene, of Deerfield, N. H. She d. in Melrose, Mass., April 19, 1877. He d. Dec. 8. 1867.

[Eighth Generation] Children:
1951. i. JOSEPH WARREN GREENE, b. April 26, 1837, in Boston, d. April 1, 1844
1952 ii. BENJAMIN FRANKLIN GREENE, b. April 23, 1839, m. June 4, 1861, Sarah F. Holmes.
1953. iii. CAROLINE JOSEPHINE GREENE, b. March 24, 1842. m. Sept. 17, 1862. Henry A. Leonard.
1954. iv. MARY A. GREENE, b. Oct. 10, 1846, m. Sept. 3, 1868, Dr. Joseph Heber Smith.

[Eighth Generation.]
1952. ii. BENJAMIN FRANKLIN GREENE, second son and child of Joseph H. and Caroline A. Babcock Greene, and grandson of Mary Childs Babcock, b. April 23, 1839, m. June 4, 1861, Sarah F. Holmes, in Melrose, Mass. She was b. in Charlestown, Mass., Nov. 8, 1839.

[Ninth Generation.] Children:
1955. i. EDITH FRANCES GREENE, b. June 12, 1863, in Melrose, Mass.
1956. ii. LILLIAN EVELYN GREENE, b. Jan. 28, 1865, in Chicago, Ill.
1957. iii. PHILLIP HOLMES GREENE, b. Sept. 2, 1869, in Chicago, Ill.
1958. iv JOSEPH GREENE, b. Jan. 29, 1872, d. June 7, 1873, in Chicago, Ill., æ. 4 mo.
1959. v. FRANKLIN BABCOCK GREENE, b. May 28, 1873, in Chicago, Ill.

[Eighth Generation.]
1953. iii. CAROLINE JOSEPHINE GREENE, eldest dau. and third child of Joseph H. and Caroline A. Babcock Greene, and granddaughter of Mary Childs and Rufus Babcock, b. in Boston, March 24, 1842, m. Sept. 17, 1862, in Melrose, Mass., Henry A. Leonard, of Taunton, Mass.

[Ninth Generation.] Children:
1960. i. HENRY FRANKLIN LEONARD, b. July 10, 1863, in Melrose, Mass.
1961. ii. CAROLINE MAY LEONARD, b. Aug. 22, 1865, in Melrose, Mass.

[Eighth Generation.]
1954. iv. MARY A. GREENE, second dau. and fourth child of Joseph H. and Caroline A. Babcock Greene, and granddaughter of Mary Childs and Rufus Babcock, b. in Boston, Mass. Oct. 10, 1846, m. in Melrose, Mass., Sept. 3, 1868, Dr. Joseph Heber Smith.

[Ninth Generation.] Children:
1962. i. ARLINE SMITH, b. Dec. 3, 1871, in Melrose, Mass.
1963. ii. CONRAD SMITH, b. Oct. 27, 1873, in Melrose, Mass.

[Fourth Generation.]

1785. v. EDWARD CHILD, fifth and youngest child of Edward and Margaret Weld Child, b. in Roxbury, Mass., Sept. 13, 1721, m. abt. 1750, a Mrs. Perrin, mother of Augustin Perrin.

[Fifth Generation.] Children:

1964. i. SARAH CHILD, b. May 19, 1746, m. by Rev. Mr. Adams, Jan. 20, 1771, James Wheaton.

1965. ii. RACHEL CHILD, b. Aug. 28, 1752, m. by Rev. Wm. Gordon, June 13, 1776, Payson Williams.

[Third Generation.]

18. iv. GRACE CHILD, fourth child and eldest dau. of Benjamin and Grace Morris Child, b. in Roxbury, Mass., Oct. 27, 1689, m. May 14, 1713, Timothy Walker, of Rehoboth, Mass., who was the son of Samuel and Martha Ide Walker, b. Sep. 14, 1687.[1] Mrs. Grace Child Walker was admitted to the church 14th June, 1724, her death occurred about five years later, 30th Oct. 1729. Mr. Walker was a man of influence in the community, and of wealth for that period; he re-married 30th Jan., 1730, Miss Rachel Beverly.

[Fourth Generation.] Children:

1966. i. ELIZABETH WALKER, b. April 26, 1714, m. March 12, 1740, Jasiel Perry, Jr.

1967. ii. MARTHA WALKER, b. April 22, 1716, d. May 1, 1733.

1968. iii. TIMOTHY WALKER, b. July 25, 1718, m. Dec. 10, 1841, Elizabeth Carpenter.

1969. iv. HULDAH WALKER, b. Jan. 19, 1721, m. Oct. 25, 1742, Josiah Carpenter.

1970. v. ALATHEA WALKER, b. Dec., 1724, m. Aug. 14, 1746, James Dexter.

1971. vi. EUNICE WALKER, b. Sept 4, 1728, m. May 11, 1749, James Hill.

1972. vii. MARTHA WALKER, 2D, b. Feb. 17, 1739, m. Stephen Hastings.

[Fourth Generation.]

1966. i. ELIZABETH WALKER, eldest child of Grace Child and Timothy Walker, b. in Rehoboth, Mass., April 26, 1714, m. March 12, 1740, Jasiel Perry, Jr., son of Jasiel and Rebecca Perry.

[Fifth Generation.] Children:

1973. i. REBECCA PERRY, b. Sept. 4, 1742, d. young, in Rehoboth, Mass.

1974. ii. TIMOTHY PERRY, b. Aug. 3, 1744, m. Huldah Hill, of Attleboro, Mass. Had three children.

1975. iii. REBECCA PERRY, 2D, b. Aug. 5, 1746, bapt. as Mehitable.

1976. iv. STEPHEN PERRY, b. May 4, 1751.

[1] The record of Grace Child who married Timothy Walker and that of her sister Mary Child, who married Peter Walker is largely obtained from "The Walker's of the Old Colony and their Descendants."

1977. v. JASIEL PERRY, JR., b. June 15, 1753, m. Betsey ———. Had eight children.

1978. vi. ELIZABETH PERRY, b. Dec. 16, 1755.

1979. vii. GRACE PERRY, b. April 7, 1758.

[Fourth Generation.]

1968. iii. Col. TIMOTHY WALKER, eldest son and third child of Grace Child and Timothy Walker, b. in Rehoboth, Mass., July 26, 1718, m. Dec. 10, 1741, Elizabeth Carpenter, dau. of Ebenezer Carpenter, of Attleboro, Mass. She was b. April 21, 1720. She d. July 2. 1780. Mr. Walker m. 2d, Mrs. Patience ———. Col. Walker was a soldier of the Revolution. He was chosen as selectman of Rehoboth, represented the town in the General Court of Massachusetts, and was a delegate to the Provincial Congress 1774–5.

[Fifth Generation.]   Children:

1980. i. LEPHA WALKER, b. Aug. 4. 1743, m. April 16, 1761, John Perry. Had six children.

1981. ii. SARAH WALKER, b. July 14. 1745, m. May 21, 1766, John Bishop. Had five children.

1982. iii. BETTY WALKER, b. April 8, 1747, d. unm.

1983. iv. LYDIA WALKER, b. May 1, 1749, m. Nov. 16, 1767, Amos Read.

1984. v. TIMOTHY WALKER, b. May 22, 1751, m. June 2, 1774, Molly Wilmarth, who had seven children, d. Sept. 7, 1791; m. 2d, July 11, 1793, Lucy Redway, who had seven children.

1985. vi HULDAH WALKER, b. April 29, 1755, m. 1791, Joseph Chaffee. Had four children.

1986. vii. MARTHA WALKER, b. June 12, 1758, m. Feb. 3. 1780, John Davis. Had nine children.

[Fourth Generation.]

1969 iv. HULDAH WALKER, third dau. and fourth child of Grace Child and Timothy Walker, b. in Rehoboth, Mass., Jan. 19, 1721, m. Oct. 25, 1742, Josiah Carpenter, son of Obadiah Carpenter. Resided in Cumberland, R. I. She d. in 1747.

[Fifth Generation.]   Children:

1987. i. CYRIL CARPENTER, b. Aug. 27, 1743, m. Nov. 28, 1765, Lucy Lang or Lane. Had eleven children.

1988. ii. JOSIAH CARPENTER, b. Jan. 5. 1747, m. Sept. 21, 1769, Hepsibeth Wilmarth. Had five children.

[Fourth Generation.]

1970. v. ALATHEA WALKER, fourth dau. and fifth child of Grace Child and Timothy Walker, b. in Rehoboth, Mass., Dec., 1724, m. Aug. 14, 1746, James Dexter, of Attleboro, Mass. Resided in Cumberland, R. I.

[Fifth Generation.] Children:

1989. i. HOPESTILL DEXTER, b. about 1747, m. Benjamin May; had seven children.

1990. ii. JAMES DEXTER, m. Rebecca Wheeler.

1991. iii. HULDITH DEXTER, m. 1st, Stephen Brown; m. 2d, Mr. Follett.

1992. iv. OLIVER DEXTER.

1993. v. MERCY DEXTER, m. Benjamin Wolcott.

1994. vi. SIMEON DEXTER, d. unmarried.

1995. vii. ESEK DEXTER, m. Margaret Coleman

1996. viii. BENJAMIN DEXTER, m. Mary Dexter.

1997. ix. NANCY DEXTER, m. Jeremiah Whipple.

1998. x. ALATHEA DEXTER, d. unmarried.

1999. xi. LUCINA DEXTER, m. Dea John Dexter

2000. xii. TIMOTHY DEXTER, m. Sarah Messenger.

[Fourth Generation.]

1971. VI. EUNICE WALKER, fifth dau. and sixth child of Grace Child and Timothy Walker, b. in Rehoboth, Mass., Sept. 4, 1728, m. May 11, 1749, James Hill, a man remarkable for his integrity and punctuality. Mrs. Hill d. Dec. 31, 1772.

[Fifth Generation.] Children:

2001. i. BARBARA HILL, d. unmarried in Rehoboth, Mass.

2002. ii. PHOEBE HILL, d. unmarried in Rehoboth, Mass.

2003. iii. EUNICE HILL, d. unmarried in Rehoboth, Mass.

2004. iv. JAMES HILL, JR., m. Freelove Andrews; had six children.

2005. v. HANNAH HILL, m. Jonathan Hayes; had nine children

2006. vi. JOHN HILL, m. Mehitable Walker; resided in Clarendon, Vt.

2007. vii. CYNTHIA HILL, m. Asa Angell; resided in New Berlin, N. Y.

2008. viii. SARAH HILL, m. John Larned; resided in Clarendon, Vt.

2009. ix. DANIEL HILL, m. Sarah Hutchins; resided in New York and had several children.

2010. x. LUCY HILL, m. David Hill; had two children.

[Third Generation.]

19. V. MARY CHILD, second dau. and fifth child of Benjamin and Grace Morris Child, b. in Roxbury, Mass., Oct. 25, 1791, m. Jan. 9, 1715, Peter Walker, who was b. Sept. 18, 1689, a son of Samuel and Martha Ide Walker. Mr. and Mrs. Walker were admitted to communion Oct. 10, 1724. Mrs. Mary Child Walker d. between 1730 and '32. Mr. Walker was twice married after—2d m. Jan. 18, 1733, Mrs. Martha Read: 3d m. Bethiah———. At his death his inventory amounted to £238.

[Fourth Generation.] Children:

2011. i. MARY WALKER, b. Aug., 1716, m. March 9, 1737, Daniel Perry.

2012. ii. SAMUEL WALKER, b. July 14, 1718, m., had 1 son, d. before 1746.

2013. iii. PETER WALKER, JR., b. July 14, 1718, m. Hannah Fuller, of Willington, Ct.; had six children.

}Twins.

2014. iv. PATIENCE WALKER, b. April 27, 1720, d. July 19, 1744.

2015. v. JOHN WALKER, b. Oct. 3, 1721, m. Molly ——.

2016. vi. HANNAH WALKER, b. March 6, 1723, m. John Peck.

2017. vii. GRACE WALKER, } Twins. } b. Dec. 14, 1724, d. Dec. 14, 1724.
2018. viii. ESTHER WALKER, {

2019. ix. MOSES WALKER, b. Nov. 2, 1725, d. Nov. 21, 1725.

2020. x. MOSES WALKER, 2D, b. Oct. 5, 1726, m. March 15, 1753, Sarah Bowen, who d. March or May 3, 1768; m. 2d. March 2, 1769, Deliverance Carpenter Read; m 3d, Mrs Jemima Walker Bishop.

2021. xi. AARON WALKER, b. Oct. 19, 1728, m. Jan. 30, 1755, Esther Carpenter: m. 2d, Dec. 22, 1763, Huldah Whittaker.

2022. xii. GRACE WALKER, b. Dec. 28, 1730.

2023. xiii. EPHRAIM WALKER, b. Dec. I, 1736, m. Dec. 26, 1771, Leatfe Ide.

[Fourth Generation.]

2011. i. MARY WALKER, eldest child of Mary Child and Peter Walker, b. in Rehoboth, Mass., August, 1716, m. March 9, 1737, Daniel Perry of Rehoboth.

[Fifth Generation.] Children:

2024. i. DANIEL PERRY, JR., b. Jan. 15, 1739.

2025. ii. EZRA PERRY, b. May 22, 1741.

2026. iii. NOAH PERRY, b. Oct. 3, 1743.

2027. iv. MARY PERRY, b. Aug. 5, 1745.

2028. v. DANIEL PERRY, b. April 3, 1748.

2029. vi. LYDIA PERRY, b. April 30, 1750.

2030. vii. ELIJAH PERRY, b. Nov. 19, 1752.

[Fourth Generation.]

2013. iii. PETER WALKER, JR., second son and third child of Mary Child and Peter Walker, b. in Rehoboth, Mass., July 14, 1718, m. Hannah Fuller of Willington, Ct.: resided in Ashford, Ct.

[Fifth Generation.] Children:

2031. i. SAMUEL WALKER, b. Sept. 2, 1748, m. Alice Case; had eleven children.

2032. ii. PETER WALKER, b. 1760, m. Sally Carpenter; had three children.

2033. iii. MARY WALKER, m. David Tuttle; had six children.

2034. iv. SARAH WALKER, m. Jonathan Peck; resided in Randolph, Vt.

2035. v. HANNAH WALKER, m. Ebenezer Cross; resided in Canada.

2036. vi. GRACE WALKER, m. Levi Wakefield; six children, resided in Stafford, Ct.

[Fourth Generation.]

2015. v. JOHN WALKER, third son and fifth child of Mary Child and Peter Walker, b. in Rehoboth, Mass., Oct. 3, 1721, m. Molly —— about 1751. He was a "Capt. and Gent." in 1788; and a noted man in Rehoboth, sergeant of the Minute

Men in Lexington alarm, from Rehoboth, and saw service in the Revolution.

[Fifth Generation.] Children:

2037. i. JOHN WALKER, JR., b. Nov. 1, 1752, d. unmarried, 1832.

2038. ii. CALVIN WALKER, b. Jan. 5, 1754, m. Feb. 10, 1780, Phœbe Cole; had eight children.

2039. iii. MOLLY WALKER, b. Dec. 6, 1756, m. Sept. 22, 17—, Caleb Ormsbee of Providence, R. I.

2040. iv. PETER WALKER, b. March 29, 1759; sailed from Providence and never again heard from.

2041. v. JOSEPH WALKER, b. Feb. 24, 1761, m. Dec. 3, 1784, Sarah Lane; resided in Nelson, N. Y.; eight children.

2042. vi. AMY WALKER, b. Feb. 24, 1762, d. young.

2043. vii. ELIZABETH WALKER, b. Feb. 27, 1763, d. in early womanhood.

2044. viii. LUTHER WALKER, b. Jan. 7, 1766, m. Mary Weaver, dau. of Capt. Lewis Weaver of Lansingburgh, N. Y.; had five children. Resided at one time in Troy, N. Y., and while there he built for himself the first two-story house in Troy.

2045. ix. LYDIA WALKER, b. Feb. 10, 1768, m. Aug. 30, 1796, Nathaniel Croade of North Providence, R. I.

2046. x. GEORGE WHITEFIELD WALKER, b. Feb. 7, 1770, m. April 14, 1796, Mehitable Bucklin; had eight children.

2047. xi. BOSWORTH WALKER, b. March 1, 1773, m. Feb. 9, 1802, Elizabeth Weaver, dau. of Capt. Lewis Weaver; had seven children.

2048. xii. WILLIAM WALKER, b. March 27, 1775, d. in infancy.

2049. xiii. ELIJAH WALKER, b. Feb. 10, 1777, d. in youth.

[Fourth Generation.]

2019. x. Lieut. MOSES WALKER, fifth son and tenth child of Mary Child and Peter Walker, b. in Rehoboth, Mass., Oct. 5, 1726. He was three times married—1st, March 15, 1753, Sarah Bowen, daughter of Peter and Susannah Bowen, she d. in 1768; m. 2d, Mch. 2, 1769, Deliverance Carpenter Read, she d. Mch. 20, 1789; m. 3d, Mrs. Jemima Walker Bishop.

[Fifth Generation.] Children:

2050. i. SUSANNAH WALKER, b. July 1, 1754, m. David Bliss; three children.

2051. ii. HULDAH WALKER, b. Sept. 20, 1756, m. Feb. 15, 1785, Isaac Brown; resided in Barnet, Vt.; seven children.

2052. iii. MOSES WALKER, b. Dec. 16, 1760, m. 1st, April 10, 1783, Anna Brown; m. 2d, Aug. 14, 1787, Mary Whittaker; m. 3d, 1790, Hannah Carpenter.

2053. iv. SARAH WALKER, b. June 13, 1763, m. Ebenezer French; resided in Halifax, Vt.

2054. v. ETHEL WALKER, b. Aug. 28, 1769, m. Nov. 25, 1795, Susannah Carpenter. He d. in Webster, Mich., "not of age but of medicine," says his son, who is an M. D.; had eleven children.

W

2055. vi. Benjamin Walker, b. Oct. 19, 1770, m. Nov. 22, 1801, Susannah Bullock. He was farmer, selectman, lister, justice of the peace and representative to state legislature; resided in Lyndon, Vt.; had 4 children

2056. vii. Aaron Walker, b. Jan. 9, 1776, m. 1800, Betsey Hoffman, who d. Oct. 18, 1826; m 2d, Feb. 25, 1827, Mrs. Sally Gould Leman. "He was first a Methodist, second of United Brethren, third a Cumberland Presbyterian, fourth a Dunkard, and fifth a Baptist." Had twelve children.

2057. viii. Dille or Delia Walker, b. Aug. 21, 1772, m. April 7, 1803, Henry Hoffman; resided in Vermont; three children.

2058. ix. Lucy Walker, b. April 3, 1774, m. Feb. 26, 1793, Abel Wilmarth; five children.

2059. x. Hannah Walker, b. Dec. 23, 1777, d. before 1806.

2060. xi. Ezra Walker, b. Oct. 28, 1780, m. 1st, Martha Blanding, who d. Sept. 1, 1816; m. 2d, Dec 1, 1819, Mary Robinson; resided in Attleboro, Mass.; had eleven children.

[Fourth Generation.]

2021. xi. Lieut. Aaron Walker, sixth son and eleventh child of Mary Child and Peter Walker, b. in Rehoboth, Mass., Oct. 19, 1728, m. 1st, Jan. 30, 1755, Esther Carpenter, dau. of Abiah and Experience Carpenter, she d. June 16, 1763; m. 2d, Dec. 22, 1763, Huldah Whittaker, dau. of Israel and Margaret W. He d. in Roxbury, at the siege of Boston, of campfever.

[Fifth Generation.] Children:

2061. i. Patience Walker, b. Mch 21, 1756, m. July 30, 1778, Ezra Reed; resided in Langdon, N. H.; had five children.

2062. ii. Hannah Walker, b. Mch. 7, 1758, m. May 29, 1777, Elkanah French; had eleven children.

2063. iii Abiah Walker, b. Mch. 2, 1760, d. unmarried about 1830.

2064. iv. Samuel Walker, b. Feb 4, 1762, m. 1784, Anna Carpenter; had five children.

2065. v. Esther Walker, b. Oct. 27, 1764, m. July 1, 1790, John White; six children.

2066. vi. Walter Walker, b. Nov. 16, 1766, m. June 11, 1801, Grace Loomis; resided in Clarendon, Vt.; had seven children.

2067. vii. Relief Walker, b June 25, 1769, m. Mch. 9, 1793, Otis Walcott; resided in Pawtucket, R. I.; seven children.

2068. viii. Nancy Walker, b. July 19, 1771, m. Dec. 30, 1793, George Sweetland of Attleboro, Mass.; two children.

2069. ix. Pamelia Walker, b. Nov. 22, 1773, m. Sept. 27, 1796, Joseph Baker; resided in Providence, R. I.; seven children.

[Third Generation.]

20. vi. Ebenezer Child, sixth child of Benjamin, Jr., and Grace Morris Child, b. in Roxbury, Mass., Sept. 7, 1693, m. Elizabeth Bacon about 1720.   Mr. Child left the Roxbury home and settled in the township then called New Roxbury,

later Woodstock—a colony of Massachusetts, till the change of boundary line gave the town to the State of Connecticut, here Lieut. Child resided many years. When his son, Ebenezer, wished to remove to Vermont, he was found ready to encounter anew the discomforts and rigors of pioneer life. Lieut. Child was a man of energetic, resolute firmness, but with a most true affection. His death occurred in 1773, at Union, Orange Co., Vt. Mrs. Elizabeth Bacon Child d. Nov. 30, 1768.

[Fourth Generation.] Children:

2070 i OBADIAH CHILD, b. in Woodstock, Aug. 30, 1721, d. Dec. 3, 1722.

2071. ii. ELIZABETH CHILD. b. in Woodstock, May 3, 1723, d. Jan. 20, 1742.

2072. iii. SUSANNA CHILD,[1] b. in Woodstock, Mch. 24, 1725, "published in bans of matrimony," April 10, 1744, to John Newell, m. Dec. 30, 1756, Peter Child. (*Record with Peter Child, page* 240.)

2073 iv. EBENEZER CHILD, JR., b. in Woodstock, April 17, 1732, m. 1st, 1754, Charity Bugbee: m. 2d. 1775, Alice Cobb

2074. v. MARY CHILD, b. in Woodstock, Feb. 24, 1733, m. Col. Freeman of Sturbridge, Mass.

2075. vi. KEZIAH CHILD, b. in Woodstock, Feb. 18, 1734, m. June 20, 1754, John Bacon.

2076. vii. HANNAH CHILD. b. in Woodstock, Jan. 12, 1735, m. June 17, 1752, Japheth Bicknell.

2077. viii. JEMIMA CHILD, b. in Woodstock. Feb. 12, 1736, m. 1764, Benjamin Freeman

2078. ix. DEBORAH CHILD, b. in Woodstock, Oct. 27, 1738.

2079. x. OBADIAH CHILD, 2D., b. in Woodstock, Oct. 23, 1740, unm.

2080. xi. MARGARET CHILD, b. ——, d. July 15, 1742.

[Fourth Generation.]

2073. iv. EBENEZER CHILD, JR., second son and fourth child of Ebenezer and Elizabeth Bacon Child, b. in Woodstock, Ct., (then called New Roxbury, Mass.,) April 17, 1732. Mr. Child was twice married—first in 1754 to Miss Charity Bugbee, who was b. in Woodstock in 1728, was the mother of his children, and a woman of most lovely character. A son writes of her, "she died as she had lived, a meek and humble christian, Dec. 20, 1772 ; she was courteous to servants, and one in whom the poor found a friend, and the needy was rarely sent empty away." The same son writes of the second mother, Alice Cobb, who m. Mr. Ebenezer Child, Jr., in 1775, as a most kind parent and lovely woman.

[1] This Susan Child who married Peter was erroneously stated to have been daughter of Nathaniel Child.

Mr. Ebenezer Child, Jr., was a man of indomitable will and when, by any stress of circumstances, diverted from the pursuit of his regular business, he immediately turned to the best work offering.   So we find him on the first winter after his removal to Leicester, Vt., when the rigors of the northern winters prevented further toil upon his farm, teaching in Rutland, Vt. The farm he had chosen was wholly unredeemed, and the cutting of large forest trees, with the sturdy strokes of the axe, was an initiative step to open the soil to the sun before any crops could be looked for.   The trees felled, a primitive plowing around the thick-standing stumps made ready the ground for corn and wheat.   Patriotic also, he was engaged in the warfare, which darkened the early years of the colonies. He served in the French war under Generals Putnam and Durkee.   The severities of exposure and labor proved too violent, and Mr. Child succumbed to an inflammatory fever and died in the town of Leicester, Addison Co., Vt., June 7, 1791 ; he had been received into the communion of the church in 1740. Upon the organization of the town, he had been chosen its first town clerk.   Mrs. Alice Cobb Child d. Mch. 22, 1801.

[Fifth Generation.]   Children:

2081. i. SOPHIA CHILD, b. Mch. 7, 1755, m. Simon Wright.

2082. ii. PENUEL CHILD, b. Mch. 7, 1757, m. 1st, Oct. 11, 1780, Charlotte Loomis; m. 2d, Oct. 22, 1815, Mrs. Sabra Henry.

2083. iii. PERLEY CHILD, b. Dec. 6, 1759, m. Lucy Symons.

2084. iv. EBENEZER CHILD, b. Nov. 12, 176 3, d. Aug. 3, 1768, in Woodstock, Ct.

2085. v. BETHIAH CHILD, b. June 22, 1765, d. Sept. 2, 1768, in Woodstock, Ct.

2086. vi. ELIZABETH CHILD, b. Dec. 29, 1767, m. Abner Brigham.

2087. vii. EBENEZER CHILD, 2D, b. Aug. 7, 1770, m. Dec. 6, 1792, Anna Grey.

[Fifth Generation.]

2081. i. SOPHIA CHILD, eldest dau. and child of Ebenezer, Jr., and Charity Bugbee Child, b. in Woodstock, Ct., Mch. 7, 1755, m. abt. 1774, Simon Wright.   Mr. Wright was b. Feb. 27, 1754, and d. Jan. 1, 1808.   Mrs. Sophia Wright d. July 12, 1819.

[Sixth Generation.]   Children:

2088. i. GARDNER WRIGHT, b. Mar. 17, 1775, m. Mch. 28, 1797, Jemima Rice.

2089. ii. CHARITY WRIGHT, b. Nov. 13, 1777, d. Dec. 20, 1803.

2090. iii. POLLY WRIGHT, b. Sept. 16, 1780, d. June 12, 1818.

2091. iv. ELIZABETH WRIGHT, b. Mch. 16, 1783, d. May 28, 1840.

2092. v. NANCY WRIGHT, b. Aug. 7, 1785, d Sept. 1829.

2093. vi. JOHN WRIGHT, b. Aug. 19, 1788.

2094. vii. LOYAL WRIGHT, b. Dec. 25, 1791.

2095. viii. WALTER S. WRIGHT, b. Aug 3, 1794, d. Aug 1829.

2096. ix. DANFORD WRIGHT, b. April 1, 1797.

2097. x. SIMEON WRIGHT, b. June 8, 1809.

[Sixth Generation.]

2088. i. GARDNER WRIGHT, eldest son and child of Sophia Child and Simeon Wright, b. in Vermont, Mch. 17, 1775, m. Mch. 28, 1797, Jemima Rice.

[Seventh Generation.] Children:

2098 i. JOSEPH W. WRIGHT, b. May 18, 1798. Resides in Kalamazoo, Mich

2099 ii. JULIA M. WRIGHT, b Mch. 16, 1800, d. Mch. 16, 1825.

2100 iii. ALFRED WRIGHT, b. Mch. 8, 1802.

2101. iv CHARITY WRIGHT, b. Jan 3, 1804, d. Feb. 21, 1841.

2102 v. BETSEY WRIGHT, b. Nov. 20, 1806, m. Mr. Knowlton, of Brandon, Vt.

2103. vi. SOPHIA CHILD WRIGHT, b. Mch. 13, 1810

2104. vii. WILLIAM B. WRIGHT, b. Nov. 26, 1814, d. Oct. 25, 1848.

2105. viii. GEORGE W. WRIGHT, b Jan. 17, 1817, d. April 15, 1849.

[Fifth Generation.]

2088. ii. PENUEL CHILD, eldest son and second child of Ebenezer and Charity Bugbee Child, b. in Woodstock, Ct., May 8, 1757, m. Oct. 11, 1780, Miss Charlotte Loomis.

While quite a young man, filled with energy and cheerful acceptance of toil and trouble, and delight in conquered obstacles, Mr. Child with his young wife found a home in the Green Mountain State, and there set up his penates. Mrs. Charlotte Loomis Child died in Brandon, Vt., Jan. 11, 1815, at the age of fifty. Mr. Child married second on the 22d October, 1815, Mrs. Sabra Cannon Henry, widow of Daniel Henry, of Brandon, Vt., and adopted daughter of Mary Winslow, all originally from Hardwick, Mass. Mrs. Sabra C. H. Child died at the home of Penuel Child, Jr., in Pittsfield, Vt., on the 7th March, 1855. Mr. Child died in the same place August 22, 1843, æ. 87.

[Sixth Generation.] Children:

2106. i. RALPHA RODOLPHA CHILD, b. in Union, Ct., Feb. 12, 1782, m. Nov. 27, 1805, Hannah Demming.

2107. ii. JOHN BURNAP CHILD, b. in Union, Ct., June 25, 1786, m. Mch. 6, 1808, Polly Ganson.

2108. iii. FREDERICK AUGUSTUS CHILD, b. Dec. 11, 1788, m. Mch. 28, 1818, Charlotte Sessions.

2109. iv. PENUEL CHILD, JR., b. May 9, 1794, m. Mch. 10, 1824, Mary Henry.

2110. v. DANIEL PUTNAM CHILD, b. Jan. 12, 1803, d. Dec. 29, 1841, at Schoolcraft, Mich.

2111. vi. HENRY LOOMIS CHILD, b. Oct. 5, 1816, m. D. B. Hale, of Middlebury, Vt.

[Sixth Generation.]

2106. i. RALPHA RODOLPHA CHILD, eldest son and child of Penuel and Charlotte Loomis Child, b. in Union, Ct., Feb. 11, 1782, m. Nov. 27, 1805, Hannah Demming, dan. of Jonathan Demming. She was b. Jan. 13, 1786, in Goshen, Mass. Mr. R. R. Child d. April 22, 1824.

[Seventh Generation.] Children:

2112. i. CHARLOTTE CHILD, b. May 9, 1807, m. Samuel Granger.

2113. ii. JAMES McCLUER CHILD, b. Mch. 31, 1809, m. Miss White, of Watertown, N. Y.

2114. iii. EMILIA CHILD, b. May 24, 1811, m. James Brainard, of Weybridge, Vt.

2115. iv. JOHN SCHUYLER CHILD, b. Sept. 19, 1813.

2116. v. LUTHER DEMMING CHILD, b. Mch. 5, 1816.

2117. vi. HENRY RODOLPHUS CHILD, b. Oct. 3, 1822; a very bright and lovely young man, who died in early manhood, at the house of his sister, Mrs. C. C. Granger, Castleton, Vt.

[Sixth Generation.]

2107. ii. JOHN BURNAP CHILD, second son and child of Penuel and Charlotte Loomis Child, b. in Union, Ct., June 25, 1786, m. Mch. 6, 1808, Polly Ganson. He d. in Pittsfield, Vt., Nov. 23, 1840. Mrs. P. G. Child d. in Brandon, Vt., Feb. 1, 1822.

[Seventh Generation.] Children:

2118. i. CHERRY CHILD, b. June 11, 1808, m. Simeon Bigelow.

2119. ii. MARY CHILD, b. July 4, 1810, m. Royal D. Far.

2120. iii. JOHN JAY CHILD, b. Aug. 12, 1814, m. Mary Smith.

2121. iv. JOSEPH PUTNAM CHILD, b. Aug. 12, 1815, m. May 12, 1844, Mary Ann Smith.

2122. v. MARTHA GERALDINE CHILD, b. Aug. 29, 1818, m. Freeman Mathews.

2123. vi. PENUEL GANSON CHILD, b. Dec. 17, 1821.

[Seventh Generation.]

2121. iv. JOSEPH PUTNAM CHILDS, second son and fourth child of John Burnap and Polly Ganson Child, b. in Pittsfield, Vt., Aug. 12, 1815, m. May 12, 1844, Mary Ann Smith, dau. of Robert Smith, of Bellingham, Mass. Mr. Childs is a florist. Residence, Woonsocket, R. I.

[Eighth Generation.] Children:

    2124. i. MARTHA EVALINE CHILDS, b. Nov. 12, 1845, d. Jan. 9, 1849.

    2125. ii. IDA EVALINE CHILDS, b. Mch. 21, 1850, d. Dec. 26, 1856.

    2126. iii. FRANK ALLEN CHILDS, b. Nov. 7, 1851, m. Nov. 4, 1875, Mary E. Ballou.

[Eighth Generation.]

    2126. iii. FRANK ALLEN CHILDS, only son of Joseph P. and Mary A. Smith Childs, b. Nov. 7, 1851, m. Nov. 4, 1875, Mary E. Ballou, dau. of Levi T. Ballou, of Cumberland, R. I. Reside in Woonsocket, R. I.

[Ninth Generation.] Children:

    2127. i. BERTHA ELOISE CHILDS, b. Nov. 25, 1876.

    2128. ii. FRANK HOWARD CHILDS, b. April 12, 1878.

[Sixth Generation.]

    2108. iii. FREDERICK AUGUSTUS CHILD, third son and child of Penuel and Charlotte Loomis Child, b. in Union, Tolland Co., Ct., Dec. 11, 1789, m. Mch. 28, 1818, Miss Charlotte Sessions, dau. of Walter and Anna Loomis Sessions. Mrs. Charlotte S. Child, b. in Union, Ct., Feb. 21, 1795, d. Oct. 3, 1875. Mr. F. A. Child d. Feb. 21, 1860, in Brandon, Rutland Co., Vt., where his home had been for many years.

[Seventh Generation.] Children:

    2129. i. CAROLINE FRANCES GULNARE CHILD, b. Oct. 18, 1818, m. Mch. 5, 1840, Moses J. Enos.

    2130. ii. An infant, unchristened, b. 1820.

    2131. iii. CHARLOTTE CHILD, b. Feb. 3, 1822, d. æ three years in Middlebury, Vt.

    2132. iv. HELEN MARIA CHILD, b. Aug. 22, 1823, m. Aug. 3, 1843, Harrison Ward.

    2133 v. ANTOINETTE MADALINE CHILD, b. June 3, 1825; resides in Forestdale, Rutland Co., Vt.; teacher.

    2134. vi. ADELIZA C. CHILD, b. July 1, 1828, m. Feb. 25, 1847, John Capen.

    2135. vii. HARRY G. CHILD, b. April 30, 1830, m. May 12, 1852, Juliette C. Allen.

    2136. viii. AUGUSTA A. CHILD, b. Jan. 29, 1832, m. Oct. 10, 1854, Major Freeman Allen.

    2137. ix. SABRINA A. CHILD, b. Oct. 28, 1834, d. Aug. 1, 1852, in Brandon, Vt.

    2138. x. GEORGE CARROLL CHILD, b. Feb. 8, 1837, unm.; resides in Forestdale, Rutland Co., Vt.

[Seventh Generation.]

    2129. i. CAROLINE FRANCES GULNARE CHILD, eldest child of Frederick Augustus and Charlotte Sessions Child, b. in Brandon, Vt., Oct. 18, 1818, m. Mch. 5, 1840, Moses J. Enos, who d. in Eagle, Wisconsin, Mch. 9, 1877. Mr. Enos was a native of Leicester, Addison Co., Vt., where he was b. Feb. 13, 1799.

[Eighth Generation.]   Children:

2139. i. FRANCES A. ENOS, b. Feb. 10, 1841, at Leicester, Vt., d. Sept. 13, 1844, at Eagle, Wis.

2140. ii CLARENCE H. ENOS, b. Nov. 28, 1845, d Dec. 24, 1854, at Eagle, Wis.

2141. iii. ADDIE ENOS, b. May 6, 1851, m. Oct. 5, 1871, S. De Witt Wilbur.

[Eighth Generation.]

2141. iii. ADDIE ENOS, third child and second dau. of Caroline F. G. Child and Moses J. Enos, b. at Eagle, Waukesha Co., Wis., May 6, 1851, m. Oct. 5, 1871, S. De Witt Wilbur, who was b. at Palmyra, Jefferson Co., Wis., July 5, 1854. Residence Eagle, Wis.

[Ninth Generation.]   Children:

2142. i. EVELYN BELL WILBUR, b. Aug. 20, 1872, at Eagle, Wis.

2143. ii. PEARL MAY WILBUR, b. Nov. 14, 1875, at Eagle, Wis.

2144. iii. MINNIE DAISY WILBUR, b. Jan 1, 1879, at Eagle, Wis.

[Seventh Generation.]

2132. iv. HELEN MARIA CHILD, fourth dau. and child of Frederick Augustus and Charlotte Sessions Child, b. in Salisbury, Addison Co., Vt., Aug. 22, 1823, m. Aug. 3, 1843, Harrison Ward, who was b. Dec. 18, 1812, and d. near Fort Elliott, Texas, Jan. 8, 1879. Their residence was in Waukesha, Wis., and Mrs. Helen M. Child Ward is yet a resident of Waukesha.

[Eighth Generation.]   Children:

2145. i. HERMAN MELANCTHON WARD, b. Jan. 5, 1845, in Eagle, Waukesha Co., Wis.; m. and resides in Oakland, Cal.

2146. ii. IDA HELEN WARD, b. Feb. 25, 1848, m. May 13, 1867, J. B. Curtiss.

2147. iii. FREDERICK AUGUSTUS WARD, b. Mch. 21, 1850, in Eagle, Wis.; resides at Fort Elliott, Texas.

2148. iv. CASSIUS CLAY WARD, b. June 6, 1852, in Eagle, Wis.; resides in Waukesha, Wis.

2149. v. WALTER CAPEN WARD, b. Oct. 7, 1854, m. Hattie Meyers.

2150. vi. HENRY BEECHER WARD, b. Feb. 11, 1857, in Waukesha, Wis., where he resides.

[Eighth Generation.]

2146. ii. IDA HELEN WARD, only dau. and second child of Helen M. Child and Harrison Ward, b. in Brandon, Vt., Feb. 25, 1848, m. in Waukesha, Wis., May 13, 1867, John Barney Curtiss.   Residence Chicago, Ill.

[Ninth Generation.] Children:
2151. i. JOHN BARNEY CURTISS, JR., b. Jan. 28, 1873, in San Francisco, Cal., d. Oct. 16, 1873.
2152. ii. HELEN CHANDLER CURTISS, b. Jan. 23, 1875, in San Francisco, Cal., d Feb. 2, 1877.

[Eighth Generation.]
2149. v. WALTER CAPEN WARD, fourth son and fifth child of Helen M. Child and Harrison Ward, b. in Eagle, Waukesha Co., Wis., Oct. 7, 1854, m. Hattie Meyers. Residence San Francisco, Cal.

[Ninth Generation.] Child:
2153. i. Infant unnamed.

[Seventh Generation.]
2134. vi. ADELIZA CHARLOTTE CHILD, sixth dau. and child of Frederick Augustus and Charlotte Sessions Child, b. in Brandon, Vt., July 1, 1828, m. Feb. 25, 1847, Hon. John Capen, who was b. in Goshen, Vt., Mch. 23, 1818, and d. Jan. 5, 1878, in Brandon, Vt. A sister-in-law writes of him, " If ever a man was perfect in all his ways and habits he was, strictly honest and upright in all his dealings. His business was that of a lumber dealer and practical land surveyor. He was elected to fill the posts of town clerk, grand juryman and justice of the peace ; he also represented the town in the State Legislature several times, and was a member of the Vermont constitutional convention. He was in early years a successful and honored instructor." Mrs. A. C. Child Capen resides in Brandon, Vt.

[Eighth Generation.] Children:
2154. i. MARY CHARLOTTE CAPEN, b. Aug. 9, 1859, d. Aug. 11, 1859, in Goshen, Vt.
2155. ii. JOHN BERNARD CAPEN, b. May 21, 1866, d. Sept. 23, 1866, in Brandon, Vt.
2156. iii. FLAVIA ANTOINETTE CAPEN, b. Aug. 11, 1867.

[Seventh Generation.]
2135. vii. HARRY G. CHILD, eldest son and seventh child of Frederick Augustus and Charlotte Sessions Child, b. in Brandon, Vt., April 30, 1830, m. May 12, 1852, Juliette C. Allen. Mr. Child removed soon after marriage to the West, is now a resident of Berlin, Green Lake Co., Wisconsin, and engaged in a large commercial business.

[Eighth Generation] Children:
2157. i. HERBERT W. CHILD, b. April 24, 1854, in Brandon, Vt.
2158. ii. HIRAM A. CHILD, b. Jan. 23, 1858, m. Jan. 13, 1878, Jennie M. Burr

[Eighth Generation.]

2158. ii. HIRAM A. CHILD, second son and child of Harry G. and Juliette C. Allen Child, b. in Kingston, Green Lake Co., Wis., Jan. 23, 1858, m. Jan. 13, 1878, Jennie M. Burr; reside in Berlin, Wis.

[Ninth Generation.] Child:
    2159. i. HARRY BURR CHILD, b. Mch. 30, 1879.

[Seventh Generation.]

2136. viii. AUGUSTA ALICE CHILD, seventh dau. and eighth child of Frederick Augustus and Charlotte Sessions Child, b. in Brandon, Vt., Jan. 29, 1832, m. Oct. 10, 1854, Major Freeman Allen of Brandon, Vt., who was b. in Rochester, Windsor Co., Vt., Dec. 20, 1829.

[Eighth Generation.] Children:
    2160. i. JOHN SCOTT ANDERSON ALLEN, b. May 17, 1861, drowned Aug. 21, 1872 in a freshet, which compelled the family to flee from their home, the boy was held by his father until exhaustion relaxed his hold, and his own life was nearly sacrificed.
    2161. ii. LOTTIE MAY ALLEN, b. Jan. 27, 1867, d. Dec. 13, 1878. Two more lovely and endearing children are rarely given to fond parents, and their early deaths have cast shadows beyond the home circle.

[Sixth Generation.]

2109. iv. PENUEL CHILD, JR., fourth son and child of Penuel and Charlotte Loomis Child, b. in Union, Ct., May 9, 1794, m. Mch. 10, 1824, Miss Mary Henry, dau. of Daniel Henry, of Brandon, Vt. Mr. Penuel Child, Jr., d. in Clinton, Wisconsin, Sept. 4, 1868. His widow resides in Edgarton, Wis.

[Seventh Generation.] Children:
    2162. i. WILLIAM WALLACE CHILD, b. Nov. 11, 1824, m. April 25, 1848, Eluthra Caroline Harrison Hatch.
    2163. ii. ROLIN RODOLPHUS CHILD, b. Oct. 21, 1827, m. May 25, 1854, Mariette Young.
    2164. iii. MARY CHILD, b. May 29, 1831, m. abt. 1859, R. R. Brown.
    2165. iv. ELLEN CHILD, b. May 15, 1835, m. abt. 1856, H. B Delong.
    2166. v. A daughter—unchristened.

[Seventh Generation.]

2162. i. WILLIAM WALLACE CHILD, eldest child of Penuel, Jr., and Mary Henry Child, b. in Brandon, Vt., Nov. 11, 1824, m. by the Rev. J. B. Clark, April 25, 1848, Eluthra Caroline Harrison Hatch, who was b. in Pittsfield, Vt., Aug. 18, 1826, dau. of Orton and Pamelia Harrison Hatch. Resides at Edgerton, Rock Co., Wisconsin. Is engaged in business as dealer and packer in leaf tobacco.

[Eighth Generation.] Children:
    2167. i. FLORENCE ELUTHRA CHILD, b. Sept. 24, 1849, at Eagle, Wis.
    2168. ii. HAROLD WALLACE CHILD, b. Nov. 16, 1851, at Eagle, Wis.

[Seventh Generation.]
    2163. ii. ROLLIN RODOLPHUS CHILD, second child and son of Penuel, Jr., and Mary Henry Child, b. in Brandon, Vt., Oct. 21, 1827, m. May 25, 1854, Mariette Young, of Lake Mills, Wis. Reside in Clinton, Rock Co., Wisconsin.

[Eighth Generation.] Children:
    2169. i. GERTRUDE MARY CHILD, b. Sept. 27, 1855, d. young.
    2170. ii. HUBERT HENRY CHILD, b. April 4, 1857, in Albion, Wis.
    2171. iii. CHARLES ROLIN CHILD, b. Oct. 6, 1861, in Albion, Wis.
    2172. iv. ELLEN ELUTHRA CHILD, b. April 3, 1863.
    2173. v. GRACE EVELYN CHILD, b. Feb. 1, 1867.
    2174. vi. CLIFTON PUTNAM CHILD, } Twins, b. Aug. 26, 1868.
    2175 vii. CLAYTON PENUEL CHILD, }
    2176. viii ISORA MARY CHILD, b. Mch. 15, 1875.

[Seventh Generation.]
    2164. iii. MARY CHILD, eldest dau. and third child of Penuel, and Mary Henry Child, b. in Pittsfield, Vt., May 29, 1831, m. R. R. Brown, abt. 1859.

[Eighth Generation.] Children:
    2177. i. PENUEL CHILD BROWN, b. Sept. 11, 1860.
    2178. ii WALLACE SCHUYLER BROWN, b. Oct. 16, 1863.
    2179. iii. MARY GERTRUDE BROWN, b. Jan. 12, 1868.
    2180. iv GEORGE RICHARD BROWN, b. Nov. 9, 1873.

[Seventh Generation.]
    2165. iv. ELLEN CHILD, second dau. and fourth child of Penuel, Jr., and Mary Henry Child, b. in Pittsfield, Vt., May 15, 1835, m. H. B. Delong, abt. 1855.

[Eighth Generation]
    2181. i. ISORA MARY DELONG, b. April 26, 1857.
    2182 ii. LILLIAN E. DELONG, b. Mch. 19, 1860.
    2183. iii. JOHN HENRY DELONG, b. Aug. 14, 1871.

[Sixth Generation]
    2111. vi. HENRY LOOMIS CHILD, youngest child of Penuel and Charlotte Loomis Child, b. in Brandon, Vt., Oct. 5, 1816, has been three times married—1st, in 1839, Diadama Burt Hale, of Middlebury, Vt.; 2d, Katherine Winter; 3d, Dec. 26, 1844, Mary Helen Post. Resides in Troy, N. Y. Occupation, that of ship carpenter.

    Mr. Child in early manhood had a vigorous constitution, and a fondness for adventure not altogether free from hardships and exposure to danger. His love for hunting wild game led

him to the Adirondac Mountains, where his winters for some
years were spent hunting the deer and other wild animals
abounding in those forests, making his mode of life an opportunity for gain in the valuable furs and hides which he was
able to bring to a paying market. Few were regarded as a
better "shot" than Mr. Child. The vigor of former years has
given place to infirmities which enfeeble his declining years.

[Seventh Generation.] Children:

2184. i. ORENNA CHILD, b. 1840.

2185. ii. PENUEL BENJAMIN CHILD, b. 1842.

2186. iii. LUCY SABRINA CHILD, b. Feb. 4, 1844, m. Mch. 27, 1864, Chas.
Vayette.

2187. iv. DANIEL HENRY CHILD, b. Feb. 27, 1846, m. Mary Webster.

2188. v. FRANCIS MARION CHILD, b. April 29, 1848, m. April 27, 1869,
Sarah Breslin.

2189. vi. WILLIAM WALLACE CHILD, b. 1860.

2190. vii. ALICE KATHARINE CHILD, b. 1865.

2191. viii. FREDERICK AUGUSTUS CHILD, b. 1868.

2192. ix. CHARLOTTE CHILD, b. 1870.

[Seventh Generation.]

2186. iii. LUCY SABRINA CHILD, second dau. and third child
of Henry Loomis and Diadama B. Hale Child, b. in Stockbridge. Vt., Feb. 4, 1844, m. by the Rev. Lewis Derush, in
Whitehall, N. Y., Mch. 27, 1864, Charles Vayette, who was b.
in Whitehall, N. Y.. Aug. 18, 1836. Mr. Vayette is a truck-
man by occupation, in Whitehall, N. Y.

[Eighth Generation] Children:

2193. i. ORAANNA VAYETTE, b. Dec. 25, 1864.

2194. ii. WILLIAM FRANCIS VAYETTE, b. Jan. 14, 1867, d. April, 1867.

2195. iii. CHARLES HENRY VAYETTE, b. July 8, 1869, d. same month.

2196. iv. GEORGE VAYETTE, b. June 24, 1870, d. July 7, 1870.

2197. v. SARAH ELIZABETH VAYETTE, b. Mch. 25, 1871, d. May, 1871.

2198. vi. WILLIAM VAYETTE, b. Jan. 24, 1873, d. July, 1873.

2199. vii. AUGUSTUS VAYETTE, b. Oct. 4, 1875.

2200. viii. EDWARD ELLSWORTH VAYETTE, b. Dec. 2, 1877.

[Seventh Generation.]

2187. iv. DANIEL HENRY CHILD, second son and fourth
child of Henry Loomis and Diadama B. Hale Child, b. in Middlebury, Vt., Feb. 27, 1846, m. Mary Webster, of East Pultney,
Vt. Resides at Sutherland Falls, Rutland Co., Vt.

[Eighth Generation.] Children:

2201. i JOHN HENRY CHILD, b. 1869.

2202. ii. MARY CHILD, b. 1873.

[Seventh Generation.]

2188. v. FRANCIS MARION CHILD, third son and fifth child of Henry Loomis and Diadama B. Hale Child, b. in Middlebury, Vt., April 29, 1848, m. April 27, 1869, by the Rev. J. J. McDonald, in Whitehall, N. Y., Sarah Breslin, who was b. in Hemingford, Canada East, July 23, 1847. Mr. F. M. Child when four years of age lost his mother, and went soon after to reside in Whitehall. He has been engaged in various kinds of business; at twelve years of age began his care of himself. He has associated himself with his brother in-law, Charles Vayette, in business, and resides in Whitehall, N. Y.

[Eighth Generation.]   Children:
    2203. i. CHARLES FRANCIS CHILD, b. Mch. 23, 1870.
    2204. ii. PATRICK HENRY CHILD, b. May 16, 1872.
    2205. iii. WILLIAM ALBERT CHILD, b. Jan. 6, 1876.
    2206. iv. MARY AGNES CHILD, b. July 26, 1878.

[Fifth Generation.]

2083. iii. PERLEY CHILD, second son and third child of Ebenezer and Charity Bugbee Child, b. in Woodstock, Ct., Dec. 6, 1859, m. Miss Lucy Symons. He d. May 30, 1812, in Pittsfield, Vt.

[Sixth Generation.]
    2207. i. POLLY CHILD, m. Mr. Farnham.
    2208. ii. SOPHIA CHILD, m. Mr. Salisbury.
    2209. iii. BETSEY CHILD, m Mr. Farnham.

[Fifth Generation.]

2086. vi. ELIZABETH CHILD, second dau. and sixth child of Ebenezer and Charity Bugbee Child, b. in Woodstock, Ct., Dec. 29, 1767, m. Abner Brigham.

[Sixth Generation.]   Children:
    2210. i. BETSEY BRIGHAM.
    2211. ii. WILLIAM BRIGHAM.
    2212. iii. SOPHIA BRIGHAM.
    2213. iv. NANCY BRIGHAM.
    2214. v. LUCIUS BRIGHAM.
    2215. vi. LOUISA BRIGHAM.
    2216. vii. ASA BRIGHAM.
    2217. viii. CHARLES BRIGHAM.

2084. v. EBENEZER CHILD, fourth son and youngest child of Ebenezer and Charity Bugbee Child, b. in Union, Ct., Aug. 17, 1770, m. at Brandon, Vt., Dec. 6, 1792, Miss Anna Gray, of Worcester, Mass.

Mr. Child had an inheritance of strong intellectual and moral qualities, and so far conquered all unpropitious surroundings as to make them contribute to the development of a strong mind, in a strong physical system. Early in life he was a puny boy, and always regarded much younger than he really was. When past ninety years of age, he writes most touchingly and tenderly of being lifted by his father to look upon the pale, silent face of the loving mother whose care he would never know, and of whom this act would prove the sole remembrance; he was then about three years old. The death of his mother, when he was so young, led to his being placed in the home of an elder married sister, with whom he remained until the second marriage of his father, and the family removed from Connecticut to Vermont, when he bravely shared the perils and deprivations, toil and loneliness of a home in the sparsely settled Green Mountain State. After aiding his father to build their log-house and gather in the grain raised around the stumps of trees on their lately cleared land in the summer and autumn of their entrance into Vermont, in the late autumn he made his way on foot and alone, to the old home and friends in Connecticut. He was then about twelve years old. With the dear kindred he spent the winter. Early spring found him on a rudely constructed vehicle, with the new mother, and their small household supplies, making his way amid cold and snow to Vermont.

His father's death occurring a few years later, Mr. Ebenezer Child settled the estate and started a new farm for himself, to which he brought his young bride, with strong courage and manly pride to carve out his own fortunes, and rear a large family. For many years, till quite past the threescore years and ten, his activities were laborious, continuous and efficient. The wonderful retention of the mental faculties until his death, when ninety-six years of age, help to prove that it is undue and extreme use which destroys. Mr. Ebenezer Child very early in life took such a decided and intelligent stand in the township upon all questions, political, religious and social, as to render him a power for good, and a frequent recognition by his fellow townsmen in the bestowal of differing offices, attested their appreciation. At the age of seventy-one, we find him to have delivered an address at Pittsfield, Vermont, on the formation of a Lyceum in that town. For many years Mr. Child was a regular contributor to certain local newspapers of articles upon most of the leading topics of the day, and as at this period, the differences of the Arminian and Calvinistic Creeds were deeply moving the New England mind. Mr. Child was especially interested and active in the discussions. The Masonic order found in him a friend and defender, and the growth and development of the young republic of the United States, awakened his deepest, heartiest enthusiasm. After passing into the four-score years some infirmities of body rendered locomotion more difficult and the amusements and occupations were limited to the use of the pen and reading. Sizeable folios were filled with copied letters and manuscripts of his composition, as legacies for his fondly cherished grandchildren, towards whom he entertained the most lavish affection, in whose progress he took pride, and whose ambition he sought to kindle for noblest effort and attainment. One or two extracts from letters addressed to the grandsons, Don Alonzo and Chas. G. Child, of New York, will evince his own clear mind, and true interest in them. From a letter bearing date Sept. 25, 1865, we give a sketch of his daily life, which he says he furnishes them as they may not be able to understand how a man so aged could pass the day, (then being ninety five):

As a great poet has said—

> 'Tis but one youth at most that mortals have,
> And one old age prepares us for the grave.'

I retire at 7 o'clock P. M., and Morpheus soon locks up the sensitive organs in quiet and balmy slumbers, which I generally enjoy until something like 4 o'clock A. M. I then return thanks to the great Author of my many blessings, and indulge half an hour in repeating and singing to myself those old hymns and psalms I used to indulge in sixty or seventy years ago. I arise about 6 A. M., after dressing myself, by the aid of my staff with some bodily exertion walk the piazza, then return to my room, wash, take half or three-fourths of a wine-glass of bitters; by this time I hear the glad voice sounding, 'Breakfast ready, Father!' of which I partake heartily. The amusements of the day you know well, when you think of reading papers, writing, and scrap-book, etc. My vacant hours of late dwell much on moral and scientific subjects. As I see the first rays of morning light breaking forth from the East, I say, here is another incontestible evidence of the being of a Supreme Creator. Nothing less than Almighty power, which creates and governs a universe of eighty millions of worlds, could keep in order this inconceivably great and mysterious machine, whereby sun and moon, stars, comets and their satellites, move in such harmony for thousands of years without the least variation.

Again he writes—

* * *   The mind of man evidently designed for progressive improvement, not to end with life, but to continue in another state of improved existence forever, if we continue to improve our intellectual faculties while living here on earth.   Youth seems to be the favorable time for
the cultivation and maturing of our moral and social natures, and ennob-
ling faculties that will enable us to become worthy and respected members
of society.   Says a great and good man: 'The youth who cultivates his
intellect and habitually obeys the precepts of christianity, will in mature
life enjoy within himself a fountain of moral and intellectual happiness, the
appropriate reward of obedience.'   Man when viewed in one aspect resem-
bles a demon, in another he bears the impress of the image of God.   When
seen in his crimes he might resemble a devil, when contemplated in his
charities, his discoveries in science, his vast combinations for the benefit of
his race, he appears a bright intelligence from heaven.   I have illustrated
these facts for your especial consideration that you may now in youth
profit by the comparison; make choice and habitually pursue a course of
life tending to refinement in mind and manners.

In another letter he writes—

November has been very mild and accommodating, though his hoarse
and hollow breath betokens his sudden dissolution, then stern and gloomy
December will usurp his iron rule and unrelenting winter follow in his
train.   These rough November blasts have already attacked this old, dilapi-
dated and decaying tenement, that has endured the chill frosts of more
than four score and ten winters and can make but feeble defence, and we
are now fortifying a place for retreat during cold winter's unwelcome
rigor, which will require a covering like the shield of Ajax, 'With seven
thick folds o'er cast of tough bull's hide, and solid brass the last.'

> 'But let chill winter bind the crystal streams,
> Withdraw from earth the sun's enlivening beams
> And scatter snow-flakes o'er the frozen sea,
> Thou canst not freeze the streams of true-eyed charity.'

We close these extracts which might be much multiplied
with his pleasant wishes for these grandsons, written them on
the incoming of a New Year—

May your happiness increase with your virtues, may generous hearts,
true friendships, peaceful and happy firesides, be the reward of your labors
of love, is the sincere desire of your old grandfather.

[Sixth Generation.]   Children:

2218. i. SALLIE WARNER CHILD, b. Oct. 19, 1793, in Brandon, Vt., d.
March, 1843, at Pittsfield, Vt : unmarried.

2219. ii. HORACE S. CHILD, b. Feb. 6, 1796, m. Oct. 15, 1817, Mary P.
Rice.

2220. iii. CHAUNCEY CHILD, b. Mch. 10. 1798, m. Frances Cecelia Morse.

2221. iv. ANNA MARIA CHILD, b. April 7, 1801, at Brandon, Vt., d. Oct.,
1867, at Castleton, Vt.; unmarried.

2222. v. EARL CHILD, b. Mch. 13, 1803, m. Louisa Keyes of Stockbridge,
Vt.

2223. vi. ALMIRA CHILD, b. Mch. 7, 1805, m. May, 1828, Edward Whitcomb.

2224. vii. ALONZO CHILD, b. July 21, 1807, m. Aug. 28, 1838, Mary Goodrich.

2225. viii. BENJAMIN FRANKLIN CHILD, b May 27, 1809, m. April 30, 187, Esther Hicks.

2226. ix. JULIA CHILD, b April 27, 1811, m. Oct. 1840, Chester Baxter.

2227. x. PEARLEY A. CHILD, b. April 8, 1813, m. 1st, April 13, 1834, Helen Pratt; m. 2d. Aug. 1877, Miss Hawley.

2228. xi. WILLIAM GRAY CHILD, b. Oct. 8, 1815, in Brandon, Vt., d. in Michigan; unmarried.

2229. xii. ELIZA GREENWOOD CHILD, b. May 12, 1819, at Brandon, Vt. Resides in Orange, N. J.; unmarried.

2230. xiii JANE BETHIA CHILD, b. Oct. 27, 1822, at Brandon. Vt., d. Jan. 16, 1862, at Castleton, Vt.; unmarried.

To all these children Mr. Ebenezer Child secured the best possible advantages for education available, in the true New England spirit considering it the surest endowment he could secure to them.

[Sixth Generation.]

2219. ii. HORACE S. CHILD, second child and eldest son of Ebenezer and Anna Gray Child, b. in Brandon, Rutland Co., Vt., Feb. 6, 1796, m. Oct. 15, 1817, Miss Mary P. Rice, of Hardwick, Worcester Co., Mass. Mr. Child, like many others of his race, found a home and final resting in the West, where he closed his long and useful life in Geneseo, Henry Co., Ill., on the 4th of March, 1872, at seventy-two years of age.

[Seventh Generation.] Children:

2231. i. HORACE RICE CHILD, b Oct. 23, 1818, m Miss Mary Lee, of Springfield, Vt.

2232. ii. ELLEN MARIA CHILD, b. Aug. 18, 1820, m. Oct. 15, 1839, Henry S. Ford.

2233. iii. ORANGE WATSON CHILD, b. Aug. 29, 1824, m. Aug. 6, 1851, Susan Stickney.

2234. iv. ANN MELISSA CHILD, b. Oct. 19, 1826, m. May 11, 1847, Benjamin F. Baker.

2235. v. SARAH JANE CHILD, b. Mch., 1830, m. Jan. 10, 1850, James G. Goodrich.

2236. vi. ALBERT ALONZO CHILD, b. June, 1832, m. Frances Page.

2237. vii. FRANCIS PEARLEY CHILD, b. Mch. 31, 1835, m. July 15, 1856, Celia Gillespie.

[Seventh Generation.]

2231. i. HORACE RICE CHILD, eldest son and child of Horace S. and May P. Rice Child, b. in Brandon, Vt., Oct. 23, 1818, m. in Springfield, Windsor Co., Vt., Miss Mary Lee.

[Eighth Generation.] Children:

2238. i. GEORGE CHILD.

2239. ii. ELIZABETH CHILD.

X

2240. iii. SARAH CHILD.
2241. iv. HERBERT CHILD, }
2242. v. HENRY CHILD. } Twins.

[Seventh Generation.]

2232. ii. ELLEN MARIA CHILD, eldest dau. and second child
of Horace S. and Mary P. Rice Child. b. in Rutland, Vt., Aug.
18, 1820, m. Oct. 15, 1839, Mr. Henry S. Ford, of Mendon, Vt.
Reside in Geneseo, Henry Co., Ill.

[Eighth Generation.] Children:

2243. i. WATSON R. FORD, b. Nov. 18, 1840, at Mendon, Rutland Co., Vt.,
d. Dec. 12, 1863, in Danville Prison, from wounds received in the war in
1861. He belonged to Co. I., 112th Illinois Volunteers.

2244. ii. SARAH E. FORD, b. April 27, 1846, m. Oct. 15, 1869, Mill P.
Parker.

2245. iii. J. DAYTON FORD, b. June 6, 1847, m. Dec. 29, 1870, Minnie K.
Weston.

2246. iv. ELLA B. FORD, b. July 11, 1849, m. Dec. 29, 1874, George W.
Beale.

2247. v. HORACE C. FORD, b. Mch. 2, 1853, m. Feb. 29, 1878, Nettie J.
Sargent.

2248. vi FANNY M. FORD, b. May 25, 1759, at Geneseo, Ill.

2249. vii. FRED L. FORD, b. July 20, 1861, at Geneseo, Ill., d. Aug. 15,
1875.

2250. viii. HENRY L. FORD, b. Mch. 31, 1865, at Geneseo, Ill., d. June 19,
1866.

[Eighth Generation.]

2244. ii. SARAH E. FORD, eldest dau. and second child of
Ellen M. Child and Henry S. Ford, b. in Mendon, Vt., April
27, 1846, m. Oct. 15, 1869, Mill P. Parker. Reside in Kinsley,
Edwards Co., Kanzas.

[Ninth Generation.] Children:

2251. i. JESSIE E. PARKER, b. Sept. 4, 1870.

2252. ii. JAMES PARKER, b. Sept. 1, 1872, d. Mch. 28. 1873.

2253. iii. GUY W. PARKER, b. Mch. 19, 1873, d. July 25, 1878.

2254. iv. F. BLANCH PARKER, b. May 18, 1874, d. Aug. 22, 1878.

2255. v. LILLIE PARKER, b. Sept. 9, 1878.

[Eighth Generation.]

2245. iii. J. DAYTON FORD, second son and third child of
Ellen M. Child and Henry S. Ford, b. in Mendon, Vt., June 6,
1847, m. Dec. 29, 1870, Minnie K. Weston.

[Ninth Generation.] Children:

2256. i. ELLEN H. FORD, b. Oct. 17, 1874.

2257. ii. HARRY T. FORD, b. April 16, 1875.

[Eighth Generation.]

2246. iv. ELLA B. FORD, second dau. and fourth child of
Ellen M. Child and Henry S. Ford, b. in Mendon, Vt., July 11,
1849, m. Dec. 29, 1874, George W. Beale.

[Ninth Generation.] Children:
2258. i. GEORGE A. BEALE, b. Dec. 26, 1875.
2259. ii. E BLANCH BEALE, b. April 5, 1879.

[Eighth Generation.]

2247. v. HORACE CHILD FORD, third son and fifth child of Ellen M. Child and Henry S. Ford, b. in Mendon, Vt., Mch. 2, 1853, m. Feb. 29, 1878, Nettie J. Sargent.
[Ninth Generation.] Child:
2260. i. GUY D. FORD, b. Mch. 8, 1879.

[Seventh Generation.]

2233. iii. ORANGE WATSON CHILD, second son and third child of Horace S. and Mary P. Rice Child, b. Aug. 29, 1824, in Castleton, Rutland Co., Vt., m. in Boonville, Oneida Co., New York, Aug. 6, 1851, Miss Susan Stickney. Mr. and Mrs. O. W. Child reside in Elizabeth, Union Co., New Jersey.

Mr. Child is largely engaged in railway enterprise, in Nassau Street, New York City—supplying railway corporations with equipments for operating their roads, such as steel and iron rails, locomotives, cars, etc. We are much indebted to Mr. Child for the interest he has taken in our work, and for essential aid in furnishing family records.
[Eighth Generation.] Children:
2261. i. WILLIAM CHILD, b. Oct. 3, 1854, d. same day in Boonville, N. Y.
2262. ii JOSEPHINE CHILD, b. Jan. 23, 1856 at Boonville, N. Y., d. Jan. 8, 1859, in St. Louis, Missouri
2263. iii. FRANK WATSON CHILD, b. Dec. 12, 1859, at Boonville, N. Y.; resides in Elizabeth, New Jersey.
2264. iv. JENNIE S. CHILD, b. Aug. 4, 1861, d. May 16, 1862, in Tarry-Town-on-the-Hudson, N. Y.

[Seventh Generation.]

2234. iv. ANN MELISSA CHILD, second dau. and fourth child of Horace S. and Mary P. Rice Child, b. Oct. 19, 1826, m. May 11, 1847, Benjamin Franklin Baker, of Pittsfield, Vt. Mr. and Mrs. Baker are now resident in Chicago, Ill.
[Eighth Generation.] Children:
2265. i. MARY EDNAH BAKER, b. Mch. 18, 1848, m. abt. 1861, Albert Smith.
2266. ii. CLARA MARIA BAKER, b. Oct. 1, 1858, at Rock Island, Ill.

[Eighth Generation.]

2265. i. MARY EDNAH BAKER, eldest child of Ann Melissa Child and Benjamin F. Baker, b. in Pittsfield, Vt., Mch. 18, 1848, m. about 1861, Albert Smith. Reside in Chicago, Ill.

[Ninth Generation.] Children:
2267. i. LATHIE E. SMITH, b. May 1, 1862, in Chicago, Ill.
2268. ii FRANK BAKER SMITH.
2269. iii. KATE STEVENS SMITH.
2270. iv. CARRIE SMITH.

[Seventh Generation.]
2235. v. SARAH JANE CHILD, third dau. and fifth child of Horace S. and Mary P. Rice Child, b. Mch. 1830, at Glens Falls, Warren Co., N. Y., m. Jan. 10, 1850, in St. Louis, Missouri, to Mr. James G. Goodrich; removed from St. Louis in 1863, to 412 Michigan Ave., Chicago, Ill., with their family.
[Eighth Generation] Children:
2271. i. MARY WALLACE GOODRICH, b. Nov. 26, 1850, at St. Louis, Mo.
2272. ii. JULIUS G. GOODRICH, b. Oct. 6, 1852, at St. Louis, Mo.
2273. iii. NELLIE GOODRICH, b. Jan. 6, 1855, at St. Louis, Mo.
2274. iv. SARAH CHILD GOODRICH,) Twins { b. Aug. 6,1857, St. Louis, Mo.
2275. v. JAMES G. GOODRICH,) (d. Sept '10, 1857.
2276. vi. HARRY GOODRICH, b. July 11, 1867, in Chicago, Ill.

[Seventh Generation.]
2236. vi. ALBERT ALONZO CHILD, third son and sixth child of Horace S. and Mary P. Rice Child, b. June, 1832, m. Frances Page, at Nashua, N. H. Mr. Child is in business in Chicago, Ill.
[Eighth Generation] Children.
2277. i. JESSIE CHILD.
2278. ii. GEORGE CHILD.
2279. iii. PAIGE CHILD.

[Seventh Generation.]
2237. vii. FRANCIS PEARLEY CHILD, fourth son and seventh child of Horace S. and Mary P. Rice Child, b. in Pittsfield, Vt., March 31, 1835, m. July 15, 1856, Celia Gillespie, and resides at present in Chicago, Ill.
[Eighth Generation.] Child:
2280. i. FRANCIS CHILD.

[Sixth Generation.]
2220. iii. CHAUNCEY CHILD, second son and third child of Ebenezer and Anna Gray Child, b. in Brandon, Rutland Co., Vt., March 10, 1798, m. Jan. 1, 1841, Miss Frances Celia Morse, at Brighton, Livingston Co., Michigan. Mr. Chauncey Child died at Staunton, Mt. Calm Co., Michigan, Nov. 26, 1875.
[Seventh Generation.] Children:
2281. i. ELIZA CECELIA CHILD, b. July 29, 1842, m. June 5, 1860, Joseph F. Jewett.
2282. ii. CHAUNCEY EUGENE CHILD, b. April 15, 1844, in Hartland, Livingston, Co., Mich., d. Jan. 10, 1845.

2283. iii. FRANCES EUGENIE CHILD, b. April 29, 1846, in Hartland, Livingston Co., Mich., d. Sept. 1, 1848.

2284. iv. EBENEZER G. CHILD, b. Mch 11, 1848, in Hartland, Livingston Co., Mich., m. at Greenville, Mich., July 3, 1877, Miss Ollie Sharp.

2285. v. EMMA LOUISA CHILD b. Oct. 14, 1850, in Hartland Livingston Co., Mich.

2286. vi. FRANKLIN GRAY CHILD, b. Oct. 1, 1852, in Hartland, Livingston Co., Mich., d. Jan. 23, 1859, in Cleveland, Ohio.

2287. vii. BURR JULIUS HERBERT CHILD, b. Mch. 13, 1855, m. Dec. 31, 1874, Alice M. Cannon.

[Seventh Generation.]

2281. i. ELIZA CECELIA CHILD, eldest dau. and child of Chauncey and Frances Celia Morse Child, b. in Hartland, Livingston Co., Mich., July 29, 1842, m. in Cleveland Ohio, June 5, 1860, Joseph F. Jewett. Reside in Cincinnati, Ohio.

[Eighth Generation.] Children:

2288. i. LAURA HEPPIE JEWETT, b Mch. 21, 1861, at Cincinnati, Ohio.

2289. ii. JENNIE LOUISE JEWETT, b. Aug 31, 1862, at Cincinnati, Ohio d. Sept. 3, 1865.

2290. iii. HELEN MARIA JEWETT, b. April 13, 1864, at Cincinnati, Ohio.

2291. iv. CARRIE LOUISE JEWETT, b. Aug. 11, 1866, at Wyoming, Ohio.

2292. v. JOSEPH F. JEWETT, JR., b. July 11, 1868, at Wyoming, Ohio.

2293. vi. GRACE ELIZA JEWETT, b. Sept. 13, 1870, at Wyoming Ohio.

2294. vii. MAX JEWETT, b. Nov. 17, 1872, at Wyoming, Ohio.

2295. viii. CECELIA CHILD JEWETT, b. Dec. 26, 1874 at Wyoming, Ohio.

[Seventh Generation.]

2287. vii. BURR JULIUS HERBERT CHILD, fourth son and seventh child of Chauncey and Frances Celia Morse Child, b. in Milford, Oakland Co., Mich., m. at Mill Brook, Mich., Dec. 31, 1874, Miss Alice M. Cannon.

[Eighth Generation.] Child:

2296. i. LEWIS HERBERT CHILD, b. Oct. 26, 1876.

[Sixth Generation]

2222. v. EARL CHILD, third son and fifth child of Ebenezer and Anna Gray Child, b. in Brandon, Rutland Co., Vt., Mch. 13, 1803, m. at Stockbridge, Vt., Nov. 4, 1827, Miss Louisa W. Keyes, who was b. in Bridgewater, Vt., Sept. 13, 1813. Mr. Earl Child died in Hartland, Mich., April 9, 1862. Mrs. Child died in Brighton, Mich., June 14, 1845.

[Seventh Generation.] Children.

2297. i. A daughter—unchristened—b Feb. 10, 1829, d. same day in Pittsfield, Vt.

2298. ii. EARL KEYES CHILD, b. Mch. 21 1830, in Pittsfield, Vt., m. May 30, 1852, Jennette Harrington.

2299. iii. A son—unchristened—b. April 5, 1832, d. same day, in Brandon, Vt.

2300. iv. Minon J. Child, b. Jan. 26, 1833, d. Jan. 31, 1833, in Leicester, Vt.

2301. v. Anna Maria Child, b. Jan. 9, 1836, m. Oct. 23, 1854, John S. Topping.

2302. vi. Helen Pratt Child, b. Feb. 21, 1839, m. Feb. 28, 1861, Robert B. Smith.

[Seventh Generation.]

2301. v. Anna Maria Child, fifth child of Earl and Louisa W. Keyes Child, b. in Green Oak, (afterwards Oakland) Mich., Jan. 9, 1836, m. Oct. 23, 1854, John S. Topping, at Tarrytown, N. Y.

[Eighth Generation] Children:

2303. i. Mary Louise Topping, b. Oct. 11, 1857, in New York City.

2304. ii. Jessie Patience Topping, b. Dec. 9, 1860, in Alton, Ill.

2305. iii. Helen Maria Topping, b. July 25, 1863, in Alton, Ill.

2306. iv. Erastus Doane Topping, b. Oct. 27, 1866, in Alton, Ill.

2307. v. Alonzo Child Topping, b. Jan. 25, 1869, in Alton, Ill.

2308. vi. Gracie Sheldon Topping, b. Oct. 19, 1871, in Alton, Ill.

2309. vii. John Ryder Topping, b. Feb. 1, 1875, in Alton, Ill.

[Seventh Generation.]

2302. vi. Helen Pratt Child, sixth and youngest child of Earl and Louisa W. Keyes Child, b. in Hartland, Livingston Co., Mich., Feb. 21, 1839, m. Feb. 28, 1861, Robert B. Smith, in Alton, Ill.

[Eighth Generation.] Child:

2310. i. Earl Clarendon Smith, b. April 26, 1862, in Alton, Ill.

[Sixth Generation.]

2223. vi. Almira Child, third dau. and sixth child of Ebenezer and Anna Gray Child, b. at Brandon, Rutland Co., Vt., March 7, 1805, m. May, 1828, Mr. Edward Whitcomb, at Pittsfield, Vt. Reside at Le Roy, Mower, Co., Minnesota.

[Seventh Generation.] Children:

2311. i. Julia Whitcomb, b. Oct. 9, 1834, in Fredonia, Chautauqua Co., New York, d. Aug. 9, 1853.

2312. ii. Helen Whitcomb, b. June 13, 1836, in Fredonia, N. Y., d. May 1844.

2313. iii. Anna Whitcomb, b. Sept. 10, 1838, in Hiram, Portage Co., Ohio, m. Sept. 20, 1856, Albert Allen, at Le Roy, Minn. Resides in California.

2314. iv. Edward B. Whitcomb, b. Oct. 5, 1841, in Spring Prairie, Wis., m. Feb. 22, 1868, Maggie Taylor, at Le Roy, Minn.

2315. v. Emma Whitcomb, b. Mch. 19, 1846, at Burlington, Wis., d. April 9, 1848.

2316. vi. Adelaide Whitcomb, b. Oct. 16, 1849, in Burlington, Wis, m. Aug. 10, 1867, Samuel Bacon, in Le Roy, Minn.

[Sixth Generation.]

2224. vii. ALONZO CHILD, fourth son and seventh child of Ebenezer and Anna Gray Child, b. in Brandon, Vt., July 21, 1807, m. Aug. 28, 1838, in Pittsfield, Vt., Miss Mary Goodrich, dau. of Mr. James Goodrich ; a Scotch family. Mrs. Goodrich, the mother of Mrs. Alonzo Child, was a Wallace, said to be in direct descent from the hero of Scotland.

Mr. Alonzo Child, like his brothers and sisters, was educated in the common schools and academies of New England, but from the rapid growth of the frame which early attained more than average stature, there resulted much physical weakness, resulting in an affection of the eyes which ultimately destroyed the sight of one. Skillful treatment from the leading physicians of Massachusetts saved him from utter blindness. Though thus tried at his entrance upon the activities of life, he was nothing daunted, but with cheerful zeal began the career which resulted for him in such pecuniary success. His debut was made in Lowell, Mass., a large manufacturing city. Hither he bent his steps, entrusted by Dr. Eliphalet Nott, President of Union College, Schenectady, N. Y., with a consignment of the stoves invented and patented by Dr. Nott, for the use of anthracite coal. The venture was an entirely successful one, attesting anew the quick apprehension of character, and whole-hearted generosity of the learned Doctor, as well as the thorough business capabilities of the young merchant. This location though pleasant to Mr. Child in many respects, did not offer the opportunity for that enlargement of business of which Mr. Alonzo Child felt capable. Closing his affairs in Lowell, Mr. Child went to the West and found in the stirring haste, and breadth of method, the kind of business atmosphere for which he was especially adapted. He made St. Louis, Missouri, the base of his operations, which proved an eminently wise decision. Mr. Child made for himself a name and position among the merchant princes of that city. His interests were wide and deep ; unostentatious in charities, he was yet always ready to help on every movement which promised elevation to his fellow-beings, either pecuniarily or morally. Many prosperous business houses to-day owe largely their success to some kindly loan or start in life from his easily sliding purse-string. With all this extreme activity, Mr. Child was a man of strong home attachments,

delighting to render his abode one of attraction from its luxury
of comforts. In the years 1843–4, Mr. Child was in Europe
combining business profits and intellectual culture. From the
year 1850, Mr. Child became a resident of Tarry-town on-the-
Hudson, not far from New York City, though continuing his
business houses in the West and usually passing a large part
of each winter in St. Louis. Of his patriotism we will permit
the accompanying resolutions to speak, premising that Mr.
Child had reached the close of his life, so full of large interests
in the West, and of pleasant, useful, honorable characteristics
in the social world of his eastern home, on the third of June,
1873. Mr. Child was trustee of the Mutual Life Ins. Co., of
New York City, and director of the Westchester Savings Bank,
aiding largely in the formation of the latter.

At a regular meeting of the Board of Trustees of the Mutual
Life Ins. Co., of New York City, held June 4, 1873, the President announced the death of Alonzo Child, a Trustee of the
company for many years. Judge Davis addressed the Chair as
follows, presenting the appended resolutions :

"*Mr. President*: The announcement you have just made of the decease of
one of the most respected and esteemed members of this Board, must fill
every heart with profound sorrow and deep sympathy. Alonzo Child has
been a useful and honored member of this Board for many years, always
faithful to duty, wise in council and ready to discharge every obligation
with fidelity and integrity. Mr. Child was distinguished for a long and
honored mercantile career. His commercial integrity was never questioned,
and he ever stood in the front ranks of those who have transacted the business affairs of our country. But I desired to refer particularly to the in-
valuable and patriotic services he rendered to the country in its late struggles for national existence. Mr. Child had a large mercantile house established at St. Louis, and through it, for more than thirty years previous to 1861,
had furnished the government with all needful supplies in the line of his
business, for its armies in the West, and the Indian tribes dependent upon
the government for their annual needs. At the commencement of the war,
his firm at St. Louis invested everything they had for the purpose of maintaining the government of the United States. They had at one time risked
over a million of dollars in supplies furnished to maintain troops in the
field They were the first to hang out the stars and stripes on Main St., in
St Louis; and were always willing to trust the government with anything
they wanted and to imperil their whole fortune in its support. The merchants in St. Louis would not sell to or trust the government, but Mr.
Child's house did, until his resident partner thought they were ready to
break, and telegraphed to Mr Child, at New York, to know if they should
go on, to which Mr. Child replied: 'Proceed to the extent of every dollar we
have, and all you can raise.' His efforts to sustain the government were

characterized by its officers as nearly superhuman, and the name of no man
should be held in more grateful remembrance than that of Alonzo Child,
for his unrequited and priceless services in sustaining this nation in its
hour of peril. I quote from the record for these facts in a case in which I
acted professionally for Mr. Child; and I shall ever blush for my country at
the *injustice* it meted out to him in the matter.

But peace to his memory. He has gone where the wicked cease from
troubling and the weary are at rest. Let us ever cherish in grateful remembrance his many virtues, his kind, genial and quiet manners, and imitate
his self-sacrifices, patriotic devotion to his country, and fidelity in the discharge of every duty."

Much more of like character was here said, and by the Trustees
of the Westchester Savings Bank, as well as by the press, one
sentiment pervading every utterance that of thorough, ready,
cordial recognition of the entire honesty of his life.

[Seventh Generation.] Children:

2317. i. DON ALONZO CHILD, b. Aug. 30, 1840, m. Dec. 12, 1865, Annie
Cromwell.

2318. ii. DAYTON CHILD, b. July, 1840, d. June, 1841, in St. Louis, Mo.

2319. iii. JULIUS PRATT CHILD, ⎰ ᵇ ⎱ Resides in Jacksonville, Fla.

⎱ ᵗ ⎰ b. Feb. 14, 1845. [Wheelwright.

2320. iv. CHARLES GARDNER CHILD, ⎰ ⎱ m. April 16, 1871, Carrie

2321. v. GEORGE FRANKLIN CHILD, b. 1847, d. 1847, in St. Louis, Mo.

2322. vi. MARY EMMA CHILD, b. April 23, 1849, at St. Louis, Mo., m. Dec.
16, 1869, Stephen C. Millett.

2323. vii. HENRY CLAY CHILD, b. May 6, 1852, at Tarrytown, N. Y., m.
July 15, 1875, Lizzie Ferguson, of New York.

2324. viii. KATE MARIA CHILD, b. Aug. 10, 1853, m. Dec. 7, 1875, Daniel
C. Millett.

[Seventh Generation.]

2317. i. DON ALONZO CHILD, eldest son and child of Alonzo
and Mary Goodrich Child, b. in St. Louis, Mis., Aug. 30, 1840,
m. Dec. 12, 1865, Miss Annie Cromwell, of Brooklyn, N. Y.
Mr. and Mrs. Don Alonzo Child reside in New York City.

[Eighth Generation.] Children:

2325. i. CROMWELL CHILD, b. July 8, 1867, in Brooklyn, N. Y.

2326. ii. MARY GOODRICH CHILD, b. Nov. 8, 1868, in Brooklyn, N. Y.

[Seventh Generation

2320. iv. CHARLES GARDNER CHILD, twin son with Julius
Pratt Child, of Alonzo and Mary Goodrich Child, b. in St.
Louis, Mo., Feb. 14, 1845, m. April 16, 1871, Miss Carrie
Wheelwright, of New York City, in which place Mr. and Mrs.
Chas. G. Child reside, at 125 W. 47th st. Mr. Charles G. Child
is a broker on Wall st., New York City.

[Eighth Generation.]   Children:

    2327. i. CHARLES GARDNER CHILD, JR., b. Mch. 1872, in New York.

    2328. ii. BESSIE WHEELWRIGHT CHILD, b. Oct. 1877, in New York.

[Seventh Generation.]

    2322. vi. MARY EMMA CHILD, eldest dau. and sixth child of Alonzo and Mary Goodrich Child, b. in St. Louis, Mo., April 23, 1849, m. Dec. 16, 1869, Stephen C. Millett. Mr. Millett died in Columbia, South Carolina, Feb. 24, 1874. Mrs. Millett resides in Orange. N. J.

[Eighth Generation.]   Children:

    2329. i. MARY GOODRICH MILLETT, b. Dec. 7, 1870, in Beaufort, S. C.

    2330. ii. KATIE CHILD MILLETT, b. Sept. 13, 1872, in Beaufort, S. C.

    2331. iii. STEPHEN COLWELL MILLETT, b. Dec. 5, 1873, in Beaufort, S. C.

[Seventh Generation.]

    2324. viii. KATE MARIA CHILD, second dau. and youngest child of Alonzo and Mary Goodrich Child, b. in Tarry-town-on-the Hudson, Aug. 10, 1853, m. Dec. 7, 1875, Daniel C. Millett, at South Orange, N. J. Mr. and Mrs. D. C. Millett reside in Milwaukee, Wis.

[Eighth Generation.]   Child:

    2332. i. ANNA GRAY MILLETT, b. Sept. 3, 1877, in Milwaukee, Wis.

[Sixth Generation.]

    2225. viii. BENJAMIN FRANKLIN CHILD, fifth son and eighth child of Ebenezer and Anna Gray Child, b. in Brandon, Vt., May 27, 1809, m. April 30, 1847, Esther Hicks, at Bennington, Vt. : died in Shiawassee Co., Mich.

[Seventh Generation.]   Children:

    2333. i. GEORGE CHILD, b. May 12, 1848, m. Dec. 1870.

    2334 ii. ALONZO P. CHILD, b. July 21, 1853, m. July 21, 1875, at Lanesburg, Mich.: d. April 29, 1877, at same place.

    2335. iii. WATSON CHILD, b. Nov. 21, 1861, at Shionapa, Mich. Resides in Lanesburg, Mich.

    2336. iv. EDWIN CHILD b. Oct. 1, 1866, at Lanesburg, Mich.

[Sixth Generation.]

    2226. ix. JULIA CHILD, fourth dau. and ninth child of Ebenezer and Anna Gray Child, b. in Brandon, Rutland Co., Vt., April 27, 1811, m. Oct. 1840, Chester Baxter, at Pittsfield, Vt., and died at Castleton, Vt., April 4, 1867, aged 56 years.

[Seventh Generation.]   Children:

    2337. i. ELLEN DANA BAXTER, b. July, 1841, in Pittsfield, Vt., m. Oct. 10 1868, John H. Langdon.

    2338 ii. ELIZABETH MORSE BAXTER, b. April, 1845, in Pittsfield, Vt., m. April 4, 1870, Benson Ferris. Resides at Princeton, Ill.

[Sixth Generation.]

2227. x. PEARLEY AUGUSTUS CHILD, sixth son and tenth child of Ebenezer and Anna Gray Child, b. in Brandon, Vt., April 8, 1813; has been twice married—1st, April 13, 1834, by Rev. Elisha Tucker, to Helen Maria Pratt, in Buffalo, N. Y., where she was b. Dec. 1, 1817. Mrs. H. M. Pratt Child died at West Exeter, N. Y., April 14, 1866. Mr. Child m. 2d, Aug., 1877, Miss Hawley, of Brooklyn, N. Y. Mr. Child is engaged in the hardware business, in the stove manufacturing department. He is a man of strong presence and genial spirit; a well proportioned man six feet in height. He was associated with his brother, Alonzo Child, in the hardware trade in St. Louis, Missouri, for some years, where they were most extensive and successful operators.

[Seventh Generation.] Children:

2339. i. HELEN PRATT CHILD, b. Mch. 8, 1835, m. Dec. 17, 1856, Lorenzo D. Colt.

2340. ii. FRANCES RACHEL CHILD, b. Nov. 12, 1836, m. Oct. 6, 1859, Clark Lockwood Carpenter.

2341. iii. PASCAL P. CHILD, b. Oct. 25, 1838, m. Nov. 10, 1861, Charlotte H. Clarke.

2342. iv. HIRAM HERENDEAN CHILD, b. Oct. 26, 1840, d. Aug. 14, 1849, at Buffalo, N. Y.

2343. v. MARILLA ALLEN CHILD, b. Aug. 2, 1842, d. Feb. 4, 1847, at Buffalo, N. Y.

2344. vi. JULIA MARIA CHILD, b. Sept. 28, 1848, m. Dec. 12, 1873, Mark L. Filley.

2345. vii. PEARLEY AUGUSTUS CHILD, JR., b. July 24, 1857, at Cleveland, Ohio.

[Seventh Generation.]

2339. i. HELEN PRATT CHILD, eldest child of Pearley Augustus and Helen M. Pratt Child, b. in Buffalo, N. Y., Mch. 8, 1835, m. in Cleveland, Ohio, Dec. 17, 1856, Lorenzo D. Colt. Resided in West Exeter, Otsego Co., N. Y., where she d. May 1, 1866.

[Eighth Generation.] Children:

2346. i. PASCAL CHESTER COLT, b. May, 1859, at West Exeter, N. Y.

2347. ii. CHARLOTTE HENRIETTA COLT, b. Nov. 21, 1860, at West Exeter, N. Y.

2348. iii. JAMES DENISON COLT, b. July, 1862, at West Exeter, N. Y.

2349. iv. LORENZO COLT, b. Dec. 1863, at West Exeter, N. Y., d. at same place Dec. 1863.

[Seventh Generation.]

2340. ii. FRANCES RACHEL CHILD, second dau. and child of Pearley Augustus and Helen M. Pratt Child, b. in Buffalo,

N. Y., Nov. 12, 1836, m. at St. Louis, Mo., Oct. 6, 1859, Clark
Lockwood Carpenter.   Reside in Lansingburgh, N. Y.

[Eighth Generation.]   Children:

2350. i. CLARK HIRAM CARPENTER, b. Dec. 29, 1860, at Kansas City, Mo.

2351. ii. PEARLEY AUGUSTUS CARPENTER, b. Aug. 19, 1862, at St. Louis,
Mo., d. Aug. 22, 1865, at West Exeter, N. Y.

2352. iii. HELEN MARIA CARPENTER, b. Aug. 13, 1864, d. Aug. 12, 1865,
at West Exeter, N. Y.

2353. iv. FREDERIC AUGUSTUS CARPENTER, b. Mch. 14, 1868, at Orange,
N. J.

2354. v. FRANCES LUCILLE CARPENTER, b. Aug. 5, 1872, at Lansingburgh,
N. Y.

[Seventh Generation.]

2341. iii. PASCAL PRATT CHILD, eldest son and third child of
Pearley Augustus and Helen M. Pratt Child, b. in Buffalo,
N. Y., Oct. 25, 1838, m. in St. Louis, Mo., Nov. 10, 1861
Charlotte H. Clarke.

[Eighth Generation.]   Children:

2355. i. PASCAL CHILD, b. 1862, and d. in St. Louis, Mo.

2356. ii. HELEN CHILD, b. July 5, 1864, in St Louis, Mo.

2357. iii. HARRY CHILD.

2358. iv. HIRAM CHILD, d. at Carlyle, Ill.

2359. v. CHARLOTTE CHILD.

2360. vi. FRANCES RENA CHILD.

2361. vii. JULIA CHILD.

[Seventh Generation.]

2344. vi. JULIA MARIA CHILD, fourth dau. and sixth child
of Pearley Augustus and Helen M. Pratt Child, b. in Buffalo,
N. Y., Sept. 28, 1848, m. at Lansingburgh, N. Y., Dec. 12,
1873, Mark L. Filley.   Reside in Lansingburgh, N. Y.

[Eighth Generation.]   Children:

2362. i. OLIVER DWIGHT FILLEY, b. Mch. 14, 1876, in Lansingburgh, N.Y.

2363. ii. MARCUS L. FILLEY, b. Sept. 18, 1878, in Lansingburgh, N. Y.

2364. iii. FREDERIC CHILD FILLEY, b. May 30, 1879, in Lansingburgh, N.Y.

[Third Generation.]

22. viii. WILLIAM CHILD, eighth child and fifth son of
Benjamin and Grace Morris Child, b. in Roxbury, Mass., Oct.
14, 1677, m. 1723, Deborah Goddard, dau. of Joseph and
Deborah Goddard.   He early removed to Woodstock, Ct.

[Fourth Generation.]   Children.

2365. i. LUCY CHILD, b in Woodstock, Ct., Sept. 30, 1729, m. April 26,
1753, Thomas May.

2366. ii. JONATHAN CHILD, b. in Woodstock, Ct, Dec. 17, 1731, m. June
12, 1755, Dinah Bacon.

2367. iii. WILLIAM CHILD, b. in Woodstock, Ct., 1733, d. 1734.

[Fourth Generation.]

2366. ii. Col. JONATHAN CHILD, second child and eldest son of William and Deborah Goddard Child, b. in Woodstock, Ct., Dec. 17, 1731, m. June 12, 1755, Dinah Bacon, dau. of Thomas Bacon. She was b. 1735, and d. Jan. 3, 1814. He d. April 5, 1814, in Thetford, Vt. He obtained his military title of colonel in the Revolutionary army. He was engaged in the battles of Bunker Hill and Bennington, as well as other battles.

Col. Jonathan Child was among the early emigrants from Woodstock, Ct., to that part of New Hampshire bordering on Vermont, and settled in Orford, N. H. At what date we are not informed, but probably between the years of 1770 and '75. Hon. William Child, of Fairlee, Vt., who is familiar with the history of that part of the State of Vermont upon which Orford borders, and who has supplied a chapter of history for a "Historical Gazetteer" of Vermont, says:

"In my researches for scraps of history for that work, I found Col. Jonathan Child, then of Orford, N. H., was with others quite prominent in the first organization of Fairlee, Vt., as a town, which was then a small parcel of the territory known as the 'New Hampshire Grant,' and as a matter of course, several of our first town meetings between the years 1770 and 1780, were warned and held in Orford, N. H. Col. Child, I think, afterwards moved to Lyme, N. H., and possibly might have crossed the river and located in Thetford, Vt. At any rate his son William, who spent a large property as commissary for the purchase of supplies for our Revolutionary soldiers, located on a river farm in Thetford, Vt., where some of his descendants are still residing."

[Fifth Generation.] Children.

2368. i. CYRIL CHILD, b. May 5, 1756. Killed in battle in Pennsylvania, July 4, 1778. A soldier of the Revolutionary war.

2369. ii. WILLIAM CHILD, b. Dec. 10, 1757, m. Sept. 28, 1780, Mary Heaton.

2370. iii. ZERIAH CHILD, b. Oct. 9, 1759.

2371. iv. PERSIS CHILD, b. Aug. 23, 1761, d. Jan. 29, 1786.

2372. v. LUCY CHILD, b. Aug. 24, 1763, m. Israel Newton, M. D.

2373. vi. AZUBAH CHILD, b. Jan. 13, 1765, d. Oct. 27, 1784.

2374. vii. ASENATH CHILD, b Dec. 29, 1767, m. —— Day. Had one daughter, Mrs. Asenath Pettibone of Muscatine, Iowa.

2375. viii. DEBORAH CHILD, b. Dec. 15, 1769, d. July 31, 1799.

2376. ix. ABIEL CHILD, b. Jan. 22, 1772, at Lyme, N. H., d. May 5, 1773.

2377. x. HANNAH CHILD, b. Oct. 31, 1774.

2378. xi. POLLY CHILD, b. July 24, 1777, m. Rev. Asa Burton.

[Fifth Generation.]

2369. ii. WILLIAM CHILD, second child and son of Col. Jonathan and Dinah Bacon Child, b. in Woodstock, Ct., Dec. 10, 1757, m. Sept. 28, 1780, Mary Heaton, who was b. in Swansey, N. H., Oct. 14, 1756, dau. of Captain William Heaton. She d. at Thetford, Vt., Dec. 23, 1836. He d. at Thetford, Vt., Aug. 27, 1843, aged 86.

Mr. Child was a Revolutionary soldier, and fought with Col. Jonathan Child, his father, in the battle of Bennington, and in other battles. He settled in Thetford, Vt., where he was an extensive property holder; a man of much influence and reliability; an earnest and self-sacrificing patriot, having spent a large share of his handsome estate in aiding the triumph of the American cause.

[Sixth Generation.]   Children:

2377. i. LUCINDA CHILD, b. in Thetford, Vt., July 4, 1781, m. 1823, Solomon Childs, of Henniker, N. H., where she d. Jan. 20, 1852, leaving 10 children.

2378. ii. OLIVE CHILD, b. in Thetford, Vt., June 3, 1782, d. June 20, 1782.

2379. iii. CYRIL CHILD, b. in Thetford, Vt., April 20, 1783, m. Polly ——.

2380. iv JONATHAN CHILD, b. in Lyme, N. H., Jan. 30, 1785, m. May 7, 1818, Sophia Eliza Rochester.

2381. v. BELA CHILD, b. in Thetford, Vt., Dec. 28, 1786, m. 1st, Feb. 28, 1812, Rosalinda Chapman, m. 2d, Feb. 3, 1834, Sally Belding Page.

2382. vi. ABIEL CHILD, b. in Thetford, Vt., Jan. 12, 1789, d. Jan. 1789.

2383 vii. AZUBAH CHILD, b. in Thetford, Vt., Jan. 10, 1790, m. Joseph Kinney.

2384. viii. PERSIS CHILD, b. in Thetford, Vt., Jan. 31, 1792, m. July 6, 1815, Benjamin Maltby.

2385. ix. EBER CHILD, b. Feb. 28, 1794, d. Jan. 10, 1795.

2386. x. ELONA CHILD, b. in Thetford, Vt., Feb. 9, 1796, d. unm., April 22, 1863.

2387. xi. EBER CHILD. 2D, b. in Thetford, Vt., July 31, 1798, m. Nancy Tyler.

[Sixth Generation.]

2379. iii. CYRIL CHILD, third child and eldest son of William and Mary Heaton Child, b. in Thetford, Vt., April 20, 1783, m. Polly ——. Had seven children: he d. April 4, 1849.

[Seventh Generation.]   Children:

2388. i. MARY CHILD, m. Mr. Thrasher.

2389. ii. LUCIUS CHILD, m. Miss Maltby.

2390. iii. MARIA CHILD, m. Mr. Maltby.

2391. iv. EMILY CHILD, m. Mr. Bickford. ⎫
2392. v. HARRIET CHILD, m. Mr. Bickford. ⎬ Same person
⎭

2393. vi. CYNTHIA CHILD, unm.

2394. vii. AZUBAH CHILD, unm.

[Sixth Generation.]

2380. iv. MAJOR JONATHAN CHILD, fourth child and second son of William and Mary Heaton Child, b. in Lyme, N. H.,

Jan. 30, 1785, m. May 7, 1818, Sophia Eliza Rochester, second dau. of Hon. Nathaniel Rochester, the founder of the city of Rochester, N. Y. He died in Buffalo, N. Y., Oct. 27, 1860, and was buried at Mt. Hope Cemetery in Rochester, N. Y. They had five sons and four daughters.

Mr. Jonathan Child descended from worthy ancestors whose nobility of birth was derived not of royal blood, but of inherited virtues, that imparted dignity, stability and commanding influence to their possessor. His history evinces traits of character that fitted him to occupy prominent and influential positions in society, both from his moral virtues and his intellectual force. The esteem in which he was held by his fellow citizens shows him to have been a sagacious, discreet and conscientious man. His record is one that his descendants may look back upon with pride, and with desire to emulate.

As a patriot, he inherited the spirit and courage of ancestors whose love of country was conspicuous in the Revolutionary War, in which father and son fought side by side. When the call went forth for volunteers in the war of 1812, Mr. Jonathan Child, (the subject of this notice) was enrolled as a volunteer, and fought in the battle of Fort Erie, and acquired the title of Major. At home he was as popular as he was influential abroad. The popular favor conferred upon him the honor of the *first* Mayor of the City of Rochester; and elected him one or more terms a member of the Legislature of the State of New York, from Ontario county. Few men have a deeper hold on the confidence and esteem of their fellow-citizens than did Mr. Child. We have been furnished with the following editorial articles, published in one of the Rochester papers, (the name of the paper was not given) on the occasion of his death, showing the estimate in which he was held in the community where he had spent the larger part of his active life:

DEATH OF EX-MAYOR CHILD.

" It will be heard with pain, but not with surprise, that our late fellow-citizen, the venerable Jonathan Child, is no more. He died at the residence of his daughter, Mrs. Asher P. Nichols, in Buffalo, at half-past one o'clock this morning. Mr. Child had been in feeble health for a year past, and for a few weeks he had been hopelessly prostrate. His disease was an affection of the heart. He had been at Buffalo some time, under the care of his daughter, whose attentions he required to smooth his pathway to the grave, and make his last moments comfortable. Mr. Child was born at

Lyme, New Hampshire, on the 30th Jany., 1785. His grandfather, bearing the same name, was a soldier of the Revolution, as was his father. His father was a soldier in the war of 1812 and Mr. Child was also in that service, having held the post of major and paymaster in the militia of the State of New York. He was, we believe, present at the battle of Lake Erie. Deceased came from New England to Utica in 1806, and there taught school, and was subsequently a clerk for Watts Sherman, an extensive merchant of that city. In 1810 Mr. Child came to what is now Monroe county, and located as a merchant at Charlotte. He subsequently removed to Bloomfield, Ontario county, and was there in the mercantile business till about 1820. He then came to Rochester, and was subsequently an extensive contractor on the canal. He had a large contract at Lockport for cutting through the mountain ridge for the canal, and he also kept a store in the village.

"In 1827, under the new village charter of Rochester, Mr. Child was chosen a trustee to represent the third ward, and he was reëlected in 1830. In 1834, when the city charter was obtained, the common council elected Mr. Child mayor. He served, however, but a short time and resigned on the 23d day of June. He was a conscientious advocate of temperance and not agreeing with the policy of the board in granting licenses, he resigned that he might not sacrifice his principles or clog the wheels of government of the new city. In his letter of resignation to the board he said: 'It becomes incumbent on me, in my official character, to sign these papers (licenses) I am constrained to act according to my most solemn convictions of moral duty and estimation of legal right in all cases connected with the office intrusted to me. When I find myself so situated in my official station as to be obliged, either on the one hand, to violate these high obligations, or, on the other, to stand in opposition to the declared wishes of a large majority of the board, and through them of their constituents—my valued friends and fellow-citizens—I dare not retain the public station which exposes me to this unhappy dilemma. I, therefore, now most respectfully resign into your hands the office of mayor of the city of Rochester.' This was nobly done, and we do not care to point to a better index of the character of Hon. Jonathan Child than this extract from his letter to the board presents.

"In the later years of the life of Mr. Child he was unfortunate in business, and was deprived of all the gains of early life, but he met all his losses with fortitude, and moved on with the same equanimity of temper and cheerfulness that characterized him in youth. In this respect he was indeed a remarkable man, and a model for his fellow-citizens. No man was more esteemed than the deceased. He had no enemies and was beloved by all. He was a sincere christian and member of St. Luke's church for many years, and up to the last hour of consciousness on earth he maintained that calmness, serenity and abiding confidence in his faith which the real christian always possesses.

[Seventh Generation.]   Children:

2395. i. MARY LOUISA CHILD, b. Feb. 8, 1819, m. Oct. 28, 1841, Washington Gibbons, Esq.

2396. ii. NATHANIEL ROCHESTER CHILD, b. in Rochester, N. Y., Nov. 20, 1820, m. June 26, 1844, Elizabeth Stone Prince.

2397. iii. WILLIAM CUMMING CHILD, b. Sept. 8, 1822, d. July 1, 1823.

2398. iv. WILLIAM CHILD, b. April 27, 1824, d. Dec. 2, 1824.

2399. v. EMILY CHILD, b. July 10, 1825, m. Aug. 13, 1851, Hon. Asher P. Nichols, comptroller of the State of New York and senator one term in New York State Legislature. No children. Mr. Nichols d. May 30, 1880.

2400. vi. SOPHIA CHILD, b. in Rochester, N. Y , Aug. 20, 1827, d. July 15, 1828.

2401 vii. JONATHAN HENRY CHILD, b. in Rochester, N. Y., Dec. 26, 1828. Mr. Child is a business man in Rochester, N. Y., and was recently editor of the Geneva *Gazette*, Geneva, N. Y.

2402. viii. CORNELIA ROCHESTER CHILD. b. Sept. 8, 1832, d. Oct. 3, 1856.

2403. ix. THOMAS COLEMAN CHILD, b. July 25, 1837, d Aug. 17. 1837.

[Seventh Generation.]

2395. i. MARY LOUISA CHILD, eldest child of Maj. Jonathan and Sophia Eliza Rochester Child, b. Feb. 8, 1819, m. Oct. 28, 1841. Washington Gibbons, Esq., attorney-at-law and city recorder in Rochester. N. Y.

[Eighth Generation] Children:

2404. i. JONATHAN CHILD GIBBONS, b. in Rochester, N. Y., Oct. 12, 1842, d March 28, 1845.

2405. ii. SOPHIA ROCHESTER GIBBONS, b in Rochester, N. Y.

2406. iii. NATHANIEL ROCHESTER GIBBONS, b. in Rochester, N. Y., June 12, 1847, d. Sept. 6, 1856.

2407. iv. MARY STAFFORD GIBBONS, b. in Rochester, N. Y., May 15, 1851, d. Dec. 17, 1858.

2408. v. MONTGOMERY GIBBONS, b. in Rochester, N. Y., Oct. 15, 1854.

2409. vi. EMILY NICHOLS GIBBONS, b. in Rochester. N. Y.

[Seventh Generation.]

2396. ii. NATHANIEL ROCHESTER CHILD. second child and eldest son of Major Jonathan and Sophia Eliza Rochester Child, b. in Rochester, N. Y., Nov. 20, 1820, m. June 26, 1844, Elizabeth Stone Prince, he d. October 8, 1848.

[Eighth Generation.] Children:

2410. i. ANNA CUTLER CHILD, b. March 8, 1845, d. 1851.

2411. ii NATHANIEL ROCHESTER CHILD, b. July 2, 1848, d. October, 1849.

[Sixth Generation.]

2381. v. BELA CHILD. fifth child and third son of William and Mary Heaton Child, b. in Thetford, Vt., Dec. 28, 1786. m. twice—1st Feb. 28, 1812, Rosalinda Chapman of Keene, N. H., she d. Oct. 3. 1831 : Mr. Child m. 2d, Feb. 3, 1834, Sally Belding Page, she d. 1879 ; he d. in Thetford, Vt., July 30, 1866.

[Seventh Generation.] Children:

2412 i. IRENE KING CHILD, b. in Thetford, Vt., July 14, 1813, d. Aug. 30, 1840, unmarried.

Y

2413. ii. WILLIAM HEATON CHILD, b. in Thetford, Vt., Oct. 6, 1814, m twice—1st, LAVINA MOREY; m. 2d, Jan. 21, 1863, Sarah Jane Howard.

2414. iii. JONATHAN CHAPMAN CHILD, b. in Thetford, Vt., April 16, 1817, m 1848, Emily Eliza Roberts.

2415. iv ELEANOR CLARINDA CHILD, b Dec. 24, 1818, unmarried.

2416. v. LUCY ANN CHILD, b. Aug. 23, 1823, unmarried.

[Seventh Generation.]

2413. ii. WILLIAM HEATON CHILD, eldest son and second child of Bela and Rosalinda Chapman Child, b. in Thetford, Vt., Oct. 6, 1814, m. Mch. 6, 1839, Lavina Morey, dau. of Alanson Morey of Thetford, Vt., she d. Jan. 13, 1860; he m. 2d, Sarah Jane Howard, Jan. 21, 1863.

[Eighth Generation.]   Children: By first marriage.

2417. i. WILLIAM ARTHUR CHILD, b Oct. 29, 1843, d. Nov. 22, 1859

2418. ii. INFANT (unchristened), b. Nov. 15, 1848, d. March 25, 1849.

2419. iii. BELA CHILD, b. May 24, 1852, m. Grace E. Lord May 24, 1879, and d. July 3, 1879.

By second marriage.

2420. iv. WILLIAM CHILD, b. April 10, 1864, d. Sept. 16, 1864.

2421. v. MARY LUCY CHILD, b. Jan. 27, 1866.

2422. vi. LIZZIE HOWARD CHILD, b. March 16, 1868.

2423. vii. JONATHAN HENRY CHILD, b. Feb., 1872.

2423a. viii. EMILY ALIDA CHILD, b. Sept. 29, 1874.

[Seventh Generation.]

2414. iii. JONATHAN CHAPMAN CHILD, third child and second son of Bela and Rosalinda Chapman Child, b. in Thetford, Vt., April 16, 1817, m. 1848, Emily Eliza Roberts, at Rochester, N. Y.

[Eighth Generation.]   Children:

2424. i. GEORGE HENRY CHILD.

2425. ii. ANNA GALE CHILD.

2426. iii. EMILY CHILD.

[Sixth Generation.]

2383. vii. AZUBAH CHILD, seventh child and third dau. of William and Mary Heaton Child, b. Jan. 10, 1790, m. Joseph Kinney; she d. in Thetford, Vt., May 9, 1867.

[Seventh Generation.]   Children:

2427. i. LORENZO CHILD KINNEY, m Sophia Strong.

2428. ii. FLORUS KINNEY, m. Laura Southworth.

2429. iii. ADINO KINNEY, m. Sabrah Southworth,

[Seventh Generation.]

2427. i. LORENZO CHILD KINNEY, eldest child of Azubah Child and Joseph Kinney, m. Sophia Strong.

[Eighth Generation.]   Children:

2430. i. JOSEPH CHILD KINNEY, m. Louisa Rugg.

2431. ii. LORENZO WILLISTON KINNEY.

2432. iii. Lucinda Azubah Kinney.

2433. iv. Charles Newton Kinney, m. Mary Sophia Snow.

2434. v. Harriet Louisa Kinney

2435. vi. Israel Strong Kinney, m. Carrie M Preston.

[Eighth Generation.]

2430. i. Joseph Child Kinney, eldest child of Lorenzo Child Kinney and Sophia Strong. m. Louisa Rugg.

[Ninth Generation.] Children:

2436. i. George Edward Kinney.

2437. ii. Phineas Child Kinney.

2436a. iii. Alice Sophia Kinney.

2437a. iv. Linda Mabel Kinney.

[Eighth Generation]

2433. iv. Charles Newton Kinney, third son and fourth child of Lorenzo Child and Sophia Strong Kinney. m. Mary Sophia Snow.

[Ninth Generation.] Children:

2438. i. Gertrude May Kinney.

2439. ii. Jessie Eveline Kinney.

2440. iii. Mabel Southworth Kinney.

[Eighth Generation.]

2435. vi. Israel Strong Kinney, fourth son and sixth child of Lorenzo Child and Sophia Strong Kinney, m. Carrie M. Preston.

[Ninth Generation.] Child:

2441. i. Ethel Maud Kinney.

[Seventh Generation.]

2428. ii. Florus Kinney, second child and son of Azubah Child and Joseph Kinney. m. Laura Southworth.

[Eighth Generation.] Children:

2438a. i. Sidney Kinney.

2439a. ii. Niram Kinney.

[Seventh Generation.

2429. iii. Adino Kinney, m. Sabrah Southworth, sister of Laura Southworth.

[Eighth Generation.] Children:

2440a. i. Fanny Fern Kinney.

2441a. ii. Lilly Kinney, d. aged 11 months.

[Sixth Generation.]

2384. viii. Persis Child, eighth child and fourth dau. of William and Mary Heaton Child, b. in Thetford, Vt., Jan. 31. 1792. m. July 5, 1815, Benjamin Maltby. The nephew and niece of this Benjamin Maltby married children of Cyril Child.

brother of Mrs. Maltby.   Persis Child Maltby, d. Jan. 5, 1865, in Thetford, Vt.

[Seventh Generation.]   Children: All died unmarried.

    2442. i. HULDAH S. MALTBY. b. May 7, 1816, d. Nov. 23, 1833.

    2443. ii. MARY CHILD MALTBY, b. April 23, 1820, d. Nov. 19, 1845.

    2444. iii. WILLIAM S. MALTBY, b. Dec. 20, 1822, disappeared September, 1844, supposed to have been drowned in Ohio river.

    2445. iv. NANCY M. MALTBY, b. Jan. 20, 1824, d. Sept. 21, 1843.

    2446 v. EBER H. MALTBY, b. Dec. 21, 1826, d. Oct. 17, 1845.

    2447. vi. ELLEN S. MALTBY, b. May 14, 1828, d. Dec. 4, 1843.

[Sixth Generation.]

    2387. xi. REV. EBER CHILD, eleventh child and youngest son of William and Mary Heaton Child, b. in Thetford, Vt, July 31, 1798, m. Nancy Tyler, about 1828.   Mr. Child pursued his academic studies in Randolph Academy, Vermont, graduated at Dartmouth College, New Hampshire, and taught for a season in Groton Academy, Massachusetts. Studied theology at Andover Theological Seminary, was licensed and ordained as an evangelist, settled as pastor in Deering, N. H., afterwards in Calais, Me., and in Byron, Genesee county, N. Y.   A portion of his active life was spent in promoting the moral reforms of the day.   He was scholarly in his attainments, possessing a good knowledge of Latin, Greek, Hebrew and French, and had much reputation as an elocutionist.   Personally he possessed warm social qualities, with sincere and earnest piety, and was deservedly influential among his acquaintances.   He died in Fulton, Wis., Dec. 15, 1847.

[Seventh Generation.]   Children:

    2448. i MARY ELIZABETH CHILD, b. April 7, 1829, d. 1847.

    2449 ii. WILLIAM HENRY CHILD, b. Sept. 6, 1830, d. in infancy.

    2450. iii HENRY Y. CHILD, b. April 27, 1832, m. Feb. 18, 1858, Angeline Adams.

    2451. iv. FRANCIS BROWN CHILD, b. Feb. 22, 1834, m. Feb., 1878, Frances M. Cheesbro.

    2452. v. CHARLES CARROL CHILD, b. Jan. 9, 1836, d. 1848.

    2453. vi. FREDERICK OBERLIN CHILD, b. Dec. 15, 1838, m. 1st, Jan. 1, 1863, Maggie G. Sax; m. 2d, Sept. 19, 1870, Mary Eastman.

    2454 vii. ELLEN LOUISA CHILD, b. Sept. 14, 1844.

[Seventh Generation.]

    2450. iii. HENRY Y. CHILD, third child and second son of Rev. Eber and Nancy Tyler Child, b. April 27, 1832, m. Feb. 18, 1858, Angeline Adams, dau. of Thomas and Charlotte

Adams, of Jefferson county, Miss.; she was b. June 29, 1837, at Vicksburg, Miss. Mr. Child d. Nov. 2, 1876. Mrs. Child resides with her family at Vicksburg, Miss. Mr. Child emigrated to the south in early manhood, and established himself in the mercantile business in Natchez, Miss. His business was prosperous for many years, until the failure of his health. He closed his life peacefully after a lingering illness, tenderly cared for by his devoted family and kind, sympathizing friends.

[Eighth Generation.] Children:

2455. i. MARY BELL CHILD, b. in Natchez, Miss., Dec. 16, 1858.

2456. ii. LOTTA C. CHILD, b. in Natchez, Miss., Oct. 14, 1860.

2457. iii. THOMAS EBER CHILD, b. in Natchez, Miss., Jan. 22, 1862.

2458. iv. BRANDON TYLER CHILD, b. at Church Hill, Miss., Oct. 7, 1864, d. Oct. 14, 1864.

2459. v. FRED. CARROL CHILD, b. at Natchez, Miss., Nov. 18, 1865.

2460 vi. ANNIE RUTH CHILD, b. at Natchez, Miss., Jan. 28, 1868.

2461. vii. ALICE JORDAN CHILD, b. at Natchez, Miss., April 16, 1870.

2462. viii. ELLA LEE CHILD, b. at Natchez, Miss., April 16, 1871.

2463. ix. STELLA HENRIETTA CHILD, b. at Natchez, Miss., March 16, 1873.

2464. x. JOHN CLIFTON CHILD, b. at Natchez, Miss., May 7, 1875.

[Seventh Generation.]

2451. iv. FRANCIS BROWN CHILD, fourth child and third son of Rev. Eber and Nancy Tyler Child, b. Feb. 22, 1834, m. Feb., 1878, Frances M. Cheesbro. On the breaking out of the rebellion Mr. Child enlisted in the 13th Wis. Vol. Regt. of Infantry in the Union army, and served three years. He held the office of first lieutenant in the Quartermaster's Guard. He is now a farmer in Emerald Grove, Wis.

[Eighth Generation.] Child:

2465. i. CARL VICTOR CHILD, b. in Emerald Grove, Wis., May 11, 1879.

[Seventh Generation.]

2453. vi. FREDERICK OBERLIN CHILD, sixth child and fifth son of Rev. Eber and Nancy Tyler Child, b. at Dummerston, Vt., Dec. 15, 1837; m. twice—1st, Jan. 1, 1863, Maggie G. Sax of Lima, Rock county, Wis.; 2d, Sept. 19, 1870, Mary Eastman of Benton Harbor, Mich., dau. of Amos and Sophronia Eastman.

[Eighth Generation.] Children: By first marriage.

2466. i. CHARLES FREMONT CHILD, b. at La Prairie, Wis.

By second marriage.

2467. ii. LUELLA MARY CHILD, b. at Bradford, Wis., Feb. 2, 1872.

2468. iii. MAGGIE CHILD, b. at La Prairie, Wis., Sept. 2, 1875.

2469. iv. HENRY Y. CHILD, b. at La Prairie, Wis., Oct. 11, 1876.
2470. v. RUTHIE SOPHRONIA CHILD, b. at La Prairie, Wis., July 10, 1879.

[Fifth Generation.]

2372. v. LUCY CHILD, fifth child and second dau. of
Col. Jonathan and Dinah Bacon Child, b. in Woodstock, Ct.,
Aug. 24, 1763, m. Dr. Israel Newton. They had seven children ;
no record is obtained of any except Persis.
[Sixth Generation.] Child:
    2471. i. PERSIS NEWTON, m. Ebenezer Boardman.

[Sixth Generation.]

2471. i. PERSIS NEWTON, m. Ebenezer Boardman ; had
three children, record only of Maria.
[Seventh Generation.] Child:
    2472. i. MARIA BOARDMAN, m. John Loveland of Norwich, Vt.

[Eighth Generation.] Children:
    2473. i MARY LOVELAND.
    2474. ii. LIZZIE LOVELAND.

[Fifth Generation.]

2378. xi. POLLY CHILD, eleventh child and seventh dau.
of Col. Jonathan and Dinah Bacon Child, b. in Woodstock,
Ct., Dec. 15, 1769, m. Rev. Asa Burton, D. D.
[Sixth Generation.] Children:
    2475. i. MERCY BURTON, m. Presbury West.
    2476. ii. ——, (daughter) m. Skinner.
    2477. iii. ——, (daughter) m. Lucius Gary of Galesburg, Ill. They had
one daughter, Lizzie Gary. They are now living at Galesburg, Ill.

[Sixth Generation.]

2475. i. MERCY BURTON, eldest child of Polly Child and
Rev. Asa Burton, D. D., m. Presbury West; reside in Lancas-
ter, N. H.
[Seventh Generation.] Children:
    2476a. i. PRESBURY WEST, Jr., m. ——.
    2477a. ii. ASA BURTON WEST, m. —— and had four children.

CHAPTER I.

PENUEL CHILD.

In few words we would call the especial attention of the reader to the founders of this branch of the Child family. As the homes in Connecticut and Massachusetts filled rapidly by the large number of children, (a fashion of that date not wholly dropped by the name even now, though not universal as of yore,) the sons and daughters went out to brave the perils and test the joys of pioneer life, as their grand-parents had done in coming to America. Indeed, we can but feel that just the kind of energy, fortitude, and unconquerableness which characterized those early Puritans, was an absolute necessity to enable them to attempt obtaining a livelihood from the Granite Hills. Nor can we doubt that the prophetic words of the Psalmist, and of Isaiah and Joel, were their strong staff : indeed, we can almost hear the sweet-voiced women reading those comfortable words, "I will lift up mine eyes unto the hills, from whence cometh my help." "For ye shall go out with joy, and be led forth with peace : the mountains and the hills shall break forth before you into singing." When the crops were like to fail did they not gain courage from these further words: "And it shall come to pass in that day that the mountains shall drop down new wine, and the hills shall flow with milk." Nor can we marvel that looking upon the bent frames and toil-worn hands which had wrung by the hardest "sweat of the brow" the small farms from amid the rocks, that later generations should joyously turn them to the luxuriant prairies and oak-openings of the Western States. [Third Generation.]

23. ix. Capt. PENUEL CHILD, sixth son and ninth child of Capt. Benjamin and Grace Morris Child, b. in Roxbury, Mass., Sept. 3, 1699, m. March 7, 1724, Dorothy Dwight, dau. of Rev. Josiah and Mary Partridge Dwight of Woodstock, Ct. Rev. Josiah Dwight, father of Mrs. Penuel Child, was in the third generation from his earliest American ancestor, John Dwight, who came to the Massachusetts colony, in 1634 or 5,

with his family then consisting of a wife and three children, one of whom was Capt. Timothy Dwight, the father of Rev. Josiah Dwight. Capt. Timothy Dwight married Anna Flint Dwight, daughter of Rev. Henry Dwight of Braintree, Mass. Rev. Josiah Dwight married Mary Partridge, daughter of Col. Samuel Partridge, of Hadley, Mass. Rev. Mr. Dwight was the first pastor of the Congregational church of Woodstock, Ct., (then New Roxbury), being settled there in the summer of 1690. Rev. Mr. Dwight was a man of strong will, perseverance, and real piety. We sketch thus specifically the parentage of Mrs. Child that test may be made of the proverb that "like begets like." Most honorable, and strictly religious, fervent and patriotic, were the ancestors of Mrs. Child. We claim no less for the projenitors of Mr. Pennel Child, the reader must be jury after the perusal of the record which will be as full and correct a portrayal of the descendants as it has been possible to obtain. It should be observed that Mrs. Child is one remove farther from her emigrating ancestor than her husband. We call attention to this fact that those possessing the most admirable "Genealogy of the Dwight Family," prepared by Rev. Prof. Dwight, D. D., LL.D., of Clinton, N. Y., may not imagine an error. In this work Mr. Child of course takes the lead, and in the other Mrs. Child follows her parents. Captain and Mrs. Pennel Child resided in Thompson, Ct. From Mr. Dwight's Genealogy we quote what he there writes of Captain Pennel Child: "He joined the church at Thompson at its organization in 1730, and was appointed, as the records state, 'quorister for us in the public worship.' The gift of song was almost universal in the Child name, though none have been especially distinguished in the musical profession. Some ten children were given to Mr. and Mrs. Child, but Capt. Child did not live to see many of them entering upon their own independent careers; he died October 24, 1760. His widow, Mrs. Dorothy Dwight Child married on November 24, 1761, Robert Goddard of Sutton, Mass.

[Fourth Generation.]   Children:

2478. i. JOSIAH CHILD, b. March 6, 1725, m. twice—1st, Feb. 6, 1745, Sarah Green of Thompson, Ct.; m. 2d, 1763, Sarah Adams of Killingly, Ct.

2479. ii. MARTHA CHILD, b. Aug. 18, 1726, m. Jan. 31, 1754, Isaac Whitmore of Thompson, Ct.

2480. iii. EUNICE CHILD, b. Oct. 7, 1728, m. March 19, 1749, Seth Hibbert of Thompson, Ct.

2481. iv. Lois Child, b. April 26, 1730, d. unmarried.

2482. v. Timothy Child, bap. Dec. 19, 1731.

2483. vi. Richard Child, bap. March 11, 1733, m. Feb. 1, 1759, Abigail Green.

2484. vii. Silence Child, bap. June 8, 1735, d. Nov. 5, 1840.

2485. viii. Eleazer Child, bap. Oct. 2, 1737.

2486. ix. Grace Child, bap. Aug. 12, 1739.

2487. x. Dorothy Child, bap. May 28, 1742.

[Fourth Generation.]

2378. i. Josiah Child, eldest son and child of Capt. Penuel and Dorothy Dwight Child, b. in Thompson, Ct., March 6, 1725. Mr. Josiah Child was married twice—1st, Feb. 6, 1745, Miss Sarah Green of Thompson, Ct., a dau. of Capt. Henry and Judith Guile Green, b. Sept. 21, 1696 : m. 2d, Sept. 1, 1763, Sarah Adams of Killingly, Ct. Mr. Josiah Child, like his father, was a tiller of the soil—one of the staid, substantial people who have given the old "Nutmeg State" its wide-spread repute for shrewd steadiness.

[Fifth Generation.] Children:

2488. i. Benjamin Child.

2489. ii. Silence Child, bap. Jan. 10, 1747, d. Nov. 14, 1751.

2490. iii. Zerviah (Gervish?) Child, bap. March 18, 1750, d. Dec. 6, 1754.

2491. iv. William Child, bap. Nov. 1, 1752.

2492. v. Silence Child, 2d., bap. Nov. 10, 1754, m. July 7, 1780, John Blackman of Woodstock, Ct.

2493. vi. Penuel Child, b. Feb 22, 1757, m. abt. 1782, Sarah Woodward.

2494. vii. Judah Child, bap. March 14, 1758.

2495 viii. Martha Child, bap. Jan. 14, 1760.

2496. ix. Dwight Child, b. about 1762.

2497. x. Jesse Child, b. about 1764.

2498. xi. Theodore Child,[1] b. about 1766.

2499. xii. Michael Child, b. about 1768.

[Fifth Generation.]

2493. vi. Penuel Child, fourth son and sixth child of Josiah and Sarah Green Child, b. Feb. 22, 1757, m. about 1782 Sarah Woodward, who was b. Oct. 22, 1761. Mr. Penuel Child removed with his father to Sand Lake, (now East Poestenkill,) Rensselaer county, N. Y., "in the year of the cold summer," said to have been the year 1816. Here Mr. Child reared a large family, and here he died Jan. 16, 1813. Mrs. Sarah W. Child died Dec. 24, 1843.

---

[1] The record of Theodore Child's family we hope to receive in season for the appendix.

[Sixth Generation.]   Children:

2500. i. LUCINDA CHILD, b. Oct. 17, 1783, m. John Amidon.

2501. ii. WILLIAM CHILD, b. June 17, 1785, m. 1st, Dec. 25, 1809, Zulma Clark; m. 2d, 1833. Sarah Whiting.

2502. iii. MATILDA CHILD, b. Nov. 7, 1787, m. about 1807, Joseph Amidon.

2503. iv. DOLLY CHILD. b. June 23, 1789. m. Otis Gould.[1]

2504. v. TRYPHOSA CHILD. b. April 27, 1792, m. Sept. 14, 1814, William Clark.

2505. vi. ILURA CHILD, b. Aug. 5, 1794, m. about 1815. David Horton.

2506. vii. LYMAN P. CHILD, b. Jan. 21, 1797, m. Jan. 5, 1822, Mary Gould.

2507. viii. JESSE CHILD, b. July 5, 1799, m. about 1827. Sarah Heath

2508. ix. SARAH CHILD, b. Dec. 8, 1803, m. Oct. 8, 1822, Phillip Amidon.

[Sixth Generation.]

2501. ii. WILLIAM CHILD, second child and eldest son of Penuel and Sarah Woodward Child. b. June 17, 1785, m. twice—1st, Dec. 25, 1809, Zulyma Clark, who was b. Oct. 10, 1792, d. July 26, 1829; m. 2d, 1833. Sarah Whiting. Mr. Child died June 2, 1868.

[Seventh Generation.]   Children:

2509. i. LYDIA R. CHILD, b. July 11, 1811, m. Jan. 13, 1841, Royal Southwick.

2510. ii. WILLIAM C. CHILD, b. June 25, 1815, m. Jan. 18, 1846, Sarah Dunham.

2511. iii. HORACE CHILD, b. June 25, 1817, m. Oct. 21, 1839, Ruby Cooley.

2512. iv. MELVIN CHILD, b. July 26, 1820, m. 1850, Rachel Ann Vosburg.

2513. v. MINERVA F. CHILD, b. June 17, 1822, m Jan. 8, 1863, Edward H. Bennett.

2514. vi. ILURA CHILD, b. Nov. 19, 1824.

2515. vii. ZULYMA CHILD, b. June 18, 1835, d. June 25, 1866.

2516. viii. AMELIA CHILD, b. July 16, 1836, m. Sherbury Calkins.

2517. ix. FRANCES E. CHILD, b. Nov. 13, 1838. m. Paul Anthony.

2518. x. GRACE E. CHILD, b. Feb. 26, 1841, m. Charlie Calkins.

2519. xi. LUCY A. CHILD, b. Jan. 28, 1843, m. David Richards.

2520. xii. SARAH J. CHILD, b. Feb. 17, 1845, m. David Byum

2521. xiii. MARY E. CHILD, b. July 13, 1847, m. John Richmond.

2522. xiv. WILBUR CHILD, b. June 1, 1849, m. —— Paul.

[Seventh Generation.]

2509. i. LYDIA R. CHILD, eldest child of William and Zulyma Clark Child, b. July 11, 1811, m. Jan. 13, 1841, Royal Southwick; reside in Somerset, Niagara county, N. Y.

---

[1]The record of the family of Dolly Child and Otis Gould is not yet obtained. Should it be sent in season it will be placed in the appendix.

[Eighth Generation] Children:

2523. i. ALICE M. SOUTHWICK, b. Aug. 5, 1842, m. March 5, 1863, William G. Williams.

2524. ii. LYDIA A. SOUTHWICK, b. Oct. 21, 1843.

2525. iii. MARY E. SOUTHWICK, b. Nov. 7, 1846, m. Feb. 18, 1869, Silas M. Oliphant.

2526. iv. MARTHA J. SOUTHWICK, b. Jan. 5, 1850.

2527. v. MARIA L. SOUTHWICK, b. Dec. 20, 1851, m. Dec, 20, 1875, Andrew Bowers.

[Seventh Generation.]

2510. ii. WILLIAM C. CHILD, eldest son and second child of William and Zulyma Clark Child, b. June 25, 1815, m. Jan. 18, 1846, Sarah Dunham.

[Eighth Generation.] Children:

2528. i. GEORGE CHILD, b. June 22, 1849.

2529. ii. WILLIAM CHILD, b. Dec. 24, 1851.

2530. iii. ELIZA ANN CHILD, b. March 3, 1854, d. Jan. 27, 1865.

2531. iv. FRANK CHILD, b. July 3, 1858

[Seventh Generation.]

2511. iii. HORACE CHILD, second son and third child of William and Zulyma Clark Child, b. in Sand Lake, Rensselaer county, N. Y., June 25, 1817, m. Oct. 21, 1839, by George Eastman, Esq. to Ruby Cooley. She was b. Dec. 19, 1820, in Murray, Orleans Co., N. Y.

Mr. Horace Child accompained his uncle, Jesse Child, to the county of Ashtabula, in Ohio, in the autumn of 1838. Here he found his wife. Soon after his marriage he returned to the State of New York, he was, however, not long content, but two years sufficied him, and he was again in Ohio. On the 30th November, 1849, he moved with his family, which consisted of a wife and four small children, to the township of Rome, Ashtabula Co., carrying his household-goods across Grand River on the stringers of a floating bridge, moving back into a heavy forest, half a mile. His house was fourteen by twenty feet, of his own building, cutting away the trees so they would not fall upon the house in the high winds; driving his cow and a few sheep nine miles round to get them to his new home. Then he began clearing off his farm, and as he had no team, he was obliged to draw his logs out from the woods by hand. But endowed with wonderful energy and perseverance, he succeeded in winning for his family a pleasant home and comfort. The hardships he endured bore heavily upon him, and before

the three-score he passed peacefully to his death.—March 7,
1874, aged 56 years, 8 months and 10 days, leaving a wife and
eight children to mourn the loss of a kind husband and indulgent parent.

[Eighth Generation.]   Children:

2532. i. WILLIAM R. CHILDS, b. Sept. 21, 1840, m. Feb. 19, 1876, Ann
E. Gould.

2533. ii. SYNTHIA J. CHILDS, b. Oct. 11, 1842, m. Jan. 1, 1863, Myron L.
Dutton.

2534. iii. MARIETTA L. T. CHILDS b. Jan. 29, 1846, in Sheffield, Ohio.

2535. iv. OREN H CHILDS, b April 23, 1848, m. Aug. 15, 1867, Josie
Alderman.

2536. v. ALICE M. CHILDS, b. Oct. 30, 1850, m. May 25. 1875, Benjamin
Baker.

2537. vi. MELVIN A. CHILDS, ⎰ ⎱ b. Feb 6, 1854, d. Nov. 23, 1874, in
                                         Rome, Ohio.
2538. vii MARY A. CHILDS, ⎰ ⎱ b. Feb. 6, 1854.

2539. viii. NELSON P. CHILDS, b. May 20, 1856, in Rome, Ashtabula Co.,
Ohio.

2540. ix. HIRAM F. A CHILDS, b Mch. 30, 1859, in Rome, Ashtabula
Co., Ohio.

[Eighth Generation.]

2532. i. WILLIAM R CHILDS, eldest child of Horace and
Ruby Cooley Child, b. in Sheffield, Ohio, Sept. 21, 1840, m.
by Noah Haskins, Esq., in Jefferson, Ashtabula Co., Ohio,
Feb. 19, 1876, to Ann E. Gould.   She was b. June 13, 1838, in
Burton, Ohio.

[Ninth Generation.]   Child:

2541. i. HORACE M. CHILDS, b. Jan. 11, 1877 d. Jan. 29, 1877.

[Eighth Generation.]

2533. ii. SYNTHIA J. CHILDS, eldest dau. and second child
of Horace and Ruby Cooley Child, b. in Pembroke, Genesee
Co., N. Y., Oct. 11, 1842, m. by Rev. E. Johnston, in Rome,
Ohio, Jan. 1, 1863, to Myron L. Dutton, who was b. Aug. 17,
1840.   Mrs. Synthia J. Childs Dutton d. in Thompson, Geauga
Co., Ohio, Nov. 22, 1870, æ. 28.

[Ninth Generation.]   Children:

2542. i. INFANT SON, unchristened, b. Dec. 10, 1863, d. Dec. 24, 1863.

2543. ii. DORA A. DUTTON, b. Feb. 14, 1865, in Thompson, Geauga Co.,
Ohio.

2544. iii. WALTER DUTTON, b. Oct. 22, 1867, in Denmark, Ohio.

2545. iv. MINNIE DUTTON, b. Feb. 15, 1870, in Thompson, Ohio.

[Eighth Generation.]

2535. iv. OREN H. CHILDS, second son and fourth child of
Horace and Ruby Cooley Child, b. in Sheffield, Ohio, April

23. 1848, m. by Rev. P. P. Pinney, in Willoughby, Lake Co., Ohio, Aug. 15, 1867, to Josie Alderman, who was b. June 5, 1845.

[Ninth Generation.] Children:

2546. i. KATY J. CHILDS, b. May 7, 1871, in Orwell, Ohio, d. Jan. 27, 1876, in Rome, Ohio.

2547. ii. WHEATON CHILDS, b. Dec. 1, 1874, in Kirtland, Lake Co., Ohio, d. March 24, 1878, in Denmark, Ohio.

2548. iii. WINA CHILDS, b. June 13, 1877, in Rome, Ashtabula Co., Ohio.

[Eighth Generation.]

2536. v. ALICE M. CHILDS, third dau. and fifth child of Horace and Ruby Cooley Childs, b. in Rome, Ashtabula Co., Ohio, Oct. 30, 1850, m. by Charles Babcock, Esq., in the same town, May 25, 1875, to Benjamin Baker.

[Ninth Generation.] Child:

2549. i. CORA M. BAKER, b. Dec 27, 1876, in Orwell, Ashtabula Co., Ohio.

[Seventh Generation.]

2512. iv. MELVIN CHILD, third son and fourth child of William and Zulyma Clark Child, b. July 26, 1820, m. 1850, Rachel Ann Vosburg.

[Eighth Generation.] Children:

2550. i. EMILY CHILD, b. June 5, 1851, in Berlin, Wis.

2551. ii. ELLA CHILD, b. June 7, 1853, m. Sept., 1879, Mr. Jackson.

2552. iii ERNEST CHILD, b. July 1858, m. Sept. 1878, Kittie Clough.

[Sixth Generation.]

2502. iii. MATILDA CHILD, second dau. and third child of Pennel and Sarah Woodward Child, b. Nov. 7, 1787, in Rensselaer Co., N. Y., m. about 1807, Joseph Amidon, b. 1782, d. 1846. Mrs. Matilda Child Amidon d. Dec. 23, 1833. Resided in Rensselaer Co., N. Y., where all their children were born.

[Seventh Generation.] Children:

2547a. i. CYRUS AMIDON, b. Aug. 13, 1808, m. 1822, Maria Uretta Cropsey; he d. Dec. 14, 1857.

2548a ii. MARTIN AMIDON, b. Sept. 9, 1812, m. July 12, 1834, Polly Burritt.

2549a. iii. ILURA AMIDON, b. Jan. 27, 1815, m. 1st, Sept. 1833, Barney Clapper; m. 2d, 1838, John Wyland.

2550a. iv. SOPHIA AMIDON, b. Jan. 21, 1817, m. 1835, Seely Burritt.

2551a. v. DEXTER A. C. AMIDON, b. April 9, 1819, m. May 1, 1839, Marandy Cropsey.

2552a. vi. JOSEPH P. AMIDON, b. Feb. 17, 1822, m. Feb. 15, 1844, Wealthy A. Wright.

[Sixth Generation.]

2504. v. TRIPHOSA CHILD, fourth dau. of Penuel and Sarah Woodward Child, b. April 27, 1792, m. Sept. 14, 1814, William B. Clark. Mrs. T. Child Clark, d. July 27, 1873.

[Seventh Generation.] Children:

2553. i. ALONZO CLARK, b. June 2, 1815, m. Feb. 8, 1840, Mary Ann Blood.

2554. ii. CLARAMOND M. CLARK, b. March 31, 1817, m. July 1, 1838, John Dunham.

2555. iii. ALVIN CLARK, b. Aug. 26, 1818.

2556. iv. WILLIAM CLARK, b. Sept. 5, 1819, m. Jan. 1, 1846, Sarah Dunham.

2557. v. FREEMAN CLARK, b. July 12, 1821.

2558. vi. EDWARD CLARK, b. June 26, 1823, m Dec. 27, 1845, Sabrina M. Bennett; residence Chesening, Mich.

2559. vii. ZEPHANIAH CLARK, b. Jan. 7, 1826.

2560. viii. MATILDA CLARK, b. Feb. 10, 1828.

2561. ix. ILURA CLARK, b. Nov. 1, 1829.

2562. x. GEORGE CLARK, b Nov. 1, 1832, d. Dec. 8, 1875.

2563. xi. ABEL R. CLARK, b. Sept. 20, 1834, m. Sept. 4, 1867, Susan Rowley; residence Carlton, Orleans Co., N. Y.

[Seventh Generation.]

2553. i. Rev. ALONZO CLARK, eldest child of Tryphosa Child and William B. Clark, b. June 2, 1815, m. Feb. 8, 1840, Mary Ann Blood. Mr. Clark is a Methodist clergyman; residence Carleton, Orleans Co., N. Y.

[Eighth Generation.] Children:

2564. i. MEHITABLE TRYPHOSA CLARK.

2565. ii. ORRIN CLARK.

2566. iii. GEORGE CLARK.

2567. iv. MARY CLARK.

2568. v. HATTIE CLARK.

[Seventh Generation.]

2554. ii. CLARAMOND M. CLARK, eldest dau. and second child of Tryphosa Child and William B. Clark, b. March 31, 1817, m. July 1, 1838, John Dunham: reside in Montrose, Mich.

[Eighth Generation.] Children:

2569. i. SARAH MINERVA DUNHAM.

2570. ii. GEORGE DUNHAM.

2571. iii. RUSSEL DUNHAM, d. in the army.

2572. iv. MORRIS DUNHAM.

[Seventh Generation.]

2556. iv. WILLIAM CLARK, third son and fourth child of Tryphosa Child and William B. Clark, b. Sept. 5, 1819, m.

Jan. 1, 1846, Sarah Dunham: reside in Carleton, Orleans Co., N. Y.

[Eighth Generation.] Children:

2573. i. DE WITT CLARK.

2574. ii. MARY CLARK.

2575. iii. ALLIE CLARK.

2576. iv. WILLIAM CLARK, JR.

[Sixth Generation.]

2505. vi. ILURA CHILD, fifth dau. and sixth child of Pennel and Sarah Woodward Child, b. Aug. 5, 1794, in Rensselaer Co., N. Y., m. about 1815, David Horton. Mrs. Ilura Child Horton d. about 1822.

[Seventh Generation.] Children:

2573b. i. MELISSA HORTON, b. 1816.

2574b. ii. DAVID HORTON, b. 1818.

2575b. iii. MARY HORTON, b. 1820

2576b. iv. ILURA HORTON, b. 1822.

[Sixth Generation.]

2506. vii. LYMAN P. CHILD, second son and seventh child of Pennel and Sarah Woodward Child, b in Sand Lake, N. Y., Jan. 21, 1797, m. Jan. 5, 1822, Mary Gould, dau. of Bezaleel Gould, formerly of Woodstock, Ct., who was b. Sept. 1, 1802. Mr. Child moved to Genesee Co., N. Y., and settled upon a farm in the parish of Corfu.

[Seventh Generation.] Children:

2577. i. DARIUS CHILD, b. Sept. 4, 1822, m May 28, 1848, Charlotte E. Patterson.

2578. ii. LUCINDA CHILD, b. April 21, 1824, m. March 18, 1840, Norman L. Knox

2579. iii. ALPHA CHILD, b April 4, 1827, m. Feb. 9, 1850, Martha B. Wigent.

2580. iv. GEORGE CHILD, b. Aug. 14, 1829, d. March 27, 1849, in Pembroke, N. Y.

2581. v. EMELINE CHILD, b. Aug. 13, 1831, d. Aug. 27, 1831, in Pembroke, N. Y.

2582. vi. CLARK CHILD, b. Aug. 16, 1833, m. 1855, Mary A. E. Campbell.

2583. vii. OPHIR CHILD, b. Aug. 17, 1835, d. May 1, 1854, in Pembroke, N. Y.

2584. viii. WILLIAM EATON CHILD, b. Nov. 1, 1837, m. Nov. 20, 1858, Emeline Wigent, dau. of Samuel Wigent.

2585. ix. OTIS CHILD, b. April 4, 1842, d. in the army, during the war of the rebellion, March, 1862.

[Seventh Generation.]

2577. i. DARIUS CHILD, eldest child of Lyman P. and Mary Gould Child, b. in Batavia, N. Y., Sept. 4, 1822, m. May 28, 1848, Charlotte E. Patterson: resides in Ohio.

[Eighth Generation.] Children:
  2586. i. GEORGE THOMAS CHILD, b. June 13, 1849.
  2587. ii. JULIETTE ISABELLA CHILD, b. May 8, 1852.

[Seventh Generation.]

2578. ii. LUCINDA CHILD, eldest dau. of Lyman P. and Mary Gould Child, b. in Pembroke, Genesee Co., N. Y., April 21, 1824, m. March 18, 1840, Norman L. Knox, who was b. Jan. 25, 1820.

[Eighth Generation.] Children:
  2588. i. JOHN T. KNOX, b. April 18, 1841.
  2589. ii. FREDERICK W. KNOX, b. Jan. 7, 1843.
  2590. iii. ELIZA A. KNOX, b. Jan. 15, 1845.
  2591. iv NORMAN L. KNOX, JR., b. Aug. 27, 1847.
  2592. v. GEORGE L. KNOX, b. July 12, 1850.
  2593. vi. JAMES P. KNOX, b. May 21, 1852.
  2594. vii. MYRON W. KNOX, b. May 1, 1855.
  2595. viii. GILBERT H. KNOX, b. March 2, 1857.
  2596. ix. DARIUS C. KNOX, b. Jan. 27, 1858.
  2597. x. MARY E. A. KNOX, b. Jan. 27, 1859.
  2598. xi. IDA B. KNOX, b. March 6, 1861.
  2599. xii. ADELBERT D. KNOX, b May 19, 1863.
  2600. xiii. WILLIE KNOX, b. March 10, 1866.
  2601. xiv. ROSA L. KNOX, b. Aug. 12, 1867.
  2602. xv. EDWARD E. KNOX, b. Sept. 13, 1870.

[Seventh Generation.]

2579. iii. ALPHA CHILDS, second son and third child of Lyman P. and Mary Gould Childs, b. in Pembroke, N. Y., April 4, 1827, m. Feb. 9, 1850, Martha B. Wigent, who was b. June 9, 1833.

[Eighth Generation.] Children:
  2603. i. ROSETT A. CHILDS, b. Dec. 19, 1851, m. Jan. 1, 1868, John McMillan.
  2604. ii. MARY A. CHILDS, b. Feb. 14, 1853, m. Sept. 13, 1871, John C. Miller.
  2605. iii. DWIGHT F. CHILDS, b Sept. 27, 1855.
  2606. iv. CHARLES A. CHILDS, b. Aug. 17, 1856.
  2607. v. LYMAN E. CHILDS, b. July 8, 1859.
  2608. vi. WILLIAM J. CHILDS, b. May 31, 1867.
  2609. vii. MARTHA E. CHILDS, b. Dec. 26, 1875.

[Seventh Generation.]

2582. vi. CLARK CHILDS, fourth son and sixth child of Lyman P. and Mary Gould Child, b. in Pembroke, N. Y., Aug. 16, 1833, m. about 1855, Mary A. E. Campbell, dau. of Homer Campbell, she was b. Aug. 31, 1834, in Barry, Orleans county, N. Y.; reside in Corfu, N. Y.

[Eighth Generation.] Children:

2610. i. GEORGE L. CHILDS, b. April 25, 1856, d. same day in Pembroke, N. Y.

2611. ii. KEZIAH L. CHILDS, b. July 24, 1857, d. Sept. 22, 1858, in Pembroke N.Y.

2612 iii. ALBERT L. CHILDS, b. Sept. 26, 1859, in Pembroke, N. Y.

2613. iv. CHARLES K. CHILDS, b. Sept. 2, 1863, in Pembroke, N. Y.

Sixth Generation.]

2507. viii. JESSE CHILD, third son and eighth child of Pennel and Sarah Woodward Child, b. in Williamstown, Mass., July 5, 1799, m. about 1827, Sarah Heath, who d. Jan. 8, 1873; he resided in Ohio and Michigan.

[Seventh Generation.] Children:

2614. i. SARAH E. CHILD, b March 18, 1829, m. Nov. 16, 1848, Alexander M. Johnson.

2615. ii. HENRIETTA CHILD, b. July 4, 1831, d. Oct. 29, 1842.

2616. iii. MATILDA CHILD, b. March 23, 1834, d. April 23, 1834.

2617. iv. SIMON P. CHILD, b. Dec. 27, 1836, d. in the army Jan. 6, 1863.

2618. v. IRVIN J. CHILD, b. Aug. 10, 1839, m. 1st, Dec. 12, 1867, Jane Briggs: m. 2d, April 24, 1873, Elizabeth R. Briggs.

2619. vi. MARY E. CHILD, b. July 11, 1841, m. Theodore Metcalf; she d. Jan. 1, 1857.

2620. vii. JAMES W. CHILD, b. Nov. 2, 1843.

2621. viii. MARTHA A. CHILD, b. Aug. 6, 1846.

[Seventh Generation]

2614. i. SARAH E. CHILD, eldest child of Jesse and Sarah Heath Child, b. in Barry, Orleans county, N. Y., March 18, 1829, m. Nov. 16, 1848, Alexander M. Johnson; resides in East Rockport, Ohio.

[Eighth Generation.] Children:

2622. i. SARAH MINERVA JOHNSON, b. Sept. 30, 1849, in Ashtabula, Ohio.

2623. ii. ALFRED A. JOHNSON, b. Nov. 17, 1853, in Paw Paw, Mich.

2624 iii. JAMES M. JOHNSON, b. March 27, 1857, in Paw Paw, Mich.

2625. iv. LAWRENCE T. JOHNSON, b Oct. 28, 1859, in Bay City, Mich.

2626 v. WALTER B. JOHNSON, b. Dec. 21, 1862, in Bay City, Mich.

[Seventh Generation.]

2618. v. IRVIN J. CHILD, second son and fifth child of Jesse and Sarah Heath Child, b. in Ashtabula, Ohio, Aug. 10, 1839, m. twice—1st, in Howell, Mich., Dec. 12, 1867, Jane Briggs; m. 2d, April 24, 1873, Elizabeth Rosling Briggs, both daughters of Thomas and Grace Briggs; resides in Fairfield, Clay county, Nebraska.

[Eighth Generation.] Children:

2627. i. JESSE CHILD, b. Sept. 4, 1870, in Howell, Mich.

2628. ii. ANNA CHILD, b. Aug. 2, 1872, in Howell, Mich

A·1

[Sixth Generation.]

2508. ix. SARAH CHILD, sixth dau. and ninth child of Pennel and Sarah Woodward Child, b. Dec. 8, 1803, in Sand Lake, N. Y., m. in Batavia, N. Y., Oct. 8, 1822, Phillip Amidon, who was b. Aug. 15, 1799, in Keene, New Hampshire; son of Philip and Jerusha Smith Amidon. Mrs. Sarah Child Amidon died July 11, 1867. Residence East Pembroke, Genesee Co., N. Y.

[Seventh Generation.]   Children:

2629. i. OTIS AMIDON, b. Sept. 4, 1823, m. Oct. 7, 1847, Grace Cooley.

2630. ii. GEORGE AMIDON, b. Aug. 22, 1825, d. Aug. 22, 1825, in Pembroke, N. Y.

2631. iii. HARRIET AMIDON, b. May 16, 1827, d. Jan. 21, 1834, in Pembroke, N. Y.

2632. iv. MALINDA AMIDON, b. Mch. 24, 1830, m. Jan. 1, 1849, Ichabod J. Case.

2633. v. MARVIN C. AMIDON, b. May 24, 1832, m. Oct. 26, 1854, Susan Fishell.

2634. vi. MATILDA J. AMIDON, b. Nov. 15, 1834, m. April 5, 1852, Albert Cups.

2635. vii. ALBERT AMIDON, b. Jan. 2, 1837, m. Mch. 12, 1868, Nancy J. Baker.

2636. viii. HARRIET A. AMIDON, b. Dec. 27, 1839, m. Feb. 2, 1859, John Gowdy.

2637. ix. SARAH A. AMIDON, b. July 15, 1842.   A teacher.

2638. x. CYRUS P. AMIDON, b. May 19, 1845, m. Oct. 4, 1867, Mary Brown.

[Seventh Generation.]

2629. i. OTIS AMIDON, eldest child of Sarah Child and Philip Amidon, b. in Batavia, N. Y., Sept. 4, 1823, m. Oct. 7, 1847, Grace Cooley, who was b. in Yates Co., N. Y., May 25, 1826. Mr. Amidon died Sept. 29, 1864.

[Eighth Generation.]   Children:

2639. i. SARAH A. AMIDON, b. July 5, 1848, d. July 30, 1848.

2640. ii. MARY J. AMIDON, b. Mch. 30, 1850, m. Dec. 23, 1875, Julius Ingalsbee.

2641. iii. GEORGE E. AMIDON, b. June 11, 1852.

2642. iv. ALICE J. AMIDON, b. Sept. 28, 1855.

2643. v. ELMER O. AMIDON, b. April 9, 1861.

[Eighth Generation.]

2640. ii. MARY J. AMIDON, second dau. of Otis and Grace Cooley Amidon, and granddaughter of Sarah Child Amidon, b. Mch. 30, 1850, m. Dec. 23, 1875, Julius Ingalsbee, who was b. Dec. 16, 1851.

[Ninth Generation.]   Children:

2644. i. FRANK INGALSBEE, b. Sept. 14, 1876.

2645. ii. EUGENE INGALSBEE, b. Jan. 26, 1878.

[Seventh Generation.]

2632. iv. MALINDA AMIDON, second dau. and fourth child of Sarah Child and Philip Amidon, b. in Pembroke, N. Y., Mch. 24, 1830, m. Jan. 1. 1849, Ichabod J. Case, who was b. Feb. 24, 1829.

[Eighth Generation.] Children:

2646. i. MARVIN J. CASE, b. Nov. 24, 1849, d. Sept. 10, 1851.

2647. ii. HELEN L. CASE, b. Sept. 18, 1851, m. July 4, 1870, Frederick Sunricker.

2648. iii. SARAH A. CASE, b. Feb. 5, 1854, m. Dec. 31, 1871, Albert King.

2649. iv. LOUIS CASE, b. Jan. 13, 1856, m. Dec. 31, 1879, Lizzie Carlisle.

2650. v. PHILLIP J. CASE, b. July 17, 1868.

[Eighth Generation.]

2647. ii. HELEN L. CASE, eldest dau. of Ichabod J. and Malinda Amidon Case, and granddaughter of Sarah Child and Phillip Amidon, b. Sept. 18, 1851, m. July 4, 1870, Frederick Sunricker, who was b. Oct. 12, 1843.

[Ninth Generation.] Children.

2651. i. JAY D. SUNRICKER, b. Oct. 6, 1872.

2652. ii. WILLIE M. SUNRICKER, b. Mch. 12, 1874.

2653. iii. LEWIS J. SUNRICKER, b. April 4, 1876.

[Eighth Generation.]

2648. iii. SARAH A. CASE, second dau. and third child of Ichabod and Malinda Amidon Case, and granddaughter of Sarah Child Amidon, b. Feb. 5, 1854, m. Dec. 31, 1871, Albert King, who was b. Nov. 18, 1848.

[Ninth Generation.] Children:

2654. i. SYLVIA J. KING, b. Nov. 24, 1872.

2655. ii. JOHN J. KING, b. Oct. 6, 1873.

2656. iii. MELINDA H. KING, b. Mch. 12, 1876.

2657. iv. LINDA C. KING, b. Feb. 12, 1879.

[Seventh Generation.]

2633. v. MARVIN CHILD AMIDON, third son and fifth child of Sarah Child and Phillip Amidon, b. in Pembroke, N. Y., May 24, 1832, m. Oct. 26, 1854, Susan Fishell, who was b. Oct. 25, 1835.

[Eighth Generation.] Children:

2658. i. FRANK AMIDON, b. Feb. 8, 1858, m. Nov. 1, 1878, Emma Tucker, who was b. Oct. 26, 1862.

2659. ii. JOHN AMIDON, b. Oct. 28, 1871, in Pembroke, N. Y.

[Seventh Generation.]

2634. vi. MATILDA J. AMIDON, third dau. and sixth child of Sarah Child and Phillip Amidon, b. in Pembroke, N. Y.,

Nov. 11, 1834, m. April 5, 1852, Albert Cups, who was b. Jan. 4, 1831. Mrs. Matilda J. A. Cups died July 14, 1874.

[Eighth Generation.] Children:
    2660. i. ORRA S. CUPS, b. July 24, 1855, m. Nov. 20, 1872, Frank Cropsy.
    2661. ii. GEORGE CUPS, b. Aug. 23, 1858.
    2662. iii. WILLIAM CUPS, b. June 13, 1863.
    2663. iv. NELLIE CUPS, b. July 4, 1865.
    2664. v. BERTIE CUPS, b. Oct. 20, 1868.
    2665. vi. LURA CUPS, b. July 4, 1875.

[Eighth Generation.

    2660. i. ORRA S. CUPS, eldest child of Matilda J. Amidon and Albert Cups, and granddaughter of Sarah Child Amidon, b. July 24, 1855, m. Nov. 20, 1872, Frank Cropsy, who was b. Oct. 27, 1842.

[Ninth Generation.] Children:
    2666. i. MUSA CROPSY, b. Oct. 25, 1873.
    2667. ii. MINA CROPSY, b. Feb. 16, 1875.
    2668. iii. COURT T. CROPSY, b. Mch. 12, 1877.
    2669. iv. FRANK G. CROPSY, b. Nov. 17, 1878.

[Seventh Generation.]

    2635. vii. ALBERT AMIDON, fourth son and seventh child of Sarah Child and Philip Amidon, b. in Pembroke, N. Y., Jan. 2, 1837, m. Mch. 12, 1868, Nancy J. Baker, who was b. Feb. 4, 1852.

[Eighth Generation.] Children:
    2670. i. BERTIE AMIDON, b. May 24, 1869.
    2671. ii. WARREN E. AMIDON, b. Mch. 26, 1871.
    2672. iii. VESTA P. AMIDON, b. Oct. 24, 1876.

[Seventh Generation.]

    2636. viii. HARRIET A. AMIDON, fourth dau. and eighth child of Sarah Child and Phillip Amidon, b. in Pembroke, N. Y., Dec. 27, 1839, m. Feb. 2, 1859, John Gowdy, who was b. July 23, 1833.

[Eighth Generation.] Children:
    2673. i. LEVI GOWDY, b. Dec. 2, 1859.
    2674. ii. EVA E. GOWDY, b. Jan. 4, 1867.
    2675. iii. JESSIE GOWDY, b. Aug. 1, 1871.

[Seventh Generation.]

    2638. x. CYRUS P. AMIDON, youngest child of Sarah Child and Phillip Amidon, b. in Pembroke, N. Y., May 19, 1845, m. Oct. 4, 1867, Mary Brown, who was b. June 20, 1846.

[Eighth Generation.] Child:
    2676. i. NELLIE AMIDON, b. July 15, 1868.

[Fifth Generation.]

2498. iii. THEODORE CHILD, third son and child of Josiah and Sarah Green Child, was b. abt. 1766, married and had the following children, but we cannot obtain further knowledge of the family.

[Sixth Generation.] Children:

2677. i. JOHN CHILD.
2678. ii. LUTHER CHILD.
2679. iii. GEORGE CHILD.
2680. iv. NATHANIEL CHILD.

[Fourth Generation.]

2479. ii. MARTHA CHILD, eldest dau. and second child of Capt. Pennel and Dorothy Dwight Child, b. in Thompson, Ct., Aug. 18, 1726, m. Jan. 31, 1754, Isaac Whitmore of that town. Mr. and Mrs. Whitmore were the parents of thirteen children, of whom we can only obtain the record of three.

[Fifth Generation.] Children:

2681. i. TAMAR WHITMORE, bapt. Feb. 2, 1755.
3682. ii. SABRA WHITMORE, bapt. Mch. 24, 1756.
2683. iii. JABEZ WHITMORE, bapt. Feb. 12, 1758, m. Sept. 20, 1781, Miss Hannah Larned.

[Fourth Generation.]

2480. iii. EUNICE CHILD, second dau. and third child of Capt. Pennel and Dorothy Dwight Child, b. in Thompson, Ct., Oct. 7, 1728, m. in the same place, Mch. 19, 1749, Mr. Seth Hibbert.

Fifth Generation.] Children:

2684. i. LOIS HIBBERT, bapt. Sept. 2, 1750.
2685. ii. GERVISH HIBBERT, b. April 15, 1755.
2686. iii. ELISHA HIBBERT, b. Jan. 13, 1758.
2687. iv. AARON HIBBERT, b. Feb. 1, 1761.

[Fourth Generation.]

2483. vi. RICHARD CHILD, third son and sixth child of Capt. Pennel and Dorothy Dwight Child, b. in Thompson, Ct., Mch. 11, 1733, m. Feb. 1, 1759, Abigail Green, dau. of Capt. Henry and Judith Guile Green, of Thompson, Ct. She was b. at Killingly, Ct., May 7, 1738, d. Aug. 1, 1830, aged 92 years, 2 mo. 24 d. Richard Child died in 1781.

[Fifth Generation.] Children:

2688. i. TIMOTHY CHILD, b. Mch. 17, 1760, bapt. June 23, 1760, m. May 15, 1788, Amy Parish.
2689. ii. HANNAH CHILD, b. July 14, 1762, m. Ezra Child, son of Peter Child of Woodstock, Ct., d. Nov. 29, 1844. Recorded with her husband.

2690. iii. EUNICE CHILD, b. July 10, and bapt. July 15, 1764, m. 1st, Mr. Gates; 2d Jan. 29, 1792, Ebenezer Demming.

2691. iv. JOHN CHILD, b. Mch. 11, 1766, and bapt. Sept. 7, m. Nov. 15, 1792, Martha Hutchins.

2692. v. MARY CHILD, b. Jan. 22, 1770, m. Jan. 3, 1795, Ebenezer Sanborn.

2693. vi. ABIGAIL CHILD, b. July 14, 1771, m. Nov. 27, 1794, Samuel West.

2694. vii. ROSE ANNA CHILD, b. Dec. 30, 1773, m. Jan. 1, 1794, Samuel Hutchins.

2695. viii. DUDLEY CHILD, b. May 7, 1776, m. April 24, 1800, Molly Weeks; m. 2d, Mrs. Nancy Child, dau. of Capt. Willard Child and widow of Elisha Child.

2696. ix. MATILDA CHILD, b. Aug. 8, 1778, m. May 15, 1798, David Weeks.

2697. x. MARTHA CHILD, b. abt. 1780.

[Fifth Generation.]

2688. i. TIMOTHY CHILD, eldest son and child of Richard and Abigail Green Child, b. in Thompson, Ct., Mch. 17, 1760, m. May 15, 1788, Miss Amy Parish, who was b in 1764.

Mr. Timothy Child, like most of his name who were of sufficient age, entered personally into the heroic struggle for national enfranchisement, and lived to enjoy the fruit of the victory, in the peaceful prosperity which speedily resulted. After his decease, his widow received a small pension in recognition of his services in the Revolutionary contest. In 1799 Mr. and Mrs. Child with their children, then numbering six, removed to Sullivan Co., New York. Here they labored, clearing off the forest trees, to make for themselves a home and farm, enduring many hardships unknown to the pioneer of to-day. "The first school established in the place," writes his youngest son, "was organized by my father's benevolence, in procuring a teacher and a few spelling-books. No grist mill nearer than Bloomingburgh, a distance of some sixteen miles, the road to which would now be hard travelling for a wood-road." The strong attachments to the New England homes, were everywhere evidenced in the repetition of the names of towns and hamlets, which were themselves in memoriam of the far away motherland. Mr. Timothy Child was no exception to this general local attachment, and gave to his new home in Sullivan county the name of his native place in Connecticut. After a life of honor and usefulness, Mr. Child died, Feb. 5, 1825. His widow survived him some twenty years, dying July 5, 1845.

[Sixth Generation.]   Children:

2698. i. LAURINDA CHILD, b. May 22, 1789, m. April 19, 1807, Benjamin Lord, of Newark, N. J.

2699. ii. BRADLEY CHILD, b. 1790, d. at the age of 21, in Riverton, N. J.

2700. iii. RICHARD DWIGHT CHILD, b. Sept. 4, 1792, m. 1st, Feb. 20, 1817, Mary Andrews; m. 2d, Dec. 13, 1857, Abigail Andrews.

2701. iv. OBADIAH CHILD, b. Dec. 25, 1794, m. May 9, 1815, Charity Thompson.

2702. v. ABIGAIL CHILD, b. 1796, d. young, in Sullivan Co., N. Y.

2703. vi. ARCHIPPUS P. CHILD, b. Dec. 31, 1797, m. Dec. 27, 1818, Margaret Sax.

2704. vii. ABIGAIL CHILD, 2ND, b. Jan. 5, 1800, m. Mch. 25, 1821, Nathan Anderson.

2705. viii. JAMES BRIGHAM CHILD, b. Dec. 24, 1802, m. 1st, 1826, Ann Willsie; m. 2d, 1861, Mrs. Weston.

2706. ix. JOHN G. CHILD, b. Oct. 10, 1805, m. 1st, 1829, Lois Ann Grant; m. 2d, May 16, 1875, Mrs. Hoyt.

[Sixth Generation.]

2698. i. LAURINDA CHILD, eldest child of Timothy and Amy Parish Child, b. in Thompson, Ct., May 22, 1789, m. April 19, 1807, Benjamin Lord, son of John Lord of Thompson, Sullivan Co., N. Y.

Mr. and Mrs. Lord shared life for forty-seven years, most of this time resident in the State of New Jersey, carefully educating and training a large family into mature years, before death came to break up the home. Mr. Lord died near Trenton, N. J., May 27, 1854. Mrs. Laurinda Child Lord survived her husband some seventeen years; attaining her own rest Jan. 9, 1871, when past fourscore. For a time Mr. and Mrs. Lord resided near Rahway, N. J., and here their first child was born; while he was an infant they removed to the immediate vicinity of Trenton, N. J., and the other eight children were born near or in that city.

[Seventh Generation.] Children:

2707. i. WILLIAM G. LORD, b. Feb. 7, 1809, m. 1st, Mch. 23, 1837, Anna Margaret Beach, who d. July 7, 1841; m. 2d, Jan. 11, 1843, Elizabeth H. Hays.

2708. ii. JOHN ALLEN LORD, b. Feb. 4, 1811, m. Nov. 1843, Amelia Morton.

2709. iii. RICHARD D. LORD, b. Jan. 24, 1813, m. Jan. 24, 1838, Jane Capner.

2710. iv. EBENEZER BRADLEY LORD, b. May 2, 1816, m. 1st, July 15, 1844, Mary Ann Hays, who d. June 9, 1850; m. 2d, June 20, 1855, Elmira Hays.

2711. v. BENJAMIN LORD, b. Aug. 21, 1819, m. 1st, May 23, 1843, Amanda Potter, who d. May 31, 1870; m. 2d, Dec. 6, 1871, Julia Fowler.

2712. vi. LAURINDA LORD, b. Nov. 9, 1821, d. Sept. 6, 1825, æ. 4 yrs 2 mo. 3 days.

2713. vii. TIMOTHY W. LORD, b. Jan. 22, 1824, m. 1st, June 3, 1846, Martha Hornell, who d. June 9, 1877; m. 2d, June 19, 1878, Ellen Fowler.

2714. viii. HEZEKIAH T. LORD, b. Sept. 11, 1826, m. June 4, 1844, Emma M. Seinor.

2715. ix. MARY LAURINDA LORD, b. Oct. 4, 1828, m. Nov. 18, 1851, Arthur Hornell.

[Seventh Generation.]

2707. i. WILLIAM G. LORD, eldest son and child of Laurinda Child and Benjamin Lord, b. near Rahway, N. J., Feb. 7, 1809. Has been twice married—1st, Mch. 23, 1837, Anna Margaret Beach, dau. of Cyrenus and Mary Beach, all of Newark, N. J. Mrs. Anna M. B. Lord d. July 7, 1841, leaving an infant only four weeks old. Mr. Lord m. 2d, Jan. 11, 1843, Elizabeth H. Hays, dau. of Michael and Elizabeth Hays, of Burlington, N. J. When about 22 years of age Dr. Lord went to Philadelphia, Pa., and studied dentistry; in March, 1834, he went to Newark, N. J., and opened a dental office. In the constant and successful pursuit of this profession Dr. Lord has passed the years succeeding, always residing in Newark. To Dr. William G. Lord we are indebted for this record of his mother and her descendants:

[Eighth Generation.] Children:

2716. i. ANNA MARGARET LORD, b. June 12, 1841, m. Mch. 17, 1870, Charles A. Boucher.

2717. ii. WILLIAM G. LORD, JR., b. Jan. 22, 1844, m. Feb. 17, 1876, Mariah Louisa Sellers, dau. of Robert F. and Mariah L. Sellers, of Pittsburg, Pa.

2718. iii. ELIZABETH HAYS LORD, b. Aug. 2, 1845, m. Oct. 19, 1870, Horace S. Squier.

2719. iv. LAURINDA AMANDA LORD, b. Nov. 28, 1847, d. Mch. 12, 1866, very suddenly, when visiting in Pittsburg, Pa.

2720. v. MARY ANN AUGUSTA LORD, b. Oct. 6, 1849.

2721. vi. CARRIE FRANCES LORD, b. Feb. 5, 1852.

2722. vii. FRANK HOWARD LORD, b. Sept. 21, 1854.

[Eighth Generation.]

2716. i. ANNA MARGARET LORD, dau. of Dr. William G. and Anna Margaret Beach Lord, and granddaughter of Laurinda Child Lord, b. in Newark, N. J., June 12, 1841, m. Mch. 17, 1860, Charles A. Boucher. Through deep waters has Mrs. Boucher been called to pass, five children have been given her, only to be transplanted to the heavenly gardens, and last her husband has entered into rest, leaving her a childless widow, in February, 1879.

[Eighth Generation.]

2718. iii. ELIZABETH HAYS LORD, eldest dau. of Dr. William G. and Elizabeth H. Hays Lord, and granddaughter of

Laurinda Child Lord, b. in Newark, N. J., Aug. 2, 1845, m. Oct. 19, 1870, Horace S. Squier, of Newark.

[Ninth Generation.] Children:
2723. i. SHELDON SQUIER.
2724. ii. LIZZIE SQUIER.

[Seventh Generation.]

2708. ii. JOHN ALLEN LORD, second son and child of Laurinda Child and Benjamin Lord, b. in Trenton, N. J., Feb. 4, 1811, m. Amelia Morton, dau. of John and Amelia Morton, of New York City, November, 1843. He died suddenly in Bergen Hill, N. J., where he resided, Nov. 23, 1861, aged 50 years. Eight children were given them, of whom six survive the father, and with their mother reside in the vicinity of New York City.

[Eighth Generation.] Children:
2725. i. WILLIAM ALLEN LORD, b. July 24, 1842, d. Aug. 12, 1842.
2726. ii. WILLIAM ALLEN LORD, 2D., b. July 24, 1843.
2727. iii. AMELIA MORTON LORD, b. Sept. 11, 1845.
2728. iv. JOHN LORD, b. July 24, 1849.
2729. v. KATE LORD, b. July 17, 1852.
2730. vi. JAMES DEMOTT LORD, b. Nov. 4, 1854.
2731. vii. ADALINE LORD, b. Aug. 30, 1856.
2732. viii. FREDERIC LORD, b. Aug. 31, 1859.

[Seventh Generation.]

2709. iii. RICHARD D. LORD, third son and child of Laurinda Child and Benjamin Lord, b. in Trenton, N. J., Jan. 24, 1813, m. Jan. 24, 1838, Jane Capner, dau. of Thomas and Jane Capner. Mr. R. D. Lord died in Trenton, December 21, 1853.

[Eighth Generation.] Children:
2733. i. LAURINDA LORD, b. Feb. 25, 1840, d. Oct. 1, 1865.
2734. ii. ANNA MARGARET LORD, b. Mch. 17, 1841.
2735. iii. SARAH JANE LORD, b. Jan. 15, 1845.
2736. iv. THOMAS CAPNER LORD, b. Sept. 2, 1847, d. Sept. 13, 1849.

[Seventh Generation.]

2710. iv. EBENEZER BRADLEY LORD, fourth son and child of Laurinda Child and Benjamin Lord, b. in Trenton, N. J., May 2, 1816, m. twice—1st m., July 15, 1844, to Mary Ann Hays, dau. of Michael and Elizabeth Hays, of Burlington, N. J. Mrs. Mary A. H. Lord d. at the home of her parents June 9 1850. Mr. Lord m. 2d, Elmira Hays, sister of his first wife, June 20, 1855. Mr. Ebenezer B. Lord d. at the residence of his father-in-law Aug. 7, 1856. His widow, Mrs. Elmira H. Lord, m. 2d, Judge Elias Doughty, of Vineland, N. J., Oct. 29, 1873.

[Eighth Generation.]   Children:
    2737. i. MARY CLARA LORD, m. Oct. 7, 1871, Nathan Irving, of Trenton, N. J.
    2738. ii. ELIZABETH HAYS LORD, d. in infancy.

[Seventh Generation.]
    2711. v. BENJAMIN LORD, JR., fifth son and child of Laurinda Child and Benjamin Lord, b. in the city of Trenton, N. J., Aug. 21, 1819, was twice married—1st m., May 23, 1843, Amanda Potter, dau. of Isaac and Abigail Potter of New Providence, N. J.   Mrs. Amanda Potter Lord d. in New York City May 31, 1870.   Dr. Lord m. 2d, Julia Fowler, dau. of Charles and Lillias Fowler, of New York City, Dec. 6, 1871. Dr. Benjamin Lord is of the dental profession, residing on West Twenty-eighth Street, New York.

[Eighth Generation.]   Children:
    2739. i. BENJAMIN POTTER LORD, b. Mch. 10, 1845, d. Mch. 13, 1845.
    2740. ii. GEORGIANA LORD, b. Oct. 2, 1846.
    2741. iii. JOSEPH EDWIN LORD, b. Feb. 6, 1848.

[Seventh Generation.]
    2713. vii. TIMOTHY W. LORD, sixth son and seventh child of Laurinda Child and Benjamin Lord, b. in Trenton, N. J., Jan. 22, 1824, m. 1st, June 3, 1846, Martha Hornell, dau. of Richard A. and Martha Hornell.   Mrs. M. H. Lord, d. June 9, 1877.   Mr. T. W. Lord m. 2d, June 19, 1878, Miss Ellen Fowler, sister of the second Mrs. Benjamin Lord.

[Eighth Generation.]   Children:
    2742. i. ANNA AMELIA LORD, b. Feb. 11, 1848, d. April 18, 1850.
    2743. ii. BENJAMIN CHILD LORD, b. Oct. 15, 1849, d. Nov. 14, 1857.
    2744. iii. RICHARD HORNELL LORD, b. Nov. 28, 1851.

[Seventh Generation.]
    2714. viii. HEZEKIAH F. LORD, seventh son and eighth child of Laurinda Child and Benjamin Lord, b. in the city of Trenton, N. J., Sept. 11, 1826, m. June 4, 1844, Emma M. Seinor, dau. of William and Catherine Seinor, of New York City.

[Eighth Generation.]   Children:
    2745. i. MARY J. LORD, b. Mch. 4, 1845.
    2746. ii. EMMA S. LORD, b. Nov. 16, 1846.
    2747. iii. BENJAMIN F. LORD, b. Feb. 12, 1848.
    2748. iv. KATE S. LORD, b. Dec. 8, 1852.
    2749. v. WILLIAM G. LORD, b. Aug. 2, 1854, d. Aug. 9, 1856.

[Seventh Generation.]
    2715. ix. MARY LAURINDA LORD, second dau. and ninth child of Laurinda Child and Benjamin Lord, b. in Trenton,

N. J., Oct. 4, 1828, m. Nov. 18, 1851, Arthur Hornell of Trenton. Mrs. Mary L. L. Hornell d. March 24, 1853.

[Eighth Generation.] Child:

2750. i. ANNA M. HORNELL, resides in Camden, N. J.

[Sixth Generation.]

2700. iii. RICHARD DWIGHT CHILD, third child and second son of Timothy and Amy Parish Child, b. in Thompson, Ct., Sept. 4, 1792, was twice married—1st, Feb. 20, 1817, Mary Andrews, who was b. April 12, 1796, dau. of Francis and Sabra Parsons Andrews, and d. Mch. 19, 1855. Mr. Richard D. Child m. 2d, Dec. 13, 1857, Abigail Andrews, who was b. in 1799, and d. Jan. 10, 1877. Mr. Child was a man of business, and so efficient in whatever he undertook, that once placed by the will of his fellow citizens in place of power or trust, they were reluctant to accept a change. We find him holding the office of supervisor of Neversink, for three years, from 1825 to 1828. In 1828 he was elected sheriff of Sullivan Co., New York. He made his home in Grahamsville, New York, residing in one home some forty-seven years.

[Seventh Generation.] Children:

2751. i. MARIA CHILD, b. Aug. 3, 1818, m. Dec. 1840, John H. Divine.

2752. ii. CLARISSA ANDREWS CHILD, b. Nov. 14, 1821, m. June 29, 1849, Nathan C. Clark.

2753. iii. BETSEY SMITH CHILD, b. June 26, 1826, d. Nov. 23, 1851.

2754. iv. HARRIET ANDREWS CHILD, b. Dec. 11, 1828, d. July 23, 1834.

2755. v. GEORGE BRADLEY CHILD, b. Feb. 9, 1838, m. 1st, July 12, 1860, Adelia Decker, who d. Mch. 30, 1869; m. 2d, Mch. 14, 1872, Nancy P. Smith.

[Seventh Generation.]

2751. i. MARIA CHILD, eldest child of Richard Dwight and Mary Andrews Child, b. in Grahamsville, Sullivan Co., N. Y., Aug. 3, 1818, m. Dec. 1840, John H. Divine, d. Nov. 14, 1850. Residence at Lochsheldrake, Sullivan Co., N. Y.

[Eighth Generation.] Children:

2756. i. DWIGHT DIVINE, b. Mch. 1842. Resides in Ellenville, N. Y.

2757. ii. JAMES DIVINE, b. June 1, 1849, d. Aug. 10, 1870.

[Seventh Generation.]

2752. ii. CLARISSA ANDREWS CHILD, second dau. and child of Richard and Mary Andrews Child, b in Grahamsville, N.Y., Nov. 14, 1821, m. June 29, 1849, Nathan C. Clark. Residence Grahamsville, N. Y.

[Eighth Generation.] Children:

2758. i. MARY HORTON CLARK, b. Aug. 18, 1855. Resides in Grahamsville.

2759. ii. RICHARD DWIGHT CLARK, b. July 11, 1857. Resides in Hurley, Ulster Co., N. Y.

2760. iii. MARIUS EUGENE CLARK, b. Aug. 12, 1863. Resides in Grahamsville.

[Seventh Generation.]

2755. v. GEORGE BRADLEY CHILD, only son and youngest child of Richard Dwight and Mary Andrews Child, b. in Grahamsville, Sullivan Co., N. Y., Feb. 9, 1838, has twice married—1st, June 12, 1860, Adelia Decker, she d. Mch. 30, 1869; m. 2d, Mch. 14, 1872, Nancy P. Smith. Mr. Child is following closely in the footsteps of his most worthy father; is a resident of Grahamsville, and has there been, like his father, supervisor of Neversink, from 1867 to 1873, some five years.

[Eighth Generation.]   Children:

2761. i. ANNA CHILD, b. July 21, 1861, d. July 27, 1864.
2762. ii. AMY CHILD, b. July 15, 1873.
2763. iii. RICHARD TIMOTHY CHILD, b. Oct. 22, 1878.

[Sixth Generation.]

2701. iv. OBADIAH CHILD, third son and fourth child of Timothy and Amy Parish Child, b. in Thompson, Ct., Dec. 25, 1794; removed from Connecticut with his father in 1799, to Sullivan Co., N. Y. In 1815, on May 9, he m. in Neversink, Charity Thompson, who was b. in Marbletown, Ulster Co., N. Y., Dec. 14, 1795, a dau. of John and Ann Thompson, of Neversink, Ulster Co., and afterwards of Homer, Cayuga Co., N. Y. A daughter of Mr. Obadiah Child (Mrs. Vrandenburg) sends us a most pleasant sketch of him:

"My father was a member of the Baptist church, an active and useful christian, always willing to make any sacrifice to attend with his family upon the services of the Sanctuary. A close student of the Bible, and remarkable or peculiar for his apt quotations of scripture in conversation. Gifted with a sweet power of melody, he delighted in the service of song, and was often the leader in this part of the services. A very favorite hymn was one commencing 'Welcome, sweet day of rest.' A fond husband, and indulgent father, he was ever ready to expend his means in the purchase of books and other methods for the education of his children; but exceedingly particular in the observance of the Sabbath. His last illness (typhoid fever) was brief but severe. On his last earthly Sabbath, a beautiful clear morning, he said: 'This is Sunday, and I am very happy.' 'The time for the singing of birds has come, and the voice of the turtle is heard in the land.' He died April 8th, 1867, at Wawarsing, Ulster Co., New York, and his memory is precious to us. Mrs. Charity Thompson Child, my mother, survived my father about nine years. She always enjoyed that 'peace which passeth understanding, from her constant trust in Jesus. She loved the New Testament with a devotion seldom witnessed; her life was an exemplification of the sweet spirit of Christ. I often thought her name suitable, for her life was love. She was very happy through her last short sickness. I asked her near the close, 'Are you happy trusting in Jesus?' her answer, 'O yes; happier than I ever expected to be,' with such a light beaming on her countenance as I never saw elsewhere. She tried to say more, we could only understand 'pure in heart,' and then she entered into 'perfect peace.' March 9th, 1875, from Neversink, Sullivan Co., N. Y."

[Seventh Generation.] Children:

2764. i. CHARLES C. CHILD, b. Dec. 26, 1819, m. twice.

2765. ii. MARY ANN CHILD, b. July 8, 1822, m. Feb. 16, 1847, John Vradenburg.

2766. iii. LORINDA CHILD, b. Nov. 19, 1825, m. Sept. 21, 1852, Herman Sarr.

2767. iv. AMY CHILD, b. Sept. 20, 1828, m. 1858, Wm. C. Carson.

2768. v. JOHN THOMPSON CHILD, b. Mch. 17, 1831, d. Aug. 30, 1849.

2769. vi. SARAH CHILD, b. Feb. 22, 1834, in Rhinebeck, Duchess Co., N.Y.

2770. vii. ABIGAIL CHILD, b. Oct. 11, 1837, m. Oct. 23, 1878, H. Atherton.

2771. viii. BRADLEY CHILD, b. Dec. 8, 1840, d. Feb. 11, 1841.

[Seventh Generation.]

2765. ii. MARY ANN CHILD, eldest dau. and second child of Obadiah and Charity Thompson Child, b. in Liberty, Sullivan Co., July 8, 1822, m. Feb. 16, 1847, Rev. John Vradenburg, at Grahamsville, Sullivan Co., N. Y. Their residence has been in New Paltz, now Clintondale, Ulster Co., N. Y. "Mr. John Vradenburg is a clergyman, most active and successful in his manifold labors, especially in revival seasons, often his duties calling him to distant fields of labor." Mrs. Mary A. Child Vradenburg is an intelligent, earnest, christian wife and mother.

[Eighth Generation.] Children:

2772. i. LOUISA VRADENBURG, b. Dec. 9, 1847, m. June 27, 1866, Eli Van-Wagner.

2773. ii. CHARLES VRADENBURG, b. Nov. 29, 1848, d. May 21, 1853.

2774. iii. JAMES VRADENBURG, b. Jan. 26, 1853, d. May 21, 1853.

2775. iv. MINNIE VRADENBURG, b. Mch. 3, 1854, m. Aug. 28, 1879.

2776. v. CARRIE VRADENBURG, b. Jan. 12, 1860.

2777. vi. JENNIE VRADENBURG, b. April 21, 1865.

[Eighth Generation.]

2772. i. LOUISA VRADENBURG, eldest child of Mary Ann Child and Rev. John Vradenburg, b. in New Paltz, Ulster Co., N. Y., m. June 27, 1866, Eli Van Wagner. In 1869 they removed to Corning, Adams Co., Iowa, where Mr. Van Wagner is engaged in mercantile business. They are active, prominent members of the Methodist Episcopal church. Mrs. Van Wagner is the Corresponding Secretary of the Women's Foreign Missionary Society.

[Ninth Generation.] Children:
  2778. i. LILLIE VAN WAGNER, b. May 21, 1867, in New Paltz, N. Y.
  2779. ii. MARY VAN WAGNER, b. July 7, 1868, in New Paltz, N. Y.
  2780. iii. LIZZIE VAN WAGNER, b. July 21, 1875, in Corning, Iowa.
  2781. iv. MAUDE VAN WAGNER, b. May 6, 1877, in Corning, Iowa.
  2782. v. Infant—unnamed—b. Sept. 11, 1879, in Corning, Iowa.

[Seventh Generation.]

  2766. iii. LORINDA CHILD, second dau. and third child of
Obadiah and Charity Thompson Child, b. in Rockland, Sulli-
van Co., N. Y., Nov. 19, 1825, m. Sept. 21, 1852. Herman
Sarr, of Grahamsville, Sullivan Co., N. Y. They reside at
Council Bluffs, Pottawattamie Co., Iowa.

[Eighth Generation.] Children:
  2783. i. MARY ALICE SARR, b. July 19, 1853, d. Sept. 21, 1854, at Fallsburgh, N. Y.
  2784. ii. VIOLA SARR, b. Aug. 6, 1855, m. 1875, J. B. Matthews.
  2785. iii. ELLEN SARR, b. Oct. 22, 1859, in Franklin, Polk Co., Iowa.
  2786. iv. JOHN SARR, b. Mch. 23, 1866, d. Dec. 7, 1866.

[Eighth Generation.]

  2784. ii. VIOLA SARR, second dau. and child of Lorinda
Child and Herman Sarr, b. in Fallsburgh, Sullivan Co., N. Y.,
Aug. 6, 1855, m. in 1875, J. B. Mathews.
[Ninth Generation.] Child:
  2787. i. HERMAN P. MATHEWS, b. April 15, 1878.

[Seventh Generation.]

  2767. iv. AMY CHILD, third dau. and fourth child of Obadiah and Charity Thompson Child, b. in Rockland, Sullivan
Co., N. Y., Sept. 20, 1828, m. April 12, 1860. William C.
Carson. Before her marriage, Mrs. Carson was a teacher in
Dubuque, Iowa, now resides at Council Bluff, Iowa.
[Eighth Generation.] Children:
  2788. i. IDA CARSON, b. April 8, 1861.
  2789. ii. ETTA CARSON, b. Sept. 11, 1863, d. May 11, 1865.
  2790. iii. EDITH CARSON, b. Feb. 17, 1865.
  2791. iv. WILLIE CARSON, b. May 30, 1868, d. Jan. 13, 1870.

[Sixth Generation.]

  2703. vi. ARCHIPPUS PARISH CHILD, fourth son and sixth
child of Timothy and Amy Parish Child, b. in Sullivan Co.,
N. Y., Dec. 31, 1797, m. in Stoddardsville, Pa., Dec. 27, 1818,
Margaret Sax, who was b. Oct. 16, 1803.

  Mr. A. P. Child upon his marriage settled in Wilkes Barre,
Luzerne Co., Pa.; two years latter he removed to Stoddardsville, and engaged in carpentry, making the building of mills.

his especial work. He built a number of steam mills in Luzerne county, Pa., both grist and saw mills, and was considered a leading mill-wright of the State. In 1839, Mr. Child moved to Hickory Run, and while resident here, rose to a fine position in his business. In 1851 he again moved, and now settled in Montoursville, Lycoming Co., Pa., where he continued his business until his death, Feb. 19, 1860, aged 62. Mrs. Margaret Sax Child survives her husband, and is residing with her son, J. Sinton Child, in Montoursville, Pa.

[Seventh Generation.] Children:

2792. i. BRADLEY CHILDS, b. Dec. 5, 1819, m. Jan. 4, 1849, Margarey S. Willson.

2793. ii. JULIAN CHILDS, b. Oct. 25, 1821, m. April 17, 1841, John C. Strong.

2794. iii. MARIA L. CHILDS, b. Aug. 15, 1824, m. June 26, 1843, George Lowman.

2795. iv. HARRIET CHILDS, b. May 5, 1827, m. July 5, 1846, William Steel.

2796. v. ISABELLA CHILDS, b. Nov. 27, 1829, in Stoddardsville, Pa., d. Dec. 3, 1849, æ. 20, in Hickory Run, Pa.

2797. vi. MARGARET CHILDS, b. April 12, 1832, m. Jan. 1, 1851, Gerard L. Staples

2798. vii. JOSEPH SINTON CHILDS, b. Sept. 24, 1835, m Jan. 13, 1865, Mary Mecum.

2799. viii. JAMES BINGHAM CHILDS, b. June 1, 1838, in Stoddardsville, Pa., d. May 13, 1844, in Hickory Run, Pa.

2800. ix. MARY CHILDS, b. April 16, 1841, in Hickory Run, d. Aug. 24, 1869, in Montoursville, Pa

[Seventh Generation.]

2792. i. BRADLEY CHILDS, eldest son and child of Archippus and Margaret Sax Child, b. in Wilkesbarre, Pa., Dec. 5, 1819, m. Jan. 4, 1849, Margarey S. Willson. Is an extensive and successful business man, resides in White Haven, Luzerne Co., Pa. Lumber manufacturer.

[Eighth Generation.] Children:

2801. i. ELIZABETH WATSON CHILDS, b. Dec. 13, 1850, d. May 22, 1852.

2802. ii. NORAH S. CHILDS, b. Aug. 29, 1852, m. May 28, 1872, George W. Koons.

2803. iii. ARCHIE PARISH CHILDS, b. Sept. 5, 1854, m. Aug. 2, 1873, Ella Bechtell.

2804. iv. ALEXANDER M. CHILDS, b. Aug. 31, 1856, d. June 6, 1862.

2805. v. BRADLEY W. CHILDS, b Sept. 2, 1858.

[Eighth Generation.]

2802. ii. NORAH S. CHILDS, second dau. and child of Bradley and Margarey S. Willson Childs, b. in White Haven, Pa., Aug. 29, 1852, m. May 28, 1872, George W. Koons.

[Ninth Generation.]   Children:
  2806. i. ALEXANDER W. KOONS, b. June 12, 1873.
  2807. ii. BRADLEY KOONS, b. Mch. 12, 1875.
  2808. iii. GEORGE WILLSON KOONS, b. Mch. 21, 1877.

[Eighth Generation.]
  2803. iii. ARCHIE PARISH CHILDS, eldest son and third child
of Bradley and Margarey S. Willson Childs, b. in White Haven,
Pa., Sept. 5, 1854, m. Aug. 2, 1873, Ella Bechtell.
[Ninth Generation.]   Children:
  2809. i. GUY B. CHILDS, b. June 21, 1874, d. Jan. 25, 1878.
  2810. ii. MARGAREY CHILDS, b. Nov. 25, 1875.

[Seventh Generation.]
  2793. ii. JULIAN CHILDS, eldest dau. and second child of
Archippus P. and Margaret Sax Childs, b. in Stoddardsville,
Pa., Oct. 25, 1821, m. April 17, 1841, John C. Strong.   Resides
in White Haven, Luzerne Co., Pa.
[Eighth Generation.]   Children:
  2811. i. JAMES STRONG, b. Feb. 16, 1842, m. Sept. 26, 1865, Amanda
Rupert.
  2812. ii. MARY MARGARET STRONG, b. Jan. 25, 1846, m. Dec. 20, 1866,
Samuel Watson.
  2813. iii. GEORGE BRADLEY STRONG, b. Oct. 4, 1849, m. Aug. 29, 1874,
Susie Waman.
  2814. iv. SARAH ISABELLA STRONG, b. Dec. 6, 1854, m. Sept. 16, 1873,
L. E. Tennant.
  2815. v. ARCHIE PARISH STRONG, b. Nov. 3, 1856.
  2816. vi. JOHN CURTIS STRONG, b. April 5, 1859.

[Eighth Generation.]
  2811. i. JAMES STRONG, eldest child of Julian Childs and
John C. Strong, b. Feb. 16, 1842, m. Sept. 26, 1865, Amanda
Rupert.
[Ninth Generation.]   Children:
  2817. i CURTIS RUPERT STRONG, b June 16, 1867, d. Sept. 3, 1867.
  2818. ii. ARCHIE MERWINE STRONG, b. Dec. 24, 1869, d. June 5, 1874.
  2819. iii. GEORGE STRONG, b. Feb. 2, 1871, d April 15, 1875.
  2820. iv. EDWARD STRONG, b. June 5, 1873.
  2821. v. CHARLIE STRONG, b Dec. 15, 1875.

[Eighth Generation.]
  2812. ii. MARY MARGARET STRONG, eldest dau. and second
child of Julian Childs and John C. Strong, b. Jan. 25, 1846,
m. Dec. 20, 1866, Samuel Watson.
[Ninth Generation.]   Children:
  2822 i. CLARABEL WATSON, b. Aug. 12, 1868.
  2823. ii. SADIE JULIA WATSON, b. July 24, 1873.
  2824. iii. JOHN CURTIS WATSON, b. April 29, 1875.
  2825. iv. ARCHIE BUTTLAR WATSON b. Dec. 28, 1878.

[Eighth Generation.]

2813. iii. GEORGE BRADLEY STRONG, second son and third child of Julian Childs and John C. Strong, b. Oct. 4, 1849, m. Aug. 29, 1874, Susie Waman.

[Ninth Generation.] Children:
   2826. i. SARAH JENNIE STRONG, b. Nov. 15, 1875.
   2827. ii. JULIANNA STRONG, b. Nov. 29, 1876.
   2828. iii. JAMES PARISH STRONG, b. Dec. 8, 1878.

[Eighth Generation.]

2814. iv. SARAH ISABELL STRONG, second dau. and fourth child of Julian Childs and John C. Strong, b. Dec. 6, 1854, m. Sept. 16, 1873, L. E. Tenant.

[Ninth Generation.] Children:
   2830. i. JOHN CURTIS TENANT, b. Nov. 18, 1874.
   2831. ii. BRADLEY CHILD TENANT, b. June 24, 1879.

[Seventh Generation.]

2794. iii. MARIA L. CHILDS, second dau. and third child of Archippus and Margaret Sax Childs, b. Aug. 15, 1824, in Stoddardsville, Pa., m. June 6, 1843, George Lowman. Resides in Troy, Bradford Co., Pa.

[Eighth Generation.] Children:
   2832. i. MARY ELIZABETH LOWMAN, b. Nov. 10, 1844, d. Feb. 2, 1847.
   2833. ii. KATE LOWMAN, b. June 5, 1846, m. Oct. 1, 1867, Herrick McReam.
   2834. iii. ARCHIE PARISH LOWMAN, b. Sept. 20, 1848, d. Feb. 5, 1849.
   2835. iv. CHARLES WESLEY LOWMAN, b. Mch. 29, 1851, m. Mch. 24, 1877, Kate McCormick.
   2836. v. JAMES B. LOWMAN, b. April 12, 1853, m. Nov. 15, 1877, Maranda Morgan.
   2837. vi. HELEN A. LOWMAN, b. Nov. 4, 1855, m. April 12, 1874, H. Baldwin.

[Eighth Generation]

2833. ii. KATE LOWMAN, second dau. and child of Maria L. Childs and George Lowman, b. June 5, 1846, m. Oct. 1, 1867, Herrick McReam.

[Ninth Generation.] Children:
   2838. i. ESSIE M. McREAM, b. Feb. 10, 1871.
   2839. ii. NELLIE M. McREAM, b. July 15, 1872, d. Oct. 3, 1879.

[Eighth Generation.]

2836. v. JAMES B. LOWMAN, third son and fifth child of Maria L. Childs and George Lowman, b. April 12, 1853, m. Nov. 15, 1877, Maranda Morgan.

[Ninth Generation.] Child:
   2840. i. ALICE M. LOWMAN, b. Sept. 16, 1879.

B-1

[Eighth Generation.]

2837. vi. HELEN ADALINE LOWMAN, third dau. and sixth child of Maria L. Childs and George Lowman, b. Nov. 4, 1855, m. April 12, 1874, H. Baldwin.

[Ninth Generation.]   Child:
   2841. i. WILLIAM F. BALDWIN, b. Sept. 29, 1879.

[Seventh Generation.]

2795. iv. HARRIET CHILDS, third dau. and fourth child of Archippus and Margaret Sax Childs, b. in Stoddardsville, Pa., May 5, 1827, m. July 5, 1846, William Steel.   Reside in Nicholson, Wyoming Co., Pa.

[Eighth Generation.]   Children:
   2842. i. EDGAR ALONZO STEELE, b. Mch. 6, 1848, m. Dec. 7, 1875, Alice Brown.
   2843. ii. MARY ALICE STEELE, b. Nov. 13, 1851, m. June 17, 1872, William Bartholomew.
   2844. iii. EMMA FRANCIS STEELE, b. July 31, 1854, m. June 28, 1873, Frank McDonald.
   2845. iv. SINTON ELROY STEELE, b. Mch. 27, 1858.

[Eighth Generation.]

2842. i. EDGAR ALONZO STEELE, eldest child of Harriet Childs and William Steele, b. Mch. 6, 1848, m. Dec. 7, 1875, Alice Brown.

[Ninth Generation.]   Child:
   2846. i. CHARLES EDGAR STEELE, b. April 2, 1878.

[Eighth Generation.]

2843. ii. MARY ALICE STEELE, eldest dau. and second child of Harriet Childs and William Steele, b. Nov. 13, 1851, m. June 17, 1872, William Bartholomew.

[Ninth Generation.]   Children:
   2847. i. BEULAH BENTON BARTHOLOMEW, b. June 29, 1877.
   2848. ii. WILLIAM HAVIE BARTHOLOMEW, b. May 2, 1879.

[Eighth Generation.]

2844. iii. EMMA FRANCIS STEELE, second dau. and third child of Harriet Childs and William Steele, b. July 31, 1854, m. June 28, 1873, Frank McDonald.

[Ninth Generation.]   Children:
   2849. i. HARRIET MAY McDONALD, b. May 9, 1874.
   2850. ii. EVA FRANCIS McDONALD, b. Oct. 20, 1877.

[Seventh Generation.]

2797. vi. MARGARET CHILDS, fifth dau. and sixth child of Archippus and Margaret Sax Childs, b. April 12, 1832, in Stoddardsville, Pa., m. Jan. 1, 1851, Gerard L. Staples.   Reside at Jersey Shore, Lycoming Co., Pa.

[Eighth Generation.] Children:

2851. i. GERTRUDE R. STAPLES, b. May 30, 1853, m. June 19, 1875, Joseph Stevenson.

2852. ii. BYRON E. STAPLES, b. April 14, 1855.

2853. iii. EDWARD EUGENE STAPLES, b. Nov. 19, 1857.

2854. iv. JENNIE S. STAPLES, b. June 20, 1862.

[Eighth Generation.]

2851. i. GERTRUDE R. STAPLES, eldest child of Margaret Childs and Gerard L. Staples, b. May 30, 1853, m. June 19, 1875, Joseph Stevenson.

[Ninth Generation.] Children:

2855. i. MAUD ESTELLA STEVENSON, b. Sept. 7, 1877.

2856. ii. FRANK N. STEVENSON, b. Aug. 10, 1879.

[Seventh Generation.]

2798. vii. JOSEPH SINTON CHILDS, second son and seventh child of Archippus and Margaret Sax Childs, b. Sept. 24, 1835, in Stoddardsville, Pa., m. Jan. 13, 1865, Mary Mecum. Resides at Jersey Shore, Lycoming Co., Pa.

[Eighth Generation.] Children:

2857. i. HARRY SINTON CHILDS, b. April 9, 1867.

2858. ii. GEORGE BRADLEY CHILDS, b. Sept. 5, 1869.

2859. iii. ROBERT OTTO CHILDS, b. June 14, 1872, d. Sept. 15, 1877.

2860. iv. IRVIE G. P. CHILDS, b. May 3, 1875, d. May 10, 1875.

2861. v. WILLIAM HESSER CHILDS, b. April 9, 1877.

2862. vi. IDA MARY CHILDS, b. Aug. 25, 1879.

[Sixth Generation.]

2704. vii. ABIGAIL CHILD, third dau. and seventh child of Timothy and Amy Parish Child, was born in Thompson, Sullivan Co., N. Y., on the 3d January, 1800, married 25th March, 1821, Nathan Anderson, son of George and Matilda Anderson. Mr. Anderson died 26th March, 1826. Mrs. Anderson resides in Philadelphia, Pa., where she "celebrated her eightieth birthday anniversary," as she writes her nephew, Dr. William G. Lord, of Newark, N. J., on the 21st January, 1880, having walked alone in her widowhood for fifty-four years.

[Sixth Generation.]

2705. viii. JAMES BRIGHAM CHILD, fifth son and eighth child of Timothy and Amy Parish Child, born in Thompson, Sullivan Co., N. Y., on December 24, 1802, married twice—1st. to Ann Willsie; m. 2d, in 1861, to Mrs. Weston, widow of Rev. Horace Weston. Mr. James B. Child began his business career in Orange Co., N. Y. In 1848 moved to Ellenville, Ulster Co., N. Y., and died there on February 14, 1878.

[Seventh Generation.] Children:

2863. i. GEORGE ROOSA CHILD, b Mch. 26, 1827.

2864. ii. NIAL TOWNLEY CHILD, b. April 13, 1830, m. twice—1st, Jan. 26. 1853, Alvira Weston, who d. April 11, 1863; m. 2d, Jan. 3, 1864, Marilla Weston.

2865. iii. JAMES BRIGHAM CHILD, JR., b. Nov. 2, 1838, m. Oct. 2, 1860, Margaret H. Brown, dau. of Rev. Paul R. Brown.

[Seventh Generation.]

2864. ii. NIAL TOWNLEY CHILD, second son and child of James Brigham and Ann Willsie Child. b. in Minisink. Orange Co.. N. Y., April 13, 1830; m. twice—1st, Jan. 26, 1853, Alvira Weston; Mrs. Alvira Weston Child d. April 11, 1863; m. 2d. Jan. 3, 1864, Marilla Weston. Mr. Child is a tanner, and resides in Nicholson, Pa.

[Eighth Generation.] Children:

2866. i. GEORGE WESLEY CHILD, b. April 15, 1854.

2867. ii. ANNA ELIZABETH CHILD, b. Mch. 8, 1856.

2868. iii. ELLEN AUGUSTA CHILD, b. April 3, 1860.

2869. iv. HORACE WESTON CHILD, b May 12, 1861.

2870. v. JAMES HOWARD CHILD, b. Aug. 15, 1869.

2871 vi WILLIAM McKINSTRY CHILD, b. Sept. 1. 1871. d. Feb. 6, 1875

[Seventh Generation.]

2865. iii. JAMES BRIGHAM CHILD. JR., third son and child of James B. and Ann Willsie Child. b. in Orange Co.. N. Y.. Nov. 2, 1838. m. Oct. 2, 1860. Margaret H. Brown. dau. of Rev. Paul R. Brown. of the New York conference, of the Methodist Episcopal Church. Mrs. Margaret H. Brown Child b. Dec. 29, 1878

[Eighth Generation.] Children:

2872. i. KATIE L. CHILD, b. Mch. 9, 1865.

2873. ii. MARY E. CHILD, b. Sept. 5. 1875.

[Sixth Generation.]

2706. ix. Judge JOHN GREENLEAF CHILD. sixth son and youngest child of Timothy and Amy Parish Child, b. in Thompson. Sullivan Co.. N. Y.. Oct. 10, 1805. Has been m. twice—1st. in 1829, to Lois Ann Grant; 2d m. May 16, 1875, Mrs. Hoyt, widow of Charles Hoyt. Judge Child is a man of position in the town of Napanock, Ulster Co.. N. Y.. a man who may be accredited most emphatically self-made. His school training continued but twenty-seven days after he was twelve years old. yet from his sixteenth year to his twenty-second he taught in the winters, working upon his father's farm in the summer. The succeeding four years he served as clerk and manager at the Ulster Iron Works. In 1835 he moved to Sullivan Co., and was appointed under sheriff and served three years, and elected sheriff. In 1863 he was elected special county judge, and special surrogate, and served six years. In 1870, Judge Child settled in Napanock, and in 1878 served as justice of the sessions. He was admitted to the bar in 1858 at Albany, having prepared himself for his examination and practice of the law without a tutor, qualifying himself in like manner as a successful surveyor. In his seventy-fifth year he is yet in the active exercise of his profession, and serving as justice of the peace.

[Seventh Generation.] Children:

2874. i JOHN T. CHILD, b. May 16, 1831, m. Louisa Holmes.
2875. ii. AMOS G. CHILD, b. Nov. 2, 1833, m. Margaret ———
2876. iii. BILLINGS G. CHILD, b. Dec. 27. 1835, m. Celia Vandermark.
2877. iv. EMILY CHILD, b. March 4, 1838.
2878. v. MARY CHILD, b. Nov. 1839.
2879. vi. ARTHUR P. CHILD, b. Oct. 1, 1843.
2880. vii. ARCHIBALD N. CHILD, b. March 11, 1846.
2881. viii. JAMES E. CHILD, b July 11, 1848.

[We have made innumerable efforts in differing ways to obtain the proper dates in the five families following, but in vain.]

[Seventh Generation.]

2874. i. JOHN TRAVERSE CHILD, eldest son and child of Judge John G. and Lois A. Grant Child, b. in Sullivan Co. on May 16, 1831, and m. ——— Louisa Holmes of Pittsburg, Pa. Mr. John T. Child was a civil engineer and served in the late war with great efficiency in this capacity. He d. in Pittsburg. Pa., in 1869.

[Eighth Generation.] Children:

2882. i. WILLIE CHILD.
2883. ii. CARRIE CHILD.

[Seventh Generation.]

2875. ii. AMOS GRANT CHILD, second son and child of Judge John G. and Lois A. Grant Child, b. in Sullivan Co. on Nov. 2, 1833, and m. Margaret ———. Mr. Amos G. Child was like his elder brother, a civil engineer, and like him did good service in the war of the rebellion. Mrs. Margaret ——— Child died.

[Eighth Generation.] Children:

2884. i. CLINTON S. CHILD.
2885. ii. A daughter.

[Seventh Generation.]

2876. iii. BILLINGS G. CHILD, third son and child of Judge John G. and Lois A. Grant Child, b. in Sullivan Co., Dec. 27, 1835, m. Celia Vandermark. Of this third son of Judge Child we can make the same record as of the two brothers elder. Mr. B. G. Child d. in Elmira, N. Y., in 1870.

[Eighth Generation.] Children:
2886. i. ANNA T. CHILD.
2887. ii. LILLIE CHILD.
2888 iii. CARRIE CHILD.

[Seventh Generation.]

2879. vi. ARTHUR PARISH CHILD, fourth son and sixth child of Judge John G. and Lois A. Grant Child, b. in Sullivan Co., N. Y., Oct. 1, 1843, m. and has three children.

[Eighth Generation.] Children:
2889. i. ANNA CHILD.
2890. ii. LOIS CHILD.
2891. iii. ANTOINETTE CHILD.

[Seventh Generation.]

2880. vii. ARCHIBALD N. CHILD. fifth son and seventh child of Judge John G. and Lois Grant Child. b. in Sullivan Co., N. Y., March 11, 1846, m. and has two children.

[Eighth Generation.] Children:
2892 i. GEORGE CHILD.
2893. ii. Infant unnamed.

[Fifth Generation.]

2691. iv. Capt. JOHN CHILD, second son and fourth child of Richard and Abigail Green Child, b. in Thompson, Conn., March 11, 1766, m. Nov. 15, 1792, Martha Hutchins, who was b. in Haverhill, Essex Co., Mass., Jan. 9, 1773. Mrs. Martha Hutchins Child was a daughter of Jeremiah Hutchins, who had removed from Massachusetts to Bath, N. H., when Mrs. Child was very young. Mr. Child was early apprenticed to Mr. John May of Woodstock, Conn., a kinsman; this transaction was, therefore, not effected in a strictly legal manner. Upon attaining his majority the remuneration for his services was referred to two friends of Mr. May and Mr. Child, who settled the affair amicably or satisfactorily to each—in the quaint phraseology of the time "chalked a like amount"— which enabled Mr. Child to provide himself with an outfit, consisting of a French horse, a saddle and bridle, a suit of clothing and a gun—the cost of all perhaps would not exceed fifty dollars. Thus equipped Mr. Child joined his brother-in-law, Mr. Ezra Child, in Bath, N. H. More surely armed with cheerful determination and strong hope, he was so well skilled that he commanded readily the highest wages of the times, viz., $8 per month. The accumulations arising therefrom enabled him to marry in the simple style of the country, with stock consisting of his horse, a black cow (said to have "given blue milk,") a black swine, and a black sheep. His competent husbandry soon increased his store and want was known only when the grain crop of one year scarce sufficed to meet the incoming harvest of the succeeding: this insufficiency of bread was met by the good black cow and plenty of potatoes. Mr. and Mrs. Child, indifferent to luxuries, found their happiness in meeting their labors with one will and heart, and trained a noble, handsome family of sons and daughters to be good citizens, true wives, and in time parents of a goodly posterity, honoring their name, and winning new honors for it in turn. Mr. Child d. in Bath, Grafton Co., N. H., April 18, 1841; Mrs. Child survived her husband some twenty-three years. For some years before her decease, her anniversary birthday was celebrated by the home gathering of children and grand-children—the last occasion observed, in 1863, her descendants numbered 112. Gathered home like the full ripened grain, when past the four score and ten, she passed from earth in the full assurance of a comfortable hope, in 1864.

[Sixth Generation.] Children:

2894. i. MEHITABLE CHILD, b. Jan. 20, 1794, d. Sept. 14, 1794.

2895. ii. ABIGAIL CHILD, b. April 22, 1798, m. Dec. 2, 1819. Hon. John Hibbard.

2896. iii. HANNAH CHILD, b. May 25, 1800, m. Sept. 11, 1822, Leonard Walker.

2897. iv. MARTHA CHILD, b. Jan. 11, 1802, m. Mch. 14, 1822, William Lang.

2898. v. LUVIA CHILD, b. Feb. 23, 1804, m. Sept. 11, 1823, Henry H. Lang.

2899. vi. JOHN MAY CHILD, b. Jan. 23, 1806, m. 1828, Sally Randall.

2900. vii. EZRA CHILD, b. Jan. 26, 1808, m. 1st, Oct. 31, 1834, Hannah Walden; m. 2d, 1864, Martha Eastman.

2901. viii. DWIGHT PENUEL CHILD, b. July 9, 1810, m. May 16, 1833, Nancy May Child.

2902. ix. ROSANNA CHILD, b. April 30, 1812, m. Mirand A. Witcher.

2903. x. SUSAN L. CHILD, b. Nov. 23, 1814, m. Jan. 1, 1835, William Lang.

2904. xi. BRADLEY G. CHILD, b. Sept. 24, 1818, m. Nov. 17, 1837, Hannah Child.

[Sixth Generation.]

2895. ii. ABIGAIL CHILD, second dau. and child of Capt.
John and Martha Hutchins Child, b. in Bath, N. H., April
22, 1798, m. Dec. 2, 1819, Hon. John Hibbard, of the same
town, b. Sept. 14, 1782. Mr. Hibbard for years represented
the town of Bath in the New Hampshire Legislature, and at
home has been one of the custodians of town affairs in the
position of selectman. He is a wealthy farmer.

[Seventh Generation.] Children:

2905. i. HANNAH C. HIBBARD, b. Mch. 8, 1821, in Bath, N. H., m. Dec.
22, 1842. Dudley Child.

2906. ii. CHESTER HIBBARD, b. Feb. 25, 1823, in Bath, N. H.

2907. iii. ADELINE HIBBARD, b. Nov. 1, 1824, in Bath, N. H.

2908. iv. JOHN HIBBARD, JR., b. Mch. 25, 1826, in Bath, N. H., d. Aug.
13, 1826.

2909. v. REBECCA HIBBARD, b. May 24, 1827, in Bath, N. H.

2910. vi. ELIHU HIBBARD, b. Jan. 7, 1829, d. Dec. 18, 1874, in Bath, N. H.

2911. vii. Infant—unchristened—b. Sept. 5, 1830, d Sept. 8, 1830, in Bath,
N. H.

2912. viii. ROSANNA C. HIBBARD, b. Feb. 5, 1832, d. April 18, 1864, in
Bath, N. H.

2913. ix. JOHN NEWELL HIBBARD, b. Nov. 19, 1833, d. Aug. 30, 1878, in
Bath, N. H.

2914. x. MARTHA J. HIBBARD, b. Jan. 1, 1836.

2915. xi. WARREN HIBBARD, b. June 19, 1837.

2916. xii. ARTHUR HIBBARD, b. Oct. 18, 1839.

2917. xiii. SERAPHINA HIBBARD, b. June 24, 1842

[Sixth Generation.]

2896. iii. HANNAH CHILD, third dau. and child of Capt.
John and Martha Hutchins Child, b. in Bath, N. H., May 25,
1800, m. Sept. 11, 1822, Leonard Walker, son of Chloe Child
and Leonard Walker, of Strafford, Orange Co., Vt. Mr. Walker
was a farmer and resided in Bath, Grafton Co., N. H., where
he died Sept. 21, 1840. Mrs. Hannah Child Walker died there
Nov. 4, 1865.

[Seventh Generation.] Children:

2918. i. CHARLES EDWIN WALKER, b. July 22, 1823, d. Sept. 13, 1826.

2919. ii. MARTHA HUTCHINS WALKER, b. Feb. 5, 1825, m. Mch. 4, 1846,
Jonathan Child. Mrs. Martha H. W. Child's record of family is given in
connection with the family of her husband.

2920. iii HANNAH LORAINE WALKER, b. July 5, 1827, d. Aug. 17, 1830.

2921. iv. FREEMAN WALKER, b. May 31, 1829, d. Aug 16, 1830.

2922. v. JOHN CHILD WALKER, b. Oct. 10, 1830, m. April 26, 1864, Jennie
C. Weeks.

2923. vi. ELIZA C. WALKER, b. Dec. 1, 1832, d. Oct. 3, 1853.

2924. vii. CHARLES LEON WALKER, b. Jan. 2, 1835, m. Nov. 12, 1864, Louisa M. Wilcox.

2925. viii. FREEMAN WALKER, 2D, b. April 13, 1837, d. Nov. 20, 1837.

2926. ix. CHLOE CHILD WALKER, b. June 3, 1839, d. June 3, 1846.

[Seventh Generation.]

2922. v. JOHN CHILD WALKER, third son and fifth child of Hannah Child and Leonard Walker, b. in Bath, Grafton Co., N. H., Oct. 10, 1830, m. April 26, 1864, Jennie C. Weeks. Mr. and Mrs. John C. Walker resided in Grinnell, Iowa. Mrs. Walker died May 10, 1879.

[Eighth Generation.] Children:

2927. i. LEONARD WALKER, b. Mch. 17, 1865.

2928. ii. CHARLES EDWIN WALKER, b. April 11, 1867.

2929. iii. ALICE LIZZIE WALKER, b. Jan. 25, 1870.

2930. iv. ERNEST WALKER, b. Dec. 25, 1871.

2931. v. BESSIE WEEKS WALKER, b. Mch. 17, 1873.

2932. vi. MARTHA WALKER, b. June 21, 1875, d. Sept. 23, 1875.

2933. vii. JOHN CHILD WALKER, JR., b. Dec. 19, 1878.

[Seventh Generation.]

2924. vii. CHARLES LEON WALKER, fourth son and seventh child of Hannah Child and Leonard Walker, b. in Bath, Grafton Co., N. H., Jan. 2, 1835, m. Nov. 12, 1864, Louisa M. Wilcox. Three children of the family of nine of Mr. and Mrs. Leonard Walker survive, two sons and one daughter. Mr. John Child Walker, Mrs. Jonathan Child and Mr. Charles Leon Walker are the survivors. Very fortunately they are not separated, though settled far from their native hills; they have their homes in the growing town of Grinnell, Iowa.

[Eighth Generation.] Children:

2934. i. CORA LOUISA WALKER, b. Feb. 17, 1867.

2935. ii. KENT STACY WALKER, b. Dec. 17, 1869.

[Sixth Generation.]

2897. iv. MARTHA CHILD, fourth dau. and child of Capt. John and Martha Hutchins Child, b. in Bath, N. H., Jan. 11, 1802, m. Mch. 14, 1822. Hon. William Lang. Mr. Lang is now a resident in Concord, New Hampshire, and like his brother-in-law, has enjoyed the honor of a seat in the State Legislature. For some eight years he acted as selectman of the town of Bath. Mrs. Martha Child Lang died in Bath, N. H., May 5, 1834,—she was the mother of four children.

[Seventh Generation.] Children:

2936. i. JOHN CHILD LANG. b. Feb. 8, 1823, in Bath, N. H.

2937. ii. MEHITABLE CHILD LANG, b. Mch. 17, 1825, in Bath, N. H.

2938. iii. WILLIAM DWIGHT LANG, b. July 27, 1827, in Bath, N. H.

2939. iv. ALICE WALKER LANG, b. July 22, 1829, in Bath, N. H.

[Sixth Generation.]

2898. v. LUVIA CHILD, fifth dau. and child of Capt. John and Martha Hutchins Child, b. in Bath, N. H., Feb. 23, 1804, m. Sept. 11, 1823, Hon. Henry H. Lang, who, like the other sons-in-law and sons of the family, was an influential man in affairs of the town ; chosen by his townsmen their representative in the State Legislature, and for years an excellent selectman.

[Seventh Generation.] Child:

2940. i. MARTHA M. C. LANG, b. Jan. 9, 1825.

[Sixth Generation.]

2899. vi. JOHN MAY CHILD, eldest son and sixth child of Capt. John and Martha Hutchins Child, b. in Bath, N. H., Jan. 23, 1806, m. 1828, Sally Randall, of Danville, Vt. A farmer, and resided at Monroe Plain, Grafton Co., N. H. Mr. John M. Child died Aug. 11, 1879.

[Seventh Generation.] Children:

2941. i. LUCINDA CHILD, b. July, 1829.

2942. ii. EDWIN W. CHILD, b. May, 1831, m. Eliza Sterling.

2943. iii. ISRAEL R. CHILD, b. 1833, d. young.

2944. iv. SUSAN CHILD, b. 1835, m. Robert Beattie.

2945. v. G. OSMORE CHILD, b. July, 1840, m. Eliza Ash.

2946. vi. SARAH CHILD, b. Jan. 1848.

[Sixth Generation.]

2900. vii. EZRA CHILD, second son and seventh child of Capt. John and Martha Hutchins Child, b. in Bath, N. H., Jan. 26, 1808, m. Oct. 31, 1834, Hannah Walden of Newbury, Vt. Mr. Child m. a second time, 1864, Martha Eastman, b. Dec. 14, 1816, and d. in 1869; he d. Sept. 17, 1870.

[Seventh Generation.] Children:

2947. i. LORAINE W. CHILD, b. March 10, 1835.

2948. ii. ABBY ANN CHILD, b. May 7, 1837, m. Nov. 23, 1866, George C. Learned.

2949. iii. FREEMAN CHILD, b. Jan. 1, 1845, d. March 10, 1845.

2950. iv. LEWIS STONE CHILD, b. April 10, 1846.

[Seventh Generation]

2948. ii. ABBY ANN CHILD, second dau. and child of Ezra and Hannah Walden Child, b. in Bath, N. H., May 7, 1837, m. Nov. 23, 1866, George C. Learned.

[Eighth Generation.] Children:

2951. i. ABBY G. LEARNED, b. Aug. 11, 1867.

2952. ii. JOHN W. LEARNED, b. Aug. 27, 1869.

2953. iii. ORWELL N. LEARNED, b. Jan. 15, 1875.

[Sixth Generation.]

2901. viii. Hon. DWIGHT PENUEL CHILD, third son and eighth child of Capt. John and Martha Hutchins Child, b. in Bath, N. H., July 9, 1810, m. May 16, 1833, Nancy May Child, b. April 8, 1814, in Exeter, Otsego Co., N. Y., a daughter of Elisha and Nancy (Child) Child. It is often said that the external surroundings of early years leave strong imprint upon the mental and moral nature. We cannot doubt this, we can equally believe that the physical system is affected by these influences: and a guerdon of personal beauty seems the gift of the mountains to those born in their shadows. Upon this family of Capt. John and Martha Hutchins Child the dower of an attractive exterior has been widely bestowed, though unaccompanied with the vigorous health we are apt to believe assured to the dwellers among the hills. Hon. Dwight P. Child makes no departure from this inheritance and has helped to pass on the gift to a large family of honorable sons and daughters. Living upon the farm his father redeemed from the wilderness, Mr. Child's dwelling faces the bold heights of the White Mountain range, not far removed, the lights and shadows ever diversifying the rugged sides and sharpened peaks afford constant interest and alluring charm. Here childhood, youth and manhood, have sped their swift years, bringing cares and troubles, but much more of joy and plenty. Fertile acres and full garners attest the joint inheritance of wise thrift and intelligent foresight. Serving his fellow-citizens for years as a town official, Hon. Mr. Child has also represented them in the halls of their State Legislature. The home has found its charm and true light in the mother whose modesty deprecates notice, but whose works praise her.

[Seventh Generation.] Children.

2954. i. WILLIAM GRAVES CHILD, M. D., b. Feb. 4, 1834, m. 1st, March 18, 1858, Caroline Buck Lang, she d. May 10, 1867; m. 2d, Sept. 3, 1868, Luvia Lang.

2955. ii. ELISHA CHILD, b. May 5, 1835, d. June 9, 1835, in Bath, N. H.

2956. iii. HENRY H. L. CHILD, b. July 22, 1836, m. Sept. 19, 1860, Abigail Kimball.

2957. iv. PARKER MORSE CHILD, b. June 10, 1838, m. Oct. 29, 1861, Abigail Hatch.

2958. v. HARRIET CHILD, b. Feb. 8, 1840, d. Aug. 17, 1846, in Bath, N. H.

2959. vi. SYLVINA THORPE CHILD, b. Sept. 8, 1841, m. William H. Sawyer of Worcester, Mass.

2960. vii. JOHN D. CHILD, b. Dec. 29, 1842, m. March 22, 1871, Julia E. Dow.

2961. viii. HENRIETTA A. CHILD, b. Oct. 3, 1844, d. May, 1862, in Bath, N. H.

2962. ix. ADELINE H. CHILD, b. Dec. 27, 1847.

2963. x. ALBERT CHILD, b. Jan. 18, 1850, d. July 23, 1853.

2964 xi. MARY JANE CHILD, b. Oct. 4, 1852.

2965. xii. JULIET CHILD, b. Nov. 1, 1857.

[Seventh Generation.]

2954. i. Hon. WILLIAM G. CHILD, M. D., eldest son and child of Hon. Dwight P. and Nancy May (Child) Child, b. in Bath, N. H. Feb. 4, 1834, and has twice married. His first marriage to Miss Caroline Buck Lang, March 18, 1858. Mrs. Caroline B. L. Child died May 10, 1867. Dr. Child m. second Miss Luvia Lang, Sept. 3, 1868; these ladies were sisters, and daughters of Sherburne and Mehitable Ricker Lang.

Dr. William G. Child read medicine in New York City, walking the hospitals there, and closed his medical course in the department of medicine of Dartmouth College, in Hanover, N. H., graduating in 1857. Dr. Child settled in Bath for his professional duties until the war of the Rebellion. Of his army life we quote the account given by Rev. Prof. B. W. Dwight in his Genealogy of the Dwight Family:

"He entered the U. S. A. of Vols., Aug. 13, 1862, as assistant surgeon in the 5th Regiment, N. H. Vols., and was commissioned surgeon in the same regiment, Nov. 4, 1864, and served until July, 1865, the close of the war. He was in the battles of South Mountain, Antietam, Fredericksburgh, Brandy Station, Gettysburgh, Chancellorsville, Cold Harbor, Petersburgh, Deep Bottom, etc. While at Point Lookout, he was detailed to superintend the hospital for rebel prisoners of war, where he often had 500 men on the sick list. He had eight assistant surgeons under him, most of them rebels. He was present in the theatre when President Lincoln was shot."

When discharged from army service, Dr. Child returned to his native place, and resumed his practice, with greatly enlarged experience, and has taken a prominent position in the medical profession of the State. Dr. Child has made a special study of diseases arising from malarial influences, and of the hereditary transmission of disease. With a widely extended ride for practice, he has found time to serve honorably his constituents in the State Legislature. A very marvellous personal resemblance to the distinguished divine in Brooklyn, N. Y., Rev. Henry Ward Beecher, has resulted in much amusement to the genial M. D.

[Eighth Generation.] Children:

2966. i. WILLIAM CLINTON CHILD, b. March 1, 1859, in Bath, N. H.

2967. ii. KATE CHILD, b. Sept. 22, 1860, in Bath, N. H.

2968. iii. BERNARD VANDERKIEFT CHILD, b. Nov. 28, 1862, in Bath N. H.

2969. iv. SUSAN WADE CHILD, b. Dec. 4, 1865, in Bath, N. H.

2970. v. JOHN LESLIE CHILD, b. Aug. 1, 1870, in Bath, N. H.

2971. vi. JAMES DWIGHT CHILD, b. May 12, 1875, in Bath, N. H.

[Seventh Generation.]

2956. iii. HENRY H. L. CHILD, third son and child of Hon. Dwight P. and Nancy M. C. Child, b. in Bath, N. H., July 22, 1836, m. Sept. 19, 1860, Abigail Kimball, who was b. in Bath, June 11, 1835, a daughter of James Kimball of that town. Mr. and Mrs. H. H. L. Child reside in Sparta, Monroe Co., Wis. Mr. Child is connected with the firm of Fisk & Irish, dealers in agricultural implements of all kinds.

[Eighth Generation.] Children:

2972. i. IRVING CHILD, b. Oct. 20, 1861, in Bath, N. H.

2973. ii. DWIGHT CHILD, b. Dec. 3, 1864, in Bath, N. H., d. Dec. 25, 1873, in Sparta, Wis.

[Seventh Generation.]

2957. iv. PARKER MORSE CHILD, fourth son and child of Hon. Dwight P. and Nancy M. C. Child, b. in Bath, N. H., June 10, 1838, m. Oct. 29, 1861, Abigail Hatch, who was b. April 11, 1841, in Bath, N. H., is a daughter of Abel Scott and Abigail Hatch of Barnet, Vt. Mr. P. M. Child is general agent of the Massachusetts Mutual Life Insurance Co., for Milwaukee, Wis.

[Eighth Generation.] Children:

2974. i. BLANCH MAY CHILD, b Jan. 17, 1863.

2975. ii. HENRY HATTON CHILD, b. Jan. 24, 1865.

2976. iii. SCOTT PARKER CHILD, b. May 30, 1867.

2977. iv. ALICE MAUDE CHILD, b. Nov. 30, 1870.

2978. v. ABBY CHILD, b. April 3, 1873, d. Sept. 16, 1873.

2979. vi. RALPH SUTHERLAND CHILD, b. March 7, 1878

[Seventh Generation.]

2959. vi. SYLVINA THORP CHILD, second dau. and sixth child of Hon. Dwight P. and Nancy M. (Child) Child, b. in Bath, N. H., Sept. 8, 1844, m. Jan. 4, 1870, William A. Sawyer of Worcester, Mass. Mrs. Sylvina T. Child Sawyer d. Sept. 23, 1872. Mr. Sawyer is an enterprising lumber merchant of Worcester.

[Eighth Generation.] Child:

2980. i. GERTRUDE MAY SAWYER, b. Feb. 13, 1871, in Worcester, Mass., d. Jan. 29, 1872.

Seventh Generation.]

2960. vii. JOHN D. CHILD, fifth son and seventh child of Hon. Dwight P. and Nancy M. (Child) Child, b. Dec. 29, 1842, in Bath, Grafton Co., N. H., m. Mch. 22, 1871, Julia E. Dow. Mr. John Child remains upon the home farm, occupying the house in which his parents dwelt during the earlier years of their married life. A noble specimen of the young manhood of the Granite State.

[Eighth Generation.] Children:

2981. i. ETTA AILINE CHILD, b. Jan. 1, 1872, in Bath, N. H.
2982. ii. EDITH MAY CHILD, b. Sept. 15, 1873, in Bath, N. H.
2983. iii. DWIGHT PENUEL CHILD, b. Oct. 1, 1877, in Bath, N. H.

[Sixth Generation.]

2903. x. SUSAN L. CHILD, seventh daughter and tenth child of Capt. John and Martha Hutchins Child, b. in Bath, N. H., Nov. 23, 1814, m. her brother-in-law, William Lang, of Warren, N. H., Jan. 1, 1835.

[Seventh Generation.] Children:

2984. i. MARTHA LANG, b. Oct. 17, 1837, in Bath, N. H.
2985. ii. CHARLES SAMUEL LANG, b. Aug. 30, 1844, in Bath, N. H.

[Sixth Generation.]

2904. x. Hon. BRADLEY G. CHILD, fourth son and eleventh child of Capt. John and Martha Hutchins Child, b. in Bath, N. H., Sept. 24, 1818, m. Nov. 17, 1837, Miss Hannah Child, third dau. and eighth child of Elisha and Nancy (Child) Child, of Exeter, Otsego Co., N. Y., she was b. May 21, 1816.

Of such uniform excellence and prominent citizenship was this family of Capt. John Child, that one might write a description of character and deed for one member and then apply it regularly to sons and sons in-law indiscriminately, and yet this oneness of success has nowhere obliterated individuality of character. Enough of sterling sound sense, keen business ability, and uprightness of character remained to supply amply the eleventh child. The piercing yet genial, kindly black eye is surmounted with ample brain room, and crowned with the early almond blossoms of a gracious age, whose decades are scarce credited by the alert step and vigorous healthful figure; a most noble specimen of the New England thoughtful farmer. Mr. B. G. Child has graced the board of selectmen for his town, and held counsel on affairs of the State in its legislative halls at Concord, N. H. Of a large family, Mr. and Mrs. Child have been called to resign many to the "Stern Reaper whose name is Death."

[Seventh Generation.] Children:

2986. i. GILBERT CHILD, b. Mch. 24, 1839, d. July 29, 1879.

2987. ii. EDGAR CHILD, b. Sept. 3, 1842, d. Aug. 23, 1853.

2988. iii. CHARLES HENRY CHILD, b. May 28, 1846.

2989. iv. FLORA E. CHILD, b. June 12, 1850, d. Sept. 28, 1853.

2990. v. MARTHA H. CHILD, b. June 15, 1852, d. Aug. 15, 1853.

2991. vi. ALICE CHILD, b. Jan. 21, 1855, m. June 3, 1880, Harry H. Jones.

2992. vii. MYRA H. CHILD, b. Sept. 17, 1858.

2993. viii. FLORA H. CHILD, b. Oct. 30, 1860.

[Fifth Generation.]

2692. v. MARY CHILD, third dau. and fifth child of Richard and Abigail Green Child, b. in Thompson, Ct., Jan. 22, 1770, m. Jan. 3, 1795, Ebenezer Sanborn, who was b. Oct. 13, 1772. Mr. E. Sanborn d. Oct. 28, 1839, aged 67 years. His occupation that of a farmer. Mrs. Mary Child Sanborn survived her husband some years, dying at the age of 83, April 13, 1853, in Jay, Vt. This family has been widely scattered, and the record is not as full as could be desired.

[Sixth Generation.] Children:

2994. i. MATILDA SANBORN, b. Mch. 2, 1796, m. Enoch Sanborn.

2995. ii. LOUISA SANBORN,) m. April 3, 1819, Nahum Downs.

2996. iii. LANSON SANBORN,) Twins b. Nov. 26, 1797. m. Mch. 26, 1833, Almira A. Dodge.

2997. iv. HENRY SANBORN, b. Dec. 19, 1799, d. Mch. 17, 1825, aged 25 yrs. 3 mo.

2998. v. ANNA SANBORN, b. Nov. 2, 1801, m. Adna Crandall.

2999. vi. HANNAH SANBORN, b. Nov. 29, 1803, m. Stoddard Meeker.

3000. vii. BRADLEY SANBORN, b. Dec. 2, 1805, m. Emeline A. Lamb.

3001. viii. MARY SANBORN, b. April 19, 1808, d. Sept. 19, 1810, aged 2 yrs. 5 mo.

3002. ix. EDMUND SANBORN, b. April 16, 1812, m. Harriet R. White.

3003. x. MARTHA SANBORN, b. May 28, 1814, m. Mch. 22, 1832, William Williams.

[Sixth Generation.]

2994. i. MATILDA SANBORN, eldest dau. and child of Mary Child and Ebenezer Sanborn, b. Mch. 2, 1796, m. about 1817, Enoch Sanborn.

[Seventh Generation.] Children:

3004. i. JANE SANBORN, b. Nov. 6, 1818, m. May, 1848, Abram Reuter. Reside at Potter, P. Q.

3005. ii. HORACE SANBORN, b. Jan. 4, 1821, m. Jan. 27, 1850, Harriet Hatch. Reside at North Troy, Vt.

3006. iii. DAVID SANBORN, b. 1824; not living.

3007. iv. CHESTER SANBORN, b. Nov. 29, 1827, m. May, 1866, Philena Walker. Reside at North Troy, Vt.

3008. v. LADORA ANN SANBORN, b. Nov. 27, 1829, m. Mch. 9, 1853, John
S. Bacon. Reside in Hatley, P. Q.

3009. vi. EMELINE SANBORN, b. 1831; not living.

3010. vii. ORRIN SANBORN, b. May 18, 1833, m. 1859, Jane Currier. Reside in Lowell, Mass.

3011. viii. JULIA SANBORN, b. June 9, 1835, m. 1855, Solomon Elkins, of
North Troy, Vt.

3012. ix. ALMIRA SANBORN, b. Oct. 23, 1838, m. 1866, Isaac Harris. Reside in Piermont, N. H.

[Sixth Generation.]

2995. ii. LOUISA SANBORN, second dau. and child of Mary
Child and Ebenezer Sanborn, b. Nov. 26, 1797, m. Feb. 3, 1819,
Nahum Downs.

[Seventh Generation.]   Children:

3013. i. AUGUSTA ANN DOWNS, b. Nov. 2, 1819, m. Mr. Gove of Whitefield, N. H.

3014. ii. LAURA DOWNS, b. Oct. 9, 1821, m. Mr. Harriman of St. Johns-
burg, Vt.

3015. iii. AZRO BUCK DOWNS, b. Sept. 1, 1823.

3016. iv. HENRY DOWNS, b. April 3, 1825.   It is reported that this family
have all died, but the dates cannot be ascertained.

[Sixth Generation.]

2996. iii. LAUSON SANBORN, twin child and first son of
Mary Child and Ebenezer Sanborn, b. Nov. 26, 1797, m. Mch.
26, 1833, Almira Azuba Dodge, who was b. in January 1807.

[Seventh Generation.]   Children:

3017. i. JOSEPHINE SANBORN, b. March 1, 1837, m. March 18, 1857, Sidney Wood; reside in Lowell, Mass.

3018. ii. MARQUANAH SANBORN, b. Feb. 25, 1840, m. Dec. 6, 1858, Charles
R. Bartlett, a wealthy farmer in Jay, Vt.

[Sixth Generation.]

2998. v. ANNA SANBORN, third dau. and fifth child of Mary
Child and Ebenezer Sanborn, b. Nov. 2, 1801, m. Adna Crandall.

[Seventh Generation.]   Children:

3019. i. MARY CRANDALL.

3020. ii. GEORGE WASHINGTON CRANDALL.

3021. iii. EBENEZER CRANDALL.

3022. iv. SYLVANUS CRANDALL.

3023. v. BRADLEY CRANDALL.

[Sixth Generation.]

2999. vi. HANNAH SANBORN, fourth dau. and sixth child of
Mary Child and Ebenezer Sanborn, b. Nov. 29, 1803, m. Stoddard Meeker.   Unable to obtain the date of the marriage or
any record of the children except their names, and that one
child married.

[Seventh Generation.] Children: (None of which are living.)

3024. i. CAROLINE MEEKER.

3025. ii. MARTHA MEEKER.

3026. iii. PERSIS MEEKER.

3027. iv. HANNAH MEEKER.

[Sixth Generation.]

3000. vii. BRADLEY SANBORN, third son and seventh child of Mary Child and Ebenezer Sanborn, b. Dec. 2, 1805, m. Mch. 20, 1833, Emeline Amanda Lamb. Mr. Sanborn d. Nov. 28, 1853; resided in Lowell, Vt.

[Seventh Generation.] Children:

3028. i. LOUISA MARIA SANBORN, b. June 1, 1834, m. Dec. 5, 1855, William C. Lyman; reside in Michigan.

3029. ii. SULLIVAN HUTCHINS SANBORN, b. Nov. 5, 1835, d. Dec. 1869.

3030. iii. MOODY EVANDER SANBORN, b. Oct. 16, 1837, m. June 11, 1872, Sarah Scott; reside at Eden, Vt.

3031. iv. AMANDA MATILDA SANBORN, b. Aug. 17, 1839, d. 1844.

3032. v. CHARLES B. SANBORN, b. Aug. 5, 1841, m. Aug. 7, 1867, Ann M. Shannon; reside in Winchester, Mass.

3033. vi. LANSON O. SANBORN, b. Oct. 5, 1843, m. Nov. 10, 1870, Inez A. Morse; reside in Lowell, Vt.

3034. vii. FRANKLIN HENRY SANBORN, b. Nov. 8, 1845, m. May 13, 1865, Ellen Ricker; reside in Lowell, Vt.

3035. viii. ADELAIDE VICTORIA SANBORN, b. Aug. 22, 1847, d. Oct. 9, 1867.

3036. ix. MADELON SANBORN, b. July 12, 1850, m. Dec. 7, 1865, John Meares; reside in Manchester, N. H.

[Sixth Generation.]

3002. ix. EDMOND SANBORN, fourth son and ninth child of Mary Child and Ebenezer Sanborn, b. April 16, 1812, m. Mch. 15, 1835, Harriet Rand White, who was b. Feb. 28, 1821. Reside in Texas.

[Seventh Generation.] Children:

3037. i. REBECCA NEWELL SANBORN, b. Dec. 15, 1835, married twice—1st, Jan. 1, 1856, Darwin Squires, who d. April 2, 1859; m. 2d, April 26, 1860, William Jaquis; reside in Colton, N. Y.

3038. ii CHARLES C. SANBORN, b. Dec. 10, 1837, m. June 5, 1865, Elizabeth Leonard; reside in Texas.

3039. iii. SARAH JANE SANBORN, b. Jan. 11, 1840, m. Oct. 20, 1859, Royal B. Squires; reside in Minnesota.

3040. iv. HENRY BRADLEY SANBORN, b. Sept. 10, 1845, m. Feb. 20, 1867, Ellen M. Wheeler; reside in Texas.

3041. v. HATTIE A. SANBORN, b. Jan. 1, 1859.

[Sixth Generation.]

3003. x. MARTHA SANBORN, sixth dau. and tenth child of Mary Child and Ebenezer Sanborn, b. May 28, 1814, m. Mch. 22, 1832, William Williams, who was b. Feb. 5, 1803. Of

C 1

the large family given to Mr. and Mrs. Williams eight have
attained maturity, and entered upon successful business
careers. Five are engaged in mercantile pursuits in Providence, R. I., two in business in Chicago, Ill. One dau. only is
living, married to a farmer in easy circumstances, and resides
near her parents, whose home is in South Troy, Vt. To Mrs.
Williams we are much indebted for her kindly aid in obtaining such statistics as we have of her brothers, and sisters and
their families.

[Seventh Generation.] Children:

3042. i. EFFINGHAM HOWARD WILLIAMS, b. June 9, 1834, m. March 28
1859, Thirza Jane Harris; reside in Providence, R. I.

3043. ii. ELIZA JANE WILLIAMS, b. Oct. 21, 1836, m. July 7, 1859, Horace
Freeman Bartlett; reside in Newport, Vt.

3044. iii. MARCELLUS DOW WILLIAMS, b. Dec. 8, 1838, m. June 7, 1870,
Hattie Jane Thompson; reside in Providence, R. I.

3045. iv. MARTHA ANN WILLIAMS, b. Sept. 8, 1840, m. March 28, 1858,
Darius Loring Hildreth. Mrs. M. A. Williams Hildreth d. in 1862 in
Newport, Vt.

3046. v. WILLIAM HARVEY WILLIAMS, b. Jan. 27, 1844, m. Sept. 25, 1869,
Abby Jane Gilpin, reside in Providence, R. I.

3047. vi. MARK BYRON WILLIAMS, b. Feb. 27, 1846, d. 1852.

3048. vii. EUGENE LOREN WILLIAMS, b. Aug. 22, 1848, m. Oct. 31, 1875,
Lucia Durell; reside in Providence, R. I.

3049. viii. OSCAR BURTON WILLIAMS, b. Sept. 14, 1851, m. May 12, 1878,
Minnie Jane Mills; reside in Providence, R. I.

3050. ix. IDA WILLIAMS, b. July 2, 1853, d. 1854.

3051. x. DON FERNANDO WILLIAMS, b. June 11, 1855; resides in Chicago, Ill.

3052. xi. CORTEZ ELMER WILLIAMS, b. May 30, 1859; resides in Chicago, Ill.

[Fifth Generation.]

2693. vi. ABIGAIL CHILD, fourth dau. and sixth child of
Richard and Abigail Green Child. b. in Thompson, Ct., July
6, 1771, m. in Strafford, Vt., Nov. 27, 1794, Samuel West,
who was b. Sept. 17, 1768. Mrs. Abigail Child West, possessed of the best qualities of head and heart, brought up
her large family to respect goodness and aim for its attainment,
to cultivate and care for mind and body as sure and certain
avenues to upright lives. A grandson, Mr. George E. West,
writes :

"My grandmother died 24 years ago, in my father's family, when I was
only 16 years of age, but I remember her very distinctly as a woman of
sterling worth, who could repeat from memory more passages of Scripture
and Watts' Hymns, than any other person I ever knew. I greatly revere

her memory, and for me to collate these records of her posterity has been indeed 'a labor of love.'"

Mr. Samuel West died Nov. 20, 1855, æ. 87. Mrs. Abigail Child West died Nov. 9, 1856, æ. 85. "Her children arise up, and call her blessed."—Prov. 31. 28. From the Vermont *Chronicle* we make the following extracts, as illustrating the public estimate of Mr. and Mrs. West. The dates of their deaths we have previously given, so will omit the statistical portion of these obituary notices; only premising that the deaths occurred almost exactly one year apart:

"Mr. West was born in Concord, N. H. When quite young his parents removed to Strafford, Vt., where, and in Bath, N. H., he resided until 1827 when he removed to Troy, Vt. He was a worthy member of the Congregational church, exemplary and punctual in all the duties both of a christian and a citizen, beloved and respected by all who knew him, and has at last, full of years, left the congregation of the church militant on earth to join, as we humbly hope, the assembly of the church triumphant in heaven." Of Mrs. West it is said: "She resided most of her life in Bath, N. H., and Troy, Vt. In early life she united with the Congregational church, of which she has been a consistent member, and died as she had lived in the faith and hope of the gospel."

[Sixth Generation.] Children:

3053. i. RICHARD CHILD WEST, b. May 29, 1795, m. July 29, 1822, Sarah Dickerson.

3054. ii. JONATHAN WEST, b. Jan. 26, 1797, m. Oct. 31, 1824, Sarah Lawrence.

3055. iii. TIMOTHY WEST, b. Oct. 28, 1798, m. March 28, 1830, Mary Gordon.

3056. iv. SAMUEL WEST, JR., b. Nov. 30, 1800, m. Feb. 21, 1828, Miss Thomas.

3057. v. ABIEL WEST, b. Nov. 13, 1802, m. 1st, Jan. 7, 1838, Sophia Ann Platt; m. 2d, Sept. 20, 1846, Louisa Ashley.

3058. vi. HARRY LOVEJOY WEST, b. May 3, 1805, m. 1st, April 7, 1827, Phœbe Dickerson; m. 2d, Oct. 8, 1851, —— ——.

3059. vii. ERASTUS WEST, b. July 17, 1807, m. Dec. 3, 1855, Maria Marsh; resides in N. Troy, Vt.

3060. viii. DUDLEY WEST, b. Oct. 15, 1809, m. Jan. 1, 1839, Mary E. Powers.

3061. ix. HANNAH WEST, b. Feb. 18, 1812, m. Feb. 24, 1856, Edward Stevens; reside in Troy, Vt.

3062. x. THERON WEST, b. Aug. 28, 1814, in Bath, N. H., d. Feb. 25, 1815, æ. 5 mo., 27 d.

3063. xi. THERON WEST, 2d, b. Aug. 15, 1816, in Bath, N. H., d. April 16, 1829, in Troy, Vt., æ. 12 y. 8 mo. 1 d.

[Sixth Generation.]

3053. i. RICHARD CHILD WEST, eldest son and child of Abigail Child and Samuel West, b. in Strafford, Vt., May 29,

1795, m. July 29, 1822, Sarah Dickerson.   He d. in 1857,
æ. 62, at Painted Post, Steuben Co., N. Y.

[Seventh Generation.]   Children:
    3064. i. CHARLES FRANCIS WEST, b. Dec. 20, 1822.
    3065. ii. RICHARD HENRY WEST, b. Jan. 9, 1825, d. July 1, 1830.
    3066. iii. JOHN WATSON WEST, b. Feb. 17, 1827, d. Aug. 13, 1828.
    3067. iv. AMANDA ROSE WEST, b. June 18, 1829.
    3068. v. HENRIETTA WEST, b. April 1832, d. 1851.
    3069. vi. MARY CAROLINE WEST.

[Sixth Generation.]

    3054. ii. JONATHAN WEST, second son and child of Abigail
Child and Samuel West, b. in Strafford, Vt., Jan. 26, 1797, m.
Oct. 31, 1824, Sarah Lawrence.   He d. Mch. 19, 1876, æ. 79,
at Port Jervis, Orange Co., N. Y.

[Seventh Generation.]   Children:
    3070. i. WILLIAM LAWRENCE WEST, b. Oct. 5, 1825.
    3071. ii. ALBERT SAMUEL WEST, b. Feb. 25, 1827.
    3072. iii. GEORGE CLINTON WEST, b. Sept. 18, 1828.
    3073. iv. HENRY FARNUM WEST, b. Sept. 18, 1830.
    3074. v. SARAH ABIGAIL WEST,   b. Feb. 19, 1832.
                                 Twins.
    3075. vi. MARY CAROLINE WEST, b. Feb. 19, 1832, d. æ. 2 w., 2 i.
    3076. vii. ANN MARIA WEST, b. Nov. 14, 1834.
    3077. viii. DUDLEY FRANCIS WEST, b. 1838.
    3078. ix. JOHN CHILD WEST, b. Dec. 28, 1839.

[Sixth Generation.]

    3055. iii. TIMOTHY WEST, third son and child of Abigail
Child and Samuel West, b. in Strafford, Vt., Oct. 28, 1798, m.
Mch. 28, 1830, Mary Gordon.   He d. Mch. 8, 1875, æ. 76 yrs.,
4 mos. 10 d., at South Hadley Falls, Mass.

[Seventh Generation.]   Children:
    3079. i. SAMUEL CURTIS WEST, b. March 25, 1831, d. March 13, 1867.
    3080. ii. MARY LUCRETIA WEST, b. Nov. 21, 1832.
    3081. iii. PHŒBE JANE WEST, b. Jan. 7, 1834, d. Dec. 27, 1836.
    3082. iv. WILLIAM EDWIN WEST, b. May 26, 1835.
    3083. v. SOPHIA ANN WEST, b. May 10, 1837.
    3084. vi. DAVID BARD WEST, b. Jan. 24, 1839.
    3085. vii. CHARLES HENRY WEST, b. Oct. 2, 1841.
    3086. viii. ABBY JANE WEST, b. June 13, 1843.
    3087. ix. RUBY EMELINE WEST, b. March 7, 1847, d. Oct. 3, 1873.

[Sixth Generation.]

    3056. iv. SAMUEL WEST, JR., fourth son and child of Abigail
Child and Samuel West, b. in Strafford, Vt., Nov. 30, 1800, m.
Feb. 21, 1828, Miss Thomas; residence Lumberland, N. Y.

[Seventh Generation.] Children:

3088. i. OSCAR THOMAS WEST, b. Dec. 11, 1828.

3089. ii. JAMES WEST, b. May 11, 1830, d. Nov. 25, 1840.

3090. iii. ALMIRA WEST, b. Feb. 16, 1832.

3091. iv. MARY CAROLINE WEST, b. 1834, d. Jan. 18, 1837, æ. 3 years.

3092. v. SARAH MATILDA WEST, b. Oct. 1835.

3093. vi. HARLAN PAGE WEST, b. April 13, 1839.

3094. vii. PHŒBE MARIA WEST, b. May 11, 1841, d. Dec. 29, 1841.

3095. viii. MARIETTA WEST, b. Nov. 13, 1843.

3096. ix. THEODORE WEST, b. Aug. 12, 1845.

[Sixth Generation.]

3057. v. ABIEL WEST, fifth son and child of Abigail Child and Samuel West, b. Nov. 13, 1802, in Strafford, Vt., married twice—1st, Jan. 7, 1838, Sophia Ann Platt; m. 2d, Sept. 20, 1846, Louisa Ashley. Mr. Abiel West d. Oct. 12, 1878, æ. 75 years, 10 months 29 days, at Glens Falls, Warren Co., N.Y.

[Seventh Generation.] Children:

3097. i. SARAH JANE WEST, b. Oct. 22, 1838, d. Nov. 7, 1839.

3098. ii. CHARLES HENRY WEST, b. Sept. 8, 1840, d. Oct. 1841.

Children by second wife:

3099. iii. GEORGE HENRY WEST, b. July 1, 1847.

3100. iv. CHANDLER ABIEL WEST, b. Aug. 5, 1849.

3101. v. NANCY ABIGAIL WEST, b. Jan. 1, 1852.

[Sixth Generation.]

3058. iv. HARRY LOVEJOY WEST, sixth son and child of Abigail Child and Samuel West, b. in Bath, Grafton Co., N. H., May 3, 1805, m. twice—1st, April 7, 1827, Phœbe Dickerson; m. 2d, Oct. 8, 1851. He d. March 31, 1868, aged 62 years, 9 months, 28 days, at Sparrowbush, Orange Co., N. Y.

[Seventh Generation.] Children:

3102. i. MARIETTA WEST, b. Nov. 21, 1827.

3103. ii. HANNAH WEST, b. June 28, 1829.

3104. iii. FREDERICK AUGUSTUS WEST, b. June 2, 1831.

3105. iv. ADALINE WEST.

3106. v. ADALINE AUGUSTA WEST, b. Aug. 25, 1836.

3107. vi. GEORGE WEST, b. July 30, 1839.

3108. vii. MARTHA JANE WEST, b. Feb. 4, 1842.

3109. viii. DELIA ANN WEST, b. Sept. 11, 1845.

[Sixth Generation.]

3060. viii. DUDLEY WEST, eighth son and child of Abigail Child and Samuel West, b. in Bath, Grafton Co., N. H., Oct. 15, 1809, m. Jan. 1, 1839, Mary E. Powers. He d. Dec. 22, 1862, aged 53 years, 2 months, 7 days, in Bath, N. H.

[Seventh Generation.] Children:

3110. i. GEORGE EDWIN WEST, b. Oct. 24, 1839. [To whom we are indebted for the record of the West family.]

3111. ii. Augustus Dudley West, b. July 13, 1841, d. May 16, 1869.
3112. iii. Dwight Lang West, b. Mch. 27, 1843.
3113. iv. Sarah Jane West, b. Feb. 25, 1845.
3114. v. Henry Green West, b. Sept. 11, 1846, d. Mch. 2, 1871.
3115. vi. Luvia Sabrina West, b. Jan. 6, 1849, d. Jan. 13, 1861.

[Fifth Generation.]

2694. vii. Rosa Anna Child, fifth dau. and seventh child of Richard and Abigail Green Child, b. Jan. 2, 1774, m. in Thompson, Windham Co., Ct., Jan. 1, 1794, Samuel Hutchins Mr. Hutchins was b. in Haverhill, Mass., in 1769. He combined mercantile and agricultural pursuits with large success, and was yet farther enriched with the patriarchal complement of children. Mr. Hutchins d. in Bath, N. H., in 1830. Mrs. Hutchins surviving him some fourteen years, d. July 10, 1844, at the age of seventy.

[Sixth Generation.]   Children:

3116. i. Hannah Hutchins, b. Sept. 29, 1794, m. May 9, 1812, Ira Goodall.
3117. ii. Ezra C. Hutchins, b. April 10, 1796, m. Feb. 7, 1821, Augusta A. F. Sinclair.
3118. iii. Samuel Hutchins, Jr., b. Dec. 26, 1797, m. 1st, Mch. 29, 1829, Martha Rix; m. 2d, Aug. 1841, Rebecca Moore.
3119. iv. Lucretia Hutchins, b. Sept. 8, 1799, m. Oct. 1819, Gen. John Wilson.
3120. v. Persis Hutchins, b. July 16, 1801, m. May 1823, John Hurd.
3121. vi. Rosanna Hutchins, b. Jan. 26, 1803, m. Luther Foote.
3122. vii. Chester C. Hutchins, b. July 6, 1805, m. Feb. 12, 1835, Jane Swan.
3123. viii. Moses P. Hutchins, b. June 8, 1808, m. 1st, Jane Johnstone; m. 2d, Eliza Morris; m. 3d, Jane Grey.
3124. ix. Horace G. Hutchins, b. July 20, 1811, m. Oct. 22, 1844, Julia Hurd.
3125. x. Martha Hutchins, b. Dec. 15, 1813, d. June 17, 1815.
3126. xi. Martha S. Hutchins, b. Mch. 1817, m. 1840, Warren D. Gookin.
3127. xii. Henry C. Hutchins, b. Aug. 1, 1820, m. Oct. 9, 1845, Mary L. Groat.

[Sixth Generation.]

3116 i. Hannah Hutchins, eldest child of Rosanna Child and Samuel Hutchins, b. in Bath, N. H., Sept. 29, 1794, m. May 9, 1812, Hon. Ira Goodall, Esq., of Bath, N. H.; a lawyer of mark in the State. Mrs. Hannah H. Goodall d. June 3, 1872, in West Philadelphia, Pa. Esq. Goodall d. Mch. 3, 1868, in Madison, Wis.

[Seventh Generation.] Children:

3128. i. DAVID G. GOODALL, b. Mch. 19, 1813, m. June 29, 1835, Maria D. French. Mr. Goodall was first resident in Lisbon, N. H., as a merchant; since removed to Beloit, Wis.

3129. ii. HANNAH C. GOODALL, b. Dec. 17, 1814.

3130. iii. LUCRETIA W. GOODALL, b. Feb. 9, 1817, m. July 1840, John L. Carleton, a lawyer of Bath, N. H.

3131. iv. ELLEN B. GOODALL, b. Nov. 27, 1818, m. Dec. 3, 1845, John H. French.

3132. v. IRA E. GOODALL, b. June 25, 1820, m. Sept. 26, 1842, Mary French.

3133. vi. SAMUEL H. GOODALL, b. Mch. 31, 1823, m. 1st, May 1850; m. 2d, Sept. 26, 1867, E. P. Nelson.

3134. vii. HORACE H. GOODALL, b. Mch. 20, 1826, d. Aug. 21, 1827.

3135. viii. HORACE H. GOODALL, b. Mch. 21, 1828, d. Aug. 23, 1829.

3136. ix. JANE E. GOODALL, b. June 17, 1830, m. Dec. 13, 1854, Thomas P. Sargent.

3137. x. JULIA R. GOODALL, b. April 14, 1833, m. Nov. 2, 1853, Alonzo P. Carpenter, Esq.; lawyer in Bath, N. H.

3138. xi. EDWARD B. GOODALL, } m. Mch. 5, 1863, Louise Bartlett.
 Twins b. Jan. 10, 1838.
3139. xii. FRANCIS H. GOODALL, } m. Aug. 24, 1865, Ophelia P. Brewer.

[Edward B. Goodall is a dentist of Portsmouth, N. H. Francis H. Goodall a lawyer, and clerk in Second Auditor's Office, Treasury Department, Washington, D. C.]

[Fifth Generation.]

2695. viii. Dea. DUDLEY CHILD, third son and eighth child of Richard and Abigail Green Child, b. in Thompson, Windham Co., Ct., May 22, 1776, m. 1st, April 24, 1800, Molly Weeks, who was b. Nov. 12, 1778, d. in 1831. Dea. Child m. 2d, Sept. 1832, Mrs. Nancy Child, widow of Elisha Child, of Exeter, Otsego Co., N. Y., and dau of Capt. Willard Child, of Woodstock, Ct.

Dea Dudley Child removed when quite a young man to Bath, N. H., sharing with his brother, Capt John Child, and his brother-in-law, Mr. Ezra Child, the privations incident to the settlement of a new country. These three families formed a nucleus around which a neighborhood of industrious, hardy and sober people gathered; laying the foundations of a prosperous community which grew rapidly in numbers and importance. When the religious element was embodied in a Congregational church, Dea. Child was early chosen an office-bearer, and served in the capacity of deacon with efficiency till his death. The Scotch element was a noticeable feature in the order and theological phase of this community, having been thus moulded by the Rev. Mr. Sutherland, a Scotch Presbyterian, whose impress remained upon this people long after the stern old divine had entered into his reward. Dea. Dudley Child died May 22, 1846. Mrs. Nancy (Child) Child died March 23, 1850. Her children were of her first marriage, Dea. Dudley's children of his union with Mrs. M. W. Child.

[Sixth Generation.] Children:

3140. i. CHARITY CHILD, b. April 11, 1801, d. Oct. 8, 1807, in Bath, N. H.

3141. ii. THEODOSIA CHILD, b. Sept. 17, 1802, m. Sept. 23, 1824, Stephen N. Bartlett.

3142. iii. DAVID CHILD, b. Mch. 29, 1805, m. Mch. 22, 1827, Charlotte Moulton.

3143. iv. LUTHERA CHILD, b. Oct. 25, 1806, m. May 6, 1827, Amos K. Heath.

3144. v. MOLLY CHILD, b. Feb. 7, 1809, d. Mch. 31, 1812.

3145. vi. DUDLEY CHILD, b. Oct. 21, 1810, d. Aug. 21, 1814.

3146. vii. WILLARD CHILD, b. Aug. 23, 1812, d. Jan. 23, 1813.

3147. viii. RICHARD CHILD, b. Feb. 20, 1814, m. Sept. 1, 1839, Adaline Smith.

3148. ix. MARY CHILD, b. Mch. 13, 1816, m. Jan. 25, 1838, Smith Moulton.

3149. x. DUDLEY CHILD, 2D, b. Mch. 27, 1819, m. Dec. 22, 1842, Hannah Hibbard.

3150. xi. JONATHAN CHILD, b. Feb. 10, 1821, m. Mch. 4, 1846, Martha N. Walker.

3151. xii. WILLARD CHILD, 2D, b. Nov. 19, 1823, d. Dec. 15, 1857, at Grinnell, Iowa.

[Sixth Generation.]

3141. ii. THEODOSIA CHILD, second dau. and child of Dea. Dudley and Mary Weeks Child, b. in Bath, N. H., Sept. 17, 1802, m. Sept. 23, 1824, Stephen N. Bartlett, by the Rev. David Sutherland. Mr. Stephen N. Bartlett is the son of Amos and Eunice K. Noyes Bartlett, of Bath, N. H. Mr. and Mrs. Stephen N. Bartlett removed to Grinnell, Iowa, in May 1855, with their family of five children, where he died 1880.

[Seventh Generation.] Children:

3152. i. ELIZA ANN BARTLETT, b. in Bath, N. H., Sept. 18, 1828, d. Oct. 27, 1864, in Grinnell, Iowa.

3153. ii. EMERY S. BARTLETT, b. in Bath, N. H., Sept. 7, 1832.

3154. iii. MOSES W. BARTLETT, b. in Bath, N. H., Feb. 26, 1834.

3155. iv. STANLEY M. BARTLETT, b. in Bath, N. H., Dec. 4, 1836.

3156. v. PHILOMELA M. BARTLETT, b. in Bath, N. H., July 23, 1839.

[Sixth Generation.]

3142. iii. DAVID CHILD, eldest son and third child of Dea. Dudley and Mary Weeks Child, b. in Bath, N. H., Mch. 29, 1805, m. Mch. 22, 1827, Charlotte Moulton, who was b. Mch. 13, 1811: is a dau. of John and Mary Moulton, of Lyman, N. H.

Mr. David Child as the elder son of a pioneer, made early acquaintance with the hardships inevitable in a new country. His surroundings, however, were not unfavorable to the development of sturdy and manly qualities, suited to fit him for a respected and useful citizenship in the town of his birth. His education was such as the town schools of that period afforded, and quite sufficient to awaken him to the full value and appreciation of good scholarship. His marriage to a worthy daughter of honorable parentage was the beginning of a new era and an added stimulus to his efforts in the life struggle. His industry and economy enabled him not only to gain a competence for himself and his growing family, but to accumulate a handsome property. In the spirit of enterprise, inherent and fostered, he left his native hills, with the honoring good-will of his townsmen, and settled in Nevada, Story Co., Iowa. Surrounded by a goodly family of sons and daughters, he expects here to spend the evening of life, trusting the honest toil of the morning will gild the sun-setting.

[Seventh Generation.] Children:

3157. i. CHESTER CHILD, b. in Bath, N. H., July 24, 1828, m. Dec. 25, 1858, Margaret A. Daley, dau. of Wilson and Margaret Daley, of Nevada, Iowa. Mr. Chester child d. at Nevada, Iowa, Oct. 24, 1867.

3158. ii. CHARITY CHILD, b. in Bath, N. H., Sept. 1830, m. Feb. 1, 1852, Theodore Lawrence, of Saratoga, N. Y.

3159. iii. GEORGE CHILD, b. Dec. 15, 1832, m. Oct. 9, 1853, Lavina Hall.

3160. iv. ELIZA CHILD, b. April 3, 1835, m. Feb. 19, 1825, S. S. Webb.

3161. v. SMITH M. CHILD, b. Oct. 5, 1836, m. June 10 1867, Rachel L. Trumbull.

3162. vi. LE ROY CHILD, b. Oct. 1, 1838, m. Dec. 27, 1864, Lida J. Heizer.

3163. vii. SAMUEL M. CHILD, b. June 27, 1840, m. June 1867, Mary E. Harding.

[Seventh Generation.]

3158. ii. CHARITY CHILD, eldest dau. and second child of David and Charlotte Moulton Child, b. in Bath, N. H., Sept. 1830, m. Feb. 1, 1852. Theodore Lawrence, of Saratoga, N. Y. Mr. and Mrs. Lawrence reside in Peoria, Ill.

[Eighth Generation.] Children:

3164. i. ALBERT LAWRENCE, b. at Peoria, Ill., June 2, 1853, d. Jan. 17, 1854.

3165. ii. HATTIE LAWRENCE, b. at Peoria, Ill., Feb. 2, 1855, unm.

3166. iii. ALVAH LAWRENCE, b. at Peoria, Ill., June 16, 1857, unm.

3167. iv. MAY CHARLOTTE LAWRENCE, b. at Peoria, Ill., May 2, 1860, unm.

3168. v. LUELLA LAWRENCE, b. at Peoria, Ill., Sept. 1, 1862, unm.

3169. vi. CORA LAWRENCE, b. at Peoria, Ill., July 2, 1865, d. Oct. 9, 1866.
3170. vii. IDA ELIZABETH LAWRENCE, b. in Peoria, Ill., Jan. 3, 1868.
3171. viii. DAVID C. LAWRENCE, b. in Peoria, Ill., July 9, 1870, d. Oct. 26, 1873.
3172. ix. WALTER CHESTER LAWRENCE, b. in Peoria, Ill., Jan. 2, 1876.

[Seventh Generation.]

3159. iii. GEORGE CHILD, second son and third child of David and Charlotte Moulton Child, b. in Bath, N. H., Dec. 15, 1832, m. Oct. 9, 1853, Lavina Hall, dau. of Alba and Elizabeth Hall, of Hanover, N. H. She was b. April 14, 1833.

[Eighth Generation.]　Children:
3173. i. FANNY CHILD, b. in Nevada, Iowa, Jan. 27, 1857, d. July 26, 1858.
3174. ii. HATTIE C. CHILD, b. in Nevada, Iowa, Oct. 6, 1859.
3175. iii. WILLIE W. CHILD, b. in Nevada, Iowa, Jan. 7, 1862.
3176. iv. GEORGE C. CHILD, b. in Nevada, Iowa, Sept. 2, 1864.
3177. v. HARRY F. CHILD, b. in Nevada, Iowa, Oct. 3, 1868.
3178. vi. BURT B. CHILD, b. in Nevada, Iowa, Feb. 2, 1871.
3179. vii. MARY E. CHILD, b. in Nevada, Iowa, Sept. 18, 1875.
3180. viii. FREDDIE E. CHILD, b. in Nevada, Iowa, Dec. 22, 1877.

[Seventh Generation.]

3160. iv. ELIZA CHILD, second dau. and fourth child of David and Charlotte Moulton Child, b. in Bath, N. H., April 3, 1835, m. Feb. 1, 1852, S. S. Webb, who was b. Aug. 15, 1824, in Charlestown, Mass. Mr. and Mrs. Webb reside at Boone, Iowa.

[Eighth Generation.]　Children:
3181. i. CHARLES P. WEBB, b. at Nevada, Iowa, June 19, 1857.
3182. ii ETTA P. WEBB, b. at Nevada, Iowa, May 6, 1861.

[Seventh Generation.]

3161. v. SMITH M. CHILD, third son and fifth child of David and Charlotte Moulton Child, b. in Bath, N. H., Oct. 5, 1836, m. June 10, 1867, Rachel L. Trumbull. Mr. and Mrs. Smith M. Child reside at Dunlap, Iowa.

[Eighth Generation.]　Children:
3183. i. CHARLOTTE M. CHILD, b. at Dunlap, Iowa, May 8, 1868, d. Oct. 23, 1870.
3184. ii. SAMUEL T. CHILD, b. at Dunlap, Iowa, Oct. 13, 1871, d. Oct. 19, 1871.
3185. iii. EDWARD A. CHILD, b. at Dunlap, Iowa, Mch. 9, 1873.
3186. iv. DAVID B. CHILD, b. at Dunlap, Iowa, June 1, 1875.

[Seventh Generation.]

3162. vi. LE ROY CHILD, fourth son and sixth child of David and Charlotte Moulton Child, b. in Bath, N. H., Dec. 17, 1838, m. Dec. 27, 1864, Lida J. Heizer, dau. of Mathew and Mary Heizer, of Indianapolis, Indiana. She was b. June 1, 1846. Mr. and Mrs. Le Roy Child reside in Indianapolis, Indiana.

[Eighth Generation.] Children:

3187. i. JESSE CHILD, b. Sept. 28, 1865, at Nevada, Iowa.

3188. ii. PEARL CHILD, b. Mch. 6, 1873, at Indianapolis, Ind.

3189. iii. FRED CHILD, b. June 20, 1875, at Indianapolis, Ind.

[Seventh Generation.]

3163. vii. SAMUEL M. CHILD, fifth son and seventh child of David and Charlotte Moulton Child, b. in Bath, N. H., Jan. 27, 1840, m. June 1867, Mary E. Harding, who was b. July 2, 1846. Mr. and Mrs. S. M. Child reside in Atlantic, Iowa.

[Eighth Generation.] Children:

3190. i. LULU CHILD, b. May 5, 1869, at Atlantic, Iowa.

3191. ii. CHARLIE C. CHILD, b. July 19, 1871, at Atlantic, Iowa.

3192. iii. LIZZIE H. CHILD, b. Aug. 15, 1873, at Atlantic, Iowa.

3193. iv. GERTIE CHILD, b. Nov. 23, 1875, at Atlantic, Iowa.

[Sixth Generation.]

3143. iv. LUTHERA CHILD, fourth child and third dau. of Dea. Dudley and Mary Weeks Child b. in Bath, N. H., Oct. 25, 1806, m. May 6, 1827, Amos K. Heath, who was b. Sept. 30, 1800.

[Seventh Generation.] Children:

3194. i. JOSEPH HEATH, b. Feb. 26, 1828, m. abt. 1859, Anna Karney.

3195. ii. DUDLEY CHILD HEATH, b. March 11, 1830.

3196. iii. MARY C. HEATH, b. Aug. 23, 1832.

3197. iv. ABNER F. HEATH, b. March 2, 1835, m. April 17, 1869, Susan Page.

3198. v. SOPHIA T. HEATH, b. Dec. 11, 1837, m. Henry O. Sargent.

3199. vi. EVERETT K. HEATH, b. April 23, 1840, m. June 6, 1872, Ella Gould.

3200. vii. WILLIAM W. HEATH, b Sept. 3, 1842, d. May 5, 1864.

3201. viii. HENRY K. HEATH, b. Jan. 30, 1845, m. March 17, 1868, Sarah Scales.

3202. ix. WILLARD C. HEATH, b. May 23, 1846, m. June 6, 1872, Anna Gould.

3203. x. EDWARD K. HEATH, b. June 17, 1849.

[Seventh Generation.]

3194. i. JOSEPH HEATH, eldest child of Luthera Child and Amos K. Heath, b. Feb. 26, 1828, m. abt. 1859, Anna Karney of Melbourne, Australia.

[Eighth Generation.] Children:

3204. i. AMOS K. HEATH, b. 1860.

3205. ii. JOSEPH HEATH, b. 1869.

[Seventh Generation.]

3199. vi. EVERETT K. HEATH, fourth son and sixth child of Luthera Child and Amos K. Heath, b. April 23, 1840. m. June 6, 1872, Ella Gould.

[Eighth Generation.] Child:

3206. i. WILLIAM W. HEATH, b. Jan. 20, 1873.

[Seventh Generation.]

3201. viii. HENRY K. HEATH, sixth son and eighth child of Luthera Child and Amos K. Heath, b. Jan. 30, 1845, m. Mch. 17, 1872, Sarah Scales.

[Eighth Generation.] Child:

3207. i. NELLIE S. HEATH, b. Sept. 4, 1872, d. Aug. 3, 1876.

[Sixth Generation.]

3147. viii. RICHARD CHILD, fourth son and eighth child of Dea. Dudley and Mary Weeks Child, b. in Bath, N. H., Feb. 20, 1814, m., by Rev. Mr. Nichols, Sept. 1, 1839, Miss Adaline Smith, who was b. Sept. 29, 1816, and is a dau. of Reuben and Lydia Hill Smith, of Lyman, N. H. Mr. Richard Child, one of the younger sons of Dea. Dudley Child spent the earlier part of his life in his native town. His struggles with the difficulties of life have thoroughly taxed his nerve and courage, but possessing an earnestly industrious temperament, he has not known want. Hoping to win more readily the smiles of fortune, Mr. Child removed with his family, in 1868, to Nevada, Story Co., Iowa, where ampler fields awaited cultivation with less severe tax upon all the vital energies, and better opportunities offered for the advancement of his children.

[Seventh Generation.] Children:

3208. i. EXCELLENCE AUGUSTA CHILD, b. April 24, 1841, m. Jan. 14, 1863, by Rev. Dudley Kimball to Ephraim Page Colby. Removed to Iowa in October 1871.

3209. ii. LYDIA ANN CHILD, b. Mch. 19, 1843, m. April 6, 1870, Joseph Bellamore.

3210. iii. MARY ARVILLA CHILD, b. Aug. 25, 1845, m. Feb. 2, 1868, by Rev. Mr. Hurd, in Indian Town, Iowa, to Abel Ruggles.

3211. iv. NANCY MARIA CHILD, b. July 28, 1847, m. Nov. 1, 1872, Albert Coffin.

3212. v. DUDLEY RICHARD CHILD, b. Jan. 17, 1849, d. Aug. 5, 1853.

3213. vi. EMILY ASENATH CHILD, b. Feb. 2, 1852, m. April 5, 1870, John P Willson.

3214. vii. REUBEN LE ROY CHILD, b. Oct. 29, 1853, m. Dec. 25, 1876, Lucy Crippen.

3215. viii. Infant—unchristened—b. Sept. 29, 1855, d. same day.

3216. ix. Infant—unchristened—b. Oct. 10, 1857, d. same day.

[Seventh Generation.]

3209. ii. LYDIA ANN CHILD, second dau. and child of Richard and Adaline Smith Child, b. in Bath, N. H.. Mch. 19, 1843. m. in Indian Town, Iowa, by Rev. Mr. Hurd, April 6, 1870, Joseph Bellamore.

[Eighth Generation.] Child:

    3217. i. ALBERT HENRY BELLAMORE. b. Oct. 31, 1874.

[Seventh Generation.]

3211. iv. NANCY MARIA CHILD, fourth dau. and child of Richard and Adaline Smith Child, b. in Bath, N. H., July 28, 1847. m. in Nevada, Story Co., Iowa, by Rev. Mr. Thompson. Nov. 1, 1872, Albert Coffin.

[Eighth Generation.] Children:

    3218. i. ALBERT R. COFFIN. b. Dec. 19, 1874.

    3219. ii. MARY ADALINE COFFIN, b. Nov. 1, 1876.

[Seventh Generation.]

3213. vi. EMILY ASENATH CHILD. fifth dau. and sixth child of Richard and Adaline Smith Child, b. in Bath, N. H.. Feb. 2, 1852. m. in Nevada, Iowa, by Rev. Mr. Williams. April 5, 1870, John P. Willson.

[Eighth Generation.] Children:

    3220. i. ADALINE ALMIRA WILLSON, b. Oct. 9, 1872

    3221. ii. MARY ELLA WILLSON, b. Sept. 1, 1874.

    3222. iii. ELIZABETH LIVINGSTON WILLSON, b. Sept. 25, 1876.

    3223. iv. RICHARD AUGUSTUS WILLSON, b. Aug. 21, 1877.

[Seventh Generation.]

3214. vii. REUBEN LE ROY CHILD. second son and seventh child of Richard and Adaline Smith Child, b. in Bath, N. H., Oct. 29, 1853. m. in Nevada, Iowa, by Rev. Mr. Reed, Dec. 25, 1876, Lucy Crippin.

[Eighth Generation.] Child:

    3224. i. EDGAR R. CHILD, b. Jan. 6, 1878.

[Sixth Generation.]

3148. ix. MARY CHILD, fifth dau. and ninth child of Dea. Dudley and Mary Weeks Child, b. in Bath. Grafton Co.. N. H., Mch. 13, 1816. m. Jan. 25, 1838. Smith Moulton.

[Seventh Generation.] Children:

    3225 i. GILLESPIE MOULTON, b. Oct. 11, 1838, d. Sept. 20, 1839

    3226. ii. CHARITY S. MOULTON, b. April 30, 1840, m. Feb. 12, 1861, R. Manson Ash.

    3227. iii. JULIA E. MOULTON, b. June 3, 1842, m. Dec. 4, 1872, James L. Cutting.

    3228. iv. MARY L. MOULTON, b. March 11, 1844, m. March 29, 1876, Henry C. Nelson.

    3229. v. DUDLEY C. MOULTON, b. Dec. 10, 1847. m. May 26, 1870, Mary J. George.

[Seventh Generation.]

3226. ii. CHARITY S. MOULTON, eldest dau. and second
child of Mary Child and Smith Moulton, b. April 30, 1840, m.
Feb. 12, 1861, R. Manson Ash.

[Eighth Generation.] Children:
    3230. i. FRANK H. ASH, b. Dec. 21, 1861.
    3231. ii. CLINTON M. ASH, b. Feb. 17, 1863, d. Feb. 23, 1872.

[Seventh Generation.

3229. v. DUDLEY CHILD MOULTON, youngest son and child
of Mary Child and Smith Moulton, b. Dec. 10, 1847, m. May
26, 1870, Mary J. George.

[Eighth Generation.] Child:
    3232. i. LIZZIE A. MOULTON, b. July 12, 1871.

[Sixth Generation.]

3149. x. DUDLEY CHILD. JR., fifth son and tenth child of
Dea. Dudley and Mary Weeks Child, b. in Bath, Grafton Co.,
N. H., Mch. 27, 1819, m. Dec. 22, 1842, Hannah Hibbard, dau.
of Hon. John and Abigail Child Hibbard.

Upon his father's decease, he was installed as possessor of
the old homestead.   From an elevation of land a few rods from
his door, with a glass, one can discern the Summit House on
Mount Washington, the highest point of ascent in the White
Mountains: while the long panorama of mountains stretch out
and up their bold, rugged peaks in full view.   Mr. Dudley
Child is the only one of his father's numerous family remaining in Bath.   The fertile prairies of the West having allured
most of them to imigrate.   Mr. Child may be regarded one of
the substantial citizens of the town: a man of steady habits, an
excellent farmer, and a cordial supporter of the institutions of
learning and religion.   He and his cousins, Hons. Dwight R.
and Bradley G. Child, share almost alternately the trustee-
ship of their school district.

[Seventh Generation.] Children:
    3233. i ELLEN M. CHILD, b. Sept. 28, 1845, d. Dec. 24, 1868, in Bath, N. H.
    3234. ii. ELISHA H. CHILD, b. June 27, 1849, d. Feb. 24, 1859, in Bath,
N. H.
    3235. iii. EDWIN W. CHILD, b. May 4, 1852, in Bath, N. H.
    3236. iv. LIZZIE J. CHILD, b. Nov. 22, 1855, m. April 6, 1880, Sanborn W.
Belden, of Brooklyn, N. Y.
    3237. v. FRANKLIN L. CHILD, b. Dec. 31, 1858, in Bath, N. H.
    3238. vi JOHN HIBBARD CHILD, b. May 1, 1862, d. 1863, in Bath, N. H

[Sixth Generation.]

3150. xi. JONATHAN CHILD, sixth son and eleventh child of Dea. Dudley and Mary Weeks Child, b. in Bath, N. H., Feb. 10, 1821, m. in the same place by Rev. David Sutherland, Mch. 4, 1846, Martha Hutchins Walker, dau. of Hannah Child and Leonard Walker, of Bath. Mr. Jonathan Child, youngest but one of twelve children, came upon the stage of life after the severities of pioneer days in Bath were passed; he escaped therefore much which the elder brothers and sisters so courageously overcame. For him life opened with more of sunshine, the progress of society in matters civil and religious, rendered all its conditions easier. His natural endowments enabled him to command the respect of his fellow-citizens in his native town, while resident there, and qualified him to win equal honors and esteem when established in the western home, to which he removed in the spring of 1868. In the flourishing town of Grinnell, Iowa, Mr. Child has made for himself an honorable position. In all the ways through which he has been called to walk, he has found a true help-meet in his wife, whose honorable parentage guaranteed all which time has wrought out.

[Seventh Generation.] Children:

3239. i. CHLOE WALKER CHILD, b. Dec. 24, 1846, in Bath, N. H., a deaf mute, educated at Hartford, Conn.

3240. ii. SYLVIA HANNAH CHILD, b. Oct. 16, 1850, d. Oct. 18, 1850.

3241. iii. ALDACE WALKER CHILD, b. Jan. 11, 1852, m. Sept. 7, 1875, Alice B. Weeks.

3242. iv. ARTHUR LEON CHILD, b. Nov. 8, 1854. An artist.

3243. v. HATTIE MARTHA CHILD, b. Dec. 12, 1858, m. July 23, 1878, Walter Ford Hammond.

3244. vi. WILLIE JAMES CHILD, b. July 17, 1861, d. July 19, 1861.

[Seventh Generation.]

3241. iii. ALDACE WALKER CHILD, eldest son and third child of Jonathan and Martha H. Walker Child, b. in Bath, N. H., Jan. 11, 1852, m. Sept. 7, 1875, Alice B. Weeks; reside in Grinnell, Iowa.

[Eighth Generation.] Child:

3245. i. CLINTON CENTENNIAL CHILD, b. July 4, 1876.

[Fifth Generation.]

2696. ix. MATILDA CHILD, sixth dau. and ninth child of Richard and Abigail Green Child, b. Aug. 8, 1778, m. May 15, 1798, David Weeks, who was b. July 14, 1774. Mr. David

Weeks d. June 11, 1842. Mrs. Matilda Child Weeks d. Oct. 3, 1847. The great grandchildren of this couple now number forty-seven.

[Sixth Generation.] Children:

3246 i. LAURA WEEKS. b. May 16, 1799, unmarried.

3247. ii. JOHN CHILD WEEKS, b. Dec. 10, 1800, m. 1st, Dec. 3, 1826, Maria Powers: m. 2d, Mch. 27, 1842, Ascenath Smith.

3248. iii. MARY CHILD WEEKS, b. Dec. 25, 1802, m. Sept. 27, 1826, Martin C. Powers.

3249. iv. DUDLEY CHILD WEEKS. b. Dec. 24. 1804, m. April 20, 1853, Lucy Topliff.

3250. v. ALFRED WEEKS. b. Dec. 12, 1806, m. Jan. 2. 1835, Candace Porter.

3251. vi. JONATHAN WEEKS, b. Dec. 2, 1808, m. Dec. 10, 1840, Betsey Chamberlain.

3252. vii. MOSES MERRISON WEEKS. b. Feb. 4. 1811. m. Dec. 29, 1840. Sally Minot.

3253. viii. WILLARD CHILD WEEKS. b. April 21, 1813, m. April 20, 1853, Lestine Merrill.

3354. ix. EZRA HUTCHINS WEEKS, b. July 21. 1816, d. Sept. 1, 1846.

3255. x. EMILY WEEKS, b. July 16, 1818, m. April 14, 1842, William Minot.

3256. xi. ELIZA WEEKS. b. April 10. 1821, m. Dec. 29, 1840. George Chamberlain.

[Sixth Generation.]

3247. ii. JOHN CHILD WEEKS, eldest son and second child of Matilda Child and David Weeks, b. in New Hampshire, Dec. 10, 1800, twice married—1st, Dec. 3, 1826, Maria Powers; m. 2d, Mch. 27. 1842. Ascenath Smith. Mr. John C. Weeks d. June 23, 1874.

[Seventh Generation.] Children.

3257. i. MARY P. WEEKS. b. Mch. 3, 1843.

3258. ii. CHARLES AUGUSTUS WEEKS, b. May 7, 1831. d. Feb. 1, 1862.

3259 iii. LUELLA WEEKS, b. Feb. 8, 1834, d. Feb. 1, 1867.

3260. iv DAVID WEEKS, b. Jan. 5, 1836.

3261. v. LUVIA LANG WEEKS, b. March 12, 1840.

3262. vi. MARIA WEEKS, b. April 9, 1842.

3263. vii. FRANKLIN WEEKS, b. July 1, 1843.

3264. viii. ELLEN FRANCES WEEKS, b. July 11, 1847, d. Dec. 30, 1862.

3265. ix. ISAAC SMITH WEEKS, b. April 15, 1856.

3266. x. MOSES W. WEEKS, b. Dec. 28, 1858.

3267. xi. HARRY EUGENE WEEKS, b. Nov. 5, 1863.

[Sixth Generation]

3248. iii. MARY CHILD WEEKS, second dau. and third child of Matilda Child and David Weeks, b. Dec. 25, 1802, doubtless considered the most perfect Christmas gift ever bestowed upon her parents. Mary Child Weeks m. Martin C. Powers, Sept. 27, 1826.

[Seventh Generation.] Children:

3268. i. CHARLES POWERS, b. Aug. 20, 1828.
3269. ii. LAURA W. POWERS, b. Aug. 30, 1831.
3270. iii. JOHN MARCUS POWERS, b. Oct. 18, 1834.
3271. iv. WALTER POWERS, b. July 19, 1836.
3272. v. MARTHA ELLEN POWERS, b. Nov. 15, 1837.
3273. vi. MARIA W. POWERS, b. Dec. 29, 1839, d. June 15, 1870.

[Sixth Generation.]

3249. iv. DUDLEY CHILD WEEKS, second son and fourth child of Matilda Child and David Weeks, b. Dec. 24, 1804, m. April 20, 1853, Lucy Topliff.

[Seventh Generation.] Children:

3274. i. HORACE WEEKS, b. Nov. 17, 1832.
3275. ii. ADALINE WEEKS, b. Oct. 15, 1834.
3276. iii. ANNETTE WEEKS, b. Sept. 29, 1836.

[Sixth Generation.]

3250. v. ALFRED WEEKS, third son and fifth child of Matilda Child and David Weeks, b. Dec. 12, 1806, m. Jan. 2, 1838, Candace Porter.

[Seventh Generation.] Children:

3277. i. LUCIA P. WEEKS, b. Jan. 23, 1841.
3278. ii. WILLARD H. WEEKS, b. Jan. 26, 1844.

Sixth Generation.]

3251. vi. JONATHAN WEEKS, fourth son and sixth child of Matilda Child and David Weeks, b. Dec. 2, 1808, m. Dec. 10, 1840, Betsey Chamberlain. Mr. and Mrs. Jonathan Weeks died within a few days of each other, in June, 1878: Mr. Weeks the 18th, Mrs. Weeks the 14th, of the month.

[Seventh Generation.] Children:

3279. i. ELIZABETH C. WEEKS, b. Sept. 1, 1842.
3280. ii. JANE C. WEEKS, b. Oct. 10, 1844.
3281. iii. ALICE B. WEEKS, b. July 7, 1848.
3282. iv. EMILY M. WEEKS, b. Feb. 10, 1853.

[Sixth Generation.]

3252. vii. MOSES MERRISON WEEKS, fifth son and seventh child of Matilda Child and David Weeks, b. Feb. 4, 1811, m. Dec. 29, 1840, Sally Minot.

[Seventh Generation.] Children:

3283. i. MINOT WEEKS, b. Dec. 31, 1841.
3284. ii. HARRIET P. WEEKS, b. Oct. 6, 1844.
3285. iii. WILMOT WEEKS, b. June 37, 1848.
3286. iv. ELBRIDGE WEEKS, b. Feb. 4, 1851.

D-1

[Sixth Generation.]

3253. viii. WILLARD CHILD WEEKS, sixth son and eighth child of Matilda Child and David Weeks, b. April 21, 1813, m. April 20, 1853, Lestine Merrill.

[Seventh Generation.] Children:

3287. i. EZRA EUGENE WEEKS, b. July 31, 1854.
3288. ii. LOWELL MASON WEEKS, b. Aug. 7, 1857.
3289. iii. NELLIE WEEKS, b. Aug. 10, 1859.
3290. iv. EFFIE WEEKS, b. Oct. 30, 1861.
3291. v. CLARA ETTA WEEKS, b. June 28, 1863.

[Sixth Generation.]

3255. x. EMILY WEEKS, third dau. and tenth child of Matilda Child and David Weeks, b. July 16, 1818, m. April 14, 1842, William Minot.

[Seventh Generation.] Children:

3292. i. ELIZA MINOT, b. May 15, 1843.
3293. ii. MARIAN B. MINOT, b. May 3, 1850.
3294. iii. MARTHA W. MINOT, b. Nov. 3, 1853.
3295. iv. JONAS MINOT, b. May 22, 1857.

[Sixth Generation.]

3256. xi. ELIZA WEEKS, fourth dau. and eleventh child of Matilda Child and David Weeks, b. April 10, 1821, m. Dec. 29, 1840, George Chamberlain.

[Seventh Generation.] Children:

3296. i. WILLARD W. CHAMBERLAIN, b. May 30, 1842.
3297. ii. EDWIN CHAMBERLAIN, b. Jan. 27, 1844.
3298. iii. SAMUEL N. CHAMBERLAIN, b. April 4, 1855.
3299. iv. JENNETTE CHAMBERLAIN, b. July 2, 1858.
3300. v. EMILIE M. CHAMBERLAIN, b. Aug. 24, 1860.

[Fourth Generation.]

2485. viii. ELEAZER CHILD, fourth son and eighth child of Capt. Penuel and Dorothy Dwight Child, b. in Thompson, Ct., Oct. 2, 1737, m. though to whom not yet ascertained.

[Fifth Generation.] Children:

3301. i. SABRA CHILD, bapt. May 18, 1763, m. Dec. 21, 178-, Ebenezer Carroll, of Killingly, Ct.
3302. ii. THANKFUL CHILD, bapt. May 18, 1763.
3303. iii. DOROTHY CHILD, bapt. Nov. 24, 1765.
3304. iv. ELIZABETH CHILD, bapt. Nov. 24, 1765.

[Third Generation.]

25. xi. Dea. THOMAS CHILD, eleventh child and eighth son of Benjamin and Grace Morris Child, b. in Roxbury, Mass., Nov. 10, 1703, m. by John Chandler, Esq., Nov. 24, 1729, Anna Morris, dau. of Dea. Edward Morris. He was one of seven brothers who emigrated from Roxbury to Woodstock ;

and was one of the early deacons in the Congregational church of Woodstock, Ct. He d. July 19, 1762, aged 59. She d. Aug. 11, 1806, in her 95th year.

[Fourth Generation.] Children: All born in Woodstock.

3305. i. MILTHEA CHILD, b. Aug. 12, 1730, bapt. Aug. 20, d. Aug. 26, 1730.

3306. ii. MARGARET CHILD, b. July 28, 1731, bapt. Aug. 29, 1731, d. July 26, 1742.

3307. iii. SYBIL CHILD, b. Mch. 3, 1733, m. Mch. 15, 1756, Edward Ainsworth.

3308. iv. ANNA CHILD, b. Aug. 17, 1734, bapt. Aug. 18, 1734.

3309. v. ALITHEA CHILD, b. Aug. 4, 1736, m. Nov. 19, 1761, Thos. Peake.

3310. vi. WILLIAM CHILD, b. May 15, 1738, bapt. July 4, 1738, d. Feb. 6, 1752.

3311. vii. DOROTHY CHILD, b. April 3, 1740, m. 1st, Oct. 23, 1763, Solomon Atherton; m. 2d, Feb. 26, 1766, Joshua Child.

3312. viii. LOIS CHILD, b. June 18, 1742, m. Nov. 17, 1768, Joseph May.

3313. ix. THOMAS CHILD, Jr., b. July 15, 1744, m. Jan. 26, 1775, Lucy Gage.

3314. x. LEMUEL CHILD, b. July 12, 1747, m. Nov. 16, 1768, Dorcas Perry.

3315. xi. HULDAH CHILD, b. Nov. 19, 1749, m. April 28, 1769, Stephen Skinner.

3316. xii. WILLIAM CHILD, 2d, b. Dec. 4, 1752, m. Dec. 29, 1784, Susannah Corbin.

[Fourth Generation.]

3313. ix. THOMAS CHILD, JR., ninth child and second son of Dea. Thomas and Anna Morris Child, b. in Woodstock, Ct., July 15, 1744, m. Jan. 26, 1775, Lucy Gage. She d. Feb. 3, 1795.

[Fifth Generation.] Children:

3317. i. WALTER CHILD, b. in Woodstock, Ct., Nov. 15, 1776.

3318. ii. ANNA CHILD, b. in Woodstock, Ct., Sept. 1, 1778.

3319. iii. ASA CHILD, b. in Woodstock, Ct., Sept. 17, 1780.

[Fourth Generation.]

3314. x. LEMUEL CHILD, tenth child and third son of Dea. Thomas and Anna Morris Child, b July 12, 1747, m. Nov. 16, 1768, Dorcas Perry. She was b. Dec. 22, 1741, d. Mch. 26, 1825. He d. May 6, 1808.

[Fifth Generation.] Children:

3320. i. HULDAH CHILD, b. in Woodstock, Ct., Aug. 19, 1769, d. Feb. 27, 1855, unmarried.

3321. ii. THOMAS PERRY CHILD, b. in Woodstock, Ct., Dec. 20, 1770, d. Nov. 27, 1773.

3322. iii. STEPHEN CHILD, b. in Woodstock, Ct., Feb. 24, 1772, d. Oct. 19, 1783.

3323. iv. ROWENA CHILD, b. in Woodstock, Ct., Dec. 3 1775, m. Nov. 26, 1795, Alba Abbott.

3324. v. NANCY CHILD, b. in Woodstock, Ct., May 20, 1778, m. Jan. 7, 1799, Willard Abbott.

3325. vi. PERRY CHILD, b. in Woodstock, Ct., Oct. 6, 1780.

3326. vii. DOLPHUS CHILD, b. in Woodstock, Ct., Mch. 25, 1785, m. Dec. 1, 1808, Chloe Jackson.

[Fifth Generation.]

3326. vii. DOLPHUS CHILD,* seventh child and fourth son of Lemuel and Dorcas Perry Child. b. in Woodstock, Ct., Mch. 25. 1785. m. Dec. 1. 1808. Chloe Jackson. He d. Mch. 1867. She d. Feb. 18, 1869, near Clymer, Chautauqua Co., N. Y.

[Sixth Generation.] Children:

3327. i. JUSTUS CHILDS. b. in Woodstock, Ct., Sept. 21, 1809. m. Sept. 21, 1834. Betsey Budlong.

3328. ii. NANCY CHILD, b. in Woodstock, Ct., Aug. 27, 1813, m. A. H. Palmer.

3329. iii. LEMUEL MORRIS CHILD, b. in Woodstock, Ct., Feb. 7, 1816, m. Amy Colgrove.

3330. iv. THOMAS PERRY CHILDS, b. in Woodstock, Ct., June 8, 1817. m. Altezera E. Eaton.

3331. v. ROWENA CHILD, b. in Woodstock. Ct., Aug. 16, 1822, m. William Burnett.

3332. vi. MARY CHILD, b. in Woodstock, Ct., July 16, 1824, m. Samuel Cooley.

[Sixth Generation.]

3327. i. JUSTUS CHILDS, eldest child of Dolphus and Chloe Jackson Child. b. in Woodstock. Ct., Sept. 21, 1809, m. Sept. 21, 1834. Betsey Budlong. dau. of Joseph Budlong, Esq., of Bridgewater, N. Y., a wealthy and influential farmer in that town. Mrs. Justus Childs was b. in Paris, Oneida Co., N. Y., Jan. 31, 1815. Mr. Childs d. May 24, 1868.

Mr. Justus Childs commenced active life as a farmer in the town of Paris, Oneida Co., N. Y., which occupation he successfully followed for a number of years, when from his accumulations he established himself in the manufacture of agricultural implements, in the city of Utica, N. Y. The business grew on his hands to large proportions. taxing his energies to an extent which seriously impared his health. In the prime of manhood and amid business activities, he fell into a decline which terminated his useful life. Mr. Childs was a man highly esteemed for his integrity. generosity and business talent.

[Seventh Generation.] Children:

3333. i. SARAH LOUISA CHILDS. b. in Bridgewater, N. Y., Nov. 18, 1835, m. Alexander B Roberts of Utica, d. Oct. 20, 1870

3334. ii JOSEPH MORRIS CHILDS, b. in Bridgewater, N Y., April 17, 1840. m. Sept. 1. 1864, Cora Brown.

3335. iii. WALLACE BUDLONG CHILDS, b. in Bridgewater, N. Y., July 8, 1842. Graduated at Hamilton College, Clinton, Oneida Co.. N. Y., in the Class of 1864: studied law and entered upon his profession. M. Sept. 15, 1869, Kate C. Van Buren of Dunkirk, N. Y., d. in Utica N. Y., in 1870.

3336. iv. ORLANDO JUSTUS CHILDS. b. in Bridgewater, N. Y., July 25, 1844, m. Dec. 10, 1874. Ella A. Jones.

3337. v. KATE ELIZABETH CHILDS, b. in Bridgewater, N. Y., July 10, 1848, m. April 13, 1872, Charles G. Bamber.

3338. vi. CHARLES HENRY CHILDS, b. in Bridgewater, N. Y.. Dec. 26, 1854.

* Two sons of Dolphus Child have added the " s " to their name.

[Seventh Generation.]

3334. ii. JOSEPH MORRIS CHILDS, second child and eldest son of Justus and Betsey Budlong Childs, b. in Bridgewater, N. Y., April 17, 1840, m. Sept. 1, 1864, Cora Brown, dau. of Charles Brown of Unadilla Forks, Otsego Co., N. Y. The eldest sons of Mr. Justus Childs, J. Morris and Orlando J., were the immediate successors of their father. The business of this house has been successfully carried on for a number of years in the hands of these brothers, who are men of integrity and thorough business habits. A recent change in the firm, by the withdrawal of Mr. O. J. Childs, leaves the business in the management of J. Morris Childs and his younger brother Charles H. Childs, as junior partner. The firm is known as extensive wholesale dealers in agricultural implements, conducting a lucrative business on Fayette street, Utica, N. Y.

[Eighth Generation.] Children:

3339. i. WALTER B. CHILDS, b. in Utica, Sept. 18, 1867.
3340. ii. FANNIE M. CHILDS, b. in Utica, June 28, 1872.

[Seventh Generation.]

3336. iv. ORLANDO J. CHILDS, fourth child and third son of Justus and Betsey Budlong Childs, b. in Bridgewater, N. Y., July 25, 1844, m. Dec. 10, 1874, Ella A. Jones, dau. of Jonathan Jones of Utica, N. Y. Mr. O. J. Childs withdrew from the old firm as before stated, to enter into new business relations, and formed a partnership with his brother-in-law, Frank Jones, under the firm name of Childs & Jones, in Utica, N. Y. They are extensive dealers in dairy apparatus and general hardware, extending their trade to the southern states.

[Eighth Generation.] Child:

3341. i. WALLACE J. CHILDS, b. in Utica, Oct. 5, 1875.

[Seventh Generation.]

3337. v. KATE ELIZABETH CHILDS, fifth child and second dau. of Justus and Betsey Budlong Childs, b. in Bridgewater, N. Y., July 10, 1848, m. April 13, 1872, Charles G. Bamber; residence Lockport, N. Y.

[Eighth Generation.] Children:

3342. i. GERTRUDE BAMBER, b. April 17, 1875.
3343. ii WILLIAM BAMBER, b. Sept. 29, 1876.
3343a iii. BESSIE BAMBER, b. 1879.

[Sixth Generation.]

3328. ii. NANCY CHILD, second child and eldest dau. of Dolphus and Chloe Jackson Child, b. Aug. 27, 1813, m. Sept. 28, 1834, A. H. Palmer; reside in Sandwich, Ill.

[Seventh Generation.] Children:

3344. i. OSCAR B. PALMER, b. Aug. 20, 1835.

3345. ii. MORRIS M. PALMER, b. Jan. 24, 1837.

3346. iii. CAMILLUS J. PALMER, b. Aug. 24, 1838, d. Feb. 24, 1839.

3347. iv. CLINTON R. PALMER, b. Dec. 13, 1839.

3348. v. CAMILLUS M. PALMER, 2D. b. Aug. 16, 1841, d. Jan. 12, 1863.

3349. vi. JAMES B. PALMER, b. Dec. 9, 1842, d. May 1, 1847.

3350. vii. FRANCES PALMER, b. Oct. 18, 1844, d. Sept. 19, 1845.

3351. viii. FRANCES PALMER, 2D, b. June 9, 1846.

3352. ix CLARA PALMER, b. Nov. 5, 1848.

3353. x MARY E. PALMER, b. May 20, 1851.

3354. xi. ISADORA PALMER, b. Dec. 21, 1854.

[Sixth Generation.]

3329. iii. LEMUEL MORRIS CHILD, third child and second son of Dolphus and Chloe Jackson Child, b. in Woodstock, Ct., Feb. 7, 1816, m. Amy Colgrove, then of Clymer, N. Y. He removed to Baxter Springs, Cherokee Co., Kansas, and d. there Aug. 9, 1878.

[Seventh Generation.] Children:

3355. i. JUSTUS CHILD: lives at Parker's Landing, Pa.

3356 ii. FRANK CHILD: lives at Baxter Springs, Kansas.

[Sixth Generation]

3330. iv. Rev. THOMAS PERRY CHILDS, fourth child and third son of Dolphus and Chloe Jackson Child, b. in Woodstock, Ct., Jan. 8, 1817, m. Sept. 21, 1840, at Troy, Ohio, Altezera E. Eaton, dau. of Rev. Zelva Eaton. Mr. Childs is a clergyman of the Baptist denomination. He is extensively and favorably known as the discoverer of a catarrh remedy called "Childs' Catarrh Specific." Much success seems to have attended his efforts in this direction, as would be indicated by the numerous flattering testimonials which have been published from those who have been benefitted by its use: resides in Troy, Ohio.

[Seventh Generation.] Children:

3357. i. ALMIRA CHILDS, b. July 22, 1841, m. Nov. 23, 1865, Dr. J. H. Green.

3358. ii. ABBOTT EATON CHILDS, b Aug. 29, 1845, m. Olive A. Shilling.

3359. iii. EDWIN DOUGLASS CHILDS, b. May 15, 1850, d Aug. 30, 1850.

3360. iv. MARY ESTHER CHILDS, b. Aug. 18, 1852, m. Dec. 25, 1873, Albert D. Knick.

3361. v. ALTEZERA CHILDS, b. June 28, 1856, d. Aug. 21, 1856

3362. vi CLARA CHILDS, ⎫ TWINS ⎧ b. July 22, 1858, d. July 28, 1858.

3363. vii CALLA CHILDS, ⎭   ⎩ b. July 22, 1858, d. Oct. 23, 1858.

3364. viii. FRANK PERRY CHILDS, b. Aug. 26, 1860.

[Seventh Generation.]

3357. i. ALMIRA CHILDS, eldest child of Rev. Thos. Perry and Altezera E. Eaton Childs, b. Jan. 22, 1841, m. Nov. 23, 1865, Dr. J. H. Green.

[Eighth Generation.] Child:
  3465. i. ANNA MARY GREEN, b. Jan. 19, 1871.

[Seventh Generation.]
    3358. ii. ABBOTT EATON CHILDS, second child and eldest son of Rev. Thos. Perry and Altezera E. Eaton Childs, b. Aug. 29, 1845, m. May 11, 1875, Olive A. Shilling; reside in Troy, Ohio.
[Eighth Generation.] Child:
  3366. i. THOMAS MAXWELL CHILDS, b. Dec. 30, 1877.

[Seventh Generation.]
    3360. iv. MARY ESTHER CHILDS, fourth child and second dau. of Rev. Thos. Perry and Altezera E. Eaton Childs, b. Aug. 18, 1852, m. Dec. 25, 1873, Albert Dye Knick; residence Troy, Ohio.
[Eighth Generation.] Child:
  3367. i. ALBERT DYE KNICK, JR., b. Dec. 6, 1875.

[Sixth Generation.]
    3331. v. ROWENA CHILD, fifth child and second dau. of Dolphus and Chloe Jackson Child, b. in Woodstock, Ct., Aug. 16, 1822, m. Mch. 10, 1844, William Bennett, b. Feb. 18, 1821, d. Oct. 15, 1853.
[Seventh Generation.] Child:
  3368. i. M. LEDRU ROLLIN BENNETT, b. Aug 19, 1846, m May 12, 1867, Dora Lamora Rogs; she was b. Aug. 20, 1846.

[Sixth Generation.]
    3332. vi. MARY CHILD, sixth child and third dau. of Dolphus and Chloe Jackson Child, b. in Woodstock, Ct., July 16, 1824, m. Nov. 1, 1859, Samuel I. Cooley, son of Job M. and Eugenie Cooley. He was b. in Pharsalia, Chenango Co., N. Y., March 6, 1831.
[Seventh Generation.] Children:
  3369. i. DOLPHUS JOB COOLEY, b. Sept. 6, 1861.
  3370. ii. CARROLL ABBOTT COOLEY, b. July 28, 1863.
  3371. iii. CLARENCE DANA COOLEY, b. July 30, 1865.
  3372. iv. CHLOE EUGENIE COOLEY, b. Jan. 3, 1869.

[Fourth Generation.]
    3316. xii. WILLIAM CHILD, 2D, twelveth child and fourth son of Dea. Thomas and Anna Morris Child, b. in Woodstock, Ct., Dec. 4, 1752, m. Dec. 29, 1780, Susannah Corbin.
[Fifth Generation.] Children:
  3373. i. LILLIE CHILD, b. in Woodstock, Ct., Sept. 16, 1781.
  3374. ii. ABIGAIL LILLIE CHILD, b. in Woodstock, Ct., March 23, 1786.

CHAPTER VI.

JOSHUA CHILD.

The reader who has become familiar with the name of Mr. Isaac Child of Boston, who gathered much of the early statistics embodied in this work, will observe his descent from Benjamin the emigrant, through the Joshua Child who heads this Chapter.

[Second Generation.]

5. iii. JOSHUA CHILD, third child and son of Benjamin Child, the emigrant, b. in Roxbury, Mass., 1658. We learn the "Apostle Elliot" laid upon his head the consecrating waters of baptism, giving to him the name Joshua, on the 20th of June, 1658; at the same time, in like manner enfolding the elder sons Ephraim and Benjamin. The happy union of his brother Benjamin with Grace Morris, brought Joshua into pleasant friendship with the Morris family, and resulted in his alliance May 9, 1685, with Elizabeth Morris, a sister of Grace, she was born March 26, 1666. A memorandum upon a legal paper belonging to Mr. Benjamin Child, signed by Mr. Joshua Child, states that he had received his full part of the estate of his late father some time before; bestowed upon him doubtless by his father at the time of his marriage, with a view to his comfortable establishment in life. Mr. Joshua Child made his home a short distance west of the old homestead in the now pleasant village of Brookline, Mass. Here generation after generation of the family lived and died for nearly two hundred years. Mr. Joshua Child was a man much respected, and held numerous offices of importance and honor in this town up to the time of his decease. His health became much impared, and entire loss of sight shadowed his latter days, so that his death on the 18th of January, 1729, was unto him indeed an entrance into light. The full patriarchal number of children graced this home, though not all of the twelve grew to maturity. Mrs. Elizabeth Morris Child died March 6, 1754, aged 88.

[Third Generation.] Children:

3375. i. JOSHUA CHILD, JR., b. June 20, 1687, m. Sept. 6, 1715, Deborah Weld.

3376. ii. ISAAC CHILD, b. Dec. 20, 1688, m. 1st, 1713, Sarah Newell; m. 2d, 1716, Elizabeth Weld.

3377. iii. ELIZABETH CHILD, b. July 20, 1691, m. Dec. 18, 1711, John May of Roxbury, who removed to Woodstock, Ct.

3378. iv. MEHITABLE CHILD, b. Oct. 27, 1693.

3379. v. JOSEPH CHILD, b. Jan. 7, 1696, m. Nov. 29, 1722, Abigail Bridges.

3380. vi. ABIGAIL CHILD, b. Mch. 15, 1698, m. Nov. 12, 1719, Jas. Draper.

3381. vii. ANN CHILD, b. April 8, 1700, m. Joshua Murdock, of Newton, Mass.

3382. viii. DOROTHY CHILD, b. May 5, 1701, m. May 2, 1723, Ebenezer Draper.

3383. ix. PRUDENCE CHILD, b. July 22, 1703.

3384. x. SAMUEL CHILD, b. Nov. 7, 1705, d. young.

3385. xi. SAMUEL CHILD, 2D, b. Feb. 4, 1707.

3386. xii CALEB CHILD, b. Sept. 16, 1709, m. Oct. 19, 1728, Rebecca Dana.

[Third Generation.]

3375. i. JOSHUA CHILD, JR., eldest child of Joshua and Elizabeth Morris Child, b. June 20, 1687, m. Sept. 6, 1715, Deborah Weld.

[Fourth Generation.] Children:

3387. i. ABIJAH CHILD, b. Feb. 24, 1717, d. Dec. 3, 1719.

3388. ii. MARY CHILD, b. Dec. 24, 1718, d. Dec. 21, 1719.

3389. iii. ABIJAH CHILD, 2D, b. Nov. 21, 1720, d. young.

3390. iv. JOSHUA CHILD, JR., b. April 21, 1722, d. young.

3391. v. JOSHUA CHILD, 2D, b. April 22, 1726.

[Third Generation.]

3376. ii. ISAAC CHILD, second child of Joshua and Elizabeth Morris Child, b. Dec. 20, 1688, m. 1st, 1713, Sarah Newell; m. 2d, 1716, Elizabeth Weld.

[Fourth Generation.] Children. By Sarah Newell:

3392. i. SARAH CHILD, b. April 11, 1715, m. Ezra Davis, of Roxbury, Mass.

By Elizabeth Weld:

3393. ii. ISAAC CHILD, JR., b. April 30, 1717, in Brookline, Mass., d. yg.

3394. iii. ELIZABETH CHILD, b. June 12, 1718, in Brookline, Mass., m. June 15, 1738, John Payson.

3395. iv. ESTHER CHILD, b. in Brookline, Mass., Feb. 17, 1720, d. young.

3396. v. ISAAC CHILD, 2D, b. in Brookline, Mass, May 1, 1722, m. Dec. 12, 1745, Elizabeth Weld.

3397. vi. ESTHER CHILD, 2D, b. in Brookline, Mass, Nov. 14, 1724, m. Josiah Murdock, of Newton. He d. May 23, 1794.

3398. vii. ABIGAIL CHILD, b. in Brookline, Mass., April 15, 1727.

3399. viii. ANNA CHILD, b. in Brookline, Mass., April 24, 1730.

[Fourth Generation.]

3396. v. ISAAC CHILD, JR., fifth child of Isaac and Elizabeth Weld Child, b. May 1, 1722, m. Dec. 12, 1745, Elizabeth Weld. He d. May 23, 1794.

[Fifth Generation.] Children:

3400. i. DAVID CHILD, b. in Brookline, Mass., Nov. 2, 1740, d. Oct. 16, 1766.

3401. ii ABIJAH CHILD, b. in Brookline, Mass.. Dec 7, 1748, m. Lois Davis, of Roxbury. She was b. Oct. 9, 1748, d. July 24, 1830.

3402. iii. MARY CHILD, b. in Brookline, Mass., May 2, 1750. m. Daniel White, of Brookline.

3303. iv. ABIGAIL CHILD, b. in Brookline, Mass., Feb. 5, 1752, m. John Colburn, of Sturbridge, Mass.

3404. v. DANIEL CHILD, b. in Brookline, Mass., Feb. 19, 1754, m. Oct. 29, 1781, Rebecca Richards.

3405. vi. ELIZABETH CHILD, b. in Brookline, Mass., Feb 8, 1756, d yg.

3406. vii. ELIZABETH CHILD, 2D, b. in Brookline, Mass., July 23, 1758, d. young.

3407. viii. SARAH CHILD, b. in Sturbridge, Mass , May 1, 1760, d. young

3408. ix. ANN CHILD, b. in Sturbridge, Mass., Jan. 11, 1761, d. young.

3409. x. ISAAC CHILD, b. in Sturbridge, Mass., May 2, 1763, m. Esther Bardwell.

3410. xi. JOSEPH CHILD, b. in Sturbridge, Mass , Oct. 16, 1765.

3411. xii. DAVID WELD CHILD, b. in Sturbridge, Mass., Feb. 19, 1772. m. April, 1801, Abigail Dorr, dau. of Ebenezer Dorr, merchant.

[Fifth Generation.]

3401. ii. ABIJAH CHILD, second child of Isaac and Elizabeth Weld Child, b. in Brookline, Mass., Dec. 7, 1748, m. abt. 1777, Lois Davis, of Roxbury, who was b. Oct. 25, 1749, d. May 1, 1824. Mr. Abijah Child first settled in Roxbury, Mass., and thence removed to Sturbridge, Mass.

[Sixth Generation.] Children:

3412. i. MARY CHILD, b. July 5, 1778, m. Peres Walker, of Sturbridge, Mass.

3413. ii. WILLIAM CHILD, b. in Sturbridge, Mass., April 15, 1780, unm.

3414. iii. SARAH CHILD, b. in Sturbridge, Mass., Mch. 1, 1782, m. Lyman Morse, of Sturbridge, Mass.

3415. iv. AMASA CHILD, b. in Sturbridge, Mass., Mch. 21, 1784, m. Dec. 1, 1808, Cynthia Freeman, dau. of Comfort Freeman. She was b. Oct. 9, 1784, d. July 9, 1830. He d. Dec. 27, 1828.

3416. v. NANCY CHILD, b. in Sturbridge, Mass., June 30, 1786, m. Lyman Johnson.

[Sixth Generation]

3412. i. MARY CHILD, eldest child of Abijah and Lois Davis Child, b. July 5, 1778, m. Perez Walker, of Sturbridge, Mass.

[Seventh Generation.] Children:

3417. i. LOUISA WALKER, b. Feb. 23, 1800.

3418. ii. MARY WALKER, b. Oct. 28, 1804.

3419. iii. CHESTER WALKER, b. Oct. 28, 1802.

3420. iv. CLORINDA WALKER, b. Mch. 26, 1809.

[Sixth Generation.]

3413. ii. WILLIAM CHILD, second child of Abijah and Lois Davis Child. Was a leading and successful merchant in Baltimore, Maryland. He was never married, but has left memorials in his successful and useful life, which his friends will be glad to preserve in these records. The knowledge of the history of Mr. Child as a representative man of the branch to which he belonged, obtained from one of the line, will justify some pleasant inferences:

It is a prominent feature in the characteristics that distinguish the family surname, that practical life partakes of the sober and robust cast, derived from the age in which the Puritans lived, and gave complexion to the moral and social phases of society. The successes of life, though not remarkably striking, with few exceptions have grown out of the vitalizing and enduring elements, which underlie the structure of substantial and prosperous communities. We find this happily illustrated in the brief history of Mr. William Child, second son of Mr. Abijah Child, of the 5th generation. His personal virtues were the basis of his active and useful life. They won for him the esteem and confidence of his fellow citizens, and made him a benefactor to his race. His kinsmen may proudly cherish the memory of so worthy a representative of their line. The estimate in which he was held as a citizen of Baltimore may be seen in an article copied from the Baltimore *American*, on the occasion of his death February 11, 1862. It says:

" No citizen was more remarkable for his punctuality and uniformly regular deportment than the deceased, and his amiable and benevolent disposition was well known and endeared him to a large circle of intimate friends. The regularity of his habits may well be judged of when we state that for forty-eight years he never failed to appear at his counting room before breakfast, and during that long period he was never once known to be absent from his pew in church. For the city of his adoption Mr. Child entertained the liveliest feelings of affection and regard; and when the invasion by the British took place, in 1814, he stood manfully in its defence in Fort McHenry. Cherishing warmly the principles of christian philanthropy he shaped the whole action of his life by the golden rule of ' doing unto others as he would be done by.' "

[Fifth Generation.]

3414. iii. SARAH CHILD, third child of Abijah and Lois Davis Child, b. Mch. 1, 1782, m. Lyman Morse of Sturbridge, Mass.

[Sixth Generation.] Children:

3421. i. WILLIAM CHILD MORSE, b. in Sturbridge, Mass., Feb. 23, 1805.
3422. ii. JULIA MORSE, b. in Sturbridge, Mass., March 29, 1809.
3423. iii. SAMUEL MORSE.
3424. iv. LYMAN MORSE, JR., d. 1858.
3425. v. SARAH MORSE, d. 1863.

[Sixth Generation.]

3415. iv. Capt. AMASA CHILD, fourth child and second son
of Abijah and Lois Davis Child, b. in Sturbridge, Mass., Mch.
21, 1784. m. Dec. 1, 1808, Cynthia Freeman, dau. of Comfort
Freeman of Sturbridge. Of the substantial men of the period
Mr. Child ranked among the most popular of his fellow townsmen for intelligence, sturdy principles and general prosperity.
As a tiller of the soil he was prosperous, and successful in
securing the means for a comfortable independence for himself
and family. As a patriot he gave to his country willing and
unconstrained service at the time of the British invasion of
1812. In this war he held a captain's commission and served
to its close, when he was honorably discharged to serve his
country in a civil capacity. His public services, as a representative from the town of Sturbridge, for a term of years in succession in the Massachusetts Legislature, are proofs of the
confidence reposed in him by his fellow townsmen. He died
in mature manhood, bequeathing to a large family of interesting sons and daughters the virtues of a worthy father.

[Seventh Generation.] Children:

3426. i. ALPHONSO CHILD, b. in Sturbridge, Mass., Sept. 10. 1809, d.
Aug. 28 1830.

3427. ii. AMANDA CHILD, b in Sturbridge. Mass., Nov. 15, 1811, m. May
4, 1831, Fitzhugh Morse.

3428. iii. CYNTHIA FREEMAN CHILD, b. in Sturbridge, Mass., Sept. 15,
1812, m. Oct. 6, 1836, Howard Upham.

3429. iv. ABIJAH CHILD, b. in Sturbridge, Mass., Dec. 8, 1815, m. Sept.
24, 1840. Hannah Upham.

3430. v ANNA CHILD, b. in Sturbridge. Mass., March 30, 1819.

3431. vi. ADDISON CHILD, b. in Sturbridge, Mass., Jan. 30, 1821, m.
Abbie Cunningham Child.

3432. vii. ADALINE SOPHIA CHILD, b. in Sturbridge, Mass., March 19,
1823, m. May 16, 1855, Henry Porter.

3433. viii CLARINDA CHILD, b. in Sturbridge, Mass., Oct. 25, 1826, d.
Feb. 3, 1827.

3434. ix. AMASA DAVIS CHILD, b. in Sturbridge, Mass., July 21, 1828,
d. July 14, 1829.

[Seventh Generation.]

3427. ii. AMANDA CHILD, eldest dau. and second child of
Amasa and Cynthia Freeman Child, b. in Sturbridge, Mass.,
Nov. 15, 1811. m. May 4, 1831. Fitzhugh Morse: she d. April
17, 1867.

[Eighth Generation.] Children:

3435. i. HENRY ALPHONSO MORSE, b. March 27, 1832, m. Sept. 29, 1857,
Joey D. Cunningham.

3436. ii. AMASA CHILD MORSE, b. Oct. 24. 1833, m. 1858, Mary Ann Southwick.

3437. iii. FITZ ALBERT MORSE, b. May 25, 1839, m. May, 1875, Helen D. Colting.

3438. iv. ELLEN EUGENIA MORSE, b. Oct. 20, 1844, m. Sept. 29, 1870, Rev. Richard Metcalf.

[Eighth Generation.]

3435. i. HENRY ALPHONSO MORSE, eldest child of Amanda Child and Fitzhugh Morse, b. Mch. 27, 1832, m. Sept. 29, 1857, Joey D. Cunningham.

[Ninth Generation.] Children:
3439. i. RUTH MORSE, b. 1858.
3440. ii. ABBA CHILD MORSE, b. 1861.
3441. iii. GERTRUDE MORSE, b. 1864.

[Eighth Generation.]

3436. ii. AMASA CHILD MORSE, second child and son of Amanda Child and Fitzhugh Morse, b. Oct. 24, 1833, m. 1858, Mary Ann Southwick.

[Ninth Generation.] Children:
3442 i. WILLIAM CHILD MORSE, b. 1859.
3443. ii. ANNA SOUTHWICK MORSE, b. 1860.
3444. iii. EDNA SOUTHWICK MORSE, b. 1862.
3445. iv. HENRY ALPHONSO MORSE, b. 1870.

[Eighth Generation.]

3437. iii. FITZ ALBERT MORSE, third child and son of Amanda Child and Fitzhugh Morse, b. May 25, 1839, m. May, 1875, Helen D. Colting.

[Ninth Generation.] Children:
3446. i. ROBERT CUNNINGHAM MORSE, b. 1877.
3447. ii. ALBERT CHILD MORSE, b. 1878.

[Seventh Generation.]

3428. iii. CYNTHIA FREEMAN CHILD, third child and second dau. of Amasa and Cynthia Freeman Child, b. Sept. 15, 1813, m. Oct. 6, 1836, Howard Upham: she d. 1873.

[Eighth Generation.] Children:
3448. i. LUCIUS EVERETT UPHAM, b. 1838, m. 1858, Emily Dorman.
3449. ii ADDISON CHILD UPHAM, b. 1842.

[Seventh Generation.]

3429. iv. ABIJAH CHILD, fourth child and second son of Amasa and Cynthia Freeman Child, b. in Sturbridge, Mass., Dec. 8, 1815, m. Sept. 24, 1840, Hannah Upham: he d. Dec. 11, 1875.

[Eighth Generation.] Children:
3450. i. ALPHONSO FREEMAN CHILD, b. 1841, d. Aug. 20, 1864, a prisoner of war at Andersonville.

3451. ii. FLORENCE C. CHILD, b. 1845, m. William ———.
3452. iii. WILLIAM CHILD, b. 1846.
3453. iv. ADA LOIS CHILD, b. 1848.
3454. v. HANNAH CLARA CHILD, b. 1850, m. Clarence Shumway.

[Seventh Generation.]

3430. v. ANNA CHILD, third dau. and fifth child of Amasa and Cynthia Freeman Child, b. in Sturbridge, Mass., Mch. 30, 1819. She was a teacher of pleasant memory, in Virginia and California; she died in the latter State Aug. 6, 1865, greatly respected and lamented, as well for her philanthropy as for her capacity as an instructor. The Boston *Christian Register* of September 3, 1865, pays the following deserved tribute to the memory of Miss Child:

" The subject of this notice. Miss Anna Child, whose death we chronicle to-day, was a native of Sturbridge, Mass. She became early in life a teacher in the South, but living in the midst of slavery her views in regard to it became gradually so much at variance with those with whom she daily associated that she found she must veil her sentiments, and sacrifice either her personal feelings or her sphere of usefulness there. She chose the latter and returned to the North, although in so doing she parted with many warm and estimable personal friends there. After spending some years at home, she determined to seek a new and enlarged sphere of doing good, and went to California, in 1859, in the same steamer that carried out our lamented Star King and family. She opened a school for girls there, which she continued to the time of her last illness, oftentimes receiving and instructing such as were unable to pay for it. She was a constant and sincere worshipper at the Unitarian church, and was an efficient and conscientious teacher in the Sunday-school, during Mr. King's ministry and since, and as Mr Stebbins writes, 'found her own happiness in making others happy.' Her funeral was in the Unitarian church, Aug. 7, attended by many members of the Sunday-school and a goodly number of those who had been attracted by her unselfish goodness. At the regular teachers' meeting, held Aug. 14th, the following preamble and resolutions were passed:

'God in his infinite wisdom has removed one of our number by death. Miss Anna Child was for many years connected with this Sunday-school, and by her faithful and untiring service, her gentle disposition and unfailing love for the school, had won the esteem and affection of all who knew her. When we miss her from her sphere of duty, and wonder why one so useful should be so suddenly taken away; it is at least some consolation to believe that for her ' to die is gain,' still it is becoming us to recognise our loss, and to tender our sympathy to her bereaved friends. Therefore, *Resolved*, That the Superintendent be instructed to convey to the friends and family of Miss Child our sense of her worth, and the loss we have sustained in her death, and offer our sympathy with them in their bereavement.'

SAN FRANCISCO, CAL., Aug. 14, 1865.   SAMUEL S. CUTTER,
Supt. Pilgrim Sunday School."

[Seventh Generation.]

3431. vi. ADDISON CHILD, third son and sixth child of Amasa and Cynthia Freeman Child, b. in Sturbridge, Mass.,

Jan. 30. 1821. m. Abbie Cunningham Child, dau. of Joshua and Lucretia Dorr Child, who was b. 1817, d. May 20, 1874.

Mr. Addison Child is a thorough Anglo-Saxon in personnel, six feet in height, symmetrical in figure, and of a fine presence. A goodly inheritance of strong physical and mental qualities, have been developed and cultivated. The advantages of home and foreign travel have enlarged his powers, and in the refinement of cultured society he finds his true home. His literary attainments are finely shown in the able articles over his signature in the earlier part of this book. Of the mercantile house of Lewis Audenraid & Co., Boston, Mass., he has made his financial success a means of enjoying the delights of genuine rural life, in St. Lawrence Co., New York, devoting time and means to the best development of a wooded, hilly township. Looking to the future, he has stocked the lakes and streams from the fish nurseries of Western New York.

[Seventh Generation.]

3432. vii ADALINE SOPHIA CHILD, fourth dau. and seventh child of Amasa and Cynthia Freeman Child, b. in Sturbridge, Mass., Mch. 19, 1823, m. May 16, 1855, Henry Porter.

[Eighth Generation.] Child:

3455. i. THEODORE CHILD PORTER, b. 1860.

[Fifth Generation.]

3404. v. DANIEL CHILD, fifth child and third son of Isaac and Elizabeth Weld Child, b. in Brookline, Mass., Feb. 19, 1754, m. Oct. 29, 1781, Rebecca Richards, who was b. Dec. 18, 1760, d. May 10, 1826. He d. Oct. 27, 1844.

[Sixth Generation] Children:

3456. i BETSEY CHILD b. in Brookline, Mass., Jan. 24, 1772, m. May 5, 1803, Oliver Fisher, of Boston. He was b. Feb. 28, 1778, d. April 6, 1830, she d. Oct. 17, 1858.

3457. ii. RICHARDS CHILD, b. in Brookline, Mass., Dec. 9, 1783, m. Oct. 4, 1812, Elizabeth Richards.

3458. iii. JOSHUA CHILD, b. in Brookline, Mass., Dec. 28, 1785, m. Aug. 5, 1815, Lucretia Dorr.

3459 iv. JOHN RICHARDS CHILD, b. in Brookline, Mass., Aug. 28, 1788, m. in 1820, Hannah Richards.

3460. v. ISAAC CHILD, b. in Brookline, Mass, Mch. 15, 1791, d. April 4, 1791.

3461. vi. ISAAC CHILD, 2D, b. in Newton, Mass., May 1, 1792, m. 1st, Eliza Billings: m. 2d, Maria M. Eastman: m 3d, Abigail Baker.

3462. vii. HANNAH CHILD, b. in Newton, Mass., Aug. 3, 1794, d. Feb. 27, 1809.

3463. viii. CATHARINE RICHARDS CHILD, b. in Newton, Mass, Feb. 27, 1797, d. Oct. 19, 1873, unmarried.

3464. ix. JULIA CHILD, b. in Roxbury, Mass., June 27, 1799, d. Sept. 25, 1800.

3465. x. DAVID CHILD, b. in Roxbury, Mass., July 15, 1801, d. in Cincinnati, Ohio, 1840, unmarried.

3466. xi. DANIEL FRANKLIN CHILD, b. in Roxbury, Mass., May 16, 1803, m. Nov. 14, 1839, Mary Davis Guild.

3467. xii. HANNAH CHILD, 2D, b. Mch. 17, 1809, d. by drowning in a well.

[Sixth Generation]

3457. ii. RICHARDS CHILD, second child and eldest son of Daniel and Rebecca Richards Child, b. in Brookline, Mass., Dec. 9, 1783, m. Oct. 4, 1812, Elizabeth Richards, dau. of Paul Dudley and Anna May Richards. She was b. Aug. 18, 1781, d. in Boston, Dec. 13, 1878. Mr. Child d. Nov. 28, 1840. The following obituary from the Boston *Daily Journal* of Mrs. Child will be read with interest :

"DEATH OF A REMARKABLE OLD LADY.—Mrs. Elizabeth Child, one of the oldest residents of Boston, died at her residence, No. 1 Hollis street, Friday morning, at the age of 97 years, 3 months, 25 days. About one year ago she ceased to go down stairs, but she has been able to walk about her chambers until within three months. She did not take her bed until within a short time of her decease, and she possessed her faculties until the last.

Mrs. Child was the daughter of Paul Dudley Richards, who died in 1832, at the age of 82 years, and was a descendant in a direct line of Thomas Dudley, one of the first Governors of the Province of Massachusetts Bay, the connecting links in the genealogical chain being Governor Joseph Dudley, William Dudley, Elizabeth Dudley Richards and Paul Dudley Richards. She was born August 18 1781, on Bennet street, near the corner of Washington, her parents having but one other child, Joseph, who died in 1822. Marrying Mr. Richards Child, of this city, she had two children, both of whom she outlived. These children were Elizabeth, wife of the late Dr. Abel Ball (deceased in 1856), and Henry R. Child (deceased in 1847). Her husband died in 1840. At the present time her nearest living relatives are her grandson, Mr. Dudley R. Child of this city, and several nephews and nieces. For many years she has lived in the old house at the corner of Hollis and Washington streets, which was built by her father in 1790, he having purchased the land soon after the great fire of 1787, paying therefor the sum of £160 She has always lived within 200 yards of this spot. Mrs. Child was a woman of much intelligence, and retained her mental faculties to the last, not only possessing vivid recollections of old-time events but taking an interest in current events which led her to keep fully informed concerning them. Her eyesight was remarkable, and she *never* was obliged to use glasses, but up to a few weeks before her death she read for herself the news of the time as given in the columns of *The Daily Journal*, to which she has been a constant subscriber since 1861, at which time she gave up the *Courier* on account of its secession proclivities, which did not accord with her old-fashioned " Whig " sentiments. She was a devout christian and a member of the Hollis Street Church, in which she owned a pew inherited from her ancestors. She held pleasant memories of her former pastors,

Rev. Mr. Wight, Rev. Samuel West, Rev. Horace Holly, and others. Among her memories of general events was that of having seen Gen. Washington on Orange street, now Washington street, when she was about twelve years of age. In her charities Mrs. Child was unostentatious and actuated by good judgment. Her way of living was quiet and her disposition peaceful, and to these facts, together with her possession of a sound constitution, may be attributed the great length of her life. In some respects she was peculiar, never having been inside an omnibus horse-car or steam-car. Still she has visited the White Mountains, the State of Maine, and various parts of this State, always traveling, however, in a carriage or stage coach. Given to industry throughout her life, she was able to sew and knit to within a short time of her death. Her last days have been comforted by the tender ministrations of her faithful companion, Miss Lydia Ball, who has resided with her over twenty-seven years. She was in many respects a very remarkable woman, and her decease removes one more of those who are living ties between the last century and the present."

[Seventh Generation.] Children:

3468. i. ELIZABETH CHILD, b. in Boston, Mass., July 24, 1813, m. June 24, 1845, Dr. Abel Ball, of Northborough, Mass., son of Dr. Stephen Ball, of Northborough, Mass. He was b. in 1810. We are without the date of his death. The following brief notice is from the *New England Historical and Genealogical Register:*

"Dr. Ball studied medicine with his father in Northborough Mass. He received the degree of M. D. from Bowdoin College in 1837, since which he has been in the practice of dentistry. He married Elizabeth R. Child. The death of Dr. Ball was very sudden. He was on a visit to Philadelphia, and had attended the Centennial Exhibition during the day, and on his return to the Globe Hotel he fell dead in the wash-room in the act of putting his hand to the water faucet. The cause of his death was disease of the heart.

His relative and friend, Mr. Isaac Child, says of him: "His reputation for skill in his profession was very high. He was truly a man whom to know was to love. He had a heart as tender as a child, and his sympathies were ever ready to flow out to every one who needed them. His amiable and affectionate nature bound his friends to him in the strongest ties, and deep and universal will be the mourning for his sudden and unexpected departure." He was admitted a member of the New England Historical Genealogical Society in Nov. 4, 1865.

3469. ii. HENRY CHILD, b. in Boston, Mass., July 17, 1815, d. April 6, 1816.

3470. iii. HENRY CHILD, 2D, b. in Boston, Mass., July 25, 1816, m. June 24, 1844, Sarah Shurtliff Freeman, dau. of Dr. Benjamin Shurtliff and widow of Benjamin Freeman. Mr. Child was a merchant in Hillsboro, Ill. Mrs. Child was b. in 1813, d. Aug. 8, 1876.

[Eighth Generation.] Child:

3471. i. DUDLEY RICHARDS CHILD, b. June 2, 1845, m. Oct. 13, 1866, Missouri Stockwell.

[Ninth Generation.] Children of Dudley Richards and Missouri Child:

3472. i. DUDLEY RICHARDS CHILD, JR., b. Sept. 16, 1867.

3473. ii. EDITH CHILD, b. Sept. 27, 1870.

3474. iii. BESSIE CHILD, b. March 5, 1879.

[Sixth Generation.]

3458. iii. JOSHUA CHILD, third child and second son of Daniel and Rebecca Richards Child, b. in Brookline, Mass.,

E-1

Dec. 28, 1785, m. Aug. 5, 1816, Lucretia Dorr, dau. of Ebenezer Dorr, of Boston; she was b. June 19, 1781, d. Dec. 16, 1863.
[Seventh Generation.] Children:

3475. i. ABBIE CUNNINGHAM CHILD, b. in Boston, Mass., Sept. 10, 1817, m. Addison Child, son of Amasa and Cynthia Freeman Child, d. May 24.*1874.

3476. ii. HENRY DORR CHILD, b. ——, d. May 24 1874, in Florence, Italy, unmarried. It is considered a remarkable coincidence that Mr. Henry Dorr Child and his sister, Abbie Cunningham Child, wife of Mr. Addison Child, should have died about the same time though 3,000 or 4,000 miles apart and in different countries.

[Sixth Generation.]

3459. iv. JOHN RICHARDS CHILD, fourth child and third son of Daniel and Rebecca Richards Child, b. in Brookline, Mass., Aug. 28, 1788, m. 1820, Hannah Richards, dau. of Joshua and Deborah Davis Richards; she was b. April 13, 1797. Mr. Child removed to Cincinnati, O., where he was engaged for many years in a prosperous business. He was a man of large benevolence, esteemed for his manly and noble qualities; he d. Aug. 24, 1866.
[Seventh Generation.] Children:

3477. i. ELIZABETH FISHER CHILD, b. in Boston, Mass., 1821, m. George Henry Davis; lived in Cincinnati and New York City.

3478. ii. JOHN RICHARDS CHILD, JR., b. in Boston, Mass., Jan. 29, 1823, m. Frances Wood of Cincinnati, O.

3479. iii. CAROLINE FRANCES CHILD, b. in Cincinnati, O., Jan. 15, 1825, d. Sept. 27, 1826.

3480. iv. JOSHUA RICHARDS CHILD, b. in Cincinnati, O., May 22, 1828, d. March 30, 1829.

3481. v. RICHARD E. CHILD, } b. in Cincinnati, O., Aug. 3, 1838,
 - Twins. {d. June 28, 1840.
3482. vi. WARREN HARTSHORN CHILD, } b. in Cincinnati, O., Aug. 3, 1838, m. 1865, Molly Edmondston.

[Seventh Generation.]

3477. i. ELIZABETH FISHER CHILD, eldest child of John Richards and Hannah Richards Child, b. in Boston, Mass., 1821, m. about 1845, George Henry Davis; they reside in New York City.
[Eighth Generation.] Children:

3483. i. HENRY DAVIS, b. Jan. 8, 1847.

3484. ii. CARLTON C. DAVIS, b. June 18, 1848, m. Jan. 12, 1875, Julia Helen Force.

3485. iii. WALTER JOHN DAVIS, b. May 18, 1860.

[Eighth Generation.]

3484. ii. CARLTON C. DAVIS, second child and son of Elizabeth Fisher Child and George Henry Davis, b. in Cincinnati,

* On page 407, the date of death of Mrs. Abbie Cunningham Child is given May 20, 1874. The discrepancy is owing to different dates in the record sent us—discovered too late to be remedied.

Isaac Child

O., June 18, 1848, m. Jan. 12, 1875, Julia Helen Force of Pittsburg, Pa.; she was b. in Pittsburg, Pa., Nov. 12, 1853. She is the dau. of William and Mary A. Force. Mr. Child resides in Denver, Col.

[Ninth Generation.] Child:

3486. i. CARLTON CHARLES DAVIS, b. in Denver, Col., Nov. 26, 1876.

[Seventh Generation.]

3478. ii. JOHN RICHARDS CHILD, second child and eldest son of John Richards and Hannah Richards Child, b. in Boston, Mass., Jan. 29, 1823, m. about 1846, Frances Wood.

[Eighth Generation.] Children:

3487. i. WILLIAM WOOD CHILD, b. in Cincinnati, O., Aug. 8, 1847.
3488. ii. JOHN RICHARDS CHILD, JR., b. in Cincinnati, O., Feb. 16, 1849.
3489. iii. HANNAH FRANCES CHILD, b. in Cincinnati, O., 1853.

[Sixth Generation.]

3461. vi. ISAAC CHILD, 2D, sixth child and fifth son of Daniel and Rebecca Richards Child, b. in Newton, Mass., May 1, 1792, m. three times—1st, Nov. 22, 1821, Eliza Billings, dau. of Benjamin and Susanna Weld Billings of Roxbury, Mass., she was b. 1798; m. 2d, July 4, 1848, Maria M. Eastman, dau of Phineas and Judith Gale Eastman of Franklin, N. H., she d. April 3, 1853, and he m. 3d, May 31, 1854, Abigail Baker, dau. of Eli Forbes Baker, Esq., of Steuben, Me., she was b. Mch. 7, 1816. Mrs. Eliza Billings Child was intered at West Roxbury, Mass., and Mrs. Maria Eastman Child at Forest Hill Cemetery, Roxbury.

Mr. Isaac Child by reason of his great age, eligible family connections, and many years of special devotion to genealogical research relating to our family name, is justly entitled to a pleasant notice in this connection. He was born in Roxbury, Mass., on the first of May, 1792, making his age at this date (Sept. 1, 1880,) 88 years and 4 months. One possessed of the physical and intellectual stamina, which it has been the fortune of Mr. Child to inherit from a robust ancestry, could scarcely live to his age without an instructive history of much interest. We should look for intelligence and manliness, and all the best results of an industrious and virtuous life. The channel of Mr. Child's activities has brought him in contact with men of intelligence and culture, and enabled him to have memories which future generations will contemplate with no little interest. His early life was spent in mercantile pursuits either in his own interest or that of others, which was characterized by efficiency and entire uprightness. During these many years of business employments, his reading and observation have been quite extensive, resulting in humane and benevolent views of life, as well as in the adoption of opinions and theories on moral and religious questions, which have drawn him aside from the generally accepted current systems of the present day. Without detracting from his moral worth he might be regarded as somewhat eccentric. Whether his *medi- nmistic* tendencies should be classed among his eccentricities we express no opinion. He claims, to quote his own language, " a foretaste of the future life as immediately connected with the present, as fully exhibited by the whole character of Jesus . . . . overlooked or evaded by the christian world of the present times." We discover in this no very great advance in christian experience over the rest of the christian world. And he adds: "Universal kindness, forgiveness, goodness, and unselfishness in every possible way are sure to raise us toward God and a happy future." There can be no doubt that these attainments are the legitimate fruits of true faith in Christ, which is the common belief of the bulk of professing christians. His moral honesty cannot be questioned. The drift of his researches for many years have been in the direction of genealogical lore and antique curiosities. Specimens of the latter constitute an unclassified cabinet full of interest. Here one lives among the ancients. The lessons afforded are suggestive of instructive and amusing events. It would be folly to call some of the results of a long life thus displayed, a waste of time, and a proof of an aimless life—each man fills a sphere, no man lives in vain. His emanations are full of instructive lessons that should be used to make us wiser and better. In the line of genealogical investigations in behalf of our family name, Mr. Child has been indefatigable. While bodily infirmities are bowing his once noble form, his mental powers are still remarkable for vigor. His domestic felicities have been shared and enhanced by three successive companions in holy wedlock, whose intelligence, amiability and moral worth have constituted no small part of his home comforts; the last of whom still lives to sympathize with and care for his declining years.

[Seventh Generation.] Children of Isaac Child by 1st marriage:

3490. i. SOPHIA BUCKLAND CHILD, b. in Boston, Mass., Aug. 11, 1822, m. Sept. 15, 1842, James Guild, son of Samuel Guild, of Roxbury, Mass. She d. Dec. 2, 1857. They had no children.

By second marriage:

3491. ii. SUSAN REBECCA CHILD, b. in Boston, Mass., Sept. 21, 1855, d. Aug. 1858, at Steuben, Me. This was a remarkably mature child, and gave great promise for the future.

3492. iii. ELIZABETH BALL CHILD, b. June 1, 1858, d. July 30, 1860.

[Sixth Generation.]

3466. xi. DANIEL FRANKLIN CHILD, eleventh child and seventh son of Daniel and Rebecca Richards Child, b. in Roxbury, Mass., May 10, 1803, m. Nov. 4, 1839, Mary Davis Guild, dau. of Samuel and Mary Mears Guild. She was b. Dec. 23, 1807, d. Jan. 25, 1864. He d. suddenly Oct. 18, 1876.

Mr. Daniel F. Child is so thoroughly presented in the obituary notices of him in three of the leading papers of Boston, the *Commonwealth, Transcript* and *Advertiser*, that we feel we cannot do better than make excerpts therefrom:

"He was connected with the Boston locomotive works and the Hinkley and Drury locomotive works, as treasurer, more than forty years. He was favored from youth to manhood with ample means for early training and education; whoever shared in the noble and characteristic justice of this man was made better and more happy for life thereby. Hospitable to new truth, though not carried away by delusion, he examined every new theory in physics and morals; and if his faith waned he was as frank in its abandonment as he had been chivalrous in its defence. A parishoner and warm friend of Theodore Parker; exceedingly tenacious of opinion, and firm as steel in his protest against public wrong. Mr. Child was in his private relations the most gentle and genial of men. He

"Never found fault with you, never implied
Your wrong by (his) right; and yet men at (his) side
Grew nobler, girls purer."

His nature seemed proof against trial; strong and sweet to the core. Some of the happiest hours of his life were passed in solitary visits to his farm in West Roxbury. He was on his way to this favorite haunt when, without a sigh, he passed away in the railway train, on the 18th October, 1876."

[Seventh Generation.] Children:

3493. i. MARY LOUISA EVERETT CHILD, b. in Boston, Mass., May 27, 1841, m. Oct. 5, 1863, Francis Bush.

3494. ii. FRANKLIN DAVID CHILD, b. in Boston, Mass., Nov. 24, 1842, m. at the St. James Hotel, Boston, Mass., by Rev. Minot J. Savage, Nov. 6, 1879, Eliza C. Howard, dau. of the late William H. Howard.

3495. iii. GEORGE FREDERICK CHILD, b. in Boston, Mass., Aug. 9, 1844.

3496. iv. SAMUEL GUILD CHILD, b. in Boston, Mass., July 21, 1849.

3497. v. SOPHIA CHILD, b. in Boston, Mass., June 3, 1853.

[Fifth Generation.]

3409. x. ISAAC CHILD, JR., tenth child and fourth son of Isaac and Elizabeth Weld Child, b. in Sturbridge, Mass., May

2, 1763, m Sept. 30, 1792, Esther Bardwell. She d May 3, 1835. He d. April 5, 1840. This family removed to Craftsbury, Vt.: at what date is not given.

[Sixth Generation.] Children:

3498. i. ESTHER CHILD, b. in Sturbridge, Mass., July 22, 1793, d. same day.

3499. ii. DAVID CHILD, b. in Sturbridge. Mass., Aug. 23, 1794, m. Jan. 1, 1822, Abigail Jones.

3500. iii. CHARLES LEWIS CHILD. b. in Sturbridge, Mass., Jan. 24, 1796, d. young.

3501. iv. ABIJAH CHILD, b. in Sturbridge, Mass., Mch. 7, 1798, d. same day.

3502. v. CHARLES LEWIS CHILD, 2D. b. in Sturbridge, Mass., Sept. 5, 1800, m. twice—1st, April 10, 1823, Harriet Leach; m. 2d, Dec. 16, 1827, Malinda Leach.

3503. vi. AZUBAH BARDWELL CHILD. b. in Sturbridge, Mass., Dec. 5, 1803, d. Nov. 4, 1821.

3504. vii. ELIZABETH BARDWELL CHILD, b. in Sturbridge, Mass., Jan. 18, 1808, m. Mch. 16, 1828, Ansel Robbins.

[Sixth Generation.]

3499. ii. DAVID CHILD, second child and eldest son of Isaac and Esther Bardwell Child, b. in Sturbridge, Mass., Aug. 23, 1794, m. Jan. 1, 1822, Abigail Jones. She was b. July 3, 1801. Lived in Craftsbury, Vt., and removed to Union Centre, Ohio.

[Seventh Generation.] Children:

3505. i. MARIAN WINFIELD CHILD. b. June 12, 1826. d. June 5, 1829.

3506. ii. ISAAC CHILD, b. June 15, 1830, m. Mch. 24, 1864, Clarissa S. Downer.

3507. iii. SIMON BARDWELL CHILD, b. April 2, 1834, m. April 14, 1859, Susan Michael.

3508. iv. WILLIAM MASON LEWIS CHILD, b. July 10, 1838, d. May 2, 1839.

3509. v. MARY CHILD, } Twins. } b. Sept. 24, 1846.
3510. vi. MARTHA CHILD,

[Seventh Generation.]

3507. iii. SIMON BARDWELL CHILD, third child and second son of David and Abigail Jones Child, b. April 2, 1834, m. April 14, 1859, Susan Michael.

[Eighth Generation.] Children:

3511. i. CARRIE CHILD. b. Jan. 30, 1860, d. Aug. 8, 1863.

3512. ii. HATTIE M. CHILD, b. Jan. 1, 1862, d. May 18, 1864.

[Sixth Generation.]

3502. v. CHARLES LEWIS CHILD, 2D, fifth child and fourth son of Isaac and Esther Bardwell Child, b. Sept. 5, 1800, m. twice—1st, April 10, 1823, Harriet Leach: she d. Jan. 14, 1825 ; m. 2d, Dec. 16, 1827, Malinda Leach, sister of the first wife; she d. Aug. 7, 1879. Mr. Child d. Mch. 8, 1880, in Decorah, Iowa. Mrs. Sallee, a daughter, writes of her father as a great but patient sufferer in the last months of his life;

but they were brightened and cheered by the prospect of a happy future in his anticipated surroundings in the spirit world. He was an upright man, well informed on the general topics of the day : a man of genial temperament and pleasant humor. He was one of the first settlers in Decorah, Iowa, having located there in 1853 : was active in the affairs of town and county.

[Seventh Generation.] Children. By first marriage :

3513. i. SYLVANUS LEACH CHILD, b. Dec. 16, 1824, d. Mch. 31, 1841.

By second marriage :

3514. ii. JOHN KILLUM CHILD, b. Sept. 3, 1828, d. Sept. 4, 1830.

3515. iii. SARAH JEMIMA CHILD, b. Feb. 17, 1830, m. Jan. 11, 1849, James B. Hartgrave.

3516. iv. MARY ANN CHILD, b. Mch. 19, 1833, m. Dec. 25, 1851, John B. Davin.

3517. v. ESTHER CHILD, b. May 25, 1835, m. May 25, 1856, Daniel C. Jerold.

3518. vi. DARIUS CHILD, b. July 17, 1837, m. Dec. 25, 1861, Amanda Malvina Moore.

3519. vii. GEORGE CHILD, b. April 7, 1840, d. Mch. 4, 1849.

3520. viii. ELIZABETH CHILD, b. April 30, 1842, m. Oct. 11, 1865, William Sallee.

3521. ix. AMASA CHILD, b. Aug. 24, 1844, m. Mary A. Jenkins.

[Seventh Generation.]

3515. iii. SARAH JEMIMA CHILD, eldest dau. of Charles Lewis and Malinda Leach Child, b. in Sturbridge, Mass., Feb. 17, 1831, m. Jan. 11, 1849, James B. Hartgrave. Mrs. Hartgrave d. Nov. 1, 1875, in Floyd, Floyd Co., Iowa, to which place the family removed from Tazwell Co., Ill. Mr. Hartgrave is by occupation a blacksmith.

[Eighth Generation.] Children :

3522. i. HARRIET LEACH HARTGRAVE, b. in Tazwell, Co., Ill., Oct. 18, 1849, m. Henry Lawrence Inman.

3523. ii. CHARLES LEWIS HARTGRAVE, b. in Allamakee Co., Ill., May 8, 1853 m. Sept. 19, 1879, Geneva Gifford. Resides in Wellington, Kansas.

3524. iii. SUSAN JANE HARTGRAVE, b. in Decorah, Iowa, May 8, 1855, m. July 14, 1872, Lewis Miller.

3525. iv. PAMELIA REBECCA HARTGRAVE, b. in Decorah, Iowa, Nov. 2, 1856, m. Dec. 25, 1873, Charles Sibley.

3526. v. LUCIA MALINDA HARTGRAVE, b. in Decorah, Iowa, Sept. 4, 1858.

3527. vi. ISABELL MARION HARTGRAVE, b. in Decorah, Iowa, Mch. 22, 1862.

3528. vii. SARAH SENORA HARTGRAVE, b. in Decorah, Iowa, Feb. 22, 1865.

3529. viii. JAMES HARTGRAVE, b. in Decorah, Iowa, Dec. 14, 1868, d. same day.

[Eighth Generation.]

3522. i. HARRIET LEACH HARTGRAVE, eldest child of Sarah Jemima Child and James B. Hartgrave, b. in Tazwell Co., Ill., Oct. 18, 1849, m. Mch. 27, 1869, Henry Lawrence Inman of Winter, Burton Co., Iowa : reside in Wellington, Sumner Co., Kansas.

[Ninth Generation.]   Children:
    3530. i. AUSTIN JAMES INMAN, b. in Winter, Iowa, Jan. 20, 1870.
    3531. ii. NORABELL INMAN, b. in Winter, Iowa, Aug. 31, 1871.
    3532. iii. HENRY LAWRENCE INMAN, JR., b. in Winter, Ia, Mch. 6, 1873.
    3533. iv. SARAH MELVINA INMAN, b. in Floyd, Iowa, Mch. 9, 1876.
    3534. v. HATTIE LEONICE INMAN, b. in Wellington, Sumner Co., Kansas, Dec. 11, 1879.

[Eighth Generation.

    3524. iii. SUSAN JANE HARTGRAVE, third child and second dau. of Sarah Jemima Child and James B. Hartgrave, b. in Decorah, Winneshiek Co., Iowa, May 8, 1853, m. July 14, 1872, Lewis Miller of Floyd, Floyd Co., Iowa: they reside in Floyd, Iowa.

[Ninth Generation.]   Children:
    3535. i. PEARLA C. MILLER, b. in Floyd, Iowa, May 14, 1873.
    3536. ii. JAMES MILLER, b. in Floyd, Iowa, Aug. 1875.
    3537. iii. CORAL BELLE MILLER, b. in Floyd, Iowa, April 7, 1878.

[Eighth Generation.]

    3525. iv. PAMELIA REBECCA HARTGRAVE, fourth child and third dau. of Sarah Jemima Child and James B. Hartgrave, b. in Decorah, Winneshiek Co., Iowa, Nov. 2, 1856, m. Dec. 25, 1873, Charles Sibley.

[Ninth Generation.]   Children:
    3538. i. FREDDIE SIBLEY, b. Nov. 1874.
    3539. ii. GRACE SIBLEY, b. May 1877.

[Seventh Generation.]

    3516. iv. MARY ANN CHILD, second dau. of Charles Lewis and Melinda Leach Child, b. Mch. 19, 1833, m. Dec. 25, 1851. John Henry Davin of Tazwell Co., Ill.; reside in Urbana, Burton Co., Iowa.

[Eighth Generation.]   Children:
    3540. i. EMILY JANE DAVIN, b. in Decorah, Iowa, April 28, 1853, m. John Gunn, Dec. 23, 1875; reside in Jewell, Jewell Co., Kansas.
    3541. ii. ELIZABETH DAVIN, b. in Decorah, Iowa, Oct. 4, 1855, m. March 1876, Spencer Johnson.
    3542. iii. ELVIRA MALINDA DAVIN, b. in Decorah, Iowa, Jan. 1, 1858.
    3543. iv. ANN DAVIN, b. in Decorah, Iowa, June 26, 1860.
    3544. v. CLARA DAVIN, b. in Decorah, Ia., Sept. 3, 1863, d. Sept. 10, 1865.
    3545. vi. PHILIP DAVIN, b. in Burton Co., Iowa, May 23, 1866, d. Oct. 8, 1866.
    3546. vii. AMASA DAVIN, b. in Burton Co., Iowa, Feb. 17, 1868.
    3547. viii. MALVINA DAVIN, b. in Burton Co, Iowa, Feb. 23, 1871.

[Eighth Generation.]

    3541. ii. ELIZABETH DAVIN, second child and dau. of Mary Ann Child and John Henry Davin, b. in Decorah, Iowa, Oct. 4, 1855, m. March 1876, Spencer Johnson: they reside near Winter, Iowa.

[Ninth Generation.] Children:
3548. i. ELSIE JOHNSON, b. Jan. 17, 1877.
3549. ii. CHARLES LESLIE JOHNSON, b. Dec. 1878.

[Seventh Generation.]

3517. v. ESTHER LUCINDA CHILD, third dau. of Charles Lewis and Malinda Leach Child, b. May 25, 1835, m. May 25, 1856, Daniel C. Jerold of Decorah, Iowa; reside in Lime Springs, Howard Co., Iowa.

[Eighth Generation.] Children:
3550. i. SARAH MATILDA JEROLD, b. in Decorah, Iowa, Nov. 2, 1857.
3551. ii. EMMA MALINDA JEROLD, b. in Decorah, Iowa, Dec. 11, 1861, d. June 14, 1862.
3552. iii. SAMUEL ELMER JEROLD, b. in Tioga Co., Pa., June 2, 1864.
3553. iv. DANIEL AMASA JEROLD, b. in Tioga Co., Pa., Oct. 22, 1867

[Seventh Generation.]

3518. vi. DARIUS CHILD, fifth child of Charles Lewis and Malinda Leach Child, b. July 17, 1837, m. Dec. 25, 1861, Amanda Malvina Moore.

[Eighth Generation.] Children:
3554. i. ETTA LUCIA CHILD, b. Dec. 14, 1862, in Decorah, Iowa.
3555. ii. JAMES LEWIS CHILD, b April 3, 1865, in Decorah, Iowa.
3556. iii. LAURA ELIZABETH CHILD, b. March 13, 1867, in Decorah, Iowa.
3557. iv. GEORGE LESLIE CHILD, b. Sept. 9, 1871, in Decorah, Iowa.

[Seventh Generation.]

3520. viii. ELIZBETH CHILD, fourth dau. of Charles Lewis and Malinda Leach Child, b. in Craftsbury, Vt., April 30, 1842, m. Oct. 11, 1865, William Sallee, of Decorah, Iowa. He d. Sept. 27, 1880. He was sergeant in Co. H. 9th Iowa Vet. Vol.; wounded at Pea Ridge. Mrs. Sallee resides in Decorah, Iowa.

[Eighth Generation.] Children:
3558. i. CHARLES WILBER SALLEE, b. in Emmet, Iowa, Oct. 7, 1866.
3559. ii. DARIUS ABRAM SALLEE, b. in Benton Co., Iowa, April 13, 1868.
3560. iii. ALMA MALINDA SALLEE, b. in De Pue, Bureau Co., Ill., Dec. 31, 1874.

[Seventh Generation.]

3521. ix. AMASA CHILD, fifth son of Charles Lewis and Malinda Leach Child, b. in Craftsbury, Vt., Aug. 24, 1844, m. about 1873. Mary A. Jenkins. Residence Decorah, Iowa.

[Eighth Generation.] Children:
3561. i. ESTELLA MAY CHILD, b. in Juniata, Adams Co., Nebraska, Jan. 27, 1874.
3562. ii. CHARLES LEWIS CHILD, b. May 7, 1875, in Juniata, Neb.
3563. iii. ALICE ROSAMOND CHILD, b. June 11, 1877, in Juniata, Neb.
3564. iv. ADDIE CORA CHILD, b. Nov. 15, 1878, in Juniata, Neb.

[Fifth Generation.]

3411. xii. DAVID WELD CHILD, twelfth child and seventh
son of Isaac, Jr., and Elizabeth Weld Child, b. in Sturbridge,
Mass., Feb. 19, 1792, m. April 1801, Abigail Dorr. dau. of
Ebenezer and Abigail Cunningham Dorr, a merchant of Boston.
[Sixth Generation] Children:

3565. i. DAVID CHILD, b. in Boston, Mass., June 6, 1802, d. young.

3566. ii. EDWARD VERNON CHILD, b. in Boston, Mass , March 13, 1804,
m. in 1831, Malinda Katharine Lee.

3567. iii. ABIGAIL DORR CHILD, b. in Boston, Mass., Aug. 10, 1806, d.
Sept. 27, 1807.

3568. iv. WILLIAM HENRY CHILD, b. in Boston, Mass., Dec. 22, 1809, d.
Nov. 12, 1811.

[Sixth Generation.]

3566. ii. EDWARD VERNON CHILDE, second child and son of
David Weld and Abigail Cunningham Dorr Child, b. in Boston, Mass., Mch. 13, 1804, m. 1831, Malinda Katharine Lee,
dau. of General Henry Lee of Baltimore, Md. : she d. 1861, in
Paris, France. Reside in Paris, France.

[Seventh Generation.] Children.

3569. i. EDWARD LEE CHILDE, b. in Baltimore, Md., 1832, m. 1868,
Blanche De Triquite of Paris, France.

3570. ii. ARTHUR CHILDE, b. in Boston, Mass., 1834, d. in Munich,
Bavaria.

3571. iii. FLORENCE CHILDE, b. in Florence, Italy, 1838, m. 1853, Count
Henry Soltyk of Cracow, Poland.

3572. iv. MARY CHILDE, b in Paris, France, 1841, m. 1859, Robert Hoffman of Baltimore, Md., she d. 1865.

[Seventh Generation.]

3571. iii. FLORENCE CHILDE, third child and eldest dau. of
Edward Vernon and Katharine Lee Childe, b. 1838, in Florence, Italy, m. 1853, Count Henry Soltyk of Cracow, Poland.

[Eighth Generation.] Child:

3573. i. STANISLAUS SOLTYK, b. in 1854. He is a midshipman in the
Austrian Navy.

[Third Generation.]

3377. iii. ELIZABETH CHILD, third child and eldest dau. of
Joshua and Elizabeth Morris Child, b. in Roxbury, Mass., July
20, 1691, m. Dec. 18, 1711, John May, of Roxbury, Mass. He
was b. 1686.

Immediately after marriage Mr. May removed to Woodstock,
where he spent a long and useful life. We are indebted to the
diary of this Mr. May, covering the years of 1711-12-13, for
establishing the identity of John Child of Woodstock, who
m. Elizabeth ———, as the tenth child of Benjamin Child the

emigrant. Mr. John May was of the fourth generation in descent from his emigrant ancestor. His father was John May, born in Roxbury, Mass., May 19, 1663, married Prudence Bridge. His grandfather was John May, who was born in England, 1631, who, with his brother, Samuel, emigrated with their father to America. His great grandfather, John May, was born in May-field, Sussex Co., England, 1590. He came to America in 1640, and settled in that part of Roxbury, Mass., known as Jamaica Plains. He married twice, the name of first wife, or date of marriage, is not given. She died 1651. Her death is mentioned by the "Apostle Elliot" where he says "Sister Maye died a very gracious and savory christian." His second marriage was to Sarah ———. According to tradition, Mr. May, was master of the vessel called The James, which, as early as 1635, sailed between the port of London and New England. He died April 28, 1670. Mrs. May died the same year.*

[After giving the descendants of John May, who married Elizabeth Child, we shall give some account of his brother, Nehemiah, the eighth child of John and Prudence Bridge May.]

[Fourth Generation.] Children. All the children were b. in Woodstock, Ct:

** i. Elizabeth May, b. Oct. 18, 1712.

** ii. John May, Jr., b. Sept. 9, 1714. He and one of his brothers were killed in bed by lightning.

** iii. Joshua May, b. Oct. 16, 1716, m. Anna Bacon.

** iv. Caleb May, b. Sept. 13, 1719, m. twice—1st, Elizabeth Child; m. 2d, Mehitable Holbrook.

** v. Stephen May, b. Nov. 10, 1721, m. Mary Child.

** vi. Thomas May, b. Feb. 14, 1723, m. Lucy Goddard Child.

** vii. Prudence May, b. Mch. 22, 1725, d. 1728.

** viii. Esther May, b. Jan. 7, 1727, d. July 6, 1729.

** ix. Prudence May, 2d, b. 1728.

** x. Esther May, 2d, b. 1729, d. young.

** xi. Prudence May, 3d, b. April 11, 1730.

** xii. Joseph May, b. April 3, 1732.

[Fourth Generation.]

** iii. Joshua May, third child and second son of Elizabeth Child and John May, b. in Woodstock, Ct., Oct. 16, 1716, m. Jan. 20, 1741, Anna Bacon.

*We are indebted to Henry A. May, Esq., of Boston, who is revising a Genealogy of the May Family, for this item of history. The record of Elizabeth Child May and her descendants reached us too late for the regular numbering.

[Fifth Generation.]   Children:
   *** i. JOSEPH MAY, b. in Woodstock, Ct., Feb. 28, 1743, m. Lois Child.
   *** ii. HANNAH MAY.
   *** iii. JOHN MAY, b. in Woodstock, Dec. 29, 1749, m. Hannah Bugbee.
   *** iv. HARMON MAY.
   *** v. JOSHUA MAY.
   *** vi. WALTER MAY.

[Fifth Generation.]
   *** iii. JOHN MAY, third child and second son of Joshua and Anna Bacon May, b. in Woodstock, Dec. 29, 1749, m. Mch. 12, 1778, Hannah Bugbee; she was b. June 6, 1755, d. Nov. 15, 1857.

[Sixth Generation.]   Children:
   **** i. MARY MAY, b. in Woodstock, Jan. 23, 1779, m. Luther Rawson.
   **** ii. PENUEL MAY, b. in Woodstock, April 19, 1781, d. Sept. 20, 1759.
   **** iii. ERASTUS MAY, b. in Woodstock, Feb. 8, 1783, d. Feb. 8, 1787.
   **** iv. CHARLES MAY, b. in Woodstock, April 17, 1785, m. Mrs. Maria Chandler.
   **** v. JOHN B. MAY, b. in Woodstock, Jan. 7, 1787, m. Sylvia Alba.
   **** vi. SOPHIA MAY, b. in Woodstock, Nov. 30, 1789, d. Mch. 2, 1794.
   **** vii. BETSEY MAY, b. in Woodstock, Dec. 11, 1791, d. 1806.
   **** viii. SALLY MAY, b. in Woodstock, Oct. 15, 1793, m. Asa May.
   **** ix. ERASTUS MAY, 2D, b. in Woodstock, Nov. 2, 1796, m. Lydia M. Child. (For children see page 195, No. 911.)
   **** x. SOPHIA MAY, 2D, b. Oct. 3, 1798, m. Dexter W. Jones.

[Sixth Generation.]
   **** viii. SALLY MAY, eighth child of John May and Hannah Bugbee, and granddaughter, of Elizabeth Child and John May, b. in Woodstock, Ct., Oct. 15, 1793, m. Mch. 1819, Asa May.

[Seventh Generation.]   Children:
   ***** i. ELIZABETH MAY, b. July 10, 1821, m. Luther Rawson.
   ***** ii. CHARLES HARRIS MAY, b. Feb. 2, 1823, m. Mch. 20, 1856, Harriet F. Child, dau. of Stephen and Abigail Carter Child. (For children see p. 171.)
   ***** iii. EZRA C. MAY, b. Oct. 13, 1825, m. Elsie E. Chamberlain.
   ***** iv. CARLO MAY, b. Sept. 3, 1829, m. Mch. 23, 1853, Sarah M. Child, dau. of Dea. William and Sophia Selby Child. (For children see p. 252.)

[Fourth Generation.]
   ** iv. CALEB MAY, fourth child and third son of Elizabeth Child and John May, b. in Woodstock, Ct., Sept. 13, 1791, m. twice—1st, Oct. 15, 1751, Elizabeth Child, dau. of Ebenezer and Elizabeth Child, of Woodstock, Ct.; she was b. May 3, 1723; m. 2d, Mehitable Holbrook.

[Fifth Generation.]   Children:
   *** i. HANNAH MAY, b. in Woodstock, Ct., 1752.
   *** ii. ABIGAIL MAY, b. in Woodstock, Ct., Jan. 24, 1753.

[Fourth Generation.]

** v. STEPHEN MAY, fifth child and fourth son of Elizabeth Child and John May, b. in Woodstock, Ct., Nov. 10, 1721, m. June 11, 1747, Mary Child, dau. of Ephraim and Priscilla Harris Child. She was b. April 1, 1721, d. Mch. 18, 1807. He d. May 3, 1794.

[Fifth Generation.] Children:

*** i. ELIZABETH MAY, b. in Woodstock, Ct., Nov. 10, 1748, m. Aaron Lyon.

*** ii. LUCY MAY, b. Mch. 6, 1750.

*** iii. MARY MAY, b. Aug. 25, 1752, m. Mch. 21, 1777, Alpha Child, son of Nathaniel and Jemima Bugbee Child, of Woodstock, Ct. (For children see page 252, No. 1578.)

*** iv STEPHEN MAY, JR., b. in Woodstock, Ct., Mch. 23, 1755, m. Hannah Murray.

*** v. JOANNA MAY, b. Feb. 8, 1757.

*** vi EPHRAIM MAY, b. in Woodstock, Ct., Nov. 22, 1759, m. Abigail Chandler.

*** vii. SARAH MAY, b. in Woodstock, Ct., Nov. 21, 1761, m. Col. Chester Child; she d. Feb., 1826. (For children see page 240.)

*** viii. ASA MAY, b. in Woodstock, Ct., Sept. 4, 1764, m. Annie Fillibrown; he d. Nov. 17, 1825.

[Fourth Generation.]

** vi. THOMAS MAY, sixth child and fifth son of Elizabeth Child and John May, b. in Woodstock, Ct., Feb. 14, 1723, m. 1755, Lucy Goddard Child, dau. of William and Deborah Goddard Child, she d. Dec. 17, 1790.

[Fifth Generation.] Children:

*** i. SILAS MAY, b. in Woodstock, Ct., 1753, d. 1805.

*** ii. WILLIAM MAY, b. in Woodstock, 1760, d. Dec. 12, 1849.

*** iii. ABEL MAY, b. in Woodstock, 1762, d. Oct. 10, 1767.

*** iv. CHLOE MAY, b. in Woodstock, 1764, d. Sept. 17, 1767.

*** v. PRUDENCE MAY, ⎰ b. in Woodstock, 1766, d. June 24, 1831.
Twins.
*** vi. JONATHAN MAY, ⎱ b. in Woodstock, 1766, d. 1836.

*** vii. ABIGAIL MAY, b. in Woodstock, m. Cyril Carpenter.

*** viii. THOMAS MAY, b. in Woodstock, m. Mary Hunt Mills.

We notice also Nehemiah May, a brother of the John May who married Elizabeth Child, as some of his descendants have married into the Child family. He emigrated with his brother John to Woodstock, Ct., where he reared a family of seven children. His youngest son, Eliakim May, married Martha Lyon, daughter of Mehitable Child and Nehemiah Lyon. Eliakim and Martha Lyon May had six children (see page 198). His second child, Nehemiah May, married Nancy Morse, daughter of Dr. David Morse, of Woodstock, Ct. Nehemiah and Nancy Morse May had six children; their second child, Trenck May, married Cynthia Child, daughter of Capt. Willard Child. (For record of Trenck May, see page 199.)

[Third Generation.]

3379. v. JOSEPH CHILD, fifth child and third son of Joshua and Elizabeth Morris Child, b. in Roxbury, Mass., Jan. 7, 1696, m. Nov. 29, 1722, Abigail Bridges. Removed to Woodstock, Ct., where the births of his children are recorded. He d. 1765, aged 69. She d. Jan. 24, 1788.

[Fourth Generation.]   Children:

3574. i. ANNA CHILD, b. in Woodstock, Ct., June 17, 1725, m. Nathaniel Johnson, Jr.

3575. ii. ABIGAIL CHILD, b. in Woodstock, Ct., Jan. 15, 1727, m. Oct. 5, 1752, Ebenezer Haven.

3576. iii. PRUDENCE CHILD, b. in Woodstock, Ct., July 22, 1729, m. July 15, 1752, Uriah Allard.

3577. iv. RELIEF CHILD, b. in Woodstock, Ct., Feb. 12, 1830.

3578. v. REBECCA CHILD, b. in Woodstock, Ct., April 11, 1733, d. Oct. 18, 1736.

3579. vi. FRANCIS CHILD, b. Dec. 28, 1735, d. April 10, 1738.

3580. vii. REBECCA CHILD, 2D, b. in Woodstock, Ct., Mch. 13, 1838.

3581. viii. JOSEPH CHILD, JR., b. in Woodstock, Ct., Mch. 4, 1739, m. Abigail ——. He d. Oct. 26, 1760, at Greenbush, N. Y. She m. again, Nov. 19, 1767, Nathaniel Blake, of Woodstock, Ct.

3582. ix. ABEL CHILD, b. Feb. 24, 1746, d. Mch. 5, 1751.

[Fourth Generation.]

3574 i. ANNA CHILD, eldest child of Joseph and Abigail Bridges Child, b. in Woodstock, Ct., June 17, 1725, m. April 1, 1756, Nathaniel Johnson, Jr.; she d. Aug. 29, 1804.   Mr. Johnson was army nurse in the Revolutionary war, and died of small-pox at Fishkill, N. Y., where he was buried.

[Fifth Generation.]   Children: All born in Woodstock, Ct.

3583. i. STEPHEN JOHNSON.

3584. ii. WILLIAM JOHNSON, b. Oct. 13, 1760.

3585. iii. PETER JOHNSON.

3586. iv. SILAS JOHNSON, b. June 29, 1763, m. March 31, Huldah Beckwith.

3587. v. LEVI JOHNSON, b. March 25, 1766, m. —— Bishop.

3588. vi. SARAH JOHNSON, m. —— Morse.

3589. vii. ASA JOHNSON, b. Oct. 16, 1767, m. at Bolton, Ct., April 24, 1794, Clarissa Carver.

3590. viii. ANNA JOHNSON, b. Dec. 25, 1771, m. Nathaniel Brown.

3591. ix. MARY JOHNSON, b. ——, m. —— Lyons.

3592. x. NATHANIEL JOHNSON, JR., b. June 5, 1775, m. Lydia Chandler, d. Dec. 31, 1851.

3593. xi. DOLLY JOHNSON, b. Aug. 23, 1776.   Of the seven sons of Nathaniel Johnson, Jr., four were patriot soldiers of the Revolution—Peter was first-lieutenant.

[Fifth Generation.]

3589. vii. ASA JOHNSON, seventh child and sixth son of Anna Child and Nathaniel Johnson, Jr., b. Oct. 16, 1767, m.

April 24, 1794, Clarissa Carver, of Bolton, Ct. Clarissa Carver was a descendant of Gov. Carver, of the Plymouth colony, and a decided christian woman.

[Sixth Generation.] Children:

3594. i. CLARISSA JOHNSON, b. in Bolton, Ct., Jan. 25, 1796, m. Capt. Asa Lawrence.

3595. ii. MARY JOHNSON, b. in Bolton, Ct. Sept. 24, 1798, unmarried.

3596. iii. PAMELIA JOHNSON, b. in Deerfield, Mass., June 23, 1800, d. Dec. 31, 1858, unmarried.

3597. iv. ASA JOHNSON, JR., b. in Deerfield, Mass., Feb. 13, 1802, m. July 4, 1830, Julia Warner Sadd.

3598. v. CARVER JOHNSON, b. in Deerfield, Mass., June 30, 1804, d. April 9, 1868.

3599. vi. HARVEY CHILD JOHNSON, b. in Deerfield, Mass., Sept. 30, 1806, d. Mch. 15, 1858.

3600. vii. NATHANIEL TRUMBULL JOHNSON, b. in Deerfield Mass., Nov. 17, 1808.

3601. viii. EBENEZER JOHNSON, b. in Deerfield, Mass., April 10, 1811.

[Sixth Generation.]

3597. iv. Rev. ASA JOHNSON, fourth child and eldest son of Asa and Clarissa Carver Johnson, and grandson of Anna Child and Nathaniel Johnson, Jr., b. in Deerfield, Mass., Feb. 13, 1802, m. July 4, 1830, Julia Warner Sadd, dau. of Dea. Chauncey and Cynthia Barbour Sadd of Windsor, Ct. Mrs Johnson died March 23, 1852, at Goshen, Ind. Rev. Mr. Johnson graduated at Union College, Schenectady, N. Y., in 1827, and at Auburn Theological Seminary, in 1830. His pastorates as a Presbyterian clergyman have been in Cape Gerardeau, Mo.; Richmond and Nunda, N. Y.; Peru, Ind.; Adel and Redfield, Iowa. He resides with his son, Rev. E. P. Johnson, in Marshall, Mich.; four children.

[Seventh Generation.] Children:

3602. i. CYNTHIA MARIA JOHNSON, b. May 3, 1831, m. June 14, 1860, Rev. Francis Z. Rossiter, son of Rev. Dudley Denison Rossiter and Eliza Woodbridge Rogers. Rev. Mr. Rossiter was b. in Boston, Mass., June 8, 1831. He graduated at Marietta College, Ohio, in 1850, and at Lane Theological Seminary in 1859. His pastorates as a Presbyterian clergyman have been in Huron, Ohio; Oshkosh and Omro, Wis : no children.

3603. ii. ELEANOR EMERSON JOHNSON, b. Oct. 22, 1833, m. Sept. 25, 1855, Rev. F. S. McCabe D. D., of Topeka, Kansas. Dr. McCabe was successor of his father-in-law, Rev. Asa Johnson, in Peru, Ind.

3604. iii. Rev. EDWARD PAYSON JOHNSON, b. Jan. 26, 1850, m. March 23, 1878, Cora Brown. Mr. Johnson has been settled at Sandy Hill, N. Y., and is now the pastor of the Presbyterian church in Marshall, Mich.

3605. iv. MARY CLARISSA JOHNSON, b. June 5, 1855.

[Third Generation.]

3382. viii. DOROTHY CHILD, eighth child and fifth dau. of Joshua and Elizabeth Morris Child, b. in Roxbury, Mass., May 5, 1701, m. May 2, 1723, Ebenezer Draper.

[Fourth Generation.] Children:

3606. i. DOROTHY DRAPER, b. Feb. 1, 1724.

3607. ii. ANN DRAPER, b. May 23, 1725.

[Third Generation.]

3386. xii. CALEB CHILD, twelfth child and sixth son of Joshua and Elizabeth Morris Child, b. in Roxbury. Mass., Sept. 16, 1709, m. Oct. 19, 1736, Rebecca Dana.

[Fourth Generation.] Children:

3608. i. ANNA CHILD, b. Dec. 16, 1739, d. Oct. 15, 1747.

3609. ii. MEHITABLE CHILD, b. Mch. 23, 1740, d. Sept. 28, 1747.

3610. iii. ABIGAIL CHILD, b. Aug. 10. 1744, d. Nov. 10, 1745.

3611. iv. CALEB CHILD, JR., b. Sept. 17, 1746, d. Oct. 16, 1747.

3612. v. PHINEAS CHILD, bapt. Sept. 3, 1749, m. abt. 1775, Elizabeth Briggs.

3613. vi. SOLOMON CHILD, b. Sept. 13, 1752, m. 1803, widow William Wiswell.

3614. vii. CALEB CHILD, JR., 2D, b. May 7, 1759, m. 1799, Sarah Bramhall.

[Fourth Generation.]

3612. v. PHINEAS CHILD, fifth child and second son of Caleb and Rebecca Dana Child, bapt. Sept. 3, 1749, m. abt. 1775, Elizabeth Briggs, dau. of James Briggs, of West Roxbury, Mass. Mr. Child d. 1814. Mrs. Child d. Sept. 28, 1800.

[Fifth Generation.] Children:

3615. i. PHINEAS CHILD, JR., b. April 25, 1777, m. Sept. 20, 1801, Susanna Whitney.

3616. ii. THOMAS CHILD, b. Jan. 10. 1779, m. 1803, Harriet Williams; lived in Cambridge, Mass.

3617. iii. SOLOMON CHILD, b. Jan. 30, 1781, d. at Putnam. Ct., May, 7, 1816

3618. iv. BETSEY CHILD, b. Dec. 3, 1782, m. Nov. 8, 1812, Aaron Rhodes.

3619 v. REBECA CHILD, b Nov. 21, 1784, m. Dec. 14, 1807, William Tucker, of Boston. Mass.; she d. Sept. 10, 1842.

3620. vi. POLLY CHILD, b. Oct. 15. 1786, d. Dec. 14, 1867, unmarried.

3621. vii. ABIGAIL CHILD, b May 17, 1789, d. May 10, 1795.

3622. viii ANNA CHILD, b. July 13, 1792, m. Thomas Dillaway; she d. in Boston, July 1829.

3623. ix. SARAH CHILD, b. Dec. 6, 1795, m. Andrew Hyde, of Prescott, Mass., d. Jan 4, 1847.

[Fifth Generation.]

3615. i. PHINEAS CHILD, JR., eldest child of Phineas and Elizabeth Briggs Child, b. April 25, 1877, m. Sept. 20, 1801, Susanna Whitney, of Warwick, Mass. She was b. Jan. 31, 1773. Resided in Warwick.

[Sixth Generation.] Children:

3624. i. PHINEAS CHILD, JR., b. March 18, 1804, d. Jan. 16, 1852.

3625. ii. DANIEL CHILD, b. Dec. 20, 1805, d. Jan. 2, 1828, unmarried

3626. iii. SUSANNA CHILD. b. Sept 27. 1807, unmarried.

[It is with very sincere regret that I learn upon the issue of my last circulars, announcing the completion of my work, that the record sent me of the descendants of Joshua Child, is quite incomplete, and also that numerous errors in dates and names are found in other families of this line, besides those herewith amended, yet too late to correct.

When I was preparing the material sent me of the Caleb Child who married Sarah Bramhall, I felt that there should be later report, and wrote to Mr. Isaac Child for some address by which I might obtain it, but could get none. In sending my last circulars I have found the grandchildren of this Rev. Caleb Child, and I most gladly welcome from them, especially Mr. Ethan Allen Doty, the following most interesting account of this talented man and his worthy and honorable descendants.

It may not be amiss to state in connection with this supplement that I have compared the record sent me of *early* history, with copies made personally, or by agents, of town records, in Woodstock, Ct., Upton, Deerfield, Rutland and Boston, Mass., and of the Roxbury church records.]

Rev. CALEB CHILD, M. D., whose record is very brief on page 425, was b. May 13, 1759, and m. July 21, 1799, Sarah Bramhall. In 1792 he went to Albany, N. Y., and opened a school there, with a recommendation signed by " Samuel West, minister of the Church of Christ, Hollis street, Boston." " William Heath, late Major General in the American army, Roxbury," "and twenty other persons of respectability" to the effect that, " Mr. Caleb Child, the bearer, has taught school to general satisfaction, and with great success, in the neighborhood of this place for five years past, during which time he has occasionally supplied the pulpit at the Third Parish in Roxbury, having at a proper time, and in a regular manner, entered on the work of the Gospel ministry." In June, 1795, Deacon Caleb Child was recommended for admittance to the Order of Priests, by a certificate signed by Bishop Seabury and the Standing Committee of the Episcopal Church in Connecticut, and addressed to the Bishop of New York. He was granted a certificate as physician by Gilbert Livingston, Master in Chancery at Poughkeepsie, June 1, 1798, and March 3, 1803, was appointed by the Governor, " Surgeon of the Reg't of Militia in the county of Dutchess." From this time until his death he preached the Gospel, practicing at the same time as a physician, and for at least a portion of the time while residing in Troy, N. Y., kept an apothecary store. Rev. Dr. Child could not have filled all these varied callings, had he not been a very methodical man : a large volume of sermons in manuscript testifies to his power as a minister, as well as to his neatness as a penman. A medallion portrait of him on ivory, taken apparently about his fortieth year, remains in the family : it represents him in clerical costume, with a pleasing and attractive face, and strong characteristics. His marriage to Miss Bramhall was not pleasing to her parents, and the service was performed by William Lathrop, Esq., at the home of her uncle Elisha Barlow, Esq., the brother of her mother. The Bramhalls and Barlows were among the earliest settlers of Amenia, N. Y., the Bramhalls having come from Plymouth, Mass., and the Barlows from Sandwich on Cape Cod.

[Fifth Generation.] Children:

i. EDMUND BRAMHALL CHILD, b. Dec. 23, 1800, m abt. 1823, Fanny N. Lockwood.

ii. CALEB CHILD, b May 31, 1803, in Poughkeepsie, N. Y. He received a fair education and became a printer. In 1832, he left New York City for the South. He died at New Orleans, La., of yellow fever, Oct. 9, 1833, just as he had been called to the editorship of a newspaper in Mobile, Ala. He was a man of varied attainments, and died greatly regretted.

iii. MARY ELIZA CHILD, b. in Poughkeepsie, Oct. 25, 1805, d. at Troy, N. Y., May 30, 1841.

iv. REBECCA ANNA CHILD, b April 4, 1808, m. May 2, 1847, Isaac D. Wetsell.

v. SARAH MEHITABLE CHILD, b. Sept. 19, 1810, m. Oct. 15, 1839, Warren S. Doty.

vi. SOLOMON CHILD, b. in Troy, N. Y., July 19, 1813. Became a printer; left New York City in 1832, and settled finally in Montgomery, Ala., where he became editor and part owner of the Montgomery *Advertiser*; at that time the second in value of newspapers in the State. He died there, unmarried, 1838 or '39.

vii. JOSEPH BRAMHALL CHILD, b June 8, 1815, m. 1858, Sarah B. Hamlin.

[Fifth Generation.]

EDMUND BRAMHALL CHILD, the eldest son and child of Rev. Caleb and Sarah Bramhall Child, b. in Stamford, Ct., Dec. 23, 1800, m. about 1823, Fannie N. Lockwood, dau. of Millington Lockwood, of Albany, N. Y. The family of Dr. Caleb Child inherit the literary tastes and talents of the father, three of the sons becoming journalists. Mr. E. B. Child was for several years connected with the Albany *Argus*. He published the *Escretor*, a masonic paper, also the *American Masonick Record* in that city. He was the publisher of the Albany Directory for a number of years. He died in Albany in 1840.

[Sixth Generation.] Children:

i. HENRY CLAY CHILD, b April 25, 1824, m. Jan. 30, 1848, Georgiana T. H. Bowman.

ii. EDMUND BRAMHALL CHILD, b. Sept. 2, 1826, m. Oct. 7, 1855, Rebecca Anna Harystman

iii. JANE LOCKWOOD CHILD, b. Aug. 5, 1830, m. Capt. John Baxter of Cape Cod. Two children, son and daughter; names not sent.

iv. CHARLES AUGUSTUS CHILD, b. Sept. 13, 1834, m. and has four children; names not given. Mr. Child is President of the American Union Express Co., New York City.

[Sixth Generation.]

i. HENRY CLAY CHILD, eldest child of Edmund Bramhall and Fanny N. Lockwood Child, b. in Albany, N. Y., April 25, 1824, m. Jan. 30, 1848, by Rev. William Adams, D. D., of Central Presbyterian Church, New York City, Georgiana T. H. Bowman. Residence, 35 8th street, Hoboken, N. J. A printer.

[Seventh Generation.] Children:

i. FANNY MILLINGTON CHILD, b. in New York City, Dec. 24, 1848, m. Jan. 8, 1868, James H. Wilson. She d. May 6, 1869, without children.

ii. EMMA BERTHA CHILD, b. in New York City, Aug. 6, 1851, m. Oct. 25, 1876, David B. Idell.

iii. LAURA AMELIA CHILD, b in Hoboken, N. J., Aug. 20, 1853, d. May 2,

iv. ELLA GERTRUDE CHILD, b. in Hoboken, N. J., April 7, 1857.   [1857.

v. GRACE CHARLOTTE CHILD, b. in Hoboken, N. J., Sept. 8, 1859.

vi. JENNIE LOUISE CHILD, b. in Hoboken, N. J, April 22, 1864.

vii. GEORGE HENRY CHILD, b. in Hoboken, N. J., Nov. 30, 1866.
viii. FRANK MALCOMB CHILD, b in Hoboken, N. J., Jan. 1870.

[Sixth Generation.]
  ii. EDMUND BRAMHALL CHILD, b. Saturday Sept. 2, 1826, in Albany, N. Y., m. Oct. 7, 1855, on Sunday, at the home of the bride, in Morrisania, Rebecca Anna Harystman, dau of Arthur Berryhill and Katherine Eliza Drummond Harystman, who were among the original settlers of Morrisania, now a part of the City of New York, an active participant in public affairs, was elected and re-elected to various offices, and was for many years Justice of the Peace. Mr. E. B. Child attended the schools of Mr. Morse and Mr. Steele of Albany. Learned the printing business; became an editor and publisher in New York City. Actuary of Mechanics Institute in that city several years, and much valued in that position for his efficiency. Is a democrat in politics. Is a writer for the press. Engaged in Fire Ins. business. Residence, New York City.

[Seventh Generation.] Child:
  i. EDMUND BRAMHALL CHILD, JR., b. Monday, July 11, 1864, in Morrisania, N. Y. Attended Miss Coyles' school, and the "Suburban Seminary" of Rev. Edwin Johnson.

[Fifth Generation.]
  iv. REBECCA ANNA CHILD, second dau. of Rev. Caleb and Sarah Bramhall Child, b. in Poughkeepsie, N. Y., April 4, 1808, m. May 2, 1847, Isaac Dennison Wetsell of Albany, N.Y. He was b. in Catskill, N. Y., Nov. 21, 1811 ; son of James and Katherine Van Bergen Van Valtenberg Wetsell. Mrs. R. A. C. Wetsell d. Nov. 10, 1879.

[Sixth Generation.] Child:
  i. SARAH HARRIET WETSELL, b. Oct. 27, 1849. m. Oct. 20, 1874, John T. Bramhall.

[Sixth Generation.]
  i. SARAH HARRIET WETSELL, only child of Rebecca Anna Child and Isaac D. Wetsell, b. in Albany, N. Y., Oct. 27, 1849, m. Oct. 20, 1874, John Tobias Bramhall, who was b. Oct. 6, 1849, at Ghent, Columbia county, N. Y. : son of Charles Hurlburt and Eliza Hogeboom Bramhall.

[Seventh Generation.] Children:
  i. LAURA ELBERTJE BRAMHALL, b. in Falls Church, Va., Oct. 14, 1875.
  ii. LIDA MARTIN BRAMHALL, b. in Albany, N. Y., Oct. 25 1877.
  iii. FREDERIC DENNISON BRAMHALL, b. in Albany, N. Y., April 16, 1880.

[Fifth Generation.]
  v. SARAH MEHITABLE CHILD, third dau. of Rev. Caleb and Sarah Bramhall Child, b. Sept. 19, 1810, in Troy, N. Y., m. at Niscayuma, Albany county, N. Y., Oct. 15, 1830, Warren Samuel Doty, who was b. in Rensselaer county, N. Y., May 6, 1810 ; a son of Ethan Allen and Keturah Tompkins Doty. He was a lineal descendant of Edward Dotey, one of the original pilgrims of the "Mayflower." Mrs. Doty was early thrown on her own resources by the death of her parents ; was a woman of superior natural gifts, self-reliant, energetic, and thoroughly devoted to the care of her family circle. Mr. and Mrs. Doty removed, in 1831, to New York City, and for several years both worked as map mounters in the map establishment of the Coltons,

Mr. Doty later went into the business of engraving and printing, in which he continued until his death : he was a successful business man, and won the respect and esteem of all who knew him. He died at Brooklyn. N. Y., Nov. 14, 1855. Mrs. Sarah M. C. Doty died at Brooklyn, N.Y., July 23, 1878, aged 68. Funeral services were held Thursday the 25th, from her late residence 97 St. Felix street. She was buried in the family lot at Greenwood beside her husband. Affectionate, kind and devoted parents, their memory will ever be cherished by their children.*

[Sixth Generation.] Children:

i. MARY ELIZA DOTY, b. in New York City, July 5, 1831, unm: merchant: lives in Brooklyn, N. Y.

ii. GEORGE WASHINGTON DOTY, b. in New York City, Oct. 5, 1834, d. in Brooklyn, Nov. 6, 1879. Clerk: unmarried.

iii. ETHAN ALLEN DOTY, b. in New York, June 14, 1837, m. Jan. 22, 1861, Ellie Eliza McFarlan, who was b. in Brooklyn, Aug. 23, 1839; dau. of James and Margaret Cronk McFarlan. Mr. Doty was educated at the public schools and college of New York City, where he is now a merchant and manufacturer, of the firm of Doty & McFarlan.+

iv. CATHERINE LONG DOTY, b. in New York, Nov. 5, 1839, m. Feb. 15, 1861, Gilbert R. Lindsay.

v. REBECCA ANNA DOTY, b. in New York, April 10, 1842, unm. Resides in Brooklyn, N. Y.

vi. SARAH MEHITABLE DOTY, b. in New York, June 7, 1845, d. in Brooklyn, July 6, 1849.

vii. WARREN SAMUEL DOTY, b. in Brooklyn, Sept. 22, 1848, unm: clerk. Lives in Brooklyn.

[Sixth Generation.]

iv. CATHERINE LONG DOTY, second dau. of Sarah M. Child and Warren S. Doty, b. in New York City, Nov. 5, 1839, m. in Brooklyn, Feb. 15, 1861, Gilbert Robertson Lindsay, who was b. in New York, Jan. 31, 1834, son of Gilbert Robertson and Susanna Brower Lindsay. Reside in Rahway, N. J., where he is a practicing lawyer and Superintendent of Public Schools.

[Seventh Generation.] Children:

i. KATE LINDSAY, b. Oct. 5, 1865, in Brooklyn.

ii. ROBERT LINDSAY, b. Sept. 14, 1869, in Rahway, N. J.

iii. SARAH AGNES LINDSAY, b. Aug. 19, 1875, in Rahway, N. J.

[Fifth Generation.]

JOSEPH BRAMHALL CHILD, seventh and youngest child of Rev. Caleb and Sarah Bramhall Child, was a printer, received a fair education. In June, 1847, he left New York City as a sailor and was not heard from till his return to the city in 1852, having in the mean time sailed mainly between the coasts of Africa and England. About 1855 he removed to Grand Detour, Ogle county, Ill., where he married, in 1858, a widow whose maiden name was Sarah B. Hamlin (first husband's name unknown). Mr. Child died in the autumn of 1864, in Grand Detour. Communications have failed to reach his family since 1866.

[Sixth Generation.] Children:

i. MARY ELIZA CHILD, b Mch. 13, 1859,

ii IDA FRANCES CHILD, b. July 5, 1860,

iii. EDMUND BRAMHALL CHILD. b. 1862.

iv. A daughter, b. Dec. 10, 1864.

*The brief mention of Mrs. Doty's death is from an "In memoriam" card.
+ Is collecting material for the Genealogy of the "Dotey or Doten family."

3627. iv. ELIZABETH CHILD, b. Jan. 25, 1810, m. Ebenezer Bird of Framingham. Mass.; she d. July 20, 1860.

3628. v. ANN MARIA CHILD b. Aug. 26, 1812, m. May 21, 1841, Harvey Barber; they lived in Warwick. Mass.

3629. vi. SOPHIA WHITNEY CHILD, b. June 23, 1815, d. July 18, 1816.

3630. vii. WILLIAM THOMAS CHILD, b. Oct. 6, 1817, m. Sept. 10, 1847, Mary R. Watts.

[Sixth Generation.]

3630. vii. WILLIAM THOMAS CHILD, seventh and youngest child and third son of Phineas and Susanna Whitney Child, b. Oct. 6, 1817, m. Sept. 10, 1847, Mary R. Watts. Reside at Gates, Mo.

[Seventh Generation.] Child:

3631. i. ANN MARIA CHILD, b. in Gates, Mo., May 1, 1849, m. Mch. 11, 1868, Milton Barnes

[Fourth Generation.]

3613. vi. SOLOMON CHILD, sixth child of Caleb and Rebecca Dana Child, b. Sept. 13, 1752, m. 1803, the widow of William Wiswell, of Newton. Mass.

[Fifth Generation.] Children:

3632. i. BULAH CHILD, b. 1804.

3633. ii. MARY ANN CHILD, b. 1805.

3634. iii. REBECCA CHILD, b. 1806.

[Fourth Generation.]

3614. vii. CALEB CHILD, 2D, seventh child and fourth son of Caleb and Rebecca Dana Child, b. May 7, 1759, m. 1799, Sarah Bramhall, dau. of Edmund and Mehitable Bramhall of Armenia, Dutchess Co., N. Y. She d. 1806, at Canaan, Columbia Co., N. Y. Mr. Child was a graduate of Harvard University, Cambridge, Mass. He lived and died in Albany, N. Y.

[Fifth Generation.] Children:

3635. i. EDMUND BRAMHALL CHILD, b. in Albany, N. Y., Dec. 23, 1800, m. Isabella ———.

3636. ii. CALEB CHILD, JR., b. in Albany, N. Y., May 31, 1803, d. of yellow fever, at Mobile, Ala: unmarried.

3637. iii. MARY ELIZA CHILD, b. in Poughkeepsie, N. Y., 1806, d. 1811.

3638. iv. REBECCA ANN CHILD, b. in Poughkeepsie, N. Y., April 4, 1808, m. Dennison Weskell, of Albany, N. Y.

3639. v. SARAH MEHITABLE CHILD, b. in Troy, N. Y., Sept. 18, 1810, m. Warren Doty; now lives in New York City, and has six children, names and dates of birth not given.

3640. vi. SOLOMON CHILD, b. July 18, 1813; lives in Texas; unmarried.

3641. vii. JOSEPH BRAMHALL CHILD, b. June 8, 1815, d. in Illinois a few years since, after an adventurous life.

F 1

CHAPTER VII.

JOHN CHILD

It seems necessary to introduce this line with a preface, as there has been some question as to its paternity, and it becomes us to state the premises and our reasons for the conclusion we have reached in the matter. Our first point will be the fact that Benjamin and Mary Child of Roxbury. Mass., emigrants to America, had a son John, their tenth child and fifth son. The second point is to identify said John and his descendants, as there are found two lines quite distinct in their homes and families who have been supposed to be his posterity. We will give then, here, the reasons for the conclusion attained.

We find that by far the larger number of the descendants of Benjamin Child, emigrant, removed from Roxbury to the colony established in the town now called Woodstock in Connecticut, though we have no evidence that any of his sons went there unless it should seem that his younger son John did go there. If we find John did go to Woodstock our perplexity ends. We have upon the Woodstock records the births of a large family of children to John and Elizabeth Child. At the time of the sending of the second delegation from Roxbury to the colony then called New Roxbury, seven sons of Benjamin Child, the second son of the Emigrant of that name, were old enough to go. some were married, others married after removing: John. the younger son of the emigrant, was not much the senior of some of his nephews, and might have felt he could better establish a family in the newer country. A very strong point in the presumptive proof (for we cannot call it positive) is that the families from those earlier times always held themselves to be closely allied: a stronger proof comes to us from an old diary of one John May. who married in 1711 Elizabeth Child. the daughter of Joshua Child, (Joshua being the son of Benjamin Child, the emigrant.) In this diary, which we have carefully read. we find Mr. May calls the John Child of Woodstock, Ct., "Uncle John," (as he would be the uncle of his wife Elizabeth Child May, if he

were the son of the emigrant and so the brother of Joshua,)
while Ephraim, Benjamin, &c., the grandchildren of the emigrant, he always calls "cousin." Others beside ourselves have
examined the Woodstock records on this point, and entertain
no doubt that the John whom we place at the head of this
chapter, and whose long line of posterity we record, is the son
of Benjamin Child, the emigrant. We therefore register him
as we have done the others.

[Second Generation.]

12. x. JOHN CHILD, fifth son and tenth child of Benjamin
and Mary Child, b. in Roxbury, Aug. 1, 1671, m. about 1696
or 1697 Elizabeth ———. Removed to New Roxbury, afterwards Woodstock, Ct.; his children settled in that part of the
town called West Woodstock, and here at a good old age he
was "gathered to his father's" in 1764.

[Third Generation.] Children:

3642. i. JOHN CHILD, JR., b. in Roxbury abt. 1698, m. Dec. 7, 1721,
Abigail Ainsworth.

3643. ii. NATHANIEL CHILD, b. in Woodstock, Ct., Sept. 3, 1699, m. Dec.
8, 1726, Dorothy Johnson.

3644. iii. SAMUEL CHILD, b. Sept. 25, 1700, d. same week.

3645. iv. SAMUEL CHILD, 2D, b. Jan. 27, 1702, m. May 27, 1727, Keziah
Hutchins.

3646. v. JACOB CHILD, b April 25, 1703, m. April 18, 1728, Dorcas Ainsworth.

3647. vi. JOSIAH CHILD, b. Oct. 11, 1705, d. same month.

3648. vii. ELIZABETH CHILD, b. Sept. 10, 1708.

3649. viii HANNAH CHILD, b. Nov. 12, 1709, m. July 30, 1738, John
Chamberlain.

3650. ix. ABIGAIL CHILD, b. May 17, 1711, d. June 19, 1790.

3651. x. MARTHA CHILD, ⎱ TWINS. ⎰ b. June 10, 1712, d. June 20, 1712.
3652. xi. MARY CHILD. ⎱   ⎰   d. June 10, 1712.

[Third Generation.]

3642. i. JOHN CHILD, JR., eldest child of John and Eliza
beth Child, b. probably in Roxbury, Mass., abt. 1697 or 1698,
m. Dec. 7, 1721, Abigail Ainsworth.

[Fourth Generation.] Children:

3653. i. DOROTHY CHILD, b. in Woodstock, Ct., Oct. 6, 1722.

3654. ii. SARAH CHILD, b. in Woodstock, Ct., May 12, 1724.

3655. iii. ABIJAH CHILD, b. in Woodstock, Ct., Sept. 17, 1726, m. twice—
1st, Oct. 29, 1748, Priscilla Morse; m. 2d, Abigail Johnson.

3656. iv. ABIGAIL CHILD, b. in Woodstock, Ct., Jan. 1, 1728, m. Oct. 10,
1740, Nathan Ainsworth.

3657. v. JOHN CHILD, JR., b. in Woodstock, Ct., Aug. 8, 1733, m. Jan. 22,
1756, Sybil Bugbee.

3658. vi. SHUBAEL CHILD, b. in Woodstock, Ct, Aug. 13, 1735, m. Dec.
27, 1759, Abigail Bowen.

3659. vii. BENAIAH CHILD, b. in Woodstock, Ct., April 17, 1740.

3660. viii. HANNAH CHILD, b. in Woodstock, Ct., Oct. 3, 1742.

[Fourth Generation.]

3655. iii. ABIJAH CHILD, third child of John and Abigail Ainsworth Child, b. in Woodstock, Ct., Sept. 17, 1726, m. 1st, Priscilla Morse, Oct. 29, 1748; m. 2d, abt. 1750, Abigail Johnson.

[Fifth Generation.] Children: By first marriage.

3661. i. ABIJAH CHILD, JR., b. in Woodstock, Ct., Sept. 3, 1749, m. Feb. 17, 1774, Sarah Mascraft.

By second marriage.

3662. ii EUNICE CHILD, b in Woodstock, Ct., May 3, 1750, m. May 17, 1770, Samuel Ruggles.

3663. iii. SARAH CHILD, b. in Woodstock, Ct., Feb. 18, 1752, m. Jan. 19, 1775, Elijah Mason.

3664. iv. HANNAH CARPENTER CHILD, b. in Woodstock, Ct., April 26, 1754.

3665. v. BENAIAH CHILD, b. in Woodstock, Ct., April 19, 1756.

3666. vi. FANNY CHILD, b. in Woodstock, Ct., April 6, 1759.

3667. vii. ASA CHILD, b. in Woodstock, Ct., June 18, 1761, m. April 20, 1791, Abigail Adams.

[Fifth Generation.]

3661. i. ABIJAH CHILD, JR., eldest child of Abijah Child and Priscilla Morse, b. in Woodstock, Ct., Sept. 3, 1749, m. Feb. 17, 1774, Sarah Mascraft, in Pomfret, Ct., and removed to Pomfret, Vt., which town began to be settled in 1770.

[Sixth Generation.] Children:

3668. i. JACOB CHILD, b. Feb. 11, 1775, m. March 3, 1800, Abigail Drew.

3669. ii. SARAH CHILD, b. Sept. 13, 1776, m. Dec. 1, 1796, John Lamb.

3670. iii ABIJAH CHILD, JR., b. May 18, 1778, unmarried.

3671. iv. SANFORD CHILD, ⎰ b. Mch. ⎱ m. Dec. 4, 1806, Polly Conant.
3672. v. CLARINDA CHILD, ⎱ Twins ⎰ 3, 1780, ⎰ m. Mch. 5, 1810, John Wood.

3673. vi. GARDNER B. CHILD, b. Feb. 22, 1782, m. Mch. 27, 1816, Isabella Martin.

3674. vii. JOHN CHILD, b. Dec. 14, 1783, m. 1812, Lorain Meigs.

3675. viii. IRENA CHILD, b. May 27, 1794, m. Aug. 22, 1822, Truman Dixon.

[Sixth Generation.]

3668. i. JACOB CHILD, eldest son and child of Abijah and Sarah Mascraft Child, b. in Pomfret, Vt., Feb. 11, 1775, m. Mch. 3, 1800, Abigail Drew; removed soon after his marriage to Franklin Co., N. Y.

[Seventh Generation.] Children:

3676. i. ANGELINA CHILD, b. Nov. 6, 1800, m. April 8, 1817, John Cargin.

3677. ii. JOHN CHILD, b. March 29, 1802, m. Sybil Clark.

3678. iii. JACOB CHILD, JR., b. Feb. 13, 1804, m. Samantha Sumner.

3679. iv. MARY F. CHILD, b. Oct. 8, 1808.

3680. v. GEORGE CHILD, b. June 2, 1812, m. 1st, July 1836, Mary C. Nutter; m. 2d, Calista Cofferin.

3681. vi. CHAUNCEY CHILD, b. June 5, 1814, m. May 11, 1837, Caroline Taylor.

3682. vii. WILLIAM S. CHILD, b. Dec. 21, 1815, m. March 16, 1841. Sophronia Coonley.

3683. viii. CAROLINE A. CHILD, b. Dec. 16, 1821, m. Feb. 2, 1841, Truman Hale of Chateaugay, N. Y.

[Seventh Generation.]

3677. ii. JOHN CHILD, second child and eldest son of Jacob and Abigail Drew Child, b. in Pomfret, Vt., Mch. 29, 1802, m. May 20, 1824, Sybil Clark. Mr. Child d. Dec. 21, 1836, Mrs. Child m. 2d, July 23, 1844, Joseph Pike, and d. Feb. 27, 1879. Residence Castle Rock, Minnesota.

[Eighth Generation.] Children:

3684. i. CLARK CHILD, b Jan. 10, 1826, m. Dec. 24, 1848, Mary Goke.

3685. ii. TEMPLE CHILD, b. April 23, 1828, m. Sept. 27, 1852, Cornelia M. Hastings.

3686. iii. HENRY D. CHILD, b Oct. 17, 1830, m. July 3, 1856, Eliza R. Howell.

3687. iv. MELINDA CHILD, b. April 16, 1833, m. May 7, 1851, George P. Smith.

3688. v. LUCINDA CHILD, b. April 18, 1835, d. June 1, 1853.

[Eighth Generation.]

3686. iii. HENRY D. CHILD, third son and child of John and Sybil Clark Child, b. Oct. 17, 1830, m. July 3, 1856, Eliza R. Howell. Residence East Castle Rock, Dakota Co., Minn.

[Ninth Generation.] Children:

3689. i. JOHN H. CHILD, b. July 12, 1857.

**** ii. HERBERT E. CHILD, b. Jan. 1, 1860.

**** iii. TEMPLE A. CHILD, b. Nov. 9, 1872.

[Seventh Generation.]

3678. iii. JACOB CHILD, JR., second son and third child of Jacob and Abigail Drew Child, b. in Pomfret, Vt., Feb. 13, 1804, m. about 1831, Samantha Sumner, of Malone, N.Y. Mr. Child d. Sept. 13, 1873. Mrs. S. S. Child d. in Constable, Franklin Co., N. Y., May 28, 1846.

[Eighth Generation.] Children:

3690. i. DELIA CHILD, b. April 5, 1832, m. Nov. 18, 1857, Nahum B. Robbins, of Constable.

3691. ii. DANIEL CHILD, b. June 18, 1833.

3692. iii. GEORGE W. CHILD, b. April 3, 1835, m. Sept. 19, 1861, Arabel Wentworth.

3693. iv. CLARISSA CHILD, b. Sept. 6, 1836, m. George W. Shears.

3694. v. JOHN F. CHILD, b. Dec. 27, 1837.

3695. vi. BETSEY CHILD, b Oct. 14, 1839, m. John Watson.

3696. vii. PUTNAM F. CHILD, b. Dec. 27, 1841

3697. viii. WILLIAM A. CHILD, b. Oct. 14, 1844.

[Eighth Generation.]

3692. iii. GEORGE W. CHILD, second son and third child of Jacob, Jr., and Samantha Sumner Child, b. April 3, 1835, m. Sept. 19, 1861, Arabel Wentworth.   Reside in Constable, N.Y.

[Ninth Generation.]   Children:

3698. i. ALICE B. CHILD, b. Aug. 22, 1862, in Constable, N. Y.

3699. ii. CARRIE E. CHILD, b. Oct. 3, 1864, in Constable, N. Y.

3700. iii. WARREN H. A. CHILD, b. July 8, 1868, in Constable, N. Y.

3701. iv. GEORGE W. CHILD, JR., b. June 6, 1870, in Constable, N. Y., d. Oct. 6, 1873.

[Seventh Generation.]

3680. v. GEORGE CHILD, third son and fifth child of Jacob and Abigail Drew Child, b. in Windsor Co., Vt., June 2, 1812, m. twice—1st, July 1836, Mary C. Nutter; m. 2d, Calista Cofferin.   Mr. Child resided in Malone, Franklin Co., N. Y: In 1853 he removed to Illinois, and resided near Belvidere, in Boon Co., from thence he removed to Colorado, thence to California, in 1858.

[Eighth Generation.]   Children:

3702. i. GEORGE ALBION CHILD, b. 1840 d. ——.

3703. ii. MARY ELZADIE CHILD, b. 1842, d. ——.

3704. iii. ROBERT A. CHILD, b. Mch. 22, 1845, m. Dec. 24, 1873, Mary E. Cofferin.

3705. iv. HENRY FRANKLIN CHILD, b. 1846.   Resides in Decatur, Ill.

3706. v. JOHN SAMUEL CHILD, b. ——, d. at Higgins Place, Arkansas, Oct. 1870.

3707. vi. ORANGE SCOTT CHILD.

3708. vii. CORYDON CHILD, ⎰ ⎱ Resides at Dubuque, Iowa.
3709. viii. CORNELIA CHILD, ⎱ TWINS ⎰ d. aged 4 years.

3710. ix. ABBIE CHILD.

[Eighth Generation.]

3704. iii. ROBERT A. CHILD, second son and third child of George and Mary C. Nutter Childs, b. in Antwerp, Jefferson Co., N. Y., Mch. 22, 1845, m. Dec. 24, 1873, in Normal, McLean Co., Illinois, by Rev. Mr. Leonard, Mary E. Cofferin, dau. of William W. G. and Helen E. Lester Cofferin.   Mr. William W. G. Cofferin died Sept. 1866.   Mrs. H. E. L. Cofferin resides with her daughter, Mrs. Robert A. Child, in Hinsdale, Ill.   Mr. Robert A. Child enlisted March, 1861, in the Federal army, and served until August, 1865, in the armies of the Mississippi and the Cumberland, respectively, under Generals Fremont, Hunter, Grant, Sherman, and Thomas.

[Ninth Generation.]   Children:

3711. i. LESTER COFFERIN CHILD, b. Oct. 11, 1874, in Hinsdale, Ill.

3712. ii. WILLIAM ROBERT CHILD, b. Sept. 27, 1876, in Hinsdale, Ill.

[Seventh Generation.]

3681. vi. CHAUNCEY CHILD, fourth son and sixth child of Jacob and Abigail Drew Child, b. June 5, 1814, m. May 11, 1837, Caroline Taylor. Residence Malone, Franklin Co., N.Y.

[Eighth Generation.] Children:

3713. i. EDSON R. CHILD, b. May 28, 1838.

3714. ii. CORNELIA C. CHILD, b. Oct. 29, 1839.

3715. iii. MALVINA J. CHILD, b. Jan. 28, 1840.

3716. iv. MARION CHILD, b. Aug. 22, 1843, d. Feb. 4, 1859.

3717. v. AUGUSTA J. CHILD, b. July 22, 1845.

[Seventh Generation.]

3682. vii. DR. WILLIAM S. CHILD, fifth son and seventh child of Jacob and Abigail Drew Child, b. Dec. 21, 1815, m. Mch. 16, 1841, Sophronia Coonley, of Constable, N. Y. Mr. Child studied for the medical profession with Dr. George Darling of Constable, N. Y. Settled in Chateaugay, Franklin Co., N. Y.; commenced practice as a surgeon and physician, and gained the reputation of being skillful in his profession; a worthy and esteemed citizen. He died Aug. 21, 1846.

[Eighth Generation.] Children:

3718. i. SARAH A. CHILD, b. Oct. 3, 1843, m. 1871, William Lockley, of Boston.

3719. ii. WILLIAMINE S. CHILD, b. Jan. 13, 1847, in Chateaugay, N. Y.

[Sixth Generation.]

3671. iv. SANFORD CHILD, third son and fourth child of Abijah and Sarah Mascraft Child, b. in Pomfret, Vt., Mch. 3, 1780, m. Dec. 4, 1806, Polly Conant. Removed early to Franklin Co., New York.

[Seventh Generation.] Children:

3720. i. GARDNER A. CHILD, b. May 14, 1808, m. 1st, Dec. 27, 1836, Adelia M. Berry; m. 2d, Adelaide Parker.

3721. ii. LEONARD C. CHILD, b. July 23, 1809, m. 1st, May 15, 1837, Betsey B. Peck; m. 2d, Nov. 6, 1843, Elvira White.

3722. iii. LUCY CHILD, b. July 12, 1811, m. July 26, 1836, Enoch Miller.

3723. iv. JUSTIN CHILD, b. June 27, 1813, m. Dec. 25, 1839, Delilah Daggett.

3724. v. MARY CHILD, b. Sept. 17, 1816, d. unm. 1859.

3725. vi. BENJAMIN F. CHILD, b. Jan. 14, 1819, d. unm. Nov. 1, 1842.

3726. vii. CHARLES CHILD, b. May 7, 1821, d. unm. 1847.

3727. viii. THOMAS J. CHILD, b. July 4, 1823, d. unm. 1845.

3728. ix. CATHERINE E. CHILD, b. Dec. 30, 1827, m. Wilhelm Alexander.

[The last seven of these children have been teachers of the public schools in this State. The three elder sons are farmers in Malone, Franklin Co., N. Y.]

[Seventh Generation.]

3720. i. GARDNER A. CHILD, eldest child of Sanford and Polly Conant Child, b. in Pomfret, Vt., May 14, 1808, m.

twice—1st, Dec. 27, 1836, Adelia M. Berry; m. 2d, Adelaide Parker; residence Malone, Franklin Co., N. Y.: a farmer.

[Eighth Generation.] Children:

3729. i. SANFORD A. CHILD, b. Oct. 3, 1837, in Malone, N. Y., m. Oct. 25, 1871, Esther Keeler.

3730. ii. HIRAM G. CHILD, b. Sept. 25, 1841, in Malone, N. Y., m. Nov. 1866, Elizabeth Mott.

3731. iii. DELIA A. CHILD, b. Oct. 5, 1862.

3732. iv. FRED. P. CHILD, b. Sept. 5, 1866.

[Eighth Generation.]

3729. i. SANFORD A. CHILD, eldest child of Gardner A. and Adelia M. Berry, b. in Malone, N. Y., Oct. 3, 1837, m. Oct. 25, 1871, Esther Keeler; residence Malone, N. Y.

[Ninth Generation.] Children:

3733. i. SARAH A. CHILD, b. Aug. 13, 1872, in Malone, N. Y.

3734. ii. HIRAM R. CHILD, b. Oct. 21, 1873, in Malone, N. Y.

3735. iii. LUCY M. CHILD, b. Nov. 1, 1875, in Malone, N. Y.

3736. iv. CLARA C. CHILD, b. May 28, 1878, in Malone, N. Y.

[Eighth Generation.]

3730. ii. HIRAM G. CHILD, second son and child of Gardner A. and Adelia M. Berry Child, b. in Malone, N. Y., Sept. 25, 1841, m. Nov. 1866, Elizabeth Mott, in Chateaugay, N. Y., where they resided, and in that place Mr. H. G. Child d. Nov. 14, 1873.

[Ninth Generation.] Child:

3737. i. CORA CHILD, b. Sept. 2, 1868, in Chateaugay, N. Y.

[Seventh Generation.]

3721. ii. LEONARD C. CHILD, second son and child of Sanford and Polly Conant Child, b. in Pomfret, Vt., July 23, 1809, m. twice—1st, May 15, 1837, Betsey B. Peck; m. 2d, Nov. 6, 1843, Elvira White. He is a tanner and shoemaker.

[Eighth Generation.] Children:

3738. i. CLARINDA CHILD, b. Jan. 28, 1839, m. May 13, 1862, Rodney S. Bell.

3739. ii. DORCAS CHILD, b. May 13, 1845.

3740. iii. ELMINA CHILD, b. April 27, 1847, d. April 17, 1848.

3741. iv. CATHERINE E. CHILD, b. May 18, 1849, m. July 2, 1868, Daniel H. Tarble.

3742. v. MARY P. CHILD, b. March 13, 1851, d. April 2, 1851.

3743. vi. FLAVEL H. CHILD, b. May 20, 1852, m. Nov. 14, 1876, Angeline Purdy.

3744. vii. FRANK L. CHILD, b. Nov. 28, 1854.

[Seventh Generation.]

3723. iv. JUSTIN CHILD, third son and fourth child of Sanford and Polly Conant Child, b. in Pomfret, Vt., June 27,

1813. m. Dec. 25, 1839, Delilah Daggett: residence Malone, Franklin Co., N. Y.*

[Eighth Generation.] Children:

3745. i. ELLA R. CHILD, b. Dec. 6, 1846, m. April 15, 1874, James M. Gregory.

3746. ii. ALICE E. CHILD, b. Dec. 30, 1848, d. May 18, 1852.

3747. iii. FRED. D CHILD, b. Oct. 16, 1850, m. May 1, 1872, Lizzie Burch.

3748. iv. LUCY E. CHILD, b. Dec. 14, 1852.

[Eighth Generation.]

3745. i. ELLA R. CHILD, eldest child of Justin and Delilah Daggett Child, b. in Malone, N. Y., Dec. 6, 1846, m. April 15, 1874, James M. Gregory of Stockton, Cal. Mrs. E. R. Child Gregory d. in San Jose, Cal., April 11, 1876.

[Ninth Generation.] Child:

3749. i. ARCHIE GREGORY, b. April 24, 1875.

[Eighth Generation.]

3747. iii. FRED. D. CHILD, only son of Justin and Delilah Daggett Child, b. in Malone, N. Y., Oct. 16, 1850, m. May 1, 1872, Lizzie Burch.

[Ninth Generation.] Children:

3750. i. LOUIS CHILD, b July 4, 1875.

3751. ii. ELLA R. CHILD, b. Oct. 10, 1876.

3752. iii. WILLIAM CHILD, b. Jan. 26, 1878.

[Sixth Generation.]

3672. v. CLARINDA CHILD, second dau. and fifth child of Abijah and Sarah Mascraft Child, b. in Pomfret, Vt., March 3, 1780, a twin with her brother, Sanford Child. She m. March 5, 1810, John Wood of Malone, Franklin Co., N. Y. Mrs. Clarinda Child Wood moved to Janesville, Wis., with her elder dau. Mrs. Trowbridge, abt. 1855 or 1856, but survived only a year or two the change of climate.

[Seventh Generation.] Children:

3753. i. SARAH WOOD, b. in Malone, N. Y., m. Pardon Trowbridge of Bombay, Franklin Co., N. Y. They removed to Wisconsin, but lived only two or three years in the new home, leaving several small children orphans by their early demise. But one name of these little ones has reached us, Safford Trowbridge.

3754. ii ELIZA WOOD, m. Melvin Allen of Constable, Franklin Co., N. Y., and about 1837 or 1838 removed to Michigan.

[Sixth Generation.]

3674. vii. JOHN CHILD, fifth son and seventh child of Abijah and Sarah Mascraft Child, b. in Pomfret, Windsor Co., Vt., m. in 1812, Lorain Meigs, and moved to Franklin Co., N. Y.

* To Mr. Justin Child we are largely indebted for the statistics of this family, descendants of Abijah and Sarah Mascraft Child.

[Seventh Generation.] Children:

3755. i. ORPHA CHILD, b. Dec. 1814, m. May 24, 1849, David F. Berry of Malone.

3756. ii. HULDAH CHILD, b. Jan. 1816, m. 1846, Joshua Lewis of Huntington, Canada East, and d. May 1850.

[Fourth Generation.]

3657. v. JOHN CHILD, fifth child and second son of John and Abigail Ainsworth Child, b. in West Woodstock, Aug. 8, 1733, m. Jan. 22, 1756, Sybil Bugbee.   He d. 1768.

[Fifth Generation.] Children:

3757. i. ELIAS CHILD, b. in West Woodstock, Ct., Jan. 7, 1758, m. Jan. 25, 1791, Polly Dewing.

3758. ii. OLIVE CHILD, b. in West Woodstock, Ct., Sept. 23, 1759, m. Nov. 9, 1779, Elias Keyes, of Ashford, Ct.

3759. iii. IRENE CHILD, b. in West Woodstock, Ct., April 10, 1762, m. Oct. 28, 1799, Elijah Perry.

3760. iv. JONATHAN CHILD, b. in West Woodstock, Ct., Meh. 6, 1764, d. April 10, 1793.

3761. v. ESTHER CHILD, b. in West Woodstock, Ct., April 4, 1766.

3762. vi. JOHN CHILD, JR., b. in West Woodstock, Ct., (Posthumous) Aug. 29, 1768, m. April 29, 1800, Betsey Thayer.

[Fifth Generation.]

3757. i. ELIAS CHILD, eldest child of John and Sybil Bugbee Child, b. in West Woodstock, Ct., Jan. 7, 1758, m. Jan. 25, 1791, Polly Dewing.

[Sixth Generation.] Children:

3763. i. ALMIRA CHILD, b. in West Woodstock, Ct., May 30, 1792, m. June 3, 1811, Waldo Fox.

3764. ii. SALLY CHILD, b. in West Woodstock, Ct., Oct. 4, 1793.

3765. iii. SOPHIA CHILD, b. in West Woodstock, Ct., Jan. 16, 1797, m. Daniel Perry.

3766. iv. ELIAS CHILD, JR., b. in West Woodstock, Ct., April 2, 1799, m. Dec. 8, 1825, Nancy Perrin.

3767. v. HORATIO NELSON CHILD, b. in West Woodstock, Ct., Aug. 1, 1802, m. Jan. 30, 1826, Dolly M. Paine.

3768. vi. MARIAH CHILD, b. in West Woodstock, Ct., June 1805.

3769. vii. CAROLINE CHILD, b. in West Woodstock, Ct., June 24, 1806, m. July 23, 1844, Anson Pani, of Canada.

[Sixth Generation.]

3765. iii. SOPHIA CHILD, third child of Elias and Polly Dewing Child, b. in West Woodstock, Ct., Jan. 16, 1797, m. Daniel Perry.

[Seventh Generation.] Child:

3770. i. WM. H. PERRY, (date of birth not obtained) of Wheeler & Wilson M'fg Co.   Two other children, but names not obtained.

[Sixth Generation.]

3766. iv. ELIAS CHILD, JR., fourth child and eldest son of Elias and Polly Dewing Child, b. in Woodstock, Ct., April 2,

1799, m. Dec. 8. 1825, Nancy Perrin, dau. of David Perrin. Mr. Elias Child d. 1866.

[Seventh Generation.] Children:

3771. i. MYRTIS C. CHILD, b. in West Woodstock, Ct., Dec. 2. 1827, m. John McClay Smith.

3772. ii. ALMIRA CHILD, b. in West Woodstock, Ct., Nov. 1, 1829, m. May 3, 1847, J. H. Morse.

3773. iii. MARY AUGUSTA CHILD, b. in West Woodstock, Ct., Sept. 12, 1831, m. Aug. 1854, J. H. Lee.

3774. iv. EMMA CHILD, b. Mch. 1833, d. June 1834.

3775. v. EMMA J. CHILD, b. in West Woodstock, Ct., 1835, m. Nov. 13, 1861, Allen F. Phillips.

3776. vi. HENRY F. CHILD, b. in West Woodstock, Ct., Nov. 12. 1839. Resides in Newark, N. J.; unmarried. Agent for Wheeler & Wilson Mr'fg Co., 827 Broad St., Newark.

[Seventh Generation.]

3771. i. MYRTIS C. CHILD, eldest child of Elias and Nancy Perrin Child, b. in West Woodstock, Ct., Dec. 2, 1827, m. 1852, John McClay Smith, merchant of Peoria, Ill. She d. Mch. 17, 1866.

[Eighth Generation.] Children:

3777. i. ARTHUR MCCLAY SMITH, b. July 17, 1853, m. 1875, Kittie Jackson.

3778. ii. FREDERICK A. SMITH, b. Jan. 23, 1857, d. Sept. 15, 1874.

3779. iii. HERBERT C. SMITH, b. Dec. 21, 1858. All the above children were born in Peoria, Ill.

[Seventh Generation.]

3772. ii. ALMIRA CHILD, second child of Elias and Nancy Perrin Child, b. in West Woodstock, Ct. Nov. 1, 1829, m. May 3, 1847, J. H. Morse, son of A. C. Morse of Belchertown, Mass. Mr. Morse is a jeweler, in Jacksonville, Ill.

[Eighth Generation.] Children:

3780. i. EMMA A. MORSE, b. Mch. 13, 1848, m. July 1, 1869, John T. Chandler.

3781. ii. JOHN C. MORSE, b. Oct. 13, 1850, in Peoria, Ill.; is a druggist.

3782. iii. JAMES M. MORSE, b. in Peoria, Ill., Aug. 22, 1853, m. Oct. 13, 1875, Agnes Armstrong, of Peoria, Ill. He is a lawyer.

3783. iv. CHARLES MORSE, b. Jan. 24, 1856, in Peoria, Ill.; is a lumber merchant.

3784. v. FRANK MORSE, b Oct. 9, 1858, in Peoria, Ill.; is a machinist.

3785. vi. VAN HORN MORSE, b. Aug. 21, 1862, in Peoria, Ill., d. Aug. 15, 1866.

3786. vii. IRVING J. MORSE, b. June 10, 1870, in Peoria, Ill.

[Eighth Generation.]

3780. EMMA A. MORSE, eldest child of Almira Child and J. H. Morse, b. Mch. 13, 1848, m. July 1, 1869, John T. Chandler, son of Clarissa Child and Dr. Charles Chandler of Chandlerville, Ill.; a druggist in Jacksonville, Ill.

[Ninth Generation.]   Children:
   3787. i. CHARLES CHANDLER, b. in Chandlersville, Ill., Jan. 27, 1870.
   3788. ii. MYRTIS CHILD CHANDLER, b. in Chandlersville, Ill., May 27, 1873

[Seventh Generation.]

   3773. iii. MARY AUGUSTA CHILD, third child and dau. of
Elias and Nancy Perrin Child, b. in Woodstock, Ct., Sept. 12,
1831, m. Aug. 1854, J. H. Lee: mercantile agent in New
York City.
[Eighth Generation.]   Child:
   3789. i. HATTIE A. LEE, b. in New York City, July 17, 1855, d. soon.

[Seventh Generation.]

   3775. v. EMMA J. CHILD, fifth child and dau. of Elias and
Nancy Perrin Child, b. in West Woodstock, Ct., 1835, m. Nov.
13, 1861, Allen F. Phillips, of West Woodstock, Ct.
[Eighth Generation.]   Children:
   3790. i. HUBERT C. PHILLIPS, b. in West Woodstock, Ct., Nov. 16, 1864.
   3791. ii. MYRTIS PHILLIPS, b. in New York City, Oct. 19, 1867.
   3792. iii. IDA A. PHILLIPS, b. in Rockford, Ill., Mch. 22, 1877.

[Sixth Generation.]

   3767. v. HORATIO NELSON CHILD, fifth child of Capt. Elias
and Polly Dewing Child, b. in West Woodstock, Ct., Aug. 1,
1802, m. Jan. 30, 1826, Dolly M. Paine, dau. of Abram W. Paine
Mr. Child d. Oct. 18, 1844.   Mrs. Child lives with her daughter, Mrs. Foster, in Worcester, Mass.
[Seventh Generation.]   Children:
   3793. i. SARAH CHILD, b. in West Woodstock, Ct., Jan. 22, 1827, m. twice
—1st, Nov. 1846, Otis Stetson; m. 2d, 1862, C. C. Foster.
   3794. ii. FRANK P. CHILD, b. in West Woodstock, Ct., Jan. 29, 1830, m.
Feb. 1856, Emma Weber.
   3795. iii. SIDNEY E. CHILD, b. in West Woodstock, Ct., Feb. 7, 1833, m.
1857, Sarah Van Sickle.
   3796. iv. EDWIN M. CHILD, b. in West Woodstock, Ct., Sept. 10, 1837, m.
1858, Mary Cox.

[Seventh Generation.]

   3793. i. SARAH CHILD, eldest child of Horatio Nelson and
Dolly M. Paine Child, b. in W. Woodstock, Ct., Jan. 22, 1827,
m. 1st, 1846, Otis Stetson; he d. 1860, and she m. 2d, by Rev.
J. Sessions, May, 1862, C. C. Foster.   Mr. and Mrs. Foster
are both teachers in the public schools in Worcester, Mass.
[Eighth Generation.]   Children: By first marriage.
   3797. i. CHARLES NELSON STETSON, b. Dec. 1847, d. Aug. 22, 1864.
                By second marriage:
   3798. ii. SADIE M. FOSTER, b. March 12, 1863, d. Feb. 12, 1864.

[Seventh Generation.]

3794. ii. FRANK P. CHILD, second child and eldest son of Horatio Nelson and Dolly Mason Child, b. in Woodstock, Ct., Jan. 29, 1830, m. Feb. 1856, Emma Weber, dau. of Geo. R. Weber. Mr. Child is a teacher.

[Eighth Generation.] Child:
3799. i. SADIE M. CHILD, b. Oct. 1860.

[Seventh Generation.]

3795. iii. SIDNEY E. CHILD, third child of Horatio Nelson and Dolly M. Paine Child, b. in Woodstock, Ct., Feb., 7, 1833, m. twice—1st, 1857, Sarah Van Sickle; m. 2d, 1874, Susie Van Sickle, sister of first wife. Mr. Child resides in Gaysville, Deadwood Mines, in the Black Hills, Col.

[Eighth Generation.] Children:
3800. i. FRANK PAINE CHILD, b. in Aurora, Ill., Dec. 25, 1858.
3801. ii. WILLIE E. CHILD, b. in Aurora, Ill., 1859.
By second wife.
3802. iii. GRACE MARY CHILD, b. Sept. 1875.

[Seventh Generation.]

3796. iv. EDWIN M. CHILD, fourth child and third son of Horatio Nelson and Dolly M. Paine Child, b. Sept. 10, 1837, in W. Woodstock, Ct., m. 1858, Mary Cox, dau. of John Cox. Mr. Child is a teacher.

[Eighth Generation.] Children:
3803. i. CHARLIE N. CHILD.
3804. ii. ALICE M. CHILD.

[Fifth Generation.]

3762. vi. JOHN CHILD, sixth child and third son of John and Sybil Bugbee Child, b. Aug. 29, 1768, m. April 29, 1800, Betsey Thayer.

[Sixth Generation.] Children:
3805. i. WILLIAM NORRIS CHILD, b. in W. Woodstock Aug. 6, 1801, d. Jan. 23, 1802.
3806. ii. RUSSELL CHILD, b. in W. Woodstock Jan. 31, 1803, m Caroline Marrone.
3807. iii. GORDON HICKS CHILD, b. in W. Woodstock Aug. 1, 1804, m. Julia Richards.
3808. iv. ELIZA CHILD, b. in W. Woodstock March 22, 1807, m. John Paine.
3809. v. WILLIAM EDWIN CHILD, b. in W. Woodstock May 12, 1808, m. Eliza Tait.

[Sixth Generation.]

3806. ii. RUSSELL CHILD, son of John and Betsey Thayer Child, b. in W. Woodstock, Ct., Jan. 31, 1803, m. abt. 1835, Caroline Marrone.

[Seventh Generation.] Children:
   3810. i. SARAH CHILD, d. in infancy.
   3811. ii. EMMA CHILD, b. April 6, 1838, d. July 6, 1844.
   3812. iii. WILLIAM S. H. CHILD, b. Feb. 18, 1840, m. Maria Eversley.
   3813. iv. JULIA ELIZABETH CHILD, b. Nov. 13, 1843, m. Edwin Bennett.

[Seventh Generation.]

   3812. iii. WILLIAM S. H. CHILD, only son and third child of
Russell and Caroline Marrone Child, b. Feb. 18, 1840, m. Nov.
16, 1864, Maria Eversley.
[Eighth Generation.] Children:
   3814. i. EVERSLEY CHILD, b. Feb. 5, 1867.
   3815. ii. RUSSELL CHILD, b. Dec. 28, 1872, d. Dec. 3, 1873.
   3816. iii. WILLIAM MARRONE CHILD, } TWINS { b. April 11, 1877.
   3817. iv. HAROLD BENNETT CHILD, }

[Seventh Generation.]

   3813. iv. JULIA ELIZABETH CHILD, dau. of Russell and
Caroline Marrone Child, b. Nov. 13, 1843, m. Oct. 25, 1865,
Edwin Bennett.
[Eighth Generation.] Children:
   3818. i. EDWIN BENNETT, JR., b. June 1, 1866, d. June 5, 1866.
   3819. ii. WILLIE R. BENNETT, b. Nov. 17, 1867.
   3820. iii. JULIA ANNA BENNETT, b. Oct. 31, 1870.
   3821. iv. ALICE BENNETT, b. June 30, 1874, d. July 5, 1874.

[Sixth Generation.]

   3807. iii. GURDON HICKS CHILD, third son and child of
John and Betsey Thayer Child, b. Aug. 1, 1804, m. Aug. 5,
1829, Julia Richards; resides in West Hartford, Ct.
[Seventh Generation.] Children:
   3822. i. EMERY E. CHILD, b. in W. Woodstock Jan. 8, 1832, m. Mary Van
Slyck.
   3823. ii. JULIA ELIZABETH CHILD, b. in W. Woodstock Sept. 26, 1834, d.
Oct. 6, 1836.
   3824. iii. ALBERT THAYER CHILD, b. in W. Woodstock Feb. 21, 1844, m.
Julia Larkham.
   3825. iv. FRANK RUSSELL CHILD, b. in W. Woodstock April 29, 1846, d.
May 21, 1872.
   3826. v. CARRIE ELIZABETH CHILD, b. in W. Woodstock April 29, 1851.
   3827. vi. WILLIAM HAMLIN CHILD, b. in W. Woodstock March 7, 1857.

[Seventh Generation.]

   3822. i. EMERY E. CHILD, son and first child of Gurdon
and Julia Richards Childs, b. Jan. 8, 1832, m. June 3, 1858,
Mary E. Van Slyck.
[Eighth Generation.] Children:
   3828. i. JAMES VAN SLYCK CHILD, b. Feb. 26, 1859.
   3829. ii. GRACE CHILD, b. Nov. 16, 1862.
   3830. iii. MARY CHILD, b. Dec. 12, 1865.

[Seventh Generation.]

3824. iii. ALBERT THAYER CHILD, second son and third child of Gurdon Hicks and Julia Richards Child, b. Feb. 21, 1844, m. Dec. 3, 1869, Julia C. Larkham.

[Eighth Generation.] Children:

3831. i. ERNEST L. CHILD, b. Feb. 29, 1868.

3832. ii. BERTIE CHILD, b. March 10, 1871.

[Sixth Generation.]

3809. v. WILLIAM EDWIN CHILD, son of John and Betsey Thayer Child, b. May 12, 1808, m. June 1, 1837, Eliza Tait, who d. April 1, 1876.

[Seventh Generation.] Children:

3833. i. ANNA ELIZA CHILD, b. July 18, 1843, m. July 19, 1870, Thomas Henry Osborn.

3834. ii. JULIA HELEN CHILD, b. Oct. 11 1844.

3835. iii. EDWIN M. G. CHILD, b. July 11, 1846, m. Jan. 11, 1876, Ida Nora Woodruff.

3836. iv. CHARLES SIDNEY CHILD, b. Dec. 3, 1849, d. Dec. 23, 1852.

3837. v. EMERY THAYER CHILD, b. Jan. 12, 1851, m. Ophelia Woodruff.

3838. vi. WILLIAM CLENDENNING CHILD, b. June 15, 1854, d. Aug. 25, 1854.

[Seventh Generation.]

3833. i. ANNA ELIZA CHILDS, dau. of William Edwin and Eliza Tait Childs, b. July 18, 1843, m. Thomas Henry Osborn July 19, 1870.

[Eighth Generation.] Child:

3800a. i. WILLIAM TAIT OSBORN, b. Aug. 15, 1871.

[Seventh Generation.]

3835. iii. EDWIN M. G. CHILD, son of William Edwin and Eliza Tait Child, b. July 11, 1846, m. Jan. 11, 1876, Ida Nora Woodruff.

[Eighth Generation.] Child:

3801a. i. RAY EDWARD CHILD, b. Nov. 30, 1876.

[Seventh Generation.]

3837. v. EMERY THAYER CHILD, fifth child of William Edwin and Eliza Tait Child, b. Jan. 12, 1851, m. March 15, 1874, Ophelia Woodruff.

[Eighth Generation.] Children:

3802a. i. IDA WILDE CHILD, b. July 6, 1875, d. Oct. 5, 1875.

3803a. ii. MARY CHILD, b. July 30, 1877, d. same day.

[Fourth Generation.]

3658. vi. Doct. SHUBAEL CHILD, sixth child and third son of John and Abigail Ainsworth Child, b. in West Woodstock, Ct., Aug. 13, 1735, m. Dec. 27, 1759, Abigail Bowen. She d. May 14, 1788. He d. June 7, 1811.

[Fifth Generation.] Children:

3804b. i. CYNTHIA CHILD, b. in West Woodstock, Ct., Oct. 26, 1760.

3805b. ii. CHARLES CHILD, b. in West Woodstock, Ct., May 9, 1762.

3806b. iii. ERASTUS CHILD, b. in West Woodstock, Ct., Nov. 17, 1763.

3807b. iv HANNAH CHILD, b. in West Woodstock, Ct., Nov. 26, 1765.

3808b. v. EPAPHRAS CHILD, b. in West Woodstock, Ct., Sept. 1, 1767, m. about 1796, Sally ——.

3809b. vi. LYDIA CHILD, b. in West Woodstock, Ct., April 3, 1769.

3810b. vii. NOADIAH CHILD, b in West Woodstock, Ct , Feb. 15, 1771.

3811b. viii. A son—unchristened—b. in West Woodstock, Ct., Jan. 26, 1773.

3812b. ix. MARY CHILD, b. in West Woodstock, Ct., Jan. 1, 1776.

3813b. x. PRENTICE CHILD, b. in West Woodstock, Ct., Dec. 16, 1777.

3814b. xi. JARED CHILD, b. in West Woodstock, Ct , Nov. 25, 1779.

[Fifth Generation.]

3808b. v. EPAPHRAS CHILD, fifth child and third son of Doct. Shubael and Abigail Bowen Child, b. in West Woodstock, Ct., Sept. 1, 1767, m. about 1796, Sally ——.

[Sixth Generation.] Children:

3815b. i. BETSEY CHILD, b. in West Woodstock, Ct., Oct. 12, 1797.

3816b. ii. GEORGE CHILD, b. in West Woodstock, Ct., Mch. 2, 1799.

3817b. iii. SETH CHILD, b. in West Woodstock, Ct., Mch. 5, 1802.

3818b. iv. SALLY CHILD, b. in West Woodstock, Ct., Nov. 21, 180-.

3819b. v. EMELINE CHILD, b. in West Woodstock, Ct., Oct. 14, 180-.

3720b. vi. JOHN PRENTISS CHILD, b. in West Woodstock, Ct., Feb. 18, 1814.

3821b. vii. MARY CHILD, b. in West Woodstock, Ct., Jan. 13, 1817.

[Third Generation.]

3643. ii. NATHANIEL CHILD, second son and child of John and Elizabeth Child, b. in Woodstock, Ct., Sept. 3, 1699, m. Dec. 8, 1726, Dorothy Johnson.   Mr. Nathaniel Child removed to Thompson, in the same county (Windham), and there reared a large family.   But of several of his children we obtain no certain data, and can present but two sons with their descendants.   These, however, rank with the noblest of the name for alert intelligence and probity.

[Fourth Generation.] Children:

3839. i. NATHANIEL CHILD, b. abt. 1730, m. abt. 1765, Susannah Williams.

3840. ii. ELIJAH CHILD, b. April 11, 1737, m. Mch. 24, 1759, Rachel Palmer.

[Fourth Generation.]

3839. i. NATHANIEL CHILD, son of Nathaniel and Dorothy Johnson Child, b. abt. 1730, m. abt. 1765, Susannah Williams, of Burrelville, Rhode Island : a descendant of Roger Williams. Mr Child passed his long life of some ninety-six years in Thompson, Ct.; his occupation was that of a farmer.

[Fifth Generation.] Children:
   3841. i. JESSE CHILD, m. Lydia Brown.
   3842. ii. LYDIA CHILD, m. Asa Winter.
   3843. iii. HANNAH CHILD, m. Martin Spencer.
   3844. iv. ARINDA CHILD, m. June 22, 1790, Elijah Corbin.
   3845. v. DOLLY CHILD, m. Chester Upham.
   3846. vi. CHLOE CHILD, m. Mr. Chapman.
   3847. vii. OLIVE CHILD, m. Mr. Brown.
   3848. viii. NATHANIEL CHILD, JR., b. Nov. 8, 1779, m. May 31, 1804,
Nancy Whitford.

[Fifth Generation.]

   3841. i. JESSE CHILD, son of Nathaniel and Susannah Williams Child, b. in Thompson, Ct., and settled in Webster, Mass. He m. Lydia Brown. Six of their eight children reached years of maturity, and married.*

[Sixth Generation.] Children:
   3849. i. ALVAN CHILD.
   3850. ii. CLARISSA CHILD, m. Smith.
   3851. iii. LAVINIA CHILD, m. John Albee.
   3852. iv. ALMIRA CHILD, m. Gideon Brown.
   3853. v. HARRIET CHILD, m. Thomas Pope.
   3854. vi. EMILY CHILD, m. Otis Stone.
   3855. vii. ZIBA CHILD.
   3856. viii. WILLARD CHILD.

[Fourth Generation.]

   3845. v. DOLLY CHILD, fourth dau. of Nathaniel and Susannah Williams Child, b. in Thompson, Ct., m. Chester Upham, of the same place, to whom were given three sons and three daughters.

[Fifth Generation.] Children:
   3857. i. ARAD UPHAM.
   3858. ii. CHESTER UPHAM.
   3859. iii. DAVIS UPHAM.
   3860. iv. POLLY UPHAM.
   3861. v. AREIDA UPHAM.
   3862. vi. JULIA UPHAM.

[Fourth Generation.]

   3848. viii. NATHANIEL CHILD, youngest son of Nathaniel and Susannah Williams Child, b. in Thompson, Ct., Nov. 8, 1779, m. May 31, 1804, Nancy Whitford, dau. of Joseph and Nancy Rawson Whitford. Mr. and Mrs. Child, through their long and useful lives, were residents of their native town. Mr.

*We have been informed that many of this family are living. We have sought them by advertising in the Webster, Mass., papers, and by correspondence, but vainly.

G-1

Nathaniel Child died April 11, 1864. Mrs. Nancy Whitford Child was born in Dudley, Mass., April 15, 1777, and died in Thompson, Ct., May 21, 1877, more than rounding out a century of life by thirty-six days.

[Fifth Generation.] Children:

3863. i. WALDO CHILD, b. June 24, 1805, m. Dec. 24, 1848, Ursula Young, dau. of Brazil and Melvina Young, of Killingly, Ct. They were married by Rev. Isaac Day. Mr. Waldo Child was a machinist. His death occurred April 27, 1878.

3864. ii. MARCUS CHILD, b. Mch. 30, 1807, m. Sept. 16, 1830. Chloe Talbot.

3865. iii. OTIS CHILD, b. May 25, 1809, m. Mch. 30, 1834, Mary E. Rice, who d. Feb. 4, 1861; m. 2d. June 2, 1863, Mrs. Louisa Kingsbury.

3866. iv. ELSEA D. CHILD, b. July 11, 1811, m. Anthony Emlott.

3867. v. SILAS CHILD, b. May 9, 1814, m. Jan. 1, 1839, Lucina Leavens.

3868. vi. NANCY W. CHILD, b. Mch. 12, 1817, m. Anthony Emlott.

[Fifth Generation.]

3864. ii. Hon. MARCUS CHILD, second son and child of Nathaniel and Nancy Whitford Child, b. in Thompson, Ct., Mch. 30, 1807, m Sept. 16, 1830, by the Rev. Abial Williams of Hadley, Mass., Chloe Talbot, dau. of Simeon and Nancy Leach Talbot, of Killingly, Ct.   Mr. Marcus Child resides in Wilsonville, a parish of the town of Thompson, Ct., and is both a farmer and manufacturer.   He has twice represented the town in the State Legislature.

[Sixth Generation.] Children:

3869. i. JAMES L. CHILD, b. May 31, 1832, d. Sept. 6, 1832, at Webster, Mass.

3870. ii. ELSIE D. CHILD, b. Feb. 1, 1834, m. Oct. 7, 1853, William De Witt.

3871. iii. NATHANIEL CHILD, b. June 17, 1836, at Killingly, Ct., m. by the Rev. Justin S. Barrows, Nov. 25, 1858, at Chicopee, Mass., Miss Annie A. Scott, daughter of Sylvester and Mary Ann White Scott, of Chicopee. Mr. Nathaniel Child enlisted on January 4, 1864, in the 14th unattached Co, of Mass. Heavy Artillery, afterwards Co. I, 3d Regt. Heavy Artillery, (acting engineers and pontoons).   Served until mustered out in September, 1865, at the close of the war, thus adding another name to the long roll of patriots, who have honored the Child blood and name.   Mr. Child is by occupation a moulder, and is also a farmer in Thompson, Ct.

3872. iv. HATTIE ANN CHILD, b. June 3, 1841, m. Feb. 22, 1864, John A. Moulton.

3873. v. JOSEPH B. CHILD, b. Mch. 11, 1851, m. Sept. 11, 1871, Annie E. Moseley, of Elgin, Ill, where Mr. Child resides.

[Sixth Generation.]

3870. ii. ELSIE D. CHILD, second child and eldest dau. of Hon. Marcus and Chloe Talbot Child, b. in Webster, Mass., Feb. 1, 1834, m. by Rev. Mr. Chapin, in Thompson, Oct. 7, 1853, to William De Witt, who was b. Jan. 5, 1825; the son of Hollis and Sarah Harris De Witt, of Oxford, Mass.

[Seventh Generation.] Children:

3874. i. FRANK DE WITT, b. in Fiskville, R. I., Feb. 25, 1855, married and resides in Elgin, Ill.

3875. ii. ADA JANE DE WITT, b. in Thompson, Ct., Jan, 12, 1856, d. Sept. 29, 1857, at Oxford, Mass.

3876. iii. CLINTON DE WITT, b. in Thompson, Ct., Dec. 3, 1858.

3877. iv. WILLIAM DE WITT, JR., b. March 6, 1860; resides in Webster, Mass.

3878. v. ELMER L. DE WITT, b. in Chicopee, Mass., Oct. 1, 1861.

[Sixth Generation.]

3872. iv. HATTIE ANN CHILD, second dau. and fourth child of Marcus and Chloe Talbot Child, b. in Killingly, Ct. June 3, 1841, m. in Thompson, Ct., by Rev. Anthony Palmer, Feb. 22, 1864, John H. Moulton of Westminster, Mass.. Mr. and Mrs. Moulton reside in Elgin, Ill.

[Seventh Generation.] Child:

3879. i. HATTIE L. MOULTON, b. June 3, 1865.

[Fifth Generation.]

3865. iii. OTIS CHILD, third son and child of Nathaniel and Nancy Whitford Child, b. in Thompson, Ct., May 25, 1809, m. March 30, 1834, by Rev. John Francis, Mary E. Rice, dau. of Luke and Mary Davis Rice of Southbridge, Mass. Mrs. Mary E. Rice Child d. in Thompson Feb. 4, 1861. Mr. Otis Child m. 2d, June 2, 1863, by Rev. Anthony Palmer, Mrs. Louisa Kingsbury, dau. of Mark and Sallie Barnes Elwell of Dudley, Mass. Mr. Child is a machinist and farmer, residing in Dudley, Mass.

[Sixth Generation.] Children:

3880. i. GERSHOM P. CHILD, b. March 14, 1835, m. May 12, 1858, Eliza J. Dennison.

3881. ii. FRED. R. CHILD, b. in Thompson, Ct., Oct. 20, 1853. Remembering that though it is said "Man shall not live by bread alone," yet that it is also said by the same authority, "In the sweat of thy face shalt thou eat thy bread," Mr. Fred. Child caters for the "inner man" of his fellow-citizens by baking, amid the heat, their "daily bread."

[Sixth Generation.]

3880. i. GERSHOM P. CHILD, eldest son of Otis and Mary E. Rice Child, b. in Sturbridge, Mass., March 14, 1835, m. in Mystic, Ct., May 12, 1858, by Rev. Ebenezer Blake, Eliza J. Dennison, who was b. in Norwich, Ct., March 22, 1840, dau. of John J. and Olive Jillson Dennison of Groton, Ct. Like many others of this family Mr. Child has a double occupation, attending to a farm and superintending the weaving in one of the innumerable manufactories which cause the perpetual hum of industry with which the New England States resound.

[Seventh Generation.] Children:

3882. i. MINNIE D. CHILD, b. in Thompson, Ct., Oct. 11, 1861.

3883. ii. LENNIE J. CHILD, b. in Thompson, Ct., March 4, 1865.

[Fifth Generation.]

3867. v. SILAS CHILD, fourth son and fifth child of Nathaniel and Nancy Whitford Child, b. in Thompson, Ct., May 9, 1814, m. Jan. 1, 1839, by Rev. Mr. Robinson, Lucina Leavens, dau. of Oliver and Anna Talbot Leavens of Killingly, Ct. Mrs. Lucina Leavens Child was b. in Thompson, May 8, 1821. Mr. and Mrs. Silas Child reside in Thompson, Ct., where his business is that of machinist.

[Sixth Generation.] Children:

3884. i WILLARD H. CHILD, b. Aug. 29, 1840, m. 1st, Maria Darling; m. 2d, ———

3885. ii. GEORGE D. CHILD, b. Oct. 2, 1843, d. Oct. 12, 1862, in Thompson, Ct.

3886. iii. LUTHER M. CHILD, b. Aug. 17, 1848, m. April 19, 1870, Ella F. Upham.

[Sixth Generation.]

3886. iii. LUTHER M. CHILD, third child and son of Silas and Lucina Leavens Child, b. in Thompson, Ct., Aug. 17, 1848, m. in Thompson, April 19, 1870, by Rev. Alfred Presley, Ella F. Upham, who was b. in Thompson, Sept. 26, 1848, a dau. of William J. and Mary Underwood Upham. Mr. Child is a musician, residing in Webster, Mass.

[Seventh Generation.] Children:

3887. i. MERTON L. CHILD, } TWINS } b. in Norwich, Ct., April 17, 1848.
3888. ii. MYRA L. CHILD. }

[Fourth Generation.]

3840. ii. ELIJAH CHILD, son of Nathaniel and Dorothy Johnson Child, b. in Thompson, Ct., April 11, 1737, m. March 24, 1759, Rachel Palmer of Dudley, Mass. As the children attained their majority they removed to the State of Vermont; and about the year 1796 Mr. and Mrs. Elijah Child, with such of their family as had not preceded them, completed the exodus settling in Sharon, Vt. Mrs. Rachel Palmer Child was a more than ordinarily gifted woman, especially in her metrical talent. A poem of hers upon the celebrated "Dark Day," whose shadows fell at noon-tide and whose weird gloom she witnessed, was considered of much merit. It is unfortunately lost, so we may not hand it down to her descendants.

[Fifth Generation.] Children:

3889. i. ASA CHILD, b. Jan. 7, 1761. Enlisted in the Revolutionary army under legal age for a soldier, and fell a victim to the small-pox in 1777.

3890. ii. RACHEL CHILD, b. April 5, 1762, d. young in Thompson, Ct.

3891. iii. STEPHEN CHILD, b. 1763, m. Zilpha Brooks.

3892. iv. DAVID CHILD, b. Feb. 25, 1764, m. 1st, Ruth Brown: m. 2d, Mrs. Billingsby.

3893. v. MARY CHILD, b. July 24, 1767, d. 1797 unmarried.

3894. vi. SIMEON CHILD, b. Oct. 31, 1769, m. Miss Perry.

3895. vii. ABNER CHILD, b. April 13, 1772, m. 1st, Jan. 23, 1800, Achsah Carpenter: m. 2d, Dolly ———

3896. viii. ARTEMAS CHILD, b. Jan. 16, 1775, m. Dec. 3, 1796, Hannah Ormsby.

3897. ix. DANIEL CHILD, b. Nov. 10, 1777, m. Rebecca Howe.

3898. x. ELIAS CHILD, b. April 22, 1780, m. abt. 1803, Tamar Vincent.

3899. xi. RACHEL CHILD, 2D, b. May 6, 1783, m. May 20, 1800, Jepther Keith.

[Fifth Generation.]

3891. iii. STEPHEN CHILD, third child and second son of Elijah and Rachel Palmer Child, b. in Thompson, Ct., in 1763, m. Zilpha Brooks: was settled first in Morristown, Vt., removed to Sharon, and from thence to Pomfret, in the same State, where he died. After his decease his family removed to Massachusetts.

[Sixth Generation.] Children:

3900. i. MATILDA CHILD.

3901. ii. HANNAH CHILD.

3902. iii. ELIZABETH CHILD.

3903. iv. THEDA CHILD.

3904. v. WILLARD CHILD.

[Fifth Generation.]

3892. iv. CAPT. DAVID CHILD, third son and fourth child of Elijah and Rachel Palmer Child, b. in Thompson, Ct., Feb. 25, 1764, was twice m.—m. 1st, abt. 1782, Ruth Brown: m. 2d, Mrs. Billingsby. Mr. Child early removed to the State of Vermont, and settled in Sharon, Windsor Co. Mr. David Child was drowned in White River, near Sharon, July 22, 1824.

[Sixth Generation.] Children:

3905. i. NATHAN CHILD, b. Feb. 9, 1783, m. May 28, 1807, Belinda Hayes.

3906. ii. ELIJAH CHILD, b. Nov. 15, 1785, m. 1st, Jan. 15, 1810, Eliza Brownell, who d. Oct. 10, 1823; m. 2d, Jan. 29, 1824, Phœbe Carr.

3907. iii. DAVID CHILD, b. Sept. 15, 1787, m. 1808, Susanna Tinkham.

3908. iv. RUTH CHILD, b. April 7, 1789, m. Nov. 26, 1807, Isaiah Tinkham.

3909. v. ABNER CHILD, b. Jan. 13, 1793, m. June 12, 1817, Rhoda Fay, of Pomfret, Vt.

3910. vi. POLLY CHILD, b. Oct. 1793, m. Feb. 18, 1813, Roland Leonard.

3911. vii. JOEL CHILD, b. May 16, 1796, m. Oct. 4, 1833, Electa Colling.

3912. viii. HULDAH CHILD, b. May 3, 1798, m. Nov. 1817, Gamaliel Leonard.

3913. ix. LYMAN CHILD, b. 1799.

3914 x. AMITY CHILD, b. April 9, 1801, m. 1st, Mch. 12, 1823, Levi Rodgers; m. 2d, Mch. 8, 1834, Elijah Russell.

3915. xi. SYLVANUS CHILD, b. Jan. 19, 1805, m. Nov. 16, 1837, Harriet Warren, who was b. Mch. 22, 1809. Mr. Sylvanus Child d. Mch. 18, 1870.

3916 xii. ROXANNA CHILD, b. June 6, 1808, m. May 2, 1827, Parker Morse.

3917. xiii. FANNY CHILD.

[Sixth Generation.]

3905. i. NATHAN CHILD, eldest son and child of Capt. David and Ruth Brown Child, b. in Sharon, Vt., Feb. 9, 1783, m. May 28, 1807, Belinda Hayes, who was b. Jan. 27, 1786. Mr. Child d. Aug. 7, 1828. Mrs. Child d. April 29, 1853, surviving her husband some twenty-five years.

[Seventh Generation.] Children:

3918. i. Infant, dau. (unchristened) b. Dec. 25, 1808, d. same day.

3919. ii. PHILANDA CHILD, b. Dec. 14, 1810, m. Aaron Fales.

3920. iii. NATHAN CHILD, JR., b. Feb. 12, 1813, d. Mch. 14, 1826.

3921. iv. LUCINDA CHILD, b. July 3, 1816, m. Horace Church.

3922. v. MARY E. CHILD, b. May 21, 1826, m. Bushrod R. Gibson.

[Sixth Generation.]

3906. ii. ELIJAH CHILD, second son and child of Capt. David and Ruth Brown Child, b. in Sharon, Vt., Nov. 15, 1785, m. twice—1st, Jan. 15, 1810, Eliza Brownell, who d. in Sharon, Oct. 10, 1823; m. 2d, Jan. 29, 1824, Phœbe Carr, who was b. Mch. 6, 1796. Mr. Elijah Child d. Nov. 7, 1872.

[Seventh Generation.] Children:

3923. i. ORAN CHILD, b. Dec. 14. 1812, d. April 5, 1815, in Sharon, Vt.

3924. ii. LUCIUS CHILD, b. Dec. 15, 1814, m. April 1840, Frances Maria Bragg.

3925. iii. RUFUS B. CHILD, b. Dec. 4, 1816, m. Oct. 28, 1855, Hannah B. Hamilton.

3926. iv. ALEXANDER B. CHILD, b. Dec. 10, 1819, m. Mch. 1, 1846, Sarah E. Ballard.

3927. v. DAVID V. CHILD, b. Dec. 4, 1824, m. July 4, 1856, Angenette Knickerbocker.

3928. vi. ELIZA M. CHILD, b. June 12, 1826, m. May 3, 1858, Edward Turner.

3929 vii. CHARLES H. CHILD, b. Sept. 30, 1827, m. Oct. 6, 1853, Esther A. Hawkins.

3930. viii. JOSEPH C. CHILD, b. Jan. 25, 1830, m. 1st, Dec. 12, 1854, Nancy M. Burnham, who d. May 1859; m. 2d, July 4, 1862, Christiana S. Clark.

3931. ix. ROSELLA CHILD, b. Mch. 22, 1831, m. Nov. 15, 1758, Ezra Ferris.

3932. x. RUTH CHILD, b. Mch. 31, 1834, d. Nov. 4, 1837, in Warren, Vt.

3933. xi. CATHERINE M. CHILD, b. Feb. 1, 1837, m. Jan. 26, 1864, Abner Lull.

3934. xii. HULDAH A. CHILD, b. May 14, 1841, m. April 30, 1859, Leuman C. Ackley.

[Seventh Generation.]

3924. ii. LUCIUS CHILD, second child and son of Elijah and Eliza Brownell Child. b. in Sharon, Vt., Dec. 14, 1814, m. April 1840, Frances Maria Bragg, who was b. Mch. 12, 1818. Mr. Lucius Child, d. in Granville, Vt., Nov. 12, 1863. Mrs. F. M. B. Child d. in Waitsfield, Vt., Feb. 23, 1852.

[Eighth Generation.] Children:

3935. i. ANNORA CHILD, b. Sept. 1847, d. Jan. 24, 1854.

3936. ii. AUGUSTUS F. CHILD, b. Feb. 15, 1852, m. Aug. 18, 1875, Emma E. Bruce.

[Seventh Generation.]

3925. iii. RUFUS B. CHILD, third son and child of Elijah and Eliza Brownell Child. b. in Sharon, Vt., Dec. 4, 1816, m. Oct. 28, 1855, Hannah B. Hamilton, who was b. in Birds Run, Guernsey Co., Ohio, Dec. 13, 1836. Mr. and Mrs. Rufus B. Child reside in Parkersburg, Butler Co., Iowa.

[Eighth Generation] Children:

3937. i. CHARLES W. CHILD, b. April 26, 1858, in Hope, Bartholomew Co., Illinois.

3938. ii. M. ADA CHILD, b. May 28, 1861.

[Seventh Generation.]

3926. iv. ALEXANDER B. CHILD, fourth son and child of Elijah and Eliza Brownell Child. b. in Sharon, Vt., Dec. 10, 1819, m. Mch. 1, 1849, Sarah E. Ballard, who was b. Nov. 15, 1828. Mr. and Mrs. Alexander B. Child reside in Granville, Vt. Mr. Child has been very efficient in collecting and forwarding data of his branch of the family for this book ; but for his very cordial aid much would have been lacking.

[Eighth Generation.] Child:

3939. i. MARY E. CHILD, b. Aug. 27, 1850, in Pomfret, Windsor Co., Vt.

[Seventh Generation.]

3927. v. DAVID V. CHILD, fifth son of Elijah and eldest child of Elijah and Phœbe Carr Child, b. in Sharon, Vt., Dec. 4, 1824. m. July 4, 1856, Angenette Knickerbocker, who was b. Mch. 2, 1838. Reside in Moreau Parish, South Glens Falls, Saratoga Co., N. Y.

[Eighth Generation.] Children:

3940. i. GEORGE H. CHILD, b. May 18, 1857, m. Aug. 11, 1878, Jemima Jones.

3941. ii. FABYAN CHILD, b. Mch. 16, 1860, d. Sept. 26, 1862.

2942 iii. ELMARE E. CHILD, b. Feb. 28, 1862.

3943. iv. HERBERT S. CHILD, b. Feb. 13, 1864.

3944. v. FABAN E. CHILD, b. Sept. 9, 1867, d. Aug. 12, 1873.

3945. vi. ANGENETTA CHILD, b. July 24, 1869.

3946. vii. ALBERT E. CHILD, b. May 23, 1876.

[Seventh Generation]

3928. vi. ELIZA M. CHILD, eldest dau. of Elijah and Phœbe Carr Child, b. in Sharon, Vt., June 12, 1826, m. May 3, 1858, Edward Turner, who was b. in Cornwall, England, June 4, 1832. Mr. Turner d. Nov. 30, 1878. Family reside in Tomhannock, Rensselaer Co., N. Y.

[Eighth Generation.] Children:

3947. i. IDA L. TURNER, b. Mch. 19, 1859.

3948. ii. LIBBIE M. TURNER, b. July 31, 1861, in Malta, Saratoga Co., N. Y., m. May 2, 1876, Robert Hudson. Reside in Iowa.

3949. iii. JOHN TURNER, b. Aug. 14, 1865, in Jay, Essex Co., N. Y.

3950. iv. EDDIE TURNER, b. July 18, 1866, in Jay, Essex Co., N. Y.

3951. v. HATTIE TURNER, b. Feb. 24, 1870, in Peru, Clinton Co., N.Y.

[Seventh Generation.]

3929. vii. CHARLES H. CHILD, seventh child of Elijah and third child of Elijah and Phœbe Carr Child, b. in Sharon, Vt., Sept. 30, 1827, m. Oct. 6, 1853, Esther A. Hawkins, who was b. Feb. 10, 1835. Mr. and Mrs. Charles H. Child reside at Ash Grove, Iroquois Co., Illinois.

[Eighth Generation.] Children:

3952. i. CHARLES H. CHILD, JR., b. Sept. 7, 1854, at Ash Grove, Ill.

3953. ii. PHŒBE E. CHILD, b. Sept. 17, 1856, d. Aug. 31, 1860, in Ash Grove, Ill.

3954. iii. LOUISA CHILD, b. Mch. 31, 1858, m. July 9, 1876, Edwin Ash.

3955. iv. JOHN C. CHILD, b. Mch. 27, 1860, d. June 17, 1860, at Ash Grove, Ill.

3956. v. SARAH J. CHILD, b. Dec. 29, 1861, d. Mch. 12, 1864, at Ash Grove, Ill.

3957. vi. LEWIS G. CHILD, b. May 3, 1866, d. Oct 3, 1869, at Ash Grove, Ill.

3958. vii. ROBERT L. CHILD, b. June 26, 1868, d. Nov. 15, 1869, at Ash Grove, Ill.

3959. viii. HULDAH A. CHILD, b. Oct. 28, 1869, at Ash Grove, Ill.

3960. ix. WESLEY CHILD, b. Mch 31, 1872, at Ash Grove, Ill.

3961. x. WILLIAM CHILD, b. Feb. 22, 1874, d. Feb. 24, 1874, in Ash Grove, Ill.

[Eighth Generation.]

3954. iii. LOUISA CHILD, third child and second dau. of Charles H. and Esther A. Hawkins Child, b. at Ash Grove, Iroquois Co., Ill., March 31, 1858, m. July 9, 1876, Edwin Ash, who was b. in Lancashire Co., England. Reside in Illinois.

[Ninth Generation.] Children:

3962. i. ROSANNA ASH, b. April 4, 1877.

3963. ii. JOHN ASH, b. Dec. 14, 1878.

[Seventh Generation.]

3930. viii. JOSEPH C. CHILD, eighth child of Elijah and fourth of Elijah and Phœbe Carr Child, b. in Sharon, Vt, Jan.

25, 1830, m. Dec. 12, 1854, Nancy W. Burnham, who d. May
1859. Mr. Child remarried July 4, 1862, Christiana S. Clark.
Reside in Hanover, N. H.

[Eighth Generation.] Children.

    3964. i. ARTHUR B. CHILD, b. Dec. 18, 1858.
    3965. ii. MABEL H. CHILD, b. Nov. 25, 1865.
    3966 iii. MYRTIE C. CHILD, b. Oct. 1, 1867.
    3967. iv. MARCELLUS C. CHILD, b. June 15, 1876.

[Seventh Generation.]

    3933. xi. CATHERINE M. CHILD, eleventh child of Elijah
and seventh of Elijah and Phœbe Carr Child, b. in Sharon,
Vt., Feb. 1, 1837, m. Jan. 26, 1864, Abner Lull, who was b.
May 31, 1836. Residence Granville, Addison Co., Vt.

[Eighth Generation.] Children:

    3968. i. DORA P. LULL, b. April 1, 1868.
    3969. ii. LULA E. LULL, b. Jan. 8, 1872.
    3970. iii. INA ALBERTHA LULL, b. Aug 9, 1875.

[Seventh Generation.]

    3934. xii. HULDAH ANN CHILD, twelfth child of Elijah and
eighth child of Elijah and Phœbe Carr Child, b. in Thurman,
Warren Co., N. Y., May 14, 1841, m. April 30, 1859, Lehman
C. Ackley, who was b. Nov. 25, 1837. Mr. and Mrs. Ackley
reside at Glens Falls, Warren Co., N. Y.

[Eighth Generation.] Children:

    3971. i. CHARLES E. ACKLEY, b. April 21, 1860, d. March 31, 1862.
    3972. ii. EDWARD C. ACKLEY, b. Oct. 19, 1863, d. Aug. 6, 1865.
    3973. iii. LANETTA S. ACKLEY, b. July 21, 1866
    3974. iv. FRANK E. ACKLEY, b. Oct. 24, 1868.
    3975. v. FRED. C. ACKLEY, b. Nov. 10, 1871.
    3976. vi. ELBERTHA ACKLEY, b. Feb. 20, 1875.

[Sixth Generation.]

    3907. iii. DAVID CHILD, JR., third son and child of Capt.
David and Ruth Brown Child, b. in Sharon, Vt., Sept. 15, 1787,
m. in 1808 Susanna Tinkham, who was b. in Pomfret, Vt., May
20, 1791. Mr. David Child, Jr., died in Sharon, Nov. 24,
1862; Mrs. Susanna T. Child died June 27, 1870.

[Seventh Generation.] Children:

    3977. i. ALVIN CHILD, b. Jan. 30, 1809, m. March 9, 1830, Clarinda Hall.
    3978. ii. ORLANDO CHILD, b. Jan. 2, 1812, m Sept. 14, 1837, Luth L.
Pere.
    3979. iii. JUSTIN L. CHILD, b. July 28, 1815, m. Aug. 16, 1836, Elvira
Shacher.
    3980. iv. DAVID LORENZO CHILD, b Aug. 28, 1816, m. Nov. 26, 1839,
Margaret L. Dysart.
    3981. v. ALICE S. CHILD, b. April 2, 1822, m. March 21, 1839, Austin
Leonard.

3982. vi. LORIETTE A. CHILD. b. Jan. 20. 1833, m. March 24, 1851. James G. Jackman.

[Seventh Generation.]

3977. i. ALVIN CHILD. eldest child of David. Jr., and Susanna Tinkham Child. b. in Sharon. Vt., June 30. 1809. m. March 9. 1830. Clarinda Hall. Mr. Alvin Child resides in Claremont. N. H., but his early home and the birthplace of his children was Pomfret, Vt.. in which place Mrs. Clarinda Hall Child died June 5. 1877.

[Eighth Generation.] Children:

3983. i. LUTHERA CHILD. b. May 2. 1831. m. Isaac Allen.

3984. ii. VICTORIA CHILD. b. Dec. 10. 1832. m. Calvin Washburn.

3985. iii. RUSSELL CHILD. b. Sept. 18. 1834. d. 1836.

3986. iv. OSCAR CHILD. b. Dec. 3. 1837.

3987. v. ALVIN CHILD. JR., b. Nov. 21. 1844.

3988. vi. AMELIA CHILD. b. Feb. 4. 1846. m. Albro Martin.

[Seventh Generation.]

3978. ii. ORLANDO CHILD. second son and child of David. Jr., and Susanna Tinkham Child. b. in Sharon. Vt., Jan. 2. 1812. m. Sept. 14. 1837. Luth L. Pere. Reside in Hanover. N. H.

[Eighth Generation.] Children:

3989. i. EDWIN O. CHILD. b. Jan. 9. 1841. d. June 29. 1842.

3990. ii. EMILY L. CHILD. b. July 10. 1843. d. May 22. 1845.

3991. iii. ELLIS T. CHILD. b. Mch. 12. 1846. d. Sept. 7. 1847.

3992. iv. LURA A CHILD. b. Aug. 6. 1848. d. Nov. 15. 1849.

3993. v. EDWIN W. CHILD. b. Sept. 1. 1850. d. Aug. 9. 1852.

3994. vi. ALICE C. CHILD. b. Feb. 4. 1854. m. Dec. 24. 1875. Max K. Walker.

[Eighth Generation.]

3994. vi. ALICE C. CHILD. only child of six of the family of Orlando and Luth L. Pere Child who lived to maturity. b. Feb. 4. 1854. m. Dec. 24. 1875. Max K. Walker. who was b. Mch. 4. 1852.

[Ninth Generation.] Child:

3995. i. MAX O. WALKER. b. Mch. 18. 1877.

[Seventh Generation.]

3979. iii. JUSTIN L. CHILD. third son and child of David. Jr., and Susanna Tinkham Child. b. July 28. 1815. m. Aug. 16. 1836. Elvira Shacher. who was b. Dec. 25. 1816. Reside in West Randolph. Vt.

[Eighth Generation.] Children:

3996. i. EDGAR A. CHILD. b. Aug. 14. 1839. d. May 2. 1840. at Granville. Ill.

3997. ii. OSCAR B. CHILD. b. June 4. 1841. at Pomfret. Vt., m. Sept. 27. 1867. Mary L. Badger.

3998. iii. ELSIE V. CHILD. b. March 5. 1852.

3999. iv. HERBERT GLENN CHILD b. June 20. 1861. d. March 6. 1864.

[Eighth Generation.]

3997. ii. OSCAR B. CHILD, second son and child of Justin L. and Elvira Shacher Child, b. in Pomfret, Vt., June 4, 1841, m. Sept. 27, 1867, Mary L. Badger, who was b. June 16, 1841. Reside in West Randolph, Vt.

[Ninth Generation.] Children:
4000. i. LELIA MAY CHILD, b. Nov. 17, 1870, at Bethel, Vt.
4001. ii. MARY BADGER CHILD, b. Oct. 20, 1874, at West Randolph, Vt.

[Seventh Generation.]

3980. iv. DAVID LORENZO CHILD, fourth son and child of David, Jr., and Susanna Tinkham Child, b. Aug. 28, 1816, m. Nov. 26, 1839, Margaret L. Dysart. Mr. David L. Child d. April 29, 1871, in Granville, Ill.

[Eighth Generation.] Children:
4002. i. SUSAN E. CHILD, b. May 23, 1842.
4003. ii. CLARINDA CHILD, b. April 22, 1844.
4004. iii. LUCINDA A. CHILD, b. Aug. 27, 1846.
4005. iv. DAVID W. CHILD, b. Nov. 9, 1848.
4006. v. ARCHIBALD P. CHILD, b. July 19, 1850.
4007. vi. KATE L. CHILD, b. Dec. 25, 1852.

[Seventh Generation.]

3981. v. ALICE S. CHILD, eldest dau. and fifth child of David, Jr., and Susanna Tinkham Child, b. April 2, 1822, m. March 21, 1839, Austin Leonard, who was b. Jan. 30, 1820. Reside in Rochester, Windsor Co., Vt.

[Eighth Generation.] Children:
4008. i. LEONORA LEONARD, b. 1840.
4009. ii. CAROLINE S. LEONARD, b. March 23, 1842, m. Feb. 4, 1864, George E. Marsh.
4010. iii. ELMER J. LEONARD, b. Aug. 5, 1844, was killed in the recent war on March 3, 1864.

[Eighth Generation.]

4009. ii. CAROLINE S. LEONARD, second dau. and child of Alice S. Child and Austin Leonard, b. in Rochester, Vt., Mch. 23, 1842, m. Feb. 4, 1864, George E. Marsh, who was b. June 4, 1839. Reside in Hancock, Vt.

[Ninth Generation.] Children:
4011. i. CARRIE M. MARSH, b. Mch. 21, 1865.
4912. ii. CLINNIE E. MARSH, b. Sept. 25, 1867.
4013. iii. LESLIE L. MARSH, b. June 29, 1868, d. Feb. 17, 1869.
4014. iv. DANA G. MARSH, b. Aug. 20, 1874.

[Seventh Generation.]

3982. vi. LORIETTE A. CHILD, second dau. and sixth child of David, Jr., and Susanna Tinkham Child, b. Jan. 29, 1833,

in Pomfret. Vt., m. Mch. 24, 1851. James G. Jackman, of Enfield Centre, N. H., who was b. Oct. 21, 1826. Reside in Enfield, N H.

[Eighth Generation.]   Children:
 4015. i. JAMES C. JACKMAN, b. Aug. 2, 1853.
 4016. ii. FLORENCE JACKMAN, b. Aug. 24, 1856.
 4017. iii. LORAN CHILD JACKMAN, b. Oct. 2, 1858.
 4018. iv. LURA A. JACKMAN, b. Feb. 20, 1864.
 4019. v. ALLEN H. JACKMAN, b. Sept. 8, 1866.

[Sixth Generation.]

 3908. iv. RUTH CHILD, eldest dau. and fourth child of Capt.
David and Ruth Brown Child. b. in Sharon, Vt., April 7, 1789,
m. Nov. 26, 1807, Isaiah Tinkham. who was b. June 15, 1782.
Mr. Tinkham d. Oct. 14, 1851.   Mrs. Ruth Child Tinkham d.
May 2, 1859.

[Seventh Generation.]   Children:
 4020. i CHARLES TINKHAM, b. Nov. 23, 1808, m. 1837, Amanda Baron;
reside at Queechee, Vt.
 4021. ii. RUTH TINKHAM, b. Jan. 8, 1810, m. 1838, W. L. Bragg; reside
at Queechee, Vt.
 4022. iii. EMILY TINKHAM, b. Jan. 26, 1813, m. Oct. 20, 1832, Otis Warren.
 4023. iv. CELIA TINKHAM, b Feb. 4, 1817, m. Feb. 2, 1840, G. W. Martin;
reside at West Randolph, Vt.
 4024 v. JANE TINKHAM, b. May 25, 1818, m. Feb 21, 1844, H L. Williams; reside at Woodstock, Vt.

[Sixth Generation.]

 3909. v. ABNER CHILD, fourth son and fifth child of Capt.
David and Ruth Brown Child, b. in Sharon, Vt., Jan. 13, 1793,
m. June 12, 1817, Rhoda Fay, who was b. in Sharon, Vt., June
13, 1797.   Mr. Abner Child d. in Pomfret. Vt., Aug. 9, 1872,
Mrs. Rhoda Fay Child d. in the same place Nov. 30, 1873.

[Seventh Generation]   Children:
 4025. i. MOSES FAY CHILD, b. Mch. 3, 1818, m. May 4, 1841, Lucinda
Fails.
 4026. ii. MARCELLUS CHILD, b. Mch. 17, 1819, m. Feb. 1, 1848, Desde-
mona Udal; resides in Pomfret, Vt.
 4027. iii MARCIA M. CHILD, b. Oct. 17, 1820, m. June 17, 1840, Philander
Cook.
 4028. iv. ALBA CHILD, b. April 18, 1822, m. twice—1st, Dec. 6, 1844,
Hester Ann Rogers; m. 2d, Aug. 7, 1853, Adeline Robinson.
 4029. v. ZERA CHILD, b. Mch. 9, 1824, m. Oct. 10, 1848, Caroline Torrey.
He d. Oct. 6, 1852; resided in Weymouth, Mass.
 4030 vi. CHAUNCEY CHILD, b. Dec. 2, 1826, m. Jan, 6, 1848, Jane
Howard.
 4031. vii. QUINCY A. CHILD, b. Oct. 19, 1828, d. July 13, 1847, in Sharon, Vt
 4032. viii. MELINDA S. CHILD, b. Oct. 2, 1830, m. Nov. 29, 1849, Lorenzo
Church.
 4033. ix. EDWIN W. CHILD, b. Oct. 28, 1833, m. Oct. 28, 1859, Diantha
Harrington, of Pomfret, Vt.   He d. Nov. 7, 1865, in Sharon, Vt.

4034. x. JASPER H. CHILD, b July 21, 1838, was drowned in White River, Sharon, Vt., near the spot where his grandfather lost his life, thirty years before. Mr. Jasper Child was drowned Aug. 5, 1857.

[Seventh Generation.]

4025. i. MOSES FAY CHILD, eldest son and child of Abner and Rhoda Fay Child, b. in Sharon, Vt., Mch. 3, 1818, m. May 4, 1841, Lucinda Fails, and removed to Hancock, Addison Co., Vt., where he now resides.

[Eighth Generation.] Children:

4035. i. EDWIN A. CHILD, b. April 20, 1846, d. Sept. 20, 1857, in Hancock, Vt.

4036. ii. MOSES ALBA CHILD, b. Dec. 26, 1847, in Hancock, Vt. Resides in Hillsborough Bridge, N H.

4037. iii. EDWIN R. CHILD, b. Aug. 1, 1850, in Hancock, Vt. Resides in Hillsborough, N. H.

4038. iv. CAROLINE CHILD, b. Jan. 10, 1853, in Hancock, Vt.

[Seventh Generation.]

4027. iii. MARCIA M. CHILD, eldest dau. and third child of Abner and Rhoda Fay Child, b. Oct. 17, 1820, in Sharon, Vt., m. June 17, 1840, Philander Cook. Mr. and Mrs. Cook resided some years in Holyoke, Mass., removing thence to Bureau Co., Ill., where Mrs. Cook d. Aug. 28, 1848.

[Eighth Generation.] Children:

4039. i. MARCELLUS COOK, b June 24, 1841; resides in Bureau Co., Ill.

4040 ii LUCIA M COOK, b. Sept. 18, 1843, m. a Mr. Blanchard; has one child, Ida Blanchard

4941. iii. ARTHUR COOK, b. May 7, 1845; resides in Bureau Co., Ill.

4042. iv. ALBA COOK, b. July 10, 1848, d. July 30, 1848.

[Seventh Generation.]

4028. iv. ALBA CHILD, third son and fourth child of Abner and Rhoda Fay Child, b. April 18, 1822, in Sharon, Vt., m. twice—1st, Dec. 6, 1844, Hester Ann Rogers, who d. July 22, 1852, ae. 26 years; m. 2d, Aug. 7, 1853, Adeline W. Robinson.

[Eighth Generation.] Child:

4043. i. INEZ CHILD, b. Sept. 4, 1850, m Dec. 11, 1878, A. D. Whitmore; resides at Spring Prarie, Walworth Co., Wis.

[Seventh Generation.]

4030. vi. CHAUNCEY CHILD, fifth son and sixth child of Abner and Rhoda Fay Child, b. Dec. 2, 1826, in Sharon, Vt., m. Jan. 6, 1848, Jane Howard. Resides in Pomfret, Vt.

[Eighth Generation.] Children:

4044. i. QUINCY E. CHILD, b. Aug. 2, 1848, m. Nov. 16, 1869, Sarah Frink.

4045. ii. EDWIN C. CHILD, b. March 4, 1850, m. Fanny King of Pomfret, Vt.; reside in Cottonwood Falls, Kansas.

4046. iii. WINFIELD SCOTT CHILD, b. June 3, 1852, m. Jan. 12, 1874, Jennie Brooks.

4047. iv. EDITH CHILD, b. July 2, 1872.

[Eighth Generation.]

4044. i. QUINCY E. CHILD, eldest son and child of Chauncey and Jane Howard Child, b. in Pomfret, Vt., Aug. 2, 1848, m. Nov. 16, 1869, Sarah Frink. Removed to Kansas.

[Ninth Generation.] Child:

4048. i. WAYNE CHILD, b. 1871.

[Eighth Generation.]

4045. iii. WINFIELD SCOTT CHILD, third son and child of Chauncey and Jane Howard Child, b. in Pomfret, Vt., June 3, 1852, m. Jan. 12, 1874, Jennie Brooks, of Pomfret, where they reside.

[Ninth Generation.] Child:

4049. i. FLORENCE CHILD, b. Feb. 5, 1877.

[Seventh Generation.]

4032. viii. MELINDA S. CHILD, second dau. and eighth child of Abner and Rhoda Fay Child, b. in Sharon, Vt., Oct. 2, 1830, m. Nov. 29, 1849, Lorenzo Church. Mr. Church d. Feb. 7, 1855, aged 30 years. Mrs. Church m. 2d, May 29, 1857, George Snow. Mrs. Snow d. Aug. 28, 1863.

[Eighth Generation] Children:

4050. i. EFFIE MAY CHURCH, b. Dec. 4, 1853, d. Sept. 12, 1855.

4051. ii. JASPER HERBERT SNOW, b. May 18, 1858.

4052. iii. ELLEN SNOW, b. Dec. 8, 1862.

[Sixth Generation.]

3910. vi. POLLY CHILD, second dau. and sixth child of Capt. David and Ruth Brown Child, b. Oct. 1793, in Sharon, Vt., m. Feb. 18, 1813, Roland Leonard. Mrs. Polly Child Leonard d. March 8, 1878. Their residence was in Rochester, Windsor Co., Vt., where all their large family were born.

[Seventh Generation.] Children:

4053. i. AN INFANT (unchristened), b. April 29, 1814, d. in Rochester, Vt., May 10, 1814.

4054. ii. AN INFANT (unchristened,) b. March 12, 1815, d. soon in Rochester, Vt.

4055. iii. LEANDER LEONARD, b. in Rochester, Vt., Jan. 29, 1816.

4056. iv. ALECTA LEONARD, b. Nov. 29, 1817.

4057. v. LOUISA LEONARD, b. Oct. 22, 1819.

4058. vi. EUNICE LEONARD, b. March 29, 1821.

4059. vii. AGRO LEONARD, b. April 10, 1823.

4060. viii. AURILLA LEONARD, b. Jan. 29, 1825.

4061. ix. ORPH. LEONARD, b. Oct. 5, 1827.

4062. x. ALVOSA LEONARD, b. Nov. 20, 1828.

4063. xi. MARY LEONARD, b. Oct. 30, 1830.

4064. xii. ALBERT LEONARD, b. May 1, 1832.

4065. xiii. MARY J. LEONARD, b. Sept. 30, 1834.

4066. xiv. EDGAR B. LEONARD, b. Dec. 19, 1837.

[Sixth Generation.]

3911. vii. JOEL CHILD, fifth son and seventh child of Capt David and Ruth Brown Child, b. in Sharon, Vt., May 16, 1796, m. Oct. 4, 1833, Electa Colling of Derby, Vt., who was b. Feb. 11, 1812. Mr. Joel Child d. Oct. 3, 1877.

[Seventh Generation.] Children:

4067. i. MYRON CHILD, b. Aug. 3, 1834, m. Sept. 14, 1861, Sophia Spaulding.

4068. ii. MARY ANN CHILD, b. Sept. 15, 1836, m. June 5, 1857, N. C. Davis.

4069. iii. BELINDA J. CHILD, b. in Coventry, Vt., Nov. 7, 1839, m. July 23, 1861, Eugene L. Barnes. Mrs. B. J. Child Barnes d. April 11, 1862.

4070. iv. CYNTHIA H. CHILD, b. Nov. 2, 1842, m. Aug. 24, 1870, S. A. Lewis.

4071. v. ELLA M. CHILD, b. June 20, 1855, m. May 5, 1872, Francis Lamb.

[Seventh Generation.]

4067. i. MYRON CHILD, eldest son and child of Joel and Electa Colling Child, b. in Coventry, Vt., Aug. 3, 1834, m. Sept. 14, 1861, Sophia Spaulding. Reside in California.

[Eighth Generation.] Children:

4072. i. FRANK E. CHILD, b. May 4, 1866.

4073. ii. FLORIBELL CHILD, b. March 13, 1870.

4074. iii. ALFRED H. CHILD, b. Dec. 20, 1872.

4075. iv. RENETTA M. CHILD, b. May 10, 1877.

[Seventh Generation.]

4068. ii. MARY ANN CHILD, eldest dau. and second child of Joel and Electa Colling Child, b. in Coventry, Vt., Sept. 15, 1836, m. June 5, 1857, N. C. Davis. Mrs. Mary A. Child Davis d. Feb. 3, 1871.

[Eighth Generation.] Child:

4076. i. FLORIBELL DAVIS, b. Aug. 9, 1858, d. March 5, 1865.

[Seventh Generation.]

4070. iv. CYNTHIA H. CHILD, third dau. and fourth child of Joel and Electa Colling Child, b. in Coventry, Vt., Nov. 2, 1842, m. Aug. 24, 1870, S. A. Lewis.

[Eighth Generation.] Children:

4077. i. FRANK H. LEWIS, b. Feb. 18, 1875.

4078. ii. GRACE J. LEWIS, b. July 12, 1877.

[Seventh Generation.]

4071. v. ELLA M. CHILD, fourth dau. of Joel and Electa Colling Child, b. in Pomfret, Vt., June 20, 1855, m. May 5, 1875, Francis Lamb.

[Eighth Generation.] Child:

4079. i. GEORGE A. LAMB, b. at Randolph, Vt.

[Sixth Generation.]

3912. viii. HULDAH CHILD, third dau. and eighth child of Capt. David and Ruth Brown Child, b. in Sharon, Vt., May 3, 1798, m. Nov. 1817, Gamaliel Leonard. Mr. Leonard d. Oct. 28, 1850; Mrs. Huldah Child Leonard d. Oct. 25, 1865.

[Seventh Generation.] Children:

4080. i. AMANDA LEONARD, b. Aug. 11, 1819, d. Sept. 20, 1819.

4081. ii. PHŒBE LEONARD, b. July 13, 1820, m. Jan. 21, 1845, Chauncey Perry.

4082. iii. RUTH C. LEONARD, b. Nov. 23, 1821, m. Jan. 4, 1847, Lester Perry.

4083. iv. AMANDA LEONARD, 2D., b. Dec. 23, 1823, m. June 6, 1840, Reuben Munsell.

4084. v. AMITY A. LEONARD, b. March 29, 1826, m. Jan. 4, 1847, Gilbert D. Allen.

4085. vi. HARVEY LEONARD, b. Oct. 6, 1827, m. April 23, 1854, Josephine E. Davis.

4086. vii. LAURA LEONARD, b. Jan. 15, 1833, d. Ap. 7, 1841, at Sharon, Vt.

4087. viii. DANIEL H. LEONARD, b. May 23, 1837, d. Aug. 3, 1863, at Sharon, Vt.

4088. ix. DAVID E. LEONARD, b. Aug. 18, 1844, d. in Douglas Hospital, Washington, D. C., Aug. 13, 1864.

[Seventh Generation.]

4082. iii. RUTH C. LEONARD, third dau. and child of Huldah Child and Gamaliel Leonard, b. in Sharon, Vt., Nov. 23, 1821, m. Jan. 4, 1847, Lester Perry, who d. Feb. 15, 1859.

[Eighth Generation.] Child:

4089. i. LUVILLA E. PERRY, b. Oct. 25, 1852, m. Oct. 25, 1871, Francis S. Snow of Sharon, Vt.

[Ninth Generation.] Child:

4090. i. LUVIA MARIA SNOW, b. April 7, 1875.

[Seventh Generation.]

4083. iv. AMANDA LEONARD, 2D, fourth dau. and child of Huldah Child and Gamaliel Leonard, b. in Sharon, Vt., Dec. 23, 1823, m. June 6, 1840, Reuben Munsell of Sharon, who d. Jan. 28, 1866.

[Eighth Generation.] Children:

4091. i. JOHN MUNSELL, b. June 28, 1843, m. Susie Butler.

4092. ii. RUBY A. MUNSELL, b. Jan. 9, 1846, m. July 29, 1866, Stephen F. Ramsdell.

4093. iii. LAURA J. MUNSELL, b. Dec. 27, 1847, d. Oct. 18, 1850.

4094. iv. CLARA MUNSELL, b. Sept. 21, 1850, m. May 16, 1874, Henry C. Towne, of Boston.

4095. v. CAROLINE MUNSELL, b. Aug. 10, 1852, d. Sept. 27, 1867.

4096. vi. ABBIE J. MUNSELL, b. Feb. 6, 1855, m. Aug. 15, 1876, Charles M. Hazen.

4097. vii. SARAH B. MUNSELL, b. Dec. 31, 1856, d. Nov. 6, 1873.

4098. viii. WILLIAM W. MUNSELL, b. July 28, 1859.

4099. ix. CLINTON R. MUNSELL, b. April 19, 1863.

4100. x. CHESTER MUNSELL, b. Aug. 8, 1865, d. Jan. 12, 1866.

[Eighth Generation.]

4091. i. JOHN MUNSELL, eldest child of Reuben and Amanda Leonard Munsell, and grandchild of Huldah Child Leonard, b. in Sharon, Vt., June 28, 1843, m. Susie Butler, of Lowell, Mass.

[Ninth Generation.] Children:
4101. i. MINA MAY MUNSELL.
4102. ii. FAY WILLIS MUNSELL, b. April 9, 1878.

[Eighth Generation.]

4092. ii. RUBY A. MUNSELL, eldest dau. and second child of Reuben and Amanda Leonard Munsell, and granddaughter of Huldah Child Leonard, b. in Sharon, Vt., Jan. 9, 1846, m. July 29, 1866, Stephen F. Ramsdell, of St. Louis, Missouri.

[Ninth Generation.] Children:
4103. i. STEPHEN L. RAMSDELL, b. July 18, 1867, d. Feb. 29, 1868.
4104. ii. SUSIE F. RAMSDELL, b. Aug. 14, 1870.
4105. iii. STEPHEN G. RAMSDELL, b. April 27, 1878.

[Eighth Generation.]

4096. vi. ABBIE J. MUNSELL, fifth dau. and sixth child of Reuben and Amanda Leonard Munsell, and granddaughter of Huldah Child Leonard, b. in Sharon, Vt., Feb. 6, 1855, m. Aug. 15, 1876, Charles M. Hazen, of West Hartford, Vt., where they reside.

[Ninth Generation.] Children:
4106. i. CLARA A. HAZEN, b. Sept. 29, 1877.
4107. ii. EMMA ELIZA JANE HAZEN, b. April 18, 1879.

[Seventh Generation.]

4084. v. AMITY A. LEONARD, fifth dau. and child of Huldah Child and Gamaliel Leonard, b. in Sharon, Vt., Mch. 29, 1826, m. Jan. 4, 1847, Gilbert D. Allen, of Pomfret, Vt.

[Eighth Generation.] Children:
4108. i. ETHAN U. ALLEN, b. Oct. 11, 1847, in Granville, Vt., m. Aug. 28, 1873, Mary A. Vaughn.
4109. ii. LAURA M. ALLEN, b. Aug. 20, 1849, in Pomfret, Vt.

[Eighth Generation.]

4108. i. ETHAN U. ALLEN, eldest son and child of Gilbert D. and Amity A. Leonard Allen, and grandson of Huldah Child Leonard, b. in Granville, Vt., Oct. 11, 1847, m. Aug. 28, 1873, Mary A. Vaughn, of Woodstock, Vt.

[Ninth Generation.] Children:
4110. i. FLORENCE E. ALLEN, b. Nov. 20, 1875, in Pomfret, Vt.
4111. ii. LUCY E. ALLEN, b. July 25, 1877, in Pomfret, Vt.

H-1

[Seventh Generation.]

4085. vi. HARVEY LEONARD, eldest son and sixth child of Huldah Child and Gamaliel Leonard, b. in Sharon, Vt., Oct. 6, 1827, m. April 23, 1854, Josephine E. Davis, of Sharon.

[Eighth Generation.] Children:
  4112. i. HOWARD G. LEONARD, b. July 20, 1857, in Royalton, Vt.
  4113. ii. JASPER D. LEONARD, b. May 15, 1860, in Bridgewater, Ct.

[Sixth Generation.]

3014. x. AMITY A. CHILD, fourth dau. and tenth child of David and Ruth Brown Child, b. in Sharon, Vt., April 9, 1801, m. 1st, Mch. 12, 1823, Levi Rodgers, who was b. Mch. 19, 1800; Mr. Rodgers, d Dec. 1, 1833. Mrs. Amity Child Rodgers m 2d, Mch. 8, 1834, Elijah Russell. Mrs. Amity A. Child Russell d. Jan. 8, 1871. Mr. Russell d. Dec. 3, 1844.

[Seventh Generation.] Children:
  4114. i. ALMIRA RODGERS, b. July 2, 1824, d. Jan. 23, 1848, at Norwich, Vt.
  4115. ii. GEORGE D. RODGERS, b. April 22, 1826, d. Aug. 12, 1862, at Mayfield, N. Y.
  4116. iii. JANE E. RODGERS, b. Sept. 25, 1828, d. Feb. 18, 1852, at Mayfield, N. Y.
  4117. iv. SARAH E. RUSSELL, b. Mch. 12, 1836, m. June 9, 1855, Augustus Vinton.
  4118. v. LEVI H. RUSSELL, b. Oct. 2, 1838, in Rochester, Vt.

[Seventh Generation.]

4117. iv. SARAH E. RUSSELL, fourth child of Amity Child and eldest child of Amity Child and Elijah Russell, b. in Rochester, Vt., Mch. 12, 1836, m. June 8, 1855, Augustus Vinton. Reside in Granville, Vt.

[Eighth Generation.] Children:
  4119. i. LE ROY A. VINTON, b. Jan. 31, 1857, at Granville, Vt.
  4120. ii. WILLIE R. VINTON, b. Aug. 27, 1861, at Granville, Vt.
  4121. iii. HATTIE E. VINTON, b. Aug. 16, 1867, at Granville, Vt.

[Sixth Generation.]

3916. xii. ROXANNA CHILD, fifth dau and twelfth child of David and Ruth Brown Child, b. in Sharon, Vt., June 6, 1806, m. May 2, 1827, Parker Morse, who was b. in New Hampshire, 1803, d. Mch. 7, 1877.

[Seventh Generation.] Children:
  4122. i. JOSEPH MORSE, }
  4123. ii. MARY MORSE, } TWINS. } b. 1830, in Metamora, Ill.
  4124. iii. MARTHA MORSE, b. 1832, in Metamora, Ill.

[Fifth Generation.]

3894. vi. SIMEON CHILD, fourth son and sixth child of Elijah and Rachel Palmer Child, b. in Thompson, Ct., Oct. 31, 1769, m. 1797, Miss Perry.

[Sixth Generation.] Children:

4125. i. SARAH CHILD, b. 1798, m. Stephen Gibbs.

4126. ii. RACHEL CHILD, b. 1800, m. Emery Ashley.

4127. iii. MARY CHILD, b. 1802, m. 1st. —— Simons, of Hartford, Vt.; m 2. —— Morse, of Haverhill, N. H.

4128. iv. BETSEY CHILD, b. 1804, m. Seth Hodges.

4129. v. ANNIE CHILD, b. 1806, m. Jotham Howe.

4130. vi. SAREPTA CHILD, b. 1808, m. James Culver.

4131. vii. RUTH CHILD, b. 1810, m. Albert Freeman.

4132. viii. SIMEON CHILD, JR., b. Jan. 15, 1812. Has been for many years a much respected and honored member of the community of Shakers, at Enfield, Grafton Co., N. H. To him, through another member of the community, we are much indebted for the record of the family.

4133. ix. Infant daughter (unchristened) b. 1814.

[Sixth Generation.]

4125. i. SARAH CHILD, eldest dau. and child of Simeon and — Perry Child, b. in Royalton, Vt., in 1798. m. Stephen Gibbs of Pomfret, Vt. From Vermont they went west to reside, but we do not know where, and have only a slight report.

[Seventh Generation.] Children:

4134. i. NORMAN CHILD GIBBS.

4135. ii. LAURA GIBBS

[Sixth Generation.]

4126. ii. RACHEL CHILD, second dau. and child of Simeon and — Perry Child, b. in Royalton, Vt., in 1800. m. Emery Ashley of Hartland, Windsor Co., Vt.

[Seventh Generation.] Children:

4136. i. ALBERTUS ASHLEY, } TWINS.
4137. ii. ALMIRA ASHLEY, }

4138. iii. SAREPTA ASHLEY.

4139. iv. CAROLINE ASHLEY.

4140. v. CHARLES ASHLEY.

[Sixth Generation.]

4129. v. ANNIE CHILD, fifth dau. and child of Simeon and — Perry Child, b. in Royalston, Vt., in 1806, m. Jotham Howe of Enfield, N. H.

[Seventh Generation.] Children:

4141. i. LAURA HOWE.

4142. ii. JANE HOWE.

[Sixth Generation.]

4130. vi. SAREPTA CHILD, sixth dau. and child of Simeon and — Perry Child, b. in Royalston, Vt., in 1808, m. James Culver of Pomfret, N. H.

[Seventh Generation.] Children:

4143. i. WILLIAM CULVER.

4144. ii NEWTON CULVER.

4145. iii. JOHN CULVER.

4146. iv. ARTHUR CULVER.

[Sixth Generation.]

4131. vii. RUTH CHILD, sixth dau. and child of Simeon and — Perry Child. b. in Royalston. Vt., in 1810. m. Albert Freeman of Lebanon, N. H. [We believe there were other children, but have not obtained the names.]

[Seventh Generation.] Child:

4147. i. CHARLES FREEMAN.

[Fifth Generation.]

3895. vii. ABNER CHILD, fifth son and seventh child of Elijah and Rachel Palmer Child, b. in Thompson, Ct., April 13, 1772, m. 1st, Jan. 23, 1800, Achsah Carpenter, who was b. in Coventry, Ct., Aug. 16, 1780, d. April 9, 1823. Mr. Abner Child m. 2d, Dolly Franklin. Mr. Child d. June 8, 1859; Mrs. Dolly Franklin Child d. March 1, 1860. Mrs. Achsah Carpenter Child was one of fourteen children who grew up, married, and had large families.

[Sixth Generation.] Children:

4148. i. IRENE CHILD, b. Sept. 22, 1801, m. Aug. 25, 1822, Eber H. Baxter.

4149. ii. EBER CARPENTER CHILD, b. Dec. 24, 1803, m. May 7, 1829. Fanny Hazletine.

4150. iii. BETSEY CHILD, } TWINS { b. Mch. 7, 1806, } { d. Mch. 23, 1806.

4151. iv. PAMELIA CHILD, } { m. Jan. 1, 1858, Ezra M. Hutchinson, d. May 11,1875.

4152. v. MARY CHILD, b. Mch. 9, 1810, m. Jan. 22, 1839, Stephen Goodspeed.

4153. vi. ACHSAH CHILD, b. Mch. 31, 1812, d. May 16, 1813.

4154. vii. DENNIS CHILD, b. Dec. 22, 1814. m. Sept. 20, 1837, Frances A. Straus.

4155. viii. ZILLAH CHILD,.b. Jan. 16, 1820, d. June 16, 1820.

4156. ix. ROSWELL CHILD, b. June 19, 1821, m. Nov. 22, 1843, Abigail Goodspeed.

4157. x. JERUSHA CHILD. b. Mch. 25, 1823, d. April 7, 1823.

[Sixth Generation.]

4148. i. IRENE CHILD, eldest child of Abner and Achsah Carpenter Child, b. in Sharon, Vt., Sept. 22, 1801, m. in Moretown. Aug. 25, 1822, Eber Hubbard Baxter, who was b. in Berlin, Vt., on Sept. 25, 1799. Is now (1879) residing in Cascade, Kent Co., Mich. Mr. Baxter is a man of strongly marked characteristics, noticeably successful in the results attending their development. Skeptical of the good wrought by physicians in the usual practice of the profession, he has not called one to prescribe in his family for fifty years; but has meantime reared a family of thirteen children, to man and womanhood. While yet residing in Vermont Mr. Baxter, beside holding many township offices, was chosen to represent the town of Fayston, Washington Co., Vt., in the State Legislature for several terms. In the year 1851 Mr. Baxter, with his family, removed to Michigan, and has remained there in the enjoyment even now of unusual mental and physical vigor.

[Seventh Generation.] Children:

4158. i. ALBERT BAXTER, b. Aug. 3, 1823, m. Feb. 22, 1849, Elvira E. Guild.

4159. ii. BERNARD BAXTER, b. July 6, 1824, m. Oct. 27, 1844, Harriet J. Brigham.

4160. iii CELIA BAXTER, b. March 16, 1826, m. June 20, 1849, Elisha Aldis Brigham.

4161. iv. ORMAN BAXTER, b. Aug. 16, 1827, m. Dec. 11, 1866, Hettie M. Olmstead.

4162. v. ROSINA BAXTER, b. April 4, 1829, m May 1, 1854, Oren N. Cadwell

4163. vi. EDWIN BAXTER, b. March 9, 1831, m. April 30, 1860, Carrie A. Keyes.

4164. vii. URI J. BAXTER, b. Jan. 20, 1833, m. 1865, Maggie Lowry.

4165. viii. ZADA BAXTER, b. in Fayston, Vt., March 28, 1835, m. May 10, 1870, Isaac Coeman, in Lowell, Mich.

4166. ix. SABRINA BAXTER, b. Dec. 17, 1836, m. Jan. 1, 1875, Justice Cooper.

4167. x. IRA C. BAXTER, b. in Fayston, Washington Co., Vt., Nov. 13, 1838. Enlisted in the Union Army, in 21st Michigan Infantry Regiment, in the war of the Rebellion, and was killed in battle at Chickamauga, Sept. 20, 1863.

4168. xi. MILO BAXTER, b. Aug. 15, 1841, m. Jan 20, 1867, Ellen Celia Rich.

4169. xii. DOLLY F. BAXTER, b June 12, 1845, m. Oct. 18, 1870, Silas Beckey; occupation farming, reside in Cascade, Mich.

4170. xiii. VIENNA IRENE BAXTER, b Feb. 21, 1848, m. July 25, 1878, Isaac Coeman, a farmer, and cousin of Zada Baxter's husband. Reside in Lowell, Mich.

[Seventh Generation.]

4158. i. ALBERT BAXTER, eldest child of Irene Child and Hon. Eber Hubbard Baxter, b. in Moretown, Vt., Aug. 3, 1823, m. in Fayston, Vt., Feb. 22, 1849, Elvira E. Guild. Mrs. E. E. Guild Baxter, d. Oct. 27, 1855. Mr. Baxter has not remarried. A boyhood in the vitalizing air of the Green Mountains, was strengthened in muscle by the farm training, and tutored in mind at the village school, with brief drill at higher academies. Albert Baxter began life for himself, as so many of his race have done, by wielding the birch, and doubtless teaching the youth of his native State. But he could not

content himself with such a career, and soon after reaching his
majority he left Vermont for that El Dorado of New England
youth, the West. For a time he was an instructor in Wisconsin, but made his way to Grand Rapids, Mich. Of two trades
he made himself master, but his real work was in neither.
Buoyant with the hopes of early manhood, and fired by the
very spirit of '76, Mr. Baxter entered the political arena in the
Peninsula State, joined with spirits akin to his own in their
fervid zeal for righting wrongs, and turning the nation from
that oppression of thousands which nullified her claim as a
free republic. The minds of many had been almost unconsciously tending to an overturn in political sentiment, when
these zealous souls sounded their bugle note, under a new banner, a host were found ready to join their ranks, and the republican party was a fact. Now Mr. Baxter found in journalism
his true sphere, and the Grand Rapids *Daily Eagle* has winged
forth the strong, earnest words of a broad patriotism, throughout the State of his adoption. The brief synopsis of the life
of Mr. Albert Baxter has a moral, worthy of the study of all
young men who desire to make their mark in the world. And
if it is no higher motive than an ambition not to be excelled,
the true method is contained in this history. But a worthier,
higher motive seems to have prompted Mr. Baxter in his activities. His life has been marked by a steady devotion to
honest principles, the love of country, and a desire for the
highest good of the race. The strength of a matured manhood has not been wasted on impracticable theories. The
steady aim of life with him has been the defence of right, and
the maintenance of a truly republican form of government as
instituted by the fathers. It is a noble life which all may
gladly emulate.

[Seventh Generation]

4159. ii. BERNARD BAXTER, second son and child of Irene
Child and Hon. Eber H. Baxter, b. in Moretown, Vt., July 6,
1824, m. Oct. 27, 1844, Harriet J. Brigham.

[Eighth Generation.] Children:

4171. i. WILLIAM A. C. BAXTER, b. Oct. 15, 1845, d. young.

4172. ii. AURILLA S. D. BAXTER, b. Mch. 12, 1847, m. Jan. 12, 1866, Thos.
J. Hulbert, at Cascade, Mich.

4173. iii. BERNARD NELSON BAXTER, b. June 11, 1855, in Moretown, Vt.,
d. in Cascade, Mich., about 1868.

4174. iv. LUCY IRENE BAXTER, b. Jan. 15, 1852, m. 1873, Wm. Hall.

4160. iii. CELIA BAXTER, eldest dau. and third child of Irene Child and Hon. E. H. Baxter, b. in Moretown, Vt., Mch. 16, 1826, m. June 20, 1849, Elisha Aldis Brigham, a farmer of Fayston, Vt. Mr. and Mrs. Brigham reside in Chippewa, Mecosta Co., Mich. Mrs. Brigham has written many poems for the press, but no compilation of them has been made.

[Eighth Generation.] Children:

4175. i. ZIBA WHITTIER BRIGHAM, b. May 8, 1850, m. Mattie J. Clark; have one son.

4176. ii. ELISHA KOSSUTH BRIGHAM, b. Dec. 23, 1851, m. Maria C. Green.

4177. iii. EDWIN BAXTER BRIGHAM, b. Oct. 1, 1857.

4178. iv. ROSINA BRIGHAM, b. April 4, 1859, d. June 5, 1878.

4161. iv. ORMAN BAXTER, third son and fourth child of Irene Child and Hon. E. H. Baxter, b. in Moretown, Vt., Aug. 16, 1827, m. Dec. 11, 1866, Hettie M. Olmstead, at Grand Haven, Mich. Mr. Baxter combines farming and market-gardening.

[Eighth Generation.] Children:

4179. i. Infant (unchristened) d. young.

4180. ii. Infant (unchristened) d. young.

4181. iii. CELIA ARVILLA BAXTER, b. May 17, 1872.

4162. v. ROSINA BAXTER, second dau. and fifth child of Irene Child and Hon. Eber H. Baxter, b. in Moretown, Vt., April 4, 1829, m. in Paris, Mich., May 1, 1854, Oren N. Cadwell. Went to California about 1869, and reside in Santa Barbara Co. Mr. Cadwell is a farmer and horticulturist.

[Eighth Generation.] Children:

4182. i. ANDREW IRVING CADWELL, b. Feb. 17, 1855.

4183. ii. INA IRENE CADWELL, b. Nov. 23, 1860.

4184. iii. LINNIE BANKS CADWELL, b. Jan. 21, 1863.

4185. iv. Infant daughter (unchristened) b. 1866, d. 1870.

4163. vi. EDWIN BAXTER, fourth son and sixth child of Irene and Hon. E. H. Baxter, b. in Moretown, Vt., March 9, 1831, m. 1st, at Grand Rapids, Mich., April 30, 1860, Carrie A. Keyes; Mrs. Carrie A. K. Baxter d. Dec. 3, 1866; m. 2d, at Stanbridge, Quebec Province, Canada, May 23, 1868, Ellen L. Scagel. Mr. Edwin Baxter served in the recent war as a Captain, in Michigan Regt. mechanics and engineers. He is a lawyer in successful practice; at present Circuit Court Commissioner of Ottawa Co., Mich. His residence is in Grand Haven, Mich.

[Eighth Generation.] Children:

4186. i. Infant (unchristened) d. young.

4187. ii. MINNIE S. BAXTER, b. July 22, 1861.

4188. iii. EDWIN CHILDS BAXTER, b. Sept. 12, 1878.

[Seventh Generation.]

4164. vii. URI J. BAXTER, fifth son and seventh child of Irene Child and Hon. Eber H. Baxter, b. in Payston, Vt., Jan. 20, 1833, m. in Cascade, Mich., in 1865, Maggie Lowry. When about eighteen, Mr. Uri Baxter began teaching, and continued in that profession for some years: he then devoted himself to journalism for a time. For fourteen years has held various positions of trust and responsibility, in the general land office in Washington, D. C. Mr. U. J. Baxter is a lawyer, graduate of the Columbia Law School of New York City. Was admitted to the bar by the Supreme Court of the U. S. Is at present Acting Chief of Indian Division, Interior Dept. Resides at Linden, Maryland.

[Eighth Generation.] Child:

4189. i. JENNIE BAXTER, b. about 1866.

[Seventh Generation.]

4166. ix. SABRINA BAXTER, fourth dau. and ninth child of Irene Child and Hon. Eber H. Baxter, b. in Fayston, Washington Co., Vt., Dec. 17, 1836, m. Jan. 31, 1875, Justice Cooper, who was b. in Wright, Schoharie Co., N. Y., May 7, 1834. A farmer, residing in Evart, Osceola Co., Mich.

[Eighth Generation.] Children:

4190. i. BAXTER GIFFORD COOPER, b. Feb. 10, 1876, in Evart, Osceola Co., Mich.

4191. ii. INEZ COOPER, b. June 28, 1879, in Evart, Osceola Co., Mich.

[Seventh Generation.]

4168. xi. MILO BAXTER, seventh son and eleventh child of Irene Child and Hon. E. H. Baxter, b. in Fayston, Vt., Aug. 15, 1841, m. Jan. 20, 1867, Ellen Celia Rich, of Rutland, Barry Co., Mich. He enlisted in the 21st Mich. Inf. Regt.: was wounded in the same battle at Chickamauga as his brother, Ira C. Baxter. His wounds, however, were healed, and he served through the war. He resides now at Abilene, Dickenson Co., Kansas. Is engaged in farming.

[Eighth Generation.] Children:

4192. i. EBER ESTES BAXTER, b. Nov. 18, 1867.

4193. ii. SHERMAN ALBERT BAXTER, b. May 27, 1872.

4194. iii. Louise Pearl Baxter, b. Dec. 9, 1873.
4195. iv. Adan Baxter, b. 1869.

[Sixth Generation.]

4149. ii. EBER CARPENTER CHILD, second child and eldest son of Abner and Achsah Carpenter Child, b. at Moretown, Vt., Dec. 24, 1803, m. in Moretown, May 7, 1829, Fanny Hazeltine. Mr. Eber C. Child seems to have inherited some of the poetic talent of his grandmother, Mrs. Rachel Palmer Child, and cheers his hours of solitude by turning his meditations into verse, even now, when fourscore years have blanched his hair, and dimmed somewhat the keenness of his vision.

[Seventh Generation.] Children:
4196. i. Ruthven Ferdinand Child, b. Jan. 11, 1830.
4197. ii. Cornelia J. Child, b. Sept. 19, 1832, m. Jan. 20, 1856, Allen Campbell Baker.
4198. iii. Jerusha B. Child, b. May 27, 1836.

[Seventh Generation.]

4197. ii. CORNELIA J. CHILD, eldest dau. and second child of Eber Carpenter and Fanny Hazeltine Child, b. in Moretown, Vt., Sept. 19, 1832, m. Jan. 20, 1856, Allen Campbell Baker, of Granville, Washington Co., N. Y. Mr. Baker has been a most agreeable, and successful teacher in high schools and academies.

[Eighth Generation.] Children:
4199. i. Ellen Louise Baker, b. Feb. 27, 1856.
4200. ii. George Wordsworth Baker b. Dec. 16, 1859.
4201. iii. Kate Campbell Baker, b. Oct. 19, 1862.
4202. iv. Fanny Hazeltine Baker, b. Mch. 6, 1867, d. Oct. 15, 1870.
4203. v. Charles Evarts Baker, b. June 19, 1870.
4204. vi. Grace Lillian Baker, b. Feb. 13, 1876.

[Sixth Generation.]

4152. v. MARY CHILD, fourth dau. and fifth child of Abner and Achsah Carpenter Child, b. Mch. 9, 1810, m. Jan. 22, 1839, Stephen Goodspeed, of Moretown, Vt.

[Seventh Generation.] Children:
4205. i. Samuel A. Goodspeed, b. Dec. 25, 1839, d. Feb. 9, 1845, at Moretown, Vt.
4206. ii. Myron R. Goodspeed, } twins { m. Jan. 1, 1871, Cynthia Lamb, b. Jan. 31, 1844.
4207. iii. Myra R. Goodspeed, } { m. Moses Palmer.
4208. iv. Ruth V. Goodspeed, b. Aug. 9, 1849, m. Feb. 15, 1874, Frank C. Lamb.

[Seventh Generation.]

4208. iv. RUTH V. GOODSPEED, second dau. and fourth child of Mary Child and Stephen Goodspeed, b. at Warren, Vt., Aug. 9, 1849, m. Feb. 15, 1874, Frank C. Lamb, of Granville, Vt.

[Eighth Generation.] Children:
4209. i. MAMIE R. LAMB, b. Mch. 15, 1875, d. Oct. 21, 1877.
4210. ii. MABEL F. LAMB, b. Oct. 21, 1876.

[Sixth Generation.]
4145. vii. DENNIS CHILD, second son and seventh child of
Abner and Achsah Carpenter Child, b. in Moretown, Vt., Dec.
22, 1814, m. in the same place Sept. 20, 1837, Frances A.
Straus.
[Seventh Generation.] Children:
4211. i. RUTH FRANKLIN CHILD, b. July 22, 1838, m. Feb. 24, 1858,
Charles W. Bushnell.
4212. ii. OREN D. CHILD, b. Feb. 28, 1840, m. Nov. 5, 1868, Jennie
Goodell.
4213. iii. ANNA M. CHILD, b Dec. 16, 1841, d. March 3, 1842.
4214. iv. ASAHEL S. CHILD, b. May 6, 1843, m. Dec. 21, 1865, H. A.
Hamilton.
4215. v. ALPHEUS A. CHILD, b. Aug. 27, 1846.
4216. vi. EUNICE A. CHILD, b. Sept. 11, 1850, m. Nov. 12, 1871, C. F.
Remington.
4217. vii. MARY CHILD, b. Nov. 26, 1859, at Omro, Wis.

[Seventh Generation.]
4211. i. RUTH FRANKLIN CHILD, eldest dau. and child of
Dennis and Frances A. Straus Child, b. in Moretown, Vt.,
July 22, 1838, m. at Omro, Wis., Feb. 24, 1858, Charles W.
Bushnell.
[Eighth Generation.] Children:
4218. i. DE WITT BUSHNELL,) TWINS. (b. June 12, 1860.
4219. ii. DE ETT BUSHNELL. (
4220. iii. ETHEL BUSHNELL, b. Oct. 25, 1862.

[Seventh Generation.]
4214. iv. ASAHEL S. CHILD, second son and fourth child of
Dennis and Frances A. Straus Child, b. in Moretown, Vt.,
May 6, 1843, m. Dec. 21, 1865, H. A. Hamilton.
[Eighth Generation.] Children:
4221. i. HATTIE CHILD, b. Nov. 20, 1866, d. young.
4222. ii. MYRTLE CHILD, b. Feb. 11, 1868.
4223. iii. RALPH CHILD, b. Oct. 10, 1874.

[Seventh Generation.]
4216. vi. EUNICE A. CHILD, third dau. and sixth child of
Dennis and Frances A. Straus Child, b. in Moretown, Vt.,
Sept. 11, 1850, m. Nov. 12, 1871, C. F. Remington.
[Eighth Generation.] Children:
4224. i. ANGIE C. REMINGTON, b. Nov. 15, 1871.
4225. ii. LILLIAN M. REMINGTON, (TWINS. (b. June 5, 1878.
4226. iii. INFANT (unchristened), ((d. same day.

[Sixth Generation.]

4156. ix. ROSWELL CHILD, third son and ninth child of Abner and Achsah Carpenter Child, b. in Moretown, Vt., June 19, 1821, m. Nov. 22, 1843, Abigail Goodspeed, who was b. April 16, 1820, in Sharon, Vt. Mr. Roswell Child has always resided in Moretown, Vt., and has been a man much respected by his fellow-citizens, though unambitious of honors or office. He has been much interested to advance this work, for which we tender him our most cordial thanks.

[Seventh Generation.] Children:

4227. i. HENRY FRANKLIN CHILD, b. Nov. 29, 1844, m. July 4, 1874, Lizzie M. Harrison.

4228. ii. EMMA FRANCES CHILD, b. Aug. 2, 1846, m. Feb. 19, 1867, George E. Spaulding.

4229. iii. ABNER CARPENTER CHILD, b. Dec. 23, 1849, m. Feb. 14, 1872, Ella A. Howes.

4230. iv. ELLA GERTRUDE CHILD, b. July 10, 1854, m. Sept. 13, 1871, John W. Eagan.

4231. v. UDIN PERCY CHILD, b. April 12, 1856.

4232. vi. LEON ALBERT CHILD, b. March 3, 1860.

4233. vii. MATTIE MIONA CHILD, b. Oct. 20, 1861.

4234. viii. MERRIL ROSWELL CHILD, b. March 25, 1865.

[Seventh Generation.]

4227. i. HENRY FRANKLIN CHILD, eldest son and child of Roswell and Abigail Goodspeed Child, b. in Moretown, Vt., Nov. 29, 1844, m. July 4, 1874, Lizzie M. Harrison.

[Eighth Generation.] Child:

4235. i. CHARLES HENRY CHILD, b. Nov. 6, 1876, d. March 13, 1878.

[Seventh Generation.]

4229. iii. ABNER CARPENTER CHILD, second son and third child of Roswell and Abigail Goodspeed Child, b. in Moretown, Vt., Dec. 23, 1849, m. Feb. 14, 1872, Ella A. Howes.

[Eighth Generation.] Children:

4236. i. MYRTIE ELLA CHILD, b. June 23, 1873.

4237. ii. ESTELLA MAY CHILD, b. Feb. 26, 1878.

[Seventh Generation.]

4230. iv. ELLA GERTRUDE CHILD, second dau. and fourth child of Roswell and Abigail Goodspeed Child, b. in Moretown, Vt., July 10, 1854, m. Sept. 13, 1871, John W. Eagan.

[Eighth Generation.] Children:

4238. i. HERBERT JOHN EAGAN, b. June 14, 1873.

4239. ii. MARY ELLA EAGAN, b. Aug. 8, 1875.

4240. iii. ABBIE EMMA EAGAN, b. April 27, 1877.

[Fifth Generation.]

3896. viii. ARTIMAS CHILD, sixth son and eighth child of Elijah and Rachel Palmer Child, b. in Thompson, Ct., Jan. 15,

1775, m. Dec. 3, 1796, Hannah Ormsby, who was b. Sept. 23, 1776. Mr. Artimas Child resided in Sharon, Vt., where he d. Oct. 5, 1852. Mrs. Hannah Ormsby Child d. Feb. 15, 1868.

[Sixth Generation.]   Children:

4241. i. ROSWELL CHILD, b. Sept. 17, 1797, d. June 24, 1828, when bathing in a mill pond, belonging to his father.

4242. ii. HARVEY CHILDS, b. Dec. 3, 1799, m. Feb. 18. 1829, Clarissa Little.

4243. iii. CHARLES CHILDS, b. Dec. 14. 1802, m. Dec. 12. 1837. Sally Abbott.

4244. iv. NANCY CHILDS, b. May 23, 1805, m. April 24, 1837, Elijah Brigham.

4245. v. LUCINDA CHILDS, b. Aug. 10, 1807, m. Oct. 17, 1840, Asahel Brigham.

4246. vi. LAURA CHILDS, b. Mch. 3, 1811, m. Oct. 13, 1841, Solomon Robinson.

4247. vii. EMILY CHILDS. b. Mch. 13. 1814, m. June 21, 1841, Harvey B. Gilbert.

4248. viii. MARY ANN CHILDS, b. Jan. 27, 1824, d. Feb. 28, 1875, unm.

[Sixth Generation.]

4242. ii. HARVEY CHILDS, second son and child of Artimas and Hannah Ormsby Childs, b. in Sharon, Vt., Dec. 3, 1799, m. Feb. 18, 1829, Clarissa Little, who was b. in Norristown, Vt., Feb. 9, 1808. Mr. Childs aided his father in clearing one of the densely wooded farms of Vermont. He built a saw-mill, which enabled them to dispose of the felled trees with profit; he also became noted as a mill-wright and builder of bridges. In 1838 he removed with his family to Illinois, settling in Mendota, La Salle Co. He is a thorough business man, a prosperous farmer, highly esteemed for honesty and fair dealing; has been postmaster, and for thirty years justice of the peace; now engaged in money loaning and land speculation.

[Seventh Generation.]   Children:

4249. i. CHARLES CHILDS, b. Jan. 28, 1830, m. Sept. 28, 1858. Ann Eliza Smith.

4250. ii. ORSON CHILDS, b. April 10, 1831, m. Dec. 31, 1860, Julia M. Dix.

4251. iii. EDMOND SHERMAN CHILDS, b. March 29. 1834, m. Nov. 9, 1858, Eleanor Dix

4252. iv. CLARISSA MARIAH CHILDS, b July 31, 1841, d. Nov. 4, 1854.

4253. v. HIRAM LITTLE CHILDS, b. at Perkins Grove, Ill., Jan. 26, 1847. Emigrated to California in 1867; editor for three years of the *Inyo Independent;* is now Deputy U. S. Revenue Collector. Resides in Bodie, Mono Co., Cal.

[Seventh Generation.]

4249. i. CHARLES CHILDS, eldest son and child of Harvey and Clarissa Little Childs, b. in Sharon, Vt, Jan. 28, 1830, m. Sept. 28, 1858, Eliza A. Smith of Conway, Mass.   He helped his father in opening out several prairie farms. Is a successful architect and builder: now resident upon a farm in Lee, Lee Co., Ill.

[Eighth Generation.] Children:

4254. i. VIOLA ALVARETTA CHILDS, b. in Lamoille, Ill., June 25, 1859.

4255. ii. FRANK LESLIE CHILDS, b. Oct. 8, 1860, in Lamoille, Ill.

4256. iii. LYMAN WHEELOCK CHILDS, b. Oct. 1, 1867, in Willow Creek, Ill.

4257. iv. NELLIE ELIZA CHILDS, b. May 16, 1869, in Willow Creek, Ill.

[Seventh Generation.]

4250. ii. ORSON CHILDS, second son and child of Harvey and Clarissa Little Childs, b. in Sharon, Vt., April 10, 1831, m. Dec. 31, 1860, Julia M. Dix. When seventeen he left home and learned a carpenter's trade, which he prosecuted some years dilligently. He afterwards purchased a farm, and for some years resided upon it. Is a resident of Mendota, Ill.

[Eighth Generation.] Children:

4258. i. DANA O. CHILDS, b. April 18, 1863, d. Oct 1, 1864, in Clarion, Ill.

4259. ii. DELLA M. CHILDS, b. Oct. 2, 1865, in Clarion, Ill.

4260. iii. BERTHA E. CHILDS, b. April 18, 1870, in Clarion, Ill.

4261. iv. MINNIE DIX CHILDS, b. Dec. 1, 1874, in Clarion, Ill.

[Seventh Generation.]

4251. iii. EDMOND SHERMAN CHILDS, third son and child of Harvey and Clarissa Little Childs, b. in Norristown, Vt., Mch. 29, 1834, m Nov. 9, 1858, Eleanor Dix, of Wilmington, Vt. In early life Hon. E. S. Childs was a helper to his father in farm labors in the prairie state. Became an architect, and later the owner of one of the beautiful prairie farms. Has traveled extensively in the United States. Elected supervisor of La Salle Co., Ill., in 1873. Is now (1880) mayor of Mendota, Ill.

[Sixth Generation.]

4243. iii. CHARLES CHILDS, third son and child of Artimas and Hannah Ormsby Child, b. in Sharon, Windsor Co., Vt., Dec. 14, 1802, m. Dec. 12, 1837, Sallie Abbott, dau, of the late Daniel and Sallie Abbott, of Mantville, Medina Co., Ohio.

For the first thirty years of his life, Mr. Charles Childs remained with his father, when old enough to do so aiding in the culture of the farm, and in the operation of a saw-mill. One who has never seen a farm in New England can scarce apprehend one of the most unceasing labors of farming in that region, the removal of stone from the fields, which the plough yearly upturns with a persistant uniformity unequaled by the

crops sown after the ploughing ; to gather up the stones was
an early task for the farmers' boys, and those returning from
the soft, alluvial loam culture of the West to look upon the
old homesteads, marvel at the courage which continues to cultivate the stony hills and valleys. To this labor Mr. Childs
was early inured, and the limited scope of the country school-
ing, snatched at intervals from farm toil and mill tending, was
all the training he received. But it proved sufficient to develope
in him earnestness, thoroughness and practical skillfulness.
The very atmosphere imparted vigor, and the moral surroundings wrought out true nobility and sterling integrity. In the
spring of 1833, Mr. Childs bade farewell to New England and
purchased him a farm in La Fayette, Medina Co., Ohio. Here
he became soon a prominent citizen, noted for his excellent
judgment, wise counsels, indomitable energy and a rare gift
of "keeping his own counsel." "Early in the history of the
township, he was elected to the position of justice of the peace,
and retained the office some thirty years. For many years
postmaster ; and while ever true to his political party (republican), he was cordially esteemed by all. In the home relations
he proved himself equally the true man, loving tenderly, wife
and children. He was heartily lamented when he 'ceased from
his labors' at threescore years and ten, on the first of March,
1873."

[Seventh Generation.]   Children :

4262. i. CHARLES FRANKLIN CHILDS, b. Sat. Sept. 8, 1838, m. April 12.
1863, Mary Jane Chapin.

4263. ii. CORNELIA VICTORIA CHILDS, b. Tues. Sept. 29, 1840, m. Sept. 3,
1865, Peter Miller.

4264. iii. CORDELIA MALVINA CHILDS, b. Thurs. Aug. 18, 1842, m. May 3,
1866, Amos Sheldon.

4265. iv. LAURA JANE CHILDS, b. Fri. Nov. 29, 1844, m. Jan. 17, 1875,
Calvin Brown.

4266. v. WILLIAM HERMAN CHILDS, b. Sun. Sept. 13, 1846, m. April 1,
1877, Lillie Foster.

4267. vi. EMMA ELIZA CHILDS, b. Tues. Oct. 12, 1848, m. Dec. 28, 1874.
Joseph McClennan Campbell.

4268. vii. INFANT (unchristened),)
4269 viii.   "   "   } Triplets. b. Sept. 19, 1850, d. same day.
4270. ix.   "   "   )

4271. x. VIOLA ADELLA CHILDS, b. Wed. Dec. 31, 1851.

4272. xi. ELLA ALVATTA CHILDS, b. Mon. July 10, 1854.

[Seventh Generation.]

4262 i. CHARLES FRANKLIN CHILDS, eldest son and child of
Charles and Sallie Abbott Childs, b. in La Fayette, Medina Co.,

Ohio, Saturday Sept. 8, 1838, m. April 12, 1863. Mary Jane Chapin, dau. of Dea. Henry and Mary Mansfield Chapin of La Fayette. Ohio. The ancestors of Mrs. Mary Jane Chapin Childs came to America about twelve years later than those of Mr. Childs. The emigrant ancestor of Mrs. Childs was a Dea. Samuel Chapin, who settled in Springfield. Mass., in 1642, from Derbyshire. England, though considered of Welsh origin. The accompanying brief chronological descent of Mrs. Childs places her one generation farther removed from the first of her family resident in America than her husband:

1st Gen.—Dea. Samuel Chapin, 1642.	5th Gen.—Ebenezer Chapin.
2d " Japhet Chapin.	6th " Timothy Chapin.
3d " Ebenezer Chapin.	7th " Henry Chapin.
4th " Ebenezer Chapin.	8th " Mary Jane Chapin, 1879.

Upon their marriage Mr. and Mrs. C. F. Childs removed to Benzonia. Mich. In the autumn of 1866 they left Michigan for Durant, Cedar Co., Iowa. Remained there about two years, when for better educational advantages for their children they again changed their home and settled, as they think, permanently in Grinnell, Iowa, in which place Iowa College opens its doors for the higher training of the young in that growing State. Mr. and Mrs. Childs became united with the Congregational church in 1859.

[Eighth Generation.] Children:

    4273. i. ELLA VIOLA CHILDS, b. Aug. 14, 1864.

    4274. ii. ARTHUR CHAPIN CHILDS, b. June 1, 1867.

    4275. iii. MARY EVELYN CHILDS, b. June 1, 1872.

    4276. iv. CHARLES HENRY CHILDS, b. Jan. 12, 1875, d. Feb. 8, 1875.

[Seventh Generation.]

    4263. ii. CORNELIA VICTORIA CHILDS, eldest dau. and second child of Charles and Sally Abbott Childs, b. in La Fayette, Ohio, Sept. 29, 1840, m. Sept. 3, 1865. Peter Miller, son of Jacob and Sarah Miller. Mr. Peter Miller was one of the first to respond to President Lincoln's call for 75,000 troops. He served through the war, holding the office of first lieutenant. After the peace, Mr. Miller returned to his family, and in the spring of 1868, settled upon a farm in Mitchellville, Polk Co., Iowa.

[Eighth Generation.] Children:

    4277. i. FRED L. MILLER, b. Aug. 24, 1866.

    4278. ii. CHARLES E. MILLER, b. Nov. 20, 1868.

    4279. iii. OLA B. MILLER, b. May 9, 1873.

    4280. iv. EDITH M. MILLER, b. April 1, 1875.

    4281. v. ALMOND D. MILLER, } TWINS { b. Dec. 29, 1877, d. July 16, 1878.

    4282. vi. EDMOND G. MILLER, } { b. Dec. 29, 1877.

[Seventh Generation.]

4264. iii. CORDELIA MALVINA CHILDS, second dau. and third child of Charles and Sally Abbott Childs, b. in La Fayette, Ohio, Aug. 18, 1842, m. May 3, 1866, Amos Sheldon, son of Hiram and Irene Sheldon, of the same place. Mr. and Mrs. Sheldon reside in La Fayette, Medina Co., Ohio, where he is engaged in farming ; is also a county surveyor.

[Eighth Generation.] Children:

4283. i. MAY ELVIRA SHELDON, b. July 11. 1867.
4284. ii. EMMA IRENE SHELDON, b. Jan. 1, 1870.
4285. iii. BIRT CHARLES SHELDON, b. Jan. 7, 1873.
4286. iv. WILLIAM HIRAM SHELDON, b. Sept. 27. 1875.

[Seventh Generation.]

4265. iv. LAURA JANE CHILDS, third dau. and fourth child of Charles and Sally Abbott Childs, b. in La Fayette, Medina Co., Ohio, Nov. 29, 1844, m. Jan. 17, 1875, Calvin F. Brown, son of E. H. and Eliza Brown. Mr. Brown is a farmer, and their home is in Mitchellville, Iowa.

[Eighth Generation] Child:

4287. i. BESSIE MAY BROWN, b. Nov. 13, 1875.

[Seventh Generation.]

4266. v. WILLIAM HERMAN CHILDS, second son and fifth child of Charles and Sally Abbott Childs, b. in La Fayette, Ohio, Sept. 13, 1846. m. April 1, 1877, Lillie Foster of Creston, Iowa, where he has made his home. His occupation is farming.

[Eighth Generation.] Child:

4288. i. CHARLES MATHEW CHILDS, b. March 9, 1878, d. July 18, 1878.

[Seventh Generation.]

4267. vi. EMMA ELIZA CHILDS, fourth dau. and sixth child of Charles and Sally Abbott Childs, b. in La Fayette, Medina Co., Ohio, m. Dec. 28, 1874, Joseph McClennan Campbell of Kansas. Mr. and Mrs. Joseph McClennan Campbell reside at Smith Centre, Smith Co., Kansas, where he is engaged in farming.

[Eighth Generation.] Children:

4289. i. JESSIE CAMPBELL, b. Oct. 17, 1875.
4290. ii. MARIE CAMPBELL, b. July 5, 1877.

[Sixth Generation.]

4244. iv. NANCY CHILD, eldest dau. and fourth child of Artimas and Hannah Ormsby Child, b. in Sharon, Vt., May 23, 1805, m. April 24, 1837, Elijah Brigham. Reside in Craftsbury, Vt. A farmer.

[Seventh Generation.] Children:

4291. i. EMILY PAULINA BINGHAM, b. Mch. 16, 1835.

4292. ii. LUCIAN HARVEY BINGHAM, b. July 5, 1840. Mr. L. H. Bingham was a student of the University at Burlington, Vt. Left his studies and enlisted as a soldier in the recent war, on the third of December, 1863. He was wounded on the 6th of May following, and died from his wounds on the 28th May, 1864, at Campbell Hospital, Washington, D. C. His graduation would have been in the August succeeding, but he had entered the Higher School of suffering, and from it was promoted to the ranks of Patriot Martyrs.

[Sixth Generation.]

4245. v. LUCINDA CHILDS, second dau. and fifth child of Artimas and Hannah Ormsby Child, b. in Sharon, Vt., Aug. 10, 1807, m. Oct. 17, 1840, Asahel Bingham. Mr. and Mrs. Bingham left Vermont and settled for a time in Ohio, from thence removed to Roanoke, Woodford Co., Ill., where they lived upon a farm. Mr. Asahel Bingham died Aug. 22, 1874.

[Seventh Generation.] Child:

4293. i. EMERY EDWARD BINGHAM, b. April 11, 1845.

[Sixth Generation.]

4246. vi. LAURA CHILDS, third dau. and seventh child of Artimas and Hannah Ormsby Child, b. in Sharon, Vt., March 3, 1811, m. Oct. 13, 1841, Solomon Robinson. Reside in Morrisville, Vt.

[Seventh Generation.] Children:

4294. i. LAURA ELLEN ROBINSON, b. Jan. 8, 1845, m. March 6, 1867, James Tyler Jewett: reside in Morristown, Vt.

4295. ii. GEORGE PLATT ROBINSON, b. March 21, 1852, m. June 23, 1873, Ida Ellen Cheney: reside in Walcott, Vt.

[Sixth Generation.]

4247. vii. EMILY CHILDS, fourth dau. and seventh child of Artimas and Hannah Ormsby Child, b. in Sharon, Vt., March 23, 1814, m. Jan. 21, 1841, Harvey B. Gilbert, in Princeton, Ill. Mr. Gilbert was an officer in the Baptist church. He d. Oct. 4, 1868. Mr. and Mrs. Gilbert resided for some time in Cordova, Ill., and from thence went to Burlington, Iowa.

[Seventh Generation.] Children:

4296. i. LIBBIE C. GILBERT, b. July 5, 1842, m. Oct. 31, 1865, Joseph Johnston.

4297. ii. CELINA J. GILBERT, b. July 19, 1846, m. Dec. 31, 1868, James Dickie.

4298. iii. AMANDA M. GILBERT, b. June 10, 1850, m. March 23, 1869, S. S. Bronson.

4299. iv. GEORGE W. GILBERT, b Oct. 11, 1858.

[Seventh Generation.]

4297. ii. CELINA J. GILBERT, second dau. and child of Emily Childs and Harvey B. Gilbert, b. July 19, 1846, m.

4·1

Dec. 31, 1868, James Dickie. Mr. Dickie is engaged in the lumber business, and resides in Montrose, Iowa.

[Eighth Generation.] Children:

4300. i. EMILY E. DICKIE, b. Aug. 29, 1870.

4301. ii. ELEANOR CHILDS DICKIE, b. Jan. 1, 1874.

[Seventh Generation.]

4298. iii. AMANDA M. GILBERT, third dau. and child of Emily Childs and Harvey B. Gilbert, b. June 10, 1850, m. March 23, 1869, S. S. Bronson. Reside in Marshalltown, Iowa.

[Eighth Generation.] Child:

4302 i. ETHELYN J. BRONSON, b. Jan. 15, 1872.

[Fifth Generation.]

3897. ix. DANIEL CHILD, seventh son and ninth child of Elijah and Rachel Palmer Child, b. in Thompson, Ct., Nov. 10, 1877, m. Rebecca Howe. Mr. and Mrs. Child resided for a time in Sharon, Vt., then removed to Potsdam, St. Lawrence Co., N. Y.

[Sixth Generation.] Children:

4303. i. AVERY CHILD.

4304. ii. ZEBINA CHILD.

4305. iii. DILLANY CHILD.

4306. iv. HANNAH CHILD.

4307. v. CHASSENDA CHILD.

4308. vi. POLLY CHILD.

4309. vii. SIMEON CHILD.

[Fifth Generation.]

3898. x. ELIAS CHILD, eighth son and tenth child of Elijah and Rachel Palmer Child, b. in Thompson, Ct., April 22, 1780, m. abt. 1803, Tamar Vincent. Mr. Elias Child made several removes. We find him to have resided in Rochester, N. Y., then in Ohio, and lastly in Kalamazoo, Mich., where he d. Nov. 3, 1847. Tamar Vincent Child was b. Aug. 12, 1781, d. Aug. 19, 1865.

[Sixth Generation.] Children:

4310. i. ASA CHILD, b. April 3, 1804.

4311. ii. TAMAR OLIVE CHILD, b. July 19, 1806.

4312. iii. CENITH CHILD, b. Oct. 28, 1808.

4313. iv. RHODA CHILD.

4314. v. LAURA CHILD.

4315. vi. TIMOTHY V. CHILD, b. Jan. 29, 1820. Mr. Timothy V. Child is one of those men who possess an active brain, much executive ability, and find happiness in a diversity of employment. Accordingly he grinds out bread and boards in his differing mills, sells all sorts of commodities at his store, carries on a farm, the products of which aid him to verify the smartness of the family by keeping an hotel.

[Fifth Generation.]

3899. xi. RACHEL CHILD, third dau. and eleventh child of Elijah and Rachel Palmer Child, b. in Thompson, Ct., May 5, 1783, m. in Pomfret, Vt., May 20, 1800, Jeptha Keith, who was b. in Bridgewater, Mass., March 15, 1774. Mrs. R. C. Keith was the only dau. in this large family who married. Her residence was in Sharon, Vt.; she d. in Topsham, Vt., June 6, 1842. Mr. Keith d. in Enfield, N. H., Aug. 9, 1856.

[Sixth Generation.] Children:

4316. i. JOSEPH KEITH, b. Nov. 6, 1801, m. Nov. 25, 1828, Mrs. Hannah Harding Smith.

4317. ii. CYRIL KEITH, b. Jan. 1, 1804, m. Oct. 23, 1828, Susan King.

4318. iii. JONATHAN KEITH, b. March 5, 1806, m. Feb. 12, 1844, Polly P. Willson.

4319. iv. ICHABOD KEITH, b. April 19, 1808, d. in Sharon, Vt., Jan. 30, 1830.

4320. v. MATILDA KEITH, b. June 20, 1810, m. abt. 1831, Joel Bixby.

4321. vi. ARTEMAS KEITH, b. Jan. 24, 1813; resides in Topsham, Vt , unm.

4322. vii. SUSANNAH KEITH, b. June 18, 1815, d. at Enfield, N. H., Nov. 5, 1847.

4323. viii. OSCAR F. KEITH, b. July 10 1818, d. at Sharon, Vt., April 5, 1827.

4324. ix. ELIJAH CHILD KEITH, b. Jan. 6, 1821, m. July 7, 1843, Margaret B. Roker.

[Sixth Generation.]

4316. i. JOSEPH KEITH, eldest child of Rachel Child and Jeptha Keith, b. in Sharon, Vt., Nov. 6, 1801, m. Nov. 25, 1828, Mrs. Hannah Smith, widow of Jesse Smith, and dau. of Joseph and Hannah Baker Harding of Wellfleet, Mass., where she was b. Jan. 15, 1805. Mr. Joseph Keith d. in Lowell, Mass., April 18, 1879.

[Seventh Generation.] Children:

4325. i. JESSE SMITH KEITH, b. in Sharon, Vt., July 8, 1830; after seven years of blindness, died March 13, 1853.

4326. ii. EMILY ANN KEITH, b. in Sharon, Vt., May 24, 1833, d. in Boston, Mass., Feb. 14, 1836.

4327. iii. LAURAETTE KEITH, b. in Sharon, Vt., Dec. 10, 1834, m. Oct. 6, 1856, Lucian Carlos Tyler, who was b. Jan. 20, 1834. Boot and shoe dealer and resides in Arlington, Mass.

4328. iv. EMILY KEITH, b. Feb. 21, 1842, m. April 18, 1864, Wesley Milton Merritt, who d. June 29, 1868; m. 2d, Feb. 28, 1877, Robert Skeing Young.

4329. v. JOSEPH HARDING KEITH, b. April 18, 1848, m. Dec. 7, 1873, Alma Enna Carter.

[Seventh Generation.]

4328. iv. EMILY KEITH, third dau. and fourth child of Joseph and Hannah Harding Smith Keith, and granddaughter of Rachel Child and Joseph Keith, b. in Sharon, Vt., Feb. 21,

1842, m. 1st, in Lowell, Mass., April 16, 1864, Wesley Milton
Merritt, who was b. in Sharon, Vt., and d. in Fitchburg, Mass.,
June 29, 1868: Mrs. Merritt m. 2d, Feb. 28, 1877, Robert
Skeing Young, who was b. in Montreal, P. Q., May 28, 1838.
Reside in Lowell.   Mr. Young is a printer for J. C. Ayer & Co.
[Eighth Generation.]   Child:
    4330. i. WALTER JOSEPH MERRITT, b. Jan. 29, 1867, in Lowell, Mass.

[Seventh Generation.]

    4329. v. JOSEPH HARDING KEITH, second son and fifth
child of Joseph and Hannah Harding Smith Keith, b. in Sharon,
Vt., April 18, 1848. m. in Kearney, Nebraska, Dec. 7, 1873.
Alma Enna Carter, who was b. in Lowell, Mch. 13, 1856. Re-
side in Omaha, Nebraska.   Watchmaker.
[Eighth Generation.]   Child:
    4331. i. JET OMA KEITH, b. April 22, 1879, in Omaha, Nebraska.

[Sixth Generation.]

    4317. ii. CYRIL C. KEITH, second son and child of Rachel
Child and Jeptha Keith, b. in Sharon, Vt., Jan. 1, 1804, m.
Oct. 23, 1828, Susan King, who was b. Aug. 27, 1805, a
daughter of Solomon and Susan King.   Mr. Cyril C. Keith d.
Mch. 25, 1856.
[Seventh Generation.]   Children:
    4332. i. JOSEPH OSCAR KEITH, b. Feb. 27, 1830, m. 1855, Sophia Spear.
    4333. ii. EDWIN SYLVESTER KEITH, b. Feb. 22, 1832, m. 1856, Sarah Ann
Butman.
    4334. iii. AMANDA MALVINA KEITH. b. Nov. 6, 1834.
    4335. iv. MARY ARILDA KEITH, b. Sept. 3, 1838. m. Dec. 8, 1857, Joseph
E. Loomer
    4336. v. FRANCES MIRAETTA KEITH,   b. Feb.   m. July 1, 1866,
                                    (TWINS) 1, 1842.   Edwin L. Tis-
    4337. vi. BENJAMIN FRANKLIN KEITH,   dale.
    4338. vii. MARTHA JANE KEITH, b. Dec. 28, 1843, m. Dec. 9, 1863, James
W. Porter.

[Seventh Generation.]

    4335. iv. MARY A. KEITH, second dau. and fourth child of
Cyril and Susan King Keith, and granddaughter of Rachel
Child Keith, b. Sept. 3, 1838, m. Dec. 8, 1857, Joseph E.
Loomer.
[Eighth Generation.]   Children.
    4339. i. FLORENCE BIANCA LOOMER, b. Sept. 19, 1858.
    4340. ii. CARLOSS EDWIN LOOMER, b. April 14, 1860.
    4341. iii. JULIA LILLIAN LOOMER, b. Aug. 23, 1862.
    4342. iv. FRED CLARENCE LOOMER, b. Dec. 30, 1865.

[Seventh Generation.]

4336. v. FRANCES MIRAETTA KEITH, third dau. and fifth child of Cyril C. and Susan King Keith, and granddaughter of Rachel Child Keith, b. Feb. 1, 1842, m. July 1, 1868, Edwin L. Tisdale. Reside in Rockford, Ill.

[Eighth Generation.] Children:

4343. i. SUSAN INA TISDALE, b. April. 1, 1869.

4344. ii. EDWIN SYLVESTER TISDALE, b. Mch. 18, 1873.

4345. iii. MYRON EDWIN TISDALE, b. Mch. 10, 1876.

[Seventh Generation.]

4338. vii. MARTHA JANE KEITH, fourth dau. and seventh child of Cyril C. and Susan King Keith, and granddaughter of Rachel Child Keith, b. Dec. 28, 1843, m. Dec. 9, 1863, James W. Porter.

[Eighth Generation.] Children:

4346. i. EFFIE IRENE PORTER, b. Oct. 13, 1864.

4347. ii. WALTER WINEARLS PORTER, b. Feb. 18, 1866.

4348. iii. CHARLOTTE ELIZABETH PORTER, b. Sept. 19, 1868.

4349. iv. CLARK AVERY PORTER, b. Jan. 1, 1871.

4350. v. LAURA ALICE PORTER, b. July 23, 1876.

4351. vi. SUSAN KING PORTER, b. June 19, 1878.

[Sixth Generation.]

4318. iii. JONATHAN KEITH, third child and son of Rachel Child and Jeptha Keith, b. Mch. 5, 1806, in Sharon, Vt., m. Feb. 12, 1844, Polly P. Willson, who was b. Sept. 19, 1813. Residence in Pomfret, Windsor Co., Vt.

[Seventh Generation.] Children:

4352. i. MARION ADELA KEITH, b. Jan. 12, 1845.

4353. ii. CHARLES EDWARD KEITH, b. Mch. 22, 1846, m. Jan. 26, 1871, Marion A. Gear, who was b. Dec. 19, 1839.

4354. iii. JONATHAN WILLARD KEITH, b. June 4, 1848.

4355. iv. WILLIAM SABIN KEITH, b. Aug. 25, 1852.

4356. v. FREDERICK EUGENE KEITH, b. Mch. 2, 1854, m. Oct. 18, 1877, Nora A. Vradenburg, b. Dec. 24, 1858.

4357. vi MARY ALANTHA KEITH, b. June 7, 1856.

[Sixth Generation.]

4320. v. MATILDA KEITH, eldest dau. and fifth child of Rachel Child and Jeptha Keith, b. in Sharon. Vt., June 20, 1810, m. about 1831, Joel Bixby. Mrs. Bixby d. in Topsham, Vt., Dec. 9, 1847.

4358. i. JONATHAN NELSON BIXBY, b. Dec. 26, 1833, m. Sarah Willey. He d. Mch. 19, 1863.

4359. ii. LUCY BIXBY, b. Dec. 30, 1835, d. Dec. 30, 1855.

4360. iii. JASON BIXBY, b. Nov. 9, 1837, d. Dec. 9, 1861.

4361. iv. JEPTHA KEITH BIXBY, b. Jan. 22, 1840.

4362. v. RACHEL ADELAIDE BIXBY, b. Feb. 26, 1842, d. Feb. 19, 1863.

4363. vi. MARGARET MARIA BIXBY,) m. June 7, 1862, John Avery, who
   { TWINS, } b. Nov. 28, 1846.   was b. Feb. 27, 1838.
4364. vii. MARY MARANDA BIXBY,) m. Hosea Chase.

[Eighth Generation.]

4324. ix. ELIJAH CHILD KEITH, seventh son and ninth
child of Rachel Child and Jeptha Keith, b. in Sharon, Vt., Jan.
16, 1821, m. in Fitchburgh. Mass., July 7, 1843, Margaret
Butler Roker, dau. of Daniel and Margaret Butler Roker, of
Appleton, Me. Mrs. Roker is a kinswoman of General Butler
of Massachusetts. Mr. and Mrs. Elijah Child Keith reside in
Bala, Riley Co., Kansas. Mr. Child has in his possession a
little brown cream jug, or pitcher, bought by his grandmother,
Rachel Palmer Child, when she was sixteen years of age, about
eighty-one years ago : and his grandfather, Elijah Child's shav
ing cup. These relics of the early times of our colonies, are
becoming increasingly valuable to the descendants.

[Seventh Generation.]   Children:

4365. i. ALWILDA M. KEITH, b. in Topsham, Me., May 4, 1846, m. July
11, 1869, Joseph H. Mitchell, at Deloir, Iowa.

4366. ii. IRWIN E. KEITH, b. Jan. 3, 1848, at New Salem, Me., m. Mch.
14, 1869, Jennie E. Dobson, at Deloir, Iowa. Reside at Neligh, Antelope
Co., Nebraska.

4367. iii. MELVIN S. KEITH, b. April 21, 1851, in Union, Me Resides on
a farm in Neligh, Neb.; unmarried.

4368. iv. ADELPHUS B. KEITH, b. April 24, 1855, at Appleton, Me., m.
July 3, 1875. Carrie Bieber, of Deloir, Iowa. Reside in Denison, Iowa.
Editor of the *Crawford Co. Bulletin*, and professor of practical phrenology;
also lectures upon physiology, anatomy, etc.

[Fourth Generation.]

3645. iv. SAMUEL CHILD, fourth child and son of John and
Elizabeth Child, b. in Woodstock, Ct., Jan. 27, 1702, m. May
27, 1727, Keziah Hutchins, of Killingly, Ct   Samuel d May
21, 1764.

[Fifth Generation.]   Children:

4369. i. ANNA CHILD, b. in Woodstock, Ct., Dec. 28, 1728, m. Jan. 4,
1747, Asa Morris, son of Edward Morris.

4370. ii. SILAS CHILD, b. in Woodstock, Ct, Feb. 7, 1731, m. Jan. 20,
1756, Jedidah Allen.

4371. iii. SAMUEL CHILD, JR., b. in Woodstock, Ct., May 1, 1733, m.
July 8, 1762. Elizabeth Weld, of Pomfret. Ct.

4372. iv. STEPHEN CHILD, b. in Woodstock, Ct., May 4, 1736, d. Oct. 14,
1758.

4373. v. TABITHA CHILD, b. in Woodstock, Ct., June 21, 1738, m. July
28. 1762, Lieut. Richard Peabody, of Pomfret, Ct.

4374. vi. MARY CHILD, b. in Woodstock, Ct., July 6, 1740, m. July 20,
1759, Darius Ainsworth.

4375. vii. ESTHER CHILD, b. in Woodstock, Ct., May 2, 1743, m. July
1767, Ebenezer Paine.

4376. viii. JACOB CHILD, b. in Woodstock, Ct., April 23, 1746, m. 1st, 1773, Sybil Sumner; she d. Aug. 10, 1777; m. 2d, Sept. 23, 1779, Meletiah Curtis

4377. ix. KEZIAH CHILD, b. in Woodstock, Ct., Dec. 20, 1748.

4378. x. ELIZABETH CHILD, b. in Woodstock, Ct., Jan. 17, 1750.

4379. xi. MARTHA CHILD, b. in Woodstock, Ct., July 2, 1753, d. Nov. 17, 1754.

[Fifth Generation.]

4370. ii. SILAS CHILD, second child and eldest son of Samuel and Keziah Hutchins Child, b. in Woodstock, Ct., Feb. 7, 1731, m. Jan. 20, 1756, Jedidah Allen.

[Sixth Generation.] Children:

4380. i. PHINEAS CHILD, b. in Woodstock, Ct., Aug. 16, 1757.

4381. ii. TIMOTHY CHILD, b. in Woodstock, Ct., Nov. 27, 1759.

4382. iii. MOLLY CHILD, b. in Woodstock, Ct., Oct. 20, 1761.

4383. iv. PAMELIA CHILD, b. in Woodstock, Ct., Dec. 29, 1764.

4384. v. HERMI CHILD, b. in Woodstock, Ct., Aug. 2, 1767.

4385. vi. STEPHEN CHILD, b. in Woodstock, Ct., April 24, 1769.

4386. vii. JEDIDAH CHILD, b. in Woodstock, Ct., Nov. 21, 1770.

[Fifth Generation.]

4371. iii. SAMUEL CHILD, JR., third child and second son of Samuel and Keziah Hutchins Child, b. in Woodstock, Ct., May 1, 1733, m. July 8, 1762, Elizabeth Weld, of Pomfret, Ct., d. May 1, 1783.

[Sixth Generation.] Children:

4387. i. AZUBA CHILD, b. in Woodstock, Ct., Jan. 10, 1763, m. 1st, Moses Chandler; m. 2d, Elias Taylor.

4388. ii. HARBA CHILD, b. in Woodstock, Ct., April 28, 1764, m. Polly Lee.

4389. iii. LUCINDA CHILD, b. in Woodstock, Ct., May 27, 1766, m. Adin Williams.

4390. iv. BELINDA CHILD, b. in Woodstock, Ct., July 31, 1768, m 1st, Paul Davidson; m. 2d, Mr. Short. She d. March 23, 1806.

4391. v. ANNA CHILD, b. in Woodstock, Ct., April 6, 1770, m. Silas Coburn.

4392. vi. ROXALANA CHILD, b. in Woodstock, Ct., Nov. 20, 1772, m. Jacob Weed.

4393. vii. SARAH CHILD, b. in Woodstock, Ct., Dec. 31, 1775, m. Roswell Lee.

4394. viii. WALDO CHILD, b. in Woodstock, Ct., Aug. 15, 1777, m. Mary Nicholson.

4395. ix. EZRA CHILD, M. D., b. in Woodstock, Ct., Dec 6 1781, m. Betsey Bellows. He was by profession a physician, a man of much prominence; settled in Indiana, was a member of the Indiana State Legislature for two terms; died leaving a family, of whom little is known.

[Sixth Generation.]

4388. ii. HARBA CHILD, second child and eldest son of Samuel and Elizabeth Weld Child, b. in Woodstock, Ct., April 28, 1764, m. abt. 1786, Polly Lee of Pomfret, Ct., she

was b. 1767.   Soon after marriage they removed to Hartland.
Vt., where their children were born, except the youngest, Dr.
Seth Child.   The parents removed, in 1805, to the town of
Barnston, in Canada.   Mr. and Mrs. Child d. in Rome, N. Y.,
1814.

[Seventh Generation.] Children:

4396. i. SAMUEL CHILD, b. in Hartland, Vt., Feb. 27, 1787. m. Nancy
Drew: she was b. in Maine, Jan. 26, 1785.

4397. ii. SALLY CHILD, b. in Hartland, Vt., 1791, m. Jonathan Waterman.

4398. iii. LUCY CHILD, b. in Hartland, Vt., 1796, m. 1st, Ruel Taylor:
m. 2d, Joseph Rollins. Both died in San Jose, Cal., a few years since.

4399. iv. CHARLES CHILD, b. in Hartland, Vt., 1798; m. ── Hemstraught.

4400. v. STEPHEN CHILD, b. in Hartland, Vt., 1800, m. Hannah Lyman:
settled in Illinois.

4401. vi. BETSEY CHILD, b. in Hartland, Vt., 1802, m. P. Loosa: settled
in Illinois.

4402. vii. SETH CHILD, b. probably in Barnston, Canada, April 4, 1811.
m. March 23, 1836. Juliette Wood.

[Seventh Generation.]

4396. i. SAMUEL CHILD, eldest child of Harba and Polly
Lee, b. in Hartland, Vt., Feb. 27, 1787, m. Nancy Drew about
1814.   Settled in Barnston, Canada, where he now resides.

[Eighth Generation.] Children:

4403. i. MARY CHILD, b. in Barnston, Canada, April 30, 1815.

4404. ii. HARBA CHILD, b. in Barnston, Canada, June 26, 1816.

4405. iii. NANCY CHILD, b. in Barnston, Canada, Dec. 25, 1817.

4406. iv. SAMUEL CHILD, JR, b. in Barnston, Canada, June 9, 1819.

4407. v. MARCUS CHILD, b. in Barnston, Canada, Sept. 6, 1821.

4408. vi. BETSEY CHILD, b. in Barnston, Canada, June 10, 1824

4409. vii. ISAAC CHILD, b. in Barnston, Canada, Oct. 4, 1826.

4410. viii. ABIGAIL M. CHILD, b. in Barnston, Canada, June 12, 1830.

[Eighth Generation.]

4404. ii. HARBA CHILD, eldest son and second child of
Samuel and Nancy Drew Child, m. 1st, Adaline Bowley: m.
2d, Jane Emerson of Alexandria, N. H.   He settled in Bradford, P. Q.   He was a man of much prominence, and held
various offices of trust and responsibility, and has been actively engaged in public affairs much of his life.   He had one
child only, which died young.

[Eighth Generation.]

4407. v. MARCUS CHILD, fifth child and third son of Samuel
and Nancy Drew Child, b. in Barnston, Canada, Sept. 6, 1821,
m. abt. 1856.   Mr. Child was for a number of years a successful teacher; is now engaged in municipal affairs in Dixville.

Stanstead, P. Q., his present residence. Is justice of the peace, postmaster, and acting treasurer of the municipality. [We are much indebted to him for the record of this family.]

[Ninth Generation.] Children:

4411. i. MARCUS L. CHILD, b. in Dixville, P. Q., 1857, d. 1862.

4412. ii. HARBA CHILD, b. in Dixville, P. Q., July 18, 1862.

4413. iii. IRA L. CHILD, b. in Dixville, P. Q., Nov. 17, 1863.

[Seventh Generation.]

4399. iv. CHARLES CHILDS, fourth child and second son of Harba and Polly Lee Child, b. 1798, m. —— Hemstraught, she was b. near Campville, Tioga Co., N. Y., 1800, d. 1873 at Owego.

[Eighth Generation.] Children:

4414 i. CHARLES CHILDS, JR., b. in Scott, N. Y., 1821.

4415. ii. LUCY CHILDS, b. in Scott, N. Y., 1824, m. 1st, Z. C. Moore; m. 2d, D. H. Whitney.

4416. iii. ELIAS WALDO CHILDS, b. in Scott, N. Y., Feb. 1, 1827, m. June 5, 1865, Diadama Hawley.

4417. iv. SAMUEL A. CHILDS, b. Jan. 25, 1830, m. May 9, 1853, Lucelia O. Whiting.

4418. v. MARCUS CHILDS, b. in 1835, unmarried. Mr. Childs has been a teacher for eleven years in the public schools in Barton, N. Y.

[Eighth Generation.]

4414. i. CHARLES CHILDS, JR., eldest child of Charles and —— Hemstraught Childs, b. in Scott, N. Y., 1821, m. ——. Resides in Cleveland, O.

[Ninth Generation.] Child:

4419. i. FRANCES CHILDS, b. 1858.

[Eighth Generation.]

4415. ii. LUCY CHILDS, second child and eldest dau. of Charles and —— Hemstraught Childs, b. 1824 in Scott, N. Y., m. 1st, 1841, Zopher C. Moore; m. 2d, D. H. Whitney. She had five children, only one lived.

[Ninth Generation.] Child:

4420. i. GEORGE G. MOORE, b. 1852, m. Margaret Fulmer of Campville, Tioga Co., N. Y.

[Eighth Generation.]

4416. iii. ELIAS W. CHILDS, third child and second son of Charles and —— Hemstraught Childs, b. in Scott, Cortland Co., N. Y., Feb. 1, 1827, m. Jan. 5, 1865, Diadama Hawley, dau. of Rev. Francis Hawley of Cazenovia, N. Y., (now living in Westfield, Mass.) Mrs. Childs had one sister, Mrs. Jared Pettibone of Vernon Centre, N. Y., and one brother, Gen. J. R. Hawley of Hartford, Ct. Mrs. Childs d. July 23, 1873.

[Ninth Generation.]   Children:

4421. i. A Son, who d. in infancy.

4422. ii A Daughter, b. Sept. 1869, d. Oct. 13, 1870.

[Eighth Generation.]

4417. iv. Hon. SAMUEL A. CHILDS, fourth child and third son of Charles and —— Hemstraught Childs, b. in Campville, Tioga Co., N. Y., June 25, 1830, m. May 9, 1853, Lucelia O. Whiting, dau. of Anson L. Whiting of Scott, N. Y.   Resides in Scott, Cortland Co., N. Y.   Mr. Child was a member of the New York State Legislature from Cortland Co in 1880.

[Ninth Generation.]   Children:

4423. i. ERNEST W. CHILDS, b. in Scott, N. Y., Dec. 31, 1854.

4424. ii. HENRY W. CHILDS, b. in Scott, N. Y., July 31, 1856; resides in Owego, N. Y., and is school commissioner for Tioga Co , N. Y.

4425. iii. HAROLD CHILDS, b. Nov. 3, 1860, d. Feb 1877.

[Seventh Generation.]

4400. v. STEPHEN CHILD, fifth child and third son of Harba and Polly Lee Child, b. in Waitsfield, Vt., June 12, 1802. He removed with his parents to Barnston, P. Q., in 1806. In 1815 they removed to Hartland, Windham Co., Vt., where both parents d. in 1820. Stephen went to Potsdam, St. Lawrence Co., N. Y., and engaged in school teaching. He m. March 4, 1826, Hannah Lyman, who was b. in Brookfield, Vt., Sept. 15, 1808. After the birth of their elder children, they removed, with a colony of fifty-two persons, to Sangamon Co., Ill., Oct. 26, 1833, and settled in the village of Sangamon, Ill. Mr. Child was a farmer and teacher through life. He was early identified with the party organized for the emancipation of the enslaved colored race. Was an active and efficient agent of the Underground railroad, and hundreds of colored people, while fleeing from bondage, found in him a friend and protector. And it was a matter of great satisfaction to Mr. Child that he lived to see the day of emancipation of the colored bondsmen. His death occurred Sept. 4, 1875. His widow still lives in Sangamon, Ill., with one of her sons.

[Eighth Generation.]   Children:

4412a. i. JOHN L. CHILD, b. in Potsdam, St. Lawrence Co., N. Y., Mch. 23, 1827, m. Feb. 17, 1859, Mary E. Anderson.

4413a. ii. MARY L. CHILD, b. in Potsdam, N.Y., Sept. 27, 1831, m. G. B. Seeley.

4414a. iii. MARTHA CHILD. b. in Sangamon Co., Dec. 8, 1833, m. Dec. 25, 1852, T. F. Anderson.

4415a iv. STEPHEN CHILD, JR., b. April 14, 1848, in Sangamon Co., Ill.; lives in Sangamon.

4416a. v. HANNAH CHILD, b. in Sangamon, Ill., Nov. 29, 1850, d. in 1853.

[Eighth Generation.]

4412*a*. i. JOHN L. CHILD, eldest child of Stephen and Hannah Lyman Child, b. in St. Lawrence Co., N. Y., Mch. 23, 1827, m. Feb. 17, 1859, Mary E. Anderson.

[Ninth Generation.] Children:
4417*b*. i. FRANK CHILD.
4418*b*. ii. CHARLIE CHILD.

[Eighth Generation.]

4414*a*. iii. MARTHA L. CHILD, third child and second dau. of Stephen and Hannah Lyman Child, b. in Sangamon, Ill., Dec. 8, 1833, m. Dec. 25, 1852, T. F. Anderson.

[Ninth Generation.] Children:
4419*c*. i. CHARLES ANDERSON, m. and lived in Kansas; was killed 1879.
4420*c*. ii. EDWARD ANDERSON.
4421*c*. iii. HENRY ANDERSON.
4422*c*. iv. TAVNER ANDERSON.
4423*c*. v. HATTIE ANDERSON.
4424*c*. vi. LAURA ANDERSON.

[Seventh Generation.]

4402. vii. Doct. SETH CHILD, seventh child and fourth son of Harba and Polly Lee Child, b. in Barnston, Canada, April 14, 1811, m. Mch. 23, 1836, Juliette Wood, dau. of Rev. Luke and Anna Wood. She was b. June 27, 1818. Doct. Child is a practicing physician in East Hartford, Ct.

[Eighth Generation.] Children:
4426. i. JULIETTE CHILD, b. in Hartford, Ct., Mch. 4, 1837, m. May 1, 1856, Rev. E. Baldwin.
4427. ii. HENRY THEODORIC CHILD, b. in Durham, Ct., Oct. 13, 1838, d. 1839.
4428. iii. MARY TAYLOR CHILD, b. in Durham, Ct., Jan. 18, 1841, d. Feb. 3, 1844.
4429. iv. HENRY EDWARDS CHILD, b. in Durham, Ct., Aug. 30, 1844, m. Feb. 3, 1869, Ella Wilcox, of Springfield, Mass.
4430. v. MARY LEE CHILD, b. in East Hartford, Ct., Dec. 23, 1846.
4431. vi FRANCIS RUSSELL CHILD, b. in East Hartford, Ct., April 19, 1849.
4432. vii. SAMUEL BERESFORD CHILD, b. in East Hartford, Ct., Nov. 5, 1861.

[Eighth Generation.]

4426. i. JULIETTE CHILD, eldest child of Doct. Seth and Juliette Wood Child, b. in Hartford, Ct., Mch. 4, 1837, m. May 1, 1856, Rev. Elijah Baldwin, of New Britian, Ct. She d. Feb. 23, 1857, at Milford, Ct.

[Ninth Generation.] Child:
4433. i. JULIA CHILD BALDWIN, b. at Milford, Feb. 23, 1857.

[Sixth Generation.]

4394. viii. WALDO CHILD, eighth child and second son of
Samuel and Elizabeth Weld Child, b. in Woodstock, Ct., Aug.
15, 1777, m. abt. 1811, Mary Nicholson, eldest dau. of Wm
B. Nicholson, a Revolutionary soldier; who removed from the
East to Norwich, Chenango Co., N. Y., about 1806. His
daughter, Mrs. Annah Amelia Child Randall, wife of Rev.
Silas G. Randall of Providence, R. I., gives the following inter-
esting sketch of her father and family :

"When he was six years of age his father died: and when he was ten his
mother, with her numerous family, moved to Hartland, Vt. He had six
sisters and two brothers. The sisters married in Vermont and most of them
reared large families. When a young man, Waldo commenced teaching school,
often having a hundred or more pupils, and as books were scarce, he was obliged to give them problems and lessons of his own originating, and for this he
was fully competent, being a man of broad culture, a close thinker, and of a
retentive memory. Though slender in person, he had indomitable courage
and perseverance, combined with great social qualities and affable manners,
which made him hosts of friends. In 1806, he made his way westward into
the almost unknown portion of New York, the Chenango Valley. Where
the flourishing village of Norwich now stands, one log hut alone marked the
place. Five miles west of Norwich, in the town of Preston, he took up a
tract of land, cleared off and improved many acres, and nearly paid for it,
when to his consternation he discovered the agent to be a rascal. And after
repeated efforts at great cost to retain it, he was obliged to lose it all.
Nothing daunted, he took up more land and worked with renewed energy
to make for himself a home. In 1811, he married Mary, eldest daughter of
Wm B Nicholson, a soldier of the Revolution, who emigrated with his
family from the East about the same time with himself. Here they lived
happily many years, rearing a large family of children, eleven in number.
In the winter of '45, the typhoid fever, like a scourge, swept through the
place, in a few weeks taking four from their number."

[Seventh Generation.]   Children:

4434. i. ELIZABETH CHILD, b. in Preston, Chenango Co., N.Y., 1812, m.
1868, Lucius Aldrich, of Green, N. Y.

4435. ii. ROXALANA CHILD, b. in Preston, N. Y., 1813, d. 1845.

4436. iii. LOUISA CHILD, b. in Preston, N. Y., 1815. Resides at Green
with Mrs. Aldrich.

4437. iv. LUCIA CHILD, b. in Preston, N. Y., 1816, d. 1830.

4438. v. MARCIA CHILD, b. in Preston, N. Y., 1818, d 1845.

4439. vi. MARY CHILD, b. in Preston, N. Y., 1820, m. David R. Randall,
a lawyer of some eminence of Scranton, Pa. She d. 1855, leaving one son,
having his father's profession, and resides in Washington, D. C.

4440. vii. EZRA CHILD, b. in Preston, N. Y., 1822, d. 1833.

4441. viii. ANNA AMELIA CHILD, b in Preston, N. Y., 1827, m. 1865,
Rev. Silas G. Randall, son of Rev. Benjamin Randall of West Cornwall, Vt.
They reside in Providence, R. I.

4442. ix. JACOB CHILD, b. in Preston, N. Y., 1829, d. 1845.

4443. x. CHARLES CHILD, b. in Preston, N.Y., 1831. Went south in 1848. In 1861, m. Victoria Atkins of Louisana. When last heard from, in 1868, lived on Bayou Almander, 60 miles from New Orleans.

4444. xi. SAMUEL CHILD, b. 1833, d. 1837.

[Fifth Generation.]

4376. viii. JACOB CHILD, eighth child and fourth son of Samuel and Keziah Hutchins Child, b. in Woodstock, Ct., April 23, 1746, m. 1st, 1773, Sybil Sumner, b. 1751, she d. Aug. 10, 1777; m. 2d, Sept. 23, 1779, Miletiah Curtis. He d. July 20, 1822.

[Sixth Generation.] Children:

4445. i. BENJAMIN CHILD, b. in Woodstock, Dec. 18, 1774, m. 1802 or 3, Matilda Bolles.

By second wife.

4446. ii. ASA CHILD, b. in Woodstock, Sept. 13, 1781, m. Mch. 11, 1807, Alathea Stowell.

4447. iii. SYBIL CHILD, b. in Woodstock, Aug. 28, 1783, d. Aug. 29, 1809.

4448. iv. SAMUEL CHILD, b. in Woodstock, Nov. 10, 1785, m. Mch. 26, 1811, Almira Hastings, of Lebanon, N. Y.

4449. v. CHESTER CHILD, b. in Woodstock, Sept. 27, 1787, m. May 3, 1820, Mary Blanchard, of Boston, Mass., b. 1794, d. Oct. 15, 1858.

4450. vi. ELIZABETH CHILD, b. in Woodstock, Ct., June 22, 1788, m. Abijah Sessions.

4451. vii. STEPHEN CHILD, { m. Sept. 23, 1819, Louisa Dean, of b. Mch. 14, 1791. [Ashford, Ct.

4452. viii. JACOB CHILD, JR., { d. March, 1817. } TWINS.

4453. ix. DYER CHILD, b. in Woodstock, Ct., Nov. 19, 1792, m. but had no children.

4454. x. MORRIS CHILD, b. in Woodstock, Ct., April 11, 1794, m. had one child, Helen or Ellen. He d. 1857.

4455. xi. ROXANA CHILD, b. in Woodstock, Ct., June 20, 1796, m. Dec. 20, 1820, Increase Sumner of Ashford, Ct. She d. July 6, 1860.

4456. xii. HIRAM CHILD, b. in Woodstock, Ct., Oct. 18, 1798, m. twice; had no children, one wife was Caroline H. Chandler. He d. Aug. 1878, æ. 80.

[Sixth Generation.]

4445. i. BENJAMIN CHILD, only child of Jacob Child by his wife Sybil Sumner, b. in West Woodstock, Ct., Dec. 18, 1774, m. about 1803, Matilda Bolles, dau. of David and Susanna Bolles. She was b. Sept. 22, 1783. Her father is said to have been the founder of the first Baptist church in Woodstock, Ct., whose organization occurred in February, 1766. (See Ammidown's Historical Sketches.) He was an active and influential member of the church. Two of his sons, (as we are informed by one of his descendants) Rev. Dr. Lucius and Rev. Mathew Bolles, were prominent Baptist clergymen in Boston. His daughter, Mrs. Benjamin Child, adhered to her father's form of faith, while her husband was not less attached to the doctrines and forms of the Congregational church in which he had been educated. But their different church relations seem not to have interrupted their domestic happiness. Mr. Child more christian than sectarian in his feelings, like a good husband as he was, would on the hour of Sabbath service, drive some distance past the Congregational church and tenderly hand out his charming wife at the door of the Baptist church, and return and worship in the Congregational church, each regardful of the others conscience, not to say sectarian tenacity.

[Seventh Generation.] Children:

4457. i. DANFORTH CHILD, b. in West Woodstock, Ct., Sept. 18, 1804, m. Nov. 24, 1831, Clarissa Perrin.

4458. ii. LUCIUS CHILD, b. in West Woodstock, Ct., Sept. 20, 1809, m. Oct. 30, 1834, Mary Wing.

[Seventh Generation.]

4457. i. DANFORTH CHILD, eldest child of Benjamin and Matilda Bolles Child, b. Sept. 18, 1804, m. Nov. 24, 1831, Clarissa Perrin. He d. July 11, 1855.

[Eighth Generation.] Children:

4459. i. MARY CLARISSA CHILD, b. in West Woodstock, Ct., Dec. 16, 1832, d. Mch. 15, 1838.

4460. ii. LUCIUS N. CHILD, b. in West Woodstock, Ct., Feb. 22, 1834.

4461. iii. MARY E. CHILD, b. in West Woodstock, Ct., Feb. 9, 1839.

4462. iv. JERUSHA CHILD, b. in West Woodstock, Ct., Oct. 6, 1843.

[Seventh Generation.]

4458. ii. LUCIUS CHILD, second child of Benjamin and Matilda Bolles Child, b. Sept. 20, 1809, m. Oct. 30, 1834, Mary Wing, of Hartford, Ct.

[Eighth Generation.] Child:

4463. i. FRANCES AMELIA CHILD, b. July 17, 1839.

[Sixth Generation.]

4446. ii. ASA CHILD, second child of Jacob and eldest child of Jacob and Miletiah Curtis Child, b. in West Woodstock, Ct., Sept. 13, 1781, m. March 11, 1807, Alathea Stowell of Stafford, Ct. He d. July 1854; Mrs. Child d. Aug. 11, 1879. Four years after his marriage Mr. Child migrated to the town of Eaton, Madison Co., N. Y., and settled on a farm, where he resided for eleven years, when he removed to the town of Lenox, Madison Co., N. Y., and purchased a home, where he spent the balance of his life. The country was new and the settlers were exposed to many hardships. Mr. Child possessed the requisites for a successful pioneer—courage, energy and physical endurance. Among the early settlers of the township, he was an efficient element in laying the foundations of a prosperous community.

At an early day a Presbyterian church was organized in the town, of which he was constituted a ruling elder. For many years he was active and efficient in promoting its growth and usefulness, when party feeling, in 1834, rose high on the anti-slavery question and led to a rupture in the church. Mr. Child was a man of thorough convictions, and allowed his conscience to control his actions. In the belief that the church was derelict in its duty on this question, he left it and connected himself with a new organization known as a "Union church." He was a patriot in the fullest sense of the word, as well as a philanthropist. He was esteemed for his unselfish and manly characteristics.

[Seventh Generation.] Children:

4464. i. Royal Hibbard Child, b. in West Woodstock, Ct., Jan. 17, 1809, m. 1st, Jan. 14, 1835, Cornelia De Gaass Gates; m. 2d, Servilia Gilbert Benedict.

4465. ii. Mary Child, b. in Eaton, N. Y., May 22, 1814, m. May 8, 1841, Julius Duncan.

4466. iii. Luvan Child, b. in Eaton, N. Y., July 18, 1819, m. July 22, 1846, Aulton A. Briggs.

4467. iv. Eliza Child, b. in Eaton, N. Y., May 26, 1821, m. March 26, 1843, Thomas McCleary.

4468. v. Benjamin Child, b. in Lenox, N. Y., June 1, 1823, m. Aug. 1849, Celestia E. Child.

4469. vi. Roxy Ann Child, b. in Lenox, N. Y., June 28, 1826, m. Dec. 12, 1850, Elbridge Flower.

4470. vii. Emily Child, b. in Lenox, N. Y., Sept. 26, 1829, m. May 26, 1852, Frank Whitney.

[Seventh Generation.]

4464. i. Royal Hibbard Child, eldest child of Asa and Alathea Stowell Child, b. in West Woodstock, Ct., Jan. 17, 1809, m. 1st, Jan. 1, 1835, Cornelia De Gaass Gates of Lebanon, N. Y.; she was b. in Lebanon, N. Y., Sept. 25, 1814, d. Oct. 2, 1868. He m. 2d, Servilia Gilbert Benedict, dau. of Stephen Benedict of Lebanon, N. Y. His children were by his first marriage. In his youth Mr. Child enjoyed the ordinary educational advantages of the period, and attained to a degree of intelligence that fitted him for responsible positions in life. At mature manhood he established a home of his own, as a farmer in the town of Lenox, Madison Co., N. Y., which yielded him fair accumulations. He identified himself in all the progressive movements inaugurated for the benefit of society, and shaped his conduct by deep and honest convictions of the right. In the anti-slavery agitations of an early period he is found in full sympathy with the bondman, and until his manicles were stricken from his limbs by the proclamation of the martyred President Lincoln, the wrongs of the slave ceased not to burden his heart. Following his honest convictions, he severed his connections with the church of his early relations and connected himself with an organization in church fellowship which held no communion with slaveholders or their sympathizers. Conscientious and upright, his christian influence has been stable and effective in the circles of his acquaintance. He has a quiet and pleasant home in the village of Canastota, Madison Co., N. Y.

[Eighth Generation.] Children:

4471. i. GEORGE G. CHILD, b. in Lenox, Madison Co., N. Y., Jan. 5, 1837, d. Jan. 11, 1852.

4472. ii. CYRENE N. CHILD, b, in Lenox, Madison Co., N. Y., Aug. 29, 1847.

4473. iii. EZRA G. CHILD, b. in Lenox, Madison Co., Aug. 8, 1854, m. May 16, 1878, Etta Zeh of Albany, N. Y.; he resides in Moravia, Cayuga Co., N. Y., and is in the butchering business.

[Seventh Generation.]

4465. ii MARY CHILD, second child and eldest dau. of Asa and Alathea Stowell Child, b. in Eaton, N. Y., May 22, 1814, m. May 8, 1841, Julius Duncan, of Lenox, N. Y. He was b. Nov. 28, 1814.

[Eighth Generation.] Child:

4474. i. CHARLES DUNCAN, b. 1851, m. Jan. 23, 1877, Ella Loucks.

[Seventh Generation.]

4466. iii. LUVAN CHILD, third child and second dau. of Asa and Alathea Stowell Child, b. in Eaton, N. Y., July 18, 1819, m. July 22, 1846, Aulton Briggs, a farmer in Leroy, Benton Co., Mo. He d. in Iowa: date of death not given. Mrs. Briggs resides in Leroy, Mo.

[Eighth Generation.] Children:

4475. i. ANSEL CHILD BRIGGS, b. in Boardman, Story Co., Iowa, Sept. 10, 1847. He is a clergyman connected with the M. E. church, South.

4476. ii. CARONA HIBBARD BRIGGS, b. July 27, 1849, in Elkador, Iowa, m. Sept. 14, 1876, Mattie A. Wyatt; is a clergyman of the M. E. church, South.

4477. iii. RHODA DULCIS BRIGGS, b. in Elkador, Iowa, Sept. 2, 1851, m. June 13, 1875, A. J. McDonald.

4478. iv. WILLIAM FLOYD BRIGGS, b. in Elkador, Iowa, Mch. 2, 1855; is a M. E. clergyman, connected with Southern church.

4479. v. JOHN CHARLES FREMONT BRIGGS, b. in Elkador, Iowa, Oct. 11, 1856, d. same day.

4480. vi. AULTON FRANK BRIGGS, b. in Centralia, Marion Co., Ill., Sept. 14, 1857; is a M. E. clergyman in the Southern church. These four sons are said to be young men of fine natural abilites, and give great promise of usefulness in their profession.

4481. vii. WARD POTTER BRIGGS, b. in Milton, Tazwell Co., Ill., Oct. 26, 1859, d. in Leroy, Mo., Aug. 16, 1873.

4482. viii. ALATHEA BRIGGS, b. in Centralia, Ill., Sept. 24, 1862.

[Eighth Generation.]

4476. ii. Rev. CARONA HIBBARD BRIGGS, second child and son of Luvan Child and Aulton Briggs, b. in Elkador, Iowa, July 27, 1849, m. Sept. 14, 1876, Mattie A. Wyatt of Warren Co., Mo.

[Ninth Generation.] Child:

4483. i. FRANK ANSEL WYATT BRIGGS, b. Aug. 18, 1877, in Brownsville, Saline Co., Mo.

[Seventh Generation.]

4467. iv. ELIZA CHILD, fourth child and third dau. of Asa and Alathea Stowell Child, b. in Eaton, N. Y., May 26, 1821, m. Mch. 26, 1843, Thomes McCleary, who was b. Mch. 21, 1814; was a farmer in the town of Sullivan, Madison Co., N.Y. He, d. Feb. 23, 1853.

[Eighth Generation.] Children: .

4484. i. MARY McCLEARY, b. in Sullivan, Madison Co., N. Y., Dec. 28, 1843, m. Oct. 19, 1870, Mortimer Petrie.

4485. ii. BETSEY McCLEARY, b. in Sullivan, Madison Co., N. Y., Jan. 25, 1846, m. July 1, 1869, Battese Revoir.

4486. iii. SAMUEL McCLEARY, b. in Sullivan, Madison Co., N. Y., Aug. 10, 1847, m. and no further account.

4487. iv. ANNA McCLEARY, b. in Sullivan, Madison Co., N. Y., Jan. 4, 1850.

4488. v. EMMA McCLEARY, b. in Sullivan, Madison Co., N. Y., May 5, 1852, m. Sept. 4, 1875, Leroy Trumball.

[Eighth Generation.]

4484. i. MARY McCLEARY, eldest child of Eliza Child and Thomas McCleary, b. in Sullivan, N. Y., Dec. 28, 1843, m. Oct. 19, 1870, Mortimer Petrie. She d. Jan. 28, 1875, leaving two children.

[Ninth Generation.] Children:

4489. i. BLANCHE PETRIE, b. Feb. 26, 1872.

4490. ii. GERTIE PETRIE, b. Oct. 25, 1873.

[Eighth Generation.]

4485. ii. BETSEY McCLEARY, second child and dau. of Eliza Child and Thomas McCleary, b. in Sullivan, N. Y., Jan. 25, 1846, m. July 1, 1869, Battese Revoir. Residence Syracuse, N. Y.

[Ninth Generation.] Child:

4491. i. BERTIE REVOIR, b. Sept. 20, 1877.

K·1

[Eighth Generation.]
4488. v. EMMA McCLEARY, fifth child and fourth dau. of
Eliza Child and Thomas McCleary, b. in Sullivan, N. Y., May
5, 1852, m. Sept. 4, 1875, Leroy Trumball.   Residence Oneida
Lake, N. Y.
[Ninth Generation.]   Children:
    4492. i. BESSIE TRUMBALL, b. July 20, 1876.
    4493 ii. INFANT (unchristened), d. at six months.

[Seventh Generation.]
4468. v. BENJAMIN CHILD, fifth child and second son of
Asa and Alathea Stowell Child, b. in Lenox, Madison Co.,
N. Y., June 1, 1823, m. Aug. 17, 1849, by Rev. Mr. Stickney,
Celestia E. Child, dau. of Ephraim and Armenia Higgins
Child.   Ephraim Child was the eldest son of Charles Thomp-
son and Clarissa (Child) Child of Exeter, Otsego Co., N. Y.
Mrs. Benjamin Child was b. Oct. 20, 1831, d——.   Resided
in Lenox, N. Y.
[Eighth Generation.]   Children:
    4494. i. ALICE CHILD, b. in Lenox, N. Y., June 3, 1850, m. March 3, 1868.
E. D. Benedict.
    4495. ii. FRANK W. CHILD, b. in Lenox, N. Y., Nov. 28, 1851.
    4496. iii. LUCY A. CHILD, b. in Lenox, N. Y., Sept. 26, 1855.

[Eighth Generation.]
4494. i. ALICE CHILD, eldest child of Benjamin and Celestia E. Child, b. in Lenox, N. Y., June 3, 1850, m. March 3,
1868, E. D. Benedict.
[Ninth Generation.]   Child:
    4497. i. ERNEST BENEDICT, b. May 29, 1872.

[Seventh Generation.]
4469. vi. ROXY ANN CHILD, sixth child and fourth dau. of
Asa and Alathea Stowell Child, b. in Lenox, N. Y., Jan. 28,
1826, m. Dec. 12, 1850, Elbridge W. Flower of Lenox, N. Y.
They emigrated to the West in 1869, and settled in Warren.
Jo Davis Co., Ill.   In 1873 they removed to Montgomery
Co., Iowa.
[Eighth Generation.]   Children:
    4498. i. ALATHEA FLOWER, b. in Oneida Co., N. Y., May 23, 1852, m.
1872, John K. Vint of Du Page Co. Iowa; removed to Montgomery Co.,
Iowa: she d. Sept. 30, 1878.
    4499. ii. EMILY E. FLOWER, b. in Madison Co., N. Y., July 4, 1855, d.
July 11, 1856.
    4500 iii. JESSIE FLOWER, b. in Onondaga Co., N. Y., March 4, 1857, m.
April 1878, Wayne K. Frake.
    4501. iv GROVE L. FLOWER, b. in Onondaga Co., N. Y., Nov. 2, 1858.

4502. v. LIZZIE L. FLOWER, b. in Onondaga Co., N. Y., April 2, 1861.
4503. vi. MARK FLOWER, } TWINS. b. in Monroe Co., N. Y., Jan. 25, 1866.
4504. vii. MATTIE FLOWER, }
4505. viii. INFANT (unchristened), d. young.

[Seventh Generation.]

4470. vii. EMILY CHILD, seventh child and fifth dau. of Asa and Alathea Stowell Child, b. in Lenox, N. Y., Sept. 26, 1829, m. May 26, 1852, Frank Whitney of Lenox, N. Y. Mr. W. d. in Cleveland, Oswego Co., N. Y., 1854, and Mrs. W. m. 2d, 1857, Marcus Weaver of Syracuse, N. Y. Mrs. Weaver d. Nov. 1860.

[Eighth Generation.] Children: (No children by first marriage.)
4506. i. ELLA WEAVER.
4507. ii. MATTIE WEAVER.
4508. iii. GEORGE WEAVER.

[Sixth Generation.]

4449. v. CHESTER CHILD, fifth child and third son of Jacob and Milatiah Curtis Child, b. in West Woodstock, Ct., Sept. 27, 1787, m. May 3, 1820, Mary Blanchard Malcom of Boston, Mass. Mrs. Child d. Oct. 15, 1858. Mr. Child is still living with his daughter, Mrs. Mary C. Platt, wife of the late Rev. William Platt, at Ludlowville, N. Y., in his 94th year. Mrs. Platt has furnished the following sketch of her father, written December 1877:

"My father, Mr. Chester Child, is still living, in his 91st year, in perfect health and spirits—can work or walk all day long whenever he chooses. His hearing is but slightly impaired (some days not all perceptibly); his eyesight without glasses is dim, but with them he reads the *Evening Post* through every day of his life. Never misses a meal at the table, nor a night's rest. He takes a sponge bath of the whole person in cold water every morning before dressing, summer and winter, and sleeps in a cold room. He has a good set of natural teeth, upper and under, and a thick, heavy head of hair. He toasts his feet at the fire for more than two hours every night before retiring. This he has done for more than fifty years. At about forty years of age he gave up the use of his cigar (the only form in which he ever used tobacco), and has never resumed it since. Uses no liquors; is very simple in his diet; very neat and methodical in his habits. He has been so industrious in his whole long life, that he cannot bear any one who does not work. He wrote a Christmas letter to his son yesterday more broken than this, but quite as legible and distinct. I think I may safely presume that among your list of many names you can hardly have many whose age and comforts have exceeded my father's. He was engaged most of his life in New York City in active business, until about eight years ago, when he came into the country and made his home in my family, where he will probably spend the remainder of his days.

"Yours respectfully, MARY C. PLATT."

In a postcript Mrs. Platt further adds:

"My father travels alone every summer from here to New York to visit his son, and from thence to Woodstock, Ct., to visit the old homestead, which is still in possession of his brother Hiram; and while upon this trip he takes in Boston and several other places where relatives live."

As intimated by the writer few can show a better record than Mr. Chester Child, the subject of this notice. And this little sketch furnishes a lesson in favor of correct habits, and daily occupation in some useful employment. Well may descendants be proud of so worthy an ancestor.

[Seventh Generation.]   Children:

4509. i. CHARLES MALCOM CHILD, b. Mch. 1821, m. July 29, 1845, Augusta Platt.

4510. ii. MARY CAROLINE CHILD, b. Sept. 26, 1823, m. May 15, 1848, Rev Wm. K. Platt.

4511. iii. CHESTER HAMILTON CHILD, b. Mch. 23, 1827, d in Kansas City, Mo., Feb. 23, 1872; no children.

4512. iv. FRANCIS HENRY CHILD, b. Dec. 14, 1828, d. Dec. 19, 1846.

4513. v. EVALINE CHILD, b. Dec. 21, 1831. d. May 2, 1835.

[Seventh Generation.]

4509. i. CHARLES MALCOM CHILD, eldest son and child of Chester and Mary Blanchard Malcom Child, b. Mch. 1821, m. July 21, 1845, Augusta Platt, dau. of Richard and Harriet Platt. He is a dealer in oils and paints, of the firm of Jessup & Childs, 225 Pearl street, New York City.

[Eighth Generation.]   Children:

4514. i. ELLA LOUISA CHILDS, b. May 9, 1846, m. Henry Hurlburt, Jr., a broker in New York City.

4515. ii. FRANCIS HENRY CHILDS, b. April 16, 1849. Clerk in his father's office.

4516. iii. CHARLES AUGUSTUS CHILDS, b. May 28, 1851. Clerk in his father's office.

4517. iv. HARRIET ESTELLE CHILDS, b. Jan 12, 1854, d. Nov. 2, 1857.

4518. v. FREDERICK MALCOM CHILDS, b. Mch. 15, 1856.

4519. vi. CLARA AUGUSTUS CHILDS,   / ⚥ (b. Nov. / d. April 25, 1861.
4520. vii CLARENCE AUGUSTUS CHILDS. \ TWINS / 9, 1860. (d. Aug. 21, 1861.

4521. viii. AUGUSTUS DENSMORE CHILD, b. Mch. 22, 1864.

[Seventh Generation.]

4510. ii. MARY CAROLINE CHILD, eldest dau. and second child of Chester and Mary Blanchard Malcom Child, b. Sept. 1823, m. May 15, 1848, Rev. Wm. K. Platt, son of Richard and Harriet Platt. Residence Ludlowville, Tompkins Co., New York.

Mr. Platt was a respected Presbyterian clergyman. A native of New York City, in youth he united with Rev. Dr. William

Adam's church in Broom street, graduated at Union College, Schenectady, in 1840, and later at Union Theological Seminary, New York City, and was ordained by New York Presbytery. As a pastor he was beloved for his devotion, his efficiency and tender ministrations. Disciplined by sore affliction and bodily infirmities, his heart was touched at the sufferings of others, which awakened his sympathies and called forth from his lips words of consolation and assurance. His life terminated peacefully at his home, October 30th, 1880.

[Eighth Generation.] Children:

4522. i. MARY EVELINE PLATT, b. April 12, 1849, d. April 29, 1853.

4523. ii. HARRIET NEWELL PLATT, b. Jan. 24, 1851, d. Dec. 14, 1857.

4524. iii. FRANCES AUGUSTA PLATT, b. Feb. 14, 1853, d. Oct. 3, 1857.

4525. iv. CHARLES MALCOM PLATT, b. Feb. 21, 1855. A graduate of Williams College.

4526. v. CHESTER CHILDS PLATT, b. Oct. 30, 1857; a druggist in Ludlowville.

4527. vi. MARION R. PLATT, b. Aug. 5, 1860, d. Nov. 16, 1861.

4528. vii. MARY HATTIE PLATT, b. Oct. 5, 1862.

4529. viii. WILLIAM ADAMS PLATT, b. Feb. 20, 1865.

4530. ix. CLARENCE HENRY PLATT, b. Feb. 6, 1868.

[Third Generation.]

3645. v. JACOB CHILD, fifth child and son of John and Elizabeth Child, b. in Woodstock, Ct., April 25, 1703, m. April 18, 1728, Dorcas Ainsworth.

[Fourth Generation.] Children:

4531. i. JACOB CHILD, JR., b. in Woodstock, Ct., Nov. 2, 1729, d. Sept. 6, 1739.

4532. ii. NATHAN CHILD, b. in Woodstock, Ct., Sept. 19, 1733, m. Oct. 29, 1760, Dorcas Green.

[Fourth Generation.] Children:

4532. ii. NATHAN CHILD, second child and son of Jacob and Dorcas Ainsworth Child, b. Sept. 19, 1733, m. Oct. 9, 1760, Dorcas Green.

[Fifth Generation.] Children. All born in Woodstock, Ct:

4533. i. MARY CHILD, b. July 20, 1761.

4534. ii. CHLOE CHILD, b. Sept. 1, 1762, d. Nov. 26, 1762.

4535. iii. JACOB CHILD, b. April 15, 1764.

4536. iv. JOHN CHILD, b. Jan. 17, 1766.

4537. v. NATHAN CHILD, JR., b. Sept. 17, 1767.

4538. vi. CHLOE CHILD, 2D, b. Feb. 18, 1770.

4539. vii. CYRIL CHILD, b. Sept. 15, 1771.

4540. viii. CYNTHIA CHILD, b. Oct. 25, 1776.

CHAPTER VIII.

WILLIAM CHILD.

[First Generation.]

4541. MR. WILLIAM CHILD, one of the early emigrants to the Massachusetts colony, appears from such evidence as we can attain, to have been the brother of Ephraim Child, and to have come to America either with his brother or shortly before him. We have again to state that the necessity for a quiet leaving the mother country, led to most incomplete lists of the passengers in the sailing vessels, and compels the historian of to-day to obtain dates by a comparison of events and deeds. Mr. William Child was made freeman in 1634, and was a man of some landed estate. He seems to have married in England, and probably his son Joseph was born there, as we have no record of his birth, while Richard and John are found on the Watertown records as born in that town in the years 1631 and 1636. Mr. Child seems to have died early, a victim to the severe climate. His widow is mentioned in the will of Mrs. Elizabeth Palmer Child, who leaves to her some of her wardrobe, which was more ample and luxurious than that of most of the colonists. Mr. Ephraim Child was a true friend to these nephews while living, and left them portions of his estate upon his decease, though his grand-nephew and namesake, Ephraim Child, son of Benjamin Child of Roxbury, was his acknowledged heir.

[Second Generation.] Children :

4542. i. JOSEPH CHILD, b. about. 1629, m. 1654, Sarah Platt.

4543. ii. RICHARD CHILD, b. in Watertown, Mass., 1631, m. 1st, Mch. 30, 1662, Mehitable Dimmick; m. 2d, Jan. 16, 1678, Hannah Traine.

4544. iii. JOHN CHILD, b. in Watertown, Mass., 1636, m. 1st, about 1662, Mary ———: m. 2d, May 29, 1668, Mary Warren.

[Second Generation.]

4542 i. JOSEPH CHILD. eldest son of William Child, b. in England, about 1629, came in infancy with his parents to America, and m. in 1654, Sarah Platt.

[Third Generation.] Child:

4545. i. JOSEPH CHILD, JR., b. in Watertown, Mass., Jan. 7, 1659, m. 1st, Sept. 2, 1680, Sarah Norcross: m. 2d, July 26, 1705, Ruth Maddock.

[Fourth Generation.] Children:

4546. i. SARAH CHILD, b. Nov. 11, 1684, m. Nov. 13, 1710, Daniel Howard of Malden, Mass.

4547. ii. JOSEPH CHILD, b. June 21, 1685, m. July 8, 1713, Mary Thacher.

4548. iii. MARY CHILD, b. April 11, 1687, d. 1688, in Watertown, Mass.

4549. iv JOHN CHILD, b. Mch. 29, 1689, m. 1715, Thankful Fuller.

4550. v. SAMUEL CHILD, b. Mch. 29, 1695, d. 1707, in Watertown, Mass.

4551. vi. ISAAC CHILD, b. Mch. 5, 1700, m. July 2, 1729, Eunice Pierce.

4552. vii. LYDIA CHILD, b. June 2, 1706, m. Dec. 9, 1729, James Fay, of Weston, Mass.

4553. viii. ABIGAIL CHILD, b. Sept. 19, 1708.

4554. ix. EBENEZER CHILD, b. Jan. 19, 1712.

[Fourth Generation.]

4547. ii. JOSEPH CHILD, eldest son and second child of Joseph and Sarah Norcross Child, b. in Watertown, Mass., June 21, 1685, m. July 8, 1713, Mary Thacher.

[Fifth Generation.] Children:

4555. i. JONATHAN CHILD, b. July 3, 1714, m. about 1737, Elizabeth ——.

4556. ii. SAMUEL CHILD, b. Mch. 30, 1716, m. Feb. 17, 1740, Elizabeth Berry.

4557. iii. MARY CHILD, b. Feb. 26, 1718, m. April 19, 1739, Joseph Whiting.

4558. iv. JOSEPH CHILD, JR., b. Oct. 28, 1720, d. May 9, 1774.

[Fifth Generation.]

4555. i. JONATHAN CHILD, eldest child of Joseph and Mary Thacher Child, b. in Watertown, Mass., July 3, 1714, m. about 1737, Elizabeth ——, d. 1774.

[Sixth Generation.] Children. Born in Watertown, Mass:

4559. i. ELIZABETH CHILD, b. Jan. 1, 1738, m. Jan. 6, 1757, Josiah Norcross.

4560. ii. ABIGAIL CHILD, b. Nov. 2, 1743.

4561. iii. JONATHAN CHILD, JR., b. Feb. 25, 1747, m. Elizabeth Mason.

4562. iv. MARY CHILD, b. Nov. 25, 1751, m. April 28, 1782, David Learned.

4563. v. JOSEPH CHILD, b. Dec. 17, 1761, m. Oct. 3, 1782, Lucy Parmenter.

[Sixth Generation.]

4561. iii. JONATHAN CHILD, JR., third child second son of Jonathan and Elizabeth Child, b. Feb. 25, 1747, m. abt. 1775, Elizabeth Mason.

[Seventh Generation.] Children born in Watertown, Mass:

4564. i. JONATHAN CHILD, b Feb. 4, 1776.

4565. ii. ABIGAIL CHILD, b. Mch. 26, 1779, d. April 16, 1855, at Weston.

4566. iii. ELIZABETH CHILD, b. Dec. 13, 1778.

4567. iv HANNAH CHILD, b. Aug. 20, 1783.

4568. v. SUSANNA CHILD, b. June 3, 1788.

[Sixth Generation.]

4563. v. JOSEPH CHILD, fifth child and second son of Jonathan Jr., and Elizabeth Child, b. in Watertown, Dec. 17, 1761.

m. Oct. 3, 1782, Lucy Parmenter: resided in Lexington, Mass.
[Seventh Generation.] Child:

4569. i. MOSES CHILD, b. in Lexington, Mass., June 13, 1787, m. Aug. 8, 1810, Mary Ball Williams, of Marlboro, Mass. She was b. April 4, 1786, d. 1807. She was a direct descendant of Abraham Williams, an original proprietor of Marlboro.

[Eighth Generation.] Children:

4570. i. LUKE CARTER CHILD, b. in Lexington, Mass., Mch. 16, 1811, m. Dec. 10, 1835, Rebecca A. Hale.

4571. ii. ELIZA W. CHILD, b. in Lexington, Dec. 22, 1812.

[Eighth Generation.]

4570. i. LUKE CARTER CHILD, eldest child and only son of Moses and Mary Ball Williams Child, b. in Lexington, Mass., Mch. 16, 1811, m. Dec. 10, 1835, Rebecca A. Hale. Was a business man in Boston for several years: withdrew from business and settled in Lexington on a farm, in the year 1849.

[Ninth Generation.] Children, born in Boston, Mass.

4572. i. CAROLINE R. CHILD, b. Dec. 3, 1836, d. Feb. 21, 1838.

4573. ii. HENRY M. CHILD, b. May 15, 1839, d. Nov. 16, 1844.

4574. iii. ELLEN R. CHILD, b. Oct. 17, 1841, d. Sept. 14, 1849.

4575. iv. MARY E. CHILD, b. Sept. 19, 1843.

4576. v. EDWARD H. CHILD, b. April 23, 1846, d. Sept. 12, 1849.

4577. vi. FRANK C. CHILD, b. April 21, 1849.

[Fifth Generation.]

4556. ii. SAMUEL CHILD, second son and child of Joseph and Mary Thacher Child, b. in Watertown, Mass., Mch. 30, 1716, m. Feb. 5, 1740, Elizabeth Berry.

[Sixth Generation.] Children, born in Watertown, Mass.

4578. i. MARY CHILD, b. July 13, 1741.

4579. ii. SARAH CHILD, b. Mch. 28, 1743.

4580. iii ELIZABETH CHILD, b. Feb. 7, 1746.

4581. iv. SAMUEL CHILD, JR., b. Feb. 10, 1748.

4582. v. LYDIA CHILD, b. July 22, 1750.

4583. vi. EBENEZER CHILD, b. April 25, 1753.

[Fourth Generation.]

4549. iv. JOHN CHILD, fourth child and second son of Joseph and Sarah Norcross Child, b. in Watertown, May 29, 1689, m. 1715, Thankful Fuller.

[Fifth Generation.] Children, born in Watertown, Mass.

4584. i. BETSEY CHILD, b. June 13, 1716, d. 1717.

4585. ii. EPHRAIM CHILD, b. Sept. 16, 1718.

4586. iii. ROBERT CHILD, b. Feb. 28, 1720, m. 1761, Margaret Woodstock.

4587. iv. CALEB CHILD, b. Sept. 10, 1721, m. May 29, 1744, Lucy Greenwood of Weston.

4588. v. THANKFUL CHILD, b. Sept. 4, 1726, m. Mch. 1752, John Capel of Waltham.

4589. vi. HANNAH CHILD, b. Jan. 27, 1828.

4590. vii. JOSIAH CHILD, b. April 14, 1731, m. 1st, 1759, Rebecca Segar; m. 2d, Lucy Osgood.

4591. viii. SARAH CHILD, b. Feb. 6, 1733, d. 1755.

4592. ix. LYDIA CHILD, b. April 3, 1736, m. 1754, Thomas Williams, Jr.

[Fifth Generation.]

4586. iii. ROBERT CHILD, third child of John and Thankful Fuller Child, b. in Watertown, Mass., Feb. 28, 1720, m. 1761, Margaret Woodstock, of Needham, Mass. He settled in Newton.

[Sixth Generation] Child:

4593. i. JOHN CHILD, b. in Newton, Mass., May 16, 1762.

[Fifth Generation.]

4590. vii. JOSIAH CHILD, seventh child of John and Thankful Fuller Child, b. in Watertown, April 14, 1731, m. 1st, 1759, Rebecca Segar; m. 2d, 1765, Lucy Osgood.

[Sixth Generation.] Children, born in Newton, Mass.

4594 i. REBECCA CHILD, b. May 18, 1760.

By second marriage

4595. ii. ELIZABETH CHILD, b. July 4, 1766.

4596. iii FANNY CHILD, b. Mch 9, 1768.

4597. iv. SPENCER CHILD, b. May 2, 1770.

4598. v. DAVID CHILD, b. Aug. 27, 1772.

4599. vi. LUCY CHILD, b. Sept. 18, 1774.

4600. vii. ABNER CHILD, b. Sept. 19, 1776, m. June 4, 1800, Betsey Richards.

[Sixth Generation.]

4600. vii. ABNER CHILD, third son and seventh child of Josiah and Lucy Osgood Child, b. in Newton, Mass., Sept. 19, 1776, m. June 4, 1800, Betsey Richards. She was b. July 19, 1779, dau. of Ebenezer and Hannah Wiswall Richards; she d. Jan. 1, 1875. Resided in Roxbury, Mass.

[Seventh Generation.] Children:

4601. i. ANNA PARKER CHILD, b. in Roxbury, Mass., April 27, 1801, m. Oct. 18, 1824, Benjamin Parker, a merchant in Baltimore, Md.

4602. ii. SARAH CHILD, b. Feb. 2, 1804, in Roxbury, Mass., d. Aug. 20, 1806.

4603. iii. ABNER CHILD, JR., b. Dec. 20, 1808, in Roxbury, Mass.

[Fourth Generation.]

4551. vi. ISAAC CHILD, sixth child, fourth son of Joseph and Sarah Norcross, b. in Watertown, Mass., Mch. 5, 1700, m. July 2, 1729, Eunice Pierce. He was a turner by trade. He d. Feb. 7, 1789. She d. Sept. 1, 1793. They lived in Waltham, Mass.

[Fifth Generation] Children born in Waltham, Mass.

4604. i. PHINEAS CHILD. b. April 26, 1730. m. 1st, June 2. 1757, Louisa Dakin: m. 2d. April 15, 1770, Ruth Wheeler.

4605. ii ISAAC CHILD, JR., b Jan. 26, 1733, m. 1st, 1753, Sarah ——: m. 2d, Hannah ——, of Lincoln: m. 3d. Lydia ——.

4606. iii. EUNICE CHILD, b. April 6, 1734.

4607 iv. THADDEUS CHILD. b. April 13, 1736, m. July 29. 1762, Hepsibah Warren, of Lincoln.

4608. v. ABIJAH CHILD, b. April 23, 1739. m Oct. 27. 1763, Sarah Cutler.

4609. vi. ABRAHAM CHILD. b. Aug. 12. 1741. m. April 2. 1767. Rebecca Stowell.

4610. vii. RUTH CHILD.

4611. viii. DAVID CHILD. bapt. 1746, d. June 21. 1767.

4612. ix. LUCY CHILD. bapt. April 29. 1749.

[Fifth Generation.]

4604. i. PHINEAS CHILD. eldest child of Isaac and Eunice Pierce Child, b. in Waltham. Mass., April 26. 1730, m. 1st. June 2. 1756, Louisa Dakin: m. 2d, April 15, 1770. Ruth Wheeler. They resided in Weston. Mass.

[Sixth Generation.] Children, born in Weston. Mass.

4613. i. PHINEAS CHILD. JR, b. Sept. 5, 1757.

4614. ii. MOLLY CHILD, b. Oct. 3, 1759.

4615 iii. JONAS DAKIN CHILD. b. April 9, 1762, m. May 10. 1837. Susan Elms.

4616. iv. AMOS CHILD, b. July 5, 1764.

4617. v. LOUISE CHILD. { TWINS { b. July 6, 1766. { m. Mch. 15, 1785,
4618. vi. CATHARINE CHILD. { { { John Flagg. Jr.

[Fifth Generation.]

4605. ii. ISAAC CHILD. JR.. second child and son of Isaac and Eunice Pierce Child. b. in Waltham. Mass.. Jan. 26. 1733. m. 1st. 1753. Sarah ——: m. 2d. Hannah —— of Lincoln. Mass.: m. 3d. Lydia ——. Resided in Lincoln, Mass.

[Sixth Generation.] Children, born in Waltham and Lincoln, Mass :

4619. i. DANIEL CHILD, b. in Waltham. Mass.. Nov. 24. 1754. d. Sept. 19, 1756.

4620. ii. TIMOTHY CHILD, b. Sept 9. 1756, d. same day.

4621. iii. ABEL CHILD. b. April 10. 1757. m. 1st. 1785. Polly ——: m. 2d, Lydia ——.

4622. iv. SOLOMON CHILD. b. Nov. 1. 1762. m. April 26. 1804. Betsey Sanderson.

4623. v. MATILDA CHILD. b. April 18, 1764. m. Feb. 23, 1786. William Hobbs of Weston, Mass.

4624. vi LYDIA CHILD. b. in Lincoln, Mass.. Sept. 9, 1768, pub. Dec. 27. 1787, to Nathan Hobbs of Weston, Mass.

4625 vii. POLLY CHILD, b. Sept. 17, 1771, m. Sept. 13, 1798, Edward Fisk.

4626. viii. PRENTICE CHILD, b. Dec. 14. 1774. d. young.

4627. ix. PRENTICE CHILD, 2D, b. Dec 1, 1775, m. April 2, 1811. Harriet Livermore.

4628. x. ISAAC J. CHILD. JR., b. Feb. 7, 1778. m. June 26. 1804. Betsey Wellington.

[Sixth Generation.]

4621. iii. ABEL CHILD. third son and child of Isaac and Sarah Child, b. in Waltham, Mass., April 10, 1757, m. 1st, 1785, Polly ——; m. 2d, Lydia ——. Resided in Lincoln, Mass.

[Seventh Generation.] Children:

4629. i. POLLY CHILD, b. in Lincoln, Mass., March 29, 1786.

4630. ii. MARY CHILD, b. in Lincoln, Mass., Nov. 9, 1787.

[Sixth Generation.]

4622. iv. SOLOMON CHILD, fourth child and son of Isaac Child, by his second wife Hannah ——, b. in Waltham, Mass., Nov. 1, 1762, m. April 26, 1804, Betsey Sanderson.

[Seventh Generation.] Children:

4631. i. LEONARD CHILD, b. in Waltham, Mass., Feb. 5 or 7, 1805, m. Feb. 1, 1867, Lydia Livermore.

4632. ii. SOLOMON CHILD, JR., b. in Waltham, Mass., Sept. 6, 1808, d. Aug. 13, 1855, unmarried.

4633. iii. SARAH JANE CHILD, b. in Waltham, Mass., July 7, 1812, m. April 18, 1850, Reuben Wyman.

[Seventh Generation.]

4631. i. LEONARD CHILD, eldest child of Solomon and Betsey Sanderson Child, b. in Waltham or Watertown, Mass., Feb. 5 or 7, 1805, m. Feb. 1, 1867, Lydia Livermore.

[Eighth Generation.] Children:

4634. i. LYDIA ELIZABETH CHILD.

4635. ii. THOMAS LIVERMORE CHILD.

[Sixth Generation.]

4627. ix. PRENTICE CHILD, 2D, ninth child of Isaac Child, it may be by Lydia, b. in Waltham or Lincoln, Mass., Dec. 1, 1775, m. April 2, 1811, Harriet Livermore, she was b. Sept. 25, 1787, d. July 3, 1865; he d. May 15, 1857.

[Seventh Generation.] Child:

4636 i. WILLIAM PRENTICE CHILD, b. in Waltham, Mass., Nov. 11, 1817, m. 1st, Dec. 13, 1840, Eunice M. Fuller, she d. March 11, 1846; m. 2d, Jan. 14, 1847, Esther E. Hollis; he d. Sept. 7, 1877.

[Eighth Generation.] Children, born in Waltham, Mass.:

4637. i. HARRIET L. CHILD, b. Oct. 27, 1841, m. Dec. 24, 1874, Edward P. Smith.

4638. ii. WILLIAM GARLAND CHILD, b. Feb. 12, 1843, m. Oct. 7, 1869, Ellen Pierce.

4639. iii. ELLEN EUNICE CHILD, b. April 7, 1845, d. Jan. 16, 1868.

4640. iv. OLIVER PRENTICE CHILD, b. June 30, 1848, d. Aug. 11, 1871.

4641. v. MELVIN LATHROP CHILD, b. July 3, 1849, m. Dec. 20, 1871, Sophia George.

4642. vi. SARAH JANE CHILD, b. June 22, 1860.

[Eighth Generation.]

4638. ii. WILLIAM GARLAND CHILD, second child and eldest son of William Prentice and Eunice M. Fuller Child, b.

in Waltham. Mass., Feb. 12. 1843. m. Oct. 27, 1869, Ellen Pierce.

[Ninth Generation.] Children, born in Waltham, Mass.:
  4644. i. ARTHUR CHILD. b. April 4, 1871.
  4645. ii ALICE PIERCE CHILD, b. May 4, 1873.
  4646. iii. WILLIAM BENJAMIN CHILD, b. Feb. 4. 1876.

[Sixth Generation.]

4628. x. Capt. ISAAC CHILD, JR., tenth child of Isaac Child, possibly by his third wife Lydia ——, b. Feb. 7. 1778. m. June 26. 1804. Betsey Wellington: she was b. Feb. 4. 1784, d. July 30. 1865.

[Seventh Generation.] Children, born in Waltham, Mass.:
  4647. i. DARIUS CHILD, b. Oct. 13, 1805. m. Dec. 26. 1830. Lydia H. Chandler.
  4648. ii. EVALINA CHILD, b. June 1807. m. Oct. 16, 1828. Thomas Noxon.
  4649. iii. ELIZABETH CHILD, b. Dec. 1. 1809. m. April 8. 1837. Joseph Howe.
  4650. iv. ISAAC CHILD, JR., b. Oct. 9, 1813. m. April 7. 1835. Mary Ann Smith.
  4651. v. PRENTICE CHILD, b. Jan. 14. 1815, m. Jan. 14, 1847, Esther Hollis.
  4652. vi. AUGUSTUS CHILD, b. Oct. 9. 1818. m. March 9, 1853, Eliza Ann Blodgett.
  4653. vii. MARY MATILDA CHILD. b. Aug. 5. 1820. m. April 16, 1840. James Wellington.
  4654. viii. MARTHA CHILD. b. Oct. 11, 1824. m. Feb. 10, 1847. Billings Smith.

[Seventh Generation.]

4647. i. DARIUS CHILD, eldest child of Capt. Isaac and Betsey Wellington Child. b. in Waltham. Mass.. Oct. 13, 1805. m. Dec. 26. 1830. Lydia H. Chandler.
[Eighth Generation.] Children:
  4655. i. WILLIAM H. CHILD.
  4656. ii. SARAH CHILD.

[Seventh Generation.]

4648. ii. EVALINA CHILD. second child of Capt. Isaac and Betsey Wellington Child. b. in Waltham. Mass.. June 1807. m. Oct. 16, 1828, Thomas Noxon.
[Eighth Generation.] Children:
  4657. i. ELIZABETH NOXON.
  4658. ii. THOMAS P. NOXON.

[Seventh Generation]

4649. iii. ELIZABETH CHILD, third child and second dau. of Capt. Isaac and Betsey Wellington Child, b. Dec. 1. 1809, m. April 8. 1837. Joseph Howe.

[Eighth Generation.] Children:
    4659. i. MARY B. HOWE.
    4660. ii. WARREN B. HOWE.
    4661. iii. JOSEPH M. HOWE.
    4662. iv. LIZZIE C. HOWE.
    4663. v. WILLIAM S. HOWE.

[Seventh Generation.]

4650. iv. ISAAC CHILD, JR., fourth child and second son of Capt. Isaac and Betsey Wellington Child, b. in Waltham, Mass., Oct. 9, 1813, m. April 7, 1835, Mary Ann Smith, d. June 26, 1862.

[Eighth Generation.] Children:
    4664. i. EMILY J. CHILD.
    4665. ii. ANNA D. CHILD.
    4666. iii. THOMAS W. CHILD.

[Seventh Generation.]

4651. v. PRENTICE CHILD, fifth child of Capt. Isaac and Betsey Wellington Child, b. in Waltham, Mass., Jan. 14, 1815, m. Jan. 14, 1847, Esther Hollis; he d. 1862.

[Eighth Generation.] Children:
    4667. i. AUSTIN C. CHILD.
    4668. ii. LYDIA M. CHILD.
    4669. iii. MARY M. CHILD.
    4670. iv. BETSEY E. CHILD.

[Seventh Generation.]

4652. vi. AUGUSTUS CHILD, sixth child of Capt. Isaac and Betsey Wellington Child, b. in Waltham, Mass., Oct. 9, 1818, m. March 9, 1853, Eliza Ann Blodgett.

[Eighth Generation.] Children:
    4671. i. CHARLIE CHILD.
    4672. ii. CARLTON CHILD.

[Seventh Generation.]

4653. vii. MARY MATILDA CHILD, seventh child of Capt. Isaac and Betsey Wellington Child, b. Aug. 5, 1820, m. April 16, 1840, James Wellington.

[Eighth Generation.] Children:
    4673. i. HERBERT J. WELLINGTON.
    4674. ii. ARTHUR P. WELLINGTON.
    4675. iii. WARREN H. WELLINGTON.

[Seventh Generation.]

4654. viii. MARTHA CHILD, eighth child of Capt. Isaac and Betsey Wellington Child, b. in Waltham, Mass., Oct. 11, 1824, m. Feb. 10, 1847, Billings Smith.

[Eighth Generation.] Children:
    4676. i. BILLINGS SMITH, JR.
    4677. ii. LUCY R. SMITH.
    4678. iii. WILLIE SMITH.
    4679. iv. RALPH SMITH.
    4680. v. ALICE M. SMITH.

[Fifth Generation.]

    4607. iv. THADDEUS CHILD, fourth child, third son of Isaac
and Eunice Pierce Child, b. in Waltham, April 13, 1736, m.
July 29, 1762, Hepzebah Warren of Lincoln, Mass., where he
settled.

[Sixth Generation.] Children, born in Lincoln, Mass.
    4681. i. SILAS CHILD, b. Feb. 1, 1763.
    4682. ii. JOEL CHILD, b. Jan. 20, 1765.
    4683. iii. NATHAN CHILD, b. May 20, 1770.
    4684. iv. ANNA CHILD, b. July 3, 1772.
    4685. v. AARON CHILD, b. Sept. 17, 1775.
    4686. vi. SALLY CHILD, b. Feb. 3, 1782.

[Fifth Generation.]

    4608. v. ABIJAH CHILD, fifth child fourth son of Isaac and
Eunice Pierce Child, b. in Waltham, Mass., April 23, 1739,
m. Oct. 27, 1763, Sarah Cutler, dau. of Benjamin and Mary
Cutler of Lexington, Mass. She was b. June 17, 1736, d.
Mch. 3, 1812. He d. Aug. 3, 1808. "He settled in Lexington
and was admitted to the church 1764. He was a respectable
citizen, and filled several town offices. Mr. and Mrs. Abijah
Child were called to pass through a scene of affliction which
rarely falls to the lot of parents, as will be seen by the records.
Six of their children were taken from them by death in twelve
days. They were buried in the old graveyard, and one large
stone tells the sad tale."—*Hudson's History of Lexington.*

[Sixth Generation.] Children, born in Lexington, Mass.:
    4687. i. SARAH CHILD, b. Dec. 17, 1764, d. Aug. 28, 1778.
    4688. ii. EUNICE CHILD, b. May 13, 1766, d. Aug. 23, 1778.
    4689. iii. ABIJAH CHILD, JR., b. Aug. 1, 1767, d. Aug. 29, 1778.
    4690. iv. ABIGAIL CHILD, b. June 18, 1771, d. Aug. 29, 1778.
    4691. v. BENJAMIN CHILD, b. Nov. 16, 1773, d. Aug. 24, 1778.
    4692. vi. MOSES CHILD, b. Sept. 1, 1776, d. Aug. 19, 1778.
    4693. vii. ISAAC CHILD, b. Oct. 11, 1777, d. Nov. 11, 1811.

[Fifth Generation.]

    4609. vi. CAPT. ABRAHAM CHILD, sixth child and fifth son
of Isaac and Eunice Pierce Child, b. in Waltham, Mass., Aug.
12, 1741, m. April 2, 1767, Rebecca Stowell.

[Sixth Generation.] Children born in Watertown, Mass.

4694. i. DANIEL CHILD, b. Nov. 29, 1767, m. July 1792, Phœbe Hobbs.

4695. ii. JONATHAN CHILD, b. Mch. 5, 1769.

4696. iii. WILLIAM CHILD, b. Sept. 16, 1770.

4697. iv. ABIGAIL CHILD, b. May 26, 1772.

4698. v. REBECCA CHILD, b. Sept. 18, 1773.

4699. vi. ABRAHAM CHILD, JR., b. Feb. 16. 1775.

4700. vii. THOMAS CHILD, b. April 21, 1777.

[Second Generation.]

4543. ii. RICHARD CHILD, second son and child of William
Child, b. in Watertown, Mass., in 1631, m. 1st, at Waltham,
Mass., March 30, 1662, Mehitable Dimmick, dau. of Thomas
Dimmick of Barnstable. Their union of fourteen years was
blessed with eight children. Mrs. M. D. Child d. Aug. 1, 1676,
and Mr. Child m. 2d, Jan. 16, 1678, Hannah Traine, youngest
dau. of the first John Traine. Five children were added in
this marriage—all were born in Watertown. Mr. Child shared
with his brothers in the legacies of the Uncle Ephraim Child.
We find he took the oath of fidelity upon attaining his majority. He d. Nov. 11, 1694.

[Third Generation.] Children:

4701. i. RICHARD CHILD, JR., b. March 30, 1663, m. Dec. 30, 1686, Mary
Flagg; he d. 1691.

4702. ii. EPHRAIM CHILD, b. Oct. 9, 1664, d. Feb. 1665.

4703. iii. SHUBAEL CHILD, b. Dec. 19, 1665, m. Oct. 27. 1687, Abigail
Saunders.

4704. iv. MEHITABLE CHILD, b. 1666, m. July 18, 1691, Edward Garfield.
Mehitable was admitted to the First Church April 27, 1690.

4705. v. EXPERIENCE CHILD, b. Feb. 26, 1669, m. Sept. 20, 1689, Benjamin Flagg.

4706. vi. ABIGAIL CHILD, b. Jan. 16, 1672, m. 1695, Joseph Lathrop of
Barnstable.

4707. vii. EBENEZER CHILD, ⎰ ⎱ d. 1675.
⎱TWINS.⎰ b. Nov. 10, 1674.   [Barnstable.
4708. viii. HANNAH CHILD, ⎰ ⎱ m. July 30, 1702. Joseph Blish of
4709. ix. ELIZABETH CHILD, b. July 4, 1681.

4710. x. JOSHUA CHILD, b. Dec. 30, 1682, m. abt. 1720, Sarah ——.

4711. xi. MARGARET CHILD, ⎰ ⎱ m Dec. 25, 1701, Joseph Priest.
⎱TWINS.⎰ b. May 16, 1687.
4712. xii. JOHN CHILD, ⎰ ⎱ m. Experience Fuller.

4713. xiii. REBECCA CHILD, b. Feb. 4, 1693.

[Third Generation.]

4703. iii. SHUBAEL CHILD, third son and child of Richard
and Mehitable Dimmick Child, b. in Watertown, Mass., Dec.
19, 1665, m. Oct. 27, 1687, Abigail Saunders. After the birth
of two children, Mr. Child suffered from mental aberration.
Very great ignorance or apathy, rendered the condition of the

insane at this period, and even at a later date, one of much
needless suffering. Sympathy with this greatest possible misfortune, was lost in terror of the possible acts of the victims:
even the medical faculty did little to cure, or alleviate the disease. No suitable retreats were provided; and when the disease
became violent in its demonstrations, close confinement in some
subterranean room, or prison cell was the doom of the unfortunate. Mr. Shubael Child was condemned to this fearful fate,
and died from exposure to the rigors of a New England winter,
in an unwarmed cell of the county prison. On the tenth of
July, 1694, a petition was presented in the Court: in the quaint
phraseology of the day, "In behalf of Shubael Child, *formerly
out of his head*, who was frozen in the county prison." Of
the exact nature of this address we are not apprised, but as
Mr. Child could not then be benefitted thereby, we presume it
in the interest of the widow and children so grievously afflicted.
The two children grew to manhood, the elder, Mr. Richard
Child, named for his grandfather, died when only twenty-two.
[Fourth Generation.] Children:

4714. i. RICHARD CHILD, b. April 9. 1690, d. 1712.

4715. ii. SHABUEL CHILD, JR., b. Sept. 8, 1693, m. abt. 1717, Mary ——.

[Fourth Generation.]

4715. ii. SHABUEL CHILD, JR., second son and child of
Shubael and Abigail Saunders Child, b. in Watertown, Mass.,
Sept. 8. 1693, m. abt. 1717, Mary ——. Resided in Weston,
Mass., where their children were born. We are dependent
upon the baptismal register for this record.
[Fifth Generation.] Children:

4716. i. RICHARD CHILD, bapt. Sept. 17, 1719.

4717. ii. MARY CHILD, bapt. Sept. 17, 1719.

4718. iii. SHUBAEL CHILD, bapt. July 17, 1721, m. Feb. 14, 1744, Sarah
Stratton.

[Fifth Generation.]

4718. iii. SHUBAEL CHILD, third child and second son of
Shubael and Mary Child, b. in Weston, Mass., bapt. July 17,
1721, m. Feb. 14, 1744, Sarah Stratton. [The custom of very
early christenings prevailed in New England, so failing the
exact date of birth, we approximate very nearly from the
record of baptism.]
[Sixth Generation] Children:

4719. i. MARY CHILD, b. in Watertown, Mass., Nov. 1743, m. Dec. 22,
1752, Joseph Allen.

4720. ii. SARAH CHILD, b. in Watertown, Mass., Jan. 16, 1748, m. Sept.
20, ——. Jonathan Stratton, Jr.

[Third Generation.]

4711. x. JOSHUA CHILD. tenth child of Richard and second of Richard and Hannah Traine Child, b. Dec. 30, 1682, m. abt. 1720, Sarah ———. Resided in Worcester.

[Fourth Generation.] Children:

4721. i. SARAH CHILD, b. Feb. 2, 1721.

4722. ii. JOSHUA CHILD, JR., b. Sept. 26, 1725, m. June 2, 1748, Mary Hinds.

4723. iii. THOMAS CHILD, b. Sept. 26, 1726, m. Nov. 23, 1753, Anna Bullard.

4724. iv. HANNAH CHILD, b. Oct. 10, 1727, m. May 18, 1758, Peter Newton.

4725. v. JOSIAH CHILD, ⟩ TWINS. ⟨ b. Dec. ⟩ m. Aug. 3, 1753, Experience
4726. vi. MARY CHILD, ⟩ ⟨ 20, 1728. ⟩ Read.

4727. vii. ABRAHAM CHILD, b. April 26, 1732.

[Fourth Generation.]

4723. iii. THOMAS CHILD, second son and third child of Joshua and Sarah Child, b. Sept. 26, 1726, m. Nov. 23, 1753, Anna Bullard. Thomas Child resided in Rutland, Worcester Co., Mass., where he d. Feb. 1, 1812, aged 86 years.

[Fifth Generation.] Children, born in Rutland, Mass.

4715a. i. ABIATHER CHILD, b. Sept. 15, 1754, m. 1st, Mch. 13, 1780, Sarah Ames; m. 2d, Mch. 6, 1826, Eliza Newton.

4716a. ii. ANNA CHILD, b. Jan. 27, 1760, m. Nov. 21, 1782, Hezekiah Metcalf.

4717a. iii. MARY CHILD, m. Sept. 5, 1777, Moses Clark of Hubbardston.

4718a. iv ELIZABETH SHEPHERD CHILD, b. Jan. 21, 1772, d. April 9, 1827, aged 55 years.

[Fifth Generation.]

4715a. i. ABIATHER CHILD, eldest child of Thomas and Anna Bullard Child, b. in Rutland, Mass., Sept. 14, 1754, m. 1st, Mch. 13, 1780, Sarah Ames; m. 2d, Mch. 2, 1826, Eliza Newton, being in his seventy-second year at the time of his last marriage, and his bride eighteen. Mr. A. Child d. in Rutland, Oct. 1, 1833.

[Sixth Generation.] Children, born in Rutland, Mass.

4719b. i. JACOB CHILD, b. Aug. 19, 1781, m. April 19, 1807, Nancy Bowker.

4720b. ii. BENJAMIN CHILD, b. June 22, 1782.

4721b. iii. SARAH CHILD, b. Aug. 12, 1785, m. April 3, 1825, Luther Wheeler.

4722b. iv. ANNA CHILD, b. Mch. 15, 1787.

4723b. v. MARY CHILD, b. Mch. 17, 1789.

4724b. vi. ISABEL CHILD, b. April 29, 1790.

4725b. vii. SUSANNA CHILD, b. July 17, 1793, m. July 4, 1814, Cyprian Stratton.

4726b. viii. CURTIS CHILD, b. June 21, 1795.

4727b. ix. JAMES MADISON CHILD, b. Feb. 27, 1827.

L-1

[Third Generation.]

4712. xii. JOHN CHILD, sixth son and twelfth child of Richard and Hannah Traine Child, b. in Watertown, Mass., May 16, 1687, m. about 1714, Experience Fuller, who d. in 1770. Mr. Child resided in Newtown, Mass., where all his children were born.

[Fourth Generation.] Children:

4728. i. RICHARD CHILD, b. Jan. 16, 1716.
4729. ii. JOHN CHILD, b. Oct. 6, 1717, m 1738, Tabitha Segar.
4730. iii. ABIGAIL CHILD, m. Jonas Ward.

[Fourth Generation]

4729. ii. JOHN CHILD, second son and child of John and Experience Fuller Child, b. in Newton, Mass., Oct. 6, 1717, m. 1738, Tabitha Segar. Mr. Child settled in Worcester, Mass., and there his children were born: he d. Nov. 10, 1745.

[Fifth Generation.] Children:

4731. i. TABITHA CHILD, b. Feb. 14, 1742.
4732. ii. JOHN CHILD, JR., b. Feb. 15, 1744.

[Second Generation.]

4544. iii. JOHN CHILD, third son and child, as it appears, of William Child was born after his parents removal to America, in 1636, in Watertown, Mass.: m. 1st, Mary ——: m. 2d, May 29, 1668, Mary Warren, who was b. Nov. 29, 1651, and was a granddaughter of John Warren, who came to America in the "Arabella" with Governor Winthrop, in 1630. As it has been deemed probable from certain circumstantial evidence that Ephraim Child, of Watertown, came to New England with Gov. Winthrop; it is also presumable that William accompained his brother. Mr. Warren, the grandfather of Mrs. M.W. Child, was one of the selectmen of Watertown, and a prominent citizen, though some amusing entries found in the town records, which were also church records, would indicate the source whence some of his descendants have drawn their independence of character, and departure from the early established orthodox views. First, we find "John Warren fined, Oct. 1651, twenty shillings for an offence against the laws of baptism"; second, "John Warren fined, April 4, 1654, for neglect of public worship, fourteen Sabbaths, at five shillings each, total £3 10s." Absenting oneself from church in those days a somewhat expensive luxury. The Warren family was most creditably and prominently known in the colonial and state history of

Massachusetts, notwithstanding the eccentricities of their ancestor. Mr. John Child took a prominent part in the affairs of town and colony, and was chosen representative to the General Court of Massachusetts. He became the head of a large line of posterity, who have honored the name. By a nuncupative will, witnessed by his brother Richard and two others, he left to his eldest son, John, his "dwelling house with its lot of twelve acres, also some meadow lands," and "the reversion of all lands upon the little plains." His youngest son, Daniel, received his farm lands. Mr. Child died Oct. 15, 1676, æ. 40. Mrs. Child remarried; and d. May 12, 1734, æ. 83.

[Third Generation.] Children:

4733. i. MARY CHILD, b. Jan. 8, 1663.
4734. ii. JOHN CHILD, b. Apr. 25, 1669, m. Oct. 5, 1693, Hannah French.
4735. iii. ELIZA CHILD, b. July 24, 1670.
4736. iv. DANIEL CHILD, b. June 5, 1677, m. Jan. 29, 1702, Beriah Bemis.

[Third Generation.]

4734 ii. JOHN CHILD, eldest son of John Child, and eldest child of John and Mary Warren Child, b. in Watertown, Mass., April 25, 1669, m. Oct. 5, 1693, Hannah French, dau. of Capt. William French, who was the first representative of the town of Billerica, Mass., to the General Court in 1666. Mr. Child resided in the west precinct of Watertown, of which he was chosen, in 1721, one of the "committee to manage the prudentials." This precinct was, in 1730, incorporated a separate town, called Waltham, and he was of the committee chosen "to take effectual care that learning shall be advanced." He possessed property in Waltham and Weston. He d. in Waltham, 1743, æ. 73. Mrs. H. F. Child d. Jan. 2, 1766, æ. 90. Mr. Child had been a representative, like his father, in the General Court. His children were born in Watertown.

[Fourth Generation.] Children:

4737. i. JOHN CHILD, JR., b. Aug. 5, 1694, m. 1721, Abigail ——.
4738. ii. JONATHAN CHILD, b. April 26, 1696, m. Oct. 2, 1729, Abigail Parker.
4739. iii. SARAH CHILD, bap. Nov. 19, 1704.
4740. iv. ABIGAIL CHILD, bap. Nov. 4, 1705.
4741. v. ISAAC CHILD, bap. March 24, 1706, m. 1st, Dec. 7, 1727, Anna Adams; m. 2d, 1747, Hannah Goddin.
4742. vi. PRUDENCE CHILD, bap. July 16, 1708, m. Nov. 17, 1737, Allen Flagg.
4743. vii. LYDIA CHILD, bap. Oct. 7, 1711.
4744. viii. JONAS CHILD, bap. June 14, 1713.
4745. ix. RUTH CHILD, bap. Aug. 27, 1715, in Weston, Mass.
4746. x. MEHITABLE CHILD, b. Jan. 13, 1717.

[Fourth Generation.]

4738. ii. JONATHAN CHILD, second son and child of John and Hannah French Child, b. in Watertown, Mass., April 26, 1696, m. Oct. 1729, Abigail Parker, who was b. Sept. 9, 1711. Miss Parker is thought to be a descendant of Capt. James Parker, a noted citizen of Groton, Mass. Some notice of him is found in the history of that town by Butler. Mr. and Mrs. Child settled in Grafton, Worcester Co., Mass., where they reared a large family. Mrs. A. P. Child d. Mch. 3, 1756. The following quaint epitaph is upon the head stone now standing in one of the ancient cemeteries of Grafton, which marks the last resting place of Mr. Jonathan Child.*

> "Here lies buried the body of Mr. Jonathan Child,
> Who departed this life Sept. 8th, 1787, in the 92 year of his age.
> Behold and see as you pass by,
> As you are now so once was I,
> As I am now so you must be,
> Prepare for death and follow me."

[Fifth Generation.]   Children:

4747. i. JOSIAH CHILD, b. Oct. 17, 1730, m. April 24, 1755, Elizabeth Ball.

4748. ii. ABIGAIL CHILD, b. Aug. 28, 1732, in Grafton, Mass.

4749. iii. ELIZABETH CHILD, b. Oct. 28, 1735, in Grafton, Mass.

4750. iv. JONATHAN CHILD, JR., b. Feb. 14, 1738, m. April 16, 1767, Eunice Smith.

4751. v. RUTH CHILD, b. Oct. 2, 1740.

4752. vi. SOLOMON CHILD, b. Jan. 31, 1744, m. April 16, 1767, Martha Rice.

4753. vii. SARAH CHILD, b. Aug. 13, 1746.

4754. viii. JOSEPH CHILD, b. Jan. 29, 1753.

[Fifth Generation.]

4738. i. JOSIAH CHILD, eldest son and child of Jonathan and Abigail Parker Child, b. in Grafton, Mass., Oct. 17, 1730, m. April 24, 1755, Elizabeth Ball of Westboro, Mass. About 1760 Mr. and Mrs. Child removed to Upton, Mass., where he purchased a farm, and was ever after known as one of the substantial and reliable citizens, though not found much in public affairs. It may be with propriety mentioned here that part of the descendants of Mr. Josiah Child use the terminal "s" upon their name; it is found that in the later years of Mr. Child's life some records of business on the Upton town books have the "s," and a like statement may be made of his son Asa Child. A descendant of Mr. Asa Child, Mr. Walter Childs of

* We are indebted to the courtesies of Mr. A. A. Ballou of Grafton, Mass., and J. Wilmarth, M. D., of Upton, for our statistics in this line.

San Francisco, Cal., (who sends us the pleasing narratives in his line,) expresses the very earnest hope that "a return to the more correct and euphonious mode of spelling and speaking the name will not be delayed." Upon these venerated ancestors the blame rests, and between them we must divide the responsibility. Three of Mr. Child's children were born in Grafton, the others after his removal to Upton. Mrs. Elizabeth Ball Child d. Aug. 23, 1793, æ. 69. Mr. Josiah Child d. Oct. 14, 1806, æ. 76.

[Sixth Generation.] Children:

4755. i. ABIGAIL CHILD, b. in Grafton, Mass., May 3, 1756.

4756. ii. STEPHEN CHILD, b. in Grafton, Mass., Oct. 18, 1757.

4757. iii ELIZABETH CHILD, b. June 21, 1759, m. May 9, 1780, Joseph Potter.

4758. iv. JOHN CHILD, b. Feb. 3, 1765, m. Oct. 5, 1786, Lois Taft.

4759. v. ASA CHILD, b. June 19, 1767, m. 1st, Oct. 21, 1784, Rebekah Taft; m. 2d, June 1, 1799, Clarissa P. Ide.

4760. vi. JOSIAH CHILD, b. Feb 2, 1762

[Sixth Generation.]

4757. iii. ELIZARETH CHILD, second dau. and third child of Josiah and Elizabeth Ball Child, b. in Grafton, Mass., June 21, 1759, was published in banns of matrimony, April 5, 1780, m. May 9, 1780, to Joseph Potter of Upton, Mass.

[Seventh Generation.] Child:

4761. i. SARAH B. POTTER, b. Nov. 28, 1780.

[Sixth Generation.]

4758. iv. JOHN CHILD, second son and fourth child of Josiah and Elizabeth Ball Child, b. in Upton, Mass., Feb. 3, 1765, m. Oct. 5, 1786, Lois Taft. Mr. Child remained in his native place an honored citizen through life. He d. Feb. 18, 1837.

[Seventh Generation.] Children:

4762. i. JOEL CHILDS, b. Sept. 21, 1787, m. Nov. 17, 1806, Mehitable Flagg.

4763. ii. LEWIS CHILDS, b. July 23, 1789, d. Mch. 2, 1796, in Upton, Mass.

4764. iii. LEVINA CHILDS, b. Jan. 15, 1792, m. April 20, 1818, David Bachelor.

4765. iv. ELIJAH CHILDS, b Jan. 8, 1794, m. Dec. 19, 1818, Elizabeth Jenkins.

4766. v. LEWIS CHILDS, 2D, b. Dec. 9, 1796, d. Sept. 25, 1823.

4767. vi. SANFORD CHILDS, b. Mch. 9, 1801, m. Dec. 2, 1824, Harriet Le Sure. Sanford Childs d. July 22, 1875.

4768. vii. FISHER H. CHILDS, b. Mch. 2, 1803, m. May 12, 1823, Adaline Turner.

4769. viii. BETSEY CHILDS, b. Jan. 25, 1805, m. May 24, 1825, Hammon Torry.

4770. ix. JULIA CHILDS, b. July 1808, m. Jan. 1, 1829, Samuel S. Le Sure.

4771. x. JUDSON T. CHILDS, b. Aug. 21, 1811, m. Nov. 20, 1838, Hannah A. Taft.

[Seventh Generation.]

4762. i. JOEL CHILDS, eldest son and child of John and Lois Taft Child, b. in Upton, Mass., Sept. 21, 1787, m. Nov. 17, 1806, Mehitable Taft of Upton, Mass., where they resided.

[Eighth Generation.] Children:

4772. i. EMILIA C. CHILDS, b. Feb. 21, 1807.

4773. ii. CHANDLER F. CHILDS, b. in Upton, Mass., Sept. 22, 1808, m. Sept. 29, 1828, Louisa McFarland.

[Ninth Generation.] Children:

4774. i. ANN A. CHILDS, b. Nov. 10, 1829.

4775. ii. CHARLES E. CHILDS, b. Mch. 29, 1830, d. Dec. 21, 1831.

4776. iii. JOEL C. CHILDS, b. Nov. 5, 1831, d. May 19, 1838.

4777. iv. CHARLES W. CHILDS, b. Dec. 3, 1833.

4778. v. SARAH H. CHILDS, b. May 17, 1835, m. Jan. 30, 1853, Charles H. Chamberlain, and have several children, names not obtained.

4779. vi. ADELIZA F. CHILDS, b. April 21, 1837, d. July 1, 1846.

4780. vii. JANE D. CHILDS, b. July 29, 1838, m. John Q. A. Olney. Two children.

4781. viii. LUCY M. CHILDS, b. June 16, 1840, d. June 25, 1846.

4782. ix. GEORGE E. CHILDS, b. Nov. 19, 1842, m, Feb. 23, 1867, Lucy M. Aldrich. Have several children.

4783. x. LUCY A. CHILDS, b. 1853, m. July 15, 1870, Eldred H. Prentice. Two children.

[Seventh Generation.]

4764. iii. LEVINA CHILDS, eldest dau. and third child of John and Lois Taft Childs, b. in Upton, Mass., Jan. 15, 1792, m. April 20, 1818, David Bachelor of Upton.

[Eighth Generation.] Children:

4784. i. JOEL DEXTER BACHELOR, b. April 5, 1822, m. Sept. 23, 1843, Clarissa G. Saunders. One child.

4785 ii. DAVID FISK BATCHELOR, b. July 16, 1832, m. Nov. 21, 1866, Sarah Jane Taft. One child.

[Seventh Generation.]

4765. iv. ELIJAH CHILDS, third son and fourth child of John and Lois Taft Childs, b. in Upton, Mass., Jan. 8, 1794, m. Dec. 19, 1818, Elizabeth Jenkins.

[Eighth Generation.] Children:

4786. i. HARRIET CHILDS, b. Oct. 18, 1819.

4787. ii. OTIS CHILDS, b. Jan. 27, 1821.

[Seventh Generation.]

4768. vii. FISHER H. CHILDS, sixth son and seventh child of John and Lois Taft Childs, b. in Upton, Mass., Mch. 2, 1803, m May 12, 1823, Adaline Turner of Leicester, Mass. Mr. Childs d. Sept. 30, 1845.

[Eighth Generation.] Children:

4788. i. HORACE CHILDS, b. Sept. 19, 1823, d. June 17, 1826.

4789. ii. ALMON CHILDS, b. May 18, 1826, m. Oct. 17, 1847, Martha M. Fay.

4790. iii. JANE CHILDS, b. Dec. 11, 1830, m. Aug. 5, 1852, John Goulding.

[Eighth Generation.]

4789. ii. ALMON CHILDS, second son and child of Fisher H. and Adaline Turner Childs, b. in Upton, Mass., May 18, 1826, m. Oct. 17, 1847, Martha M. Fay of Grafton, Mass. Resides in Norwich, Ct. Engaged in straw bleaching.

[Ninth Generation.] Children:
4791. i. ANNA MARIA CHILDS, b. Aug. 13, 1850, d. Sept. 10, 1857.
4792. ii. IDA ESTELLA CHILDS, b. Mch. 1, 1853.
4793. iii. FRANK DEXTER CHILDS, b. June 2, 1857.

[Eighth Generation.]

4790. iii. JANE CHILDS, only dau. of Fisher H. and Adaline Turner Childs, b. in Upton, Mass., Dec. 11, 1830, m. Aug. 5, 1852, John Goulding.

[Ninth Generation.] Child:
4794. i. VICTOR GOULDING.

[Seventh Generation.]

4769. viii. BETSEY CHILDS, second dau. and eighth child of John and Lois Taft Childs, b. in Upton, Mass., Jan. 25, 1805, m. May 24, 1825, Hammon Torrey.

[Eighth Generation.] Children:
4795. i. ALMIRA TORREY.
4796. ii. LOUIS TORREY, m. Wakeman.
4797. iii. JANE TORREY, d. young.

[Seventh Generation.]

4770. ix. JULIA CHILDS, third dau. and ninth child of John and Lois Taft Childs, b. in Upton, Mass., July 1808, m. Jan. 1, 1829, Samuel G. Le Sure.

[Eighth Generation.] Children:
4798. i. SARAH M. LE SURE, b. Sept. 8, 1832, d. Nov. 17, 1865.
4799. ii. WILLIAM G. LE SURE, b. 1836, m. Dec. 3, 1863, Clara M. Bachelor.
4800. iii. AUGUSTINE F. LE SURE, b. Aug. 19, 1840, d. Oct. 19, 1859.
4801. iv. ORLANDO F. LE SURE, b. Oct. 1, 1845.

[Eighth Generation.]

4799. ii. WILLIAM G. LE SURE, second son and child of Julia Childs and Samuel G. Le Sure, b. in Upton, Mass., in 1836, m. Dec. 3, 1863, Clara M. Bachelor. Resides in Boston, Mass.

[Ninth Generation.] Children:
4802. i. WILLIE AUGUSTINE LE SURE, b. Dec. 7, 1868.
4803. ii. JENNIE MARION LE SURE, b. Dec. 9, 1870.
4804. iii. FLORENCE JULIA LE SURE, b. April 15, 1875.
4805. v. SARAH MINNIE LE SURE, b. Jan. 24, 1878, d. April 17, 1878.

[Seventh Generation.]

4771. x. JUDSON T. CHILDS, seventh son and youngest child of John and Lois Taft Childs, b. in Upton, Mass., Aug.

21, 1811, m. Nov. 20, 1838, Hannah A. Taft. Residence
Upton.

[Eighth Generation.] Children.

4806. i. BETSEY R. CHILDS, b. Jan. 29, 1840, m. Nov. 16, 1864, Edward
P. Hopkins.

4807. ii. ELLEN E. CHILDS, b. Nov. 11, 1841.

4808. iii. ANNA CHILDS, b. July 7, 1843, d. Oct. 23, 1843.

4809. iv. EDWIN CHILDS, b. Feb. 11, 1846, d. March 29, 1846.

4810. v. HENRY M. CHILDS, b. April 7, 1850.

4811. vi. MARY A. CHILDS, b Dec. 31, 1851.

4812. vii. FRANK L. CHILDS, b. May 21, 1858

[Eighth Generation.]

4806. i. BETSEY R. CHILDS, eldest child of Judson T. and
Hannah A. Taft Childs, b. in Upton, Mass., Jan. 29, 1840, m.
Nov. 16, 1864, Edward P. Hopkins of Northbridge.

[Ninth Generation.] Children:

4813. i. FRANK B. HOPKINS, b. May 16, 1869.

4814. ii. CHARLES G. HOPKINS, b. April 26, 1871, d. Sept. 1877.

[Sixth Generation.]

4759. v. Col. ASA CHILDS, third son and fifth child of
Josiah and Elizabeth Ball Child, b. in Upton, Mass., June 19,
1767, m. 1st, Oct. 21, 1784, Rebekah Taft; m. 2d, June 1,
1799, Mrs. Clarissa Partridge Ide. Mrs. R. T. Childs was the
dau of John Taft, Esq., town treasurer of Upton, and a neice
of Capt. Robt. Taft of the army of the Revolution. At the
time of his first marriage Col. Childs was about seventeen
years of age, his bride not fifteen. Mrs. R. T. Childs d. in
1798. A touch of romance attended the acquaintance with
the second wife. Some time before meeting her Col. Childs
dreamed one night that he was riding, and came in view of a
house which he felt impelled to enter, upon doing so he was
captivated by the sight of the woman he was to marry, and
then awoke. The vividness of the dream, which abode with
him some time, was fading, when renewed by a curious experience. Business called him to Norfolk Co.; he was riding
upon a road new to him, but was impressed by its strange
familiarity, for which he could not account until he saw before
him the house of his dream, which he determined at once to
verify. Dismounting he made easy pretext for entering, and
actually met with the fair lady of the vision, who was none
other than Mrs. Clarissa P. Ide. The attraction was mutual.
Mrs. Ide was the widow of Gregory Ide, and a descendant in
the fifth generation from William Partridge, one of the pro-

Col. ASA CHILD.
(From an oil Portrait.)

prietors of Medway, Mass., in 1650. Mrs. C. P. I. Childs was b. June 14, 1775.

Col. Childs' boyhood was ennobled and enriched by the thrilling events of the War of the Revolution. A lad of eight years, mounted upon a horse in his father's field, he was startled by the firing in the memorable Concord fight of April 19, 1775. Sept. 4, 1792, we find he was commissioned Ensign of the 2d Mass. Inf.; on Sept. 10, 1780, made Lieut.; and Captain Sept. 29, 1801. April 22, 1805, made Major, and further promoted Lieut. Col. and Commandant of the Regiment in 1809. His military service extending through the administrations of Governors Hancock, Adams, Sumner, Gill, Strong, Sullivan, Lincoln and Gore. A commission in the regular army, tendered him in recognition of his military ability, he was compelled to decline.

Col. Childs was a man of superior personal appearance, six feet one inch in height, finely proportioned, and of erect carriage. Social, affectionate, full of humor, and affable in manner, he readily made and retained friends. He was fond of fine horses, and appeared at his best when mounted; even in his eighty-first year he used to ride a spirited grey, and contests between rider and steed were said to have been exhibitions of rare horsemanship.

Col. Childs was early a successful business man, and before 1808 possessed a comfortable fortune; at that time he became security for a friend who was engaged in the manufacture of arms, under a government contract. The embargo of 1807 so raised the price of materials as to embarrass the friend, and lead to his failure. Col. Childs assumed the contract and completed it, though at the loss of almost his entire fortune. This unsettled him in home and business relations. For three years we find him seeking opportunity to retrieve his losses. For brief periods he was in Pawtucket and Providence, R. I., and in New York City. Unsatisfied with the openings for business, Col. Childs determined, in 1817, to go to the far West. In the summer of that year he went with his family to Buffalo, and thence to the upper waters of the Alleghany river. Here a flat boat was procured, laden with his household effects; and with his family he embarked, intending, if necessary, to go to the Mississippi to secure a home. Upon reaching Pittsburgh, Pa., the illness of one of the children compelled them to stop for medical aid. The boat was anchored opposite the Alleghany arsenal, whose commandant, Major Abram R. Wooley, proved a very true friend. Stone buildings were in process of erection at the arsenal, and Major Wooley offered Col. Childs the superintendency of the government quarries. This position was gladly accepted, and proved the turning of the tide of misfortunes. For two years Col. Childs retained this post under Major Wooley. Subsequently he leased a large farm in the suburbs of Birmingham, but left it for more lucrative business in Pittsburgh, in 1822. Here, through the success of his sons, he was again in the enjoyment of an easy competence, and his later years were passed in the love and honor of his posterity, and the respect of his fellow-citizens. On Nov. 4, 1849, his cherished wife was called suddenly to the heavenly home, after a loving companionship of half a century. So great was the bereavement Col. Childs could not support it, and about two months later, Jan. 9, 1850, they were reunited.

[Seventh Generation.] Children:

4815. i. DANIEL CHILDS, b. March 13, 1785, m. May 24, 1807, Anna Wood.

4816. ii. BETSEY CHILDS, b. Jan. 14, 1787, d. May 4, 1796.

4817. iii. OTIS CHILDS, b. Jan. 16, 1789.

4818. iv. JONATHAN CHILDS, b. Dec. 29, 1790.

4819. v. LUCRETIA CHILDS, b. Oct. 14, 1792.

4820. vi. WILLARD CHILDS, b. Oct. 4, 1794.

4821. vii. NATHANIEL CHILDS, b. Aug. 22, 1798.

4822. viii. AUSTIN CHILDS, b. Jan. 1, 1800.

4823. ix. HARVEY CHILDS, b. March 10, 1802, m. Jan. 5, 1829, Miss Jane Bailey Lowrie.

4824. x. ASA PARTRIDGE CHILDS, b. Dec. 13, 1804, m. 1st, Sept. 4, 1827, Frances C. Bradley: m. 2d, Jan. 3, 1851, Martha Howard.

4825. xi. LYMAN CHILDS, b. July 14, 1809, m. June 13, 1838, Anne Lougher.

4826. xii. EDSON CHILDS, b. 1811, d. in three months.

4827. xiii. CHARLES CHILDS, b. Dec. 1816, d. in Pittsburg, Pa., Dec. 20, 1820.

[We very much regret that of the first eight children of Col. Asa Childs, we have no record but the date of birth, with the exception of the following brief data of the eldest child:]

[Seventh Generation.]

4815. i. DANIEL CHILDS, eldest son and child of Col. Asa and Rebekah Taft Child, b. in Upton, Mass., March 13, 1785, m. May 24, 1807, Anna Wood. Mr. Daniel Childs d. in Upton, Mass., April 21, 1825.*

* For much data in this line we are indebted to Jerome Wilmarth, M. D., of Upton, Mass.

[Eighth Generation.] Child:

4828. i. ANNA CHILDS, b. in Upton, Mass., d. Aug. 21, 1837.

[Seventh Generation.]

4823. ix. HARVEY CHILDS, ninth child of Col. Asa and second child and son of Col. Asa and Clarissa P. Childs, b. in Upton, Mass., Mch. 10, 1802, m. Jan. 5, 1829, Jane Bailey Lowrie, eldest dau. of Hon. Mathew B. Lowrie of Pittsburgh, Pa. The losses sustained by Col. Asa Childs from 1808 to 1814, made it possible for him to furnish his sons, Harvey and Asa P., with but little pecuniary capital for their start in life : this proved but a temporary disadvantage. Possessed of winning social qualities, and trained to regard honor and honesty first, and success as secondary in the life race, these young men were not long in gaining friends and the confidence of the growing community which had become their home. Devotedly attached to each other, their intercourse was ever characterised by a courtesy which was the rivet in the loving kindness of their daily lives, as charming to witness as it was rare : indeed this harmony and trust contributed in no small degree to the success attending the various enterprises in which they were interested.

The brothers began business in Pittsburgh as boot and shoe merchants, in 1826. Their near neighbor, Mr. John Albree of Boston, (who married a daughter of Stephen Child, Esq. of Boston—recorded on page 282,) came to Pittsburgh in 1817, and established the first wholesale boot and shoe house west of the Allegheny Mountains. In 1830, Mr. Albree, who had closely observed the young Childs' firm, extended the compliment of an offer of partnership to the elder brother, Mr. Harvey Childs. In 1831, Mr. Childs, with Mr. Albree, began a business career noted for sterling integrity and prosperous development. This was before the days of railways, and tranfers of commodities from the east were made by "Conestoga wagons," over the now almost forgotten national road. The firm enjoyed for several years the monopoly of their specialty, and did a large and profitable business. Mr. Childs made frequent trips by stage to Boston, to purchase goods, and frequently obliged the Pittsburgh banks by carrying their eastern remittances, concealed within his personal baggage. In 1841, Mr. Albree, having amassed a fortune, returned to Boston. Mr. Harvey and Mr. Asa P.

Childs formed a new partnership which continued until the failing health of Mr. A. P. Childs, in 1860, led to his withdrawal from business. Mr. Harvey Childs remained at the head of the house sixteen years longer, leaving then his son, Harvey Childs, Jr., to continue the well established house. Fifty years of active business life, in which Mr. Childs held many positions of honor and trust, closely identified with many of the prominent industries which have developed the resources of western Pennsylvania. In 1836, the Exchange Bank was founded (now the wealthiest corporation of its kind in the city). Mr. Childs was elected a director. In 1847, he was elected trustee of the Western Theological Seminary, and in 1863, to the same office in the Western University. He was a director of the Allegheny Insurance Co., at its organization in 1859, an incorporator of the Real Estate Savings Bank ; holding all of these positions until his death, in some cases forty years. He was a founder and manager of the Penn. Cotton Mill, Pearl Flouring Mill, Wampum Iron Furnace, Hope Cotton Mills and Union Woolen Mills, all large manufactories. With all these enterprises, demanding each more or less of personal attention, it will be seen that Mr. Childs was both a man of business and a busy man. Yet there was no fact regarding his character more striking than that he never allowed business to become the master. He was never too busy to be polite, though the interruption came from a beggar. His reputation as a benevolent and public-spirited man, arose from a truer source than mere external generosity of purse and time ; only those conversant with his daily life can estimate the amount of self-sacrifice cheerfully rendered to all who were unfortunate. His ready sympathy and geniality endeared him especially to young men, and enabled him to exercise over them a most beneficent influence. He regarded a thorough education, combined with honorable principles, the noblest and surest endowment, and to his children secured the choicest advantages. Mr. Harvey Childs died at "Shadyside," Pittsburgh, Pa., May 17, 1876. Expressions, both public and private, of regret and respect, were numerous in the city where he was so much beloved, and with whose interests he had been identified for half a century ; during which time he never failed to meet an obligation, nor abused a trust reposed in him. A prominent Pittsburgh journal briefly expressed the general sentiment :

"In all his personal intercourse, a charming amenity was ever observed. Millions of values have passed through his hands, and his name has never been tarnished by a doubt of his high-toned, sterling integrity. No man of his day was more truthful and conscientious in every word and deed."

[Eighth Generation.] Children:

4829. i. LOWRIE CHILDS, b. April 24, 1830, m. Dec. 2, 1851, Margaret Louise Lightner.

4830. ii. CHARLES HENRY CHILDS, b. Jan. 14, 1832, d. in infancy.

4831. iii. JAMES HARVEY CHILDS, b. July 4, 1834, m July 14, 1857, Mary Howard Howe.

4832. iv. EMMA CHILDS, b. Nov. 7, 1837, d. Oct. 1, 1868.

4833. v. ALBERT HENRY CHILDS, b. Nov. 29, 1839, m. Oct. 6, 1864, Nannie McD. Price.

4834. vi. CLARA COURTNEY CHILDS, b. June 8, 1842, m. June 7, 1866, Oliver McClintock.

4835. vii. WALTER CAMERON CHILDS, b. Oct. 28, 1845, m. Oct. 5, 1879, Edith Worcester Smith.

4836. viii. HARVEY CHILDS, JR., b. Feb. 20, 1848, m. Feb. 1, 1872, Mary Zug.

[Eighth Generation.]

4829. i. LOWRIE CHILDS, eldest child of Harvey and Jane Lowrie Childs, b. in Pittsburgh, Pa., April 24, 1830, m. Dec. 2, 1851, Margaret Louise Lightner, eldest dau. of John Lightner, Esq. Mr. Childs graduated at the Western University, and entered at once upon the study of the law. Is now in the practice of his profession : residing in Topeka, Kan.

[Ninth Generation.] Children:

4837. i. HARVEY LIGHTNER CHILDS, b. Sept. 3, 1852.

4838. ii. HENRY KING CHILDS, b. Dec. 25, 1858.

4839. iii. EMMA LOWRIE CHILDS, b. Aug. 31, 1862.

4840. iv. ALBERT COOLIDGE CHILDS, b. Sept. 9, 1868.

[Eighth Generation.]

4831 iii. Col. JAMES HARVEY CHILDS, third son and child of Harvey and Jane B. Lowrie Childs, b. in Pittsburgh, Pa., July 4, 1834, m. July 14, 1857, Mary Howard Howe, eldest dau. of Hon. Thomas M. Howe of Pittsburgh.

Six feet in height, Col. Childs' distinguished personnel, combined with a manly grace and frank sociability, won for him quick confidence and esteem from every rank in life. Graduating from Miami College, Oxford, Ohio, with the class of 1852, he spent the succeeding year with the corps of engineers in surveying the route of the Pittsburgh and Connellsville railway. Col. Childs soon after entered regular business life, becoming a partner in a large manufacturing establishment. The breaking out of war, in 1861, found him enrolled with the

first to respond to the call for troops, in the 12th Regt., Penna.
Volunteers. During the three months' service he was first
lieutenant of the "City Guard" Co. of Pittsburgh. Upon the
disbandment of the 12th Regiment, though surrounded by every
home allurement, Col. Childs quickly arranged his affairs for an
indefinite absence; quietly saying to his family that "a man's
first duty is to his country, and that no alternative presented
itself to him but to remain in the field until relieved by death
or the close of the war." On Oct. 18, 1861, he was again mustered into service as Lieut. Col. of the 4th Penna. Cavalry, and
at once joined his regiment. His soldierly bearing and personal qualities soon won the admiration and respect of his
comrades, and he was presented with a sash, belt and sabre of
fine workmanship, accompanied with a complimentary letter
from the officers of the regiment. While encamped near
Washington, D. C., Col. Childs was appointed provost marshal
of Georgetown, a post demanding tact and executive ability,
which he clearly displayed. At the unanimous request of the
regiment, he was, on March 12, 1862, promoted to the
Colonelcy. Wearied with the tedium of an encampment, Col.
Childs sought service near Richmond where conflict was daily
expected, and rejoiced when the summons came to proceed to
the Peninsula. Upon arriving he was ordered with the Pennsylvania Reserves to the front, and took position the night
before the series of terrible struggles known as the "seven
days battles." An incident of the first day is worthy of note,
as it established his reputation for cool judgment. His regiment, and the 5th Regt., Cav., were ordered to fall back from
a charge upon the enemy's infantry, who were found impreg-
nably entrenched against cavalry. The regulars left the field
at a trot; Col. Childs to the surprise of the division forced his
men to leave at a walk. When asked his reason, he replied it
might do to trot off a regiment accustomed to fire, but such an
experiment tried on untested troops like his would result in
the trot becoming a gallop, and the gallop a stampede, and he
did not propose to have his men run from the first fire. A
few days later his undaunted firmness saved his command
from disastrous route. Did the limits of our book permit
many other characteristic deeds could be related of him. By
the illness of Gen. Averill, to whose brigade the 4th Penna.

Cav. was attached, Col. Childs came into command, and was ordered by Gen. McClellan to pursue the flying column of the enemy's cavalry. Returning from the pursuit on the day of the battle of South Mountain, the brigade advanced to the Antietam river. The following morning, Sept. 17, 1862, was fought the sanguinary battle of Antietam. Col. Childs, while leading his brigade under a heavy fire, was struck in the thigh by a solid shot and hurled from his horse. Recognizing the fatal nature of the wound, he dispatched an aid to Gen. Pleasanton to tell him that he was dying, gave other needed official orders, then turning to his adjutant and personal friend, Capt. King of Pittsburg, confided to him his farewell messages of love to his wife and family. To his little son, Howe, he sent his watch and said, "Tell him to be a good boy and a useful man, and true to his country." A few minutes later death released him from all pain. He was, said Lieut. Hughes. "All that we could desire as an officer and a gentleman; a braver man never lived, and never braver died." The death of Col. Childs awakened deep feeling in his native city. From one of the many tributes to his memory in the city press, we quote:

"We have already announced the death of this brave young officer on the bloody field of the Potomac. From the very beginning of the war he has been a devoted soldier of the republic. Surrounded by all that makes life pleasant, wealth, social ties of the most sacred character, in the prime of manhood and usefulness, he left all to fight for the constitution of his country and restoration of the Union. He went into the field a true soldier. Modest and unassuming, he went to fight in what ever position he might be placed. He sought no notoriety. His aim was to do his duty to his fellow-men, his country and his God. He has left a glorious name, one of which his children will be proud, and has died the death of a soldier."

Born on the anniversary of our national independence, he closed his short noble life on the anniversary day of the adoption of the federal constitution.

[Ninth Generation.] Children:

4841. i. THOMAS HOWE CHILDS, b. May 21, 1858.

4842. ii. MARY ROBINSON CHILDS, b. Oct. 28, 1859.

4843. iii. JEANIE LOWRIE CHILDS, b. July 30, 1861.

[Eighth Generation.]

4833. v. ALBERT HENRY CHILDS, fourth son of Harvey and Jane B. Lowrie Childs, b. in Pittsburgh, Pa., Nov. 29, 1839, m. Oct. 6, 1864, Nannie McDowell Price, dau. of Judge J. W. Price of Hillsboro, Highland Co., Ohio. Mr. Childs is an iron merchant. Resides in Pittsburgh, Pa.

[Ninth Generation.] Children:
    4844. i. STARLING WINSTON CHILDS, b. Mch. 25, 1870.
    4845. ii. CLARA COURTNEY CHILDS, b. Sept. 13, 1872.
    4846. iii. JENNIE LOWRIE CHILDS, b. Nov. 27, 1876.

[Eighth Generation.]

    4834. vi. CLARA COURTNEY CHILDS, second dau. and sixth child of Harvey and Jane B. Lowrie Childs, b. in Pittsburgh, Pa., June 28, 1842. m. June 7, 1866, Oliver McClintock, eldest son of Washington McClintock, Esq., of Pennsylvania.
[Ninth Generation.] Children:
    4847. i. NORMAN McCLINTOCK, b. June 13, 1868.
    4848. ii. WALTER McCLINTOCK, b. April 15, 1870.
    4849. iii. EMMA McCLINTOCK, b. Sept. 25, 1874.

[Eighth Generation.]

    4835. vii. WALTER CAMERON CHILDS, fifth son of Harvey and Jane B. Lowrie Childs, b. in Pittsburgh, Pa., Oct. 28, 1845, m. Oct. 5, 1879, Edith Worcester Smith, dau. of Willard Smith, Esq., of San Francisco, Cal. Mr. Childs is a graduate of Yale College, and now president of the Yuma Mill and Mining Co. of San Francisco, and at present a resident of California. [To Mr. Childs we are indebted for the sketches of his grandfather, father and others of his family, and for most of the material of the Lowrie family.*]
[Ninth Generation.] Child:
    4850. i. BEATRICE WALTON CHILDS, b. July 31, 1880. in Pittsburgh, Pa.

[Eighth Generation.]

    4836. viii. HARVEY CHILDS, JR., youngest child of Harvey and Jane B. Lowrie Childs, b. in Pittsburgh, Pa., Feb. 20, 1848, m. Feb. 1, 1872, Mary Zug, dau. of Christopher Zug, Esq., of Pittsburgh. Mr. Childs is a wholesale shoe dealer, having inherited the business of his father, in Pittsburgh, Pa.
[Ninth Generation.] Children:
    4851. i. JEANETTE LOWRIE CHILDS, b. Feb. 15, 1874.
    4852. ii. JAMES HAROLD CHILDS. b. July 5, 1878.

[Seventh Generation.]

    4824. x. ASA PARTRIDGE CHILDS, tenth child of Col. Asa, and third son and child of Col. Asa and Clarissa Partridge Childs, b. in Upton, Mass., Dec. 13, 1804, m. 1st, Sept. 4, 1827, Frances C. Bradley, dau. of Rev. Joshua Bradley of Randolph, Mass.; she was b. Mch. 16, 1808, and d. Mch. 17, 1848; m. 2d, Jan. 3, 1851, Martha Howard, who was b. Nov. 5, 1823.

*The sketches of the Lowrie family will be found in the appendix.

The full sketch of the elder brother, Mr. Harvey Childs, portrays the business careers of both ; therein, we find, urbanity of manner and strictest integrity to have been characteristic of each. Of the personal appearance, or individual peculiarities of Mr. A. P. Childs, we are not informed, but we learn that he was the father of a large family, and found in the later years of his life, enjoyment and ease in the society of his children, amid the refinements of his suburban residence, "Pennsylvan"; there he died May 11, 1878.

[Eighth Generation.] Children:

4853. i. OTIS BRADLEY CHILDS, b. Jan. 23, 1829, m. Jan. 8, 1856, Frances McCook.

4854. ii. CEPHAS AUGUSTUS CHILDS, b. Feb. 20, 1831, d. in infancy.

4855. iii. HARVEY GIFFORD CHILDS, b. July 28, 1833, d. Mch. 25, 1864.

4856. iv. CORNELIA CHILDS, b. Jan. 14, 1836, m. June 17, 1856, Jos. R. Hunter.

4857. v. WILLIAM RIDDLE CHILDS, b. Feb. 18, 1838, m. Mch. 31, 1864, Mary Acheson.

4858. vi. HELEN CHILDS, b. April 23, 1840, d. in infancy.

4859. vii. GEORGE ASA CHILDS, b. Mch. 23, 1842, d. May 17, 1864.

4860. viii. FANNIE CHILDS, b. April 6, 1844, m. Nov. 15, 1864, Edward P. Carpenter.

4861. ix. LYMAN BEECHER CHILDS, b. Nov. 20, 1847, m. Mch. 14, 1876, Annie Levy, dau. of J. P. Levy, Esq., of Philadelphia.

4862. x. HOWARD CHILDS, b. Feb. 7, 1852.

4863. xi. JENNIE CHILDS, b. Aug. 20, 1853, d. in infancy.

4864. xii. MARTHA HOWARD CHILDS, b. Jan. 15, 1855.

4865. xiii. ASA PARTRIDGE CHILDS, JR., b. Nov. 10, 1856.

4866. xiv. MARSHALL CHILDS, b. March 14, 1858.

4867. xv. ADELAIDE CHILDS, b. Dec. 16, 1859.

4868. xvi. JAMES ASA CHILDS, b. Aug. 4, 1865.

[Eighth Generation.]

4853. i. OTIS BRADLEY CHILDS, eldest child of Asa P. and Frances C. Bradley Childs, b. in Pittsburgh, Pa., Jan. 23, 1829, m. Jan. 8, 1856, Frances McCook, dau. of Dr. George McCook of Pittsburgh, and a cousin of the distinguished Generals McCook. Residence Pittsburgh, Pa.

[Ninth Generation.] Children:

4869. i. LIZZIE WALLACE CHILDS, b. Oct. 28, 1856

4870. ii. OTIS HART CHILDS, b. June 25, 1859.

[Eighth Generation.]

4856. iv. CORNELIA CHILDS, eldest dau. of Asa P. and Frances C. Bradley Childs, b. in Pittsburgh, Pa., Jan. 14, 1836, m. June 17, 1856, Jos. R. Hunter. Residence Pittsburgh, Pa.

M-1

[Ninth Generation.]   Children:

4871. i. FANNIE REBECCA HUNTER, b. April 26, 1857, m. Oct. 16, 1877, B. Gifford Bakenwell.

4872. ii. CORNELIA ELLA HUNTER, b. Oct. 14. 1866.

[Ninth Generation.]

4871. i. FANNIE REBECCA HUNTER. eldest child of Cornelia Childs and Jos. R. Hunter, b. in Pittsburg, Pa., April 26, 1857. m. Oct. 16, 1877, B. Gifford Bakenwell of Pittsburgh.

[Tenth Generation.]   Child:

4873. i. CORNELIA C. BAKENWELL, b. July 5, 1878.

[Eighth Generation.]

4857. v. Dr. WILLIAM RIDDLE CHILDS. fourth son of Asa P. and Frances C. Bradley Childs, b. in Pittsburgh, Pa., Feb. 18, 1838, m. March 31, 1864, Mary Acheson, dau. of Hon. Alexander W. Acheson of Washington. Pa. Mrs. Mary A. Childs d. May 8, 1877. Residence Pittsburgh, Pa.

[Ninth Generation.]   Children:

4874. i. JENNIE ACHESON CHILDS. b. Dec. 3. 1864.

4875. ii. ALEXANDER ACHESON CHILDS. b. Jan. 7. 1871.

4876. iii. HELEN CHILDS. b. May 14, 1873.

[Eighth Generation.]

4859. vii. Sergt. Major GEORGE ASA CHILDS. fifth son of Asa P. and Frances C. Bradley Childs, b. in Pittsburgh, Pa., March 23. 1842, d. from wounds received in battle May 17, 1864.

Securing his father's permission to enter the army at the age of twenty, he at once enlisted as a private in the 14th Penna. Cavalry. commanded by his friend, Col. Jas. A. Schoonmaker of Pittsburgh. From the interesting account given by Col. Schoonmaker, of the army career of Sergt. Major Childs, we extract the following:

"George enlisted July 3, 1863, while I was upon a short leave of absence at Pittsburgh, and the next day started with me for Beverly. W. Va. Upon reaching Grafton, news came that the enemy had attacked the Fourteenth, and my horse was in waiting. Here George first showed his pluck, by insisting upon accompanying me to the front, although the only available horse was unprovided with either saddle or bridle. These George improvised by means of a blanket and rope, and thus equipped he rode forty miles in half a day. On the 8th July, 1862, George was promoted to be sergeant major of the regiment, and assigned to headquarters for special duties. This appointment was fortunate, for George possessed brilliant qualifications for adjutant duty, while his gaiety and good-fellowship made him a universal favorite not only with the officers of the Fourteenth, but throughout the brigade.

"George participated in the 'Rocky Gap Raid,' but it was not until November 1st, at the fight of Droop Mountain, that he had an opportunity to take part in a general engagement, and I saw what was in him. The enemy was entrenched with artillery at the summit of a pass, and the obstructions rendered it necessary to dismount and fight our way on foot. The summit was carried by assault, and George's conspicuous gallantry on this occasion, won the admiration of the old soldiers, and satisfied all that he was a boy in years only. In December we were ordered upon the expedition known as Averell's Salem Raid, which was eminently successful, although the return was one of constant peril and much suffering. The weather was intensely cold. Streams easily forded in the advance were found swollen and full of ice. The horses were smooth shod and could not be ridden, and the men had to drag the cannons and ambulances. Many of the men reached Beverly half naked and crippled for life. Averell says in his report, 'My command has marched, climbed, slidden and swam 345 miles since the 8th, throughout this terrible retreat.' George was the life of us all at headquarters. No suffering could dishearten him, and he never failed in his duty. He took charge of the entire regimental records, carrying them in a haversack upon his back.

"On the 2d of April, 1864, the brigade again took the field. On the 10th of May we encountered Morgan, and the bloody battle of Cove Gap was fought. During the engagement I gave George a pressing dispatch to be conveyed to the general. He bowed in assent, and the next thing I saw of the boy, he was dashing straight across the field in the face of the enemy, who was advancing at short range. Averell, who had witnessed his coming with some anxiety, demanded why he had not made a détour to escape the balls, to which George, saluting, delivered the dispatch with 'Excuse me, general; but I thought a straight line was the shortest distance between the two points.' The adjutant and both staff orderlies had been shot down, and when George returned from the general, I assigned him to the position of adjutant. He was assisting me, with his accustomed dash and gallantry, to reform our line of battle, when he was shot in the right side, the bullet passing through the intestines and lodging just under the skin on the left side. Despite the wound, he straightened up upon his horse and wished to remain in action, but I directed an orderly to conduct him to the rear. The enemy's artillery coming up, decided the day against us, and in the retreat, which lasted all night, over mountain roads, George kept on his horse. The next day we were forced to bid him farewell in the enemy's country, for suffering and weakness at last conquered, and he could ride no further. All that could be done was to carry him into a neighboring farm-house, dress his wound and arrange to have a doctor called from the nearest town. We offered to leave a soldier to take care of him, but this he refused, saying that any one remaining would be exposed to capture. We were compelled to leave him, and he never returned to receive the commission so well earned, as death ensued about a month later."

From a northern lady, a Miss Delano, who was living at Mechanicsburg and who showed the wounded soldier much kindness, his family afterwards learned that Sergt. Major Childs was rallying, with a fair prospect of recovery, when a band of guerrillas came to the house and subjected him to the most brutal treatment, robbing him of money and everything of

value, even to his clothing and threatening to hang him. They finally left
him so nearly dead that a relapse ensued, and he expired the following day.

"As an adjutant," says Col. Schoonmaker, 'I have never known his
superior. His dispatches, written in the midst of action, were models of
terseness and comprehensiveness. Perfectly cool in every emergency I
never knew him to manifest the slightest fear, nor lose the habitual courtesy of his demeanor."

[Eighth Generation.]

4860. viii. FANNIE CHILDS, third dau. of Asa P. and
Frances C. Bradley Childs, b. in Pittsburgh, Pa., April 6, 1844,
m. Nov. 15, 1864, Edward P. Carpenter of Connecticut.

[Ninth Generation.] Children:

4877. i. HERBERT BANCROFT CARPENTER.
4878. ii. EDWARD PAYSON CARPENTER.
4879. iii ANNIE CHILDS CARPENTER.

[Fifth Generation.]

4752. vi. SOLOMON CHILD, third son and sixth child of
Jonathan and Abigail Parker Child, b. in Grafton, Mass., Jan.
31, 1744, m. April 16, 1767, Martha Rice of Westboro, Mass.

Animated by the restless spirit and tireless energy which
makes the best pioneer material, he could not content him to
remain in the Massachusetts colony, then becoming an old
community as it had always been a staid one, but found his
way into the "Granite State" and settled in the hill country, so
thickly wooded, of Henniker, Merrimac Co. The first emigrants
to this State were largely from the north of Ireland, transplanted Scotch, sent there from Scotland to leaven the Roman Cath-
olicism of the Emerald Isle, failing which, they found sweet
refuge in the wilds of this mountainous region, whose scenery
and climate were akin to their loved Scotia. In a community
thus penetrated with the sincere piety, sterling sense, and physical vigor for which the Scots are eminent, Mr. Child found a
congenial home. Mrs. Martha Rice Child d. in Henniker, Aug.
20, 1804, aged 56 years. Mr. Solomon Child m. 2d, Mrs. Sarah
Goodell Ward of Henniker, widow of Capt. Josiah Ward of
that town, and dau. of Nathan and Persis Whitney Goodell of
Marlborough, Mass. Mr. S. Child d. Feb. 1826, aged 84 years,
leaving quite a family to honor his memory and emulate his
virtues.

[Sixth Generation.] Children:

4880. i. ELIJAH CHILD, b. Oct. 10, 1768, in Grafton, Mass.
4881. ii. ELIZABETH CHILD, b. June 6, 1769, d. June 2, 1777.
4882. iii. MOSES CHILD, b. Sept. 10, 1772, d. Oct. 14, 1775.

4883. iv. MARTHA CHILD, b. April 5, 1773, d. Dec. 20, 1774.

4884. v. AARON CHILD, b. Mch. 4, 1774, m. 1st, Sally Joslyn; m. 2d, Lucy Ward.

4885. vi. MARTHA CHILD, 2d, b. Nov. 2, 1777, m. Mch. 1, 1803, William Heaton.

4886. vii. SOLOMON CHILD, JR., b. July 30, 1782, m. Sept. 21, 1806, Mary Long of Hopkinton, N. H. She d. Feb. 13, 1823; he m. 2d, in 1824, Lucinda Child of Vt.

4887. viii. JOSIAH CHILD, b. Oct. 11, 1784, m. 1805, Abigail Ward.

4888 ix. LUCY CHILD, b. Aug. 19, 1787, d. Dec. 10, 1789 in Henniker, N. H.

4889. x. SALLY CHILD, b. Aug. 5, 1792, m. James Heaton of Thetford, Vt. Mr. Heaton d. Nov. 17, 1857. Mrs. Heaton d. Aug. 23, 1858.

[Sixth Generation.]

4884. v. DEACON AARON CHILD, third son and fifth child of Solomon and Martha Rice Child, b. in Henniker, N. H., Mch. 4, 1774, m. 1st, abt. 1790, Sally Joslyn; m. 2d, abt. 1799, Lucy Ward. Mr. Child resided in Henniker during his early manhood, and until after his second marriage, when he removed to Livonia, Livingston, Co., New York. Mrs. Sally Joslyn Child had two children, but one survived her, her death occurring on the 29th April, 1798. Dea. Child was a man of sound judgment and earnest piety ; he died in Indiana, whither he had removed with his son, Rev. Ward Child.

[Seventh Generation.] Children:

4890. i LUCY CHILD, b. abt. 1792, d. young.

4891. ii. JAMES CHILD, b. abt. 1795, m. 1825, Hannah Hildreth.

4892. iii. WARD CHILD, b. Oct. 31, 1800, m. 1823, Martha Stevenson.

4893. iv. MARTHA CHILD, b. Dec. 17, 1802, m. Nov. 3, 1819, Oliver Parsons.

4894. v. LUCY CHILD, b. Feb. 2, 1805, m. 1828, Rev. Joel Goodell.

4895. vi. WILLIAM H. CHILD, b. April 1, 1807, m. 1st, April 15, 1828, Laura Amsden; m. 2d, Sept. 13, 1865, Mrs. Elizabeth Blake.

4896. vii. JULIA A. CHILD, b Dec. 3, 1810, d. at the age of 14.

4897. viii. ASA B. CHILD, b. Mch. 8, 1815, of whom the brother, William H. Child, writes: "This youngest son of my father's family died at Oberlin College, Ohio, aged about twenty two years, while preparing to be a missionary of the foreign field, to which service he had consecrated himself. He lived a beautiful christian life, and died a most triumphant death."

[Seventh Generation.]

4891. ii. JAMES CHILD, eldest son and second child of Dea. Aaron and Sally Joslyn Child, b. in Henniker, N. H., about 1795, m. 1825, Hannah Hildreth, dau. of Abijah and Hannah Hildreth. Mr. James Child d. April 27, 1858. Mr. James Child was an ingenious and skillful mechanic, the inventor and patentee of one of the first if not the first cooking-stove ever manufactured in the State of New Hampshire. The date of his receiving the patent-right was about 1832. His only surviving son writes: "Among my earliest recollections is learning to read my father's name upon our kitchen stove." An inheritance of the genuine spirit of loyalty cannot be unexpected in these children, nor can we marvel that one of them should be willing to lay down his life for his country. Mrs. Hannah Hildreth Child was the daughter of a revolutionary soldier, who was wounded in the battle of Bunker's Hill, and preserved from capture by the British, through the fidelity of a brave comrade, who lifted him upon his back and bore him from the field, when the Americans retreated. The oft repeated stories of the adventures of those trying days, were the solace of many a winters' night to the eager children.

[Eighth Generation.] Children:

4898. i. ELZINA CHILD, b. June 23, 1826, m. Nov. 29, 1845, Dr. Henry Wheeler of Royalton, Vt. Reside in Manchester, N. H.

4899. ii. JAMES NEWTON CHILD, b. 1828, d. Dec. 22, 1837.

4900. iii. WILLIAM FRANKLIN CHILD, b. Jan. 24, 1831, m. May 11, 1853, Julia E. Fisher, dau. of Joshua and Minerva Fisher of Asscott Township, Prov. of Quebec.

4901. iv. ELSIE JANE CHILD, b. July 3, 1833, m. Nov. 26, 1853, Charles Dyer, who was b. in Holyoke, Mass., and d. in Sherbrooke, Prov. of Quebec, Mch. 26, 1867.

4902. v. HORACE JOSLYN CHILD, b. April 12, 1835, d. June 23, 1839.

4903. vi. JASON CHILD, b. Nov. 7, 1839, m. Feb. 25, 1864, Hattie A. Fitz of Chester, New Hampshire. Mr. Child entered the United States service in the recent war, was captured by the opposing forces in June, 1864, while with the army under General Wilson, in a raid upon the Welden Railway, and died from exposure in a southern prison. He was corporal of Co. K., 1st New Hampshire Cavalry. With others he was removed from Andersonville to Florence, South Carolina, to be exchanged, too late to save his ebbing life. He died in Florence, South Carolina, on the 3d of December, 1864, three days after reaching there.

[Seventh Generation.]

4892. iii. REV. WARD CHILD, eldest son of Dea. Aaron and his second wife, Lucy Ward Child, b. in Henniker, N. H., Oct. 31, 1800, m. in 1823, Martha Stevenson of Canandaigua, Ontario Co., New York, who was b. April 10, 1801. Rev. Mr. Ward Child d. Dec. 1855, at Chagrin Falls, Ohio. Mrs. Martha S. Child d. Dec. 1875, in Selma, Ohio. Mr. Child's life was one of many changes. His ministry an earnest and laborious one. His temperament such that he was sensitive to those trials peculiar to the ministerial life. His first settlement was at Onondaga Hill, New York; he removed speedily to the State of Ohio, and had settlements in one or two places in the "Western Reserve." His health after some years requiring release from the sedentary habit of his profession, Mr. Child settled upon a farm in Strykersville, Wyoming Co., New York, but he did not entirely relinquish preaching. Returning to the Western Reserve he there closed his most active and useful life.

[Eighth Generation.] Children:

4904. i. JAMES EUGENE CHILD, b. 1824, d. in infancy.

4905. ii. JAMES EUGENE CHILD, 2b, b. July 1, 1825, in Lockport, N.Y., m. Mary Kirkpatrick of Geneva, Kanzas, where both died in 1870.

4906 iii. JULIA LOUISE CHILD, b. Oct. 23, 1828, m. April 1853, M. P. Ozanne.

4907. iv. NEWELL WARD CHILD, b. Nov. 18, 1830, in Morgan, Ohio. Resides, unmarried, at Des. Moines, Iowa.

4908. v. EDWIN WILLIAM CHILD, b. June 18, 1832, m. July 6, 1860, Helen S. Force.

4909. vi EMMA S. CHILD, b. Feb. 24, 1834, unm. Resides in Cleveland, Ohio.

4910. vii. MARTHA W. CHILD, b. Sept. 20, 1835, m. Isaac G. Thorne; lives in Selma, Ohio.

[Eighth Generation.]

4906. iii. JULIA LOUISE CHILD, third child and eldest dau. of Rev. Ward and Martha Stevenson Child, b. at Onondaga Hill, N. Y., Oct. 23, 1828, m. April 1853, M. P. Ozanne. Resides in Cleveland, Ohio.

[Ninth Generation.] Children:

4911. i. FLORENCE LOUISE OZANNE, b. Oct. 13, 1855, in Chagrin Falls, Ohio.

4912. ii. CHARLES EUGENE OZANNE, b. April 14, 1865, in Cleveland, Ohio.

4913. iii. Infant daughter (unchristened), b. Sept. 12, 1870, d. same day in Cleveland, Ohio.

[Eighth Generation.]

4908. v. REV. EDWIN WILLIAM CHILDS, fifth child and fourth son of Rev. Ward and Martha Stevenson Child, b. at Morgan, Ohio, June 18, 1832, m. July 6, 1860, Helen S. Force. Rev. E. W. Childs is a clergyman of the Presbyterian church, now settled in Jonesville, Hillsdale Co., Michigan.

[Ninth Generation.] Children:

4914. i. MARY LOUISE CHILDS, b. Nov. 13, 1863.

4915. ii. LIZZIE B. CHILDS, b. Mch. 10, 1868.

4916. iii. EDDIE P. CHILDS, b. April 15, 1870.

[Eighth Generation.]

4910. vii. MARTHA WARD CHILD, seventh child and third dau. of Rev. Ward and Martha Stevenson Child, b. in Warsaw, N. Y., Sept. 20, 1835, m. Aug. 21, 1865, Isaac G. Thorne, and resides in Selma, Clark Co., Ohio.

[Ninth Generation.] Children:

4917. i. ISABEL EMMA THORNE, b. April 19, 1867.

4918. ii. BERTHA CHILDS THORNE, b. Nov. 12, 1870.

[Seventh Generation.]

4893. iv. MARTHA CHILD, eldest dau. and fourth child of Dea Aaron and Lucy Ward Child, b. in Livonia, Livingston Co., N. Y., Dec. 17, 1802, m. Nov. 3, 1819, Dea. Oliver Parsons, at Lewiston, Niagara Co., N. Y. Mrs. Martha Child Parsons d. at Winnebago, Wisconsin, Jan. 20, 1878.

[Eighth Generation.] Children.

4919. i. HARRIET MATILDA PARSONS, b. Sept. 21, 1821, m. Oct. 14, 1841, Charles S. Moss.

4920. ii. MARIA LOUISE PARSONS, d. in infancy.

4921. iii. WILLIAM GOODELL PARSONS, b. Jan. 7, 1825, m. Oct. 28, 1857, Hannah D. Conover.

4922. iv. EDWIN CHARLES PARSONS, b. July 1827, d. July 1831, at Lockport, N. Y.

4923. v. JULIA ANN PARSONS, b. Jan. 29, 1831.

4924. vi. LUCY PARSONS, d. in infancy, in Lockport, N. Y.

4925 vii. EDWIN BURTON PARSONS, b. Feb. 16, 1836, m. Dec. 31, 1864, Abbie L. Fay.

4926. viii. OLIVER MORRIS PARSONS, b. Aug. 19, 1840, was lost on Lake Michigan, by the "Lady Elgin" disaster, Sept. 8, 1860.

4927. ix. MARY EMMA PARSONS, b. Mch. 31, 1846, m. Sept. 26, 1865, Rev. M. S. Crosswell. Rev. and Mrs. Crosswell resided for a while in California, since in Amboy, Lee Co. Ill. Rev. Mr. Crosswell is a Congregational clergyman.

[Eighth Generation.]

4919. i. HARRIET MATILDA PARSONS, eldest dau. of Martha Child and Dea. Oliver Parsons, b. in Lockport, N.Y., Sept. 21, 1821, m. Oct. 14, 1841, Mr. Charles S. Moss. Mr. and Mrs Moss had five children. Mrs. Moss d. in Lockport, April 5, 1855.

[Ninth Generation.] Children:

4928. i. WILLIAM MOSS, d. in infancy.

4929. ii. CHARLES MOSS, d. in infancy.

[Three other children whose names are not obtained.]

[Eighth Generation.]

4921. iii. WILLIAM GOODELL PARSONS, eldest son and third child of Martha Child and Dea. Oliver Parsons, b. in Lockport, N. Y., Jan. 7, 1825, m. Oct. 28, 1857, Miss Hannah D. Conover. Resides in Milwaukee, Wisconsin.

[Ninth Generation.] Children:

4930. i. WILLIAM CONOVER PARSONS, b. Nov. 17, 1869.

4931. ii. CHARLES MORRIS PARSONS, b. Nov. 22, 1871.

4932. iii. MARY LA MYRA PARSONS, b. July 4, 1877.

[Eighth Generation.]

4925. vii. CAPT. EDWIN BURTON PARSONS, third son and seventh child of Martha Child and Dea. Oliver Parsons, b. in

Lockport, N. Y., Feb. 16, 1836, m. Dec. 31, 1864, Miss Abbie L. Fay. Capt. Edwin and Mrs. Parsons reside in Milwaukee, Wisconsin.

[Ninth Generation.] Children:

4933. i. ABBIE FAY PARSONS, b. Sept. 23, 1867.
4934. ii. ALICE GERTRUDE PARSONS, b. May 24, 1869.
4935. iii. OLIVER EDWIN PARSONS, b. Nov. 8, 1877.

[Seventh Generation.]

4894. v. LUCY CHILD, second dau. and fifth child of Dea. Aaron and Lucy Ward Child, b. Feb. 2, 1805, in Livonia, N. Y., m. Rev. Joel Goodell. Rev. Mr. and Mrs. Goodell early entered upon the Home Mission work. In 1829, Mrs. Goodell "finished her course," received the "Well done, good and faithful servant," and entered into "rest," leaving one little infant who so soon followed her that together they await the Resurrection morn.

[Seventh Generation.]

4895. vi. WILLIAM H. CHILDS, second son of Dea. Aaron and Lucy Ward Child, b. in Livonia, Livingston Co., N. Y., April 1, 1807, m. 1st, April 15, 1828, Miss Laura Amsden of Phelps, Ontario Co., N. Y.; m. 2d, Sept. 13, 1865, Mrs. Elizabeth Blake. Mr. Wm. H. Childs has been for nearly half a century an active business man. The first ten years he was a merchant, and since that period engaged as a General Insurance Agent. Genial, hospitable, of large and warm heart, he is an honorable representative of his race, of which he is justly proud. Some few years since he gathered beneath his own roof a most goodly assemblage of kindred, from eight different states—one coming to the meeting of that portion of the tribe from sunny Florida; and it was asked on the occasion, "if they knew *one* of the Childs family who would be a discredit to the name?" The universal response was, No! Mr. Childs attested his patriotism in giving up one of his noble sons on the altar of freedom, and finds "no cause to blush as he looks upon his other children and grandchildren." He writes, "We are proud of every one of them; there is not a *black* or *speckled* one in the whole flock, in fact I believe there is Royal blood in the *Childs family*." We hope the future chronicler may be able to report as honorable a character in the possession of the descendants of these cherished grandchildren. Mrs. Laura Amsden Childs d. at Niagara Falls, N. Y., May 3, 1865.

[Eighth Generation.] Children:

4936. i. JULIA CHILDS, b. April 13, 1829, m. Mch. 15, 1854, at Niagara Falls, John Fowler: she d. Feb. 7, 1856, in California.

4937. ii. JOEL CHILDS, b. Mch. 14, 1831, m. July 20, 1854, Laura Morrison.

4938. iii. WILLIAM H. CHILDS, JR., b. Feb. 8, 1833, m. Feb. 14, 1855, Emma Blake of Chicago, Ill.

4939. iv. LAURA B. CHILDS, b. July 22, 1835, m. May 21, 1856, Dr. F. L. Andrews.

4940. v. AUGUSTA CHILDS, b. June 1, 1837, m. April 23, 1860, John Fowler.

4941. vi. EDWARD CHILDS, b. Aug. 22, 1839, d. Sept. 1, 1860, unm.

4942. vii. GERTRUDE CHILDS, b. Nov. 14, 1841, m. Oct. 8, 1862, Julius Ives, Jr.

[Eighth Generation.]

4937. ii. JOEL CHILDS, eldest son and second child of William H. and Laura Amsden Childs, b. Mch. 14, 1831, m. July 20, 1854, Miss Laura Morrison.   Mr. Joel Childs, kindled by the enthusiasm of patriotic fervor so universally developed during the period of the late war, inheriting perchance some of the warlike characteristics of his early ancestry, enlisted in the 45th Regiment of Illinois Volunteers, in the very opening of the contest, and laid down his life in the freshness of his young manhood, April 6, 1862, at the battle of Shiloh.   Mr. Childs left two sons to bear his name and repeat his praise.   Mrs. Laura M. Childs has since married, Capt. Rufus Ford of Buda, Illinois.

[Ninth Generation.] Children:

4943. i JOEL A. CHILDS, b. Jan. 20, 1855.

4944. ii. WILLIAM M. CHILDS, b. Dec. 11, 1856.

4945 iii. ASA M. CHILDS, d. in infancy.

[Eighth Generation.]

4938. iii. WILLIAM H. CHILDS, JR., second son of William H. and Laura Amsden Childs, b. Feb. 8, 1833, in Geneva, N. Y., m. Feb. 14, 1855, Miss Emma Blake, of Chicago, Ill.   Mr. Childs d. Dec. 29, 1863, and his widow m. Prof. Geo. H. Bangs, of Lima, Livingston Co., N. Y.   One son survives Mr. Childs, and will, it is fondly believed, make his place in the life arena so early vacated, an honored one.

[Ninth Generation.] Children:

4946. i. JULIA AGNES CHILDS, d. in infancy.

4947. ii. ELIZABETH H. CHILDS, b. Sept. 17, 1857.

4948. iii. FRANK B. CHILDS, b. Oct. 3, 1859.

[Eighth Generation.]

4939. iv. LAURA B. CHILDS, second dau. and fourth child of William H. and Laura Amsden Childs, b. July 22, 1835, m. May 21, 1856, Dr. F. L. Andrews.   She d. in Creston, Iowa, leaving seven children. But the lovely twins upon whose birth she gave up her own life soon went to her.

[Ninth Generation.] Children:

4949 i. LANGDON C. ANDREWS, d. in infancy.
4950. ii. JOHN FOWLER ANDREWS, b. Jan. 25, 1859.
4951. iii. DAISY ANDREWS, b April 22, 1860.
4952. iv. EDDIE CHILDS ANDREWS, b. June 23, 1862.
4953. v. HERBERT BLAKE ANDREWS, b. Aug. 23, 1863.
4954 vi. LAURA CHILDS ANDREWS, b. Sept. 23, 1867.

[Eighth Generation.]

4940. v. AUGUSTA CHILDS, third dau. and fifth child of William H. and Laura Amsden Childs, b. June 1, 1837, m. her brother-in-law, Mr. John Fowler, April 23, 1860. Mr. and Mrs. Fowler reside in California.

[Ninth Generation.] Children:

4955. i. WILLIAM CHILDS FOWLER, b. April 11, 1861.
4956. ii. EDWARD LANGDON FOWLER, b. Dec. 18, 1862.
4957. iii. ANNIE LAURA FOWLER, b. Aug. 4, 1865.
4958. iv. AUGUSTA MAY FOWLER, b. Dec. 9, 1868.

[Eighth Generation.]

4942. vii. GERTRUDE CHILDS, youngest dau. and child of William H. and Laura Amsden Childs, b. Nov. 14, 1841, m. Oct. 8. 1862. Julius Ives, Jr. Mr. and Mrs. Ives reside in Brooklyn, N Y.

[Ninth Generation.] Children:

4959. i. CHARLES TAYLOR IVES, b. April 8, 1864.
4960. ii. WILLIAM CHILDS IVES, b. June 18, 1865.
4961. iii. HOWARD COLBY IVES, b. Oct. 11, 1867.
4962. iv. THEODORE EDWARD IVES, b. Dec. 31, 1870.
4963. v. FLORENCE ACTEN IVES, b. April 28, 1876.

Sixth Generation.]

4885. vi. MARTHA CHILD, third dau. and sixth child of Solomon and Martha Rice Child, b. in Henniker. N. H., Nov. 2. 1777. m. Mch. 1, 1803, William Heaton, of Thetford, Vt. Mr. Heaton was b. Jan. 12, 1767, and d. Mch. 7, 1849. Mrs. Martha C. Heaton d. Mch. 29, 1860.

[Seventh Generation.] Children:

4964. i. WILLIAM CHILDS HEATON, b. Dec. 6, 1806, m. Aug. 14, 1838, Maria D. Wharford, of New York.
4965. ii. LUCY CHAPMAN HEATON. b. Mch. 20, 1809, m Jan. 4, 1830, Dr. H. H. Niles.
4966. iii. ELIZA RICE HEATON, b. April 10, 1811, m. Mch. 16, 1864, Daniel Dodge, of Post-Mills, Vt. Mr. Dodge not living.
4967. iv. SOLOMON GOODELL HEATON, b. June 21, 1813, m. July 17, 1843, Julia Annette Goodwin.
4968. v. AUSTIN CARPENTER HEATON, b. May 28, 1815, m. Nov. 2, 1861, Ariana Jones.

4969 vi. CALVIN PAGE HEATON, b. Aug. 20, 1817, m. Nov. 24, 1846, Margaret J. Evans.

4970. vii MARTHA SOPHIA HEATON, b. Mch. 1, 1820, m. Sept. 3, 1851, Horace Billings, of Beardstown, Ill.

4971. viii. MARY MARIA HEATON. b. Dec. 22, 1823, m. July 29, 1852, Thomas Porter Baldwin.

[Seventh Generation.]

4964. i. WILLIAM CHILDS HEATON, eldest son of Martha Child and William Heaton, b. Dec. 6, 1806, m. Aug. 14, 1838. Maria D. Wharford, of New York.

[Eighth Generation.] Child:

4972. i. CLARENCE D. HEATON, b. Dec. 26, 1841, m. Oct. 11, 1865, Anna Maria Gilchrist.

[Eighth Generation.]

4972. i. CLARENCE D. HEATON, son of William Childs and Maria D. Wharford Heaton. b. Dec. 26, 1841, m. Oct. 11, 1865, Anna Maria Gilchrist, dau. of John W. and Darietta Gilchrist. Mr. Heaton has long been identified with the Irvings Savings Bank, at 96 Warren St., New York City, and is a man of trusted integrity, giving the interest of the banking house ever the pre-eminence, indeed subordinating all personal ambitions to its advancement in the most honorable manner. His conscientious service is honorably esteemed by the officers of the Institution.

[Ninth Generation.] Children:

4973. i. WILLIAM C HEATON, b. Aug. 13, 1866

4974. ii. HENRY HEATON, b, July 23, 1872.

[Seventh Generation.]

4965. ii. LUCY CHAPMAN HEATON, eldest dau. of Martha Child and William Heaton. b. Mch. 20, 1809, m. Jan. 4, 1830, Dr. H. H. Niles. Mrs. L. C. Heaton Niles d. Sept. 30, 1864.

[Eighth Generation.] Children:

4975. i. ELIZABETH K. NILES, b. Nov. 3, 1833, m. Col. James Low of Charlestown, Mass. Has two children.

4976. ii. FRANCES M. NILES, b. April 7, 1840, m. William A. Dodge. Has one child.

4977. iii MARTHA KATE NILES, b. Sept. 2, 1851, m. Edwin F. Garey of Charlestown, Mass. Has two children.

[Seventh Generation.]

4967. iv. SOLOMON GOODELL HEATON, second son and fourth child of Martha Child and William Heaton, b. June 21, 1813, m. July 17, 1843, Julia Annette Goodwin. Resides at Post Mills village, Orange Co., Vt.

[Eighth Generation.] Child:

4978. i. EDWARD N. HEATON, b. April 7, 1846, m. Mrs. Nannie C. Sturgis.

[Seventh Generation.]

4968. v. REV. AUSTIN CARPENTER HEATON, D. D., third son and fifth child of Martha Child and William Heaton, b. in Thetford, Orange Co., Vt., May 28, 1815, m. Nov. 2, 1861, Ariana Frazier Jones. Mr. Heaton commenced his studies preparatory to his profession, at the Academy in his native town, making further preparation for college in like schools in New Hampshire, and graduated from Dartmouth College, in Hanover, Grafton Co., N. H., in 1840. Almost immediately he removed to Virginia, and for some nine years was an unusually successful teacher of a classical and mathematical school in Alexandria. While resident in Alexandria, received the degree of A. M. from his Alma Mater. In the year 1849 we find him pursuing his theological studies at the Theological Seminary of Princeton, New Jersey. His licensure was granted him by the Presbytery of New Brunswick, N. J., in the spring of 1850. For four years following he was settled over a Presbyterian church at Harpers Ferry, Virginia, thence called to the third Presbyterian church of Baltimore, Maryland. His stay was brief in Baltimore. In 1855, Dr. Heaton accepted a call to the church of his denomination in Princess Anne, Somerset Co., Maryland, where he has since remained. Some six years after his settlement at Princess Anne, his marriage to Miss A. F. Jones occurred. " Mrs. Heaton was a lady of most exalted character, and finished culture, and of a most respectable and ancient family." Her death, which was on the first of January, 1878, was an irreparable loss to her family. The degree of D. D. was conferred upon Rev. Mr. Heaton by the University of Delaware, in 1877.

[Eighth Generation.] Children:

4979. i. AUSTIN CARPENTER HEATON, JR., b. Oct. 30, 1863.
4980. ii. SAMUEL WILSON HEATON, b. April 16, 1866.
4981. iii. ARIANA STUART HEATON, b. Aug. 28, 1868, d. July 27, 1870.
4982. iv. SALLY STUART HEATON, b. Dec. 17, 1870.
4983. v. MARTHA CHILDS HEATON, b. Nov. 6, 1873.
4984. vi. WILLIAM PAGE HEATON, b. Aug. 23, 1877, d. June 15, 1878.

[Seventh Generation.]

4969. vi. CALVIN PAGE HEATON, fourth son and sixth child of Martha Child and William Heaton, b. in Thetford, Orange Co., Vt., Aug. 20, 1817. In 1836, he went to Illinois, and in the autumn of that year settled in Carrolton, Green Co.; m. Nov. 24, 1846, Miss Margaret J. Evans, dau. of John Evans,

Esq., of Carrolton, by the Rev. Hugh Barr. In October, 1852,
Mr. and Mrs. Heaton removed from Carrolton to Virden,
Macoupin Co., Ill., where he resided until the time of his death,
which was upon Sunday, the 26th of May, 1868. Mr. C. P.
Heaton was one of the partners in the banking house of Dubois,
Heaton & Chesnut; a citizen full of effective interest and activ-
ity in all affairs of the municipality. At a meeting of the
Board of Trustees of the town of Virden, on the day following
Mr. Heaton's decease, sincere expressions of regret were made
by leading members, and resolutions passed commendatory of
his noble life and true citizenship, and of heartfelt condolence
with his family in their great bereavement.

[Eighth Generation.]   Children:

4985. i. WILLIAM LEWIS HEATON, b. June 10, 1849, m. Sept. 9, 1875, Bessie
D. McArthur.

4986. ii. CHARLES PAGE HEATON, b. April 5, 1851, m. Oct. 19, 1870, Kate
Lane.

4987. iii. FRANK DILLER HEATON, b. Jan. 3, 1853, m. Mch. 10, 1875, Ella
V. Brooks.

4988. iv. HARRY EVANS HEATON, b. Dec. 21, 1857, m. Sept. 27, 1876, Delia
Wilson.

4989. v. AUSTIN HEATON, b. June 10, 1859, d. Aug. 7, 1859.

4990. vi. HORACE BILLINGS HEATON, b. Sept. 5, 1860, d. Oct. 9, 1860.

4991. vii. MAGGIE CHILDS HEATON, b. Feb. 2, 1864, d. Sept. 12, 1865.

4992. viii. LUCY LEONARD HEATON, b. Mch. 12, 1866, d. Sept. 16, 1867.

4993. ix. ANNA BARBER HEATON, b. April 13, 1868, d. June 7, 1868.

[Seventh Generation.]

4970. vii. MARTHA SOPHIA HEATON, third dau. and seventh
child of Martha Child and William Heaton, b. in Thetford,
Vt., Mch. 1, 1820, m. Sept. 3, 1851, Horace Billings of Beardstown, Ill. Mr. Billings was largely engaged in mercantile pursuits, and was personally interested in many of the public
improvements of central Illinois, accumulating a very considerable wealth. His death occurred on the 22d of February, 1873,
at Jacksonville, Ill., where he had been a resident two years.
The property which Mr. Billings supposed would shield his
small family from all care, with the ignis fatuus character it
often manifests, took to itself wings and fled away. Very fortunately Mrs. Billings possessed a wealth of cultured intellect
which enabled her to meet these adverse circumstances. The
ill health of her only surviving child, led her after a few years,
to the Pacific coast, where mother and daughter are instructors.
Mrs. Billings is in the "State Institution for the Deaf, Dumb

and Blind," at Berkely near Oakland, California. Miss Ellen
E. Billings, has charge of the department of instrumental music
in the Napa Ladies' Seminary, at Napa City, California.

[Eighth Generation.] Children:

4994. i. MARTHA HEATON BILLINGS, b. Jan. 21, 1854, d. Oct. 21, 1854.

4995. ii. ELLEN ELIZABETH BILLINGS, b. June 26, 1856.

4996. iii. HORACE HEATON BILLINGS, b. July 22, 1858, d. July 21, 1860.

[Seventh Generation.]

4971. viii. MARY MARIA HEATON, fourth dau. and eighth
child of Martha Child and William Heaton, b. in Thetford,
Vt., Dec. 22, 1823, m. July 29, 1852, Thomas Porter Baldwin.

[Eighth Generation.] Child:

4997. i. MARY P. BALDWIN, b May 3, 1853, m. Frederick A. McDonald
of Jacksonville, Illinois.

[Sixth Generation.]

4886. vii. SOLOMON CHILD, JR., fourth son of Solomon and
Martha Rice Child, b. in Henniker, N. H., July 30, 1782, m.
1st, Sept. 21, 1806, Miss Mary Long of Hopkinton, N. H.; m.
2d, 1824, Lucinda Child, dau. of William and Mary Heaton
Child of Thetford, Vt. Mrs. Mary Long Child d. Feb. 13,
1823. Mr. Solomon Child, Jr., survived both wives; Mrs.
Lucinda (Child) Child, d. Jan. 20, 1852, her husband Oct. 19,
1865, when five years past his fourscore.

[Seventh Generation.] Children:

4998 i. HORACE CHILD, b. Aug. 10, 1807, m. Matilda R Taylor of Lemp-
ster, New Hampshire.

4999. ii. ENOCH LONG CHILD, b. Oct. 6, 1808, m. Oct. 6, 1840, Harriet
Long. Graduated from Yale College in 1840, and taught for several years.
Resides in Concord, Merrimack Co., N. H.

5000. iii. MARY LONG CHILD, b. April 17, 1810, m. Oct. 2, 1850, Asa
Whitney of Henniker, N. H.

5001. iv. WARREN STORY CHILD, b. Oct. 12, 1811, m. Nov. 27, 1839, Sarah
T. Lane of Candia, N. H.

5002. v. MARTHA CLEAVELAND CHILD, b June 13, 1813, m. Sept 20, 1838,
Benjamin Colby of Henniker, N. H.

5003. vi. DAVID CHILD, b. June 4, 1815, d. April 6, 1816.

5004. vii. Infant Son, b. June 10, 1816, d. same day.

5005. viii. CELESTIA M. CHILD, b. Oct. 11, 1817, d. Nov. 1, 1817.

5006. ix. DAVID CURTIS CHILD, b. Oct. 8, 1818, d. Dec. 12, 1837.

5007. x. JULIA ANN CHILD, b. Feb. 26, 1821, d. July 30, 1854.

5008. xi. CAROLINE SAWYER CHILD, b. Jan. 25, 1823, m. Sept. 1846, John
J. Stillman of Bridgeport, Ct.

[Seventh Generation.]

5000. iii. MARY LONG CHILD, eldest dau. of Solomon, Jr.,
and Mary Long Child, b. in Henniker, N. H., April 17, 1810;
m. Oct. 2, 1850, Mr. Asa Whitney, of the same place. Mr.

Whitney d. in 1857. Mrs. Whitney resides in Cambridge, Mass., with her daughter, Mrs. Eugene Brooks.

[Eighth Generation.] Children:

    5009. i. ENOCH LONG WHITNEY, b. Jan. 8, 1852, d Jan. 13, 1852.

    5010. ii. SARAH MATILDA WHITNEY, b. Sept. 15, 1855, m. Feb. 12, 1874, Eugene D. Brooks of Cambridge, Mass.

[Eighth Generation.]

    5010. ii. SARAH MATILDA WHITNEY, dau. of Mary Long Child and Asa Whitney, b. Sept. 15, 1855, m. Feb. 12, 1874, Eugene D. Brooks of Cambridge, Mass.

[Ninth Generation.] Children:

    5011 i. MARION REBECCA BROOKS, b. Mch. 27, 1875.

    5012. ii. LYMAN WARREN BROOKS, b. Nov. 9, 1876.

    5013. iii. EDITH D. BROOKS, b. Sept. 19, 1878.

[Seventh Generation.]

    5001. iv. WARREN STORY CHILD, third son of Solomon, Jr., and Mary Long Child, b. Oct. 12, 1811, m. Nov. 27, 1839, Miss Sarah F. Lane of Candia, N. H.

[Eighth Generation.] Children:

    5014. i. RICHARD LANE CHILD, b. Aug. 2, 1843, m. Nov. 19, 1877, Kate Gutterson.

    5015. ii. CURTIS BENSON CHILD, b. Aug. 25, 1845. Graduated at Dartmouth College, Hanover, N. H.

    5016. iii. MARY ABBY CHILD, b. Aug. 29, 1849, m. Aug. 2, 1873, Francis Ensor Pendergast.

    5017 iv FREDERIC WARREN CHILD, b. June 17, 1853, d. Aug. 26, 1854.

[Eighth Generation]

    5014. i. RICHARD LANE CHILD, eldest son of Warren Story and Sarah T. Lane Child, b. in Henniker, N H. Aug. 2, 1843, m. Nov. 19, 1877, Miss Kate Gutterson

[Ninth Generation.] Child:

    5018. i. ANNA LOIS CHILD, b. Oct. 25, 1878.

[Eighth Generation.]

    5016. iii. MARY ABBY CHILD, only dau. of Warren Story and Sarah T. Lane Child, b Aug. 29, 1849, m. Aug. 2, 1873, Francis Ensor Pendergast of Dublin, Ireland.

[Ninth Generation] Children:

    5019. i An infant daughter, b. at De Pere, Wisconsin, d. young.

    5020. ii. JEFFERY JOSEPH PENDERGAST, b. Aug. 30, 1875, at De Pere, Wis.

    5021. iii. FRANCIS FREDERIC PENDERGAST, b. July 1, 1878, at Hastings, Adams Co , Nebraska.

[Seventh Generation.]

    5002. v. MARTHA CLEAVELAND CHILD, second dau. of Solomon, Jr., and Mary Long Child, b. June 13, 1813, m. Sept. 20, 1838, Benjamin Colby of Henniker, N. H.

[Eighth Generation.] Children:

5022. i. JULIA LAWRENCE COLBY, b. Dec. 5, 1839, m. Garland Blanchard.

5023. ii. FRANKLIN EDSON COLBY, b. Mch. 31, 1842, d. Sept. 17, 1845.

5024. iii. ALMA EDSON COLBY, b. Jan. 28, 1845, m. Mch. 1867, John S. Gerry.

5025. iv. ENOCH LONG CHILD COLBY, b. Jan. 15, 1854, m. July 11, 1877, Helen S. Gove of Charlotte, Monroe Co., N. Y.

[Eighth Generation.]

5022. i. JULIA LAWRENCE COLBY, eldest dau. of Martha Cleaveland Child and Benjamin Colby, b. in Henniker, N. H., Dec. 5, 1839, m. S. Garland Blanchard of Hillsboro, N. H. Mrs. Blanchard d. June 20, 1866.

[Ninth Generation.] Child:

5026. i. BELLE BLANCHARD.

[Eighth Generation.]

5024. iii. ALMA EDSON COLBY, second dau. of Martha Cleaveland Child and Benjamin Colby, b. in Henniker, N. H., Jan. 28, 1845, m. Mch. 1867, John S. Gerry.

[Ninth Generation.] Child:

5027. i. JULIA GERRY.

[Eighth Generation.]

5025. iv. ENOCH LONG CHILD COLBY, second son of Martha Cleaveland Child and Benjamin Colby, b. Jan. 15, 1854, m. July 11, 1877. Helen S. Gove of Charlotte, Monroe Co., N. Y.

[Ninth Generation.] Child:

5028. i. CARRIE ALMA COLBY, b. Oct. 23, 1878.

[Seventh Generation.]

5008. xi. CAROLINE SAWYER CHILD, eleventh child and fifth dau. of Solomon, Jr., and Mary Long Child, b. in Henniker, N. H., Jan. 25, 1823, m. Sept. 1846, John J. Stillman of Bridgeport, Ct. Mrs. Stillman d. at Dover, Delaware, July 26, 1867.

[Eighth Generation.] Children:

5029. i. HORACE CHILDS STILLMAN, b. June 30, 1847, m. 1869, Anna Loomis.

5030. ii. WILLIAM ASHBEL STILLMAN, b. Sept. 10, 1849, m. Nov. 7, 1872, Maria Morrison of New York City. Three infants who d. young.

5031. iii. JULIA LONG STILLMAN, b. July 1851, d. Oct. 1851.

5032. iv. AUGUSTUS MUNGER STILLMAN, b. Nov. 9, 1854, m. Nov. 10, 1877, Mary Coburn of Hartford, Ct., where they reside.

5033. v. CARRIE BELL STILLMAN, b. Sept. 17, 1856, m. May 26, 1875, Sidney Eames

5034. vi. JOSEPH TOWNE STILLMAN, b. Nov. 12, 1858, d. by drowning, 1862, at the age of four.

5035. vii. CLARA JUDSON STILLMAN, b. Dec. 12, 1860.

5036. viii. MARY EMILY STILLMAN, b. Oct. 7, 1863.

N-1

5037. ix. JOHN JAMES STILLMAN, b. July 8, 1867, d. on the 28, and was laid with his mother.

[Eighth Generation.]

5029. i. HORACE CHILDS STILLMAN, eldest son of Caroline Sawyer Child and John J. Stillman, b. in Bridgeport, Ct., June 30, 1847, m. in 1869, Anna Loomis of Byron, New York. Mr. and Mrs. Stillman reside in California.

[Ninth Generation.]   Child:
5038. i. MAE SAWYER STILLMAN, b. Nov. 7, 1873.

[Eighth Generation.]

5033. v. CARRIE BELL STILLMAN, second dau. of Caroline Sawyer Child and John J. Stillman, b. in Bridgeport, Ct., Sept. 17, 1856, m. May 26, 1875, Sidney Eames of Bridgeport, Ct., where they reside.

[Ninth Generation.]   Child:
5039. i. HARRY HERBERT EAMES, b. May 23, 1876.

[Sixth Generation.]

4887. vii. JOSIAH CHILD, fourth son and seventh child of Solomon and Martha Rice Child b. in Henniker, Oct. 11, 1784. m. 1805, Abigail Ward, dau. of Capt. Josiah and Sarah Goodell Ward and step-daughter of Mr. Solomon Child. Mr. Josiah Child d. Feb. 1, 1862. Mrs. Child d. Jan., 1870. Mr. Child was an office-bearer in the church, and one of those who largely contributed, by his personal qualities and in the virtues developed under his pious care in his offspring to swell the number of whom one of the family writes, " A godly ancestry, and almost without exception a godly generation, men and women if not brilliant, yet living to bless the world." Nor was Mrs. Child at all behind her husband in the possession of most genial and christian characteristics, as her children most fondly attest. Mr. and Mrs. Josiah Child were blessed with eleven children.*

[Seventh Generation.]   Children:
5040. i. AARON CHILDS, b. Dec. 1, 1806, m. April 11, 1833, Hannah F. Bemis.

5041. ii. IRA GOODELL CHILDS, b. Feb. 6, 1809, m. April 6, 1834, Abigail Wilder.

5042. iii. JOSIAH CHILDS, b. Mch. 1, 1811, m. May 16, 1843, Louisa Toombs.

5043. iv. CARLOS CHILDS, b. ab't 1813, m. 1849, Paulina Brackett, dau. of William Brackett of Colebrook, N. H.

5044. v. ROSELLA CHILDS, b. Aug. 24, 1815, m. April, 1837, Capt. John Whitney of Lancaster, Mass.; m. 2d, John Edgarton of same place.

---

* The final s added by the children in this line.

5045 vi. WILLIAM CAREY CHILDS, b. Nov. 1817, d. Oct. 31, 1841. Of devout and earnest character Mr. Childs early consecrated his life to the Saviour, and died while pursuing his studies preparatory to the work of the ministry.

5046. vii. SERENO AUSTIN CHILDS, b. 1819, m. Nov. 7, 1849, Mary Lowe, dau. of Stephen Lowe of Fitchburg, Mass.

5047. viii. ADDISON CHILDS, b. Oct., 1821, d. Nov. 5, 1844 Like his brother William he felt that he could best " work for Jesus " in the clerical profession, and had but "girded on his armor" when the captain of his choice called him to work in the " Church Triumphant."

5048. ix. SARAH CHILDS, b. April, 1824, d. Aug., 1826.

5049. x. JAMES WEBSTER CHILDS, b. June 16, 1826, m. Aug., 1848, Lucy Hubbard, dau. of John Hubbard of Claremont, N. H.

5050. xi MARY ELIZABETH CHILDS, b. Aug. 24, 1829, m. Dec. 21, 1852, Calvin Lowe of Fitchburg, Mass.

[Seventh Generation.]

5040. i. HON. AARON CHILDS, eldest son and child of Dea. Josiah and Abigail Ward Childs, b. in Henniker, N. H., Dec. 1, 1806, m. April 11, 1833, Hannah F. Bemis, dau. of Jonathan Bemis of Windham, Vt. All the children of Dea. Josiah and Mrs. Abigail Ward Child, were born in his own native place in the Granite State, but as Daniel Webster said of it, "New Hampshire was an excellent State to emigrate from," so it appeared to this large household of sons. The eldest set the example. The year after his marriage Mr. Childs with his bride removed to the then wilds of Michigan, he purchased a tract of land in Washtenaw Co. and established a home. His daughter writes, " For many years he experienced the manifold trials incident to pioneer life, at that period. From the organization of the township in which he resides, he has been connected with it in official capacities. For fifteen years he was its Supervisor. In 1870 he was elected a member of the State Legislature." Though privation of luxuries may have been the unavoidable lot of these early settlers of the Peninsular State, long since ease and plenty have crowned their toils, and none are held in more thorough esteem than the Hon. Aaron Childs and his numerous family.

[Eighth Generation.] Children:

5051. i. JONATHAN CHILDS, b. Mch. 14, 1834, m. 1st, May 29, 1866, Frances Crawford; m. 2d, 1873, Fannie Ganse.

5052. ii. LEWIS E. CHILDS, b. May 25, 1836, m. June 12, 1866, Frances Richardson.

5053. iii. LAVINIA L. CHILDS, b. Jan. 21, 1841, m. Aug. 21, 1861, Robert Campbell, Jr.

5054. iv. WILLIAM K. CHILDS, b. July 12, 1843, m. Dec. 2, 1868, Fidelia Cate.

5055. v. EUGENE M. CHILDS, b May 28, 1846, m. Sept. 17, 1873, Emma A. Osborne.

5056. vi. ALMA C. CHILDS. b. April 3, 1850, in Augusta, Mich.*

5057. vii. ELLEN A. CHILDS, b. June 12, 1851, m. May 25, 1874, Villiam G. Osborne.

5058. viii. HANNAH R. CHILDS. b. Oct. 11, 1854, d. Nov. 19, 1854, in Augusta, Mich.

5059. ix. ELVIRA CHILDS, b. Feb. 5, 1856, d. Feb. 29, 1856, in Augusta, Mich.

[Eighth Generation.]

5051. i. COL. JONATHAN CHILDS, eldest son and child of Hon. Aaron and Hannah F. Bemis Childs, b. at Laoni, Chatauqua Co., N. Y., Mch. 14, 1834. Col. Childs m. 1st, May 29, 1866, Miss Frances Crawford, at Appalachicola, Florida ; she d. in Jacksonville. Fla., Dec., 1871. In 1873 he m. Miss Fannie Ganse. "Col. Jonathan W. Childs, at the beginning of the war of the Rebellion, was appointed Major in the 4th Mich. Infantry. Afterwards Lieut. Col. and Col. of the same Reg't. He passed through many of the severe battles of the Army of the Potomac." At the close of the war he went to Florida, where he resided several years. In 1876 he removed to Anderson, Howard Co., Maryland. Mrs. Fannie Ganse Childs is a relative of the late minister to Russia, the Hon. Bayard Taylor.

[Ninth Generation.] Children:

5060. i. ELAINE CHILDS, b. Mch. 5, 1874. in Richmond, Va.

5061. ii ABBIE BLANCHE CHILDS, b. April 9, 1876, in Washington, D. C. d. June 3, 1876.

[Eighth Generation.]

5052. ii. CAPT. LEWIS E. CHILDS, second son and child of Hon. Aaron and Hannah F. Bemis Childs, b. in Augusta, Mich., May 25, 1836, m. at Fitchburg, Mass.. June 12, 1866, Frances Richardson, dau. of William Richardson. Captain Childs, at the beginning of the late war, joined the 11th Mich. Infantry. He served three years in the Army of the Cumberland. At the battle of Chickamauga, Sept. 2, 1863, he was severely wounded and taken prisoner, afterwards exchanged. He now resides in Ypsilanti, Mich.

[Ninth Generation.] Children:

5062. i. HERBERT WARD CHILDS, b. Sept. 8, 1867, at Fitchburg, Mass.

5063. ii. HAROLD HAZLETINE CHILDS, b. Mch., 1869, d. Aug., 1869, at Ypsilanti, Mich.

* To Miss Alma C. Childs we are indebted for much of our material in her immediate line.

5064. iii. WILLIAM ROSCOE CHILDS, b. Jan. 1870, d. Aug. 1870, at Ypsilanti, Mich.

5065. iv. MABEL FRANCES CHILDS, b. Nov. 1873, d. July 1874, at Ypsilanti, Mich.

[Eighth Generation.]

5053. iii. LAVINIA L. CHILDS, eldest dau. and third child of Hon Aaron and Hannah F. Bemis Childs, b. in Augusta, Washtenaw Co., Mich., Jan. 21, 1841, m. Aug. 21, 1861, Robert Campbell, Jr. of Augusta, from which place Mr. and Mrs. Campbell removed to Pittsfield, in Hillsdale Co. Mr. Campbell is descended from a sister of Oliver Cromwell ; and also a kinsman of Thomas Campbell, the poet.

[Ninth Generation.] Children :

5066. i. WALTER WEBSTER CAMPBELL, b. May 4, 1862, in Augusta, Mich.

5067. ii. ELIZABETH ALMA CAMPBELL, b. Aug. 7, 1868, in Pittsfield, Mich.

[Eighth Generation.]

5054. iv. WILLIAM K. CHILDS, third son and fourth child of Hon. Aaron and Hannah F. Bemis Childs, b. in Augusta, Mich., July 12, 1843, m. in Highland, Mich, Dec. 2, 1868, Miss Fidelia Cate. dau. of Franklin Cate. William K Childs was no whit behind his elder brothers in patriotism, and was himself a soldier in the Western Division of the Northern Army. He is at present serving his second term as Sergeant-at-arms in the House of Representatives of the State Legislature, at Lansing, Michigan.

[Ninth Generation.] Children:

5068. i. WALLIS L. CHILDS, b. Oct 4. 1870, in Pittsfield, Mich.

5069. ii. LELIA M. CHILDS, b. June, 1875, in Pittsfield, Mich.

[Eighth Generation.]

5055. v. EUGENE M. CHILDS, fourth son of Hon. Aaron and Hannah F. Bemis Childs, b. in Augusta, Mich., May 28, 1846, m. Sept. 17, 1873, to Miss Emma A. Osborne, dau. of Rev. William F. Osborne. Reside in Augusta, Mich.

[Ninth Generation.] Children :

5070. i. EDITH M. CHILDS, b. Feb. 4, 1875, in Augusta, Mich.

5071. ii. ADDIE WINIFIED CHILDS, b Mch 3, 1877, in Augusta, Mich.

[Eighth Generation.]

5057. vii. ELLEN A. CHILDS, third dau. and seventh child of Hon. Aaron and Hannah F. Bemis Childs, b. in Augusta, Michigan, June 12, 1851, m. May 25. 1874, William G. Osborne of Grand Rapids, Mich., where they now reside.

[Ninth Generation.] Children:

5072. i. Roy William Osborne, b. May 11, 1875, d. Sept. 15, 1875.

5073. ii. Alma Childs Osborne, b. July 3, 1878, at Dover, Allegan Co., Mich.

[Seventh Generation.]

5041. ii. Ira Goodell Childs, second son and child of Dea. Josiah and Abigail Ward Childs, b. in Henniker, N. H., Feb. 6, 1809, m. April 6, 1834, Abigail Wilder, dau. of John Wilder of Lancaster, Mass. Mr. Childs was a man "revered and loved by all who knew him. He passed away in the prime of an honorable and useful life, on the 19th of August, 1859," in Augusta, Michigan, where he had early joined his elder brother, Hon. Aaron Childs. In 1861, Mrs. A. W. Childs m. Israel Trask of Beverly, Mass., whom she survived several years. She d. Mch. 20, 1874.

[Eighth Generation.] Children:

5074. i. Josiah Goodell Childs, b. Dec. 20, 1835, in Lancaster, Mass., d. June 1, 1836, in Augusta, Mich.

5075. ii. Josiah Ward Childs, b. June, 1, 1838, m. Oct. 19, 1870, Phebe Ann Sherman.

5076. iii. Sarah Ann Childs, b Jan. 5, 1841, m. Nov. 30, 1876, John Francis Bowditch.

[Eighth Generation.]

5075. ii. Josiah Ward Childs, second son and child of Ira Goodell and Abigail Wilder Childs, b. in Lancaster, Mass., June 1, 1838, m. in Braintree, Mass., Oct. 19, 1870, Phebe Ann Sherman, dau. of William Sherman. She was b. Sept. 27, 1844. Residence Braintree, Norfolk, Co., Mass.

[Ninth Generation.] Children:

5077. i. Annie Wilder Childs, b. July 12, 1872, in Braintree, Mass.

5078. ii. William Sherman Childs, b May 26, 1875, in Braintree, Mass.

5079. iii. Richard Ward Childs, b. Jan. 17, 1877, in Braintree, Mass.

[Eighth Generation]

5076. iii. Sarah Ann Childs, only dau. of Ira Goodell and Abigail Wilder Childs, b. in Lancaster, Mass., Jan. 5, 1841, m. Nov. 30, 1877, John Francis Bowditch of Boston, Mass., who was b. Oct. 17, 1847. Residence Boston, Mass.

[Ninth Generation.] Child:

5080. i. John Clinton Bowditch, b. Nov. 4, 1878, in Boston, Mass.

[Seventh Generation]

5042. iii. Dea. Josiah Childs, third son and child of Dea. Josiah and Abigail Ward Childs, b. in Henniker, N. H., March 1, 1811, m. May 16, 1843, Louisa Toombs, dau. of Lewis Toombs of Lancaster, Mass. Dea. Childs removed to Augusta

Mich., whither his two elder brothers had preceded him. "A man of eminent character and piety, his influence in the community where he resides is attested by the numerous offices of trust to which he has been elected." Resides in Augusta.

[Eighth Generation.] Children:

5081. i. ADDISON CHILDS, b. June 10. 1844, m. Dec. 7, 1870, Juliette Smith

5082. ii. ANNA G. CHILDS, b. July 17, 1846. m. Nov. 25, 1871, David Horner.

5083. iii. LOUISA A. CHILDS, b. July 27, 1848, m. Dec. 31, 1872, Orville Hawkes of Elmira, N. Y.

5084. iv. JOSIAH SELWYN CHILDS, b. Nov. 23, 1850, m. Mch. 2, 1875, Charlotte A. Smith.

5085. v. SERENO A. CHILDS, b. Aug. 19, 1852, d. June, 1862, in Augusta, Mich.

5086 vi. ROSELLA CHILDS, b. Feb. 18, 1855.

5087. vii. IRA GOODELL CHILDS, b. Feb. 15, 1858, d. June, 1862, in Augusta, Mich.

[Eighth Generation.]

5081. i. ADDISON CHILDS, eldest child of Dea. Josiah 2d, and Louisa Toombs Childs, b. in Augusta, Mich., June 10, 1844, m. in the same place Dec. 7, 1870, Juliette Smith, dau. of Daniel Smith. Removed to Ypsilanti, Mich.

[Ninth Generation.] Children.

5088. i. HORACE CHILDS, b. Sept. 1871, in Augusta, Mich.

5089. ii HAROLD CHILDS, b. Nov. 1878, in Ypsilanti, Mich.

[Eighth Generation.]

5082. ii. ANNA G. CHILDS, eldest dau. and second child of Dea. Josiah 2d and Louisa Toombs Childs, b. in Augusta, Mich., July 17, 1846, m. Nov. 25, 1871, David Horner of Ypsilanti, Washtenaw Co., Mich.

[Ninth Generation.] Child:

5090. i. GERTRUDE CHILDS HORNER, b. May 13, 1875, in Ypsilanti, Mich.

[Eighth Generation.]

5084. iv. JOSIAH SELWYN CHILDS, second son and fourth child of Dea. Josiah 2d and Louisa Toombs Childs, b. in Augusta, Mich., Nov. 23, 1850, m. Mch. 2, 1875, Charlotte A. Smith, dau. of Daniel Smith of Augusta, in which place they continue their home.

[Ninth Generation.] Child:

5091. i. ELLEN LOUISA CHILDS, b. Jan. 1, 1878, in Augusta, Mich.

[Seventh Generation.]

5044. v. ROSELLA CHILDS, eldest dau. and fifth child of Dea. Josiah and Abigail Ward Childs, b. in Henniker, N. H., Aug. 24, 1815, m. 1st, in April, 1837, Capt. John Whitney of Lancaster, Mass.; m. 2d, John Edgarton of Lancaster.

[Eighth Generation.] Child:

5092. i. WALTER HENRY KNOX WHITNEY, b. in 1845, at Clinton, Mass., m. in 1867, Emma Hadley of Sterling, Mass. Mr. Walter H. K. Whitney d. Oct. 8, 1872, in Worcester, Mass., leaving one child.

[Ninth Generation.] Child:

5093. i. GERTRUDE P. WHITNEY, b. July 8, 1869.

[Seventh Generation.]

5046. vii. SERENO AUSTIN CHILDS, sixth son and seventh child of Dea. Josiah and Abigail Ward Childs, b. in Henniker, N. H., in 1819, m. Nov. 7, 1849, Mary Lowe, dau. of Stephen Lowe of Fitchburg, Mass., where Mr. Childs has made his residence

[Eighth Generation.] Child:

5094. i. FREDERICK A. CHILDS, b Sept. 5, 1856.

[Seventh Generation.]

5049. x. JAMES WEBSTER CHILDS, eighth son and tenth child of Dea. Josiah and Abigail Ward Childs, b. in Henniker, N. H., June 16, 1826, m. Aug. 1848, Lucy Hubbard, dau. of John Hubbard of Claremont, N. H. Mr. and Mrs. James W. Childs removed at once to Michigan.

[Eighth Generation.] Children:

5095. i. CARLOS WEBSTER CHILDS, b. June 10, 1855, m. April 24, 1878, Ella Hazleton.

5096. ii. MARY A. CHILDS, b. Aug. 2, 1858.

[Eighth Generation.]

5095. i. CARLOS WEBSTER CHILDS, eldest child of James Webster and Lucy Hubbard Childs, b. in Augusta, Mich., June 10, 1855, m. April 24, 1878, Ella Hazleton of Hartford, Mich.

[Ninth Generation.] Child:

5097. i. EDNA ELLA CHILDS, b. Feb. 22, 1879.

[Seventh Generation.]

5050. xi. MARY ELIZABETH CHILDS, third dau. and eleventh child of Dea. Josiah and Abigail Ward Childs, b. in Henniker, N. H., Aug. 24, 1829, m. Dec. 31, 1852, Calvin Lowe of Fitchburg, Mass., removed to Michigan the same year and settled in Augusta, Washtenaw Co., where they now reside.

[Eighth Generation.] Children:

5098. i. EDWARD GOODELL LOWE, b. Mch. 3, 1854, d. Jan. 6, 1877.

5099. ii. AUSTIN CHILDS LOWE, b Feb. 12, 1856, m. Mch. 31, 1879, Mary Angeline Davis of Ypsilanti, Mich.

5100. iii. ABBIE LOUISA LOWE, b. April 25, 1858, d. May 19, 1875.

5101. iv. LUCY ROSELLA LOWE, b. Jan. 5, 1861, d. May 4, 1865.

5102. v. MARY LAVINA LOWE, b. Oct. 22, 1862, d. Feb. 3, 1863.

5103 vi. LUCY EDITH LOWE, b April 13, 1867.

5104. vii. JAMES WEBSTER LOWE, b. Feb. 22, 1869.
5105. viii. CARLOS WILLIAM LOWE, b. Mch. 2, 1871.
5106. ix. MARY ELIZABETH LOWE, b. Jan. 22, 1873, d. Aug. 18, 1873.

[Fourth Generation.]

4741. v. ISAAC CHILD, fifth child and third son of John and
Hannah French Child, b. in Watertown, Mass., Mch. 21, 1706,
m. 1st, Dec. 7, 1727, Anna Adams; she d. Feb. 16, 1746; m.
2d, April 1, 1747, Hannah Goddin. He d. in Waltham, Mass.,
Feb. 16, 1788.

[Fifth Generation.] Children:
5107. i. NATHANIEL CHILD, b. in Waltham, Mass., Oct. 31, 1728, d. May
15, 1731.
5108. ii. MOSES CHILD, b. in Waltham, Mass., April 6, 1731, m. Mch. 28,
1758, Sarah Styles.
5109. iii. EUNICE CHILD, b. in Waltham, Mass., April 14, 1734.
5110. iv. AMOS CHILD, b. in Waltham, Mass., ab't 1753, m. ab't 1778.

[Fifth Generation.]

5108. ii. MOSES CHILD, second son and child of Isaac and
Anna Adams Child, b. in Waltham, Mass., April 6, 1731, m.
Mch. 28, 1758, Sarah Styles. She was born in Lunenburgh,
Mass., June 13, 1734, d. June 3, 1818. He d. Feb. 8, 1793.

The record of Moses Child is derived from two sources.
One account furnished by Mr. Isaac Child of Boston, whose
manuscripts are gathered mostly from Boston records, gives
his birth as the son of Isaac Child of Waltham, Mass., in 1731,
and m. to Sarah Styles of Waltham. The other account furnished by a descendant of Moses Child, gives him as the son
of an English emigrant, who landed in Casco Bay, Maine, in
1730, and that he was born on ship-board in the bay. We
have not been able to verify fully these records. He may
have been born in a vessel and in Casco Bay, even if it had not
sailed from England. His parents may have been among the
emigrants from Massachusetts who were seeking new settlements in Maine, as we know many of the family name went
and settled in Maine from the earlier settled portions of Massachusetts. Both agree substantially as to date of birth, and to
details of his subsequent history. The fact that these descendants cannot give any names of the emigrating parents, and no
such are found, or any of their records, renders it more probable that he is the son of Isaac and Anna Adams Child of
Waltham, Mass., who might have been on their way to Maine
to settle, or visit those resident there, at the time of his birth;
rendered the more probable, that communication with Maine

was then by water more than by land. He was a prominent citizen of his day. He was commissioned a lieutenant in the old French War, by Gov. Shirley, and bore the same rank in our Revolutionary struggle. He was at the capture of Gen. Burgoyne, previous to which he received a commission from Gen. Washington to repair to East Maine and Nova Scotia to inquire into the condition of those colonies. The following is a copy of the commission:

"*By his Excellency, Geo. Washington, Esq., Commander in-Chief of the United Colonies.*

To MOSES CHILD, ESQ:

"The Honorable, the Continental Congress, having lately passed a Resolve, contained in the following words, to wit: That two persons be sent at the expense of these Colonies, to Nova Scotia, to inquire into the state of that Colony, the disposition of the inhabitants towards the American cause, and the condition of the fortifications, dock yards, the quantity of the war-like stores, and the number of soldiers, sailors and ships of war there; and to transmit the earliest intelligence to Gen. Washington.

"I do thereby constitute and appoint you, the said Moses Child, to be one of the persons to undertake this business. And as the season is late, and this a work of great importance, I entreat and request that you will use the utmost dispatch, attention, and fidelity in the execution of it. The necessity of acting with a proper degree of caution and secrecy is too apparent to need recommendation. You will keep an accurate account of your expenses, and upon your return you will be rewarded in a suitable manner for the fatigue of your journey and the services you render your country, by conducting and discharging this business with expedition and fidelity. Given under my hand this 24th day of Nov. 1775.

"GEORGE WASHINGTON."

[Sixth Generation.] Children, born in Waltham and Grafton, Mass.:

5111. i. ASA CHILD, b. April 8, 1753, d. Feb. 8, 1759.

5112. ii. SARAH CHILD, b. Mch. 26, 1760, d. May 25, 1760.

5113. iii. JAMES CHILD, b. April 4, 1762, m. 1781, Hannah Cushing.

5114. iv. SARAH CHILD, 2d, b. June 26, 1763.

5115. v. SUSANNA CHILD, b. July 23, 1766, m. Judge Ebenezer Champney.

5116. vi. ELISHA CHILD, b. Oct. 31, 1767, m. Feb. 17, 1795, Martha Abbott.

5117. vii. PRUDENCE CHILD, b. Aug. 30, 1769, d. Sept. 6, 1805.

5118. viii. BETSEY CHILD, b. Nov. 2, 1771, m. 1st, —— Spaulding; m. 2d, —— Spalter.

5119. ix. ISAAC CHILD, b. July 27, 1774, m. 1st, Sarah Rockwood; m. 2d, Polly Kimball.

5120. x. ANNA CHILD, b. Sept. 27, 1779, d. Oct. 17, 1779.

[Sixth Generation.]

5113. iii. JAMES CHILD, third child and second son of Moses and Sarah Styles Child, b. in Grafton, Mass., April 4, 1762. He resided in Grafton, Mass., in Hallowell, Maine, and

in Augusta, Maine.   He m. in 1781, Hannah Cushing, dau. of
Adam and Sarah Reed Cushing of Abbington, Mass.   She
was b. April 10, 1762, and d. at Augusta, Maine, Nov. 20,
1842.   Mr. Child emigrated to Hallowell when the country
was almost a wilderness, bringing with him as his only patrimony, a good name, a sound and robust constitution, high
principles of honor and integrity.   He was accompanied by a
brother-in-law with whom he engaged in the mercantile business.   Their first stock of goods was purchased on credit of a
Boston firm.   Connecting the fur trade with the Indians with
their other business, they were quite successful in the results
of their first purchase, realizing an amount of profits nearly
sufficient to pay the bills they had contracted.   Mr. Child
went to Boston, paid his bills and obtained from the same
house a new supply of goods.   In returning to his place of
business the vessel bearing himself and goods was wrecked on
the coast, his goods were a total loss, and his own life was
scarcely saved.   On reaching his home he found other misfortunes had befallen him, which left him penniless, caused by
the absconding of his partner.   With the burden of debt
incurred in the last purchase resting upon his shoulders, together with the entire lack of family supplies for the winter
which was just upon him, and no resources but his own energies, he addressed a note to his Boston creditors giving a full
statement of the case, asking for their forbearance, and promising full payment for his purchases as fast as his earnings in
some business would allow.   His creditors gave him their sympathies and their assurances that they would not trouble him.
This nerved him afresh for new enterprise.   He established a
tannery as promising remunerative returns for his labors.   His
lack of practical knowledge was supplied by the kindness of a
clerical friend, Rev. Jason Livermore, who had been reared a
practical tanner.   This enterprise proved a success ; he re-
trieved his lost fortune, and liquidated his entire indebtedness.
This turning point in his financial affairs was the beginning of
prosperity, which followed him through after life.   In later
years his home seems to have been in Augusta, Me.   He was
among the organizers of the first Congregational church of
that town, and contributed largely to the erection of a house
of worship, at whose altars he worshiped till his death.   He

was one of the organizers of the first bank in Augusta, Me., and for years a director. Public confidence gave him various offices of trust—such as inspector, justice of the peace, and for thirteen years town treasurer. Of a cheerful temperament, he was facetious, full of amusing and instructive anecdote, modest of his own abilities, social and benevolent. In practical life he possessed inflexible honesty and uprightness. His christian character was consistent, exemplary and cheerful.

[Seventh Generation.] Children:

5121. i. ANNA CHILD, b. in Groton, Mass., Dec. 23, 1782, d. at Calais, Me.

5122. ii. GREENWOOD CUSHING CHILD, b. in Groton, Mass., June 24, 1785, m. Nov. 17, 1815, Lucy Howe Palmer.

5123. iii. JAMES LORING CHILD, b. May 31, 1792, m. Nov. 10, 1822, Jane Hale of Portland, Me.

5124. iv. HANNAH CHILD, b. abt. 1795, m. Nov. 12, 1814, Francis Swan.

5125. v. ELISHA CHILD, b. Nov. 12, 1797, m. Dec. 4, 1822, Maria Palmer.

5126. vi. JOHN CHILD, d. in infancy.

5127. vii. SARAH CHILD, d. ——.

[Seventh Generation.]

5122. ii. GREENWOOD CUSHING CHILD, second child of James and Hannah Cushing Child, b. in Groton, Mass., June 24, 1785, m. Nov. 17, 1815, Lucy Howe Palmer of Augusta, Me., she d. in Massachusetts May 17, 1866. He resided in Augusta, Me., and d. July 24, 1855. He was a merchant of extensive business, was characterized by an exceeding largeness and uprightness of dealing. He bequeathed a large estate to his widow and children; with an utter distaste for mingling in public affairs he declined all office.

[Eighth Generation.] Children, born in Augusta, Me.

5128. i. SARAH REED CHILD, b. Dec. 12, 1816, m. July 25, 1844, Wm. L. Walker. They have no children. Reside in Braintree, Mass.

5129. ii. LUCY PALMER CHILD, b. Feb. 14, 1819, m. June 17, 1843, Capt. Samuel Gore. An underwriter; they reside in Europe.

5130. iii. MARY CHILD, b. Mch. 17, 1821, m. Oct. 4, 1860, Mark F. Duncklee. He was b. in Greenfield, N. H., Dec. 9, 1824; is a lawyer by profession. Residence, Braintree, Mass.

5131. iv. GEORGE ALBERT CHILD, b. July 6, 1823, m. Jan. 9, 1849, Charlotte N. Marshall. He d.—no date—leaving one dau., living in Monson, Me.

5132. v. JAMES RUFUS CHILD, b. Oct. 7, 1825, m. Aug. 25, 1859, Margaret Bridge. He was a cotton planter in Georgia; d. leaving three daughters.

5133. vi. WILLIAM CHILD, b. Nov. 8, 1827. Resides in Augusta; unm.

5134. vii. MARCIA GREENWOOD CHILD, b. April 30, 1830. Resides in Braintree. Mass.

5135. viii. HELEN CUSHING CHILD, b. July 3, 1832, d. Feb. 21, 1833.

[Seventh Generation.]

5123. iii. JAMES LORING CHILD, third child of James and Hannah Cushing Child, b. in Augusta, Me., May 31, 1792, m. Nov. 10, 1822, Jane Hale of Portland, Maine.

Mr. James L. Child, after the usual common school training, entered the Hallowell Academy, designing to fit for college. A casualty seriously injuring his knee disabled him for months and changed his plans. Upon his recovery he entered at once upon the study of the law, which he was obliged to make a long term of five years. With a taste for belles lettres, he was a writer of some most pleasing prose and verse. He also made a practical study of surveying. His first legal partnership was with Hon. Thomas Rice of Winslow, Me.; the election of Mr. Rice as representative in Congress, caused an early dissolution of this firm; but Mr. Child retained the lucrative business of the office. At this period, 1812, the war with Great Britian awakened much military enthusiasm. In January, 1814, Gov. Strong of Massachusetts, appointed Mr. Child captain of the Augusta militia; and justice of the peace for Kennebec. Ill health soon rendered change of scene and rest imperative, and Mr. Child travelled both in the United States and abroad. An acquaintance formed in England led Mr. Child to form a commercial partnership in Charleston, S. C.; the failure in Liverpool of Mr. Witherspoon, a brother of Mr. Child's partner, abruptly terminated the business. Mr. Child returned to Augusta, Me., and resumed his professional duties, and was not long after an active participator in the ceremonies and labors attending the separation of Maine from Massachusetts, and the formation of a distinct state government: this was in 1820. Mr. Child had won so fine a reputation for business dispatch, that he was at once chosen Clerk of the House of Representatives of the new State, a post he held for eleven years. Later he was made a Councillor of the United States District Court of Maine. He was elected a member of the State Legislature, but declined to serve. In all municipal interests he was an active and able organizer and director. He was one of the directors of the Augusta bank, and in uniform attendance till the day before his death, which occurred in 1862. His life was marked by great energy, versatility of talent and executive ability.

[Eighth Generation.] Children, born in Alna and Augusta, Me.:

5136. i. DANIEL CARLTON CHILD, b. Oct. 27, 1823, was drowned in Columbia river, Oregon, Mch. 25, 1851.

5137. ii. ANN ELIZA CHILD, b. Mch. 26, 1825, m. Aug. 31, 1843, Lieut. Robert Auchmuly Wainwright, U. S. A.

5138. iii. JAMES LORING CHILD, JR, b Feb 20, 1827, m. Nov. 19, 1848, Mrs. Elizabeth McCrea.

5139. iv. GRENVILLE HALE CHILD, b. Jan. 30, 1829, m Charlotte N. Ballard.

5140. v. REBECCA JANE CHILD, b. Sept. 2, 1830, d. Feb 26, 1833.

5141. vi. REBECCA JANE CHILD, 2D, b. Oct. 3, 1833, m. Sept. 3, 1853, Gardner H. Cushing.

5142 vii. HANNAH SWAN CHILD, b. Oct. 2, 1836, m. May 17, 1857, Henry Wells Severance.

5143. viii. HORACE CHILD, b. July 25, 1840, d. Jan. 4, 1845.

5144. ix. ALICE WAINWRIGHT CHILD, b. Jan. 8, 1844, d. Jan. 13, 1844.

5145. x. ROBERT WAINWRIGHT CHILD, b. Jan. 15, 1846, m. Anna Carey. He had two children, both died. He is a lumber surveyor of Boston, Mass.

[Eighth Generation.]

5137. ii. ANN ELIZA CHILD, second child of James Loring and Jane Hale Child, b. in Alna, Me., Mch. 26, 1825, m. Aug. 21, 1843, Lieut. Robert A. Wainwright, U.S.A. He was b. at Newport, R. I., d. at Benicia Arsenal, Cal., Dec. 22, 1866

[Ninth Generation] Children:

5146. i. ROBERT D. WAINWRIGHT, now Lieut. of the Marine Corps U. S. N.

5147. ii. ISABELLA M. WAINWRIGHT. d. in Detroit. Mich , 1871.

[Eighth Generation.]

5138. iii. REV. JAMES LORING CHILD, b. in Alna, Me., Feb. 20, 1827, m. Nov. 19, 1848, Mrs. Elizabeth McCrea of New York City ; was a clergyman of the M. E. church. He resided in Michigan ; d. 1873, in Denver, Colorado.

[Ninth Generation.] Children. They reside in Leavett, Mich.

5148. i. BENJAMIN WAINWRIGHT CHILD.

5149. ii. JANE HALE CHILD.

5150. iii. ISABELL KIMBALL CHILD.

5151. iv. FRANKLIN ARTHUR CHILD.

5152. v. CAROLINE AMELIA CHILD.

5153. vi. ANNA FARGO CHILD.

[Seventh Generation.]

5125. v. ELISHA CHILD, fifth child of James and Hannah Cushing Child, b. Nov. 12, 1797, m. Dec. 4, 1822, Maria Palmer. Both d. in Augusta, Me.

[Eighth Generation] Children, born in Augusta, Me.

5154. i. CHARLOTTE ELIZABETH CHILD, b. 1825, m. Daniel Fales of New York City. Merchant.

5155. ii. HANNAH MARIA CHILD, b Jan. 27, 1828, m. Dec. 9, 1852, Samuel W. Jaques. Lawyer, Biddeford, Me.

5156. iii. PAULINA PALMER CHILD, b. May 21, 1830, m. Llewllyn W. Lithgow of Augusta, Me.

5157. iv. MARGARET E. CHILD, b. 1833, unm.

5158. v. EDWARD STYLES CHILD, b. Sept. 17, 1834, d. Oct. 3, 1844.

[Sixth Generation.]

5116. vi. ELISHA CHILD, sixth child and third son of Moses and Sarah Styles Child, b. in Groton, Mass., Oct. 31, 1767, m. Feb. 17, 1795, by Rev. Abel Fisher, Martha Abbott, of Wilton, N. H. She was b. Dec. 11, 1772. Resided in Temple, N. H. He d. April 5, 1853. She d. Dec. 15, 1861.

[Seventh Generation.] Children, born in Temple, N. H.

5159. i. MOSES CHILD, b. Jan. 30, 1796, d. June 29, 1796.

5160. ii. PATTY CHILD, b. May 16, 1797, d. Feb. 29, 1868, unm.

5161. iii. SARAH H. CHILD, b. Mch. 22, 1799, m Nov. 24, 1825, James Killam.

5162. iv. POLLY CHILD, b. Mch. 25, 1801, m. May 17, 1825, Nathaniel Ford Locke

5163. v. JAMES CHILD, b. Sept. 20, 1802, m. May 10, 1827, Mary Locke Laws.

5164. vi. NAHUM CHILD, b. July 3, 1805, m. Nov. 12, 1833, Betsey Wright.

5165. vii. HARRIET CHILD, b. July 9, 1807, m. Mch. 5, 1829, Samuel Mitchell

5166. viii. BETSEY CHILD, b. April 8, 1809, m. Sept. 9, 1829, Francis Killam of Temple, N. H.

[Seventh Generation.]

5161. iii. SARAH H. CHILD, third child of Elisha and Martha Abbott Child, b. in Temple, N. H., Mch. 22, 1799, m. Nov. 24, 1825, James Killam.

[Eighth Generation.] Children:

5167. i. RODNEY A. KILLAM, b. July 11, 1828.

5168. ii. JAMES O. KILLAM, b. June 27, 1831.

5169. iii. ELIZA M. KILLAM, b. Nov. 28, 1841

[Seventh Generation.]

5162. iv. POLLY CHILD, fourth child, third dau. of Elisha and Martha Abbott Child, b. in Temple, N. H., Mch. 25, 1801, m. May 17, 1825, Nathaniel Ford Locke of Peterborough, N. H.

[Eighth Generation.] Children:

5170. i. MARTHA C. LOCKE, b. July 28, 1827.

5171. ii. ALMENA FRANCES LOCKE, b. May 16, 1832.

5172. iii. ALBERT D. LOCKE, b. Feb. 3, 1836.

[Seventh Generation.]

5163. v. JAMES CHILD, fifth child, second son of Elisha and Martha Abbott Child, b. in Temple, N. H., Sept. 20, 1802, m. May 10, 1827, Mary Laws. She was b. Jan. 19, 1799, in Billerica, Mass. She was the dau. of Thomas and Mary Locke Laws. Resided in Peterborough, ~~Mass.~~ N. H.

[Eighth Generation.] Child:

5173. i. NAHUM ABBOTT CHILD, b. Nov. 9, 1828, in Temple, N. H., m. April 11, 1860, Ellen Sargent. She was b. Nov. 28, 1836.

[Ninth Generation.]   Children
    5174. i. JAMES EDWARD CHILD, b. in Temple, N. H., Feb. 13, 1861.
    5175. ii. SAMUEL MITCHELL CHILD, b. Sept. 10, 1862, in Temple, N. H.
    5176. iii. MARTHA JANE CHILD, b. in Temple, N. H., April 18, 1865.
    5177. iv. Infant, (unchristened) b. Sept. 13, 1872, d. soon.

[Seventh Generation.]

    5164. vi. NAHUM CHILD, sixth child and third son of Elisha and Martha Abbott Child, b. July 3, 1805, m. Nov. 12, 1833, Betsey Wright.

[Eighth Generation.]   Child:
    5178. i. MARY CHILD.

[Seventh Generation.]

    5165. vii. HARRIET CHILD, seventh child and fourth dau. of Elisha and Martha Abbott Child, b. in Temple, N. H., July 9, 1807, m. Mch. 5, 1829, Samuel Mitchell of Hancock, N. H.

[Eighth Generation.]   Children:
    5179. i. GEO. F. A. MITCHELL, b. May 17, 1838, d. May 8, 1863.
    5180. ii. FRANCIS MITCHELL, b. ———— d. May 6, 1857, at Lawrence, Kansas.
    5181. iii. BETSEY C. KILLAM MITCHELL, b. ————, m. Nov. 26, 1859, John M. Graham of Waterloo, Kansas.

[Sixth Generation.]

    5119. ix. ISAAC CHILD, ninth child, fourth son of Moses and Sarah Styles Child, b. in Watertown or Waltham, 1774, m. 1st, 1808, Sarah Rockwood. She was b. in 1781, d. Oct. 17, 1815 ; m. 2d, April 5, 1816, Polly Kimball. She was b. Feb 10, 1795.

[Seventh Generation.]   Children, born in Lancaster, Mass.
    5182. i. RUFUS CHILD, b. Dec. 9, 1809.
    5183. ii. SARAH PEASE CHILD, b. April 3, 1811.
    5184. iii. JAMES E. CHILD, b. Sept. 9, 1818, d. Feb. 22, 1822.
    5185. iv. MARY C. CHILD, b. Nov. 11, 1820, d. July 14, 1836.
    5186. v. JAMES CHILD, b. June 30, 1823.
    5187. vi. GEORGE CHILD, b. Oct. 13, 1824, m. Sept. 4, 1858, Louisa Edwards.
    5188. vii. JANE A. CHILD, b. June 11, 1827.

[Fifth Generation.]

    5110. iv. AMOS CHILD, child of Isaac and Hannah Goddin Child, b. abt. 1753-4, m. abt. 1778-9. He lived in Lincoln, Mass., and Nelson, N. H.

[Sixth Generation.]   Children:
    5189. i. AMOS CHILD, JR., b. abt. 1780, m. Naomi Hartshorn.
    5190. ii. JONAS CHILD, b. Sept. 26, 1782, in Nelson, N. H., m. Patty Bassett, abt. 1807.
    5191. iii. SALLY CHILD, unmarried.

    5189. i. AMOS CHILD, JR., eldest child of Amos and ———— Child, b. abt. 1780, m. Naomi Hartshorn.

[Seventh Generation.] Children:

5192. i. Amos Child, Jr.

5193. ii. Hannah Child.

[Sixth Generation.]

5190. ii. Jonas Child, second child of Amos and Hannah Goddin Child, b. in Nelson, N. H., Sept. 26, 1782, m. about 1807, Patty Bassett. Lived in Boston, Mass.

[Seventh Generation.] Children:

5194. i. Samuel Bassett Child, b. June 19, 1808, in Boston. Lived in Indiana; m. five times.

5195. ii. Priscilla Griffin Child, b. in Boston, Sept. 27, 1809, m. J. Kingsbury of the "Choctaw Mission."

5196. iii. Martha Belding Child, b. in Boston, Mass., Feb. 23, 1811, m. Joseph Longley, Keene, N. H.

5197. iv. Jonas Dakin Child, b. Feb. 23, 1811, m. May 11, 1837, Susan Elms. } TWINS.

5198. v. William Lawson Child, b. in Boston, May 25, 1814, m. Elma Alford.

5199. vi. Nathan Madan Child, b. Dec. 29, 1815, in Boston, m. a Miss Springer. Reside at Keene, N. H.

5200. vii. Betty Bassett Child, b. in Boston, Mch. 25, 1826, d. soon.

5201. viii. Sarah Jane Child, b. in Boston, April 18, 1827, m. Emanuel Small, New Liberty, Ky.

[Third Generation.]

4736. iv. DANIEL CHILD, fourth child, second son of John and Mary Warren Child, b. in Watertown, 1677, m. Jan. 29, 1702, Beriah Bemis. He d. 1724. His widow m. Aug. 12, 1736, Joseph Pierce. She d. aged 88.

[Fourth Generation.] Children, born in Watertown, Mass.

5202. i. Sarah Child, b. Sept. 14, 1702, m. June 13, 1734, John Fisk.

5203. ii. Susanna Child, b. Mch. 6, 1705.

5204. iii. Elizabeth Child, b. Feb. 18, 1707, m. July 21, 1725, Dea. Isaac Stearns of Waltham, Mass.

5205. iv. Daniel Child, Jr., b. April 9, 1709, m. Jan. 13, 1729, Mary Bright.

5206. v. David Child, b. Dec. 27, 1711, m. 1st, Oct. 23, 1737, Grace Brown. Settled in Shrewsbury; m. 2d, Mehitable Richardson.

5207. vi. John Child, b. Dec. 2, 1713, m. Aug. 15, 1758, Ruhama Pierce.

5208. vii. Joshua Child, b. Mch. 2, 1717, m. April 30, 1741, Grace Bemis. On Oct. 23, 1774, they were transferred from the church of Watertown to that of Lincoln.

5209. viii. Samuel Child, b. Feb. 7, 1719, m. 1st, Oct. 19, 1745, Mary Ball; m. 2d, Esther ———; m. 3d, April 8, 1799, Mrs. Elizabeth Stimpson.

5210. ix. Elisha Child, b. Feb. 16, 1721, m. 1st, Mary ———; m. 2d, Mehitable Garfield.

5211. x. Mary Child, b. June 10, 1722, m. Mch. 11, 1743, Joseph Whitney of Weston.

[Fourth Generation.]

5205. iv. DANIEL CHILD, JR., fourth child, eldest son of Daniel and Beriah Bemis Child, b. in Watertown, Mass., April

O 1

9, 1709, m. Jan. 13. 1729, Mary Bright, dau. of Nathaniel Bright. He was a selectman of Waltham.

[Fifth Generation.]   Children, born in Waltham, Mass.

5212. i. ANNA CHILD, b. July 6, 1730.

5213. ii. DANIEL CHILD, b. April 26, 1732, d. May, 1733.

5214. iii. ABIJAH CHILD, b. Jan. 12, 1734, m. 1st, Dec. 15, 1759, Beulah Harrington: m. 2d, Dec. 2, 1790, Ann Bemis.

5215. iv. DANIEL CHILD, 2D, b. Feb. 21, 1736.

5216. v. LYDIA CHILD, b. Feb. 25, 1738, m. Oct. 26, 1758. William Flagg.

5217. vi. SARAH CHILD, b. Aug. 11, 1740, m. Jan. 2, 1760, Wm. Benjamin.

5218. vii. JONAS CHILD, b. Sept. 30, 1743, m. Jan. 11, 1770, Hannah Sanderson.

5219. viii. MARY CHILD, b. Oct. 14, 1745, m. Oct. 6, 1763. Wm. Hagar of Waltham.

5220. ix. BETTIE CHILD, b. Mch. 9, 1748, d. Sept. 24, 1751.

5221. x. JOSIAH CHILD, b. June 17, 1750, d. Sept. 24, 1757.

5222. xi. EPHRAIM CHILD, bapt. June 30, 1754.

[Fifth Generation.]

5214. iii. ABIJAH CHILD, third child, second son of Daniel, Jr. and Mary Bright Child, b. in Waltham, Jan. 12, 1734, m. 1st, Dec. 15, 1759, Beulah Harrington ; m. 2d, Dec. 2, 1790, Ann Bemis. He was captain in 25th Regt. of the Continental army of the Revolution in 1775. He was selectman of Waltham, Mass., in the years 1774–5 and 1787.

[Sixth Generation.]   Children born in Waltham, Mass.

5223. i. EPHRAIM CHILD, b. July 26, 1760, m. Nov. 6, 1784, Lydia Livermore.

5224. ii. ABIJAH CHILD, JR., b. Jan 14, 1762, ⎰ TWINS ⎱ d. young. [Benjamin,
5225. iii. BEULAH CHILD, b. Jan. 14, 1762, ⎱ ⎰ m. Feb. 16, 1786, Wm.

5226. iv. SARAH CHILD, b. June 2, 1764, d. July 14, 1769.

5227. v. DANIEL CHILD, b. July 3, 1766, m. Jan. 7, 1787, Phebe Parks.

5228. vi. WILLIAM CHILD, b. May 14, 1768.

5229. vii. PHEBE CHILD, b. Nov. 4, 1769.

523). viii. EDWARD CHILD, b. Jan. 12, 1772.

5231. ix. ELIZABETH CHILD, b. Dec. 8, 1773, m. Nov. 23, 1802, Antepas Maynard.

5232. x. ANNA CHILD, b. Nov. 8, 1775, m. April 1, 1791, Nathaniel Carter.

5233. xi. ABIJAH CHILD, JR, b. Jan. 25, 1779, m. 1807, Polly Sanderson.

[Sixth Generation.]

5223. i. EPHRAIM CHILD, eldest child and son of Abijah and Beulah Harrington Child, b. July 26, 1760, m. Nov. 6, 1784, Lydia Livermore. Ephraim first resided in Waltham, then he removed to Livermore, Maine, or more probable he removed to Livermore after the birth of his fifth child, Amos, b. 1794, in Waltham, Mass.

[Seventh Generation.] Children, born in Waltham, Mass.:

5234. i. POLLY CHILD, b. April 20, 1785.

5235. ii. LYDIA CHILD, b. April 11, 1788.

5236. iii. WILLIAM CHILD, b. July 7, 1790.

5237. iv. EPHRAIM CHILD, JR., b. Mch. 22, 1792.

5238. v. AMOS CHILD, b. May, 16, 1794.

[Fifth Generation.]

5218. vii. JONAS CHILD, seventh child and fourth son of Daniel, Jr. and Mary Bright Child, b. in Waltham, Sept. 30, 1743, m. Jan. 11, 1770, Hannah Sanderson. She d. 1808.

[Sixth Generation.] Children, born in Waltham, Mass.

5239. i. ABIGAIL CHILD, b. 1770, d. soon.

5240. ii. JOSIAH CHILD, b. Aug. 2, 1771.

5241. iii. FRANCIS CHILD, b. Aug. 11, 1774.

5242. iv. HANNAH CHILD, b. Nov. 17, 1776, m. Feb. 21, 1799, Jonas Green.

5243. v. MARY CHILD, b. April 6, 1779, m. Oct. 27, 1796, Daniel Tower.

5244. vi. JONATHAN CHILD, b. April 16, 1781.

5245. vii. JOHN CHILD, b. Dec. 8, 1783.

5246. viii. JONAS CHILD, JR., b. April 6, 1786, m. Hannah ———.

5247. ix. Thomas Child, b. Feb. 4, 1791.

[Sixth Generation.]

5246. viii. JONAS CHILD, JR., eighth child of Jonas and Hannah Sanderson Child, b. in Waltham, Mass., April 6, 1786, m. about 1803, Hannah ———.

[Seventh Generation.] Child:

5248. i. JOSIAH CHILD, b. in Waltham, Mass., Jan. 1804, d. July 26, 1804.

[Fourth Generation.]

5206. v. DAVID CHILD, fifth child and second son of Daniel and Beriah Bemis Child, b. in Watertown, Mass., Dec. 27, 1711, m. 1st, Oct. 23, 1737, Grace Brown. Settled in Shrewsbury, Mass.: m. 2d, Nov. 29, 1759, Mehitable Richardson of Worcester.

[Fifth Generation.] Children, born in Shrewsbury, Mass:

5249. i. BEULAH CHILD, b. June 4, 1739, m. Feb. 27, 1766, Samuel Lee of Rutland, Vt.

5250. ii. SUSANNA CHILD, b. June 6, 1741.

5251. iii. DAVID CHILD, JR., b. Jan. 30, 1745, m. 1774, Lydia Stevens.

5252. iv. ZACHARIAH CHILD, b. Nov. 19, 1763, m. in 1784, Lydia Bigelow.

5253. v. AMOS CHILD, b. Aug. 27, 1765.

[Fifth Generation.]

5252. iv. ZACHARIAH CHILD, eldest child of David and his second wife Mehitable Richardson Child, b. Nov. 19, 1763, m. 1784, Lydia Bigelow, dau. of David Bigelow of Worcester, Mass. He was a Revolutionary soldier and lived at West Boylston, Mass.

[Sixth Generation.] Children:

5254. i. MARCUS CHILD, b. ab't 1790, m. Lydia Chadwick. "He went to Stanstead, Canada, P. Q. at an early day of its settlement, and was employed by Levi Bigelow as a clerk. At a later period he became a partner with Mr. Bigelow in the drug business on Stanstead Plains. Mr. Child became very prominent and held many offices. He represented the County of Stanstead in the Provincial Parliament for a number of years. In the Revolution of 1837-9 he was identified with the Radical and Reformatory Party, and for a time was proscribed and compelled to leave the country. His party came again into power, and he returned and was again elected to the Provincial Parliament for Stanstead county. He removed to Coatacook and died there. He left a son at Coatacook by the name of Geo. M. Child."

5255. ii. LEVI B. CHILD, b. ab't 1792, m. ——.

5256. iii. DAVID LEE CHILD, b. July 8, 1794, m. Oct. 28, 1828, Lydia M. Francis.

5257. iv. JOHN CHILD, b. ab't 1802, m. 1st, Mch. 13, 1832, Laura Dwight: m. 2d, Oct. 23, 1856, Ellen W. Healy.

5258. v. WALTER CHILD, b. 1803, d. in Watertown, Mass..

5259. vi. ANNIS CHILD, b. 1805, m. —— Howe, d. in Derby, Vt.

5260. vii. LYDIA CHILD, b 1807, d. unm. in West Boylston, Mass.

5261. viii. SUSAN CHILD, b. 1809, m. ——Andrus of Derby Vt.

5262. ix. MARIA CHILD, b. 1811, m.——Haskins, West Boylston, Mass

[Sixth Generation.]

5255. ii. LEVI B. CHILD, b. 1792, m.——.

[Seventh Generation.] Children:

5263. i. CHARLES B. CHILD, lives in Cincinnati, O.

5264. ii. JOHN STARK CHILD, in Carson City, Nevada.

5265. iii. WM. HOWE CHILD, Gainsville, Ala

5266. iv. SUSAN PARIS CHILD, m. J. W. Kelley, Manchester, Iowa.*

5267. v. ANN M. CHILD, m.—— White; d. in Indiana.

5268. vi. KATIE F. CHILD, m.—— Martin, lives in Carson City, Nevada.

5269. vii. RUTH M. A. CHILD, m. —— Frazier, West Derby, Vt.

[Sixth Generation.]

5256. iii. DAVID LEE CHILD, third son and child of Zachariah and Lydia Bigelow Child, b. in West Boylston, Mass., July 8, 1794, m. Oct. 28, 1828, Lydia Maria Francis, who was b. in Medford, Mass., in 1802.

Mr. and Mrs. David L. Child merit at our hands an especial notice, for by their philanthropic and literary labors they have attained deserved notability. Mr. Child was educated for the legal profession, but was more devoted to journalism and other literary work than to the practice of the law. "For several years Mr. Child was the editor of the *Massachusetts Journal*, published in Boston. In 1841, Mr. Child and his gifted wife removed to New York City, and became joint-editors of the newspaper called the *Anti-Slavery Standard.* He published a large pamphlet on the taking of Texas from Mexico, called

* We are indebted to Mr. J. W. Kelley for this record.

Naboth's Vineyard, also a small volume on the manufacture of beet sugar; pamphlets and articles for various papers and magazines mostly on political topics of the day."*

Mrs. Child has for some years resided in Wayland, Mass., in one of the cosy homes surrounded by noble elms, so frequent in New England. Mrs. Lydia M. Child was the daughter of Mr. David Francis of Medford, Mass. Mr. Francis was somewhat widely known in New England as the manufacturer of a sort of biscuit called the Medford cracker; he was a man of good mind, and, with his wife's efficient aid, gave to his children the best advantages for education, with an inheritance of good intellectual powers. Their earliest American ancestor of the name, settled in Medford in 1636. Rev. Convers Francis, D. D., of Harvard University, a clergyman of the Unitarian church, is an elder brother of Mrs. Child, and was largely instrumental in the development of her "early love of literature." In the home of Dr. Francis, Mrs. Child wrote her first romance, "Hobomok," suggested to her by the perusal of Dr. Palfrey's article on Yamoydan in the North American Review. The succeeding year was issued "The Rebels; A Tale of the Revolution." In this work are found two gems,—a speech which she makes James Otis utter, is so full of patriotism and strength as to have been often declaimed as Otis' own words; and a sermon of Whitefield which many presumed the genuine work of the great divine. In 1826, Mrs. Child edited a monthly magazine, the *Juvenile Miscellany*, which she sustained eight years. She also wrote a cook book, "The Frugal Housewife," "The Girl's Own Book," "The Mother's Assistant." These were followed by a " History of the Condition of Women in all Ages," "Philothea, a Greek Romance," of the time of Pericles. During the residence of Mrs. Child in New York, she became the close friend of Isaac T. Hopper, so widely known as the friend of the slave, and after his death Mrs. Child wrote the very fascinating story of his life. We cannot mention all her writings, but "collectively they number over a hundred." We close our brief notice of this most noble and thoroughly practical, true, loveable woman in the words of the North American Review :

"We are not sure that any woman in our country would outrank Mrs. Child. This lady has long been before the public as an author with much

* These items of Mr Child's public life were received from the p·n of Mrs. L. M. Child, his widow.

success, and she well deserves it, for in all her works we think that nothing can be found which does not commend itself by its tone of healthy morality and good sense. Few female writers, if any, have done more or better things for our literature in its lighter or graver depths."

On the 20th of October, 1880, Mrs. Lydia Maria Child died at her home in Wayland. Funeral services were conducted in a most quiet, unostentatious manner as she had wished. Rev. Mr. Salter of Roxbury officiated, taking for his text portions of Mrs. Child's latest book, "Aspirations of the World." Hon. Wendell Phillips pronounced a chaste and just eulogy.

By will Mrs. Child left $50,000 to the Hampton Agricul tural College of Virginia, and $9,000 to several charitable in- stitutions.

[Sixth Generation.]

5257. iv. CAPT. JOHN CHILDE,* fourth child and son of Zach- ariah and Lydia Bigelow Child, b. in West Boylston, Mass., Aug. 30, 1802, m. Mch. 13, 1832, Laura Dwight, b. Dec. 23, 1809, dau. of James Scott and Mary Sanford Dwight of Spring- field, Mass. Mr. Childe added the terminal "e" to his name, which is really the only correct addition to be made. He was a graduate of West Point. He was 1st Lieut. and Capt. in the U. S. army, and a superior civil engineer. He constructed "The Western Railroad," (from Pittsfield to Albany) the "Con- necticut River Railroad," and also "The Cleaveland & Colum- bus Railroad," and "The Mobile & Ohio Railroad," the last (three hundred miles long) being his great work as an engineer. He was a man of high toned character, well educated, very energetic, and generous in the use of his means. Mrs. Laura D. Childe was lost in the "Arctic," Sept. 27, 1854, with her daughter, Lelia Maria Childe, on her return voyage from a tour of pleasure through Europe. He m. Oct. 23, 1856, his second wife, Ellen Wills Healy. Capt. John Childe d. at Springfield, Mass., Feb. 2, 1858.

[Seventh Generation.] Children:

5270. i. FRANCIS DWIGHT CHILDE, b. Jan. 18, 1833, d. Sept. 20, 1833.

5271. ii. LELIA MARIA CHILDE, b. April 11, 1835; was lost at sea in the "Arctic," Sept. 27, 1854.

5272. iii. MARY DWIGHT CHILDE, b. Aug. 9, 1845.

By second wife:

5273. iv. JOHN HEALY CHILDE, b. Jan. 18, 1858.

* This account is taken from Dr. B. W. Dwight's Genealogy of the Dwight Family.

[Fourth Generation.]

5208. vii. JOSHUA CHILD, seventh child, fourth son of Daniel and Beriah Bemis Child, b. in Watertown, Mass., Mch. 2, 1717, m. April 30, 1741, Grace Bemis. Dismissed in 1774 from the church in Watertown to that in Lincoln.

[Fifth Generation.] Children, born in Waltham, Mass.

5274. i. ANNA CHILD, b. Nov. 13, 1741.

5275. ii. LUCY CHILD, b. Mch. 1, 1744.

5276. iii. JOSHUA CHILD, JR., b. Mch. 26, 1749, m. Feb. 24, 1781, Elizabeth Hammond.

5277. iv. DANIEL CHILD, b. Dec. 24, 1752, m. Molly ———, ab't 1777.

5278. v. BETTY CHILD, b. Sept. 1, 1755.

5279. vi. BERIA CHILD, b. Feb. 5, 1758, d. unm. 1816.

5280. vii. ELIJAH CHILD, b. Nov. 17, 1760, m. 1st, Sept. 3, 1807, Mary Knight; she d. 1809. He m. 2nd, Nov. 29, 1810, Anna Hosmer.

5281. viii. MICAL CHILD, b. July 15, 1756, d. Feb. 1773.

[Fifth Generation.]

5276. iii. JOSHUA CHILD, JR., third child and eldest son of Joshua and Grace Bemis Child, b. Mch. 26, 1749, in Watertown, Mass., m. Feb. 24, 1781, Elizabeth Hammond, dau. of Jonathan and Lydia Stratton Hammond of Waltham, Mass. She d. May, 1824.

[Sixth Generation.] Children, born in Lincoln, Mass.

5282. i JOHN CHILD, b. Oct. 19, 1781, d. July 13, 1825.

5283. ii. POLLY CHILD, b. April 13, 1784.

5284. iii. JOSHUA CHILD, JR., b. June 25, 1785.

5285. iv. ELIZABETH CHILD, b. April 10, 1788.

[Fifth Generation.]

5277. iv. DANIEL CHILD, fourth child, second son of Joshua and Grace Bemis Child, b. in Watertown, Mass., Dec. 24, 1752, m. ab't 1777, Molly ———.

[Sixth Generation.] Children:

5286. i WILLIAM CHILD, b. in Watertown, Mass., Nov. 23, 1778.

5287. ii. DANIEL CHILD, JR., b. in Watertown, Mass., Sept. 22, 1780.

5288. iii. POLLY CHILD.

5289. iv. TIMOTHY CHILD.

5290. v. CYNTHIA CHILD.

5291. vi. BETSEY CHILD.

5292. vii. NATHANIEL CHILD.

5293. viii. HARRIET CHILD.

5294 ix. JONAS CHILD.

5295. x. LUCY CHILD.

5296. xi. FRANCES CHILD.

[Fourth Generation.]

5209. viii. ENSIGN SAMUEL CHILD, fifth son and eighth child of Daniel and Beriah Bemis Child, b. in Watertown, Mass.,

Feb. 7, 1719, m. 1st, Oct. 19, 1745, to Mary Ball, who d. Nov. 18, 1748; m. 2nd, in 1750, Esther ——, who d. Sept. 10, 1778; m. 3rd, April 8, 1779, Mrs. Elizabeth Stimpson. In the later years of his life Ensign Child removed with his large family of children and grand-children to Vermont, and became thus the pioneer settlers of Addison county in that State. There, surrounded by a most noble, cherished line of descendants, he sleeps, after a long and useful life. He d. Dec. 18, 1803, æ. 85 yrs. 10 mos. Mrs. E. S. Child d. April 8, 1803.

[Fifth Generation.] Children:

5297. i. DANIEL CHILD, b. Nov. 13, 1748, d. Feb. 1749 in Weston, Mass.

5298. ii. ESTHER CHILD, b. April 18, 1751, m. Sept. 9, 1773, Benjamin Hagar.

5299. iii. MARY CHILD, b. Jan. 12, 1753, m. April 21, 1773, Roger Bigelow.

5300. iv. LUCY CHILD, b. April 18, 1755, d. Feb. 1756, in Weston, Mass.

5301. v LUCY CHILD, 2nd, b. April 11, 1757, m. Oct. 24, 1777, John Sheppard.

5302. vi. MOSES CHILD, b. Aug. 8, 1858 in Weston, Mass.

5303. vii. ANNA CHILD, b. Mch. 26, 1759, d. y'g in Weston, Mass.

5304. viii. EUNICE CHILD, b. Nov. 6, 1760, m. Dec. 15, 1784, Daniel Twitchell.

5305. ix. SAMUEL CHILD, JR., b. Nov. 1, 1762, m. 1st, Aug. 8, 1784, Abigail Sheppard, m. 2nd, Nov. 9, 1789, Hannah Lamson.

5306. x. ANNA CHILD, 2d, b. Nov. 2, 1766 in Weston. Mass.

[Fifth Generation.]

5298. ii. ESTHER CHILD, eldest dau. and second child of Ensign Samuel and Esther Child, b. in Weston, Mass., April 18, 1751, m. Sept. 9, 1773, Benjamin Hagar, who was b. Jan. 26, 1749. After the birth of their children Mr. and Mrs. Hagar removed to Weybridge, Vt., from Waltham, Mass., where they had resided. Mrs. Esther Child Hagar d. in Weybridge, Vt., in 1837.

[Sixth Generation.] Children:

5307. i. BENJAMIN HAGAR, JR., b. Feb. 23, 1774, m. Jan. 16. 1801, Sarah Martin.

5308. ii. BETSEY HAGAR, b. Jan. 3, 1776, m. —— Stearns.

5309. iii. ESTHER HAGAR, b. July 12, 1778, d. young.

5310. iv. JONATHAN HAGAR, b. Sept. 12, 1779, m. Jan. 1808, Louise Tradeaux.

5311. v. THOMAS HAGAR, b. Oct. 19, 1781, m. Jan. 26, 1802, Polly Fitch.

5312. vi. ABNER HAGAR, b. Jan. 31, 1784, m. Aug. 1816, Hannah Barker.

5313. vii. LUTHER HAGAR, b. Oct. 8, 1786, m. Aug. 25, 1813, Sarah Adams.

5314. viii. CALVIN HAGAR, b. May 2, 1789, m. Dec. 12, 1822, Sarah Commers.

5315. ix. JONAS HAGAR, b. May 21, 1791, d. Dec. 10, 1791.

5316. x. JONAS HAGAR, 2nd, b. Sept. 10, 1793, m. Nov. 29, 1822, Elmira M. Mishar.

[Sixth Generation.]

5307. i. BENJAMIN HAGAR, JR., eldest child of Esther Child and Benjamin Hagar, b. in Waltham, Mass., Feb. 23, 1774, m. Jan. 16, 1801, Sarah Martin, who was b. Jan. 28, 1803, and d. May 2, 1865, in Weybridge, Vt.   Mr. B. Hagar, Jr., d. in Berbice, South America, Jan. 29, 1821.

[Seventh Generation.] Children:

5317. i. BENJAMIN HAGAR, JR, b. Feb. 8, 1802, d. Oct. 6, 1827.

5318. ii. LUTHER MARTIN HAGAR, b. Sept. 24, 1804, m. Feb. 19, 1827. Clarissa Read.

5319. iii. JONATHAN HAGAR, b. Feb. 19, 1807, m. and had two children. He d. Nov. 16, 1879.

5320. iv. HANNAH HAGAR, b. Dec 1, 1899, m. Wm. Green; d. Dec. 6, 1870, at Marion, N. Y. Left two daughters.

5321. v. HENRY WILLIAM HAGAR, b. Aug. 24, 1812, m., and d. April 24, 1853, at Weybridge, Vt. Left three children.

5322. vi. ABNER HAGAR, b. Dec 28, 1814, m. Dec. 2, 1841, Tamson Hubbard and has been a successful physician for some years, in Marengo, Ill.

[Seventh Generation.]

5317. i. BENJAMIN HAGAR, eldest child of Benjamin and Sarah Martin Hagar, and grandson of Esther Child Hagar, b. Feb. 8, 1803, d. Oct. 6, 1827, in Washington, D. C. " He was a fine scholar, a graduate of Middlebury College, Vt., and had studied medicine. He was principal of a school for young ladies in Washington at the time of his death."

[Seventh Generation.]

5318. ii. LUTHER MARTIN HAGAR, second son and child of Benjamin and Sarah Martin Hagar, and grandson of Esther Child Hagar, b. Sept. 24, 1804, m. Feb. 19, 1827, Clarissa Read. Mr. Hagar was fitted for college, but after the death of his father, was led to change his plans, went to Sherburne, Vt., and entered a store: he became a successful merchant in that town. In 1842 he removed to Burlington, Vt., with his family who were all born in Sherburne, Vt.

[Eighth Generation.] Children:

5323. i. SARAH CLARA HAGAR, b Dec. 3, 1827. Resides in Europe.

5324. ii. MARIA ELLEN HAGAR, b. Sept. 18, 1829.

5325. iii. JULIUS MARTIN HAGAR, b. July 5, 1831. Resides in Boise City, Ada Co., Idaho.

5326. iv. KATHERINE ALMIRA HAGAR,*)   (b. July 21, 1833.
5327. v. CAROLINE FRANCES HAGAR,) TWINS (d. June 8, 1856.

5328. vi. GEORGE INGERSOLL HAGAR, b Oct. 1835, m. Sept. 27, 1868, Lucia Lyon. Has five children.

* We are indebted to Miss Katherine A. Hagar of Burlington, Vt., for this account of the descendants of Esther Child and Benjamin Hagar.

[Seventh Generation.]

5319. iii. Of JONATHAN HAGAR, third son and child of Benjamin and Sarah Martin Hagar, and grandson of Esther Child Hagar, we have only outlines. We know that he was b. Feb. 19, 1807, was m. and had two children, and that his death occured on Nov. 16, 1879, in Plainfield, Ill. : but this extract from an obituary notice is appended, because it is said to express the general characteristics of the Hagar family. "By good business management, excellent investments, economy and industry, Mr. Hagar succeeded in amassing considerable wealth, a portion of which he judiciously invested in real estate. He was a member of the Congregational church at Plainfield, an earnest, energetic christian who believed that a religion worth having, was worth praying and working for, and his liberal donations to the church, and all other worthy objects, as well as his zeal in the cause of temperance, attested the sincerity of his belief, and the purity of his religious character." One of the family, Miss K. A. Hagar, while doubting the claim made for them, that they were "men of mark," says, "they are usually very honest, often very pious, refined, cultivated, kind-hearted men."

[Sixth Generation.]

5308. ii. BETSEY HAGAR, eldest dau. and second child of Esther Child and Benjamin Hagar, b. in Waltham, Mass., Jan. 3, 1776, m. Mr. Stearns.

[Seventh Generation.] Children:

    5329. i. ABIJAH STEARNS.
    5330. ii. JOHN STEARNS.
    5331. iii. SYLVIA STEARNS.
    5332. iv. ELIZA STEARNS.
    5333. v. KATHERINE STEARNS.

[Sixth Generation.]

5310. iv. JONATHAN HAGAR, second son and fourth child of Esther Child and Benjamin Hagar, b. in Waltham, Mass., Sept. 12, 1779, m. Jan. 1808, Louise Tradeaux. They had fifteen children ; eight dau. lived and m., seven died in infancy. Mr. and Mrs. Jonathan Hagar resided in Middlebury, Vt., and there he died, in April 1855.

[Seventh Generation.] Children:

    5334. i. MARY LOUISE HAGAR, m Gias Seymour.
    5335. ii. ESTHER HAGAR, m. Nelson Rogers.
    5336. iii. CLARA J. HAGAR, m. B. F. Niles.

5337. iv. SYBIL A. HAGAR, m. Charles D. Nash.
5338. v. JULIA HAGAR, m. Mason Perkins.
5339. vi. ELECTA N. HAGAR, m. Walter Johnson.
5340. vii. EMMA S. HAGAR, m. Samuel Marshall.
5341. viii. HARRIET H. HAGAR, m. Louis Ricard.

[Sixth Generation.]

5311. v. THOMAS HAGAR, third son and fifth child of Esther Child and Benjamin Hagar, b. in Waltham, Mass., Oct. 19, 1781, m. Jan. 26, 1802, Polly Fitch. Lived in Montreal, Canada.

[Seventh Generation.] Children:
5342. i. GEORGE HAGAR.
5343. ii. EMELINE HAGAR.
5344. iii. CHARLES HAGAR.
5345. iv. CLARA HAGAR.
5346. v. EDWARD HAGAR.

[Sixth Generation.]

5312. vi. ABNER HAGAR, fourth son of Esther Child and Benjamin Hagar, b. in Waltham, Mass., Jan. 31, 1784, m. Aug. 2, 1816, Hannah Barker. Lived and died at Plantagenet, Canada.

[Seventh Generation.] Children:
5347. i. EMMA HAGAR, d. young.
5348. ii. ABNER HAGAR, JR., d. young.
5349. iii. AMELIA HAGAR, d. aged 16 years.
5350. iv. ALBERT HAGAR, member of the Canadian Parliament at Ottawa.
5351. v. MARIA HAGAR.

[Sixth Generation.]

5313. vii. LUTHER HAGAR, fifth son of Esther Child and Benjamin Hagar, b. in Waltham, Mass., Oct. 8, 1786, m. Aug. 25, 1813, Sarah Addams. Lived and died at Cumberland Head, N. Y.

[Seventh Generation.] Children:
5352. i. CHARLES HAGAR.
5353. ii. JONATHAN HAGAR.
5354. iii. MARIA HAGAR, deceased.
5355. iv. ALBERT HAGAR.

[Sixth Generation.] Children:

5314. viii. CALVIN HAGAR, sixth son and eighth child of Esther Child and Benjamin Hagar, b. in Waltham, Mass., May 12, 1789, m. Dec. 22, 1812, Sarah Commers. Resided in Whitehall, Lynn Co., Ill. Died in 1846.

[Seventh Generation.] Children:
5356. i. CAROLINE HAGAR, deceased.
5357. ii. CALVIN HAGAR, JR., m. A dau. of this Calvin Hagar and grand-daughter of Esther Child Hagar, "was one of the army of heroic

nurses who served in the hospital of St. Louis during the greater part of the war. She was commissioned at her own request to work under the National Freedmen's Aid Commission of New York, in Vicksburg, in the winter of 1864. In April she was taken sick with malarial fever and died May 3, 1864."

[Sixth Generation.]

5316. x. JONAS HAGAR, 2d, eighth son of Esther Child and Benjamin Hagar, b. in Waltham, Mass., Sept. 10, 1793, m. Nov. 29, 1822, Elmira M. Mishar. Resided in New Brunswick, N. J.

[Seventh Generation.] Children:
5358. i. HENRY HAGAR, deceased.
5359. ii. FISHER HAGAR.
5360. iii. JONAS HAGAR, lives in Boston, Mass.
5361. iv. EMMA HAGAR, m. Mr. Rogers.

[Fifth Generation.]

5304. viii. EUNICE CHILD, sixth dau. and eighth child of Ensign Samuel and Esther Child, b. in Weston, Mass., Nov. 6, 1760, m. Dec. 15, 1784, Daniel Twitchell of Newton, Mass. Mr. Daniel Twitchell was a soldier in the war of the Revolution, beginning in the battle of Lexington. He nearly lost his life in recapturing a cannon taken by the enemy. Mr. and Mrs. Twitchell formed a part of the band, composed of her parents, grand parents, brothers and sisters with their families, who removed to Vt., and settled in Addison county. Mr. Twitchell was severely injured by the fall of a heavy limb from a tree, upon his head; after months and years of great suffering he died, in 1800, leaving his widow with seven children to train up aright, and a farm upon which was a large indebtedness. Mrs. E. C. Twitchell was a woman of great energy of body and mind, and equal to the great burden cast upon her. Her farm she cleared from debt, her children were brought up to become self-reliant, upright, honorable, successful members of society. In early life Mrs. Twitchell united with the Methodist church, but subsequently joined the Society of Friends, of which body she was an efficient, faithful member, being endowed with rare gifts of speech. Unusual physical strength was hers throughout her life, enabling her when fully fourscore to attend to her dairy, milking her cows, and making butter without aid; indeed from choice she lived alone in the later years of her life, communing with high and holy thoughts. She died in 1844 aged 84 years. For this sketch of one of the noblest, truest christian women of the Child family we are largely indebted to her grand-daughter Mrs. Weltha P. T. Griswold of Greenfield, Ill.

[Sixth Generation.] Children:

5362. i. LYDIA TWITCHELL, b. April 18, 1785, m. Dec. 2, 1810, David E. Griswold.

5363. ii. DANIEL TWITCHELL, JR., b. 1787, m. Sara Clark.

5364. iii. SAWIN TWITCHELL, b. 1789, d. 1791 in New Haven, Vt.

5365. iv. TIMOTHY W. TWITCHELL, b. 1791, m. 1813, Pamelia Marsh.

5366 v. SOPHIA TWITCHELL, b. 1794, d. 1803 in New Haven, Vt.

5367. vi. JONAS TWITCHELL, b. Feb. 29, 1796, m. May 3, 1820, Sarah Weeks.

5368. vii. JOHN TWITCHELL, b. 1798, m. 1818, Anna Sandford.

[Sixth Generation.]

5362. i. LYDIA TWITCHELL, eldest child of Eunice Child and Daniel Twitchell, was b. in Weston, Mass., April 18, 1785, m. Dec. 2, 1810, David Evarts Griswold, who was b. Dec. 18, 1789. This marriage took place in New Haven, Vt. Mr. and Mrs. Griswold, with her brother Mr. John Twitchell and wife, emulating the example of their parents, sought a home in a new country, and with their families took up many acres of uncultivated land at Apple Creek Prairie, Green Co., Ill., where they became opulent farmers, and have left their families in ease and comfort. Mrs. Lydia T. Griswold died near Whitehall Aug. 17, 1845. Mr. Griswold died at the same place Aug. 24, 1874. Mr. Griswold married a second time, in 1846, we do not know to whom.

[Seventh Generation.] Children:

5369. i. MELISSA A. GRISWOLD, b. Aug. 5, 1812, m. 1832, William P. Burroughs.

5370. ii. SOPHIA L. GRISWOLD, b. Dec. 8, 1813, m. Sept. 14, 1834, Ransom Swallow.

5371. iii. OSCAR DAMON GRISWOLD, b. Dec. 12, 1815, m. Dec. 11, 1834, Lutheria Swallow.

5372. iv. HILON GRISWOLD, b. July 25, 1817, d. Dec. 5, 1818.

5373. v. EDGAR GRISWOLD, b. Jan. 20, 1820, m. Mch. 12, 1840, Lucy North.

5374. vi. EDWIN GRISWOLD, ⎫ TWINS. ⎧ m. 1844, Weltha P. Twitchell. b. Dec. 7, 1822.

5375. vii. EVARTS GRISWOLD, ⎭ ⎩ d. Oct. 24, 1823.

5376. viii. Infant unchristened, b. Jan. 19, 1825, d. same day.

[Seventh Generation]

5369. i. MELISSA A. GRISWOLD, eldest child of David E. and Lydia T. Griswold, b. in Vermont, Aug. 5, 1812, m. in 1832, William P. Burroughs. Settled near Greenfield, Green Co., Ill., where they became wealthy land owners.

[Eighth Generation.]   Children:

5377. i. DAVID BURROUGHS, m. and has two children.

5378. ii. A dau. now Mrs. Smith Jaques.

[Seventh Generation.]

5370. ii. SOPHIA L. GRISWOLD, second dau. and child of
David E. and Lydia T. Griswold, b. in Vermont, Dec. 8, 1813,
m. Sept. 14, 1834, Ransom Swallow. Mr. Swallow was a successful merchant and farmer. He d. Feb. 22, 1845, in Manchester, Scott Co , Ill., where their home had been for some
years. Mrs. Swallow still resides there.

[Eighth Generation.]   Children:

5379. i. GEORGE R. SWALLOW, b. Aug. 21, 1832, m. Virginia Davis, dau.
of Abijah Davis of Jerseyville, Ill. Mr. Geo. R. Swallow was in business
in Vincennes, Ind., at the time of the late war. He joined the 7th Ind.
Battery, Sept. 21, 1861, as a private, was soon promoted, upon the resignation of the captain to his post. After the battle of Missionary Ridge joined
the 10th Ind. Cavalry and was successively advanced to a Colonelcy; was
wounded in Tennessee, but served till the close of the war. Mr. Swallow is
now cashier of the National Bank of Trinidad, Colorado, where he resides.
Mr. and Mrs. Swallow are active members of the Presbyterian church.

5380. ii ALBERT L SWALLOW, b. July 14, 1842, m Sept. 5, 1865, Maggie
Heaton. Had six children.

5381. iii. LYDIA ANNA SWALLOW, b. Feb. 22, 1845, m. Feb. 25, 1868, Virgil
A. Stuart of Fairmount, Fillmore Co., Nebraska, where they reside. Mr.
Stuart deals largely in grain, cattle, &c Mr. and Mrs Stuart are members
of the Presbyterian church, and earnest workers in the Sabbath school in
Fairmount, to which place they removed in 1871. They have five living
children.

[Seventh Generation.]

5371. iii. OSCAR DAMON GRISWOLD, eldest son and third
child of Mrs. Lydia T. and Daniel E. Griswold, and grandson
of Mrs. Eunice Child Twitchell, b. in New Haven, Vt., Dec.
12, 1815, m. Dec. 11, 1834. Lutheria Swallow, who was b. in
West Windsor, Vt., Nov. 18, 1817. Mr. O. Damon Griswold
died near Whitehall, Ill., Aug. 24, 1854.

[Eighth Generation.]   Children:

5382. i. OSCAR GRISWOLD, b. Nov. 4, 1835, d. May 15, 183-, in Castleton,
Vt.

5383. ii. FREDERICK GRISWOLD, b Oct. 23, 1842, was drowned while
crossing the Platte river on his way to California, May 29, 1852.

5384. iii. ALICE GRISWOLD, b. Aug 6, 1849, m. 1870, William C. Baker.

[Eighth Generation.]

5384. iii. ALICE GRISWOLD, only dau. of O. Damon and
Lutheria Swallow Griswold, b. near Whitehall, Ill., Aug. 6,
1849, m. 1870, William Baker, who was b. near Winchester,
Scott Co., Ill., Aug. 16, 1848. Mr. and Mrs. Baker reside on
the homestead near Whitehall, Ill.

[Ninth Generation.] Children, born near Whitehall, Ill:

5385. i. MABEL E. BAKER, b. June 30, 1871.

5386. ii. FREDERICK E. BAKER, b. July 1, 1873.

5387. iii. EDGAR D. BAKER, b. May 27, 1875.

5388. iv. CHARLES BAKER, b. Aug. 8, 1877, d. Dec. 29, 1877.

5389. v. NELLIE BAKER, b. Dec. 8, 1878.

[Seventh Generation.]

5373. v. EDGAR GRISWOLD, third son and fifth child of
David E. and Lydia T. Griswold, and grand-son of Mrs.
Eunice Child Twitchell, b. in New Haven, Vt., Jan. 30, 1820,
m. Mch. 12, 1840, Lucy North, who was b. Mch. 12, 1822,
near Whitehall, Ill.   Mr. Griswold accompanied his parents
on their removal to the West, and is now resident on the
home place near Whitehall, Ill.

[Eighth Generation.] Children:

5390. i. PERRY D. GRISWOLD, b. April 14, 1842, m. July 24, 1864, Olive
Stone.

5391. ii. SETH N. GRISWOLD, b. Jan. 18, 1843, m. Dec. 11, 1871, Etta
Whiteside, who was b. Sept. 17, 1849.   Reside at Whitehall, Ill.

5392. iii. CHESTER S. GRISWOLD, b. Dec. 22, 1844, d. Oct. 8, 1845.

5393. iv. MARY E. GRISWOLD, b. Aug. 17, 1847, m. Dec. 13, 1870, Edward
S. Boulton.

5394. v. SYLVIA J. GRISWOLD, b. Jan. 19, 1850.

5395. vi. MARTHA A. GRISWOLD, b. Sept. 10, 1852, d. Sept. 25, 1853.

5396. vii. DAMON A. GRISWOLD, b. Oct. 31, 1855, m. July 11, 1875, Etna
Baldwin.

5397. viii. LYDIA GRISWOLD, b. May 7, 1858, d. Sept. 1, 1858.

5398. ix. * CAROLINE GRISWOLD, b. Oct. 16, 1859.

5399. x. GEORGE A. GRISWOLD, b. Aug. 15, 1863, d. Aug. 23, 1866.

5400. xi. EDWARD A. GRISWOLD, b. June 26, 1866.

[Eighth Generation.]

5390. i. PERRY D. GRISWOLD, eldest son and child of Edgar
and Lucy North Griswold, b. in Whitehall, Ill., April 14,
1841, m. in Sonoma Co., California, July 24, 1864, Olive Stone,
who was b. Nov. 8, 1844, in Kalamazoo Co., Mich.   "Mr.
Perry D. Griswold started for California April 9, 1862, accompanied by Frederick Griswold, his cousin, son of Damon Griswold, and several others.   While crossing the Platte river,
Frederick and others of the party were drowned.   The rest
of the party continued their saddened journey.   Mr. Griswold
remained some years in California, returned for a time to
Whitehall, Green Co., Ill., his old home, but has now settled
in or near Solomon City, Kansas."

* We are much indebted to Miss Caroline Griswold for enabling us to
make this record so complete.

[Ninth Generation.] Children:

5401. i. RUBIE GRISWOLD, b. Aug. 5, 1865, in Mendocino Co., Cal.

5402. ii. EMMA F. GRISWOLD, b. May 12, 1868, in Sonomo Co., Cal.

5403. iii. EDGAR G. GRISWOLD, b. May 23, 1870, in Sonomo Co., Cal.

5404. iv. HUBERT GRISWOLD, b. June 7, 1872, in Green Co., Ill.

5405. v. LUCY E. GRISWOLD, b. June 1, 1874, in Green Co., Ill.

5406 vi. WALTER H. GRISWOLD, b Aug. 27. 1876, in Ottawa Co., Kansas.

5407. vii. MARCUS GRISWOLD, b. Nov. 30, 1878, in Ottawa Co., Kansas.

[Eighth Generation.]

5393. iv. MARY E. GRISWOLD, eldest dau. and fourth child of Edgar and Lucy North Griswold, b. at Whitehall, Aug. 17, 1847, m. Dec. 13, 1870, Edward Spellon Boulton, who was b. in Orleans Co., N. Y., May 14, 1837. Occupation, farmer, carpenter. Residence Greenfield, Green Co., Ill.

[Ninth Generation.] Child:

5408. i. STANTON STOCKWELL BOULTON, b. Feb. 28, 1874, near Palmyra, Macoupin Co., Ill.

[Eighth Generation.]

5396. vii. DAMON A. GRISWOLD, fourth son and seventh child of Edgar and Lucy North Griswold, b. in Whitehall, Green Co., Ill., Oct. 31, 1855, m. July 11, 1875, Etna Baldwin, who was b. Mch. 29, 1856. Farmer by occupation.

[Ninth Generation.] Children:

5409. i. LEWIS E. GRISWOLD. b July 5, 1876, in Whitehall, Ill.

5410. ii. LUCY H. GRISWOLD, b. Jan. 7, 1878. in Bluemound, Macon Co., Illinois.

[Sixth Generation.]

5365. iv. TIMOTHY W. TWITCHELL, third son and fourth child of Eunice Child and Daniel Twitchell, b. in Weston, Mass., 1791, m. in 1813, Pamelia Marsh.

Mr. Twitchell purchased a comfortable house near his mother's home, here his children were born and here he dwelt for many years. He was an extensive contractor for the erection of factories and other large buildings and covered bridges. He was a man of great energy, excellent habits and noble character, one who was always held in the highest esteem by the large circle of his acquaintance. For twenty-two years he held the office of justice of the peace; was also often in other posts of honor as the choice of his townsmen. A fall, resulting in a fractured hip, compelled a temporary rest, and gave him time to think of visiting some of his elder children who had removed to the West. Not daunted by his lameness, or his wife's precarious health, he took her with him to Illinois

and was so charmed with the country he remained, and wrote
to his children in Vermont to sell the home and come to him.
For a few weeks he was rejoicing in the reunion of his eight
children in their new home; suddenly the Asiatic cholera came
and swept away "the choice ones of the flock," a son, (the
youngest) a fine young man of twenty years, and a most promising daughter of seventeen. A few weeks later another son,
twenty-three years old, died of quick consumption; this was
followed not long after by the death of his wife. Chastened,
but sustained in his sorrows by his christian hope, Mr. Twitchell
lived on, like his mother, in earnest work, and patient waiting
until nearly fourscore and two years of age. The last months
of his life, intense suffering from the injury of years previous,
shadowed his days, but no murmur was permitted to escape
his lips. He died Nov. 1872.

[Seventh Generation.] Children:

5411. i. JULIUS SAWIN TWITCHELL, b. Jan. 26, 1818, m. Dec. 30, 1847,
Emily Robley.

5412. ii. MELVIN TWITCHELL, b. Dec. 29, 1819, m. Sept. 29, 1852, Elizabeth Brendel.

5413. iii. EMULIUS TWITCHELL, b. 1822, in Weybridge, Vt.; moved to Illinois. Is a wealthy man, unmarried.

5414. iv. WELTHA P. TWITCHELL, b. 1824, m. 1844, Edwin Griswold.

5415. v. CYNTHIA J. TWITCHELL, b. 1826, m. 1st, 1849, Remsen Prindle;
m. 2d, 1876, Stephen Ostrander.

5416. vi. CYRUS TWITCHELL, b. Nov. 1832, d. April 1856, of lung disease.

5417. vii. MYRON A. TWITCHELL, b. Mch 1834, d. Aug. 1855, of cholera.

5418. viii. JULIA SOPHIA TWITCHELL, b. 1837, d. Aug 1855, of cholera.

[Seventh Generation.]

5411. i. JULIUS SAWIN TWITCHELL, eldest child of Timothy
and Pamelia Marsh Twitchell, and grandson of Mrs Eunice
Child Twitchell, b. in Weybridge, Vt., Jan. 26, 1818, m. Dec.
30, 1847, Emily Robley, dau. of Capt. Richard and Desire
Griswold Robley, b. April 22, 1825, in Illinois. He d. Oct.
8, 1872. Mrs. E. R. Twitchell d. Sept. 22, 1872.

[Eighth Generation.] Children:

5419. i. MARY ALICE TWITCHELL, } TWINS { b. May 17, 1850, d. July 25,
1851. [ton Wilder.

5420. ii. MARIE ALLETTA TWITCHELL, } { m. Aug. 28, 1873, John Mil-

5421. iii. LORA TWITCHELL, b. June 18, 1853.

5422. iv. ADAH ELLEN TWITCHELL, b. Feb. 11, 1856, m. Sept. 27, 1877,
George Washington Melvin.

5423. v. RALPH ROBLEY TWITCHELL, b. July 16, 1859.

5424. vi. JULIUS GRANT TWITCHELL, b. June 12, 1864.

P-1

]Eighth Generation.]

5422. iv. ADAH ELLEN TWITCHELL, fourth dau. and child of Julius S. and Emily Robley Twitchell, and great.granddaughter of Mrs. Eunice Child Twitchell, b. Feb. 11, 1856, m. Sept. 27, 1877, George W. Melvin. A farmer, in Illinois.

[Ninth Generation.]   Child:

5425. i. EMILY LUELLA MELVIN, b. Aug. 4, 1878.

[Seventh Generation.]

5412. ii. MELVIN TWITCHELL, second son and child of Timothy and Pamelia Marsh Twitchell, and grandson of Mrs. Eunice Child Twitchell, b. Dec. 29, 1819, in Weybridge, Vt., m. Sept. 29, 1852, in Audubon, Ill., Elizabeth Brendel. Farmer. Residence Lemars, Plymouth Co., Iowa.

[Eighth Generation.]   Children:

5426. i. MYRWIN EUGENE TWITCHELL, b. Sept. 29, 1853 in Audubon, Ill Resides with his father. A teacher.

5427. ii. CYRUS TWITCHELL, b. July 11, 1855, m. Nov. 5, 1879, Matilda Jane Rigley. Resides in Concordia, Cloud Co., Kansas. Grocer and carpenter.

5428. iii. MYRON ANSON TWITCHELL, b. Jan. 31, 1857, near Greenfield Green Co., Ill. Teacher.

[Seventh Generation.]

5414. iv. WELTHA P. TWITCHELL, eldest dau. and fourth child of Timothy and Pamelia Marsh Twitchell, and granddaughter of Mrs. Eunice Child Twitchell, b in Weybridge, Vt., 1824, m. 1844, Edwin Griswold, son of David E. and Lydia Twitchell Griswold, and grandson of Mrs Eunice Child Twitchell, b. Dec. 7, 1822. Of eight children born of this marriage but two survive.*

[Eighth Generation.]   Children:

5429. i. ARTHUR GRISWOLD, b. 1847.

5430. ii. ALBERT M. GRISWOLD, b. 1849. These sons remain with their parents upon their large farm in Greenfield, Green Co., Ill.

[Seventh Generation.]

5415. v. CYNTHIA J. TWITCHELL, second dau. and fifth child of Timothy and Pamelia Marsh Twitchell, and granddaughter of Mrs. Eunice Child Twitchell, b. in Weybridge, Vt., in 1826, m. 1st, in 1849, Remsen Prindle, son of Elder Lyman Prindle. Mr. Remsen Prindle died of consumption in 1860. Mrs. Prindle m. 2d, in 1876, Stephen Ostrander, and resides in West Plattsburg, N. Y.

[Eighth Generation.]   Children:

5431. i. LINNIE PRINDLE, b. 1850, in Addison Co., Vt. Graduated from a Normal School and became principal of the High School of Whitehall, Ill.

* To Mrs. W. P. T. Griswold we are much indebted for data of her branch.

Married Miss Kate Bowman, and resides in Kansas. Has one son and one daughter; is engaged in farming.

5432. ii. LYMAN PRINDLE, b. 1857. Has been a teacher, is now wholesale dealer in earthern ware.

[Sixth Generation.]

5367. vi. JONAS TWITCHELL, fourth son of Eunice Child and Daniel Twitchell, b. in Middlebury, Vt., Feb. 29, 1796. m. May 3, 1820, Sarah Weeks, who was b. April 13, 1803.

Early life was passed in the pioneer times of the Green Mountain State, inured thus to meeting deprivations and overcoming obstacles, there seemed to him no need to fear the trials incident to western migrations. In 1831, Mr. and Mrs. Twitchell with their children moved to Michigan, and resided there some years. His son, Dr. R. W. Twitchell, having established himself in Minnesota, desired his father to be with him, and again Mr. Twitchell made removal to a new country, but with all cheer. An exceedingly industrious and upright man, he would never seek wealth but through open, legitimate methods. His life closed in a quiet sleep on the 27th of September, 1877, in Chatfield, Minn. Mrs. Twitchell was a native of Long Island, her parents belonged to the Society of Friends: she died on the 19th of November, 1847. Mr. Jonas Twitchell died at the home of his son, R. W. Twitchell, M. D., in Chatfield, Minn., in his 82d year. A fitting memorial notice was contributed to the county paper by one who knew him well, summing up the characteristics of the man and the varied experiences of his life, commending the industry which was untiringly manifested and the integrity always maintained. Closing with an account of the end, which we think can be most fittingly described in the words of the Psalmist, "So He giveth His beloved sleep."

[Seventh Generation.] Children:

5433. i. EUNICE SARAH TWITCHELL, b. Feb. 27, 1821, m. Jan. 3, 1839, Ebenezer Prindle.

5434. ii. REFINE WEEKS TWITCHELL, b. Mch. 29, 1823, m. May 23, 1852, Martha J. Carpenter.

5435 iii. ELLEN TWITCHELL, b. Jan. 27, 1825, d. Jan 30, 1825.

5436. iv. JACOB W. TWITCHELL, b. Feb. 21, 1826, d. Jan. 17, 1827.

5437. v. JOHN J. TWITCHELL, b. May 30, 1828, d. Sept. 25, 1829.

5438. vi. WILLIAM PENN TWITCHELL, b. Sept. 6, 1830, d. Feb. 1836, in Greenville, Ohio.

5439. vii. DANIEL SAWIN TWITCHELL, b. April 11, 1833.

5440. viii. ANN ELIZA TWITCHELL, b. May 3, 1835, m. Sept. 8, 1853, Norman Case.

[Seventh Generation.]

5433. i. EUNICE SARAH TWITCHELL, eldest child of Jonas and Sarah Weeks Twitchell, and grandchild of Eunice Child Twitchell, b. Feb. 27, 1821, m. Jan. 3, 1839, Ebenezer Prindle, who was b. June 22, 1817.   Mr. Prindle is a real estate and insurance agent, in Evanston, Ill.   Mrs. Prindle d. Jan. 20, 1872.

[Eighth Generation.]   Children:

5441. i. LEWIS EBEN PRINDLE, b. Oct. 23, 1840.   Resides in Kansas City, Mo.   Bank teller.

5442. ii. LEICESTER CORYDON PRINDLE, b. Oct. 8, 1842.   Resides in Evanston, Ill.   Cashier Western Branch Hartford Fire Ins. Co., Chicago, Ill.

5443. iii. WILLIAM PENN PRINDLE, b. Sept. 13, 1846.   Resides in Dakota. Farmer.

5444. iv. THEODORE REFINE PRINDLE, b. Aug. 16, 1849, d. Feb. 10, 1874.

5445. v. SARAH ELLA PRINDLE, b. May 15, 1855.   Resides in Evanston, Ill.   Instructor in preparatory department of Northwestern University.

5446. vi. EMMA MAY PRINDLE, b. Feb. 17, 1860.   Resides in Evanston, Ill.   Student.

[Seventh Generation.]

5434. ii. DR. REFINE W. TWITCHELL, eldest son and second child of Jonas and Sarah Weeks Twitchell, and grand-son of Eunice Child and Daniel Twitchell, b. in Middlebury, Vt., Mch. 29, 1823, m. May 23, 1852, Martha J. Carpenter of Baldwinsville, N. Y.   When eight years old Dr. Twitchell left Vermont with his father and went to Michigan, where he spent his boyhood and early manhood.   In 1854 with his wife and one child, Dr. Twitchell removed to Chatfield, Minnesota: his second child was the first child born in that town.   During the late war, Dr. Twitchell served as surgeon through the four years, the first two years connected with a Minnesota reg't and the last two in the Volunteer Dep't of the U. S. A.   At the close of the war Dr. Twitchell returned to Minnesota, and has ever since devoted himself to his profession with great assiduity and success.

[Eighth Generation.]   Children:

5447. i. SARAH EDNA TWITCHELL, b. Sept. 1853, in Somerset, Mich.

5448. ii. HERBERT EUGENE TWITCHELL, b Mch. 29, 1855, in Chatfield, Minn : now a medical student in Cincinnati, Ohio.

5449. iii. Stephen Carpenter Twitchell, b. April 8, 1857, d. Sept. 11, 1857, in Chatfield, Minn.

5450. iv. CARPIE CARPENTER TWITCHELL, b. Feb. 24, 1859.

5451. v. MARTHA A. TWITCHELL, b. Aug. 7, 1867.

[Seventh Generation.]

5440. viii. ANN ELIZA REBECCA TWITCHELL, third dau. and eighth child of Jonas and Sarah Weeks Twitchell, and grand-daughter of Mrs. Eunice Child Twitchell, b. in Sylvan, Washtenaw Co., Mich., May 3, 1835, m. Sept. 8, 1853, Norman Case, in Sylvan, Mich. Present residence Minneapolis, Minn. Mrs. A. E. R. T. Case has quite a local distinction for her rendition of Shakespeare and other authors. Mr. Case d. Jan. 5, 1871.

[Eighth Generation.] Children:

5452. i. ALICE E. R. CASE, b Aug. 27, 1854, d. Nov. 23, 1869, in Mich.

5453. ii. WILLIE D. CASE, b. Mch. 7, 1856, d. Oct. 15, 1869, in Michigan.

5454. iii. CARRIE LEANORE CASE, b. Aug. 27, 1858, in Michigan.

5455. iv. JOHNNIE WEEKS CASE, b. Aug. 15, 1860, in Michigan.

5456. v. CLAUD M. CASE, b. Mch. 19, 1866, in Minnesota.

[Sixth Generation.]

5368. vii. JOHN TWITCHELL, fifth son and seventh child of Daniel and Eunice Child Twitchell, b. in Weybridge, Vt., 1798, m. 1818, Anna Sandford. Mr. and Mrs. Twitchell settled in New Haven, Vt., on their marriage, and here four of their children were born; they moved to Waltham about 1825, four more children were born to them in Waltham. In 1831, the family removed to Illinois; in 1833, Mr. Twitchell "entered land" in what is now known as Jersey Co., Ill. On the 10th of August, in that year, he died, leaving his widow with seven small children to endure the hardships of a new country. But the patient care and struggle have been successful, and all have attained to manhood and womanhood with comfortable homes.

[Seventh Generation.] Children:

5457. i. GASTON D. TWITCHELL, b. 1819, in New Haven, Vt. Resides unmarried with his mother in Virden, Ill.

5458. ii. MARY ANN TWITCHELL, b. in New Haven, Vt., 1820, m. 1842, Augustus Stearns.

5459. iii. LYDIA TWITCHELL, b. 1822, in New Haven, Vt. Resides in Virden, Ill.; unmarried.

5460. iv. ANJANETTA TWITCHELL, b. 1824, in New Haven, Vt., d. 1827, in Waltham, Vt.

5461. v. LORETTE TWITCHELL, b. 1826, m. 1846, Nathan Chamberlin.

5462. vi. SIDNEY L. TWITCHELL, b. 1827, m. 1st, 1851, Celia C. Sanders, who d. Dec. 3, 1861; m. 2d, 1873, Mrs. Augusta V. Cox.

5463. vii. JANE S. TWITCHELL, b 1829, m. 1856, John Ryan.

5464. viii. LORANE H. TWITCHELL, b. 1831, in Waltham, Vt. Resides with her mother in Virden, Ill.

[Seventh Generation.]

5458 ii. MARY ANN TWITCHELL, eldest dau. of John and Anna Sandford Twitchell, and grand-daughter of Eunice Child Twitchell, b. in New Haven, Vt., 1820, m. 1842, Augustus Stearns.

[Eighth Generation.] Children:

5422*a.* i. LUCY A. STEARNS, b. 1843, m. 1864, Mr. Murphy.
5423*a.* ii. ALICE J. STEARNS, b. 1848, m. 1868, Mr. Kayser.
5424*a.* iii. CHARLES D. STEARNS. b. 1853, m. 1879.
5425*a.* iv. ELLA C. STEARNS, b. 1857, m. 1879, Mr. Ellas.

[Eighth Generation.]

5422*a.* i. LUCY A. STEARNS. eldest child of Mary A. Twitchell and Augustus Stearns, b. 1843, m. 1864, Mr. Murphy.
[Ninth Generation.] Children:

5426*b.* i. ALICE L. MURPHY, b. 1865.
5427*b.* ii. MARY J. MURPHY, b. 1867, d. 1867.
5428*b.* iii. MATILDA I. MURPHY, b 1870, d. 1874.
**** iv. HERMON M. MURPHY, b. 1871.
5429*b.* v. JULIA L. MURPHY, b. 1873.
5430*b.* vi. GEORGE A. MURPHY, b. 1874.
5431*b.* vii. LYDIA L. MURPHY, b. 1876.
5432*b.* viii. RUTH L. MURPHY, b. 1877.
5433*b.* ix. CHARLES D. MURPHY, b. 1879, d. 1879.
5434*b.* x. HELLEN E. MURPHY, b. 1889.

[Eighth Generation.]

5423*a.* ii. ALICE J. STEARNS, second dau. of Augustus and Mary Ann Twitchell Stearns. and grand-daughter of Eunice Child Twitchell, b. 1848, m. about 1868, Mr. Kayser.
[Ninth Generation.] Children:

5435*b.* i. EFFIE KAYSER, b. 1869.
5436*b.* ii. ALBERT C. KAYSER, b. 1870.
5437*b.* iii. EMMA KAYSER, b. 1873.

[Eighth Generation.]

5424*a.* iii. CHARLES D. STEARNS, great-grandson of Eunice Child Twitchell and son of Mary A. Twitchell and Augustus Stearns, b. 1853, m. about 1879.
[Ninth Generation.] Child:

5438*b.* i. GASTON D. STEARNS, b. 1880.

[Eighth Generation.]

5425*a.* iv. ELLA C. STEARNS, youngest child of Augustus and Mary A. T. Stearns, and great grand-daughter of Eunice Child Twitchell, b. 1857, m. about 1878-9, Mr. Ellas.
Ninth Generation.] Child:

5439*b.* i MABEL ELLAS, b. 1889.

[Seventh Generation]

5461. v. LORETTE TWITCHELL, fourth dau. of John and Anna Sandford Twitchell, and grand-daughter of Eunice Child Twitchell. b. in Waltham. Vt., 1826. m. 1846, Nathan. Chamberlin. Residence, Virden, Ill. Mrs. L. T. Chamberlin d. Oct. 18. 1880.

[Eighth Generation.] Children:

5440a. i. EDGAR G. CHAMBERLIN, b. 1846, d. 1861.

5441a. ii. LEONORA L. CHAMBERLIN, b. 1848.

5442a. iii. JULIA W CHAMBERLIN, b. 1849, d. 1861.

5443a. iv. ANNIE J CHAMBERLIN, b. 1853, m. about 1873, Mr. Turner.

5444a. v. DAVID H CHAMBERLIN, b. 1855, d. 1856.

5445a. vi. ELLA E. CHAMBERLIN, b. 1856.

5446a. vii. MINNIE F. CHAMBERLIN, b. 1862.

5447a. viii. CARRIE H. CHAMBERLIN, b. 1864.

[Eighth Generation.]

5443a. iv. ANNIE J. CHAMBERLIN. third dau. of Nathan and Lorette Twitchell Chamberlin, and great grand-daughter of Eunice Child Twitchell, b. 1853, m. about 1873, Mr. Turner.

[Ninth Generation.] Children:

5448b. i. MARY L. TURNER, b. 1874.

5449b. ii. GEORGE N. TURNER, b. 1876.

[Seventh Generation.]

5462. vi. SIDNEY L. TWITCHELL. second son of John and Anna Sandford Twitchell, and grand-son of Eunice Child Twitchell, b. in Waltham, Vt., 1827, m. 1st, 1851, Celia C. Sanders, who d. Dec. 3, 1861; m. 2d. 1873, Mrs. Augusta V. Cox.

[Eighth Generation.] Children:

5450a. i. ALLENA L. TWITCHELL, b. 1853.

5451a. ii. RANSOM L. TWITCHELL, b. 1855, m. about 1879.

5452a. iii GEORGE S. TWITCHELL, b. 1857, d. 1860.

5453a. iv. ERNEST W. TWITCHELL, b. 1859.

5454a. v. CLARA I. TWITCHELL, b. 1860, d. 1860.

5455a. vi. ALBERT TWITCHELL, b. 1874, d. 1874.

5456a. vii. JOHN TWITCHELL, b. 1878.

5457a. viii. EUGENE TWITCHELL, b. 1879.

[Eighth Generation.]

5451a. ii. RANSOM L. TWITCHELL. eldest son of Sidney L. Twitchell, and great grand-son of Eunice Child Twitchell, b. 1855, m. about 1879.

[Ninth Generation.] Child:

5458b. i. EDITH S. TWITCHELL, b. 1880.

[Seventh Generation.]

5463. vii. JANE S. TWITCHELL. fifth dau of John and Anna Sandford Twitchell, and grand-daughter of Eunice Child Twitchell, b. 1829, in Waltham, Vt., m. 1856, John Ryan.

[Eighth Generation.] Children:

5459a. i. JENNIE M. RYAN, b. 1857.

5460a. ii. JOHN H. RYAN, b. 1858.

5461a. iii. EMMA A. RYAN, b. 1859

5462*a*. iv. CHARLES G. RYAN, b. 1860.
5463*a*, v. FLORA O. RYAN, b. 1862.
5364*a*. vi. EDGAR RYAN, b. 1863.
5465*a* vii. JAMES E. RYAN, b. 1865.

[Fifth Generation.]

5306. ix. SAMUEL CHILD, JR., third son and ninth child of
Ensign Samuel and Esther Child, b. in Weston, Mass., Nov. 1,
1762, m. 1st, Aug. 8, 1784, Abigail Sheppard of Newton, Mass.:
m. 2d. Nov. 19, 1789, Hannah Lamson.   Ensign Samuel
Child, accompanied by his son, Samuel and family, and the
families of his daughters, Mrs. Esther Child Hagar, Mrs. Mary
Child Bigelow, Mrs. Lucy Child Sheppard and Mrs. Eunice
Child Twitchell, early moved to Vermont and settled in Addison Co., and their descendants have been the most influential
citizens, giving tone and weight to the entire county.   Mr.
Samuel Child was a man of more education than was usual in
that region at that period.

[Sixth Generation.]   Children:

5465. i. ALEXANDER CHILD, b. Feb. 22, 1785, m. 1813, Betsey Haskins.

5466. ii MALINDA CHILD, b —, m. 1812, Joseph Boies.

5467. iii. JULIA CHILD, b. 1792, d. 1800, aged 8 years.

5468. iv. BETSEY CHILD, b. Oct. 31, 1794, m. Oct. 5, 1813, John G. Rider.

5469. v. JOHN CHILD, b. Dec. 8, 1796, m. 1st, Nov. 1, 1826, Abigail Wright:
m. 2d, Feb. 18, 1844, Mahala B. Pratt

5470. vi. EBENEZER CHILD, b. Oct. 8, 1799, m. 1822, Aurelia Hunt.

5471. vii. SAMUEL CHILD, b. 1800, m. 1830, Roxana Winch.

[Sixth Generation.]

5465. i. ALEXANDER CHILD, eldest son and child of Samuel,
Jr., and Abigail Sheppard Child, b. in Weston, Middlesex Co.,
Mass., Feb. 22, 1785, m. in Highgate, Vt., in 1813, Betsey Haskins.   Mr. Alexander Child died in Manasha, Wisconsin, Aug.
4, 1863.   Mrs. Betsey Haskins Child died in the same place
Nov. 1st, 1866.   Mrs. Child was descended from the Litch-
fields of Connecticut, a family of prominence and worth, and
most patriotic.   Her father, "Seth Haskins, enlisted and served
as an artificer in the war of 1812."   Gifted with a poetic imagin-
ation. Mr. Haskins wrote some pieces of considerable merit.
Mrs. Child inherited the gift of song.   The wandering mania
which impels many to encounter the hardships and overcome
obstacles incident to a pioneer life, seemed to have taken a strong
hold upon Mr. Child, leading him into eastern New York.   Several removes within that State resulted in a settlement in Barre.

Orleans Co., where he made his home for some twenty years, engaged in agricultural pursuits—this was at the time the Erie canal was being made, and its construction brought farm products into a wider market. Not however satisfied with the slow accumulations of this small town, Mr. Child concluded to make another move, and went with his large family to Joliet, Ill. A very fatal epidemic prevailing in that vicinity determined him to pitch his tent elsewhere, and in Milwaukee, Wis., he once more sought a home. Here a number of his children were engaged in brick making, others taught. The nomadic life had interfered with the education of the family, somewhat, but all appreciated the advantages of higher culture and have sought to secure it for their children. In the year 1848 or '49, the entire family emigrated to the Fox River Valley in Wisconsin, and are there permanently located. Mr. Alexander Child was not a religious man, but a man of integrity and uprightness. Mrs. Child was a very earnest christian, and her sincere piety has proved a rich dower to her large family of children.

[Seventh Generation.] Children:

5472. i. SIDNEY SMITH CHILDS, b. Jan. 18, 1814, m. 1862, Katie E. Linch.

5473. ii. SAMUEL B. CHILDS, b. 1815, m. 1846, Malinda Church.

5474. iii. JOHN W. CHILDS, b. 1817, m. 1847, Sarah E. Marshall.

5475. iv. NELSON B. CHILDS, b. 1819, m. 1st, 1843, ——; m. 2d, 1848, Jane Church.

5476. v. ABIGAIL S. CHILDS, b. 1821, m. 1839, George Gerty.

5477. vi. SETH HASKINS CHILDS, b. 1823, m. 1st, 1845, Elsie Stevens; m. 2d, 1852, Lavina Church.

5478. vii. SYBIL D. CHILDS, b. 1826, m. 1st, 1850, Darius Newman; m. 2d, Hugh Gear.

5479. viii. ALEXANDER CHILDS, JR., b. 1828, d. 1859.

5480. ix. CHARLES B. CHILDS, b. 1831, m. 1859, Charlotte McMinnen.

5481. x. JULIA CHILDS, b. 1834, m. 1854, John Hodgdon.

[Seventh Generation.]

5472. i. SIDNEY SMITH CHILDS, eldest child of Alexander and Betsey Haskins Childs, b. in New Haven, Vt., Jan. 18, 1814, m. in 1862, Katie E. Linch. Resides in Menasha, Winnebago county, Wis.

[Eighth Generation.] Children:

5482. i. ALEXANDER CHILDS, b. 1863.

5483. ii. WILLIAM CHILDS, b. 1865, d. 1869.

5484. iii. FREDERICK CHILDS, b. 1868.

5485. iv. WILLIS CHILDS, b. 1871.

[Seventh Generation.]

5473. ii. SAMUEL B. CHILDS, second son and child of Alexander and Betsy Haskins Childs, b. in Hadley, N. Y., in 1815, m. 1846, Malinda Church. Resides in Wrightstown, Brown county, Wis.

[Eighth Generation.] Children:

    5486. i. WILLARD CHILDS, b. 1846.
    5487. ii. BETSEY CHILDS, b. 1848, m. 1866, George Burt.
    5488. iii. SAMUEL B. CHILDS, JR., b. 1850, m. 1879.
    5489. iv. FRANKLIN CHILDS,   } Twins. } b. 1852.
    5490. v. WASHINGTON CHILDS, }
    5491. vi. TRUMAN CAILDS, b. 1854.
    5492. vii. EVA CHILDS, b. 1856, m. 1875, Robert Murry.
    5493. viii. LUCIAN CHILDS, b. 1858.
    5494. ix. CARLOUS CHILDS, b. 1860.
    5495. x. ALICE CHILDS, b. 1864.

[Seventh Generation.]

5474. iii. JOHN W. CHILDS, third son and child of Alexander and Betsy Haskins Childs, b. in Richmond, N. Y., 1817, m. in 1847, Sarah E. Marshall. Mrs. Child d. in 1873. Residence Roscobell, Wis.

[Eighth Generation.] Children:

    5496. i. EMMA CHILDS, b. 1851, m. 1870, Oscar Angle.
    5497. ii. ALBERT CHILDS, b. 1853. Resides in Independence, Iowa.
    5498. iii. JOHN CHILDS, b. 1855. Resides in Vood River, Nebraska.
    5499. iv. LEWIS G. CHILDS, b. 1857. Resides in Independence, Iowa.
    5500. v. LAURA CHILDS, b. 1860, m. 1878, Daniel Pallado.
    5501. vi. ADDIE R. CHILDS, b. 1862.
    5502. vii. SARAH M. CHILDS, b. 1864.
    5503. viii. ELLA M. CHILDS, b. 1868.
    5504. ix. RANSOM CHILDS, b. 1871.

[Seventh Generation.]

5475. iv. NELSON B. CHILDS, fourth son and child of Alexander and Betsy Haskins Childs, b. in Lima, N. Y., in 1819, m. 1st, 1843, ——; m. 2d, 1848, Jane Church. Mrs. N. B. Childs d. in 1847.

[Eighth Generation.] Children:

    5505. i. Infant, (unchristened.)
    5506. ii. Infant, (unchristened.)
    5507. iii. ALVIRA CHILDS, b. 1849, m. 1876, Frederick Hillman.
    5508. iv. CHARLES CHILDS, b. 1851, m. 1877.
    5509. v. SIDNEY CHILDS, b. 1852, m. 1878.
    5510. vi. MARY CHILDS, b. 1856, m. 1876, Charlie Watson.
    5511. vii. JANE CHILDS, b. 1858, m. 1877, Charles Williams.
    5512. viii. ADELAIDE CHILDS, b. 1861, m. 1877.
    5513. ix. JAMES CHILDS, b. 1863.

5514. x. CARLOUS CHILDS, b. 1867.
5515. xi. ELLA CHILDS, b. 1869.

[Seventh Generation.]

5476. v. ABIGAIL SHEPPARD CHILDS, eldest dau. and fifth child of Alexander and Betsey Haskins Childs, b. in 1821, m. in 1839, George Gerty. Residence Kaukauna, Outgamie Co., Wisconsin.

[Eighth Generation.] Children:
5516. i. MATILDA GERTY, b. 1840, m. 1857, Simon Clough.
5517. ii. GEORGE GERTY, b. 1842, m. 1869.
5518. iii. BARNEY GERTY, b. 1845, m. 1867.
5519. iv. ABIGAIL GERTY, b. 1849, m. 1857, Lewis McAbee.
5520. v. BETSEY GERTY, b. 1851, m. 1870, John Powers.
5521. vi. MAGGIE GERTY, b. 1856, m. 1872, Peter Duban. She d. 1873.
5522. vii. SALLY GERTY, b. 1859, m. 1877, John Savine.

[Seventh Generation.]

5477. vi. SETH HASKINS CHILDS, fifth son of Alexander and Betsy Haskins Childs, b. in Barre, N. Y., in 1823, m. 1st, 1845, Elsie Stevens, who d. the following year: m. 2d, 1852, Lavina Church.

[Eighth Generation.] Children:
5523. i. ELSIE CHILDS, b. 1854, m. 1874, Robert Hamilton.
5524. ii. ALEXANDER CHILDS, b. 1857.
5525. iii. GEORGE CHILDS, b. 1873.

[Seventh Generation.]

5478. vii. SYBIL D. CHILDS, second dau. of Alexander and Betsey Haskins Childs, b. in Barre, N.Y., in 1826, m. 1st, 1850, Darius Newman, who d. in 1855: m. 2d, 1857, Hugh G. Gear. Residence Menasha, Wis.

[Eighth Generation.] Children.
5526. i. HENRY CLAY NEWMAN, b. 1852. Residence Wood River, Neb.
5527. ii. CLARIE NEWMAN, b. 1854, d. 1863.
5528. iii. BETSY ANN GEAR, b. 1860.
5529. iv. CHARLES CHILDS GEAR, b. 1861.
5530. v. WILLIE HUGH GEAR, b. 1863.

[Seventh Generation.]

5480. ix. CAPT. CHARLES B. CHILDS, seventh son of Alexander and Betsey Haskins Childs, b. in 1831, m. in 1859, Charlotte McMinnen. Captain Charles Childs is supposed to have been lost from a government steamer wrecked on the Pacific coast in 1877. Mrs. Childs resides at 1803 Madison street, Chicago.

[Eighth Generation.] Child:
5531. i. MINNIE CHILDS, b. 1859, d. 1864.

[Seventh Generation.]

5481. x. JULIA CHILDS, third dau. of Alexander and Betsy Haskins Childs, b. in Barre, N. Y., in 1834, m. in 1854. John Hodgdon.

[Eighth Generation.] Children:

5532. i. INEZ HODGDON, b. June 10, 1855.
5533. ii. WILLIE HODGDON, b. Sept. 13, 1857.
5534. iii. ALICE M. HODGDON, b. Feb. 12, 1860.
5535. iv. GEORGE HODGDON, b. Mch. 27, 1862.
5536. v. JOHN W. HODGDON, b. May 4, 1865.

[Sixth Generation.]

5468. iv. BETSEY CHILD, third dau. of Samuel and Hannah Lamson Child, b. in Weybridge, Addison Co., Vt., Oct. 31 1794, m. Oct. 5, 1813, John G. Rider of New Haven, Vt. Mr. and Mrs. Rider moved to western New York at that period sparsely settled, and more remote from the luxuries of life than are many of our territories to-day. The daughter, Mrs. D. L. Taylor, writing us, says:

"Our mother was a woman of great worth; through all the hardships and vicissitudes incident to a pioneer life, she ever maintained a high and noble character. As a mother, she was affectionate and true, and no children could hold in higher esteem a mother than do hers, their mother. She ever retained her love for her native State, and dwelt much on the delights of her Green Mountain home."

Mr. J. G. Rider d. in Le Roy, Genesee Co., N. Y., Aug. 12, 1874. Mrs. Betsey Child Rider d. in the same place Dec. 18, 1878.

[Seventh Generation.] Children:

5532*a*. i. JULIA CHILD RIDER, b. April 21, 1815, m. May 20, 1839, William A. Kelsey.
5533*a*. ii. LOUISA RIDER, b. Dec. 14, 1819, m. May 7, 1837, C. S. Taylor.
5534*a*. iii. BETHIAH CLARK RIDER, b. Feb. 18, 1821, m. June 3, 1840, James S. Tew.
5535*a*. iv. HANNAH JANE RIDER, b. Jan. 18, 1823, m. Dec. 13, 1842, C. S. Taylor.
5536*a*. v. DORCAS LORENA RIDER, b. Aug. 12, 1826, m. Aug. 26, 1846, A. B. Taylor.
5537. vi. VANNESSE RIDER, b. April 8, 1830, d. April 10, 1832.
5538. vii. EBENEZER RIDER, b. Sept. 3, 1833, m. Sept. 14, 1854, Fanny Hovey.
5539. viii. ELIZABETH RIDER, b. Sept. 13, 1837, d. Sept. 27, 1838.

[Seventh Generation.]

5532*a*. i. JULIA CHILD RIDER, eldest dau. and child of Betsey Child and John G. Rider, b. in Addison Co., Vt., April 21, 1815, m. May 20, 1839, William A. Kelsey, in Chili, N. Y. Residence Le Roy, New York. Mrs. J. C. R. Kelsey d. in Le Roy, N. Y., Feb. 28, 1880.

[Eighth Generation.] Children:

5540. i. JOHN RIDER KELSEY. b. Aug. 30. 1841. m. Sept. 1864, Sarah Brown.

5541. ii. HERBERT SARTELLO KELSEY, b. June 17, 1844, m. Dec. 24, 1879, Ida Joslin.

5542. iii. ELEANORA MALINDA KELSEY, b. Sept. 14, 1849, m. Dec. 24, 1866, John L. Sawyer.

5543. iv. ALBION HALL KELSEY. b. Aug. 9, 1851. m. Nov. 24, 1879, Dora Powers.

[Eighth Generation.]

5540. i. JOHN RIDER KELSEY. eldest child of Julia Child Rider and William A. Kelsey, b. in Le Roy. Genesee Co., N. Y., Aug. 30, 1841, m. Sept. 1864, Sarah Brown of Cortland, Ill., where they now reside.

[Ninth Generation.] Children:

5544. i. STELLA MAY KELSEY, b. July 13, 1865, in Cortland, Ill.

5545. ii. CLARA ESTHER KELSEY, b. Sept. 6, 1871, in Bristol. Ind.

5546. iii. JOHN ALBION KELSEY, b. Aug. 21, 1876.

[Eighth Generation.]

5542. iii. ELEANORA MALINDA KELSEY. only dau. of Julia Child Rider and William A. Kelsey, b. in Le Roy, N. Y., Sept. 14, 1849, m. Dec. 24, 1866, John L. Sawyer.

[Ninth Generation.] Children:

5547. i. CORWIN SAWYER.

5548. ii. CHARLES SAWYER.

5549. iii. WILLIAM SAWYER.

5550. iv. VERNA GRACE SAWYER.

5551. v. GERTIE SAWYER.

[Seventh Generation.]

5533a ii. LOUISA RIDER, second dau. and child of Betsey Child and John G. Rider, b. in Le Roy, Genesee Co., N. Y., Dec. 14. 1819, m. in the same place. May 7, 1837, C. S. Taylor. Mrs. L. R. Taylor d. Oct. 12, 1841.

[Eighth Generation.] Children:

5552. i. CELESTIA TAYLOR. b. Dec. 12, 1839, m. Dec. 23, 1867, Dr. John Ellison Best.

5553. ii. LOUISA TAYLOR. b. Oct. 3, 1841, m. May 1, 1863, Lyman H. Smith.

[Eighth Generation.]

5552. i. CELESTIA TAYLOR. eldest child of Louisa Rider and C. S. Taylor. and granddaughter of Betsey Child Rider, b. in Le Roy, N. Y., Dec. 12, 1839, m. Dec. 23, 1867, Dr. John Ellison Best. in McHenry Co., Ill.

[Ninth Generation.] Children:

5554. i. EMMA BEST, b. Dec. 9, 1873.

5555. ii. BRUCE TAYLOR BEST, b. Dec. 3, 1876.

[Eighth Generation.]

5553. ii. LOUISA TAYLOR, second dau. and child of Louisa Rider and C. S. Taylor, and granddaughter of Mrs. Betsey Child Rider, b. in Le Roy, N. Y., Oct. 1841, m. in Huntley, McHenry Co., Ill., May 1, 1863, Lyman Henry Smith, who was b. in Conneaut, Ashtabula Co., Iowa, July 22, 1841. Residence Elgin, Ill.

[Ninth Generation.] Children:

5556. i. Daughter, (unchristened,) b. and d. Jan. 31, 1865, in Woodstock, Ill.

5557. ii. HOWARD TAYLOR SMITH, b. Nov. 25, 1868, in Elgin, Kane Co., Ill.

[Seventh Generation.]

5534a. iii. BETHIA CLARK RIDER, third dau. and child of Betsey Child and John G. Rider, b. in LeRoy, N. Y., Feb. 18, 1821, m. June 3, 1840, James S. Tew. Mrs. B. C. R. Tew d. at her father's home in LeRoy, Aug. 5, 1872.

[Eighth Generation.] Child:

5558. i. BETSEY RIDER TEW, b. 1841, m. Nov. 11, 1861, Major Frank F. Peats, sheriff of Winnebago Co., Ill. Residence, Rockford, Ill.

[Ninth Generation.] Child:

5559. i. MABEL PEATS, b. May 13, 1869, in Rockford, Ill.

[Seventh Generation.]

5535a. iv. HANNAH JANE RIDER, fourth dau. and child of Betsey Child and John G. Rider, b. in LeRoy, Genesee Co., N. Y., Jan. 18, 1823, m. Dec. 13, 1842, her brother-in-law, Chauncey S. Taylor. Reside in Belvidere, Ill.

[Eighth Generation.] Children:

5560. i. Infant son unchristened, b. Feb. 3, 1844, d. Feb. 9, 1 44.

5561. ii. CELIA M. TAYLOR, b. Sept. 19, 1849, in Elk Grove, d. April 2, 1852, in Chicago, Ill.

5562. iii. EDNA JANE TAYLOR, b. Oct. 1, 1850, in Pleasant Valley, Ill.

[Seventh Generation.]

5536a. v. DORCAS LORENA RIDER, fifth dau. and child of Betsey Child and John G. Rider, b. in LeRoy, N. Y., Aug. 12, 1826, m. in same place Aug. 26, 1846, A. B. Taylor. Residence. Helena, Montana Territory.

[Eighth Generation.] Children:

5563. i. ALBION RIDER TAYLOR, b. Dec. 4, 1848, in Chicago, Ill., d. Feb. 29, 1849, in Chicago, Ill.

5564. ii. LEAH LORENA TAYLOR, b. Dec. 25, 1854, in Rockford, Ill., d. Oct. 22, 1859.

5565. iii. VERNA ELIZABETH CHILD TAYLOR, b. Mch. 9, 1859, in LeRoy, N. Y., m. April 18, 1878, Wm. C. Swett, in Helena, Montana Territory.

5566. iv. MARA SIGOURNEY TAYLOR, b. June 15, 1863, in Rockford, Ill.

[Seventh Generation.]

5538. vii. EBENEZER RIDER, second son and seventh child of Betsey Child and John G. Rider, b. in LeRoy, Genesee Co., N. Y., Sept. 5, 1833, m. Sept. 14, 1854, Fanny Hovey. Mr. Rider resides on the old homestead, in LeRoy, purchased by his father in the early part of the present century.

[Eighth Generation.] Children:

5567. i. CARRIE ADELE RIDER, b. July 25, 1855, m. May 11, 1875, George W. Kelsey.

5568. ii. FRANK LEROY RIDER, b. Aug. 10, 1856.

5569. iii. CELIA VERNEPO RIDER, b. Dec. 15, 1857.

5570. iv. HATTIE LOUISA RIDER, b. Aug. 29, 1861.

5571. v. JAY G. RIDER, b. April 4, 1869.

5572. vi. CHARLIE HOVEY RIDER, b. Aug. 29, 1875.

5573. vii. CORA ANTOINETTE Rider, b. Feb. 23, 1877.

[Eighth Generation.]

5567. i. CARRIE ADELE RIDER, eldest child of Ebenezer and Fanny Hovey Rider, and grand-daughter of Betsey Child Rider, b. in LeRoy, Genesee Co., N. Y., July 25, 1855, m. May 11, 1875, George W. Kelsey.

[Ninth Generation.] Children:

5574. i. FLORA ADELIA KELSEY, b. Mch. 1876.

5575. ii. FLORENCE MAY KELSEY, b. May 1877.

[Sixth Generation.]

5469. v. HON. JOHN CHILD, second son of Samuel and eldest son of Samuel and Hannah Lamson Child, b. in Weybridge, Vt., Dec. 8, 1796, m. 1st, Nov. 1, 1826, Abigail, only dau. of Daniel and Bathsheba Frost Wright of New Haven, Vt.; m. 2nd, Feb. 18, 1844, Mrs. Mahala Briggs Pratt, widow of Elisha R. Pratt of Weybridge, and dau. of Apollos and Stella Briggs of Rochester, Vt. "Mr. John Child received his education at the common school, supplemented by instruction by his father, who at that time was reputed to be the best educated man in that town. When thirty years of age he married his first wife, who was but seventeen years old; the young wife was naturally ambitious, and developed strength of character, with great executive ability and an amiable disposition, which rendered her truly a help-meet. The children of this union were three sons and five daughters, four of whom died in girlhood; one daughter and the sons are still living. During the first fourteen years of his married life Mr. Child resided in Panton, Vt.; May 7, 1840, he removed to Weybridge, where he remained until his death. On July 26, 1843, the wife and mother was

taken from her family by death, leaving her husband and eight
children to mourn her loss. This great void was filled the
following year by Mr. Child's second marriage to Mrs. Pratt,
a woman of fine presence, and large benevolence. She combined
the rare traits of character which fitted her to fill the difficult
and responsible position of step mother, to a large family in
such a way as to make her respected and beloved by the whole
circle. The children of this marriage were three sons, two of
whom died in boyhood. Soon after his first marriage John
Child united with the Methodist Episcopal church of which
he was an active member till his death. He gave generously
to support the gospel and for benevolent objects, contributing
largely for the erection of the present M. E. church edifice in
Weybridge. As a business man he was successful in accumulating a large property, which was never lessened or wasted by
speculation or mismanagement. He was by occupation a gen-
tleman-farmer, and during his later years indulged much in
piscatorial sports of which he was always passionately fond.
In politics he was an ardent Republican, a firm believer in
sound currency, a protective tariff, and honest men for official
stations ; he filled at times most of the various town offices,
and was a member of the Vermont assembly in 1852–3. At
the age of 75 he was stricken with pneumonia and died Mch.
27, 1872, beloved and respected by all for his sterling traits of
character, not least among them his compassion for and generosity in assisting the poor. His widow, four sons and one
daughter survive him."*

[Seventh Generation.] Children:

5576. i. JULIA ABIGAIL CHILD, b. in Panton, Vt., Oct. 1, 1827, d. July
31, 1843.

5577. ii. JOHN ADAMS CHILD, b. June 20, 1829. m. Mch. 10, 1852, Sarah
Louisa Drake.

5578. iii. LOUISA MELISSA CHILD, b. in Panton, Vt., Oct. 3, 1831, d. Oct.
22, 1846.

5579. iv. ESTHER MARY CHILD, b. in Panton, Vt., Nov. 22, 1833, d. Sept.
13, 1847.

5580. v. ANDREW JACKSON CHILD, b. Feb. 7, 1836, m. June 1, 1862,
Mary E. Burt.

5581. vi. HARRIET HANNAH CHILD, b. April 23, 1838, m. Dec. 21, 1856,
Charles Carroll Colby.

5582. vii. DANIEL WRIGHT CHILD, b. June 12, 1840, m. Sept. 13, 1870,
Nevada Chase.

5583. viii. JULIA ABIGAIL CHILD, 2D, b. in Weybridge, Vt., Feb. 20,
1843, d. Sept. 20, 1847.

* This pleasing sketch of a noble man and his beloved wives is furnished us by his elder
son, Hon. John J. Child of Weybridge, Vt.

5584. ix. SAMUEL EBENEZER CHILD, b. in Weybridge,Vt., June 22, 1846, d. Sept. 1, 1847.

5585. x. SAMUEL PRATT CHILD, b. in Weybridge, Vt, Jan. 26, 1849, d. Jan. 9, 1857.

5586. xi. GEORGE EDWARD CHILD, b. Feb. 22, 1851, m. Jan. 25, 1879, Susan H. Wright.

MARY ELLEN PRATT, only child of Mrs. Mahala B. Pratt Child, by her marriage to Elisha R. Pratt, died in Weybridge, Vt., July 23, 1848, aged about 11 years.

[Seventh Generation.]

5577. ii. HON. JOHN A. CHILD, eldest son of Hon. John and Abigail Wright Child, b. in Panton, Vt., June 20, 1829, m. Mch. 10, 1852, Sarah Louisa Drake, eldest dau. of Dea. Elijah G. and Harriet Brewster Drake, b. in Weybridge, Vt., May 10, 1830. Mrs. Sarah L. D. Child received an academic education at Royalton, Vt., the residence of an uncle, Rev. Cyrus B. Drake, for forty years pastor of the Congregational church of that place : at the age of sixteen she became a teacher, in which occupation she continued until her marriage. The cause of education being of deep interest with her, the somewhat unusual compliment, in Vermont, of appointing ladies to office was tendered her, in repeated elections to the position of school superintendent. Energetic and active in matters of moral reform, the temperance cause finds in her an untiring and efficient supporter. Early in life she united with the Congregational church of Weybridge, and continues prominent among its members, and as a teacher in the Sabbath school. Mr. J. A Child received an academic education at Vergennes, Vt. In the autumn of 1853, Mr. and Mrs. J. A. Child located in Weybridge, where they now reside. Mr. Child is by occupation a farmer, and breeder of fine horses, and merino sheep, the last named being with him a specialty. His religious sympathies are with the Congregational denomination, with which church he united soon after marriage. In politics he is Republican to the core, and for the past twenty years has labored earnestly for the maintenance of the principles of that party. Prominent among the offices bestowed upon him is that of town clerk, to which he was elected in 1867, and has held continuously to the present time, 1880."

[Eighth Generation.] Children, born in Weybridge, Vt.:

5587. i. WILLIS BRYANT CHILD, b. Jan. 12, 1854, m. Nov. 12, 1877 Flora Effie Mott, eldest dau. of Rev. John S. and Maria Gregg Mott, of the M. E. Troy Conference. She was b. Nov. 17, 1854, in Cambridge, Vt.; received an academic education, music being made a specialty. A lady of rare execu-

R-1

tive ability, high moral principle, engaging manners and amiable disposition; she carries sunshine to the hearts of all her friends. Mr. Willis B. Child received a thorough academic training. His minority, except a year spent in travel in the west, was spent with his parents, and with them he continues to reside since his marriage. By occupation, a farmer, devoting special attention to the breeding of fine horses. A true son of the Green Mountain State, in politics he is soundly Republican.

5588. ii. Infant daughter, d. young.

5589. iii. HARRIET EMILY CHILD, b Sept. 23, 1857, m. Oct. 1, 1879, Charles Sumner Crysler, a rising young lawyer of Independence, Mo. Mrs. H. E. Child Crysler was educated at the Stanstead, P. Q., Female College, devoting much time to drawing and painting, for which she evinced decided talent. Portrait painting and crayoning were her special favorites, and to better perfect herself in these branches she spent a year at the St. Louis School of Design. Endowed with rare gifts and winning manners, and possessing the sterling qualities of mind and heart that command respect, she is a favorite with all who know her.

[Seventh Generation.]

5580. v. COL. ANDREW JACKSON CHILD, second son and fifth child of Hon. John and Abigail Wright Child, b. in Panton, Addison Co., Vt., Feb. 7, 1836, m. June 1, 1862, Mary Eliza Burt, dau. of Henry and Edna Boynton Burt. She was b. in Ticonderoga, N. Y., Oct. 5, 1835.

Col. Child was educated at Fort Edward, N. Y., Collegiate Institute. He went into service with the 14th Regt., Vermont Vols., in Oct. 1862, as Second Lieutenant, and served until mustered out in 1863. He was promoted successively as First Lieut., Major, and Lieut. Col. of Militia in 1864–5. Moved to Independence, Missouri, in 1869. In 1876 he again moved, and has settled in St. Louis, Mo. A man of energy, buoyancy of spirit, and earnest purpose, Col. Child honors the ancestry, he is proud to descend from. He is at present purchasing agent for the Missouri State Grange.

[Eighth Generation.] Children:

5590. i. PHILIP SHERIDAN CHILD, b. Oct. 24, 1864, in Weybridge, Vt.

5591. ii. JOHN HENRY CHILD, b. Dec. 20, 1865, in Weybridge, Vt.

5592. iii. CARROLL COLBY CHILD, b. May 8, 1868, in Weybridge, Vt.

5593. iv. CHARLES JEWETT CHILD, b. Jan. 16, 1870, in Independence, Mo.

[Seventh Generation.]

5581. vi. HARRIET HANNAH CHILD, only surviving dau. of Hon. John and Abigail Wright Child, b. in Panton, Addison Co., Vt., April 23, 1838, m. in Weybridge, Vt., Dec. 21, 1858, Charles Carroll Colby. Residence Stanstead, P. Q., Canada.

[Eighth Generation.] Children:

5594. i. ABBY LEMIRA COLBY, b. Sept. 27, 1859.

5595. ii. JESSIE MAUD COLBY, b. Nov. 11, 1861.

5596. iii. EMILY STEWART COLBY, b. Feb. 1, 1864, d. Sept. 17, 1865.

5597. iv. CHARLES WILLIAM COLBY, b. Mch. 25, 1867.

5598. v. CARROLL CHILD COLBY, b. Sept. 7, 1869, d. Sept. 28, 1869.
5599. vi. HARRIET ALICE COLBY, b. Sept. 5, 1870, d. Aug. 30, 1871.
5600. vii. JOHN CHILD COLBY, b. Nov. 24, 1873.

[Seventh Generation.]

5582. vii. DANIEL WRIGHT CHILD, third son of Hon. John and Abigail Wright Child, b. in Weybridge, Vt., June 12, 1840, m. in Independence, Jackson Co., Mo., Sept. 13, 1870, Nevada Chase. Residence Greenhorn, Pueblo Co., Colorado.
[Eighth Generation.] Children:
    5601. i. RUTH CHASE CHILD, b. June 26, 1874, d. May 3, 1878.
    5602. ii. CHARLES DANIEL CHILD, b. May 21, 1876.
    5603. iii. THOMAS EDWARD CHILD, b. Feb. 25, 1879.

[Seventh Generation.]

5586. xi. GEORGE EDWARD CHILD, youngest child of Hon. John and Mahala B. P. Child, b. in Weybridge, Vt., Feb. 22, 1851, m. Jan. 25, 1877, Susan H. Wright, dau. of Edwin S. and Sarah L. Brevoort Wright. She was b. May, 1855. Most thoroughly educated, she is a lady of refinement and culture, and much esteemed by a large circle of friends. Mr. George Edward Child was educated at the Fort Edward Institute, N. Y.; his minority, when not at school, was spent in the paternal home. He resides at the "Child Homestead" in Weybridge; is by occupation a farmer and dealer in merino sheep, and has also an extensive sheep ranch in Heurfano Co., Colorado. His religious sympathies are with the Methodist Episcopal church, to which he is a liberal contributor. Like his father, he is a staunch Republican
[Ninth Generation.] Child:
    5604. i. CECIL MAUD CHILD, b. Nov. 15, 1878.

[Sixth Generation.]

5470. vi. EBENEZER CHILD, second son and fifth child of Samuel and Hannah Lamson Child, b. in Weybridge, Vt., Oct. 8, 1799, m. in 1822, Aurelia Hunt, who d. Feb. 20, 1878.

In 1826, Mr. Ebenezer Child moved from Vermont to De-Kalb, St. Lawrence Co., N. Y., making the removal with a pair of oxen to draw his large covered wagon in which were closely stowed his wife and two small children, with most of their household effects. He moved slowly over the rough roads driving two cows. The following year Mr. Child returned to Vermont for a few things left behind them, and for a sum of one hundred dollars which his brother John paid him for his "birth-right." With about two hundred dollars of money he started on his farm, then all woods. By industry and economy he has come into the enjoyment of a farm of some three hundred acres, well stocked, and money at interest, and in his latter days can rest without anxiety. The patient toil and strong courage required at the time Mr. Child and his young wife entered the woods of St. Lawrence Co., fifty-four years since, can scarce be understood by those who yearly visit it now (1880) for pleasure and escape from the weary round of toil in our large cities, at that period many of them only small villages.

[Seventh Generation.] Children:

5605. i. CLARA JANE CHILD, b. June 3, 1823, m. Nov. 1, 1848, R. D. Rider.

5606. ii. BRAINERD E. CHILD, b. Aug. 19, 1825, d. Mch. 22, 1845.

5607. iii. SAMUEL M. CHILD, b. July 20, 1828, d. Mch. 29, 1845.

5608. iv. JULIA F. CHILD, b. about 1830, m. Sept. 1854, J. E. Barber.

5609. v. SEYMOUR P. CHILD, b. July 6, 1835, d. Oct. 5, 1839.

5610. vi. SIDNEY O. CHILD, b. June 6, 1838, m. Dec. 31, 1867, Lovina S. Murdock.

5611. vii. EMMA A. CHILD, b. Aug. 17, 1841, m. Nov. 1865, William H. Bentley.

[Seventh Generation.]

5605. i. CLARA JANE CHILD, eldest child of Ebenezer and Aurelia Hunt Child, b. in Weybridge, Vt., June 3, 1823, m Nov. 1, 1848, R. D. Rider of Weybridge, where they reside. Mr. Rider is a farmer.

[Eighth Generation.] Children:

5612. i. LUCY JANE RIDER, b. Sept. 9, 1849: Prof. of Natural Sciences in Kendree College, Lebanon, Ill.

5613. ii. EBENEZER CHILD RIDER, b. Oct. 19, 1855, m. Oct. 8, 1879, Emma A. Allard: occupation farming. Residence Weybridge, Vt.

5614. iii. ELLSWORTH RIDER, b. June 1862: attending school in Lebanon, Ill.

[Seventh Generation.]

5608. iv. JULIA F. CHILD, second dau. and fourth child of Ebenezer and Aurelia Hunt Child. b. in St. Lawrence Co., N. Y., about 1830, m. in Sept. 1854, J. E. Barber, a farmer residing in Rensselaer Falls, N. Y.

[Eighth Generation.] Child:

5615. i. LILLIAN A. BARBER, b. about 1855, m. Oct. 30, 1878, Morris D. Thompson, clerk on boat upon the Chippewa river, Wis.

[Seventh Generation.]

5610 vi. SIDNEY O. CHILD, fourth son and sixth child of Ebenezer and Aurelia Hunt Child, b. in St. Lawrence Co., N. Y., June 6, 1838, m. Dec. 31, 1867, Lovina S. Murdock. Mr. Child is resident with his father upon the home farm in Rensselaer Falls, N. Y.

[Eighth Generation.] Child:

5616. i. ERNEST M. CHILD, b. Nov. 14, 1876.

[Sixth Generation.]

5471. vii. SAMUEL CHILD, third son and sixth child of Samuel and Hannah Lamson Child, b. in Weybridge, Vt., Feb. 20, 1803, m. Mch. 18, 1829, in Pittsford, Rutland Co., Vt., Roxana Winch. She was b. in Framingham, Mass., Aug. 18, 1802, a dau. of Bijah and Rebecca Winch. Mr. Samuel Child d. in Cherry Valley, Ashtabula Co., Ohio, Sept. 18, 1870, having moved there from Weybridge, Vt., in the fall of 1834.

[Seventh Generation.] Children:

5617. i. ROXANA REBECCA CHILD, b Feb. 1, 1830, m. July 25, 1848, Elisha Hall, Jr.

5618 ii. EMILY CHILD, b. Feb. 9, 1833, m. Dec. 31, 1849, Charles Edward Petrie.

5619. iii. EUNICE MELVINA CHILD, b. Oct. 10, 1836, m. Jan. 1, 1857, Pulaski James Wood

5620. iv. MELISSA CHILD, b. Dec. 20, 1841, d. Feb. 16, 1842, in Cherry Valley, Ohio.

[Seventh Generation.]

5617. i. ROXANA REBECCA CHILD, eldest child of Samuel and Roxana Winch Child, b. in Weybridge, Vt., Feb. 1, 1830, m. July 25, 1848, Elisha Hall, Jr. Mrs. R. R. C. Hall d. Mch. 23, 1867, in Cherry Valley, Ohio, having returned to this place some three years previous, from California.

[Eighth Generation.] Children:

5621. i. SAMUEL ARTHUR HALL, b. May 3, 1852, in New Lyme, O., m. Jan. 1874, Cornelia Tomas.

5622. ii. ROMULUS STRONG HALL, b Nov. 27, 1856, in San Francisco, Cal., d. Nov. 28, 1868, in Chicago, Ill.

[Seventh Generation.]

5618. ii. EMILY CHILD, second child and dau. of Samuel and Roxana Winch Child, b. in Weybridge, Vt., Feb. 9, 1833, m. Dec. 31, 1849, Charles Edward Petric. Reside in Cherry Valley, Ashtabula county, Ohio.

[Eighth Generation.] Children:

5623. i. WALTER HENRY PETRIE, b. July 5, 1855, m. Nov. 27, 1877, Martha Heath.

5624. ii. EARNEST CHARLES PETRIE, b. Jan. 23, 1861.

5625. iii. IVA MELVINA PETRIE, b. Dec. 10, 1868, d. Sept. 4, 1875.

[Eighth Generation]

5623. i. WALTER HENRY PETRIE, eldest child of Emily Child and Charles E. Petric, b. in Cherry Valley, Ohio, July 5, 1855, m. Nov. 27, 1877, Martha Heath.

[Ninth Generation.] Child:

5626. i. ALTON FERN PETRIE, b. Oct. 9, 1878.

[Seventh Generation.]

5619. iii. EUNICE MELVINA CHILD, third dau. and child of Samuel and Roxana Winch Child, b. in Cherry Valley, Ohio, Oct. 10, 1836, m. Jan. 1, 1857, Pulaski James Wood. Residence Cherry Valley, Ashtabula county, Ohio.

[Eighth Generation.] Children:

5627. i. HUBERT PULASKI WOOD, b. May 22, 1861.
5628. ii. EMILY ROXANA WOOD, b. Dec. 30, 1866.

[Fourth Generation.]

5210. ix. ELISHA CHILD, ninth child, sixth son of Daniel and Beriah Bemis Child, b. in Watertown, Mass., Feb. 16, 1721, m. 1st, Mary — ; m. 2nd, June 1, 1760, Mehitable Garfield.

[Fifth Generation.] Children, born in Watertown, Mass.

5629. i. MARY CHILD, b. Sept. 30, 1753.
5630. ii. BEULAH CHILD, b. June 2, 1754.
5631. iii. WM. LINCOLN CHILD, b. June 16, 1759.
5632. iv. NABBY CHILD, b. Aug. 31, 1761.
5633. v. SARAH CHILD, b. May 18, 1763, d. soon.
5634. vi. SARAH CHILD, 2nd, b May 17, 1764.
5635. vii. ELISHA CHILD, Jr., b. Feb. 28, 1770, m. about 1790, Abigail —; she d. Oct. 27, 1877. He d. July 19, 1823.

[Fifth Generation.]

5635. vii. ELISHA CHILD, JR., fourth child of Elisha and Mehitable Garfield Child, b. Feb. 28, 1770, m. about 1790, Abigail —.

[Sixth Generation.] Children, born in Watertown, Mass.

5636. i. POLLY CHILD, b. Sept. 8, 1791.
5637. ii. ELISHA CHILD, JR., b. Mch. 24, 1794.
5638. iii. JONAS CHILD, b. July 24, 1796.
5639. iv. ABIGAIL CHILD, b. 1798.

[This record should have been placed immediately after that of the descendants of Josiah Child on page 524, but it was not obtained until other matter had been placed in the printers' hands. We therefore bring it into as close order as possible.]

[Fifth Generation.]

4750. iv. JONATHAN CHILD, JR., second son of Jonathan and Abigail Parker Child, b. in Grafton, Mass., Feb. 14, 1738, m. April 16, 1787, Eunice Smith of Westboro, Mass. Mr. and Mrs. Child were people of earnest piety, and so trained their children that they too grew into most devout christians, and to the third and fourth generations, the blessings have descended, as we learn from a grand-daughter, Mrs. Hannah Child Whiting of West Medway, Mass., from whom we learn that her grand-father "resided through his long life in one house, and there died in the town of Westboro, Mass., in 1808, æ 70 : his widow died 1813, æ 75.

[Sixth Generation.] Children:

5640. i. ESTHER CHILD, b. 1768, m. Thomas Smith.

5641. ii. ELIZABETH CHILD, b. about 1769, d. unmarried.

5642. iii. SAMUEL CHILD, b. about 1770, d. unmarried.

5643. iv. EPHRAIM CHILD, b. 1772, m. Nov. 6, 1794, Katherine Whitney.

5644. v. A son, name not ascertained.

5645. vi. SARAH CHILD, m. Capt Christopher Nason : three children, one son, Charles Nason, m. Martha Stone of Groton, Mass.

[Sixth Generation.]

5640. i. ESTHER CHILD, eldest dau. of Jonathan, Jr. and Eunice Smith Child, b. in Westboro, Mass., 1768, m. Thomas Smith and resided in Smithfield, R. I., where her children were born, and she died leaving two daughters, (two sons died young,) who, with their father went to the West and cannot be traced.

[Seventh Generation.] Children.

5646. i. ELIZABETH SMITH.

5647. ii. EUNICE SMITH.

[Sixth Generation.]

5643. iv. EPHRAIM CHILD, second son and fourth child of Jonathan, Jr., and Eunice Smith Child, b. in Westboro, Mass., about 1770, m. Nov. 6, 1794, Katherine Whitney of Grafton. Mr. Child resided in Sturbridge, Mass., a few years, then at the request of his father returned to Westboro, and remained during the life of his father.

[Seventh Generation.] Children:

5648. i. POLLY CHILD, b. Aug. 9, 1795, m. 1819, Lawson Graves.

5649. ii. LUCY CHILD, b. May 27, 1797, d. Mch. 1, 1830, a most lovely christian.

5650. iii. HANNAH CHILD, b. Oct. 16, 1798, m. July 10, 1851, Mason Whiting.

5651. iv. EPHRAIM CHILD, JR., b. April 27, 1802, m. Sept. 17, 1825, Durenda Holt.

5652. v. ABIGAIL CHILD, b. Oct. 25, 1803, m. Nov. 29, 1820, Joseph H. Muzzy.

5653. vi. ELI W. CHILD, b. June 23, 1809, m. July 4, 1830, Maria M. Morse. Mr. Child d. April 7, 1843. His widow m. 2nd, Samuel Banister; she d. 1846: no children.

5654. vii. MARY CHILD, b. Nov. 15, 1810, d. Mch. 19, 1819.

5655. viii. SIMEON CHILD, b. 1812, d. Oct. 30, 1813.

[Seventh Generation.]

5648. i. POLLY CHILD, eldest child of Ephraim and Katherine Whitney Childs, b. in Sturbridge, Mass., Aug. 9, 1795, m.

1819, Lawson Graves. Eleven children were given them, three died in infancy; and as we have no dates of birth may not have given them in due chronological order.

[Eighth Generation.] Children:

5656. i. ELI WHITNEY GRAVES, went to California and died on his return, in New York City, aged 25 years.

5657. ii. WILLIAM B. GRAVES, m. Jane Frost of Hubbardston, Mass.; had three children, one died in infancy; a son and daughter living. Mother died 1875.

5658. iii. SIMON W. GRAVES, removed to the State of New York.

5659. iv. HENRY GRAVES, resides in Worcester, Mass.

5660. v. CATHERINE GRAVES, m. William Frost; four children, two daughters died 1877. Mother died 1875.

5661. vi. MARIA GRAVES, m. Elon G. Higgins.

5662. vii. ALBERT P. GRAVES, m. 1st, Elvira Bonney; m. 2d, Matilda Randolph. Mr. Graves prepared for the ministry and was settled over the Greenwood Church, Brooklyn, N. Y. After some years labor in the pastorate, Mr. Graves felt it his duty to enter upon the work of an Evangelist; and in this way has labored in many States with eminent success. Upon the death of his first wife, leaving two young sons, he devotedly watched over and educated them.

[Eighth Generation.]

5661. vi. MARIA GRAVES, second dau. of Polly Child and Lawson Graves, b. in Worcester, Mass., m. Elon G. Higgins, a merchant of Worcester, Mass. Four sons are with their father in business.

[Ninth Generation.] Children:

5663. i. FREDERICK HIGGINS, d. 1879, aged 23 years.

5664. ii. CHARLES HIGGINS.

5665. iii. FRANK HIGGINS.

5666. iv. WILLIAM HIGGINS.

5667. v. EDWARD L. HIGGINS.

5668. vi. ETHA E. HIGGINS.

5669. vii. ARTHUR HIGGINS.

5670. viii. Infant son, (unchristened.)

5671. ix. Infant daughter, (unchristened.)

[Seventh Generation.]

5650. iii. HANNAH CHILD, third dau. and child of Ephraim and Katherine Whitney Child, b. in Sturbridge, Mass., Oct. 16, 1798, m. in Worcester, Mass., July 10, 1851, Mason Whiting. Mrs. Whiting, now in her 83d year, has kindly furnished us much of her line. She is the last of her generation in the household of her father. Delicate from childhood, she has long survived the more rugged, and still performs the domestic duties of her household. Through her long life she has tenderly watched over the sick and dying, lovingly ministering to their physical and spiritual necessities. With her beloved husband she awaits the "Inasmuch as ye have done it unto one of the least of these my brethren, ye have done it unto me." Reside in West Medway, Norfolk county, Mass.

[Seventh Generation.]

5651. iv. EPHRAIM CHILD, JR., eldest son of Ephraim and Katherine Whitney Child, b. in Sturbridge, Mass., April 27, 1802, m. Sept. 17, 1825, Durenda Holt of Holden, Mass. Mr. Child died at Rutland, Mass., Jan. 6, 1847. Three sons in this family, in mature years, changed their christian names : in our record we give both. Mrs. D. H. Childs resides in West Boylston, Mass.

[Eighth Generation.] Children:

5672. i. SIMON W. CHILDS, (now George Childs) b. Oct. 7, 1826, m. Feb. 24, 1850, Ellen Wallace. Resides in California. Three children.

5673. ii. MARY CHILDS, b. Sept. 24, 1829, d. April 28, 1838, in Worcester, Mass.

5674. iii. JOEL (now William) CHILDS, b. July 15, 1831, in Worcester, Mass., m. July 21, 1860, Mrs. Jane A. Hall. He mysteriously disappeared from a diving-bell scow at the government works at Hell Gate, about 1868.

5675. iv. DANIEL CHILDS, b. Nov. 8, 1833, d. May 10, 1838, in Worcester, Mass.

5676. v. ELI INDEPENDENCE (now George Eli) CHILDS, b. May 10, 1836, m. Nov. 25, 1861, Mrs. Julia A. Knapp.

5677. vi. NANCY MARIA CHILDS, b. Feb. 13, 1838, m. 1st, April 14 1856, Samuel S. Stevens; m. 2d, May 1, 1865, John W. Adams.

5678. vii. DAVID E. CHILDS, b. Oct. 22, 1839, m. Dec. 25, 1865, Anna Newell.

5679. viii. HENRY W. CHILDS, b. Oct. 7, 1841, m. Oct. 7, 1866, Mary P. Robbins of Nova Scotia. Two children.

5680. ix. JONATHAN E. CHILDS, b. at Rutland, Mass., Aug. 13, 1843. On his nineteenth birth-day, Aug. 13, 1862, enlisted in the 10th Mass. Battery, Light Artillery, and died in an army hospital in Washington, D. C., Nov. 15, 1862.

5681. x. EHHRAIM PRESCOTT CHILDS, b. in Worcester, Mass., April 23, 1847, d. Oct. 5, 1868, in same place.

[Eighth Generation.]

5676. v. GEORGE ELI CHILDS, fourth son and fifth child of Ephraim and Durenda Holt Childs, b. in Worcester, Mass., May 10, 1836, m. Nov. 25, 1861, Mrs. Julia A. Knapp of Fitchburgh. On his marriage to Mrs. Knapp, Mr. Child adopted her son of the previous marriage and gave him his name.

[Ninth Generation.] Child:

5682. i. FRANK CHILDS, of Fitchburgh.

[Eighth Generation.]

5677. vi. NANCY MARIA CHILDS, second dau. and sixth child of Ephraim and Durenda Holt Childs, b. in Worcester, Mass., Feb. 13, 1838, m. 1st, in Worcester, Mass., April 14, 1856,

Samuel S. Stevens of Washington, D. C.: m. 2d, May 1, 1865, at West Brookfield, Mass, John W. Adams. Residence West Rutland, Mass.*

[Ninth Generation.] Children:

5683. i. FRANK ELMER ADAMS, b. April 6, 1867, at West Rutland, Mass.

5684. ii. MARY EDITH ADAMS, b. May 12, 1871, d. May 21, 1874, in West Rutland.

[Eighth Generation]

5678. vii. DAVID E. CHILDS, fifth son of Ephraim and Durenda Holt Childs, b. in Worcester, Mass., Oct. 22, 1839, m. Dec. 25, 1865, Anna Newell of Springfield, Mass., who was b. Feb. 29, 1840. Resides in New Haven, Ct.; is a mechanic.

[Ninth Generation.] Children:

5685. i. MARY BELLE CHILD, b. Feb. 6, 1870, d Mch. 27, 1870, in Springfield, Mass.

5686. ii. EDDIE PRESCOTT CHILD, b. June 4, 1871, d. Aug. 1, 1871, in Springfield, Mass.

5687. iii. HARRY LINWOOD CHILD, b. Mch. 13, 1872, in New Haven, Ct.

5688. iv. WEBB NEWELL CHILD, b. Mch. 29, 1877, d. July 10, 1877, in New Haven, Ct.

5689. v. FRANK HOLT CHILD, b. Aug. 6, 1878, in New Haven, Ct.

[Eighth Generation.]

5679. viii. HENRY W. CHILDS, eighth child and sixth son of Ephraim, Jr., and Durinda Holt Childs, b. in Worcester, Mass., Oct. 7, 1841, m. Oct. 7, 1866, Mary Porter Robbins of Nova Scotia, of Scotch and English parentage. Mr. Childs resides in Worcester, Mass., at No. 8 Portland street: is shipping agent for several manufacturing firms in Worcester.

[Ninth Generation.] Children:

** i. JOHN FREEMONT CHILDS, b. April 9, 1867.

** ii. JENNIE MAY CHILDS, b. May 1, 1872.

** iii. A SON, b. May 22, 1876, d. soon.

** iv. A SON, b. Oct. 23, 1878, d. soon.

[Seventh Generation.]

5652. v. ABIGAIL CHILD, fourth dau. of Ephraim and Katherine Whitney Child, b. in Sturbridge, Oct. 25, 1803, m. Nov. 27, 1820, Joseph H. Muzzy. Mr. Muzzy d. Nov. 21, 1843, aged 46 years.

[Eighth Generation.] Children:

5690. i. MARY CATHERINE MUZZY, b. Dec. 10, 1836, d. Sept. 3, 1846.

5691. ii. ADOLPHUS THEODORE MUZZY, b. 1829, m. T. Emma Streatton. Reside in Boston.

*To Mrs. Adams we are indebted for most valuable information of her family, and an addition to our number of copies of the coats of arms held in the family name.

CHAPTER IX.

JOHN CHILD OF BOSTON.

The evidence is so strong which points to the John Child of Woodstock, Ct., who married Elizabeth ——, as the son John of Benjamin Child the emigrant, that it has been accepted and so recorded. We are, therefore, compelled to search the early records and find, if we can, some progenitor for the family in Boston and vicinity who have been supposed hitherto in this Benjamin line. We find no less than three of the name of John Child on the early records, from any one of whom this line may have come. One is a John Child, a brother of Dr. Robert Child, who distinguished himself in Boston, as elsewhere recorded. These brothers are supposed to be of the family of Sir Joshua and Sir John Child of London and India. Another John Child gave testimony at the age of twenty-five, in 1653. And a third was a somewhat noted tailor of the times, a man of property, some of whose descendants removed to Maine. There has been a supposition that John Child who married Elizabeth ——, may have married for his second wife Sarah Blake, thus making him identical with John Child of Boston ; but this could not be, for John Child of Boston was married to Sarah Blake in 1710, while the youngest child of John and Elizabeth was born in 1712. There is another hypothesis quite reasonable and not impossible, that John Child of Boston may have been a descendant of Joseph Child who was born 1674, the youngest son of Benjamin the emigrant, of whose life we have no record. We strongly incline to the latter theory from the frequent repetition of the name Joseph among the descendants, the like custom noticeable in other lines. We cannot establish the direct line at present, but time may reveal the missing link. We therefore record the following name as in the second generation.

[Second Generation.]

5692. i. JOHN CHILD, b. in Boston, Mass., Aug. 1, 1671, m. by Rev. Benjamin Wadsworth, Feb. 10, 1710, Sarah Blake.

[Third Generation.] Children:

5693. i. JOHN CHILD, JR., b. in Boston, Mass., Feb. 8, 1714, m. Dec. 23, 1736, Jane Lawrence.

5694. ii. SARAH CHILD, b. in Boston, Mass., Mch. 1716.

[Third Generation.]

5693. i. JOHN CHILD, JR., eldest child of John and Sarah Blake Child, b. Feb. 8, 1714, m. Dec. 23, 1736, Jane Lawrence.

[Fourth Generation.] Children, born in Boston, Mass.

5695. i. JOHN CHILD, JR., b. Sept. 13, 1737. He was killed in battle at the siege of Lewisburg or Bell Isle.

5696. ii. JOSEPH CHILD, b. Dec. 21, 1739, d. young.

5697. iii. NATHANIEL CHILD, b. Mch. 15, 1741.

5698. iv. JOSEPH CHILD, 2D, b. July 15, 1744, d young.

5699. v. SARAH CHILD, b. Feb. 2, 1746.

5700. vi. JAMES CHILD, b. June 12, 1748.

5701. vii JOSEPH CHILD, 3D, b. Oct. 29, 1749, m. 1st, Anna Brett; m. 2d, Susan Gray.

5702 viii. BENJAMIN CHILD, b. Sept. 1, 1751.

[Fourth Generation.]

5701. vii. JOSEPH CHILD, seventh child and sixth son of John and Jane Lawrence Child, b. Oct. 29, 1749, m. 1st, Anna Brett; m. 2d, Susan Gray.

[Fifth Generation.] Children:

5703. i. ANN BRETT CHILD, d. young.

5704. ii. JOHN CHILD, b. April 13, 1784, m. Nov. 1808, Lucy Howard.

5705. iii. HANNAH CLOUGH CHILD, b. Sept. 10, 1787, d. Oct. 29, 1875. aged 87.

5706. iv. JANE LAWRENCE CHILD, b. June 25, 1790.

5707. v. JOSEPH CHILD, JR., b. Aug 19, 1792, m. 1st, Mary James; m. 2d, Maria Fisk, who d. April 2, 1879.

5708. vi. NATHANIEL CHILD, b. 1795, m. April 26, 1821, Katharine Stimpson of Charlestown, Mass.

5709. vii. BENJAMIN GRAY CHILD, b. Dec. 19, 1797, m. 1821, Eliza Treadwell. She d. June 26, 1866.

5710. viii. NICHOLAS GRAY CHILD, b. Sept. 4, 1802, m. Sept. 1823, Catherine Colwell.

5711. ix. ELIZA TREADWELL CHILD, b. 1805, d. Aug. 9, 1876, unm.

5712. x. ANN BRETT CHILD, 2D, b. 1808, d. July 31, 1876, unm.

[Fifth Generation.]

5704. ii. JOHN CHILD, eldest son of Joseph and Susan Gray Child, b. April 13, 1784, m. Nov. 1808, Lucy Howard.

[Sixth Generation.] Children, born in Boston. Mass.

5713. i. GEORGE HOWARD CHILD, b. 1809, m. May 21, 1835, Abigail Duren.

5714. ii. HENRIETTA CHILD, b. 1811, m. Thomas Comer. Had two or three children.

5715. iii. AMELIA CHILD, b. about 1813, d. young.

5716. iv. JOHN CHILD, b. about 1815, d. young.

5717. v. ELLEN CHILD, b. about 1817, m. Timothy House.

5718. vi. ADALINE CHILD, b. about 1819, m. in New York or Brooklyn.

5719. vii. ANN JANE CHILD, b. 1821, d. young.

5720. viii. JOHN CHILD, JR., b. May 30, 1826, d. unm.

[Sixth Generation.]

5713. i. GEO. HOWARD CHILD, b. in Boston, Mass., 1809, m. May 21, 1835, Abigail Duren. He d. Nov. 6, 1867.

From the Boston *Transcript*, of Nov. 7, 1867, we copy the following notice of Mr. Child on the occasion of his death :

"Mr. Geo. H. Child died yesterday P. M., after a lingering illness, at his residence in Dover street. He was a gentleman widely known and respected. His genial nature, generous disposition and rare varied information made him a universal favorite. In early manhood he was treasurer of the Old Tremont Theatre; afterward, for years, the chief clerk of Mr. Jonas Chickering, and Chickering & Sons. During the war he had charge of an important branch of the military department of the government (State). In all these positions he was found adequate to the most pressing exegency. Through his long and painful illness he was cheered by the warm sympathies and attention of hundreds of devoted friends."

[Seventh Generation.] Child:

5721. i ELIZA F. CHILD, b. April 4, 1836, m. Nov. 20, 1854, Francis L. Tileston.

[Seventh Generation.]

5721. i. ELIZA F. CHILD, only child of George Howard and Abigail Duren Child, b. in Boston, Mass., April 4, 1836, m. Nov. 20, 1854, Francis Tileston, son of Edmund Tileston of Dorchester, Mass. Mrs. Eliza F. Child Tileston resides in Dorchester, Mass.

[Eighth Generation.] Children :

5722. i. HELEN McLEAN TILESTON, b. Aug. 18, 1855.

5723. ii. EDMUND PITT TILESTON, b. Aug. 18, 1857.

[Sixth Generation.]

5717. v. ELLEN CHILD, third dau. of John and Lucy Howard Child, b. in Boston, Mass., abt. 1817, m. Timothy House.

[Seventh Generation.] Child:

5724. i. EDWARD HOWARD HOUSE, a man of letters, now resident in Japan.

[Fifth Generation.]

5707. v. JOSEPH CHILD, JR, fifth child and second son of Joseph and Susan Gray Child, b. Aug. 19, 1792, m. 1st, 1819, Mary James. She d. Sept. 1839 ; m. 2d, Maria Fisk, d. Oct. 2, 1879. He d. Sept. 20, 1878.

[Sixth Generation] Children, born in Boston, Mass.

5725. i. MARY ANN JAMES CHILD, b. April 30, 1820, m. 1842, William Winslow Emerson.

5726. ii. WM. CAPERS CHILD, b. Feb 5, 1822, m. 1843, Mary Emeline Smith.

5727. iii. FRANCIS JAMES CHILD, b. Feb. 1, 1825, m. 1862, Elizabeth Ellery Sedgwick.

5728. iv. SARAH CHILD, b. Aug. 12, 1827, m. Benjamin Delmont Lock.

5729. v. JOSEPH CHILD JR., b. May 4, 1829, m. 1860, Frances Ellen Sullivan.

5730. vi. ELIZA JANE CHILD, b. May 19, 1831, m. 1852, John Ware Davis.

5731. vii. ANNETTE CHILD, b. May 24, 1834.

5732. viii. CAROLINE CHILD, b. Mch. 7, 1837, m. Oct. 27, 1870, Amos K. Fiske of New York.

[Sixth Generation.]

5725. i. MARY ANN JAMES CHILD, eldest child of Joseph, Jr., and Mary James Child, b. in Boston, Mass., April 30, 1820, m. 1842, Wm. Winslow Emerson.

[Seventh Generation] Children:

5733. i. MARY FRANCES EMERSON, b. May 26, 1843.

5734. ii. WILLIAM HERBERT EMERSON, b. Dec. 30, 1846, m. Dec. 1871, Helen Shearer.

[Seventh Generation.]

5734. ii. WM. HERBERT EMERSON, second child and only son of Mary Ann James Child and Wm. Winslow Emerson, b. Dec. 30, 1846, m. Dec. 1871, Helen Shearer.

[Eighth Generation.] Children:

5735. i. ROBERT LEONARD EMERSON.

5736. ii. HELEN EMERSON.

5737. iii. ELLIOT EMERSON.

[Sixth Generation.]

5726. ii. WILLIAM CAPERS CHILD, second child and eldest son of Joseph, Jr., and Mary James Child, b. in Boston, Mass., Feb. 5, 1822, m. Nov. 19, 1843, Mary Emeline Smith of Saugus, Mass., who was b. Aug. 1, 1822.

[Seventh Generation.] Children, born in Boston, Mass.

5728. i. WM. SWEETSER CHILD, b. July 31, 1844, m. Nov. 13, 1867, Isadore Eleanor Stearns.

5739. ii. CHARLES KIMBALL CHILD, b. May 20, 1849, m. May 18, 1873, Maria Louisa Rogers.

[Seventh Generation.]

5738. i. WILLIAM SWEETSER CHILD, eldest child of Wm. Capers and Mary Emeline Smith Child, b. July 31, 1844, m. Nov. 13, 1867, Isadore Eleanor Stearns. She was b. in Boston, Dec. 21, 1844.

[Eighth Generation.] Children:

5740. i. WARREN JACOBS CHILD, b. in Medford, Mass., Jan. 24, 1869.

5741. ii. HENRY TYLER CHILD, b. in Medford, Mass., July 31, 1876.

[Seventh Generation.]

5739. ii. CHARLES KIMBALL CHILD, second child and son of Wm. Capers and Mary E. Smith Child, b. in Boston, Mass., May 20, 1849, m. May 18, 1873, Maria Louisa Rogers.

[Eighth Generation.] Children:

5742. i. WM. HENRY CHILD, b. in Medford, Mass., April 8, 1876.

5743. ii. ALICE KIMBALL CHILD, b. in Medford, Mass., Aug. 11, 1878.

[Sixth Generation.]

5727. iii. PROF. FRANCIS J. CHILD, Ph. D., third child and second son of Joseph, Jr., and Mary James Child, b. in Boston, Mass., Feb. 1, 1825, m. 1862, Elisabeth Ellery Sedgwick. She was b. in New York City Jan. 7, 1825.

Professor Child was graduated at Harvard University, Cambridge, Mass., in 1846. He was tutor in mathematics for some time in the same institution. In 1848, Harvard College gave him the position of tutor in rhetoric and history. In 1851, he was advanced to a professorship in rhetoric and oratory. In 1876, he was still further promoted to the Chair of English Literature, a position which he still fills. In 1854, the honorary degree of Doctor of Philosophy was conferred upon him by the "University of Gottengen." In 1849, he visited Europe, where he spent two years in study and travels. He is especially distinguished for his thorough acquaintance with early English literature. As a Chaucer scholar, he has perhaps no superior in America or Europe. He is the author of the admirable article on "Ballard Poetry" in Johnson's Encyclopedia. Dr. Child is also the compiler of "English and Scottish Ballads," in 8 vols., Boston, 1860, which contains all but two or three of the ancient ballads, known to scholars, and is a most valuable and rare collection.

[Seventh Generation.]   Children:

5744. i. HELEN MARIA CASTILIA CHILD, b. in Cambridge, Mass., Oct. 12, 1863, m. Timothy House.

5745. ii. SUSAN SEDGWICK CHILD, b. in Cambridge, Mass., Aug. 14, 1866.

5746. iii. HENRIETTA ELLERY CHILD, b. in Cambridge, Mass., Nov. 2, 1867.

5747. iv. FRANCIS SEDGWICK CHILD, b. in Cambridge, Mass., June 12, 1869.

[Sixth Generation.]

5729. v. JOSEPH CHILD, JR., 2D. fifth child and third son of Joseph and Mary James Child, b. in Boston, Mass., May 4, 1829, m. Mch. 29, 1860, Frances Ellen Sullivan. She was b Mch. 18, 1837, in Exeter, N. H.; dau. of Thomas and Frances Ann Sullivan. Residence in West Cambridge, Mass.

[Seventh Generation.]   Children:

5748. i. MARY JANE CHILD, b. in West Cambridge, Jan. 15, 1861.

5749. ii. ALICE CHILD, b. Feb. 28, 1863, d. May 29, 1870.

5750. iii. EDITH FRANCES CHILD, b. May 25, 1867.

5751. iv. ARTHUR WARREN CHILD, b. Nov. 30, 1868.

[Sixth Generation.]

5730. vi. ELIZA JAMES CHILD, sixth child and third dau. of Joseph and Mary James Child, b. in Boston, Mass., Mch. 19,

1831, m. Nov. 10, 1852, John Ware Davis, who was b. in Boston, Mass., Jan. 19, 1830. She d. Mch. 30, 1874.

[Seventh Generation.]   Child:

5752. i. CHARLES LOWELL T. DAVIS, b. in Cambridgeport, Aug. 14, 1853, d. Mch. 27, 1873.

[Sixth Generation.]

5732. viii. CAROLINE CHILD, eighth child and fifth dau. of Joseph, Jr., and Mary James Child, b. in Boston, Mass., Mch. 7, 1837, m. Oct. 27, 1870, Amos Kidder Fiske of New York City.

[Seventh Generation.]   Children:

5753. i. PHILIP SIDNEY FISKE, b. Sept. 27, 1872.

5754. ii. ANNETTE FISKE, b. Oct. 13, 1873.

5755 iii. MARGUERITE FISKE, b. Jan. 28, 1876.

[Fifth Generation.]

5708. vi. NATHANIEL CHILD, sixth child and third son of Joseph and Susan Gray Child, b. in 1795, m. April 26, 1821, Catharine Simpson of Charlestown, Mass. She was b. May 1, 1793, and d. Jan. 17, 1880. Mr. Child d. Sept. 1, 1821. The following obituary of Mrs. Child is from a Boston paper.

The death of Catherine Stimpson Child, which occurred in this district on Thursday evening, removes from our midst one whose gentle kindness and devoted life made her dearly loved, and will cause her departure to be sincerely mourned. She was born in Charlestown in 1793, and her life was a busy and active one, in every duty of which she was faithful and sincere. Her purity of thought and action, her sweetness of disposition endeared her to all who knew her, and no one can forget the tenderness of her sympathy for all who needed it. Hers was a life well spent through all its length, and the reward of good service on this earth was certainly gained by her. She could trace directly her descent from George Bunker, from whom the noted battle site of the Revolution derives its name, John Stimpson having married a Rebecca Bunker, in 1709. She leaves one son, Francis Child, of this district.

[Sixth Generation.]   Child:

5756. i. FRANCIS CHILD, b. in Boston, Mass., July 28, 1820, m. Feb. 2, 1840, Juliet Dearing.

[Sixth Generation.]

5756. i. FRANCIS CHILD, only child of Nathaniel and Catherine Simpson Child, b. in Boston, Mass., July 28, 1820, m. Feb. 2, 1840, Juliet Wilcox Dearing of Charlestown, Mass.; she was born Mch. 9, 1824. Residence, Charlestown, Mass. Mr. Child is recognized in the circle of his acquaintance as a man of intelligence and culture, possessing good business talent, a man of strict integrity, and engaged in successful mercantile

Francis Child

business in the firm of Childs & Lane, dealers in carpets, Tremont street, Boston. In municipal and State affairs he has evinced a capacity for wisely counselling and securing the best results for the public benefit. In the years of 1859–60 and '61, he held the office of Inspector in the Massachusetts State Prison. In 1862 and '63, he was a member of the Board of Aldermen in Charlestown, Mass.: the same year he was trustee of the Charlestown Public Library: in 1863–64, he was a member of the Massachusetts State Senate, commissioner for the erection of the soldiers' monument of Charlestown, Mass.; for ten years trustee and vice president of the Winchester home for aged women: a member of the Mystic Water Board eight years: a member of Gov. Rice's executive council for 1877–8: Master of the Henry Prince Lodge of Masons for 1869–70 and 71: District Deputy Grand Master of Massachusetts Grand Lodge for 1878–9 and '80: all these positions he could not hold were not his qualifications superior.

[Seventh Generation.] Children:

5757. i. JULIA FRANCIS CHILD, b. June 5, 1841, m. July 26, 1861, Charles Gilbert Pease.

5758 ii. GEORGE THEODORE CHILD, b. Sept. 7, 1842, m. Sept. 19, 1866, Ella Byrnes.

5759. iii. MARIA LOUISA CHILD, b. Nov. 27, 1843, d. in infancy.

5760. iv. NATHANIEL CHILD, b. Feb. 8, 1847.

5761. v. RUBY MOORE CHILD, b. June 22, 1848, m. Herbert E. Burrage.

5762. vi. CATHARINE STIMPSON CHILD, b. April 22, 1851, m. C. M. Buxton.

5763. vii. MARY LOUISA CHILD, b. Aug. 26, 1853.

5764. viii. CARRIE MADELINE CHILD, b. Aug. 6, 1855, m. Dec. 1876, Charles W. Porter.

5765. ix. FRANK CHILD, b. July 19, 1858.

[Seventh Generation.] Children:

5757. i. JULIA FRANCIS CHILD, eldest child of Francis and Juliet W. Dearing Child, b. June 5, 1841, m. July 26, 1861, Charles Gilbert Pease, b. Aug. 6, 1835.

[Eighth Generation] Children:

5766. i. ALICE BARTLET PEASE, b. 1864.

5767. ii. FRANCIS CHILD PEASE, b. 1866.

5768. iii. CHARLES FRANCIS PEASE, b. 1868.

5769. iv. HERBERT PEASE, b. 1870.

5770. v. WILLIAM HENRY PEASE, b. 1872.

5771. vi. HARRY PEASE, b. 1875.

[Seventh Generation.]

5758. ii. GEO. THEODORE CHILD, second child and eldest son of Francis and Juliet W. Dearing Child, b. Sept. 7, 1842, m. Sept. 19, 1866. Lucy Ella Byrnes, b. Oct. 22, 1842.

[Eighth Generation.] Children:
　　5772. i. ARTHUR FRANCIS CHILD, b. Sept. 10, 1868.
　　5773. ii. JULIET NEILSON CHILD, b. Mch. 21, 1870.
　　5774. iii. MABEL BRIGHAM CHILD, b. Dec. 16, 1872
　　5775. iv. ANNA CHILD, b. 1874.
　　5776. v. HAROLD CHILD, b. April 7, 1879.

[Seventh Generation.]

5761. v. RUBY MOORE CHILD, fifth child and third dau. of Francis and Juliet W. Dearing Child, b. June 22, 1848, m. 1869, Herbert E. Burrage.

[Eighth Generation.] Children.
　　5777. i. FRANCIS J. BURRAGE, b. 1870.
　　5778. ii. HARRY L. BURRAGE, b. 1872.
　　5779. iii. ALICE B. BURRAGE, b. 1874.

[Seventh Generation.]

5762. vi. CATHARINE STIMPSON, CHILD, sixth child and fourth dau. of Francis and Juliet W. Dearing Child, b. April 22, 1851, m. Mch. 3, 1876, C. M. Buxton.

[Eighth Generation.] Children:
　　5780. i. HORACE C. BUXTON, b. Jan. 15, 1877.
　　5781. ii. EDWARD G. BUXTON, b. May 20, 1879.

[Seventh Generation.]

5764. viii. CARRIE MADELINE CHILD, eighth child, sixth dau. of Francis and Juliet W. Dearing Child, b. Aug. 6, 1855, m. Dec. 7, 1876, Charles W. Porter.

[Eighth Generation.] Children:
　　5782. i. WILLIAM F. PORTER, b. Dec. 7, 1877.
　　5783. ii. CHARLES I. PORTER, b. May 12, 1879.

[Fifth Generation.]

5709. vii. BENJAMIN GRAY CHILD, seventh child and fourth son of Joseph and Susan Gray Child, b. in Boston, Mass., Dec. 19, 1797, m. 1821, Eliza Treadwell; she d. Jan. 26, 1866. Mr. Child resides in St. Louis, Mo.   In a letter written to Mr. Isaac Child of Boston dated Jan. 1868, Mr. Benjamin Gray Child speaks of "the loved ones who have flown from time" in early infancy and winning childhood, showing a remarkable instance of mortality, equaled perhaps by one case only recorded in this volume.

[Sixth Generation.] Children:

5784. i. RICHARD D. CHILD, b. Aug. 12, 1822, d. Sept. 26, 1823.

5785. ii. ELIZA CHILD, b. Aug. 17, 1823, d. May 5, 1825.

5786. iii. ELIZA CHILD, 2D, b. Feb. 9, 1825, d. Jan. 18, 1827.

5787. iv. BENJAMIN GRAY CHILD, JR., b. April 11, 1827, d. Sept. 6, 1828.

5788. v. MARIA J. CHILD, b. May 11, 1829, d. April 27, 1839.

5789. vi. ELIZABETH I. CHILD, b. Dec. 27, 1839.

5790. vii. MARY CHILD, b Jan. 24, 1833, d. April 9, 1839.

5791. viii. EMMA CHILD, b. Mch. 3, 1835, d. April 17, 1839.

5792. ix. BENJAMIN GRAY CHILD, 2D, b. June 2, 1837, d. April 19, 1839.

5793. x. AMELIA CHILD, b. Jan. 24, 1840.

5794. xi. HALCYON CHILD, b. May 6, 1842, m. Charles F. Child of Warren. He d. Feb. 15, 1866. Mr. Charles F. Childs was a man highly respected for literary and other attainments.

[Fifth Generation.]

5710. viii. NICHOLAS GRAY CHILD, seventh child and fifth son of Joseph and Susan Gray Child, b. Sept. 4, 1802, m. Sept. 1823, Catharine Caldwell. He is a professional chemist. Resides in Cambridge, Mass.

[Sixth Generation.] Children, born in Cambridge, Mass.

5795. i. SARAH JANE CHILD, b Feb. 10, 1824; m. Dec. 10, 1844, Reuben Sherburne.

5796. ii. RICHARD DEVANS CHILD, b. 1826, m. July 16, 1851, Martha A. Sawyer.

5797. iii. CATHARINE CHILD, b. Nov. 23, 1829, m. Nov. 17, 1850, Stephen B. Chandler.

5798. iv. JAMES BONTICON CHILD, b. Nov. 21, 1831, m. Nov. 30, 1852, Fannie L. Dodge.

5799. v. NATHANIEL GRAY CHILD, b. Nov. 19, 1834, m. 1855, Mary Emma Freemantle.

[Sixth Generation.]

5795. i. SARAH JANE CHILD, eldest child of Nicholas Gray and Catharine Caldwell Child, b. in Charlestown, Mass., Feb. 10, 1824, m. Dec. 10, 1844, Reuben Sherburne of Boston, Mass.

[Seventh Generation.] Children:

5800. i. EDWARD CHILD SHERBURNE, b. in Boston Jan. 24, 1850, m. Oct. 21, 1873, Emma S. Dimmie of Cambridge, Mass. ⎫ Twins.

5801. ii. FRANK STAPLES SHERBURNE, b. Jan. 24, 1850. ⎭

[Sixth Generation.]

5796. ii. RICHARD DEVANS CHILD, second child of Nicholas Gray and Catharine Caldwell Child, b. 1826, m. July 16, 1851, Martha A. Sawyer of Palmyra, Maine, dau. of John and Thankful Sawyer. Mr. R. D. Child is an agent in Boston Water Works Office.

[Seventh Generation.] Children, born in Charlestown, Mass

5802. i. GEO. SHERBURNE CHILD, b. July 24, 1853, m. Mch. 25, 1875, Frances L. M. Lawrence.

5803. ii. RICHARD GRAY CHILD, b. Mch. 3, 1856, d. July 3, 1859.
5804. iii. JOHN HOWARD CHILD, b. Mch. 13, 1860.

[Seventh Generation.]

5802. i. GEO. SHERBURNE CHILD, eldest child of Richard Devans and Martha A. Sawyer Child, b. in Charlestown, Mass., July 24, 1856, m. Mch. 25, 1875, Frances Laurella Margaret Lawrence.

[Eighth Generation.] Child:

5805. i. RICHARD DEVANS CHILD, b. Nov. 2, 1878, d. May 10, 1879.

[Sixth Generation.]

5797. iii. CATHARINE CHILD, third child of Nicholas Gray and Catharine Caldwell Child, b. in Cambridge, Mass., Nov. 23, 1829, m. Nov. 15, 1850, Stephen Baker Chandler of New Hampshire.

[Seventh Generation.] Children:

5806. i. WALTER SHERWOOD CHANDLER, b. Oct. 8, 1851, d. Aug. 7, 1853.
5807 ii. HERBERT HAMILTON CHANDLER, b. Nov. 5, 1853.
5808. iii. LIZZIE ADELAIDE CHANDLER, b. Dec. 6, 1855.
5809. iv. EDWARD DANA CHANDLER, b. April 4. 1859.
5810 v. SARAH JANE CHANDLER, b. June 21, 1862.
5811. vi. HARRY WINTHROP CHANDLER, b. Mch. 31, 1869.
5812. vii. FRANK SHERBURNE CHANDLER, b. Sept. 14. 1871.

[Sixth Generation.]

5798. iv. JAMES BONTICON CHILD, fourth child of Nicholas Gray and Catharine Caldwell Child, b. in Cambridge, Mass., Nov. 21, 1831, m. Nov. 30, 1852, Fannie S. Dodge. He resides in Charlestown, Mass.

[Seventh Generation.] Children, born in Charlestown, Mass.

5813. i. FREDERICK E. CHILD, b. Nov. 30, 1853.
5814. ii. FRANK CHILD, b. 1856.
5815. iii. ELLA FRANCES CHILD, b. 1861.

[Sixth Generation.]

5799. v. NATHANIEL GRAY CHILD, fifth child of Nicholas Gray and Catharine Caldwell Child, b. in Cambridge, Mass., Nov. 19, 1834, m. 1855, Mary Emma Freemantle. He d. June 19, 1862.

[Seventh Generation.] Children:

5816. i. FREDERICK S. CHILD, b. July, 1856.
5817. ii. EMMA ADELAIDE CHILD, b. Dec. 9, 1862.

CHAPTER X.

SAMUEL CHILD AND DESCENDANTS.

This chapter introduces an emigrant, undoubtedly allied to the Roxbury *families*, but in what degree we have no record to determine. We rely upon the ancient public records for much information of this line, and they do not furnish as much detail as we could desire. A conflicting of opinions seems to exist between "Freeman" and "Savage," two authorities upon colonial matters, in regard to the Richard Child who heads the following large posterity: From "Freeman" we are led to believe him the son of Samuel Child, while "Savage" regards him as a brother of said Samuel. If Richard was born in America, as the record of the date of his birth would indicate, (stated to have been in 1624,) then we must conclude that "Freeman" is correct, and Samuel Child was the emigrant. If this is true, it also makes Samuel Child the first of the name who came to the colony of Massachusetts. In that case the Samuel Child slain by the Indians, March 26, 1675, would probably have been a brother of Richard, as the father would have been too aged, it would seem, to have undertaken to go into battle. Yet we have a statement from "Freeman" that Samuel Child was slain by the Indians at Rehoboth March 25, 1675; in the same battle was also slain a Samuel Linnet, brother of his son Richard's wife, Mary Linnett; while "Savage" in his Genealogical Collections, page 285, gives Richard Child as one of the early settlers of Barnstable, and brother of Samuel Child.

Richard Child's ancestry is, therefore, in somewhat the same obscurity as that of Benjamin Child of the Roxbury line of descendants, and that of the Watertown line. But the fact and date of this marriage we have. A large line of descendants are traced directly from his son Richard, who are found in western Massachusetts, on leaving Cape Cod, and thence spreading into Vermont and westward. Another line of descendants of Richard, the elder, it is supposed are found in Maine. As the first settlement of Plymouth colony was in 1620, if Richard Child was born in 1624, in New England, we know that his father must have been an emigrant of the Plymouth Colony; and "Freeman" states him to have been the Samuel Child who was slain by the Indians. As no other person competes for the paternity of Richard Child, we accept Samuel Child, therefore, as the *head* of this long Barnstable line.

[Second Generation.]

5818. i. RICHARD CHILD, the accepted son of Samuel Child, b. 1624, m. Oct. 15, 1649, Mary Linnett of Barnstable, Mass.

[We are able at present to give but one child of Richard and Mary Linnett Child, though probably they had others.]
[Third Generation.] Child:

5819. i. RICHARD CHILD, JR., son of Richard and Mary Linnett Child, b. in Barnstable, Mass., Mch. 1653, m. about 1678, Elizabeth Crocker, dau. of John Crocker. She was b. Oct. 7, 1660, d. Jan. 15, 1716.

"Freeman" in his "History of Cape Cod" gives Richard a second wife, Hannah ——. Richard Child ranked among the prominent citizens of Barnstable, and was an honored deacon in the Congregational church of that place. He died Jan. 15, 1716.

[Fourth Generation.] Children, born in Barnstable, Mass.

5820. i. SAMUEL CHILD, b. Nov. 6, 1679, m. July 7, 1709, Hannah Barnard.

5821. ii. ELIZABETH CHILD, b. Jan. 25, 1681.

5822. iii. THOMAS CHILD, b. Jan. 10, 1682, m. Mary ——.

5823. iv. HANNAH CHILD, b. —— 22, 1684, m. July 30, 1702, Joseph Blish.

5824. v. TIMOTHY CHILD, b. Sept. 22, 1686, m. Nov. 26, 1719, Hannah Chapin.

5825. vi. EBENEZER CHILD, b. Mch. 1691, m. Hope ——.

5826. vii. ELIZABETH CHILD, 2D, b. June 6, 1692.

5827. viii. JAMES CHILD, b. Nov. 6, 1694, m. Sept. 27, 1722, Elizabeth Crocker.

5828. ix. MERCY CHILD, b. May 7, 1697.

5829. x. JOSEPH CHILD, b. Mch. 5, 1699, m. April 23, 1724, Deliverance Hamblin.

5830. xi. THANKFUL CHILD, b. Aug. 15, 1702, m. Oct. 25, 1722, Ebenezer Hamblin.

[Fourth Generation.]

5820. i. DEA. SAMUEL CHILD, eldest child of Richard and Elizabeth Crocker Child, b. in Barnstable, Mass., Nov. 6, 1679, m. 1st, July 7, 1709, Hannah Barnard. She d. May 16, 1727; m. 2d, about 1729, Experience ——. Experience d. May 25, 1744; m. 3d, according to one record, June 25, 1750, Sarah Philip Mattoon Field, widow of Zachariah Field of Northfield, Mass. She d. Mch. 21, 1752, aged 63 years. Dea. Samuel Child d. Mch. 18, 1756, aged 77. He removed from Barnstable to Deerfield at an early period, where he was esteemed as a man of character and influence, being a deacon of the Congregational church and prominent in town affairs. He was a blacksmith by occupation.

[Fifth Generation.] Children, born in Deerfield,* Mass.

5831. i. HANNAH CHILDS, b. July 8, 1710, m. Nov. 30, 1732, Moses Smith.

5832. ii. SAMUEL CHILDS, JR., b. Sept. 20, 1712, m. Dec. 13, 1739, Sarah Wright.

5833. iii. ASA CHILDS, b. Jan. 3, 1715, m. Oct. 31, 1737, Rhoda Wright.

5834. iv. DAVID CHILDS, { m. Feb. 28, 1744, Rebecca Arms.
{ TWINS. { b. March 23, 1718.
5835. v. JONATHAN CHILDS, { m. Rebecca Scott.

5836. vi. EBENEZER CHILDS, b. Nov. 11, 1720, m. abt. 1750, Rachel ——.

5837 vii. ELIZABETH CHILDS, b. Aug. 5, 1724, m. Mch. 19, 1750, Nathaniel Phelps.

5838. viii. EXPERIENCE CHILDS, b. June 7, 1730, m. July 11, 1751, Jonathan Hoit.

[Fifth Generation.]

5832. ii. SAMUEL CHILDS. JR., second child and eldest son of Samuel and Hannah Barnard Child, b. Sept. 20, 1712, m. Dec. 13, 1739, Sarah Wright. He, like his father, was a deacon of the Congregational church in Deerfield, Mass. He d. Jan. 15, 1786. Mrs. Sarah Wright Childs d. Nov. 26, 1797.

[Sixth Generation] Children, born in Deerfield, Mass.

5839. i. AMZI CHILDS, b. Sept. 21, 1740, m. Jan. 22, 1762, Submit Wright.

5840. ii. SARAH CHILDS, b. Sept. 27, 1742.

5841. iii. SAMUEL CHILDS, JR., b. Oct. 28, 1745, m Nov. 29, 1770, Mary Nims.

5842. iv. HANNAH CHILDS, b. Sept. 29, 1749, m. Dec. 3, 1771, David Field.

5843. v. SIMEON CHILDS, b. April 25, 1753, d. Dec. 12, 1755.

5844. vi. EXPERIENCE CHILDS, b. Feb. 20, 1757, d. Sept. 28, 1758.

[Sixth Generation.]

5839. i. AMZI CHILDS, eldest child of Samuel Jr., and Sarah Wright Childs, b. Sept. 21, 1740, m. Jan. 22, 1767, Submit Wright. He d. Nov. 2, 1817. Submit Wright Childs, d. Sept. 2, 1824.

[Seventh Generation.] Children, born in Deerfield, Mass.

5845. i. ELIZABETH CHILDS, b. Dec. 29, 1767, d. April 29, 1768.

5846. ii ELIZABETH CHILDS, 2D, b. Feb. 17, 1769, m. Feb. 6, 1794, Selah Root of Montague, Mass.

5847. iii. DAVID WRIGHT CHILDS, b. May 12, 1771, d. May 21, 1771.

5848. iv. SIMEON CHILDS, b. June 9, 1772, d. Jan. 24, 1834.

5849. v. AMZI CHILDS, JR., b. Oct. 1, 1774.

5850. vi. SUBMIT CHILDS, b. Dec. 6, 1776, d. April 26, 1833.

5851. vii. DAVID WRIGHT CHILDS, 2D, b. Nov. 27, 1778, m. Jane —.

5852. viii. JAMES CHILDS, b. Nov. 10, 1780, d. Oct. 2, 1806.

5853. ix. ERASTUS CHILDS, b. Oct. 31, 1782, m. Jan. 8, 1811, Mercy Hawks.

5854. x. HENRY CHILDS, b. Feb. 27, 1784, m. Matilda —.

*In the Deerfield records we usually find the name written with the terminal "s," though never on the Barnstable records.

5855. xi. SARAH CHILDS, b. Aug. 2, 1787, m. Giles Hubbard of Leverett, Mass. She d. Oct. 20, 1831.

5856. xii. ALVAN CHILDS, b. Aug. 11, 1789, m. Sophia —.

5857 xiii. CHARLOTTE CHILDS, b. Aug. 11, 1792, m. Sept. 19, 1830, Samuel Billings of Wooster, Ohio. She d. Oct. 29, 1831.

[Seventh Generation.]

5851. vii. DAVID WRIGHT CHILDS. 2D, seventh child and fourth son of Amzi and Submit Wright Childs, b. Nov. 27, m. 1778, Jane —. She d. Sept. 28, 1867.

[Eighth Generation.] Children, born in Deerfield, Mass.:

5858. i. MARIAN E. CHILDS, b. —: m. Aug. 12, 1853, B. Zebina Stebbins.

5859 ii. HENRY SEYMOUR CHILDS, b. Sept. 4, 1844, m. Dec. 7, 1865, Lucy E. Grout.

[Eighth Generation.]

5858. i. MARIAN CHILDS, b. in Deerfield, Mass., m. Aug. 12, 1853, B. Zebina Stebbins.

[Ninth Generation.] Children, born in Deerfield, Mass.

5860. i. RYLAND ZEBINA STEBBINS, b. Aug. 4, 1854, d. Jan. 10, 1855.

5861. ii. FANNY MARIA STEBBINS, b. Jan. 14, 1856.

5862. iii. FREDERICK R. STEBBINS, b. July 15, 1857.

5863. iv. BENJAMIN ZEBINA STEBBINS, JR., b. Oct. 16, 1865.

[Eighth Generation]

5859. ii. HENRY SEYMOUR CHILDS, second child of David Wright and Jane Childs, b. Sept. 4, 1844, m. Dec. 7, 1865, Lucy E. Grout.

[Ninth Generation.] Children, born in Deerfield, Mass.

5864. i. HERBERT LESLIE CHILDS, b. Jan. 4, 1867.

5865. ii. JENNIE LAURA CHILDS, b. Feb. 12, 1869.

5866. iii. RALPH DAVID CHILDS, b. April 18. 1872.

5867. iv. HARRY GROUT CHILDS, b. Feb. 21, 1874, d. Sept 28, 1874.

5868. v. ALFRED CHILDS, b. Feb. 29, 1876.

[Seventh Generation.]

5853. ix. ERASTUS CHILDS, ninth child and sixth son of Amzi and Submit Wright Childs, b. in Deerfield, Mass., Oct. 31, 1782, m. Jan. 8, 1811, Mercy Hawks. He d. Feb. 17, 1858. She d. Dec. 28, 1854.

[Eighth Generation.] Children, born in Deerfield, Mass.

5869. i. HANNAH DICKENSON CHILDS, b. Oct. 22, 1811, m. April 7, 1836, Boyden Arms.

5870. ii. JAMES CHILDS, b. July 31, 1813.

5871. iii. RHODOLPHUS CHILDS, b. Oct. 18, 1815.

5872. iv. CALISTA CHILDS, b. July 15, 1819, m. Nov. 26, 1840, Nathaniel Hitchcock.

5873. v. RALPH CHILDS, b. Feb. 5, 1822, m. Louisa W. Benham.

5874. vi. ROBERT CHILDS, b. April 22, 1824, m. Jan. 8, 1851, Mary Ann Warner.

[Eighth Generation]

5872. iv. CALISTA CHILDS, fourth child and second dau. of Erastus and Mercy Hawks Childs, b. July 15, 1819, m. Nov. 26, 1840, Nathaniel Hitchcock.

[Ninth Generation.] Child:

5875. i. JAMES CHILDS HITCHCOCK, b. in Deerfield Nov. 28, 1841, d. Sept. 18, 1864; a soldier of our army, died at Andersonville, Geo.

[Eighth Generation]

5873. v. RALPH CHILDS, fifth child and third son of Erastus and Mercy Hawks Child, b. in Wapping (Old Deerfield), Mass., Feb. 5, 1822, m. April 16, 1844, Louisa W. Benham. She was b. at New Haven, Ct. Jan. 27, 1825. Mr. Childs d. Dec. 12, 1867. Mr. Childs had a somewhat eventful life, but the incidents which make up a brief history, served to develop manly characteristics. His youth was spent in labor on his father's farm, where habits of industry were formed and practical business knowledge acquired which served him in coming years. After a series of varied fortunes in several business enterprises, we find him, in the meridian of life, rendering military service to his country. In 1864 he entered the Union army and joined the 1st Massachusetts "Light Battery." Soon after reaching the battle-field he was appointed inspector of "repairs," a trust which he faithfully fulfilled, and his services recognized by his colonel, in the presentation of a valuable horse and equipments; also a sword. He was a favorite among his comrades on account of his kind and obliging disposition. Before the close of the war he was badly kicked by a horse from which injury he never fully recovered. He was with difficulty removed to his home, where the sympathy and tender care of his family and friends partially restored his health; at length he was attacked with typhoid fever which terminated his life. Mr. Childs was a man of warm and abiding friendships. He was esteemed and loved for his manly and generous qualities.

Mrs. Childs was left at the death of her husband with a family of young children dependent upon her exertions for support and education, a care which required courage, energy and enduring patience. She proved herself equal to the task. Her children have grown to maturity under a discipline and culture, through a christian mother's guiding counsels and provident care, which qualify them for useful and responsible positions in life.

[Ninth Generation.] Children

5876. i. RALPH STEBBINS CHILDS. b. in Deerfield, Mass , Aug 11 1845. unmarried. General insurance agent for the Benefit Life Co., Rhode Island Mr Childs has for many years been identified with the temperance reform; has rendered much active service in the cause; is recognized as a leader in this department of benevolent work; has been promoted to the highest offices in the different orders in that organization in the State of Rhode Island and has resolved to make the service in this cause his life work. Mr. Childs resides in Providence, R. I.

5877. ii. CHARLES H. CHILDS, b. in Deerfield, Mass., July 17. 1847, d. April 25, 1853.

5878. iii. HOMER B. CHILDS, b. Aug. 7, 1850, d. April 27, 1853.

5879. iv. IDA L. CHILDS, b. at Shelburne Falls, Mass., May 11, 1854, d. July 20, 1858.

5880. v. ISABELLA J. CHILDS, b. in Shelburne Falls, Mass., Nov. 13, 1856, d. July 22, 1858.

5881. vi. CHARLES H. CHILDS, 2D, b. in Shelburne Falls, Mass , Nov. 12, 1858. Is a printer.

5882. vii. HOMER B. CHILDS, 2D. b. in Colerane, Mass., June 11, 1862. Is a jeweller.

5883. viii. JULIA L. CHILDS, b. in Colerane, Mass., Feb. 7, 1865.

[Eighth Generation.]

5874. vi. ROBERT CHILDS, sixth child and fourth son of Erastus and Mercy Hawks Childs, b. April 22, 1824, m. Jan. 8, 1851, Mary Ann Warner. She d. June 8, 1870, and he m. 2d, April 22, 1873, Mrs. Phebe B. Atwell Childs.

[Ninth Generation.] Children, born in Deerfield, Mass.

5884. i. A dau. unchristened, b. July 25, 1854, d. —.

5885. ii. ROBERT WARNER CEILDS. b. May 28, 1862.

5886. iii. FRANCIS R. CHILDS, ⎰ ⎱ b. Sept. 26, 1875.
5887. iv. ALICE ELIZA CHILDS, ⎰ TWINS ⎱

[Seventh Generation.]

5854. x. HENRY CHILDS, tenth child and seventh son of Amzi and Submit Wright Childs, b. Feb. 27, 1784, m. Matilda — about 1816. Matilda d. June 11, 1825, and he m. 2d, Catharine —, who d. a widow Oct. 12, 1870

[Eighth Generation.] Children, born in Deerfield, Mass.

5888. i. AMZI CHILDS. b. Nov. 1, 1817.

5889. ii HENRY CHILDS, JR., b. July 18, 1819, m. Aug. 19, 1847.

5890. iii. DEXTER CHILDS, b. June 13, 1822, m June 6, 1860, Elizabeth Briggs.

5891. iv. MATILDA CHILDS, b. June 19, 1824, m. Dec. 20, 1848, Evander G. Stebbins.

[Eighth Generation.]

5890. iii. DEXTER CHILDS, third child and son of Henry and Matilda Childs, b. June 13, 1822, m. June 6, 1860, Elizabeth Briggs.

[Ninth Generation.] Child:

5892. i. Son unchristened, b. Dec. 22, 1862, d —,

[Eighth Generation]

5891. iv. MATILDA CHILDS, fourth child and only dau. of Henry and Matilda Childs. b. June 19, 1824, m. Dec. 20, 1848. Evander G. Stebbins.

[Ninth Generation.] Children, born in Deerfield, Mass.

5893. i. WILLIAM STEBBINS, b. Dec. 6, 1848.

5894. ii. CHARLES HENRY STEBBINS, b. June 24, 1859.

[Seventh Generation.]

5856. xii. ALVIN CHILDS, twelfth child and eighth son of Amzi and Submit Wright Childs. b. Aug. 11, 1789, m. 1st, about 1819, Sophia —. Sophia d. July 12, 1835: m. 2d, May 4, 1836. Lucretia B. Clark of Montague, Mass.

[Eighth Generation.] Children, born in Deerfield, Mass.

5895. i. CYNTHIA CHILDS, b. Aug. 15, 1820.

5896. ii. LUCY CHILDS, b. Mch. 7, 1822, d. June 10, 1824.

5897. iii. ISRAEL CHILDS, b. Jan. 27, 1824, m. Jan. 12, 1859, Elizabeth J. Adams.

5898. iv. JARVIS CHILDS, b. Feb. 20, 1827.

5899. v. SIMEON CHILDS, b. Mch. 5, 1837.

[Sixth Generation.]

5841. iii. SAMUEL CHILDS, JR., third child, second son of Samuel and Sarah Wright Childs. b. in Deerfield, Mass., Oct. 28, 1745, m. Nov. 29, 1770, Mary Ninns. He d. Oct. 27, 1808. She d. Jan. 7, 1821.

[Seventh Generation.] Children, born in Deerfield, Mass.

5900. i. MARY CHILDS, b. Sept. 22, 1771.

5901. ii. ISRAEL CHILDS, b June 17, 1773, d. Aug. 8, 1777.

5902. iii. EXPERIENCE CHILDS, b. June 3, 1775, d. Aug. 2, 1777.

5903. iv. SAMUEL CHILDS, JR., b. July 1, 1777, m Anna —.

5904. v. ISRAEL CHILDS, 2D, b. July 25, 1779, removed to Shelburne.

5905. vi. WILLIAM CHILDS, b. Oct. 12, 1781, d. Jan. 5, 1812.

5906. vii. EXPERIENCE CHILDS, 2D, b. Jan. 27, 1784, m. Jan. 19, 1808, Ebenezer Barnard of Waitsfield, Vt.

5907. viii. RUFUS CHILDS, b. Feb. 28, 1786.

5908. ix. SOPHIA CHILDS, } Twins. { b. July 21, 1788.

[Henderson, N. Y.

5909. x. CLARISSA CHILDS, { Twins. { m. Oct. 23, 1810, Shubal Allerton of

5910. xi. SARAH CHILDS, b. May 14, 1791, m. Dec. 11, 1828, Giles Hubbard of Leverett, Mass.

[Seventh Generation.]

5903. iv. SAMUEL CHILDS, JR., fourth child, second son of Samuel and Mary Ninns Childs, b. July 1, 1777, m. Anna —, about 1805. He d. May 24, 1830. She d. July 31, 1854.

[Eighth Generation.] Children, born in Deerfield, Mass.

5911. i. MARY CHILDS, b. Jan. 6, 1806.

5912. ii. MINERVA CHILDS, b. Jan. 16, 1808 { m. Nov. 17, 1830, Alfred O.

5913. iii. MARTHA CHILDS, b. Jan 19, 1810. { Goodenough. The record is not clear.

5914. iv. PHIDELIA CHILDS, b. April 15, 1812, m. Nov. 27, 1837, Gorham Hamilton of Conway, Mass.

5915. v. SAMUEL CHILDS, JR , b. Oct. 4, 1815, m. Nov. 26, 1837, Mary Sheldon.

5916. vi. ANN CHILDS, b. Mch. 17, 1818.

[Eighth Generation.]

5912. ii. MINERVA CHILDS, second child and second dau. of Samuel Jr., and Anna Childs. Or,

5913. iii. MARTHA CHILDS, third child and dau. of Samuel Jr., and Anna Childs. One of these sisters m. Nov. 17, 1830, Alfred O. Goodenough, and died May 10, 1847.

[Ninth Generation.] Children, born in Deerfield, Mass.

5917. i. MARY ETTA GOODENOUGH, b. 1831, d. Mch. 6, 1857, æ 19 years.

5918. ii. ALFRED GOODENOUGH, b. Sept. 5, 1844, d. Aug. 5, 1863, at Mound City, Arkansas; a soldier in the Union army in the war of the Rebellion.

[Eighth Generation.]

5915. v. SAMUEL CHILDS, JR., fifth child and only son of Samuel and Anna Childs, b. in Deerfield, Mass., Oct. 4, 1815, m. Nov. 26, 1837, Mary Sheldon. He d. Feb. 17, 1874.

[Ninth Generation] Children:

5919. i. ALONZO CHILDS, b. —; m. Oct. 27, 1864, Melissa A. Rice.

5920. ii. SAMUEL CHILDS, b. —; m Nov. 26, 1868, Harriet E. Mason.

5921. iii. MARY E. CHILDS, b. Nov 29, 1852, m. Nov. 17, 1860, Andrew B. Jackson.

5922. iv. HATTIE M. CHILDS, b. —; m. Oct. 30, 1873, Stephen C. Kingsley.

[Ninth Generation.]

5919. i. ALONZO CHILDS, eldest child of Samuel and Mary Sheldon Childs, m. Oct. 27, 1864, Melissa A. Rice.

[Tenth Generation.] Children, born in Deerfield, Mass.

5923. i. HARRY STEPHEN CHILDS, b. Aug. 1, 1866, d. Feb. 27, 1868.

5924. ii. LOVELL ALONZO CHILDS, b. April 5, 1871.

5925. iii. MERRILL FERBUSH CHILDS, b. July 26, 1872.

[Ninth Generation.]

5920. ii. SAMUEL CHILDS, JR., second child and son of Samuel and Mary Sheldon Childs, m. Nov. 26, 1868, Harriet E. Mason. She d. April 26, 1876.

[Tenth Generation.] Children, born in Deerfield, Mass.

5926. i. ANNA FIDELIA CHILDS, b. July 15, 1870.

5927. ii. A son unchristened, b. Dec. 10, 1873, in Dublin, N. H.

5928. iii. HARRY E. CHILDS, b. Mch 15, 1876, d. July 25, 1876.

[Fifth Generation.]

5833. iii. ASA CHILDS, third child and son of Samuel and Hannah Barnard Childs, b. in Deerfield, Mass., Jan. 3, 1715, m. Oct. 31, 1736, Rhoda Wright.

[Sixth Generation.] Children, born in Deerfield, Mass.

5929. i. CHARITY CHILDS, b. 1737, m. June 13, 1757, Daniel Nims.

5930. ii. ASA CHILDS, JR., b. Oct. 3, 1738, m. Dec. 22, 1768, Elizabeth Hawks.

5931. iii. LIBBEUS CHILDS, b. Oct. 3, 1740, m. Oct. 4, 1767, Sarah Walker.

5932. iv. SAMUEL CHILDS, b. Nov. 12, 1742, m., Sept. 27, 1768, Eunice Wright.

5933. v. RHODA CHILDS, b. April 30, 1746, m. Oct. 25, 1768, Moses Hawks.

[Sixth Generation.]

5929. i. CHARITY CHILDS, eldest child of Asa and Rhoda Wright Childs, born in Deerfield, Mass., 1737, m. June 13, 1757, Daniel Nims.

[Seventh Generation.] Children, born in Deerfield, Mass.

5934. i. ABIGAIL NIMS, b. April 29, 1758.

5935. ii. ASA NIMS, b. Jan. 11, 1860.

5936. iii. DANIEL NIMS, b. Nov. 9, 1761.

5937. iv. LUCINDA NIMS, b. Nov. 14, 1763.

[Sixth Generation.]

5931. iii. LIBBEUS CHILDS, third child and second son of Asa and Rhoda Wright Childs, b. in Deerfield, Mass., Oct. 3, 1740, m. Oct. 4, 1767, Sarah Walker. After the birth of his two eldest children he removed to Conway, Mass.

[Seventh Generation.] Children:

5938. i. DAVID CHILDS, b. in Deerfield, Mass., April 19, 1768.

5939. ii. ENOS CHILDS, b. in Deerfield, Mass., Mch. 23, 1770.

5940. iii. OLIVER CHILDS, b. in Conway, Mass., July 27, 1783, m. 1st, Electa Whitmore.

[Seventh Generation.]

5940. iii. OLIVER CHILDS, third child and third son (as given in this record) of Libbeus and Sarah Walker Childs, b. in Conway, Mass., July 27, 1783, m. 1st, Electa Whitmore, dau. of Oliver Whitmore of Seneca, Ontario county, N. Y. She d. Aug. 2, 1816, leaving no children; m. 2d, Nancy Hart, dau. of Joseph and Huldah Hart of Seneca, N. Y. She d. April 30, 1831; m. 3d, Betsey Gilbert, dau. of John Gilbert of Seneca, N. Y.

[Eighth Generation.] Children, b. in Seneca, N. Y. By second marriage:

5941. i. ELECTA EMELINE CHILDS, b. April 17, 1809, d. —.

5942. ii. THERON HART CHILDS, b. Mch. 26, 1812, m. 1st, Esther Tallman; m. 2d, Caroline Benjamin.

5943. iii. AUGUSTUS WALSTEIN CHILDS, b. Mch. 22, 1814, m. Amytis Warner.

5944. iv. EDMUND CHILDS, b. June 7, 1816, m. Eunice Richardson.

5945. v. BENJAMIN CHILDS, b. April 8, 1819, m. Laura Sherwood.

5946. vi. EMELINE CHILDS, b. June 26, 1821.

5947. vii. Joseph Childs, b. Oct. 8, 1823, m. Julia A. Belding.
5948. viii. Gilbert Childs, b. April 20, 1826.
By third wife:
5949. ix. Bradley Alonzo Childs, b. May 19, 1832.
5950. x. Nancy Augusta Childs, b. Aug. 23, 1833.
5951. xi. Oliver Porter Childs, b. Nov. 12, 1838.

[Eighth Generation.]

5942. ii. THERON HART CHILDS, second child and eldest son of Oliver and Nancy Hart Childs, b. in Seneca, N.Y., Mch. 26, 1812, m. 1st, Dec. 31, 1832, Esther Tallman, dau. of John and Clarissa Vrooman Tallman. She d. Feb. 11, 1848 ; m. 2d, May 23, 1849, Caroline Benjamin, dau. of Nathan and Jerusha Webster Benjamin of Phelps, N. Y. Both marriages by Rev. Stephen Porter of Geneva, N. Y. Mr. Theron H. Childs d. Oct. 18, 1859.

[Ninth Generation.] Children, born in Seneca, N. Y.

5952. i. Julia Ann Childs, b. Oct. 12, 1833, m. Oct. 5, 1858, Ira Milton Judd, son of Joseph M. Judd. Mr. Judd is conductor on the Ithaca, Cortland & Elmira Railroad. Residence Freeville, Tompkins county, N. Y.

5953. ii. Sarah Frances Childs, b. Feb. 24, 1837, m. May 1, 1860, E. Payson Porter, son of Rev. Stephen Porter. Mr. Porter is Statistical Secretary of the Sunday School Union in Chicago, Ill.

5954. iii. Theron Tallman Childs, b. Aug. 17, 1843, m. Aug. 17, 1868, Emma Augusta Brown.

[Ninth Generation.]

5954. iii. THERON TALLMAN CHILDS, third child and only son of Theron Hart and Esther Tallman Childs, b. in Seneca, N. Y., Aug. 17, 1843, m. Aug. 17, 1868, by Rev. B. B. Grey of Canandaigua, N. Y., Emma Augusta Brown, dau. of Dr. Talcott Russell and Electa Hart Brown of Geneva, N. Y. Mr. Theron Tallman Childs is a telegraph operator in Chicago, Ill.

[Tenth Generation.] Children, born in Chicago, Ill.

5955. i. Winnefred Esther Childs, b. June 22, 1870.
5956. ii. Jesse Hart Childs, b. Feb. 9, 1874.
5957. iii. Frances Judd Childs, b. Aug. 25, 1876.

[Eighth Generation.]

5943. iii. AUGUSTUS WALSTEIN CHILDS, third child and second son of Oliver and Nancy Hart Childs, b. in Seneca, N. Y., Mch. 22, 1814, m. May 27, 1841, Amytis Warner, dau. of Russell and Mary Warner. Mr. Childs is a farmer, and resides in Hudson, Lenawee county, Mich.

[Ninth Generation.] Children, born in Hudson, Mich.

5958. i. Augustus Oliver Childs, b. July 21, 1844.
5959. ii. Delora Adelle Childs, b. Nov. 27, 1847.
5960. iii. Frank Marion Childs, b. Nov. 30' 1849.

5961. iv. WILLIE CHILDS, b. June 6, 1851.

5962. v. THERON CHARLES CHILDS, b. June 8, 1853.

5963. vi. GRACIE M. CHILDS, b. April 4, 1861.

5964. vii. JENNIE AUGUSTA CHILDS, b. Nov. 16, 1864.

[Eighth Generation.]

5944. iv. EDMUND CHILDS, fourth child and third son of Oliver and Nancy Hart Childs, b. in Seneca, N. Y., June 7, 1816, m. in Marathon, Cortland county. N. Y., by Rev. Wm. Bradford, April 9, 1841, Eunice Richardson, dau. of Jacob and Lucy Tilden Richardson of Lebanon, N. H. He removed to Michigan the same year and settled in Wheatland, Hillsdale county. In 1845, he returned to New York. In 1849, he went again to Michigan where he now resides, a farmer in the town of Wheatland.

[Ninth Generation.] Children:

5965. i. EMELINE CELESTIA CHILDS, b. in Wheatland, Mich., Aug. 27, 1842.

5966. ii. HARRIET JONES CHILDS, b. in Wheatland, Mich., May 27, 1844.

5967. iii. EUGENE CHILDS, b. in Seneca, N. Y., July 2, 1846.

5968. iv. LEANDER HOBERT CHILDS, b. in Seneca, N. Y., May 14, 1848.

5969. v. EDMUND CHILDS, JR., b. in Wheatland, Mich., July 6, 1850.

5970. vi. EUNICE FOX CHILDS, b. in Wheatland, Mich., Mch. 12, 1853.

5971. vii. CHARLES HENRY CHILDS, b. in Wheatland, Mich., Feb. 10, 1855.

5972. viii. SAMUEL PEASE CHILDS, b. in Wheatland, Mich., Nov. 12, 1857.

[Eighth Generation.]

5945. v. BENJAMIN CHILDS, fifth child and fourth son of Oliver and Nancy Hart Childs, b. in Seneca, N. Y., April 8, 1819, m. May 29, 1843, by Rev. Geo. Hyde, Laura Sherwood, dau. of Homer and Electa Hotchkiss Sherwood of Fairfield, Vt. He d. Jan. 27, 1878, in the town of Seneca, N. Y.

[Ninth Generation.] Children, born in Phelps, Ontario Co., N. Y.

5973. i. HOMER SHERWOOD CHILDS, b. May 23, 1845.

5974. ii. ALBERT SHERWOOD CHILDS, b. Sept. 18, 1852.

5975. iii. HATTIE ELECTA CHILDS, b. Sept. 29, 1857.

[Eighth Generation.]

5947. vii. JOSEPH CHILDS, seventh child and fifth son of Oliver and Nancy Hart Childs, b. in Seneca, Ontario county, N. Y., Oct. 8, 1823, m. by Rev. Mr. Russell of Seneca, N. Y., to Julia A. Belding, dau. of Wm. and Clarissa Belding of Seneca, N. Y. Mr. Childs is a farmer and resides in Seneca, New York.

[Ninth Generation] Children:

5976. i. WILLIAM EZRA CHILDS, b. in Seneca, N. Y., Jan. 15, 1848, m. Nellie E. Tiffany.

5977. ii. MARY E. CHILDS, b. in Seneca, N. Y., April 24, 1859.

[Ninth Generation.]

5976. i. WILLIAM EZRA CHILDS, eldest child of Joseph and Julia A. Belding Childs, b. in Seneca, N. Y., Jan. 15, 1848, m. in Phelps, Ontaria county, N. Y., Nellie E. Tiffany, dau. of Lamont and Sophia Tiffany of Phelps, N. Y.

[Tenth Generation.] Child:

    5978. i. JOSEPH L. CHILDS, b. in Seneca, N. Y., Oct. 5, 1878.

[Sixth Generation.]

5932. iv. SAMUEL CHILDS, fourth child and third son of Asa and Rhoda Wright Childs, b. in Deerfield, Mass., Nov. 12, 1742, m. Sept. 27, 1768. Eunice Wright. He d. Mch. 1, 1814.

[Seventh Generation] Children, born in Deerfield, Mass.

    5979. i. NOAH WRIGHT CHILDS, b. Aug. 20, 1769, m. Dec. 19, 1791, Mary Graves.

    5980. ii. ASA CHILDS, b. Aug. 23, 1771, m. Jan. 25, 1798, Polly Grandy.

    5981. iii. ESTHER CHILDS, b. Aug. 16, 1773, d. Jan. 15, 1799.

    5982. iv. RHODA CHILDS, b. Sept. 5, 1775, d. Oct. 2, 1775.

    5983. v. RHODA CHILDS, 2D, b. Oct. 13, 1776.

    5984. vi. EUNICE CHILDS, b. Aug. 17, 1778, m. April 25, 1799, Oliver Morton.

    5985. vii. TIRZA CHILDS, b. July 12, 1780, m. Jan. 7, 1824, Dea. Janes of Northfield, Mass.

    5986. viii. LEMUEL CHILDS, b. Aug. 28, 1782, d. Feb. 25, 1808.

    5987. ix. SAMUEL CHILDS, JR., b. Sept. 8, 1784, m. about 1812, Electa —.

    5988. x. CEPHAS CHILDS, b. Feb. 2, 1787, m. Eleanor —.

    5989. xi. CAROLINE CHILDS, b. Mch. 1, 1790.

[Seventh Generation.]

5979. i. NOAH WRIGHT CHILDS, eldest child of Samuel and Eunice Wright Childs, b. in Deerfield, Mass., Aug. 26, 1769, m. Dec. 19, 1791, Mary Graves of Sunderland, Mass. She was b. Mch. 30, 1773, d. Sept. 10, 1859. He d. Oct. 4, 1825. A record received from a descendant of Noah Childs writes the middle name *Webster*, while the Deerfield records give it as *Wright*: and this descendant says Noah's mother was a relative of Noah Webster the Lexicographer, and that Mary Graves was of Huguenot origin. At what date Mr. Childs removed from Deerfield, Mass., we are not informed. Eight of his eleven children are recorded in the Deerfield, Mass., town records as born in that town; the youngest of these in 1804. His removal was after this date. He went from Deerfield to the town of Sullivan, Madison county, N. Y., and purchased a large tract of land, connected with which were grist, saw and plaster mills. In the war with England, in 1812, he was called into service in the U. S. army, and held the office of sergeant in the division stationed at Buffalo, N. Y.

[Eighth Generation] Children:

5990. i. THEODORIC CHILDS, b. Mch. 30, 1792, m. May 14, 1814, Jane Crawford. He had three sons and five daughters living in Fairview and that vicinity. He d. July 16, 1834.

5991. ii. WILLIAM PARSONS CHILDS, b. May 14, 1793, m. 1st, Dec. 12, 1823, Mabel Worcester; m. 2d, Minerva Blackman; m. 3d, Betsey Rose. He had two sons and two daughters. Edward Childs, his eldest son, lives in Warren Centre, Iowa. One daughter is living in Albany, N. Y. One son and and daughter have died. Mr.Wm. Parsons Childs d. April 13, 1871.

5992. iii. HARRIET CHILDS, b. Jan. 13, 1795, d. Feb. 24, 1796.

5993. iv. HARRIET CHILDS, 2D, b. Oct. 6, 1796, d. Jan. 9, 1860.

5994. v JULIA F. CHILDS, b. April 13, 1798, m. May 7, 1834, Ward Walton. They had four children, one son and three daughters; all dead except one daughter who is married to Frederick Childs and lives in Kenton, Hardin county, Ohio.

5995. vi. JAMES HECTOR CHILDS, b. Nov. 16, 1801, m. Oct. 28, 1829, Lucy Hayden; d. Sept. 7, 1866, leaving no children.

5996. vii. CALISTA CHILDS,)
5997. viii. CARLOS CHILDS, (Twins. } b. April 23, 1804; Carlos d. Sept. 5, 1825; Calista d. Sept 18, 1860,

5998. ix. GEORGE MORRIS CHILDS, b. May 13, 1808, m. Palmyra P. Wadsworth; had one son, Theodoric Childs living in Bridgeport, Madison county, N. Y.

5999. x. ALONZO W. CHILDS, b. April 4, 1811, m. 1st, Mch. 5, 1833, Catharine M. Marvin; 2d and 3d m. not known; had four sons and one dau. Resides in Minnesota.

6000. xi. EDWARD CHILDS, b. July 15, 1813, m. 1st. June 22, 1841, Clara Gross Burr; m. 2d, Nov. 5, 1866, Martha Nichols.

[Seventh Generation.]

6000. xi. EDWARD CHILDS, eleventh child and seventh son of Noah W. and Mary Graves Childs, b. July 15, 1813, m. 1st, June 22, 1841, Clara Gross Burr: she d. July 19, 1866: m. 2d, Nov. 5, 1866, Martha L. Nichols: she d. Sept. 29, 1874 at Norwich, N. Y. Mr. Childs was sheriff of Chenango county, N. Y., for the years 1861-2 and '63. He served two terms previously as under sheriff. He was also special agent and Deputy Provost Marshal of the 19th New York district during the civil war. Mr. Childs was killed Sept. 29, 1874, by a collision on the Delaware. Lackawanna & Western RR., acting at the time as mail agent between Utica and Binghamton. His residence was in Utica.

6001. i. CHARLES EDWARD CHILDS, b. Sept. 29, 1843, m. Sept. 27, 1866, Hattie E. Close of Johnstown, N. Y. Mr. Childs resides in Norwich, N. Y.

Ninth Generation.] Children, born in Norwich, N. Y.

6002. i. CLARA LOUISE CHILDS, b. 1867.

6003. ii. EDWARD STUART CHILDS, b. 1868.

6004. iii. CATHARINE PERLEE CHILDS, b. 1872

T-1

[Seventh Generation.]

5980. ii. ASA CHILDS, second son and child of Samuel and
Eunice Wright Childs, b. in Deerfield, Mass., Aug. 23, 1771,
m. Jan. 25, 1798, Polly Grandy.

[Eighth Generation.] Children, born in Deerfield, Mass.
6005. i. CHARLES CHILDS, b. Feb. 14, 1799, m. April 25, 1822, Eliza
Wells.
6006. ii. LEWIS CHILDS, b Oct. 29, 1800.
6907. iii. ESTHER CHILDS, b. Nov. 3, 1802.
6008. iv. MARY CHILDS, b. Jan. 14, 1805.
6009. v. CATHARINE CHILDS. b. Dec. 17, 1806.
6010. vi. LUCINDA CHILDS, b. Jan. 24, 1809, m. Dec. 17, 1857. Medad
Alexander.

[Seventh Generation.]

5987. ix. SAMUEL CHILDS, ninth child and fourth son of
Samuel and Eunice Wright Childs, b. Sept. 8, 1784. m. it appears about 1812, Electa — ; she d. Jan. 29, 1876.

[Eighth Generation.] Children, born in Deerfield, Mass.
6011. i. ALBERT CHILDS, b. Dec. 28, 1814, m. about 1852, Martha L. —.
6012. ii. THEODORE CHILDS, b. April 1. 1818.
6013. iii. SUSAN GATES CHILDS, b. Aug. 10, 1821, m. May 25. 1848, Caleb
A. Starr.

[Eighth Generation.]

6011. i. ALBERT CHILDS, eldest child of Samuel and Electa
— Childs, b. Dec. 28, 1814, m. about 1852, Martha L—.

[Ninth Generation.] Children, born in Deerfield, Mass
6014. i. THEODORE CHILDS, b. Mch. 16. 1853.
6015. ii. A daughter unchristened, b. Dec. 19, 1854.
6016. iii. ANNA S. CHILDS, b. Sept. 27, 1857.

[Eighth Generation.]

6013. iii. SUSAN GATES CHILDS, third child and only dau.
of Samuel and Electa Childs. b. Aug. 10, 1821, m. May 25,
1848. Caleb A. Starr.

[Ninth Generation.] Children, born in Deerfield, Mass.
6017. i. MARY HOUGHTON STARR, b. April 18. 1849.
6018. ii. WILLIAM WESLEY STARR, b. Jan 9. 1851.

[Seventh Generation.]

5988. x. CEPHAS CHILDS, tenth child and fifth son of Samuel and Eunice Wright Childs, b. Feb. 2, 1787, m. about 1809,
Eleanor Root. He d. April 14, 1831. She d. Sept. 13, 1866.

[Eighth Generation.] Children, born in Springfield and Deerfield, Mass.
6019. i. LEMUEL CHILDS, b. May 13, 1810, m. 1847, Almira Allen.
6020. ii. FRANKLIN CHILDS, b. Oct. 21, 1812, d. June 8, 1849.
6021. iii. GEORGE CHILDS, b. Dec. 13, 1814.
6022. iv CAROLINE CHILDS, b Nov. 10, 1818.

6023. v. JONATHAN ROOT CHILDS, b. May 10, 1822.
6024. vi. CEPHAS ROOT CHILDS, b. Aug. 26, 1824.

[Eighth Generation.]
6019. i. LEMUEL CHILDS, eldest child of Cephas and Eleanor
Robert Childs, b. in Springfield, Mass., May 13, 1810, m. about
1847, Almira Allen.
Ninth Generation.] Children, born in Deerfield, Mass.
6025. i. EDWARD SMEAD CHILDS, b. Mch 22, 1848.
6026. ii. GEORGE FRANKLIN CHILDS, b. Jan. 30, 1850.
6027. iii. JULIA ELLA CHILDS, b. Dec. 14, 1852, m. Dec. 28, 1870, Walter
Arnold.
6028. iv. MARY JANE CHILDS, b. Oct. 14, 1854
6029. v. JONATHAN R. CHILDS, b. June 27, 1862, in Springfield, Mass.

[Ninth Generation.]
6027. iii. JULIA ELLA CHILDS, third child and eldest dau.
of Lemuel and Almira Allen Childs, b. Dec. 14, 1852, m. Dec.
28, 1870, Walter Arnold.
[Tenth Generation.] Child:
6030. i. ELLA MAUD ARNOLD, b. Jan. 1878.

[Fifth Generation]
5834. iv. DAVID CHILDS, fourth child and third son of Samuel and Hannah Barnard Childs, b. in Deerfield, Mass., Mch.
23, 1718, m. Feb. 28, 1744, Rebecca Arms. He d. May 8, 1760.
[Sixth Generation.] Children, born in Deerfield, Mass.
6031. i. REBECCA CHILDS, b. Feb 8, 1745.
6032. ii. ABIGAIL CHILDS, b. Dec. 21, 1747, m. Dec. 17, 1767, Wait-
still Hawks.
6033. iii. DAVID CHILDS, b. April 11, 1750, d. June 13, 1760.
6034. iv. LEMUEL CHILDS, b. Mch. 24, 1752, m. Rebecca —.
6035. v. RUTH CHILDS, b. Aug. 12, 1754, m. Dec. 10, 1773, Israel Nims.
6036. vi JOANNA CHILDS, b. Sept. 29, 1757, m. Feb. 18, 1778, Peter
Gates.

[Sixth Generation.]
6034. iv. LEMUEL CHILDS, fourth child and second son of
David and Rebecca Arms Childs, b. Mch. 24, 1752, m. about
1778, Rebecca —.
[Seventh Generation.] Children, born in Deerfield, Mass.
6037. i. JOANNA CHILDS, b Sept. 5, 1779.
6038. ii. REBECCA WARNER CHILDS, b. Jan. 15, 1781.

[Sixth Generation.]
6035. v. RUTH CHILDS, fifth child and third dau. of David
and Rebecca Arms Childs, b. Aug. 12, 1754, m Dec. 10, 1773,
Israel Nims.
[Seventh Generation.] Children, born in Deerfield, Mass.
6039. i. JEREMIAH NIMS, b. Mch. 2, 1776.
6040. ii. REBECKAH NIMS b. Nov. 10, 1777, d. Dec. 13, 1778.

6041. iii. REBECKAH NIMS, 2D, b. Sept. 2, 1779.

6042. iv. PLINY NIMS, b July 12, 1791.

[Fifth Generation.]

5835. v JONATHAN CHILDS, fourth son (or twin with David Childs), of Samuel and Hannah Barnard Childs, b. Mch. 23, 1718, m. about 1739, Rebecca Scott, who was b. Jan. 9, 1707. Mr. Jonathan Childs was born in Deerfield, but early removed to Hardwick, Worcester county, Mass., where he died Mch. 18, 1793, æ 75. Mrs. Rebecca Childs was a woman of marvellous health and strength, and lived to more than round the hundred and first year. It is said she could lift a barrel of cider from the cart outside the door, and bring it into the house without help. She died in 1809.*

[Sixth Generation.] Children:

6043. i. JESSIE CHILDS, b. Oct. 1740.

6044. ii. HANNAH CHILDS, b. Sept. 17, 1742.

6045. iii. EBENEZER CHILDS, b. Jan. 25, 1744, m. Nov. 15, 1769, Abigail Willis.

6046. iv. JOSEPH CHILDS, b. Mch. 2, 1746, m. Susanna Trask.

6047. v. JONATHAN CHILDS, JR., b. Oct. 13, 1748, d. young.

6048. vi. ELIZABETH CHILDS, b. Nov. 29, 1750.

6049. vii. MOSES CHILDS, b. April 3, 1752.

6050. viii. SARAH CHILDS, b. April 2, 1755.

6051. ix. JONATHAN CHILDS, 2D, b. Oct. 24, 1756, m. 1st Deliverance Freeman; m. 2d, Anna Thompson.

6052. x. REBECCA CHILDS, b. Oct. 8, 1758.

6053. xi. DAVID CHILDS, b Nov. 16, 1760, m. about 1786, Lydia Hemmenway.

6054. xii. SARAH CHILDS, 2D, b. April 22, 1763.

[Sixth Generation.]

6045. iii. EBENEZER CHILDS, third child and second son of Jonathan and Rebecca Scott Childs, b. Jan. 25, 1744, cried in Hardwick for marriage to Abigail Willis, Nov. 15, 1769. He d. Mch. 7, 1809. She d. Dec. 25, 1810.

[Seventh Generation] Children:

6055. i. BETSEY CHILDS, b. at New Salem, Mass, May 27, 1772, d. 1870.

6056. ii. BENJAMIN WILLIS CHILDS, b at Barre, Mass., Oct. 5, 1774, m. Anna Washburn.

6057. iii. MOSES CHILDS, b at Barre, Mass., July 6, 1777.

6058 iv. EBENEZER CHILDS, JR, b. at Hardwick, Mass., Mch. 21, 1784, d. Mch. 7, 1786.

6059. v. EBENEZER CHILDS, 2D, b. at Hardwick, Mass., July 2, 1787, m. 1st, Hannah Lowell; m. 2d, Pede Johnson; m 3d, Mary Bullen.

6060. vi. ANNA CHILDS, b. —; m. — Tenney of Barre, Mass.

* We have failed to obtain as complete a record of the descendants of Jonathan and Rebecca Scott Childs as we could wish, though no suitable effort on our part has been wanting.

[Seventh Generation.]

6056. ii. BENJAMIN W. CHILDS, eldest son and second child of Ebenezer and Abigail Willis Childs, b. Oct. 1774, m. about 1798, Anna Washburn. She was b. May 24, 1780, and d. Oct. 1844. They lived for several years in Barre, Mass., and raised a large family. He was for many years a deacon in the Congregational church in Barre, and held in high esteem; he died Jan. 13, 1838.

[Eighth Generation.] Children, born in Barre, Mass.

6061. i. BENJAMIN WILLIS CHILDS, JR., b. Nov. 6, 1799, m. Jan. 24, 1827, Elizabeth Southworth.

6062. ii. TRYPHENIA CHILDS, b. Aug. 13, 1801, m. Ely Cooley.

6063. iii. AURELIA CHILDS, b. June 28, 1803, m. Wm. Burnap.

6064. iv. EVELINA CHILDS, b. May 28, 1805, d. Jan. 31, 1842.

6065. v. FRANKLIN L. CHILDS, b. Sept. 10, 1807, m. Margaret Marsh.

6066. vi. TYLER CHILDS, b. June 18, 1809, m. Nancy Williams.

6067. vii. MARTIN LUTHER CHILDS, b. June 2, 1811, m. Jan. 6, 1840, Mercy Holmes Chapin.

6068. viii. ANN W. CHILDS, b. May 26, 1813, m. 1st, Oct. 18, 1832, Lyman Hawks; m. 2d, 1840, Elias Ayres.

6069. ix. JULIA ANN CHILDS, b. April 5, 1815, m. Oct. 1838, Rev. Gideon Dana of Amherst. They had only one child which died in infancy.

6070. x. ALEXANDER HANSON CHILDS, b. Feb. 26, 1817, m. Phebe Stevens.

6071. xi. WILLIAM ALLEN CHILDS, b. June 2, 1820, m. Oct. 29, 1845, Olive Hinckley.

6072. xii. ELIZABETH HOYT CHILDS, b. Jan. 21, 1826, d. 1850.

[Eighth Generation.]

6061. i. BENJAMIN WILLIS CHILDS, JR., eldest child of Benjamin W. and Anna Washburn Childs, b. in Barre, Mass., Nov. 6, 1799, m. Jan. 24, 1827, Elizabeth Southworth. He died in 1867.

[Ninth Generation.] Children:

6073 i. ANNA CHILDS, b. Dec. 19, 1827, unmarried.

6074. ii. A son unchristened.

6075. iii. FANNY CHILDS, b. Mch. 21, 1834, m. Barnard Vassall; no children.

6076. iv. BENJAMIN WILLIS CHILDS, JR., b. Jan. 15, 1839, m. Sept. 20, 1865, Maria Chamberlain.

[Ninth Generation.]

6076. iv. BENJAMIN WILLIS CHILDS, JR., fourth child and second son of Benjamin W. and Elisabeth Southworth Childs, b. Jan. 15, 1839, m. Sept. 20, 1865, Maria Chamberlain.

[Tenth Generation.] Children:

6077. i. THOMAS CHILDS, b. Aug. 13, 1866.

6078. ii. FANNIE MARIA CHILDS, b. Jan. 3, 1868.

6079. iii. ALICE LOUISE CHILDS, b. Aug. 23, 1873.

6080. iv. MABEL CHAMBERLAIN CHILDS, b. Nov. 13, 1875.
6081. v. ANNIE C. CHILDS, b. Sept. 29, 1877.

[Eighth Generation.]

6062. ii. TRYPHENIA CHILDS, second child and eldest dau.
of Benjamin W. and Anna Washburn Childs, b. in Barre,
Mass., Aug. 13, 1801, m. Feb. 16. 1829, Eli Cooley of South
Deerfield, Mass.

[Ninth Generation.]   Children:
6082. i. DENNIS COOLEY, b. Dec. 15, 1829, m. May 11, 1855, Celestia M.
Hawks.
6083. ii. MARIA F. COOLEY, b. Sept. 4, 1832, m. Aug. 7, 1852, Alfonso K.
Graves.
6084. iii. CHARLES COOLEY, b. Nov. 19, 1834, m —.
6085. iv. TERTIUS C. COOLEY, b. Oct. 24, 1837, m. Nov. 19, 1868, Mary A.
Bates of Wisconsin.
6086. v. EMILY G. COOLEY, b. Jan. 20, 1840, m. Augustus Bates of Hadley
Mass.
6087. vi. HARRIET N. COOLEY, b. May 9, 1843, m. Jan. 21, 1869, Geo.
W. Clark of East Hampton, Mass.

[Ninth Generation.]

6082. i. DENNIS COOLEY, eldest child of Tryphenia Childs
and Eli Cooley, b. Dec. 15, 1829, m. May 11, 1855, Celestia
M. Hawks.

[Tenth Generation.]   Child:
6088 i. EMMA C. COOLEY, b. April 24, 1858, d. July 29, 1859.

[Ninth Generation.]

6083. ii. MARIA F. COOLEY, second child and eldest dau. of
Tryphena Childs and Eli Cooley. b. Sept. 4, 1832, m. Aug. 7,
1852. Alfonso K. Graves.

[Tenth Generation.]   Children:
6089. i. EMMA T. GRAVES, b. Oct. 4, 1855.
6090. ii. RAYNOLD C. GRAVES, b. July 14, 1857.
6091. iii. HATTIE GRAVES, b. Oct. 24, 1860.

[Ninth Generation.]

6085. iv. TERTIUS C. COOLEY, fourth child and third son of
Tryphenia Childs and Eli Cooley. b. Oct. 24, 1837, m. Nov. 19,
1868. Mary A. Bates.

[Tenth Generation.]   Child:
6092. i. JESSIE IDA COOLEY, b. April 5, 1872.

[Ninth Generation.]

6087. vi. HATTIE N. COOLEY, sixth child and third dau. of
Tryphena Childs and Eli Cooley, b. May 9, 1843, m. Jan. 21,
1869, Geo. W. Clark.   She died Nov. 28, 1874.

[Tenth Generation.] Children:

6093. i. ARTHUR CLARK,) TWINS. (b. Jan. 10,) d. June 14, 1870
6094. ii. ANNIE CLARK. ( ) 1870,)

6095. iii. HATTIE L. CLARK, b. Nov. 21, 1871.

[Eighth Generation.]

6063. iii. AURELIA CHILDS, third child and second dau. of Benjamin W. and Anna Washburn Childs, b. in Barre, Mass., June 28, 1803, m. Wm. Burnap of Paxton, Mass. She died Mch. 8, 1868.

[Ninth Generation.] Child:

6096. i. JULIA BURNAP.

[Eighth Generation.]

6065. v. FRANKLIN L. CHILDS, fifth child and second son of Benjamin W. and Anna Washburn Childs, b. in Barre, Mass., Sept. 10, 1807, m. Oct. 6, 1840, at Urbana, Champaign county, Ohio, Margaret Marsh of Beekmantown, Clinton county, N. Y. Resides at Marysville, Ohio.

[Ninth Generation.] Children:

6097. i. MARTHA E. CHILDS, b. in Urbana, O., Aug. 2, 1842, d. at Marysville, Mch. 17, 1864.

6098. ii. ANNA E. CHILDS. b. in Urbana, O., Aug. 26, 1844, m. Jan. 3, 1866, Professor T. S. Evans.

6099. iii. ESTHER A. CHILDS, b. in Woodstock, O., Mch. 25, 1848, m. Sept. 9, 1869, W. T. Caldwell, and resides in Chicago, Ill.

6100. iv. CHARLES H. CHILDS, b. in Marysville, O., Dec. 23, 1861. Resides in Marysville, O.

[Eighth Generation.]

6066. vi. TYLER CHILDS, sixth child and third son of Benjamin W. and Anna Washburn Childs, b. in Barre, Mass., June 18, 1809, m. Nancy Williams of Vermont. Is in the milk trade. Residence, Springfield, Mass.

[Ninth Generation.] Children:

6101. i. FRANCIS LEE CHILDS, b. in Montague, Mass., July 3, 1831, m. Sept. 26, 1858 Olive W. Markham, dau. of Vine and Polly Markham of Albion, Calhoun county, Mich. Mr. and Mrs. Markham were among the first settlers in Albion and much esteemed for moral worth, and for their efficiency in laying the foundations of a prosperous society in the infancy of this town. Mrs. Markham, whose death occurred July 26, 1880, at the house of her daughter Mrs. F. L. Childs, in Rockford, Ill., at 80 years of age, was one of the charter members of the Presbyterian church of Albion, Mich., organized in 1836-7. She was an earnest, energetic lady, whose christian zeal and self-sacrificing effort imparted life and growth to the church.

Mr. Childs was married in Iowa City, Iowa, by Rev. Peter S. Van Est. Mr. Childs graduated at the Normal school of Westfield, Mass., Feb. 27, 1855. With the characteristic energy of his race, he started out in life with the laudable ambition of building his fortune from the application of his energies to such enterprises as promised the best results. For ten years he followed school teaching as professor in Worcester, Brookfield, and Brimfield, Mass. and later in Iowa City, Iowa, where he erected a building for school purposes in which he taught for several years. He became identified in all material interests in this growing town, and a leader in all active movements promising general prosperity, such as organizing and conducting Sabbath schools, and giving tone to the observance of religious institutions. After several years of thorough pioneer labor in this town he returned to Massachusetts and devoted himself to teaching and trade for a while, when he returned to the West and entered upon teaching in the city of Detroit, Mich., under very auspicious circumstances; his pupils numbering 850, and requiring a large corps of efficient assistants. In the height of his success his health failed, when he was compelled to give up his school and seek for restoration of health in less exacting duties. The Northwest, in the region of Lake Superior, opened a new field for future work in the line of the book trade which bears a kinship to all his habits of life.

6102. ii. JULIA AUGUSTA CHILDS, b. June 18. 1838.

6103. iii. GEO. CHAMBERLAIN CHILDS, b. Sept. 15, 1844, was drowned in the Connecticut river. Sept. 18, 1862.

6104. iv. HATTIE L. CHILDS, b. Feb. 7, 1863.

[Eighth Generation.]

6067. vii. DEA. MARTIN LUTHER CHILDS, seventh child and fourth son of Benjamin W. and Anna Washburn Childs, b. in Barre. Mass., June 2. 1811, m. Jan. 6, 1840. Mercy Holmes Chapin. She was b. Aug. 17. 1816. He was one of the first deacons in the Second Congregational church in Holyoke, Mass. He is largely engaged in the manufacture of brick. Residence. Springfield. Mass.

[Ninth Generation.] Children:

6105. i. AUGUSTUS LUTHER CHILDS, b. in Fitchburg. Mass., Oct 28, 1840, m. Jan. 1, 1868, Martha Rice.

6106. ii. HENRY MARTIN CHILDS, b. in Springfield. Mass., June 11, 1845, d. Sept. 17, 1845.

6107. iii. ELLEN JULIA CHILDS, b. in Springfield. Mass., Nov. 24, 1846, m. Dec 10, 1868. Henry L. Searle

6108. iv. FREDERICK LYMAN CHILDS, b. in So. Hadley Mass. Oct. 22, 1851; a machinist in Brattleboro. Vt

6109. v. ALBERT CHAPIN CHILDS, b. in Springfield, Mass. Jan. 17. 1860; is a book-keeper for a wholesale grain firm in Wilbraham. Mass.

[Ninth Generation.]

6105. i AUGUSTUS LUTHER CHILDS. eldest child of Dea. Martin L. and Mercy Holmes Chapin Childs. b. in Fitchburg. Mass., Oct. 28. 1840. m. Jan. 1. 1868. Martha Rice.

[Tenth Generation] Children, born in Springfield. Mass.

6110. i. WILLIS AUGUSTUS CHILDS. b Nov. 9, 1869.

6111. ii ARTHUR RICE CHILDS, b. 1871, d. same year.

6112. iii. ROBERT PRENTISS CHILDS, b. May 31. 1874

[Ninth Generation.]

6107. iii. ELLEN JULIA CHILDS, third child and eldest dau. of Dea. Martin Luther and Mercy Holmes Chapin Childs, b. in Springfield. Mass., Nov. 24. 1846, m. Dec. 10. 1868. Henry Lyman Searle. He was b. Oct. 24. 1846. Residence. Springfield. Mass.

[Tenth Generation.]

6113. i. FREDERICK ALBERT SEARLE, b. Dec. 15, 1869.

6114. ii. FRANKLIN HENRY SEARLE, b. Dec. 16. 1871.

6115. iii. ALFRED LUTHER SEARLE, b. Mch 6, 1875.

[Eighth Generation.]

6068. viii. ANN W. CHILDS, eighth child and fourth dau. of Benjamin W. and Anna Washburn Childs, b. in Barre, Mass., May 26, 1813, m. 1st, Oct. 1, 1832, Lyman Hawks. He d. Feb. 18, 1839 ; m. 2d, in 1840, Elias Ayres. She resides in Prince Williams county, Va.

[Ninth Generation.] Children : By 1st marriage.

6116. i GEORGE C. HAWKS, b. Mch. 10, 1836, d. Sept. 25, 1863, unm.

6117. ii. ELVIRA CHILDS HAWKS, b. July 11, 1838, m. April 4, 1866, Henry Ayres.

By 2d marriage.

6118. iii. MARTHA A. AYRES, b. Feb. 12, 1845, m. Jan. 6, 1869, Charles E. Donehue.

6119. iv. ELLEN E. AYRES, b. Mch. 31, 1847, unmarried.

6120. v. EMMA V. AYRES, b Mch 25, 1849, unmarried.

6121. vi. JAMES T. AYRES, b. June 22, 1851, unmarried.

6122. vii. DANIEL W. AYRES, b. Feb. 17, 1853, unmarried.

[Ninth Generation.]

6117. ii. ELVIRA C. HAWKS, second child of Ann W. Childs and Lyman Hawks, b. July 11, 1838, m. April 4, 1866, Henry J. Ayres.

[Tenth Generation.]

6123. i ANNA W. AYRES, b. Aug. 3, 1871.

6124 ii. MARY ELLEN AYRES, b. Feb. 24, 1873.

6125. iii. EVA V. AYRES, b. Dec. 8, 1874.

6126. iv. GEO HAWKS AYRES, b. Nov. 7, 1876.

6127. v. J WILBUR AYRES, b. Nov. 22, 1878

[Ninth Generation.]

6118. iii. MARTHA A. AYRES, third child of Ann W. Childs and eldest by Elias Ayres, b. Feb. 12, 1845, m. June 6, 1869, Charles E. Donehue.

[Tenth Generation.] Children :

6128. i. ALVAN T. DONEHUE, b. Oct. 18, 1869.

6129. ii. EMMA E. DONEHUE, b. June 20, 1871.

6130. iii. MAUD E. DONEHUE, b. Sept. 4, 1872.

6131. iv. GERTRUDE B. DONEHUE, b. Nov. 26, 1873.

6132. v. SALLIE A. DONEHUE, b. Jan. 5, 1875.

6133. vi. CHARLES J. DONEHUE, b. Oct. 13, 1877.

6134. vii. MARY E. DONEHUE, b. Mch. 20, 1879.

[Eighth Generation.]

6070. x. DEA. ALEXANDER HANSON CHILDS, tenth child and fifth son of Benjamin W. and Anna Washburn Childs,

b. in Barre, Mass., Feb. 26, 1817, m. Nov. 28, 1839, Phebe Stevens. Is a coal dealer in Holyoke, Mass.

[Ninth Generation.] Children:

6135. i. LEVI ALEXANDER CHILDS, b. Oct. 31, 1840, m. May 21, 1862, Laura Farr.

6136. ii. MARY ANN CHILDS, b. Aug. 14, 1845, m. June 3, 1869, Robert Prentiss. No children.

[Ninth Generation.]

6135. i. LEVI ALEXANDER CHILDS, eldest child of Deacon Alexander Hanson and Phebe Stevens Childs, b. Oct. 31, 1840, m. May 21, 1862, Laura Farr.

[Tenth Generation.] Child:

6137. i. VIOLA L CHILDS, b. Oct. 30, 1863.

[Eighth Generation.]

6071. xi. WILLIAM ALLEN CHILDS, eleventh child and sixth son of Benjamin W. and Anna Washburn Childs, b. in Barre, Mass., Jan. 2, 1820, m. Oct. 29, 1845, Olive A. Hinkley.

[Ninth Generation.] Children:

6138. i. HENRY H. CHILDS, b. July 19, 1847, m. Jan. 1, 1868.

6139. ii. BENJAMIN HANSON CHILDS, b. Oct. 17, 1848, m. July 21, 1875, Iantha M. Smith.

6140. iii. CHARLES HANSON CHILDS, b. Sept. 28, 1850, unmarried.

6141. iv. AMY ELIZABETH CHILDS, b. Dec. 8, 1854, d. —.

6142. v. CARRIE AURELIA CHILDS, b. Sept. 11, 1859, d. —.

6143. vi. ELMER ELLSWORTH CHILDS, b. Sept. 11, 1861.

[Ninth Generation.]

6138. i. HENRY H. CHILDS, eldest son of William Allen and Olive A. Hinkley Childs, b. July 19, 1847, m. Jan. 1, 1868. —.

[Tenth Generation.] Children:

6144. i. GERTRUDE FRANCES CHILDS, b. Dec. 24, 1868.

6145. ii. GEORGE E. CHILDS, b. July 9, 1870.

6146. iii. OLIVE E. CHILDS, b. Dec. 1, 1872.

6147. iv CHARLES H. CHILDS, b. Sept. 13, 1874

6148. v. WILLARD T CHILDS, b. July 29, 1876.

6149. vi. FREDERICK H CHILDS, b. Feb. 28, 1878

6150. vii. ROBERT S. CHILDS, b. Dec. 26, 1879.

[Ninth Generation.]

6139. ii. BENJAMIN HANSON CHILDS, second child and son of William Allen and Olive A. Hinkley Childs, b. Oct. 17, 1848, m. July 21, 1875, Iantha M. Smith.

[Tenth Generation] Children:

6151 i. WILLIAM HERBERT CHILDS, b. Oct. 22, 1876.

6152. ii. BERNICE CHILDS, b. Aug. 7, 1878.

[Seventh Generation.]

6059. v. EBENEZER CHILDS, 2D, fifth child and fourth son of Ebenezer and Abigail Willis Childs, b. in Hardwick, Mass., July 2, 1787, m. 1st, Hannah Lowell; she d. July 16, 1834, leaving no children; m. 2d, Pede Johnson, who d. Jan. 30, 1854, æ 54 years; m. 3d, Mary Bullen, who d. Feb. 14, 1876. He d. Sept. 1, 1871, æ 87. Mr. Childs bore a conspicuous part in the war of 1812 with Great Britain. He held the office of Captain in the 9th Reg't U. S. Regulars, and fought in the battles of Sacketts Harbor and Fort Erie, receiving wounds which entitled him to a pension of $240 a year which he continued to draw for over fifty years. Mr. Childs was a man of much public spirit, known as a hard shell Baptist, and influential in that denomination. He contributed liberally towards the building of the 1st Baptist church at Farmington, Maine, where he died.

[Eighth Generation.] Children: By his 2d marriage.
   6153. i. CALVIN NEWTON CHILDS, b. Jan. 15, 1838.
   6154. ii. JAMES UPHAM CHILDS, b. Oct. 19, 1840.

[Sixth Generation.]

6046. iv. JOSEPH CHILD, fourth child and third son of Jonathan and Rebecca Scott Child, b. in Hardwick, Mass., 1746, m. Susanna Trask.

[Seventh Generation.] Children:
   6155. i. SAMUEL CHILD.
   6156. ii. ABIGAIL CHILD.
   6157 iii HANNAH CHILD.
   6158. iv. ELIJAH CHILD.
   6159. v. SUSANNA CHILD, b. April 1781, m. 1800, John Horr.
   6160 vi. MOSES CHILD, b. in New Salem, Mass., June 25, 1783, m. April 3, 1816, Sarah French.
   6161. vii. ELIZA CHILD.
   6162. viii. LYDIA CHILD, b. June 1790.
   6163. ix LORAIN CHILD, ⎱ TWINS, ⎰ b. July, 1792.
   6164. x. DIADAMA CHILD, ⎰ ⎱
   6165. xi. JOSEPH CHILD, JR., b. June 1796.
   6166. xii. Infant unchristened.

[Seventh Generation.]

6159. v. SUSANNA CHILD, fifth child of Joseph and Susanna Trask Child, b. in New Salem, Mass., April 1781, m. 1800, John Horr.

[Eighth Generation.] Children:
   6167. i. ISAAC HORR, b. in New Salem, Mass., Mch. 12, 1801.
   6168. ii. LOT HORR, b in New Salem, Mass., Sept. 8, 1803.

6169. iii. SUSANNA HORR, b. in Ware, Mass., Jan. 20, 1806, m. May 18, 1826, Lilley S. Manly.

[Eighth Generation.]

6169. iii. SUSANNA HORR, third child and only dau. of Susanna Childs and John Horr, b. in Ware, Mass., Jan. 20, 1806, m. May 18, 1826, Lilley S. Manly.

[Ninth Generation] Children, born in Hardwick, Mass.

 6170. i. ADALINE MANLY, b. Mch. 10, 1827.
 6171. ii. DWIGHT MANLY, b. Nov. 11, 1828, d. —.
 6172. iii. GEORGE MANLY, b. Oct. 17, 1830.
 6173. iv. CARLINA MANLY, b. Jan. 29, 1833.
 6174. v. ELUTHERIA MANLY, b. Feb. 13, 1835.
 6175. vi. FANNY MANLY, b. Nov. 5, 1836.
 6176. vii. CLARISSA MANLY, b. Jan. 11, 1839.
 6177. viii. DWIGHT MANLY, 2D. b. May 13, 1841.
 6178. ix. BENJAMIN MANLY, b. Mch. 8, 1843.
 6179. x. JAMES MANLY, b Sept. 16, 1845.
 6180. xi. CHARLES MANLY, }
 6181. xii. ELLEN MANLY, } TWINS. } b. Dec. 25, 1849.

[Seventh Generation.]

6160. vi. MOSES CHILDS, son of Joseph and Susanna Trask Childs, b. in New Salem, Franklin county, Mass., June 25, 1783, m. April 3, 1816, Miss Sarah French of Amherst, N. H. Mr. Moses Childs died April 30, 1839, in Cabotville, Mass., aged 56, leaving three children. Mrs. Sarah F. Childs was married Aug. 13, 1844, to Mr. Joseph Carr of Boston, and upon his death, married in Feb. 1863, Mr. Nathaniel Sawtell of Boston, whom she survived, and died in the family of her eldest son, in Niles, Mich., Oct. 13, 1879, a 82 years, 9 mo.

[Eighth Generation.] Children:

 6182. i MOSES F CHILDS, b. Jan. 4, 1818, m. May 22, 1842, Nancy Van Horn.
 6183. ii. EPHRAIM F. CHILDS. b. Dec. 25, 1821, m. April 6, 1845, Mary Ann Aldrich.
 6184 iii. SARAH MARIA CHILDS, b. Aug. 16, 1827, m. Sept. 1, 1850, George D. Baldwin.
 6185. iv. GEORGE ALBERT CHILDS, b Jan. 17, 1836, d. Aug. 2, 1837, in Cabotville, Mass.

[Eighth Generation.]

6182. i. MOSES F. CHILDS, eldest son and child of Moses and Sarah French Childs, b. in Baltimore, Md., Jan. 4, 1818, m. in Cabotville, Mass., May 22, 1842, Miss Nancy Van Horn. Resides in Niles, Berrien county, Mich. Occupation, carpenter and joiner.

[Ninth Generation.] Children:

 6186. i. GEORGE A. CHILDS, b. Mch. 4, 1845, in Cabotville. Mass.
 6187. ii. EMMA ELIZABETH CHILDS, b. Aug. 9, 1853, in Howard, Mich.

[Eighth Generation.]

6183. ii. EPHRAIM F. CHILDS, second son and child of Moses and Sarah French Childs, b. in Ware, Mass., Dec. 25, 1821, m. in Niles, Mich., April 6, 1845, Miss Mary Ann Aldrich. Mr. Ephraim F. Childs removed from Massachusetts to Michigan in the spring of 1840, where he resided until the autumn of 1878, when he removed to Omaha, Nebraska, where he now resides.

[Ninth Generation.] Children:

6188. i. GEORGE R. CHILDS, b. Nov. 16, 1846, in Bertram, Mich., m. Feb. 17, 1876, Eunice Eliza Abbott, of South Bend, Ind. Resides in Avoca, Pottawattamie county, Iowa.

6189. ii. CHARLES W. CHILDS, b. Oct. 12, 1848, m. Sept. 9, 1874, Julia E. Riddle.

6190. iii. JENNIE E. CHILDS, b. April 2, 1851, m. Jan. 27, 1877, Chauncey W. Reed.

6191. iv. FRANK F. CHILDS, b. Dec. 17, 1857, d. Oct. 7, 1865, in Howard, Mich.

6192. v. LUMBARD B. CHILDS, b. Mch. 23, 1860, in Howard, Mich. Resides in Omaha, Neb.

6193. vi. NELLIE MARIA CHILDS, b. July 8, 1862, d. July 13, 1864, in Howard, Mich.

[Ninth Generation.]

6189. ii. CHARLES W. CHILDS, second son and child of Ephraim F. and Mary Ann Aldrich Childs, b. in Howard, Mich., Oct. 12, 1848, m. in Niles, Berrien county, Mich., Sept. 9, 1874, Julia E. Riddle. Reside in Omaha, Nebraska.

[Tenth Generation.] Child:

6194. i. GRACE IRENE CHILDS, b. Feb. 4, 1876, in Howard, Mich.

[Eighth Generation.]

6184. iii. SARAH MARIA CHILDS, only dau. of Moses and Sarah French Childs, b. in Ware, Mass., Aug. 16, 1827, m. Sept. 1, 1850, in Boston, Mass., George D. Baldwin, son of Dr. Dexter and Caroline Peabody Baldwin of Antrim, N. H. Mr. and Mrs. George D. Baldwin reside on Michigan avenue, Chicago, Ill.

[Ninth Generation.] Children:

6195. i MARIA LOUISE BALDWIN, b. Dec. 18, 1851, m. Oct. 14, 1875, Charles N. Barrett.

6196. ii. GEORGE FREDERICK BALDWIN, b. Oct. 27, 1853, m. Feb. 27, 1879, May Scott of Boston.

6197. iii. FANNIE CAROLINE BALDWIN, b. Aug. 5, 1855, d. Jan. 16, 1857.

6198. iv. FANNIE FLORENCE BALDWIN b. Feb. 10, 1859, d. Aug. 27, 1860.

6199. v. FRANK WARD BALDWIN, b. Feb. 20, 1866, d. Mch. 5, 1868.

[Sixth Generation.]

6051. ix. MAJOR JONATHAN CHILDS, fifth son of Jonathan and Rebecca Scott Childs, b. in Hardwick, Mass., Oct. 24, 1756,

m. 1st, Deliverance Freeman, who d. Dec. 30, 1785 æ. 25 : m. 2d, 1786, Anna Thompson, who was b. Feb. 29, 1764. Major Childs died July 31, 1819; his widow Mrs. Anna Thompson Childs, died Oct. 3, 1838. Major Childs left Massachusetts when quite young and settled in Wilmington, Vt., where he dwelt the remainder of his long and active life, embracing the most thrilling and soul-stirring period in the history of the American Republic, when passing from colonial dependence upon Great Britain to the independent position of a separate and unique na tionality. The strong mental forces of such a man would inevitably make themselves felt a power for good or ill. A true patriot, Major Childs took most decided stand for the liberties of the young confederacy of American colonies. Possessed of the warm, enthusiastic temperament characteristic of the name, Major Childs made his country's welfare his own, and was one of those Vermont braves whose patriotism was a proverb. His commission as Sergeant of the 5th Company of Infantry, of the State of Vermont, Judah Moore, Captain, and Josiah Fish, Colonel, in command of the 3d Reg't in the 2d Brigade, is lovingly cherished by his venerating grand-children. The quaint phraseology and embellished page, render it deserving a fac simile transcript in this volume, thus placing it in the keeping of each descendant. Major Childs home was upon a farm some two miles from the village of Wilmington, upon the bank of the Deerfield river, rendered now a most attractive, beautiful, and restful site, by the stately, graceful elms which so thrive in the New England soil ; many of these noble trees were set out by Major Childs' own hand. Major Childs had two children of his first marriage, but we have been unable to learn much of them, beyond the fact that the daughter became a Mrs. Sage.

[Seventh Generation.] Children :

6200. i. A dau. who m. a Mr. Sage.

6201. ii. A son.

6202. iii. BETSEY CHILDS, b. May 6, 1787, m. Feb. 9, 1815, Thomas Wait.

6203. iv. JAMES CHILDS, b. Feb. 19, 1790, m. Betsey Jones.

6204. v. CLARISSA CHILDS, b. Feb. 5, 1792, m. April 13, 1814, Spencer Alvord.

6205. vi. JONATHAN CHILDS, JR., b. Aug. 4, 1794, m. June 2, 1822, Cynthia Lask

6206. vii. FREEMAN CHILDS, b. Feb. 17, 1797, m. Dec. 18, 1833, Elizabeth Root.

6207. viii. ADNAH B. CHILDS, b. Feb. 3, 1799, m. Mch. 9, 1826, Hannah Lamb.

6208. ix. WILLIAM CHILDS, b. July 8, 1802, m. May 10, 1829, Marilla Lamb

[Seventh Generation.]

6202. iii BETSEY CHILDS, eldest dau. of Major Jonathan and Anna Thompson Childs, b. in Wilmington, Vt., May 6, 1787, m. Feb. 9, 1815, Thomas Wait, of Coventry, R. I. Mrs. Betsey Childs Wait died in Charlestown, Mass., on Oct. 18, 1871. Mr. Wait died in Troy, N. Y., Dec. 30, 1830. Mrs. Wait was a woman of great energy, some traits of her strong character were of that positive and projective nature, which we term eccentric.

[Eighth Generation.] Children:

6209. i ELIZA ANN WAIT, b. May 26, 1816, d. Mch. 11, 1838.

6210. ii HARRIET J. WAIT, b. Jan. 5, 1819, at Rodman, Jefferson county, N. Y., m. 1st, April 8, 1847, Francis Dana Hyde; m. 2d, Sept. 23, 1857, Willard Gorham; m. 3d, June 13, 1877, Calvin Wales Alvord.

6211. iii. ORVIS C. WAIT, b. Sept. 13, 1821, d. Mch. 15, 1859.

[Seventh Generation.]

6203. iv. JAIRUS CHILDS, eldest son of Jonathan and Anna Thompson Childs, b. in Wilmington, Windham county, Vt., Feb. 19, 1790, m. about 1814, Betsey Jones, who was b. Nov. 19, 1795, in Dover, Vt. Mr. Jairus Childs resided in his native town, and there reared a goodly family, now widely scattered. Mrs. Betsey Jones Childs died Mch. 10, 1836. Mr. Childs survived but a short time dying July 3, 1837.

[Eighth Generation.] Children:

6212. i. LABAN JONES CHILDS, b. Mch. 31, 1815, m. Aug 3, 1837, Betsey Bassett.

6213. ii. ADEN THOMPSON CHILDS, b. April 27, 1817, m. in Whitingham, Vt., Sarah Roberts.

6214. iii. LORENZO WHITNEY CHILDS, b, July 31, 1819, m. April 11, 1847, Mary Emma Morse.

6215. iv. JAIRUS FRANKLIN CHILDS, b. June 10, 1822, m. Maria Crossett of Bennington, Vt. Mr Childs is a Baptist clergyman and resides in Des Moines, Polk county, Iowa.

6216 v. FRANCIS LEROY CHILDS, b. Sept. 22, 1825, m. Betsey Johnson.

6217. vi. MARY ANN CHILDS, b. Feb. 18, 1827, m. Dr. Wakley and resides in Wheaton, DuPage county, Ill.

6218. vii. HENRY CLAY CHILDS, b. May 2, 1829, m. Catharine Parmalee of Wilmington, Windham county, Vt. Mr. and Mrs. Childs removed to the West and reside near Colorado Springs; their P. O. address being Manitou, Paso county, Colorado.

6219. viii DeWITT CLINTON CHILDS, b. Jan. 22, 1833, d. Aug. 18, 1851.

6220. ix. BETSEY CLARISSA CHILDS, b. Jan. 31, 1836, d. Mch. 15, 1836.

[Eighth Generation.]

6212. i. LABAN JONES CHILDS, eldest son of Jairus and
Betsey Jones Childs, b. in Wilmington, Windham county, Vt.,
Mch. 31, 1815, m. Aug. 3, 1837, by the Rev. Dr. Dana Hyde in
Brattleboro, Vt., Miss Betsey Bassett.   For two years after his
marriage Mr. Childs resided at the homestead ; but the Bedouin
element of which we have made mention as entering somewhat
largely into the general mental constitution of the Childs family, was working upon Mr. Childs' spirits and made itself manifest by a removal to Jacksonville, Vt., where Mr. Childs was
engaged in mercantile business.   Bound to make good his
claim to the talent requisite (according to the proverb), Mr.
Childs returned to Wilmington in 1845, built and kept a hotel
for some six years.   The glowing pictures of Western life
were too alluring for his contentment, and in Sept. 1852, the
family removed to St. Charles, Kane county, Ill., and became
agriculturists : but Illinois was becoming a central State, and
the rich farming lands of the rapidly growing State of Iowa
were so attractive, that again Mr. Childs became a pioneer, and
invested in a large farm about fifteen miles from the city of
Council Bluffs, in Pottawattamie county, Iowa.   About thirteen
years since Mr. Childs made, as he thinks, his last remove and
became a resident of the thriving city of Council Bluffs.
Two children, a son and daughter, were given to Mr. and Mrs.
Laban J. Childs, but the daughter was early called to the
heavenly home.

[Ninth Generation.]   Children :
    6221. i. FRANCIS LABAN CHILDS, b. Feb. 26, 1843, m. Mch. 1865, Miss
Margaret Dewey.
    6222 ii. BETSEY ELLEN CHILDS, b. Nov. 22, 1859, d. Sept. 10, 1863.

[Ninth Generation.]

6221. i. FRANCIS LABAN CHILDS, only son of Laban Jones
and Betsey Bassett Childs, b. in Jacksonville, Vt., Feb. 26,
1843, m. Mch. 1865, Miss Margaret Dewey.   Mr. Childs resides
upon the farm which his father laid out in 1857 not far from
Council Bluffs.

[Tenth Generation.]   Children :
    6223. i. ELLEN CHILDS.
    6224. ii. FORDY CHILDS.
    6225. iii. GEORGE CHILDS.

[Eighth Generation.

6214. iii. LORENZO WHITNEY CHILDS, third son of Jairus
and Betsey Jones Childs, b. July 31, 1819, in Wilmington,

Windham county, Vt., m. April 6, 1847, Miss Mary Ermina
Morse of New Fane, Vt. Catching the wandering mania quite
diffused through this family of sons, Mr. Lorenzo W. Childs
followed his two elder brothers westward, and established himself in Villisca, Montgomery county, Iowa, where he serves
"Uncle Sam" in the post-office department in that town.

[Ninth Generation.] Children:

6226. i. ABBIE ADELL CHILDS b. Jan. 16, 1848, m. Mch. 18, 1869, Austin
E. Mitchell of Chardon, Ohio. Reside now in Villisca, Iowa.

6227. ii. FRANK CLINTON CHILDS, b. July 12, 1852, in Wilmington, Vt.,
d. Nov. 30, 1853, in Chicago, Ill.

6228. iii. MARY FRANCIS CHILDS, b. May 8, 1855, in Chicago, Ill., m. July
25, 1873, Henry H. McCartney of Villisca, Iowa, d. Sept. 6, 1873, aged 18
years.

6229. iv. ESTELLE MARIA CHILDS, b. Sept. 10, 1857, in Wheaton, Ill., m
May 4, 1878, Arnold B. McCourtie of Chicago, Ill.

6230. v. KATIE ADAH CHILDS, b. Oct. 1, 1865, d. May 15, 1867, in
Wheaton, Ill.

6231. vi. LORENZO A. CHILDS, b. Dec. 10, 1868, in Wheaton, Ill

6232. vii. FREDDIE MATHER CHILDS, b. May 8, 1870, in Villisca, Iowa.

[Ninth Generation.]

6229. iv. ESTELLE MARIA CHILDS, third dau. and fourth
child of Lorenzo Whitney and Mary E. Morse Childs, b. in
Wheaton, DuPage county, Ill., Sept. 10, 1857, m. May 4, 1878,
in Villisca, Montgomery county, Arnold B. McCourtie. Residence, Chicago, Ill.

[Tenth Generation.] Child:

6233. i. FRANKIE BELL McCOURTIE, b. April 16, 1879, in Chicago, Ill.

[Eighth Generation.]

6216. v. FRANCIS LEROY CHILDS, fifth son of Jairus and
Betsey Jones Childs, b. in Wilmington, Vt., Sept. 22, 1825,
m. Miss Betsey Johnson of Shaftesbury, Vt. Not to be out-
done by his brothers, Mr. Childs pressed toward the sun-setting,
and with the redoutable watch-words echoing in his ear, "Go
West young man," settled upon a farm in Greeley, Colorado.

[Ninth Generation.] Children:

6234. i. CHARLES LABAN CHILDS, b Sept. 15, 1866, d. Aug. 25, 1868.

6235. ii. ELLEN DEWEY CHILDS, b. May 8, 1869.

6236 iii. RATFORD FRANK CHILDS, b. July 27, 1874.

6237. iv. GEORGE CHILDS, b. Jan. 19, 1877.

[Seventh Generation.]

6204. v. CLARISSA CHILDS, second dau. of Major Jonathan
and Anna Thompson Childs, b. in Wilmington, Windham
county, Vt., Feb. 5, 1792, m. April 13, 1814, Spencer Alvord.

U·1

[Eighth Generation.] Children:

6238. i. ORPHEUS SIDNEY ALVORD, b. about 1815, m. 1st, Oct. 1839, Sophia Hastings: m. 2d, Oct. 2, 1855, Clarissa Hastings.

6239. ii. ORSAMUS ADNAH ALVORD, b. —; m. Aug. 18, 1844, Sarah Sophia Bissell, dau. of Asabel and Polly Bissell.

6240. iii CLARISSA FREEMAN ALVORD, b.—; m. Sept. 8, 1844, Samuel Jones Hitchcock. Mrs. Alvord died in 1870.

6241. iv. RHODA MARIA ALVORD, b —; m. Aug. 23, 1845, Jonathan Smith. Resides in Brattleboro, Vt.

6242. v. BARBARA ANN ALVORD. b.—; m. May 10, 1864, Freeman Lathrop.

[Eighth Generation.]

6238. i. ORPHEUS SIDNEY ALVORD, eldest son and child of Clarissa Childs and Spencer Alvord, b. in Wilmington, Vt., m. 1st, Oct 1839, Sophia Hastings: m. 2d, Oct. 1855, Clarissa Hastings, sister of the first wife.

[Ninth Generation] Child:

6243. i. ORPHEUS H. ALVORD, b. Nov. 27, 1843, m. Jan. 22, 1866, Vilowa Carroll of Dover, Vt. He died in New York Sept. 6, 1875.

[Eighth Generation.]

6242. v. BARBARA ANN ALVORD, third dau. and fifth child of Clarissa Childs and Spencer Alvord, m. May 10, 1864, Freeman Lathrop, who was b. July 23, 1837, in Hawley, Mass.; a son of George and Mary Lathrop.

[Ninth Generation.] Children:

6244. i. CLARA MAY LATHROP, b. Oct. 8, 1866.

6245. ii. JESSIE GROVER LATHROP, b. Jan. 15, 1868.

6246. iii. SIDNEY GEORGE LATHROP, b. Dec. 14, 1871.

[Seventh Generation.]

6205. vi. JONATHAN CHILDS, fourth child and second son of Major Jonathan and Anna Thompson Childs, b. in Wilmington, Windham county, Vt., Aug. 4, 1794, m. about 1822, Cynthia Lusk. Mr. and Mrs. Jonathan Childs resided some years in Pittsford, Monroe county, N. Y. Later in life they removed to Pottawattamie county, Iowa, where they died.

[Eighth Generation.] Children:

6247. i. JOHN LUSK CHILDS, b. Mch. 2, 1823, m. Jan. 15, 1851, Sara Van Derlip Merriam.

6248. ii. GEORGE CHILDS.

6249. iii. WM. F. CHILDS, b. Aug. 6, 1834, m. April 4, 1860, Adelphia J. Snelson.

6250. iv. FREDERICK C. CHILDS, b. Sept. 20, 1842, m. Nov. 7, 1866, Elizabeth King.

[Eighth Generation.]

6247. i. JOHN LUSK CHILDS, eldest son of Jonathan and Cynthia Lusk Childs, b. in Williamstown. Mass., Mch. 2, 1823, m. Jan. 15, 1851, Sara Van Derlip Merriam, dau. of

A. B. Childs

Isaac Merriam. The character of John L. Childs has been drawn in manner most fitting and chaste by his last pastor, Rev. J. O. Means of Boston Highlands, in a small volume, entitled " Everywhere a Christian," from which we make some extracts. The parents of Mr. Childs removed to Pittsford, Monroe county, N. Y., when he was about five years old, and such opportunities as the village public school, and good home training afforded were his until he was fourteen, when at his own request he was permitted to enter a store as clerk : here very strong temptations were about him, but he was delivered and enabled to acquire a reputation for perfect integrity and more than usual ability. At this period he adopted Chancellor Kent's course of reading, and to this in after years ascribed his literary tastes and culture. His eighteenth year was spent in the High School of Rochester, N. Y., with a quickened understanding and love for study which insured him success. From these pursuits he was recalled by the creditors of his late employer, (whose affairs had become embarrassed) for upon examination of the books kept by him, they were anxious to put the business into his hands to be closed, a task he accomplished most satisfactorily. At this time he became deeply impressed with the duty of personal acceptance of the truths of christianity, and thereafter his life-light shone with steadily increasing lustre till merged in the brighter light of heaven.

Mr. Childs went to Boston, in 1844, and entered a jobbing house, upon a salary so small as to be inadequate to his needs but for previous economy. He promptly connected himself with the church of which Dr. Edward N. Kirk was pastor, and soon became the close friend and frequent assistant of Dea. Daniel Safford, a man well known in New England for his piety and benevolence. In 1851, the year of his marriage, we find him a partner in the dry-goods house of Whitney & Fenno, a position attained by his intelligent, upright business habits. Severe sickness two years later compelled him to withdraw from the business, and seek health in a warmer climate, and he was restored. For a period he resided at the West, and everywhere left a strong impress of his rarely beautiful living. GENTLENESS, COURTEOUSNESS, CHEERFULNESS and HUMILITY were noticeable characteristics of Mr. Childs, while they came in some measure by nature they came more largely by grace, and they were sedulously cultivated as important elements of the Christ life. He made it a matter of prayerful self-discipline to correct infelicities of temper, and overcome peculiarities which might annoy others. Courteousness perhaps does not so well as *humaneness*, designate the large consideration he had for the feelings of others, and his carefulness by no tone of voice, or coldness of manner, or momentary forgetfulness. and by no impatience of attitude, no omission of the civilities of speech to fail in the amenities of social intercourse. At home, to his children and those employed in his household, there was the same unvarying gentleness and courtesy. " Religion was not with him a Sabbathday garb," writes one qualified to speak, " it was everything." One who did not share Mr. Childs' religious opinions, but who knew him through and through, from long business acquaintance, and who had seen him wrong-side out and seam-side out if there was such a side to his character, when he heard of his death. exclaimed: " He was the best man I ever knew : I believe he was the best man that ever lived." It was his good fortune to accumulate some wealth ; from the age of twenty-one he consecrated a tenth to the Lord, and often exceeded the amount in special benefactions. His last activity was the purchase of many valuable books wherewith to entertain and improve the young, especially young men. He was about to enter a new home in Easthampton, Mass., where he hoped to do much for Christ, among the young men gathered in the schools of that town, but the insidious disease consumption, which had been for years subtily undermining his strength, wrought out its sure course, from earthly repose into that blessed sleep which God giveth to "His beloved." Mr. Childs entered the everlasting rest Nov. 16, 1868.

[Ninth Generation.] Children:

6251. i. FREDERICK MERRIAM CHILD, b. in Boston, Jan. 23, 1852, was drowned when bathing in Lake Michigan at Milwaukee,Wis., Aug. 15, 1862.

6252. ii. HARRIET NEWELL CHILD, b. in Council Bluffs, Iowa, July 23,1856.

6253. iii. JAMES MERRIAM CHILD, b. in Boston, Aug. 28, 1858.

6254. iv. JENNIE LOUISA CHILD, b. in Milwaukee, Wis., Sept. 28, 1861.

[Eighth Generation.]

6249. iii. WILLIAM F. CHILDS, third son of Jonathan and Cynthia Lusk Childs. b. at Pittsford, Monroe county, N. Y., Aug. 6, 1834. m. April 4, 1860. Miss Adelphia J. Snelson, at Council Bluffs, Iowa.

[Ninth Generation.] Children:

6255. i. FREDERICK J. CHILDS, b. Oct. 22, 1861.

6256. ii. WILLIAM H. CHILDS, b. Dec. 8, 1862, d. May 16, 1871.

6257. iii. ANNA CHILDS, b. Nov. 24, 1865, d. Oct. 27, 1868.

6258. iv. FANNIE CHILDS, b. Mch. 20, 1869.

6259. v. IDA W. CHILDS, b. July 14, 1871, d. Sept. 3, 1872.

6260. vi. WILL CHILDS, b. Feb. 6, 1875.

[Eighth Generation.]

6250. iv. FREDERICK C. CHILDS, fourth son of Jonathan and Cynthia Lusk Childs, b. in Pittsford, Monroe county, N. Y., Sept. 20, 1842, m. Nov. 7, 1866, Elizabeth King, at Council Bluffs, Iowa.

[Ninth Generation.]

6261. i. HARRIET K. CHILDS, b. Aug. 27, 1867.

6262. ii. WILLIAM F. CHILDS, b. Oct. 31, 1869.

6263. iii. FRANK CHILDS, b. Feb. 23, 1874.

[Seventh Generation.]

6206. vii. FREEMAN CHILDS, third son and fifth child of Major Jonathan and Anna Thompson Childs, b. in Wilmington, Vt., Feb. 17, 1797, m. Dec. 18, 1833, Miss Elizabeth Root of Montague, Mass. Freeman Childs d. in Wilmington, Vt., Feb. 12, 1849.

[Eighth Generation.] Children, born in Wilmington, Vt.

6264. i. EDWARD VINCENT CHILDS.

6265. ii. ELLEN ELIZABETH CHILDS, m. Aug. 1860, Orra Stebbins, she d. in Greenfield, Mass.

6266. iii. ADELAIDE A. CHILDS, m. Orra Stebbins.

6267. iv. BRAINARD FREEMAN CHILDS, m. —.

[Seventh Generation.]

6207. viii. ADNAH B. CHILDS, fourth son and eighth child of Major Jonathan and Anna Thompson Childs, b. in Wilmington, Vt., in the last year of the eighteenth century, Feb. 17, 1799, m. Mch. 19, 1826, Miss Hannah Lamb, dau. of Major Jonathan and Hannah Hoyt Hamilton Lamb.

So admirable a sketch was given at the time of his decease, of the man and of his position in life, that we feel we cannot improve upon it, and can only say that such characters won't portray in words; the look and tone so frequent with humor, and true-hearted sunshine, must have been seen and heard to be known We give therefore entire the article referred to:

"Major A. B. Childs departed this life at his residence in Wilmington, on the 8th day of January, 1874, aged 74 years, 11 months and 5 days. The deceased was a native of Wilmington, and has been one of its most noted and influential citizens. He was the first merchant in the village; a prominent Free Mason for fifty-three years; post-master under every Democratic administration, beginning with President Jackson's, holding the office twenty-four years. He was also deputy sheriff many years, and held other places of trust, in all of which he performed his duties with great exactness and perfect fidelity. But in his social connection, more especially, we feel to regret his loss. He was one of the original founders of the Universalist Society in Wilmington, and afterwards of the church connected therewith. He was decided, but not bitter, in his religious and political sentiments, and catholic in his bearing towards all. Strictly honest in his business transactions and temperate in his personal habits. His home has been a favorite resort of bright and pleasant people, and there the penniless wanderer found abundance of cheer. His intercourse with the community was always cheerful and peculiarly genial. Mr. Childs married young to a most estimable lady, Miss Hannah Lamb, also a native of Wilmington, whose death preceded his in August 28, 1870. They were blessed with a family of twelve children, ten of whom still survive to mourn their departure. In his family none could set better examples or manifest more devotedness to the interests, moral and pecuniary, of all its members, and these children now rise up and bless his memory. Without a murmur or complaint, in perfect resignation to the Providence of God and full of hope and faith in the universal redemption of the race, he passed away

'Like one who folds the drapery of his couch about him,
   And lies down to pleasant dreams.'"

The appreciation in which the subject of this notice was held, was fully evinced by the multitude that gathered to pay their tribute of respect on the occasion of his obsequies.

[Eighth Generation.]   Children:

6268. i. JOHN MURDOCK CHILDS, b. Ap. 16, 1827, m. Nov. 20, 1849, Martha Anna Winchester.

6269. ii. WILLIAM HENRY CHILDS, b. in Boston, Sept. 17, 1828, m. Sept. 24, 1854, Anna Parker Goodrich.

6270. iii. HANNAH ANN CHILDS, b. Aug. 26, 1830, m. 1st, Ap 9, 1851, Wells S. Snow, he d. Oct. 28, 1863; she m. 2d, Nov. 14, 1874, Harry Long Williams.

6271. iv. JANE MARY CHILDS, b. July 16, 1832, m. Ap. 9, 1850, Edwin Thayer.

6272. v. ADNA LYMAN CHILDS, b. Aug. 26, 1834, m. Jan. 6, 1861, Annette Fox.

6273. vi. HELEN MARILLA CHILDS, b. Aug. 8, 1836, m. Sept. 3, 1856, John E. Clary.

6274. vii. GEORGE LEWIS CHILDS, b. May 10, 1838. Drowned in Clear Lake in Minnesota, June 4, 1857. "He was a young man of much promise, beloved by all who knew him, noble-hearted, generous and manly; he gave up his own life in the vain effort to save the life of a companion. His remains were recovered, and rest with kindred dust in the Green Mountain State."

6275. viii. ASAPH PARMALEE CHILDS, b. June 10, 1840, m. July 8, 1873, Sarah Cady.

6276. ix. ESTHER MARIA CHILDS, b. Mch. 9, 1843, m. July 1, 1860, Kittredge Haskins.

6277. x. ROLLIN SKINNER CHILDS, b. Oct. 11, 1845, m. May 2, 1872, in Wilmington, Vt., Miss Julia Esterbrooks, dau. of George and Anna Esterbrooks. Mr. Childs is associated with his brother, **A. P.** Childs, in the insurance business in Bennington, Vt.

6278. xi. SARAH MARTHA CHILDS, b. Aug. 13, 1847, m. Feb. 17, 1876, Mr. Charles D. Kidder of Springfield, Mass., son of Dwight and Kate Kidder.

6279. xii. FREDERICK WILLIARD CHILDS, b. Sept. 16, 1849, m. Jan. 8, 1878, Emma Maria Fullerton.

[Eighth Generation.]

6268. i. JOHN MURDOCK CHILDS, eldest son and child of Maj. A. B. and Hannah Lamb Childs, b. in Wilmington, Vt., April 16, 1827, m. Nov. 20, 1849, Miss Martha Ann Winchester of Marlboro, Vt. Mr. Childs d. July 2, 1869, and Mrs. C. Sept. 15, 1876.

[Ninth Generation.] Children:

6280 i. WALTER HENRY CHILDS, b. Aug. 5, 1852, m. May 2, 1875, Clara Davis.

6281. ii. LIZZIE JANE CHILDS, b. Feb. 16, 1856, d. Aug. 17, 1856.

6282. iii. ARTHUR WINCHESTER CHILDS, b. Mch. 29, 1859.

[Ninth Generation.]

6280. i. WALTER HENRY CHILDS, eldest son and child of John M. and Martha Ann Winchester Childs, b. in Wilmington, Vt., Aug. 5, 1852, m. May, 1875, Miss Clara Davis, dau. of John B. Davis of Brattleboro, Vt. Mr. Childs is of the business house of Estey & Co., organ manufacturers.

[Tenth Generation.] Child:

6283. i. CHARLES FREDERICK CHILDS, b. Feb. 1876.

[Eighth Generation.]

6269. ii. WILLIAM HENRY CHILDS, second son of Major A. B. and Hannah Lamb Childs, b. in Boston, Mass., Sept. 17, 1828, m. Miss Anna Parker Goodrich, dau. of Capt. James Goodrich of Portsmouth, N. H., who was born Sept. 7, 1830. Mr. William Childs left school and home at the age of 17, entering a dry-goods store, in Roxbury, Mass.; his employer Edwin Lamist, Esq., after a time was chosen postmaster, and young Childs was placed in the post-office. A few years later he went into a banking house in Boston, Mass., where he continued until impaired health compelled a change of climate. With his wife Mr. Childs removed to St. Paul, Minnesota, in the winter of 1855, and entered upon pioneer life with enthusiasm, locating his home in Lexington, Minn., upon the shore of a charming lake. Identifying himself with energy in the advancement of the new territory, Mr. Childs made for himself a place of honor and was by his fellow-citizens placed in many offices of responsibility. An invasion of the Sioux upon the settlement, shadowed and endangered every home: women and children were placed in safety, while fathers, husbands and brothers, remained to save the homes. This experience, almost immediately succeeded by the war of the Rebellion, necessitated changes, and many pioneer homes were deserted. Mr. Childs entered the service of the American and U. S. Express Co.'s, and settled with his family in St. Paul, Minn. Some ten years later, about 1873, another removal led him to the shores of the Pacific, whence his next transfer will be no doubt to Japan, or Australia. In San Francisco, Mr. Childs serves his country under "Uncle Sam" as store keeper.

[Ninth Generation.] Child:

6284. i. IDA AGNES CHILDS, b. Oct. 26, 1856, in Wilmington, Vt.

[Eighth Generation.]

6270. iii. HANNAH ANN CHILDS, eldest dau. of Major A. B. and Hannah Lamb Childs, b. Aug. 26, 1830, in Wilmington, Vt., m. 1st, April 9, 1851, Wells S. Snow, in Wilmington, Vt.; Mr. Snow died in Oct. 1863, leaving one son; m. 2d, Mr. Harry Long Williams, engineer of the U. S. Armory, Springfield, Mass.

[Ninth Generation.] Children:

6285. i. CHARLES LEWIS SNOW, b. Sept. 1853.
6286. ii. FREDERICK CHILDS WILLIAMS, b. Nov. 30, 1875.

[Eighth Generation.]

6271. iv. JANE MARY CHILDS, second dau. and fourth child of Major A. B. and Hannah Lamb Childs, b. July 16, 1832, in Wilmington, Vt., m. April 9, 1850, Edwin Thayer of Greenfield, Mass.

[Ninth Generation.] Children:

6287. i JENNIE MARIA THAYER, b. Oct. 27, 1853, in Greenfield, Mass.
6288. ii. WILLIAM LYMAN THAYER, b. Oct 8, 1855, in Wilmington, Vt.

[Eighth Generation.]

6272. v. ADNA LYMAN CHILDS, third son and fifth child of Maj. A. B. and Hannah Lamb Childs, b. in Wilmington, Vt., Aug. 26, 1834, m. Jan. 6, 1861, Miss Annette Fox, daughter of Alonzo and Calista Fox of Woodford, Vt. Mr. Childs is in business in his native place, catering for the home-comforts of his townsmen.

[Ninth Generation.] Child:

6289. i. FRANK FOX CHILDS, b. Feb. 1865.

[Eighth Generation.]

6273. vi. HELEN MARILLA CHILDS, third dau. and sixth child of Maj. A. B. and Hannah Lamb Childs, b. in Wilmington, Aug. 8, 1836, m. Sept. 3, 1856, Mr John E. Clary of Deerfield, Mass. Mr. Clary died in Wilmington, Sept. 4, 1861, and Mrs. Helen M. Childs Clary resides with her children, in Deerfield, Mass.

[Ninth Generation.] Children:

6290. i. GEORGE LEWIS CLARY, b. Aug. 21, 1857, in Deerfield, Mass.
6291. ii. MILLIE ALICE CLARY, b. Nov. 30, 1858.

[Eighth Generation.]

6275. viii. ASAPH PARMALEE CHILDS, fifth son and eighth child of Maj. A. B. and Hannah Lamb Childs, b. June 10,1840, Graduated at Powers Institute, Bernardston, Mass., in 1858. On the breaking out of the late civil war, Mr. Childs enlisted in Company F, of the 16th Vermont Regiment ; was detailed into Quartermaster Woodford's office. He served three years. After the war Mr. Childs entered upon the study of the law, and graduated with high honors from the Columbian Law School, Washington, D. C. Mr. Childs has not practiced law actively, but is associated with a brother in Insurance. During the period of Centennial anniversary celebrations in Vermont, Mr. A. P. Childs and a younger brother published a small paper containing addresses, accounts of festivities, notices of valued and valuable relics of the revolutionary period and association, and other items incident to such times and deeds ; very readable little sheets, deserving preservation for reference at the next Centennial. Mr. A. P. Childs married in July, 1873, Miss Sarah P. Cady, daughter of David Cady, Esq., of Bennington, where they now reside.

[Ninth Generation.] Children:

6292. i. ETHEL CHILDS, b. Aug 30, 1874.
6293. ii. LUCIA LAMB CHILDS, b. Dec. 14, 1876.

[Eighth Generation.]

6276. ix. ESTHER MARIA CHILDS, fourth dau. and ninth child of Maj. A. B. and Hannah Lamb Childs, b. March 9, 1843, in Wilmington, Windham county, Vt., m. July 1, 1860, Kittredge Haskins, Esq., counsellor at law, now of Brattleboro, Vt., son of Asaph and Amelia Haskins of Dover, Vt. Mr. Haskins is a commendable exemplification of the native American power to conquer circumstances, and make fate, unaided by adventitious surroundings. He studied law in Wilmington, and was admitted to the bar in 1854. In 1861, with wonted enthusiasm, he enlisted with the nine months troops in Co. I. of the 16th Vt. Regt.; was advanced to Lieut. and Acting Quartermaster while in service. Upon his return to Vermont he removed to Brattleboro, ever since his home, and has become one of the leading men of his State, serving in different posts most honorably to his constituents and creditably to himself. Mrs. Haskins possesses most markedly the Child characteristics, full of the bonhommie and ready repartee which rendered her father so attractive in the social circle, with a most felicitous use of the pen; and serving the Master with heart and voice in the beautiful chants of the church.

[Ninth Generation.]   Child:

6294. i. JOHNNIE ADNA CHILDS HASKINS, b. June 1, 1861, in Williamsville, Vt., d. March 27, 1864.

[Eighth Generation.]

6279. xii. FREDERICK WILLARD CHILDS, the sixth son, the twelfth and youngest child of Maj. A. B. and Hannah Lamb Childs, b. Sept. 16, 1849, in Wilmington, Vt., m Jan. 8, 1878, Emma Maria Fullerton, dau. of the late Frederick E. and Philette Wentworth Fullerton, and granddaughter of the Hon. Merrick Wentworth of Chester, Vt. There seems throughout the Child family, in the different branches, a strong desire to have all the world *insured* against something; whether this arises from the large philanthropy of the race, or no, we leave others to judge. It will be found a noticeable pursuit of the living members of this great tribe, and we find Mr. F. W. Childs, after a training of some years, in the military school of Prof. Charles Niles of Brattleboro, Vt., and the Williston Seminary in East Hampton, Mass. has devoted himself to thus preserving the lives and property of others, as well as his own.

[Ninth Generation.]   Child:

6295. i. RUTH WENTWORTH CHILDS, b. June 27, 1880, "at 1:10 o'clock P. M." The father in a telegram says: "She is bright as a button, hair black as coal, large blue eyes. Baby's for Hancock and English!" [*Poor, dear child, begins life in disappointment in the result of her first vote!*— E. C.]

[Sixth Generation.]

6053. xi. DAVID CHILDS, fifth son and eleventh child of Jonathan and Rebecca Scott Childs, b. in Hardwick, Worcester county, Mass., Nov. 16, 1760, m. abt. 1785, Lydia Hemmen-

way of Prescott, Mass., who was b. June 20, 1766. Mr. Childs
d. at New Salem, Franklin county, Mass., in 1858, aged 97.

[Seventh Generation.] Children:
6296. i. POLLY CHILDS, b. Nov. 11, 1787, m. Mr. Ballard, d. Aug. 8, 1822.
6297. ii. RHODA CHILDS, b. Jan. 5, 1789.
6298. iii. ABIGAIL CHILDS, b. July 6, 1791.
6299. iv. ABIGAIL CHILDS, 2d, b. April 5, 1794.
6300. v. FANNY CHILDS, b. Sept. 7, 1796, m. Mr. Squires of New Haven,
Ct., d. Mch. 23, 1835.
6301. vi. LYDIA CHILDS, b. Mch. 21, 1800, m. Dec. 1837, Smith Kelley.
6302. vii. SAMUEL CHILDS, b. Dec. 20, 1804, d. Sept. 10, 1875.

[Seventh Generation.]

6301. vi. LYDIA CHILDS, sixth dau. and child of David and
Lydia Hemmenway Childs, b. in New Salem, Mass., Mch. 21,
1800, m. Dec. 1837, Smith Kelley of Greenwich, Mass. Mr.
Kelley is a wealthy farmer of that town. Mrs. Lydia Childs
Kelley d. Sept. 23, 1879.

[Eighth Generation.] Children:
6303. i. CARRIE ADELIA KELLEY, b. Nov. 30, 1838, m. Jan. 14, 1868,
George Washington Wheeler.
6304. ii. SOPHIA CELESTINA KELLEY, b. Feb. 28, 1841, m. 1st, Mch. 5, 1871,
Hiram Leavens, who d. July 1871; m. 2d, May 21, 1876, Merrick Sly of
Dudley, Mass.
6305. iii. MARY FRANCES KELLEY, b. Mch. 12, 1847, d. Feb. 13, 1865.

[Eighth Generation.]

6303. i. CARRIE ADELIA KELLEY, eldest child of Lydia
Childs and Smith Kelley, b. in Greenwich, Mass., Nov. 30,
1838, m. Jan. 14, 1868, George Washington Wheeler. She d.
Aug. 2, 1873.

[Ninth Generation.] Child:
6306. i. ESTELLE WHEELER, lived a few hours.

[Fifth Generation.]

5836. i. EBENEZER CHILD, sixth child and fifth son of
Samuel and Hannah Barnard Child, b. in Deerfield, Mass.,
Nov. 11, 1720, m. about 1750, Rachel —, and removed to
Shutesbury, Mass. He was prominent in church and town
affairs, for many years a worthy deacon in the Congregational
church. He removed from Shutesbury to Shelburne, Mass.,
about 1774, or '5, and with his wife joined the Congregational
church in that town. He died in Shelburne in 1774. The
Shutesbury Town Clerk says:

"Ebenezer Child was selectman for about ten years, proprietor clerk
about twelve years, two or three years town clerk and was of great note in
town affairs, in those days, as I find his name in almost all town business."

Deacon Ebenezer Child is on the certified list of tax payers in Shelburne with his son Ebenezer; the father paying £2, and the son £1, annual tax. In furnishing some account of this family, Rev. Theophilus Packard, says:

"I could furnish some further particulars and dates concerning nearly all of the above named, and some of their descendants also I can furnish you by consulting my notes, and various documents, if such materials are what you wish for the Child's genealogy. But though I have many valuable statistics as to the tribes of the Childses, I will gladly and gratuitously furnish them to you if you deem them suitable for your profound work. Still as I may not live to answer a letter to you, I will name a few persons with their address, who can give particulars."

Then follow the names with the address. Letters addressed to them were never answered and the particulars desired never obtained. The aged, infirm and our unseen friend probably did not live to render further aid, as letters subsequently addressed to him were not answered, with one or two exceptions.

[Sixth Generation.] Children: Four children are recorded in the town records of Shutesbury, Mass., there may have been more.

6307. i. MERCY CHILD, b. April 28, 1753, in Shutesbury, Mass.

6308. ii. EBENEZER CHILD, JR., b. Aug. 22, 1756, m. Jan. 1778, Elizabeth Frary.

6309. iii. DAVID CHILD, b. Nov. 4, 1760, m. Mch. 1784, Clarissa Dickenson.

6310. iv. RACHEL CHILD, b. Mch. 23, 1764, d. Jan. 27, 1768, in Shutesbury.

[Sixth Generation.]

6308. ii. Dr. EBENEZER CHILD, second child and eldest son of Ebenezer and Rachel Child, b. Aug. 22, 1756, in Shutesbury, Mass., m. Jan. 1778, Elizabeth Frary of Deerfield, Mass. Rev. Mr. Packard says:

"They joined the Shelburne church by profession in 1778. Mrs. Child was a most excellent and godly woman. Dr. Child was long a highly respected physician in Shelburne. I knew him well and have taken his pills when a boy. My father, who lived a while in his family, has told me interesting incidents respecting him." He d. Nov. 13, 1813, æ. 57; she d. in 1834.

[Seventh Generation.] Children. The descendants of this branch add the terminal "s," and were all born in Shelburne, Mass.

6311. i. ELIZABETH CHILDS, b. 1780, d. Mch. 29, 1782.

6312. ii. NATHAN CHILDS, b. 1783, d. 1795.

6313. iii. EBENEZER CHILDS, JR., b. 1786. This son was a physician, and practiced in Shelburne, Mass., many years. He had several children, of whom were Albertus and Eben Childs, reported to be residents of Lincolton, Lincoln county, N. C., with whom the father is said to have lived some three years since at 90 years of age. Our efforts to obtain a fuller account of this branch have been unavailing.

6314. iv. CHARLES DOOLITTLE CHILDS, b. 1788, m. Catharine Arms.

6315. v. LINUS CHILDS, b. 1790, d. unm. in the State of New York many years since.

6316. vi. LLOYD CHILDS, b. 1792, d. young.

6317. vii. THANKFUL CHILDS, b. 1794, d. in 1834, in York, Livingston county, N. Y.

6318. viii. BETSEY CHILDS, b. 1796, m. Sylvanus Allen of Shelburne, Mass; lived and died in the State of New York.

6319. ix. RACHEL CHILDS, b. 1778, m. Appleton Skinner, of Shelburne, Mass., where they lived and died, leaving one daughter, Maria Childs Skinner, who died a number of years since, while teaching in the State of New York.

[Seventh Generation.]

6314. iv. CHARLES DOOLITTLE CHILDS, fourth child and third son of Dr. Ebenezer and Elizabeth Frary Childs, b. in Shelburne, Mass., July, 1788, m. Feb. 13, 1813, Catharine Arms of Greenfield, Mass. He emigrated to the State of New York in 1827, and settled in the town of York, Livingston county, N. Y. He was a tanner and currier by trade. After his removal to the State of New York, he was not confined to this branch of business, but engaged in other enterprises which rewarded his foresight and well-laid plans for legitimate and handsome accumulations. A man of enlarged views, of high and noble aims, his influence was efficiently and happily felt in the community, and no good moral and religious enterprise lacked his hearty support. Mrs. Childs was not less highly esteemed for her personal virtues, her genial disposition, her firmness of principle, her devotion to the interests of her household and conscientious discharge of all christian duties. They had five children, all born and baptized in Shelburne, Mass.

[Eighth Generation.] Children:

6320. i. HARRIET NEWELL CHILDS, b. June 15, 1816, d. Aug. 1821. A remarkably amiable and attractive child; died by swallowing a fish-bone.

6321. ii. CATHARINE ARMS CHILDS, b. May 9, 1818, m. July 17, 1845, Rev. Edwards Marsh.

6322. iii. CHARLES DWIGHT CHILDS, b. June 5, 1820, m. 1st, Jan. 12, 1843, Louisa Hamilton; m. 2d. Elizabeth Illender.

6323. iv. HARRIET NEWELL CHILDS, 2D, b. Oct. 27, 1821, m. Dec. 10, 1850, D. W. Vittum.

6324. v. GEORGE ARMS CHILDS, b. Mch. 27. 1825, m. Mch. 4, 1856, Susan Doty of Lockport, N. Y.

[Eighth Generation.]

6321. ii. CATHARINE ARMS CHILDS, second child and dau. of Charles Doolittle and Catharine Arms Childs, b. in Shelburne, Mass., Mch. 9, 1818, m. July 17, 1845, Rev. Edward Marsh. Mr. Marsh was born of christian parents. His father was an honored minister of the Presbyterian church, whose ancestry is traced to Oliver Cromwell. This son was reared amid the influences of happy domestic relations and favorable conditions of society, for bringing out the best elements of

character, all conspiring to fit him for healthful and efficient
public life. Known to us during his preparatory studies for
professional life, it is our pleasure to speak of him as a man
and a christian, of the best characteristics. He carried in his
face the marks of an ingenuous and unselfish nature, almost
sure to captivate the favor and confidence of any one who
could appreciate the signs of a noble heart. Earnest as a
christian, laborious as a minister, his life was by no means a neg-
ative one. His influence was positive, aggressive. The results of his earnest, active life, are favorably known in the
fields of labor which he successfully cultivated till he was
called by the Master to the higher life.

Mr. Marsh was twice married, fortunately in both instances.
His first marriage to a Miss Thompson, a niece of Rev. Dr.
Perine, Professor in Auburn Theological Seminary, under
whose training in part Mr. Marsh received his theological education. By this marriage he had five children. It would be
our pleasure to record their names had they been given us.

His second marriage to Miss Catharine Arms Childs was
not less fortunate. She was the daughter of a worthy and
esteemed family of the New England stamp, which brought
to their new home in Western New York, the refining and elevating influences of thorough christian training. The position
of her family secured for her education and refinements, which
justly gave her influence in society, and rendered her a valued
companion to her worthy husband. There were no children
by this marriage.

[Eighth Generation.]

6325. iii. CHARLES DWIGHT CHILDS, third child and eldest
son of Charles Doolittle and Catharine Arms Childs, b. in Shelburne, Mass., June 5, 1820, m. 1st, Jan. 12, 1843, Louisa Hamilton; m. 2d, April 29, 1866, Elizabeth Illender. Residence
of Mr. Childs, Ionia, Mich.

In boyhood and early youth Mr. Childs enjoyed the advantages of an ordinary education. Having been trained by a
judicious father in habits of industry, he was qualified for
positions of much responsibility. He obtained employment
as a clerk in a store where he developed the essential characteristics of a successful business man. He was not long in securing
promotion in business relations. Though naturally diffident

and retiring, he possessed sufficient self-reliance to assume responsibilities which never suffered at his hands. His industry, his perseverence and integrity in work furnished him, won the confidence of thorough business men who knew the value of such habits in a trusted agent and associate. It has been no part of the purpose of his life to live solely for himself. Whatever has been vital to the progress of sound morality and religion has enlisted his sympathies and his cordial support. He holds the offices of auditor and general purchasing agent of the Detroit & Lansing Railroad Company, Michigan.

[Ninth Generation.] Children. By first wife:

6325. i. HARRIET LOUISA CHILDS, b. Nov. 30, 1845, d. Feb. 25, 1870.

6326. ii. GEORGE EUGENE CHILDS, b. Jan. 27, 1847. Resides at Flint, Mich.

6327. iii. CHARLES D. CHILDS, JR., b. Feb. 14, 1856. Resides at Flint, Mich.

[Eighth Generation.]

6320. iv. HARRIET NEWELL CHILDS. 2D, fourth child, third dau. of Charles Doolittle and Catharine Arms Childs, b. in Shelburne, Mass., Oct. 29, 1821, m. Dec. 19, 1850, D. W. Vittum. Mr. Vittum is from an honorable family in New Hampshire. He went to Illinois when quite young; ultimately engaged in the mercantile business. Identified himself with every good enterprise for the proper development of the country and for the promotion of morality and religion. They have three children, names not ascertained. The family reside in Canton, Ill.

[Eighth Generation.]

6324. v. GEORGE ARMS CHILDS. second son of Charles Doolittle and Catharine Arms Childs, b. Mch. 27, 1825, in Shelburne, Mass., m. Mch. 4, 1856. Susan E. Doty of Lockport, N. Y., she was b. Dec. 8, 1833. For many years Mr. Childs was a prosperous hardware merchant in Des Moines, Iowa; later he removed to Chicago, Ill., and opened a banking house. The home training by intelligent christian parents shaped his character, and gave a healthful direction to his life habits. Among his prominent characteristics was unswerving integrity; his business was conducted upon principles of highest honesty. He d. Mch. 31, 1878, at Chicago, Ill.

[Ninth Generation.] Children, born in Des Moines, Iowa, and reside in Chicago.

6328. i. FREDERICK WILLIAM CHILDS, b. Jan. 3, 1857.

6329. ii. CATHARINE ARMS CHILDS, b. Mch. 10, 1861.

6330. iii. WILLIAM DOTY CHILDS, b. July 27, 1862.

[Sixth Generation.]

6309. iii. DAVID CHILDS, third child and second son of Ebenezer and Rachel Childs, b. Nov. 4, 1760, in Shutesbury, Mass., m. March, 1784, Clarissa Dickenson of Hatfield, Mass., she was b. July 21, 1762. Mr. Childs d. Mch. 15, 1828, æ 68; Mrs. Childs d. April 7, 1844. They resided in Conway, Mass.

[Seventh Generation.]   Children, born in Conway, Mass.

6321. i. POLIXANA CHILDS, b. Jan. 2, 1785, m. June 1806, Stephen Sanderson.

6332. ii. CALISTA CHILDS, b. Feb. 18, 1787, m. Oct. 7, 1812, Geo. Rogers.

6333. iii. OTIS CHILDS, b. Ap. 4, 1790, m. 1st, Jan 13, 1813, Sally Field. m. 2d, Dec. 14, 1820, Electa Clary; m. 3d, Feb. 22, 1827, Lois Parsons; m. 4th, Aug. 28, 1844, Mrs. Ann Dickenson.

6334. iv. SILAS DICKENSON CHILDS, b. May 29, 1794, m. Roxana Parker; they left no children.

6335. v. JUSTUS CHILDS, b. Oct. 6, 1799, d. June 18, 1828, æ 29 years.

6336. vi. FRANKLIN CHILDS, b. June 28, 1802, m. 1st, July 24, 1828, Laurinda Field; m. 2d, July 12, 1868, S. Clary.

[Seventh Generation.]

6331. i. POLIXANA CHILDS, eldest child of David and Clarissa Dickenson Childs, b. in Conway, Mass., June 2, 1785, m. Jan. 1806, Stephen Sanderson of Whately, Mass.; he was born Jan. 18, 1782; he died in Conway, Mass., May 31, 1823. She died Mch. 28, 1847, æ 62 years.

[Eighth Generation.]   Children, born in Conway, Mass.

6337. i. EDWARD SANDERSON, b. April 28, 1807, d. July 21, 1809.

6338. ii. ORPHEUS SANDERSON, b. April 13, 1809, m. Aug. 19, 1830, Sally C. White.

6339. iii. RICHARD MONTAGUE SANDERSON, b. Jan. 3, 1811, m. Mch. 16, 1837, Mary A. Thwing.

6340. iv. CHARLES SANDERSON, b. April 7, 1813, m. June 27, 1839, Maria Morse.

6341. v. AUSTIN SANDERSON, b. Mch. 28 1815, m Aug. 23, 1838, Charlotte G. Wells.

6342. vi. DIADAMA SANDERSON, b. April 24, 1817, d. Mch. 24, 1840.

6343. vii. TRYPHENIA SANDERSON, b. Aug. 11, 1819, d. Feb. 12, 1840.

6344. viii. MARY SANDERSON, b. Oct. 6, 1821. Now living in Vineland, New Jersey.

[Eighth Generation.]

6345. ii. OLPHEUS SANDERSON, second child and second son of Polixana Childs and Stephen Sanderson, b. in Conway, Mass., July 13, 1809, m. Aug. 19, 1830, Sally C. White of Southport, N. Y. She was b. Oct. 21, 1814.

[Ninth Generation.]   Children:

6345. i. MARY ELIZABETH SANDERSON, b. in Elmira, N. Y., June 17, 1831, m. Dec. 27, 1850. Lives in Lavonia, N. Y.

6346. ii. CHARLES M. SANDERSON, b. in Wells, Pa., Jan. 15, 1833, m. in Corning, N. Y., June 19, 1855.

6347. iii. TRYPHENA POLIXANA SANDERSON, b. in Elmira, N. Y., Feb. 8, 1834, m. July 3, 1849, in Catharine, N.Y., d. in Havana, N.Y., May 11, 1852.

6348. iv. SETH WHITE SANDERSON, b. in Veteran, N. Y., Feb. 29, 1836.

6349. v. JOSEPHINE DIADAMA SANDERSON, b. in Elmira, N. Y., Aug. 24, 1837, d. in Veteran, N. Y., Sept. 17, 1839.

6350. vi. LORETTA ELVIRA SANDERSON, b. in Veteran, N.Y., Aug. 7, 1839, m. in Tioga, Pa., June 17, 1855.

6351. vii. EMILY ORLINA SANDERSON, b. in Elmira, N. Y., Dec. 6, 1842.

6352. viii. ELLEN ISADORE SANDERSON, b. in Elmira, N. Y., June 27, 1847.

6353. ix. AUSTIN ALANSON SANDERSON, b. in Catharine, N.Y., Jan. 4, 1848.

6354. x. FRANKLIN CHILDS SANDERSON, b. in Corning, N. Y., Aug. 6, 1850.

6355. xi. MARQUIS DE LAFAYETTE SANDERSON, b. in Tioga, Pa., April 11, 1854.

[Eighth Generation.]

6339. iii. RICHARD MONTAGUE SANDERSON, third child and son of Polixana Childs and Stephen Sanderson, b. in Conway, Mass., Jan. 3, 1811, m. Mch. 16, 1837, Mary A. Thwing. She was b. July 20, 1809. He d. April 19, 1838, aged 27. She m. 2d, Sept. 28, 1844, Randall Graves of Whately. He was b. July 28, 1800.

[Ninth Generation.] Child:

6356. i. RICHARD SANDERSON, b. in Conway, Mass., Mch. 18, 1838: now lives in Vineland, N. J.

[Eighth Generation.]

6340. iv. CHARLES SANDERSON, fourth child and son of Polixana Childs and Stephen Sanderson, b. April 7, 1813, m. June 27, 1839, Maria Morse. She was b. April 1, 1815, in Leominster, Mass. Resided in Leominster where he died June 8, 1846, aged 33.

[Ninth Generation.] Children, born in Leominster, Mass.

6357. i. MARY JANE SANDERSON, b. April 3, 1840.

6358. ii. ELLEN MARIA SANDERSON, b. April 7, 1843.

6359. iii. ANTOINETTE ELVIRA SANDERSON, b. Jan. 17, 1845.

[Eighth Generation.]

6341. v. AUSTIN SANDERSON, fifth child and son of Polixana Childs and Stephen Sanderson, b. Mch. 28, 1815, in Conway, Mass., m. Aug. 23, 1838, in Guilford, Vt., Charlotte G. Wells, she was b. Ap. 4, 1819, in Greenfield. Austin Sanderson d. Dec. 27, 1850, in Conway, æ. 35.

[Ninth Generation.] Children:

6360. i. TRYPHENA JENNETTE SANDERSON, b. Dec. 1, 1840, in Conway, Mass., m. and resides in Amherst, Mass.

6361. ii. STEPHEN WELLS SANDERSON, b. Feb. 25, 1842, in Conway, Mass., d. Sept. 5, 1842.

W-1

[Seventh Generation.]

6332. ii. CALISTA CHILDS, second child and second dau. of David and Clarissa Dickenson Childs, b. Feb. 18, 1787, in Conway, Mass., m. Oct. 7, 1812, George Rogers, he was b. Aug. 6, 1779, in Tisbury, Mass. She d. Sept. 11, 1850, æ. 63,; he d. June 8, 1852, æ. 73.

[Eighth Generation.] Children, born in Conway, Mass.

6362. i DAVID CHILDS ROGERS, b. May 25, 1813, m. Nov. 28, 1838, Amelia Ann Foot.

6363. ii. JOSHUA KNOWLTON ROGERS, b. Dec. 21, 1814, m. Jan. 1, 1842, Pamelia Bartlett.

6364. iii. CLARISSA DICKENSON ROGERS, b. June 14, 1817, m. Nov. 28, 1839, Rodolphus Clark.

6365. iv. CALISTA CHILDS ROGERS, b. July 5, 1819, d. Mch. 3, 1820.

6366. v. EDWIN ROGERS, b. July 1, 1821, m. Nov. 27, 1844, in North Adams, Schuett S. Stevens of Swansey, N. H., where she was b. Sept. 5, 1820. Mr. Rogers, a man of cordial hospitalities, has long been one of the leading business men of North Adams, for many years he has been the popular postmaster of the town, in which capacity he has served the public with fidelity and acceptance, and by his courteous and obliging manners has won the esteem of the community.

6367. vi. CALISTA CHILDS ROGERS, 2D, b. Oct. 23, 1823.

6368. vii. GEORGE ROGERS, JR., b. July 13, 1826, d. Oct. 11, 1844, æ 18.

[Eighth Generation.]

6362. i. DAVID CHILDS ROGERS, eldest child of Calista Childs and Geo. Rogers, b. in Conway, Mass., May 25, 1813, m. in same place, Nov. 28, 1838, Amelia Ann Foot, daughter of David Foot. She was born in Peru, Mass., April 25, 1813. Reside in Greenfield, Mass. Mr. Rogers has for many years been one of the leading business men of Greenfield, recently retired, leaving a lucrative manufacturing business to his son.

[Ninth Generation.] Children:

6369. i. MARTHA ANN ROGERS, b. in West Springfield, Oct. 10, 1839, m. Charles G. Parsons.

6370. ii. FRANCES NASH ROGERS, b. in West Springfield, Mass., May 20, 1842, m. April 18, 1880, —.

6371. iii. GEORGE EDWIN ROGERS, b. in North Adams, June 10, 1849, m. Clara Clark.

[Ninth Generation.]

6369. i. MARTHA ANN ROGERS, eldest child of David Childs and Amelia Ann Foot Rogers, and grand-daughter of Calista Childs Rogers, b. in West Springfield, Mass., Oct. 10, 1839, m. Charles G. Parsons of Boston, Mass.

[Tenth Generation.] Children:

6372. i. GEORGE PARSONS.

6373. ii. MATTIE R. PARSONS.

[Ninth Generation.]

6371. iii. GEORGE EDWIN ROGERS, third child and only son of David Childs, and Amelia Ann Foot Rogers, b. in North Adams, June 10, 1849, m. Clara Clark. Mr. Rogers is a manufacturer.

[Tenth Generation.] Child:

6374. i. ETHEL C. ROGERS, b. Nov. 8, 1877.

[Eighth Generation.]

6363. ii. JOSHUA KNOWLTON ROGERS, second son and child of Calista Childs and George Rogers, b. Dec. 21, 1814, m. Jan. 1, 1842. Pamelia Bartlett, who was born in Conway, Feb. 5, 1817.

[Ninth Generation.] Children, born in North Adams, Mass.

6375. i. CALISTA CHILDS ROGERS, b. Oct. 8, 1845.

6376. ii. SARAH BARTLETT Rogers, b. Jan. 14, 1848.

6377. iii. ELLEN PAMELIA ROGERS, b. April 4, 1850.

[Eighth Generation.]

6364. iii. CLARISSA DICKENSON ROGERS, third child of Calista Childs and George Rogers, b. in Conway, Mass., June 14, 1817, m. Nov. 28, 1839, Rodolphus Clark. He was b. Feb. 16, 1815, in Conway, Mass. Reside in Dubuque, Iowa.

[Ninth Generation.] Children, born in Conway, Mass.

6378 i. SARAH GRIFFETH CLARK, b. Sept. 25, 1841.

6379. ii. ANNA BARTLETT CLARK, b. Jan. 27, 1844.

6380. iii. Infant son, (unchristened,) b. July 15, 1846, d. Aug. 3, 1846.

6381. iv. CLARA ELIZABETH CLARK, b. Jan. 29, 1850.

6382. v. MARY CALISTA CLARK, b. Oct. 18, 1852, d. July 2, 1853.

[Seventh Generation.]

6333. iii. OTIS CHILDS, third child and eldest son of David and Clarissa Dickenson Childs, b. in Conway, Mass., April 4, 1790, m. 1st, Jan. 13, 1813, Sally Field. She was b. Mch. 27, 1791, d. Dec. 29, 1819, aged 28; m. 2d, Dec. 14, 1820, Electa Clary, b. June 6, 1795, d. July 28, 1826, aged 31 years; m. 3d, Feb. 22, 1827, Lois Parsons, b. Mch. 8, 1795, d. Feb. 22, 1844; m. 4th, Aug. 28, 1844, in Buffalo, N. Y., Mrs. Ann Dickenson, b. in Rome, N. Y., Feb. 14, 1798.

[Eighth Generation.] Children,—by 1st marriage—born in Conway, Mass:

6383. i. EDWARD CHILDS, b. Dec. 31, 1813, m. 1st, May 6, 1841, Sarah Adams; m. 2d, May 5, 1852, Emily Porter.

6384. ii. WILLIAM SULLIVAN CHILDS, b. May 28, 1816, m. June, 1839, Lydia Frary.

6385. iii. HENRY CHILDS, b. Jan. 28, 1818, m. 1st Sept. 22, 1842, Mary A. Graves; m. 2d, Jan. 13, 1852, Esther L. Kinsley.

6386. iv. SARAH FIELD CHILDS, b. Dec. 21, 1819, m. Oct. 5, 1842, Samuel W. Barber.

By second marriage:

6387. v. CHARLES CHILDS, b. Jan. 20, 1822, m. Nov. 17, 1847, Elizabeth W. Webster.

6388. vi. Infant, b. Oct. 23, 1823, d. young.

6389. vii. SILAS DICKENSON CHILDS, b. July 19, 1826, m. April 11, 1850, Harriet A. Warren.

6390. viii. ELECTA C. CHILDS, b. Jan. 24, 1828. She was the eldest child of Otis and Lois Parsons Childs She m. Sept. 20, 1848, E. Fisher Ames. He was b. in Amherst, Mass., May 10, 1822. Mrs. Electa Childs Ames d. in Conway, Mass , Aug. 11, 1850, leaving no children. Mr. Ames m. again Aug. 4, 1853, in Elizabeth, N. J., Caroline Brown. She was b. in New York, Nov. 29, 1822.

6391. ix. DAVID CHILDS, b. Nov. 11, 1830, m. Sept. 27, 1855, M. Elizabeth Ladd.

6392. x. LOIS PARSONS CHILDS, b. July 15, 1833, d. Nov. 5, 1833.

6393. xi. LOIS P. CHILDS, 2D. b. Sept. 28, 1838. m ——— Wood.

[Eighth Generation.]

6383. i. EDWARD CHILDS, eldest child of Otis and Sally Field Childs, b. in Conway, Mass. Dec. 31, 1813, m. 1st, May 6. 1841. Sarah A. Adams, who was b. Feb. 23, 1815, d. in Montreal, Canada, Oct. 14, 1850, æ 35 : m. 2d, in Northampton, Mass., May 6, 1852, Emily Porter, who was born in Chesterfield, Mass., July 18, 1814.

[Ninth Generation.]   Children:

6394. i. EDWARD ADAMS CHILDS, b. in North Adams, Mass., Sept. 9, 1842.

6395. ii. OTIS FIELD CHILDS, b. in North Adams, Mass., May 7, 1844.

6396. iii. SARAH ANN CHILDS, b. in North Adams, Oct. 6, 1847, d. in Guilford, Vt , Aug. 22, 1852.

6397. iv. MARY LUCEBA CHILDS, b. in Montreal, Canada, Nov. 11, 1849.

By second marriage.

6398. v. WALTER ALBERT CHILDS, b. in Guilford, Vt., July 3, 1854, d. Sept. 10, 1854.

6399. vi. SARAH EMILY CHILDS, b. in Toronto, Canada, Nov. 15, 1856.

[Eighth Generation.]

6384. ii. WILLIAM SULLIVAN CHILDS, second child and son of Capt. Otis and Sally Field Childs, b. in Conway, Mass., May 28, 1816, m. June 4, 1839, Lydia Frary of Whately, Mass. She was b. Mch. 4, 1820.

[Ninth Generation] Children:

6400. i. ELLEN IRENE CHILDS, b. in Conway, Mass., July 19, 1840, m. Jan. 6, 1866, Dr. James Alfred Bazin.

6401. ii. LYDIA SIGOURNEY CHILDS, b. in Whitehall, N. Y., Aug. 29, 1843, m. William B. Gifford

6402. iii. WILLIAM SULLIVAN CHILDS, JR., b. in Montreal, P. Q., Oct. 16, 1846, d. Oct 27, 1847.

6403. iv. WILLIAM FREDERICK CHILDS, b. in Montreal, P Q., Nov. 3, 1852. He resides in Victoria Ellis county, Kansas.

[Ninth Generation.]

6400. i. ELLEN IRENE CHILDS. eldest child of William Sullivan and Lydia Frary Childs, b. in Conway, Mass., July

19, 1840, m. at Montreal, P. Q., Canada, Jan. 6, 1866, Dr. James Alfred Bazin of Boston, Mass.

[Tenth Generation.] Children, born in Montreal, P. Q., Canada

6404. i. An infant daughter, b. Feb. 28, 1868, d. same day.

6405. ii. MARY IRENE BAZIN, b. Mch. 3, 1869.

6406. iii. LYDIA CAROLINE BAZIN, b. June 19, 1870.

6407. iv. ALFRED TURNER BAZIN, b. Dec. 31, 1872.

6408. v. A Son, b. Oct. 15, 1879.

[Ninth Generation.]

6401. ii. LYDIA SIGOURNEY CHILDS, second child and dau. of William Sullivan and Lydia Frary Childs, b. in Whitehall, N. Y., Aug. 29, 1843, m. Jan. 16, 1868, at Montreal, P. Q., Canada, William Benjamin Gifford of New York City. They reside in Montreal, P. Q.

[Tenth Generation.] Children, born in Montreal, P. Q.

6409. i. MIRIAM CHILDS GIFFORD, b. Oct. 23, 1868.

6410. ii. ALFRED WILLIAM GIFFORD, b. Feb. 10, 1873.

[Eighth Generation.]

6385. iii. HENRY CHILDS, third child of Otis and Sally Field Childs, b. in Conway, Mass., Jan. 28, 1818, m. 1st, Sept. 22, 1842, Mary A. Graves: m. 2d, Jan. 13, 1852, Esther L. Kinsley of Stoughton, Mass.: she d. Aug. 28, 1872: m. 3d, Feb. 18, 1874, Mary D. Phillips of Northampton, Mass. Mr. Childs is of the firm of Bridgman & Childs of Northampton, Mass., blank book manufacturers and book sellers, a connection of more than forty-five years continuance.

[Ninth Generation.] Children, born in Northampton, Mass.

By first marriage:

6411. i SARAH ELIZA CHILDS, b., Jan. 28, 1844, m Sept. 10, 1873, Herbert B. Murlless.

6412. ii. MARY LOUISA CHILDS, b. April 27, 1845, m. Jan. 18, 1869, Edward C. Crafts.

6413. iii. ALBERT BATES CHILDS, b. July 24, 1846, d. June 9, 1848.

6414. iv. ALBERT BATES CHILDS, 2D, b. Oct. 5, 1848, d Aug. 29, 1849.

By second marriage:

6415. v. ELLA KINSLEY CHILDS, b. in Oct. 26, 1852, m. Sept. 6, 1876, William Warnock.

6416. vi. EDITH DUNBAR CHILDS, b. Dec. 5, 1867.

[Ninth Generation.]

6411. i. SARAH ELIZA CHILDS, eldest child of Henry and Mary A. Graves Childs, b. in Northampton, Mass., Jan. 28, 1844, m. Sept. 10, 1873, Herbert B. Murlless of Rockville, Ct.

[Tenth Generation.] Child:

6417. i. HERBERT CHILDS MURLLESS, b. Oct. 5, 1877.

[Ninth Generation.]

6412. ii. MARY LOUISA CHILDS, second child and dau. of Henry and Mary A. Graves Childs, b. April 27, 1845, m. Jan. 28, 1869, Edward C. Crafts. He d. May 12, 1874.

[Tenth Generation.] Children:

6418. i. HARRY CLINTON CRAFTS, b. Feb. 8, 1870.

6419. ii. DAVID CHILDS CRAFTS, b. Dec. 24, 1871.

[Ninth Generation.]

6415. v. ELLA KINSLEY CHILDS, dau. of Henry and Esther L. Kinsley Childs, b. Oct. 26, 1852, m. Sept. 6, 1876, William Warnock.

[Tenth Generation.] Child:

6420. i. HENRY CHILDS WARNOCK, b. Nov. 8, 1877.

[Eighth Generation.]

6386. iv. SARAH FIELD CHILDS, fourth child and eldest dau. of Otis and Sally Field Childs, b. in Conway, Mass., Dec. 21, 1819, m. Oct. 5. 1842. Samuel W. Barber, b. in Charlemont, Mass., Sept. 28, 1812.

[Ninth Generation] Children, born in Heath, Mass.

6421. i. ALBERT CHILDS BARBER, b. Aug. 16, 1843, d. July 31, 1854, aged 11 years.

6422. ii. HENRY DWIGHT BARBER, b. Jan. 3, 1845.

6423. iii. MARY ABBIE BARBER, b. Mch. 10, 1852, d. April 17, 1852.

[Eighth Generation]

6387. v. CHARLES CHILDS, fifth child and fourth son of Otis and eldest child of Otis and Electa Clary Childs, b. in Conway, Mass., Jan. 20, 1822, m. Nov. 18, 1847, Elizabeth W. Webster. b. in Goshen, Mass., April 24, 1822. Live at Montreal, Canada.

[Ninth Generation.] Child:

6424. i. ELECTA CLARY CHILDS, b. in Conway, Mass., Sept. 29, 1850, m. Nov. 17, 1875, Wm. Stephen Patterson of Montreal, P. Q.

[Ninth Generation.]

6424. i. ELECTA CLARY CHILDS, dau. of Charles and Elizabeth Williams Webster Childs, b. in Conway, Mass., Sept. 29, 1850, m. Nov. 17, 1875, Wm. Stephen Patterson of Montreal, P. Q., Canada.

[Tenth Generation.] Children, b. in Montreal, P. Q., Canada·

6425. i. KATE ELIZABETH PATTERSON, b. Sept. 20, 1876.

6426. ii. ROBERT CHILDS PATTERSON, b. April 29, 1878.

[Eighth Generation.]

6389. vii. SILAS D. CHILDS, seventh child of Otis and second son of Otis and Electa Clary Childs. b. in Conway. Mass.,

July 19, 1826, m. in Montreal, April 11, 1850, Harriet A. Warren, b. Aug. 9, 1834, in Providence, R. I. He d. in Montreal, Canada, 1860.

[Ninth Generation.] Child:

6427. i. WILLIAM HENRY CHILDS, b. in Montreal, P. Q., Canada, June 2, 1851, m. Dec. 13, 1877, Charlotte E. Cable of New York City; is salesman in a wholesale dry-goods house in New York City.

[Eighth Generation.]

6391. ix. DAVID CHILDS, ninth child of Otis and eldest son of Otis and Lois Parsons Childs, b. Nov. 11, 1830, m. Sept. 27, 1855, M. Elizabeth Ladd. She was b. in Newbury, Vt., Dec. 21, 1830, dau. of Peabody W. and Eliza Lowell Johnson Ladd. He d. at Newbury, Vt., Dec. 22, 1863. Mrs. David Childs resides at Newbury, Vt.

[Ninth Generation.] Child:

6429. i. CHARLES EZRA CHILDS, b. Oct. 22, 1856, at Montreal, P. Q., Canada; resides at Chicopee Falls.

[Eighth Generation]

6393. xi. LOIS P. CHILDS, youngest child of Otis and Lois Parsons Childs, b. in Conway, Mass., Sept. 28, 1838, m. — Wood, and resides at Newbury, Vt.

[Ninth Generation] Children:

6430. i. WALTER WOOD.
6431. ii. ALLIE WOOD.
6432. iii. LYMAN WOOD. } TWINS. }
6433. iv. CLARENCE WOOD. }

[Seventh Generation.]

6334. iv. SILAS DICKENSON CHILDS, second son of David and Clarissa Dickenson Childs, b. in Conway, Mass., May 29, 1794, m. Roxana Parker of Utica, N. Y.

The following tribute to the memory of Mr. Childs is taken from "Historical Sketches of Presbyterianism" within the bounds of the Synod of Central New York, by Rev. Dr. Fowler:

Mr. Childs commenced a clerkship in his native place; removed to Utica in 1816. He first took a place in the dry-goods store of Stalham Williams, then went as a book-keeper to the office of Jason Parker, widely known as the proprietor of extensive stage lines. Marrying the daughter of his employer, he was admitted, together with the Hon. Theodore S. Faxton, to a partnership with him in 1820; his business associations with Mr. Faxton lasting for forty years, and their stage business till 1836. Alive to the public welfare he attended to the public interests in such stations as bank and factory, and railway directorships, and as trustee of the Female Academy and the Orphan Asylum and Cemetery Association. Upright, faithful, honorable, kind and sympathising, he was always the quiet, modest and dignified gentleman, never suffering taint or suspicion. Dropping instantly dead in a banking-room, the whole community felt the shock and shared the bereavement and grief. He made liberal donations to public institutions. Among them $30,000 endowing a professorship,* called "Childs," for Hamilton College, Clinton, N. Y., to which Mrs. Childs sympathising with her husband, added $60,000, also erecting at her own expense a beautiful chapel for the Utica cemetery.

[Seventh Generation.]

6336. vi. FRANKLIN CHILDS. sixth and youngest child of David and Clarissa Dickenson Childs, b. in Conway, Mass., June 28, 1802, m. July 24, 1825, Lurinda Field, who was b. in Conway, June 8, 1798, d. Mch. 4, 1868; m. 2d, S. Clary. He d. in Conway, Mass., Mch. 1880.

[Eighth Generation.] Children:

6434. i. JUSTUS CHILDS, b. in Conway, Mass., Sept. 11, 1832, d. July 13, 1866.

6435. ii. ELLEN L. CHILDS, b. in Williamsburg, Sept. 28, 1840.

[Fifth Generation.]

5838. viii. EXPERIENCE CHILDS, eighth child of Samuel and only dau. of his second wife, Experience — Childs, b. June 7, 1730, m. 1751, Jonathan Hoit. He d. May 7, 1813. She d. Jan. 28, 1814.

[Sixth Generation.] Children, born in Deerfield, Mass.

6436. i. CLEMENT HOIT, b. Dec. 8, 1751.

6437. ii. BETURAH HOIT, b. Feb. 18, 1753.

6438. iii. EXPERIENCE HOIT, b. Nov. 11, 1754, d. Sept. 19, 1758.

6439. iv. CEPHAS HOIT, b. Dec. 19, 1756, d. Oct. 19, 1758.

6440. v. CEPHAS HOIT, 2D, b. July 3, 1759.

6441. vi. EXPERIENCE HOIT, 2D, b. May 2, 1761, drowned Sept. 19, 1762.

6442. vii. ABIGAIL HOIT, b. Sept. 11, 1763.

6443. viii. HANNAH HOIT, b July 27, 1765.

6444. ix. EXPERIENCE F. HOIT, b. May 11, 1767.

6445. x. SARAH HOIT, b April 26, 1770.

[Fourth Generation.]

5822. iii. THOMAS CHILD, third child of Richard and Elizabeth Crocker Child, b. in Barnstable, Mass., Jan. 10, 1682, m. about 1710, Mary —.

[Fifth Generation.] Children, born in Barnstable, Mass.

6446. i. DAVID CHILD, b. July 20, 1711, m. Jan. 29, 1734, Hannah Cobb.

6447. ii. JONATHAN CHILD, b. Nov. 27, 1713, m. May 19, 1757, Thankful Howland.

6448. iii. SILAS CHILD, b. Mch. 10, 1715, and removed to Rhode Island.

6449. iv. HANNAH CHILD, b. July 29, 1720, m. Prince Taylor of Conn.

6450. v. BENJAMIN CHILD, b. Dec. 4, 1727, (Willis says 1731,) m. Rebecca —, of Portland, Maine. ("Freeman" says he m. 2d, Hannah —.)

* A professorship of Agriculture and Chemistry.*

† A very large, fine picture of Mr. Childs adorns with those of other prominent men, contributors to the fund of the college, the walls of the college library.

6451. vi. THOMAS CHILD, JR., b. Sept. 10, 1731. m. 1772, Mary Freeman.
6452. vii. MARY CHILD, b. April 1, 1733.

[Fifth Generation.]

6446. i. DAVID CHILD, eldest child of Thomas and Mary — Child, b. July 20, 1711, m. Jan. 29, 1734, Hannah Cobb.

[Sixth Generation.] Children, born in Barnstable, Mass.

6453. i. DAVID CHILD, JR., b. Feb. 7, 1735, m. April 4, 1758, Hannah Davis.
6454. ii. JONATHAN CHILD, b. Dec. 25, 1737.
6455. iii. ANNAH CHILD, b. Aug. 18, 1739.
6456. iv. ASENATH CHILD, b. Feb. 28, 1741, m. — Linnett.
6457. v. JOSIAH CHILD, b. Sept. 7, 1745, m. — Lewis of Sturgis.
6458. vi. EDWARD CHILD, b. Sept. 13, 1747, m. Mary Lathrop.

[Sixth Generation.]

6453. i. DAVID CHILD, JR., eldest child of David and Hannah Cobb Child, b. in Barnstable, Mass., Feb. 7, 1735, m April 4, 1758, Hannah Davis.

[Seventh Generation.] Children, born in Barnstable, Mass.

6459. i. SUSANNA CHILD, b. July 30, 1762.
6460. ii. ASENATH CHILD, b. Sept. 2, 1765.
6461. iii. JOB CHILD, b. Sept 8, 1767.
6462. iv. HANNAH CHILD, b. Nov. 17, 1769.
6463. v. ANNA CHILD, b. Nov. 4, 1771.
6464. vi. JOSIAH CHILD, b. Dec. 14, 1773.
6465. vii. DAVID CHILD, JR., b. July 8, 1775.
6466. viii. SHUBAEL DAVIS CHILD, b. Dec. 16, 1777.
6467. ix. BENJAMIN CHILD, b. Aug. 11, 1779.
6468. x. EDWARD CHILD, b. Mch. 9, 1783.

[Fifth Generation.]

6450. v. BENJAMIN CHILD, fifth child and fourth son of Thomas and Mary — Child, b. in Barnstable, Mass., Dec. 4, 1727, m. 1751, Rebecca — of Portland, Me., to which place he removed. "Freeman" says he m. 2d, Hannah —.

[Sixth Generation.] Children:

6469. i. THOMAS CHILD, b. Sept. 25, 1752.
6470. ii. ISAAC CHILD, b. Feb. 10, 1755.
6471. iii. REBECCA CHILD, b. Mch. 3, 1769.

[Fifth Generation.]

6451. vi. THOMAS CHILD, JR., sixth child and fifth son of Thomas and Mary — Child, b. in Barnstable, Mass., Sept. 10, 1731, m. 1772, Mary Freeman, dau. of Enoch Freeman.

Willis, in his History of Portland, Me., says:

"Thomas Child was born in Boston, Mass., in 1731; removed to Portland, Maine, 1764; entered Government service in the Custom House, in 1769, in which he continued till his death, first as "Land Waiter," "Weigher and Gauger," and as Naval officer under the Government of Massachusetts. In 1772, he married Mary Freeman, daughter of Enoch Freeman. She was b. 1752. Mr. Child died Dec. 1787, and his widow died in Boston, 1832."

[Sixth Generation.] Children:

6472. i. SUSANNA CHILD, b. Nov. 16, 1773, d. May 25, 1856.

6473. ii. THOMAS CHILD, JR., b. Sept. 8, 1775, d. young.

6474. iii. MARY CHILD, b. Sept. 15, 1776, m. David Haile.

6475. iv. ISABELLA CHILD, b. May 9, 1778.

6476. v. THOMAS CHILD, 2D., b. June 5, 1782, m. June 22, 1805, Charlotte Buckman.

[Sixth Generation.]

6476. v. THOMAS CHILD, JR., fifth and youngest child of Thomas and Mary Freeman Child, b. June 5, 1782, m. June 22, 1805, Charlotte Buckman.

[Seventh Generation.] Children:

6477. i. CHARLOTTE ANN CHILD, b. Mch. 23, 1806, m. Aug. 15, 1831 John, L. Clendenning.

6478. ii. THOMAS HAILE CHILD, b. Sept. 15, 1808, m. Nov. 24, 1846, Mrs. Almira J. Melcher Appleton.

6479. iii. CHARLES WILLIAM CHILD, b. Aug. 15, 1810, m. Jan. 19, 1832, Harriet Thaxton.

6480. iv FREDERICK CHILD, b. Jan. 11, 1813, d. Mch. 2, 1842.

6481. v. GEORGE HENRY CHILD, b. Nov. 12, 1814, d. Aug. 21, 1847.

6482. vi. EDWARD BUCKMAN CHILD, b. Sept. 21, 1817, m. Dec. 29, 1840, Ann D. Buckley.

[Seventh Generation.]

6477. i. CHARLOTTE ANN CHILD, eldest child of Thomas and Charlotte Buckman Child, b. Mch. 23, 1806, m. Aug. 15, 1831, John L. Clendenning.

[Eighth Generation.] Children:

6483. i. ELLEN PORTER CLENDENNING, b. Sept. 3, 1832.

6484. ii. CHARLOTTE SUSIE CLENDENNING, b. Feb. 26, 1835, d. Sept. 22, 1836.

6485. iii. JOHN EDWARD CLENDENNING, b. Aug. 15, 1840, d. Dec. 24, 1844.

[Seventh Generation.]

6478. ii. THOMAS HAILE CHILD, second child and eldest son of Thomas and Charlotte Buckman Child, b. Sept. 15, 1808, m. Nov. 24, 1846, Mrs. Almira Melcher Appleton.

[Eighth Generation.] Children:

6486. i. THOMAS FREDERICK CHILD, b. Oct. 6, 1847.

6487. ii. WILLIAM B. B. CHILD, b. May 6, 1851, m. Oct. 16, 1872, Clara Williams Potter.

[Eighth Generation.]

6487. ii. WILLIAM B. B. CHILD, second child of Thomas Haile and Mrs. Almira Melcher Appleton Child, b. May 6, 1851, m. Oct. 16, 1872, Clara Williams Potter.

[Ninth Generation.] Child:
  6488. i. ARTHUR WARREN CHILD, b. Oct. 22, 1873.

[Seventh Generation.]
  6479. iii. CHARLES WILLIAM CHILD, third child and second son of Thomas and Charlotte Buckman Child, b. Aug. 15, 1810, m. Jan. 19, 1832, Harriet Thaxton.
[Eighth Generation.] Children:
  6489. i. CHARLES T. CHILD, b. Nov. 8, 1833.
  6490. ii. HARRY A. CHILD, b. Mch. 6, 1838.
  6491. iii. ALBERT W. CHILD, b. Mch. 10, 1840.
  6492. iv. HARRIET LOUISA CHILD, b. 1842, d. 1844.
  6493. v. ELLA A. CHILD, b. Jan. 1, 1851.

[Seventh Generation.]
  6482. vi. EDWARD BUCKMAN CHILD, sixth child, fifth son of Thomas and Charlotte Buckman Child, b. Sept. 21, 1817, m. Dec. 29, 1846, Ann D. Buckley. He died May 26, 1869.
[Eighth Generation.] Children:
  6494. i. FRANCIS D. CHILD, b. June 24, 1842.
  6495. ii. JAMES M. B. CHILD, b. Oct. 23, 1844.

[Fourth Generation.]
  5824. v. TIMOTHY CHILDS, fifth child and third son of Richard and Elizabeth Crocker Child, b. in Barnstable, Mass., Sept. 22, 1868; removed to Deerfield, Mass., m. Nov. 26, 1719, Hannah Chapin Sheldon, dau. of Japhet Chapin and widow of John Sheldon of Deerfield. She is said to have been at the burning of Deerfield by the Indians and the French, and to have jumped from the old Indian House and sprained her ancle, and was captured and taken to Canada with other prisoners. She died Sept. 30, 1765. Timothy Childs died July 26, 1776.
[Fifth Generation.] Children, born in Deerfield, Mass:
  6496. i. TIMOTHY CHILDS, JR., b. Sep 18, 1720, m. July 12, 1744, Mary Wells.
  6497. ii. ANNA CHILDS, b. Aug. 2, 1723, m. Dec. 5, 1740, Dr. Thomas Williams.

[Fifth Generation.]
  6496. i. CAPT. TIMOTHY CHILDS, eldest child of Timothy and Hannah Chapin Sheldon Childs, b. in Deerfield, Mass., Sept. 18, 1720, m. July 12, 1744, Mary Wells. [Very much of the minutiæ of the following records, apart from its dates, is kindly furnished by Mrs. Dr. Geo. S. Boardman, great granddaughter of Capt. Timothy Childs.]
  Capt. Timothy Childs, of Deerfield, was a distinguished patriot of the Revolution. He led a company of minute men from Deerfield on receiving the news of the battle of Lexington, (Mass.) His son, Dr. Timothy Childs

of Pittsfield, Mass., was marching as Lieut. with a similar corps at the same time from Pittsfield.

[Sixth Generation.]   Children, born in Deerfield, Mass.

6498. i. TIMOTHY CHILDS, JR., d. young.

6499. ii. MARY CHILDS, b. Jan. 21, 1746.

6500. iii. TIMOTHY CHILDS, JR., 2D, b. April 9. 1748. m. Feb. 1, 1778, Rachel Easton of Pittsfield, Mass.

6501. iv. JONATHAN CHILDS, b. Nov 21, 1750.

6502. v. ELIPHAZ CHILDS, b. Oct. 1, 1752.

[Sixth Generation.]

6500. iii. DR. TIMOTHY CHILDS, third child and second son of Capt. Timothy and Mary Wells Childs, b. in Deerfield, Mass., April 9, 1748, m. Feb. 1, 1778, Rachel Easton, dau. of Col. James Easton of Pittsfield. Mass., who commanded the troops under Ethan Allen in the storming of Ticonderoga. Col. Easton sacrificed his whole fortune, with the most uncalculating patriotism, in the service of his country.   Mrs. Boardman writes :

"Dr. Timothy Childs, with his father, was in the battle of Lexington commanding a company of minute men, like his father, though but a Lieutenant, and was noted for his bravery and patriotism.   He was an ardent advocate of the people's rights, and of our Republican form of Government. During the struggle for independence he participated actively and zealously by every means in his power, to promote the views and the objects of the heroes and patriots of the Revolution.   As a physician, Dr. Timothy Childs was eminently successful and useful   As a public man he was faithful and able.   As a testimony of the people's confidence, they for many years elected him to represent them in the Legislature of Massachusetts, both in the House and in the Senate; which stations he filled to the perfect satisfaction of his friends.   He died at the age of 76, having long enjoyed the confidence and esteem of his fellow citizens.   His death was regarded as a public loss.   Dr Timothy Childs and his noble wife reared a family of eight children, five sons and three daughters, whose public record, particularly that of the five sons, has obtained an honorable eminence."

Mrs. Dr. Powers of Coldwater, Mich., a grand-daughter of Dr. Timothy and Rachel Easton Childs, and daughter of Mrs. Sophia Childs Ledyard, in a letter to her cousin, Mrs. Dr. Boardman, writes :

"I feel a great pride in my mother's family, as I recall them coming and going at the old home in Pittsfield, the years I was there; I did not take it all in then. the significance of all they said and did, but the facts made an indelible impression and as I recall them now I know that the actors were a company of superior men and women.   Grandma Childs was a woman of great pride in family and education, consequently those two points have been the foundation of my estimate of people ever since.   If money comes with them well and good, it is a great blessing, but gold makes vulgarity more vulgar, and ignorance more unbearable.   Grandpa and grandma Childs had spent their lives in contact more or less with the best stamp of New England people, and grandma had great good sense, and freshness of character, which led her into sympathy with us girls, and made her very watchful of our tendencies. I bless her dear memory every day of my life, for what she did for me, and my child also reaps the benefit of it, and so on to the generations yet to come, if so be there are any."

This charming sketch of the characters, and characteristics of one of the quiet homes of New England, and the light evermore radiating therefrom, is one more blessed fulfillment of the fifth command of the Decalogue with its unfailing, gracious promise.

[Seventh Generation.] Children, born in Pittsfield, Mass.

6503. i. PERRY G. CHILDS, b. about 1779, m. in 1807, Catharine Ledyard.

6504. ii. DAVID W. CHILDS, b. 1781, m. Susan Trowbridge of Utica, N. Y.

6505. iii. HENRY H. CHILDS, b. Jan. 7, 1783, m. Sarah Allen.

6506. iv. TIMOTHY CHILDS, b. 1785, m. Miss Dickenson.

6507. v. SOPHIA CHILDS, b. Oct. 4, 1789, m. Jan. 15, 1816, Samuel Ledyard.

6508. vi. MARY W. CHILDS, b. 1791, m. Mr. Bowers.

6509. vii. ANN CHILDS, b. 1793, d. unmarried in Pittsfield, Mass.

6510. viii. THOMAS CHILDS, b. 1796, m.—

[Seventh Generation.]

6503. i. PERRY G. CHILDS, eldest child of Dr. Timothy and Rachel Easton Childs, b. in Pittsfield, Mass., 1779, m. 1807, Catharine Ledyard, dau. of Benjamin Ledyard of Aurora, N.Y. Mrs. Boardman, the third daughter, writes:

" He was one of the most esteemed and influential citizens of Cazenovia, N. Y., in which town he settled in his early active life. He was a lawyer by profession, a man of fine talents and finished education, and as a public man he was not only esteemed in his immediate circle, but his influence was happily felt far beyond the village where he resided. His death was regarded as a public loss, which occurred in his fifty-sixth year. He left three sons and four daughters.

[Eighth Generation.] Children, born in Cazenovia, N. Y.:

6511. i. CATHARINE CHILDS, m. Augustus W. Smith.

6512. ii. HELEN CHILDS, m. Sidney L. Fairchild.

6513. iii. HENRY CHILDS, d. in Mobile, Ala., of yellow fever, 1838 or 9.

6514. iv. SOPHIA L. CHILDS, m. Rev. Geo. S. Boardman, D. D.

6515. v. JANE S. CHILDS, m. R. N. Gurtreau of Cazenovia, N. Y.

6516. vi. PERRY G. CHILDS, JR., lives in San Francisco, Cal.

6517. vii. I. D. LEDYARD CHILDS, m. Eunice L. Litchfield, Cazenovia, N.Y.

[Eighth Generation.]

6511. i. CATHARINE CHILDS, eldest child of Perry G. and Catharine Ledyard Childs, b. in Cazenovia, N. Y., m. Hon. Augustus Smith. Mr. Smith was a professor in the Naval Academy at Annapolis, Maryland, and died there in 1866.

[Ninth Generation.]   Children:

   6518. i. PERRY G. SMITH, lives in Appleton, Wis.

   6519. ii. AUGUSTUS L. SMITH, lives in Appleton, Wis.

   6520. iii. HELEN F. SMITH, is lady principal in Wells College at Aurora, New York.

   6521. iv. CATHARINE SMITH, m. Professor Hill, of the Torpedo Station, R. I.

[Eighth Generation.]

   6512. ii. HELEN CHILDS, second child of Perry G. and Catharine Ledyard Childs, b. in Cazenovia, N. Y., m. Hon. Sidney L. Fairchild, who was for several terms Attorney General of the State of New York.

[Ninth Generation.]   Children:

   6522. i. CATHARINE FAIRCHILD, m. Jno. Stebbins of Cazenovia, N. Y.

   6523. ii. SOPHIA C. FAIRCHILD.

   6524. iii. CHARLES S. FAIRCHILD, m. Helen Lincklaen of Cazenovia, N.Y.

[Eighth Generation.]

   6514. iv. SOPHIA L. CHILDS, fourth child and third dau. of of Perry G. Childs and Catharine Ledyard, m. Rev. Geo. S. Boardman, D. D.   Dr. Boardman was for many years pastor of the Presbyterian church in Cazenovia.   They have no children.

   Dr. George S. Boardman was a divine of the Presbyterian church, well known and beloved.   Born in Albany, N. Y., on the 29th Dec. 1796.   At sixteen years of age he entered Union College, Schenectady, N. Y.   When twenty-three years old he graduated from Princeton Theological Seminary, N. J., and entered at once upon the work of the ministry.   With earnest zeal for two years he labored in an evangelistic form in the States of Ohio and Indiana.   His first settlement was in Watertown, N. Y., and from various causes he was led to make several changes, at one time settled in Rochester, N. Y.   His last pastorate was in the beautiful village of Cazenovia, N. Y. A residence there of fifteen years, closed in 1865, at which time he went to Europe with his wife, returning after fourteen months absence, rested and strengthened.   Rev. Dr. Torry, Dr. Boardman's successor in Cazenovia, says of him in a memorial pamphlet, containing Dr. Boardman's last sermon preached on the 29th Dec. 1876, (his eightieth birthday):

   "His preaching has been characterized by a freshness and vigor of thought, and a fullness of intellectual strength, and an elegance and eloquence of style sometimes, and a fire of earnestness and animation in the delivery, which have been frequently spoken of as wonderful by those who have heard him."

Dr. Boardman "went home" on the 7th of February, 1877.

[Eighth Generation.]

6515. v. JANE S. CHILDS, fifth child and fourth dau. of Perry G. and Catharine Ledyard Childs, b. in Cazenovia, m. R. N. Guitreau of Cazenovia, N. Y. They reside in Farmington, Minnesota.

[Ninth Generation.] Child:

6525. i. FANNY GUITREAU, m. a Mr. Wood of St. Paul, Minn.

[Eighth Generation.

6517. vii. I. D. LEDYARD CHILDS, seventh child and third son of Perry G. and Catharine Ledyard Childs, m. Eunice L. Litchfield of Cazenovia, N. Y. He d. in Litchfield, Ill., about 1859.

[Ninth Generation.] Child:

6526. i. PERRY G. CHILDS, lives in Cazenovia, N. Y.

[Seventh Generation.]

6504. ii. DAVID WELLS CHILDS, second child and son of Dr. Timothy and Rachel Easton Childs, b. in Pittsfield, Mass., 1781, m. Susan Trowbridge. For the following interesting history of Mr. Childs we are indebted to Dr. Bagg's "Pioneers of Utica":

"David Wells Childs, son of Dr. Timothy of Pittsfield, Mass., was born 1781. Was graduated at Williams College in 1800. Four years later he established himself in law in Utica, N. Y. Was clerk of the first board of trustees of the village. Director of the Bank of Utica, 1812; bank's attorney and notary public. His profession and other business secured for him much wealth. He was an extensive real estate owner in the village. His residence was on Whitesboro street, now occupied by John F. Seymour, Esq. He was a man highly esteemed for his integrity and liberality. He died July 27, 1826, of consumption. By his will, provisions were made for legacies to the following institutions: $250 to the Utica Sunday School; legacies to Auburn Theological Seminary, Western Education Society, and American Bible Society, $500 each. His wife died Dec. 14, 1820."

[Eighth Generation.] Children, born in Utica, N. Y.

6527. i. RACHEL CHILDS, b. —; m. Bushrod Burch. Mr. Burch is in Treasury Department, Washington.

6528. ii. SARAH CHILDS.

6529. iii. MARY CHILDS.

6530. iv. SUSAN CHILDS, b. —; m. Mr. Blackburn, Rock Island, Ill.

6531. v. Name not ascertained.

[Seventh Generation.]

6505. iii. DOCTOR HENRY H. CHILDS, third child and third son of Dr. Timothy and Mary Easton Childs, b. in Pittsfield, Mass., Jan. 7, 1783, m. Sarah Allen of Pittsfield, Mass. He died 1868. "He graduated at Williams College, Mass., 1802.

Entered the medical profession, and became eminent as a physician distinguished in medical science, and was the founder of Berkshire, Mass., Medical Institute, which became a college in 1837, in which he was professor of the theory and practice of medicine and president until 1863 He was a Jeffersonian Democrat. In the affairs of State he was justly influential, and promoted to official positions where statesmanship and patriotism were essential qualifications : having served in the legislative halls of Massachusetts and once filled the office of Lieut.-Governor. He had several children but all died before him except Mrs. Elias Merwin of Boston, Mass." (*See Dict. of Am. Biog. page* 183.

[Eighth Generation.] Child.

6531*a*. i. MRS. ELIAS MERWIN, Boston, Mass.

6507. v. SOPHIA CHILDS, eldest dau. of Doctor Timothy and Mary Easton Childs, b. in Pittsfield, Mass., Oct. 4, 1789, m. Jan. 15, 1816, Samuel Ledyard, who was born Jan. 29, 1782. Mr. Ledyard died at Pultneyville, N. Y., Nov. 27, 1866. Mrs. Sophia Childs Ledyard brought to her Western home the refinement and culture of New England's best, and reared her large family in the love of things noble and true, and now (1881) the harvest of her early cares and love is returned to her in the affectionate devotion of her children and grand-children. More than fourscore years and ten have been allotted her, yet she awaits the lengthening of the shadows in sweet peace.

[Eighth Generation] Children :

6532. i. RACHEL CHILDS LEDYARD, b. Dec. 10, 1816, m. Oct. 4, 1837, Lysander B. Wilcox.

6533. ii. BENJAMIN LEDYARD, b. April 27, 1819.

6534. iii. SAMUEL FOREMAN LEDYARD, b. Feb. 27, 1821, m April 10, 1850, Virginia Hunter.

6535. iv. TIMOTHY CHILDS LEDYARD, b. Aug. 3, 1822, m. June 22, 1848, Jane A. Bell.

6536. v. JOHN HENRY LEDYARD, b. May 17, 1824, m. Dec. 26, 1859, Lizzie M. Field.

6537. vi. T. SCOTT LEDYARD, b. June 12, 1827, m. 1st, Oct. 12, 1852, Augusta Todd; m. 2d, Sept. 10, 1861, Ellen M. Nichols.

6538. vii. MARGARET CUYLER LEDYARD, b. June 14, 1830, m. June 1850, Dr. David C. Powers.

6539. viii. GLEN CUYLER LEDYARD, b. June 21, 1834.

[Eighth Generation]

6532. i. RACHEL CHILDS LEDYARD, eldest child of Sophia Childs and Samuel Ledyard, b. Dec. 10, 1816, m. Oct. 4, 1837, Lysander B. Wilcox of New York.

[Ninth Generation.] Children:
6540. i. LEDYARD WILCOX.
6541. ii. HORATIO THROOP WILCOX.
6542. iii. SOPHIA CHILDS WILCOX.
6543. iv. WILLIAM J. WILCOX.
6544. v. JENNIE LEDYARD WILCOX.

[Eighth Generation.]
6534. iii. SAMUEL FOREMAN LEDYARD, third child and second son of Sophia Childs and Samuel Ledyard, b. Feb. 27, 1821, m. April 10, 1850, Virginia Hunter of Virginia.
[Ninth Generation.] Children:
6545. i. HUNTER P. LEDYARD.
6546. ii VIRGINIA CHILDS LEDYARD.

[Eighth Generation]
6535. iv. TIMOTHY CHILDS LEDYARD, fourth child and third son of Sophia Childs and Samuel Ledyard. b. Aug. 3, 1822, m. June 22, 1848, Jane A. Bell of Pa.
[Ninth Generation.] Children:
6547. i. HENRY CHILDS LEDYARD.
6548. ii. HELEN K. LEDYARD.
6549. iii. FRANK BELL LEDYARD.
6550. iv. MARY LEDYARD.

[Eighth Generation]
6536. v. JOHN HENRY LEDYARD, fifth child and fourth son of Sophia Childs and Samuel Ledyard, b. May 17, 1824, m. Dec. 26, 1859, Lizzie M. Field of Mass.
[Ninth Generation.] Child:
6551. i. HENRY FIELD LEDYARD.

[Eighth Generation]
6537. vi. T. SCOTT LEDYARD, sixth child and fifth son of Sophia Childs and Samuel Ledyard. b. June 12, 1827, m. 1st, Oct. 12. 1852. Augusta P. Todd : m. 2d, Sept. 10, 1861, Ellen M. Nichols of New York.
[Ninth Generation.] Children:
6552. i. GRACE LEDYARD.
6553. ii. MAUD LEDYARD.
6554. iii. FRED CHILDS LEDYARD.

[Eighth Generation.]
6538. vii. MARGARET CUYLER LEDYARD, seventh child and second dau. of Sophia Childs and Samuel Ledyard, b. June 14, 1830, m. June 1850, Dr. David Cooper Powers.

Mrs. M. C. L. Powers was educated at one of the best schools in New England, in Pittsfield, Mass., residing at the time in the family of her grandmother, Mrs. Dr. Timothy Childs, a woman

X-1

of most noble nature and admirably qualified to guide, and
elevate those with whom she was associated. To the wise and
loving counsels, and beautiful daily life of her grandmother,
Mrs. Powers delights to attribute her best ambitions and
noblest qualities. Dr. David Cooper Powers is a native of
Croydon, Sullivan county, N. H.; his grandfather David
Powers, was one of four brothers who removed from Massachusetts to New Hampshire in 1766. The Cooper family was
also a leading one in the same town, and from each family
there are found individuals taking prominent parts in the Revolutionary struggle. The Powers family were characterized
by giant frames, great physical strength and vigorous intellects.
Mr. Powers' father removed to the State of New York in 1830,
and settled in Cayuga county. At the Cayuga Academy,
Auburn N. Y., Dr. Powers was educated. He read medicine
in the office of his brother-in-law, Dr. Nathaniel Leavitt, and
graduated at the Berkshire Medical College, Pittsfield, Mass.,
in 1848. The years 1848 and '49 he spent in California: in
1850 he returned and resided in Auburn, N. Y., but in 1853
went again to the Pacific coast for two years. In 1855-6 he
settled in Coldwater, Mich., where he yet resides in the lucrative practice of his profession. At the period of the late war,
he was enrolled, as a surgeon attached to Loomis Battery, and
was in active service for three years in the field or in charge of
hospitals in the army of the Cumberland at Huntsville and
Nashville, Tenn. Devoted to his profession, Dr. Powers has
found little time for public affairs, but for some years has been
a director of the Southern Michigan National Bank, and for a
much longer time a member of the Board of Education, for
three years mayor of the city. Always interested for public
improvements and actively zealous in word and deed in the
support of church interests. He is held in high esteem by the
medical fraternity and his patrons for his skill and caution,
and regarded by the community as a most honorable and high
minded citizen.

[Ninth Generation.] Children:

6555. i. MARY L. POWERS, died.
6556. ii. SOPHIA CHILDS POWERS, died.
6557. iii HELEN LEDYARD POWERS.

[Seventh Generation.]

6506. iv. TIMOTHY CHILDS, fourth son of Dr. Timothy and Mary Easton Childs, b. in Pittsfield, Mass., 1785. m. Miss Dickenson. Settled as a lawyer in Rochester, N. Y. He was a man of much culture, and successful in his profession. He represented his district one or more sessions in U. S. Congress, also held the office of judge. A man of great integrity and usefulness. He left no children. (See *Dict. Am. Biog.*)

[Seventh Generation.]

6510. viii. GENERAL THOMAS CHILDS. son of Dr. Timothy and Mary Easton Childs, b. in Pittsfield, Mass., 1796, m Jan. 5, 1819, Ann Eliza Coryton, only child of Josiah and Catharine Coryton of Alexandria, Va. He died Oct. 8, 1853, a 57. General Thomas Childs has a brilliant army record which has been furnished to us by his daughter, Mrs. General Woodbury, as also that of her husband, as found in General Geo. W. Cullum's "Lives of Officers of the Army:"

" Major Childs was cadeted in the war of 1812 with Great Britain, in the campaign of 1814. On the Niagara frontier, engaged in the capture of Fort Erie; afterwards in the defence of Fort Erie until the siege was raised by the successful sortie from it Sept. 17, 1814, for which a brass quadrant, captured from a gun by him, was presented to him by Government, in the Florida war, 1836-42. Made Brevet Major Aug. 21, 1836, for planning the attack on the Indians at Fort Drane, Florida, and good conduct in that affair. Made Brevet Lieutenant Colonel Feb. 1, 1841, for gallant conduct and repeated successes in the war against the Florida Indians. Was Colonel of the artillery batallion in the military occupation of Texas, the " Army of Occupation" as it was called, from 1845 to 1847. In the war with Mexico was made Brevet Colonel May 9, 1846, for gallant conduct in the battles of Palo Alto and Resaca de la Palma; was in the battle of Monterey, Sept. 21; siege of Vera Cruz, Mch. 9, 1847; battle of Cerro Gordo, April 17, 1867; skirmish of La Hoya June 20; defence of Peubla where he commanded from Sept. 13, to Oct. 12. Military Governor of Jolapa, Made Brevet Brigadier General Oct. 12, 1847, for gallant and meritorious conduct in the defence of Peubla, Mexico; was General commanding in the military operations in East Florida, where he died Oct. 8, 1853."

Of nine children of General Thomas Childs three only lived to adult age.

[Eighth Generation.] Children:

6558. i. CATHARINE RACHEL CHILDS, b. —; m. Dec. 22, 1845, General P. Woodbury.

6559. ii. FREDERICK LYNN CHILDS, b. —; m. June 12, 1856, Mary Hooper Anderson.

6560. iii. MARY VIRGINIA CHILDS, b. —; m. Dec. 27, 1855, Dr. Wm. W. Anderson.

[Eighth Generation.]

6558. i. CATHARINE RACHEL CHILDS, dau. of General Thomas and Ann Eliza Coryton Childs, b. —, m. Dec. 12, 1845, at Southville, N. C., Gen'l Daniel P. Woodbury, U. S. Corps of Engineers. He d. at Key West, Florida, of yellow fever, while in command of the department of Key West and Tortugas, Aug. 15, 1864, aged 52 years.

"General Woodbury graduated at West Point, and was appointed a First Lieut. in the Corps of Engineers, July 7, 1838. Served as assistant engineer in the construction of the defence of Washington, 1861–'62. Participated in the Manassas campaign, making important reconnoissance in which was based the order of battle of Bull Run, which led Colonel Hunter's column to pass the enemy's left flank. In the Virginia Peninsula campaign, also in command of the Engineer Brigade, participating in the siege of Yorktown April and May, 1862, and in the subsequent operations of the campaign in the construction of roads, field works and bridges, particularly for the passage of the army in its immense trains over the Chickahominy river, White Oak Swamp, and on the retreat to Harrisons Landing. Made Brevet Colonel July 1, 1862, for gallant and meritorious services during the Peninsula campaign. He was engaged in the battle of Fredericksburg, in throwing pontoon bridges for the advance and retreat of the army of the Potomac across the Rappahannock. He was made Brevet Brig. General Dec. 13, 1862, for gallant and meritorious services at the battle of Fredericksburg, Va. He had command of the troops in the district of Key West and Tortugas. Promoted Brevet Major General for gallant and meritorious services during the Rebellion. General Woodbury was the author of a work on Sustaining Walls, 1845, and on the Theory of the Arch, in 1858. Died Aug. 15, 1864, aged 52 years."

[Ninth Generation.] Children:

6561. i. ANN ELIZA WOODBURY, m. May 30, 1866, Gerardus H. Wynkoop, M. D.

6562. ii. THOMAS CHILDS WOODBURY, Lieut. U. S. army

6563. iii. CORYTON MESSENGER WOODBURY, m June 26, 1879, Mary S. Nicoll, dau. of William Nicoll, Esq., Islip, L. I., New York.

6564. iv. KATE DEROSSER WOODBURY.

[Ninth Generation.]

6561. i. ANN ELIZA WOODBURY, eldest child of Catharine Rachel Child and Gen. Daniel P. Woodbury, m. May 30, 1866, Gerardus H. Wynkoop, M. D., of New York City.

[Tenth Generation.] Children:

6565. i. GERARDUS WYNKOOP, d. young.

6566. ii. GERARDUS WYNKOOP, 2D.

6567. iii. KATE WYNKOOP.

6568. iv. DANIEL WYNKOOP.

6569. v. ELIZABETH HELLIS WYNKOOP.

[Eighth Generation.]

6559. ii. FREDERICK LYNN CHILDS, second child and only surviving son of Gen'l Thomas and Ann Eliza Coryton Childs, m. June 12, 1856, Mary Hooper Anderson, dau. of W. W. Anderson of Stateburg, S. C.

[Ninth Generation.] Children:

6570. i. WILLIAM WALLACE CHILDS.
6571. ii. ANNIE CORYTON CHILDS.
6572. iii. THOMAS CHILDS.
6573. iv. MARY McKENZIE CHILDS.

[Eighth Generation.]

6560. iii. MARY VIRGINIA CHILDS, youngest child of General Thomas and Ann Eliza Coryton Childs, m. Dec. 27, 1855, Dr. William W. Anderson of the U. S. army.

[Ninth Generation.] Children:

6574. i. ELIZABETH WATERS ANDERSON.
6575. ii. ANN CATHARINE ANDERSON.
6576. iii. WILLIAM WALLACE ANDERSON.
6577. iv. MARY VIRGINIA ANDERSON.
6578. v. BENJAMIN MACKENZIE ANDERSON.

[Fourth Generation.]

6497. ii. ANNA CHILDS, second child of Timothy and Hannah Sheldon Childs, b. in Deerfield, Mass., Aug. 2, 1723, m. Dec. 5, 1740, Dr. Thomas Williams.

Dr. Williams was born at Newton, Mass., April 10, 1718. He received the honorary degree of Master of Arts from Yale College, about the year of 1737. Studied medicine with Dr. Wheat of Boston; settled in Deerfield, Mass., as surgeon and physician, about the year 1739. (See the Williams Genealogy.) Dr. Thomas Williams was a brother of Col. Ephraim Williams, Jr., the founder of Williams College, and brother to Abigail Williams, whose first husband was Rev. John Sargeant, and whose second husband was Gen'l Joseph Dwight, father of Col. Elijah Dwight. Mrs. Ann Childs Williams d. May 17, 1746.

[Fifth Generation.] Children, born in Deerfield, Mass.

6580. i. ELIZABETH WILLIAMS, b. Aug. 25, 1741, m. Dr. Lemuel Barnard, at Sunderland, Mass., Nov. 25, 1804.
6581. ii. ANNA WILLIAMS, b. Sept. 16, 1743, m. Elijah Dwight, Esq.
6582 iii. THOMAS WILLIAMS, b. May 5, 1746, d. July 10, 1776.

[Fifth Generation.]

6581. ANNA WILLIAMS, second child of Anna Childs and Dr. Thomas Williams, b. in Deerfield, Mass., Sept. 16, 1743,

m. Col. Elijah Dwight of Gt. Barrington, Mass. Col. Dwight
was the son of Gen'l Joseph Dwight and Mary Pynchon. He
was first Clerk of Court for the county of Berkshire, and later
Judge of the Court of Common Pleas. At the early age of
eighteen, he was lieut. of his father's brigade, sent to reduce
Ticonderoga in 1758. He died at Brookfield, June 12, 1794,
on his way to Boston. Mrs. Anna Williams Dwight sustained
the character of a highly sensible and religious woman. Active,
universal benevolence was one of her characteristics. She died
Feb. 21, 1710, at Deerfield, Mass. [Of the nine children given
them only four survived more than a few hours. Commencing
with the sixth child.]

[Sixth Generation.]   Children, born in Gt. Barrington, Mass.

6583. vi. ELIJAH DWIGHT, b. Jan 12, 1778, d. May 28, 1788.

6584. vii HORACE DWIGHT, b. Sept. 13, 1780, d. Dec. 25, 1780.

6585. viii THOMAS DWIGHT, b. June 22, 1782, d. Oct. 4, 1782.

6586. ix COL. JOSEPH DWIGHT, b. Sept. 13, 1785, m. Oct. 29, 1814, Catha-
rine Clark, dau. of Rev. Henry Clark of Brookfield, Madison county, N. Y.
He left his property to the Roman Catholic church. He resided in Utica.
(*See Dwight's Genealogy*)

[Fourth Generation.]

5825. vi. DEACON EBENEZER CHILD, sixth child and fourth
son of Richard and Elizabeth Crocker Child, b. in Barnstable,
Mass., Mch. 1691, m. about 1719, Hope —.

[Fifth Generation]   Children:

6587. i. ELIZABETH CHILD, b. in Barnstable, Mass., July 18 1720, d.
Sept. 18, 1720.

6588. ii EBENEZER CHILD, JR., b. in Barnstable, Mass., April 10, 1723,
m. 1st, Jan. 15, 1746, Hannah Crocker; m. 2d, Abigail Freeman.

6589. iii. RACHEL CHILD

6590. iv. MARY CHILD.

6591. v. MERCY CHILD.

[Fifth Generation.]

6588. ii. EBENEZER CHILD, second child and eldest son of
Dea. Ebenezer and Hope Child, b. in Barnstable, Mass., April
10, 1723, m. 1st, Jan. 15, 1746, Hannah Crocker; she d. Feb.
25, 1755; m. 2d, Abigail Freeman.

[Sixth Generation.] Children, born in Barnstable, Mass.

6592. i EBENEZER CHILD, JR., b. Nov. 3, 1747.

6593. ii JOSEPH CHILD, b. Aug. 8, 1749.

6594. iii. HANNAH CHILD, b. Sept. 10, 1751.

6595. iv DAVID CHILD, b. Mch. 2, 1754.

6596. v. JONATHAN CHILD, b. May 13, 1757.

6597. vi. ABIGAIL CHILD, b. Dec. 26, 1758.

6598. vii. HOPE CHILD, b. Jan. 21, 1761.

[Fourth Generation.]

5827. viii JAMES CHILD, eighth child and fifth son of Richard and Elizabeth Crocker Child, b. in Barnstable, Mass., Nov. 6, 1694, m. Sept. 27, 1722, Elizabeth Crocker.

[Fifth Generation.] Children, born in Barnstable, Mass.:

6599 i. SAMUEL CHILD, b. July 15, 1723.

6600. ii. JAMES CHILD, JR., b June 5, 1755, m. April 22, 1725, Mary Parker.

6601. iii. ELIZABETH CHILD, b. Dec. 20, 1730, m. May 29, 1748, Daniel Crocker.

6602 iv. SARAH CHILD, b. April 9, 1736, m. May 2, 1754, Jonathan Crocker.

6603. v. THANKFUL CHILD, b. Aug. 4, 1741, m. Mch. 27, 1760, Joseph Lawrence.

6604. vi. RICHARD CHILD, b. Mch. 22, 1743, m Mary —. He d. 1808.

[Fourth Generation.]

5829. x. JOSEPH CHILD, tenth child and sixth son of Richard and Elizabeth Crocker Child, b. in Barnstable, Mass., Mch. 5, 1699, m. April 23, 1723, Deliverance Hamblin.

[Fifth Generation.] Children, born in Barnstable, Mass.:

6605. i. JOSEPH CHILD, JR., b. Aug. 17, 1724.

6606. ii. JAMES CHILD, b. Mch. 4, 17—.

[Sixth Generation] can be found in the town
the records. One child of Samuel & 1723
as above, had wife Mary (widow of
James Berkeley) whom he m. Feb. 1, 1752.
Children were

[Seventh Generation] Samuel b. July 1, 1758.
Elijah b. Oct 24, 1762. Ebenezer Jun 18, 1766.

ELC

CHAPTER XI.

REUBEN CHILDS AND DESCENDANTS.

Unfortunately the connecting link of this branch, between Reuben Childs, its known head and his emigrant ancestor has been lost. Much effort has been made to trace this line, by members of it and by ourselves; the impression has prevailed in the family that they were of the Deerfield line or Barnstable branch, as we term it. We have procured an accredited transcript of the Deerfield, Mass., town-records, as relating to the Childs name, but we fail to find there the birth or parentage of the Reuben Childs whose descendants we here give. It is quite possible that this family may belong to what we term the Watertown branch : there were those in this line (Watertown) who would have been contemporary with the father of said Reuben Childs, who married, but whose descendants we fail to trace. It is known that members of these families moved into the middle and western counties of Massachusetts and made new settlements ; another coincident is found in the fact that some of the Watertown families, like the Deerfield, added the terminal "s." We give these incidents as possible clues. We have linked many living members by following clues as slight.

6607. REUBEN CHILDS, (father unknown) m. about 1780, Thankful Bliss. He was a soldier in the Revolutionary army. Was at the battle of Bunker Hill, and also in the expedition to Ticondaroga, 1776 or '77. We place him in the fifth generation.

[Sixth Generation.] Children:
  6608. i. SETH CHILDS, m. Emily Kneeland.
  6609 ii. JOSHUA CHILDS, b. Nov. 29, 1784, m. Jan. 30, 1810 Susan King.
  6610. iii. SOPHIA CHILDS, unmarried.
  6611. iv. DENNIS CHILDS, m. Clarence Keyes.
  6612. v. HORACE BLISS CHILDS, m. Mary Clark Jenney.
  6613. vi. SYLVESTER CHILDS, m. Mary Keyes.
  6614. vii. THANKFUL CHILDS, m. Oliver Smith.

[Sixth Generation.]

  6609. ii. JOSHUA CHILDS, second child and son of Reuben and Thankful Bliss Childs, b. Nov. 29, 1784, m. Jan. 30, 1810,

Susan King, dau. of Asaph and Mary Robbins King. She was b. in Wilbraham, Mass., April 14, 1789, d. Mch. 25, 1872. Mr. Childs d. in Springfield, Mass., Mch. 28, 1847.

[Seventh Generation.] Children:

6615 i OTIS CHILDS, b. in Wilbraham, Mass., Mch. 19, 1811, m. Feb. 14, 1838, Abby Holman.

6616. ii. MARY KING CHILDS, b. in Wilbraham, Mass., Mch. 10, 1813, m. Oct. 3, 1833, Hon. Walter Lowrie.

6617. iii. CHARLES CHILDS, b. in Springfield, Mass., Mch. 25, 1815, m. 1st. Nov. 13, 1838, Hannah Loomis, at Pompey, N. Y.; m. 2d, Catharine J. McCaslin, at Beloue, Nebraska. Reside at Omaha, Nebraska.

6618. iv. SUSAN K. CHILDS, b. in Springfield, Mass., Dec. 8, 1816, m. Oct. 18, 1838, Joseph Ingle.

6619. v. ASAPH KING CHILDS, b. in Springfield, Mass., Dec. 9, 1820, m. Jan. 17, 1856, Susan Ingle.

6620. vi. THOMAS SPENCER CHILDS b. in Springfield, Mass., Jan. 19, 1825, m. 1st. Mch. 7, 1855, Mary E. Porter; m. 2d, Aug. 24, 1864, Jane Lawrence Perkins.

[Seventh Generation.]

6615. i. OTIS CHILDS, eldest child of Joshua and Susan King Childs, b. at Wilbraham, Mass., Mch. 19, 1811, m. Abby Holman, dau. of Samuel and Mary Warriner Holman of Springfield, Mass. She was born in Wilmington, Vt., Dec. 7, 1813, d. Sept. 23, 1879. Mr. Childs is a jeweller and resides at Newton, Mass.

[Eighth Generation.] Children:

6621. i. MARY LOWRIE CHILDS, b. at Milledgeville, Ga., Oct. 11, 1841, d. at Wilbraham, Mass., Sept. 19, 1848.

6622. ii. NELLY SARGEANT CHILDS, b at Milledgeville, Ga., May 21, 1843, m. Oct. 16, 1867, Thomas Weston, Jr.

6623. iii. ELIZABETH DELANCY CHILDS, b at Milledgeville. Ga., Nov. 13, 1845, d. at Milledgeville, Ga., Sept. 26, 1847.

6624. iv. EDWIN OTIS CHILDS, b. at Milledgeville, Ga., Sept. 29, 1847, m June 25, 1874, Caroline A. Chaflin

6625. v. CHARLOTTE CLIFFORD CHILDS, b. at Springfield, Mass., May 24, 1850, d. at Springfield, Aug. 1, 1851.

6626. vi. CLARA HAMILTON CHILDS, b at Springfield, Mass., Feb. 6, 1852.

6627. vii. ANNA CLIFFORD CHILDS, b. at Springfield, Mass., Mch. 11, 1854, d. Aug. 14, 1854.

6628. viii. RALPH WARRINER CHILDS, b. at Springfield, Mass., Aug. 29, 1855, merchant in Springfield, Mass.

[Eighth Generation.]

6622. ii. NELLY SARGEANT CHILDS, second child and dau. of Otis and Abby Holman Childs, b. at Milledgeville, Ga., May 21, 1843, m. Oct. 16, 1867, Thomas Weston, Jr., son of Thomas and Thalia Weston of Boston, Mass. Mr. Weston is a lawyer and resides in Newton, Mass.

[Ninth Generation.] Children:
6629. i. GRACE WESTON, b. at Springfield, Mass., May 15, 1870.
6630. ii. ABBY CHILDS WESTON, b. at Newton, Mass., July 21, 1873.
6631. iii THOMAS WESTON, JR., b. at Newton, Mass., Aug 12, 1875.

[Eighth Generation.]

6624. iv. EDWIN OTIS CHILDS, fourth child and eldest son of Otis and Abby Hohman Childs, b. at Milledgeville, Ga., Sept. 29, 1847, m. at Newton, Mass., June 25, 1874, Caroline A. Chaffin, dau. of Edwin and Caroline A. (Gore) Chaffin of Newton, Mass. Mr. Childs is City Clerk.

[Ninth Generation.] Children, born in Newton, Mass.
6632. i. MARY CHAFFIN CHILDS, b June 19, 1875.
6633. ii. EDWIN OTIS CHILDS, JR., b Aug. 10, 1876.
6634. iii. CARRIE HELFENSTINE CHILDS, b. Nov. 22, 1878.

[Seventh Generation.]

6616. ii. MARY KING CHILDS, second child and eldest dau. of Joshua and Susan King Childs, b. in Wilbraham, Mass., Meh. 10, 1813, m. Oct. 3, 1833, Hon. Walter Lowrie, second son of John and Catharine Cameron Lowrie. Mrs. Mary King Childs Lowrie was born in the home of her maternal ancestry, with the very beautiful scenery of the Connecticut valley to educate her budding powers, and with like surroundings she grew to womanhood. Her father's home was in Springfield, Mass. With most helpful moral and intellectual atmosphere she attained an early and gracious maturity. At the age of fifteen she opened a private school and was so manifestly gifted as an instructor, that three years later she was called to the charge of a select school in Washington, D. C. In the metropolis she met Dr. Lowrie and became his wife and the very conscientious, loving mother of his children, winning their hearts and training them with fond tenderness; they ever reverenced her. Mrs. Lowrie was of strong affections, and intense inner life; her early religious training developed a rarely symmetrical character, and it is difficult to specify excellencies, where the harmony was so entire. Thoroughly united with Mr. Lowrie in his very single-eyed devotion to the Master's service, she very cordially and quietly accepted the self-denials brought upon her thereby. Upon the removal to New York City, the home of Mr. and Mrs. Lowrie became the headquarters of the missionaries, whether en-route to the distant homes with hopeful zeal, or returning, worn with toils and discouragements.

A thoroughly ordered household, where a wise economy rendered possible a generous hospitality, was the result of Mrs. Lowrie's systematic mind ; her equable temper and genial spirit made a sunny home. The correspondence of Mrs. Lowrie with the sons in the mission fields, has furnished not only a story of their experiences otherwise unknown, but most sweet expression of their fond love and reverence for her. Mrs Lowrie made time also for numerous interests outside the home ; she was for years the accurate and efficient treasurer of " The House of Industry ;" and much interested in the establishment of the Presbyterian Home for Aged Women. The services of the Sabbath were deemed a privilege not to be easily relinquished. One writes : " In the winter of her last sickness this seemed to me a weekly miracle. She received strength to dress and walk to church by half past ten, while every other day she was overcome by sleep until about eleven." Very earnestly she prayed for strength to care for her husband through his life, and it was given her. The disease which had been for years subtilely undermining her powers was stayed until her loved husband was taken home ; then it overpowered her and she sank speedily. During these last months she was in the home of her brother Rev. Thomas S. Childs, D. D. of Norwalk. Ct., (now of Wooster, Ohio) the sweet trust and hope of her life was darkened ; and for a time she was filled with doubts, but at " evening time it was light," and the loving friends watched her quietly enter into peace. We gather these facts from an interesting memorial prepared for private distribution, and sent us by Dr. Thomas S. Childs, the brother of Mrs. Lowrie, in whose home she spent the last months of life. The accompanying sketch of her husband is sent to us by Mr. Walter C. Childs of San Francisco, Cal.

Hon. Walter Lowrie was the second son of John and Catherine Cameron Lowrie, and was born in Edinburgh, Scotland, Dec. 10, 1784 ; came to America in his ninth year. He first married Miss Amelia McPherrin of Butler, Pa. ; second marriage to Miss Mary King Childs. During his early years he manifested a most earnest love of study ; his attainments were not confined to the English branches, he made the study of Latin, Greek and Hebrew a delight, and in later years was versed in the Chinese language. He designed to enter the ministry but was by circumstances kept in secular life.

From a memorial address by the Rev. Wm. M. Paxton of New York City, we extract:

"His life was such as to win the confidence and esteem of the community in which he lived. In 1811, at the age of twenty-seven, he was elected representative to the Legislature of Pennsylvania, a position he held for seven years. During this time he so rose in the confidence of the people that in 1818 he was made United States Senator for six years. This was a period of great interest in the history of our country from the importance of the measures agitated and the great men who guided the councils of the nation. Webster, Clay, Calhoun, Randolph, Benton and others, only less illustrious, were members of the Senate. Among these distinguished statesmen Walter Lowrie occupied a position of honorable prominence. I am informed by one who was present at that time, that he was regarded by the Senators who knew him best, as an authority upon all questions of political history and constitutional law. During the discussion of the Missouri compromise he made a speech which is described as of great power and force of argument, in which he took strong grounds against the extension of slavery, and uttered his protest against the establishment of slave labor upon a single foot of free territory. Upon the expiration of his term as Senator, he was elected secretary of the U. S Senate; in this office he continued twelve years. He had but two predecessors in office, each continued till death. Very much surprised, therefore, were the friends of Hon. Mr. Lowrie to learn of his resignation in 1836. His reason for so doing was that he might devote his life to the cause of missions, which he thenceforth served with untiring zeal and self-sacrifice, giving to it his time, his means, and his sons. Hon. Walter Lowrie died Dec. 14, 1868, aged 84. His eldest son, Dr. John C. Lowrie, labored in India His third son, Rev. Walter M. Lowrie, entered the field in China, where he lost his life at the hands of Chinese pirates, Aug. 18, 1847. He was regarded a man of fine talents, and an accomplished scholar. The fourth son, Rev. Reuben Lowrie, succeeded his brother in China, but after six years fell a victim to the climate.

Rev. Dr. John C. Lowrie returned from India and was his father's successor in the secretaryship of the Presbyterian Board of Missions; a post the father had most efficiently filled for thirty years."

[Seventh Generation.]

6618. iv. SUSAN K. CHILDS, fourth child and second dau. of Joshua and Susan King Childs, b. in Springfield, Mass., Dec. 8, 1816, m. Oct. 18, 1838, Joseph Ingle of Washington, D. C. She d. at Washington, D. C., Sept. 14, 1855.

[Eighth Generation.] Children:

6635. i. EDWARD H. INGLE.
6636. ii. SUSAN INGLE, died.
6637. iii. MARY P INGLE, died.
6638. iv. JOSEPH LOWRIE INGLE.

We were unable to obtain dates of birth of these children. Edward H. Ingle is an Episcopal clergyman in Athens, Ga. Joseph Lowrie Ingle is a physician in Baltimore, Md.

[Seventh Generation.]

6619. v. ASAPH KING CHILDS, fifth child and third son of Joshua and Susan King Childs, b. in Springfield, Mass., Dec. 9, 1820, m. Jan. 17, 1856, in Christ church, Washington, D. C., Susan B. Ingle, dau. of John P. Ingle of Washington, D. C.

Mr. Childs left his native place in early youth and went to Milledgeville Ga., where he spent ten years as clerk in a jewelry store. In 1846, he went to Athens, Ga., and commenced business for himself. Here he was prosperous and accumulated a handsome property, but the civil war swept nearly all away. At the close of the war, in 1864, he established himself in business again in the hardware trade. For the last five years he has held the office of president of the Northeastern Railroad of Georgia. His residence is Athens, Ga.

[Eighth Generation.] Children, born in Athens, Ga.

6639 i. FANNIE INGLE CHILDS, b. Oct. 18, 1857, m. Feb. 5, 1879, Prof. David C. Barrow, Jr.

6640 ii. WALTER LOWRIE CHILDS, b. June 29, 1859

6641 iii SUSAN KING CHILDS, b. Nov. 9, 1866, d. in Washington, D. C., June 2, 1872.

[Seventh Generation.]

6620. vi. REV. THOMAS SPENCER CHILDS, D. D., sixth child and fourth son of Joshua and Susan King Childs, b. in Springfield, Mass., Jan. 19, 1825, m. 1st, Mch. 7, 1855, in Hartford, Ct., Mary E. Porter, dau. of Haynes Lord Porter, a descendant of Gov. Haynes, the first Governor of Connecticut; m. 2d, Aug. 24, 1864, Jane Lawrence Perkins, at Boston Highlands, Mass.

The surroundings of Dr. Childs from childhood have been eminently favorable to the development of the best elements of a manly character. Always living in the atmosphere of intelligent and refining influences, his training and culture have lacked nothing to give strength to a well balanced intellect. That there has been no waste of appliances, the fruits of an industrious and beneficent career bear ample testimony. His preparatory studies for entering college were pursued under Rev. Sanford Lawton of Springfield, Mass. In 1843, he entered the University of the City of New York, and graduated with first honors in 1847, the part of Valedictorian having been assigned him. He entered the same year Princeton Theological Seminary and graduated in 1850. Spending a fourth year in the Seminary in special studies, he was licensed to preach by the Presbytery of New York, April 17, 1850. His first ministry

was brief in Berkeley county, Va., and Southampton, L. I.
In 1851, he commenced ministerial labors in Hartford, Ct., and
in 1852, at the organization of the First Presbyterian church
in that city, he was ordained its pastor, where he continued till
1865, when he was called to the First Congregational church
in Norwich, Ct., the pastorate of which he filled till 1870, when
he was elected professor of Biblical and Ecclesiastical History
in the Theological Institute of Connecticut, at Hartford, where
he continued till 1878. In 1880, he was elected professor of
Mental and Moral Science in the University of Wooster, at
Wooster, Ohio. The esteem in which Dr. Childs is held as a
private and public man in Hartford, Ct., is indicated by a brief
notice in the Hartford *Times* of his appointment to the Wooster
University Professorship:

"The many friends of the Rev. Dr. Thomas S. Childs, of this city, will hear
with interest that he has accepted a professorship in the Presbyterian University at Wooster, Ohio. This institution, though young in years, is pros-
pering greatly, and already has, in its various departments, between four
and five hundred students. Dr. Childs takes the chair of Mental and Moral
Science—a position of responsibility, and one which calls for just such intellectual ability, sound moral principle and careful training as Dr. Childs has,
in a marked degree. While regretting to part with him here, his numerous
friends will rejoice to know that he is going into so good a position. Dr.
Childs will spend the winter, with his family, in Washington City, where
he has an engagement to preach in the Western Presbyterian church, near
Lafayette Square. His practical duties in the college will begin later on in
the coming year."

Dr. Childs is publicly and favorably known through his
published articles: various sermons, tracts, pamphlets and articles in the Princeton *Review*, and the "Heritage of Peace," are the
issues of his pen. One of his late articles is a lecture delivered
in the spring of 1880, to the Unitarian congregation of Hartford, Ct., at their request—topic, CHRIST HIS OWN WITNESS,—
published in the Hartford *Times*, and printed in tract form by
the Presbyterian Board of Publication, as a valuable item of
religious literature adapted for general circulation. The high
esteem entertained for Dr. Childs by those holding differing
religious opinions from himself, is proof of his candor in the defence of his christian faith, and of his ability to convince and win
an honest inquirer after truth. Personally, Dr. Childs is gifted
with characteristics which render his social life attractive. Ac-
cessible, affable and communicative, he finds his way easily to
the confidence of all who are drawn within reach of his influence.

Of Mrs. Childs, his first wife, to whose memory a fitting tribute has been paid and preserved in a little volume, from which we quote, it may be said she possessed qualities of heart and mind, not less marked than some of those which give the Dr. deserved prominence.

Mrs. Mary Porter Childs b. in Hartford, Ct., April 11, 1826, only dau. of Haynes L. Porter, Esq., of that city, and a descendant of Governor Haynes of Connecticut and Massachusetts, a family of honor in both States at an early period. For her native city and state, Mrs. Childs cherished an especial fondness, she counted it one of the joys of her life that she was permitted always to dwell in it. She completed her school education under the able tuition of Rev. Thomas H. Gallaudet, and continued to cultivate her mind by careful and extensive reading. To a few choice friends she gave a most ardent love, but the fondest affection was for her mother. It will not seem strange, therefore, that in her home she found greater charm than in society; a distrust of her own powers contributed to her shrinking from prominence anywhere. When just past fifteen, in 1841, she was taken into the church of the Rev. Dr. Hawes. Her religious life was one of earnestness and conscientiousness, though her doubts and native reticence hindered expression of faith, while her natural buoyancy hid with a gleeful manner much of her depth of experience. In her marriage Mrs. Childs was peculiarly happy, the doubts which had shadowed her christian life fled away, and in her home she was the cheerful christian wife and mother, finding fullness of joy in her cares and quiet pleasures. The chastening hand of the Lord which she had keenly felt before, and to which she had learned to bow in the high attainment of a cheerful submission, came into her tenderly loved fold and bore away one of her lambs—even now she sorrowed in hope. In 1863 another child was given her, but after a few days she became alarmingly ill, her sufferings were most intense—a gleam of hope came, only to be shrouded. The fears and doubts of life disappeared, and in sweet calm she bade her loved ones farewell, and "walked with God." The accompanying lines of the gifted Mrs. L. H. Sigourney, on the occasion of her death, will most fittingly close our brief sketch:

"MRS. MARY PORTER CHILDS,
Wife of the Rev. Dr. Childs, and only daughter of Haynes L. Porter, Esq.
Died at Hartford, April 4, 1863."

Her lip no longer tastes
Our cup of cares and pains;
The pale king vaunts his shaft no more;
The struggle and the pang are o'er:
The victory remains.

Her's was the home-delight
In woman's sphere that lies,
The love of life,—yet fearless trust
That looks complacent on the dust
From whence the soul shall rise.

Self-forgetful, and serene,
Guiltless of ambition's sway,
Her's were those duties free from strife,
That make a faithful Pastor's wife
The blessing of his way.

Babe,—that in thy Father's arms
Her coffin-bed beside,
Dost take the dear, baptismal seal
On thy fair brow, too young to feel
What loss doth thee betide.

May its crystal wash away
Sinning, sorrowing tears,
And guide thee like a golden thread,
In thy blest mother's steps to tread,
Through all the coming years.

Little daughters, in your hearts
Plant the germ of Christian love,
Spreading, ripening more and more,
Till you find the opening door
Leading to her Home above.

Tuesday, April 7, 1863.   L. H. SIGOURNEY.

[Eighth Generation.] Children: By 1st marriage.

6642. i. MARY LOWRIE CHILDS, b. in Hartford, Ct., Jan. 1856.

6643. ii. FANNY GRAHAM CHILDS, b. in Hartford, Ct., Jan. 28, 1857.

6644. iii. ALICE LEE CHILDS, b. May 16, 1858, in Hartford, Ct., d. April 12, 1859.

By 2d marriage.

6645 iv. THOMAS CHILDS, b. March 24, 1866, in Norwalk, Ct., d. in infancy.

[Sixth Generation.]

6612. v. HORACE BLISS CHILDS, fourth son of Reuben Childs, m. Mary Clark Jenney. Resided in Conway, Mass.

[Seventh Generation.] Children:

6639*. i. EDWIN L CHILDS, m. Harriet Newell Towne.

6640*. ii. MARY ELIZABETH CHILDS.

We much regret that we are unable to link the following names with the ancestor Richard or Samuel Child of Barnstable. Mr. George A. Childs of San Francisco, sent us the accompanying items of his immediate family, and we have endeavored vainly to obtain further intelligence; those possessing the data being negligent in sending it in season. We are compelled, therefore, having waited to the last moment to print this incomplete record. We head the family with the late

6641*a*. CAPT. ALEXANDER C. CHILDS of Cotuit, Barnstable county, Mass.

[Second Generation.] Children:

6642*b*. i. A daughter.

6643*b*. ii. GEORGE ALEXANDER CHILDS, b. in Cotuit, Barnstable county, Mass., m. in San Francisco, Cal., July 24, 1872, Miss Susan L. C. Nye, dau. of Albert G. Nye, Esq., of that city, and formerly of Pocasset, Mass. Mr. George A. Childs is of the California furniture manufacturing company.

[Third Generation.] Children:

6644*c*. i. CORA ASHLEY CHILDS, b. July 8, 1875, d. Aug. 8, 1875, in San Francisco.

6645*c*. ii. LOUISE CHRISTINE CHILDS, b. Dec. 25, 1876. May she live to see her anniversary birthday on Christmas, 1976, and keep our second centennial.*

---

* The generations here are given from the parties known. Could we make the link they would be very different.

CHAPTER XII.

JEREMIAH CHILD OF SWANSEA AND DESCENDANTS.

[First Generation.]

6646. JEREMIAH CHILD. The first known of Jeremiah Child is what is gathered from the town records of Swansea, Mass., that he was born in 1645. Who his parents were we are not informed. His marriage is recorded and birth of his children and numerous descendants to the present day. He was a man of considerable prominence; became a "freeman" in 1680; a selectman in 1682; is possessed of real estate drawn by lot in 1686; conveys to his son John a tract of land in Warren, R. I., costing £8 16s., as recorded in the town records of Taunton, Mass. Married Martha —.

George W. Chase, Esq., of Providence, R. I., one of the descendants, in answer to inquiries as to the ancestor of Jeremiah Child, says:

"I have been unable to trace the origin of Jeremiah Child. He had three children that we know of, possibly he had more. He was probably twice married. In a deed dated 1689, he refers to "my now wife" Martha. In one deed he is called an innkeeper; in another a merchant. He was admitted "freeman" of Plymouth Colony, June 1, 1681, having been a resident of Swansea for some years previous."

Mr. Chase says:

„He married 2d, Elizabeth Thurber Estabrook, widow of Thomas Estabrook and daughter of John and Mary Thurber; his first wife was mother of all his children."

[Second Generation.] Children:

6647. i. JOHN CHILD, b. in Swansea, Mass., 1672, (G. W. Chase says, 1671). m. Margery Howard, about 1692.

6648. ii. JEREMIAH CHILD, JR., b. in Swansea, Mass., Sept. 2, 1683. Jeremiah Child, Jr., is mentioned by Savage and the date of his birth given as the son of Jeremiah and Martha Child of Swansea.

6649. iii. MARGARET CHILD.

[Second Generation.]

6647. i. JOHN CHILD, eldest child of Jeremiah and Martha —Child, b. in Swansea, Mass., 1672, m. Margery Howard, about 1692. She was b. 1673, d. Sept. 6, 1726. He d. Jan. 16, 1739, leaving an estate, bequeathed to him by his father, to his descendants which is held by them to the present time. In a letter written about 1864, Mr. John Throop Child says:

"My grandfather's record says, his grandfather John Child, died Jan. 16, 1739, æ 67 years. In the ancient graveyard at Kickemuit in Warren, R. I. is a stone in memory of Margery, wife of John Child, who died Sept. 12, 1726, æ 53, and near it another grave, probably her husband's."

[Third Generation.] Children, born in Swansea, Mass.:

6650. i. SARAH CHILD, b. April 3, 1693.

6651. ii. MARGARET CHILD, b. Jan. 6, 1696.

6652. iii. SUSANNA CHILD, b. Jan. 26, 1699, m. John Luther. She d. Aug. 12, 1791. He d. Jan. 4, 1771.

6653. iv. JOHN CHILD, b. 1702, m. Abigail Eddy.

6654. v. PATIENCE CHILD, b. 1704.

6655. vi. MARTHA CHILD, b. Sept. 7, 1706.

6656. vii. JAMES CHILD, b. Sept. 5, 1708, m. June 3, 1729, Sarah Haile.

6657. viii. MARY CHILD, b. Aug. 10, 1710, m. Mch. 26, 1730, David Wood.

6658. ix. OLIVER CHILD, b. April 2, 1714.

6659. x. CROMWELL CHILD, b. Jan. 14, 1716.

6660. xi. BETHIA CHILD, b. June 15, 1718.

[Third Generation.]

6653. iv. JOHN CHILD, fourth child and eldest son of John and Margery Child, b. 1702, in Swansea, m. Abigail Eddy, dau. of Rev. Michael Eddy of Newport, R. I. John Child d. Jan. 17, 1788. She d. Mch. 7, 1794.

[Fourth Generation.] Children:

6661. i. CROMWELL CHILD, m. 1st, — Miller; m. 2d, — Turner.

6662. ii. CALEB CHILD, m. twice, both times a Cole.

6663. iii. WILLIAM CHILD, m. —.

6664. iv. JAMES CHILD, m. twice.

6665. v. JEREMIAH CHILD, m. Patience Cory. He d. Dec. 29, 1825.

6666. vi. ABIGAIL CHILD, m. Edward Eddy.

6667. vii. ANN CHILD, m. a Cole.

6668. viii. A daughter, m. a Salisbury.

[Fourth Generation.]

6661. i. CROMWELL CHILD, first child of John and Abigail Eddy, m. 1st, — Miller; m. 2d, — Turner, in Warren, R. I.

[Fifth Generation.] Children:

6669. i. JOHN CHILD, killed by the Indians.

6670. ii. A daughter, married a Varnum.

6671. iii. ANN CHILDS, married a Bowen.

6672. iv. A daughter, married a Turner.

6673. v. A daughter, married a Turner.

[Fourth Generation.]

6662. ii. CALEB CHILD, second child of John and Abigail Eddy Child, m. twice, a Cole each time.

[Fifth Generation.] Children:

6674. i. CALEB CHILD, JR.

6675. ii. CROMWELL CHILD, m. Sally Luther.

6676. iii. CHRISTOPHER CHILD, b. 1775, m. Aug. 17, 1798, Mary Reynolds Child.

6677. iv. SHUBAEL PECK CHILD, b. 1779, m. Priscilla Bradford Child.

6678. v. DANIEL COLE CHILD, b. 1782.

6679. vi. SAMUEL COLE CHILD, b. 1787, m. Mary Jenny.

6680. vii. A daughter, who d. young.

[Fifth Generation.]

6676. iii. CHRISTOPHER CHILD, third child of Caleb and — Cole Child, b. 1775: m. August 17, 1798, Mary Reynolds Child, dau. of Sylvester and Priscilla Bradford Child: he d. in Smithfield, Pa.

[Sixth Generation.] Children:

6681. i. CHRISTOPHER CHILD, JR., b. abt. 1800, m. 1831, Harriet M. Wright: had three sons.

6682. ii. ROBERT CHILD, b. 1802, d. at sea, 1822.

[Fifth Generation.]

6677. iv. SHUBAEL PECK CHILD, fourth child and son of Caleb Child and — Cole Child, m. 1st Priscilla Child, dau. of Sylvester and Priscilla B. Child: she d. Dec. 1840: m. 2d, May 1843, Adaline Croad. Resided in Rehoboth and Warren, R. I.

[Sixth Generation.] Children:

6683. i. MARY COLE CHILD.

6684. ii. CHARLES THOMPSON CHILD.

6685. iii. HARRIET NEWELL CHILD.

6686. iv. ⎱ Twins. ⎱ daughters, d. young.
6687. v. ⎰   ⎰

[Fifth Generation.]

6679. vi. SAMUEL COLE CHILD, sixth child and son of Caleb Child and — Cole, his wife, b. 1787, in Warren, R. I.: went to Baltimore, Md.: m. Mary Jenny of Baltimore, Md., she was b. 1792 and d. 1862: he d. Oct. 18, 1826. Resided in Baltimore, Md.

[Sixth Generation.] Children:*

6688. i. REBECCA W. CHILD.

6689. ii. DANIEL CHILD.

6690. iii. JOSEPH CHILD.

6691. iv. SOPHIA CHILD.

[Third Generation.]

6656. vii. JAMES CHILD, seventh child of John and Margery Child, b. in Swansea, Mass., Sept. 5, 1708, m. June 3, 1729 Sarah Haile, dau. of Bernard and Abigail Haile. Began housekeeping in Warren, R. I., Feb. 10, 1730. She was b. 1713. James Child d. Feb 10, 1738. Sarah m. 2d, John Throop, Jr. of Bristol, R. I. Had by him two children.

* Much time and effort have been put forth to obtain dates in the lines without avail.

[Fourth Generation.] Children, born in Warren, R. I.:

6692. i. SYLVESTER CHILD, b. Mch. 16, 1730, at 1 P. M., m. 1st, Abigail Miller, she d Oct. 31, 1757; m. 2d, Dec 28, 1858, Joanna Barnaby; she d. May 18, 1773; m. 3d, Jan. 13, 1775, Priscilla Bradford.

6693. ii. LYDIA CHILD, b. July 12, 1731, at 10 P. M., m. Elisha Burr of Rehoboth, Mass. She d. Mch. 7, 1790. He d. Nov. 7, 1815.

6694. iii. J. JOHN CHILD, b. Jan. 20, 1733, one hour before sunrise, Saturday morning. m. Nov. 23, 1758, N. S., Rosabella Cole.

6695. iv. HEZEKIAH CHILD, b. Aug. 3, 1732, m. Jan. 13, 1756, Patience Barton.

6696. v. PATIENCE CHILD, b. June 21, 1737, on Tuesday, "A. M., sun one hour high."

6697. vi. JAMES CHILD, JR, b. Sept. 3, 1738, "on Sabbath morning, sun one hour high." m. Hannah Kelley.

Fourth Generation.]

6692. i. SYLVESTER CHILD, eldest child of James and Sarah Haile Child, b. in Warren, R. I., Mch. 17, 1730, m. 1st, about 1748, Abigail Miller; she d. Oct. 31, 1757; m. 2d, Dec. 28, 1758, Joanna Barnaby; she d May 18. 1773; m. 3d, Jan. 13, 1775, Priscilla Bradford.

[Fifth Generation.] Children, born in Warren, R. I.

6698. i. PRUDENCE CHILD, b. Aug. 5, 1749, m. Barnard Salisbury.

6699 ii. JAMES CHILD, b. Mch. 6, 1751, m. Miss Short, dau. of James Short of Swansea; removed to Westford, Otsego county, N. Y., about 1790.*

6700. iii. SARAH CHILD, b. Aug. 7, 1752, m. Rev. Charles Thompson.

6701. iv. ABIEL MILLER CHILD, b. Oct 16, 1756, d. Aug. 8, 1759.

6702. v. ABIGAIL CHILD, b. Sept. 5, 1759, d. Nov. 29, 1761.

6703. vi. GARDINER CHILD, b. April 9, 1761.

6704. vii. SYLVESTER CHILD, JR., b. Sept. 11, 1764, m. Patience Luther, dau. of Martin Luther. She d. Jan. 29, 1851. He d. Sept. 4, 1828.

6705 viii. ELIZABETH CHILD, b. July 2, 1766, m. John Croade; she d. Aug. 24, 1841.

6706. ix. LYDIA CHILD, b. Oct. 22, 1768 m. Joseph Adams. He d. April 30, 1827. She d. Sept. 28, 1860, aged 91 years.

6707. x. JOHANNA CHILD, b. June 27, 1771, d. Dec. 4, 1790.

6708. xi. A dau. unbaptized, d. Aug. 9, 1774.

6709. xii. ROBERT CHILD, b. Feb. 1777, d. April 23, 1794.

6710. xiii. MARY REYNOLDS CHILD, b. May 26, 1779, m. Aug. 1798, Christopher Child.

6711. xiv. PRISCILLA CHILD, b. May 27, 1781, m. Shubael Peck Child. He d. Dec. 1840.

[Fourth Generation.]

6294. iii. J. JOHN CHILD, third child of James and Sarah Haile Child, b. in Warren, R. I., Jan. 20, 1733, m. Nov. 23, 1758, N. S. Rosabella Cole, dau. of Ebenezer Cole. She was b. Jan. 4, 1739, d. May 19, 1820. He d. Sept. 29, 1819.

* The descendants of James Child are yet in Otsego Co., but we have been unable to obtain their record for proper insertion.

[Fifth Generation.]   Children, born in Warren, R. I.

6712. i. ABIGAIL MILLAR CHILD, b. Sept. 26, 1759, m. Dec. 3, 1772, Wm. Davis of Boston, Mass.

6713. ii. JOHN THROOP CHILD, b. Nov. 6, 1761, m. Dec. 9, 1787, Molly T. Millar.

6714. iii. SAMUEL CHILD, b. June 21, 1765, m. Jan. 20, 1790, Nancy Luther. She d. April 16, 1841.   He d. April 11, 1831.

6715. iv. NATHAN CHILD, b. July 18, 1767, m. Nov. 17, 1793, Dorcas Tibbitts. She d. Oct. 5, 1853.   He d. Sept. 29, 1829.

6716. v. ROSABELLA CHILD, b. July 25, 1769, m. Feb. 20, 1803, Edward Gardiner, who was b. 1770, d. July 21, 1824.   She d. Aug. 20, 1855.

[Fifth Generation.]

6713. ii. JOHN THROOP CHILD, eldest son and second child of J. John and Rosabella Cole Child, b. in Warren, R. I., Nov. 6, 1761, m. Dec. 29, 1787, Molly Turner Millar.   They had one child—if more, they are not given.

[Sixth Generation.]   Child:

6717. i. JOHN THROOP CHILD JR., b. in Warren, R. I., May 7, 1790, m. 1st, Sept. 19, 1811, Betsey Millar Burr.   She was b. in Pittstown, N. Y., Dec. 7, 1791, d. Sept. 5, 1852: m. 2d, 1852, Mary Ann Mason, dau. of James Mason, who was b. April 3, 1827.

The documents furnished by Mr. Isaac Child contain the following history of Mr. John Throop Child:

"Capt. John Throop Child was an eminent ship-master of Warren, R. I., and has very kindly aided in collecting the statistics of his family herein given.   In the account of his family he writes: 'My wife, Betsey Millar Burr Child, began to sail with me on Dec. 16, 1816, and continued with me on my numerous voyages until Oct. 1834, when we retired to Warren, R. I.' Thus sailing with her husband eighteen years.   Capt. Throop, if living at this date, (1880) is 90 years old.

[Seventh Generation.]   Children, by second wife; born in Warren, R. I.:

6718. i. Infant son, (unchristened), b. Dec. 26, 1853, d. young.

6719. ii. Infant son, (unchristened), b. Nov. 6, 1855, d. young.

6720. iii. MOLLY TURNER CHILD, b. Jan. 11, 1858.

6721. iv. BETSEY MILLAR CHILD, b. May 11, 1859, drowned 1861.

[Fourth Generation.]

6695. iv. HEZEKIAH CHILD, fourth child of James and Sarah Haile Child, b. in Warren, R. I., Aug. 3, 1734, m. Jan. 13, 1756, Patience Barton, dau. of Samuel and Lillie Barton.   She was b. 1744, d. Feb. 14, 1846.   He d. Dec. 4, 1798.

[Fifth Generation.]   Children, born in Warren, R. I.:

6722. i. BENJAMIN CHILD, b. Sept. 13, 1757, d. 1807, unmarried.

6723. ii. HAILE CHILD, b. Jan. 23, 1759, m. Jan. 13, 1780, Amy Kinnicut.

6724. iii. WILLIAM CHILD, b. Mch. 29, 1761, m. Betsey Ormsbee.   He was lost at sea in 1798.

6725. iv. LILLIE TURNER CHILD, b. Jan. 30, 1763, m. Seth Beck.

6726. v. PATIENCE CHILD, b. June 23, 1765, m. Jonathan Hicks.

6727. vi. NANCY CHILD, b. Oct. 3, 1767, m. Levi Clark.

6728. vii. MARY CHILD, b. Oct. 2, 1769, m. Edward Eddy.

6729. viii. SARAH THROOP CHILD, b. Nov. 5, 1771, m. Josiah Roe.

6730. ix. LYDIA CHILD, b. Mch. 29, 1774, m. Benjamin Barton.

6731. x. REBECCA CHILD, b. Nov. 14, 1776, m. James Barnes.

6732. xi. RUTH CHILD, b. Feb. 16, 1778, m. Levi Clark.

6733. xii. JAMES CHILD, b. Aug. 16, 1780, d. Mch. 14, 1787.

6734. xiii. ABIGAIL CHILD, b. Aug. 23, 1783, m. 1st, Sherebiah Talbot; m. 2d, Lawton Spencer.

[Fifth Generation.]

6723. ii. CAPT. HAILE CHILD, second child of Hezekiah and Patience Barton Child, b. in Warren, R. I., Jan. 23, 1759. Lived in Higganum, Ct; m. Jan. 13, 1780, Amy Kinnicutt. She was b. Feb. 8, 1761, d. Mch. 23, 1841. He d. Feb. 10, 1815.

[Sixth Generation.] Children, born in Warren, R. I.

6735. i. LYDIA CHILD, b. Nov. 25, 1781, m. Oct. 31, 1802, Lewen Cranston. She d. June 6, 1864.

6736. ii. WILLIAM CHILD, b. April 10, 1784, m. Mch. 7, 1808, Lucinda Thurber.

6737. iii. GARDINER CHILD, b. April 8, 1786, m. Oct. 21, 1811, Millie —. Both d. 1864. She was of Newbern, N. C. No children.

6738. iv. JAMES CHILD, b. Oct. 7, 1788, m. Nov. 8, 1810, Betsey Pettis.

6739. v. HAILE CHILD, JR., b. April 19, 1891, m. June 22, 1823, Mary Ann Burnett. He d. May 6, 1863.

6740. vi. JOHN KINNICUT CHILD, b. June 10, 1794, m. August 16, 1819, Mary Ann Newhall.

6741. vii. DANIEL CHILD, b. Oct. 29, 1796, m. July 11, 1819, Mary Ann Cole.

6742. viii. NATHAN CHILD, b. Jan. 21, 1799, m. Jan. 11, 1830, Louisa Child Clark. Both lived in Providence, R. I.; had one child, d. at six months.

6743. ix. HENRY CHILD, b. Mch. 5, 1801, unmarried; d. of consumption.

6744. x. GEORGE CHILD, b. Sept. 1803, m. May 11, 1824, Sarah M. Beverley.

[Sixth Generation.]

6735. i. LYDIA CHILD, eldest child of Capt. Haile and Amy Kinnicutt Child, b. in Warren, R. I., Nov. 25, 1781, m. Oct. 31, 1802, Lewen Cranston. She d. 1864. Had two children.

[Seventh Generation.] Children:

6745. i. MARY CRANSTON, dead.

6746. ii. LYDIA CRANSTON, b. —, m. a Mr. Hoffman.

[Sixth Generation.]

6736. ii. WILLIAM CHILD, second child of Capt. Haile and Amy Kinnicutt Child, b. in Warren, R. I., April 10, 1784, m. Mch. 7, 1808, Lucinda Thurber. He d. Sept. 20, 1831. She d. 1864.

[Seventh Generation.] Children, born in Warren, R. I.:

6747. i. ELIZA ANN CHILD, b. Jan. 13, 1809, m. July 1, 1829, Jacob M. Smith. She d. in California, Mch. 18, 1863.

6748. ii. GARDINER CHILD, b. Jan. 20, 1811, d. Oct. 11, 1811.

6749. iii. LYDIA CHILD, b. June 25, 1813, m. 1st, Patrick Ryan: m. 2d, a Mr. Fraiser.

6750. iv. HAILE CHILD, b. May 18, 1816, d. Sept. 1, 1840.

6751. v. AMY KINNICUT CHILD, b. April 25, 1819, d. Oct. 22, 1838.

6752. vi. HENRY CHILD, b. July 24, 1823, m. Jan. 22, 1848, Minerva D. Jenckes.

6752a. vii. MARY MARIA CHILD, b. Jan. 1, 1826, m. Sylvester B. Atwood.

6753. viii. LEWIS WILLIAM CHILD, b. Aug. 19, 1828, d. July 19, 1850.

[Sixth Generation.]

6738. iv. JAMES CHILD, fourth child of Haile and Amy Kinnicut Child, b. Oct. 7, 1788, m. Nov. 8, 1810, Betsey Pettis.
[Seventh Generation.] Children, born in Warren, R. I. They reside in New York City:

6754. i. MARY CHILD, b. Nov. 28, 1811.

6755. ii. LAURA CHILD, b. April 19, 1813, m. May 14, 1837, Nelson Parmerlee.

6756. iii. JAMES H. CHILD, b. May 29, 1815, m. Sept. 15, 1846, Roena Allen. He d. Oct. 23, 1867.

6757. iv. NOAH CHILD, b. Feb. 14, 1817, d. Sept. 18, 1855.

6758. v. BETSEY CHILD, b. Dec. 20, 1818, m. Sept. 20, 1842, Levi Tiffany.

6759. vi. GARDINER CHILD, b. Jan. 26, 1820, d. Mch. 18, 1846.

6760. vii. JOHN H. CHILDS, b. Mch. 5, 1823, d. Jan 9, 1872.

6761. viii. AMY CHILD, b. Nov. 6, 1825, d. Sept. 6, 1855.

6762. ix. GEORGE H. CHILD, b. Dec. 6, 1827, m. July 4, 1847, Josephine Tiffany.

[Sixth Generation.]

6740. vi. JOHN KINNICUT CHILD, sixth child of Capt. Haile and Amy Kinnicut Child, b. June 10, 1794, m. Aug. 16, 1819, Mary Ann Newhall. He d. May 2, 1855.
[Seventh Generation.] Children, born in Warren, R. I.

6763. i. JOHN NEWHALL CHILD, b. Feb. 7, 1821, m. Dec. 1, 1846, Waity S. Luther Bates.

6764. ii. HETTY N. CHILD, b. April 27, 1824, m. Ebenezer Allen.

6765. iii. HENRY CHILD, b. July 4, 1827, m. Julia White. He d. May 8, 1859.

[Sixth Generation.]

6741. vii. DANIEL CHILD, seventh child of Haile and Amy Kinnicut Child, b. Oct. 29, 1796, m. July 11, 1819, Mary Cole dau. of Jonathan and Betsey Cowan Cole. He d. July 18, 1860.
[Seventh Generation.] Children, born in Warren, R. I.

6766. i. MARY CHILD, b. Feb. 9, 1821, m. Sept. 14, 1840, Edward S. Chase.

6767. ii. BETSEY COLE CHILD, b. Oct. 8, 1822, d. Dec. 18, 1822.

6768. iii. ABBIE COLE CHILD, b. Nov. 4, 1823, m. Carl Kugler. She d. April 7, 1871.

6769. iv. JULIA ANN CHILD, b. April 14, 1826 m. Henry Smith.

6770. v. REBECCA ELLIS CHILD, b. Feb. 13, 1828, m. Oliver Snow.

6771. vi. ROBERT HENRY CHILD, b. June 14, 1830, m. Sarah Chadburn.
6772. vii. CHARLES EDWIN CHILD, b. Oct. 26, 1832, d. Jan. 8, 1835
6773. viii. ANTOINETTE CHILD, b. April 9, 1835; unmarried.
6774. ix. CHARLES EDWIN CHILD, 2D, b. Dec. 16, 1836, m. Arintha Acker.
6775. x. GEO. WILLIAM CHILD, b. April 2, 1838, m. Rachel Tripp.

[Seventh Generation.]

6766. i. MARY CHILD, eldest child of Daniel and Mary Cole
Child, b. in Warren, R. I., Feb. 9, 1821, m. Sept. 14, 1840,
Edward S. Chase of Newport, R. I. They have two children.

[Eighth Generation.] Children:
6776. i. THEODORE F. CHASE.
6777. ii. GEO. W. CHASE.

[Seventh Generation.]

6768. iii. ABBIE COLE CHILD, third child of Daniel and
and Mary Cole Child, b. in Warren, R. I., Nov. 4, 1823, m. Oct.
29, 1853, Charles Kugler. She d. April 7, 1871.

[Eighth Generation.] Children:
6778. i. GEO. ERNST KUGLER, b. Aug. 9, 1854, d. Jan. 20, 1857.
6779. ii. ANNIE LOUISA KUGLER, b. Feb. 24, 1857.
6780. iii. HARRIET AUGUSTA KUGLER, b. Aug. 25, 1860.
6781. iv. EMMA LAURA KUGLER, b. Sept. 1, 1862, d. Mch. 1, 1864.
6782. v. OTTO ERNEST KUGLER, b. Oct. 30, 1864.

[Seventh Generation.]

6769. iv. JULIA ANN CHILD, fourth child and dau. of
Daniel and Mary Cole Child, b. in Warren, R. I., April 14,
1826, m. Sept. 1843, Henry W. Smith of Norton, R. I.

[Eighth Generation.] Children:
6783. i. MINERVA C. SMITH.
6784. ii. WALTER HENRY SMITH.
6785. iii. MARILLA HODGES SMITH.
6786. iv. FRANK SMITH.
6787. v. MINNIE SMITH.
6788. vi. MARY SMITH.

[Seventh Generation.]

6770. v. REBECCA ELLIS CHILD, fifth child and dau. of
Daniel and Mary Cole Child, b. Feb. 13, 1828, m. May 1, 1848,
Oliver Snow of Nantucket.

[Eighth Generation.] Children.
6789. i. MARY LOUISA SNOW, b. Feb. 26, 1849, d. Jan. 13, 1851.
6790. ii. MARY HATTIE SNOW, b. Aug. 22, 1851, d. May 11, 1859.

[Seventh Generation.]

6774. ix. CHARLES EDWIN CHILD, 2D, ninth child and third
son of Daniel and Mary Cole Child, b. in Warren, R. I., Dec.

16, 1836, m. Arintha Acker of New York. He is clerk in
New York City post office.

[Eighth Generation.] Child:

6791. i. CHARLES EDWIN CHILD, JR.

[Seventh Generation.]

6775. x. GEORGE WILLIAM CHILD, tenth and youngest
child of Daniel and Mary Cole Child, b. in Warren, R. I.,
April 2, 1838, m. Nov. 25, 1857, Rachel S. Tripp of Westport,
Mass. He was in the Union Army in the late war of the Rebellion, was in the 29th Massachusetts Reg't, Co. F. ; was taken
prisoner at Savage Station, Virginia, and imprisoned in Richmond, Va. Three children of whom the father says he is justly
proud.

[Eighth Generation.] Children:

6792. i. TULLIE F. CHILD, b. Oct. 23, 1858, in South Dartmouth, Mass.
6793. ii. ETTA LOUISE CHILD, b. June 30, 1862, in Taunton, Mass.
6794. iii. MINERVA CHILD, b. Nov. 1865, in Westford, Mass.

[Sixth Generation.]

6744. x. CAPT. GEORGE CHILD, youngest and tenth child of
Capt. Haile and Amy Kinnicut Child, b. in Warren, R. I., Sept.
18, 1803, m. May 11, 1824, Sarah Maria Beverley of Providence, R. I., a descendant of the Ogdens of England. Capt.
Child was a boy of twelve years at the time of his father's decease. He developed a love for the sea and rose to the command of one of the best of the Long Island Sound steamers.
At the time of the burning of the "Lexington" he was her
commander and nobly sacrificed his own life to save the lives of
the passengers.

[Seventh Generation.] Children:

6795. i. FRANCES VIRGINIA CHILD, m. Henry F. Miller.
6796. ii. GEORGE HENRY CHILD, m. Rosalie Boyd.
6797. iii. EDWIN FOREST CHILD, m. Sarah Wilbur.
6798. iv. THOMAS TREUSDELL CHILD, m. twice.
6799. v. JANE BEVERLY CHILD, m. Edward R Crowell.
6800. vi. WILLIAM COMSTOCK CHILD, m. Mary MacFarlane.

[Seventh Generation.]

6795. i. FRANCES VIRGINIA CHILD, eldest child of Capt.
George and Sarah M. Beverley Child, m. Henry Franklin Miller,
manufacturer of organs and piano-fortes, Boston, Mass. From
Mrs. Miller, through her son Edwin Child Miller, we have received our record of this immediate line, though without the
dates so desirable.

[Eighth Generation.]   Children:
  6801. i. HENRY FRANKLIN MILLER, JR., m. Mary Ann Gavett.
  6802. ii. WALTER HERBERT MILLER, m. Mary Alice Edwards.
  6803. iii. FRANCES VIRGINIA MILLER, m. George Smith Burton.
  6804. iv. JAMES COOK MILLER, m. Fannie Lamson Rockwood.
  6895. v. EDWIN CHILD MILLER.
  6806. vi. WILLIAM THOMAS MILLER.
  6807. vii. ALICE OGDEN MILLER.

[Eighth Generation.]

  6801. i. HENRY FRANKLIN MILLER, JR., eldest son and child of Frances Virginia Child and Henry F. Miller, b. in Boston, Mass ; m. in that city to Mary Ann Gavett.
[Ninth Generation.]   Child:
  6808. i. MARGARET OGDEN MILLER.

[Eighth Generation.]

  6802. ii. WALTER HERBERT MILLER, second son and child of Frances V. Child and Henry F. Miller, b. in Boston, m. Mary Alice Edwards, dau. of James R. Edwards, late of Baltimore, Maryland, and a descendant of the Frye family.
[Ninth Generation.]   Children:
  6809. i. MARY ALICE MILLER.
  6810. ii. FRANCES VIRGINIA MILLER.

[Eighth Generation.]

  6803. iii. FRANCES VIRGINIA MILLER, eldest dau. of Frances V. Child and Henry F. Miller, b. in Boston, m. George Smith Burton.   The Burton family have been gathered into a genealogical work by one of its members.
[Ninth Generation.]   Child:
  6811. i. ETHEL BURTON.

[Eighth Generation.]

  6804. iv. JAMES COOK MILLER, third son of Frances Virginia Child and Henry F. Miller, b. in Boston, m. Fannie Lamson Rockwood.
[Ninth Generation.]   Children:
  6812. i. BURTON ROCKWOOD MILLER.
  6813. ii. FLORENCE HALE MILLER.

[Seventh Generation.]

  6796. ii. GEORGE HENRY CHILD, eldest son of Capt. George and Sarah Maria Beverley Child, m. Rosalie Boyd, and died some years since.
[Eighth Generation.]   Child:
  6814. i. MARION CHILD.

[Seventh Generation.]

6797. iii. EDWIN FORREST CHILD, second son of Capt. George and Sarah M. Beverley Child, m. Sarah Wilbur of Providence, R. I. Resides in San Francisco, Cal.

[Eighth Generation.] Children:

6815. i. HARRY WILBUR CHILD.
6816. ii. GEORGE BEVERLEY CHILD.
6817. iii. KATE CHILD.
6818. iv. EDWIN CHILD.
6819. v. FLORENCE CHILD.

[Seventh Generation.]

6798. iv. THOMAS TREUSDELL CHILD, third son of Capt. George and Sarah M. Beverley Child, was twice married but we cannot learn to whom. Mr. Child is a most earnest business man, residing at 538 Washington St., San Francisco, Cal.

[Eighth Generation.] Children:

6820. i. CHARLES CHILD, d. young.
6821 ii. Name not ascertained.

[Seventh Generation.]

6799. v. JANE BEVERLEY CHILD, second dau. of Capt. George and Sarah M. Beverley Child, m. Edward R. Crowell of Providence, R. I., where they reside.

[Eighth Generation.] Children:

6822. i. IDA CROWELL.
6823. ii. ANNIE OGDEN CROWELL.
6824. iii. EDWARD CROWELL.
6825. iv. JENNIE BEVERLEY CROWELL.
6826. v. MARGARET CROWELL.
6827. vi. FLORENCE MARY CROWELL.

[Seventh Generation.]

6800. vi. WILLIAM COMSTOCK CHILD, youngest child of Capt. George and Sarah M. Beverley Child, m. Mary MacFarlane. Residence Helena, Montana.

[Eighth Generation.] Children:

6828. i. ALTA CHILD.
6829. ii. FANNIE CHILD.

[Fifth Generation.]

6724. iii. WILLIAM CHILD, third child of Hezekiah and Patience Barton Child, b. in Warren, R. I., Mch. 29, 1761, m. about 1783, Betsey Ormsbee. He was lost at sea 1798.

[Sixth Generation.] Children, born in Warren, R. I.

6830. i. JOSEPH CHILD, ⎫ Twins. ⎬ b. Jan. 1785.
6831. ii. BENJAMIN CHILD, ⎭
6832. iii. SAMUEL SMITH CHILD, b. 1787.
6833. iv. WILLIAM HENRY CHILD. b. 1789.

6834. v. BETSEY CHILD, b. 1791.

6835. vi. NANCY CHILD, b. 1794.

6836. vii. WILLIAM BURTON CHILD, } TWINS, } b. 1796.
6837. viii. EZRA ORMSBEE CHILD,

6838. ix. AMANDA CHILD, b. 1798.

6839. x. SALLY CHILD, b. 1800.

[Fourth Generation.]

6697. vi. JAMES CHILD, JR., sixth and last child of James and Sarah Haile Child, b. in Warren, R. I., 1738, removed to Higganum, Ct., about 1765, m. about 1760, Hannah Kelly. She died Mch. 2, 1817. He died same day.

[Fifth Generation.] Children, b. in Warren, R. I. and Higganum, Ct.

6840. i. MARGARET CHILD, b. June 12, 1762.

6841. ii. JAMES KELLY CHILD, b. Aug. 30, 1763, m. three times.

6842. iii. THOMAS CHILD, b. April 18, 1765, m. —.

6843. iv. SYLVESTER CHILD, b. Nov. 10, 1766, m. May Cone.

6844. v. LYDIA M. CHILD, b. Aug. 7, 1768.

6845. vi. JOHN CHILD, b. Mch. 10, 1770, m. Clara Griswold.

6846. vii. SARAH CHILD, b. Mch. 8, 1773.

6847. viii. PATIENCE CHILD, b. Jan. 20, 1775.

6848. ix. SAMUEL CHILD, b. Sept. 6, 1777, disappeared, supposed to have been abducted.

6849. x. HANNAH CHILD, b. Jan. 10, 1779.

6850. xi. GARDINER CHILD, b. June 6, 1781, m. 1st, Sept. 1, 1802, Fanny Doane; m. 2d, Nov. 1824, Mrs. Esther Higgins Tyler.

6851. xii. HEMAN CHILD, b. June 12, 1784, m. about 1804, Sally Thomas.

[Fifth Generation.]

6841. ii. JAMES KELLY CHILD, second child of James and Hannah Kelly Child, b. Aug. 30, 1763, m. 1st, Prudence Brainard; m. 2d, Jane Brainard; m. 3d, Amelia Crane.

[Sixth Generation] Children, born in Higganum, Ct.:

6852. i. WEALTHY CHILD, b. Oct. 6, 1786 m. 1812, Geo. W. Smith, a Revolutionary soldier. Resided in Alexandria, La.

6853. ii. WILLIAM CHILD, b. Jan. 7, 1788, m. Ann Clark, Utica, N. Y.

6854. iii. HANNAH CHILD, b. Feb. 4, 1790, d. 1792.

6855. iv. CHAUNCEY CHILD, b. Jan. 17, 1792, m. Betsey Clark.

6856. v. CYNTHIA CHILD, b. Jan. 13, 1794, unmarried.

6857. vi. BEULAH CHILD, b. April 18, 1796, unmarried.

6858. vii. HEZEKIAH CHILD, b. April 10, 1798, m. Concurrence Seward Wilcox. Lived in Higganum.

6859. viii. DIODATE CHILD, b. Mch. 19, 1800. Resided at Carrolton, Ala., where he died 1838, unm. Was at one time Marshal of the State of Ala.

6860. ix. GEORGE GILBERT CHILD, b. Dec. 2, 1802, m. Lucinda Child Mitchell.

6861. x. HARVEY CHILD, b. Aug. 20, 1804, unm., and resided with his two sisters at the old homestead.

6862. xi. THEODORE CHILD, b. June 19, 1806, m. Mary Church of Haddam, Connecticut.

* To Mrs. Laura Dewey Child we are indebted for these dates in her husband's family.

[Sixth Generation.]

6853. ii. WILLIAM CHILD, second child of James Kelly and Prudence Brainard Child, b. in Higganum, Jan. 7, 1788, m. Ann Clark of Utica, N. Y. Resided in Springfield, Mass., since 1815.

[Seventh Generation.] Children:

6863. i. CYNTHIA ANN CHILD, b. Nov. 12, 1813, m. June 6, 1838, Henry Brown of Springfield, Mass. A druggist.

6864. ii. HARRIET JENKS CHILD, b. July 29, 1815, m. Oct. 24, 1834, Edward Ingersoll.

6865. iii. JAMES KELLY CHILD, b April 17, 1817, in Springfield, Mass., m Sept. 16, 1856,* Laura Dewey of Palmer, Mass., where he resided and where he died Aug. 22, 1873.

6866. iv. WILLIAM CLARK CHILD, b. April 13, 1820, m. Sept. 8, 1845, Martha E. Dewey.

[Seventh Generation.]

6864. ii. HARRIET JENKS CHILD, second dau. and child of William and Ann Clark Child, b. in Springfield, Mass., July 29, 1815, m. Oct. 29, 1834, Edward Ingersoll, paymaster in the U. S. Army.

[Eighth Generation.] Children:

6867. i. HARRIET JENKS INGERSOLL, b. Oct. 1, 1835, m. Aug. 13, 1856, Charles P. H. Ripley.

6868. ii. CAROLINE PHELPS INGERSOLL, b. Feb. 1, 1838, m. April 18, 1872, Richard S. Ely.

6869. iii. WM. EDWARD INGERSOLL, b. in Springfield, Mass., Sept. 22, 1842, m. May 16, 1872, Anna Gardiner Hart.

6870. iv. JOHN MARTIN INGERSOLL, b. Jan. 26, 1845, m. Nov. 13, 1872, Sabria Anna Arnold.

6871. v. JAMES CHILD INGERSOLL, b. Sept. 27, 1848, m. June 4, 1873, Nellie Newell.

6872. vi. ISABELLA INGERSOLL, b. in Springfield, Mass., Sept. 12, 1850, m. June 4, 1872, George Endicott Wilder.

[Eighth Generation.]

6867. i. HARRIET JENKS INGERSOLL, eldest child and dau. of Harriet Jenks Child and Edward Ingersoll, b. in Springfield, Mass., Oct. 1, 1835, m. Aug. 13, 1856, Charles P. H. Ripley of Brooklyn, N. Y.

[Ninth Generation.] Children:

6873. i. CHARLES STEDMAN RIPLEY, b. in Brooklyn, N. Y. June 20, 1857.

6874. ii. EDWARD INGERSOLL RIPLEY, b. Nov. 16, 1858.

6875. iii. JAMES HUNTINGTON RIPLEY, b. Oct. 3, 1859.

6876. iv. HENRY BROWN RIPLEY, b. in New York City, May 22, 1863, d. at Springfield, Mass., Sept. 10, 1864.

[Eighth Generation.]

6868. ii. CAROLINE PHELPS INGERSOLL, second child and dau. of Harriet Jenks Child, and Edward Ingersoll, b. at

Savannah Ga., Feb. 1, 1838, m. in Springfield, Mass., April 18, 1872, Richard S. Ely of New York.

[Ninth Generation.] Children, born in New York City.
6877. i. RICHARD FENWICK ELY, b. Nov. 4, 1874.
6878. ii. MAUD INGERSOLL ELY, b. Feb. 29, 1876.

[Eighth Generation.]
6870. iv. JOHN MARTIN INGERSOLL, second son, fourth child of Harriet Jenks Child and Edward Ingersoll, b. in Springfield, Mass., Jan. 26, 1845, m. in Haddam, Ct., Nov. 13, 1872, Sabria Anna Arnold.

[Ninth Generation.] Children, born in Haddam, Ct.
6879. i. HARRIET ARNOLD INGERSOLL, b. Aug. 17, 1875.
6880. ii. CHARLES ARNOLD INGERSOLL, b. Aug. 8, 1878.

[Eighth Generation.]
6871. v. JAMES CHILD INGERSOLL, fifth child, third son of Harriet Jenks Child and Edward Ingersoll, b. in Springfield, Mass., Sept. 27, 1848, m. in Springfield, June 4, 1873, Nellie Newell.

[Ninth Generation.] Children, born in Springfield, Mass.
6881. i. ROBERT NEWELL INGERSOLL, b. Jan. 29, 1875.
6882. ii. ELIZABETH MARTIN INGERSOLL, b. Aug. 2, 1877.

[Seventh Generation.]
6866. iv. WM. CLARK CHILD, fourth child, second son of William and Ann Clark Child, b. April 13, 1820, m. in Palmer, Mass., Sept. 18, 1845, Martha Emily Dewey. He d. in Palmer, Mass., Feb. 18, 1861; his wife died June 27, 1873.

[Eighth Generation.] Children:
6883. i. WILLIAM ALONZO CHILD, b. Nov. 15, 1848, m. 1st, Feb. 23, 1875, Sophronia Shepard; she d. April, 1875; m. 2d, Sept. 1875, Mary Cowan.
6884. ii CHARLES DEWEY CHILD, b. at Palmer, Mass., May 22, 1856, d. Mch. 4, 1858.
6885. iii JAMES BREWER CHILD, b. at Palmer, Mass., June 9, 1858, d. Mch. 7, 1865.

[Eighth Generation.]
6883. i. WM. ALONZO CHILD, eldest son and child of Wm. Clark and Martha E. Dewey Child, b. in Palmer, Mass., Nov. 15, 1848, m. 1st, Feb. 23, 1875, Sophronia Shepard; m. 2d. Sept. 1875, Mary Cowan.

[Ninth Generation.] Child:
6886. i. JAMES BREWER CHILD, b. May 29, 1876.

[Sixth Generation.]
6855. iv. CHAUNCEY CHILD, fourth child, second son of James Kelley and Prudence Brainard Child, b. in Higganum,

Ct., Jan. 17, 1792, m. about 1820, Betsey Clark of Utica, N. Y.; she was b. in Utica, 1793, and died at Higganum, Oct. 2, 1861.

[Seventh Generation.] Children:

6887. i. CHARLES CHAUNCEY CHILD, b. Aug. 1, 1822, m. Mary E. Manning of Sault St. Mary, Mich.

6888. ii. CARTON CLARK CHILD, b. in Higganum, Ct., Oct. 3, 1824, d. at sea, Dec. 28, 1854, four days out from Batavia on the island of Java, West Indies.

[Sixth Generation.]

6858. vii. HEZEKIAH CHILD, seventh child of James Kelley and Prudence Brainard Child, b. in Higganum, Ct., April 10, 1798, m. Concurrence Seward Wilcox.

[Seventh Generation.] Children:

6889. i. CORNELIA JOSEPHINE CHILD, m. Stephen Sears Smith of Middletown, Ct., reside in California.

6890. ii CARLOS OSCAR CHILD, b. in Higganum, Ct., Nov. 26, 1827, m. Mary Gillett of Painsville, Ohio. Carlos Child is a merchant in Maysville, Wisconsin, connected with the North Western Iron Company.

6891. iii. GUSTAVUS CHILD, b. in Higganum, Ct, May 8, 1833, d. July 22, 1834.

6892. iv. MARY EMILY CHILD, b. in Higganum, Ct., June 27, 1836.

[Sixth Generation.]

6860. ix. GEORGE GILBERT CHILD, ninth child and fifth son of James K. and Prudence Brainard Child, b. in Higganum, Ct., Dec. 2, 1802, removed to Alabama in 1822, m. 1828, Lucinda Child Mitchell. He was sheriff of Pickens county, Ala., from 1834 to 1840. He removed to Mobile, Ala., in 1840, where he resided till 1879. He died in New Orleans, April 19, 1879, while on a visit to that city.

[Seventh Generation.] Children:

6893. i. BEULAH MARIA CHILD, b. at Pickensville, Ala., 1829, m. 1850, Young Burt Olive, a planter in Alabama.

6894. ii. JAMES K. CHILD, b. 1831, in Pickensville, Ala., d. young.

6895. iii. DUFF DEWITT CHILD, b. 1833, in Pickensville, Ala., m. 1864, Frances Baurr, in Birmingham, Ala.

6896. iv. GEORGE GILBERT CHILD, JR., b. at Carrolton, Ala., Feb. 7, 1838, m. May 1, 1861, Christine DePras Reside in Augusta, Ga.

6897. v. WILLIAM FRANKLIN CHILD, b. at Cottage Hill, April 1, 1843. Resides at Mobile, Ala.; unmarried.

6898. vi. MARY JOSEPHINE CHILD, b. at Cottage Hill, Ala., 1848, d. at Mobile, Ala., 1860.

[Seventh Generation.]

6893. i. BEULAH MARIA CHILD, eldest child of George Gilbert and Lucinda C. Mitchell Child, b. in Pickensville, Ala., 1829, m. 1850, Young Burt Olive. Residence, Camden, Madison county, Miss.

[Eighth Generation.] Children:
6899. i ANDREW VINCENT OLIVE, b. 1856.
6900. ii GEORGE BURT OLIVE, b. 1862.
6901 iii. MARY JOSEPHINE OLIVE, b. 1864.

[Seventh Generation.]

6896. iv. GEORGE GILBERT CHILD, JR., fourth child, third son of George Gilbert and Lucinda C. Mitchell Child, b. in Carrolton, Ala., Feb. 5, 1838, m. May 1, 1861, Christine DePras. Residence, Augusta, Ga.
[Eighth Generation.] Children:
6902. i. GILBERT CHILD, b. June 1, 1862.
6903. ii. JOHN CHILD, b. Feb. 1864.
6904. iii. LATHAM CHILD, b. Feb. 22, 1868.
6905. iv. ANNA DePRAS CHILD, b. June 26, 1870.

[Sixth Generation.]

6862. xi. THEODORE CHILD, eleventh child and seventh son of James Kelley and Prudence Brainard Child, b. June 19, 1806, in Higganum. Ct., m. Mary Church of Haddam, Ct.
[Seventh Generation.] Child:
6906. i. JAMES HARVEY CHILD.

[Fifth Generation.]

6842. iii. THOMAS CHILD, third child, second son of James and Hannah Kelley Child, b. April 18, 1765, m. about 1787, to whom not ascertained.
[Sixth Generation.] Children, born in Warren, R. I.
6907. i. THOMAS CHILD, JR., b. Feb. 2, 1788, m. May 1810, Fanny Gridley.
6908. ii. BULKLEY CHILD, b. Aug. 5, 1789, m. Aug. 31, 1811, Sally Tracy.
6909. iii. OLIVIA CHILD, b. 1791.
6910. iv. DAVID TRYON CHILD, b. Nov. 4, 1796, m. Dec. 12, 1822, Almeda Alden.
6911. v. WILLIAM HENRY CHILD, b. Oct. 12, 1800.

[Sixth Generation.]

6907. i. THOMAS CHILD, JR., eldest child of Thomas Child, b. in Warren, R. I., Feb. 2, 1788, m. May 10, 1810, Fanny Gridley of Middletown, Ct., and removed to Rochester, N. Y., in 1825; died in 1835.
[Seventh Generation.] Children:
6912. i. ELIZABETH CHILD, m. Elbert Cranston of Rochester, N. Y.
6913. ii. HARRIET CHILD, m. John Winslow of Rochester, N. Y.
6914. iii. FRANCES CHILD, m. Albert Walker of Rochester, N. Y.
6915. iv. SARAH JANE CHILD, m. Dellon Dewey of Rochester, N. Y.
A-2

[Sixth Generation.]

6908. ii. BULKLEY CHILD, second son of Thomas Child, b. Aug. 5, 1789, m. Aug. 31, 1811, Sally Tracy of Colchester, Ct. She died Dec. 6, 1837.

[Seventh Generation.] Children:

6916. i. HANNAH TRYON CHILD, m. G. W. Harris of Middletown, Ct. She d. May 13, 1840.

6917. ii. EMILY JOHNSON CHILD, m. Benjamin B. Worthington. She d. Jan. 9, 1859.

6918. iii. HARRIET WETMORE CHILD, m. William W. White of Hartford, Ct.

6919. iv. SARAH JANE CHILD, m. Charles C. Larkum.

6920. v. MARY GARDINER CHILD, m. John A. Burnham of Hartford, Ct.

6921. vi. SUSAN ELIZA CHILD, m. John S. Sperry.

6922. vii. THOMAS CHILD, m. Fannie A. Rogers of Hartford, Ct.

6923. viii. DANIEL TRACY CHILD, m. Sarah Amanda Harvey of Hartford, Ct.

6924. ix. MARTHA AMELIA CHILD, m. Abram G. Pettibone of Hartford, Ct.

[Seventh Generation.]

6922. vii. THOMAS CHILD, seventh child of Bulkley and Sally Tracy Child, m. Fannie A. Rogers of Hartford, Ct.

[Eighth Generation.] Children:

6925. i. MAURICE W. CHILD, b. in Warren, R. I., and lived in Hartford, Ct.

6926. ii. CHARLOTTE LOUISA CHILD.

6927. iii. MAGGIE WILLIAMS CHILD.

[Seventh Generation.]

6923. viii. DANIEL TRACY CHILD, eighth child of Bulkley and Sally Tracy Child, m. Sarah Amanda Harvey.

[Eighth Generation. Children:

6928. i. NELLIE CHILD.

6929. ii. CLARA BELL CHILD.

6930. iii. HATTIE CHILD.

[Sixth Generation.]

6910. iv. DAVID TRYON CHILD, fourth child of Thomas Child, b. in Warren, R. I, Nov. 4, 1796, m. Dec. 12, 1822, Almeda Alden of Stafford, Ct. He died 1855.

[Seventh Generation.] Children:

6931. i. ADALINE E. CHILD, m. John Carrier of Middle Haddam, Ct.

6932. ii. EVELYN AUGUSTA CHILD.

6933. iii. JOHN ALDEN CHILD.

6934. iv. SOPHIA LOUISA CHILD.

6935. v. ALMEDA ALDEN CHILD.

6936. vi. HELEN LOUISA CHILD.

6937. vii. HENRY EUGENE CHILD.

6938. viii. FREDERICK AUGUSTUS CHILD.

[Fifth Generation.]

6843. iv. SYLVESTER CHILD, fourth child of James Child, Jr., and Hannah Kelly, his wife, b. in Warren, R. I., Nov. 10, 1766, m. Mary Cone: she was b. 1758, d. 1803. He d. Dec. 19, 1794.

[Sixth Generation.] Children:

6939. i. SAMUEL CHILD, m. 1st, Charlotte Bailey: m. 2d, Fanny Cotton.

6940. ii. BETSEY CHILD.

6941. iii. NANCY CHILD, b. Jan. 1792.

6942. iv. SARAH CHILD, b. June 2, 1794, m. May 20, 1813, Rutger Clark. He was b. 1792.

[Sixth Generation.]

6939. i. SAMUEL CHILD, eldest child of Sylvester and Mary Cone Child, m. 1st, 1810, Charlotte Bailey of Middletown, Ct.; m. 2d, Fanny Cotton. He d. Sept. 18, 1826.

[Seventh Generation.] Children: By first marriage:

6943. i. SARAH STARR CHILD.

6944. ii. FRANCIS CHILD.

6945. iii. ELIZABETH CHILD.

By second marriage:

6946. iv. SYLVESTER CHILD.

6947. v. LUCRETIA CHILD.

[Fifth Generation.]

6845. vi. JOHN CHILD, sixth child of James and Hannah Kelly Child, b. in Higganum, Mch. 10, 1790, m. Clara Griswold of Haddam.

[Sixth Generation.] Child:

6948. i. JULIA CHILD, m. John Tyler, d. at Mobile, Alabama, leaving three sons.

[Fifth Generation.]

6850. xi. GARDINER CHILD, eleventh child and fifth son of James, Jr., and Hannah Kelley Child, b. in Higganum, Ct., June 6, 1781, m. 1st. Sept. 1, 1802, Fanny Doane; she was b. Mch. 31, 1782, d. May 4, 1824; m. 2d, Nov. 1824, Mrs. Esther Higgins Tyler. He d. Dec. 2, 1832. He resided in Haddam, Ct.; was a ship builder.

[Sixth Generation.] Children, born in Haddam, Ct.;

6949. i. JONATHAN DOANE CHILD, b. May 5, 1803, m. Dec. 1824, Charlotte Stewart of Middle Haddam.

6950. ii. FANNY MARIAH CHILD, b. Aug. 1, 1805, m. 1828, Erastus Bidwell.

6951. iii. GARDINER CHILD, JR., b. Nov. 3, 1807, d. Nov. 27, 1827.

6952. iv. GARDINER CHILD, JR., 2d, b. April 2, 1809, m. 1st, Enza Goodrich of Rocky Hill; she d. on day of marriage: m. 2d, Eliza Cook of Brooklyn, N. Y.

6953. v. PHEBE HORTON CHILD, b. Oct. 29, 1811, m. Feb. 22, 1835, Oliver P. Smith of Haddam.

6954. vi. SAMUEL BOWEN CHILD, b. June 13, 1814, m. Adaline Bevins of E. Haddam, Ct.

6955. vii. EVALINE KELLEY CHILD, b. June 28, 1817; was residing in 1864, at Sandwich Islands.

6956. viii. RALPH POST CHILD, b. Dec. 8, 1819.

By second marriage:

6957. ix. SARAH ELEANOR CHILD, b. Dec 2, 1831, m. Philo J. Warner of Chicago, Ill.

[Fifth Generation.]

6851. xii. HEMAN CHILD, twelfth child of James, Jr., and Hannah Kelley Child, b. in Higganum, Ct., June 12, 1784, m. about 1804, Sally Thomas. Resided in Derby, Ct.

[Sixth Generation]   Children, born in Derby, Ct.:

6958. i. GEORGE A. CHILD, b. Sept. 28, 1805, m. about 1831, Abigail Allen.

6959. ii. PATIENCE CHILD, b. Aug. 17, 1807, d. Oct. 17, 1817.

6960. iii. HEMAN CHILD, JR., b. Feb. 15, 1809, m. Jan. 1, 1835, Jul'ette White.

6961. iv. ALEXANDER CHILD, b. Mch. 12, 1812, m. Nov. 24, 1839, Eunice Frances Standish.

6962. v. MARY A. CHILD, b. Dec. 17, 1814.

6963. vi. HANNAH CHILD, b. Mch. 12, 1815, m. Feb. 28, 1837, M. DeForest Canfield, b. April 21, 1809; a machinist.

6964. vii. JOHN CHILD, b. Dec. 25, 1818, m. Nov. 16, 1848, Jennette R. Post.

6965. viii. EDWIN CHILD, b. Dec. 17, 1821, d. young.

6966. ix. EDWIN CHILD, 2D, b. Feb. 28, 1824.

[Sixth Generation.]

6958. i. GEORGE A. CHILD, eldest child and son of Heman and Sally Thomas Child, b. in Derby, Ct., Sept. 28, 1805, m. about 1831, Abigail Allen. He was a carpenter.

[Seventh Generation.]   Children, born in Derby, Ct..

6967. i. ALEXANDER N. CHILD, b. Mch. 12, 1832.

6968. ii. SARAH ANN CHILD, b. Mch. 17, 1834, d. Sept. 28, 1835.

6969. iii. GEORGE HENRY CHILD, b. April 17, 1836.

6970. iv. MARY R. CHILD, b. Dec. 25, 1839, m. Jan. 8, 1859, John R. Kelley.

6971. v. GEORGE EDGAR CHILD, b. Dec. 3, 1841.

[Sixth Generation.]

6960. iii. HEMAN CHILD, JR., third child and second son of Heman and Sally Thomas Child, b. Feb. 15, 1809, m. Jan. 1, 1835, Juliette White.

[Seventh Generation.]   Children, born in Derby, Ct.:

6972. i. EVELYN L. CHILD, b. Jan. 19, 1836.

6973. ii. FRANCES J. CHILD, b Mch. 31, 1839.

6974. iii. SARAH J. CHILD, b. May 12, 1842.

6975. iv. JOHN C. CHILD, b. May 22, 1847.

6976. v. EDWARD M. CHILD, b. Mch 19, 1849.

6977. vi. WILLIE A. CHILD, b. Feb. 24, 1852.

6978. vii. CHARLES C. CHILD, b. July 4, 1854, d. Jan. 16, 1857.

6979. viii. ELLEN A. CHILD, b. 1857.

(Sixth Generation.)

6961. iv. ALEXANDER CHILD, fourth child, third son of Heman and Sally Thomas Child, b. in Derby, Ct., Mch. 12, 1812, m. Nov. 24, 1839, Eunice Frances Standish; she was b. Jan. 10, 1820. He was a woodturner by trade.

[Seventh Generation.] Children, born in Derby, Ct.:
    6980. i. HARRIET FRANCES CHILD, b. July 22, 1844.
    6981. ii. ISABELLA CHILD, b. Aug. 5, 1847.
    6982. iii. ALEXANDER FRANKLIN CHILD, b Sept. 16, 1849.
    6983. iv. ROTHSCHILD CHILD, b. June 3, 1854.
    6984. v. CHARLES FREMONT CHILD, b. Aug. 20, 1856.
    6985. vi. HERBERT STANDISH CHILD, b. April 27, 1859.
    6986. vii. WINFIELD SCOTT CHILD, b. Feb. 21, 1861.

[Sixth Generation.]

6964. vii. JOHN CHILD, seventh child, fourth son of Heman and Sally Thomas Child, b. in Derby, Ct., Dec. 25, 1818, m. Nov. 16, 1848, Jennette R. Post.

[Seventh Generation.] Children, born in Derby, Ct.
    6987. i. GEORGE HENRY CHILD, b. Jan. 16, 1851.
    6988. ii. JOHN RUSSELL CHILD, b. Nov. 10, 1855.
    6989. iii. SARAH JENNETTE CHILD, b. April 29, 1860.
    6990. iv. EDGAR AMBROSE CHILD, b. Mch 5, 1862.

[Second Generation.]

6648. JEREMIAH CHILD, JR., second child of Jeremiah and Martha Child, b. in Swansea, Sept. 2. 1683, m. 1st, Mary — ; she d. Feb. 23, 1734, æ 41 ; m. 2d, June 26, 1735, Mary Hatch : she d. Oct. 29, 1753, æ 63. His children were by the first wife.

Jeremiah was admitted freeman in May, 1729. The town records of Newport, R. I., where he resided, were destroyed during the Revolutionary War, and hence we have little information of the members of this family. Jeremiah was at first a cooper by trade, later a baker. On his gravestone appears the following quaint epitaph :

> " Whether we rest or labour, work or play,
> The world and glory of it pass away:
> This day is past or near its even grown,
> The next succeeding is to us unknown."

[Third Generation.] Children:
    6991. i. JEREMIAH CHILD, m. July 24, 1739, Elizabeth Dyer.
    6992. ii. ESTHER CHILD, b. 1720, m. July 11, 1838, David Lindsay; she d. July, 1802 æ 82.
    6993. iii. MARTHA CHILD, m. June 10, 1740, Saals Carr.
    6994. iv. THOMAS CHILD, m. May 17, 1738, Mary Toman.
    6995. v. MARY CHILD, b. 1728, d. April 1730.

BENJAMIN CHILD OF WATERTOWN.

This is one of the instances where we have not been successful in establishing the connection with the emigrant ancestor. The earliest record found verified, is that of Benjamin Child born in 1697, in Watertown, and resided probably in Newton, Mass. Married May 24, 1722, Elizabeth Greenwood. This renders it probable that his ancestor was among the early settlers of the name in Watertown, and allied to those whose birthplace is traced to that town. The future may reveal the further history which will lead to the exact facts in the case. We conclude therefore to place Benjamin in the generation of his contemporaries.

[Third Generation.]

6996. BENJAMIN CHILD, of Watertown, Mass., b. in 1697, m. May 24, 1722, Elizabeth Greenwood of Newton, Mass.; she d. 1769. He was a turner by trade.

[Fourth Generation.] Children, born in Watertown, Mass.:

6997. i. SAMUEL CHILD. b. April 28, 1723, m. 1745. Elizabeth Winchester.

6998. ii. ELIZABETH CHILD. b. Feb. 23, 1729, d. 1732.

6999. iii. HANNAH CHILD, b. Jan. 3, 1731, m. Feb. 14, 1750, William Nason of Newton, Mass., and Lexington and Dedham, according to Dr. Harris; she d. Jan. 6, 1817.

7000. iv. ELIZABETH CHILD, 2D, b. Jan. 4, 1733.

7001. v. JAMES CHILD. b. April 17. 1735. d. same year.

7002. vi. AARON CHILD,   ⎫ ⎧ m. Phebe Jackson.
                          ⎬ TWINS ⎨ b. Sept. 14, 1736.
7003. vii. MIRIAM CHILD, ⎭ ⎩ d. Dec. 1744.

[Fourth Generation.]

6997. i. SAMUEL CHILD, eldest child and son of Benjamin and Elizabeth Greenwood Child, b. in Watertown, April 28, 1723, m. in 1745, Elizabeth Winchester; she d. 1786.

[Fifth Generation.] Children, born in Newton, Mass.:

7004. i. BENJAMIN CHILD. b. Dec. 24, 1745.

7005. ii. ISAAC CHILD, b. 1747, d. young.

7006. iii. MIRIAM CHILD, b. Aug. 10, 1748.

7007. iv. MARY CHILD, b. Nov. 6, 1749.

7008. v. SAMUEL CHILD, JR., b. Jan. 13, 1751.

7009. vi. ISAAC CHILD, 2D, b. Jan. 20, 1753.

7010. vii JONATHAN CHILD, b. Nov. 6, 1756.

7011. viii. ELIZABETH CHILD, b. July 27, 1760.

7012. ix. SIMEON CHILD, b. Aug. 25, 1764, m. about 1788, Grace Winship.

[Fifth Generation.]

7012. x. SIMEON CHILD, tenth and last child of Samuel and Elizabeth Child, b. in Newton, Mass , Aug. 25, 1764, m. about

1788, Grace Winship of Lexington, Mass. She was b. May 17, 1761, and died at Cambridge, in 1831. He died at Temple, N. H., Feb. 1, 1816, from injuries received when felling a tree.

[Sixth Generation.] Children:

7013. i. SIMEON CHILD, JR., b. in Concord, Mass., April 8, 1789, m. June 16, 1822, Maria Little.

7014. ii. GRACE HURD CHILD, b. in Temple, N. H., Mch. 25, 1791, m. 1820, Mr. Smith, son of a Capt. Smith of the Revolutionary army. She died Dec. 6, 1866. He died 1854.

7015. iii. ISAAC STEPHEN CHILD, b. in Billerica, Mass., 1794, m. 1833, a Miss Norton; removed to Cincinnati, Ohio; has a family, children not given.

7016. iv. ABIGAIL CHILD, b. in Wilton, N. H., Mch. 26, 1796, m. 1818, Ralph Richardson.

7017. v. NEHEMIAH KIDDER CHILD, b. in Temple, N. H., Mch. 2, 1798, m. April 26, 1832. Lydia B. Norton.

7018. vi. MOSES WINSHIP CHILD, b. in Temple, N. H., 1809, m. Rebecca Child. He d. at Stoneham, Mass., 1865.

7019. vii. BENJAMIN CHILD, b. in Temple, N. H., 1802, d. unmarried Dec. 7, 1870.

[Sixth Generation.]

7013. i. SIMEON CHILD, JR., eldest child of Simeon and Grace Winship Child, b. in Concord, Mass., April 8, 1789, m. June 16, 1822, Maria Little of East Marshfield, Mass. He d. April 8, 1815, at Dunallen, N. J.

[Seventh Generation.] Children, born in Boston, Mass.

7020. i. CYRUS CHILD, b. Aug. 12, 1823, m. 1st, Mch. 1, 1843, Emily A. Dearborn; she d. April 26, 1844; m. 2d, Nov. 2, 1846, Elizabeth Parsons; m 3d, 1865, Linda Wright.

7021. ii. ANDREW CHILD, b. April 15, 1825, m. April 11, 1854, Alice Lowell.

7022. iii. HIRAM CHILD, b. Feb 28, 1827, d. June 3, 1827.

7023. iv. ELLEN MARIA CHILD, b. Nov. 24, 1828, m. April 26, 1848, John T. Pierson.

7024. v. MARY CAROLINE CHILD, b. Nov. 14, 1832, m. 1st, Oct. 18, 1850, Charles Gifford. He d. May 17, 1861. She m. 2d, Nov. 1864, Dr. Carl Lewthstrom.

7025. vi. AUGUSTUS CHILD, b. Dec. 29, 1833, d. Dec. 13, 1834.

7026. vii. ALPHA CHILD, b. Mch. 24, 1836, m. Mch. 11, 1869, at Rome, N.Y., Estelle Clement. He d. in Milwaukee, April 30, 1870.

7027. viii. LUCY ELIZABETH CHILD, b. Dec. 16, 1839.

[Seventh Generation.]

7020. i. CYRUS CHILD, eldest child of Simeon and Maria Little Child, b. in Boston, Aug. 12, 1823, m. 1st, Mch. 7, 1843, Emily A. Dearborn; she d. April 26, 1844; m. 2d, Nov. 2, 1846, Elizabeth Parsons; m. 3d, 1865, Linda Wright.

[Eighth Generation.] Children. By first marriage:

7028. i. FREDERICK WILLIS CHILD, b. in Boston, Jan. 1, 1844, m. 1869, Clara Olmstead of New Canaan, Ct., where they reside.

By second marriage:

7029. ii. GARDINER DAVIS CHILD, b. in Delafield, Wis., May 21, 1848, m. Nov. 18, 1867, Josie Bloomfield.

7030. iii. EMILY FRANCIS CHILD, b. in Milwaukee, Wis., Oct. 3, 1851, m. June 16, 1872, John Evans. Reside in Chicago, Ill. She was married in Dunallen, N. J., at the anniversary of her grandfather's golden wedding.

7031. iv. HORACE ANDREW CHILD, b. in Milwaukee, Wis., Oct. 6, 1853.

7032. v. STANTON CHILD, b. in Milwaukee, Wis., Jan. 18, 1862.

By third marriage:

7033. vi. HOMER CHILD, b. in Franklin, Pa., April 2, 1866.

[Eighth Generation.]

7029. ii. GARDINER DAVIS CHILD, second child and son of Cyrus and first by Elizabeth Parsons, b. in Delafield, Wis., May 21, 1848, m. Nov. 1867, Josie Bloomfield of Dunallen. They reside in Brooklyn, N. Y.

[Ninth Generation.] Child.

7034. i. FREDERICK CHILD, b. in Brooklyn, N. Y.

[Seventh Generation.]

7021. ii. ANDREW CHILD, second son and child of Simeon and Maria Little Child, b. in Boston, April 15, 1825, m. April 11, 1854, Alice Lowell of Milwaukee, Wis.

[Eighth Generation.] Children:

7035. i. CHARLES LOWELL CHILD, b. in New York, July 6, 1858.

7036. ii. CLARA JOSEPHINE CHILD, b. in Dunallen, N. J., Jan. 29, 1866.

[Seventh Generation·]

7023. iv. ELLEN MARIA CHILD, fourth child and eldest dau. of Simeon and Maria Little Child, b. in Boston, Nov. 24, 1828, m. April 26, 1848, John T. Pierson.

[Eighth Generation.] Children:

7037. i. EDWARD CLARENCE PIERSON, b. in Newburyport, Mass., April 7, 1849.

7038. ii. ALICE PIERSON, b. in Delafield, Wis., June 1850, d. in New York, Dec. 18, 1854.

7039. iii. WALTER FREEMONT PIERSON, b. in Morrisania, N. Y., Sept. 15, 1856.

7040. iv. ARTHUR PIERSON, b. in Plainfield, N. J., 1866, d. same year.

7041. v. EVA PIERSON. b. in Plainfield, N. J., 1868.

[Seventh Generation.]

7024. v. MARY CAROLINE CHILD, fifth child and second dau. of Simeon and Maria Little Child, b. in Boston, Nov. 14, 1832, m. 1st, Oct. 18, 1850, Charles Gifford; he d. May 17, 1861; m. 2d, Nov. 1864, Dr. Carl Lewthstrom.

[Eighth Generation.] Children, born in Milwaukee, Wis.:

7042. i. EDITH GIFFORD, b. Oct. 15, 1851.

7043. ii. ARTHUR GIFFORD, b. April 25, 1853.

7044. iii. BESSIE GIFFORD, b. Dec. 19, 1854.

7045. iv. HAROLD GIFFORD, b. Oct. 18, 1858.

[Sixth Generation.]

7016. iv. ABIGAIL CHILD, fourth child, second dau. of Simeon and Grace Winship Child. b. in Wilton, N. H., Mch. 26, 1796, m. 1818, Ralph Richardson, who d. 1855, at Sandgrove, Vt. She d. 1861.

[Seventh Generation.] Children:

7046 i. GEORGE WASHINGTON RICHARDSON, b. 1820.

7047. ii. ELMIRA MINERVA RICHARDSON, b. Mch. 25, 1822, m. Ezra Green.

7048. iii. LEWIS BOARDMAN RICHARDSON, b. Sept. 16, 1824, d. Mch. 10, 1871.

7049. iv. HENRY L. RICHARDSON, b. Mch. 12, 1826.

7050. v. ANN AUGUSTA RICHARDSON, b. Dec. 5, 1828, m. Gilbert L. Hilliard, who was slain at Fort Hudson, 1863. She d. June 20, 1857.

7051. vi. FRANCES FREELOVE RICHARDSON, b. April 19, 1831, m. Geo. S. Parker. Reside at Pultney, Vt.

7052. vii. JOSEPH R. RICHARDSON, b. April 30, 1833. Resides at Chester, Vt.

7053 viii. SERREL ALLEN RICHARDSON, b. Feb. 1835. Resides at Londonderry, N. H.

[Sixth Generation.]

7017. v. NEHEMIAH KIDDER CHILD, fifth child, third son of Simeon and Grace Winship Child, b. Mch. 2, 1798, in Temple, N. H., m. April 26, 1832, Lydia B. Norton. She was b. Oct. 22, 1807, in Newburyport, Mass. They reside in Somerville, Mass.

[Seventh Generation.] Children:

7054. i. SARAH E. CHILD. b. in Cambridge, Mass., Feb. 14, 1833, m. Nov. 30, 1858, Joseph H. Clark.

7055. ii. HARRIET M. CHILD, b. in Cambridge, Mass., April 5, 1835. Reside in Somerville, Mass.

7056. iii. FRANCES L. CHILD, b. in Boston, Mass., Dec. 29, 1836

7057. iv. GEORGE W. CHILD, b. in Boston, Mass., April 26, 1839, d. at Somerville, Mass., Oct. 2, 1868.

7058. v. JOSEPHINE CHILD, b. in Boston, Mass., Mch. 16, 1842, d. April 8, 1842.

7059. vi. CHARLES E. CHILD, b. in Boston, Mass., May 18, 1844, m. Sept. 12, 1869 Sophia Vickory.

7060. vii. JOSEPH H. CHILD, b. Aug. 6, 1847, d. Mch. 18, 1851.

7061. viii. FRANK A. CHILD, b. Dec. 24, 1849.

[Seventh Generation.]

7054. i. SARAH E. CHILD, eldest child of Nehemiah Kidder and Lydia B. Norton Child, b. in Cambridge, Mass., Feb. 14, 1833, m. Nov. 30, 1858, Joseph H. Clark : she resides at Somerville.

[Eighth Generation.] Children, born in Somerville, Mass.

7062. i. SARAH ADELAIDE CLARK, b. April 29, 1860.

7063. ii. HARRIET FRANCES CLARK, b. Mch. 18, 1863, d. Aug. 30, 1863.

[Seventh Generation.]

7059. vi. CHARLES E. CHILD, sixth child, third son of Nehemiah Kidder and Lydia B. Norton Child, b. May 18, 1844, m. in Boston, Sept. 12, 1869, Sophia Vickory.

[Eighth Generation.] Children, born in Boston, Mass.

> 7064. i. EDWARD LORING CHILD, b. Sept. 11, 1870.
> 7065. ii. CHARLES HERBERT CHILD, b. Oct. 8, 1873, d. April 5, 1874.

[Fourth Generation.]

7002. vi. AARON CHILD, sixth child of Benjamin and Elizabeth Greenwood Child, b. in Watertown, Mass., Sept. 14, 1736, m. 1761, Phebe Jackson, dau. of Michael Jackson : she was b. Mch. 28, 1738, d. 1817.

[Fifth Generation.] Children, b. in Watertown, Mass

> 7066. i. AMARIAH CHILD, b. July 28, 1765, m. 1st, Ruth Larkin; m. 2d, Mrs. Ann Larkin; m. 3d, Betsey Larkin.
> 7067. ii. PHEBE CHILD, b. Oct. 22, 1775, m. — Dixon of Plymouth, Mass.
> 7068. iii. MIRIAM CHILD, b. 1777, m. Mr. Coen of Dorchester, Mass.

[Fifth Generation.]

7066. i. AMARIAH CHILD, eldest child of Aaron and Phebe Jackson Child, b. in Watertown, Mass., July 28, 1765, m. 1st, 1791, Ruth Larkin : she was b. Aug. 1, 1765, d. July 8, 1813 ; m. 2d, Mrs. Ann Larkin, an English lady, widow of his first wife's brother,—her maiden name was Rogers : she d. 1818 ; m. 3d, 1820, Betsey Larkin, sister of his first wife ; she d. in Malden, in 1854. He d. in Lynn, Mass., Jan. 21, 1846.

[Sixth Generation.] Children, born in Lynn, Mass.

> 7069. i. ELIZA JACKSON CHILD, b. Oct. 27, 1792, m. April 8, 1813, Caleb Wiley.
> 7070. ii. MARIAH OLIVIA CHILD, b. June 1794, m. Elijah Bigelow.
> 7071. iii. REBECCA CHILD, } TWINS { m. Rev. Ebenezer Nelson.
> 7072. iv. RUTH CHILD, } { b. Aug. 23, 1795. } { d. 1872, at Hyde Park, unm. æ 78.
> 7073. v. AMARIAH L. CHILD, b. Aug. 23, 1797, d. 1824, at Calcutta, East Indies, unm., æ 22 years.
> 7074. vi. EBEN LARKIN CHILD, b. May 6, 1799, m. 1st, 1826, Sarah P. Larkin; m. 2d, Oct. 23, 1872, Mrs. Eliza Bayne.
> 7075. vii. ISAAC CHILD, b. Feb. 1, 1801, m. Oct. 10, 1838, Susan Hathorne.
> 7076. viii. CATHARINE CHILD, b. Dec. 20, 1802, m. Sept 14, 1825, Daniel Breed.
> 7077. ix. MARY ANN CHILD, b. June 25, 1807, d. unm. in Jackson, Tenn, 1831, aged 24 years.
> 7078. x. SAMUEL CAPEN CHILD, b. May 22, 1809, m. Mary Burditt of Lynn.
> 7079. xi. GEORGE EDWIN CHILD, b. Oct. 12, 1814, m. Sarah Reed, d. about 1855, in Jeffersonville, Ind.
> 7080. xii. SOPHIA LINCOLN CHILD, b. Aug. 14, 1821, m. 1845, Wm. W. Webster.
> 7081. xiii. M. ELIZABETH CHILD, b. July 6, 1823, m. Wm. J. Eames.

[Sixth Generation.]

7069. i. ELIZA JACKSON CHILD, eldest child of Amariah and Ruth Larkin Child, b. in Lynn, Mass., Oct. 27, 1792, m. April 8, 1813, Caleb Wiley of Lynn, Mass., d. Nov. 5, 1869, in Lynn, Mass., aged 78. Had ten children.

[Seventh Generation.] Children, born in Lynn, Mass.

7082. i. HENRY G. WILEY, b. Oct. 27, 1792, m. Lizzie Perry.

7083. ii. RUTH ANN WILEY, m. Ezra Hathorne.

7084. iii. REBECCA CHILD WILEY, m. Thomas Cowden.

7085. iv. MARIA O. WILEY, m. Theodore Prentice.

7086. v. ELIZA C. WILEY, m. Rev. Jos. H. Towne.

7087. vi. CALEB W. WILEY, m. Georgia Nutting.

7088. vii. CATHARINE LUCY WILEY, m. L. W. Spooner. Three children, names not ascertained.

7089. viii. MARY ANN WILEY, m. Thomas McPhail. No children.

7090. ix. ELIZABETH LARKIN WILEY, m. Joshua Cobb.

7091. x. CAROLINE A. WILEY, m. Clarence Gay. One child, name not ascertained.

[Seventh Generation.]

7082. i. DR. HENRY G. WILEY, eldest child of Eliza J. Child and Caleb Wiley, b. in Lynn, Mass., Oct. 27, 1792, m. Lizzie Perry.

He was a physician of much prominence in his profession in Boston, and a citizen highly respected. The following extract from an article in Calvin Cutler's "Treatise on Anatomy and Physiology," (published in a school book,) gives the peculiar circumstances of his death :

"The highly respected Dr. Wiley of Boston, lost his life by poisonous matter from the body of a patient, subjected to a post-mortem examination. He removed from his finger, previous to the examination, a hang-nail, and the poison from the dead body was brought into contact with the denuded part, and through the agency of the lymphatics, it was conveyed into the system." He left no children.

[Seventh Generation.]

7083. ii. RUTH ANN WILEY, second child of Eliza Jackson Child and Caleb Wiley, m. Ezra Hathorne.

[Eighth Generation.] Children.

7092. i. IDA HATHORNE.

7093. ii. MARY HATHORNE.

[Seventh Generation.]

7084. iii. REBECCA CHILD WILEY, third child of Eliza J. Child and Caleb Wiley, m. Thomas Cowden.

[Eighth Generation.] Children :

7094. i. HENRY W. COWDEN.

7095. ii. ANNIE COWDEN.

7096 iii. CAROLINE COWDEN.

[Seventh Generation.]

7085. iv. MARIA O. WILEY, fourth child of Eliza J. Child and Caleb Wiley. m. Theodore Prentice.

[Eighth Generation.] Child:

7097. i. THEODORE PRENTICE, JR.

[Seventh Generation.]

7086. v. ELIZA CHILD WILEY, fifth child of Eliza J. Child and Caleb Wiley, m. Rev. Joseph H. Towne. Had six children.

[Eighth Generation.] Children:

7098. i. JOSEPH H. TOWNE. JR.
7099. ii. JOSHUA TOWNE.
7100. iii. ARTHUR TOWNE.
7101. iv. KATE W. TOWNE.
7102. v. WALTER TOWNE.
7103. vi Name not sent.

[Seventh Generation.]

7087. vi. CALEB W. WILEY, sixth child of Eliza J. Child and Caleb Wiley, m. Georgia Nutting.

[Eighth Generation.] Child:

7104. i. REBECCA WILEY.

[Seventh Generation.]

7090. ix. ELIZABETH LARKIN WILEY. ninth child of Eliza J. Child and Caleb Wiley, m. 1st, Joshua Cobb: m. 2d. — Abbott.

[Eighth Generation.] Children:

7105. i. CALEB COBB.
7106. ii. CLARENCE COBB.

[Sixth Generation.]

7070. ii. MARIA OLIVIA CHILDS. second child of Amariah and Ruth Larkin Childs. b. in Lynn. Mass. June 1794. m. Elijah Bigelow. She resided in Jackson. Tenn.. and died there in 1872.

From the daughters of Mrs. Maria O. Childs Bigelow. we receive a beautiful tribute to the worth and talents of their mother :

"Our parents were pioneers of this State (Tennessee). and first met in Nashville. Tenn. My mother, on the completion of her education, came to Tennessee and taught in the Nashville Academy. then one of the first institutions of the South. After six years my mother was married, and with her husband removed to Jackson. Tenn. Our father was a graduate of Harvard University. Cambridge. Mass. He built the first brick residence in the town. Five years after their marriage our father died. leaving my mother with three children. I must especially record my mother's indomitable energy and devotion to her children. whom she educated until my brother went to college."

For forty years Mrs. Bigelow was engaged in teaching after her marriage.

[Seventh Generation.] Children:

7107. i. ELIZA MARIA BIGELOW, m. Dr. Mason.

7108. ii. AMANDA C. BIGELOW, b. Dec. 20, 1829, m. April 2, 1857, Dr. Jones.

7109. iii. ELIJAH CHILDS BIGELOW, b. Oct. 1, 1861.

Elijah Childs Bigelow was "educated by his mother until he entered college, where he displayed such intelligence and fine abilities as to induce our mother to consent to his studying law. Whilst thus engaged he was seized with hip disease and after three years suffering died, just twenty-one years of age Not once did he murmur; beautiful and cheerful was that sick room; he died triumphant. 'He being dead yet speaketh.'"

[Seventh Generation.]

7107. i. ELIZA MARIA BIGELOW, eldest child of Maria O. Childs and Elijah Bigelow, b. in Jackson, Tenn., m. Dr. Joseph D. Mason of that place, son of Daniel and Dorothy L. Smith Mason. The father of Dr. Mason was a cousin of Gen. Winfield Scott; the family were of English descent. When fifteen years of age, Miss Bigelow went to Washington, D. C., to visit her uncle, Eben L. Child, of the U. S. Postoffice, and while there was confirmed by Bishop Whittingham of Maryland. From Washington she went to Boston and its vicinity to visit her relatives, and in Boston received instruction in music, for which she inherited an especial fondness. Returning to Jackson, she married Dr. Mason, and has been blessed with a lovely gifted family of children.

[Eighth Generation] Children:

7110. i. MARIA F. MASON, m. Mr. Nolan. "She came like a flower, and so passed away, when a young wife and mother, and with her infant son awaits the resurrection of the just."

7111. ii. MARY S. MASON, "distinguished by her excellent and finely cultivated voice and dignified manners, and firmness of character."

7112. iii. GEORGIA A. MASON. "A heart of gold, full of peace and good will, full of energy. A most acceptable teacher of music on piano and guitar, in Troy, Tennessee.

7113. iv. HATTIE MASON, d. young.

7114. v. EUNICE MASON, d. young.

7115. vi. AMANDA MASON, d. young.

7116. vii. CASSITY MASON, "most talented and highly educated; her special gift is for art, and her instructor pronounces her abilities most superior."

7117. viii. JOSEPH DANIEL MASON, "generous, truthful, and talented."

7118. ix. IDA BIGELOW MASON, a bright little girl who promises to equal in gifts and graces her elder sisters.*

* By some unintentional oversight the dates of this family were not sent.

[Seventh Generation.]

7108. ii. AMANDA C. BIGELOW, second dau. and child of Maria Olivia Childs and Elijah Bigelow, b. in Jackson, Tenn., Dec. 20, 1829, m. April 2, 1857, Rev. A. W. Jones, D. D., a clergyman of the Methodist Episcopal church: a graduate of Randolph College, Macon, Virginia. For more than a quarter of a century Dr. Jones has been the president of the Memphis Conference Female Institute, in Jackson, Tenn.

[Eighth Generation.] Children:

7119. i. IDA BIGELOW JONES, b. Jan. 28, 1858. "Graduate of the insti tute of which her father is President, she has in the Conservatory of Music in Boston continued her education, with special instruction in elocution."

7120. ii. GEORGE CHILD JONES, b. Aug. 29, 1859. "Graduating from the South Western University of Jackson, Tenn., before he was 17, he en tered the Vanderbilt University at Nashville, Tenn., and graduated with the degree of A. M., after three years study, not having attained his twenti eth year. He expects to devote his talents to the service of the Master."

7121. iii. EDWIN TURNER JONES, b. June 24, 1864, d. Oct. 11, 1866.

7122. iv. CHARLES FULLER JONES, b. Oct. 10, 1867, d. Oct. 15, 1867.

7123. v. AMMATILLE C. JONES, b. Dec. 8, 1869, "a bright, precocious child."

[Sixth Generation.]

7071. iii. REBECCA CHILD, third child and twin dau. of Amariah and Ruth Larkin Childs, m. Dec. 11, 1822. Rev. Ebenezer Nelson, a Baptist clergyman, d. at Hyde Park, Mass., 1876, aged 82 years. Mr. Nelson held pastorates of differing lengths in Lynn, West Cambridge and Middleboro, Mass.

[Seventh Generation.] Children:

7124. i. REBECCA R. C. NELSON, b. Sept. 7, 1823, m. Geo B. Richmond.

7125. ii. ELIZA FISKE WILLIAMS NELSON, b. Mch. 5, 1825, m. Rev. Alex. Carr.

7126. iii. ANN MARY NELSON, b. at Lynn, Mass., July 6, 1827, d. July 13, 1832.

7127. iv. AMARIAH C. NELSON, b. at West Cambridge. Mass., May 8, 1829, m. at Mt. Hope, Alabama, Annie Simmons.

7128. v. ABBIE M. NELSON, b. April 4, 1831, m. Wm. Read Bush.

7129. vi. EBEN LARKIN NELSON, b. Dec. 3, 1834, m. Nov. 1854, Miss Emma Cobb Mott. d. Dec. 4, 1859. No children.

[Seventh Generation.]

7124. i. REBECCA R. C. NELSON, eldest dau. of Rebecca Child and Rev. Ebenezer Nelson, b. Sept. 7, 1823, m. Geo. B. Richmond, b. Nov. 9, 1822, in New Bedford. Mass. : she d. July 31, 1863, in New Bedford, Mass.

[Eighth Generation.] Children:

7130. i. WILLIAM TALLMAN RUSSELL RICHMOND, b. at New Bedford, Oct. 7. 1845.

7131. ii. GEO. N. RICHMOND, b. in Middleboro, Sept. 3, 1848, d. July, 1851.

7132 iii. EMMA CLINTON RICHMOND, b. at New Bedford, Jan. 9, 1851.

7133. iv CHARLES NELSON RICHMOND, b. at New Bedford, May 6, 1853.

7134. v. GEORGE BARSTOW RICHMOND, b. at New Bedford, July 24, 1856

7135. vi. HENRY JACKSON RICHMOND, b. at New Bedford, May 1, 1863, d. July, 1865.

[Seventh Generation.]

7125. ii. ELIZA FISKE WILLIAMS NELSON, second child of Rebecca Childs and Rev. Ebenezer Nelson, b. in Lynn, Mass., Mch. 5, 1825, m. Aug. 7, 1850, Rev. Alexander Waterman Carr, a Baptist clergyman: has been settled in Rowley, Framingham, Medfield and Dighton, Mass., a most acceptable pastor.

[Eighth Generation.] Children, born in Rowley, Mass.

7136. i. ALLAN PERCY CARR, b. Feb. 16, 1852, m. Feb. 21, 1873, Sarah Eliza Bullard of Medfield, Mass.

7137. ii. CORA C. CARR, b. May 29, 1857, m. Oct. 14, 1875, Hubert Francis Morse.

7138 iii. ALICE W. CARR, b. May 9, 1860, d. Oct. 8, 1863, in Framingham, Mass.

[Seventh Generation.]

7128. v. ABBIE M. NELSON, fifth child of Rebecca Child and Rev. Ebenezer Nelson, b. at W. Cambridge, Mass., April 4, 1831, m. Oct. 1, 1855, Wm. Read Bush of Fall River, Mass.

[Eighth Generation.] Children, born at Fall River, Mass.

7139. i. WALTER NELSON BUSH, b. Sept. 12, 1856.

7140. ii. ARTHUR RICHMOND BUSH, b. April 30, 1859.

7141. iii. ANNIE CHILD BUSH, b. April 18, 1867.

7142. iv. GEORGIE BRAYTON BUSH, b. June 30, 1871.

7143. v. LIZZIE LINCOLN BUSH, b. Aug. 18, 1875.

[Sixth Generation.]

7074. vi. EBEN LARKIN CHILD, sixth child and second son of Amariah and Ruth Larkin Child, b. in Lynn, Mass., May 6, 1799, m. 1st, 1826, Sarah P. Larkin, his cousin and dau. of Mr. — Larkin of Portsmouth, N. H., a descendant also on her mother's side of the Wentworth's of New Hampshire. Mrs. Child was one of twenty-three children, of one father and mother, but of whom there are no male descendants to perpetuate the name. Married 2d. Oct. 23, 1872, Mrs. Eliza Speiden Bayne. He died while on his wedding tour, on the 29th of the same month in Albany, N. Y. He was for many years connected with the General Postoffice, Washington, D. C., in the division termed the Dead Letter Department. He was highly valued for his fidelity and efficiency as a public officer, and greatly esteemed for his personal qualities.

[Seventh Generation.] Child:

7144. i. REV. WENTWORTH LARKIN CHILD, b. in Portsmouth, N. H., 1827, m. 1855, Louisa Murdock, dau. of Wm. C. Murdock, Esq., of Bellvue,

D. C. He d. 1860, leaving no children. He was a man of fine intellect and thorough education. but not of a robust constitution. He was a clergyman of much promise in the Episcopal church. He stood high in the esteem of his associates in the ministry and was greatly beloved by a large circle of personal friends. He was an only child, the idol of his parents, who felt keenly their loss in his comparatively early death.

[Sixth Generation.]

7075. vii. ISAAC CHILD, seventh child and third son of Amariah and Ruth Larkin Child, b. in Lynn, Mass., Feb. 1, 1801, m. Oct. 10, 1838, Susan H. Hathorne of Lynn, Mass.

[Seventh Generation.] Child:

7145. i. ISAAC HERBERT CHILD, b. in Lynn, Mass., June 29, 1839, m. Julia Ann Hathorne. She was b. Oct. 7, 1845.

[Sixth Generation.]

7076. viii. CATHARINE CHILD, eighth child of Amariah and Ruth Larkin Child, b. Dec. 20, 1803, m. Col. Daniel N. Breed of Lynn, Mass. Residence Sacramento, Cal. Col. Breed d. at San Francisco, Cal., Sept. 13, 1868.

[Seventh Generation.] Children, born in Lynn, Mass.

7146. i. KATE ANN BREED, b. Aug. 14, 1826, m. Aug. 14, 1859, Jos. D. Lord.

7147. ii. H. MARIA BREED, b. Jan. 12, 1828, m. Samuel K. White.

7148. iii. HARRIET OTIS BREED, b. April 17, 1831. d. Mch. 23, 1832.

7149. iv. DANIEL CHILD BREED, b. June 8, 1834 m Aug. 23. 1864, Nellie E. Hastings

[Seventh Generation.]

7146. i. KATE ANN BREED, eldest child of Catharine Child and Col. Daniel N. Breed. b. in Lynn, Mass., Aug. 14, 1826, m. Aug. 24, 1859, Joseph D. Lord of Sacramento, Cal.

[Eighth Generation] Children:

7150. i. EMMA MARIA LORD, b. in Sacramento, Jan. 19, 1861. Graduated at Sacramento Seminary, May, 187-.

7151. ii. FREDERICK RREED LORD, b. in Grass Valley, Cal., June 19, 1867.

7152. iii. JOSEPH D. LORD, JR., b. in Sacramento, Cal., Nov. 16, 1869.

[Seventh Generation]

7147. ii. H. MARIA BREED, second child of Catharine Child and Col. Daniel Breed, b. in Lynn, Mass., Jan. 12, 1828, m. 1st, Sept. 14, 1853, at Lynn. Mass., Samuel K. White of Charlestown, Mass.; Mr. White d. May 5, 1854; Mrs. White m. 2d, June 24, 1863, Rev. Charles R. Hendrickson, D. D., at San Francisco, Cal. They reside in Jackson. Tenn.

[Eighth Generation.] Children:

7153. i. CHARLES BREED HENDRICKSON, b. at Stockton, Cal., June 17. 1864, d. May 3, 1865.

7154. ii. GRACE HENDRICKSON, b. at Stockton, Cal., Nov. 21, 1866, d. at San Francisco, Cal., Mch. 20, 1870

7155. iii. EDWARD BREED HENDRICKSON, b. at San Francisco, Cal., Jan. 7, 1869, d. Dec. 25, 1869.

[Seventh Generation.]

7149. iv. DANIEL CHILD BREED, fourth child of Catharine
Child and Col. Daniel N. Breed, b. at Lynn, Mass., June 8,
1834, m. Aug. 23, 1864, Nellie Hastings, at San Francisco, Cal.
Reside at San Francisco, Cal.

[Eighth Generation.] Children, born at San Francisco, Cal.:
7156. i. ARTHUR HASTINGS BREED, b Nov. 27, 1865.
7157. ii. HERBERT LINCOLN BREED, b. May 24, 1878.

[Sixth Generation.]

7078. x. SAMUEL CHAPIN CHILD, tenth child and fourth
son of Amariah and Ruth Larkin Child, b. May 22, 1809, m.
Mary Burdell of Lynn, Mass. Resided in California, died at
Stockton, Cal., 1869, æ 60 years.

[Seventh Generation.] Children:
7158. i. EDWARD CHILD, killed in the battle of Chickamauga, Va., in
the war of the Rebellion.
7159. ii. CATHARINE CHILD.

[Sixth Generation.]

7080. xii. SOPHIA LINCOLN CHILD, twelfth child of Ama
riah and Ruth Larkin Child, b. in Lynn, Mass., Aug. 14,
1821, m. 1845, William W. Webster. Had three children.

[Seventh Generation.] Children:
7160. i. Name not given, died.
7161. ii. ISABEL WEBSTER, b. in Boston, Mass., Dec. 10 1847, m. Oct. 6,
1869, Judge W. E. Green.
7162. iii. REGINAL WEBSTER, b. in Boston, Mass., Jan. 23, 1857.

[Seventh Generation.]

7161. ii. ISABEL WEBSTER, dau. of Sophia Lincoln Child
and William W. Webster, b. Dec. 10, 1847, m. Oct. 6, 1869,
Judge W. E. Green of Oakland, Cal. Had four children.

[Eighth Generation.] Children, born in Oakland, Cal.:
7163. i. CARLTON W. GREEN, b. Aug. 4, 1870.
7164. ii. MABEL E GREEN, b. July 26, 1872.
7165. iii. ETHEL A. GREEN, b. Aug. 31, 1877.
7166. iv. Unnamed b. June 1, 1879.

[Sixth Generation.]

7081. xiii. ELIZABETH CHILD, thirteenth child of Amariah
and Ruth Larkin Child, b. in Lynn, Mass., July 6, 1823, m.
Wm. J. Eames of Malden. Resides in Jersey City, N. J.

[Seventh Generation.] Children:
7167. i. WALLACE EAMES, b. July, 1853.
7168. ii. MALCOLM EAMES.
7169. iii. ARTHUR EAMES.
7170. iv. GRACE EAMES.
7171. v. BESSIE EAMES.

B-2

AMHERST CHILD AND DESCENDANTS.

The first record we obtain of Amherst Child is in the town of Rutland, Mass., where his marriage is registered ; and eight years later (1798) the town records state him to be the owner of land valued at $412. We have followed all known clues to ascertain his parentage, or birthplace, unavailingly. He may be of the Barnstable or Watertown lines, as descendants of each are found in Rutland. We give these in the generations of their contemporaries in other lines.

[Fifth Generation.]

7172. AMHERST CHILD, b. Aug. 1, 1769, m. June 20, 1790, Lucy Moore ; she was b. in Rutland, Dec. 1, 1769. The eldest child was born in Worcester, Mass., the others in Rutland.

[Sixth Generation.] Children :

7173. i. GARDNER CHILD, b. April 28, 1791, m. June 27, 1815, Lucy Wilson.

7174. ii. NATHANIEL B. CHILD, b. Feb. 12, 1793, m. abt. 1830, Jane Hall.

7175. iii. ELEANOR CHILD, b. Oct. 31, 1795, d. Nov. 4, 1876.

7176. iv. SAMUEL CHILD, b. Aug. 26, 1796.

7177. v. AMHERST CHILD, b. June 5, 1799, m. Nov. 12, 1828, Lavissa Southwick.

7178. vi. MARY M. CHILD, b. June 1, 1801.

7179. vii. ROXY CHILD, b. Feb. 6, 1803.

7180. viii. SUBMIT S. CHILD, b. Oct. 2, 1804, m. Enos Kent.

7181. ix. LUCY W. CHILD, b. Nov. 25, 1806, m. William Beal.

7182. x. TYRUS M. CHILD, b. Mch. 27, 1809

7183. xi. EUNICE C. CHILD, b. Aug. 16, 1811.

[Sixth Generation.]

7173. i. GARDNER CHILD, eldest child of Amherst and Lucy Moore Child, b. in Worcester, Mass., April 28, 1791, m. June 27, 1815, Lucy Wilson, who was b. April 8, 1794. Gardner Child d. May 18, 1871, his widow Mch. 23, 1879.

[Seventh Generation.] Children :

7184. i. GEORGE A. CHILDS, b. May 28, 1816.

7185. ii. STEPHEN W. CHILDS, b. May 4, 1821, m. July 3, 1841, Penina Langdon.

7186. iii. GARDINER C. CHILDS, b. Dec. 22, 1822, m. 1st, July 1, 1845, Susan Sherman; m. 2d, Nov. 1849, Mary Ellenwood.

7187. iv. WILLIAM K. CHILDS, b. Sept. 23, 1824.

7188. v. MARY M. CHILDS, b. Oct. 2, 1826, d. Dec. 12, 1836.

7189. vi. DAVID M. CHILDS, b. Feb. 12, 1829, m. Jan. 13, 1856, Elizabeth Lemon.

7190. vii. TYRUS M. CHILDS, b. Aug. 27, 1833, d. Mch. 4, 1837.

[Seventh Generation.]

7186. iii. DR. GARDNER C. CHILDS, third son and child of Gardner and Lucy Wilson Childs, b. Dec. 24, 1822, m. 1st,

Susan P. Sherman, July 1, 1845, who d. June 1847; m. 2d, Nov. 1847, Mary A. Ellinwood. Resides in Clyde, Wayne county, N. Y.

[Eighth Generation.] Children:
    7191. i. KITTIE F. CHILDS.
    7192. ii. JOHN H. CHILDS.
    7193. iii. CORA S. CHILDS.

[Seventh Generation.]

    7189. vi. DAVID M. CHILDS, fifth son and sixth child of Gardner and Lucy Wilson Childs, b. Feb. 12, 1829, m. Jan. 13, 1856, Elizabeth Lemon, who was b. Sept. 1, 1830.

[Eighth Generation.] Children:
    7194. i. LUCY E. CHILDS, b. Nov. 25, 1856, d. Nov. 20, 1865.
    7195. ii. ALICE MAY CHILDS, b. Mch. 18, 1859.
    7196. iii. LOUISA BELLE CHILDS, b. Oct. 12, 1862.
    7197. iv. AMHERST LEMON CHILDS, b. July 23, 1867.
    7198. v. GALA DAVID CHILDS, b. Dec. 8, 1873.

[Sixth Generation.]

    7174. ii. NATHANIEL B. CHILDS, second son and child of Amherst and Lucy Moore Child, b. in Rutland, Mass., Feb. 12, 1793, m. about 1831, Jane Hall. Mr. N. B. Childs died Dec. 21, 1865.

[Seventh Generation.] Children:
    7199. i. GEORGE CHILDS, b. May 6, 1832.
    7200. ii. JOHN CHILDS, b. Jan. 12, 1834.
    7201. iii. LUCY JANE CHILDS, b. Feb 12, 1836.
    7202. iv. CAROLINE CHILDS, b. Mch. 21, 1838.
    7203. v. HENRY OTIS CHILDS, b. Oct. 17, 1841.
    7204. vi. WILLIAM ALBERT CHILDS, b. Aug. 24, 1846.

[Sixth Generation.]

    7177. v. DR. AMHERST CHILDS, fifth child and fourth son of Amherst and Lucy Moore Childs, b. in Rutland, Mass., June, 1799, m. Nov. 12, 1828, Lavissa Southwick, daughter of Major David Southwick, one of the pioneers of Seneca county, New York. Mrs. Lavissa S. Childs was born April 1, 1811. Mr. Childs came to Seneca county, N. Y., about the year 1820, entered the Fairfield Seminary, in Fairfield, Herkimer county, and graduated from the medical department. He also studied medicine with Dr. Gardner Welles of Waterloo, Seneca county, and attended lectures in Albany. Dr. Childs was for many years a successful and honored practitioner in Waterloo; here he married, as we find, in 1828, and here closed the laborious life of a country physician, whose ride is often of many miles, June 17, 1869.

Seventh Generation.] Children:

7205. i. DAVID AMHERST CHILDS, b. Aug. 12, 1830, d. Dec. 4, 1830.

7206. ii. JANE E. CHILDS, b. June 15, 1832, m. 1st, May 18, 1853, Norman P. Childs, who d. June 23, 1865; m. 2d, April 12, 1869, Elias Ronig.

7207. iii. EUNICE MARIA CHILDS, b. Aug. 5, 1834, m. May 13, 1857, S. H. Gridley, Jr.

7208. iv. HENRY AMHERST CHILDS, b. Nov. 7, 1836, d. Oct. 3, 1864, after a life of invalidism.

7209. v. ALBERT LUCAS CHILDS, b. April 12, 1840.

7210. vi. LUCY M. CHILDS, b. Nov. 6, 1843, m. Jan. 4, 1864, John S. Herrick.

7211. vii. ANNIE F. CHILDS, b. Mch. 17, 1848.

[Seventh Generation.]

7206. ii. JANE E. CHILDS, second child and eldest dau. of Dr. Amherst and Lavissa Southwick Childs, b. in Waterloo, Seneca county, N. Y., June 15, 1832, m. 1st, May 18, 1853, Norman Parsons Child; m. 2d, April 12, 1869, Elias Ronig of Waterloo. Mr. N. P. Childs was a son of Benjamin N. Childs of Worcester, Mass., b. June 4, 1827. For several years Mr. Childs was in practice as a dentist in Waterloo, N. Y. He returned to his native city and engaged in the manufacture of wire. In 1865, Mr. Childs accompanied by his family, removed to Jacmel, Hayti, West Indies. A form of yellow fever appeared on the island and one daughter died of this disease ; returning at once to the United States, but bringing with him the fatal epidemic, Mr. Childs died in the Boston hospital two days after landing, June 23, 1865. Mr. Norman P. Childs is doubtless of the Watertown line.

[Eighth Generation.] Children:

7212. i. EDWARD PAYSON CHILDS, b. at Waterloo, N. Y., July 22, 1854, prepared for college at Wilbraham Academy, Mass. Entered Williams College, Sept. 1877, with the ministry in view.

7213. ii. FRANCES MARIA CHILDS, b. at Worcester, Mass., Oct. 17, 1859, d. at Jacmel Hayti, West Indies, May 27, 1865.

7214. iii. JESSIE PARSONS CHILDS, b. at Worcester, Mass., July 1st, 1863. Lives with her mother Mrs. Ronig in Waterloo, N. Y.

[Seventh Generation.]

7207. iii. EUNICE MARIA CHILDS, third child and second dau. of Dr. Amherst and Lavissa Southwick Childs, b. in Waterloo, Seneca county, N. Y., Aug. 5, 1834, m. May 13, 1857, S. H. Gridley, Jr., son of Rev. Samuel Hart Gridley, D. D. and Mary Ann Hart. Mr. Gridley is a produce dealer in Waterloo, N. Y. Rev. Dr. Gridley the father has been forty years pastor of the Presbyterian church of Waterloo, N. Y.

[Eighth Generation.] Children:

7215. i. MARY LARISSA GRIDLEY, b. Feb. 8, 1861.

7216. ii. LAURA MARIA GRIDLEY, b. Mch. 6, 1863.

7217. iii. AMHERST CHILDS GRIDLEY, b. Feb. 12, 1870, d. Aug. 10, 1870.
7218. iv. SAMUEL CHILDS GRIDLEY, b Sept. 2, 1871, d. Mch. 21, 1873.

[Seventh Generation.]

7209. v. HON. ALBERT LUCAS CHILDS, third son and fifth child of Dr. Amherst and Lavissa Southwick Childs, born at Seneca Falls, N. Y., April 12, 1840. Received an early physical training upon a farm, which also fitted him to graduate, in 1861, at Hamilton College, Clinton, N. Y. He studied law in the office of Hon. S. G. Hadley, and was admitted to practice in 1865. Was a member of the State Legislature for Seneca county in 1877. He has delivered a number of lectures, and is well known as a public speaker throughout Western New York. At present is editor and proprietor of the *Seneca County News*, a very lively, spicy sheet, that is a general favorite in Seneca county and vicinity. A. L. Childs has held a number of positions of trust and responsibility. Has been U. S. gauger a number of years; clerk of the superintendent of Cayuga and Seneca canal; justice of the peace, &c., positions which he has filled with credit and ability. Is author of a poem-lecture, the "Song of the Shoe," of a humorous nature, that has found favor before many audiences. The accompanying little poem, one of many flowing from the facile pen of the Hon. editor, we insert as a specimen of his humorous rythmical gifts:

"THE SHOE IS ON THE OTHER FOOT."

We always when in fine array,
　The best foot forward try to put,
Yet often find to our dismay
　The shoe is on the other foot.

One morning when the Sabbath bell
　Was tolling with a solemn sound,
Inviting sinners by its call,
　From all the peaceful village round:

The gentle folk with guarded talk
　And faces dignified, serene;
In Sunday-dress with measured walk
　All moving toward the church were seen.

By some misfortune unrevealed,
　Old Deacon Marble, clever soul,
Was hurrying churchward through the field,
　Because the bell had ceased to toll!

But soon he reached the meadow brook,
　And stopped and laid his Bible down;
The swollen stream with laughter shook
　To see the Deacon wear a frown.

A single leap would not suffice,
　And Deacon had no time to lose:

To jump a stream of such a size
  Would take the polish from his shoes!

He eyed his shoes with troubled look,
  And hesitated, sore perplexed;
And wondered could he wade the brook
  In time to hear the Parson's text!

A happy thought came by and by;
  One shoe and stocking off he took,
And thought with one bare foot to try
  And cross this saucy laughing brook!

With one foot bared, and one foot dressed,
  With shoe and stocking and his book,
Our Deacon with an earnest zest
  Prepares to cross the swollen brook.

By this economy, thought he,
  I soon the other side shall reach,
And then to church will safely be
  In time to hear the Parson preach.

Such Sunday work is sure no sin;
  But never did the Deacon dream
That he might put the wrong foot in
  The middle of the laughing stream.

By this mild bit of compromise
  I'll keep one foot from getting wet;
So back the Deacon steps and tries
  Upon the other side to get.

Now up he comes with lively leap,
  Most eagerly the task to try,
But dumps the wrong foot in the deep,
  And lands the bare foot high and dry!

With sorry phiz he sighs to see
  His Sunday stocking all wet through.
While giggling, rippling brook with glee
  Pokes fun at Deacon's dripping shoe!

Too late he now counts up the cost,
  Because the wrong foot in was put;
The text and sermon both are lost,
  The shoe was on the other foot!

So, often we in fine array,
  Our best foot forward try to put,
And often find to our dismay,
  The shoe is on the other foot!

[Seventh Generation.]

7210. vi. Lucy M. Childs, third dau. and sixth child of
Dr. Amherst and Larissa Southwick Childs, b. in Waterloo,
Seneca county, N. Y., Nov. 6, 1843, m. Jan. 4, 1864, John T.
Herrick, a civil engineer, and lived several years in Denver,
Colorado. Mrs. Lucy M. Childs Herrick died at Clifton
Springs Water-Cure, where she had gone for her health, Aug.
14, 1871.

[Eighth Generation.] Child:

7219. i. Larissa Childs Herrick, b. Jan. 10, 1865, d. Oct. 5, 1865.

CHARLES CHILD.

We must preface this group of the Child name, and the two succeeding with the same regretful unlinking to an emigrant ancestor. Several of these groups would doubtless come rightly in other positions, for there is presumptive evidence of their relationship. We have had strong hope to find the missing links, and while writing up the other parts of the work, have been constantly following every thread presented, if it might be, the labyrinth should be revealed.

The three following branches, unknown perhaps to each other are, we cannot doubt, the descendants of John and Elizabeth Child of Woodstock, Ct., (see page 427,) through their son Nathaniel who is with his *known* children given on page 440; as we there state, Nathaniel is known to have had a large family of children, but we find and trace but two sons We have deemed it wise to place these lines in such order of generation as we find their contemporaries to be whose line of descent we are able to trace connectedly, as being more nearly correct, than to place them in the first and second generations and so on from the earliest known of the particular line.

[Sixth Generation.]

7220. CHARLES CHILD, b. probably in Woodstock, Ct., (no date given of birth.) m. 1st, abt. 1783, Olive Hammond; m. 2d, Olive Griffith of Hampton, Ct.

[Seventh Generation.] Children: By first marriage.

7221. i. OLIVER CHILD, b. April 7, 1785, d. Oct. 18, 1802

7222. ii. HANNAH CHILD, b. June 18, 1786, m. Dr. Charles Eldridge.

7223. iii. MATILDA CHILD, b. Mch. 15, 1788. m. abt. 1818, Charles Henshaw.

7224. iv. HORACE CHILD, b. Jan. 6, 1791, d. July 9, 1791.

7225. v. JULIA CHILD, b. July 17, 1793, d. April 5, 1806.

7226. vi. SARAH CHILD, b. Oct. 9, 1795, d. Oct. 18, 1802.

7227. vii. CHARLES CHILD, JR., b. Jan. 31, 1798, d. Oct. 16, 1802.

7228. viii. Infant, (unchristened,) b. Nov. 15, 1801, d. young.

7229. ix. CHARLES HORACE CHILD, b. Dec. 28, 1802, d. Aug. 16, 1819.

7230. x. ELISHA CHILD, b. Mch. 19, 1805, m. 1st, Mch. 31, 1828; m. 2d, Sophia M. Aldrich.

[Seventh Generation.]

7222. ii. HANNAH CHILD, second child, eldest dau. of Charles and Olive Hammond Child, b. June 18, 1786, m. Dr. Charles Eldridge of Brookline, Ct. Settled in East Greenwich, R. I. She d. Oct. 24, 1819.

[Eighth Generation.] Children:

7231. i. CHARLES ELDRIDGE, m. Sarah Pierce, d. 1846 or '47; five children.

7232. ii. LUCY GALLUP ELDRIDGE, m. Israel Sheldon of Orange, N. J.: have no children.

7223. iii. JAMES ELDRIDGE, m. Anna T. A. Henshaw; have two children.

[Eighth Generation.]

7233. iii. DR. JAMES ELDRIDGE, third child of Dr. Charles and Olive Hammond Child Eldridge, m. Anna T. A. Henshaw.

[Ninth Generation.] Children:

7234. i. ANNIE ELDRIDGE.

7235. ii. EMILY ROLF ELDRIDGE, m. — Holbrook, and lives in Minneapolis, Minnesota.

[Seventh Generation.]

7223. iii. MATILDA CHILD, third child of Charles and Olive Hammond Child, b. Mch. 15, 1788, m. about 1818, Charles Henshaw of Boston, Mass.

[Eighth Generation.] Children:

7236. i. LAURA MATILDA HENSHAW, b. April 15, 1819, m. Oct. 24, 1855, John M. Crane.

7237. ii. CHARLES CHILD HENSHAW, b. Mch. 30, 1821, m. 1st, Oct. 27, 1843. Elizabeth Fisher of Boston; she d. Mch. 1849; m. 2d, Georgiana Hammond, dau. of Edward and Eliza Smith Hammond. Charles C. Henshaw died Jan. 11, 1868, of cancer. Mrs. H. died Jan. 10, 1872.

7238. iii. Infant unchristened.

7239. iv. DAVID HENSHAW b. July 19, 1824, m. Jan. 28, 1847, Frances A. Daniels.

7240. v. JOHN HENSHAW, b. Aug. 16, 1826, d. in East Medway, Sept. 17, 1876 of consumption.

7241. vi. GEORGE HENSHAW, b. Jan. 1, 1829. Resides in Boston, unm.

[Eighth Generation.]

7236. i. LAURA MATILDA HENSHAW, eldest child of Matilda Child and Charles Henshaw, b. April 15, 1819, m. Oct. 24, 1855, John Martin Crane, son of Rev. Silas Axtelle and Mary Elizabeth Martin Crane of East Greenwich, R. I.

[Ninth Generation.] Children:

7242. i. CHARLES HENSHAW CRANE, b. Aug. 30, 1857, d. May 1, 1863.

7243. ii. HENRY AXTELLE CRANE, b. Oct. 30, 1858, m. May 29, 1879, Ida Louise Mason of East Medway, Mass.

7244. iii. CLARENCE MITCHELL CRANE, b. June 7, 1862.

[Eighth Generation.]

7239. iv. DAVID HENSHAW, second son of Matilda Child and Charles Henshaw, b. July 19, 1824, m. Jan. 28, 1847, Frances A. Daniels of Chester, Ct. He d. in Boston, Mch. 16, 1872. Mrs. H. resides in Boston, Mass.

[Ninth Generation.] Children:

7245. i. FRANCES MATILDA HENSHAW, b. Dec. 2, 1848, m. April 25, 1872, Alonzo M. Codman.

7246. ii. CHARLES DANIELS HENSHAW, b. Mch. 11, 1850.

7247. iii. DAVID HENSHAW, JR., b. Nov. 24, 1852.

7248. iv. WILLIAM ISAAC HENSHAW, b. Aug. 4, 1854.

[Ninth Generation.]

7245. i. FRANCES MATILDA HENSHAW, eldest child of David and Frances A. Daniels Henshaw, and grand daughter of Matilda Child Henshaw, b. Dec. 2, 1848, m. April 25, 1872, Alonzo Mortimer Codman of Hillsboro, N. H.

[Tenth Generation.] Child:

7249. i. CHARLES HENSHAW CODMAN.

[Seventh Generation.]

7230. x. ELISHA CHILD, tenth and youngest child of Charles and Olive Hammond Child, b. Mch. 9, 1805, m. 1st, Mch. 21, 1828, Lora Davison ; she was b. Sept. 13, 1803 ; m. 2d, Sophia M. Aldrich, b. 1856. He d. Dec. 14, 1878.

[Eighth Generation.] Children, born in Pomfret, Ct.

7250. i. CHARLES HENSHAW CHILD, b Mch. 18, 1829, d. Mch 26, 1847
7251. ii. OLIVE ANN CHILD, b. Jan. 31, 1831, m. John McClellan.
7252. iii. GEORGE CLINTON CHILD, b. Jan. 27, 1833, m. Eliza A F. Congdon.
7253. iv. EMILY MATILDA CHILD, b. Oct. 18, 1834, d. Mch. 30, 1838.
7254. v. LAURA MATILDA CHILD, b. Oct. 14, 1836, d. Feb. 13, 1837.
7255. vi. ELIZABETH CHILD, b. Nov. 21, 1838, d. Mch. 8, 1842
                        By second marriage :
               [Williams, dau. of Calone Williams of Pomfret, Ct.
7256. vii. FREDERICK MARCY CHILD, } TWINS { m. Nov. 14, 1877, Mattie A.
                                                    b. June 12, 1857.
7257. viii. ELLEN CHILD,   d. Sept. 10, 1857.
7258. ix. MARY CHILD, b. Mch. 7, 1858,
7259. x. HORACE CHILD, b. July 27, 1860.

[Eighth Generation.]

7251. ii. OLIVE ANN CHILD, second child, eldest dau. of Elisha and Lora Davison Child, b. Jan. 31, 1831, at Pomfret, Ct., m. Feb. 16, 1859, John McClellan of Woodstock, Ct

[Ninth Generation.] Children, born in Woodstock, Ct.:

7260. i. JOHN McCLELLAN, JR , b. Dec. 20, 1859, d. July 15, 1863.
7261. ii. MARY TRUMBULL McCLELLAN, b. June 31, 1861, d. July 13, 1863.
7262. iii. JESSE TRUMBULL McCLELLAN, b. Aug. 30, 1863.
7263. iv. PERCY TELL McCLELLAN, b. June 6, 1865.
7264. v. GEORGE ELDRIDGE McCLELLAN, b. Oct. 16, 1868.

[Eighth Generation.]

7252. iii. GEORGE CLINTON CHILD, third child of Elisha and Lora Davison Child, b. in Pomfret, Ct , Jan. 27, 1833, m. Jan. 22, 1857, Eliza A. F. Congdon of Hopeville, Ct. : she was b. in Thompson, Ct., June 27, 1834. Reside in Oxford, Mass.

[Ninth Generation.] Children :

7265. i. CHARLES C. CHILD, b. Nov. 2, 1857, d. July 4, 1862.
7266. ii. EZRA L. W. CHILD, b. Oct. 4, 1859, d. July 2, 1861.
7267. iii. FRANK S. CHILD, b. Dec. 7, 1860.
7268. iv. MARY A. W. CHILD, b. Dec. 9, 1862.
7269. v. GEORGE C. CHILD, JR., b. Jan. 4, 1868.
7280. vi. LORA F. CHILD, b. Sept. 26, 1869, d. Jan. 16, 1873.
7271. vii. EDWIN W. CHILD, b. Feb. 19, 1872, d. Dec. 28, 1872.

ISSACHAR CHILD AND DESCENDANTS

[Fifth Generation.]

7272. In the town records of Woodstock, Ct., is found re corded the name of Issachar Child, m. Nov. 20, 1766, Alathea Moffat. He was b. 1749 and d. July 13, 1797. She d. Oct. 5, 1812, æ 68. We have been unable to trace his ancestry. There is little doubt that he was of the Roxbury, Mass., line of emigrants.

This record is supplemented by one of his descendants Casper C. Childs, Esq. of New York City. Mr. C. adds the "s:" it is not a terminal in the Woodstock records.

[Sixth Generation.]   Children:

7273. i. EVANDER CHILD, b. in Woodstock, Ct., May 16, 1767, m. 1st, May 11, 1790, Margaretta Bush, dau. of Charles and Catharine Bush: m 2d, May 18, 1800, Mary Vermilyea.

7274. ii. ISSACHAR CHILD, JR., b. in South Brimfield, Mass., Aug. 23, 1768.

7275. iii. EPAPHRAS CHILD, b. in Stafford Springs, Ct., Mch. 17, 1770.

7276. iv. CASPER CHILD, b. in Stafford Springs, Ct. July 15, 1772, d. July 15, 1797.

7277. v. LEMUEL CHILD, b. in Schenectady, N. Y., Aug. 12, 1774, d. Aug. 12, 1795.

7278. vi. ALATHEA CHILD, b. in Albany, N. Y., June 1, 1776, d. June 9, 1776.

[Sixth Generation.]

7273. i. EVANDER CHILD, eldest child of Issachar and Alathea Child, b. in Woodstock, Ct., May 16, 1767, m. 1st, May 11, 1790, Margaretta Bush : m. 2d, May 18, 1800, Mary Vermilyea. Margaretta Child died Aug. 3, 1797. Mary Vermilyea Child, died April 28, 1841. He died Jan. 1851.

[Seventh Generation.]   Children. By first marriage:

7279. i. CHARLES BUSH CHILDS, b. Dec. 20, 1791, died.

7280. ii. CHARLES BUSH CHILDS, 2D. b Nov. 2, 1793.

7281. iii. CATHARINE CHILDS, b Dec. 19, 1795, d. April 5, 1876.

By 2d marriage.

7282. iv. CASPER C. CHILDS, b. Dec. 3, 1803, m. 1st, July 23, 1826, Sophronia Horton: m. 2d, June 13, 1871, Sarah C. Ball.

7283. v. EVANDER CHILDS, JR., b. Oct. 30, 1805.

7284. vi. AUGUSTUS F. CHILDS, b. Mch. 11, 1808.

7285. vii. WALTER L. CHILDS, b. Nov. 21, 1811.

7286. viii. JOHN V. CHILDS, b. Nov. 15, 1813.

7287. ix. MARY V. CHILDS, b. Nov. 6, 1817.

[Seventh Generation.]

7282. iv. CASPER C. CHILDS, fourth child and third son of Evander and Mary Vermilyea Child, b. Dec. 3, 1803, m. 1st, July 23, 1826, Sophronia Horton: m. 2. June 13, 1871, Mrs. Sarah C. Ball.

[Eighth Generation.] Children:

7288. i. MARY V. CHILDS, b. April 30, 1827, m. about 1858, Mr. Bliss.
7289. ii. SOPHRONIA CHILDS, b. Dec. 31, 1828.
7290. iii. CASPER C. CHILDS, JR., b. Aug. 13, 1830.
7291. iv. LOUISA CHILDS, b. Mch. 16, 1832, m. about 1862, Mr. Bell.
7292. v. CLARISSA CHILDS, b. June 22, 1835.
7293. vi. SARAH ANN CHILDS, b. Dec. 11, 1837.
7294. vii. CHARLES B. CHILDS, b. Feb. 9, 1841.
7295. viii. WALTER L. CHILDS, b. 1843.

[Eighth Generation.]

7288. i. MARY V. CHILD, eldest child of Casper C. and Sophronia Horton Childs, b. April 30, 1827, m. about 1858, Mr. Bliss.

[Ninth Generation.] Children:

7296. i. FRANK BLISS, b. Jan. 12, 1859.

7297. ii. ANDREW K. BLISS, b. April 2, 1863.

[Eighth Generation.]

7291. iv. LOUISA CHILDS, fourth child of Casper C. and Sophronia Horton Childs, b. Mch. 16, 1832, m. abt. 1862, Mr. Ball.

[Ninth Generation.] Child:

7298. i. EDWARD B. BALL, b. April 12, 1863.

JOHN P. CHILD AND DESCENDANTS.

[Fifth Generation.]

7299. JOHN P. CHILD, somewhat like Melchizedech without father or mother, is yet found to have married Judith Williams.

[Sixth Generation.] Child.

7300. BENJAMIN CHILD, b. Dec. 18, 1789, in Pomfret, Ct., m. in Killingly, Ct., Jan. 27, 1825, by Rev. Roswell Whitmore, Mary Foote, dau. of Israel and Mary Hale Foote of Marlboro, Ct., where she was b. Mch. 20, 1798. They removed from Marlboro, Ct., to Pomfret, Ct., in 1828. They removed from Pomfret to Killingley, in 1868. He died there in 1872. Mrs. Child resides with her son Geo. D. Child at 4342 Bellevue avenue, Chicago, Ill., to which place she removed in 1876.

[Seventh Generation.] Child:

7301. i GEO D. CHILD, b. at Pomfret, Ct., Sept. 17, 1831, m. Dec. 23, 1855, Cordelia Lumbard, dau. of Corlis and Armina Stoddard Lumbard of Pomfret, Ct. Mr. Lumbard died at Pomfret, Ct., Feb. 4, 1857. Mrs. Armina Lumbard resides with her daughter Mrs Geo. D. Child, at 4342 Bellevue avenue, Chicago. A commendable obedience to the Fifth Commandment. Thus caring for parents who have cared for them in their infancy. Mr. Child is a Western traveling agent for the Worcester, Mass., Corset Co.

[Eighth Generation.] Child:

7302. i. MARY ELLA CHILD, b. in Freeport, Ill., April 28, 1862.

CHAPTER XIII.

HENRY CHILD AND DESCENDANTS.

This line of the Child name in America is the only one of any considerable numbers whose home in the mother country is known with certainty.

7303. HENRY CHILD resided in Coldshill, in the parish of Rindersham, Hertford county, England; or as another account says, at Horring Crook, England. He had quite a family of children, only one of whom seems to have emigrated to the New World. The family were of the society of Friends, as many of them still are. From William Penn, Henry Child made purchase of 500 acres of land, for which he paid £10 on the 20th of January, 1687. Henry Child accompanied his young son Cephas to America, in 1693, and the purchased land was then located in Plumstead, Bucks county, Pa., near the headwaters of the Neshamony. Cephas Child was placed for a time in some family in Philadelphia, where he was taught the carpenter's trade. In 1715, Henry Child, "for the love and affection he beareth to his son Cephas," gave the above mentioned five hundred acres of land to him. With the deed Cephas, and some others, went from Baltimore to Philadelphia on foot. Cephas Child married Mary Atkinson and settled in Plumstead, Pa. Henry Child did not remain long in America. We have the copies of two most loving letters addressed by him to his son Cephas, which we would give entire for the interest to descendants did our space permit. Each of these letters date from Horring Crook, the first date: " Ye 2d of 4 mo. 1729 "; the second:

" YE 22D OF 3 MO., 1738.

"DEAR CHILD:—I thought I might have had a line from thee by some at our yearly meeting. I should be glad to hear what family thou hast, and how things prosper with thee. I desire thou mayest seek the Lord above all, that His wisdom may guide thee in all thy undertakings, that His name and truth may be honored by thee, that His blessings and mercies may be with thee, through the great mercy of the Lord. I and my family are in health, and thy sisters and their families. I gave thee account of thy brother's departure in my last letter to thee; so with love to thee and thy wife and friends, in the truth of our Lord Jesus Christ, I rest thy loving father,   HENRY CHILD,

We felt the gracious words of this epistle from the father of this line, would prove a genuine benison for his descendants, having lost none of its sweetness in the one hundred and forty-three years since it was penned.

[Second Generation.]

7304. CEPHAS CHILD, son of Henry Child of Hertford county, England, was born in England and came to America in 1693, and married Feb. 1716, Mary Atkinson. A most sad fate befell the first four children, they were burned in the accidental conflagration of the homestead.

Third Generation.] Children:

7305. i. HENRY CHILD, b. Jan. 22, 1717.
7306. ii. CEPHAS CHILD, b. Oct. 30, 1718.   } These four died by burn-
7307. iii JOHN CHILD, b June 10, 1720.   } ing.
7308. iv. ISAAC CHILD, b. 1, 1722.   }

7309. v. ABRAHAM CHILD, b. 1724.

7310. vi. HENRY CHILD, 2D, b. Jan. 1, 1725-6.

7311. vii. CEPHAS CHILD, JR., 2D, b. Jan. 18, 1727-8, m. 1st, Percilla Naylor; m. 2d, Mary Cadwallader.

7312. viii. JOHN CHILD, 2D, b. June 14, 1730, m. Sept. 12, 1751, Sarah Shoemaker.

7313. ix. ISAAC CHILD, 2D, b. Mch. 14, 1734, m. 1759, Rachel Bradshaw.

[Third Generation.]

7311. vii. CEPHAS CHILD, JR., seventh son and child of Cephas and Mary Atkinson Child, b. 1727, in Plumstead, Bucks county, Pa., m. 1st, about 1750, Percilla Naylor; m. 2d, about 1775, Mary Cadwallader. Of the sons, Abraham and Henry, elder than Cephas, we have no direct record, though we think some of their descendants are living in and about Baltimore, Md. He d. July 12, 1815, aged 88, in Plumstead, Pa.

[Fourth Generation.] Children:

7314 i. MARY CHILD, b. Nov. 31, 1751.

7315. ii. JOSEPH CHILD, b. Oct. 29, 1753, m. Dec. 27, 1780, Hannah Burgess.

7316. iii. CEPHAS CHILD, JR., b. April 10, 1755.

7317. iv. WILLIAM CHILD, b. Feb. 9, 1757.

7318. v. JANE CHILD, b. Feb. 20, 1759.

7319. vi. RICHARD CHILD, b. Jan. 3, 1761.

7320. vii. NAYLOR CHILD, b. July 15, 1762.

7321. viii. PERCILLA CHILD, b. May 15, 1768.

7322. ix. CADWALLADER CHILD, b. Aug. 18, 1776, m. 1800, Elizabeth Ray or Rea.

[Fourth Generation.]

7315. ii. JOSEPH CHILD, eldest son of Cephas, Jr., and Percilla Naylor Child, b. in Plumstead, Pa., Oct. 29, 1753, m.

Dec. 27, 1780, Hannah Burgess of Fallsington, Bucks county, Pa. He moved to Jefferson county, New York, in 1804, and dwelt there till his death, which occurred in Le Ray, Feb. 24, 1829, at the age of 77. Mrs. H. B. Child d. Mch. 22, 1830, aged 77.

[Fifth Generation.]   Children:

7323. i. DANIEL CHILD, m. Anne Gardner.

7324. ii. SAMUEL CHILD, m. 1st, Anna Brownel; m. 2d, Hannah Curby; m. 3d, Rachel Gardner.

7325. iii. JOSEPH CHILD, JR., m. Lois Howland.

7326. iv. MOSES CHILD, b. May 12, 1789, m. May 24, 1814, Nancy Burdick.

[Fifth Generation.]

7323. i. DANIEL CHILD, eldest son and child of Joseph and Hannah Burgess Child, b. about 1782, in Bucks county, Pa., m. Anne Gardner.*

[Sixth Generation.]   Children:

7327. i. LOIS CHILD, unmarried.

7328. ii. PHEBE CHILD, deceased.

[Fifth Generation.]

7324. ii. SAMUEL CHILD, second son and child of Joseph and Hannah Burgess Child, b. about 1784, in Plumstead, Pa., m. 1st, Anna Brownel; m. 2d, Hannah Curby; m. 3d, Rachel Gardner.

[Sixth Generation.]   Children.   By first marriage:

7329. i. PHEBE CHILD, m. George Hart.

7330. ii. RACHEL CHILD, m. William C. Burdick.

7331. iii. THOMAS CHILD, m. Margaret Middleton.

7332. iv. EUNICE CHILD, m. Stephen Roberts.

7333. v. MARY CHILD, m. Aylor Barber.

7334. vi. WILLIAM CHILD, m. 1st, Irene Barber; m. twice after, but we have neither the names of the wives or children.

By second marriage:

7335. vii JOSEPH CHILD, b. Jan. 18, 1825, m. 1st, April 3, 1851, Mary Jane Cory; m. 2d, July 11, 1863, Mary E. Carey.

7336. viii. ANNA CHILD, deceased.

By third marriage:

7337. ix. LYDIA CHILD.

[Sixth Generation.]

7329. i. PHEBE CHILD, eldest child of Samuel and Anna Brownel Child, b. in Bucks county, Pa., m. George Hart.

[Seventh Generation.]   Children:

7338. i. EUNICE HART, m. Hiram Howland.

7339. ii. MARY HART, m. and has one child, names not known.

7340. iii ELIZA HART, m. Stephen Howland.

* We much regret that we could obtain so few dates in this line.

7341. iv. LUCY HART, m. Ebenezer Fredenburgh.
7342. v. CHARLES HART.
7343. vi. THOMAS HART.

[Seventh Generation.]

7338. i. EUNICE HART, eldest child of Phebe Child and George Hart, b. in Pennsylvania, m. Hiram Howland.

[Eighth Generation.] Children:
7344. i. PHEBE HOWLAND.
7345. ii. AMOS HOWLAND.
7346. iii. JOSEPH HOWLAND.
7347. iv. ERVINE HOWLAND.

[Sixth Generation.]

7330. ii. RACHEL CHILD, second dau. and child of Samuel and Anna Brownel Child, b. in Bucks county, Pa., m. William C. Burdick.

[Seventh Generation.] Children:
7348. i. ANNA BURDICK, m. Winchester Wright.
7349. ii. HANNAH BURDICK, m. Curtis Corey.
7350. iii. EPHRAIM BURDICK, m. Rosilla —.
7351. iv. MERCY JANE BURDICK, deceased.

[Seventh Generation.]

7349. ii. HANNAH BURDICK, second daughter and child of Rachel Child and William C. Burdick, b. in Pennsylvania, m. Curtis Corey.

[Eighth Generation.] Children:
7352. i. WILLIAM COREY.
7353. ii. MARGARET COREY, and four others, names not known.

[Sixth Generation.]

7331. iii. THOMAS CHILD, eldest son and third child of Samuel and Anna Brownel Child, b. in Pennsylvania, m. Margaret Middleton.

[Seventh Generation.] Child:
7354. i. ANDREW CHILD, m. 1st, Mary Hoyle; m. 2d, Emma Hicks.
[Eighth Generation.] Children: By second wife:
7355. i. THOMAS CHILD.
7356. ii. EDWARD CHILD.
7357. iii. MARY CHILD.

[Sixth Generation.]

7332. iv. EUNICE CHILD, third dau. and fourth child of Samuel and Anna Brownel Child, b. in Pennsylvania, m. Stephen Roberts.

[Seventh Generation.] Children:
7358. i. SAMUEL ROBERTS, m. and has children, names not ascertained.
7359. ii. ADELAIDE ROBERTS.
7360. iii. ELIZA ROBERTS, m. Francis Plank.

[Eighth Generation.]   Child:
7361. i. ELIZABETH PLANK.

[Sixth Generation.]
7333. v. MARY CHILD, fourth dau. and fifth child of Samuel and Anna Brownel Child, b. in Pennsylvania, m. Aylor Barber.

[Seventh Generation.]   Children:
7362. i. THOMAS BARBER, married.
7363. ii. CHARLES BARBER, married.
7364. iii. Infant.
7365. iv. WILLIAM BARBER, deceased.

[Sixth Generation.]
7335. vii. JOSEPH CHILD, eldest son and child of Samuel and his second wife, Hannah Curby Child, b. in Le Raysville, N. Y., Jan. 18, 1825, m. 1st, April 3, 1851, Mary Jane Cory, who was b. May 8, 1830, d. May 24, 1862 ; m. 2d, July 11, 1863, Mary E. Carey, who was b. Feb. 7, 1838, in Wilna, Jefferson county, N. Y.   Reside in Le Ray, N. Y.

[Seventh Generation.]   Children:
7366. i. BYRON MADISON CHILD, b. June 5, 1853.   Resides at 330 Hudson Ave., Albany, N. Y.
7367. ii. SAMUEL CHILD, b. April 10, 1857.   Resides in Le Ray.

[Fifth Generation.]
7325. iii. JOSEPH CHILD, JR., third son and child of Joseph and Hannah Burgess Child, b. in Le Ray, Jefferson county, N. Y., m. Lois Howland.

[Sixth Generation.]   Child:
7368. i. HANNAH CHILD, unmarried.

[Fifth Generation.]
7326. iv. MOSES CHILD, fourth son and child of Joseph and and Hannah Burgess Child, b. May 12, 1789, m. May 24, 1814, at Mayfield, Montgomery county, N. Y., Nancy Burdick.

[Sixth Generation.]   Children:
7369. i. AMOS CHILD, b. June 19, 1815, deceased.
7370. ii. LYDIA CHILD, b. May 13, 1817, deceased.
7371. iii. HANNAH B. CHILD, b. Oct. 25, 1822, m. May 18, 1848, Daniel B. Price.
7372. iv. JAMES CHILD, b. Feb. 6, 1825, m. 1st, Mch. 3, 1848, Susan Dopp; m. 2d, Elizabeth Lewis.
7373. v. AMOS CHILD, 2D, b. Sept. 18, 1827, deceased.
7374. vi. MOSES CHILD, JR., b. Dec. 25, 1831, m. Susan —.
7375. vii. MAHLON M. CHILD, b. Mch. 19, 1835, m. Mary W. Barton.

[Sixth Generation.]
7371. iii. HANNAH B. CHILD, third child and second dau. of Moses and Nancy Burdick Child, b. in Jefferson county

N. Y., Oct. 25, 1822, m. at Le Raysville, N. Y., May 18, 1848, Daniel B. Price. Resides at Fallsington, Bucks county, Pa.[*]

[Seventh Generation.] Children:

7376. i. R. ANNA PRICE.
7377. ii. CLINTON PRICE, deceased.
7378. iii. ELIZABETH PRICE.
7379. iv. MARY C. PRICE.

[Sixth Generation.]

7372. iv. JAMES CHILD, second son and fourth child of Moses and Nancy Burdick Child, b. in Henderson, N. Y., Feb. 6, 1825, m. 1st, at Western, Oneida county, N. Y., Mch. 3, 1848, Susan Dopp; m. 2d, Mrs. Mary Elizabeth Lewis. Resides in Henderson.

[Seventh Generation.] Children:

7380. i. NANCY CHILD, b. May 1852, m. Feb. 17, 1868, William Williams.
7381. ii. WILLARD CHILD, b. April 6, 1855; fitting himself to teach.
7382. iii. STELLA CHILD, b. Dec. 27, 1860.

[Seventh Generation.]

7380. i. NANCY CHILD, eldest child of James and Susan Dopp Child, b. May 1852, in Henderson, N. Y., m. Feb. 17, 1868, William Williams. He d. 1872.

[Eighth Generation.] Children:

7383. i. WALTER WILLIAMS, b. 1869.
7384. ii. SUSAN WILLIAMS, b. 1871.

[Sixth Generation.]

7374. vi. MOSES CHILD, fourth son of Moses and Nancy Burdick Child, b. Dec. 25, 1831, m. Susan —.

[Seventh Generation.] Children:

7385. i. WILLIAM D. CHILD.
7386. ii. CARRIE LOUISA CHILD.

[Sixth Generation.]

7375. vii. MAHLON M. CHILD, fifth son and seventh child of Moses and Nancy Burdick Child, b. in Jefferson county, N. Y., Mch. 19, 1835, m. Mary W. Burton. Mr. M. M. Child is a real estate broker and conveyancer in Wilmington, Delaware. A most genial gentleman.

[Seventh Generation.] Children:

7387. i. WILLIAM LEE CHILD, b. about 1858.
7388. ii. HENRY CHILD, deceased.
7389. iii. LUCY CHILD, b. about 1867.

[Fourth Generation.]

7322. viii. CADWALLADER CHILD, eighth child of Cephas Child and only son of Cephas and Mary Caldwallader Child,

* To Mrs. H. B. Child Price we are indebted for much information in her line, and regret only that she could not send more dates.

b. in Plumstead, Bucks county, Pa., Aug. 18, 1776. He received as good an English education as the schools of the period afforded. Working upon his father's farm in the intervals of school terms. When twenty years of age he became himself a teacher, and was thus employed four years. In 1800 he was married to Elizabeth Rea, daughter of John and Jane Forman Rea, of Philadelphia, Pa. Some five years later he moved with his family to Philadelphia, Jefferson county, N. Y., "took up" 440 acres of land, and settled for life. During the earlier years of his residence in Jefferson county he was employed as agent and surveyor by Mr. James LeRay De Chemont, a wealthy land-holder of France. Mr. Cadwallader Child died April 3, 1851, æ 74 years, 7 months, 15 days. Mrs. E. R. Child died Dec. 27, 1863, æ 90.

[Fifth Generation.] Children:

7390. i. AARON CHILD, b. Jan. 19, 1801, m. Mary Hicks.

7391. ii. JOSEPH A. CHILD, b. Sept. 1, 1803, m. May 9, 1827, Merriam Wattson.

7392. iii. OLIVER CHILD, b. Feb. 16, 1807, m. 1st, July 29, 1830, Edith Shaw; m. 2d, Sept. 12, 1844, Eliza Shepard.

7393. iv. MARY CHILD, b. Mch. 30, 1809, m. July 8, 1845, Amos Evans.

7394. v. GAINOR CHILD, b. June 6, 1812, d. unmarried Feb. 19, 1847, at Philadelphia, Jefferson county, N. Y.

7395. vi. NAYLOR CHILD, b. Dec. 25, 1815, m. Aug. 22, 1864, Julia Rogers.

[Fifth Generation.]

7390. i. AARON CHILD, eldest child of Cadwallader and Elizabeth Rea Child, b. in Bucks county, Pa., Jan. 19, 1801, m. Mary Hicks.

[Sixth Generation.] Children:

7396. i. JOSEPH CHILD, m. Asenath Mosure.

7397. ii. OLIVER CHILD.

7398. iii. NOAH CHILD.

7399. iv. HENRY CHILD.

7400. v. JEMIMA CHILD.

[Fifth Generation.]

7391. ii. JOSEPH AMBLER CHILD, second son and child of Cadwallader and Elizabeth Rea Child, b. in Bucks county, Pa., Sept. 1, 1803, m. May 9, 1827, Merriam Wattson. In the autumn of 1870, Mr. Joseph A. Child removed to Iowa, and resides with his elder son.

[Sixth Generation.] Children:

7401. i. WATTSON CHILD, b. April 14, 1832, m. Nov. 10, 1859, Drusilla Sheldon.

7402. ii. VINCENT CHILD, b. May 15, 1835, m. Dec. 29, 1863, Helen F. Pierce.

[Sixth Generation.]

7401. i. WATTSON CHILDS, eldest child of Joseph A. and Merriam Wattson Child, b. in Le Ray, Jefferson county, N.Y., April 14, 1832, m. at the Willet House, Rome, N. Y., by the Rev. William E. Knox, Nov. 10, 1859, Drusilla Sheldon of Lee, Oneida county, N. Y. Mr. Wattson Childs* settled in Iowa in February, 1855 ; is now a resident of Manchester, Delaware county, Iowa.

[Seventh Generation.] Children:

    7403. i. CLARA H. CHILDS, b. Dec. 29, 1863.
    7404. ii. EDITH L. CHILDS, b. July 23, 1867.
    7405. iii. WILBERT V. CHILDS, b. Sept. 26, 1871.
    7406. iv. ELMER W. CHILDS, b. Aug. 20, 1874.
    7407. v. ROBERT E. CHILDS, b. June 13, 1876.

[Sixth Generation.]

7402. ii. VINCENT CHILDS, second son and child of Joseph A. and Merriam Wattson Child, b. in Jefferson county, N. Y., May 15, 1835, m. Dec. 29, 1863, Helen F. Pierce of West Union, Iowa. Mr. Childs was a member of the legal fraternity. He d. Mch. 18, 1873.

[Seventh Generation.] Child:

    7408. i. GEORGE W. CHILDS, b. Oct. 18, 1864.

[Fifth Generation.]

7392. iii. OLIVER CHILD, third son and child of Cadwallader and Elizabeth Rea Child, b. in Brownville, Oneida county, (now Jefferson county,) N. Y., Feb. 16, 1807, m. 1st, by Peter Cooper, Esq., of Lehigh county, Pa., July 27, 1830, Edith Shaw : Mrs. Edith S. Child d. 1842 ; m. 2d, Sept. 12, 1844, Eliza Shepard of St. Lawrence county, N. Y. Mr. Child d. Feb. 28, 1878. Mrs. Eliza S. Child resides in Philadelphia, N. Y.

[Sixth Generation.] Children:

    7409. i. HAMILTON CHILD, b. Mch 17, 1836, m. Jan. 8, 1861, Eunice M. Read.
    7410. ii. MARY J. CHILD, b. Aug. 26, 1838, m. May 3, 1869, Edward J Stannard.
    7411. iii. LEWIS J. CHILD, b. Aug. 12, 1840, m. Oct. 23, 1867, Lydia M. Wait.

[Sixth Generation.]

7409. i. HAMILTON CHILD, eldest son and child of Oliver and Edith Shaw Child, b. in Philadelphia, Jefferson county, N. Y., Mch. 17, 1836, m. Jan. 8, 1861, Eunice M. Read of Utica, Oneida county, N. Y. Mr. Child is an active business man, and has made his extensive acquaintance in his native

* Mr. Wattson Childs writes that he and his brother added the "s" to their names.

State an efficient aid to the compilation of this Genealogy. He is the publisher of the "Peoples' Comprehensive Diaries." Residence, Syracuse, N. Y.

[Seventh Generation.] Children:

7412. i. JENNIE EDITH CHILD, b. April 13, 1862, d. April 13, 1863, at Ogdensburgh, N. Y.

7413. ii. CARRIE LOUISA RACHEL CHILD, b. Nov. 1, 1865, in Philadelphia, Jefferson county, N. Y.

7414. iii. EDITH MARY SHEPARD CHILD, b. Feb. 15, 1873, in Syracuse, N. Y.

[Sixth Generation.]

7410. ii. MARY JANE CHILD, only dau. of Oliver and Edith Shaw Child, b. in Philadelphia, N. Y., Aug. 26, 1838, m. May 3, 1869, Edward Judson Stannard, who was b. Dec. 12, 1829. His parents were Heman and Minerva Smith Stannard, and were married Sept. 5, 1809. Mr. and Mrs. E. J. Stannard reside at Broadaxe, Montgomery county, Pa.

[Seventh Generation.] Children:

7415. i. ETHLYN MINERVA STANNARD, b. July 7, 1870.

7416. ii. OLIVER EDWARD STANNARD, b. Nov. 2, 1871.

7417. iii. LEWIS JUDSON STANNARD, b. May 3, 1875.

7418. iv. EDITH STANNARD, b. Feb. 18, 1877, d. Aug 26, 1877.

[Sixth Generation.]

7411. iii. LEWIS J CHILD, second son and third child of Oliver and Edith Shaw Child, b. in Philadelphia, Jefferson county, N. Y., Aug. 12, 1840, m. Oct. 23, 1867, Lydia M. Wait. Mr. L. J. Child resides on the homestead, a portion of the land purchased by his grandfather Cadwallader Child, in the town of Philadelphia, Jefferson county, N. Y.   To him we are indebted for the first regular record of this line, most cordially sent us.

[Seventh Generation.] Child:

7419. i. LEWIS EUGENE CHILD, b. July 30, 1868, in Philadelphia, N. Y.

[Fifth Generation.]

7393. iv. MARY CHILD, only dau. of Cadwallader and Elizabeth Rea Child, b. in LeRay, Jefferson county, N. Y., Mch. 30, 1809, m. July 8, 1845, Amos Evans of Evans Mills, N. Y.

[Sixth Generation.] Children:

7420. i. CEPHAS JOHN EVANS, b. Jan. 27, 1847.

7421. ii. ELIZA GAINOR EVANS, b. Oct. 22, 1849, m. Nov. 27, 1871, Galard DeLancy.

7422. iii. CLARA ABBEY EVANS, b. July 19, 1852, m. Dec. 22, 1877, Byron Jackson.

[Sixth Generation.]

7421. ii. ELIZA GAINOR EVANS, eldest dau. and second child of Mary Child and Amos Evans, b. in Philadelphia,

Jefferson county, N. Y., Oct. 22, 1849, m. Nov. 27, 1871, Galard DeLancey of Orleans county. Residence, Medina, Orleans county, N. Y.

[Seventh Generation.] Child:

7423. i. MAUD DELANCEY, b. July 15, 1872.

[Sixth Generation.]

7422. iii. CLARA A. EVANS, second dau. and third child of Mary Child and Amos Evans, b. in LeRay, Jefferson county, N. Y., July 19, 1852, m. Dec. 22, 1877, Byron Jackson, at Carthage, and resides in Champion, Jefferson county, N. Y.

[Seventh Generation.] Child:

7424. i. BERTHA MAY JACKSON, b. Nov. 20, 1878.

[Fifth Generation.]

7395. vi. NAYLOR CHILD, youngest child of Cadwallader and Elisabeth Rea Child, b. in Philadelphia, Jefferson county, N. Y., Dec. 25, 1815, m. Aug. 22, 1864, Julia Rogers, dau. of Samuel and Rachel Rogers. Mr. Naylor Child is a farmer in easy circumstances. Resides in Masonville, Iowa.

[Sixth Generation.] Children:

7425. i. WILLIAM STANLEY CHILD, b. June 8, 1865.

7426. ii. FRANK HENRY CHILD, b. Aug. 2, 1867.

7427. iii. MARY ANNELLA CHILD, b. Nov. 11, 1870.

7428 iv. IRVING HOWARD CHILD, b. Dec. 24, 1876.

[Third Generation.]

7312. viii. JOHN CHILD, eighth son and child of Cephas and Mary Atkinson Child, b in Plumstead, Bucks county, Pa., June 14, 1739, m. Sept. 19, 1751, Sarah Shoemaker, dau. of George and Grace Shoemaker of Warrington, Pa.; they were married at Friends meeting. He d. 1801, at Frankfort, Pa.

[Fourth Generation.] Children:

7429. i. HENRY CHILD, b. Oct. 12, 1752, m May 22, 1788, Sarah Kirk.

7430. ii GRACE CHILD, b. Jan. 31, 1754, d. in her sixth year.

7431. iii. SARAH CHILD, b. Nov. 20, 1755, m. Benjamin Lloyd.

7432. iv. ELISABETH CHILD, b. Nov 15, 1757, m. Thomas Parry.

7433. v. MARY CHILD, b. Nov. 19, 1759, m. Caleb Hallowell, d. July 5, 1842.

7434. vi. ISRAEL CHILD, b. Dec 6, 1761, d. in his third year.

7435. vii ABRAHAM CHILD, b. Mch. 4, 1764 d. in his sixth year.

7436 viii. GRACE CHILD, 2D, b. Dec. 26, 1765, m. Joseph Kirk.

7437. ix. JOHN CHILD, JR., b. Nov. 25, 1768, d. in his second year.

7438. x. HANNAH CHILD, b. Oct. 28, 1770, m Thomas Walton, d. May 18, 1797.

[Fourth Generation.]

7429. i. HENRY CHILD, eldest child of John and Sarah Shoemaker Child, b. Oct. 12, 1752, m. May 22, 1788, Sarah

Kirk, dau. of Isaac and Mary Kirk of Upper Dublin Township, Montgomery county, Pa., at Abington Meeting.

[Fifth Generation.] Children:

7439. i. JOHN CHILD, b. Sept. 20, 1789, m. about 1811, Rachel Teas.

7440. ii. MARY CHILD, b. Nov. 30, 1793, d. 1804.

7441. iii. ELISABETH CHILD, b. Aug. 20, 1797, m. Isaac K. Wright, d. Nov. 4, 1856.

[Fifth Generation.]

7439. i. JOHN CHILD, eldest child of Henry and Sarah Kirk Child, b. Sept. 20, 1789, m. about 1811, Rachel Teas, d. June 18, 1876.

[Sixth Generation.] Children:

7442. i. JOHN TEAS CHILD, b Dec. 14, 1812, d. Aug. 24, 1832, of cholera.

7443. ii. SAMUEL TEAS CHILD, b. Oct. 6, 1814, m. Mch. 25, 1840, Sarah Lloyd.

7444. iii. HENRY TEAS CHILD, b. Aug. 16, 1816, m. 1st, Mch. 28, 1839, Anna R. Pickering: m. 2d, April 25, 1843, Sarah Ann Nicholson, m. 3d, Jan 18, 1854, Ellen M. Hancock.

7445. iv. ISAAC T. CHILD, b. Oct. 29, 1818, d. Aug. 15, 1832, of cholera.

7446. v. THOMAS T. CHILD, b. Aug. 15, 1820, m. 1st, Dec. 25, 1843, Elisabeth Kenderdine; m. 2d, Oct. 13, 1847, Anna Martin.

7447. vi. MARY T. CHILD, b. Dec. 27, 1824, m. June 26, 1845, Hector C. Ivins.

[Sixth Generation.]

7443. ii. SAMUEL TEAS CHILD, second son and child of John and Rachel Teas Child, b. Oct. 6, 1814, m. Mch. 25, 1840, Sarah Lloyd.   Supposed to reside in Philadelphia, Pa.

[Seventh Generation.] Children:

7448. i. HARRY L. CHILD, b. Jan. 23, 1841.

7449. ii. MARY T. CHILD, b. Dec. 8, 1846.

7450. iii. ALICE B. CHILD, b. Jan. 9, 1855, d. June 18, 1868.

[Sixth Generation.]

7444. iii. HENRY TEAS CHILD, M. D., third son and child of John and Rachel Teas Child, b. Aug. 16, 1816, m. 1st, Mch. 28, 1839, Anna R. Pickering: she d. May 19, 1840 : m. 2d, April 25, 1843, Sarah Ann Nicholson ; she died Dec. 5, 1852 : m. 3d, Jan. 18, 1854, Ellen M. Hancock.   Residence, Philadelphia, Pa.   Dr. Child furnished the descendants so far as we have them of John and Sarah Shoemaker Child.

[Seventh Generation.] Children: By first marriage.

7451. i. ANNA R. CHILD, b. May 13, 1840, d. Dec. 24, 1840.

By second marriage:

7452. ii. ANNA R. CHILD, 2D, b. Jan. 23, 1844, d. Dec. 24, 1850.

7453. iii. LIZZIE N. CHILD, b Nov. 24, 1845.

7454. iv. JOHN M. CHILD, b. Sept. 22, 1847.

7455. v. WILLIAM H. CHILD, b. Mch. 11, 1851, d. Mch. 12, 1851.

7456. vi. SARAH ANN CHILD, b Nov. 11, 1852, d. same day.

By third marriage:

7457. vii. WILLIAM HENRY CHILD, b. April 5, 1855.

7458. viii. ANNA MARIA CHILD, b. Dec. 18, 1857, d. Jan. 10, 1858.

7459. ix. EDWARD SOUTHWICK CHILD, b. Feb. 21, 1859.

7460. x. THOMAS HANCOCK CHILD, b. Dec. 20, 1860.

[Sixth Generation.]

7446. v. THOMAS TEAS CHILD, fifth son and child of John and Rachel Teas Child, b. Aug. 15, 1820, m. 1st, Dec. 25, 1843, Elisabeth Kenderdine; she d Dec. 1, 1844; m. 2d, Oct. 13, 1847, Anna Martin.

[Seventh Generation.] Children:

7461. i. ELISABETH K. CHILD b. Aug. 21, 1848, d. same day.

7462. ii. GEORGE C. CHILD, b. Mch. 5, 1851.

7463. iii. ELISABETH K. CHILD, 2D, b.Oct. 26, 1853, d. Feb. 22, 1860.

7464. iv. RACHEL ANN CHILD, b. Sept. 21, 1856.

[Sixth Generation.]

7447. vi. MARY TEAS CHILD, only dau. of John and Rachel Teas Child, b. Dec. 27, 1824, m. June 26, 1845, Hector C. Ivins; he d. Jan. 17, 1869.

[Seventh Generation.] Children:

7465. i. ARTHUR C. IVINS, b. Sept. 15, 1845.

7466. ii. THOMAS C. IVINS, b. Sept. 26, 1848.

7467. iii. RACHEL C. IVINS, b. Dec. 27, 1850, d. June 1, 1866.

7468. iv. MARGARET IVINS, b. Aug. 9, 1855.

[Third Generation.]

7313. ix. ISAAC CHILD, youngest child and son of Cephas and Mary Atkinson Child, b. in Plumstead, Bucks county, Pa., Mch. 14, 1734, m. 1759, Rachel Bradshaw. Isaac Child was a minister among the Friends, and possessed of unusual spiritual gifts and grace. In 1757 he had a "vision" a full record of it is in the possession of one of his descendants: we would gladly have given some portion of it, or abstract, had it been in our power. Upon the descendants of Isaac Child a most loving, devout spirit has been transmitted. Isaac Child died April 5, 1769.

[Fourth Generation.] Children:

7469. i. JONATHAN CHILD, b. June 13, 1761, m. Feb. 2, 1799, Deborah Michener.

7470. ii. RACHEL CHILD, b. Feb. 9, 1763, m. Joseph Atkinson.

7471. iii. ISAAC CHILD, JR., b. July 20, 1765, d. Sept. 9, 1802, unmarried, in New York City, or Philadelphia, Pa.*

7472. iv. RUTH CHILD, b. May 4, 1767, m. Jonathan Brown.

7473. v. ISRAEL CHILD, b. Mch. 28, 1769, m. —.

* An acrostic by this son of Isaac Child will be found in the appendix—not being obtained in season to be placed elsewhere.

[Fourth Generation]

7469. i. JONATHAN CHILD, eldest son and child of Isaac and Rachel Bradshaw Child, b. in Plumstead, Bucks county, Pa., June 13, 1761, m. Feb. 7, 1799, Deborah Michener.

[Fifth Generation.] Children:

7474. i ISAAC CHILD, b. Dec. 15, 1799, m. but we do not learn to whom, and have no account of his descendants. He has sent us the letters of his ancestor, Henry Child of England, and the acrostic.

7475. ii. GEORGE M. CHILD, b. Mch. 27, 1801, m. Nov. 26,1829, Sarah H. Wood.

7476 iii. RACHEL B. CHILD, b. April 1, 1803, m. Nov. 11, 1836, David Hutchinson, M. D.

7477. iv. ISRAEL CHILD, b. Jan. 16, 1805, m. Nov. 11, 1831, Ann Ambler.

7478. v. JONATHAN CHILD, JR., b. May 26, 1807, d. Oct. 9, 1821.

7479. vi. JOSHUA CHILD, b. Aug. 3, 1810, d Aug. 3, 1837.

[Fifth Generation]

7475. ii. GEORGE M. CHILD, second son and child of Jonathan and Deborah Michener Child, b. Mch. 27, 1799, m. Nov. 26, 1829, Sarah H. Wood, daughter of James and Tacy Wood. She died Oct. 19, 1846.

[Sixth Generation.] Children:

7480. i. RANDOLPH CHILD, b. Mch. 4, 1836, d. Aug. 24, 1836

7481. ii. MARY T. CHILD, b. April 12, 1838, m. Oct. 13, 1870, Joseph B. Walter, M. D.*

[Fifth Generation]

7476. iii. RACHEL B. CHILD, only dau. of Jonathan and Deborah Michener Child, b. April 1, 1803, m. Nov. 11, 1836, David Hutchinson, M. D., who d. Dec. 31, 1871.

[Sixth Generation.] Children:

7482. i. ELIZABETH HUTCHINSON, b. Dec. 23, 1837, d. April 11, 1842.

7483. ii. GEORGE W. HUTCHINSON,   ⎰ TWINS. ⎱ d. 1841.

7484. iii. EDWARD MANLEY HUTCHINSON,   b. Feb. 7, 184–. m. 1869 or '70, Clay Anna Lloyd. Have two children: reside at Cannelton, W. Virginia.

7485. iv. JAMES PEMBERTON HUTCHINSON, b. Oct. 3, 1843.

[Fifth Generation.]

7477. iv. ISRAEL CHILD, third son of Jonathan and Deborah Michener Child, b. Jan. 16, 1805, m. Nov. 11, 1831, Ann Ambler, she d. Nov. 1, 1853.

[Sixth Generation.] Children:

7486. i. EDWARD HENRY CHILD, b· Feb 12, 1833, m. Mch 16, 1866, Margaret P. Brown.

7487. ii. THOMAS BROMLEY CHILD, b. July 31, 1834, m. 1st, Louise M. Linkfield; m. 2d, Oct. 31, 1878, Sallie Curtis.

7488. iii. HANNAH CHILD, b. Aug. 24, 1836, d. young.

7489. iv. JOHN M. CHILD, b. Nov. 16, 1837, d. May 29, 1870, in Austin, Nevada.

7490. v. MARIETTA H. CHILD, b. Mch. 13, 1841, d. June 6, 1864.

* To Mrs. M. T. Child Walter we are indebted for much in this line, and courteously tender our thanks.

[Sixth Generation.]

7487. ii. THOMAS BROMLEY CHILD, second son and child of Israel and Ann Ambler Child, b. July 31, 1834, m. 1st, Louise M. Linkfield, who d. Dec. 1, 1869; m. 2d, Oct. 31, 1878, Sallie Curtis. Reside in Austin, Nevada.

[Seventh Generation.] Children:

7491. i. Infant, d. young
7492. ii. HAROLD CHILD, b. Nov. 16, 1879.

[Fourth Generation.]

7470. ii. RACHEL B. CHILD, eldest dau. of Isaac and Rachel Bradshaw Child, b. Feb. 9, 1763, m. Joseph Atkinson of Bristol, Pa.

[Fifth Generation.] Children:

7493. i. ISAAC ATKINSON.
7494. ii. SALLIE ATKINSON, m. Mr. Hough.
7495. iii. RACHEL ATKINSON.
7496. iv. RUTH ATKINSON, m. William Moody of Baltimore. Had five children, all are dead.

[Fifth Generation.]

7494. ii. SALLIE ATKINSON, eldest dau. of Rachel Child and Joseph Atkinson, m. Mr. Hough.

[Sixth Generation.] Child:

7497. i. MARIETTA SOPHIA HOUGH, resides in Baltimore, Md.

[Fourth Generation.]

7472. iv. RUTH CHILD, second dau. of Isaac and Rachel Bradshaw Child, b. May 4, 1767, m. Jonathan Brown. Resided in Rahway, N. J.

[Fifth Generation.] Children:

7498. i. MARY BROWN.
7499. ii. ANDREW BROWN.
7500. iii. SARAH BROWN.

[Fourth Generation.]

7473. v. ISRAEL CHILD, youngest son and child of Isaac and Rachel Bradshaw Child, b. Mch. 28, 1769, m. Permelia —.

[The account of this family was to come through one of the sons, Henry C. Child of Freeport, Stevenson county, Ill. We have deferred to our latest possible time the arranging of this record, trusting the intended communication should reach us; we are compelled most regretfully to publish the incomplete report, presuming some unforseen occurrence has delayed or prevented the expected record.]

[Fifth Generation.]　Children:

7501. i. HENRY C. CHILD.

7502. ii. ISAAC CHILD, b. July 15, 1809, m. Mch. 16, 1837. Susanna W. Devers. We understand there were other children but do not receive the names, nor do we know if those given are in due chronological order.

[Fifth Generation.]

7502. ii. ISAAC CHILD, son of Israel and Permelia Child, b. July 15, 1809, m. Mch. 16, 1837. Susanna W. Devers. Isaac Child d. May 16, 1875.

[Sixth Generation.]　Children:

7503. i. ELIZABETH D. CHILD, b. Jan. 17, 1838, m. Mch. 19, 1865, Frederick Morley.

7504. ii. RUTHANNA CHILD, b. Oct. 5, 1839, m. Mch. 29, 1862, Benjamin M. Collins.

7505. iii. JOHN W. CHILD, b. May 17, 1841, m. April 6, 1870, Lavinia S. Early.

7506. iv. ALICE D. CHILD, b. May 10, 1845, m. Dec. 24, 1868, Joseph T. Hart.

[Sixth Generation.]

7503. i. ELIZABETH D. CHILD, eldest child of Isaac and Susanna W. Devers Child, b. Jan. 17, 1838, m. Mch. 19, 1865, Frederick Morley.

[Seventh Generation.]　Children:

7507. i. AGNES S. MORLEY, b. April 26, 1866, d. Jan. 5, 1872.

7508. ii. MARTHA M. MORLEY, b. Dec. 30, 1870.

[Sixth Generation.]

7504. ii. RUTHANNA CHILD, second dau. and child of Isaac and Susanna W. Devers Child, b. Oct. 5, 1839, m. Mch. 29, 1862, Benjamin M. Collins.

[Seventh Generation.]　Children:

7509. i. EMMARETTA K. COLLINS, b. June 16, 1863.

7510. ii. REBECCA S. COLLINS, b. April 27, 1865, d. Aug. 8, 1867.

7511. iii. MARY ANNA COLLINS, b. Nov. 16, 1866, d. July 17, 1867.

7512. iv. ALDEN M. COLLINS, b. Mch. 10, 1869.

[Sixth Generation.]

7505. iii. JOHN W. CHILD, only son of Isaac and Susanna W. Devers Child, b. May 17, 1841, m. April 6, 1870, Lavinia S. Early.

[Seventh Generation.]　Children:

7513. i. and ii. Twin sons, d. young.

7514. iii. ALBERT R. CHILD, b. Mch. 11, 1874.

[Sixth Generation.]

7506. iv. ALICE D. CHILD, youngest child of Isaac and Susanna W. Devers Child, b. May 10, 1845, m. Mch. 19, 1865, Joseph T. Hart. Residence Solebury, Bucks county, Pa.

[To Mrs. Hart we are happy to acknowledge our indebtedness for our record so far as we possess it of the descendants of Israel and Permelia Child.]

[Seventh Generation.] Children:

7515. i. John C. Hart. b. Nov. 14, 1870, d. Mch. 26, 1873.
7516. ii. Charles H. Hart, b. Dec. 20, 1872.
7517. iii. Isaac C. Hart, b. Mch. 21. 1875.
7518. iv. Susanna C. Hart, b. Mch. 4, 1877.
7519. v. Mercy H. Hart. b. Mch. 7. 1879.

We give next all we have received of another branch of this line, doubtless descendants of Abraham or Henry Child, sons of Cephas and Mary Atkinson Child, born in Plumstead, Bucks county, Pa., in the years 1724 and 1726. It is known to those now living in Morristown, Pa., that their grandfather came from Bucks county, and was of the society of Friends: his name was John Child, and he had brothers named George and Jesse, this is all we know of them. We therefore place the known head of this family in the fourth generation, as he would be if the son of one of the two brothers mentioned.

[Fourth Generation.]

7520. John Child, b. in Plumstead, Bucks county, Pa., about 130 or 140 years ago, m. Mary Phipps, daughter of a neighbor. "They left Bucks county, and settled near Plymouth Meeting in Montgomery county, about 110 years ago; had twelve children (all now deceased), eight of whom lived to be men and women.

[Fifth Generation.] Children:

7521. i. Mary Child, m. Mr. Pitt of Delaware county, had a large family, and has many descendants, not traced.

7522. ii. Petar Child, m. twice.

7523. iii. Sarah Child, m. John Conrad, raised a family of twelve children, nine sons and three daughters. Nine still living, married and with large families are settled near their old home at Plymouth Meeting, Pa.

7524. iv. James Child, unmarried, lived to be nearly 70 years old.

7525. v. Tacy Child, unmarried, lived to be over 70.

7526. vi. Elizabeth Child, m. John Robinson, moved to Ohio: had two children, a son and daughter, neither of them living and only one descendant, a great-grandson, 3 or 4 years old. (1880.)

7527. vii John Child, Jr., m. 1824, Ann Moore

7528. viii. Margaret Child, m. John Davis of Delaware county, had four children who grew up but have since died, leaving, it is believed, no issue.

[Fifth Generation.]

7522. ii. Petar Child, eldest son of John and Mary Phipps Child, b. probably in Montgomery county, Pa., and twice married, but we possess no dates, neither the names of his wives.

[Sixth Generation.] Children:

7529. i. JAMES CHILD, m. and has two daughters, names not sent.

7530. ii. SARAH CHILD, m. and has a family, no data thereof.

7531. iii. S. P. CHILD, m. and has three sons and three daughters, names and dates deficient.

[Fifth Generation.]

7527. xii. JOHN CHILD, JR., youngest child of John and Mary Phipps Childs, b. in Montgomery county, Pa., 1796, m. Feb. 1822. Ann Moore, and d. Mch. 1825. We had written him as the seventh child, as in that order he had been named, and as no dates were given we could not tell where he should come. Have since learned he was the twelfth child.

[Sixth Generation.] Children:

7532. i. JACOB CHILD, m. and has two sons and two daughters. From Mr. Child we receive all this record, and greatly regret that he did not send the names of his children. To him we express our indebtedness for his pleasant response.

7533. ii. Infant son died young.

GEORGE WILLIAM CHILDS—Philadelphia, Penn.

One of the leading descendants of Henry Child of Colds Hill, Eng., whose record we have just closed, writes us that George William Childs is of their line. For this reason we place him in juxtaposition to this branch. It is pleasant to think that Mr. Childs belongs to so noble a branch.

The record we have of Mr. Childs is mainly that of extracts from printed sketches of his life, which have been called forth by such incidents as have marked his history. He was born in Baltimore, Md., in 1829.

HIS BOYHOOD.

Mr. James Parton in a sketch written in 1870, says :

His early friends in Baltimore do not depict him as in the least resembling the ideal boy of modern novels—the Tom Browns, who put forth their whole soul in foot-ball and cricket, and bestow the reluctant residue upon the serious business of school. With sincere deference to our honored guest, Mr. Thomas Hughes, I must beg leave to state, that superior men, who learn to govern themselves and direct affairs, do not spend their boyhood so. Not in the Rugby style do the Jeffersons, Franklins, Pitts, Peels, Watts, nor the great men of business, nor the immortals of literature and art, pass the priceless hours of boyhood and youth. Such boys do not despise the oar and the bat, but they do not exalt the sports of the play-ground

George W. Childs

to the chief place in their regard. This boy certainly did not. He exhibited, even as a child, two traits seldom found in the same individual: a remarkable aptitude for business, and a remarkable liberality in giving away the results of his boyish trading. At school he was often bartering boyish treasures—knives for pigeons, marbles for pop-guns, a bird-cage for a book; and he displayed an intuitive knack in getting a good bargain by buying and selling at the right moment. At a very early age he had a sense of the value of time, and a strong inclination to become a self-supporting individual. He has told his friends that, in his tenth year, when school was dismissed for the summer, he took the place of errand-boy in a bookstore, and spent the vacation in hard work. This was not romantic, but it was highly honorable to a little fellow to be willing thus to work for the treasures that boys desire. At thirteen he entered the U. S. Navy, and spent fifteen months in the service; an experience and discipline not without good results upon his health and character.

He was a favorite among his boyish friends. One of them, Hon. J. J. Stewart, of Maryland, has recently said: " He was then what you find him now. His heart was always larger than his means. There is but one thing he always despised, and that is meanness; there is but one character he hates, and that is a liar. When he left Baltimore, a little boy, the affectionate regret of all his companions followed him to Philadelphia; and the attachment they felt for him was more like romance than reality in this every-day world. . . . I remember that he wrote to me years ago, when we were both boys, that he meant to prove that *a man could be liberal and successful at the same time.*"

Let us see if the career of the man has fulfilled the dream of the boy.

Upon reaching Philadelphia, a vigorous lad of fourteen, he knew but one family in the city, and they, soon removing, left him friendless there. He found employment in his old vocation of shop-boy in a bookstore. Paying strict attention to business, working early and late for his employer, disdaining no honest service, he soon had an opportunity, young as he was, of showing that he possessed the rarest faculty of a business man—*judgment*. After shutting up the store in the evening, he was entrusted by his employer with the duty of frequenting the book auctions and making purchases; and by the time he was sixteen, it was he who was regularly deputed to attend the book trade-sales at New York and Boston

BUSINESS.

After serving in this capacity for four years, being then eighteen years of age having saved a few hundred dollars capital, and accumulated a much larger capital in character, in knowledge of business, and in the confidence of business men, he hired a small slice of the Ledger building, and set up in business for himself. Already he felt that his mission was to conduct a great daily paper; already, he had said to himself, that paper shall be the *Public Ledger.*

ENTRANCE UPON BUSINESS AT EIGHTEEN YEARS OF AGE.

In his narrow slip of a store in the Ledger building, he bestirred himself mightily and throve apace. Faculty is always in demand; and I say again, a young man generally gets a step forward in his career about as soon as he is able to hold it.

BECOMES A MEMBER OF THE FIRM OF R. E. PETERSON & CO.

Before he was quite twenty-one, we find him a member of that publishing firm which afterwards obtained so much celebrity and success under the title of Childs & Peterson. The intelligent head of the old firm of R E. Peterson & Co. had the discernment to see his capacity, and sought an alliance with him. It was a strong firm; for the talent it contained was at once great and various. Mr. Peterson and his family had considerable knowledge of science and literature, and Mr Childs possessed that sure intuitive judgment of the public taste and the public needs without which no man can succeed as a publisher. He had, also, that strong confidence in his own judgment which gave him courage to risk vast amounts of capital, and even the solvency of the firm, upon enterprises at which many a more experienced publisher would have shaken his head.

There is no business so difficult as that of publishing books. Few succeed in it, and still fewer attain a success at all commensurate with the energy and risk which it demands. In the firm of Childs and Peterson there was much of both kinds of judgment—that which comes of general knowledge, and that which results from a knowledge of the world. Consequently, nearly all of its ventures were successful. They published few books, but they frequently contrived to make a great hit once a year. Mr. Peterson compiled a work from various sources called " Familiar Science," which Mr. Childs' energy and tact pushed to a sale of two hundred thousand copies, and secured for it a footing in many schools, which it retains to this day. We all remember with what skill and persistence Mr. Childs trumpeted the brilliant works of Dr Kane upon " Arctic Explorations," and how he made us all buy the volumes as they appeared at five dollars, and how glad we were we *had* bought them when we came to read them. Nor was Dr. Kane ill-pleased to receive a copy-right of about $70,000.

Among the massively useful books bearing his imprint, there is that truly extraordinary enterprise, " Dr. Allibone's Dictionary of English and American Authors," which is dedicated to Mr. Childs. It is questionable if there has ever been produced by one man a book involving a greater amount of labor, or one containing a smaller proportion of errors, than this colossal dictionary. Often as I have had occasion to use it, I have never done so without a new sense of its wonderful character. Probably when Mr. Childs undertook its publication, there was hardly another publishing house in the world that would have given the laborious author any encouragement; and it is safe to add that but for the outbreak of the war, he would have pushed it to a compensating sale. Other costly works published by Mr. Childs are " Bouvier's Law Dictionary," " Bouvier's Institutes of American Law," " Sharswood's Blackstone," " Fletcher's Brazil," and " Lossing's Illustrated History of the Civil War."

POWER TO MAKE FRIENDS.

His career has not been all triumph; nor can he, any more than other men, justly claim that his success is due to his unassisted powers. The strongest man needs the aid of his fellows, and he is the strongest man who knows best how to win and deserve that assistance. Such a man as Mr. Childs makes friends. It belongs to his hearty, hopeful, and generous nature to inspire regard in kindred minds; and even minds that have little in common with his own, love to bask in the sunshine of his influence. It so chanced that, among the friends who were drawn to him, early in his Philadelphia career, was the celebrated banker, Mr. Anthony J. Drexel, a gentleman whose name in the metropolis of Pennsylvania is suggestive of everything honorable, liberal, and public spirited. Mr. Childs is proud to acknowledge that, at many a crisis in his life, Mr. Drexel's sympathy and ever-ready help have been a tower of strength to him.

In the long run, however, a man stands upon his own individual merits. No external aid can long avail if there are radical deficiencies in his own character. It is his own indomitable heart and will that carry every man forward to final victory.

PERSONAL HABITS.

"Meanness," says Mr. Childs, "is not necessary to success in business, but economy *is*." He has been an economist, not only of money, but of his health, his strength, his vital force, the energy and purity of his brain. It has been his happiness to escape those habits which lower the tone of the bodily health and impair the efficiency of the mind—such as smoking and drinking—which, at this moment, lessen the useful energies of civilized man by, perhaps, one-half! He tells the young men about him that Franklin's rule for success in business is about the best that can be given—simple as it is. It consists of three words: "Temperance, industry, and frugality."

PURCHASE OF THE PUBLIC LEDGER.

Rev. Dr. Prime, editor of New York *Observer*, says:

In 1864, the *Public Ledger*, a daily penny paper, rapidly losing money, was for sale, and Mr. Childs bought it.

He converted it at once. This is *the* point, and for this only is this letter written. Mr. Childs excluded from the paper all details of disgusting crime; all reports of such vice as may not be with propriety read aloud in the family; that poison the minds of young men, inflame the passions and corrupt the heart; all scandal and slang, and that whole class of news which constitutes the staple of many daily papers. The same rule was applied to the advertising columns, and from them was excluded all that, in any shape or form, might be offensive to good morals. The friends of the new publisher predicted an early and total failure, and the more speedy because he doubled the price of the paper and increased the rates of advertising. The effect of this sudden change was at first to sink the sinking concern still lower. A class of readers and advertisers fell off. A less conscientious and a less courageous man would have staggered in the path he had marked. Not so with Mr. Childs. He employed the best talent, and paid fair wages for good work. He published six days in the week only, and on the seventh day he rested from his labors. His paper and his principles began to obtain recognition in the city. He made it a family journal. It gained the confidence of the best people, who became its daily readers, and *therefore* it was sought as the best medium of advertising.

PUBLIC LEDGER BUILDING.

The following description of this magnificent building is taken from the *Paper World*, published at Holyoke, Mas., June 1880.

On the 20th of June, 1867, a new *Ledger* building was formly opened, which, for magnificence and the completeness of all its appointments, is without a rival among newspaper establishments in the world. It is literally an industrial palace—one of the finest architectural adornments of Philadelphia, and planned throughout with special reference to the health and comfort of those who are employed in it. The warming, lighting and ventilation are as perfect as they can be made, while at frequent intervals throughout the structure are well-appointed bath rooms for every class of employes. The business office is probably the most elegant apartment of the kind on the continent, and the editorial rooms are fitted up in luxurious style, more after the manner of an author's private study than the typical sanctum.

In this connection we may conveniently speak of Mr. Childs' superb library, "the like of which is not to be found in this country, if in the world." His wide and intimate acquaintance among the literary men of his time, joined to his ample means, have afforded him such opportunities to become possessed of the rarest souvenirs of literature as are seldom enjoyed. In a noble room on the first floor of his elegant Walnut street home are enshrined the choicest of these treasures. It is a place where one who knows "the sure companionship of books" might well love to linger. In the center of the apartment is a massive and well-loaded library table, made of ebony brought from Africa for Mr. Childs by Paul Du Chaillu. By it stands the library chair, also of ebony, and a fac simile of William Beckford's chair at Fonthill. Against the walls, which are further adorned with portraits in oil of George Peabody and Henry W. Longfellow, are richly-wrought ebony book-cases, rising six feet from the floor, and filled with rare volumes, containing autographic inscriptions by their authors. But it is in a beautifully carved cabinet, standing between the two windows, that the most precious of these works are shielded from dust and careless touch. Here we find the original manuscript of a sermon by Cotton Mather, written in a fine neat hand, and dated May 17, 1703. Near it is a copy of the rare Moxon edition of Leigh Hunt's poetical works, containing the autograph inscription, "Charles Dickens, from his constant admirer and obliaged friend, Leigh Hunt." With this is a copy of Hood's "Comic Annual" for 1842, with a poetical inscription in Hood's handwriting. Other works, of yet greater interest, are: The original manuscript of Nathaniel Hawthorne's "Consular Experiences," written in the author's own beautiful hand throughout; the original manuscript, complete, of Charles Dickens' "Our Mutual Friend," dated "Thursday, Fourth January, 1866," and prefaced by an outline skeleton of the story, such as Dickens always sketched before entering on the final composition; the manuscript, written by herself and adorned with portraits, of Harriet Martineau's "Retrospect of Western Travel;" William Cullen Bryant's manuscript of his first book of the "Iliad;" portions of the original manuscript of Mary Cowden Clarke's "Complete Concordance to Shakspeare," and the original manuscript draft of General Grant's address at the opening of the Centennial Exhibition, May 10, 1876. All of these, besides many priceless manuscripts and letters of Moore, Byron, Gray, Burns, Pope, Coleridge, Schiller, Lamb and others, are elegantly bound in folios or quartos, in a manner befitting their inestimable value.

PUBLIC LIFE.

Speaking of Mr. Childs in the use of his wealth, Mr. Frank H. Norton, assistant librarian Astor Library, New York, says:

But there are more ways of dispensing wealth to public advantage than by charity alone. By freely opening his elegant residence in hospitality to visitors from foreign lands, Mr. Childs has doubtless done much for the credit of his country in this particular, while he has brought about associations among distinguished personages which could scarcely fail to inure to the public benefit in some way. Probably no such gathering of distinguished and notable people was ever collected together in the parlors of a private citizen in this country as met by invitation at Mr. Childs' Philadelphia residence on the evening of May 10th, 1876, the day of the opening of the Centennial Exhibition in Philadelphia. On this occasion there were present President Grant, with his wife; all the members of his Cabinet, with their wives; the Chief Justice and Associated Justices of the Supreme Court of the United States, and their wives; the Emperor and Empress of Brazil; the Diplomatic and other representatives of Great Britain, France, Spain, Austria, Prussia, Russia, Italy, Belgium, Turkey, Japan, China, and other powers of Europe and Asia; the governors of Maine, New Hampshire, Massachusetts, Rhode Island, Kentucky, Pennsylvania, New Jersey, Delaware, and Maryland, with their staff officers; leading members of the United States Senate and House of Representatives; Generals Sherman, Sheridan, Hancock, McDowell; Admirals Porter, Rowan, Scott, Lardner, Turner, Jenkins, Alden; Centennial Judges and Commissioners from foreign countries and the United States; famous military and naval officers, eminent judges, leading lawyers, prominent divines, presidents of colleges, authors, journalists, artists; in fact, men famous in every branch of professional and private life. And this instance, except in the remarkable comprehensiveness of its scope, as to the guests, merely illustrates the rule in Mr. Childs' social life. Scarcely a prominent visitor from abroad arrives in this country who is not furnished with letters of introduction to Mr. Childs, and entertained by him. Compare such generous courtesy to the representatives of foreign aristocracy, wealth, and intelligence, with the refinement of delicate appreciation which induced Mr. Childs, during the continuance of the Centennial, to furnish with the means to visit the great fair not only numbers of poor women who would otherwise not have seen it, but also as many as two thousand children who, through Mr. Childs' liberality, were sent happy-hearted to the wonderful Exhibition at Fairmount, and furnished with good dinners while there enjoying the show. Children of the Philadelphia Deaf and Dumb Asylum, the Church Home, and those of other public institutions of that city were thus favored, and in the case of the House of Refuge, it illustrates the peculiar quality of his thoughtfulness that he made a special request that its inmates should be permitted to lay off the uniform, which is their badge, while visiting the Exposition, and wear new suits to be supplied and paid for by him. It is in his peculiar happy faculty for discrimination in the awarding of his benefits and in his methods of distribution, as much as in the lavishness with which he yields up to public and private uses such a large portion of his fortune, that

D 2

Mr. Childs is specially distinguished. Not an unsuitable illustration of this characteristic, possibly, was his gift of a memorial window in Westminster Abbey in honor of the poets George Herbert and William Cowper. This munificent gift was merely occasioned by the receipt on the part of Mr. Childs of a circular from the committee of English gentlemen who had the matter in hand.

In considering this instance of the refinement of generosity, it should be remembered that it illustrates the patriotism of the man, no less than his liberal impulses. The placing of an elegant stained glass memorial window in Westminster Abbey—the shrine of all the memories that by the English-speaking population of the world are held dearest—was a truly graceful act, associating the American people with their English brethren in a most generous and most fitting tribute to names the world delights to honor.

At the time of the appointment of its official representatives at the Centennial Exposition, the British Government honored Mr. Childs by designating him to the service referred to in the following highly complimentary acknowledgment on the part of the Duke of Richmond and Gordon, Lord President of the Council:

[Copy.]

LONDON,
4th January, 1877.

SIR: I have heard with much pleasure from Colonel Sandford of the valuable and important assistance you have rendered me, as one of the Honorary Commissioners for Great Britain, her Colonies and Dependencies, at the Philadelphia International Exhibition of 1876.

It will gratify you to know that Her Majesty's Government have expressed their highest approval of the administration of the British section, towards the success of which in America you have been good enough so much to contribute.

I have the honor to be, sir, your obedient servant,
(Signed)　　　　RICHMOND AND GORDON.
GEORGE W. CHILDS, ESQ.
Honorary Commissioner for the United Kingdom.

We close our extracts with an item from the pen of Col. J. W. Forney, which furnishes a sort of resumé of the life of Mr. Childs:

No charity appeals to Mr. Childs in vain; no object of patriotism; no great enterprise; no sufferer from misfortune, whether the ex-Confederate or the stricken foreigner. He enjoyes the confidence of President Grant, and yet was among the first to send a splendid subscription to the monument to Greeley. He, more than any other, pushed the subscription of over $100,000 for the family of the dead hero, George G. Meade, and yet Alexander H. Stephens, of Georgia, has no firmer friend. His list of unpublished and unknown benevolences would give the lie to the story that he craves notoriety. When I carried letters from him to Europe in 1867, his name was a talisman, and it was pleasant to see how noblemen like the Duke of Buckingham honored the endorsement of an American who, thirty years ago, was a poor boy. He made his money himself, not by speculation or office, and got none by inheritance. He coins fortune like a magician, and spends it like a man of heart. He likes society, and lives like a gentleman. He is as temperate as ever Horace Greeley was, and yet he never denies his friends a generous glass of wine   His habits are as simple as Abraham Lincoln's, and yet his residence is a gem bright with exquisite decoration and rich in every variety of art.   He gives a Christmas dinner to newsboys and bootblacks, and dines travelling Dukes and Earls with equal ease and familiarity.   He never seems to be at work, goes everywhere, sees everybody, helps everybody, and yet his great machine moves like a clock under his constant supervision.

NATHANIEL CHILD and Descendants.

The succeeding account is without doubt that of another branch of the descendants of Cephas and Mary Atkinson Child. Though it is equally possible that they may be descendants of a Thomas Child, who at the age of 30, was one of a "number who had taken the oath of allegiance in London, England, and was transported in the 'Speedwell' to Virginia, May 28, 1635." This does not imply anything derogatory even then, it only proves that in leaving England he was no political refugee, as were so many in those troublous days: but we find him possessed of property: that persons were sent him from the mother country, sold for debt as was a custom, into temporary or perpetual servitude.   He is also found to be the owner of land and slaves at the Barbadoes, in the parish of St. Michaels. The tradition prevailing in this family that their earliest American ancestor was the personal friend of William Penn, leads to the belief (with other corroborating circumstances,) that they are descendants of Henry Child who leads this line and chapter.   We place the Nathaniel Child first known in the same generation as his contemporaries.   His descendants add the "s."

[Fourth Generation.]

7534. NATHANIEL CHILD, born about 1745.   At the age of twenty three he was married to Tamer Brown, in the year 1768, and resided in Elkton, Cecil county, Maryland.   He was a blacksmith and carried on the business of his trade.   His death occurred in 1793.

[Fifth Generation.]   Children:

7535. i. THOMAS CHILDS, m. Temperance Atkinson Inloes.

7536. ii. NATHANIEL CHILDS, b. 1778, m. 1802. Ann Jessop.

7537. iii. BENJAMIN CHILDS, d. in his 20th year.

7538. iv. REBECCA CHILDS, m. Captain Nathaniel Sewell.

7539. v. MARY CHILDS, m. Mr. Adair; removed to Kentucky and lost sight of.

7540. vi. SARAH CHILDS, m. Captain William McNeil.

[Fifth Generation.]

7535. i. THOMAS CHILDS, eldest son and child of Nathaniel
and Tamer Brown Child, b. in Elkton, Cecil county, Md.
m. in 1800, Temperance Adkinson Inloes. Resided in Baltimore, Md. He was a master builder, and the first person in
that city to invent and manufacture pressed brick for the fronts
of houses. He died in Baltimore, in 1837.

[Sixth Generation.] Children:

7541. i. WILLIAM CHILDS, d. at Key West, Florida, in his 22d year, of
yellow fever.

7542. ii. GEORGE CHILDS, was lost at sea in his 24th year, having been
washed overboard in a storm

7543 iii. ELIZA CHILDS, d. in her 18th year, of consumption; a girl of
rare beauty and great intellectual promise.

7544. iv. TEMPERANCE CHILDS.

7545. v. MARGARET AMANDA CHILDS, emigrated West in 1835, and opened
a store in Louisville, Kentucky. She was a woman of great energy of character, and accumulated a fortune. She travelled abroad, and married an
English gentleman by the name of Pattison, and lives at this date, 1879, in
St. Pierre, Martinique, French West Indies.

7546. vi. HENRY CHILDS, m., no names or dates.

7547. vii. ELLINOR ATKINSON CHILDS, b. Sept. 8, 1819, m. Nov. 20, 1838,
Henry L. Clark.

7548. viii. EDWARD CHILDS, settled in the South; killed in the late war.

7549. ix. THOMAS CHILDS, settled in the South; killed in the late war.

7550. x. JOSEPH CHILDS, planter in Arkansas or Texas.

[Sixth Generation.]

7546. vi. DR. HENRY CHILDS, third son and sixth child of
Thomas and Temperance Inloes Childs, b. in Baltimore, Md. He
learned the trade of boot and shoe making, carried on the trade
for several years in Baltimore, then removed to Philadelphia, Pa.,
where he studied medicine and graduated from the University
of Pennsylvania. In that city he married and removed thence
to Iowa. He settled on a farm in the valley of the DesMoines
river of that State, and cultivated his farm, and practiced his
profession. He is very successful as a physician, and has a
large practice. He is also a man of great religious influence,
being a local Methodist preacher; he fills appointments all over
the surrounding country. During the late war, he served as
surgeon of the Sixth Iowa Regiment of Volunteers. The
name of his wife has not reached us nor any facts of his family.

[Sixth Generation.]

7547. vii. ELLINOR ATKINSON CHILDS, fourth dau. and
seventh child of Thomas and Temperance Inloes Childs, b. in
Baltimore, Md., Sept. 8, 1819, m. Nov. 20, 1838, Henry L.

Clark, for many years and now secretary of the Wiggins Ferry Company, at St. Louis, Mo. She died at St. Louis, June 23, 1844, æ 25.

[Seventh Generation.] Child:

7551. i. JAMES LESLIE CLARK b. Nov. 7, 1838, in St. Louis, Mo., unmarried. Resides at DeLassus, St. Francois county, Mo.

[Fifth Generation.]

7536. ii. NATHANIEL CHILDS, second son and child of Nathaniel and Tamer Brown Child, b. in Elkton, Cecil county, Md., 1778, m. 1802, Ann Jessop, who was b. in Baltimore, Maryland, Feb. 10, 1789.

"He learned the trade of a tailor, and came to Baltimore in 1799, with a capital of seventy five cents in his pocket. He worked in the slop shop of Thomas Tennent for several years, and then opened a store of his own, on Fells Point, Baltimore, and engaged in the business of furnishing sailors' clothing for ships going to sea; in this he was successful, and now ventured to marry Miss Ann Jessop, a daughter of William Jessop, a flour merchant of Rowley's Wharf, Baltimore. In this marriage he was greatly blessed in securing a woman of great personal beauty and excellent worth, who entered heartily into all his business and social pursuits, and proved the crowning glory of his life. By her he had fourteen children, who grew up to man and womanhood. In 1811, he purchased a farm in the neighborhood of Gunpowder Forest, in Baltimore county, sixteen miles from the city. At this farm he raised this large family of children, and when they began to marry and move away, most of them to the West, he concluded to sell his farm and follow his children. This he did in 1840, and settled in St. Louis, Mo., where he engaged in business until 1851; he died in that city on the 17th of October, 1851, surrounded by most of his children. His wife, Mrs. Ann Jessop Childs, survived him ten years, dying in August, 1862, in her 74th year.

Mr. Nathaniel Childs was, while resident in Maryland, a slave-holder, owning at one time some seven men and more women. One of these men accompanied him with his command in the war of 1812, and stood with him in the battle of North Point, Sept. 12, 1814. When he died, some time later, he was carfully buried upon the farm at home. The estate is now in possession of strangers, but the grave of the faithful slave is preserved with care. When Mr. Childs removed to St. Louis, Mo., from Maryland, he set all his slaves free. Two accompanied him to the West and one remained with the family until his death. The other made his home with Mr. Nathaniel Child, Jr., to whom he was much attached, and whom he had rescued from drowning when Mr. Nathaniel, Jr., was a child; nor was the affection all on one side, loving though the African heart was. When years and infirmities came, the 'young master' sorrowed, and at his death gave him comfortable burial in the Methodist cemetery in St. Louis, and mourned the true old friend.

Mr. Nathaniel Childs represented his party in the State Legislature three terms, and ever commanded the respect and admiration of his fellow-citizens."

[Sixth Generation.]   Children:

7552. i. ARIETTA CHILDS, b. Aug. 1804, m. 1826, Josiah Small.

7553. ii. WILLIAM CHILDS, b. 1806, m. Ellinor Carter.

7554. iii. SARAH CHILDS, b. 1807, d. 1835.

7555. iv. NATHANIEL CHILDS, b. April 24, 1810, m. 1st, 1837, Eliza J. Stibbs; m. 2d, 1852, Margarette Whitlocke.

7556. v. DOMINIC CHILDS, b. 1812, m. 1840, Elizabeth Miller; both dead.

7557. vi. EDWARD CHILDS, left home to seek his fortune, in 1840, and never heard from again; by trade a tanner and currier

7558. vii. MARY CHILDS, b. Feb. 10, 1816; a woman of superior intellect. She d. Aug. 1852, in her 36th year.

7559. viii. ANN ELIZABETH CHILDS, b. 1816, d. 1838, of consumption, in her 22d year.

7560. ix. JOSHUA J. CHILDS, m. Mary Baker.

7561. x. CALEB C. CHILDS, b. Jan. 17, 1822, m. 1st, Feb. 23, 1843, Ann King; she d. May 2, 1857; m. 2d, Feb. 24, 1858, Mrs. Sophronia F. Bacon.

7562. xi. REBECCA SEWELL CHILDS, b. Mch. 12, 1821, d. April 29, 1875, at Cincinnati, Ohio.

7563. xii. CATHARINE CECILIA CHILDS, b. Jan. 8, 1826, m. 1848, Austin S. Reeves.

7564. xiii ELIZA JANE CHILDS, b. Nov. 15, 1826, m. Alexander Lyons.

7565. xiv. CHARLES JESSOP CHILDS, b Mch. 12, 1826, m. Mch. 15, 1847, Elizabeth Agnew Baldridge.

[Sixth Generation.]

7552. i. ARIETTA CHILDS, eldest child of Nathaniel and Ann Jessop Childs, b. in Baltimore, Md., in Aug. 1803, m. in 1826, Josiah Small of that city.

[Seventh Generation.]   Children:

7566. i. JOSIAH SMALL, JR.

7567. ii. WILLIAM SMALL.

7568. iii. SARAH SMALL.

7569. iv. MARY SMALL.

7570. v. EDWARD SMALL.
7571. vi. GEORGE SMALL.
7572. vii. CHARLES SMALL.
7573. viii. ROBERT SMALL.

[Sixth Generation.]

7553. ii. WILLIAM CHILDS, eldest son of Nathaniel and Ann Jessop Childs, b. in Baltimore, Md., Aug. 8, 1806, m. Oct. 15, 1842, Eleanor E. Carter of St. Louis, Mo. Mrs. Eleanor E. C. Childs was a grand-daughter of Bettie Lewis, the only daughter of General Washington's only sister. Resides now at Castroville, Monterey county, Cal.

[Seventh Generation.] Children:

7574. i. WILLIAM WARD CHILDS, b. Dec. 6, 1843. Resides in St. Louis, Mo.

7575. ii. FIELDING CARTER CHILDS, b. Aug. 13, 1846. Attorney, Notary Public, and Real Estate Agent, Scheli city, Vernon county, Mo.

[Sixth Generation.]

7555. iv. NATHANIEL CHILDS, JR., second son of Nathaniel and Ann Jessop Childs, b. in Baltimore, Md., April 24, 1810, m. 1st, in 1837, Eliza J. Stibbs, dau. of Christopher Stibbs of Bath, England; Mrs. E. J. S. Childs d. Aug. 1850, in St. Louis, Mo.; m. 2d, in 1842, Margarette A. Whitlocke of St. Louis. Mrs. M. A. Whitlocke Childs d. Feb. 17, 1880. A woman of rare graces. Upon her union with Mr. Childs, she most graciously and winningly assumed the duties of a second wife and mother. So exceeding was her devotion, and so gentle her authority, that she won the love and esteem of the children, and no home possessed more charming attractiveness. After a time she became deeply impressed with the thought that a more conscious possession of the Holy Spirit in daily, hourly life was possible for all; that some were attaining to this higher inner life, and that she might reach this blessedness. Her attendance at this time was upon the services of the " Foundry Methodist Episcopal Church," Washington, D. C. Very great earnestness attended her prayers, and the result was wonderful; her peace was like a broad, deep river, rich, full, assured; in this she dwelt evermore, until she entered the life of blessedness with her Master.[*] Mr. Nathaniel Childs, like most residents of Maryland, was at one time a slaveholder. In 1852 he set his slaves free, but felt that some

* These facts in the life of Mrs. Childs, were gathered from an interesting obituary notice of her, in the "Central Christian Advocate" of St. Louis, Mo.

of them were not at all benefitted by the gift of freedom, making their liberty an excess, and shortening their lives thereby. Mr. N. Childs writes us:

" Rev. Mr. Revels, now of Mississippi, the first man of color elected to the United States Senate since the war, was sent from Kentucky to Missouri, by the Bishop of the A. M. E. Church, to take charge of the Green street Methodist congregation of colored people in St. Louis. The law of the State of Missouri, at that time, forbade a man of color to enter the State without giving bonds for his good behaviour. Mr. Revels was arrested. He was a stranger. I went into court, and signed his bond in the penalty of $1,000. Afterward he went South and I never met him until he came to Washington, as U. S. Senator from the State of Mississippi. I attended a reception given him; when he saw me he put his arms around my neck and wept, and then told the company, among whom was Senator Henry Wilson of Mass., the circumstance of his arrest, and my coming to his rescue. This is only one of many incidents in my history with slave life."

Mr. Childs is at present in the office of the second assistant Postmaster General in Washington, D. C.

[Seventh Generation.] Children:

7576. i. NATHANIEL CHILDS, JR., d. young.

7577. ii. MARY ADELAIDE CHILDS, b. Mch. 4, 1840, m. John T. Field. Resides in St. Louis, Mo

7578 iii. THEODORE FRANCIS CHILDS, b Oct 19, 1841, m. Dec. 20, 1871, Henriella Kent Mosher.

7579. iv. ARIETTA CHILDS, b June 1843, d. 1860, in St. Joseph, Mo., aged 17 years.

7580. v. ANN ELISABETH CHILDS, b. 1845, m. Nov. 19, 1874, Frank Rudd.

7581. vi. WILLIAM CHILDS, d. young.

7582. vii. EMOGENE CHILDS d young.

7583. viii HENRY SLICER CHILDS, b. Aug. 10, 1853. Is a clerk in the U. S. Pension Office, Washington, D. C.

7584. ix. SALLIE SMALL CHILDS, b Aug. 10, 1855. Teacher in the public schools, Washington, D. C.

[Seventh Generation]

7578. iii. THEODORE FRANCIS CHILDS, second son and third child of Nathaniel, Jr., and Eliza J. Stibbs Child, b. Oct. 19, 1841, m. Dec. 20, 1871, in Springfield, Ill., Henriella Kent Mosher, daughter of George Mosher of Clarksville, Mo. Mrs. Childs was b. April 20, 1850. Mr. T. F. Childs is an Attorney at Law of the St. Louis Bar, and Deputy Collector of Internal Revenue in the first District of Missouri. It is said of Mr. Childs, that "he is the best informed man upon the Revenue laws of the United States in the city of St. Louis," where he resides.

[Eighth Generation.] Children, born in St. Louis, Mo.:

7585. i. BERTHA CHILDS, b. Aug. 18, 1873.

7586. ii. MABEL CHILDS, b. June 13, 1875.
7587. iii. EDITH CHILDS, b. Mch. 11, 1877.
7588. iv. Infant son, b. Oct. 27, 1878.

[Seventh Generation.]

7589. v. ANNIE ELIZABETH CHILDS, third dau. and fifth child of Nathaniel, Jr., and Eliza J. Stibbs Childs, b. in St. Louis, Mo., in 1845, m. Nov. 19, 1874, Frank Rudd, an attorney in New York City, of the firm of Blair, Snow & Rudd, Broadway. Reside in Brooklyn, E. D.

[Eighth Generation.] Child:

7589. i. UNA RUDD, b. Oct. 3, 1875, d. Aug. 4, 1878.

[Sixth Generation.]

7560. ix. JOSHUA J. CHILDS, fifth son and ninth child of Nathaniel and Ann Jessop Childs, b. in Maryland, m. Mary Baker of Missouri. Mrs. Mary B. Childs d. of cholera in New Orleans, in 1856. Mr. Joshua J. Childs was killed during the late war. He belonged to Jackson's Brigade of the Confederate army, and met his death in the battle of Malvern Hill, on the peninsula of Virginia, when in front of McClelland's command. Their children, left orphans at a tender age, found a home for a time in a French family in New Orleans; they ran from their home, and were conveyed to relatives in St. Louis, Mo., by a kindly steamboat captain who knew their father.

[Seventh Generation.] Children:

7590. i. THOMAS BAKER CHILDS, d. young.
7591 ii. BEVERLY WARREN CHILDS.
7592. iii. PETER CAMDEN CHILDS.

[Sixth Generation.]

7561. x. CALEB BOSLEY CHILDS, sixth son and tenth child of Nathaniel and Ann Jessop Childs, b. Jan. 17, 1822, m. 1st, Feb. 23, 1843, Ann King, of English birth, who d. May 2, 1857, in St. Louis, Mo.; m. 2d, Feb. 24, 1858, Mrs. Sophronia F. Bacon, daughter of Col. Benjamin Allen, who emigrated to Missouri from Vermont in 1818. His second wife died May 29, 1873. Mr. Caleb B. Childs is a farmer in New Hope, Lincoln county, Missouri.

[Seventh Generation.] Children:

7593. i. NOAH GORSUCH CHILDS, b. April 12, 1844, d. Oct. 16, 1845.
7594. ii. CHARLES EDWARD CHILDS, b. Oct. 4, 1845, d. Aug. 6, 1846.
7595. iii. DOMINIC JESSOP CHILDS, b. Dec. 22, 1846, d. April 1865.
7596. iv. JOSIAH SMALL CHILDS, b. May 22, 1852, d. Dec. 25, 1860.
7597. v. ANN REBECCA CHILDS, b. Feb. 6, 1854.

7598. vi. NETTIE SMALL CHILDS, b. Sept. 24 1855.
7599. vii. SALLIE ELIZABETH CHILDS, b. May 1, 1857, d. May 9, 1857.
7600. viii IMOGEN ALLEN CHILDS, b. Dec. 1 1860.
7601. ix. HARRY W. HALLOCK CHILDS, b Oct. 2, 1862
7602. x. JULIA FANNIE KATE CHILDS, b. Sept. 3, 1864.
7603. xi ELLEN JANE GORSUCH CHILDS, b Jan. 10, 1867.
7604. xii. AMA FARRIS CHILDS, b June 26 1869

[Sixth Generation.]

7564. xii. CATHARINE CECILIA CHILDS, sixth dau. and twelfth child of Nathaniel and Ann Jessop Childs, b. Jan. 8, 1826, m. in 1848, Austin S. Reeves of Cincinnati, Ohio. Four sons and four daughters have blessed this union. The eldest son a popular preacher in the Kentucky Conference of the Methodist Episcopal Church South. Residence Coventry, Ky.

[Seventh Generation]   Children:
7605. i. JOHN REEVES, b. July 10, 1849, m. Aug. 2, 1877, Emma De Garis.
7606. ii. ANNIE CHILDS REEVES, b. April 4, 1851, m. E. A. Mulford.
7607. iii. GEORGE NATHANIEL REEVES, b. May 3, 1853, m. Sept. 29, 1879, Susie V. Thompson.
7608. iv. MARY ADELAIDE REEVES, b. May 23, 1855.
7609. v. ELIZABETH BROWN REEVES, b. June 20, 1857, in Cincinnati, Ohio.
7610. vi. JEANETTE FISK REEVES, b. Sept. 28, 1859, d. Aug. 5, 1859, in Cincinnati, Ohio.
7611. vii. EDWARD THEODORE REEVES, b Mch. 22, 1861, d. May 24, 1868, in Cincinnati, Ohio.
7612. viii. AUSTIN ALBERT REEVES, b. April 29, 1862.
7613. ix KATE CECILIA REEVES, b Feb 7, 1864.
7614. x. FREDERICK REEVES, b July 30, 1866.

[Seventh Generation.]

7605. i. REV. JOHN REEVES, eldest child of Catherine C. Childs and Austin Reeves, b. in St. Louis, Missouri, July 10, 1849, m. Aug. 2d, 1877, Emma DeGaris. Rev. Mr. Reeves is a clergyman of the Methodist Episcopal Church South, and highly esteemed by his Conference.

[Eighth Generation.]   Children:
7615. i DeGaris REEVES, b. Aug. 16, 1875.
7616. ii. WALKER REEVES, b. Mch. 27, 1879.

[Seventh Generation]

7605. ii. ANNIE CHILDS REEVES, eldest dau. and second child of Catherine C. Childs and Austin S. Reeves, b. in St. Louis, Mo., April 4, 1851, married E. A. Mulford.

[Eighth Generation] Children:
7617. i. EDWARD APLIN MULFORD, JR., b. Aug. 16, 1875.
7618. ii. BESSIE MULFORD, b. Nov. 3, 1876.

[Sixth Generation.]

7564. xiii. ELIZA JANE CHILDS, seventh dau. and thirteenth child of Nathaniel and Ann Jessop Childs, b. near Baltimore, Md., m. Nov. 20, 1845, Alexander Lyons. Mr. Lyons is a native of Germany. Mrs. Eliza J. Childs Lyons d. at Madison, Ind., in 1852.

[Seventh Generation.] Children:

7619. i. ANNIE CHILDS LYONS, b. Nov. 20, 1846, d. July 10, 1848.

7620. ii. BLANCHE LYONS, b. July 13, 1848, m. Dec. 24, 1868, George Woolley.

7621. iii. ALEXANDER G LYONS, b. Mch 17, 1851, in New Haven, Ct

[Seventh Generation.]

7620. ii. BLANCHE LYONS, second dau. and child of Eliza Jane Childs and Alexander Lyons, b. July 13, 1848, m. Dec. 24, 1868, George Woolley.

[Eighth Generation.] Children:

7622. i EDWARD WOOLLEY, b. Oct. 7, 1869.

7623. ii. CHARLES WOOLLEY, b. Feb 4, 1871.

7624. iii GEORGE WOOLLEY, JR., b. Aug. 17, 1875.

7625. iv. ADELAIDE WOOLLEY, b. Sept. 17. 1879.

[Sixth Generation]

7564. xiv. CHARLES JESSOP CHILDS, M. D., seventh son and fourteenth child of Nathaniel and Ann Jessop Childs, b. near Baltimore, Md., Mch. 12, 1826, graduated at the Eclectic Medical College in Cincinnati, Ohio, Mch. 12, 1847, m. Mch. 15, 1847, Elizabeth Agnew Baldridge, daughter of Alexander Holmes Baldridge, M. D. Dr. Childs was an officer of the 5th Reg't, Illinois Cavalry during the war; served under Generals Steel and Curtis; resigned in 1863, and was elected Major of 142d Reg't of Volunteer Infantry; served with General A. J. Smith; was mustered out at the close of the war, with his Reg't at Chicago. Resides now in Coultersville, Randolph county, Ill., in the successful practice of his profession.

[Seventh Generation.] Children:

7626. i. MARY ANN CHILDS, b. Mch. 18, 1848, d. June 19, 1848.

7627. ii. EMMA FLORENCE CHILDS, b. Mch 22, 1850.

7628. iii. NATHANIEL CHILDS, b. Mch. 13, 1855. A lawyer.

7629. iv. CHARLES ALEXANDER CHILDS, b. June 6, 1857.

7630. v. LIZZIE MAY CHILDS, b. July 19 1859.

7631 vi. SALLIE JANE CHILDS, b. Dec. 29, 1861

7632. vii. THOMAS ALLEN CHILDS, b Feb 26, 1865.

7633. viii. WILLIAM HOLMES CHILDS, b. Feb. 25, 1869, d. July 28, 1869.

[Fifth Generation.]

7538. iv. REBECCA CHILDS, eldest dau. of Nathaniel and

Tamer Brown Childs, b. in Elkton, Cecil county, Md., m Nathaniel Sewell; resided in Baltimore, Md., where her children and other descendants are prominent and wealthy citizens. Each of Rebecca Childs Sewell's seven children married and reared large families, and these again have married and are numerously and respectably represented in Baltimore and New York.

[Sixth Generation.]   Children:

    7634. i. THOMAS SEWELL.

    7635. ii. JAMES SEWELL.

    7636. iii. NATHANIEL SEWELL, JR.

    7637. iv. JOHN SEWELL.

    7638. v. SARAH SEWELL.

    7639. vi. MARY SEWELL.

    7640. vii. RICHARD SEWELL.

Rev. James Sewell, second son of Rebecca Childs and Richard Sewell, became a famous Methodist preacher. His services were sought in all parts of the country. He filled pulpits by special transfer for the purpose, in Savannah, Georgia; Charleston, South Carolina; Philadelphia, Pa.; Brooklyn, New York; St. Louis, Missouri, and in all the principal appointments of the Baltimore Conference. He died a few years since, honored and loved by all who knew him

[Very much which has been promised us in this line has failed to reach us, and after repeated efforts to make the line complete, we are compelled to print without doing so.]

UNATTACHED FAMILIES.

The family here sketched is that of the Rev. John Childs and some of his descendants. It is possible that they belong to the American descendants of Henry Child of Hertfordshire, England. A tradition is recalled by one of the grandchildren, that her Aunt Sarah said "two brothers and two sisters came to America together, one of the sisters bearing the name Cassie;" we have found similar traditions in almost every line, yet facts overthrow them.

7641. "REV. JOHN CHILD, was born in Calvert county, Md., but we have not the date of his birth or marriage, or the name of his wife. Very early in life Mr. Childs was licensed by the Methodist Episcopal Church as a "local preacher." In 1789, he was by the Baltimore Annual Conference appointed upon the Montgomery circuit. His labors in the ministry were interrupted for some years. In 1816, he was again in the active ministry, serving for a year or more in the Lancaster Baltimore, Montgomery, Great Falls, Carlisle and Chambersburg circuits respectively. In 1823, he was appointed a local preacher once more, but he preferred the other line of service and was again made a circuit minister. In 1829, he received a superannuated relation and retired among his friends in the District of Columbia. Too late, however, to recuperate his wasted energies on earth. He died at the house of Mr. Thos. Jacobs in Alexandria, D. C., expressing his entire confidence in God his Saviour."

Mr. Childs was the owner at one time of a number of slaves, but at the age of twenty-one he set them all free and gave to each several acres of land.

[Of his family we can give but two children, though we understand there were more.]

[Seventh Generation.] Children:

7642. i. SARAH A. CHILDS, m. Mr. Jacobs of Langley, Fairfax county, Va.

7643. ii. JOHN W. CHILDS, b. Aug. 1, 1800, m. 1834, Martha S. Rives.

[Seventh Generation.]

7643. ii. REV. JOHN W. CHILDS, son of Rev. John Childs, b. Aug. 1, 1800, m. 1834, Martha S. Rives. Rev. Mr. John W. Childs d. May, 1850, when his children were so young that they had not heard him speak of his ancestry at all, and as they were thereafter with their mother's relatives they are unable to make a full record. At the time of the late war the family Bible in which were recorded the dates of births, deaths, etc., was stolen by the negroes and the records destroyed.

[Eighth Generation.] Children:

7644. i. MARGARET E. CHILDS, b. 1835, d. Oct. 1851.

7645 ii. MARY A. CHILDS, b. Oct 1839.

7646. iii. ANN V. L. CHILDS, b. Dec. 1841, m. Oct. 17, 1876, R H. Aylor.

7647. iv. SARAH M. CHILDS, b. Feb. 1843, d. May 1851.

7648. v. JOHN W. CHILDS, JR., b. Jan. 1845.

7649 vi. SAMUEL WESLEY CHILDS, b. July 1847, m. Dec. 2, 1879, Clara Thomas.

7650. vii. CHARLES T. CHILDS, b. Aug. 1850, d. July 1851.

[Eighth Generation.]

7646. iii. ANN V. L. CHILDS, third dau. and child of Rev. John W. and Martha S. Rives Childs, b. Dec. 1841, m. Oct. 17, 1876, R. H. Aylor. To Mrs. Aylor we are indebted for the record of her family, and regret much that we cannot give a fuller report of a family so true and devout. Residence, Oak Park, Virginia.

[Ninth Generation] Children:

7651. i. JOHN CHILDS AYLOR, b. Aug. 1877.

7652. ii. MARY RIVES AYLOR, b. Feb. 1879

JOHN CHILDS.

The latest known emigrant to America of the name, and the only emigrant with the terminal " s " attached to the name.

[First Generation.]

7653. JOHN CHILDS, b. in England Mch. 10, 1753, m. Jan. 1, 1785, Mary Gragg. She was b. in County Antrim, Ireland, Oct. 12, 1763. She came to this country at 13 years of age. His mother's name was Rachel Cornton: his father's name we do not obtain. He came to America and settled near Danville, Montour county, Pa. He died May 31, 1804, near Danville, Pa.

[The record of this branch we receive from Hiram A. Childs, Esq., of Lock Haven, and his brother Franklin P. Childs of Ottawa, Ill., grandsons of John Childs.]

[Second Generation.] Children:

7654 i. ESTHER CHILDS, b. Feb. 28, 1785, m. John Lanning, d. May 28, 1849.

7655. ii. JOHN CHILDS, b. Feb. 12, 1788, d. Dec. 12, 1867.

7656. iii. ANDREW CHILDS, b. June 13, 1789, m. Margaret Arnwine.

7657. iv. NANCY CHILDS, b. Mch. 25, 1791, m. Isaiah Blue and had several children: d. Sept. 27, 1868.

7658. v. JAMES CHILDS, b. June 16, 1793, d. Jan. 10, 1871, leaving children.

7659. vi. MARY CHILDS, b July 17, 1795, m. Daniel Cameron, uncle to Simon Cameron of Pennsylvania.

7660. vii. RACHEL CHILDS, b. Mch. 22, 1798, m. Hugh Pursel and left children.

7661. viii. MARGARET CHILDS b. Oct. 16, 1801, d. Oct. 16, 1834, unm.

7662. ix. ELIZABETH CHILDS, b. June 8, 1803, m. John Taggart, and resides in Watsontown, Northumberland county, Pa. Had a large number of children. Mr. Taggart died 1878, or '79.

[Second Generation.]

7656. iii. ANDREW CHILDS, third child and second son of John and Margaret Gragg Childs, b. in New Jersey, June 13, 1789, m. Margaret Arnwine, (sometimes called "Irving," "Irvine," "Irwin"). She was b. Nov. 17, 1798; is still living on the old farm. He died May 7, 1864, on a farm near Danville, Pa.

[Third Generation.] Children:

7663. i. JOHN G CHILDS, b. Feb. 1, 1816, m. abt. 1870, Mary McCracen. Residence Parkville, St Joseph county, Mich.

7664. ii. JAMES W. CHILDS b. July 4, 1817, m. 1st, 1849, Mary Campbell: m. 2d, about 1856, Sarah King.

7665. iii. SARAH J. CHILDS, b. Aug. 12, 1818, m. George W. Pierce. She d. Aug. 10, 1868, at Ottawa City, Ill., leaving no children.

7666. iv. WILLIAM B. CHILDS, b. Oct. 8, 1819. Wm. B. Childs left home quite early: married and lived in Wisconsin: had two children. His wife and children died. He went to the far West and was not heard from for seven years, the family supposed him dead, when his mother had a letter from him written from Idaho. Some few years later his brother, Franklin P. Childs, received a letter from him, he was then in New Mexico. Two or three years later his mother received another letter from him, he was then in Texas. No further tidings have come from him.

7667. v. MARY E. CHILDS, b. Dec. 14, 1820. Lives in Danville, Montour county, Pa.

7668. vi. ANDREW J. CHILDS, b. July 11, 1822, m. Emily Smith. No children. Resides in Lee's Summit, Jackson county, Mo.

7669. vii. FRANCIS CHILDS, b. May 28, 1825, d. Mch. 26, 1826

7670. viii. FRANKLIN P. CHILDS, b. April 28, 1826, m. Sept. 23, 1858 Maggie M. Price

7671. ix. HIRAM A. CHILDS, b. Aug. 3, 1828 Lawyer; unmarried. Resides in Lock Haven, Clinton county, Pa

7672. x. HARRIET M. CHILDS, b. June 13, 1830, m. Dr. Isaac D. Howard.

7673. xi. MARGARET R. CHILDS, b. Mch. 14, 1832, unm.; is a teacher. Resides in Montour county, Pa.

7674. xii. LUCINDA A. CHILDS, b. Oct. 19, 1834, unm. Lives at Danville, Pennsylvania.

7675. xiii. CYRUS CHILDS, b. May 31, 1837, m. Sarah Ann Williams. Has a large family of children Reside in Montour county, Pa

7676. xiv. DAVID R. P. CHILDS, b. Oct. 16, 1838, unm. Residence Montour county, Pa. Carries on the home farm.

7677. xv. REBECCA H. CHILDS b. Nov 7, 1840, d. Mch. 10, 1846.

[Third Generation.]

7664. ii. JAMES W. CHILDS, second son and child of Andrew and Margaret Arnwine Childs, b. in Danville, Pa., July 4, 1817. m. 1st, in 1849, Mary Campbell; m. 2d, in 1856, Sarah King. In the spring of 1847, Mr. J. W. Childs went to St. Joseph county, Mich. and took up a farm near Three Rivers, where he has since lived. P. O. address, Parkville, St. Jo. Co., Mich.

[Fourth Generation.] Children:

7678. i. MAGGIE J. CHILDS.

7679. ii. FRANCIS MARION CHILDS.

7680. iii. CHARLIE CHILDS.

7681. iv. DELLA CHILDS.

7682. v. FRANK CHILDS.

[Third Generation.]

7670. viii. FRANKLIN PETRICAN CHILDS, eighth child of Andrew and Margaret Arnwine Childs, b. April 28, 1826, in Montour county, Pa., m. in Ottawa City, Ill., Sept. 23, 1858, Maggie M. Price. She was b. May 16, 1827, in Fayette county, Pa. Mr. Childs first engaged in farming in Marshall county, until the spring of 1864, when he bought a farm near Ottawa, Ill., where he resided till the fall of 1871, when he purchased property, in the town, on which he now resides, a man of leisure.

[Fourth Generation.] Children:

7683. i. CORA LIEOLEN CHILDS, b. Jan. 18, 1860, graduated from High School of Ottawa, Ill., June 27, 1879, graduated from the Cincinnati Wesleyan College, June 16, 1880.

7684. ii. WINNIE VELLETTA CHILDS, b. Mch. 23, 1863, is a member of the High School, Ottawa, Ill.

[Second Generation.]

7658. v. JAMES CHILDS, fifth child of John and Mary Gragg Childs, b. June 16, 1793; m. 1st, Rachel Appleman; m. 2d, Susan McBride; m. 3d, Elizabeth Bouch; d. Jan. 10, 1871.

[Third Generation.] Children:

7685. i. JAMES H. CHILDS, m. and has two children. Resides in Stillwater, Washington county, Minn.

7686. ii. JOHN CHILDS.

7687. iii. CORDELIA CHILDS, m. — Smith. Resides at Schoolcraft, Mich.

7688. iv. APPLEMAN CHILDS, m. has two children. Lives in Dansville, Montour county, Pa.

7689. v. HANNAH CHILDS.

7690. vi. MARIA CHILDS.

7691. vii. OSCAR CHILDS, m. Resides in Iowa.

7692. viii. JACOB SIMEON CHILDS.

7693. ix. ANN CHILDS, m. Elisha W. Smith. Lives in Muncy, Lycoming county, Pa.

[Fifth Generation.]

7694. WILLIAM CHILD, removed to Maine with the family of Mr. David Marshall from Massachusetts, in 1771, and settled in what was then called Sudbury, Canada, now Bethel, Maine. Attacked by the Indians the inhabitants were compelled to flee, and this family were located in Minot, Maine. Here Mr. Child married, about 1790, Miss Anna Washburn, and removed to Livermore, in the same State, where he settled upon a farm.

[Sixth Generation.] Children:

7695. i. LEWIS WASHBURN CHILD, b. 1793, shipped with Decatur's fleet in 1815, sailed to the Mediterranean, and was never afterward heard from.

7696. ii. JOSEPH CHILD, b. Jan. 5, 1795, m. 1st, 1816, Olive Woodsum; m. 2d, 1841, Dorcas Andrews.

7697. iii. WILLIAM CHILD, JR., b. April 1797, m. 1816, Lucinda Woodsum.

7698. iv. ANNA CHILD, b. 1799, m. John Perham.

7699. v. TRUE WOODMAN CHILD, b. 1802, m. Miss Smith

7700. vi. ELISHA CHILD, b. 1804, drowned when about 20 years of age.

7701. vii. GRANVILLE CHILD, b. 1806, m. Esther Godding; twelve children, names not sent.

7702. viii. MARSHALL CHILD, b. 1808, m. about 1830, Olive Stetson.

7703. ix. AURELIA CHILD, b 1810, m. Elijah Parrington.

7704. x. ELIZA CHILD, b. 1813, m. Sulivan Andrews.

7705. xi. ADELPHIA CHILD, b. 1816, m. 1st, William Bradford; m. 2d, 1843, John Gordon.

[Sixth Generation.]

7696. ii. JOSEPH CHILD, second son and child of William and Anna Washburn Child, b. in Livermore, Maine, Jan. 5, 1795, m. 1st, in 1816, Olive Woodsum of Saco, who d. in 1840 ; m. 2d, in 1841, Dorcas Andrews of Paris, Me. Mr. Child was a farmer by occupation, was for a time resident in Turner, then in Hartford, and finally settled in Paris, all these homes in the State of Maine. Here Mr. Childs died in Dec. 1875.

[Seventh Generation.] Children:

7706. i. LEWIS W. CHILD b. 1817, m. 1844, Emily M. Reed.

7707. ii. MIRANDA CHILD, b. 1819, m. 1838, John B. Stetson.

7708. iii. ELISHA N. CHILD, b 1820, m. 1850, Elizabeth Martin of Providence. R. I. Reside in Worcester; seven children, names not sent.

7709. iv. JULIA ANN CHILD, b. 1822, m. Harrison Hayford. Resides in Belfast, Me.

7710. v. WILLIAM CHILD, b. 1826, m.—.

7711. vi. TRUE W. CHILD, b. 1828, m. 1st. about 1855, Eliza Gleason; m. 2d, Emily White.

7712. vii. OLIVE W CHILD. b. 1831, m. 1st, Mr. Sprague of Abington; m. 2d, Mr. Hans of Brookfield, Mass.

7713. viii. ROSCOE G. CHILD, b. 1834 d. at the Isle of France, 1862, unm.

7714. ix. JOSEPH F. CHILD, b. 1845.

7715. x. JOSEPHINE CHILD, b. 1847.

7716. xi. PERSIS A CHILD, b. 1849.

[Seventh Generation.]

7706. i. LEWIS W. CHILD, eldest son and child of Joseph and Olive Woodsum Child, b. in Maine, 1817, m. May, 1844, Emily M. Reed of Hartford, Me Settled upon a farm in Paris, Me.

[Eighth Generation.] Children :

7717. i. HENRY A. CHILD, b. 1845, m 1870, Mattie Little.

7718. ii. EMILY H. CHILD, b. Nov. 8, 1848, unm. A teacher in Stevens Seminary, Glencoe, Minnesota.

7719. iii. ELISHA ADRIAN CHILD, b. Aug. 10, 1850. Joiner and dealer in farm machinery, Chicago, Ill.

7720. iv. CHARLES A. CHILD, b. Aug. 8, 1853. Upholsterer, (Chicago, Ill.)

7721. v. CORYDON L. CHILD, b. Jan. 13, 1857. Farmer, Milton, Me.

7722. vi. TRUE W. CHILD, b. Oct. 22, 1858, m. about 1877, May Stevens.

7723. vii. SAMPSON R. CHILD, b. Sept 21, 1860. A teacher.

7724. viii. DANA CHILD, b. Mch. 22, 1862.

7725. ix. DELLIE JOSEPHINE CHILD, b. Aug 29, 1867.

[Eighth Generation.]

7717. i. HENRY A. CHILD, eldest son of Lewis W. and

E-2

Emily M. Reed Child, b. in Paris, Me., 1845. Served four years in the army; studied law, and established himself in Glencoe, Minn. Married in 1870, Mattie Little, d. in Chaska, Minn., in 1878.

[Ninth Generation.] Children:
    7726. i. IDA CHILD, b. 1871.
    7727. ii. LEWIS H. CHILD, b. 1873.
    7728. iii. DAN. CHILD, b. 1874.
    7729. iv. ALICE CHILD, b. 1876.

[Eighth Generation.]

7722. vi. TRUE W. CHILD, fifth son and sixth child of Lewis W. and Emily M. Reed Child, b. in Paris, Me., Oct. 22, 1858, m. about 1877, May Stevens of Rumford, Me. Resides in Milton, Me.

[Ninth Generation.] Child:
    7730. i. GRACE CHILD, b. Oct. 5, 1879.

[Seventh Generation.]

7710. v. WILLIAM CHILD, third son and fifth child of Joseph and Olive Woodsum Child, b. in Maine, in 1826, m. in Abington, Mass., and remained in Abington until 1872, when he removed to Layfayette, Indiana.

[Eighth Generation.] Children:
    7731. i. WILLIAM CHILD.
    7732. ii. ROSCOE CHILD.

[Seventh Generation.]

7711. vi. TRUE W. CHILDS, fourth son and sixth child of Joseph and Olive Woodsum Child, b. in Maine in 1828, m. 1st, about 1855, Eliza Gleason of Millbury, Mass., who d. in 1859; m. 2d, Emily White of New Hampshire. Resides in Toledo, Ohio; is of the business firm of Fuller, Childs & Co., 112 and 114 Summit St., Toledo, Ohio.

[Eighth Generation.] Children:
    7733. i. CLINTON A. CHILDS, b. Dec. 1856, m. 1879, Ida L. White of Toledo, Ohio.
    7734. ii. AUSTIN CHILDS, b. 1868.
    7735. iii. GRACE CHILDS, b. 1870.

[Sixth Generation.]

7697. iii. WILLIAM CHILD, JR., third son and child of William and Anna Washburn Child, b. in Livermore, Me., in April 1797, m. in 1816, Lucinda Woodsum of Saco. Reside in Hartford, Me. A farmer and carpenter.

[Seventh Generation.] Children:
    7736. i. WILLIAM AUGUSTUS CHILD, b. 1819, m. Elizabeth White.

7737. ii. ADRIAN CHILD, b. 1821, m. —.

7738. iii. MERINDA CHILD, m. George Smith of Cohasset, Mass.

7739. iv. ALBION CHILD, d. at sea.

7740. v. CLINTON CHILD, d. in Terra Haute, Ind.

7741. vi MARSHALL CHILD, b. in Hartford, Me., m Emily Turner of Livermore, Me.: has three children names not received.

[Seventh Generation.]

7736. i. WILLIAM A. CHILD, eldest son and child of William Jr. and Lucinda Woodsum Child, b. in Hartford, Me., in 1819, m. Elizabeth White of Whitefield, Me.

[Eighth Generation] Child:

7742. i. WILLIAM CHILD, married and resides in Boston, Mass.

[Seventh Generation.]

7737. ii. ADRIAN CHILD, second son and child of William, Jr., and Lucinda Woodsum Child, b. in Hartford, Me., 1821, m. — of Rockland, Me. Removed to Terre Haute, Indiana, and died there.

[Eighth Generation.] Child:

7743. i. WILLIAM CHILD, resides in Bois City, Colorado.

[Sixth Generation.]

7699. v. TRUE WOODMAN CHILD, fourth son and fifth child of William and Anna Washburn Child, b. in 1802, in Livermore, Me., m. a Miss Smith of Boston, Mass.

[Seventh Generation.] Child:

7744. i. CHARLES CHILD.

[Sixth Generation.]

7702. viii. MARSHALL CHILD, seventh son of William and Anna Washburn Child, b. in Livermore, Me., Jan. 25, 1808, m. 1830, Olive Stetson of Hartford, Me.

[Seventh Generation.] Children, born in Livermore, Maine:

7745. i. MARTHA CHILD, b. Jan. 2, 1834, d. Mch. 24, 1864.

7746. ii. HIRAM CHILD, b. Aug. 18, 1835.

7747. iii. ASA CHILD, b. Aug. 14, 1837. A soldier in the Union service, late war.

7748. iv. HOMER CHILD, b. Sept. 2, 1839.

7749. v. MARTHA F. CHILD, b. April 21, 1841.

7750. vi. HARRIET E. CHILD, b. May 26, 1844.

7751. vii. EMERSON CHILD,) TWINS. { b. May 11, 1846, d. in U. S. service.
7752. viii. ELIHU CHILD,) { d. in U. S. service.

7753. ix ALBERT CHILD, b. Feb. 17, 1849, d. April 20, 1864.

7754. x. ELMER P. CHILD, b. Dec. 12, 1850, d. Dec. 19, 1865.

7755. xi. FRANCIS O. CHILD, b. Mch. 13, 1854, d. July 23, 1855.

7756 xii. ALBERT M. CHILD, b. Jan. 2, 1867.

7757. DR. DANIEL CHILD. We cannot connect Dr. Child with his ancestor. He is reported as having been born in Massachusetts, Oct. 8, 1747, and as marrying in 1777, Rebeckah —, and removing to Maine. We place him in the Fourth Generation.

[Fifth Generation.] Children, born in Pembroke and Turner, Me.

  7758. i. DANIEL CHILD, JR. b. Jan. 12, 1778.
  7759. ii. RUTH CHILD, b. April 24, 1779.
  7760. iii. ANNA CHILD, b. Nov. 24, 1780.
  7761. iv. ASA CHILD, b. Nov. 9, 1788.
  7762. v. CASSIARELLA CHILD, b. Dec. 4, 1784.
  7763. vi. HOWLAND CHILD, b. Jan. 16, 1787, m. May 27, 1805, Acsah —.
  7764. vii. LYMAN CHILD,   }TWINS. { b. Jan. 18, 1789.
  7765. viii. Infant unchristened,   d. Jan. 27, 1789.
  7766. ix. LYDIA CHILD, b. April 15, 1791.

[Fifth Generation.]

  7763. vi. HOWLAND CHILD, sixth child and third son of Dr. Daniel and Rebeckah Child, b. Jan. 16, 1787, in Turner, Me., m. May 27, 1805, Achsah —. She was born in Sandwich, Me., Sept. 20, 1786. He died Jan. 6, 1840.

[Sixth Generation.] Children:

  7767. i. ARNOLD CHILD, b. in Livermore, Me., Aug. 10, 1806, m. —.
  7768. ii. STEPHEN CHILD, b. in Turner, Me., Oct. 30, 1807, m. June 12, 1831, Lydia Chandler.
  7769. iii. MARY ANN CHILD, b. in Turner, Me., Nov. 28, 1808.
  7770. iv. EMELINE CHILD, b. in Turner, Me., April 10, 1810, d. July 18, 1842.
  7771. v. MARY JANE CHILD, b. in Livermore, Me., April 12, 1812.
  7772. vi. ZIRA ANN CHILD, b. in Jay, Me., June 4, 1813.
  7773. vii. HOWLAND CHILD, JR., b. in Jay, Me., Feb. 16, 1815, d. July 18, 1816.
  7774. viii. ANNA CHILD, b. in Jay, Me., Sept. 19, 1816, d. Dec. 1861.
  7775. ix. LEONARD CHILD, b. in Jay, Me., Feb. 10, 1819, d. April 12, 1838.
  7776. x. GRANVILLE CHILD, b. in Jay, Me., Sept. 11, 1820, d. July 1, 1849.
  7777. xi. ALBION H. P. CHILD, b. July 22, 1822, m. Nov. 29, 1849, Lucy A. Keyes.
  7778. xii. COLUMBUS CHILD, b. in Canton, Me., July 21, 1825, d. May 9, 1826.
  7779. xiii. LYMAN CHILD, b. in Jay, Me., Nov. 16, 1826.

[Sixth Generation.]

  7768. ii. STEPHEN CHILD, second child and son of Howland and Achsah Child, b. in Turner, Me., Oct. 30, 1807, m. June 12, 1831, Lydia Chandler, daughter of Peleg Chandler; she was b. Sept. 4, 1813.

[Seventh Generation.] Children, all but the eldest born in Jay, Me.:

  7780. i. ANDREW A. CHILD, b. in Middleboro, Mass., Mch. 13, 1833, m. Aug. 1862, Helen Adams. A.A. Child was a physician. They had no children.

7781. ii. MARY J. B. CHILD, b. May 28, 1836, m. Feb. 28, 1861, Daniel Briggs; no children. Mrs. Briggs d. Dec. 24, 1865.

7782. iii. ELIZA A. CHILD, b. July 27, 1838, d. Oct. 31, 1849.

7783. iv. LYSANDER C. CHILD, b. April 15, 1841, m. July 16, 1865, Paulina Rawson, d. Nov. 28, 1865; no children.

7784. v. LUCY S. CHILD, b. Mch. 13, 1844, d. Sept. 28, 1847.

7785. vi. ABBIE D. CHILD, b. Feb. 9, 1846, m. June, 1875, Moses B. Thomas.

7786. vii. LUCY S. CHILD, 2D, b. July 9, 1848, m. Feb. 1867, Daniel Briggs; she d. June 24, 1872, leaving two children.

7787. viii. LYDIA A. CHILD, b. May 31, 1850, m. Jan. 1, 1873, Rose Fuller.

7788. ix. CONVERSE S. CHILD, b. Oct. 15, 1852, m. May 21, 1877, Florence Spaulding. Converse S. Child is a physician.

7789. x. JOHN L. CHILD, b May 13, 1856.

7790. xi. NELLIE CHILD, b. July 13, 1858.

[Sixth Generation.]

7777. xi. DR. ALBION H. P. CHILD, eleventh child and sixth son of Howland and Achsah Child, b. in Jay Me., July 22, 1822. m. Nov. 29, 1849, Lucy A. Keyes. He died July 19, 1856.

[Seventh Generation.] Children, born in Jay, Me.

7791. i. LUCY ELLA CHILD, b. Oct. 21, 1850, d. July 17, 1861.

7792. ii. NAOMI L. CHILD, b. Sept. 6, 1856.

[We have found some difficulty in determining whether the terminal " s " was used by Dr. Daniel Child and his descendants ; but from the light we have, we have decided to write the name without the " s."]

EPHRAIM CHILDS.

This family we suppose to be of the Watertown line. but if so, we fail to find the immediate paternity of this Ephraim Childs. We place him and his descendants with other unlinked families, trusting time may supply the lost links.

7793. EPHRAIM CHILDS of Princeton, Mass., b. April 24, 1787, m. Aug. 29, 1811, Hannah Cowden of Rutland, Mass. He d. May 7, 1818, aged, 31, in Rutland : his widow d. June 5, 1875, aged 84, in Hubbardston, Mass.

[Seventh Generation.] Children :

7794. i. JAMES COWDEN CHILDS, b. July 11, 1812, m. July 5, 1840, Susan M. Ripley.

7795. ii. WILLIAM GILMOR CHILDS, b. Oct. 1, 1814, d. July 4, 1816.

7796. iii. GEORGE CHILDS, b. Nov. 1, 1817, d. 1822.

[Seventh Generation.]

7794. i. JAMES COWDEN CHILDS, eldest son of Ephraim and Hannah Cowden Childs, b. in Rutland, Mass., July 11, 1812, m. in Vernon, Vt., July 5, 1840, Susan Malvina Ripley

[Eighth Generation.] Children, born in Princeton, Mass.

7797. i. PERSIS EMELINE CHILDS, b. June 19, 1841, m May 15, 1867, Charles E. Reid.

7798. ii. ALBERT AUGUSTIN CHILDS, b. Sept. 1, 1842, d. Mch. 9, 1843.

7799 iii. WALTER MAYNARD CHILDS, b Feb. 9, 1844, m Fannie Parker.

7800. iv. ADDISON ELLINWOOD CHILDS, b. Mch. 22, 1846, m. Sept. 15, 1879, Susan E. Grout.

7801. v. ADALINE LOUISA CHILDS, b. Feb. 16, 1849, m. Feb. 20, 1870, George W. Handy.

[Eighth Generation.]

7799. iii. WALTER MAYNARD CHILDS, second son of James C. and Susan M. Ripley Childs, b. in Princeton, Mass., Feb. 9, 1844, m. about 1878, Fannie Parker.

[Ninth Generation.] Child:

7802 i. LILLA MAY CHILDS, b. Mch. 2, 1880.

[Eighth Generation.]

7801. v. ADALINE LOUISA CHILDS, second dau. and youngest child of James Cowden, and Susan M. Ripley Childs, b. in Princeton, Mass., Feb. 16, 1849, m. Feb. 20, 1870, George W. Handy.

[Ninth Generation.] Children:

7803. i. GEORGIA EDITH HANDY, b. Oct. 3, 1871.

7804. ii. WILFRED LESTER HANDY, b. Jan. 1, 1872.

7805. iii. CHARLES LEROY HANDY, b. Feb. 17, 1875, d. in Mch. 1875.

ISAAC CHILDS OF BRATTLEBORO, VT.

The following record is furnished by Mr. Winchester Child of Cooperstown, N. Y., a son of Isaac Childs.

7806. ISAAC CHILDS, lived in Brattleboro, Vt.; removed in 1804, and settled in Worcester, Otsego county, N. Y., where he spent the balance of his life. He is said to have had seven children.

[Sixth Generation.] Children:

7807. i. WINCHESTER CHILDS, b. in Brattleboro, Vt., 1802, m. Amanda Cuppernal.

7808. ii. BENJAMIN CHILDS, b in Brattleboro, Vt., 1803.

7809. iii. POLLY CHILDS.

7810. iv. PHEBE CHILDS.

7811. v. ISAAC CHILDS.

7812. vi. AMASA CHILDS.

7813. vii. SUKEY CHILDS.

[Sixth Generation.]

7807. i. WINCHESTER CHILDS, the eldest child of Isaac Child, m Amanda Cuppernal and settled in Cooperstown,

N. Y., where he has for more than 40 years resided, and where he still lives.

[Seventh Generation.] Child:

7814. i. MARY A. CHILD, m. a Mr. Crandall; they reside in New York City.

[Sixth Generation.]

7808. ii. BENJAMIN CHILDS, second child of Isaac Childs, m. and lives in Pennsylvania: name of town not given.

[Seventh Generation.] Children:

7815. i. DAVID CHILDS.
7816. ii. GEORGE CHILDS.
7817. iii. HENRY CHILDS.
7818. iv. MARY CHILDS.
7819. v. CAROLINE CHILDS.
7820. vi. JANE CHILDS

LATEST EMIGRANTS.

7821. JOSEPH AND MARY CHILD, lived and died in St. Ives, Eng. They had one son named Joseph, b. in St. Ives, Eng., Oct. 21. 1789, m. Oct. 21, 1813, Penelope Tingle, dau. of Thomas Tingle of Kettering, Eng. Joseph Child, Jr., removed from England to the City of New York in Sept. 1824, and died April 1829. Mrs. Penelope Child died in Brooklyn, Jan 11. 1863. He was a boat builder by occupation.

[Second Generation.] Children:

7822. i. MARY CHILD, b. in St. Ives, Eng , July 18, 1814, m. June 1835, by Rev. E. F. Hatfield, William S. Alexander, son of John Alexander. Residence, Brooklyn; died 1877.

7823. ii. SUSAN CHILD b in St. Ives, Eng., Sept. 21, 1815, m. 1st, Simeon Decker; he d. 1876; m. 2d, in Brooklyn. N. Y., by F. Bailey, May 2, 1878, James H. Holmes. She died July 1878, in Buffalo, N. Y.

7824. iii. JOSEPH CHILD, JR, b in St. Ives, Eng., June 1, 1817, m. 1st, Aug. 13, 1845, Fidelia Dunning; m. 2d, July 6, 1853, Agnes Johnston.

7825. iv. PENELOPE CHILD, b. in St. Ives, Eng., and died early.

7826. v. THOMAS CHILD, b. in St. Ives, Eng., d. early.

7827. vi. PENELOPE CHILD, 2D, b. in St. Ives, Eng., d. early.

7828 vii CHARLOTTE CHILD, b. in Saffron, Waldron, Eng , June 16, 1822, m. 1853, in Brooklyn, N.Y., Mathew J. Clough; he d. in New Orleans, 1866; she d. in Brooklyn, 1874.

7829. viii. THOMAS CHILD, b. in Saffron, Waldron, Eng , in 1823, d. early.

7830. ix. ELLEN CHILD, b. in New York City, 1825, m. in Brooklyn, 1853, Joseph Harrison; removed to San Francisco, Cal. Mr. Harrison died in Nevada, Col. She m. 2d, in Brooklyn, Brittian Holmes, and resides in Buffalo, N. Y.

7831. x. GEORGE HENRY CHILD, b. in New York City, 1828, d. 1829.

[Second Generation.]

7824. iii. JOSEPH CHILD, JR., third child and eldest son of Joseph and Penelope Tingle Child, b. in St. Ives, Eng., June 1, 1817, m. 1st, Aug. 13, 1845, in Fenton, Mich., by Rev. Ira Dunning, Fidelia Dunning, daughter of the officiating clergyman; she d. Aug. 13, 1850, in New York; m. 2d, in Brooklyn, N. Y., in 1853, by Rev. James Johnston, Agnes Johnston, daughter of the officiating clergyman. Mr. Child was formerly engaged in mercantile business. Residence in Troy, N. Y.

[Third Generation.] Children. By first marriage:

7832. i. FIDELIA MATILDA CHILD, b. in Fenton, Mich., June 1, 1846, m. by Rev. Theodore L. Cuyler, D. D., in 1874, Alexander M. Davenport, son of Julius Davenport, Brooklyn, N. Y. Residence, Brooklyn, N. Y.

7833. ii. CAROLINE CHILD, b. in Brooklyn, N. Y., May 16, 1848, m. 1870, Elias S. Platt of Brooklyn, N. Y. Residence, Smithtown, N. Y.

7834. iii. MILTON D. CHILD, b. in Brooklyn, N. Y., Mch. 2, 1850. Was a clerk; died in Lansingburg, N. Y., Feb. 16, 1872.

By second marriage:

7835. iv. JAMES J. CHILD, b. in Brooklyn, N. Y., April 22, 1854. He is a book-keeper in Lansingburg, N. Y.

7836 v. AGNES CHILD, b. in Brooklyn, N. Y., Feb. 15, 1856.

7837. vi. EUPHEMIA CHILD, b. in Brooklyn, N. Y., Jan. 11, 1858.

7838. vii. JOSEPHINE CHILD, b. in Brooklyn, N. Y., July 29, 1859.

7839. viii. KATE CHILD, b. in Brooklyn, N. Y., June 24, 1861.

7840. ix. SUSAN CHILD, b. in Lansingburg, N. Y., Mch. 6, 1863, removed to New Lebanon, N. Y.

7841. x. MINNIE CHILD, b. in Lansingburg, N. Y., July 1, 1865, removed to New Lebanon. N. Y.

The following record is exceedingly incomplete as we know not when the family or any member of it came to America. We understand that those of the first and second generations, as hereafter recorded, did not come to America, but are sent as the progenitors of those now in America.

7842. THOMAS CHILD, resided in Ewhurst, Surrey county, England, and had two sons of whom we have report.

[Second Generation.] Children:

7843. i. THOMAS CHILD, JR.

7844. ii. SOLOMON CHILD.

[Second Generation.]

7843. i. THOMAS CHILD, JR., eldest son of Thomas Child of Ewhurst, England, married and had several children.

[Third Generation.] Children:

7845. i. JAMES CHILD.

7846. ii. THOMAS CHILD, JR.
7847. iii. SAMUEL CHILD.

[Third Generation.]
7845. i. JAMES CHILD, eldest son of Thomas Child, Jr.,
married and had children.

[Fourth Generation.] Children:
7848. i. JAMES CHILD, JR.
7849. ii. THOMAS CHILD.
7850. iii. WILLIAM CHILD.
7851. iv. SAMUEL CHILD.

[Fourth Generation.]
7850. iii. WILLIAM CHILD, third son of James Child, b.
about 1807. Resides at Red Bank, N. J.

[Fifth Generation.] Children:
7852. i. JOSEPH W. CHILD.
7853. ii. HENRY J. CHILD.

[Second Generation.]
7844. ii. SOLOMON CHILD, second son of Thomas Child of
Ewhurst, Surry county, England, married.

[Third Generation.] Children:
7854. i. EDWARD CHILD.
7855. ii. SOLOMON CHILD.
7856. iii. JOSEPH CHILD.

Had this record been received in season, it would have been
placed in its due chronological order on page 248, after number
1544.

[Sixth Generation.]
1500. iii. SALLY or SARAH CHILD, third dau. and child of
Cephas and Martha (Child) Child, b. in West Fairlee, Vt.,
Sept. 7, 1788, m. 1813, Andrew Luce.

[Seventh Generation.] Children:
7857. i. BENJAMIN C. LUCE, b. Nov. 15, 1815, m. Feb. 11, 1840, Mrs.
Rebecca Brown.
7858. ii. CHARLES M. LUCE, b. June 10, 1818, m. June 1, 1845, Jerusha
E. Walton.
7859. iii. LOUISA LUCE, b. Nov. 8, 1820, m. Mch. 1840, John M. Reese.
7860. iv. MARINDA LUCE, b. Mch. 3, 1823, m. Feb. 5, 1843, Egbert B.
Van Vlack.
7861. v. NANCY W. LUCE, b. Aug. 9, 1825, m. June 20, 1853, Otis
Saunders.
7862. vi. CAROLINE LUCE, b. Mch. 30, 1831, m. Dec. 11, 1854, Alvin B.
Barnes.

[Seventh Generation.]

7857. i. BENJAMIN C. LUCE, eldest son and child of Sally Child and Andrew Luce, b. Nov. 15, 1815, m. Feb. 11, 1840, Mrs. Rebecca Brown. Resides at Half Day, Lake county, Ill. To Mr. B. C. Luce we are indebted for the record of this line.

[Eighth Generation.] Children:

7863. i. MARY M. LUCE, b. Dec. 2, 1840, m. July 1857, d. Aug. 12, 1858.
7864. ii. GEORGE A. LUCE, b. Aug. 18, 1842, m. Aug. 29, 1862, Julia A. Lutzel.
7865. iii. VALERIA C. LUCE, b. May 12, 1844, m. Dec. 25, 1865, Henry J. Merrill.
7866. iv. OREN J. LUCE, b. April 7, 1847, m. Aug. 31, 1869, Kate S. Herrick.

[Eighth Generation.]

7864. ii. GEORGE A. LUCE, eldest son and second child of Benjamin C. and Rebecca Brown Luce, and grandson of Mrs. Sally Child Luce, b. Aug. 18, 1842, m. Aug. 29, 1862, Julia A. Lutzel.

[Ninth Generation.] Children:

7867. i EARNEST M. C. LUCE, b. July 14, 1864.
7868. ii. MARY LEONA LUCE, b. Jan. 16, 1868.
7869. iii. GEORGIE A. LUCE, b. Oct. 2, 1871, d. Aug. 11, 1873.
7870. iv. MYRTIE L. LUCE, b. Mch. 15, 1875.

[Eighth Generation.]

7865. iii. VALERIA C. LUCE, second dau. and third child of Benjamin C. and Rebecca Brown Luce, and grand-daughter of Mrs. Sally Child Luce, b. May 12, 1844, m. Dec. 25, 1865, Henry J. Merrill.

[Ninth Generation.] Children:

7871. i. HATTIE L. MERRILL, b. Jan. 28, 1867.
7872. ii. CLARA E MERRILL, b. July 12, 1868.
7873. iii. ANNIE R. MERRILL, b. Feb. 2, 1870.
7874. iv. ARTHUR H. MERRILL, b Oct. 12, 1871.
7875 v. CHARLES L. MERRILL, b. Mch. 18, 1879

[Eighth Generation.]

7866. iv. OREN J. LUCE, second son and fourth child of Benjamin C. and Rebecca Brown Luce, and grandson of Mrs. Sally Child Luce, b. April 7, 1847, m. Aug. 31, 1869, Kate S. Herrick.

[Ninth Generation] Children:

7876 i EUGENE LUCE, b. June 9, 1872.
7877. ii. GILBERT LUCE, b. May 21, 1874.

[Seventh Generation.]

7858. ii. CHARLES M. LUCE, second son and child of Sally Child and Andrew Luce, b. June 10, 1818, m. June 1, 1845, Jerusha E. Walton.

[Eighth Generation.] Children:
7878. i. JULIUS C. LUCE, b. Mch. 5, 1846.
7879. ii. JEROME E. LUCE, b. Oct. 8, 1847, d. Jan. 19, 1854.
7880. iii. THOMAS U. LUCE, b. Sept. 6, 1850, m. Dec. 25, 1876, Clara E. Skinner.
7881. iv. GEORGE C. LUCE, b. Mch. 18, 1852.
7882. v. CHARLES W. LUCE, b. Mch. 9, 1854, m Oct. 17, 1878, Edna A. Nillis.
7883. vi. FAYETTE J. LUCE, } TWINS. } b. Oct. 10, 1856.
7884. vii. FREMONT L. LUCE, {
7885. viii. ERNST R. LUCE, b. Nov. 11, 1858.
7886. ix. ELMER E. LUCE, b. Sept. 6, 1861.
7887. x. GRANT LUCE, b. April 9, 1864, d. Oct. 3, 1864.
7888. xi. GERTRUDE R. LUCE, b. Aug. 8, 1868, d. July 28, 1869.

[Eighth Generation.]
7880. iii. THOMAS U. LUCE, third son and child of Charles
M. and Jerusha E. Walton Luce, and grandson of Mrs. Sally
Child Luce, b. Sept. 6, 1850, m. Dec. 25, 1876, Clara E. Skinner.
[Ninth Generation.] Child:
7889. i. GRACIE A LUCE, b. Dec. 5, 1878.

[Eighth Generation.]
7882. v. CHARLES W. LUCE, fifth son and child of Charles
M. and Jerusha E. Walton Luce, and grandson of Mrs. Sally
Child Luce, b. Mch. 9, 1854, m. Oct. 17, 1878, Edna A. Nillis.
[Ninth Generation.] Child:
7890. i CLAUDE U. LUCE, b. June 20, 1879.

[Seventh Generation.]
7859. iii. LOUISA LUCE, third child and eldest dau. of Sally
Child and Andrew Luce, b. Nov. 8, 1820, m. Mch. 1840, John
M. Reese. Mrs. Louisa L. Reese d. July 24, 1852.
[Eighth Generation.] Children:
7891. i. SYLVIA REESE, b. 1841, d. at two months of age.
7892. ii. EMILY REESE, b. Jan. 1843.
7893. iii ELLINOR REESE, b. Dec. 2, 1845.
7894. iv. ANDREW REESE, b. 1848, d. 1853.

[Seventh Generation.]
7860. iv. MARINDA LUCE, second dau. and fourth child of
Sally Child and Andrew Luce, b. Mch. 3, 1823, m. Feb. 5, 1843,
Egbert B. Van Vlack.
[Eighth Generation.] Children:
7895. i. ALTA VAN VLACK, b. 1843, d. same year.
7896. ii. CLARK VAN VLACK, b. Feb. 27, 1845, m. April 20, 1868.
7897. iii HOMER VAN VLACK, b Oct. 22, 1849, m Sept 25, 1871.
7898. iv. CHARLES U. VAN VLACK, b. Sept. 22, 1853, d. July 12, 1862.
7899. v. CLARA LOUISA VAN VLACK, b. Aug. 11, 1857, d. April 20, 1863.

[Eighth Generation.]
7896. ii. CLARK VAN VLACK, eldest son and second child
of Marinda Luce and E. B. Van Vlack, and grandson of Mrs.
Sally Child Luce, b. Feb. 27, 1845, m. April 20, 1868.
[Ninth Generation.] Child:
7900. i. EDGAR VAN VLACK, b. Sept. 28, 1878.

[Eighth Generation.]

7897. iii. HOMER VAN VLACK, second son and third child of Marinda Luce and E. B. Van Vlack, and grandson of Mrs. Sally Child Luce, b. Oct. 22, 1849, m. Sept. 25, 1871. —.

[Ninth Generation.]   Children:
   7901. i. WILLARD VAN VLACK, b. Sept. 25, 1873.
   7902. ii. PHILLIP A. VAN VLACK, b. Oct. 24, 1876.
   7903. iii. GEORGE E. VAN VLACK, b. June 10, 1880.

[Seventh Generation.]

7861. v. NANCY W. LUCE, third dau. and fifth child of Sally Child and Andrew Luce, b. Aug. 9, 1825, m. June 20, 1853, Otis Saunders.

[Eighth Generation.]   Children:
   7904. i FRANK B. SAUNDERS, b. Aug. 18, 1854, m. Oct. 21, 1879, Jennie M. Haggett.
   7905. ii. FREDERICK U. SAUNDERS, b. Sept. 2, 1856, d. Aug. 18, 1858.
   7906 iii. FRANCIS A. SAUNDERS, b. July 13, 1858.
   7907. iv. FOREST L. SAUNDERS, b July 24, 1861.
   7908 v. FLORA E. SAUNDERS, b. Aug. 27, 1863.

[Seventh Generation.]

7862. vi. CAROLINE LUCE, fourth dau. and sixth child of Sally Child and Andrew Luce, b. Mch. 30, 1831, m. Dec. 11, 1854, Alvin B. Barnes.

[Eighth Generation]   Children:
   7909. i. WILLIE B. BARNES, b. Aug. 29, 1855.
   7910. ii MARY C. BARNES, b. Oct. 22, 1857, d. Mch. 8, 1860
   7911. iii. CARRIE L. BARNES, b. Mch 24, 1860.
   7912. iv. HATTIE A. BARNES, b. May 21, 1862.
   7913. v. MARY M. BARNES, b. June 23, 1866.
   7914. vi. FANNIE BARNES, b. May 25, 1869.

The succeeding record is furnished by George L. Child of Troy, N. Y. We are not able to connect the family with its early ancestry ; it is no doubt of either the line of Benjamin Child of Roxbury, through some of the Connecticut descendants, or that of Jeremiah Child of Swansea, through some of the Rhode Island families.

7915. ABEL CHILD, thought to have been born in New York City between 1790 and 1800. Removed early to Troy, N. Y., where he was for many years extensively engaged in the coffee trade ; in this business he was succeeded by his son. If there were other children we do not learn of them.

[Seventh Generation.]   Child:
   7916. i. AUSTIN CHILD, b. in New York City, Aug. 10, 1822, m. 1st, Eliza Ann Lent of Troy, N. Y.; m. 2d, Mary Elizabeth Lawton of Stuyvesant Falls. Resided at Green Island, Troy, N. Y., where he died Jan. 7, 1873.

[Eighth Generation.]   Children:
   7917. i. AUSTIN CHILD, JR., d. young.
   7918. ii. CHARLOTTE LOUISA CHILD, b. about 1845, m. J. Harney.

7919. iii. ALICE EMMA CHILD, b. 1852, d. aged 6 years.
7920. iv. GEORGE L. CHILD, b. Sept. 31, 1854, unm. Resides at Green Island, Troy; is a book-keeper for F. Cluet, 269 River street, Troy, N. Y.

[Eighth Generation]
7918. ii. CHARLOTTE LOUISA CHILD, eldest dau. of Austin and Eliza Ann Lent Child, b. in Troy, about 1845, m. J. Harney, carriage manufacturer in Sandy Hill, N. Y.

[Ninth Generation.] Child:
7921. i. MARY HARNEY, b Oct. 26, 1876.

_____

There is little doubt this line belongs to Jeremiah Child of Swansea, a most numerous family of whom we have but partial reports.

7922. JONATHAN CHILD, b. Sept. 5, 1806, in Rhode Island, (as his son F. J. believes), m. Rebecca Lay, dau. of Joseph Lay of Chatham, N. Y., about 1833. Mr. Child was Postmaster in West Troy for some years. He died Oct. 5, 1874.

[Eighth Generation.] Children:
7923. i. JOSEPH CHILD, b. 1834, or '35, m. Lois Tripp.
7924. ii. FRANK J. CHILD, b. Sept. 5 1838, m June 18, 1864, Harriet Deyo.
7925. iii. WILLIAM R. CHILD, b. Sept. 28, 1843, m. Aug. 22, 1867, Sarah Hampson, dau. of Thomas Hampson Mr. Child is a hotel keeper at Cohoes, N. Y.
7926. iv. MARY CHILD, b. 1845 m. Sept. 1863, Martin Deyo.
7927. v. CORNELIA CHILD, b. 1848. Resides in New York City, unm.
7928. vi. EMMA CHILD, b. 1852, m. 1876, Mr. Ashley, a lawyer. Reside in New York City.

[Eighth Generation.]
7923. i. JOSEPH CHILD, eldest son of Jonathan and Rebecca Lay Child, b. in Chatham, N. Y., in 1834–5, m. Lois Tripp, who died 1874.

[Ninth Generation.] Child:
7929. i. FRANK CHILD, d. 1856.

[Eighth Generation.]
7924. ii. FRANK J. CHILD, second son and child of Jonathan and Rebecca Lay Child, b. in Chatham, N. Y., Sept. 5, 1838, m. June 18, 1864, Harriet Deyo, dau. of Richard Deyo of Chatham, Columbia county, N. Y. Mr. Child is associated with his brother in a hotel at Cohoes, N. Y.

[Ninth Generation.] Child:
7930. i. CHARLIE CHILD, b. 1865.

[Eighth Generation.]
7926. iv. MARY CHILD, eldest dau. of Jonathan and Rebecca Lay Child, b. in Chatham, N. Y., in 1845, m. Sept. 1863, Martin Deyo. Reside in West Troy, N. Y.

[Ninth Generation.] Children:
   7931. i. MARTHA DEYO.
   7932. ii. WILLIE DEYO.

   7933. THOMAS B. CHILDS,—North Adams, Mass. The record of Mr. Childs and descendants is furnished by his son, Luther, of North Adams, Mass. He was b. Aug. 1, 1798, in Vermont; his parentage is not given. He m. Oct. 20, 1819, Polly Hitchcock, daughter of Arthur Hitchcock of Holly, Mass; she was b. Mch. 2, 1799, she d. April 9, 1859; he d. Mch. 9, 1872, in North Adams.

[Seventh Generation.] Children:
   7934. i. DIANTHA CHILDS, b. in Holly, Mass., Aug. 28, 1820, d. May 8, 1837.
   7935. ii. HENRY CHILDS, b. May 15, 1822, m. 1st, Jan. 8, 1843, Harriet M. Bliss; m. 2d, Sept. 9, 1854, Elizabeth Winton of Easton, N. Y.
   7936. iii. POLLY (or MARY) CHILDS, b. May 17, 1824, m. Mch. 13, 1840, Robert W. Lytle
   7937. iv. THOMAS B. CHILDS, JR., b. Sept. 6, 1826, d. Dec. 23, 1834.
   7938. v. LUTHER CHILDS, b. Feb. 9, 1829, m. July 4, 1850, Sarah M. Roberts.
   7939. vi. EDWIN B. CHILDS, b May 13, 1831, m. 1st, Dec. 31, 1851, Sophia A. McLoud; m. 2d. Oct. 14, 1854, Eliza Corbit.

[Seventh Generation.]
   7935. ii. HENRY CHILDS, second child and eldest son of Thomas B. and Polly Hitchcock Childs, b. May 25, 1822, m. 1st, Jan. 8, 1843, Harriet M. Bliss, b. in Florida, Mass.; m. 2d, Sept. 9, 1854, Elizabeth Winton of Easton, N. Y., dau. of James and Mary Winton.

[Eighth Generation.] Children:
   7940. i. AMELIA A. CHILDS, m. Robert Nordaby.
   7941. ii. THOMAS CHILDS, m. 1876, Elizabeth Jewell of Titusville, Pa.; had one child.
   7942. iii. HELEN CHILDS, m. Alonzo Holmes.
   7943. iv. EUGENE CHILDS.
   7944. v. Infant unchristened.
            By second marriage.
   7945. vi. CHARLES W. CHILDS, b. July 11, 1851.
   7946. vii. FANNIE E. CHILDS, b. Nov. 20, 1857, m. Oct. 11, 1877, Charles E. Brace.
   7947. viii. MARY E. CHILDS, b. April 25, 1858, m. 1876, Heber D. Pierce.
   7948. ix. EVA JANE CHILDS, b. July 20, 1863.

[Eighth Generation.]
   7940. i. AMELIA A. CHILDS, eldest child of Henry and Harriet M. Bliss Childs, m. Robert Nordaby.

[Ninth Generation.] Children:
   7949. i. HARRIET ANN NORDABY, b. in Titusville, Pa.
   7950. ii. ROBERT NORDABY, died young.
   7951. iii. Infant unchristened.

[Seventh Generation.]
   7936. iii. POLLY (or MARY) CHILDS, third child and second dau. of Thomas B. and Polly Hitchcock Childs, b. May 17,

1824, m. Mch. 13, 1840, Robert W. Lytle; she d. April 11. 1855.

[Eighth Generation.] Children:
    7952. i. CHARLES HENRY LYTLE, b. Feb. 23. 1842, d. Sept. 12, 1862.
    7953. ii. EMILY ANN LYTLE, b. Feb. 25, 1844, m. Oct. 1861. Joseph R. White.
    7954. iii. SARAH JANE LYTLE, b. Oct. 3, 1846, d. Mch. 28, 1847.
    7955 iv. JAMES EDWARD LYTLE, b. Aug. 1, 1848, m. April 1872, Catharine Douglass. He d. Oct. 22, 1874.
    7956. v. WILLIAM FAILING LYTLE, b. Sept. 1853, m. June 3, 1874, Eugenia Smith.

[Eighth Generation.]
    7953. ii. EMILY ANN LYTLE, eldest dau. of Mary Childs and Robert W. Lytle, b. Feb. 25, 1844, m. Oct. 1861. Joseph R. White.

[Ninth Generation.] Children:
    7957. i. ANNA WHITE.
    7958. ii. LOTTIE WHITE.
    7959. iii. JENNIE WHITE.
    7960. iv. CARRIE WHITE.
    7961. v. GERTIE WHITE.

[Eighth Generation.]
    7956. v. WILLIAM FAILING LYTLE, fifth child and third son of Mary Childs and Robert W. Lytle, b. Sept. 18, 1853, m. June 3, 1874. Eugenia Smith ; he d. June 8, 1879.

Mr. Lytle was a young man of excellent qualities of heart and mind. He was early left an orphan and reared under the care of a most estimable aunt. Miss Jane Lytle, whose care for him and an elder brother, most tenderly supplied the place of a mother. At the time of his death he was employed as clerk in a wholesale dry-goods establishment in Troy, N. Y., and held in high esteem for his fidelity and efficiency. He was a consistent and devoted member of Christ's Episcopal Church, Troy, N. Y.

[Ninth Generation.] Children:
    7962. i. CHARLES HENRY LYTLE, b. Jan. 17, 1875.
    7963. ii. WILLIAM LE ROY LYTLE, b. May 27, 1877.
    7964. iii. EUGENE LYTLE, b June 8, 1878.

[Seventh Generation.]
    7938. v. LUTHER CHILDS, fifth child and third son of Thomas B. and Polly Hitchcock Childs, b. Feb. 9, 1829, m. July 4. 1850, Sarah M. Roberts, dau. of Abner and Mary A. Roberts of Stamford, Bennington county, Vt. Resides in North Adams, Mass.

[Eighth Generation.] Children:
    7965. i. GEO. DWIGHT CHILDS, b. Feb. 5, 1853, in Adams, Mass., d. 1857.
    7966. ii. EMMA JANE CHILDS, b. Feb. 5, 1857, unm.
    7967. iii. WM. EDWARD CHILDS, b. Jan. 27, 1861; lives in N. Adams.
    7968. iv. WALTER ABNER CHILDS, b. May 27, 1864; lives in N. Adams.

[Seventh Generation.]

7939. vi. EDWIN B. CHILDS, sixth child and fourth son of
Thomas B. and Polly Hitchcock Childs, b. May 13, 1831, m.
1st, Dec. 31, 1851, Sophia A. McLoud; she d. July 1853; m.
2d, 1854, Elvira Corbit of Adams, Mass.

[Eighth Generation.] Children. By first marriage;
    7969. i. EDWIN CHILDS, d. young.
                By second marriage:
    7970. ii. HERBERT D. CHILDS, b. May 13, 1857, m. 1877, Marie Burdett
of New London.
    7971. iii. CHARLES EDWIN CHILDS, b. in Adams, July 17, 1861.

7972. JONATHAN WILLARD CHILD, b. about 1798, probably
in Cheshire, Mass. He was an only son, but of his parentage
we have no report from his son, W. A. Child. Mr. Child
married about 1819, Susan Aylesworth, daughter of Warner
Aylesworth of Adams, Mass.

[—— Generation.] Children:
    7973. i. ZILPHA M. CHILD, b. about 1820.
    7974. ii. WARNER A. CHILD, b 1823, m. Mch. 24, 1845, Hannah Taft of
Troy, N. Y. Mr. Child has been engaged in mercantile affairs a portion of
his life; is now a man of leisure in easy circumstances. Resides in North
Adams, Mass.
    There were two other children unchristened.

The accompanying brief record is sent us by Dr. William
R. Childs, for many years a resident of Deposit, N. Y.:

" WILLIAM RODERICK CHILDS, of Philadelphia, Pa., my father, was a sea
captain, he was a great, good and worthy man. He married a daughter of
Michael and Sarah Broade of Philadelphia, Pa. My father was drowned
on a return voyage from the West Indies, whence he was bringing a cargo
of oranges. My mother afterward married Dea. William Hawley of Deposit,
N. Y., and had one son, Ezra Sherman Hawley, who married and had
several children; he is a merchant of the firm of Hawley, Burk & Co., of
Nebraska. Mrs. Hawley died some years since.

[Children of Capt. W. R. Childs:]
    i. WILLIAM RODERICK CHILDS, married but had no children. Has
studied both the medical and legal professions.
    ii. THEODORE D. CHILDS, married.
    iii. ANGELINE H. CHILDS, married Henry Freeman, has three child-
ren, the eldest daughter married Mr. Price. Mr. Freeman was a railway
agent, and was killed by some accident on the railway at Deposit, N. Y.
    iv. PRISCILLA CHILDS, married Dr. Campbell of Nebraska; a man
of wealth. Has several children.
    ii THEODORE D. CHILDS, married. He is a druggist and grocer; a
well educated and worthy man; has two sons living. He resides in Walton,
Delaware county, N. Y.
    i. WILLIAM CHILDS, resides in Wyoming Territory.
    ii. JAMES CHILDS, married and has a family; resides Wyoming
Territory."

The succeeding record, a correction and filling out of the record found on page 326, has come to us just as we supposed we had printed our last records for the body of the work. As we found we could supplement it as we had done one other tardily received report, we concluded to do so instead of placing it in the appendix.

[Sixth Generation.]

2379. iii. CYRIL CHILD, eldest son of William and Mary Heaton Child, b. in Thetford, Vt., April 20, 1783, m. Dec. 23, 1807, Mary Collins, she was b. Sept. 20, 1780, in Springfield, Mass., and d. in Greigsville, town of York, Livingston county, N. Y., Nov. 15, 1863. Mr. Child d. in the same place April 4, 1848.

[Seventh Generation.] Children:

2388. i. LUCIUS COLLINS CHILD, b. Oct. 26, 1808, m. Feb. 6, 1834, Sarah Jane Maltby.

2389. ii. MARY CHILD, b. June 15, 1810, m. 1830, John B. Thrasher.

2390. iii. MARIA NEWTON CHILD, b. April 13, 1812, m. Nov. 12, 1832, Stephen L. Maltby.

2391. iv. HARRIET ATWOOD CHILD, b. July 14, 1814, m. 1st, Jan. 3, 1839, Austin Cross; m 2d, Oliver E. Wolcott.

2392. v EMILY CHILD, b. Oct. 21, 1816, m. Sept. 1834, Darius Bickford.

2393. vi. CYNTHIA R. CHILD, b. Oct. 27 1818, unmarried.

2394. vii. AZUBAH H. CHILD, b. Dec. 21, 1821, unm.; resides at Greigsville, York, Livingston county, N. Y.

[Seventh Generation.]

2388. i. LUCIUS COLLINS CHILD, only son and eldest child of Cyril and Mary Collins Child, b. Oct. 26, 1808, m. Feb. 6, 1834, Sarah Jane Maltby, a neice of his aunt, Mrs. Persis Child Maltby. He d. Feb. 25, 1854.

[Eighth Generation] Children:

7975. i. JULIA ANN CHILD, b. Dec. 7, 1834, d. May 17, 1856.

7976. ii. EDWARD PAYSON CHILD, b. May 25. 1838, m. Sept. 10. 1861, Lucy H. Mitchell.

[Eighth Generation.]

7976. ii. Hon. EDWARD PAYSON CHILD, only son of Lucius Collins and Sarah Jane Maltby Child, b. May 25, 1838, m. Sept. 10, 1861, Lucy H. Mitchell of Missouri. Judge Child resides at Lincoln, Neb., is a man of commanding presence, being over six feet in height, and weighing 225 lbs. He has been a county judge in Missouri for three years, and a member of the Nebraska legislature. Judge Child commanded a battery during the Indian war in 1864 ; chief of artillery for the Department of the Plains. He possesses those strong and sterling qualities which are essential in the right development of the new States of the western republic.

F-2

[Ninth Generation] Children:
7977. i. BERTHA CHILD, b. Sept. 2, 1864.
7978. ii. RETA LOUISE CHILD, b. Nov. 2, 1866.
7979. iii. ANNA CHILD, b. Dec. 26, 1869.
7980. iv. JULIA CHILD, b. March 18, 1872.
7981. v. FREDERICK CHILD, b. Feb. 17, 1875.
7982. vi. WILLIAM ARTHUR CHILD, b. Nov. 1878.

[Seventh Generation.]

2389. ii. MARY CHILD, eldest dau. of Cyril and Mary Collins Child, b. June 15, 1810, m. 1830, John B. Thrasher; she d. 1870. Of the five children living, we learn that they are married and that there are twelve grandchildren, but the names of the husbands and wives and their children are not forwarded.

[Eighth Generation.] Children:
7983. i. FRANCES MARIA THRASHER, d. in 1850.
7984. ii. CYRIL CHILD THRASHER.
7985. iii. MARY JANE THRASHER, d. 1839.
7986. iv. EMMA ROXANNA THRASHER.
7987. v. HARRIET THRASHER, d. 1849.
7988. vi. LUCY ANN THRASHER, d. 1845.
7989. vii. AZUBAH THRASHER.
7990. viii. LUCIUS THRASHER.
7991. ix. WILLIAM H. THRASHER.

[Seventh Generation.]

2390. iii. MARIA NEWTON CHILD, second dau. of Cyril and Mary Collins Child, b. April 13, 1812, m. Nov. 12, 1832, Stephen L. Maltby, nephew of her aunt, Mrs. Persis Child Maltby.

[Eighth Generation.] Children:
7992. i. SARAH PRESCOTT MALTBY.
7993. ii. MARTHA SOPHIA MALTBY.
7994. iii. HARLAN PAGE MALTBY.
7995. iv. LUCIUS CHILD MALTBY.
7996. v. SUPLER MALTBY.

[Seventh Generation.]

2391. iv. HARRIET ATWOOD CHILD, third dau. and fourth child of Cyril and Mary Collins Child, b. July 14, 1814, m. 1st, Jan. 3, 1839, Austin Cross, he d. Sept. 23, 1842; m. 2d, Oliver E. Walcott.

[Eighth Generation.] Children:
7997. i. HENRY A. CROSS, b. Feb. 1, 1840, m. Sept. 29, 1874, Mary Moffatt of Brooklyn, E. D
7998. ii. SARAH E. CROSS, b. Nov. 2, 1842, m. Nov. 2, 1859, A. G. Doremus of Brooklyn, E. D. They have children now at school in Geneseo, N.Y.
7999. iii. HORACE CLARK WALCOTT.
8000. iv. WILLIS OSCAR WALCOTT.

[Seventh Generation.]

2392. v. EMILY CHILD, fourth dau. of Cyril and Mary Collins Child, b. Oct. 21, 1816, m. Sept. 1834, Darius Bickford.

[Eighth Generation.] Children:

8001. i. EDWARD O. BICKFORD.
8002. ii. LEONARD BICKFORD.
8003. iii. MARIA LOUISA BICKFORD.
8004. iv. EMILY E. BICKFORD.

REV. J. ASPENWALL HODGE, D. D.

(See page 265.)

At the time of printing the record of Charlotte G. Morse, dau. of Richard Cary and Louisa Davis Morse, who married Rev. J. Aspenwall Hodge, D. D., we lacked the dates of the birth of her children, and were ignorant of the fact that her husband was a clergyman. For this reason the names of the children are here repeated. We also correct the date of Mrs. Hodge's birth and give the date of her marriage, which is omitted in the former record—her birth occurring May 28, 1833, and her marriage May 14, 1857. Rev. Dr. Hodge is pastor of the Presbyterian church and society in Hartford, Ct., and a member of the Presbytery of New York.

Children:

1703. i. JAMES BAYARD HODGE, b. July 19, 1859, d. Sept. 21, 1860.
1704. ii. J. ASPENWALL HODGE, JR., b. March 9, 1861.
1705. iii. HUGH LENOX HODGE,) TWINS (b. May 25, 1864.
1706. iv. RICHARD MORSE HODGE,)   (
1707. v. SAMUEL COLGATE HODGE, b. April 28, 1867.

8005. GEORGE CHILD. The record of George Child is obtained from his son, George Child, who resides in Albany, N. Y., and is a painter by occupation. The father died in Rochester, N. Y., 1873, leaving four children.

8006. i. GEORGE CHILD, JR., b. in 1851, in Rochester, N. Y., m. Anne Welch, in Albany, N. Y., and have one child, Nellie, b. July 13, 1876. Mr. C. resides at 338 Pearl street, Albany, N. Y.
8007. ii. JOHN CHILD, b. about 1854.
8008. iii. ANNIE CHILD, b. about 1856.
8009. iv. HENRY CHILD, b. about 1859.

The father of George Child may have been Jonathan Child, who resided in Pittsford, N. Y., and afterwards removed to Council Bluffs, Iowa, who had a son George, and may have been the father of George, Jr.

1590. i. SAMUEL CHILD, (see page 252) eldest child of Dea.
William and Sally Lyon Child, b. in Woodstock, Ct., Aug. 1,
1816. m. Jan. 29, 1840. S. A. T. Perry, dau. of John and
Thankful Perry, of Woodstock, Ct., b. June 2, 1820. Mr.
Child d. June 9, 1868.

[Eighth Generation.]   Children:
   8010. i. ANNA P. CHILD, b. Feb. 24, 1841, m. July 1, 1868, James Bracken.
   8011. ii. HERRICK M. CHILD, b. Jan. 21, 1845, m. Feb. 11, 1866, Olive S.
Angell.

[Eighth Generation.]

   8010. i. ANNA P. CHILD, eldest child of Samuel and S. A. T.
Perry Child, b. Feb. 24, 1841, m. July 1, 1868, James Brack-
en.   Residence Webster, Mass.

[Ninth Generation.]   Child.
   8012. i. HOWARD W. BRACKEN, b. Oct. 15, 1869.

[Eighth Generation.]

   8011. ii. HERRICK M. CHILD, second child of Samuel and
S. A. T. Perry Child, b. Jan. 21, 1845, m. Feb. 11, 1866, Olive
S. A. Angell, dau. of John C. and Phœbe A. Angell, of Sin-
clairville, Chautauqua county, N. Y.   Residence, Worcester,
Mass.

[Ninth Generation.]   Children:
   8013. i. MATELINE A. CHILD, b. Dec. 22, 1866.
   8014. ii. EDITH P. CHILD, b. May 22, 1879.

POTTSTOWN PA. BRANCH.

THOMAS AND MARY CHILD. This family, being unable to trace their line beyond Thomas Child, the father of William Child, of Pottstown, Pa., we are left in doubt as to their paternity. Similarity of name and proximity of residence point to the Thomas Child mentioned on page 757, who was a property-holder in Virginia in the early part of the seventeenth century; or, the family may belong to that recorded on pages 766-7, the tradition of whose paternity varies but little from that handed down by this and other lines. Or, again, they may be descendants of Cephas Child, page 734, the posterity of several of his large family not having been found in our researches.

Mr. William Child, of Marietta, Pa., who has for many years been connected with the Auditor's office, in Washington, D. C., sends the following account of Thomas Child, the earliest ancestor of whom he has any knowledge; it reached us after many of the copies were bound and sent out. He says: "I understand that Thomas Child was one of three brothers, who came to this country and settled in Pottstown, Pa. My father, William Child, was the son of Thomas and Mary Child, b. Jan. 2, 1795, in Pottstown, Pa. He married Mary Williams, daughter of Joshua and Sarah Williams, b. Sept. 3, 1783. She died in Marietta, Pa., Aug. 25, 1849; he died Oct. 24, 1873.

Children:

i. SARAH MARIA CHILD, b. Oct. 8, 1807, in Pottstown, Pa., d. Sept. 9, 1860, unmarried.

ii. THOMAS CHILD, b. in Marietta, Pa., Nov. 23, 1809; m. 1st, Susan V. Gratiot, of Gratiot's Grove, Wis. She d. 1845. He m. 2d, Mrs. May Ann Neal, of Baltimore, Md. He d. Nov. 12, 1873. They had two children, son and daughter: Willie H., b. 1843; Mary, b. 1850, died young. The son was killed by a sharp-shooter during the Rebellion, in front of Petersburgh, Va. He was a Lieutenant in the forty-fifth Regt. Penn. Vol., and had served over three years. Was twenty-one years old at the time of his death.

iii. WILLIAM CHILD JR., b. in Marietta, Pa., Mar. 6, 1812; m. June 4, 1833, Susan Kepler.

iv. JOSHUA CHILD, b. in Marietta, Pa., Aug. 24, 1814; d. April 18, 1867, unmarried, in Cal.

v. EDWARD CHILD, b. Jan. 5, 1819; d. July 10, 1820, in Marietta, Pa.

vi. RUSSELL ALBERTUS CHILD, b. in Marietta, Pa., Aug. 22, 1820; m. ——; d. July 13, 1871.

vii. CHARLES FRANKLIN CHILD, b. Nov. 28, 1826; d. Jan. 22, 1828.

viii. MARGARET G. CHILD, b. Mar. 31, 1823, unmarried.

WILLIAM CHILD, third child and second son of William and Mary Child, b. in Marietta, Pa., Mar. 6, 1812; m. June 4, 1833, Susan Kepler, dau. of Jacob and Elizabeth Kepler, who was b. May 4, 1811.

Children:

i. CHARLES CARROLL CHILD, b. in Marietta, Pa., April 24, 1835; d. Oct. 9, 1835.

ii. SULLIVAN SUMPTION CHILD, b. in Marietta, Pa., Mar 5, 1836; m. Nov. 19, 1861, Annie Biehel, of Harrisburg, Pa. They had two children, one son and one daughter; dau. d. yg., son, George Bergner, b. Sept. 28, 1862.

iii. SARAH CECILIA ALINDA CHILD, b. Sept. 23, 1836, in Marietta, Pa.; m Sept. 8, 1859, H. S. Hoover, of Waverly, Bremer Co., Iowa, where they reside. They have three children: one son, Elmer Ellsworth, b. May 16, 1861; two daughters: Miriam b. Nov. 28, 1865; Katie b. Jan. 8, 1867.

iv. MARY ELIZABETH CHILD, b in Marietta, Pa., Sept. 26, 1840; m. Sept. 25, 1866. E. G. Herr, of Goshen, Ind. They have one son, Charles Child Herr, b. June 19, 1861.

v. EMMA VICTORIA CHILD, b. Aug. 23, 1842, in Marietta, Pa.; m. Aug. 23, 1864, A. S. Pomeroy, of Waterloo, Black Hawk Co., Iowa. They have one son, William Jesse, b. June 20, 1865; two daughters, Anna May, b. May 1, 1867; Emma Clara, b. Nov. 30, 1868.

vi. MIRIAM ADEL CHILD, b. July 13, 1845; m. June 1, 1870, W. A. Ripley, of Newark, N. J. They have one son, Wainwright, b. Oct. 29, 1871.

vii. MAGGIE ANN CHILD, b. April 20, 1849; m. June 4, 1872, A. D. Wike, of Marietta, Pa. They have two sons and one daughter; William Jacob, b. Feb. 27, 1873; Susan Child, b. Nov. 19, 1878; Albert Chester, b Dec 27, 1880."

APPENDICES.

CAPT. WILLARD CHILD. [See page 178.]

The following obituary of Capt. W. Child was found by his daughter, Mrs C. C. May, after the printing of his family record in the body of the work, and is prefaced by a brief note of the editor of the Boston paper in which it was published at the time of his decease:

"The subject of the following obituary notice has been for many years well known to many of our readers. The old patriot having fought a good fight as a soldier of his country and as a christian, died full of years on the spot of his birth. He was on Dorchester Heights the morning the British forces evacuated Boston. From those heights, where he had worked all night long throwing up embankments, he saw the British fleet, as the sun rose in the morning, slowly sailing out of Boston harbor. Capt. Child was also with the army of the North at the surrender of Burgoyne."—*Ed. Cour.*

Died in Woodstock, Ct., on the 13th inst. (Nov. 1844) Mr. Willard Child, father of Rev. Willard Child of Norwich, Ct., aged 86 years.

The following are extracts from the sermon preached at his funeral:

"The subject of these solemnities was a christian in early life. He made a public profession of religion, and a long subsequent christian career has proved that he was in reality what he professed to be. He has been ever since a useful and consistent member of the Christian Church, and by his labors, his prayers and benefactions, and examples, has aided to sustain and carry forward the institutions of religion. Even in his last days his Church, and the whole Church of Christ, were the objects of his interest, love and prayers. He said to me a few days since, 'O, there is not a day passes but I pray for the Church.' He went down to the tomb like a shock of corn in its season—ripe in years, ripe for heaven—like a sun that sets behind the horizon without a cloud. He died the death of the righteous, and his last end was like his. On the morning of his death, in answer to several inquiries, he said: 'I feel no alarm in view of death: my hope rests on Jesus—it enters into that within the veil'; 'I feel that I love the Saviour more than any thing else.' There was no rapture, no triumph, but settled, calm, christian confidence. His death was like his life, especially like his closing weeks, serene and peaceful. In the midst of dearest earthly friends, who affectionately ministered to his latest wants, he peacefully breathed his last. There are but few, comparatively, who leave behind them at their death so numerous an offspring as he has left. Of nine children who reached maturity, eight still survive. All these are members of the Christian Church. One (Rev. Willard Child) is a minister of the gospel, of whose success and usefulness it does not become me here to speak. The number of his grandchildren are seventy-seven, about sixty of whom are living. The number of great-grandchildren is about forty, and, if I am rightly informed, the far-greater proportion of these are members of the Christian Communion; so that he could say in his last hour, with Simeon of old, 'Lord, now lettest thou thy servant depart in peace, for mine eyes have seen thy salvation.' He expected to meet them in heaven, to present them to his Master, to hear their voices in the choir of the redeemed, and to dwell with them forever where no tie is sundered and no 'farewell tear is shed.' Let me die the death of the righteous, and let my last end be like his." —*Com.*

HON. CALVIN GODDARD CHILD. [See page 141.]

At the commencement of the preparation of this volume, more than three years since, Hon. Calvin G. Child was among the earliest to express himself in favor of the enterprise, and up to the time of his decease, looked forward with much interest to its completion. In the Providence of God he has been called to enter upon new scenes where his brilliant intellect and benevolent heart find wider scope in a higher sphere of activities. In a letter I received from one of his daughters, in response to one sent her mother on the occasion of his death, she writes: "We are very grateful for your sympathy in our great sorrow, and shall be much pleased to have you insert the notice of his death in the Genealogy, in which my father was much interested." His service to his country for many years has been one of honor and usefulness. If pride of birth is ever justifiable, Mr. Child had an indisputable right to cherish such distinction. His paternal ancestors for generations bore the stamp of men of robust, physical powers with decidedly strong intellectual characteristics; men of positive opinions, men of intelligence and unquestioned executive abilities. From his maternal ancestry also he inherited largely advantages in birth, culture and position, the Goddards, the Hales and the Bellamys, who have adorned the bar, the pulpit, the judicial bench and the halls of legislation, head the line, to be connected with whom is an honor and a benediction. Such have been the antecedents of Hon. Calvin Goddard Child.

The esteem in which he was held by his fellow citizens may be gathered from utterances of the public press on the occasion of his death. The New York *Times*, Sept. 29, 1880, says:

"The Hon. Calvin Goddard Child, United States District Attorney for Connecticut, died yesterday morning at his home in Stamford, in the forty-seventh year of his age. Mr. Child was born at Norwich, Conn., and came of a family whose members attained eminent positions in public and social life in various parts of Northern New England. Prominent among his ancestors was the Hon. Calvin Goddard, whose name he bore. Shortly after leaving Yale College as one of the graduating class of 1855, Mr. Child received the appointment of Lieutenant-Colonel on the staff of Gov. Buckingham, whose private secretary he was during the rebellion. About ten years ago he was appointed United States District Attorney for Connecticut, an office in which he was thrice confirmed as his own successor, and in which he earned the entire confidence of the Judiciary and the Bar of his native State. The vigilance with which he guarded the interests of the Government did not prevent him from discharging with rare fidelity, duties devolving upon him as counsel for the New York and the New Haven Railroad Company, and other clients. His standing as a lawyer was very high, and his perfect familiarity with legal decisions relating to railroads rendered him a dangerous adversary in the trial suits instituted in the higher courts of this State, as well as at the Bar of Connecticut. In private life Mr. Child was a gentleman whose striking amiability and gentleness attracted many friends, who in common with the members of the profession which he adorned, will deeply feel his loss. His old college mates, by whom he was particularly beloved, on hearing the news of his illness, a few weeks since, suspended the yearly festivities of their class and sent him a telegraphic message of sympathy, and expressed their regret that his sickness had prevented him from attending their twenty-fifth anniversary. Mr. Child was married to Kate, daughter of Jonathan Godfrey, of Southport, Conn. His funeral will take place at 2 P. M. to-morrow from St. John's Episcopal Church of Stamford, and the interment will be at Southport."

Of his efficiency and trustworthiness as a legal adviser, the New York *Tribune* says:

"He has been counsel for the New York and New Haven Railroad Company for the past fifteen years, and had acted as attorney for other corporations in suits of importance. He was very careful and painstaking in the preparation of his cases, and showed great skill and judgment in their trial. As an officer of the Government, he was zealous and faithful in the discharge of his trust; as a lawyer, he was devoted to the interests of his client; and as a citizen he commanded the respect and esteem of all who knew him Among his more intimate friends he was regarded with feelings of affection for his geniality of manner and kindness of heart, as well as for his unvarying courtesy and good nature."

The Stamford *Herald* says:

"The Hon. Calvin G. Child, one of Stamford's most valued and beloved citizens, is dead. His health during the last two years has been far from good. A slight stroke of apoplexy last March caused his friends great alarm, and was the first premonition of the disease which during the last month developed into softening of the brain, from which he died about 5 o'clock yesterday morning

Calvin Goddard Child, son of Asa Child, a distinguished member of the Connecticut Bar, and grandson of Judge Calvin Goddard, one of Connecticut's most distinguished jurists, was born at Norwich, Conn., April 6, 1834. He was graduated at Yale College in the class of 1855, pursued his legal studies at the Harvard Law School, was admitted to the bar at Boston in February, 1858, and at once commenced the practice of law in Norwich, where he remained until 1864. During his residence in Norwich he was for a time Judge of the City Court in that city, and also held the office of executive secretary to Governor Buckingham, a position which at that time, during the thick of the rebellion, was peculiarly onerous and exacting, and the duties of which he discharged with great fidelity and efficiency. Later he was appointed an aid on the staff of Governor Buckingham with the rank of Colonel. In 1864, he removed to Southport, practicing law in New York City in partnership with Hon. Thomas E. Stewart until 1867, when he removed to Stamford, and with Hon. Joshua B. Ferris formed the firm of Ferris & Child, and has since resided in this place.

He was appointed United States District Attorney for Connecticut by President Grant in February, 1870, a position which he held at the time of his death, his third term expiring in 1882. During his occupancy of this office the business pertaining to it has been so systematized, and conducted with such efficiency and at the same time so little friction, that the District of Connecticut has come to be regarded as a model one at Washington. For the last twelve years Mr. Child had been of counsel to the New York and New Haven Railroad, conducting all its litigation in Fairfield county and the city of New York. He achieved marked success in this branch of his practice, and was frequently retained by and against other corporations.

He had also a large general practice, and was universally acknowledged to stand in the front rank of his profession in this State. His clients found in him not only a faithful and judicious counsellor, but an earnest friend as well, and while no one could be more prompt and zealous in defending their strict legal rights against wrongful encroachment, he was continually striving to settle all controversies if possible by amicable adjustment on broad equitable principles. While lacking in none of the departments of his profession, he particularly excelled as an advocate, in the trial and presentation of causes either to court or jury, and his public speaking, whether forensic or otherwise, was justly admired for its chaste and elegant English, as well as its force and directness.

During his residence in Stamford, Mr. Child identified himself with the interests of the town, and actively engaged in many projects for the advancement of its material and s cial interests. At the time of his death he was a director of the Stamford Water Company and of the Telephone Company, a trustee of the Ferguson Library and a member of the vestry of St. John's Church. He was elected by the last Diocesan Convention a delegate to the General Convention of the Protestant Episcopal Church, soon to hold its session in New York City.

Mr. Child was a man of wide reputation and had a large circle of acquaintance throughout the country, and was universally respected and esteemed. He was one whom to know was an honor and a pleasure, whom to know well was a blessing.

He was married in September, 1858, to Miss Catharine Godfrey, daughter of Capt. Jonathan Godfrey of Southport, who survives him, together with four children."

Of the estimate of his influence as a Christian man, we quote some extracts from an article by his pastor, as found in the *Churchman :*

"He was also a devout and earnest Christian, a cultivated scholar and an exact thinker. The appreciation of the rector and vestry of his own parish was shared by the Bishop and Convention of the Diocese of Connecticut; and few men have in so short a public church life acquired so much consideration and influence in a body not much given to recognize new influences. He had recently been placed on the delegation to the General Convention, and the conscientious attention which his trained legal mind had already given to the constitution and law of the church and to the special subjects which are now up for consideration, especially the tenure of church property gave great promise of usefulness as a member of that body."

We append to the notice of Hon. C. G. Child a correct list of his children by some accident not complete as given on page 142.

i. KATE GODFREY CHILD, b. Aug. 21, 1859, in Norwich, Ct.

ii. ALICE GODDARD CHILD, b. Jan. 2, 1861, in Norwich, Ct.

iii. CALVIN GODDARD CHILD, JR., b. Aug. 27, 1762, in Norwich, Ct.

iv. WILLIAM BUCKINGHAM CHILD, b. Nov. 1865, in Stamford, Ct.

v. ELISABETH CHILD, b. Aug. 20, 1868, in Stamford, Ct.

HORATIO H. CHILD. [See page 231.]

At Leonardsville, Madison county, N. Y., on the 6th Dec. 1880, died Mr. H. H. Child; suddenly called yet ready found to exchange time for eternity. Engaged in business at the time of his decease, full of cheerful activity, he daily awaited the summons, while his friends could not realise the possibility. Every detail of his affairs was in complete order, his very account books revealing his constant vigilance. Stricken with pain by the wayside, a good Samaritan took him into his house, and administered unto him, but our Lord bade him hence and he went willingly. The spiritual life had been manifestly growing, purifying and sweetening. A gracious yielding on many points not vital, but once felt by him to be tenaciously held and contended for, evidenced the attaining of the Christlikeness; yet no one could be farther removed from morbidness. Seven weeks previous to the day of his burial he attended the marriage of his son, Rev. F. S. Child, an event so wholly satisfactory to him, that he felt he could utter his nunc dimittis with a full and ready heart. One half the small family are on the farther shore awaiting those who still *labor* and *wait.*

ELISHA CHILD. [See page 229.]

His death occurred subsequent to the printing of his family record. The following extract is from an obituary notice published in the *Putnam Patriot,* Ct:

As a young man Mr. Child had good principles and steady habits. He retained this character throughout his life. He was inflexible wherever principles were at stake. Conscientious in all matters, he was particularly so in all that seemed to him duty. He enjoyed the confidence of men to an unusual degree. A few weeks before his death he was elected to the State Legislature and was especially pleased with this mark of the esteem and confidence of his fellow townsmen. The firmness of his principles is shown by the fact that for more than forty years he was a staunch believer in total abstinence, and deeply interested in all efforts to promote the cause, Genial and kind hearted by nature Mr. Child enjoyed meetings for social intercourse, and his pleasant smile and the kindly vein of humor in his nature made him a welcome member of such gatherings. The freshness of his feelings was shown by his interest in the young people, and their high regard for him. But the great charm of the man lay in the simple christian character which surrounded him as an atmosphere. His faith was strong, but simple as that of a child, and it had been chastened and deepened by the many trials and sorrows of his life. He had many christian graces but the crown of them all was his deep humility. For, while to others he seemed to grow riper and riper, he seemed to himself to become more conscious of his needs as a sinner, and so he cast himself entirely upon the grace of God in Jesus Christ. For over forty-two years he was a member of the Congregational church in North Woodstock, and at his death, as for many previous years, held the office of deacon. Liberal, according to his means, in maintaining public worship; a constant and active attendant at the weekly prayer meeting; above all, confessedly sincere and exemplary in his christian walk, he was indeed a "pillar" of the church. He died Dec. 15, 1880, aged 68 years, 6 months. Funeral services were held in the church at North Woodstock, on the Sunday afternoon following his death, and the large attendance drawn from all parts of the town showed how wide and deep was the appreciation of those that knew his life.

The following brief obituary is given for several reasons. The residence of Mr. Child was in the county in England from which most of the emigrant ancestors are supposed to have come. The Baldwins were of kindred blood to the Child family, which led to the assumption on the part of the late baronet of their arms and name; the arms being the same given in this book. The death occurring as we are upon this work, we think it fitting to place it here, for the association of Mr. Child with men of note of his time in letters and statesmanship.

WILLIAM LACON CHILDE. M. P.

One of the oldest ex-members of the British Parliament, Mr William Lacon Childe, of Kinlet Hall, Shropshire, and of Kyre, Worcestershire, who in three weeks more would have attained the age of ninety-five, died in England on the 14th inst. He was the only son of the late Mr. William Baldwin (who assumed the surname and arms of Childe only), by his marriage with Annabella, second daughter of Sir Charlton Leighton, of Loton Park, Shropshire, and was born on the 3d of January, 1786. He was educated at Harrow, where he was school fellow of the late Lord Palmerston, Sir Robert Peel, Lord Byron and the late Duke of Sutherland. He afterward entered Christ Church, Oxford. He sat in the House of Commons in the conservative interest, as member for Wenlock, in the first Parliament of George IV. He moved the address in reply to the King's speech in February, 1823. Mr. Childe was a magistrate and deputy lieutenant for the counties of Worcester and Salop, and served as high sheriff of the latter county in 1859. He was also a magistrate for the county of Hereford. He married in 1807 Harriet, second daughter of the late Mr. William Cludde, of Orleton, Shropshire, by whom he has left a family. He is succeeded in his estates by his eldest son and heir, Mr William Lacon Childe, who was born in 1810, and married in 1839 Barbara, daughter of the late Mr. Thomas Giffard, of Chillington, Staffordshire.—*Herald, Dec.* 26, 1880.

Page 372. No. 2966.—William Clinton Child, died in Bath, N. H., Oct. 25, 1880, in his 21st year.

See page 216.—Mrs. Almira Holmes Child, wife of Charles Child, died Sept. 21, 1880.

Page 145, No. 597.—Mrs. Lavinia Lyon Child Ingalls, died Dec. 1879, at 71 years.

Page 171, No. 780.—Mrs. Sophia (Child) Child, widow of Abel Child, Jr., died Aug. 6, 1880, in Boston, Mass., was buried in East Woodstock, Ct.

Page 665, No. 6427.—On Ash Wednesday, Mch. 2, 1881, Mrs. Charlotte E. Cable Childs, wife of Wm. Henry Childs, died in New York City, leaving an infant of a few hours old.

Page 289, No. 1905.—Edith May Childs, died in New York City, March 13, 1881.

Page 785, No. 7956.—Mrs. Eugenia Smith Lytle, widow of William F. Lytle, died in Troy, N. Y., Feb. 22, 1881.

APPENDIX II.—SKETCHES.

When preparing the record of the children of Hon. John Child, (see page 583,) of Weybridge, Vt., we were informed that Mrs. Harriet H. Child Colby, (see page 586,) the only surviving daughter, and her husband, Hon. C. C. Colby, were gifted, cultured people, and we awaited so long as we could the facts herewith given: by some unfortuitous circumstances they were in season only for the appendix:*

"Mrs. H. H. Child Colby was educated at the Fort Edward Institute, N. Y., where she graduated with the highest honors Nov. 19, 1856. In 1857 she accepted the position of preceptress of the Stanstead, P. Q., Female Seminary, and resigned the following year to become the wife of Charles Carroll Colby, then a rising young lawyer of Stanstead. During her school days she developed a poetic talent, which won high encomiums, and some of her published poems, written at that time, are pronounced by critics 'very gems.' After marriage the cares and duties of a wife and mother with her had higher claims, and the exercise of this talent was discontinued. Endowed with refined sensibility, and superior intelligence, from extensive and varied reading, brilliant conversational powers and the most amiable disposition, combined with high moral attributes, Mrs. Colby is truly fitted to adorn the highest social circles. The religious sympathies of Mr. and Mrs. Colby are with the Wesleyan Methodists, having united with that church soon after their marriage."

A writer in the *Richmond Guardian*, P. Q., of January 21, 1881, under the head of "Our Leaders" "The Eastern Township's Group," speaks of Mr. Colby as follows:

Charles Carroll Colby, M. P. for Stanstead, the senior of the group, who was first returned to Parliament in 1867. A member of the House for so many years his complete recognition as a leader in debate, has been of comparatively recent date, and he has grown slowly and naturally into the position he now occupies as one of the acknowledged leaders in debate, and an authority on all topics which pertain to political economy. Mr. Colby is an extremely modest man, and has not been a frequent speaker. The political economists of the House are few in number:—Sirs R. Cartwright, and Tilley, Messrs Mackenzie, T. White, Charlton McCarthy, Mills, and Colby are the prominent representatives of the school. Alike, yet not akin; differing from each other in the breadth and sympathies yet apt scholars in the domain of study they have made their own. As a rule this

* This sketch and that of Daniel W. Child, (see page 587,) are from the pen of the elder brother, Hon. John A. Child, of Weybridge, Vt.

school of politicians are zealous in their conceits, passionately wedded to abstractions and tyrannical in their insistence upon the adaptability of their cherished theories to all conceivable conditions of society, and admitting of no exceptions. It is therefore refreshing to be able to lay one's hand upon a *doctrinaire* of the sect who can intelligently and effectively apply the principles of political economy in their essence, yet in that modified form called for by an exceptional condition of national life, without doing violence to those axiomatic truths which it is the purpose and function of that, by no means exact science to inculcate. Mr. Colby is preëminently a political economist of this type.

There is a saying of the poet Pope: "One science only will one genius fit," and this learned essayist, furthermore, says, that not only is the genius of any particular individual "limited to particular arts," but that his knowledge is also "confined to single parts of the particular art" in which he may be proficient. This is emphatically true of the political economist. Mr. Colby is an exceptional instance of one of the school, who while grasping the essential principles is able to apply them to special and exceptional circumstances, extending to the minutest detail without in the slightest way compromising admitted truths of the science. There is moreover, in his speeches an invigorating sense of honesty, of outspokenness, and of candor; and they afford evidence of extensive erudition and accurate knowledge; uniting happily great reading with that solid judgment and discrimination which turns the learning of others to liberal account without the least compromise of their freedom of thought; and his language is always pure, melodious, and nervous. He gives his opinions free vent and is not afraid of his convictions. His sentences all abound with the fervor and fullness of feeling which constitutes the highest form of oratory; and on this account he is always listened to with pleasure and advantage, and will hold the attention of a wearied and listless auditory when an impassioned and fervid speaker would fail to secure a hearing. He is not an impassioned speaker, nor imaginative; rarely poetical, and never pathetic. Yet he is an orator. He speaks with an ease and readiness which suggest an accurate and comprehensive acquaintance with his subject. He is not apt with metaphor but is always happy with his illustrations and quotations, though he rarely uses them; and he never fails to carry conviction.

Mr. Colby is a close student. If you are in search of him during a sitting of the House, you will find him in the Library looking up the facts for a meditated speech. When *he is prepared* he will speak; for rather than fail to do full justice to his theme he will forego the contemplated deliverance; he will have it all at his fingers' ends, and will be greedily listened to as well by "the other side of the House" as his own. A reply to him is very rarely attempted. He always has something new to say, and that something is true and terse; he invariably presents his case with modesty, yet, withal, with that confidence and symmetry of proportions which characterizes the master-hand of an expert. He is a logical debater and travels closely in company with his subject; observing an order of arrangement which, like the scale in a musical gamut, leads up evenly and uniformly to the predicated conclusion. He is moreover, a moderate man—never overdoing himself, or overreaching his theme, and is one of the most amiable of disputants. Though he has a great command of language, and that keen perception which enables the logical mind to penetrate a sophistry, he never belittles an opponent or exults in the weakness of his argument. He possesses in a remarkable degree the happy faculty of being able to make his most subtle ideas perfectly plain to others by the use of simple, yet striking language. When he has done speaking it is felt that the argument is complete; no loopholes are left, no patching up necessary; one feels that a master has spoken, that the deliverence is complete;—every part of it jointed together with the mathematical exactness of a mosaic panel.

It is needless to say that Mr. Colby is a conservative; but he is by no means a strong party man. When principles divide men into groups he is a tower of strength in the ranks of those who are in sympathy with him, but where principles are absent personal likings nor the traditions of association will secure his co-operation. Like the great Robert Hall who "would not cross the street to make a Baptist, but would go a long way to make a Christian." Mr. Colby would go much "out of his way" to make a patriot, but would not turn over his hand to make a conservative. He is also a con istent politician. In days like the present, which witness such startling changes in the actions and votes of whole parties, as well as in the opinions of individuals consistency of conduct and fidelity of principle are qualities which claim atten ion by their very rarity, and impress the student of the history of our times with feelings of esteem and confidence. Press and people, alike, whatever be their differences in political opinion, agree with remarkable unanimity in their estimate of the honorable members for Stanstead. Partizanship will frequently discover and proclaim blemishes in an opponent, but when, as in Mr. Colby's case these are spoken of accompanied by expressions of good will and respect, a far more valuable compliment is paid than would be any ready tribute from a friendly admirer. That portion of the press which delights to direct its shafts against the faults — often more imagined than real—of our public men, has spared Mr. Colby, and the townships have just reason to pride themselves on having,—in the eyes of his political adversaries—at least one public man who is regarded as being, like Cæsar's wife, "above suspicion."

Mr. Colby is by profession a lawyer. He was born at Derby, Vt., in 1827. His father, Dr. Colby, represented Stanstead for many years in the old Parliament, before the Union of 1841. He is a graduate of Dartmouth College, N. H., and is known to be an accomplished scholar. He has been twice returned by acclamation, but at the last General Election was forced to go through the ordeal of a contest, the "frivolous and vexatious" character of which was shown by the enormous majority which was rolled up in his favor by his enthusiastic constituents.

Miss Abby Lemira Colby, eldest daughter of Charles C. and Harriet (Child) Colby, was educated at Stanstead Female College, piano-forte music being made a specialty, in which she became very proficient. Her school days have also been supplemented with the advantages of American and foreign travel. Her fine intellectual culture, captivating manners, with much beauty of person, and amiable traits of character, renders her at once the favorite of the social circle and an ornament to the best society.

Miss Jessie Maud Colby, second daughter of Charles C and Harriet (Child) Colby, received her education at Stanstead Female College, where she graduated with the highest honors in the class of 1878, receiving at that time a special degree in music. Yet the prominent feature in her college life was the high degree of attainment made in not a few but all the branches of the college course. This symmetry of development in intellectual culture finds also in her its counterpart in the development of those high moral qualities, which combined with other graces make the refined and noble woman

Daniel Wright Child, third son of John and Abigail Wright Child, received an academical education at the Vergennes,Vt , Grammar School, and Troy Conference Academy. Upon attaining his majority, he engaged in general farming, and specially in breeding and dealing in Spanish merino sheep, with marked financial success. In 1867, he, in company with his brother, Col. A. J. Child, located in Independence, Missouri, making as before the sheep business a specialty, with the addition of breeding fine blooded horses. September 13th, 1870, he was united in marriage with Nevada, eldest daughter of G. Chace of Independence, Mo.

Mrs Nevada Chace Child was born in Warren county, Ill., Sept. 13th, 1850. She received her education at Vinton, Burton county, Iowa. In 1866, Mr. Chace an i family settled in Independence, Mo., and the two years preceding her marriage was occupied in teaching in the graded school of that place. In the summer of 1872, D. W. Child and wife removed to Greenhorn near Pueblo, Colorado, making the journey across the plains, overland, with a large herd of sheep to stock his ranch. In 1873, the stock of sheep was largely augmented by thorough bred Spanish merinos from Vermont. But the lawless and desperate cattle ranchmen of the territory looked with a jealous eye upon what they considered the encroachments of the sheepmen, and speedily organized for their extermination. As the leader in maintaining the rights of the sheepmen, D. W. Child stood firm and unflinching, and the concentrated ire of the desperadoes was launched on his devoted head. During a night's absence from home the cowardly miscreants made a descent on his corrall and butchered between five and six thousand dollars worth of h.s finest sheep. This outrage of course reacted upon the perpetrators, large rewards were offered by the Governor and others for their apprehension, and they were obliged to leave the country, and the sheepmen were left in the quiet enjoyment of their rights. D. W. Child is an energetic, thorough going business man, and succeeds in what he undertakes. The breeding of fine horses (in connection with sheep farming) and more recently mining, have receiv d considerable attention.

The religious sympathies of Mr. and Mrs. Child are with the Baptist denomination (not close communion), with which church they united several years since. Being well qualified by education and culture, and having seen and experienced much of frontier life, they have contributed numerous interesting sketches and adventures to the New York *Tribune, Journal of Agriculture*, and Colorado *Farmer*. Many of the "Colorado articles" which have appeared in those prints, have been contributed by them. Republican in politics, they have done their full share in helping to build up the "Centennial State."

THE LOWRIE FAMILY.

The original name was Lawrie or Laurie, but was changed after the family came to America to Lowrie, as it was commonly pronounced. In the old family Bible, the possession of the late Chief Justice Lowrie there is a record running through five generations, from which we quote, 1st, Joseph Lowrie and Jane McGhie married April 1, 1748; 2d, John Lowrie, eldest son of Joseph and Jane Lowrie, born July 9, 1749, married Jan. 29, 1772, Catherine Cameron; 3d, Mathew Bonsall Lowrie, eldest son of John and Catherine C. Lowrie, born May 12, 1778, married May 8, 1805, Sarah Anderson; 4th, Jane Bailey Lowrie, eldest daughter of Mathew B. and Sarah A. Lowrie, born Feb. 14, 1806, married Jan. 5, 1829, Harvey Childs of Pittsburgh, Pa. We find also that Walter Lowrie, second son of John and Catherine C. Lowrie, born Dec. 10, 1784, married 1833, Mary K. Childs, daughter of Joshua and Susan King Childs of Springfield, Mass.

John Lowrie and Catherine Cameron were married by Rev. Mr. McCallan of Ardnamurchan; Catherine was of the Highland clan Cameron. The Lowries were Lowlanders. For many years John resided in Edinburgh, and there several of his children were born. In 1793, he emigrated to America, locating first in Huntingdon county, Pa., but afterwards moved to Butler county where he remained. Despite the difficulties inseperable from rural life, he secured his children an education, the tastes inherited by his posterity leading them into professional life. Mr. Lowrie was known in his new home as a man of ability, energy and integrity. He died Aug. 10, 1840, aged 91.

Hon. M. B. Lowrie, son of John and Catherine Cameron Lowrie, was born in Edinburgh, Scotland, May 12, 1778, and came to America with his parents in 1793. Married May 8, 1805, Miss Sarah Anderson, eldest daughter of James and Jane Bailey Anderson. Mr. Anderson was born in Cumberland county, Pa., in 1760, married Miss Jane Bailey in 1786.

Mr. M. B. Lowrie was a student at the University of Edinburg, when the removal of the family to America interrupted his studies. He continued his education, however, even in the classical branches, and qualified himself to become a successful teacher. In 18 7, he removed with his wife and eldest child, Miss Jane B. Lowrie, to Pittsburgh, Pa. On the way thither, in Armstrong county, his son, Walter Hoge Lowrie, was born. After reaching Pittsburgh, Mr. Lowrie established a school which he continued for several years, gaining the respect of the community for his character, education and probity. Accordingly, in 1816, when the city of Pittsburgh was chartered, he was one of the first twelve aldermen appointed by Governor Simon Snyder from among the prominent citizens, who were commissioned

for life, and from among whom the mayors of the city were to be selected
by the action of the city councils. In 1830, Mr. M. B. Lowrie was thus
chosen mayor. Hon. M. B. Lowrie died in Pittsburgh, July 28, 1850, from
a sudden attack of cholera morbus caused by returning to the city in the heat
of summer. Four sons attained manhood, Hon. Walter H. Lowrie, Dr.
Jas. A. Lowrie, Rev. Jno. M. Lowrie, D. D., and Joseph W. Lowrie.

Chief Justice Walter Hoge Lowrie, LL. D., eldest son of Hon. Mathew
B. and Jane Bailey Lowrie, born in Armstrong county, Pa., March 31,
1807; grew to manhood in Pittsburgh, here he graduated from the
Western University, June, 1826. He began at once the study of the
law in the offices of Hon. Chas. Shaler and Hon. Walter Forward, was admitted to the bar Aug. 4, 1829. For seventeen years he devoted himself
assiduously to his profession. August 20, 1846, he was appointed by Governor Shunk president judge of the District Court of Allegheny county; he
held this position until 1851, when he was elected to the Supreme Court of
Pennsylvania; of this court he was judge six years. In 1857, he became
Chief Justice of Pennsylvania, his associates were Jeremiah S. Black, George
W. Woodward, John C. Knox, and William Strong, forming a bench ever
regarded by the bar of the country as of rare distinction. At the expiration
of his term, in 1863, Judge Lowrie resumed legal practice for five years in
Pittsburgh. In 1868, he removed to Philadelphia. In 1870, was elected
president judge of Crawford county, and removed to Meadville, and there
resided in the discharge of his official duties until the time of his death,
October 14, 1876. Chief Justice Lowrie was one of Pennsylvania's most
eminent jurists. The Princeton *Review*, vol. 2, in giving a review of the
"Lowrie Opinions," states: "He is best known by his judicial opinions.
Many of them contain very thorough and philosophical discussions of com-
plicated judicial questions pervaded by a pure and decided tone of individual and social morality and order. Judge Lowrie was esteemed for his
perfect fairness and love of justice, regarding the spirit of the law and not
the letter as the law itself. As a philosophical writer, he contributed to
several journals, monthly and quarterly. The following are among his published essays: 'Inductive and Deductive Politics,' 'The Dissolution of
Empires,' 'The Natural Grounds of Civil Authority,' 'Buckley's History
of Civilization,' etc." In manners and appearance, Judge Lowrie was a
gentleman of the old school. From the tribute paid to his memory by Hon.
H. C. Richmond, before the Bar of Crawford county, we make one extract:
"We have known few men who possessed to so great an extent the power
of personal attraction. Of a fine presence and a pleasant countenance, his
qualities of head and heart were such as not only to command respect, but
to win and hold the affections. He was a learned lawyer, an erudite scholar,
a devout Christian, and, what in his exalted position was, if possible of
greater importance, an upright and impartial judge. In his judicial decisions he knew neither friend nor acquaintance, nor stranger, nor foe—if,
indeed, he had a foe." Two sons survive him, Jas. A. Lowrie, an attorney
of Denver, Colorado, and Rev. Samuel T. Lowrie, late Prof. of Exegesis and
Literature in the Western Theological Seminary of Pittsburgh.

Major James A. Lowrie, eldest son of Judge W. H. Lowrie, was born in
Pittsburgh, Pa., Jan. 25, 1833. Graduated July, 1851, from Miami University,
Oxford, Ohio, and in December, 1854, was admitted to the bar in Pittsburgh.
In 1861, he espoused the Union cause and served under Gen. Negley, with
Major Patterson's column, in Maryland and Virginia. On the 7th of Octo-
ber, 1861, he was appointed Assistant Adjutant with rank of captain, and
served on the staff of Brig Gen'l Negley, until after the battle of Chica-
mauga. After the battle of Stone River he was promoted Major and Assistant Adj Gen'l. At this time he obtained short leave of absence and was
married in Pittsburgh, Nov. 24, 1863, to Miss Mary J. Park, of that place.
He was then assigned to the staff of Brig. Gen'l Baird, in Maj. Gen'l Thomas'
Army of the Cumberland, participating in all the engagements until the
fall of Atlanta, Georgia. He then resigned and returned to his home,
resuming his profession. In 1875, he removed with his family to Colorado.

Dr. James A. Lowrie, second son of Hon. M. B. and Jane Bailey Lowrie, born in Pittsburgh, Feb. 12, 1810, graduated from the Western University of that city, and at once began the study of medicine for which he had unusual gifts. Took his medical diploma at Philadelphia in 1831. In 1832 the Asiatic cholera reached New York. Desiring to be fully prepared to grapple with the disease, he went to New York and devoted himself to its study under the best physicians and in the hospitals. He was so enthusiastic as to overwork, when exhausted he contracted a violent cold. He was a man of powerful physique, and having always enjoyed perfect health was at first disposed to make light of it. He made a voyage to the West India Islands in January, 1833, for restoration, unavailingly. He returned to Philadelphia, sunk rapidly and died May 1st, 1833.

The following brief outline of the life of Rev. John M Lowrie, D. D., is taken from his memoir written by Rev. Wm. D. Howard, D. D., of Pittsburgh, Pa.:

John M Lowrie son of Hon. Mathew B. Lowrie, was born in the city of Pittsburgh, July 16, 1817, married in April, 1843, Miss Hetty Dusenbury. Dr. Lowrie graduated with distinction from Lafayette College in the class of 1840, and afterwards pursued his theological studies at the Princeton Seminary. Oct. 18, 1843, he was ordained pastor of the church of Blairstown and Knowlton, N. J., and afterwards officiated as pastor at Wellsville, O., and at Lancaster, O. In 1856, he was installed at Fort Wayne, Ind., and there remained until the close of his life.

Dr. Lowrie was a man of much more than ordinary natural gifts. His attainments in the classics and in mathematics, and his acquaintance with history, science and general literature, were extensive and accurate. He was especially familiar with poetry, both classical and English, and was himself the author of a number of hymns which have a high degree of poetic merit. He was also the author of several works of a historical and religious character, among which are "Esther and Her Times." "The Hebrew Lawgiver," &c.

Failing health compelled him, in 1866, to give up active work and seek recovery in a European tour. The relief derived, however, was but temporary, and after returning home a steady decline set in which resulted in death on the 26th of Sept., 1867. Three sons survive him, Rev. Matthew B. Lowrie, Rev. J. Gibson Lowrie and Harry C. Lowrie.

CYRUS B. CHILDS.

In response to a note from us Mr. Childs says his father was Cyrus Wentworth Childs, his grandfather was Cyrus Childs, and his great grandfather was Ebenezer Childs, and supposes the mention of these names will give us a clue to his line of ancestry. These names, however, do not suggest his line, and the name of Ebenezer is so often used in different branches it does not indicate the family to which he belongs. Mr. Cyrus B. Childs says:

"The earliest history of the family that I am in possession of, dates back to the early portion of the present century, when their residence was eighty or one hundred miles west of Boston, Mass. From thence I trace them to western New York, to Ohio, Michigan, Illinois, and on to the great American desert, now known as Nebraska. I can give biography of my father, grandfather, and many incidents of the later portion of my great grandfather's life."

We have been unable to obtain any further information from Mr. Childs, though several communications have been sent him. Mr. Childs is an attorney at law, a real estate, collection and insurance agent, notary public and general conveyancer, residing in Riverton, Franklin county, Neb.

HOLLISTER FAMILY.

Solomon Hollister was an early emigrant from Connecticut to South Ballston, N. Y., and was the father of several sons and daughters, all born in that town. The sons were men of marked characteristics, of robust constitutions, and of sturdy principles; and gave a healthy moral and religious tone to the community. These sons were Roswell, Ezra, Joshua and Solomon. There were also two daughters—perhaps more. One married a Mr. Miller, who was a lawyer; the other married a Mr. Waterman, a well-to-do farmer of Ballston. Roswell Hollister, the father of Mrs. Melissa Hollister Child, (see page 226,) was born November 5, 1782, and married 1805, Esther Guernsey, born October 31, 1787. Mrs. Hollister was of highly respectable parentage. She was a noble christian woman, whose heart and energies were ever employed in various good works. She was a kind and affectionate mother, but sensible and judicious in the treatment of her household. She was long a widow. Mr. Hollister died June 27, 1825, and Mrs. Hollister died November 19, 1865. They had eight children: i. Melissa, born October 7, 1807, married August 29, 1831, Elias Child. She died July 18, 1832, in Tompkins, Delaware county, N. Y., and was buried in South Ballston, her native place; she had one child, died soon. ii. Alfred, born August 19, 1809, married December 30, 1835, Eliza Raymond, of Ballston Centre—there is no record at hand of any children; he died September 12, 1842. iii. Arzelia, born December 20, 1811, married October 2, 1835, James H. Spear, a hardware merchant of Ballston, Spa., N. Y.; he died some years since. Mrs. Spear lives in Goshen, Orange county, N. Y., where an only child and son, is engaged in the hardware trade. James Spear, the son, married November, 1867, Sarah Brown, daughter of Silas C. and Sarah Holbert Brown, of Orange county, N. Y. They have had four or five children, two only are living—Arzelia and Nathan. iv. Zilpha, born May 5, 1814, a sweet child and lovely christian, died March 5, 1832. v. Roswell G., born April 23, 1816, went at an early day to Savannah, Georgia, and settled; he married June 1, 1842, Catharine Wood; he has been an active business man for more than thirty years, a man of determined purpose and manly courage; he has children, but we are not informed of their names and number. vi. Nathan, born September 25, 1818, married 1st, about 1845, or 1846, Miss Jane Thurston, of Duchess county, N. Y.; married 2d, March 2, 1852, Louisa Cornelia Brown, daughter of Silas C. and Sarah Holbert Brown. Mr. Hollister has been in active mercantile business for forty years or more, in Brooklyn, Elmira, Rochester and Utica, N. Y. In the last named place has been in an extensive book trade for twenty years or more, in which he still continues. By the first marriage he had two children: 1. Alfred born November 10, 1847, married September 9, 1871, E. Evadne Halisea. They have one child, Alfred Edwin, born April 19, 1879. 2. Kate, born August 6, 1849, married April 19. 1874, George Hippard of New York City; they have two children—a daughter and son. By second marriage he had seven children: 1. Emma, born Feb. 7, 1853, died in infancy. 2. Esther Guernsey, born January 30, 1855, died August 20, 1875. 3. Lewis Brown, born February 6, 1857. 4. Jasper Thurston, born April 29, 1859, died November 16, 1861. 5. Sarah Brown, born April 6, 1861. 6. Cora May, born May 8, 1863. 7. Nathan Roswell,

born April 23, 1868. vii. Esther, born September 28, 1821, died unmarried, October 30, 1849, in South Ballston, N. Y., a bright, intelligent and beautiful girl, as lovely in disposition and christian character as she was beautiful in person; tenderly loved in the family circle; a girl of warm affections, possessing a sympathetic nature, fond of expressing itself to relieve human suffering, and add to the sum of human happiness. viii. Ezra, the youngest, born December 23, 1823, was a prompt and active lad, left his maternal home in early youth, and now for many years has not been traced.

THORP FAMILY, BUTTERNUTS, N. Y.

In connection with a brief notice of Mrs. Sylvina Thorp Child, page 226, I should not feel that I was doing justice to her memory did I not make more than a passing allusion to her parentage and family connection. Her father, Edward Thorp, Esq., was a wealthy farmer in the town of Butternuts, Otsego county, N. Y. He was born in the town of Greenwich, Ct., in 1776. At sixteen years of age he removed with his parents to Butternuts, where his long and active life was spent, dying 1869, at the age of ninety-three years. He was a man of robust constitution, of remarkable physical endurance, and not less remarkable for his intellectual vigor and love of literature. When a severe days' labor on the farm had been closed, the short hours of the night often found him absorbed in some interesting book or periodical, and in one instance a whole night was thus unconsciously spent. He was well informed upon all the current topics of the day, much beyond the average man of the period, and quite at home among the old British authors. Endowed with a retentive memory, the reading of his younger days was fresh in his mind to the latest period of his life. At ninety years of age he has been heard to repeat passages from "Watts' Lyrics," which he had committed to memory at nine years of age, with the emphasis and enthusiasm of youth. He retained his mental vigor, scarcely impaired, to the time of his death; memory reverting only with less distinctness to more recent events.

In politics he was a Federalist, a Whig, and a Republican, successively, as one form was adopted for another. A purer and more unselfish patriot could not be found. Commencing with the election of President John Adams, in 1797, when his first vote was cast, he never failed to vote at a presidential election up to the time of his death, covering a period of seventy-two years, and extending through the administrations of seventeen Presidents, including the accidental administrations of John Tyler, Millard Fillmore and Andrew Johnson. Mr. Thorp was a man of unswerving integrity, instinctively a gentleman in his intercourse with his neighbors and fellow townsmen. He despised dishonesty, trickery and vulgarity in every possible form; transparent in his own character, he could not endure the absence of frankness in others. He was a man of broad and liberal views on all public questions, yet a man of pronounced opinions. He readily comprehended the public necessities, and was an earnest advocate for all enterprises of public benefit. He was efficient in advancing the cause of general education, as might be expected of a man of his degree of enlightenment. He was a living chronology of all remarkable events connected with the history of the country, and was an authority from which few would

G-2

venture to take an appeal. He was a man of great tenacity of purpose, which, accompanied by sound judgment, rendered him one of the valuable and efficient citizens of the town.

Mr. Thorp was early married to Miss Sylvina Tremain, a lady of much personal worth, possessing qualities of heart and head which she efficiently developed in the circle of her home, and was an esteemed member of society. She died in 1844. They had eight children, all of whom lived to settle in life.

i. The eldest, Charles A. Thorp, born in 1796, was graduated at Hamilton College, in Clinton, N. Y., under President Backus. Studied law and settled in Norwich, Chenango county, N. Y., where most of his professional life was spent. He married, in 1829, Susan Avery of Oxford, Chenango county, N. Y. They had four children, all daughters. The eldest, Sarah Thorp, married Mr. William Thomas, an intelligent and active business man; now settled in the State of Arkansas, an extensive land owner. Elizabeth Thorp, the second daughter married Hon. Horace G. Prindle, of Norwich, N. Y., a prominent and successful lawyer, who for many years held the office of County Judge of Chenango county, N. Y. The third daughter, Mary Thorp, is unmarried, and lives with her father in Norwich, N. Y. The youngest daughter died young. Charles A. Thorp, Esq., when in his prime, held a high position as a lawyer at the bar of Chenango county, N. Y. The thoroughness with which he prepared his cases for court, with the power of language he displayed in arguing them, established a reputation which secured him a large patronage. Like his father, he possessed great tenacity of purpose, and seldom failed to accomplish his ends. In politics, his affiliations were with the old Whig party, and later with the Republican. His conversational powers were unusual, and he seldom failed to interest the listener. Often his topic made him forgetful of himself. We can relate an amusing anecdote without giving offence. On return from New York City, on one occasion, with several of his townsmen, to their homes, while entertaining them in conversation, he folded and twisted, and picked into atoms his railroad ticket, which he held in his hand. When the conductor called for tickets, his ticket was missing. He began a thorough search of his pockets, and of the seat, and of the floor, but no ticket could be found, till the remnants of paper on the car floor, when put together, revealed the mystery. The incident recalled the story of Sir Isaac Newton's being discovered, boiling his watch while holding in his hand the egg which he supposed was in the vessel. Mr. Thorp is spending the evening of his life in Norwich, N. Y.

ii. The second child and son of Edward and Sylvina Tremain Thorp was Lewis Edward, born in 1798. He married, in 1827, Margaret Mack. He was a farmer and lived in Butternuts. He possessed excellent native abilities and had a fair education. At sixteen years of age he had become a competent surveyor, and was often employed in surveying large tracts in and about Otsego county. He was a man of integrity and an earnest supporter of good society, and an esteemed citizen. He was a man of keen sensibilities and honorable instincts, of independent opinions, but courteous and urbane. He died in 1848, leaving no children. Mrs. Thorp died some years later.

iii. The third child and eldest daughter of Edward and Sylvina Tremain Thorp was Abigail P. Thorp, born in 1800. She married Mr. James Boyd, a merchant in the town of Laurens, Otsego county, N. Y., where he died after several years of a successful business. Mr. Boyd belonged to a highly respected family. An elder brother settled in the city of Monroe, Mich., a merchant. A prosperous business brought him handsome accumulations. He died some years since, leaving several children. One, William Boyd, a merchant who succeeded his father in the business as well as in the eldership of the Presbyterian church in Monroe. Another son, Rev. Erasmus J. Boyd, has long been at the head of a female institute in Monroe, Mich., a very efficient educator. Mr. and Mrs. James Boyd had two children, Edward and Christina, both died in youth. Mrs. Boyd is a lady much esteemed in the circle of her acquaintance, among whom she has spent a long and pleasant life. Her family passing away from her many years ago, her intellectual tastes and her literary resources have enabled her to spend a long life with less of a sense of loneliness than usually falls to the lot of those in like position. She is well posted in the history of the country, and she inherits a characteristic prominent in the family, independence in her opinions.

iv. The fourth child and second daughter of Edward and Sylvina Tremain Thorp is Caroline Matilda, born in 1804, married in 1827, Dea. Elias Foote of Brighton, N. Y., and later of Batavia, Genesee county, N. Y. Mr. Foote was a woolen manufacturer: the larger portion of his life was spent in Batavia, during which time he was an active business man and a prominent member and officer in the Presbyterian church. He was a native of Stockbridge, Mass., born May 15, 1799, and died in Batavia, Jan. 29, 1875. Mrs. Foote is a fair representative of the general characteristics, prominent in the Thorp family; with positive opinions and persistency of purpose she maintains a wise independence in the affairs of life. Early consecrating herself to the service of her Divine Master, her life has been one of true and sincere devotion to the christian faith. Mrs. Foote resides in Batavia. There were six children of this marriage: 1. Elizabeth, born Aug. 23, 1830, married May 6, 1852, Henry S. Worthington of Lenox, Mass.; he died Jan. 23, 1853; they had one child, Libbie, she died at nearly three years of age. 2. Edward, born Jan. 31, 1832, married in 1857, Helen Case of Honeoye Falls; he died Nov. 28, 1867; she died Aug. 1876. They had two children, Carrie, who died Nov. 1861, aged three years; Renee, who died in 1867, aged one year. 3. Henry, born June 28, 1834, died April 14, 1855. 4. George, born March 6, 1836, died young. 5. Fannie, born Nov. 23, 1839, married in 1860, Richard Wells a physician; they reside in Messenla, Montana, between the Rocky and Bitter Root Mountains. Their children are, Richard, aged 14; Ernest Custer, aged 3; Bruce, aged 1 year. 6. Jennie, born Aug. 23, 1846, married in 1869, James Rogers, a physician; they live in Sedalia, Mo.

v. The fifth child of Edward and Sylvina Tremain Thorp was William, born in 1806; he was married, in 1846, to Christina Bear. Mr. Thorp was up to the average man in point of capacity and intelligence; after marrying he settled in Western Pennsylvania as a lumberman and farmer; he died in 1877. Mrs. Thorp died earlier. They left one or two children; whether they are alive, we are not informed.

vi. Sylvina, (see page 226,) the sixth child and third daughter of Edward
and Sylvina Tremain Thorp, was born in 1809, and died October 5, 1865, in
the City of New York. In addition to the brief notice on page 226, it wil
not be out of place to give here a further sketch of her life. She early developed bright intellectual faculties, and an unusual fondness for books, and was
often found reading with eagerness, books beyond the comprehension of
most children of her years. Her early school discipline was under the instruction of Rev. Levi Collins, a thorough scholar and disciplinarian, and
principal of Gilbertsville Academy, in the town of Butternuts. Her graduation later, after the completion of the usual prescribed course of studies,
was from the Oxford, N. Y., Academy. Her attainments for the period
were considered of high order, and subsequently proved as substantial as
finished scholarship of the present day. Her conversational powers were so
noticeable a gift as to elicit frequent compliments from interested listeners.
An intelligent gentleman on one occasion having listened to some topic under discussion, remarked that her utterances needed no revision for the press,
her language was so well chosen, so luminous and forcible. Her manners were
dignified and courteous. She was never charged with violating the propri-
eties of life in language or manners. While independent in her opinions,
they were modestly expressed. In the domestic relations, she was amiable,
judicious and warmly sympathetic. Intelligently and devoutly christian
in feeling and sentiment, she was loved for her sincerity and consistency of
life. Of her four children three preceded her in death. The youngest, a
son, survives her, inheriting not a few of his mother's characteristics.
At the age of fifteen he entered the office of the Rochester, N. Y., Gas
Light Company as clerk, under Superintendent George W. Parsons, Esq.
Two years thereafter, at the breaking out of the war of the Rebellion, 1861,
he was advanced to the Chief Clerkship, made vacant by the enlistment of
the superintendent's son, Capt. Theron Parsons, in the Union Army. This
position he held for three years, till the close of the war, when Capt. T.
Parsons returned to his former post, and young Child went to New York
City and entered the publishing house of Ivison, Phinney & Co., now Ivison,
Blakeman, Taylor & Co., where he still remains. While connected with the
Gas Light Office, he was quite popular with the company, superintendent
and employes, and the superintendent declared his cash account for the three
years that the funds were passing through his hands, " was never a cent out
of the way " though eighty or ninety thousand dollars a year were the re-
ceipts and disbursements. On his leaving the office the employes (fifty in
number), testified their esteem for him in the presentation of a valuable
gold watch chain.

vii. Hannah was the seventh child and youngest daughter of Edward and
Sylvina Tremain Thorp. She was born in 1814, and married in 1857, Mr.
William D. Babcock of Butternuts, N. Y. Mrs. Babcock was a person of
great, good sense, well informed, of a most sweet and lovely disposition,
kind and sympathising, withal possessing the independence of character,
peculiar to the Thorp family. She died in calm, peaceful, christian hope,
in 1877, leaving no children.

viii. The eighth and youngest child of Edward and Sylvina Tremain
Thorp, is the Hon. Henry Thorp, born in 1816, and married in 1840, Mary
H. Buckley, daughter of the late John Buckley, Esq., of Unadilla, N. Y.,

and later of Freeport, Ill. Mr. Thorp is the Benjamin of the family, and occupies the homestead; a fair representative in hospitalities and social amenities of an honored father. His pleasantry and good humor have made him a favorite in his family circle; while native good sense and sound judgment have rendered him a reliable and safe counsellor. Of generous impulses and liberal views, his interest in public affairs has been a prominent feature in his activities, and by the suffrages of his fellow townsmen, has served a term as their representative in the State Legislature. Mr. and Mrs. Henry Thorp have reared a family of eight children: i. M. Augusta, who married Charles Child. (See page 229.) ii. John B., born Sept. 20, 1843; settled in Lansing, Iowa, as a merchant; married July, 1872, Eva Spenser of Lansing, Iowa, niece of Rev. Dr. Spenser, late of Brooklyn, N.Y. They have two children—1. Minnie M., born May, 1873; 2. Charles Henry, born May, 1875. iii. Edward, twin with John, born Sept. 20, 1843, died Aug. 1860. iv. James Henry, born Aug. 13, 1845, married May, 1869, Minnie Hurd, daughter of David Hurd, Esq., an extensive business man of Butternuts, N. Y. Mr. Thorp is at the homestead, a thorough farmer and business man; a citizen much esteemed for his probity and executive ability. Mr. and Mrs. J. H. Thorp have three children—1. Benjamin Hurd, born Nov. 7, 1870; 2. Mary Helen, born Aug. 10, 1872; 3. James Lewis, born Feb. 11, 1879. v. Eliza, born April 26, 1847, married Oct. 1867, James A. Mead, a physician, in Chicago, Ill. They have two children—1. Allen Henry, born Meh. 17, 1870; 2. Florence, born Sept. 1877. vi. Lewis Edward, born April 6, 1849, is a physician and surgeon, settled, but unmarried, in Gilbertsville, in the town of Butternuts, N. Y., and in a successful and lucrative practice. vii. Julia Christena, born Dec. 29, 1851. viii. William, born Feb. 11, 1854; is a lawyer, settled in Sidney, Delaware county, N. Y.

CLEAVELAND FAMILY.

The Cleaveland family is of mixed blood, French and Anglo-Saxon. A tradition has been found in the family that the Norman name was DeCliffland, but of this we have no certain data. In Great Britain the family were residents of Durham county, one of the most northern counties of England. The emigrant ancestor was "Moyses" Cleaveland who married in England, in 1648, Ann —, and removed soon after from Ipswich, Suffolk county to America, settling in that part of Massachusetts now known as Winchester, Middlesex county; a citizen esteemed for his probity and sterling mental qualities. One of the ancient slabs of dark colored stone marks his grave. "Moyses" reared a large family of sons and several daughters. His third son, Samuel Cleaveland, removed to Canterbury, Ct., and was himself the head of a numerous family of talent and worth; one of his sons, Col. Aaron Cleaveland, was a man of stalwart frame, and great executive ability. He was prominent in the affairs of the colony, and in the military operations against the Indians and French. Capt. Aaron Cleaveland, eldest son of Col. Aaron, was a "member of the State Legislature; a man of wit, humor and talent." Several of his sons were clergymen. From this line, by their mother, are descended Rev. S. Hanson Coxe, D. D., and Bishop A. Cleaveland Coxe, D. D.

Josiah Cleaveland, the eighth child of "Moyses" Cleaveland, also settled in Canterbury, Ct., in 1694, when it is said there was but one English family in the town. In 1699, he purchased 176 acres of land from Owaneco, "then being of Peagscommeck." Josiah Cleaveland, Jr., married Abigail Payne, and two of his sons, Ebenezer and John, became clergymen of the Congregationalist denomination, in Massachusetts, somewhat distinguished for the position they held in a religious movement whose followers were termed New Lights. Rev. John Cleaveland preached for a time in Boston, declining a settlement, he became a pastor in "Chebacco," now Essex, Mass.; he was a man of unusual polemic abilities; he was a chaplain in the Revolutionary war, and his camp-chest and powder-horn are now in the possession of his descendants, as well as his study chair, and the office chair of his son, Parker Cleaveland, M. D. It may not be unsuitable to mention here, that to Mrs S. P. Cleaveland Child belongs a chair given her by her father, which was brought by one of her French ancestors in 1680, from a Waldensian home; its age is pronounced by connoisseurs of the antique to be from five to six hundred years, the form being the index. Two sons of the Rev. John Cleaveland were physicians, Nehemiah and Parker, and resided in Essex county, Mass.; they were men of great stature, and with well proportioned forms. Dr. Nehemiah Cleaveland had four sons, one Rev. Elisha Cleaveland, D.D., a clergyman in New Haven, Ct., for some years; another, John Cleaveland, was a lawyer, a member of the Bar in New York City.

Parker Cleaveland, M. D., was a man of the genuine Puritan stamp, and as truly and surely administered to the souls as the bodies of his patients. He married for his second wife his cousin, Abigail Cleaveland, daughter of Aaron Cleaveland of Canterbury, Ct., and a sister of Gen. Moses Cleaveland, who purchased from the Indians the site of the city of Cleaveland, to which he gave his own name. The eldest son of Dr. P. Cleaveland was Parker Cleaveland, a graduate of Harvard University, Cambridge, Mass.; he was one of the first professors in Bowdoin College, Brunswick, Me.; a man of superior talents and scholarship, holding the Chair of Chemistry and Mineralogy; and member of several foreign scientific societies. The second son was the Rev. John Payne Cleaveland, D. D., a graduate of Bowdoin College, of whom other record is found on pages 226, 227.

He married for his first wife, Miss Susan Hurd Dole, daughter of Moses and Sarah Thurston Dole. Mr. Dole was of a most sunny disposition, never known to find fault however great the provocation. A man of the keenest wit, quick at repartee, but without satire or sarcasm. His contact with men was sure to allay asperity, and awaken pleasure, yet a man of decided characteristics. There were several children of this marriage, all of whom were naturally brilliant and talented. The only son was educated for a clergyman, and has filled a long and useful ministry in the Congregational Church. Mrs. Cleaveland was a person of rare personal beauty, a lady of brilliant intellect, superior culture. She was a pupil of Professor Emerson, an eminent teacher of his times. She was a classmate and room-mate of Mary Lyon, the founder of Mt. Holyoke Seminary, and attained an excellent scholarship. Her gentleness of disposition and refinement of manner rendered her attractive, and gave her great influence in the circle of her acquaintance. To these natural characteristics were added sincere piety and large christian sympathy. From this marriage were two children, daughters, the youngest, Caroline Worcester, a most lovely and precocious child, died at ten and a half years of age, in Ann Arbor, Washtenaw county, Mich. The elder daughter, Susan Parker, the wife of the publisher of this work, has been highly educated, and ranks among the cultured, refined and intelligent members of society. The traces of her intellectual ability will be found on the pages of this volume, without the promise of which the laborious and perplexing task of preparing this Genealogy would not have been undertaken. Dr. Cleaveland's second wife was Miss Julia Chamberlain, daughter of Capt. Samuel and Mary Tilton Chamberlain of Exeter N. H. Captain Chamberlain was for many years commander of a merchant vessel, engaged in the carrying trade between this and foreign countries. Mrs. Julia C. Cleaveland is a lady of commanding presence, of dignified manners and unusually qualified to adorn society; a lady of positive religious character and much devoted to benevolent work.

Almost the entire line is found in the medical, legal or clerical professions. Some of the families, both in England and America, have succumbed to the mania for abriding words, and omit the *a* in writing the name, though not to its improvement.

--- --

CALHOUN FAMILY.

The Calhoun family, to which Mrs. Charles Henry Childs belongs, has a prominence in the civil and religious history of the country, the brief sketch of which cannot fail to interest and gratify the friends and descendants of this alliance.

The original name was Coquhoun, then Colquhoun, which latter form is still retained by some of the descendants, and by others it is changed to Calhoun. The family is of Scotch extraction. The early ancestor, whose history is traced, is Andrew Calhoun, born March 27, 1764, in Parish Ray, Donegal county, Ireland. His parents were natives of Ayre county, Scotland—the family were probably among the early emigrants who were transplanted from Scotland under government arrangements for the benefit of Ireland's untutored population. We have not the date of his emigration to this country. He is known as a man of influence and position in this country; was settled in Boston, Mass., and was an officer in the Park Street church for many years. He had seven sons, born in Boston, Mass.: 1. Andrew Calhoun, the eldest, was much in public life—canal commissioner in the State of New York, editor, at one time clerk of the Senate of New York, and served a while in the custom house in New York. 2. Wm. B. Calhoun was a lawyer and settled in Springfield, Mass., and for a long time represented the Springfield district in Congress, and filled many offices of trust in his native State. 3. Rev. Simeon Calhoun, D. D., was one of the oldest and ablest missionaries in the Holy Land; he died in Buffalo, N. Y., a few years since, greatly lamented by the christian public. After his death, his widow returned to the missionary field. A son, after qualifying himself in both medicine and theology, has succeeded his father in missionary work in the Holy Land. 4. John Calhoun, a lawyer, has been much in political life, and under appointment by Congress as surveyor general of Kansas. 5. Charles Calhoun, a lawyer, and clerk of Massachusetts State Senate. 6. Henry Calhoun, the father of Mrs. Charles H. Childs, was a man of

large stature (I think all the sons were above medium size), of commanding presence, affable and courteous in manners and highly esteemed for his
integrity and efficiency as a public officer. The New York *Tribune* said
at the time of his decease: "Henry Calhoun was first a valued partner in a
very prominent jobbing house in New York city—afterwards received the
appointment of deputy collector of this port under Fillmore, continued for
many years with distinguished ability and faithfulness, and died in the
public service." He died May 7, 1867. 7. James Calhoun, the youngest of
the seven sons, a lawyer, was at one time a law partner of President Abraham Lincoln—an alliance of which one might be proud. Hon. John C.
Calhoun, the great southern statesman, was a cousin of Andrew Calhoun.

APPENDIX III.

MARRIAGES.

Page 232, No. 1,395.—Rev. Frank S. Child was married Oct. 21, 1880, in
the Congregational church of "Sound Beach," in the town of Greenwich,
Ct., by Rev. Samuel Scovil of Stamford, Ct., to Miss Lizzie J. Lilly, only
daughter of the late General John and Hattie A. Lilly, of Lafayette, Ind.
Mrs. Child was born in Lafayette in 1859; reared in easy circumstances,
and enjoyed the advantages of thorough education in classical schools at
home, and the wider field of travel abroad.

BIRTHS.

Page 138, No. 585.—To Anna Gertrude Child and Samson Whitemore, a
daughter, Edith Sanford Whitemore, born in Newton Highlands, Mass.,
November 27, 1879.

Page 139, No. 586.—To Willis Sandford and Nettie Griffin Child, a son,
Sanford Willis Child, Jr., born at Newbury, Kansas, August 20, 1880.

Page 190, No. 1,011.—To Herbert and Evelyn L. Hebberd Leavitt, in
Woodstock, Ct., twins, Kenneth Washburn Leavitt and Kathleen Evelyn
Leavitt, born May 3, 1880.

Page 189, No. 1,003.—To Henry Thurston and Ella E. Fitts Child, in
South Woodstock, a son, William Chapin Child, born September 12, 1880.

Page 236, No 1,439.—To Sarah Elizabeth Child and Fielding B. Webb, a
daughter, in Iowa, Grace Green Webb, born December 15, 1880.

BENJAMIN G. CHILD. (See page 602, No. 5709.)

The following were received too late to place them under the head of Obituary Notices:

Mr. Benjamin G. Child, an old Bostonian, has just died in St. Louis, Mch. 1884. He came of revolutionary stock, his father having served and been disabled in the war of the Revolution. Born at Boston, December 19, 1797, the death of his father threw him at an early age into the whirlpool of the world to fight out his way by himself. The tendency of his mind being of a mechanical turn, he took up ship-building, inventing many valuable tools used in the exercise of his craft. When the war of 1812 broke out he joined a company commanded by his brother, Joseph Child, and made the campaign. Returning to Boston he resumed his ship-building. November 18, 1821, he married Eliza Treadwell Gray, of Boston, who died in St. Louis, June 26, 1866. Owing to the financial crisis in 1837, under the effect of the banks, he felt compelled to leave Boston, and the loved associations of his early home, for Cincinnati. From Cincinnati he went to St. Louis, in 1847, still following his profession of steamboat-building, etc. During the late war he returned East, and was for five years engaged in the Brooklyn and Boston navy-yards. Since then he has been a constant resident of St. Louis, his three daughters all being teachers in the public schools. Mr. Child was a thorough Republican, a devoted Swedenborgian, and liberal in all his views. But what endeared him most to those who knew him best was his thorough kindliness and charity toward all men. He occasionally contributed to the *Commonwealth*. Indeed, he had begun, as we are informed, a series of articles detailing his early reminiscences of Boston. Prof. Francis J. Child, of Harvard, is his nephew.—*Boston Commonwealth.*

Bessie Child, born March 5, 1879, died March 17 or 18, 1881. (See page 409, No. 3474.)

WILLIAM HENRY CHILD.

The following epitome of a family of the name should have come in on page 768, as this family are probably descendants of Cephas and Percilla Naylor Child of Plumstead, Bucks County, Pa. By some oversight it failed to be placed in its natural position. The account is furnished by one of its members, Mr. George W. Child of St. Louis, Mo.

He says: " my grandfather was William Henry Child. He moved from Annapolis, Md., to a large farm near the Mogathry river. He was so accommodating as to endorse for most any friend, and had to pay all notes he endorsed, which amounted to thousands of dollars. Consequently he was broken up. His wife was a Miss Tropp.

Their children were, Elizabeth, Martha Ann, Sarah, William Henry, Jun., and Zachariah; Zachariah Child was my father, and was the youngest and is the only survivor of the family; the others died years ago. William Henry Jun., and my father were the only ones that married. My mother was a Posterfield. The children of Zachariah and —— Posterfield Child were three daughters and seven sons: Martha Ann, Elizabeth Frances, Mary Ann, William Henry, William Henry 2nd, Zachariah, Jun., Samuel Garlin, James Thomas, Charles Wesley, and George W. Child the writer. Of the children the daughters are married and are still living. Of the sons none are living except James Thomas, and Charles Wesley, both married, and myself unmarried. My grandfather had a brother Benjamin Child, who lived in Western Virginia. He had several sons and daughters, and owned the White Sulphur Springs. There are a great many of our name in that vicinity. My father's family were all born in the city of Baltimore, and reared there; my father owning a considerable property in that city."

We regret the absence of all dates in this history, which are quite essential in a complete and satisfactory Genealogical record, and that we could obtain no fuller account of the earlier ancestors. We have written, addressing the descendants of Benjamin Child, but failed to obtain any reply; the letter being returned to us from the Dead Letter Office at Washington, D. C.

FACTS OF INTEREST.

The following statistics of those of the name and descent in the various professions and pursuits is, we fear, incomplete, as in many instances we have not ascertained these particulars, though always aiming to do so. We can but presume for example the number of graduates from the various collegiate institutions to be much larger than the number we record, yet we know with certainty only of this number. The enumeration does not include any who are only allied by marriage.

Lawyers	29	Teachers	70	Physicians	43
College Graduates	45	Clergymen	45	Soldiers	100

The soldiers are found scattered through the lines. Serving in the early French and Indian Wars; the Revolutionary struggle; the later contest with Great Britain, called the War of 1812; the Mexican War; and the War of the Rebellion.

The colleges represented are:

Dartmouth,	Brown,	Harvard,	Hamilton,	Miami,
Middlebury,	Oberlin,	Union,	Yale,	Williams.

Vanderbilt University,   Western University,
University of New York.

The Ohio, Vermont and New Hampshire Medical Schools.

The Auburn,	Yale,	Cambridge,
Oberlin,	Union,	Lane,

And Andover Theological Seminaries.

The Harvard and Columbia Law Schools.

It may be of interest to the curious to preserve the following fact related of one of the name, by Sir Travers Twiss, in the meeting of the International Law Congress in London, August 14, 1879. He said: "The first Promissory Note payable to bearer, issued in England, was issued by Sir Francis Child, from the vicinity of Temple Bar, 150 years ago, who three years afterwards became Lord Mayor of London."

INDEX.—CHILD.

The names of *minors* now living, and the names of those who died young, are not given in the Index; but will be found with the record of their parents. The records of females married will be found under the name of the husband.

INDEX.—CHILDS.

The names of *minors* now living, and the names of those who died young, are not given in the Index; but will be found with the record of their parents. The records of females married will be found under the name of the husband.

INDEX --CHILDE.

The names of *minors* now living, and the names of those who died young are not given in the Index; but will be found with the record of their parents. The records of females married will be found under the name of the husband.

INDEX OF ALL ALLIED NAMES.

The names of *minors*, and of those who died young are found with the record of the parents.